Introduction

The *Time Out Eating & Drinking Guide* is the most authoritative and comprehensive guide to good restaurants, gastropubs and cafés in the capital. This is not just because we have a great passion for food, and for finding the best places to eat and drink in London. What you have in your hands is the only London guide for which anonymous critics pay for their meal and drinks just like a regular customer (Time Out then reimburses their expenses). We do not tell the restaurants we are coming, nor do we reveal who we are after the meal. Restaurants can exert no pressure on us as to the content of their reviews, and do not pay to be included in the guide. Our editors select all the establishments featured on merit and interest alone.

We want our readers to know just what the experience of eating at each restaurant might be like for them, and take pains to ensure that our reviewers remain totally objective on your behalf. Our insistence on undercover reporting means that our experience is much more likely to reflect your experience. This can't be said of well-known newspaper restaurant columnists: they often receive preferential treatment from restaurant kitchens who have their photographs pinned up to ensure the critics do not go unrecognised (and those critics are inclined to feel insulted or ill-treated if they are not recognised, adding further bias to their reviews).

Many of our reviewers have extraordinary expertise in specialist areas. Several are trained cooks or former chefs, others are well-established food and/or wine authors, and some are simply dedicated enthusiasts who have lived abroad and learned much about a particular region's cuisine. Our contributors include chefs who have worked in the grand hotels of India and in kaiseki restaurants of Japan, expert bakers and baristas, award-winning wine writers, and food lovers hailing from Iran, Russia and Malaysia.

For the weekly *Time Out London* magazine alone, our reviewers visit around 200 new places every year. Their better discoveries are then included in this guide. Reviewers also check other new openings as well as revisiting places included in previous editions. We also take in feedback and recommendations from users of the Time Out website (www.timeout.com/restaurants). Then we eliminate the also-rans to create the list of London's best eateries that this guide represents. We hope you find it useful, and that it helps you get more enjoyment from eating out in the capital.

Time Out is proud to support StreetSmart. Each November and December hundreds of top London restaurants run the StreetSmart £1 per table campaign to raise funds for the homeless. Every penny from every £1 raised will help provide comfort and hope to people who on the streets. For a full list of participating restaurants, just log on to www.streetsmart.org.uk.

STREETSMART
HELPING THE HOMELESS
Supported by

Contents

timeout.com/restaurants

Features

Restaurants

EDITION
30

Cheap Eats

Drinking

Maps & Indexes

Published by

Time Out Guides Limited
Universal House
251 Tottenham Court Road
London W1T 7AB
Tel +44 (0)20 7813 3000
Fax +44 (0)20 7813 6001
email guides@timeout.com
www.timeout.com

Editorial
Editor Cath Phillips
Deputy Editor Phil Harriss
Group Food & Drink Editor Guy Dimond
Listings Editors William Crow, Christian Kingston

Editorial Director Sarah Guy
Series Editor Cath Phillips
Management Accountant Margaret Wright

Design
Senior Designer Kei Ishimaru
Guides Commercial Senior Designer Jason Tansley

Picture Desk
Picture Editor Jael Marschner
Picture Researcher Ben Rowe
Freelance Picture Researchers Isidora O'Neill, Oliver Puglisi

Advertising
Sales Director St John Betteridge
Account Managers Deborah Maclaren, Bobbie Kelsall-Freeman @ The Media Sales House

Marketing
Group Commercial Art Director Anthony Huggins
Circulation & Distribution Manager Dan Collins

Production
Group Production Manager Brendan McKeown
Production Controller Katie Mulhern-Bhudia

Time Out Group
Chairman & Founder Tony Elliott
Chief Executive Officer Aksel Van der Wal
Editor-in-Chief Tim Arthur
Group Financial Director Paul Rakkar
UK Chief Commercial Officer David Pepper
Time Out International Ltd MD Cathy Runciman
Group IT Director Simon Chappell
Group Marketing Director Carolyn Sims

Sections in this guide were written by
African Lauren Bravo; **The Americas (North American)** Tania Ballantine, Euan Ferguson, Nora Ryan **(Latin American)** Simon Coppock, Susan Low, Neil McQuillian, Sally Peck; **Brasseries** Sarah Guy, Susan Low, Jenni Muir, Anna Norman, Cath Phillips, Nicholas Royle, Ros Sales, Shalinee Singh, Yolanda Zappaterra; **British** Jessica Cargill Thompson, Simon Coppock, Euan Ferguson, Sarah Guy, Susan Low, Jenni Muir, Cath Phillips, Nick Rider; **Caribbean** Yolanda Zappaterra; **Chinese** Tania Ballantine, Phil Harriss, Paul Murphy, Jeffrey Ng, Sally Peck; **East European** Silvija Davidson, Janet Zmroczek; **Fish** Jan Fuscoe, Anna Norman, Emma Perry; **French** Emily Boyce, Richard Ehrlich, Anne Faber, Euan Ferguson, Sarah Guy, Lisa Harris, Jenni Muir, Nick Rider, Rob Orchard, Sally Peck, Cath Phillips; **Gastropubs** Emily Boyce, Simon Coppock, Silvija Davidson, Claire Fogg, Sarah Guy, Jenni Muir, Anna Norman, Emma Perry, Cath Phillips, Nick Rider, Nick Royle, Eleanor Smallwood; **Global** Sarah Guy, Phil Harriss, Caroline Hire, Matthew Lee, Nora Ryan, Shalinee Singh, Eleanor Smallwood, Caroline Stacey; **Greek** Alexi Duggins; **Hotels & Haute Cuisine** Tania Ballantine, Silvija Davidson, Richard Ehrlich, Ruth Jarvis, Jenni Muir, Jeffrey Ng; **Indian** Tania Ballantine, Euan Ferguson, Roopa Gulati, Phil Harriss, Rashmi Narayan, Cath Phillips; **Italian** Emily Boyce, Silvija Davidson, Richard Ehrlich, Lewis Esson, Sarah Guy, Susan Low, Jenni Muir, Jeffrey Ng, Sally Peck, Celia Plender, Natasha Polyviou; **Japanese** Nigel Kendall, Kei Kikuchi, Jeffrey Ng, Sally Peck, Celia Plender, Eleanor Smallwood; **Jewish** Judy Jackson; **Korean** Celia Plender, Yolanda Zappaterra; **Malaysian, Indonesian & Singaporean** Jeffrey Ng; **Middle Eastern** Ros Sales, Cyrus Shahrad, Janet Zmroczek; **Modern European** Tania Ballantine, Emily Boyce, Claire Fogg, Sarah Guy, Phil Harriss, Ruth Jarvis, Cath Phillips, Natasha Polyviou, Nick Rider, Ros Sales, Eleanor Smallwood, Janet Zmroczek; **North African** Matthew Lee, Janet Zmroczek; **Pan-Asian & Fusion** Sarah Guy, Susan Low; **Spanish & Portuguese** Lisa Harris, Caroline Hire, Ruth Jarvis, Susan Low, Nick Rider; **Steakhouses** Tania Ballantine, Simon Coppock, Euan Ferguson, Claire Fogg, Sarah Guy, Jenni Muir, Peter Watts; **Thai** Lewis Esson, Cath Phillips, Celia Plender, Eleanor Smallwood; **Turkish** Simon Coppock, Euan Ferguson, Neil McQuillian, Jenni Muir, Ros Sales, Caroline Stacey; **Vegetarian** Charlotte Morgan, Jenni Muir, Cath Phillips, Natasha Polyviou; **Vietnamese** Euan Ferguson, Jenni Muir, Ros Sales, Eleanor Smallwood, Yolanda Zappaterra; **Budget** Tania Ballantine, Anne Faber, Sarah Guy, Lisa Harris, Neil McQuillian, Jenni Muir, Nick Royle, Ros Sales, Yolanda Zappaterra; **Cafés** Jessica Cargill Thompson, Simon Coppock, Richard Ehrlich, Janice Fuscoe, Sarah Guy, Lisa Harris, Annie Lund, Jael Marschner, Emma Perry, Cath Phillips, Elizabeth Winding; **Coffee Bars** Richard Ehrlich; **Fish & Chips** Tania Ballantine, Simon Coppock, George Faulkner, Annie Lund, Jenni Muir; **Ice-cream Parlours** Sarah Guy, Jael Marschner, Jenni Muir, Rashmi Narayan; **Pizza & Pasta** George Faulkner, Sarah Guy, Lisa Harris, Jessica Cargill Thompson, Jael Marschner, Nick Royle, Nora Ryan; **Bars** Euan Ferguson, *Time Out* magazine; **Eating & Entertainment** Ellie Kumar; **Wine Bars** Ruth Jarvis.

Additional reviews by Zena Alkayat, Tania Ballantine, Emily Boyce, Jessica Cargill Thompson, Simon Coppock, Silvija Davidson, Guy Dimond, Alexi Duggins, Richard Ehrlich, Lewis Esson, Anne Faber, Euan Ferguson, Jan Fuscoe, Roopa Gulati, Sarah Guy, Lisa Harris, Phil Harriss, Caroline Hire, Ruth Jarvis, Matthew Lee, Susan Low, Annie Lund, Jael Marschner, Jenni Muir, Neil McQuillian, Rashmi Narayan, Jeffrey Ng, Anna Norman, Sally Peck, Emma Perry, Cath Phillips, Celia Plender, Natasha Polyviou, Nick Royle, Nora Ryan, Ros Sales, Shalinee Singh, Eleanor Smallwood, Caroline Stacey, Peter Watts, Elizabeth Winding, Yolanda Zappaterra, Janet Zmroczek.

The Editor would like to thank Katy Attfield, Guy Dimond, Susie Giles, Sarah Guy, Christina Stewart, Ellie Kumar, Oliver Kay, John Watson. Thanks to our sponsor, MasterCard.

Maps JS Graphics (john@jsgraphics.co.uk). Maps 1-18 and 24 are based on material supplied by Alan Collinson and Julie Snook through Copyright Exchange. London Underground map supplied by Transport for London.

Photography pages 10 (left), 52, 57, 122 (middle), 203 (left), 220, 223 (left and middle), 307 Olivia Rutherford; 10 (middle), 102, 116 (top left and bottom), 160 (left and bottom), 236, 239, 243, 278 (middle), 286, 328 Helen Cathcart; 10 (right), 11 (middle), 17, 23 (right), 27, 28, 30, 39 (left), 40, 44, 48, 52, 73, 78 (middle), 79, 96, 98, 116 (top right), 121, 126 (bottom left and top right), 135 (top right), 139, 141 (top left), 158 (left), 195 (middle), 199, 202, 206, 219 (top), 227, 228, 242, 244, 246 (right), 247, 259 (left), 260, 265 (middle), 266, 268, 269 (middle), 274 (right), 278 (left and right), 279, 283 (left), 290 (left and middle), 291, 293, 301 (right), 312 (left and middle), 313, 314, 319, 325 (left and right) Rob Greig; 11 (bottom), 23 (left), 51 (right), 58, 60, 63 (left and middle), 111, 115, 154 (left and top right), 155 (bottom), 159, 163, 196, 320 (middle) Alys Tomlinson; 11 (top), 29, 35, 39 (right), 43, 47, 55, 83, 89 (middle), 94, 120, 131 (left), 132, 167, 271, 272, 294, 317 (top) Michael Franke; 20 (left), 65 (right), 190, 195 (left), 223 (right), 251, 252 (right), 259 (right), 263, 274 (middle), 305 (middle) Michelle Grant; 20 (middle and right), 85 (left), 86, 141 (bottom left and right), 224, 226 (middle), 233 (left and right), 259 (middle), 261 Jitka Hynkova; 21, 65 (middle), 89 (right), 105 (right), 171 (left and middle), 216 (top, bottom left and bottom right), 219 (bottom), 312 (right), 317 (bottom) Britta Jaschinski; 22, 39 (middle), 51 (middle), 65 (left), 67, 74, 75 (top right), 76, 77, 84 (right), 85 (top right), 87, 91, 105 (middle), 109, 127, 131 (middle), 136, 140 (left and middle), 171 (right), 175, 177, 183 (middle and right), 184 (right), 186 (right), 191 (middle), 194, 195 (right), 203 (middle), 205, 215, 225, 226 (right), 231, 233 (middle), 234, 246 (left and middle), 249, 256, 296, 325 (middle), 234, 295 (middle and right), 299 Ming Tang-Evans; 23 (middle), 36, 68, 75 (middle), 78 (left), 174, 252 (left), 255, 321, 323 (top right) Heloise Bergman; 24, 66, 99, 110, 186 (left), 188, 250, 280, 295 (left), 298 Tricia De Courcy Ling; 25 Ed Reeve; 49 Jason Bailey; 51 (left), 53, 180 Louise Haywood-Schiefer; 61 Ken Copsey; 71, 252 (middle), 253, 283 (right) Ed Marshall; 75 (top left and bottom), 191 (left) Katie Peters; 78 (right), 105 (left), 122 (right), 125, 140 (right), 158 (middle and right), 173, 183 (left), 193, 209, 218 (top and middle), 305 (right), 320 (left) Jonathan Perugia; 82 Cath Lowe; 89 (left), 90 (left) Franck Allais; 112, 135 (left and bottom), 301 (middle) Scott Wishart; 118 Ben Rowe; 122 (left) Kristian Buus; 131 (right), 323 (bottom and top left) Nerida Howard; 153, 166 Paul Winch-Furness; 159 Martin Daly; 157 Anne Faber; 165 Paula Glassman; 163 Stephen Barber; 186 (middle), 187 David Axelbank; 191 (right) Christina Theisen; 203 (right) Catherine Frawley; 204 Steve Wallington; 212 Neil Setchfield; 218 (bottom) Ed Reeve; 221 (middle) Keiko Oikawa; 221 (left) David Loftus; 252 (middle), 253, 305 (left), 306 Ed Marshall; 269 (left and right), 320 (right) Tom Baker; 277 Annie Armitage; 289 (top right) Paul McGough; 303 Zed Jameson; 316 (top) Paul Clarke.

The following images were supplied by the featured establishments: pages 32, 33, 37, 38, 63 (right), 64, 84 (left and middle), 85 (bottom right), 88, 90, 101, 106, 107, 122 (left), 123, 126 (middle top and top left and bottom right), 128, 142, 149, 154 (bottom right), 155 (top), 160 (middle and bottom), 172, 178, 181, 184 (left), 203 (right), 216 (middle right), 217, 221, 226 (left), 229, 232, 235, 237, 258, 265 (left and right), 267, 274 (left), 276, 288, 289, 290 (right), 292, 301 (left), 302, 304, 315, 316 (bottom), 318, 327.

Printed by Wyndeham Group.
Time Out Group uses paper products that are environmentally friendly, from well-managed forests and mills that used certified (PEFC) Chain of Custody pulp in their production.

ISBN 978-1-9050-4275-3
ISSN 1750-4643
Distribution by Comag Specialists (01895 433 800). For further distribution details, see timeout.com.

Taste Thai
Busaba
Eathai
106 Wardour Street
London W1F 0TR
020 7255 8686
22 Store Street
London WC1E 7DF
020 7299 7900
8–13 Bird Street
London W1U 1BU
020 7518 8080
35 Panton Street
London SW1Y 4EA
020 7930 0088
319 Old Street
London EC1V 9LE
020 7729 0808
Westfield
Shepherd's Bush
London W12 7GA
020 3249 1919
Bicester Village
50 Pingle Drive
Oxford OX26 6WD
01869 362 700
44 Floral Street
London WC2E 9DA
020 7759 0088
Westfield
Stratford City
London E20
020 8221 8989
356 King's Road
London SW3 5UZ
020 7349 5488
busaba.com
Takeaway available

About the guide

LISTED BY AREA
The restaurants in this guide are listed by cuisine type: British, Chinese, Indian, Middle Eastern, Modern European etc. Then, within each chapter, they are listed by geographical area: ten main areas (in this example, East), then by neighbourhood (Shoreditch). If you are not sure where to look for a restaurant, there are two indexes at the back of the guide to help: an A-Z Index (starting on p371) listing restaurants by name, and an Area Index (starting on p354), where you can see all the places we list in a specific neighbourhood.

STARS
A red star ★ means that a venue is, of its type, very good indeed. A green star ★ identifies budget-conscious eateries – expect to pay £25 per head for a three-course meal, or its equivalent (not including drinks and service).

NEW
The NEW symbol means new to this edition of the *Eating & Drinking Guide*. In most cases, these are brand-new venues.

TIME OUT HOT 50
The HOT 50 symbol means the venue is among what we consider to be London's top 50 iconic eating and drinking experiences. For details of the complete 50, *see p8.*

AWARD NOMINEES
Winners and runners-up in Time Out's Eating & Drinking Awards 2012. For more information on the awards, *see p10.*

OPENING HOURS
Times given are for last orders rather than closing times (except in cafés and bars).

PRICES
We have listed the cheapest and most expensive main courses available in each restaurant. In the case of many oriental restaurants, prices may seem lower – but remember that you often need to order several such dishes to have a full meal.

COVER CHARGE
An old-fashioned fixed charge may be imposed by the restaurateur to cover the cost of rolls and butter, crudités, cleaning table linen and similar extras.

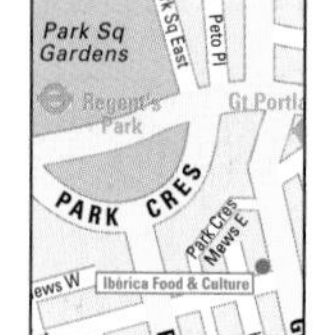

MAP REFERENCE
All restaurants that appear on our street maps (starting on p330) are given a reference to the map and grid square where they can be found.

SERVICES
These are listed below the review.

Babies and children We've tried to reflect the degree of welcome extended to babies and children in restaurants. If you find no mention of either, take it that the restaurant is unsuitable.

Disabled: toilet means the restaurant has a specially adapted toilet, which implies that customers with walking disabilities or wheelchairs can get into the restaurant. However, we recommend phoning to double-check.

Vegetarian menu Most restaurants claim to have a vegetarian dish on the menu. We've highlighted those that have made a more concerted effort to attract and cater for vegetarian (and vegan) diners.

East

Shoreditch

★ ★ Hipsters HOT 50

2011 RUNNER-UP BEST NEW CHEAP EATS

240 Old Street, EC1V 2XY (9876 4321). Old Street tube/rail. **Lunch served** 8am-noon, **dinner served** 7pm-midnight daily. **Main courses** £8-£15.50. **Set dinner** £12 2 courses, £18 3 courses. **Cover** £1. **Credit** AmEx, MC, V.

The Shoreditch bar aesthetic that has crept into the dining scene this year has its nadir at Hipsters. An unfinished factory roof makes choosing the right table a matter of real importance (though umbrellas are thoughtfully provided). Concrete ventilation tubes pipe in car fumes directly from Old Street, so that Silicon Roundabout geeks can feel as at ease. Hipsters is full of energetic branding types in clothes of neurotically appropriate casualness, as studiedly artless as the venue itself. But the set-up for this 'pop-up food and drink collaboration' is just as on-trend as the interior. Sit at one of the small reclaimed tables on an oil drum seat and the waiting staff will take your order of comfort-cum-junk food from a chalked-up board. Top of the list is the 'Deputy Dawg', which viscerally evokes the nightbus journey back west from Dalston at 4am. Have this with some 'Soppy Fries', washed down with some craft 'Dalston Rude Beer', before considering the dessert list, which includes a 'Hells Angels' Delight' of grown-up naughtiness. As is often the case with fashionable restaurants, the wait for tables is long; no bookings are taken, and you can only eat here by Twitter invitation, once you have been 'liked' by the restaurant's Facebook page.

Available for hire: fixie bikes. Bookings not accepted. Tables outdoors (6, pavement). Takeaway service. Vegetarian menu. **Map 6 Q4.**

Anonymous, unbiased reviews

The reviews in the *Eating & Drinking Guide* are based on the experiences of Time Out restaurant reviewers. Venues are always visited anonymously, and Time Out pays the bill. No payment or PR invitation of any kind has secured or influenced a review. The editors select which places are listed in this guide, and are not influenced in any way by the wishes of the restaurants themselves. Restaurants cannot volunteer or pay to be listed; we list only those we consider to be worthy of inclusion. Advertising and sponsorship has no effect whatsoever on the editorial content of the *Eating & Drinking Guide*. An advertiser may receive a bad review, or no review at all.

Photo Credit: Lianna Fowler photographed by thomas zanon-larcher, directed by Jules Wright (2010)

Time Out's Hot 50

We have picked 50 places, entirely subjectively, that we believe offer some of London's most interesting eating experiences. We're not saying these venues have the best food and drink in the capital, but we believe each adds something life-enhancing to our city. Here they are, in alphabetical order. Each review is marked with a HOT 50 symbol in the relevant chapter of the guide.

Amaya
Indian p142.
Sparkling and sophisticated modern Indian grill.

Baltic
East European p82.
Classic East European dishes are given a contemporary spin at this still-glamorous restaurant and jazz bar.

Barrafina
Spanish p237.
A pint-sized space attracting mile-long queues for its stylish, authentic tapas and fine selection of sherries and Spanish wines.

Barshu
Chinese p73.
The fiery flavours of Sichuanese cooking, served in style.

Bentley's Oyster Bar & Grill
Fish p85.
Take a seat at the art nouveau bar for freshly shucked oysters and London's best fish pie.

Bistrot Bruno Loubet
French p91.
The Zetter hotel is a colourful setting for Bruno Loubet's modern French cooking.

Bistrotheque
French p102.
Bistro food and modish bar make for an original combination at this east London hotspot.

Buen Ayre
The Americas p37.
Argentinian parrillada (steak grill) with everything from ribeyes to sweetbreads.

Le Café Anglais
Modern European p210.
Rowley Leigh's buzzy Bayswater brasserie.

Caravan
Brasseries p39.
A restaurant, bar and coffee roastery where beans are ethically sourced and expertly blended to suit the season. Now with a sibling in King's Cross.

Czechoslovak Restaurant
East European p83.
The city's only Czech restaurant and bar is a piece of living history.

Franco Manca
Pizza & Pasta p309.
One of the first eateries to open in Brixton Market, serving probably the best pizzas in London.

La Fromagerie
Cafés p280.
Dine among the deli ingredients at this charming fine food store.

Gelupo
Ice-cream Parlours p303.
Seaside hues of white and blue make this a sunny spot to enjoy superb Sicilian-style gelati and granita.

The Grill at the Dorchester
British p54.
Peerless British food, bonkers Scottish decor, in one of London's grandest hotels.

Harwood Arms
Gastropubs p111.
British country produce stars at this Fulham pub dining room.

Hawksmoor
Steakhouses p246.
Will Beckett and Huw Gott's very British steakhouse and cocktail bar – now with three branches, in Spitalfields, Covent Garden and the City.

Hix Soho
British p54.
Mark Hix's fun British restaurant with characterful downstairs bar.

Koba
Korean p186.
Spicy, sizzling Korean cooking in the middle of the West End.

Koya
Japanese p177.
This udon specialist demonstrates the beauty of keeping it simple, in both food and decor.

The Ledbury
Hotels & Haute Cuisine p138.
Thrill to the cooking of Aussie chef Brett Graham's cooking in Notting Hill.

Locanda Locatelli
Italian p161.
A sexy, lounge-like dining room serving fine Italian cuisine and impressive wines.

Lola Rojo
Spanish p239.
Bringing a slice of Spain's nueva cocina to Battersea.

Mandalay
Global p122.
Sample first-rate Burmese fare at this otherwise basic caff.

Masa
Global p126.
The Middle East meets the Indian subcontinent in an unsung corner of Harrow.

Momo
North African p223.
A great Maghrebi soundtrack, cool Marrakech decor and some of the best Moroccan food in London.

Moro
Spanish p234.
Enduringly popular Exmouth Market restaurant with a menu that stretches from Spain right along the Mediterranean.

Nahm
Thai p252.
Royal Thai cuisine served with style and grace in a glittering dining room.

NOPI
Pan-Asian & Fusion p228.
Yotam Ottolenghi's newer and smarter big brother of the Ottolenghi cafés. Pricey, though.

Petersham Nurseries Café
Modern European p222.
Greg Malouf has replaced Skye Gyngell, but the cooking is just as inventive, and the bucolic setting still gorgeous.

Poppies
Fish & Chips p299.
Retro Spitalfields chippie with top-notch frying and more than a hint of happy days.

The Providores & Tapa Room
Pan-Asian & Fusion p227.
World-beating fusion fare served all day, from banana and pecan french toast to grilled scallops with crab and quinoa dumplings.

Rasa Samudra
Indian p141.
A rare opportunity to sample the authentic and surprisingly fiery fish cookery of Kerala.

River Café
Italian p165.
The wood-fired oven takes centre stage in this world-famous, yet relaxed, Hammersmith classic.

Roka
Japanese p173.
Spectacularly designed restaurant based around a central grill, and great for Fitzrovia people-watching.

St John
British p52.
Fergus Henderson's uncompromising approach to food, and especially meat, has inspired a new generation of chefs both here and abroad.

Sakonis
Indian p157.
The original Indian vegetarian chat (snack) house, serving South Indian and Gujarati dishes.

Sketch: Lecture Room & Library
Hotels & Haute Cuisine p137.
Pierre Gagnaire's astonishing food isn't the only talking point at this stylish celebration of art and luxury.

Song Que
Vietnamese p270.
Authentic Vietnamese dishes at affordable prices.

Spuntino
The Americas p28.
A slice of New York's Lower East Side in the heart of Soho.

Sweetings
Fish p84.
Old-world bonhomie and classic British fish dishes since 1889.

Terroirs
Wine Bars p327.
Natural wines and small plates pioneer that's inspired a vat of imitators.

Towpath
Cafés p287.
Quirky waterside café in N1.

Les Trois Garçons
French p103.
Home to hippo heads, stuffed bulldogs and vintage handbags, as well as terrific French food.

Viajante
Hotels & Haute Cuisine p139.
Nuno Mendes' Bethnal Green outpost of cutting-edge cuisine.

Vinoteca
Wine Bars p327.
A model wine bar with well-priced, well-rendered cooking, and all wines to take home at retail price.

Wapping Food
Modern European p221.
Victorian pumping station museum/art-gallery serving inventive modern cooking and an Australian wine list.

Wild Honey
Modern European p207.
Anthony Demetre and Will Smith run a trio of excellent restaurants – this is our current favourite.

The Wolseley
Brasseries p42.
A decade on, and this former car showroom still feels like one of London's most exciting destinations, day or night.

Yauatcha
Chinese p73.
Still a hot destination for first-rate dim sum, served all day.

Time Out's 23rd annual Eating & Drinking Awards 2012

Lima London

Boqueria Tapas

10 Greek Street

Time Out has an unrivalled reputation for promoting the best of London's eating and drinking places – something of which we are very proud. It is not just those with the grandest credentials that we champion, either, but the little places that are, in their own field, worthy of note. This is the ethos behind our broad coverage of London's gastronomic delights – from weekly reviews in *Time Out* magazine to our numerous guides. And this is why our annual Eating & Drinking Awards take in not only London's restaurant elite, but also representatives from neighbourhood restaurants, gastropubs and cafés, as independently selected by a panel of Time Out judges.

The award categories, which vary each year, reflect the diverse needs and tastes of London's diners and drinkers; for example, this year's awards for Best New Latin American Restaurant and best New Meat Restaurant recognise the current interest in food of the Americas, notably ceviche and barbecue. With new reviews appearing each week in *Time Out* magazine (and on our website, www.timeout.com/restaurants), the list of potential candidates can seem dauntingly long. The judges visit every shortlisted venue as normal paying punters (we never accept PR invitations or freebies), so that a final decision can be reached.

And the winners are...

BEST NEW BEER BAR

WINNER
Crown & Anchor *See p316.*

RUNNERS-UP
Brewdog *See p316.*
Bull *See p316.*
Railway Tavern *See p317.*

BEST NEW CHEAP EATS

WINNER
Boqueria Tapas (Spanish & Portuguese) *See p241.*

RUNNERS-UP
Okan (Japanese) *See p181.*
Roti Chai (Indian) *See p143.*
Tuk Cho (Pan-Asian & Fusion) *See p228.*

BEST NEW DESIGN

WINNER
Mari Vanna (East European) *See p78.*

RUNNERS-UP
La Bodega Negra (Latin American) *See p32.*
The Delaunay (Brasseries) *See p40.*
Shrimpy's (North American) *See p24.*

BEST NEW LATIN AMERICAN RESTAURANT

WINNER
Lima London *See p31.*

RUNNERS-UP
La Bodega Negra *See p32.*
Ceviche *See p33.*
Sushisamba *See p31.*

BEST NEW LOCAL RESTAURANT

WINNER
Abbeville Kitchen (Modern European) *See p214.*

RUNNERS-UP
Lawn Bistro (French) *See p101.*
Potli (Indian) *See p146.*
Provender (French) *See p103.*

BEST NEW MEAT RESTAURANT

WINNER
Tramshed (British) *See p61.*

RUNNERS-UP
Duke's Brew & Que (North American) *See p29.*
Pitt Cue Co (North American) *See p27.*
Meat Liquor (North American) *See p25.*

BEST NEW NO BOOKINGS RESTAURANT

WINNER
10 Greek Street (Modern European) *See p209.*

RUNNERS-UP
Burger & Lobster (North American) *See p27.*
Pizarro (Spanish & Portuguese) *See p241.*
Polpo Smithfield (Italian) *See p159.*

BEST NEW RESTAURANT

WINNER
The Delaunay (Brasseries) *See p40.*

RUNNERS-UP
Bistro Union (Brasseries) *See p45.*
Brasserie Zédel (French) *See p96.*
Dabbous (Haute) *See p132.*

The Delaunay

Mari Vanna

Tramshed

This year's judges:
Tania Ballantine, Jessica Cargill Thompson, Guy Dimond, Alexi Duggins, Euan Ferguson, Susan Low, Cath Phillips

Where to...

Got the hunger, the people, the occasion, but not the venue? These suggestions will help you find the perfect spot to eat, drink and be merry.

The Modern Pantry

GO FOR BREAKFAST

Breakfast is offered every day unless stated otherwise. *See also* **Brasseries** and **Cafés**.

Abbeville Kitchen (Sat, Sun) Modern European p214
Albion British p61
Bentley's Oyster Bar & Grill (Mon-Fri) Fish p85
Bistrot Bruno Loubet French p91
Botanist Modern European p203
Brasserie Zédel (Café) French p96
Café Chula The Americas p37
Carluccio's Caffè Italian p159
Canteen British p57
Cecconi's Italian p161
Chiswell Street Dining Rooms Modern European p203
Cinnamon Club (Mon-Fri) Indian p146
Le Coq d'Argent (Mon-Fri) French p90
Dean Street Townhouse British p54
Delfina (Mon-Fri) Modern European p217
The Diner The Americas p30
Dishoom Indian p140
English Restaurant British p61
Fifth Floor (Café, Mon-Sat) Modern European p205
Garufa The Americas p38
Goring Hotel British p57
The Grill at the Dorchester British p54
Hix British p54
Jugged Hare Gastropubs p105
Lutyens (Mon-Fri) French p90
The Luxe Modern European p220
Mamuska! East European p82
The Modern Pantry (Mon-Fri) Pan-Asian & Fusion p226
New Asian Tandoori Centre (Roxy) Indian p156
NOPI (Mon-Fri) Pan-Asian & Fusion p228
Northall British p57
Orange Public House & Hotel Gastropubs p107
Paramount (Mon-Fri) Modern European p204
The Providores & Tapa Room Pan-Asian & Fusion p227
Queen Adelaide (Sat, Sun) Gastropubs p108
Roast (Mon-Sat) British p60
Rochelle Canteen (Mon-Fri) British p61
Sakonis (Sat, Sun) Indian p157
St John Bread & Wine British p62
Simpson's-in-the-Strand (Mon-Fri) British p55
Smiths of Smithfield Modern European p205
Sotheby's Café (Mon-Fri) Modern European p207
This Bright Field British p62
Trojka East European p82
York & Albany Modern European p222

EAT/DRINK BY THE WATERSIDE

See also the Southbank Centre branches of **Giraffe** and **Wagamama**.

Blue Elephant Thai p257
Blueprint Café Modern European p217
Dock Kitchen Modern European p210
Lido Café Cafés p283
Camino (Docklands branch) Spanish p235
Gaucho (Tower Bridge and Richmond branches) The Americas p31
Narrow Gastropubs p114
Le Pont de la Tour Modern European p217

Lido Café

Paramount

Royal China (Docklands branch) Chinese p74
Serpentine Bar & Kitchen Cafés p280
Skylon Modern European p214
Stein's Budget p277
Towpath Cafés p287
Water House Brasseries p46
Waterline British p62

ENJOY THE VIEW

Blueprint Café Modern European p217
Le Coq d'Argent French p90
Duck & Waffle Brasseries p39
Galvin at Windows Hotels & Haute Cuisine p135
Oxo Tower Restaurant, Bar & Brasserie Modern European p214
Min Jiang Chinese p74
Paramount Modern European p204
Plateau Modern European p219
Roast British p60
Rhodes Twenty Four British p52
Skylon Modern European p214
Smiths of Smithfield (Top Floor) Modern European p205
Sushisamba The Americas p31

SHARE DISHES

See also **Spanish & Portuguese**.

Bocca di Lupo Italian p163
Cannon & Cannon British p59
Caravan Brasseries p39
Caravan King's Cross Brasseries p41
Club Gascon French p91
Dinings Japanese p174

Kopapa Brasseries p41
Lalibela African p22
Made in Camden Brasseries p50
Norfolk Arms Gastropubs p106
Ottolenghi Brasseries p50
La Petite Maison French p95
Roti Chai Indian p143
Tayyabs Indian p151
Terroirs Wine Bars p327`
This Bright Field British p62
Vine Gastropubs p119
Wahaca The Americas p36

TAKE AFTERNOON TEA

See also **Cafés**.

Bistro Union Brasseries p45
Bob Bob Ricard Brasseries p42
Botanist Modern European p203
Chiswell Street Dining Rooms Modern European p203
Dean Street Townhouse British p54
The Delaunay Brasseries p40
Les Deux Salons French p93
National Dining Rooms (Bakery) British p55
Northall British p57
Quince Turkish p260
Restaurant at St Paul's British p51
Sotheby's Café Modern European p207
The Wolseley Brasseries p42

TAKE THE KIDS

See also **Cafés** and **Ice-cream Parlours**.

Adam & Eve Gastropubs p121
Bill's Brasseries p50
Blue Elephant Thai p257
Clissold Arms Gastropubs p120
Depot Brasseries p45
Duke of Cambridge Gastropubs p114
Giraffe Brasseries p50
Herne Tavern Gastropubs p109
Jamie's Italian Italian p170
Manor Arms Gastropubs p113
Marine Ices Budget p276
Masala Zone Indian p140

Bistro Union

Yipin China

PEOPLE-WATCH

A Little of What You Fancy Brasseries p47
Albion British p60
Bar Boulud French p94
Brasserie Zédel French p96
Le Café Anglais Modern European p210
Le Caprice Modern European p207
Dean Street Townhouse British p54
The Delaunay Brasseries p40
Dock Kitchen Modern European p210
Hackney Pearl Brasseries p49
Henry Root Modern European p213
Hix British p54
The Ivy Modern European p205
Meat Liquor The Americas p25
Mr Chow Chinese p67
Quo Vadis British p54
Riding House Café Brasseries p41
Roganic Hotels & Haute Cuisine p134
Scott's Fish p85
Sketch: Lecture Room & Library Hotels & Haute Cuisine p137
The Wolseley Brasseries p42
Yauatcha Chinese p73
Zuma Japanese p173

TRY UNUSUAL DISHES

Adulis African p21
Ariana II Global p126
Asadal Korean p187
Baozi Inn Chinese p70
Barshu Chinese p73
Cah Chi Korean p189
Caravan Brasseries p39
Caravan King's Cross Brasseries p41
Dinner by Heston Blumenthal Hotels & Haute Cuisine p133
Duck & Waffle Brasseries p39
Esarn Kheaw Thai p255
Faanoos II Middle Eastern p198
Hélène Darroze at the Connaught Hotels & Haute Cuisine p136
Hereford Road British p57
Hibiscus Hotels & Haute Cuisine p137
Hunan Chinese p65
KaoSarn Thai p258
Kopapa Brasseries p41
Lima London The Americas p31
Lola Rojo Spanish p239
Mandalay Global p122
Masa Global p126
The Modern Pantry Pan-Asian & Fusion p226
The Providores & Tapa Room Pan-Asian & Fusion p227
Roganic Hotels & Haute Cuisine p134
Sake No Hana Japanese p176
Song Que Vietnamese p270
Sushisamba The Americas p31
Tbilisi East European p82
Texture Hotels & Haute Cuisine p134
Viajante Hotels & Haute Cuisine p139
Yashin Japanese p178
Yipin China Chinese p76

DO BRUNCH

See also **Brasseries** and **Cafés**.

Bistrot Bruno Loubet (Sat, Sun) French p91
Le Café Anglais (Sat) Modern European p210
Christopher's (Sat, Sun) The Americas p23
Les Deux Salons (Sun) French p93
Duke's Brew & Que (Sat, Sun) The Americas p29
Empress (Sat, Sun) Modern European p220
Gilbert Scott (Sat, Sun) British p53
Joe Allen (Sat, Sun) The Americas p24
Lardo (Sat, Sun) Italian p169
Manson (Sat) British p58
The Modern Pantry (Sat, Sun) Pan-Asian & Fusion p226
Ransome's Dock (Sat, Sun) Modern European p215
Rivington Grill (Mon-Fri) British p61
Wapping Food (Sat, Sun) Modern European p221

DINE ALFRESCO

Adam & Eve Gastropubs p121
Avalon Gastropubs p113
Belvedere French p99
Clerkenwell Kitchen Cafés p278
Clissold Arms Gastropubs p120
Dock Kitchen Modern European p212
Duke of Sussex Gastropubs p108
Ealing Park Tavern Gastropubs p108
Gallery Mess Brasseries p45
Geales Fish p87
Greek Affair Greek p127

Lardo

Where to... get in first

Bubbledogs

JUST OPENED

Beard to Tail

77 Curtain Road, EC2A 3BS (www.beardtotail.co.uk).
Hot on the heels of their pop-up in June 2012, the team behind Callooh Callay have found a permanent location in Shoreditch. The restaurant serves hearty dishes such as pulled beef featherblade and slow-roasted pork rump with a sage and wild garlic crust, along with some creative cocktails.

Begging Bowl

168 Bellenden Road, SE15 4BW (7635 2627, www.thebeggingbowl.co.uk).
This no-bookings Thai restaurant in Peckham has proved a huge hit locally thanks to its very imaginative menu, good drinks list and cool-looking interior.

Bubbledogs

70 Charlotte Street, W1T 4QG (7637 7770, www.bubbledogs.co.uk).
Continuing the trend for poshed-up junk food, this Fitrovia newcomer offers various gourmet hot dogs (pork, beef or veggie) plus a fine collection of lesser-known champagnes. No bookings are taken, so expect to wait.

Chrysan

1 Snowden Street, Broadgate West, EC2A 2DQ (3657 4777, www.chrysan.co.uk).
Yoshihiro Murata, the owner of Michelin-three-star restaurant Kikunoi in Japan, has teamed up with the Hakkasan group to bring his take on traditional Kyoto cuisine to London's financial district.

Green Man & French Horn

54 St Martin's Lane, WC2N 4EA (7836 2645).
The fourth branch of the Terroirs French bistro and wine bar chain, which also specialises in so-called 'natural wines'. It's on the edge of Covent Garden, very close to the original Terroirs.

Old Bengal Warehouse

Old Bengal Warehouse, 16A & B New Street, EC2M 4TR (3503 0785, www.newstreetgrill.com; 3503 0790, www.fishmarket-restaurant.co.uk).
A massive new dining complex from D&D London, housed in an 18th-century industrial building near Bishopsgate. The restaurants are the New Street Grill (meat), Fish Market (seafood), plus the Old Bengal Bar (cocktails) and a wine bar.

Pizza East, Chicken Shop & Dirty Burger

79 Highgate Road, NW5 1TL (3310 2020, www.chickenshop.com; 3310 2000, www.pizzaeast.com).
The Soho House Group has colonised the whole of the former Grand Union pub building in Kentish Town. There's Chicken Shop, a diner-style rotisserie restaurant in the basement, the latest branch of Pizza East upstairs, and Dirty Burger (*see p250*) in a shack round the back.

Slider Bar (Lucky Chip at the Player Bar)

Player Bar, 8 Broadwick Street, W1F 8HN.
The Lucky Chip caterers seem to have found their spiritual home amid the Americana, stuffed moose head and den-style decor of this low-lit basement below Agent Provocateur. The pulled pork 'slider' (mini burger) is exemplary.

South Place Hotel

3 South Place, EC2M 2AF (3503 0000, www.southplacehotel.com).
D&D London, the people behind Skylon, Launceston Place and Quaglino's, are entering new territory with their first hotel. Located near Liverpool Street and Broadgate, the hotel includes two restaurants: all-day eatery 3 South Place and seafood restaurant Angler.

Sushi Tetsu

12 Jerusalem Passage, EC1V 4JP (3217 0090, http://sushitetsu.co.uk).
With an intimate atmosphere and well-sourced fish, this Clerkenwell sushi bar wouldn't be out of place in modern-day Tokyo. Booking is essential: with only seven counter seats, one table and one chef, it fills up fast.

DUE TO OPEN OCT 2012

Bo London

4 Mill Street, W1S 2AX.
Following on from his success in Hong Kong, Alvin Leung is back in the UK to showcase his 'X-treme Chinese cuisine' in Mayfair. Expect the likes of cod with saffron miso, Sauternes and seaweed or 'Iberico 36' (with morels, vermicelli and gazpacho), plus new specialities inspired by the British larder.

Café Colbert

50-52 Sloane Square, SW1W 8AX (www.colbertchelsea.com).
Rex Restaurant Associates re-create the all-day 'grand café' style of the Wolseley and the Delaunay (their best-known restaurants), but this time in Chelsea, rather than the West End.

John Salt

131 Upper Street, N1 1QP.
Ben Spalding, former head chef of Roganic, is set to start a six-month residency upstairs at the John Salt (formerly called Keston Lodge) in Islington. On the menu will be a mix of global ingredients cooked with innovative techniques.

Naamyaa Café

Angel Building Islington, 407 St John's Street, EC1V 4AB (www.naamyaa.com).
A Bangkok-style Thai café from the owners of popular chain restaurant Busaba Eathai.

DUE TO OPEN NOV 2012

MASH

81 Brewer Street, W1F 9ZN.
The first UK venue from the Danish-based MASH chain of modern American steakhouses is located in a historic site in Soho, which has been restored to its glamorous 1930s design.

Chicken Shop

Homa Brasseries p49
Lemonia Greek p125
Manor Arms Gastropubs p113
Mazi Greek p129
Narrow Gastropubs p114
New Cross House Gastropubs p114
El Parador Spanish p243
Petersham Nurseries Café Modern European p222
River Café Italian p165
Royal China (Docklands branch) Chinese p74
Scott's Fish p85
Towpath Cafés p287
Vine Gastropubs p119

NO BOOKINGS

Meat Liquor The Americas p25
Pitt Cue Co The Americas p27
Pizarro Spanish p241
Spuntino The Americas p28
10 Greek Street Modern European p209

TAKE A DATE

Almeida French p104
Amaya Indian p142
Andrew Edmunds Modern European p209
Angelus French p97
L'Anima Italian p158
Assaggi Italian p165
L'Autre Pied Modern European p206
The Bingham Hotels & Haute Cuisine p139
Bistrotheque French p102
Bob Bob Ricard Brasseries p42
Brasserie Zédel French p96
Le Café Anglais Modern European p210
The Delaunay Brasseries p40
Eyre Brothers Global p124
Hakkasan Chinese p67
J Sheekey Fish p84
Lamberts British p59
Locanda Locatelli Italian p161
Magdalen Modern European p217
Maze Hotels & Haute Cuisine p137
Roka Japanese p173
Sake No Hana Japanese p176
Sketch: Lecture Room & Library Hotels & Haute Cuisine p137
Theo Randall at the Intercontinental Italian p163
Les Trois Garçons French p103
Upstairs Modern European p213
Wapping Food Modern European p221

EAT AT THE BAR

Anchor & Hope Gastropubs p114
Arbutus Modern European p209
Barrafina Spanish p237
Bentley's Oyster Bar & Grill Fish p85
Bocca di Lupo Italian p163
Le Caprice Modern European p207
Eyre Brothers Global p121
J Sheekey Fish p84
Massimo Italian p164
Maze Hotels & Haute Cuisine p137
Morito Spanish p233
Moro Spanish p234
Pollen Street Social Hotels & Haute Cuisine p137
Roka Japanese p173
Salt Yard Spanish p235
Tapas Brindisa Spanish p237
Tom's Kitchen Brasseries p42
Wright Brothers Soho Fish p87
Yashin Japanese p178

GRAB A MEAL BEFORE A SHOW

Almeida French p104
Anchor & Hope Gastropubs p114
Botanist Modern European p203
Canteen (South Bank branch) British p57
Joe Allen The Americas p24
Masala Zone (Covent Garden branch) Indian p140
Le Mercury Budget p276
Ottolenghi Brasseries p50
Tas (Waterloo branch) Turkish p259
Veeraswamy Indian p144

EAT LATE

La Bodega Negra The Americas p32
Brasserie Zédel French p96
Café Chula The Americas p37
Le Caprice Modern European p207
The Delaunay Brasseries p40

Dishoom Indian p140
Joe Allen The Americas p24
Lahore Kebab House Indian p149
Mamuska! East European p82
Mangal II Turkish p260
Spuntino The Americas p28
The Wolseley Brasseries p42

LOVE THE LOOK

Amaya Indian p142
L'Anima Italian p158
L'Autre Pied Modern European p206
L'Atelier de Joël Robuchon Modern European p205
Baltic East European p82
Bob Bob Ricard Brasseries p42
La Bodega Negra The Americas p32
Brasserie Zédel French p96
Bread Street Kitchen Brasseries p39
Caravan King's Cross Brasseries p41
China Tang Chinese p68
Les Deux Salons French p93
The Delaunay Brasseries p40
Dinings Japanese p174
Gilbert Scott British p53
Hakkasan Chinese p67
Hawksmoor (Seven Dials) Steakhouses p249
Mari Vanna East European p78
The Luxe Modern European p220
Massimo Italian p164
NOPI Pan-Asian & Fusion p228
Pearl Bar & Restaurant Hotels & Haute Cuisine p133
Petersham Nurseries Café Modern European p222
Roux at the Landau Hotels & Haute Cuisine p129
Sake No Hana Japanese p176
Sketch: The Gallery Pan-Asian & Fusion p227
Sketch: Lecture Room & Library Hotels & Haute Cuisine p137
Riding House Café Brasseries p41
Les Trois Garçons French p103
Wapping Food Modern European p221
Zuma Japanese p173

Restaurants

African

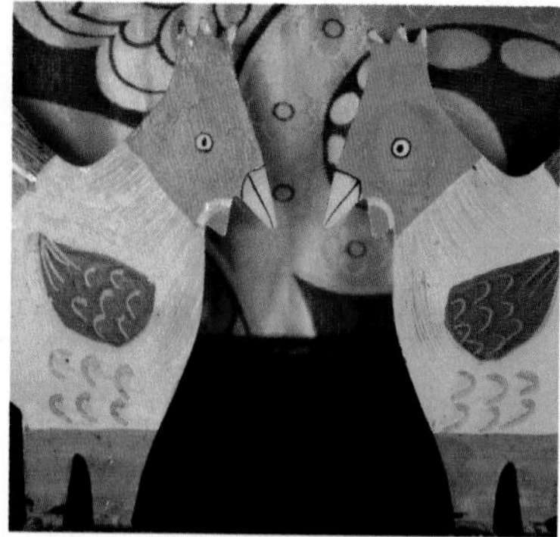

Despite the large and varied African communities spread across the capital, there aren't many restaurants catering to their needs. Best represented are the similar cuisines of Eritrea and Ethiopia: **Mosob** and **Adulis** in west and south London are our current favourites for the former, and the **Queen of Sheba** and newcomer **Muya**, both in Kentish Town, for the latter. For a change, try the Italian-influenced Somali cooking at the **Village** in Hammersmith.

The team behind the excellent food market stall Spinach & Agushi (www.spinachandagushi.co.uk) opened a small café inside Covent Garden's Africa Centre in August 2012. The **Africa Café by Jollof Pot** (38 King Street, WC2E 8JR, 7473 5666) is a small daytime operation with reheated dishes served in takeaway cartons, but it's the only place in Covent Garden you'll find jollof rice, suya chicken or spinach and agushi. For restaurants specialising in the cuisines of North Africa, *see p223*.

West

Hammersmith

★ The Village

95 Fulham Palace Road, W6 8JA (8741 7453, www.somalirestaurant.co.uk). Hammersmith tube. **Meals served** 11.30am-11.30pm daily. **Main courses** £6-£11.99. **Unlicensed** no alcohol allowed. **Credit** AmEx, MC, V.
Somali

This relaxed basement restaurant does its best to create a community atmosphere in the middle of Hammersmith, drawing a throng of Somali regulars as well as locals and the odd curious visitor from farther afield. Service during our visit was rather slow and indifferent, despite only three tables being occupied; little advice was offered with the menu. Luckily, the food stands up for itself, and we tucked into an eclectic combo of sweet chilli chicken with pineapple, and cheese-stuffed fried potato rolls, to start. Pasta features prominently due to Somalia's history of Italian occupation, as do grilled meats, seafood and even a decadent tiramisu. The more traditional African dishes are given modern twists. Lemon sole fillet was perfectly cooked and served with a rich cream sauce, on a mountain of corn maize. 'Marinated tender lamb fillet' delivered exactly that: succulent and well seasoned, though its accompaniment of Somali bread soaked in coriander sauce might divide opinion. No alcohol is served, but there are own-made fruit smoothies among the usual soft drink options. The Village's decor is scruffier than its slick website would suggest, but prices are good for the sheer quantity of food served. You're likely to have satisfied bellies, if not quite an indulgent dining experience.

Available for hire. Babies and children admitted. Takeaway service. **Map 20 C5.**

Westbourne Park

★ Mosob

339 Harrow Road, W9 3RB (7266 2012, www.mosob.co.uk). Westbourne Park tube. **Meals served** 6-11pm Mon-Thur; 6-11.30pm Fri; 3-11.30pm Sat; 3-11pm Sun. **Main courses** £7.50-£10. **Set meal** £14.95-£19.95 per person (minimum 2). **Credit** MC, V. Eritrean

If you're familiar with Eritrean food, you're likely to enjoy Mosob – but if you're new to the cuisine, all the better. Service goes beyond cheery and attentive to positively educational, with a lesson in the communal eating style for all who need it, and a book on Eritrean architecture offered to look at between courses. There are African and European beers and a decent cocktail list (including the 'sexy Mosob'), while the food centres on the staple that is injera: pleasingly sour, stretchy flatbread used to mop up meat stews, spiced split peas and vegetables. For the indecisive there are well-priced set menus covering the most popular dishes, with ample choice for vegetarians. Starters of crispy falafel and veggie injera rolls make a great introduction, served with a fiery dip and yoghurt. Next comes a belt-busting platter of lamb, chicken, split pea and veg stews, served just as happily with rice and a fork for those who don't want to get hands-on. The meat is tender, the flavours fragrant and the textures deliciously varied. Regulars drop in through the evening, each time to a rapturous welcome. Service can be slow, and you're seated pretty close to other diners, but that's all the more reason to settle in for the night and make friends.

Babies and children welcome: high chairs. Booking advisable. Separate room for parties, seats 22. Takeaway service. **Map 1 A4.**

South

Brixton

★ Asmara

386 Coldharbour Lane, SW9 8LF (7737 4144). Brixton tube/rail. **Dinner served** 5.30-11.30pm daily. **Main courses** £7.20-£9.80. **Set meal** £30 (2 people) vegetarian, £32 (2 people) meat. **Credit** MC, V. Eritrean

This low-key Brixton café – named after the capital of Eritrea – is bedecked in Eritrean artwork and table mats, and has a central bar. There's a second storey to accommodate big parties, but it's fair to point out we were the only diners in the restaurant for most of the meal, although friends and relatives of the staff did drop in. Service was smiling and attentive; the food satisfying rather than spectacular. Highlights included a beautifully spiced spinach and cottage cheese starter, smooth lentil mash, and chicken with red onions in spiced ghee – a succulent departure from the spicy stews that make up the bulk of the menu. Portions are generous, and everything is served on sour injera

pancake – although there's a good range of rice and couscous dishes as sides too. Ice-cold Castel beer was a good foil for the food, and while desserts are absent from the menu, there are fragrant teas and coffee to round off the evening. If you're looking for a comprehensive introduction to Eritrean dining then Asmara might not be the answer, but as a tasty neighbourhood local, it does the job nicely.
Babies and children welcome: high chairs. Booking advisable. Separate room for parties, seats 35. Takeaway service. Vegan dishes. Vegetarian menu. **Map 22 E2**.

Kennington

Adulis

44-46 Brixton Road, SW9 6BT (7587 0055, www.adulis.co.uk). Oval tube. **Meals served** 4-11pm Mon-Wed; noon-11pm Thur-Sun. **Main courses** £10.95-£13.95. **Credit** MC, V.
Eritrean

Adulis offers a lovely welcome, and is among the more polished of London's African eateries. The room is adorned with authentic art and trinkets, and service is swift and friendly. The restaurant's philosophy is based on the saying, 'Words are sweet, but they never take the place of food.' And while the food (flavoured with herbs and spices imported from Eritrea) takes centre stage, there's a nice buzz to the place even on a relatively quiet Monday night. Communal spiced stews are the mainstay, eaten with injera, a giant sourdough pancake – using your fingers rather than cutlery. To get the most from the abundant choice on offer, go for one of the sharing selections – our platter of vegetable and meat dishes for two could easily have fed a third. Among the highlights were kitfo, beautifully seasoned and buttered chopped beef; awaze tibsi, a potently fiery lamb stew; and timto, a pottage of spiced lentils in olive oil. There's a good list of lagers and wines, but for a more traditional tipple, try miés, a fermented honey wine. Desserts are surprisingly good, but finish with the ritual coffee ceremony. Roasting beans are wafted around the table as a prologue to the drink, which is flavoured with frankincense. Served in small clay cups, this coffee is designed to be savoured.
Babies and children welcome: high chairs. Booking advisable weekends. Separate room for parties, seats 100. Takeaway service.
Map 16 M13.
For branch see index.

Lalibela. See p22.

Menu

Accra or **akara**: bean fritters.
Aloco: fried plantain with hot tomato sauce.
Asaro: yam and sweet potato porridge.
Ayeb or **iab**: fresh yoghurt cheese made from strained yoghurt.
Berbere: an Ethiopian spice mix made with many hot and aromatic spices.
Cassava, **manioc** or **yuca**: a family of coarse roots that are boiled and pounded to make bread and various other farinaceous dishes. There are bitter and sweet varieties (the bitter variety is poisonous until cooked).
Egusi: ground melon seeds, added to stews and soups as a thickening agent.
Froi: fish and shrimp aubergine stew.
Fufu: a stiff pudding of maize or cassava (qv) flour, or pounded yam (qv).
Gari: a solid, heavy pudding made from ground fermented cassava (qv), served with thick soups.
Ground rice: a kind of stiff rice pudding served to accompany soup.
Injera, **enjera** or **enjerra**: a soft, spongy Ethiopian and Eritrean flatbread made with teff/tef (a grain originally from Ethiopia), wheat, barley, oats or cornmeal. Fermented with yeast, it should have a distinct sour tang.
Jollof rice: like a hot, spicy risotto, with tomatoes, onions and (usually) chicken.
Kelewele or **do-do**: fried plantain.
Kenkey: a starchy pudding that's prepared by pounding dried maize and water into a paste, then steaming inside plantain leaves. Usually eaten with meat, fish or vegetable stews.
Moi-moi, **moin-moin** or **moyin moyin**: steamed beancake, served with meat or fish.
Ogbono: a large seed similar to egusi (qv). Although it doesn't thicken as much, it is used in a similar way.
Pepper soup: a light, peppery soup made with either fish or meat.
Shito: a dark red-hot pepper paste from Ghana, made from dried shrimps blended with onions and tomatoes.
Suya: a spicy Nigerian meat kebab.
Tuo or **tuwo**: a stiff rice pudding, sometimes served as rice balls to accompany soup.
Ugba: Nigerian soy beans; also called oil beans.
Waakye: a dish of rice and black-eyed beans mixed with meat or chicken in gravy.
Waatse: rice and black-eyed beans cooked together.
Wot or **we'ts**: a thick, dark sauce made from slowly cooked onions, garlic, butter and spices – an essential component in the aromatic stews of East Africa. **Doro wot**, a stew containing chicken and hard-boiled eggs, is a particularly common dish.

North

Kentish Town

★ Muya NEW

13 Brecknock Road, N7 0BL (3609 0702, www.muyarestaurant.com). Kentish Town tube/rail or Camden Road rail. **Dinner served** 6-11pm Mon-Sat; 6-10pm Sun. **Main courses** £7-£12.95. Ethiopian

On fasting days – and there are no fewer than 250 of them each year – followers of the Ethiopian Orthodox church are required to avoid meat, fish, dairy and eggs. But if the fasting platter at Muya is anything to go by, abstinence need not be a chore. It included spiced lentil purée, boiled spring greens and various other vegetables, all eaten with injera, the crumpet-like spongy bread served with every meal. Decidedly non-vegan is kitfo: lean minced beef, briefly heated in spiced clarified butter and served almost raw, like steak tartare. It came topped with ayib, a ricotta-like soft cheese, and was marvellous. We also enjoyed minchet abish alicha wot, a curry-like dish characterised by turmeric and ginger, which contained beef so finely ground we could almost drink it; and key wot, a spicy stew featuring uncommonly tender lamb. Ethiopian drinks include reliable lagers Castel and St George's, though oenophiles probably won't be impressed by the country's rudimentary wines. A better choice might be tej, a traditional honey mead, which staff said should appear on the menu soon. The two-floored restaurant lacks charisma, and we'd prefer to listen to Mulatu Astatke and the Ethio-jazz luminaries rather than generic background music. However, service was friendly and informative, and the excellent-value food is the equal of anything we've eaten in Addis Ababa.
Map 26 C5.

Queen of Sheba

12 Fortess Road, NW5 2EU (7284 3947, www.thequeenofsheba.co.uk). Kentish Town tube/rail. **Dinner served** 6-11.30pm Mon-Sat; 6-10.30pm Sun. **Main courses** £7-£19.50. **Set meal** £30-£40 (2-3 people). **Credit** MC, V. Ethiopian

The Queen of Sheba is one of two Ethiopian restaurants on Fortess Road, and at first glance you might be tempted to pass it by for the bells and whistles of Lalibela, up the street. But the small, spicily scented café serves consistently good food to devoted locals and curious tourists. Service is cheerful and attentive, with plenty of advice for baffled newcomers and a squirt of sanitiser to prepare you for hands-on eating. Each dish is spooned lovingly on to your plate at the table. Vast helpings of sour, spongy injera come with every meal, used to parcel up the rich stews and transport each bite to your mouth. There's a well-chosen range of the traditional we'ts and t'ibs (sautéed meat or vegetables), with fiery and milder dishes to suit most palates. Two delicious versions of kitfo (Ethiopia's signature steak tartare) are available, and everything from the stews to the side dishes of potatoes, spinach and cottage cheese is richly buttered and beautifully fragranced. Drinks include wine or Ethiopian beer. Forget dessert and instead revel in the heady spiced coffee.

Available for hire. Babies and children welcome: high chairs. Booking advisable Fri, Sat. Takeaway service. Vegan dishes. Vegetarian menu. **Map 26 B4**.

Tufnell Park

Lalibela

137 Fortess Road, NW5 2HR (7284 0600). Tufnell Park tube or bus 134. **Dinner served** 6-10.30pm daily. **Main courses** £10.99-£11.99. **Credit** MC, V. Ethiopian

The joy of Ethiopian dining is often found in the theatre of the meal – and this cosy Tufnell Park favourite, with its two headily scented floors of authentic furniture, pictures and knick-knacks, certainly sets the scene. Service is a little slow and attention to detail has slipped over the years, but devoted locals ensure that Lalibela is still bustling on a Monday night. The vast menu might bewilder a newcomer, but it ticks all the right boxes, with plenty of variations on the traditional meaty stews. Lentils, pumpkin, aubergine and spinach provide tempting vegetarian choices too. Starters of marinated lamb kebabs and battered cauliflower 'butterfly' were tasty enough, if a little heavy-handed, but we enjoyed the main courses more. Bubbling in clay pots beside the table, mushroom and okra wot was rich and fragrantly spiced, while fried fish in a fiery red-pepper sauce tasted delicious (if slightly overcooked) – both were mopped up with stretchy, sour injera flatbread. There's a good range of wine, fruit juices and lager. End your meal with frankincense-laced Ethiopian coffee, heralded by the delicious waft of roasting beans.

Babies and children welcome: high chairs. Booking advisable. Takeaway service. Vegetarian menu. **Map 26 B3**.

Muya

The Americas

NORTH AMERICAN

There's no doubt about it – we can't get enough of the good ol' US of A. London's North American dining scene hasn't been this lively for years. Not only is *Dallas* back on the small screen, but you can hardly turn a corner without the sweet smell of barbecue smoke, or a juicy burger coming off the grill. What's more, standards are on the up, putting dishes that might once have been classed as 'junk food' on to the menus of smart, sexy restaurants. For cooking that's fresh from the 'cue, check out the carnivorous creations from newcomers (and cult favourites) **Duke's Brew & Que**, **Pitt Cue Co** and **Meat Liquor**. No-bookings restaurant **Burger & Lobster** has the best-value crustaceans in town – try the new Soho branch, which is as big as it is buzzy (making waiting times and queues less of an issue). Head to **Spuntino** for NYC-style sliders (that's mini burgers to the uninitiated), or to **Shrimpy's** for a just-this-side-of-the-border sunshine burger (this time, the burger comes filled with deep-fried soft shell crab, with a side of guacamole). Or drop by **Mishkin's** for the closest thing London has to a New York diner.

Central

City

Barbecoa

20 New Change Passage, EC4M 9AG (3005 8555, www.barbecoa.com). St Paul's tube. **Meals served** 11.45am-11pm Mon-Sat; noon-10pm Sun. **Main courses** £16-£65. **Credit** AmEx, MC, V.

There's an industrial feel to this glam shopping-centre restaurant – and we don't just mean its cavernous proportions and metallic faux-factory decor. You can almost sense the purr of the production line that delivers upmarket grills and US-style barbecue dishes from open kitchens to over 200 diners, via a bevy of perma-perky, black-shirted staff. You can also sense the business plan: draw them in with big names (Jamie Oliver and sidekick Adam Perry Lang own the joint), keep turning the tables, price optimistically (bread £5, Sierra Nevada £7) and upsell repeatedly. In return, punters get fantastic views of St Paul's, a proper buzz and some damn good meat dishes – ribs more beef than bone; smoky, savoury pulled pork; and steaks cut from Scottish and Irish beef by the in-house butcher (there's a shop downstairs). Not all dishes were as admirable: a pretty little pink tower of sea bass ceviche lacked flavour; and an otherwise good beetroot salad was overwhelmed by lazily dressed watercress. Of the desserts, only the peanut butter sundae – topped by popcorn and accompanied by a saucer of salt caramel – delivered a wow factor. On a Saturday night, the largely out-of-town, special-occasion customers were lapping it all up.

Available for hire. Babies and children welcome: high chairs; nappy-changing facilities. Booking advisable. Disabled: lift; toilet. Separate room for parties, seats 50. Tables outdoors (4, terrace). **Map 11 P6**.

Bodean's

16 Byward Street, EC3R 5BA (7488 3883, www.bodeansbbq.com). Tower Hill tube. **Meals served** noon-11pm Mon-Sat; noon-10.30pm Sun. **Main courses** £6.75-£19.95. **Credit** AmEx, MC, V.

With the recent proliferation of new pits on the block, it's easy to forget that Bodean's was once the capital's first and only destination for authentic US barbecue. Our visit to the Tower Hill branch proved this small chain is still serious about the smoke. We recommend bypassing the more pedestrian burgers, hotdogs and steaks and heading straight for the barbecued food, a sharing platter being the most efficient way to savour the array of smoked meats offered. The beauty of US barbecue is the regional subtleties that vary state to state, so as well as a plate piled high with pulled pork and baby back ribs, we also enjoyed 'burnt ends', or beef brisket, a tradition of Kansas City cooking. A standout helping of Jacob Ladder ribs saw the caramelised outer bark yielding to meltingly tender beef beneath. Furnished in the same playful decor as other outlets, this basement branch is a mix of hog-shaped door knobs, antler candelabras and luxe black leather banquettes. The ground-floor bar features an extensive list of Stateside beer and cocktails, with an emphasis on bourbon and American whiskies.

Available for hire. Babies and children welcome: children's menu; high chairs, nappy-changing facilities.. Booking advisable. Separate room for parties, seat 16. Takeaway service. **Map 12 R7**.
For branches see index.

Covent Garden

Christopher's

18 Wellington Street, WC2E 7DD (7240 4222, www.christophersgrill.com). Covent Garden tube.
Bar **Open/meals served** 11.30am-midnight Mon-Wed; 11.30am-1.30am Sat; 11.30am-10.30pm Sun.
Restaurant **Lunch served** noon-3pm Mon-Fri. **Brunch served** 11.30am-3pm Sat, Sun. **Dinner served** 5-11.30pm Mon-Sat; 5-9.30pm Sun.
Both **Main courses** £16.95-£39.95. **Set meal** (5-7pm Mon-Sat) £16.95 2 courses, £21.50 3 courses. **Credit** AmEx, MC, V.

Mishkin's

London's first licensed casino once occupied this site, but now your best bet is steak – high-quality USDA prime cuts from Nebraskan cattle, in fact. Add to the mix a menu featuring Maine lobsters and a martini list as long as your arm and there's more than a touch of Manhattan about this grand Covent Garden grill. American classics are open to interpretation at Christopher's. A cobb salad was a delicate construction of leaves, crisp bacon, blue cheese and avocado, rather than the hearty rustic portions you'd find stateside. Our pork belly and boston baked beans came flecked with cubes of feta, the tangy cheese tempering the heat of the spice-rubbed meat. The restaurant's location is enviable: a mere curtain call away from some of London's busiest West End shows, making this an attractive option for pre- and post-theatre dining. The menu offers five choices per course. We were impressed with a starter of cod cake featuring a punchy harissa rémoulade, and a main of barbecue-rubbed bavette: a cheaper cut of beef made tender by 100-day ageing. The striking dining room, all high ceilings and sweeping staircases, adds to the sense of occasion.

Available for hire. Babies and children welcome: children's menu; high chairs. Booking advisable. Separate room for parties, seats 40. **Map 18 F4.**

Joe Allen

13 Exeter Street, WC2E 7DT (7836 0651, www.joeallen.co.uk). Covent Garden tube.
Breakfast served 8-11.30am Mon-Fri. **Meals served** noon-12.30am Mon-Fri; 11.30am-12.30am Sat; 11.30am-11.30pm Sun. **Brunch served** 11.30am-4pm Sat, Sun. **Main courses** £9.50-£22.50. **Set brunch** £19.50 2 courses, £21.50 3 courses incl drink. **Set meal** (noon-3pm Mon-Fri, 5-6.45pm Mon-Sat) £16 2 courses, £18 3 courses. **Credit** AmEx, MC, V.

An old trouper that is much loved by thespians and theatregoers, Joe Allen is sadly showing its age. Not on the surface, mind: the classic brick-wall basement rooms hung with show posters look as good as ever. But the quality of the food now lags far behind what is available elsewhere in London, and the prices aren't particularly cheap. Barbecue spare ribs, served with basmati rice and black-eyed peas, and a (tasty) corn muffin can be bettered at any number of places, and the famed (off-menu) house burger was a mean, overdone portion; a generous pile of chips kept hunger at bay. Also strictly portioned was a crab and avocado starter; more substantial was a comforting bowl of black-bean soup. Baked cheesecake proved the final straw: claggy in texture, and tasting mainly of cheese. The short wine list comes on a laminated sheet. Staff range from on-the-ball to can't-be-bothered. One for loyal fans and night owls only – at least until the kitchen ups its game.

Babies and children welcome: booster seats; high chairs. Booking advisable. Entertainment: pianist 9pm-1am Mon-Sat. Tables outdoors (2, pavement). **Map 18 E4.**

★ Mishkin's NEW

25 Catherine Street, WC2B 5JS (7240 2078, www.mishkins.co.uk). Covent Garden tube.
Meals served 11am-11.30pm Mon-Sat; noon-10.30pm Sun. **Main courses** £3-£12. **Credit** AmEx, DC, MC, V.

Another hot destination from restaurateurs Richard Beatty and Russell Norman (of Spuntino and Polpo acclaim), this 1950s-themed New York diner has a Jewish-accented menu, minus the kosher ingredients. The look is suitably weathered; a half-window net-curtain frontage offers a peek on to the U-shaped bar, manned by clued-up young staff. Formica table-tops, banquettes, bare brick walls, and a tiled black and white floor add to the retro vibe. The menu is divided into sandwiches, meatballs, all-day brunch and supper choices, salads, sides and extras. Expect the likes of juicy meatballs, bagels, salt beef, latkes, schnitzels and mom's-own desserts. Un-Jewish, but lovely, our big fat pork hot dog was much appreciated for its meaty goodness, its tumble of sauerkraut and its vinegary jalapeños. Slider burgers of dinky steamed beef patties, piled high with squidgy fried onions and melted cheese, were equally satisfying – a light-bite respite from the enormous dimensions of sandwiches and hot dogs. Sadly, our salt beef sandwich, although crammed with juicy, tender meat, was let down by an overdose of abrasive lip-tingling salt. Despite such occasional glitches, Mishkin is a lively venue with attitude aplenty.

Babies and children admitted. Booking advisable. **Map 18 E4.**

King's Cross

Shrimpy's NEW

2012 RUNNER-UP BEST NEW DESIGN

The King's Cross Filling Station, Goods Way, N1C 4UR (8880 6111, www.shrimpys.co.uk). King's Cross or St Pancras tube/rail. **Meals served** 11am-10.30pm daily. **Main courses** £15-£20. **Credit** AmEx, MC, V.

Shrimpy's is run by Pablo Flack and David Waddington (of Bistrotheque, *see p102*) and occupies a former filling station destined for demolition in 2014. A makeover has enhanced the modernist look by shielding it from road traffic with rippling sheets of translucent fibreglass. On one

side is the Regent's Canal. The interior is a small, sleek dining room and bar counter; cartoonish artwork on the walls evokes mid 20th-century Americana. The menu pays homage to down-home food, yet is quite unlike it. A glazed burger bun filled with deep-fried soft-shell crab had crunch, the aroma of the fryer, and a slight seafood taste. Meaty-textured monkfish was slightly scorched by the grill, the pallid flesh offset by crimson rings of radish and zipped up with lemon and chilli. Less successful were the starters; salt-cod croquettes were mush-filled and oddly shaped, though we liked the accompanying aïoli. And the 'Peruvian ceviche' was lacklustre; our waiter couldn't tell us what fish was used, and the dominant flavours were of lime and raw onion. So, the cooking is good rather than great, and prices aren't cheap, but what makes this two-year pop-up a destination diner is the striking design and the undeniable cool factor.
Babies and children admitted. Booking advisable. Disabled: toilet. **Map 4 L2.**

Marylebone

★ Meat Liquor NEW

2012 RUNNER-UP BEST NEW MEAT RESTAURANT
74 Welbeck Street, W1G 0BA (7224 4239, www.meatliquor.com). Bond Street tube.
Meals served noon-11pm Mon-Thur; noon-1am Fri, Sat. **Main courses** £3-£8. **Credit** MC, V.

What is perhaps currently London's hippest restaurant was opened by Yianni Papoutsis after he'd spent a few years driving his Meat Wagon mobile grill around town. Along with his famed burgers, it serves up a serious side order of attitude. Wires dangle from the ceiling, walls are violently graffitied, it's eerily dark and grungy, and the rockabilly/hillbilly/garage is turned up loud. It would be a distressing environment for elderly relatives – but if granny loves a good burger, there's no better place in London to get one. Yianni has clearly done his research into the underrated artform that is the US hamburger: everything, down to the enamel tin it's served on, is pitch-perfect. Patties are 100% beef, topped with additions such as pickles, cheese, red onions, chilli or the secret 'dead hippie' sauce, and served in a glazed bun. Other dishes include sweet and spicy buffalo wings, fried pickles (very Deep South),

Shrimpy's

coleslaw and chilli dogs: kitchen roll is provided to compensate for the lack of cutlery – and you'll need it. The attention-deficit decor is not to some people's taste, and staff can sometimes appear aloof. But Meat Liquor is good value (a cheeseburger costs £6.50) and the closest you'll get to a down 'n' dirty diner without crossing the Atlantic.
Bookings not accepted. Children admitted before 6pm. Disabled: toilet. **Map 9 H6.**

Soho

★ Burger & Lobster Soho NEW

2012 RUNNER-UP BEST NEW NO BOOKINGS RESTAURANT

36 Dean Street, W1D 4PS (7432 4800, www.burgerandlobster.com). Leicester Square, Oxford Circus or Tottenham Court Road tube. **Meals served** noon-10.30pm Mon-Sat; noon-10pm Sun. **Main courses** £20. **Credit** AmEx, MC, V.

Proof that less can be more, the late 2011 launch of Burger & Lobster, with its no-nonsense, three-item menu of burger, lobster, or lobster roll, was a runaway hit. This second branch – a large Soho diner tricked out with lobster-red banquettes – is no less popular, with all the seats on our midweek visit occupied and a loud, jaunty atmosphere. While it's possible for groups or lunchtimers to book, this joint is geared towards walk-ins, with a clipboard waiting list and a cocktail bar for loitering. Food costs £20, an all-in price that includes a huge carton of thin-cut fries and even a side salad: you won't go hungry here. Our burger, cooked medium-rare as requested, came classically filled with lettuce, tomato and red onion, plus thick-cut bacon and a melted square of processed cheese. It's pretty good, but for ultimate value, choose the lobster. We had ours in the shell: a 1lb whole crustacean, first steamed, then grilled, for a terrific balance of subtle sweetness with just a lick of smoke. For an extra £10, you can upgrade to a whopping two-pounder, but we prefer to leave room for a sweet treat: the Snickers-in-a-tub pud saw rich chocolate mousse layered on to a devilish peanut-studded salt caramel. Cheery staff smooth the ride along.
Available for hire. Babies and children admitted. Booking advisable. Disabled: toilet. Tables outdoors (2, pavement). **Map 17 B3.**
For branch see index.

Pitt Cue Co NEW

2012 RUNNER-UP BEST NEW MEAT RESTAURANT

1 Newburgh Street, W1F 7RB (7287 5578, www.pittcue.co.uk). Oxford Circus tube. **Lunch served** noon-3pm, **dinner served** 6-10pm Mon-Sat. **Main courses** £9.50-£16. **Credit** MC, V.

Not long after the peripatetic Meateasy laid down roots and moved into a West End restaurant, Pitt Cue Co did the same. After spending the summer of 2011 serving superlative US-inspired dishes such as pulled pork, ribs and smoked brisket from a van, it moved into a tiny space in Soho. The dining room has space for about 20 people, and there are also a few stools around the bar area – so if you don't want to queue, avoid the busiest times. Many London restaurants take their cues from the Deep South these days, but few do it as well as Pitt Cue. The meaty ribs are unparalleled: a flavour-packed dry rub and a long, long smoking renders them dark, sweet and intense, bringing to mind steamy nights in those southern states where barbecue

Meat Liquor. See p25.

THE AMERICAS

Burger & Lobster Soho. See p27.

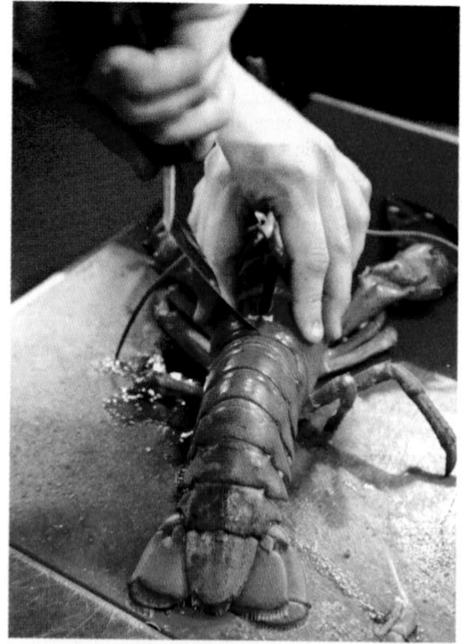

is a way of life. Other slow-cooked meats don't disappoint either – pulled pork is superb in a roll and is made even more indulgent with a jar of bone marrow mash; more unusual is the 'house sausage', chargrilled slices of a giant meat tube far removed from British bangers. Additions such as baked beans with pork, chipotle slaw and crunchy pickles are spot-on. To drink, there are cocktails made with American rye whiskey and bottled Kernal ale.
Babies and children admitted. Bookings not accepted. Takeaway service. **Map 17 A3.**

★ Spuntino HOT 50

61 Rupert Street, W1D 7PW (no phone, www.spuntino.co.uk). Leicester Square or Piccadilly Circus tube. **Meals served** 11am-midnight Mon-Sat; noon-11pm Sun. **Main courses** £5.50-£10. **Credit** AmEx, MC, V.
At lunchtime at least, the long queues that used to discourage visits to this no-phone, no-bookings and not-exactly-large retro American joint have dissipated. The lovely tiles behind the bar are original to the premises, a former butcher's shop, which partly alleviates the feeling you're in a theme restaurant: a carefully constructed London take on a New York take on road-food and Italian classics. In fact, you get some rather good-value (for the area), good-hearted cooking. Eggs receive a rare moment in the limelight: soft-boiled, on lentil and anchovy crostini; truffled, on toast; with soldiers; and in the best french toast this side of Chicago (if you like it sugar-sticky). Sliders amp up the flavour; pulled pork inauthentically but deliciously packs in crackling and pickled apple; bone marrow infiltrates ground beef. The fried chicken also holds more interest than it would down home. There are decent salads and desserts and 'plates' that include the no frills (mac 'n' cheese) and the more cultured (good mackerel, saffron and broad beans). Eat at stools at the bar (witness enthusiastic staff at play) or counters at the back (there are no tables as such).
Babies and children admitted. Bookings not accepted. **Map 17 B4.**

West

Westbourne Park

★ Lucky 7

127 Westbourne Park Road, W2 5QL (7727 6771, www.lucky7london.co.uk). Royal Oak or Westbourne Park tube. **Meals served** noon-10.30pm Mon; 10am-10.30pm Tue-Thur; 9am-11pm Fri, Sat; 9am-10.30pm Sun. **Main courses** £6.95-£12.95. **Credit** MC, V.
Tom Conran's small but well-rounded Lucky 7 plays homage to the American diner in miniature. With seating limited to six oversized vinyl booths, every inch of the remaining space is filled with chrome fittings, vintage advertising and kitsch Americana. In true diner form, there's a big emphasis on breakfast, with buttermilk pancakes, eggs 'any style' and Tex-Mex huevos rancheros. Taking a cue from our napkins, which illustrated how to build 'The perfect Lucky 7 hamburger', we

plumped for the bacon blue cheese and green chilli cheese burgers, served with ready-to-assemble slices of beef tomato, onion, pickles, lettuce and coleslaw on the side. Like our surroundings, we packed as much into the available space as physically possible. A triumph of engineering as much as taste, the burgers were glorious, the 100% Aberdeen Angus patties juicy and well seasoned. Doughnut-sized onion rings, XXX thick shakes and banana splits continue the 'big is beautiful' theme in this bijou spot. After 6pm a cocktail menu is available alongside a small selection of American beers. A concession to the 'no bookings' policy is the takeaway service, well loved by locals and doing brisk trade on our visit.
Babies and children welcome: children's menu. Bookings not accepted. Takeaway service.
Map 7 A5.

North East
Haggerston

Duke's Brew & Que NEW
2012 RUNNER-UP BEST NEW MEAT RESTAURANT
33 Downham Road, N1 5AA (3006 0795, www.dukesjoint.com). Haggerston rail. **Open** 4pm-midnight Mon-Fri; 10am-midnight Sat; 10am-11pm Sun. **Brunch served** 10am-3.30pm Sat; 11am-3.30pm Sun. **Dinner served** 6-11pm Mon-Fri; 6-10.30pm Sat; 5-10pm Sun. **Main courses** £10-£27. **Credit** AmEx, MC, V.
Barbecue in the 'burbs? Why not – the success of this slice of the Deep South in De Beauvoir Town shows that London is more than ready for a more sophisticated take on the food of the US. A former pub has been kitted out with some serious smoking equipment imported from Oklahoma and a brewing kit, resulting in the ribs 'n' beer combo so often seen in the southern states but, until recently, rare here. The menu is short: beef and pork ribs, pulled pork sliders, steak, burger. The side orders are authentic: baked beans with pork, thin fries, deep-fried pickles, mac 'n' cheese. It's all served on metal trays, which is deemed fashionable in London but is merely commonplace in the US. And the meats are as good as you could hope for. The burger and steak are decent, but make the most of the kitchen's smoking expertise and go for the ribs – charred, sticky, sweet, spiced, tender, liable to collapse from their bone at the faintest of forkings. Sliders are great too; the slightly sweet mini burger buns are stuffed with strands of slow-cooked pork, a deep-fried pickle and a blob of coleslaw. The 'brew' side of the name is properly done too. Duke's houses the fledgling Beavertown Brewery, which makes three beers; bottled beers include London breweries Meantime and Kernal as well as Chicago's Goose Island and Maryland's Flying Dog.
Available for hire. Babies and children admitted. Booking advisable. Disabled: toilet. Tables outdoors (5, pavement). **Map 6 R1.**

North
Islington

North Pole NEW
188-190 New North Road, N1 7BJ (7354 5400, www.thenorthpolepub.co.uk). Angel tube or Essex Road or Haggerston rail. **Open** 11am-11pm

Pitt Cue Co. See p27.

THE AMERICAS

Mon-Thur; 11am-midnight Fri, Sat; 11am-10.30pm Sun. **Meals served** noon-10pm Mon-Sat; noon-9pm Sun. **Main courses** £7-£14.50. **Credit** AmEx, MC, V.

After a brief spell as the North Star, this pub has reclaimed its original Victorian name and relaunched with an of-the-moment menu of real ale, craft beer and sweet, smoky US barbecue cooking (from pulled pork, ribs, and burgers to more snacky chicken wings, mac 'n' cheese and sliders). Our pulled pork roll, served with fries and coleslaw, was done well, but drinks here are done even better. Eight real ales and two ciders are on tap, including Fyne Ales's Jarl and Monty's Sunshine from Mid Wales. Choosing is made harder by the 12 beers on keg (London Fields Unfiltered Lager was there, as were representatives from Meantime, Anchor and Flying Dog). In a neat and welcome touch, bottles are available to drink in or take away with the lids on, at decent prices. Among the 20-odd on offer, standouts are Left Hand's superb Milk Stout, Anchor's Pepe Nero, brewed with black pepper, and several from cult Norwegian brewery Nogne Ø. Design-wise it will offend nobody, treading a path between gastropub and plain old pub. It's a big place, with a smart outdoor area sheltered from the busy New North Road.

Babies and children welcome: children's menu; high chairs. Tables outdoors (10, garden). Takeaway service. **Map 5 P1**.

North West

Kensal Rise

The Diner

64-66 Chamberlayne Road, NW10 3JJ (8968 9033, www.goodlifediner.com). Kensal Green or Kensal Rise tube. **Meals served** 11am-10pm Mon-Thur; 9am-11pm Fri, Sat; 9am-10pm Sun. **Main courses** £5.20-£15. **Credit** MC, V.

With its brand of crowd-pleasing American nourishment and family-friendly venues, the Diner has quietly branched out into five locations across town, one of the latest and largest occupying a prime spot on Kensal Rise's Chamberlayne Road. Our spring bank holiday visit saw groups of hungover locals and young families soaking up the sunshine on the sizeable front terrace and in the back garden. Inside, the decor, unsurprisingly, takes a cue from the restaurant's name: all spring-loaded napkin dispensers, vintage lamps and red banquettes. Don't expect to order in a hurry: there's a dizzying list of breakfasts, sandwiches, burgers, Mexican dishes and 'blue plate specials' to get through. We tested the American credentials with a shrimp po' boy, and this New Orleans staple translated well: deep-fried prawns in spicy mayo encased in a soft baguette. Western eggs came scrambled with a mix of peppers, cheese and bacon next to a portion of cubed home fries. Milkshakes are the stuff of teen B-movie dreams, served both in a glass and the ice-cold steel mixing-cup for extra top-ups. Over-18s refreshments include an impressive selection of American craft beers and booze-spiked 'hard shakes'.

Babies and children welcome: children's menu; high chair; nappy-changing facilities. Booking advisable. Disabled: toilet. Tables outdoors (7, garden; 4, terrace). Takeaway service.

For branches see index.

Duke's Brew & Que. See p29.

LATIN AMERICAN

If past years have been about Mexico, this is Peru's time to shine. Take yourself on a journey of exploration: from the weird and wonderful creations cooked up at **Lima London** (eco-dried potato stew, anyone?) to the more traditional offerings of **Tierra Peru**. Not forgetting, of course, the restaurant named after the dish of the moment: **Ceviche** (here, there are seven versions vying for your attention). City slickers with deep pockets will love **Sushisamba**, where the raw fish sits cheek-by-jowl with cooking from Peru and Brazil; the views, from the 38th floor of the City's brand-new Heron Tower, are tremendous. Elsewhere on the continent (and notably more casual) is **La Bodegra Negra**, a speakeasy-style Mexican restaurant with two entrances – one family-friendly, the other styled as the door to a sex shop. But it's not just the newcomers that deserve praise; great Argentinian steaks can be found at long-running neighbourhood joints **Buenos Aires Café** in Blackheath and **Santa Maria del Sur** in Battersea.

Central

City

Sushisamba NEW

2012 RUNNER-UP BEST NEW LATIN AMERICAN RESTAURANT

Floors 38 & 39, Heron Tower, 110 Bishopsgate, EC2N 4AY (3640 7330, www.sushisamba.com). Liverpool Street tube/rail. **Lunch served** 11.30am-2.30pm, **dinner served** 5.30-11pm daily. **Main courses** £4-£24. **Credit** AmEx, MC, V. Japanese/Peruvian/Brazilian

A Japanese-Brazilian-Peruvian restaurant may seem like a fusion too far, but there's logic to the Latin American mash-up. Peru and Brazil have large Japanese immigrant populations, and Sushisamba is Japanese food viewed through a South American prism. As well as sushi and sashimi there are South American ceviches (ours was fresh, light and tongue-zappingly zingy). Eggplant with mustard miso, cooked on a big robata grill that's as Japanese as it is South American, was similar to Japanese nasu dengaku (fried aubergine topped with miso) but with a South American accent; pleasantly, smokily umami-ish. Elsewhere the menu is peppered with Peruvian ingredients such as quinoa salad and large-kernelled Peruvian corn. Brazilian dishes get a look-in with churrasco, a big beefy barbecue. Moqueca, seafood stew with bright orange dende (palm) oil, enriched with coconut milk, was missing the crunchy farofa (toasted manioc) that's considered essential in Brazil, but was a respectable version. A Roald Dahl-esque great glass elevator whisks diners from the ground floor to the 38th with stomach-churning speed, and the views across London are so breathtaking that we had difficulty keeping our attention from straying horizon-ward. The big downer with Sushisamba, though, is the sky-high prices.

Available for hire. Babies and children welcome: high chairs. Booking essential. Disabled: lift; toilet. **Map 12 R6.**

Fitzrovia

Gaucho Charlotte Street

60A Charlotte Street, W1T 2NU (7580 6252, www.gauchorestaurants.co.uk). Goodge Street or Tottenham Court Road tube. **Meals served** noon-11pm Mon-Sat; noon-10.30pm Sun. **Main courses** £15.95-£52.50. **Credit** AmEx, MC, V. Argentinian

You don't want to feel herded at an Argentinian steak restaurant. Thankfully, despite the huge dining area and familiar cow-skin decor, this branch of the Gaucho chain maintains a personal, attentive touch. Front-of-house staff look after coats, while waiters describe the steaks with the gory aid of a board topped with raw examples. A pre-starter of complimentary rustic bread augured well for the meat; it was plain-looking but big on flavour. To follow, each portion of a ceviche sampler (prawn, trout, mackerel) was two mouthfuls at most. Beautifully presented, it was a feast primarily for the eyes. Empanadas were good but seemed overpriced. For the main event, an easy chewing bife de cuadril (rump) was superior to the more expensive bife de ancho (ribeye) in both taste and texture. Each cut can be cranked up in weight – a popular option with the expense-account diners that Gaucho attracts. Accompaniments were variable: chimichurri sauce was bland and leafy, more suited to bread dipping than as an accompaniment to grilled meat; however, chips were good, a side dish of tenderstem broccoli in wasabi dressing was cooked just-so, and the flavours of a tomato salad were robust.

Available for hire. Babies and children welcome: high chairs. Booking advisable. Disabled: lift; toilet. Dress: smart casual. Separate room for parties, seats 10. **Map 3 J5.**

For branches see index.

★ Lima London NEW

2012 WINNER BEST NEW LATIN AMERICAN RESTAURANT

31 Rathbone Place, W1T 1JH (3002 2640, www.limalondon.com). Tottenham Court Road tube. **Lunch served** noon-2.30pm, **dinner served** 5.30-10.30pm Mon-Sat. **Main courses** £16-£22. **Set lunch** (Mon-Fri) £20 3 courses. **Credit** AmEx, DC, MC, V. Peruvian

When pundits began heralding Peruvian food as the next big thing, we were sceptical, but the PR bandwagon has turned out to be a showcase for a cuisine that deserves recognition – and Lima London is our pick of Peru. The space is understated and becalmed, but the menu reads like a collection of food haikus, and the dishes crafted by chef Virgilio Martinez look like Modernist works of art. Artichokes with green lime, fava beans, tree tomato emulsion and molle pink pepper turns out to be a beauty of a dish, as impressive for its bold appearance as for its vibrant flavours. Sweet, sharp and hot are the defining tastes here, and they work as brilliant counterpoints to the soft texture and bland flavour of avocado, corn – and potatoes. Potatoes, arguably Peru's gift to humanity, figure large but in surprising guises. Eco-dried potato stew (in the Andes, a natural 'freeze-drying' process is used to preserve the tubers over the harsh winters) was spiced with chilli and topped with a grating of bittersweet chocolate. We took another leap into the unknown with cured sliced duck breast with algarrobo honey (with an intense, savoury taste), shaved foie gras and sharp-tasting little leaves called ghoa cress. The dish was a stunner, its sweet-savoury interplay enhanced with the crunch of sea salt. Lima London left us scratching our heads slightly, reaching for our dictionaries – but vowing to come back for more.

Available for hire. Babies and children welcome: high chairs. Booking advisable. Tables outdoors (4, pavement). Vegan dishes. **Map 17 B2.**

Mestizo

103 Hampstead Road, NW1 3EL (7387 4064, www.mestizomx.com). Warren Street tube or Euston tube/rail. **Meals served** noon-11pm Mon-Sat. **Lunch served** noon-4pm, **dinner served** 5-10pm Sun. **Main courses** £10-£24. **Credit** AmEx, MC, V. Mexican

Mestizo seems to be aimed slightly upmarket from London's spicy fast-food norm for Mexican restaurants. For instance, it offers a few relatively uncommon dishes – the nopales (cactus) taco, say – and a prodigious list of premium tequilas. However, Saturday night is party time, with fake sombreros and obligatory shots for birthday girls, and the silliest of mainstream Mexican 'folk' culture (cheesy costume dances) on TVs at the back. After a punchy frozen 'classic' margarita and an equally successful cucumber variety, we were set to enjoy the forced bonhomie. Sadly, neither the try-hard service (four waiters buzzed around during a short meal), nor the flavours from the surprisingly extensive menu impressed. To start, empanadas – effectively four fried pancakes, containing potato, cheese, mushroom and sweetcorn, and a vegetable mush – were little more than beer fodder. Next, both mole poblano (chicken breast in the classic Mexican sauce) and tamarind shrimp had little fire, perhaps neutered to appeal to a broader clientele. A deeply smoky salsa roja with the empanadas, and the fine beans that accompanied the mole, suggested things could have been better. Service was good too; even under pressure, the staff stayed enthusiastic.

Available for hire. Babies and children welcome: high chairs. Booking advisable weekends. Disabled: toilet. Separate room for parties, seats 60. Takeaway service. **Map 3 J3.**

Holborn

Bull Steak Expert NEW

54 Red Lion Street, WC1R 4PD (7242 0708, www.thebullsteakexpert.com). Holborn tube. **Lunch served** noon-3pm Mon-Fri. **Dinner served** 5.30-10pm Mon-Fri; 5.30-10.30pm Sat.

Sushisamba. See p31.

Main courses £16-£38. **Set meal** £27 3 courses. **Credit** AmEx, MC, V. Argentinian

The slightly clumsy name of this Argentinian restaurant was presumably given to avoid confusion with the dozens of pubs called 'the Bull'. No matter – it's the only thing that jars at this steak specialist. Rump, cooked on a custom grill, arrived rare as requested, the outside nicely browned, the interior tender, with the meat full-flavoured and well-seasoned. Order steak, and that's all you'll get. Golden-hued, crisp chips are listed as a side dish, as is chimichurri sauce. A steak burger was similarly spartan: no bun, just a patty of moist beef, though this dish did at least come with a slice of cheese, and chips on the side. The brief menu lists other Argentinian dishes: empanadas with crisp pastry encasing well-spiced minced beef, or sweetcorn centres that really are sweet. Sweetcorn is also pounded and wrapped in corn husk and grilled to give a surprisingly light side dish. Desserts include flan, the Spanish version of crème caramel. The Bull is a simply decorated place – the colour scheme of blood-red and black only subtly suggests Argentina – that lacks pretension and provides solicitous, prompt service.

Available for hire. Babies and children admitted. Booking advisable. Separate room for parties, seats 22-28. **Map 10 M5**.

Marble Arch

Casa Malevo

23 Connaught Street, W2 2AY (7402 1988, www.casamalevo.com). Marble Arch tube.
Lunch served noon-2.30pm Mon-Fri. **Brunch served** noon-3.30pm Sat, Sun. **Dinner served** 6-10.30pm daily. **Main courses** £17-£24. **Set lunch** £14.99 2 courses, £16.99 3 courses. **Credit** AmEx, DC, MC, V. Argentinian

We were surprised to be told by our sparky, smartly turned-out waitress that Casa Malevo means 'house of the nasty man': there's nothing nasty about this little restaurant. Notwithstanding wall-mounted monochrome pictures of gauchos and a soundtrack of melancholy accordion and violin, the place feels like a continental brasserie, its dark bentwood furniture nicely spaced around a central bar – but the food is pure Latin America. From the good-value set lunch, we tucked into an empanada whose crisp, flaky pastry encased an unctuous mix of sweetcorn, shallots and mozzarella; a delicious rump steak (all steaks are imported from Argentina, hence, due to EU restrictions, served off the bone) with slab-sized chips and a couple of interesting Argentinian sauces; and 'flan casero' (like crème caramel) with dulce de leche. On a return visit, we might finish with 'cheese of the day' with membrillo and oatcakes. Our à la carte choices were even better: British lamb chops grilled slowly to tenderness in their own fat; thick but exquisitely soft beef carpaccio given fruitiness by lemon and lively green olives; and a handsomely dressed salad of rocket, garlic, onions, red pepper and parmesan shavings. That name? It's just a famous tango.

Available for hire. Babies and children welcome: high chairs. Booking advisable. Separate room for parties, seats 12. Tables outdoors (3, pavement). **Map 8 F6**.

Pimlico

Rodizio Preto

72 Wilton Road, SW1V 1DE (7233 8668, www.rodiziopreto.co.uk). Victoria tube/rail.
Meals served noon-10.30pm Mon-Thur; noon-11pm Fri, Sat; noon-10pm Sun. **Buffet** £19.95 (£14.95 vegetarian). **Credit** AmEx, MC, V. Brazilian

Restaurant-rich Wilton Road is thronged with people browsing for dinner. The hook that brings them to Preto is rodízio. The genius lies in the meal's simplicity: *passadors* (servers) will keep bringing you meat until you tell them to stop. The no-messing-around vibe is echoed by the restaurant's graphics, with a menu featuring a toucan (that's South America) superimposed over Tower Bridge (that's London). It has ten pages of drinks and just two explaining the food: £14.95 for access to the buffet and salad counters, or £19.95 for the same plus a ton of meat. We asked if many people opt for the former. 'Vegetarians', came the reply. In fact, there's plenty that is meat-free here, from deep-fried cassava (mandioca frita) to Brazilian cheese breads (pão de queijo) and plentiful salads. Sit on the leafy pavement terrace or in the smart interior and prepare for the many-pronged (and skewered) meat attack. Up to a dozen types are brought to the table on rotation. Highlights were alcatra (top sirloin) and chicken hearts. Less moreish was the cupim, with its near-flabby texture; described here as 'neck', it is traditionally the hump of zebu cattle. At weekends, Preto also serves an excellent feijoada stew.

Babies and children welcome: children's menu; high chairs; nappy-changing facilities. Booking advisable weekends. Tables outdoors (7, pavement). Vegetarian menu. **Map 15 J10**.
For branches see index.

Soho

La Bodega Negra NEW

2012 RUNNER-UP BEST NEW LATIN AMERICAN RESTAURANT
2012 RUNNER-UP BEST NEW DESIGN

16 Moor Street, W1D 5NH (7758 4100, www.labodeganegra.com). Leicester Square tube.
Café-bar **Open** noon-1am Mon-Sat; noon-11.30pm Sun. **Meals served** noon-midnight Mon-Sat; noon-11pm Sun. **Main courses** £8-£12.
Restaurant-bar **Open** 6pm-1am Mon-Sat; 6-11.30pm Sun. **Meals served** 6pm-midnight Mon-Sat; 6-10.30pm Sun. **Main courses** £12-£16.
Both **Credit** AmEx, MC, V. Mexican

Beneath a lurid Soho shopfront, ablaze with neon signs screeching 'sex shop', is a new transatlantic import – the London outpost of the NYC-based La Esquina, an ultra-trendy downtown café-taqueria. As at La Esquina, La Bodega Negra is an upstairs-downstairs affair; the ground-level café (entrance on Moor Street) serves tacos, tostaditas and quesadillas, and mains such as huevos rancheros (ranch-style eggs) with black beans. The downstairs restaurant and bar (entrance in Old Compton Street) is where the main action happens. The underground space is like a Hammer Horror interpretation of a Mexican Day of the Dead fiesta, all dark alcoves and low lighting, with a few phantasmagorical artworks in the reservations-only bar area. As in the café, there's a selection of tacos (our prawn and jicama version, in a crunchy, flavourful shell, was properly punchy) and tostaditas (such as moreish tuna with smoky chipotle and avocado). The menu extends to mains such as steaks and grills, and nicely spiced chicken paillard with pumpkin seeds, served with a green moat of pumpkin seed oil. The food is more akin to Mexican-American. And it's spicy; many of the hundreds of types of chilli in Mexico put in an appearance here – raw in feisty salsas and slow-cooked in stews. The well-made margaritas make good tongue-tamers and fans of Mexican spirits will be in awe of the impressive list of tequilas and mezcals.

Bookings not accepted café; bookings essential restaurant. Children admitted (café). Disabled: toilet (café). Separate rooms for parties (restaurant), seating 30-50. **Map 17 C3.**

Ceviche NEW

2012 RUNNER-UP BEST NEW LATIN AMERICAN RESTAURANT

17 Frith Street, W1D 4RG (7292 2040, www.cevicheuk.com). Leicester Square tube. **Tapas served** noon-11.30pm Mon-Sat; noon-10.30pm Sun. **Tapas** £6.75-£13.50. **Credit** AmEx, MC, V. Peruvian

Corn, potatoes and the signature dish of ceviche – raw citrus-marinated fish (or veg), served here in seven versions – are the stars of the menu. Peruvian food may be terra incognita for many Londoners, but the country's indigenous ingredients provide common ground – even if the bar snack of cancha (large, crunchy corn kernels) bears little relationship to the more-familiar tender yellow sweetcorn niblets. Corn also finds its way into an 'alianca Lima' ceviche, along with sea bass, octopus, prawns and mussels with red onion and coriander, all held together with chilli-spiked lime juice, which 'cooks' the fish. A top version. Anticuchos (barbecued skewers of fish, chicken or beef), typical street-food, are a good option – chicken liver skewers delivered a cunning contrast of smokiness with a slow after-burn from chilli. A salad of quinoa and butter beans layered on top of crushed avocado was less successful, the quinoa grains somewhat soggy rather than firm and light. But mostly Ceviche gets it right – it's a good-time place with a colourful interior and a buzzing pisco bar at the front. The grape-based spirit is the only one served here, and staff mix a mean pisco sour, topped with a good dollop of whipped egg white.

Babies and children admitted. Booking advisable. Vegan dishes. Vegetarian menu. **Map 17 C3.**

Lima London. See p31.

West

Westbourne Grove

★ Taqueria

139-143 Westbourne Grove, W11 2RS (7229 4734, www.taqueria.co.uk). Notting Hill Gate tube. **Meals served** noon-11pm Mon-Thur; noon-11.30pm Fri, Sat; noon-10.30pm Sun. **Main courses** £3.90-£8.75. **Set lunch** (noon-4.30pm Mon-Fri) £6.50 1 course. **Credit** MC, V. Mexican

Mexican food is on the ascendancy in London, and this cheerful café serving hearty, classic (if rather plebeian) dishes, is among the city's best. The use of authentic ingredients is the key; Taqueria is owned by the same folk as Cool Chile, the Borough Market stalwarts who sell an impressive range of chillies, beans and tortillas (all available in the restaurant's kiosk). Mexican comfort food is its métier. Tortilla soup, with a classic tomato-chicken stock, was rich and attractively decorated with crisply fried tortillas. You'll find a varied choice among the 15 meat, vegetarian and fish tacos on the menu, and anything with the house-made chorizo is delicious. To drink, order a tequila, margarita or beer, or enjoy a fresh juice (watermelon is refreshing, or go for a Vampire: steeped hibiscus mixed with orange juice, a sweet and tart combination that perfectly complements the spicy food). Leave space for dessert; the churros con cajeta – doughnuts that you dip in rich chocolate sauce – are divine. The café's location on Westbourne Grove means that diners are frequently more smartly attired than the casual but pleasant dining room, where old Mexican film posters provide the decoration.

Available for hire. Babies and children welcome: high chairs. Bookings not accepted Fri-Sun. **Map 7 A6.**

South

Battersea

Santa Maria del Sur

129 Queenstown Road, SW8 3RH (7622 2088, www.santamariadelsur.co.uk). Queenstown Road rail. **Lunch served** noon-3pm daily. **Dinner served** 6-10pm daily. **Main courses** £19-£25. **Credit** MC, V. Argentinian

Before you get to the front door of this bustling neighbourhood grill, the aroma of barbecuing beef grabs you by the nostrils and lures you in, straight past the imported parrillada grill, from whence

come various cuts of the restaurant's pride and joy – prime Argentinian beef – and into the simple, red-walled, wood-floored interior. If you don't like meat, you may want to reconsider your dining options. Before various cuts of *vaca* or massive, meaty mixed grills for the main course, starters comprise chorizo, morcilla (black pudding) or ox tongue, as well as empanadas (pasty-like little savoury pies). The beef empanada, made with chopped beef and black olives, would pass muster in Mendoza. Next, ribeye was satisfyingly juicy, with a charred exterior and rich, red interior. It wasn't the most tender of steaks, but it was good, and nicely accessorised by a herby, sharp criolla sauce and a mound of crunchy chips. Desserts are typical sweet, calorific confections beloved by South Americans, such as dulce de leche ice-cream or budin (bread pudding). The all-Argentinian wine list is notable for its quality and breadth, but prices are high and the by-the-glass offering is unimaginative.
Babies and children welcome: high chairs; nappy-changing facilities. Booking advisable weekends. Entertainment: musicians, tango 8.30pm Mon. Tables outdoors (4, pavement).

La Bodega Negra. See p32.

Brixton

★ Casa Morita NEW
Unit 9, Market Row, Brixton Market, SW9 8LB (8127 5107, www.casamorita.com). Brixton tube/rail. **Meals served** 11am-5.30pm Tue, Wed; 11am-10.30pm Thur-Sat; 10am-4.30pm Sun. **Main courses** £9-£11. **Credit** AmEx, MC, V. Mexican
The bustling atmosphere of Brixton Market is the perfect spot for Casa Morita's down-home cooking and friendly atmosphere. Careful ordering can deliver a lively, tasty and affordable night out in one of London's hottest restaurant scenes. Start with a refreshing Mexican beer or tamarind soda, and creamy chilli-laden guacamole. House-fried tortilla chips were beautifully crisp without a hint of grease – perfect! But the quality of dishes varied enormously: mole tacos featured shredded chicken in a superbly sweet, fragrant spiced sauce – ideal! Tacos with chorizo had rich, spicy ground sausage enlivened with onion, coriander and guacamole garnish. Tacos de Alambre, however, supposedly inspired by Mexico's Lebanese immigrants, featured lacklustre tiny cubes of beef overcooked with red and yellow peppers and bacon and smothered in cheese; the dish tasted more like a non-kosher Philly cheesesteak than a Mexican speciality. The children's menu will suit only the very pickiest of eaters; the single plain corn taco with shredded poached chicken seemed overpriced at £2.50. Desserts of Mexican crème caramel and lime meringue pie were well worth the calories. Erratic service, a problem when the Casa launched, seems to have been sorted out; on our visit, wait staff were attentive and helpful. We expect that the menu will be similarly refined.
Available for hire. Babies and children welcome. Booking advisable. Tables outdoors (4, market). Takeaway service. **Map 22 E2**.

South East

Bermondsey

Constancia
52 Tanner Street, SE1 3PH (7234 0676, www.constancia.co.uk). Bermondsey tube or London Bridge tube/rail. **Dinner served** 6-10.30pm Mon-Sat. **Meals served** 1.30-9.30pm Sun. **Main courses** £17.60-£25. **Credit** AmEx, MC, V. Argentinian
This street's tanneries would once have had passers-by holding their nose. Ironic, then, that it's now Constancia's sweet-smelling parrilla grill that dominates this corner of SE1. The restaurant certainly needs those alluring aromas: its exterior, tucked beneath a residential block, could hardly be less enticing. Only the two potted plants by the entrance come close to evoking the pampas. The L-shaped interior is better, mixing traditional and modern elements. Deep-brown walls are decorated with a gaucho's lasso and woven mat; industrial light-fittings hang from the ceiling; and the long, blackened grill looks 100 years old. Early indications of the food weren't promising. Serrano ham had a jerky-like stiffness, and the rocket atop it was dry. Accompanying bread was cheap, sliced baguette. However, standards leapt once the charcoal grill came into play. A parrillada mixta included black pudding, sausage and provoleta cheese – each item worth its place, with only the centrepiece 11oz ojo de bife (ribeye) lacking punch. It was out-muscled by another main of 8oz churrasco, the cheapest steak on the menu. An (albeit undressed) salad of spinach, raw mushroom and parmesan made a fine foil to the meat, though accompanying chips were of staff-canteen standard, despite their garlic and parsley sprinkles.
Babies and children welcome: high chairs. Booking advisable dinner Fri, Sat. Disabled: toilet. **Map 12 R9**.

Blackheath

Buenos Aires Café
17 Royal Parade, SE3 0TL (8318 5333, www.buenosairesltd.com). Blackheath rail. **Lunch served** noon-3pm Mon-Fri; noon-4pm

Ceviche. See p33.

Sat, Sun. **Dinner served** 6-10.30pm daily. **Main courses** £9-£22. **Credit** MC, V. Argentinian

Situated on the outskirts of Blackheath Village, this relaxed Argentinian restaurant is the perfect place to while away an afternoon gazing across the heath – aim for a table outside or on the ground floor rather than in the tiny basement bar area. High ceilings and whitewashed walls are countered by reassuring clutter; every inch of the walls is covered in framed prints and wine racks well-stocked with Argentinian reds. Staff are unfalteringly welcoming, barely batting an eyelid when we arrived half an hour later than our booking. Regulars are warmly ushered in and greeted by name, making a visit here seem like dining at a friend's house. Flavoursome steaks from grass-fed Argentinian cattle dominate the menu, backed up by a number of vegetarian dishes and a pizza list. The Buenos Aires pizza is nearly as big as the table and comes loaded with ham, artichokes, peppers and olives. Takeaway pizzas are also available, if the kitchen isn't too busy – just phone ahead and ask. Own-made sauces such as aïoli and chimichurri are well-balanced, but better was a traditional Argentinian side dish of stewed corn with red pepper, onion and melted cheese – the ultimate comfort food.

Babies and children welcome: booster seats. Booking essential. Tables outdoors (4, pavement).

For branch see index.

East

Spitalfields

Boho Mexica

151-153 Commercial Street, E1 6BJ (7377 8418, www.bohomexica.co.uk). Liverpool Street tube/rail or Shoreditch High Street rail. **Lunch served** noon-2.30pm Fri. **Brunch served** 12.30-4.30pm Sat, Sun. **Dinner served** 5.30-10pm Mon, Tue; 5.30-11pm Wed-Fri; 4.30-11pm Sat; 4.30-10pm Sun. **Main courses** £9.95-£14.95. **Set brunch** £12.95. **Credit** AmEx, MC, V. Mexican

Describing itself as the 'best real Mexican in London' could be hubris on Boho Mexica's part – but judging by the number of cool young things crammed in on a weeknight, many seem to agree. The cosy space has warm ochre walls decorated with old Mexican adverts, with a long bar for drinkers, and tables close enough to irritate if your neighbours have had more than five cocktails (as ours had). It's also pretty hard to read the menu, with the only light coming from candles and a backlit screen collage of famous London landmarks watched over by Our Lady of Guadalupe. But don't let that worry you: chill, and order another margarita (100% agave tequila, triple sec, tamarind and lime) – they're good. Handmade tortilla chips with chunky guacamole make a good opener to a meal, and the prawn cocktail is pretty special too, thanks to the addition of coconut jelly. Quesadillas are joined on the menu by more unusual dishes such as pollo a la morita (chicken marinated in tamarind sauce), which turned out to be another winner. Even tacos impressed: the soft circles of dough topped with sea bass and delicious 'coleslaw' spiced up with tabasco. Friendly, if scatty, service adds to the Mexican flavour.

Available for hire. Babies and children admitted. Booking advisable. Disabled: toilet. **Map 6 R5.**

Stratford

★ Wahaca

6 Chestnut Plaza, Westfield Stratford City, E20 1GL (3288 1025, www.wahaca.co.uk). Stratford tube/rail/DLR. **Meals served** noon-11pm Mon-Sat; noon-10.30pm Sun. **Main courses** £6-£10. **Credit** AmEx, MC, V. Mexican

This steadily expanding chain made its debut in Covent Garden in 2007. It gets many things right. Dishes are to share, but also offered in large-plate versions (platos fuertes) for times when gourmet shades into gourmand, and close attention is paid to sourcing. Neither guacamole with pork scratchings nor pork pibil tacos tend to last long, and the Michelada (a hangover-trouncing beer concoction with lime and spicy tomato juice) verges on the addictive. The decor is cheerfully ad hoc, creating a relaxed feel. The downsides flow from these strengths: relaxed can drift into inattentive (on a recent visit, our waiter completely forgot one dish – but having finally delivered it, rectified his error by chalking it off the bill); and replacing imported Mexican ingredients with British alternatives (cheddar in the black bean and cheese quesadilla, crumbly lancashire cheese in the black bean tostada and grilled corn) is apt to demonstrate the superiority of the originals. Most seating at this branch is in a well at the centre, but the rest of the set-up emulates other outlets – down to the grow-your-own chilli seeds handed out with the bill.

Babies and children welcome: children's menu; high chairs; nappy-changing facilities. Bookings not accepted. Disabled: toilet. Tables outdoors (7, terrace; 12, covered terrace). Vegan dishes. Vegetarian menu.

For branches see index.

Whitechapel

Moo!

4 Cobb Street, E1 7LB (7377 9276, www.moogrill.co.uk). Aldgate or Aldgate East tube or Liverpool Street tube/rail. **Breakfast served** 8-11am Mon-Thur. **Dinner served** 5-11pm Mon-Thur, Sat. **Meals served** 8am-11pm Fri; noon-5pm Sun. **Main courses** £5-£18. **Credit** AmEx, MC, V. Argentinian

'The best steaks in the city,' the website reckons. With a shopfront hardly bigger than a cow's backside, it's no wonder that Moo! talks itself up so forcefully. The grand claims might also be influenced by this bar-restaurant's Square Mile location, where a little brashness fits right in. Inside, it looks the part; compact and characterful (thanks to chatty staff), the venue does everything you want of a good steakhouse. The decor of brick, wood and leather might almost be used as a visual guide to steak cooking times. The punchy menu offers just three steak cuts (all served with either fries or salad). A handful of other mains include sausages and Italian-inspired breaded steaks. Among the five lomitos (sandwiches) is the bells-and-whistles 'potro'. Ham, mozzarella, egg and salad snuggling up to Argentinian rump inside a ciabatta should be worthy of multiple exclamation marks, but the steak disappointed a little. The sausage and roasted pepper filling of the restaurant's 'famous' choripán sandwich was much better, and deserved its mouthy tag; empanadas were excellent value. Moo! also offers breakfast (heavy on the meat and cheese, no fruit in sight), making the most of the City location.

Babies and children admitted. Booking advisable. Parties. Takeaway service. **Map 12 R6**.

Casa Morita. See p35.

North East

Hackney

Buen Ayre HOT 50

50 Broadway Market, E8 4QJ (7275 9900, www.buenayre.co.uk). London Fields rail or bus 26, 48, 55. **Lunch served** noon-3pm Fri; noon-3.30pm Sat, Sun. **Dinner served** 6-10.30pm daily. **Main courses** £13-£25.50. **Credit** MC, V. Argentinian

Maybe it's the primordial desire to eat unfeasibly large piles of meat that explains why this local Argentinian steakhouse was crowded on the soggy Sunday night of our visit. A huge charcoal grill sizzling and hissing with plate-sized 2in-thick steaks, sausages and black puddings was doing its best to fulfil the brief, aided by genial staff chattering in Spanish and creating a lively, neighbourhood feel. The food looked impressive, served as mini grills (parrilladas) piled high with nicely charred mixed meats for larger groups, or as single steak dishes with chimichurri sauce, butter-bean and roast pepper garnish for less greedy couples. However, rather like the stark, couldn't-care-less decor, it missed the mark. Buen Ayre's steaks seemed no better than the decent meat we can buy at many supermarkets these days, their blandness not helped by a chimichurri sauce tasting predominantly of dried herbs, their borderline-obscene size emphasising quantity over quality. Generous side salads sang with flavour and offered a pleasing freshness to the meal, but lots of greasy fat garlic and parsley chips were going back to the kitchen barely touched.

Available for hire. Babies and children welcome: high chairs. Booking advisable. Disabled: toilet. Tables outdoors (5, garden).

Café Chula

North

Camden

★ Café Chula NEW

75 West Yard, Camden Lock Place, NW1 8AF (7284 1890, www.cafechula.co.uk). Camden Town tube. **Meals served** 8am-6pm Mon, Tue; 8am-9pm Wed; 8am-midnight Thur; 8am-5pm, 6pm-midnight Fri; 8am-5pm, 6pm-1am Sat; 9am-10pm Sun. **Main courses** £7.50-£9. **Credit** MC, V. Mexican

It can't be easy for a café to stand out in Camden Market, as there are scores of food stalls filling the West Yard at weekends. Nevertheless, Café Chula draws in the punters with its little covered terrace and big window looking out on to the canal. The room has a Mexican-beach feel, with faded blue, green and terracotta painted walls and 1950s diner

bar stools. The menu focuses on classic Mexican snacks – quesadillas, tacos, nachos and tortas (sandwiches). Fish tacos were excellent: crispy beer-battered tilapia goujons came snuggled in soft corn shells, drizzled with a very spicy chipotle-lime mayo. And we liked the zingy guacamole. But chicken quesadillas, although moist and bursting with cheesy chicken filling, lacked flavour. Steak tacos were better, comprising chargrilled meat cubes drizzled with an intriguing tomatillo salsa (flavours of garlic, lime and coriander were given a grainy texture by the tomatillo). Watery hot chocolate and overly crisp churros were a disappointing finale. Cocktails, however, are worth ordering; margarita flavours include a sour tamarind, a jalapeño and cucumber, and a fiery grapefruit and habanero chilli.
Available for hire. Babies and children admitted. Tables outdoors (5, balcony). Takeaway service. **Map 27 C2**.

Highbury

Garufa

104 Highbury Park, N5 2XE (7226 0070, www.garufa.co.uk). Arsenal tube. **Meals served** 10am-10.30pm daily. **Main courses** £12-£26. **Set lunch** £9.80-£12.50 1 course incl glass of wine, beer or soft drink. **Credit** MC, V. Argentinian

For a restaurant that deals squarely with the business of steak, Garufa has hit upon the ideal interior: small and brick-walled, with a low-lit colour scheme of browns and reds. You can easily picture a gaucho at one of the simple, sturdy tables. Large monochrome photographs of old Buenos Aires evoke the country's heritage. A shame, then, that our steaks didn't do it proud. The smudge of red fruit sauce alongside a bife de chorizo rivalled the meat for impact. That sauce and two others (stilton and brandy, or Malbec and pepper) are available as supplements, yet the small pot of chimichurri should be all that adorns Argentinian beef. A side of humita norteña (a rich slop of sweetcorn, onion, basil and butter) outshone the beef. The cheaper 'special' of churrasco marinado had greater flavour, and arrived with sliced boiled potato, scant rocket and parmesan: no additional sides required. There's one fish option (sea bass on this visit) and one vegetarian dish (own-made ravioli). Our starters had been better: empanadas were light and flaky; sweetbreads were succulent, delicate discs in a lemon and spring onion sauce. To drink, South American cocktails bolster an alluring Argentinian wine list.
Available for hire. Babies and children welcome: children's menu; high chairs; nappy-changing facilities. Booking advisable dinner. Entertainment: tango 8pm Mon. Takeaway service.

Islington

Sabor

108 Essex Road, N1 8LX (7226 5551, www.sabor.co.uk). Angel tube. **Dinner served** 6-10pm Tue, Wed; 6-11pm Thur, Fri. **Meals served** noon-11pm Sat, Sun. **Main courses** £12-£19. **Set lunch** £16 2 courses, £17.50 3 courses. **Credit** AmEx, MC, V. Pan-Latin American

This place's name – 'flavour' – could be its one-word manifesto. Ranging coast-to-coast across South America, cherry-picking its maximum-impact dishes and ingredients, Sabor's approach sees classics like Cuban ropa vieja share menu space with the kitchen's own creations. Sweetcorn fritters from the set menu were a simple, well-fried starter, accompanied by tangy avocado salad. An à la carte ceviche peruano wasn't available, but substitute Brazilian caldo verde soup shone. For the set menu main course, humitas (dumplings of cornmeal, sweetcorn, onions and peppers) were freshly steamed, served alongside plentiful leaf salad and palm heart. Our waiter, excellent throughout, recommended the Argentinian steak for an à la carte main, but Brazil won out again: moqueca fish stew was rich and bountiful, topped with a great shell-on prawn and slab of swordfish. Desserts included own-made rum and raisin ice-cream, and banana bread with rum caramel and guanábana (soursop) sorbet. Full-length windows next to the street give the narrow space an airy feel, while mounted Barranquilla Carnival masks, colourful tables and a sleek metallic ceiling sculpture perk up the white-walled interior.
Babies and children welcome: high chairs. Booking advisable. Vegetarian menu. **Map 5 P1**.

Tierra Peru NEW

164 Essex Road, N1 8LY (7354 5586, www.tierraperu.co.uk). Angel tube or Essex Road rail. **Meals served** noon-11pm daily. **Main courses** £9.95-£15.95. **Set lunch** (noon-3pm) £12 2 courses, £15 3 courses. **Credit** MC, V. Peruvian

Peru's diverse cuisine shares similarities with its Andean neighbours, but its London interpretation escapes the cheap-and-cheerful pigeon-holing to which, say, Mexican and Brazilian restaurants are subject. Tierra Peru aims for contemporary sophistication; good lighting, attractive art, black furniture and creative crockery smarten the long, narrow room, as do the staff's black uniforms. A dish of delicate, spicy puffed maize kernels served on arrival signals the restaurant's upmarket intentions; a short list of formally made cocktails – including pisco sour and an algarrobina (made from carob juice) – confirms them, as well as eliciting a relaxed vibe from the mixed clientele. Traditional dishes from across the country feature key ingredients: chilli, potato and other starchy roots, fish and seafood, rice and various types of corn. Marinades, herbs and sweet-sour spicing provide complexity. Ceviche had just the right texture and tang, and our tamalito starter (steamed corn mash filled with chicken or pork) shamed the Mexican version. Ostensibly simple mains of carapulcra (Andean: based on sun-dried potatoes, peanuts and rice, with chicken and pork ribs) and majarisco (coastal: mashed plantain with seafood) both looked like garnished mounds of mush, but tasted great. Desserts are tooth-achingly sweet, if delicious.
Available for hire. Babies and children welcome: high chairs. Disabled: toilet. Takeaway service. **Map 5 P1**.

Tierra Peru

North West

Kensal Green

★ Sabor Brasileiro

639 Harrow Road, NW10 5NU (8969 1149, www.saborbrasileiro.info). Kensal Green tube/rail. **Meals served** noon-7pm Tue-Sat; noon-5pm Sun. **Main courses** £1.30/100g. **Buffet** £10. **No credit cards**. Brazilian

It's not often that paying is a part of the fun. Housed in a brick and concrete block, this basic wood-panelled restaurant operates the *comida por kilo* (pay-by-weight) system that's common in Brazil. To the uninitiated, getting a good deal requires a little speculation. Pile up a dinner plate at the bain marie stand, then take it to be weighed: £1.30/100g or all you can eat for £10. On this occasion, there were just a few choices. The canteen presentation doesn't flatter the food, but there was clearly some Brazilian flair at play as dishes were tastier than they looked. Chicken lasagne was all shredded meat and cheese sauce. Slabs of stewing steak were just tender enough in their carrot-studded gravy (a workaday take on filé ao molho madeira). Battered fish chunks (iscas de peixe) and fried chicken were good, in spite of their long wait under the hot lamps. The obligatory beans and white rice were exemplary. Rodízio (eat-all-you-want grilled meat) is occasionally laid on at weekends, but phone ahead to check. Simple desserts are sometimes available, though a good alternative is one of the many fresh fruit juices: from familiar pineapple or mango to açaí, acerola and cupuaçu.
Available for hire evenings. Babies and children welcome: high chairs. Booking advisable. Takeaway service.

Brasseries

Flexibility has always been a prime attraction of true brasseries – those that serve meals, snacks and drinks throughout the day. The format lends itself to many interpretations, and London's restaurateurs have duly let their imaginations take flight; there's exciting variety to be found in this chapter. You want grand? Visit the newly opened **Delaunay**, a near-neighbour and sibling to the **Wolseley** and a peach of a venue for lavish mittel-European teas that evoke the Austro-Hungarian Empire. Or is a good-value neighbourhood hangout more your style? Adam Byatt's new Clapham venture **Bistro Union** indelibly ticks the right boxes. But two of our favourite establishments are run by highly creative chefs who use the malleable framework of a brasserie to showcase their imaginative fusion dishes: **Made in Camden**, where local boy Josh Katz raids the global larder to fine effect; and **Kopapa**, the latest plaything of fusion maestro and co-owner, New Zealander Peter Gordon. Antipodean flair is also in evidence at the brand-new branch of **Caravan**, occupying a converted Victorian warehouse in the fast-developing hotspot of King's Cross and featuring its own giant coffee roaster. Famished at 4pm? Read on.

Central

City

Bread Street Kitchen NEW

One New Change, 10 Bread Street, EC4M 9AB (7592 1616, www.breadstreetkitchen.com). St Paul's tube. **Breakfast served** 7-11am Mon-Fri. **Meals served** 11.30am-11pm Mon-Sat; 11am-8pm Sun. **Main courses** £12.50-£31. **No credit cards**.

To judge by this venue's size and the elaborate Russell Sage interiors – a mash-up of art deco and industrial – Gordon Ramsay can't be doing too badly. Bread Street Kitchen is located across the One New Change hallway from Barbecoa (*see p23*), Jamie Oliver's barbecue joint with Adam Perry Lang. Entering the cavernous upstairs bistro is sheer fun, like stepping out of the bowels of a stadium into the stands. Leather banquettes sweep through the black and white tiled space, which must be half the length of a football pitch. Starters sent out from the extraordinarily long open kitchen were flawless. Perfect piccalilli and mayonnaise-moistened strands of beef brisket were served with caraway seed-dotted crisp bread. A smoothie-textured gazpacho came enriched with basil oil; the white crab meat in its depths was simply an additional treat. Mains of roasted cod and short-rib burger were good (the chips excellent), but a slight step down. Attracting custom to the City on a Sunday is hard, but the brunch menu offers good budget-conscious options. Wine is available by the carafe: a nice touch.

Babies and children welcome: children's menu; crayons; highchairs. Booking advisable. **Map 11 O6.**

Duck & Waffle NEW

40th Floor, Heron Tower, 110 Bishopsgate, EC2N 4AY (3640 7310, www.duckandwaffle.com). Liverpool Street tube/rail. **Breakfast served** 7-10.45am Mon-Fri; 9-10.45am Sat, Sun. **Lunch served** 11.30-2.30pm, **dinner served** 5.30-11pm daily. **Main courses** £3-£10. **No credit cards**.

When compared to its blingtastic sister Sushisamba (*see p31*) two floors below, Duck & Waffle is the plainer, less expensive, sibling (though it still has an entrance bar with great views). The menu is certainly on-trend – too many trends, perhaps. Offal is everywhere, from lambs' tongues to porchetta di testa (a salami made from pig's head); there's a slider; some dishes are roasted 'in a brick oven'; others are served as large sharing dishes. Yet while Sushisamba's menu is a carnival of Latin and Asian influences, Duck & Waffle has British ingredients at its core. Barbecue-spiced crispy pig's ears showed a flair for presentation, with the thin, chewy strips of cartilage presented in a brown paper bag. 'Chip shop cod tongues' also slightly overdid the styling with some superfluous newsprint and a bottle of Sarson's vinegar on the side, but the four little bites of cod resembled scampi, served with a pleasingly sharp tartare sauce. The low point was the shellfish pot roast: overcooked seafood swamped by 'nduja flavouring. Desserts restored our faith in the kitchen, with a good peach melba and eton mess – simple, but effective dishes. Soon, 24-hour opening is promised, with waffles served by night, duck by day, but phone to check, as these hours hadn't kicked in as we went to press.

Available for hire. Babies and children welcome: high chairs. Booking essential. Disabled: lift; toilet. Separate room for parties, seats 14. **Map 12 R6.**

Clerkenwell & Farringdon

Caravan HOT 50

11-13 Exmouth Market, EC1R 4QD (7833 8115, www.caravanonexmouth.co.uk). Farringdon tube/rail or bus 19, 38, 341. **Meals served** 8am-10.30pm Mon-Fri; 10am-10.30pm Sat; 10am-4pm Sun. **Main courses** £4.50-£16. **Credit** AmEx, MC, V.

Now an Exmouth Market fixture, Caravan has matured into a lively local favourite. The restaurant/bar is an unintimidatingly modern space, with some quirky touches (check out the light fittings). When busy – which is often – it's noisy, but we've few other complaints. Staff are charming and competent, and the menu is a tempting read, comprising many small plates and a handful of larger ones. Confit rabbit and smoky

black pudding terrine comes with pickled nectarine and toast; squid pancake with Japanese brown sauce, mayonnaise and seaweed salt. More conservative diners might choose the delicious seared sirloin with anchovy dressing. We also relished a deep-fried duck egg, and a sharing plate of merguez sausage, falafel, houmous, aubergine relish, sheep's cheese, carrot pickle and pitta. Cornbread with chipotle butter is divine but super-rich; don't order it if you're interested in trying dessert. And you should – chocolate and espresso pudding with crème fraîche sorbet is just one of several classy options. Also worth having is coffee. It's roasted in the basement (where the kitchen and party table are located). A user-friendly drinks list includes cocktails and specialist teas alongside a global wine selection. For a less expensive option, head here for breakfast. *See p41* for new branch Caravan King's Cross.
Available for hire (Mon, Sun evenings only). Babies and children welcome: high chairs; nappy-changing facilities. Booking advisable dinner. Separate room for parties, seats 12. Tables outdoors (7, pavement). **Map 5 N4.**

Covent Garden

★ The Delaunay NEW

2012 WINNER BEST NEW RESTAURANT
2012 RUNNER-UP BEST NEW DESIGN
55 Aldwych, WC2B 4BB (7499 8558, www.thedelaunay.com). Covent Garden or Temple tube, or Charing Cross tube/rail. **Breakfast served** 7-11.30am Mon-Fri; 8-11am Sat. **Brunch served** 11am-5pm Sat, Sun. **Tea served** 3-6.30pm daily. **Meals served** 11.30am-midnight Mon-Sat; 11.30am-11pm Sun. **Main courses** £6.50-£27.50. **Cover** £2. **Credit** AmEx, MC, V.

As you might expect from the younger sibling of the Wolseley (*see p42*), there's glam-factor aplenty here, and the Delaunay manages to attract the intelligentsia out on smart dinner dates. Its interior provides more than a fitting setting, echoing European grand brasserie design, but also evoking Edwardian clubs and the Orient Express. The menu is far from cutting-edge, experimental or modernist; instead, it celebrates the heritage dishes of mittel-Europe, particularly Austria, Germany and France. Tarte flambée (from Alsace) arrives as thin as a crispbread, but topped like a pizza with smoked bacon and shallots cooked to softness; piping hot, it's a great appetiser. Wiener schnitzel might follow: boneless veal beaten to a thin layer with a mallet, then breadcrumbed and fried – a classic dish, perfectly created. Desserts include strudels, or for the chocolate-lover, what might well be London's best sachertorte. This is a proper brasserie operating all day, serving breakfast from 7am on weekdays, afternoon teas from £pm. The adjacent café (called the Counter) is open throughout the day, supplying snacks such as chicken soup with dumplings, or salt beef pretzels. Refreshingly, you're treated with equal decorum at the Delaunay, whether you're a big spender, a celeb, or just popping in for welsh rarebit or hot chocolate. It's a real treat of a place.
Babies and children welcome: crayons; high chairs; nappy-changing facilities. Booking advisable. Disabled: toilet. Separate rooms for parties, seating 8, 14 and 24.
Map 18 F4.

Bread Street Kitchen. See p39.

★ Kopapa

32-34 Monmouth Street, WC2H 9HA (7240 6076, www.kopapa.co.uk). Covent Garden or Leicester Square tube. **Breakfast served** 8.30-11am Mon-Fri. **Brunch served** 10am-3pm Sat, Sun. **Meals served** noon-10.45pm Mon-Fri; 3.30-10.45pm Sat; 3.30-9.30pm Sun. **Main courses** £10.50-£20. **Credit** AmEx, DC, MC, V.

Just what you want in a centre-of-town hangout, Kopapa is in turn soothing, cheerful and buzzing depending on the time of day you arrive. Food and drink options are winningly flexible, with the bonus that much of what's on offer is not just delicious but tweetable. Co-owner Peter Gordon, Britain's best exponent of fusion cooking, oversees a menu that reassures with fry-ups, burgers and steak sandwiches, while dazzling with combinations such as burrata, mint, black vinegar and medjool dates. You can order small plates to share, or traditional courses. Liquids are taken seriously (high-spec house coffee, fine wines and beers from New Zealand, lip-smacking cocktails) as is breakfast and brunch. Favourites from Marylebone's Providores appear here (the famous Turkish eggs, for example) but Kopapa has its own dishes too, including a comforting pile of chorizo hash with fried eggs, sriracha chilli sauce and crispy shallots. Spiced banana french toast was a rare missfire thanks to its intense orange-vanilla syrup, burning tamarind relish and flabby streaky bacon, but we marvelled at the heavenly cleverness of millet porridge with hazelnuts, sherry syrup and yoghurt. Stylishly unobtrusive decor (love the floor tiles), plentiful staff and a neat bar for quick visits cap off a gloriously handy place you'll want to return to frequently.

Available for hire. Babies and children welcome: high chairs; nappy-changing facilities. Booking advisable. Disabled: toilet. Tables outdoors (3, pavement). **Map 18 D3.**

Fitzrovia

Riding House Café

43-51 Great Titchfield Street, W1W 7PQ (7927 0840, www.ridinghousecafe.co.uk). Oxford Circus tube. **Breakfast served** 7.30am-noon Mon-Fri; 9am-12.30pm Sat, Sun. **Lunch served** noon-3.30pm Mon-Fri; 12.30-4pm Sat, Sun. **Dinner served** 6-9.30pm daily. **Main courses** £10.50-£25. **Credit** AmEx, MC, V.

It's pretty hard not to like this funky brasserie. You want breakfast? There's everything from bircher muesli to omelette arnold bennett. Fancy Sunday lunch? How about a roast (chicken or beef), a reuben sandwich or penne with meatballs for the kids? Lunch or dinner? The menu runs from Carlingford rock oysters to chateaubriand for two. Nor does Riding House Café come over all faux-French. It's capacious, with a 'traditional' dining room on one side and a bar area with a massive sharing table on the other. We say 'traditional' reservedly; wall sconces are made from stuffed squirrels, a private dining room is made from a loose-box, and much furniture is reclaimed. It would all be a bit acid-trip if it weren't so professionally done. The café is run by the team behind Bermondsey's Garrison, and gastropub-style main courses include smoked haddock kedgeree and 10oz ribeye with béarnaise. There are small plates too – on various visits, we've enjoyed artichoke dip with crostini, macaroni and gorgonzola gratin, cod fritters, and smoked eel with horseradish. End with richly spiced gingerbread with caramel ice-cream. A great wine list plus well-mixed cocktails round things off.

Babies and children welcome: children's menu; high chairs; nappy-changing facilities. Booking advisable. Disabled: toilet. Separate room for parties, seats 16. **Map 9 J5.**

Villandry

170 Great Portland Street, W1W 5QB (7631 3131, www.villandry.com). Great Portland Street tube.

Café/bar **Open** 8am-11pm Mon-Sat; 9am-6pm Sun. **Meals served** 8am-10pm Mon-Sat; 9am-5pm Sun. **Main courses** £11.50-£15.

Restaurant **Lunch served** noon-3pm Mon-Fri. **Dinner served** 6-10.30pm Mon-Sat. **Main courses** £11.50-£22.50. **Set meal** £30 3 courses incl coffee, £40 4 courses incl coffee.

Both **Credit** AmEx, MC, V.

Villandry has moved away from its French roots and now offers a more international menu, variations of which are available in all three dining areas. All serve small plates, platters and salads, but the light-filled café/bar also does breakfast, and a nice line in cocktails. The charcuterie bar sitting between the deli/foodstore and the restaurant is rather dark, but the restaurant has big windows overlooking Bolsover Street and remains an attractive room with quirky decor. The restaurant menu adds some main dishes to the mix (lamb cutlets, broccoli, broad beans and confit tomato, or grilled sea bass with fennel, orange and olive salad). Food is good without being exceptional: salt and pepper squid with tartare sauce was a decent small plate; a moist burger with emmental, tomato and basil salsa and excellent chips also found favour. Grilled chicken breast salad, with gem lettuce, edamame, leeks and avocado dressing was well flavoured (and startlingly green), but the chicken wasn't really grilled. A coupe of summer berries made an indulgent choice from an ice-cream-heavy range of desserts. The inexpensive wine list contains plenty by the glass. Staff couldn't have been more helpful – but on a Saturday night were slightly under-employed.

Available for hire. Babies and children welcome: children's menu; high chairs; nappy-changing facilities. Booking advisable. Tables outdoors (13, pavement). Takeaway service. **Map 3 H5.**

King's Cross

Caravan King's Cross NEW

Granary Building, 1 Granary Square, N1C 4AA (7101 7661, www.caravankingscross.co.uk). King's Cross or St Pancras tube/rail. **Breakfast served** 8am-11.30pm Mon-Fri. **Brunch served** 10am-4pm Sat, Sun. **Meals served** noon-10.30pm Mon-Fri; 5-10.30pm Sat. **Main courses** £13-£17. **Credit** AmEx, DC, MC, V.

Caravan King's Cross shares a home with Central Saint Martins College of Art, in the impressively converted, Grade II-listed Granary Building. Inside, it's the epitome of warehouse chic, with painted brick and high pipe-lined wooden ceilings. Office workers and art-school hipsters sit side-by-side at pine and metal tables, arranged canteen-style in long lines. Along one side, the chefs are visible behind a cage-like wire mesh. At the back, divided off by the bar, metal shelves are stacked with sacks of coffee beans waiting to go into the giant on-site roaster. Personable waiting staff move with ease between the spaces. As with the Clerkenwell original (*see p39*), the menu takes influences from many parts of the world; breakfast and brunch dishes are a strength. From the small-plates list a barely pink grilled quail was complemented well by a light but chunky cumin-scented houmous. Toasted pine nuts added texture to a mellow wedge of Swiss summerhimu blue cheese, while fresh figs and a sticky wine reduction balanced it with their subtle sweetness. The must-try dish, however, was chocolate and cherry trifle: simmered cherries, blanketed with dense chocolate cream, topped by espresso jelly and crowned with freshly baked mini-madeleines. Outdoor tables make this one of the best alfresco dining spots in London.

Available for hire. Babies and children welcome: high chairs; nappy-changing facilities. Booking advisable. Disabled: toilet. Tables outdoors (10, courtyard). **Map 4 L2.**

Karpo NEW

23-27 Euston Road, NW1 2SD (7843 2221, www.karpo.co.uk). King's Cross or St Pancras tube/rail. **Meals served** 7am-11pm daily. **Main courses** £9-£19. **Credit** AmEx, DC, MC, V.

One thing's for sure: you can't miss Karpo. It's housed within the Megaro Hotel, opposite King's Cross station. The Georgian building's owners daringly paid four street artists to spray-paint the brick façade with an enormous colourful mural (reputed to be the capital's largest). Inside, though, the design is less assured. The surroundings take their cues from a palette of vastly different styles, from industrial chic to French brasserie. Similarly, the menu veers from the Deep South to smart Italian, but – despite this muddle – execution is sound. A Scandinavian snack of smoked eel on dense Finnish bread impressed, as did a starter of tender, fleshy salt duck, served with tiny pickled mirabelles (a type of plum). Grits, a Southern US staple made of boiled cornmeal, came formed into a neat block, topped with shelled 'shrimps' and a buttery mushroom sauce. Another main course, of pink-middled slivers of lamb leg served with a provençal-style green beans and anchovy dressing, was simpler but no less memorable. Desserts ranged from a decent selection of cheeses, to salted caramel ice-cream or polenta cake; the wine list showcased organic and biodynamic bottles; and service was warm, engaged and accommodating.

Available for hire. Babies and children admitted. Booking advisable. Separate room for parties, seats 30. Takeaway service. Vegan dishes. Vegetarian menu. **Map 4 L3.**

Mayfair

Truc Vert

42 North Audley Street, W1K 6ZR (7491 9988, www.trucvert.co.uk). Bond Street tube. **Meals served** 7.30am-10pm Mon-Fri; 9am-10pm Sat; 9am-4pm Sun. **Main courses** £14.95-£19. **Credit** AmEx, MC, V.

Imagine a local restaurant transported by magic into Mayfair. Truc Vert is no central London sophisticate, what with the deli products on wooden shelves and the Sam Smith's beer on the menu (Heineken was offered when we asked if there was anything else). The jazz duo may have been too loud as well, but when it came to the food it was hard to find any gripes. From a menu heavy with French influences (plus the occasional Asian slant), an onion soup was creamier than the standard, with subtle flavouring, and packed with meltingly soft onions. Another starter – sautéed squid, with stir-fried beansprouts, mangetout, pak choi, egg noodle salad and harissa dressing – was a great combination, the squid soft and fresh, the harissa

adding just the right warmth. Swordfish steak with niçoise salad and coriander chilli struck a similarly fresh, fusion note, while artichoke and ricotta tortellini were dense, unctuous and deeply flavoured. Only a lemon and cinnamon custard missed the mark; it was fine, but not the luxurious pudding that suits being served in a tiny portion. But that's not much to complain about. On the whole, this was winning food.
Available for hire. Babies and children welcome: high chairs; nappy-changing facilities. Booking advisable. Entertainment: jazz 7.30-10.30pm Fri, Sat. Tables outdoors (12, pavement). Takeaway service. **Map 9 G6.**

Piccadilly

★ The Wolseley HOT 50

160 Piccadilly, W1J 9EB (7499 6996, www.thewolseley.com). Green Park tube. **Breakfast served** 7-11.30am Mon-Fri; 8-11.30am Sat, Sun. **Lunch served** noon-3pm Mon-Fri; noon-3.30pm Sat, Sun. **Tea served** 3-6.30pm Mon-Fri; 3.30-5.30pm Sat; 3.30-6.30pm Sun. **Dinner served** 5.30pm-midnight Mon-Sat; 5.30-11pm Sun. **All-day menu served** 11.30am-midnight daily. **Main courses** £6.75-£28.75. **Set tea** £9.75-£21; £29.75 incl glass of champagne. **Cover** £2. **Credit** AmEx, DC, MC, V.

Self-described 'café-restaurant in the grand European tradition', the Wolseley is one of London's premier destination restaurants, as popular for power breakfasts as it is for birthday celebrations. It takes itself seriously ('no photographs', memorabilia for sale), but the staff are nice, not just well drilled. The high-ceilinged room is a handsome homage to Viennese coffee houses. The main menu has Mittel European leanings too (excellent chopped liver and glorious, generous boiled salt beef with light herb dumplings) along with many brasserie classics (note-perfect soufflé suisse, steak frites), crustacea and a dish of the day. One of the quirkier options, mackerel panzanella, was a summery treat, whereas a salad of asparagus, rocket, broad beans and courgettes was mean with the spears and had more unadvertised peas than broad beans. Most disappointing was the hamburger: so dull it needed pepping up with ketchup and mustard – odd when the steak tartare had been so good. Puddings restored our faith: lushly alcoholic black forest gateau and deliciously tart passionfruit sorbet. Indeed, sweet things are a speciality, and include a splendid array of cakes. The wine list concentrates on Europe, providing plenty by the glass. Owners Chris Corbin and Jeremy King have built on the Wolseley's success with the Delaunay (*see p40*) and Brasserie Zédel (*see p96*) and have more ventures in the pipeline.
Babies and children welcome: high chairs; nappy-changing facilities. Booking advisable. Disabled: toilet. Separate room for parties, seats 12. **Map 9 J7.**

Soho

Bob Bob Ricard

1 Upper James Street, W1F 9DF (3145 1000, www.bobbobricard.com). Piccadilly Circus tube. **Lunch served** noon-3pm, **dinner served** 5.30-11pm Tue-Fri. **Meals served** noon-11pm Sat. **Main courses** £12-£40. **Set meal** (noon-6pm) £19.50-£24.75. **Set tea** (noon-6pm Sat) £23.50-£34.75. **Credit** AmEx, MC, V.

Opulently furnished with eccentric flourishes, Bob Bob Ricard looks like a sparkly makeover of the Orient Express. It's expensively fitted out with intimate booths, leather banquettes, chandeliers and shiny brass fittings. For bling appeal, there are quirky champagne call-buttons and sockets for electric toasters by each table. The menu defies description; take your pick from Kellogg's Corn Flakes and breakfast fry-ups, to all-day Russian specialities – caviar, chicken kiev, pickled herrings and seriously icy top-end vodkas. There are also sumptuous English afternoon teas, American diner classics, and nods to French bistro favourites. Cooking is anything but frivolous; chefs know their business and consistently deliver the goods, as does the service team. On recent visits, we've been impressed by the simplicity of grilled sea bass fillets, the decadence of stuffed little dumplings filled with porcini mushrooms, the crisp bite of french fries, and the succulence of spiced baby chicken partnered with crunchy coleslaw. Desserts are showy affairs: a marvellous makeover of eton mess emerged as a powder-pink meringue globe filled with strawberry sorbet, berries and whipped cream. The imaginative cocktails – pink-hued rhubarb gin and tonic, and lemon sherbet punch – provide nursery flavours with a grown-up twist.
Booking advisable. Children over 12 admitted. Disabled: toilet. Dress: elegant (ties not required). Separate room for parties, seats 10. **Map 17 A4.**

Kettner's

29 Romilly Street, W1D 5HP (7734 6112, www.kettners.com). Leicester Square or Piccadilly Circus tube. **Meals served** noon-11pm Mon-Wed; noon-11.30pm Thur-Sat; noon-9.30pm Sun. **Main courses** £11.50-£27.50. **Set meal** (5-6.30pm) £16.50 2 courses, £19.50 3 courses. **Credit** AmEx, MC, V.

Kettner's has long had an air of nostalgia about it, having been through several incarnations in its long history. When it was a posh version of Pizza Express, it exuded a tatty, faded glamour. Reborn as a brasserie, the shabbiness was replaced by swish decor redolent of the restaurant's 1930s heyday, with palms, mirrors and a somewhat glitzy champagne bar. The place has a definite buzz, but it seems to be more about the setting (and the closely packed tables) than the food. The menu features tried-and-tested classics – the likes of beef carpaccio, oysters and smoked salmon to start, with coq au vin, beef bourguignon and steaks to follow – with the occasional more modish dish, such as belly pork. We tried a small, rather bland piece of pollock on a bed of overcooked cabbage, and a succulent steak, cooked rare as requested, though served with a rather bijou salad. Puddings shone, however – a mango crème brûlée was a dense delight. Overall, though, we would have liked cooking with a bit more gusto, and generosity: £16.50 seemed a lot to pay for a small piece of fish, however chichi the surroundings.
Babies and children welcome: children's menu; high chairs; nappy-changing facilities. Booking advisable Thur-Sat. Disabled: toilet. Entertainment: pianist 6.30-9.30pm Tue-Sat. Separate rooms for parties, seating 12-85. **Map 17 C4.**

Princi

135 Wardour Street, W1F 0UT (7478 8888, www.princi.co.uk). Leicester Square or Tottenham Court Road tube. **Meals served** 8am-midnight Mon-Sat; 8.30am-10pm Sun. **Main courses** £5-£12. **Credit** AmEx, MC, V.

The southern reaches of Wardour Street are home to several bakers these days, giving the super-glamorous Princi a run for its money, but this Italian panetteria has upped its game accordingly and still reigns supreme. In Claudio Silvestrin's smart sandstone interior, the long black marble counters and plinths that serve as stand-up tables still gleam and sparkle, the clientele are still more stylish Milan than boho Soho, and the breads, cakes, pizze al taglio and hot dishes still stand out from the growing crowd. Presentation is classy. Wide glass cases are filled with the prettiest, most delicate Italian pâtisserie and desserts imaginable. Further down the long counter, a great selection of focaccia, pizza and hearty salads features such perfect Italian ingredients as prosciutto, fresh fennel, artichokes, milky mozzarella and bright red beef tomatoes. It's a nightmare finding a seat once you've done the self-service shuffle, and standing around with a laden tray of delicious food and nowhere to eat is annoying, but once you do find a stool and settle in, you'll feel a very long way from London, physically and gastronomically.
Babies and children admitted. Bookings not accepted. Disabled: toilet. **Map 17 B4.**

Strand

Tom's Kitchen

Somerset House, Strand, WC2R 1LA (7845 4646, www.tomskitchen.co.uk). Covent Garden or Temple tube. **Brunch served** 10am-4pm Sat, Sun. **Lunch served** noon-3pm Mon-Fri. **Dinner served** 6-9.30pm Mon-Sat. **Main courses** £12.50-£29.50. **Credit** AmEx, DC, MC, V.

The approach to Tom's Kitchen, across the grand courtyard of Somerset House, is impressive, though the restaurant itself is deliberately low-key. The second branch of chef Tom Aikens' British brasserie, it occupies a series of small rooms, the first containing a bar, the rest a mix of rustic wooden furniture and leather banquettes, including communal tables ideal for groups. Next door is Tom's Deli, a daytime café; outside, a vast riverside terrace, occupied in summer by Tom's Terrace, is a marvellous spot for alfresco drinks. The crowd-pleasing menu features brasserie stalwarts (caesar salad, macaroni cheese, burgers, shepherd's pie) alongside some seasonal dishes – though why beer-battered pollock and chips should be considered particularly summery is a mystery. Pricing isn't so democratic: it's £17 for said fish and chips, and the wine list offers little below £25. Pappardelle with chunky ceps, and grilled black bream (a miserly portion) were decent but not outstanding; a side of cauliflower cheese was watery. Puds are a highlight, from baked alaska and sherry trifle to a large slab of fluffy, creamy lemon cheesecake. There are some irritations. Everything is served on chunky wooden boards: fine for bread, allowable for a burger, but ridiculous when even a bowl of pasta comes perched on a board. And much fuss is made about suppliers, including the 'happy pigs' from Blythburgh who provide the honey-glazed pork belly – but there's no mention of the presumably less happy geese responsible for the foie gras that turns up in three dishes.
Babies and children welcome: high chairs; nappy-changing facilities. Booking advisable. Disabled: toilet. **Map 18 F5.**
For branch see index.

The Delaunay. See p40.

West

Chiswick

High Road Brasserie

162-166 Chiswick High Road, W4 1PR (8742 7474, www.highroadhouse.co.uk). Turnham Green tube. **Meals served** 7am-11pm Mon-Thur; 7am-midnight Fri; 8am-midnight Sat; 8am-10pm Sun. **Main courses** £10-£22. **Set lunch** (noon-5pm Mon-Fri) £12.50 2 courses, £15.50 3 courses. **Credit** AmEx, MC, V.

Clever Soho House group; they always seem to know what people want wherever they open in the world, and Chiswick's High Road Brasserie is no exception. A social chameleon, it transforms from bustling brunch hangout to relaxed all-day dining room (including cakes and sandwiches at teatime) and offers cocktails at the marble bar in the evenings. Menus change seamlessly as the hours go past and it always seems busy, with everyone from families to media types. In summer, the outdoor tables under the generous awning at the front are the place to be. The interior is a stylish mix of modern and retro, with beautiful coloured floor tiles, green leather banquettes, wooden chairs and fabulous light fittings. A crowd-pleasing menu offers bistro classics such as onion soup gratin, coq au vin and steak frites, mixed with Italian and modern British favourites. The pork belly bun, groaning with flavoursome meat and apple sauce, is a must-try. Having garnered strong reviews on opening, the Brasserie suffered a shaky period where service and food standards wavered, but we're pleased to report that things are back on form.

Babies and children welcome: children's menu; crayons; high chairs; nappy-changing facilities. Booking advisable dinner and weekends. Disabled: toilet. Tables outdoors (8, pavement).

Sam's Brasserie & Bar

11 Barley Mow Passage, W4 4PH (8987 0555, www.samsbrasserie.co.uk). Chiswick Park or Turnham Green tube. **Open** 9am-midnight Mon-Wed, Sun; 9am-12.30am Thur-Sat. **Meals served** 9am-10.30pm daily. **Main courses** £11.75-£20.50. **Set meal** (noon-3pm Mon-Fri; 6.30-7.30pm Mon-Thur, Sun) £13.50 2 courses, £16.50 3 courses. **Credit** AmEx, MC, V.

Sam's fulfils its brasserie brief to a T: drinkers catered for at the front bar; diners offered solid global cooking all day, in the dining area to the left; a soundtrack that's inoffensive without being bland (the Smiths to Jerry Lee Lewis); and staff who are well drilled, if not particularly warm, in dealing with Chiswick society (lone businessmen, couples, families). There's a cheap early dinner, and a menu that extends from ribeye steak clichés to Mediterranean favourites in the tapas line and even a Goan fish and prawn curry. Crisply attired staff briskly take your coat and offer jugs of tap water unprompted. Unfortunately, the kitchen's timings were out on our visit: both padrón peppers and squid were chewy, and the anchovy mayonnaise with the squid seemed rather light on salty fish. Only a full-flavoured, exceptionally creamy garlic soup starter, accompanied by bread of yeoman solidity, excelled. During a midweek dinner, the bar was livelier than the restaurant – perhaps no surprise given the long, curated wine list with options available by the 500ml carafe or glass.

Available for hire. Babies and children welcome: children's menu; high chairs; nappy-changing facilities. Booking advisable Thur-Sat. Disabled: toilet. Separate room for parties, seats 26 (mezzanine).

For branch (Harrison's) see index.

Caravan King's Cross. See p41.

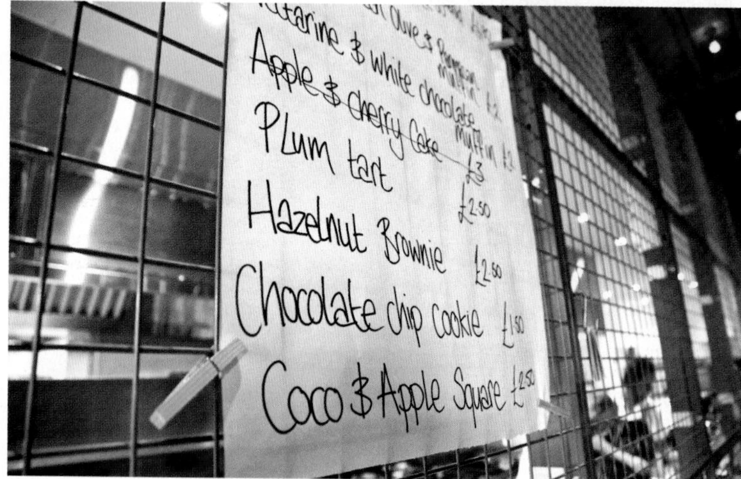

Ladbroke Grove

Electric Brasserie

191 Portobello Road, W11 2ED (7908 9696, www.the-electric.co.uk). Ladbroke Grove tube. **Breakfast served** 8am-noon daily. **Brunch served** noon-5pm Sat, Sun. **Meals served** noon-11pm Mon-Sat; noon-10pm Sun. **Main courses** £10-£28. **Set lunch** (noon-5pm Mon-Fri) £13.50 2 courses, £16.50 3 courses. **Credit** AmEx, MC, V.

The easy-going vibe and please-all menu make the Electric highly popular. It's the answer to many dining conundrums: as suitable for a solo lunch as for a family get-together or casual date. At busy times, notably weekend brunch, booking is a good idea. Timeless brasserie fittings make the place seem like it's been here for years. Tables out front are ideal for people-watching, while the dim recesses of the back room are suited to late-night dining. The breakfast menu (avocado and poached egg on sourdough, full english) runs into the all-day choices: sandwiches, small plates (chipolatas with honey mustard, devilled whitebait with lemon mayo), seafood and dishes such as macaroni cheese or duck cassoulet. We're fond of the sirloin steak sandwich, with caramelised onion and gruyère, and the smoked haddock hash (on the brunch menu). The set meal is a good deal; a well-executed three courses of chicken livers with pancetta and butternut squash, crispy-skinned pollack with pea and chervil sauce, and zabaglione with raspberries hit the spot. The drinks list is similarly varied, from superior smoothies to cocktails. Staff are courteous and proficient; a glitch was quickly rectified with a free espresso. It's part of the Soho House Group.

Available for hire. Babies and children welcome: booster seats; crayons; high chairs; nappy-changing facilities. Booking advisable Thur-Sun. Disabled: toilet. Tables outdoors (6, terrace).

Map 19 B3.

Westbourne Grove

Daylesford Organic

208-212 Westbourne Grove, W11 2RH (7313 8050, www.daylesfordorganic.com). Ladbroke Grove or Notting Hill Gate tube. **Meals served** 8am-6pm Mon-Sat; 10am-3pm Sun. **Main courses** £9.95-£14.95. **Credit** AmEx, MC, V.

The idea behind Daylesford Organic is an appealing one: to provide fresh, organic food direct from farm to city. This includes keeping the grocery, deli and bakery (located at the front of the firm's large and bright Westbourne Grove branch) stocked with impossibly shiny produce and artisanal cheeses, chutneys and pâtisserie. It also means providing the café kitchen with ample quantities of these high-quality ingredients – in partnership with similar-minded suppliers. This dedication to first-rate raw materials may, in part, account for the pricey menu, though to charge around a tenner for brunch variations on poached or scrambled eggs on toast still seems steep. Lunch offers the opportunity to indulge in some homely dishes, from loaded welsh rarebit and beetroot and bacon soup, to creamy pearl barley risotto and succulent slow-roasted lamb – though you'll often have to queue for the pleasure. Just be prepared to share the communal tables with the area's moneyed families and beautiful young couples. And don't expect too much from the waiting staff; they're far too busy to be gracious.

Babies and children welcome: crayons; high chairs; nappy-changing facilities. Bookings not accepted. Disabled: toilet. Tables outdoors (6, pavement). Takeaway service. Vegan dishes.

Map 7 A6.

For branch see index.

South West

Barnes

Depot

Tideway Yard, 125 Mortlake High Street, SW14 8SN (8878 9462, www.depotbrasserie.co.uk). Barnes Bridge or Mortlake rail or bus 209. **Brunch served** 9.30-11.30am Sat. **Lunch served** noon-3pm Mon-Fri; noon-3.30pm Sat; noon-5pm Sun. **Dinner served** 6-11pm daily. **Main courses** £10.95-£19.95. **Set lunch** (Mon-Fri) £12.95 2 courses, £15.95 3 courses. **Credit** AmEx, DC, MC, V.

Smart enough for a celebratory splurge, casual enough for a midweek supper, this Thameside brasserie pitches it just right. And the locals, mainly affluent and middle-aged, have been enjoying its charms since 1986. The long room is split into a bar and two dining areas. Polished parquet flooring, olive and mushroom coloured walls, stylish banquettes and clever lighting create an atmospheric backdrop; ask for a window table for fabulous sunset views over the water (there are a few outdoor tables in the courtyard, but none next to the river). The menu is divided by type ('veggies & salads', 'fish & shellfish'), with some dishes available in both starter and main course sizes – a helpful, flexible approach mirrored in the deft, affable service from the mainly female staff. Mediterranean and Asian influences pepper the menu, alongside more obviously British dishes. A large, crisp-coated fish cake, its fluffy interior offset by pickled beetroot and a pomegranate salsa, was a hit, as was a big bowl of skinny fries. Seared mackerel with rosemary roast potatoes and a salad of brown shrimp, cabbage and dill (from the bargain-priced set menu) was marred only by a scalding plate that turned the potatoes limp. Desserts, always a highlight, include a notably wide range of sorbets and ice-creams (top marks for the salted caramel), but our pick is eton mess, an indulgent mash-up with vanilla ice-cream, strawberry sauce and toasted almonds.

Available for hire. Babies and children welcome: children's menu; crayons; high chairs; nappy-changing facilities. Booking advisable. Tables outdoors (11, courtyard).

Georgina's NEW

56 Barnes High Street, SW13 9LF (8166 5559, www.georginasrestaurants.com). Barnes Bridge rail or 209, 283 bus. **Breakfast served** 9am-noon, **lunch served** noon-3pm Mon-Fri. **Brunch served** 11am-3pm Sat, Sun. **Dinner served** 6-10pm Mon-Sat. **Main courses** £14-£22. **Credit** AmEx, MC, V.

Georgina's looks good, making the most of an awkward, wedge-shaped site. Fold-back front doors, white walls and furniture and a glass roof mean it's bright and light, and the design is contemporary and feminine, with pretty mirrors and striking chairs. You can visit for morning coffee and pastries, afternoon tea, weekend brunch or full-blown lunch and dinner. Seasonal Mediterranean flavours dominate the menu, which runs from simple salads (chickpea, couscous and herbs) and pasta (spaghetti vongole) to the likes of barbecued sirloin and chips. Expert input has come from Adam Byatt, chef-patron of Clapham's Trinity and Bistro Union, so it promises a lot. But doesn't always deliver. Best was the lobster burger: a generous wodge of firm-fleshed crustacean inside a decent bun, plus fat, crisp onion rings and a chargrilled whole corn on the cob, leaves pulled flamboyantly back. It was messy, homely and indulgent. Less successful were the starters: a dull five-bean salad and an intriguing-sounding combo – flatbread, harissa, whitebait and mizuna – that didn't combine in any meaningful way. What sets the venture apart is the person behind it: Barnes local Nicola Horlick, the high-profile City financier dubbed 'superwoman' for managing to combine a stellar career with bringing up six children (it's named after her eldest daughter who died of leukaemia).

Available for hire. Babies and children welcome: children's menu; high chairs. Booking advisable. Disabled: toilet. Tables outdoors (4, garden). Takeaway service. Vegetarian menu.

Chelsea

Gallery Mess

Saatchi Gallery, Duke of York's HQ, King's Road, SW3 4LY (7730 8135, www.saatchi-gallery.co.uk). Sloane Square tube. **Breakfast served** 10am-1pm Sat, Sun. **Meals served** 11.30am-9.30pm Mon-Sat; 11.30am-6.30pm Sun. **Main courses** £12-£18.50. **Set tea** (2.30-6pm) £9.50, £15 for 2 people. **Credit** AmEx, MC, V.

With a clientele that's a mix of *Made in Chelsea*-ites and culture hounds visiting the Saatchi Gallery, the vibe here is posh but, thanks to the friendly staff, not intimidatingly so. A short but interesting menu keeps it simple. A starter of green pea and ham hock soup with wild garlic leaf was superb, packed with intense flavours. The sharing plates of antipasti were tempting, but we plumped for Aberdeen Angus beef burger with brioche and chips, and grilled chicken with orange, quinoa and pomegranate salad, both cooked to perfection. Arguably, the quinoa was the star of the show, as toothsome as it was healthy, although puddings – rhubarb crumble and Madagascan vanilla panna cotta with mixed berry compote – were also faultless. A short international wine selection is given ballast by a long list of cocktails, and a few bottled beers. The interior is light and bright, and the plentiful outdoor seating is well hidden from the King's Road traffic. One of the nicest pitstops in Chelsea.

Babies and children welcome: high chairs; nappy-changing facilities. Booking advisable lunch and dinner. Disabled: toilet. Separate room for parties, seats 60. Tables outdoors (24, terrace) until 5.30pm Nov-Apr; until 9.30pm May-Oct.

Map 14 F11.

South

Clapham

Bistro Union NEW

2012 RUNNER-UP BEST NEW RESTAURANT

40 Abbeville Road, SW4 9NG (7042 6400, www.bistrounion.co.uk). Clapham Common or Clapham South tube. **Open** 11am-10pm Mon-Sat; 11am-4pm Sun. **Brunch served** 11am-3pm

Sat; 11am-4pm Sun. **Lunch served** noon-3pm, **tea served** 3-6pm Mon-Fri. **Dinner served** 6-10pm Mon-Sat. **Main courses** £10-£24. **Credit** MC, V.

Casual newcomer Bistro Union may be cheaper than Trinity (chef Adam Byatt's other restaurant, *see p214*), but it is by no means a poor cousin. Unlike its classy older sibling, here you'll find no tasting menus, no starched linen. Instead, you can turn up unannounced (bookings are only taken early evening and for weekend brunch), grab one of the bare wooden tables, and order off a menu scrawled on to a hanging roll of brown paper. The dishes are British-leaning and favour the grazers – fish and meat come cured, as pâtés or potted, or there are small plates of seasonal greens. On our visit, we enjoyed the silky folds of thinly sliced pork cheek served simply with nicely charred breads and tumescent caperberries; and a small dish of salt-crusted whole broad beans from the grill (reminiscent of Japanese-style soy beans, edamame). But the larger 'main course' dishes are no less impressive: from our perfectly judged bavette steak, to a tender grilled quail served with a caesar-like salad of baby gem lettuce with anchovies plus berkswell cheese. Only our pud – a strawberry and mead trifle smothered with too much cream – showed a slight wobble in the kitchen. But attentive, amiable service and bang-on bartending did much to compensate.

Babies and children welcome: children's menu; high chairs. Bookings not accepted except 6-7.30pm Mon-Sat; 11am-12.30pm Sat, Sun. Tables outdoors (2, terrace). **Map 22 A3.**

South East

Bankside

Elliot's

12 Stoney Street, SE1 9AD (7403 7436, www.elliotscafe.com). London Bridge tube/rail. **Breakfast served** 8am-noon Sat. **Lunch served** noon-3pm Mon-Fri; noon-4pm Sat, Sun. **Dinner served** 6-10pm Mon-Sat. **Main courses** £4.50-£19. **Set meal** (Sun) £25 3 courses. **Credit** AmEx, MC, V.

There's much to like about Elliot's: a congenial atmosphere, charming staff and a short, interesting menu. But there are niggles too. The exposed brick walls, concrete floor and lack of soft furnishings mean noisiness; and prices are high for often-small portions. Starters are mainly assemblies; pecorino with chestnut honey, and radicchio, fennel and caper salad were both pleasing. Next, buttermilk fried chicken was a posh version of KFC: nicely flavoured but a small portion for £12. Also fine tasting yet diminutive was ricotta gnudi (similar to gnocchi) and asparagus. This was meant to come with chanterelles, but the kitchen had run out and neglected to tell the waiting staff (who at least removed it from the bill). We filled up on a generous portion of wild garlic and olive bread: finger-licking good, unlike the rather restrained chicken. Maybe hungry diners should order from the specials board. Our neighbours shared a 40-day-aged rib steak (£42.50 for 850g) and a side of cauliflower cheese: both big, glorious-looking portions. To finish, malt cake with spiced pumpkin sherbet sounded more alluring than it was. A modish drinks list runs from cocktails to Somerset cider brandy and includes biodynamic wines.

Booking advisable. Vegetarian menu. **Map 11 P8.**

The Table

83 Southwark Street, SE1 0HX (7401 2760, www.thetablecafe.com). Southwark tube or London Bridge tube/rail. **Meals served** 7.30am-4pm Mon-Fri. **Brunch served** 8.30am-3pm Sat, Sun. **Dinner served** 6-10pm Thur; 6-10.30pm Fri, Sat. **Main courses** £14-£25. **Credit** AmEx, MC, V.

The past year has brought a few changes to the Table café. The stylish interior with its polished concrete, bare wooden tables and huge windows remains, but there's a new chef (Cinzia Ghignoni, who's worked with Angela Hartnett) and a new wine list. The place is known for its breakfasts, both healthy and indulgent – simple bircher muesli, or brioche french toast with bacon and maple syrup – and buzzes at weekends during the popular brunches (think sweetcorn fritters with poached eggs). At lunch and dinner, the short menu of small and large plates is big on seasonal Italian ingredients and light on fuss. High point of our meal was richly flavoured, rough-hewn chicken livers on ciabatta toast, and green Italian friggitelli peppers with fresh ricotta and marjoram. Ingredients are of a high quality, but the timings can go a bit awry. A small plate of octopus with potatoes, capers and anchovies featured a somewhat tough cephalopod, and our rose veal steak with girolles was cooked well beyond the medium-rare requested. The wine list is brief – just two-dozen bottles – but all are food-friendly choices available by the glass. On Saturday evenings, the Table resounds with live jazz.

Babies and children welcome: high chairs. Disabled: toilet. Entertainment: jazz 9pm-midnight Sat. Tables outdoors (8, terrace). Takeaway service. **Map 11 O8.**

Blackheath

Chapters All Day Dining

43-45 Montpelier Vale, SE3 0TJ (8333 2666, www.chaptersrestaurants.com). Blackheath rail. **Breakfast served** 8-11.30am Mon-Fri. **Brunch served** 8am-3pm Sat; 9am-4pm Sun. **Lunch served** noon-3pm Mon-Fri. **Tea served** 3-6pm Mon-Sat; 4-6pm Sun. **Dinner served** 6-11pm Mon-Sat; 6-9pm Sun. **Main courses** £9.45-£30.50. **Set lunch** (Mon-Thur) £12.95 2 courses, £14.95 3 courses. **Set dinner** (Mon-Thur) £14.95 2 courses, £17.95 3 courses. **Credit** AmEx, MC, V.

Brunch with friends, bloody mary at the bar, date-night dinner, casual family Sunday lunch; the All Day Dining moniker is apt for this well-loved Blackheath restaurant. The menu has Modern European dishes (risotto of Watts Farm asparagus and pancetta, say, or spatchcock chicken with lemon and thyme) at affordable prices – but the atmosphere is relaxed, unlike the formal surroundings at Michelin-starred sister restaurant Chapter One in Bromley. The slick interior of the lively dining room is juxtaposed with quirky service; waiting staff are expert wind-up merchants, but efficient with it. A great-value set menu is available Monday to Thursday and often features more unusual dishes than the regular dinner menu. Juicy lambs' kidneys accompanied by own-made raisin bread and violet mustard (a French condiment made from black grapes and mustard seeds) was the best dish of the evening. Another surprise was the whole red onion in the centre of a red onion tatin, which had perfect pastry and moreish caramelised bits. The specialist Josper oven is used for meat dishes, its charcoal embers lending a subtle smokiness without losing the juices, in everything from a burger to a steak. Dinner isn't served at the pavement tables, but they're a great place to enjoy a sundowner overlooking the heath.

Available for hire. Babies and children welcome: children's menu; high chairs; nappy-changing facilities. Booking advisable. Disabled: toilet. Separate room for parties, seats 50. Tables outdoors (4, pavement).

Crystal Palace

Joanna's

56 Westow Hill, SE19 1RX (8670 4052, www.joannas.uk.com). Crystal Palace or Gipsy Hill rail. **Breakfast served** 10am-noon daily. **Meals served** noon-11pm Mon-Sat; noon-10.30pm Sun. **Main courses** £11.75-£32.50. **Set meal** (lunch Mon-Sat; dinner Mon-Wed) £12.95 2 courses, £16.95 3 courses. **Credit** AmEx, MC, V.

The navy sign and dark wood-panelled interior makes this restaurant almost invisible among a cluster of local high street shops at night, though it's been in situ since 1978. Family-run Joanna's takes its name from cockney rhyming slang – the old Joanna/piano was in frequent use in its heyday as a US-style restaurant. Thirty-something years later, American influences remain in the decor, particularly in the private booth that seats five. The menu, however, is that of a Modern European brasserie. Quality was variable: a starter of beetroot 'carpaccio' with goat's cheese fritters was bland and uninspiring. Tender roast chicken breast with braised lettuce, beans and greens was note perfect, but polenta cake with halloumi and an under-seasoned ratatouille lacked punch. For a taste of the restaurant's American-grill days, opt for a juicy burger or one of the reliable steaks. A short global wine list is partnered by ten or so cocktails. The restaurant was relatively quiet on a Sunday evening, and service was gracious and attentive. A bit hit and miss, then, but hopefully it was just a blip for this well-loved restaurant.

Babies and children welcome until 6pm: booster seats; children's menu; high chairs. Booking advisable; essential weekends. Tables outdoors (3, pavement).

East

Shoreditch

Water House

10 Orsman Road, N1 5QJ (7033 0123, www.waterhouserestaurant.co.uk). Haggerston rail or bus 67, 242. **Lunch served** noon-4pm Tue-Fri, Sun. **Dinner served** 6-10pm Tue-Sat. **Main courses** £10.50-£17. **Credit** MC, V.

In a dream location on Regent's Canal, and with laudable aims – it's a social enterprise and training restaurant – Water House hits the right notes on entry. The airy, light-filled space and waterside terrace make it feel modern, fresh and bright, much like the menu. The emphasis is Italian, with a tempting, seasonally led range of pasta and risotto dishes, including a pretty spring risotto with peas, broad beans and courgettes, and ravioli with courgettes and peas. But the young chefs don't shy away from invention; a starter of chilli paneer on lemonade bread won points for its rich marmaladey sauce of tomato and lemon peel, while a soft-shelled crab was crunchy and delicate. Mains of lamb

Bistro Union. See p45.

chops, steak and pan-fried duck breast were robust and generous, but overwrought sauces and marinades worked against the meats. Desserts too were a mixed bag; a chocolate fondant was oozily perfect, but ice-creams were too sweet. None of this detracts from a restaurant that has its heart in the right place and the kind of warm service that can't be faulted, but prices (mains at £16, sides an extra £3.50) seem a bit steep for the starter-level cooking. *Available for hire. Babies and children welcome: high chairs. Booking advisable. Disabled: toilet. Tables outdoors (8, towpath). Takeaway service. Vegetarian menu.* **Map 6 R2**.

Spitalfields

★ Breakfast Club

12-16 Artillery Lane, E1 7LS (7078 9633, www.thebreakfastclubcafes.com). Liverpool Street tube/rail or Shoreditch High Street rail. **Meals served** 7.30am-10pm Mon-Wed; 7.30am-10.30pm Thur, Fri; 9am-10.30pm Sat; 9am-9pm Sun. **Main courses** £3.50-£10.20. **Credit** AmEx, MC, V.

The Breakfast Club looks across the Atlantic for inspiration, featuring fun pop-culture references. It's kitted out in colourful 1980s kitsch, from novelty knick-knacks to a neon sign emblazoned with 'Sex and drugs and bacon rolls'. The American-leaning menu, laden with pancakes and breakfast burritos, is big on brunch; be prepared to queue at weekends. Portions are generous, and the quality is decent. A plate of chorizo, peppers and hash browns was as flavourful as its constituent parts would suggest, while a sweet and savoury combo included great pancakes, eggs cooked to your liking and sausage (the vegetarian version tasted own-made). Staff coped well, remaining alert and easy-going as they served a crowd that's a mix of the youthful and the young at heart. City bods stop by during the week; weekends draw Spitalfields Market shoppers. From lunch onwards, the menu expands to full-flavoured sandwiches (barbecue chicken, halloumi and spinach), jacket potatoes and burgers. There are cocktails in the evening. A semi-secret basement speakeasy – Mayor of Scaredy Cat Town – is hidden behind a Smeg fridge door. With branches in Soho, Hoxton and Angel, this small chain keeps its attitude light and its atmosphere vibrant. *Available for hire. Babies and children welcome: nappy-changing facilities. Bookings not accepted before 5pm weekends. Disabled: toilet. Takeaway service.* **Map 12 R5**.
For branches see index.

North East

Dalston

A Little of What You Fancy

464 Kingsland Road, E8 4AE (7275 0060, www.alittleofwhatyoufancy.info). Dalston Junction rail or bus 67, 242. **Breakfast served** 9am-noon Tue-Fri. **Lunch served** noon-4pm Tue-Fri; 10am-4pm Sat; noon-5pm Sun. **Dinner served** 7-9.45pm Tue, Wed; 7-10pm Thur-Sat. **Main courses** £12-£19. **Credit** MC, V.

Managing a fine balance between East London cool and middle-class tweeness, ALOWYF – a novelty when it opened, for being a British/Modern

Hackney Picturehouse Bar & Kitchen

European establishment on a street dominated by ethnic cuisine – is still going strong. Here, you can grab a good-quality brunch, a relaxed lunch or a neighbourhood evening meal. The informal restaurant (named after a song by Hackney music hall artist Marie Lloyd) has a subdued frontage that makes it hard to spot. Once inside, you'll find a narrow space furnished with calming, arty decor (furniture salvaged from a school, incongruous wooden boxes of lemons and oranges, and graphics on the walls). The menu (quirkily presented on a clipboard) changes regularly. Brunch dishes include the likes of eggs florentine, blueberry pancakes and smoked haddock kedgeree; dinner consists of well-presented plates such as organic rainbow trout or slow-braised oxtail. Desserts are a highlight: experimental (but normally addictive) cheesecakes, flourless chocolate cake (a favourite) and an amazing pavlova. Locally grown ingredients are often used, with some coming from neighbourhood gardens. While service can be patchy (in keeping with the laid-back vibe), staff are generally friendly. A Lot of What You Fancy might be a more apt name.
Available for hire. Babies and children welcome until 7pm: high chairs. Booking advisable Thur-Sat. Disabled: toilet. Takeaway service.

Hackney

★ Hackney Picturehouse Bar & Kitchen NEW

Hackney Picturehouse, 270 Mare Street, E8 1HE (0871 902 5734, www.picturehouses.co.uk). Hackney Central rail. **Open** 8am-11pm Mon-Thur; 8am-12.30am Fri; 9am-12.30am Sat; 10am-11pm Sun. **Meals served** 8am-10pm Mon-Fri; 9am-10pm Sat; 10am-10pm Sun. **Main courses** £7.50-£15. **Credit** MC, V.

A relaxed and airy space, in pristine black and white – apart from some long wooden tables at one end – HP is a good place to drop in for a (rather pricey) coffee. But the café, attached to Hackney's newest cinema, takes its food seriously too: a notice tells customers not to expect fast food. Casual, snacky dishes include pizzette, sharing boards (antipasti, Middle Eastern, a fish version and one with Spanish cured meats) and sandwiches. There's also a Picturehouse hot dog – carefully sourced from outdoor-raised pork, served with sauerkraut and sweet mustard – and burgers, along with a selection of small plates. We opted for a fresh, big-flavoured small-plate selection: a chunky houmous shot through with garlic, served with flatbread; some thick, chewy grilled halloumi served with a sassy salsa and red endive, and lovely (mostly) mild padrón peppers flash-fried with herbs and sea salt. Save room for the own-made cakes – a lot of love has gone into them; we even saw one decorated with fresh flowers.
Babies and children welcome: high chairs; nappy-changing facilities. Bookings not accepted. Disabled: toilet. Separate room for parties, seats 60. Tables outdoors (6, pavement). Vegan dishes.

Market Café NEW

2 Broadway Market, E8 4QG (7249 9070, http://market-cafe.co.uk). London Fields rail.
Bar **Open** 5-11pm Mon-Wed; noon-11pm Thur; noon-midnight Fri; 10am-midnight Sat; 10am-10pm Sun.
Restaurant **Meals served** 6-10.30pm Mon-Wed; noon-10.30pm Thur, Fri; 10am-4pm, 6-10.30pm Sat; 10am-10pm Sun. **Main courses** £9.50-£18.50.
Both **Credit** MC, V.

It's a step change for Broadway Market as its raffish independent eating and drinking houses are joined by this rather more engineered operation from Hugo Warner (who used to be the man behind the Benugo group). Market Café has an unhurried, friendly vibe and a brief, toothsome and clever menu. It offers mainly Italian food, with snacks (truffled rarebit, white onion soup, kidneys on toast) doubling as preludes for mains such as pea risotto or shoulder of lamb. Goat's curd on toast (bread is from the local E5 Bakehouse) served with prosciutto worked well, though the ham was bafflingly bereft of fat. Agretti (a marsh plant) with a duck egg sat on a puddle of olive oil – a delicious combination. Fish stew was decent, even though the rouille-spread hunk of bread standing as a croûton bulked up the volume a bit too much for us. Generally, given the carefully casual surroundings – Formica tables, enamel bowls, retro light fittings – prices are a bit high. But it suits the changing demographic to a T. Staff are accommodating, and there's a little counter for lone diners to perch at, a bar at the front and some pavement tables, all rammed at peak times.
Babies and children welcome: high chairs. Booking advisable. Tables outdoors (8, pavement).

Railroad

120-122 Morning Lane, E9 6LH (8985 2858, www.railroadhackney.co.uk). Hackney Central or Homerton rail. **Open** 10am-5pm Mon, Tue, Sun; 10am-11pm Wed-Sat. **Breakfast served** 10am-3.30pm, **lunch served** noon-3.30pm daily. **Dinner served** 7.30-9.30pm Wed-Sat. **Main courses** £10-£14. **Credit** MC, V.
It's safe to call Railroad a trailblazer – when it opened in late 2010 it was the only place we recommended in this still-on-the-up area of Hackney; two years later, it still is. It's a simple-looking café/restaurant, with minimal decoration and fewer than ten tables scattered around the tiny wedge of a kitchen. Owner Lizzie Parle (sister of Stevie Parle, of Dock Kitchen in west London) and her partner write a daily changing menu of breakfast, lunch and, Wednesday to Saturday, dinner; there's often only a choice of a few dishes but everything is imaginatively concocted, made with love and globe-trotting influence. Breakfast might be Moroccan baked eggs with cumin and home-made bread, say, or granola with yoghurt, accompanied by Square Mile coffee. If it's available, be sure to order a hibiscus cordial (also made by Lizzie, as pretty much everything is). Come evening, candles are lit and blinds are drawn, and the likes of potato and spinach curry, or breaded quail with Vietnamese-style fish sauce are served. The compact basement hosts poetry recitals and open-mic nights. Railroad's DIY ethos, independence and creativity make it somewhere we're happy to go back to again and again.
Babies and children welcome: high chair. Booking advisable dinner. Takeaway service.

Hackney Wick

Hackney Pearl

11 Prince Edward Road, E9 5LX (8510 3605, www.thehackneypearl.com). Hackney Wick rail. **Open** 8am-11pm Mon-Fri; 10am-11pm Sat, Sun. **Lunch served** noon-4pm, **dinner served** 6-10pm daily. **Brunch served** 10am-4pm Mon-Fri; 10am-1pm Sat, Sun. **Main courses** £10-£14. **Credit** MC, V.
Pearls require searching out, and this affable all-day café is hidden among the artists' studios and semi-industrial sprawl of Hackney Wick. There's an airy main room with an open kitchen, and a sunny terrace spilling on to the street – blocked off to cars, in enterprising Wick fashion, with a pair of benches dragged into the road. Pitched as an all-purpose neighbourhood hangout, it's a welcoming spot for coffee and own-made cake, drinks (cocktails, Meantime beers and a modestly priced wine list) or a proper meal from the short, weekly-changing menu. Simple seasonal dishes such as sourdough toast with roasted baby beetroot and goat's curd are nicely executed, but the kitchen also has a flair for more unusual combinations: a slab of tender, crackling-topped pork belly paired with punchy, cumin-spiked brinjal was a Sunday lunch standout. The service is friendly, if occasionally forgetful – the upside being that there's no pressure to leave, and you can happily linger over a glass of wine and borrowed backgammon set.
Available for hire. Babies and children welcome: high chairs; nappy-changing facilities. Booking advisable. Disabled: toilet. Tables outdoors (7, terrace). Takeaway service.

Stoke Newington

Homa

71-73 Stoke Newington Church Street, N16 0AS (7254 2072, www.homalondon.co.uk). Stoke Newington rail or bus 73, 393, 476. **Open** 9am-10.30pm daily. **Lunch served** noon-3pm Mon-Fri; noon-4pm Sat; noon-5pm Sun. **Brunch served** 10am-3pm Mon-Fri; 10am-4pm Sat, Sun. **Dinner served** 6-10.30pm Mon-Sat; 6-10pm Sun. **Main courses** £6.50-£18. **Credit** MC, V.
Homa's relaxed Italian dining and upmarket, classic brunch makes it a firm local favourite on Stoke Newington's Church Street. Buggies and families are very much in the majority in a space where reclaimed wooden furniture and wine stacked in old, open wardrobes evoke a funky family dining room. Decorative tiling leads through from a Georgian hallway, adding to the homely feel. Homa suits various dining styles: a circular, informal bar looks down on to an open bar below, and a takeaway coffee counter sits alongside the more formal restaurant and open terrace. Diners enjoying brunch, lunch or just a coffee all mingle together

Market Café

leisurely. Potato ravioli weren't as hot as they could have been, but the creamy wild mushroom sauce was rich with the nutty flavour of French ratte potatoes and woodland fungi. Poached eggs were perfectly runny for brunch, served with locally smoked salmon; you can even add champagne for sophisticated breakfast sparkle. Pizzas, from the wood-fired oven, are also available to take away, and Homa rivals other local Mediterranean restaurants with its own-made linguine and small plates of Spanish-inspired tapas.
Babies and children welcome: high chairs; nappy-changing facilities. Booking advisable. Disabled: toilet. Separate room for parties, seats 40. Tables outdoors (14, terrace). Takeaway service. **Map 25 B1**.

North

Belsize Park

★ Giraffe

196-198 Haverstock Hill, NW3 2AG (7431 3812, www.giraffe.net). Belsize Park tube. **Meals served** 8am-11pm Mon-Fri; 9am-11pm Sat; 9am-10.30pm Sun. **Main courses** £4.95-£15.95. **Credit** AmEx, MC, V.
Family-friendly Giraffe has recently evolved into several sub-species, each taking something the original does pretty well and repackaging it for a different, generally more adult market. There's now a bar and grill in Soho, a colourful burger and cocktail joint near Selfridges, and a Leon-ish counter-service spot in King's Cross called Giraffe Stop. Clearly, they're all-too-aware that not everyone can relax surrounded by kids and buggies. Yet it's the relief of finding a place that seamlessly charms children and parents that lures families to this reliable chain. Giraffe know what to offer: good sausages, penne with a tomato sauce that actually tastes nice; crayons and puzzles; a slightly more sophisticated menu for tweenies. And they're just as savvy with grown-ups. The something-for-everyone menu ranges from indulgent burgers and skin-on fries to diet food; breakfast pancakes and Union Hand-Roasted coffee to meze platters and margaritas. Oh, and 50% discount bar deals off-peak. The cuisines of Mexico, Japan, South-East Asia and the US are regularly trawled for inspiration. We were impressed with a recent salad bowl of soba noodles, tofu and edamame: the soy dressing gave it plenty of oomph, though the ingredient temperatures were inconsistent. Desserts tend to be lacklustre.
Babies and children welcome: children's menu; crayons; high chairs; nappy-changing facilities. Booking advisable. Disabled: toilet. Tables outdoors (16, terrace). Takeaway service.
Map 28 C3.
For branches see index.

Camden Town & Chalk Farm

★ Made in Camden

Roundhouse, Chalk Farm Road, NW1 8EH (7424 8495, www.madeincamden.com). Chalk Farm tube. **Lunch served** noon-2.30pm Mon-Fri. **Brunch served** 10.30am-3pm Sat, Sun. **Dinner served** 6-10.30pm Mon-Sat; 6-10pm Sun. **Main courses** £4.40-£16. **Set lunch** £10 2 courses. **Credit** AmEx, MC, V.
The Roundhouse is a surprising place to find a rocking restaurant, let alone cooking of this calibre. A note-perfect mix of concert posters, panoramic windows, dark wood and red seating counterpoints the confident fusion dishes of Camden Town boy Josh Katz (ex-Ottolenghi). Diners are advised to choose two or three plates each to share, depending on appetite. There's clearly a formula to Katz's style – a flavourful goop topped with protein, scattered with something crunchy and drizzled with a zingy sauce – but we'll forgive the repetitiveness when the combinations sing like this. Witness sumac and lemon-pepper calamares with pumpkin jam and sriracha chilli aïoli, or grilled chicken with miso carrot purée, pickled cucumber, shiitake and coconut. Fried fennel with feta, pistachio and salted caramel will convert any hater of the aniseed-flavoured bulb. The weekend brunch menu features a global grab-bag of eggy and cheesy things. We like that they aim to keep things local, serving the full range of Camden Town Brewery beers, wines from Bibendum in Primrose Hill and coffee from Caravan in Exmouth Market. We don't like coming when there's a concert on – the bar influx leads to extraordinary waits for the even simplest things.
Babies and children welcome: high chairs; nappy-changing facilities. Booking advisable. Disabled: toilet. **Map 27 B1**.

Islington

Bill's

9 White Lion Street, N1 9PD (7713 7272, www.bills-website.co.uk). Angel tube. **Breakfast served** 8am-noon Mon-Fri; 8am-1pm Sat; 9am-1pm Sun. **Meals served** noon-10.30pm Mon-Fri; 1-10.30pm Sat; 1-10pm Sun. **Main courses** £8.50-£15.95. **Credit** AmEx, MC, V.
The original Bill's opened in Lewes, East Sussex in 2001; it's expanded rapidly since being acquired by the Côte chain in 2008 and now has branches in student-heavy towns such as Brighton and Cambridge, as well as London, with more on the way. The appeal of the formula – old-fashioned deli meets country-style café/restaurant – is obvious, and women, in particular, seem to like the place, but there's definitely a corporate whiff to the operation. Chunky tables and school chairs, metal shelving full of Bill's own-label jams, chutneys and oils (for sale, of course), and hanging garlands of dried chillies and colourful tissue paper – all seem to have been ordered from Retro Design Inc. Still, the effect is vibrant and homely, aided by a funk-soul soundtrack and chummy staff. Come for breakfast (eggs benedict, porridge with banana and honey), lunch or dinner, or pop in for tea and a scone. Just don't expect too much. Pea and bean risotto was bland, soggy and could have been bettered by a competent home cook; a 'tart' of slow-roast plum tomato and artichoke wasn't the cooked quiche we were expecting, merely a pile of (average) ingredients atop a pastry rectangle. And a tin pot of skinny fries was meanly portioned. We do like the old-fashioned enamel teapots, though.
Babies and children welcome: children's menu; high chairs; nappy-changing facilities. Booking advisable Fri-Sun; bookings not accepted noon-3pm daily. Disabled: toilet. **Map 5 N2**.
For branches see index.

Ottolenghi

287 Upper Street, N1 2TZ (7288 1454, www.ottolenghi.co.uk). Angel tube or Highbury & Islington tube/rail. **Meals served** 8am-10pm Mon-Wed; 8am-10.30pm Thur-Sat; 9am-7pm Sun. **Main courses** £11-£17. **Credit** AmEx, MC, V.
Yotam Ottolenghi's cookbooks have been a worldwide hit, with even the savoury dishes, which exude healthful vitality, providing eye-candy. This branch of his four-strong London chain is the only one to serve breakfast, lunch and dinner. The sophisticated space (resembling a design studio) is made up of a takeaway section at the front and a restaurant area consisting of one long white table, at the back. The menu features dizzying combinations such as faro, arborio and wild rice with feta, courgette flower, dried Iranian lime and herbs. Lunchtime typically sees around ten salads offered alongside six main courses, though get here early to avoid queuing (no bookings taken for lunch), and to ensure all dishes are still available. A selection of four salads works well as a main course; have three if you're not so hungry. Chargrilled salmon with spicy aubergine choka (similar to baba ganoush, though less creamy) was surprisingly fridge-cold, but refreshing and delicious. Best of the salads was butternut squash with sweetcorn, feta, pumpkin seeds and chilli. Dinner sees the busy kitchen crank up several notches, turning out elegantly plated fusion combinations that add Caribbean, Japanese and Thai ingredients to the core larder of British and Mediterranean produce.
Babies and children welcome: high chairs. Booking advisable dinner; not accepted lunch. Takeaway service. **Map 5 O1**.
For branches see index.

Kentish Town

Kentish Canteen

300 Kentish Town Road, NW5 2TG (7485 7331, www.kentishcanteen.co.uk). Kentish Town tube. **Meals served** 10am-10.30pm Mon-Fri; 9am-10.30pm Sat, Sun. **Main courses** £5-£15. **Set lunch** £10 1 course incl glass of wine or beer; £13.95 2 courses. **Set dinner** £13.95 2 courses. **Credit** AmEx, MC, V.
From the founders of Covent Garden's PJ's Grill, this colourful café-bistro is a smart alternative to the caffs and boozers around Kentish Town station. The contemporary furniture is a little too formal and close-set for serious lazing over fry-ups and cappuccino but segues well to after-dark cocktails, wallet-friendly wines and a menu of mackerel ceviche and grilled steaks. It makes an ideal quick date for local parents who've snared a babysitter for the evening; daytimes see office workers, freelancers and a few mums with buggies dropping by – though the interior isn't truly child-friendly. Cooking is competent and sometimes very good indeed. Mediterranean ingredients abound – chargrilled chorizo, feta, babaganoush, Israeli couscous – but there's a decent choice of burgers, eggs benedict and Sunday roast beef too. A bargain-priced two-course lunch menu includes several top-picks from the main bill of fare so doesn't feel like a cheapskate compromise. Service is enthusiastic and kind but often elusive. Many diners aim for the front terrace tables. Despite a screen of pot plants, however, you never lose the feeling that you're right by the high road – we prefer indoors.
Available for hire. Babies and children welcome: children's menu; high chairs; nappy-changing facilities. Booking advisable Sat, Sun. Disabled: toilet. Separate room for parties, seats 45. Tables outdoors (9, terrace). Takeaway service.
Map 26 B4.

British

'Confidence' is the word best describing the transformation that British food in London restaurants has undergone. Gone are the days when our native cuisine was an embarrassment, with all but a dozen or so dishes expunged from menus across town. Now, thanks to the diligence and talent of the likes of Fergus Henderson at **St John**, an abundance of traditional dishes has been rediscovered – the ingredients sourced with care and the food expertly prepared and presented with a modern sensitivity. The 'nose to tail' approach, making use of cheap cuts and offal, also chimes with these straitened times. The template can be adapted by many types of establishment: two excellent examples being the outstandingly well-judged cuisine produced by Irishman Richard Corrigan at his top-class **Corrigan's Mayfair**; and the ingredients-led cooking at neighbourhood favourite **Lamberts** of Balham. Longstanding bastions of tradition such as the **Goring** have also flourished in these conditions, as has of-the-moment chef Mark Hix – his latest venture, **Tramshed**, is the winner of Time Out's Best New Meat Restaurant. As well as continuing favourites, such as Camden's **Market**, new practitioners continue to pop up, and this year's crop includes the voguish **Rookery** bar-diner in Clapham; Clapton's bistro-like **Shane's on Chatsworth**, where local sourcing and foraging are watchwords; British charcuterie specialist **Cannon & Cannon** in Brixton; and charming café-restaurant **This Bright Field** in Hackney. Take a bow, devilled kidneys on toast, your time has come.

Central

City

Paternoster Chop House

Warwick Court, Paternoster Square, EC4M 7DX (7029 9400, www.paternosterchophouse.co.uk). St Paul's tube. **Lunch served** noon-3.30pm Mon-Fri; noon-4pm Sun. **Dinner served** 5.30-10.30pm Mon-Fri. **Main courses** £15-£25. **Set meal** (Mon-Fri) £22 2 courses, £27 3 courses. **Set lunch** (Sun) £23 2 courses incl tea or coffee, £27 3 courses incl tea or coffee. **Credit** AmEx, MC, V.

If the name wasn't clue enough, the oversized meat cleaver visible through one window should indicate the slant of this restaurant, part of the D&D London group. Set on the edge of Paternoster Square, it offers striking views of St Paul's from the large covered terrace – a lovely spot for lunch or after-work drinks. The interior is modern and white, with a bar near the entrance and an open kitchen at the rear; the closely packed blond wood tables are invariably occupied by men in suits. The menu is a meaty affair, as you might expect – butchering is done in-house – with grills, roasts, steaks (32-day-aged Galloway or Hereford beef) and a Beast of the Day. But there's plenty of seafood and fish too, with fish caught by day boats in Cornwall. With the City location comes City pricing – most mains cost over £20 – making the set menu a comparative bargain. This yielded a starter of so-so fish cakes (salted ling and salmon) accompanied by a lovely tomato pickle, and a fisherman's pie that was suitably creamy but too heavy on the mash. Finish with Neal's Yard cheeses or a classic British dessert such as fruit crumble or rhubarb fool. Service was on the ball.

Available for hire. Babies and children welcome: high chairs; nappy-changing facilities. Booking advisable. Disabled: toilet. Separate room for parties, seats 13. Tables outdoors (20, courtyard). **Map 11 O6.**

For branch (Butlers Wharf Chop House) see index.

Restaurant at St Paul's

St Paul's Cathedral, St Paul's Churchyard, EC4M 8AD (7248 2469, www.restaurantat stpauls.co.uk). St Paul's tube.

Café **Open/meals served** 9am-5pm Mon-Sat; 10am-4pm Sun.

Restaurant **Lunch served** noon-3pm, **tea served** 3-4.30pm daily. **Set lunch** £21.50 2 courses, £25.95 3 courses. **Set tea** £9.95-£21.25.

Both **Credit** MC, V.

St Paul's crypt may not have quite the impressive architecture of nearby St Mary-le-Bow (*see p274* Café Below), but it is a delightful setting. Old terracotta floor tiles, bone-handled knives and woodwork painted in heritage green contrast pleasingly with a shiny part-open kitchen, black slate tablemats and understated contemporary seating. This spot should be offering paragon British Sunday roasts – and they are pretty good – but charging a £2.50 supplement for them over the set menu price is brazen. And with a mere four wines costing under £20 a bottle, there is a sense that it is geared to City wallets and well-to-do tourists shy of the hubbub in the adjacent café. Maybe that's why we've never found it busy. On the plus side, they do a fine job showcasing British produce, putting a modern spin on traditional combinations: Norfolk asparagus, say, with poached quail egg, spinach and lime hollandaise, or arbroath smokie on toast with fennel mayonnaise and piccalilli. There's always something lovely for vegetarians, but desserts aren't a strong point. Rhubarb and custard meringue came in a leathery pre-baked pastry shell. And the blue foam topping elderflower and gooseberry fool tasted of egg white – not heavenly at all.

Babies and children welcome: high chairs; nappy-changing facilities. Booking advisable. Disabled: lift; toilet. **Map 11 O6.**

Rhodes Twenty Four

24th floor, Tower 42, Old Broad Street, EC2N 1HQ (7877 7703, www.rhodes24.co.uk). Bank tube/DLR or Liverpool Street tube/rail. **Lunch served** noon-2.15pm, **dinner served** 6-8.30pm Mon-Fri. **Main courses** £16.50-£31. **Credit** AmEx, DC, MC, V.

Gaining entrance to Rhodes Twenty Four couldn't make it clearer that you're in the corporate otherworld of the City: in the Tower 42 lobby, you're checked through security and a scanner before catching the express lift up to the 24th floor. Once there, though, the eye is grabbed by truly awe-inspiring views of the Gherkin and other temples of power around it, and disorderly London down below. Inside, the decor is dull by comparison, and so doesn't distract from the vistas or the also-stunning food. Ultra-refined versions of vaguely recognisable trad dishes are prominent: glazed lobster omelette thermidor was full of rich, elusive flavours; fine scallops came with mustard and shallot sauce and a little pyramid of creamy mash. These were only a lead-up to our mains, a delectable mix of textures and tastes in pork loin with poached apple, pork belly and a lobster ravioli, and poached hake with supreme-quality langoustines, fabulously prepared. Having got this far it would be silly to pass on desserts, which include Gary Rhodes' signature favourites such as bread-and-butter pudding but also an utterly irresistible iced peanut parfait with lime jelly. This culinary sophistication carries a price, and costs are augmented by a City-style wine list with bankers'-bonus-scale prices. Service was charming at times but surprisingly slow and unfocused at others, leaving more time to contemplate the views.

Available for hire. Babies and children welcome: high chair. Booking essential, 2-4 weeks in advance. Disabled: lift; toilet. Dress: smart casual. Separate room for parties, seats 40. **Map 12 Q6.**

For branch (Rhodes W1) see index.

Clerkenwell & Farringdon

Medcalf

38-40 Exmouth Market, EC1R 4QE (7833 3533, www.medcalfbar.co.uk). Farringdon tube/rail or 19, 38, 341 bus. **Lunch served** noon-3pm Mon-Sat; noon-3.30pm Sun. **Dinner served** 6-10pm Mon-Thur, Sat; 6-10.30pm Fri. **Main courses** £12.50-£22. **Credit** MC, V.

Now a firm fixture on Exmouth Market's vibrant dining scene, Medcalf has character aplenty. It occupies an Edwardian butcher's shop (hence the name – the beautiful lettering on the front is original), with a wood-lined interior that seems to have got slightly smarter while retaining a charming boho vibe, thanks to dangling light bulbs and pre-loved furniture. Some battered metal tables perch on the pavement; there's also a cute back garden, and the adjacent premises are used as bar overspill and for private events. It's as much bar as restaurant, with an appealing wine list and a stellar array of beers that includes Brooklyn Beer on draught and bottled beers from nearby breweries Redchurch and London Fields. The menu is short (possibly too short) and seasonal, with an emphasis on local, sometimes foraged ingredients – witness 'Hackney leaves' and wild garlic and nettle soup: the latter pleasant, but lacking garlic flavour and with a rather gloopy consistency. Too many dishes rely on assembling rather than cooking. Smoked mackerel, radish and rocket, and butternut squash,

Hix. See p54.

goat's cheese and watercress, were ingredients that shared the same plate but didn't combine into anything more meaningful. Service was also slightly distracted, with one forgetful waitress trying to cope with too many tables.

Babies and children welcome until 7.30pm: high chairs. Booking advisable dinner. Disabled: toilet. Separate room for parties, seats 18. Tables outdoors (7, pavement; 5, garden). **Map 5 N4.**

★ St John HOT 50

26 St John Street, EC1M 4AY (3301 8069, www.stjohnrestaurant.com). Farringdon tube/rail. **Lunch served** noon-2.45pm Mon-Fri, Sun. **Dinner served** 6-10.45pm Mon-Sat. **Main courses** £13.50-£23.80. **Credit** AmEx, MC, V.

Burgers, hot dogs, barbecue, Peruvian... food trends appear in London all the time, but since 1994 St John has remained a British institution whose commitment to ingredient provenance and seasonality make more sense every year. It received a Michelin star in 2009, but is a world away from the starched and Frenchified conventions of tradition: this is a casual sort of dining experience, with chef-white-clad staff who are happy to chat. Part of the curiously shaped space – a former smokehouse – is taken by a bar, which serves snacks (welsh rarebit, bone marrow salad with parsley); the restaurant sits on a mezzanine, with packed-in tables, bare white walls and even barer floorboards. In a style copied the length and breadth of the country, dishes are described with intriguing brevity. There's no indication as to how 'black cuttlefish & onions' might be cooked or presented; likewise, 'Stinking Bishop & potatoes' and 'witch sole & tartare sole' don't give much away. But everything you'll eat here will be near-perfect, unfussy celebrations of good food, with emphasis on the underused and the overlooked. Interesting wines are available by the glass at uncynical prices – and if you really want, staff will bring you a pint from the bar, which seems to sum things up.

Babies and children welcome: high chairs. Booking advisable dinner and weekends. Separate room for parties, seats 18. **Map 5 O5.**

For branch (St John Hotel) see index.

Covent Garden

Rules

35 Maiden Lane, WC2E 7LB (7836 5314, www.rules.co.uk). Covent Garden tube. **Meals served** noon-11.30pm Mon-Sat; noon-10.30pm Sun. **Main courses** £18.95-£28.95. **Credit** AmEx, MC, V.

Ah, if the pictures of Polly Fitzroy and Laura Honey, two long-forgotten Victorian dancers, could talk... Rules has been accumulating its indescribable collection of prints, paintings, hunting trophies and other knick-knacks to look down on its diners since 1798. London's oldest restaurant attracts plenty of tourists, but is no tourist trap, retaining an admirable brio and sense of quality. The velvet booths are delightfully comfortable, service is both chattily welcoming and very on-the-ball. Superlative roast beef (a hefty £32 per person) and game (in season, from Rules' own Pennine estate) are specialities, but other dishes are impressive too. Roast quail salad with apple and turnip was a delicately meaty opener; classic smoked salmon arrived with exceptional own-baked bread. The quality of the meats, full-flavoured but delicately prepared, was again a highlight of saddle of rabbit with bayonne ham, and belly of lamb with asparagus and offset by lovely goat's curd ravioli. Desserts are not neglected either: fresh raspberries were served with an exquisite pink champagne sorbet, and the very proper summer pudding was delicious. Not a cheap spot – though the Rhone Valley-oriented wine list is reasonably priced by current West End standards – but a charming choice for an indulgent meal.

Babies and children welcome: high chairs. Booking advisable. Dress: smart casual; no shorts. Separate rooms for parties, seating 8-18. **Map 18 E5.**

Gloucester Road

Launceston Place

1A Launceston Place, W8 5RL (7937 6912, www.launcestonplace-restaurant.co.uk). Gloucester Road tube. **Lunch served**

noon-2.30pm Tue-Sat; noon-3pm Sun. **Dinner served** 6-10.30pm Mon-Sat; 6.30-9.30pm Sun. **Set lunch** £27 3 courses. **Set dinner** £46 3 courses, £60 tasting menu. **Credit** AmEx, MC, V.
Slightly hidden away in a quiet Kensington street of Regency cottages, with the snugly comfortable feel of a local favourite for affluent residents, Launceston Place is part of the D&D London group, but one of the most distinctive links in the chain. Chef Timothy Allen, formerly of the Michelin-starred Whatley Manor in Wiltshire, took over from Tristan Welch, a regular TV face, at the beginning of 2012, but has continued with a similar style of exquisitely presented modern British food. The first things to impress us in our Sunday lunch menu – exceptionally well priced, like the weekday set menus – were the details, as in a stunningly subtle appetiser of mushroom velouté with hazelnuts. After that, a starter of poached egg with pea velouté and pata negra ham was a little bland by comparison, but still very enjoyable, as was a summer salad with beetroot, piquillo-style peppers and more hazelnuts. Delicate contrasts of flavour and texture were notable in roast English lamb, with the main meat alongside an unusual lamb croquette; ultra-tender roast Longhorn beef with yorkshire pud was both classic and refined. The award-winning wine list is another high point, and the sommelier is expert, enthusiastic and, like the rest of the staff, charming.
Available for hire. Babies and children welcome: high chairs. Booking advisable. Disabled: toilet. Separate room for parties, seats 10. **Map 7 C9.**

Holborn

Great Queen Street

32 Great Queen Street, WC2B 5AA (7242 0622). Covent Garden or Holborn tube.
Bar **Open** 5-11.30pm Tue-Sat.
Restaurant **Lunch served** noon-2.30pm Mon-Sat; noon-3pm Sun. **Dinner served** 6-10.30pm Mon-Sat. **Main courses** £10.80-£22.
Both **Credit** MC, V.
Great Queen Street is a great all-rounder, which you shouldn't take to mean a restaurant that is merely reliable. The menu here always holds enough interest to seem special, but you can just slope up in your most casual strides and still feel welcome. The vibe is close to that of a gastropub – and indeed the space is a converted pub – but you're here to eat, not sink a few pints and mop them up with roast pork belly. Our last visit fizzed into life from the start with glasses of quince and prosecco, before we set about the typically hearty fare. Pig's head and ham croquettes looked neater and more refined than anticipated, but were appropriately butch in flavour; cuttlefish, peas and wild garlic was nicely balanced; and an Old Spot pork chop was cooked just right, the meat's unctuousness cut by lemon, caper and sage butter. Only the salt cod, celeriac and wild mushroom pithivier lacked excitement. Service at ground level is always friendly and usually well informed (although on this occasion staff seemed unable to describe that pithivier), but downstairs in the cellar cocktail bar we've been less than impressed.
Babies and children welcome: high chair. Booking advisable. Disabled: toilet. Tables outdoors (4, pavement). **Map 18 E3.**

King's Cross

Gilbert Scott

St Pancras Renaissance London Hotel, Euston Road, NW1 2AR (7278 3888, www.thegilbert scott.co.uk). King's Cross or St Pancras tube/rail.
Brunch served 11am-2pm Sat, Sun. **Lunch served** noon-3pm daily. **Dinner served** 5.30-11pm Mon-Sat; noon-10pm Sun. **Main courses** £16-£25. **Set meal** (noon-1pm, 5.30-6.30pm, 10-11pm Mon-Fri) £22 2 courses, £27 3 courses. **Credit** AmEx, MC, V.
Enter through the handsome bar to reach the Gilbert Scott, named after the architect of the Midland Grand Hotel and housed in the august setting of its ex-Coffee Room. Brasserie furnishings soften the high-ceilinged grandeur, and the warmly professional service does the rest. Though overseen by one of London's top chefs, Marcus Wareing, this place is anything but stuffy; when one of our party didn't order a starter, the waiter brought out a mini garlic and leek soup in lieu. The menu is a tribute to English cooks and domestic produce, and packs plenty of interest into one page; the wine list takes a more global view, though Gusbourne Blanc de Blancs from Kent was a stellar glass of fizz. Prices are restaurant-level, but the results are generally worth it. Starters run from delicate (crab with pomelo, chilli, fennel and coriander) to robust (a generous serving of mulligatawny packed with quail and onion rings). Next, a Welsh pie, pastai cocos, with ham hock, cockles and leek, lacked much seafood flavour but was otherwise excellent; chargrilled pork chop, with barbecued rib, endive and apple and celeriac purée, was a delicious, nicely balanced plateful. Star pudding was Mrs Beeton's snow egg (similar to an île flottante). After a shaky start in 2011, the Gilbert Scott seems to have got into its stride.
Babies and children welcome: high-chairs. Booking advisable. Disabled: lift; toilet. Dress: smart casual. Separate room for parties, seats 14. **Map 4 L3.**

Mayfair

★ Corrigan's Mayfair

28 Upper Grosvenor Street, W1K 7EH (7499 9943, www.corrigansmayfair.com). Marble Arch tube. **Lunch served** noon-2.30pm Mon-Fri; noon-3.45pm Sun. **Dinner served** 6-10.30pm Mon-Sat; 6-9.15pm Sun. **Main courses** £21-£38. **Set lunch** (Mon-Fri) £27 3 courses incl carafe of wine. **Set meal** (Sun) £27 3 courses. **Cover** £2. **Credit** AmEx, MC, V.
Corrigan's is everything you'd hope for from a Mayfair restaurant, right down to the ruminative pianist. The setting is reverential, but doesn't confuse serious with stiff-backed – there are feathered lampshades, stood on metal birds' feet; a portrait of Dizzy Gillespie trumpets a bouquet of flowers; even the bread is served in jocularly rustic flowerpots. Above all, the food is excellent (good value, too, on the £27 Sunday lunch menu, notwithstanding a £2 cover charge and wines priced to the lower heavens). Despite an emphasis on heavy meats and seafood, nothing is staid. The rich flavour of black pudding croquettes, perfectly combining crunch and tenderness, was neatly cut by the sweetness and sharp acidity of pickled

Quo Vadis. See p54.

vegetables; sea bream en papillote was similarly perked up with preserved lemon; and lamb cutlet with peas and broad beans oozed summer contentment. The cooking is precise too – not just for a test-case rhubarb crumble soufflé, but also creating triumphantly contrasting textures in the 'crispy hen's egg, English asparagus and onion ash'. Service manages to be attentive without becoming fussy, with even the pre-dessert crumb-scraper charmingly deployed. A place for a treat, then, and an admirable one.
Babies and children welcome: high chairs. Booking advisable. Disabled: toilet. Separate rooms for parties, seating 4-25. **Map 9 G7**.

The Grill at the Dorchester HOT 50

The Dorchester, 53 Park Lane, W1K 1QA (7629 8888, www.thedorchester.com). Hyde Park Corner tube. **Breakfast served** 7-10.30am Mon-Fri; 8-11am Sat, Sun. **Lunch served** noon-2.30pm Mon-Fri; 12.30-3pm Sat; 12.30-3.30pm Sun. **Dinner served** 6.30-10.30pm Mon-Fri; 6.30-11pm Sat; 7-10.30pm Sun. **Main courses** £19-£46. **Set lunch** (Mon-Sat) £23 2 courses, £27 3 courses. **Set dinner** (6.30-7.30pm) £29 2 courses, £33 3 courses. **Set meal** £70 tasting menu (£90 incl wine). **Credit** AmEx, DC, MC, V.
The Dorchester is not under-supplied with impressive dining places, but the Grill offers one of the most distinctively enjoyable experiences of all London's grand-hotel restaurants. First there's the look: on top of the approach through the hotel's magnificent Promenade, the room itself combines the opulent (gilded gates that could have graced a Romanov palace) and the dotty (hoots-mon Scottish-theme decor of tartan seats and giant painted laddies and lassies inspired by a monster shortbread tin). Service is exceptionally attentive without being oppressive. And the food has a very individual refinement. Trad British classics feature on the menus – a daily roast of Angus beef, game in season – but the intricate, exquisite presentation is never routine. For once, menu descriptions actually undersell their dishes: own-made buffalo cheese, mozzarella-style, with herb mayo, pears and walnuts turned out to be a stunning summer starter, with fresh asparagus and split peas also among the intertwined, sweet-and-fragrant flavours. Roast veal with an almost choucroute-like onion marmalade was similarly full of delicately pleasurable surprises, while strawberry jelly arrived with a fabulously subtle dill mousse. These were both from the set lunch, which is remarkable value, although prices rise rapidly once you order a few side dishes or get into the very grand wine list. A meal here is an extravagance, but one you don't forget.
Babies and children welcome (Sat, Sun): high chairs. Booking advisable; essential weekends. Disabled: toilet. Dress: smart casual. **Map 9 G7**.

St James's

Wiltons

55 Jermyn Street, SW1Y 6LX (7629 9955, www.wiltons.co.uk). Green Park or Piccadilly Circus tube. **Lunch served** noon-2.30pm, **dinner served** 5.30-10.30pm Mon-Fri. **Main courses** £22-£60. **Set lunch** £48 3 courses incl wine. **Set dinner** (5.30-6.30pm) £35 2 courses, £45 3 courses; (5.30-10.30pm) £80, £90 tasting menus (£155, £175 incl wine). **Credit** AmEx, DC, MC, V.
Overheard at Wilton's: 'My uncle died, up in Anglesey… he was a baronet.' Walk into the most intimate of London's grand-old-institution restaurants, founded 1742, and you can think you're entering the world of PG Wodehouse, or, for more classy literary allusions, Anthony Powell. The snugly luxurious style is timeless; besuited gents, some almost certainly peers of the realm, occupy most of the tables for lunch. The great attraction is the service: the chance to be pampered by squads of black-jacketed waiters and ladies in curious green dresses. Oysters, lobsters and other seafood, fish, meats from the grill and (in season) game in traditional British styles are the specialities, but there are also roasts, vegetarian choices and several set menus. The £48 lunch menu includes three courses, with a different glass of fine wine with the first course and main. A summer salad of quail's egg, mushrooms and seasonal vegetables was brightly refreshing. More distinctive was the holstein escalope that followed: breaded veal topped with a fried egg and powerful little strips of anchovy, and served with a Madeira sauce, the whole amounting to a rich mix of treats perfectly matched with the indulgent setting. To finish, classic summer pudding was delightfully done. Presentation throughout is, naturally, just so.
Babies and children welcome: high chairs. Booking advisable. Disabled: lift; toilet. Dress: smart; jacket required. Separate room for parties, seats 20. Vegetarian menu. **Map 17 B5**.

Soho

Dean Street Townhouse

69-71 Dean Street, W1D 4QJ (7434 1775, www.deanstreettownhouse.com). Piccadilly Circus tube. **Breakfast served** 7-11.30am, **tea served** 3-5pm daily. **Meals served** 11.30am-11.30pm Mon-Sat; 11.30am-10.30pm Sun. **Main courses** £15-£24. **Set dinner** (5-7.30pm) £17 2 courses, £21 3 courses. **Credit** AmEx, MC, V.
A hard-working, all-hours restaurant offering breakfast (plus brunch at weekends) and afternoon tea, as well as lunch and dinner, DST is part of the fashionable hotel of the same name. It's housed in handsome Georgian buildings that once also held Soho legend the Gargoyle Club; the whole complex belongs to the Soho House group. The dining room has a classical look, pepped up with modern art. A seasonal, weekly changing menu might start with ham hock broth, lancashire cheese and onion tart, or razor clams with wild boar and garlic, and move on to grilled Rye Bay plaice, roast chicken with sage and onion stuffing or a salad of smoked pigeon, scotch quail eggs and puy lentils. There's a roast on Sundays, and a vegetarian menu (though this centres on unexciting cheese and egg dishes). Food is good, if not revelatory, but then it doesn't need to be – this is a popular, buzzy place, filled with everyone from groups of creatives and theatregoers to lone business diners. All are treated to proficient service from a well-drilled crew. The drinks menu ranges wide, and thanks to the bar includes many cocktails (there's even a bloody mary list).
Babies and children welcome: high chairs. Booking essential. Disabled: toilet. Separate room for parties, seats 12. Tables outdoors (7, terrace). **Map 17 B3**.

Hix HOT 50

66-70 Brewer Street, W1F 9UP (7292 3518, www.hixsoho.co.uk). Piccadilly Circus tube. **Breakfast served** 7-11am daily. **Meals served** noon-11.30pm daily. **Main courses** £14.75-£36. **Set meal** (4.30-6.30pm, 10.30-11.30pm Mon-Sat; noon-10.30pm Sun) £17.50 2 courses, £22.50 3 courses. **Credit** AmEx, MC, V.
In his 17 years with multiple operator Caprice Holdings, Mark Hix learned a thing or two about running restaurants. His flagship in the heart of Soho retains the buzz that surrounded its opening in late 2009. YBA artworks by the likes of Damien Hirst and Tracey Emin add a modern twist to the wood-panelled room, which is packed and noisy most nights (we have known service to tail off slightly when stretched, although in general it's superb). This is still the place to sample Hix's signature seasonal British cooking and revel in the informally clubby surroundings. Staples on the breakfast-to-dinner menu include roast Woolley Park Farm free-range chicken to share, smoked salmon with 'Corrigan' soda bread (most dishes contain a name-check), or hanger steak with roast bone marrow. Specials go big on seafood (we had a great smoked haddock salad with soft-boiled egg and asparagus recently) and unusual native vegetables (samphire, say, or foraged mushrooms and herbs). Drinks can force a bill alarmingly upwards, but Mark's Bar in the basement is a great spot for a few interesting cocktails, if you can bag a table (the licence requires you to choose something from the menu too).
Available for hire. Babies and children welcome: high chairs; nappy-changing facilities. Booking advisable. Disabled: toilet. Separate room for parties, seats 10. Vegan dishes. Vegetarian menu. **Map 17 A4**.
For branches see index.

Quo Vadis

26-29 Dean Street, W1D 3LL (7437 9585, www.quovadissoho.co.uk). Leicester Square, Piccadilly Circus or Tottenham Court Road tube. **Lunch served** noon-2.30pm, **dinner served** 5.30-11pm Mon-Sat. **Main courses** £14-£18.50. **Set meal** £17.50 2 courses, £20 3 courses. **Credit** AmEx, MC, V.
Since Sam and Eddie Hart (Fino, *see p235*, Barrafina, *see p237*) bought Quo Vadis in 2008, it has been good, yet not special. But in early 2012 they brightened the (already lovely) dining room, installed champion maître d' Jon Spiteri and established Jeremy Lee (ex-Blueprint Café) in the kitchen, and suddenly this is a destination restaurant once more. Lee's food is delightfully British, but with a light, modern touch, and comes at very reasonable prices. The charmingly illustrated menu changes regularly. Young garlic with goat's curd, broad beans and tapenade followed by whole mackerel with pickled gooseberries was just the thing on a summer's evening. Proper flavours shine through. From the well-priced set menu, duck and chicken liver pâté was smooth and moreish, while lamb onglet with artichoke and gremolata made a good combo. Cold roast veal with tunny (tuna) sauce, anchovies and capers was a nice change, and a side of fat golden chips offered comforting familiarity. An assured global wine list lets you spend a little or a lot; cocktails are top-notch (there's a separate bar, with a snack menu); and service comes with a smile. It's a pleasure to see a Soho icon back in contention.
Babies and children welcome: high chairs. Booking advisable. Separate rooms for parties, seating 12 and 24-32. Tables outdoors (6, terrace). **Map 17 B3**.

Union Jacks. See p58.

Strand

Savoy Grill

Savoy Hotel, Strand, WC2R 0EW (7592 1600, www.gordonramsay.com/thesavoygrill). Embankment tube or Charing Cross tube/rail.
Lunch served noon-3pm, **dinner served** 5.30-10.45pm daily. **Main courses** £18-£38. **Set lunch** £26 3 courses. **Set dinner** (5.30-6.45pm Mon-Fri) £20 2 courses, £26 3 courses. **Credit** AmEx, DC, MC, V.

Lavish renovation of the Savoy (completed 2010) included the Grill room. With its stunning Swarovski chandeliers and tortoiseshell and chrome art deco furnishings, it evokes the hotel's inter-war glory days with real pzazz (we were affably told we had the Winston Churchill table, from where he could see who else was in the room). It's now part of the Gordon Ramsay group, a label with which you never know quite what to expect – but in our experience this is a well-run ship. Service is both charmingly relaxed and very responsive; menus are a blend of the richly traditional (especially the hefty steaks) and inventive, lighter modernity. Lunch and pre-theatre set menus are a West End bargain: from the latter, a salad of golden and ruby beetroot with goat's curd was beautifully refreshing, and chilled leek and potato soup with poached quail's egg perfectly balanced. An expert use of the best fresh ingredients, with every flavour just right, enlivened mains of haddock and king prawn fish cake with mustard sauce, and an old Brit favourite, gammon with pineapple and chips. Wine prices can be frightening, but there's a fair range of less extravagant bottles. An indulgent treat.
Available for hire. Babies and children welcome: high chairs; nappy-changing facilities. Booking advisable. Disabled: toilet. Dress: smart casual. Separate room for parties, seats 40.
Map 18 E5.

Simpson's-in-the-Strand

100 Strand, WC2R 0EW (7836 9112, www.simpsonsinthestrand.co.uk). Embankment tube or Charing Cross tube/rail. **Breakfast served** 7.15-10.30am Mon-Fri. **Lunch served** 12.15-2.45pm Mon-Sat. **Dinner served** 5.45-10.45pm Mon-Sat. **Meals served** 12.15-9pm Sun. **Main courses** £16-£33.50. **Set meal** (lunch, 5.45-7pm) £25.75 2 courses, £31 3 courses. **Credit** AmEx, DC, MC, V.

Created for 19th-century gentlemen in swelling waistcoats with gold watch chains, Simpson's magnificent Grand Divan dining room – with its wood panelling, chandeliers and Liberty-print booths – continues to draw theatregoers and tourists (our waiter's 'How are you enjoying London?' was a giveaway). Beyond the opulent Victoriana, the great attraction is the much-photographed classic roast beef, carved at table on gleaming silver-domed trolleys by white-clad chefs. Yet if you don't have the beef, it seems there's little point going, given the lofty prices: alternatives we tried were unimpressive. A starter of baked goat's cheese with herby warm potato salad (more like a potato terrine) was pleasant but unexciting; duck liver pâté was smooth, but again lacking in distinct flavour. Mains were bland too: stuffed suckling pig overwhelmed by coarsely prepared, over-sweet red cabbage; skate with a spiced crust having little flavour beyond salt. The expensive wine list has high mark-ups and what almost appears to be a deliberate shortage of accessible options. Solicitous service from abundant staff adds to the experience, though it was annoying we needed to ask specifically for the set menu. A London institution that should do more to justify its charges.
Babies and children welcome: high chairs. Booking advisable. Disabled: toilet. Dress: smart casual; no trainers, T-shirts or sportswear. Separate rooms for parties, seating 25 and 150.
Map 18 E5.

Trafalgar Square

National Dining Rooms

Sainsbury Wing, National Gallery, Trafalgar Square, WC2N 5DN (7747 2525, www.peytonandbyrne.co.uk/the-national-dining-rooms). Charing Cross tube/rail.
Bakery **Meals served** 10am-4.30pm Mon-Thur, Sat, Sun; 10am-7pm Fri. **Main courses** £8-£16.50.
Restaurant **Lunch served** noon-3pm daily. **Dinner served** 5-7pm Fri. **Main courses** £14.50-£22.50. **Set meal** £24 2 courses, £27 3 courses.
Both **Credit** MC, V.

A midday meal at this refined venue in the Sainsbury Wing of the National Gallery is everything a museum lunch should be. The restaurant occupies a quiet, sophisticated space that, with its little bucket leather armchairs and banquettes, feels part private club and part fin de siècle café. Here you'll find the quality pastries and snacks expected from a Peyton & Byrne establishment, along with an inventive restaurant menu based around seasonal British produce – lemon sole with clams, summer greens and samphire, say. The Bakery menu includes a range of tarts and pies, cheese plates and classic English dishes such as stew and prawn cocktail. Four small plates for just £12 were beautifully balanced and included perfectly crisp grilled sardines on a bed of samphire and peas, heritage carrots with peach and roasted baby beet salad and a pea houmous with superb crostini. All looked attractive, and positively sang with flavour. Drinks encompass a formidable assembly of teas and infusions (sencha fukuju, anyone?), plus a fairly priced, Old World dominated wine list with oodles of by-the-glass choice.

Babies and children welcome: children's menu; high chairs. Booking advisable. Disabled: toilet. **Map 17 C5.**
For branch (National Café) see index.

Victoria

★ Goring Hotel

Beeston Place, Grosvenor Gardens, SW1W 0JW (7396 9000, www.goringhotel.co.uk). Victoria tube/rail. **Breakfast served** 7-10am Mon-Fri; 7-10.30am Sat; 7.30-10.30am Sun. **Lunch served** 12.30-2.30pm Mon-Fri, Sun. **Dinner served** 6-10pm daily. **Set lunch** (Mon-Fri) £38 3 courses; (Sun) £44 3 courses. **Set dinner** £49.50 3 courses. **Credit** AmEx, DC, MC, V.

Hidden away in a leafy enclave near Victoria Station lies the bastion of British hospitality that is the family-owned Goring Hotel. An exemplar of well-maintained Edwardian architecture and decor, it was the world's first hotel built with en-suite bathrooms throughout. The spacious dining room, redesigned by David Linley, is a serene, almost heavenly space of ivory and white, with custom furniture – even the waiters' uniforms are in tune with the decor. Food and service match this splendour, to give diners the sensation of being pampered without feeling discomfited by the attention. Chairs are carefully manoeuvred to seat one; napkins delicately placed on your lap; glasses, cutlery and crystal obelisks glint on tables; and side dishes arrive in exquisite little copper chafing dishes. The expertly prepared food is traditional British, the menu highlighting provenance and the dishes cleverly varied to provide satisfying and memorable meals. Forgotten delights such as glazed Scottish lobster thermidor omelette, and the late Queen Mother's favourite, eggs drumkilbo, are regularly available. The set three-course Sunday lunch, at a relatively modest £44, is an excellent way to sample such delights, as well as such standards as roast sirloin of Castle of Mey beef with yorkshire pudding from the trolley. The 500-bin wine list is assembled from a stupendous cellar.

Available for hire. Babies and children welcome: high chairs. Booking essential. Disabled: toilet (hotel). Dress: smart casual. Separate rooms for parties, seating 6-40. Tables outdoors (6, terrace). **Map 15 H9.**

Waterloo

Canteen

Royal Festival Hall, Belvedere Road, SE1 8XX (0845 686 1122, www.canteen.co.uk). Waterloo tube/rail. **Meals served** 8am-11pm Mon-Fri; 9am-11pm Sat; 9am-10pm Sun. **Main courses** £8.50-£18.50. **Credit** AmEx, MC, V.

Brit concept chains have become two-a-penny since the first Canteen opened on the edge of Old Spitalfields Market in 2006, but this group – now five-strong – continues to thrive. The location of the SE1 branch (tucked into the back of the Royal Festival Hall) means it's usually busy. Although the devilled kidneys on toast have always disappointed, more familiar dishes hit the spot: macaroni cheese, sausages and mash with onion gravy, the all-day breakfast – each of which costs shy of a tenner. Otherwise, prices are no longer as appetising as they were: £18.50 for the (albeit good) 28-day-aged steak, £14.50 for a reliable, daily changing roast, and a naughty £7.50 for that favourite corner-filler, the fish-finger sandwich. You might instead choose to sit at the bar for wines by the glass or 500ml carafe, half a dozen cocktails (Bramble, Cockney Cobbler) and some touches of zaniness (hot chocolate with rum, perhaps). The virtues of the place remain constant (handsome functional decor, dishes well pitched for different occasions), but the vices are also unchanged: booths a little tight for comfort, and refectory-style designer chairs lacking proper backs, neither of which invite you to linger.

Available for hire. Babies and children welcome: colouring books; high chairs; nappy-changing. Booking advisable 5.30-8pm; not accepted lunch Sat, Sun. Disabled: toilet. Tables outdoors (30, terrace). Takeaway service. **Map 10 M8.**
For branches see index.

Cannon & Cannon. See p59.

Westminster

Northall

Corinthia Hotel, 10 Northumberland Avenue, WC2N 5AE (7930 8181, www.thenorthall.co.uk). Embankment tube. **Breakfast served** 6-10am Mon-Sat; 6-11am Sun. **Lunch served** noon-3pm Mon-Sat; noon-4pm Sun. **Tea served** 5.30-7pm, **Dinner served** 5.30-11pm daily. **Main courses** £24-£39. **Set lunch** £28 3 courses. **Set dinner** £25 2 courses, £28 3 courses. **Credit** AmEx, MC, V.

The Malta-based Corinthia hotel group spent a mint turning this ex-government building near the Embankment into its London flagship, with stunning lobbies and two high-wow-factor restaurants, Italian Massimo (*see p165*) and this one, with a modern British emphasis. Decor is a blend of classic grandeur (soaring Corinthian columns, pf course), modern glitz and old-London poshness, with very comfortable leather seating and lofty windows. It's all very dressed-up, but not so clear on where it's going. Service seemed oddly uncoordinated. Menus make great play of the origin of the quality British ingredients, but the cooking seems to lack the flair of its best grand-hotel competitors. From the three-course set lunch menu – a reasonable deal for this kind of venue – cod brandade with smoked salmon, and roast barnsley lamb chop with forest mushrooms, shallots and a pile of parsley, were both pleasant, but unexciting. Just reading the 'Afters' list had us drooling, but, sadly, vanilla parfait with cherry compote and watermelon and mint jelly had almost tasteless jelly. The wine selection is suitably grand without any special highlights, but one plus is the offer of superb Damian Allsop chocolates, for an extra charge.

Babies and children welcome: high chairs. Booking advisable. Disabled: toilet. Dress: smart casual. Separate rooms for parties, seating 24 and 34. **Map 10 L8.**

West

Bayswater

Hereford Road

3 Hereford Road, W2 4AB (7727 1144, www.herefordroad.org). Bayswater tube. **Lunch served** noon-3pm Mon-Sat; noon-4pm Sun. **Dinner served** 6-10.30pm Mon-Sat; 6-10pm Sun. **Main courses** £9.50-£14.50. **Set lunch** (Mon-Fri) £13 2 courses, £15.50 3 courses. **Credit** AmEx, MC, V.

Tramshed. See p61.

Try not to be put off by the bare interior of Hereford Road (there's not a single picture on the walls) – Tom Pemberton's British cooking provides all the visual nourishment you'll need. Pemberton worked for the ground-breaking St John Bread & Wine, and the influence of Fergus Henderson is apparent. He is not afraid to serve long-forgotten dishes such as bath chaps (cured pigs' cheeks), accompanied ever so simply, but most enjoyably, by watercress and mustard. Deep-fried devilled sprats with tartare sauce was another solid success of our meal. Slow cooking is a particular forte of the kitchen, and a braised rabbit leg with fennel and bacon was so delicious that we scraped every morsel from the plate. The menu changes daily, and seasonality plays a big part; in the spring, fresh and vibrant Yorkshire rhubarb, which had been poached, came with a textbook buttermilk pudding. Sensible pricing (the set lunch is a bargain) and willing service are further reasons why this restaurant continues to be highly popular, so it's easy to forgive wooden chairs that could be more comfortable (try to relax on the diner-style red leather sofas). The Old World wine list isn't long, but has adequate options by the glass and half-litre carafe.
Babies and children welcome: high chairs. Booking advisable. Disabled: toilet. Tables outdoors (3, pavement). **Map 7 B6.**

Chiswick

Union Jacks NEW

217-221 Chiswick High Road, W4 2DW (3617 9988, www.unionjacksrestaurants.com). Chiswick Park or Turnham Green tube. **Meals served** noon-11pm Mon-Sat; noon-10.30pm Sun. **Main courses** £4-£13.50. **Credit** AmEx, DC, MC, V.
Jamie Oliver's latest enterprise triangulates three strong London trends: sharing plates, British sourcing and, on the ground floor, casual bar-counter service. The decor, upstairs and down, is graffiti pop art, the service is engaged and informative, and everything's done with good humour – for instance, instead of being offered extra toppings, you're invited to 'pimp' your pizza. The hits of our meal were 'Juliette flatbread pizza' – a margherita, but made with westcombe jacks and lincolnshire poacher, the muscularity of the cheese neatly offset by lemon thyme and a well-judged passata – and lightly battered garlic mushrooms – snappy to the tooth, but perfectly moist within. There were, however, too many misses. Smoky chicken liver was otherwise short of flavour, and came with soldiers that contrived to be both burnt and floppy, while crunchy 'by-catch fish fingers' tasted surprisingly bland. An intriguing side dish of purple sprouting broccoli had its crushed hazelnuts, bits of bacon and roast garlic in all the wrong proportions, but a sticky treacle tart with (slightly) orange soured cream brought things to a decent conclusion. While the broad range of drinks – from draught beer via English cocktails such as damson gin fizz to own-made fizzy dandelion and burdock – shows imagination, there's insufficient attention to detail just yet.
Babies and children welcome: children's menu; high chairs; nappy-changing facilities. Booking advisable dinner Thur-Sun. Separate room for parties, seats 30-60. Vegan dishes.
For branches see index.

South West

Parsons Green

Manson

676 Fulham Road, SW6 5SA (7384 9559, www.mansonrestaurant.co.uk). Parsons Green tube. **Lunch served** noon-3pm Mon-Fri. **Brunch served** 10am-4pm Sat. **Dinner served** 6-10.30pm Mon-Fri; 7-10.30pm Sat. **Meals served** noon-4pm Sun. **Main courses** £10-£18. **Set meal** (noon-3pm, 6-7pm Mon-Fri) £13.50 2 courses, £17.50 3 courses. **Credit** AmEx, MC, V.
Although only a couple of years old, Manson feels both firmly established and refreshingly innovative. The light-filled, spacious corner room combines trad distressed leather seats and eau-de-nil panelling with big steel ceiling lamps and striking wall art. Indie background music plays, replaced later in the evening by the buzz of diners – at which point service slows. Still, the friendly staff are very helpful at the decision-making stage, explaining the more offbeat items and how dishes are cooked. This matters, as the menu descriptions are just lists of ingredients (stellar British produce including Herdwick lamb, artisan cheeses and seasonal veg). The excellent early-bird menu doesn't play it safe, featuring veal shin and black pudding among the mains; it also offers the full range of à la carte desserts. Mussels were slightly overpowered by a beer and wild garlic sauce, but the concept was interesting. Portions of roast pollock and bavette steak were generous, the accompanying potatoes (super-creamy mash and fat chips) memorable.

Sticky toffee pudding was packed with dates, and served with plenty of sauce and a scoop of subtly perfumed earl grey ice-cream. Creative cooking, priced fairly, in a stylish and convivial setting.
Babies and children admitted. Booking advisable. Tables outdoors (4, pavement).

South

Balham

★ Lamberts

2 Station Parade, Balham High Road, SW12 9AZ (8675 2233, www.lambertsrestaurant.com). Balham tube/rail. **Lunch served** 12.30-2.30pm Tue-Sat. **Dinner served** 6-10.30pm Tue-Sat. **Meals served** noon-5pm Sun. **Main courses** £10-£18. **Set dinner** (Tue-Thur) £17 2 courses, £20 3 courses; (Fri, Sat) £25 2 courses, £30 3 courses. **Set meal** (Sun) £20 2 courses, £24 3 courses. **Credit** MC, V.

Much-loved Balham favourite Lamberts never fails to please. It's the kind of place that every neighbourhood should have, ticking all the right boxes: seasonal cooking, frequently changing menus, great wine list and top-quality sourcing. Sustainably sourced fish come from local supplier Murray's Fresh Fish, game from the Denham Estate, vegetables from Secretts Farm in Surrey, and rare-breed lamb, beef and pork from Richard Vaughan's Huntsham Court Farm in Herefordshire. The restaurant looks the part too, the shopfront dining room done up in shades of taupe and caramel, with colourful canvases by local artists on the walls. Add knowledgeable, alert service, plus attractive prices, and you've got a winner. An early spring dinner menu might feature such of-the-minute ingredients as purple sprouting broccoli with duck egg and sweet mustard dressing; black bream with Jersey Royal potatoes and chicory; or a pudding of blood-orange cheesecake with honeycomb. Sunday lunch is a hit with locals, offering the likes of rare-roasted rib of Angus beef with yorkshire pudding, horseradish, roast parsnips and potatoes, or a simple-but-sensational chargrilled chicken with baby gem lettuce, peas and lemony mayonnaise.
Available for hire. Babies and children welcome: children's menu (lunch); high chairs. Booking advisable; essential weekends. Tables outdoors (3, pavement).

Brixton

Cannon & Cannon NEW

18 Market Row, SW9 8LD (7501 9152, www.cannonandcannon.com). Brixton tube/rail.
Deli **Open** 11am-5.30pm Tue, Wed; 11am-10pm Thur-Sat; 11am-4pm Sun.
Restaurant **Lunch served** 11am-3pm Tue-Thur; noon-3.30pm Sun. **Dinner served** 6-10pm Thur. **Meals served** 11am-10pm Fri, Sat. **Small plates** £5.50-£7.50. **Set platter** £12.
Both **Credit** AmEx, MC, V.

This deli-café prides itself on British charcuterie. On the ground floor, inverted bouquets of goat saucisson, picante chorizo and wild venison salami dangle above a counter filled with British cheeses. All these can be sampled in the small dining room upstairs (dubbed 'the cheese salon'). Diners can choose a combination of two cheeses, two meats and two sides, served with crusty sourdough bread. All the key produce is British. Here, charcuterie means cold-smoked mutton, wild boar salami and hot smoked pigs' cheeks; cheeses include bermondsey spa (the rind is washed with Kernel beer) and unpasteurised stichelton. Cooked dishes are limited to two a day: artichokes preserved in oil, baked with pungent, unpasteurised Dorset blue vinney cheese, and topped with hazelnuts, was a delight, as was grilled Suffolk chorizo.The British theme also spills over to the brief wine list. France and Spain get competition from a Kentish white (Ortega Gribble Bridge from Biddenden) and a Sussex red (Bolney Estates Lychgate). A few black and white photos of long-gone shopfronts adorn the premises, while thrift store furniture has been jumbled together to seat diners – like many of Brixton's new wave of eateries, this is not a place to linger all evening.
Available for hire. Babies and children welcome: high chairs. Booking advisable. Separate room for parties, seats 30. Tables outdoors (5, market). Takeaway service. **Map 22 E2.**

Clapham

Rookery NEW

69 Clapham Common Southside, SW4 9DA (8673 9162, www.therookeryclapham.co.uk). Clapham Common or Clapham South tube.
Bar **Open** 5-11pm Tue, Wed; noon-11pm Thur; noon-midnight Fri, Sat; 12.30-10.30pm Sun.
Restaurant **Lunch served** noon-2.30pm Thur, Fri; noon-3pm Sat; 12.30-4pm Sun. **Dinner served** 6-10pm Tue-Sat. **Main courses** £12-£14. **Credit** MC, V.

The Rookery opened across from Clapham Common in 2011, bringing a hipsterish vibe to this increasingly genteel neighbourhood. It's bang on-trend with its small, frequently changing Med-accented British menu; its rough-hewn, casual good looks; its staff who wouldn't look out of place in Hoxton; and its interest in craft beers from Britain and beyond (there's a good wine selection and cocktails too). The location makes it a prime destination for appreciative locals. The kitchen does a mean Sunday lunch; opt for a traditional roast of Dexter beef or Gloucestershire Old Spot pork, or a warming rabbit and bacon pie for two, made with a beautifully textured suet crust – just the thing after a brisk winter walk. In summer, the outdoor terrace is a great place for drinks and bar snacks such as own-cured goose 'ham' or ginger and garlic pork ribs. We've enjoyed the likes of that revived British classic, bath chaps (cured pigs' cheeks), roast hake with dahl and cauliflower, and rare-cooked duck breast with salsa verde. The cooking has an honesty and simplicity that keeps customers returning, and the thoroughly democratic prices help too.
Babies and children welcome: high chairs. Booking advisable. Separate room for parties, seats 30. Tables outdoors (8, terrace). **Map 22 A3.**

South East

East Dulwich

Franklins

157 Lordship Lane, SE22 8HX (8299 9598, www.franklinsrestaurant.com). East Dulwich rail. **Meals served** noon-10.30pm Mon-Sat; noon-10pm Sun. **Main courses** £13-£21. **Set lunch** (noon-5pm Mon-Fri) £13.95 2 courses, £16.95 3 courses. **Credit** MC, V.

There's always something interesting to eat at Franklins. Whether it's ox tongue, calf's faggots, sweetbreads or mutton; or the first asparagus, samphire or wild garlic of spring; or rock oysters from Colchester or cheeses from the Home Counties. Everything is handled by chefs who know what they're doing with these nose-to-tail ingredients. The menu is led by the seasons, with produce sourced as locally as possible, often via the firm's farm shop next door. Bread is baked in-house. To drink, there's beer from Sussex, English fruit gins and liqueurs, draught cider, and a pleasingly wide choice of dessert wines. Franklins was in East Dulwich years before the area got so gentrified, yet even with the extensive competition that's built up, it remains the grande dame of the local foodie scene: loved and respected in equal measure. The dining room is fresh and airy, with a semi-open kitchen creating atmosphere, but many regulars like to eat in the comfortable front bar (packed for weekend brunch), or at the pavement tables. This is a great place for an intimate dinner or celebration, and the weekday lunch menu is a steal.
Available for hire. Babies and children welcome: high chairs; nappy-changing facilities. Booking advisable. Disabled: toilet. Separate room for parties, seats 34. Tables outdoors (4, pavement). **Map 23 C4.**

Greenwich

Old Brewery

Pepys Building, Old Royal Naval College, SE10 9LW (3327 1280, www.oldbrewerygreenwich.com). Cutty Sark DLR.
Café **Meals served** 10am-5pm daily. **Main courses** £6-£16.50.
Bar **Open** 11am-11pm daily. **Lunch served** noon-5pm, **dinner served** 6-10.30pm daily. **Main courses** £6-£16.50.
Restaurant **Dinner served** 6-10pm Mon-Thur; 6-10.30pm Fri. Sat; 6-9pm Sun. **Main courses** £10.50-£19.50.
All **Credit** AmEx, MC, V.

The Old Brewery, as you might guess, is all about beer. OK, it's partly about the Grade-II listed hall and World Heritage Site location, amid the quads of the Royal Naval College (now Greenwich University). It's owned by Greenwich microbrewery Meantime, and even the decor is dominated by beer – eight copper brewing vats, a giant chandelier made of 2,000 blue bottles, and a wall frieze illustrating the history of brewing. A basic café menu is available during the day; in the evening, restaurant-standard dishes are served. The food (modern British standards emphasising local produce) often acknowledges London's hop-growing neighbour, such as the blue cheese salad with Kentish cobnuts. And there's yet more beer, both as drink pairings and incorporated into the dishes – witness London Porter-braised lamb shoulder, Meantime IPA-braised neck of Tamworth pork, crème caramel served with Meantime Chocolate Porter-soaked prunes. The result: great pub food in comfortable surroundings, with genial service. Unfortunately, prices suggest the aim is higher, and on this score it falls short. The adjoining bar is really the star, with its fantastic array of world beers and a menu served outdoors in the charming courtyard where you can fully appreciate the setting.
Babies and children welcome: high chairs; nappy-changing facilities. Booking advisable. Disabled: toilet. Tables outdoors (20, garden). Takeaway service.

London Bridge & Borough

Roast

The Floral Hall, Borough Market, Stoney Street, SE1 1TL (0845 034 7300, www.roast-restaurant.com). London Bridge tube/rail. **Breakfast served** 7-10.45am Mon-Fri; 8-11.30am Sat. **Lunch served** noon-2.45pm Mon, Tue; noon-3.45pm Wed-Sat; 11.30am-4pm Sun. **Dinner served** 6-10.30pm Mon-Sat; 4-8.45pm Sun. **Main courses** £16.50-£35. **Set meal** (Sun) £32 3 courses. **Credit** AmEx, MC, V.

Perched like a glass birdcage above Borough Market, Roast's window-lined first-floor dining room – all high ceilings, white table linen, fine glassware, piano player at the bar, attentive waiters – makes a serene contrast to the melee of the market below, an oasis of leisurely dining above London's temple of haute street food. The grand space has in the past slightly outclassed the occasionally stodgy food. But a new chef, New Zealander Marcus Verberne, has started to adapt the menu to its surroundings while staying true to British roots. It won't win awards for innovation, but a starter of sautéed mushrooms on brioche was perfectly prepared and came with a dainty poached quail's egg balanced on top. Take a hint from the restaurant's name and go for a traditional roast for main course. Pork belly was meltingly tender and rich, nicely offset by apple sauce. Satisfying roast beef with yorkshire pudding and all the trimmings was a mile away from the grey mess sometimes found at old boozers. Puddings are equally time-honoured. In such a spectacular space, some diners might long for a bit of pzazz in the food, but traditionalists won't be disappointed.

Available for hire. Babies and children welcome: children's menu; high chairs; nappy-changing facilities. Booking advisable. Disabled: lift; toilet. Dress: smart casual. **Map 11 P8.**

East

Docklands

Boisdale Canary Wharf

Cabot Place, E14 4QT (7715 5818, www.boisdale-cw.co.uk). Canary Wharf tube/DLR. **Lunch served** noon-2.30pm Mon-Fri. **Dinner served** 6-10.30pm Mon-Sat. **Main courses** £14.50-£51. **Set meal** £19.75 2 courses. **Credit** AmEx, MC, V.

This highly enjoyable member of the Boisdale triumvirate is almost laughably incongruous. On the second floor is an appropriately smart bar-diner that offers a brasserie menu and mollifying puffs in the Cigar Library or on the terrace, but the third-floor main restaurant has a cod-Scottish gentlemen's-club theme entirely at odds with the office-casual modernist architecture around it. No cliché is knowingly ducked – mounted stag's head and angling trophy, tartan carpet, table-top thistles – yet they're delivered with a cheerful wink (a slightly lascivious wink when it comes to the waitresses' tartan miniskirts). From the £19.75 'Jacobite' menu, we were content with potted mackerel, despite it arriving cold rather than warm, and relished haggis with a quenelle each of orange neep and white mash: no fussy presentation, just gut-stuffing good flavours. A la carte prices trespass on expense-account territory, but crab tian (with another quenelle: avocado, this time) and king prawn caesar salad were up to the mark, big in size and taste. After 9pm, there's a stiff cover charge to watch jazz or blues from a stage at the far end of a pewter bar counter (where there's a daunting number of fine whiskies).

Available for hire. Babies and children admitted. Booking advisable Wed-Sat. Disabled: lift; toilet. Dress: smart casual; no shorts or sportswear. Entertainment: musicians Mon-Sat. Separate rooms for parties, seating 2-40. Tables outdoors (15, terrace). **Map 24 B2.**

For branches see index.

Shoreditch

Albion

2-4 Boundary Street, E2 7DD (7729 1051, www.albioncaff.co.uk). Shoreditch High Street rail. **Breakfast served** 8am-noon Mon-Fri; 8am-12.30pm Sat, Sun. **Meals served** 8am-11pm daily. **Main courses** £8-£14. **Credit** AmEx, MC, V.

It's hard not to like somewhere that makes its own jammie dodgers and bourbon biscuits: a bit of oven art for under a pound. These are on sale in the shop portion of Terence Conran's Shoreditch gastro-palace and hotel, through which you reach the Albion, identifying en route any of the picnic-style goods you'd like to be served at your table (at a supplement), notably the fine range of own-made biscuits, and cakes. The menu proper mixes up a bit of gastropub, a bit of café and a bit of hotel

Shane's on Chatsworth. See p62.

(breakfast served all day and a late-night menu featuring welsh rarebit and hot chocolate with shortbread), with a British sensibility that's both a stance and a result of using seasonal produce and local makers. There are serious sandwiches on bread baked overnight on the premises; sharing plates of crackling, charcuterie or vividly fresh kitchen-garden vegetables; snacks such as soup (we tried turnip and squash – delicious), devilled kidneys, omelette and clever salads; and more substantial game pie, rabbit stew, kedgeree, boldly battered and very popular fish and beef-dripping chips, and old-school puddings: it's reliably good. Large, bare tables line the long room; even with its open brickwork, industrial design vibe and massive windows, it's hard to believe the building started life as a Victorian warehouse.
Babies and children welcome: high chairs; nappy-changing facilities. Bookings not accepted for fewer than 7 people. Disabled: toilet. Tables outdoors (10, pavement). Takeaway service. **Map 6 R4**.

Rivington Grill

28-30 Rivington Street, EC2A 3DZ (7729 7053, www.rivingtongrill.co.uk). Old Street tube/rail. *Bar* **Open/snacks served** 11am-1.30am Mon-Sat; 11am-midnight Sun. *Restaurant* **Brunch served** 8-11am Mon-Fri. **Meals served** 11am-11pm Mon-Sat; 11am-10pm Sun. **Main courses** £10-£33.50. **Set lunch** (11am-4pm Sun) £22.50. *Both* **Credit** AmEx, MC, V.

The three-strong Rivington chain, owned by Caprice Holdings, now extends as far as Dubai; this Shoreditch original was opened by chef Mark Hix in 2003 and his influence is still clear on the menu. It's resolutely British, with, it claims, an emphasis on 'local' sourcing (although Bannockburn rib beef is surely only local if you live in Stirlingshire; see also Shetland fish, Yorkshire game, and so on). But the dedication to home-grown ingredients, free-range meat and responsibly caught seafood is admirable, and the kitchen produces solidly rendered dishes. They're mainly reassuringly familiar (fish and chips, bangers and mash, steak, chicken pie), although often feel a bit pricey; a few show cheffier touches (such as sea trout with broccoli and clams, or ham hock with piccalilli relish and dandelion). In style, it's formal enough to lure in the City spillover for business jollies, but not to the extent of alienating the many casual creatives who populate the area. Service on our last visit did everything it needed to. The whitewashed walls, black-clad staff, crisp tablecloths and long, buffed bar make for a pleasant backdrop for breakfast, lunch or dinner, as does the East End modern art scattered around (another Hix hallmark).
Babies and children welcome: high chairs. Booking advisable. Separate room for parties, seats 34. Takeaway service. Vegetarian menu. **For branch see index.**

Rochelle Canteen

Rochelle School, Arnold Circus, E2 7ES (7729 5677, www.arnoldandhenderson.com). Shoreditch High Street rail. **Breakfast served** 9am-noon, **lunch served** noon-3pm Mon-Fri. **Main courses** £10.50-£18.50. **Unlicensed. Corkage** £5. **Credit** MC, V.

Press the buzzer to gain access to the grounds of an old Victorian school and cross the grass to the modern (once bike-) shed structure that forms Rochelle Canteen. Half of it is devoted to the

This Bright Field. See p62.

kitchen, the other to a well-lit, minimally decorated dining room usually full of local artists and designers. You'll probably be sharing a table and, whether through acoustics or customer exuberance, the place can get noisy. Food is excellent. Dishes are flavoursome and every ingredient counts: a salt cod salad starter with gem lettuce, roasted tomato and aïoli was a salty, sweet, crunchy, creamy delight. Next, skate wing with monk's beard – an Italian vegetable that looks like chive and tastes like spinach – was equally satisfying, marred only by slightly undercooked new potatoes. A hearty aubergine and chickpea stew also won favour. The menu changes daily, but desserts are often charmingly old-school, such as prune and date tart or lemon posset with rhubarb. Jugs of elderflower or acai are on offer if you haven't brought your own booze. A genuine one-off in a world of bland chains.
Available for hire (evenings only). Babies and children welcome: high chairs; nappy-changing facilities. Booking advisable Thur, Fri. Tables outdoors, (12, courtyard). **Map 6 S4**.

Tramshed NEW

2012 WINNER BEST NEW MEAT RESTAURANT
32 Rivington Street, EC2A 3LX (7749 0478, www.chickenandsteak.co.uk). Old Street tube/rail. **Meals served** noon-10pm Mon-Wed; noon-11pm Thur, Fri; noon-10.30pm Sat; noon-9.30pm Sun. **Main courses** £13.50-£20. **Credit** AmEx, MC, V.

Chef Mark Hix has always had a thing for meat, and his latest venture takes things to extremes. To be precise, you can have roast chicken for one or to share, steak, chicken salad, or steak salad. (A few 'bar snax' include ox cheek croquettes and – the sole veggie option – radishes with celery salt.) To list so few options is beyond bold, and the produce has to be beyond good, which it is. Free-range fowl comes from Woolley Park Farm in Wiltshire; beef is from traditional British cattle breeds and is aged in a 'Himalayan salt chamber', the science of which is complex but results in fabulously sweet and tender steak. What's more, unless you're starving, the whole chook will feed three people, making it £8 per head. This is great value, especially as 'chips' (actually thin-cut fries) are included in the price. All this meat is meted out in a turn-of-the-century Grade II-listed industrial building (which once housed the local tram's electricity generators), a vast room with a soaring ceiling. Light comes in through an enormous arched window, while mezzanine levels break up the floor space. In pride of place is a work by Damien Hirst: a formaldehyde-filled tank containing a preserved bullock and rooster. Puds run from sweet, fragrant strawberries with Jersey cream to a fiendishly good cheesecake rippled with raspberry coulis. Staff are some of the friendliest we've encountered in London. Limited options doesn't need to mean limited success, and Tramshed makes two ingredients go a long, long way.
Available for hire. Babies and children welcome: children's menu; high chairs; nappy-changing facilities. Booking advisable. Disabled: toilet. Separate room for parties, seats 14. Takeaway service. **Map 6 R4**.

Spitalfields

English Restaurant NEW

50-52 Brushfield Street, E1 6AG (7247 4110, www.theenglishrestaurant.com). Liverpool Street tube/rail. **Meals served** 8am-11pm Mon-Fri; 9am-11pm Sat; 8am-7pm Sun. **Main courses** £11-£19. **Set lunch** £14.50 2 courses. **Set dinner** £28 3 courses. **Credit** MC, V.

The English Restaurant also serves breakfast, lunch and afternoon tea, but we visited in the evening, when the wood panelling and booths are shown off to most romantic effect by tabletop candles. The atmosphere was winningly discreet, with a hint of whispered assignations, but the food disappointed. From the à la carte, seared scallops arrived with over-sweet pickled cauliflower rather than the advertised purée, and the pleasantly crunchy herb risotto cake was too dense and combined oddly with an underpowered ratatouille and punchy red pepper mousse. The three-course set dinner was more successful: potted duck lacked flavour slightly, but was perked up by gherkins, onion marmalade and toasted raisin bread, while guinea fowl had suitably robust accompaniment

from dauphine potatoes and sauce forestière. Our waiter was charming, but evidently new: we had to call him back to take our drinks order; a salmon mousse amuse-bouche arrived breadless; and there was a (swiftly rectified) mistake with the bill. Still, topping up the tap water without being asked always gains points. The former Market Coffee House has potential (the bar area was buzzing), but when a restaurant is charging City fringe prices, it needs to show more accomplishment.
Babies and children welcome: high chairs. Booking advisable. Disabled: toilet. Separate rooms for parties, seating 18 and 50. Vegan dishes. Vegetarian menu. **Map 12 R5.**

St John Bread & Wine

94-96 Commercial Street, E1 6LZ (7251 0848, www.stjohnbreadandwine.com). Liverpool Street tube/rail. **Breakfast served** 9-11am daily. **Lunch served** noon-6pm Mon-Fri; noon-4pm Sat, Sun. **Dinner served** 6-11pm Mon-Sat; 6-9pm Sun. **Main courses** £7.10-£17.10. **Credit** AmEx, MC, V.

The even-more-pared-down version of Fergus Henderson's pared-down St John Farringdon flagship serves breakfast, lunch and dinner of sophisticated simplicity. Its whitewashed walls, chalked-up wines and specials, and open kitchen still look classy almost a decade after opening. Menus change daily, but always read more like shopping lists than bills of fare: ham, bobby beans, hen's egg. Courgette, white beans, yogurt. Slip sole, brown butter, sea purslane. Rabbit, dandelion, aïoli. 'I could make that at home,' you think, until you taste the dishes – it's not easy to achieve such spectacular results from so little (although starting with top-drawer ingredients helps; and the St John dedication to nose-to-tail eating means you'll see the likes of blood cake, crispy pig's skin and ox heart). As the restaurant's name suggests, bread is a strong point – buy it to take away fresh from the oven – as is wine, with no shortage of interesting examples by the glass. Service is supremely casual (chefs sometimes bring out plates themselves), but remains smooth as tables fill up. The Old Spot bacon sandwich, served every day, is one of London's finest.
Available for hire. Babies and children welcome: high chairs. Booking advisable. Takeaway service.
Map 12 S5.
For branch (St John Hotel) see index.

North East

Clapton

Shane's on Chatsworth NEW

62 Chatsworth Road, E5 0LS (8985 3755, www.shanesonchatsworth.com). Homerton rail. **Open/tapas served** 5-11pm Tue-Thur; 5pm-midnight Fri; 11am-midnight Sat; 11am-10pm Sun. **Meals served** 5-9.30pm Tue-Thur; 5-10.30pm Fri; 11am-10.30pm Sat; 11am-8.30pm Sun. **Tapas** £2.50-£6. **Main courses** £10-£19. **Set meal** £25 2 courses, £30 3 courses. **Credit** MC, V.

This bijou bistro has given Clapton a proper dinner destination. Shane's claims to focus on British food, seasonality and local ingredients – all very much in line with current London gastro-pretensions, and although not able to fulfil all the criteria, at least the execution strives to match the spiel. The 'foraged salad' is picked on the Hackney Marshes, and mixed with cultivated leaves, for example. A starter of mussels with nettles set the tone: big, juicy mussels in a light white wine broth with wilted nettles was an earthy dish that surprised us with boozy depth and gentle sweetness, reminiscent of a French onion soup. Ham croquettes also exceeded expectations: crisp breadcrumbs encasing a cheesy béchamel, salty chunks of ham hock and a light hit of garlic. Pan-fried, crisp-skinned hake was served in a smoky chorizo broth, augmented by the aroma of clams – a classic Spanish combination. On the heartier side was a filleted and stuffed rabbit wrapped in bacon. The moist meat was filled with a mushroom and rabbit duxelle, the rich flavours of which went well with the buttery tarragon béarnaise sauce. Rhubarb fool provided a deliciously sweet yet tangy finish. The intimate space only has a few tables and a counter facing out into the street, so booking is essential. Wednesday is BYO night.
Available for hire. Babies and children welcome: children's menu. Booking advisable dinner. Tables outdoors (4, pavement).

Hackney

This Bright Field NEW

268 Cambridge Heath Road, E2 9DA (8880 7080, www.thisbrightfield.com). Bethnal Green tube or Cambridge Heath rail. **Meals served** 7am-6pm Mon-Wed; 7am-9.30pm Thur, Fri; 9am-9.30pm Sat; 9am-6pm Sun. **Main courses** £5.50-£10. **Set dinner** (Thur-Sat) £18 2 courses, £21.50 3 courses. **Credit** MC, V.

This new addition to Hackney's café-restaurant scene is a studiedly casual scrubbed-wood and white-tiled space filled with pretty pots of lavender. The short, appealing menu of small plates is built around seasonal produce. Lyme Bay potted mackerel with gooseberries was slathered on to crisp crostini slices, made with bread from E5 Bakehouse; the unctuousness of the fish beautifully balanced by the tart, sweet fruit. Less good were two dinky salt cod fish cakes with garlic mayo – just too salty, as was the crust of crispy Suffolk pork, though this was redeemed by a zesty tomato salad. Delicate Brixham hake with creamy saffron beans and spiced sausage was a beautifully nuanced take on the Spanish bean stew, fabada. Through all this we were charmed by the staff. Their informed enthusiasm over a drinks list that includes five London beers and a small but excellent wine selection gives the impression that the focus is as much on the drink as it is the food. Delicious desserts of gloopy strawberry soup dotted with meringue and a subtle elderflower sorbet, accompanied by glasses of white port, made a fine finish. The name? It comes from William Taylor's 2001 book about Spitalfields.
Available for hire. Babies and children welcome: high chairs. Booking advisable. Disabled: toilet. Tables outdoors (5, pavement). Takeaway service.

Haggerston

Waterline NEW

46 De Beauvoir Crescent, N1 5RY (3119 0037, www.waterlinebar.com). Haggerston rail or 67, 149 bus. **Open** 11am-11.30pm Mon-Sat; 11am-9pm Sun. **Lunch served** noon-3pm Mon-Sat; 11.30am-3.30pm Sun. **Dinner served** 6-9pm Mon-Thur; 6.30-10pm Fri, Sat. **Main courses** £12.25-£20. **Credit** AmEx, MC, V.

Housed in a Haggerston canalside development next to popular café Towpath (*see p287*), Waterline aims to offset the impersonality of the new-build premises with mismatched furniture. Despite the high ceilings and exposed ducting, it has a cosy and not unpleasantly utilitarian feel. Big windows are ready to open out on to the waterway when temperatures allow. Through the back is a darkened function room (films are shown here), and up a metal staircase is a small mezzanine. At the end of the long bar is a little open kitchen – Waterline is as much restaurant as it is bar. The menu includes the likes of leek and wild mushroom tart, and roast duck breast with pear, walnut, stilton and chicory salad; a 'duo of salads' with orange and crayfish and gravadlax may have once existed separately but were presented mixed together in a bowl. Still tasty, though. Good too was a generous portion of ribeye steak and chips. A small but thoughtful draught selection consists of Bitburger, Meantime London Lager, Hogan's cider, an Adnams and the demonically dark Black Isle stout from the Scottish Highlands. There's also a mid-range wine list.
Available for hire. Babies and children welcome: books; crayons; high chairs; nappy-changing facilities. Booking advisable. Entertainment: jazz 8pm Thur. **Map 6 R1.**

North

Camden Town & Chalk Farm

★ Market

43 Parkway, NW1 7PN (7267 9700, www.marketrestaurant.co.uk). Camden Town tube. **Lunch served** noon-2.30pm Mon-Sat; 1-3.30pm Sun. **Dinner served** 6-10.30pm Mon-Sat. **Main courses** £13-£17. **Set lunch** (Mon-Sat) £10 2 courses. **Set dinner** (6-7pm Mon-Sat) £17.50 2 courses. **Credit** AmEx, DC, MC, V.

With old school chairs, open brickwork and blackboard specials, this slim Parkway unit doffs its cap to the gastropub while sporting a more formal look. Daily-changing menus start with British traditions and ingredients and veer to the Mediterranean, such as a starter of ethereally tender baby squid served with light yet fiery romesco; or chargrilled peaches with Irish goat's cheese salad and toasted seeds. The kitchen gets details right: tortano for bread; enamel dishes of skin-on fries. Market's signature single-crusted pies are great, but need to be served with a spoon. Our steamy steak and ale number came with delightfully bouncy, chewy cabbage. Pork belly was a wowser: tender meat, not too fatty, and pristine crisp crackling. Desserts might be lavender crème brûlée or treacle tart. Early-bird deals offer two courses for £17.50 before 7pm, with the advantage that you won't need to book. The wine list features several options under £20, but we plumped for a special of Portuguese red Quinta da Espiga served chilled; beer drinkers can choose from Timothy Taylor Landlord or, even better, Camden Pale Ale. Colourful views of Boris bikes and a veritable convoy of Camden poseurs enhance this delightful London experience.
Babies and children welcome: high chairs. Booking advisable. Separate room for parties, seats 12. Tables outdoors (2, pavement).
Map 3 H1.

Caribbean

The Notting Hill carnival may still be a showcase for Caribbean cookery and culture, but the London restaurant scene that celebrates the cuisine from those sunny islands has broadened its scope beyond mere street food. This year's major opening has been **Bubbas**, where in glam surroundings fashioned out of an old railway station, chef Anthony Cumberbatch is creating visually appealing versions of classic dishes for the Tulse Hill populace. It joins Camden's **Mango Room** and Clerkenwell's newly resurgent **Cottons** (starched tablecloths and all) as venues where you can enjoy Caribbean cookery with a measure of decorum. Nevertheless, street food and upbeat, exhilarating music form an irrepressible part of this joyous culture, and in London you can glory in both at Soho's caff-like **Jerk City** and Stratford's **Caribbean Scene**, where the eat-all-you-can buffet provides a great opportunity to explore this under-represented but highly flavourful cuisine.

Central

Clerkenwell & Farringdon

Cottons

70 Exmouth Market, EC1R 4QP (7833 3332, www.cottons-restaurant.co.uk). Farringdon tube/rail or bus 19, 38, 341. **Lunch served** noon-4pm, **dinner served** 5-11pm daily. **Main courses** £12.50-£14.50. **Set meal** £19.50 2 courses, £22.50 3 courses. **Credit** MC, V.

Last year we were disappointed by the lack of authenticity and poor quality of cooking at Cottons, which seemed to be fighting a losing battle with the high-quality competition on what's surely one of London's best dining streets. After a slew of less than complimentary reviews, it has come out fighting, with new decor and, it seems, a new attitude to its cuisine. Starched white tablecloths set against dark wood in a cool, pretty space give a colonial feel. The lunchtime crowd was, surprisingly, a crowd: tables were filled with small mixed groups of friends, office colleagues, couples and solo diners. The food was equally broad-ranging, from a long menu that ran from the traditional (jerk chicken, curry goat, saltfish and ackee) to more modern fusion dishes: callaloo and goat's cheese tart, for example (a pretty tart that was acceptable but lacked depth). Luckily, the goat curry, and saltfish and ackee with dumplings, were the real deal, the former hearty and meaty, the latter's super-salty morsels of cod working beautifully with the doughy, delicate dumplings. With so few good Caribbean restaurants in London, it's heartening to see Cottons back on form.

Available for hire. Babies and children welcome: high chairs. Entertainment: DJs 9.30pm-2am Fri, Sat. Separate room for parties, seats 65. Tables outdoors (5, patio). Takeaway service. **Map 5 N4.**
For branch see index.

Soho

★ ★ Jerk City

189 Wardour Street, W1F 8ZD (7287 2878). Tottenham Court Road tube. **Meals served** noon-9pm Mon-Wed; noon-10pm Thur-Sat; noon-8pm Sun. **Main courses** £6.50-£8.50. **No credit cards.**

It's had a bit of a spruce-up, but the song remains the same at this Soho star, where the emphasis is on good soul music and even better cooking. It's a simple affair; order food at the counter from a tempting blackboard selection that includes jerk or barbecue chicken, a small range of roti, braised oxtail, brown chicken and huge bowls of soup (a bargain at a fiver). Then grab a seat at a café-style table under the hopeful gaze of Barack Obama or one of the Afro-Caribbean hero portraits, and a few minutes later take charge of a huge portion of food, courtesy of the hair-netted cooks from the tiny basement kitchen. All the curries and main meals come with your choice of rice and beans and salad or hard food – plantain, dumpling, yam – and are everything you could hope for. Flaky roti is wrapped around peppery, spicy curry; the hot pepper and herb flavour of the chargrilled jerk chicken goes through to the bone; and braised oxtail is a perfect blend of meaty and gloopy. A sweet fresh fruit punch or a more sedate Guinness punch makes the ideal accompaniment.

Takeaway service. **Map 17 B3.**

South East

Tulse Hill

Bubbas NEW

7A Station Rise, SE27 9BW (8674 4114, www.bubbasrestaurant.co.uk). Tulse Hill rail. **Dinner served** 5.30-10pm Tue-Thur; 5.30-10.30pm Fri, Sat. **Meals served** 12.30-10pm Sun. **Main courses** £11.20-£19.99. **Credit** AmEx, MC, V.

The Victorian Tulse Hill railway station building has been extensively refurbished to create London's latest destination Caribbean restaurant. The new look is bargain bling: mirrors, blue LEDs embedded into cushioned walls, wipe-clean tables. With its banal R&B soundtrack and bright lights, it feels like a nightclub when the cleaners are leaving. Chef Anthony Cumberbatch has worked in some of London's best-known restaurants. In modernising the cuisine, he hasn't messed with the good cooking, but has tried giving classic dishes more visual appeal. Saltfish and ackee (always a winning combo of 'scrambled egg' fruit texture and saltfish tang) was wrapped in deep-fried filo pastry. This, and every other dish we tried, was lavishly garnished with blobs of colour, dashes of flavour and baby

Menu

Ackee: a red-skinned fruit with yellow flesh that looks like scrambled eggs when cooked; traditionally served in a Jamaican dish of salt cod, onion and peppers.
Bammy or **bammie**: pancake-shaped, deep-fried cassava bread, often served with fried fish.
Breadfruit: this football-sized fruit has sweet creamy flesh that's a cross between sweet potato and chestnut. Eaten as a vegetable.
Bush tea: herbal tea made from cerese (a Jamaican vine plant), mint or fennel.
Callaloo: the spinach-like leaves of either taro or malanga, often used as a base for a thick soup flavoured with pork or crab meat.
Coo-coo: a polenta-like cake of cornmeal and okra.
Cow foot: a stew made from the hoof of the cow, boiled with vegetables. The cartilage gives the stew a gummy or gelatinous texture.
Curried goat: usually lamb in London; the meat is marinated and slow-cooked until tender.
Dasheen: a root vegetable with a texture similar to yam (qv).
Escoveitched (or **escovitch**) fish: fish fried or grilled, then pickled in a tangy sauce with onions, sweet peppers and vinegar; similar to escabèche.
Festival: deep-fried, slightly sweet dumpling often served with fried fish.
Foo-foo: a Barbadian dish of pounded plantains, seasoned, rolled into balls and served hot.
Jerk: chicken or pork marinated in chilli spices, slowly roasted or barbecued.
Patty or **pattie**: a savoury pastry snack, made with turmeric-coloured shortcrust pastry, usually filled with beef, saltfish or vegetables.
Peas or **beans**: black-eyed beans, black beans, green peas and red kidney beans.
Pepperpot: traditionally a stew of meat and cassereep, a juice obtained from cassava.
Phoulorie: a Trinidadian snack of fried doughballs often eaten with a sweet tamarind sauce.
Plantain or **plantin**: a savoury variety of banana that is cooked like potato.
Rice and peas: rice cooked with kidney or gungo beans, pepper seasoning and coconut milk.
Saltfish: salt cod, classically mixed with ackee (qv) or callaloo (qv).
Sorrel: not the herb, but a type of hibiscus with a sour-sweet flavour.
Soursop: a dark green, slightly spiny fruit; the pulp, blended with milk and sugar, is a refreshing drink.
Yam: a large tuber, with a yellow or white flesh and slightly nutty flavour.

leaves, even pansies. Filo was again used to create a 'top hat' brimming with goat curry: a masterpiece of slow-cooked flesh with Indian-style spicing. Okra balls were similar to bhajias; dahl puri was filled with lentils. Snapper, an entire fish chargrilled inside a banana leaf, arrived stuffed with herbs. We like Bubbas for bringing ambition to Tulse Hill. We're less convinced by the formal atmosphere and the 1990s look of the place.
Available for hire. Babies and children welcome: children's menu; high chairs. Booking advisable Fri, Sat.

East

Stratford

Caribbean Scene Family

2 Gerry Raffles Square, E15 1BG (8522 8660, www.caribbeanscene.co.uk). Stratford tube/rail/ DLR. **Breakfast served** 8-11am, **meals served** noon-10pm daily. **Main courses** £4-£9.50. **Set buffet** £9-£16.70. **Credit** AmEx, MC, V.
With its vibrant murals and thatching, plus smiley staff, inconsistent service and proper upbeat soca, Caribbean Scene makes a decent stab at island evocation. Even the rather tired-looking flooring and scuffed paintwork add to the authenticity. But it's the food that really hits the spot, taking you straight to the West Indies. Nothing does it better than the all-you-can-eat buffet, a clear favourite with the tables of diners dotted around the sprawling space. We followed the crowds to the long counter, where pan after pan of down-home dishes tempted us to go back for a refill – for more excellent fish stews and the likes of kingfish, mackerel and, of course, saltfish and ackee. There's also a dizzying range of meat dishes; the chicken selection alone included stewed, curry, jerk, pineapple and barbecued, with or without sauce. Vegetables don't let the side down either: plantain was perfectly caramelised, while callaloo, okra, stewed cabbage, macaroni pie and dumplings were all as good as you'd get served à la carte. The downside? We consumed what felt like a full week's worth of salt in one – admittedly very large – meal.
Babies and children welcome: crayons; children's menu; high chairs; nappy-changing facilities. Disabled: toilet. Takeaway service. Vegan dishes. Vegetarian menu.
For branches see index.

North

Camden Town & Chalk Farm

Mango Room

10-12 Kentish Town Road, NW1 8NH (7482 5065, www.mangoroom.co.uk). Camden Town tube. **Meals served** noon-10pm daily. **Main courses** £11.50-£15.90. **Credit** AmEx, MC, V.
While London's best Caribbean food is usually found in takeaways, sometimes you want the spiciness of jerk chicken without the plastic fork. It's here that the Mango Room delivers, with stylish decor, friendly service, pretty presentation and the kind of atmosphere that makes the venue equally appealing for a date or a mates night. What you gain in ambience you lose in authenticity, though. Take the starters of ackee and saltfish, and jerk chicken. Neatly presented, the saltfish fritter was a little too fussy and bland; the chicken wings had a sweet spicy taste yet lacked the requisite smoky chargrilled flavour. Mains were variable too. Goat curry was identifiably Caribbean in its combination of rich, pungent curry sauce with tender meat (if goat curry could ever be said to be refined, this was it). But chicken with jerk sauce was no match for the versions produced by the specialist jerk joints, where the flavour goes right through the meat; here, it felt like a two-hour marinade. In contrast, sides of rice and peas, fried plantain and roti bread were accomplished and authentically flavoured, as was a totally tropical and delicious house cocktail – a bargain at £5.
Babies and children welcome: high chairs. Booking advisable weekends. Separate room for parties, seats 20. Takeaway service. Vegan dishes.
Map 27 D2.

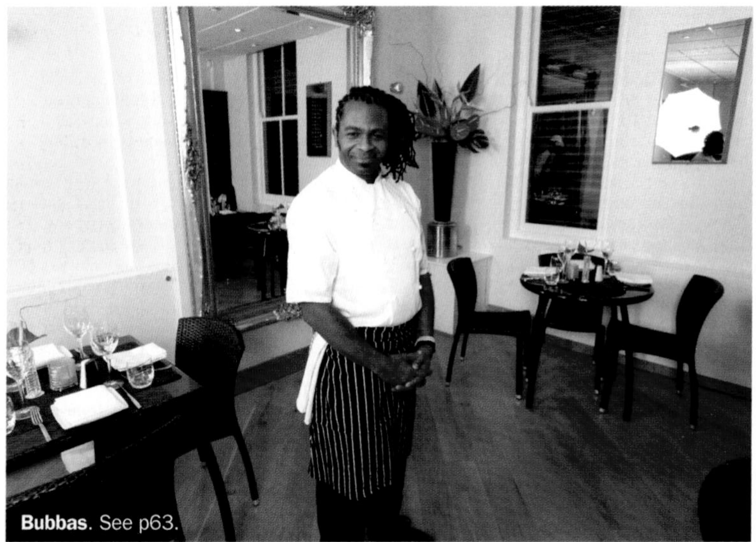
Bubbas. See p63.

Chinese

The days of frustration are almost gone, and a landmark of cross-cultural understanding is within sight. Not so long ago, many Chinese restaurateurs seemed to believe that Londoners from outside their community didn't understand or appreciate this elaborate and varied cuisine, and wanted only sweet-and-sour, chop suey takeaway fodder – which their restaurants duly provided. London's diners, on the other hand, missed out on the glories of Chinese cooking, finding their Far Eastern thrills in Japanese and South-east Asian food. All this changed when **Hakkasan** opened and Chinese venues became hip. Now, many more Londoners enjoy the delights of dim sum – surely one of the best high-quality bargains in town, with top practitioners such as **Royal China Club** and **Yauatcha** leading the way – and regional Chinese food is becoming easier to find. Cantonese cooking still predominates, due to Britain's historical links with Hong Kong, and one of our long-time favourite Cantonese establishments is Bayswater's modest **Magic Wok**. **Barshu** and its sibling **Ba Shan** remain the prime venues for Sichuan cuisine, but this year these spicy, western Chinese establishments have been joined by Hunanese specialist **Yipin China**. Food from China's eastern and northern regions, however, is still relatively scarce in London; **Shanghai Dalston** has a few eastern dishes on its menu, while **Manchurian Legends** specialises in Dongbei cooking from the north-east.

Soho's Chinatown continues to be a prime source of budget establishments (*see p70* **Chinatown on the cheap**), but here, as in nearly all parts of Chinese London, one major irritant remains. Set menus are full of the most lacklustre and ubiquitous dishes (beef in black bean sauce, chicken with cashew nuts). Ordering from a 'real' Chinese menu, balancing the textures (crisp with soft, resilient with slithery) and flavours (rich with subtle, yang with yin) is a lengthy process that's difficult for novices. A restaurant that took the strain out of choosing, by providing an exciting, well-balanced set meal, would earn our praise indeed.

Central

Belgravia

Hunan

51 Pimlico Road, SW1W 8NE (7730 5712, www.hunanlondon.com). Sloane Square tube. **Lunch served** 12.30-2pm, **dinner served** 6.30-11pm Mon-Sat. **Set lunch** £29.80 per person (minimum 2). **Set dinner** £44.80 per person (minimum 2). **Credit** AmEx, DC, MC, V.

Browsing around the farmers' market on the small square opposite Hunan helped hone our appetite. Inside, the plain white-walled dining room, furnished in pale wooden furniture, is cheered up by elegant Chinese prints and artefacts. For many years, the kitchen here has specialised in regional Chinese food – often chilli-hot, Hunanese-style; sometimes Taiwan-influenced. We were informed about the 'no choice' menu and asked how spicy we wanted our dishes. Next, a dozen tapas-sized dishes arrived in a random sequence. First was a tasty minced chicken with diced vegetables on a lettuce leaf. The portions may be small, but don't expect dinky flavours: we were never far from a garlic and chilli hit. Japanese influences came to the fore with tofu wrapped in seaweed, and then, best of all, a feather-light tempura of french beans. Stir-fried lamb with baby garlic shoots was another rousing success. The only duff note came at the end, with a chewy red-bean pancake (saved by a delicate almond-flavoured agar-agar jelly). Service is friendly, although staff can get confused with the order in which dishes appear. An enterprising wine list rounded off a splendid lunch.

Babies and children admitted. Booking essential. Vegetarian menu. **Map 15 G11**.

Chinatown

Imperial China

White Bear Yard, 25A Lisle Street, WC2H 7BA (7734 3388, www.imperial-china.co.uk). Leicester Square or Piccadilly Circus tube. **Meals served** noon-11.30pm Mon-Sat; 11.30am-10.30pm Sun. **Dim sum served** noon-5pm daily. **Main courses** £8.50-£32.50. **Dim sum** £2.60-£4. **Set meal** £19-£35 per person (minimum 2). **Minimum** £10. **Credit** AmEx, MC, V.

This Chinatown landmark was once among the area's smartest Cantonese restaurants, complete with a grand entrance and even a little bridge over a carp pond. The years, however, haven't been kind. The plump carp remain, but the 'contemporary' fixtures now look rather tired. The cooking has also lost its sparkle. On our visit, several dim sum arrived either tepid or slightly shrivelled, indicating they might have been left loitering before serving. There were other own-goals: the char siu filling in our cheung fun was overwhelmed by the thickness of the dough, while a glutinous rice parcel (wrapped in lotus leaf, then steamed) was a little bland, though the texture was spot-on. Not that there weren't moments of brilliance: from the perfection of a steamed prawn and chive dumpling, with its delicate, shimmering pastry case and aromatic,

Manchurian Legends

bouncy filling; to moreish Vietnamese spring rolls, the crunchy, golden deep-fried casing giving way to a dense, meaty centre. Factor-in the low prices for dim sum, and you can still have a decent, inexpensive lunch here, raising a cup of well-brewed oolong to the glory days. The full menu (which includes a vegetarian set meal) majors in seafood.
Babies and children welcome: high chairs. Booking advisable. Disabled: toilet. Separate rooms for parties, seating 10-70. Tables outdoors (5, courtyard). Vegetarian menu. **Map 17 C4**.

Joy King Lau

3 Leicester Street, WC2H 7BL (7437 1132, www.joykinglau.com). Leicester Square or Piccadilly Circus tube. **Meals served** noon-11.30pm Mon-Sat; 11am-10.30pm Sun. **Dim sum served** noon-5pm Mon-Sat; 11am-5pm Sun. **Main courses** £7.50-£18. **Dim sum** £2.40-£4.50. **Set meal** £11.50-£35 per person (minimum 2). **Credit** AmEx, MC, V.
Don't come to Joy King Lau expecting swanky surroundings or meek, mild-mannered service. Set on a small side street linking Chinatown with Leicester Square, this multi-level Cantonese restaurant may be a little rough around the edges, with scuffed furniture, faded carpets and staff barking instructions at one another via walkie-talkies, but what it lacks in glamour it makes up for with affordable, good-quality cooking. By night, the extensive menu covers all bases, from barbecued pork ribs or beef in black bean sauce to sliced abalone with fish lips, but a lunchtime visit also allows the varied clientele – from groups of students to suited businessmen – to select from the range of excellent dim sum. Steamed har gau were tiny, shimmering masterpieces: the translucent, expertly crimped and supple pastry giving way to a juicy filling of pale pink prawns. Equally impressive was a huge parcel of steamed glutinous rice, where the 'mixed meat' proved to be generous chunks of Chinese sausage, roast pork and beef, cooked in an intense sauce with shrimp, mushrooms and water chestnuts. Only the deep-fried yam croquettes, which arrived tepid and soggy, showed a wobble in standards. Service is frighteningly efficient.
Babies and children welcome: high chairs. Booking advisable weekends. Takeaway service. **Map 17 C5**.

★ Manchurian Legends

16 Lisle Street, WC2H 7BE (7287 6606, www.manchurianlegends.com). Leicester Square or Piccadilly Circus tube. **Meals served** 11am-11pm Mon-Wed, Sun; 11am-11.30pm Thur-Sat. **Main courses** £7.50-£12.80. **Set lunch** £5.50-£11 2 courses. **Set dinner** £18.80-£23.80 2 courses. **Credit** MC, V.
Manchurian Legends, cousin of nearby Leong's Legends, offers faithful renditions of the hearty rib-sticking cuisine of China's frosty north. Robust stews from the north-east are well executed; braised pork with glass noodles was a rich, melt-in-your-mouth slow-cooked triumph of meat and starch. Stewed chicken with tea-tree mushrooms had similarly rich and tender meat, but this time with wonderfully springy fungus. The true test of a north-western Chinese restaurant is whether it can properly execute yang rou chuan, the classic Muslim lamb kebabs that are popular – and delicious – street food throughout the People's Republic. Manchurian Legends serves the best we've had in London; the small morsels of nicely fatty lamb are cooked until the fat melts, and liberally doused in the signature chilli-cumin-sesame topping. Another Xinjiang classic, 'big plate chicken', is a wonderful symphony of spicy chicken, root vegetables and giant noodles (truly enormous: they look like tripe) in a star anise-infused broth. In July 2012, Manchurian Legends moved to Lisle Street, occupying the pleasant if cosy tented dining room that formerly housed the short-lived Wulumuchi. The elegant surroundings are a step up in class; and the food certainly transcends that produced by the previous inhabitants.
Available for hire. Babies and children welcome: high chairs; nappy-changing facilities. Booking advisable. Takeaway service. **Map 17 C4**.

New World

1 Gerrard Place, W1D 5PA (7434 2508, www.newworldlondon.com). Leicester Square or Piccadilly Circus tube. **Meals served** noon-11.45pm Mon-Thur; noon-midnight Fri; 11am-midnight Sat; 11am-11pm Sun. **Dim sum served** noon-6pm Mon-Fri; 11am-6pm Sat, Sun. **Main courses** £7-£25. **Dim sum** £2.65-£13. **Set meal** £15.90-£23.50 per person (minimum 5). **Minimum** (after 6pm) £5. **Credit** AmEx, DC, MC, V.
Having closed in 2011, New World has had a kitchen refit and is back in business. A banqueting restaurant of the old school, it's got the lot: dining rooms over several floors; red and gold rooms adorned with hanging lanterns; and a melting pot of clientele, from tourists to entire Cantonese families. It's also one of the only remaining places to offer a traditional dim sum trolley service, where everything from sliced roasted duck to egg custard tarts is on offer. Cooking, however, is inconsistent. On our visit, dishes off the trolley were often tepid, or brittle: the pastry of our cheung fun fell apart on contact, though the pieces of char sui it contained were excellent. Plates from the à la carte were equally mixed: ho fun was an overcooked, starchy mass topped with beef of dubious quality, yet the crispy noodles were exceptional, seeing a base of soft chow mein with crunchy fried edges layered with a light oyster sauce and al dente pieces of Chinese broccoli, straw mushrooms and fresh (not tinned) bamboo shoots. Service, always efficient,

veered from pushy to gracious, but costs remain low, making this iconic spot still worth a punt.
Available for hire. Babies and children welcome: high chairs; nappy-changing facilities. Bookings not accepted Sun lunch. Separate rooms for parties, seating 10-250. Takeaway service. Vegetarian menu. **Map 17 C4**.

Fitzrovia

Hakkasan

8 Hanway Place, W1T 1HD (7927 7000, www.hakkasan.com). Tottenham Court Road tube.
Bar **Open** noon-12.30am Mon-Wed; noon-1.30am Thur-Sat; noon-midnight Sun.
Restaurant **Lunch/dim sum served** noon-3pm Mon-Fri; noon-4pm Sat, Sun. **Dinner served** 6-11pm Mon-Wed, Sun; 6pm-midnight Thur-Sat. **Main courses** £16-£61. **Set lunch** £29 3 courses. **Dim sum** £3-£20.
Both **Credit** AmEx, MC, V.
Still darkly sexy, but now attracting fewer A-listers, Hakkasan's capacious basement marks the spot where Chinese dining in London became hip. Beautiful black-garbed staff, markedly more efficient than on our last visit, flit across the floor. Customers (multinational, moneyed) sit on black-leather banquettes by intricately carved dividing screens. Some chat over cocktails ordered from the impressively long bar; others drink in the nightclub-like atmosphere. Does the food match all this? On our most recent trip, just about. The set lunch offers a surprisingly broad taster of the kitchen's capabilities, beginning with a quartet of 'classics with a twist' dim sum. Best was the XO scallop ball, bursting with aromatic freshness under its translucent rice wrapper. However, venison puff wasn't an improvement on the char siu original, and the steamed morel buns (from the carte) masked the luxury ingredient with too-sweet dough. No complaints, though, about the set lunch main of succulent king prawns matched with crunchy lotus bulb in mild curry (choose steamed rice as a foil) or the outstandingly light dessert of lemon meringue pie (puddings are western in outlook). The main menu carries the innovative likes of roasted cod with champagne and honey, and black truffle roast duck. To drink, only high-rollers should venture on to the designed-to-impress wine list; we recommend the specialist teas. And for celebs, try the newer Mayfair branch.
Available for hire. Babies and children admitted. Booking essential, 3 mths in advance. Disabled: lift; toilet. Entertainment: DJs 9pm Thur-Sat. **Map 17 C2**.

Knightsbridge

Mr Chow

151 Knightsbridge, SW1X 7PA (7589 7347, www.mrchow.com). Knightsbridge tube. **Lunch served** 12.30-3pm Tue-Sun. **Dinner served** 7pm-midnight daily. **Main courses** £14.50-£38. **Set lunch** £24. **Set dinner** £45-£50. **Cover** £2. **Credit** AmEx, DC, MC, V.
Mr Chow has been playing host to the 'rich and famous' since 1968 and it continues to attract Knightsbridge's money-no-object diners – a fact evident from the number of customers on our visit. We sat in the small but glossy room on the ground floor, the space buffed up by modern art, soft leather banquettes and elegant rosewood chairs. Having pioneered the upmarket, western-friendly form of London's Chinese restaurants, Chow's remains a crowd-pleaser with its Tinseltown take on Cantonese cooking. We enjoyed a starter of minced squab chicken with diced vegetables, but turnip puffs were dry and only just saved by a garlicky chilli sauce. Beef fillet was tender, yet came with too much oyster sauce, making it a bit gloopy. Chicken served with prawns, scallops and wood-ear fungus had been sautéed with an excess of rice-wine vinegar, but the fried rice was blameless. The chatty service team have been here for a long time, and it's good to see that they have built up a relationship with the regular customers. Our request for a doggie bag was accepted without a hint of snobbishness, which went some way towards justifying the 13% service charge.
Babies and children admitted. Booking advisable; essential dinner. Separate rooms for parties, seating 20-75. **Map 8 F9**.

Marylebone

Phoenix Palace

5 Glentworth Street, NW1 5PG (7486 3515, www.phoenixpalace.co.uk). Baker Street tube.
Meals served noon-11.30pm Mon-Sat; 11am-10.30pm Sun. **Dim sum served** noon-5pm Mon-Sat; 11am-5pm Sun. **Main courses** £6.50-£25. **Dim sum** £3.20-£5. **Set meal** £20-£48 per person (minimum 2). **Credit** AmEx, MC, V.
From the welcoming red carpet to a lavish entrance lobby furnished in dark marble and rosewood furniture, Phoenix Palace is a place for special occasions. The hostess, in a fuchsia Chinese dress slit up to the thigh, led us to our table – on the higher of two tiers, in a glamorous room brimming with traditional oriental wood carvings, mirrors and splashes of gold. The full menu, with its mix of perennial favourites and lesser-seen specialities, is deservedly popular. We enjoyed a classic plate of crisp-edged egg noodles generously topped with mixed seafood (squid, scallops, prawns), colourful vegetables and a light oyster sauce. A Cantonese take on breaded veal was equally good, with succulent pieces of pan-fried meat given a crunchy, salty coating and topped with tiny morsels of baked garlic. At lunchtime, the dim sum represents the best value, though it won't set pulses racing. Classics are competently done, from the properly crimped Shanghai dumplings filled with finely minced, ginger-laced pork and a light broth, to the char siu cheung fun, which, while a tad doughy, had a terrific filling of sweet, fatty barbecued pork. Staff are efficient, and the crowd more smart than casual.

Mr Chow

Phoenix Palace. See p67.

Babies and children welcome: high chairs. Booking advisable. Separate rooms for parties, seating 12-30. Takeaway service; delivery service (over £10 within 1-mile radius). **Map 2 F4.**

★ Royal China Club

40-42 Baker Street, W1U 7AJ (7486 3898, www.royalchinagroup.co.uk). Baker Street or Marble Arch tube. **Meals served** noon-11pm; noon-11.30pm Fri, Sat; noon-10.30pm Sun. **Dim sum served** noon-4.45pm daily. **Main courses** £9.50-£120. **Dim sum** £3.80-£7. **Set meal** £40-£90 (minimum 2). **Credit** AmEx, MC, V.

Royal China Club is among the best places in London for dim sum. The elegant dining room, adorned with fine glassware and linens, and furnished in sleek black lacquer and gold decor, is an impressive place to bring guests. Both the dim sum and main menu feature plenty of luxury ingredients. If you sit at the front of the restaurant, you may find yourself eye-to-eye with a crab or lobster pottering about in the large fish tank that divides the dining area from the bar. Dishes are authentically flavoured, yet exhibit notable delicacy. Xiao long bao, the Shanghai soup dumplings often sold off a steamer on the streets of China, here get the Royal treatment by the addition of delightfully light crab to the package, rendering what in Chinatown can be a heavy, monotonous morsel into a highly complex, light and magical giant dumpling. Cantonese fish dishes are excellent too, thanks to the quality of the raw ingredients and a wonderful lightness of touch in the kitchen. You're likely to hear plenty of Cantonese spoken among diners – another stamp of approval from those in the know.

Babies and children admitted. Booking advisable Sat, Sun. Separate room for parties, seats 24. Takeaway service. **Map 9 G5.**

Mayfair

China Tang

The Dorchester, 53 Park Lane, W1K 1QA (7629 9988, www.thedorchester.com). Hyde Park Corner tube. **Meals/dim sum served** noon-midnight daily. **Main courses** £12-£48. **Dim sum** £5-£8. **Set lunch** £23. **Credit** AmEx, DC, MC, V.

London dining doesn't get much camper than China Tang. Sir David Tang's flamboyant take on Chinese design (bold colours, shiny woods, giant paintings of carp) has met its match in the art deco temple that is the Dorchester, creating the perfect subterranean scene in which to be seen. Everything – including international sugar daddies with sexy dates half their age – is gilded and lacquered to within an inch of its life. The food is mostly Cantonese, with roasted meats, stir-fries and clay-pot dishes all offered, using much higher quality meat than most Chinatown joints. Yet while the decor is splendiferous, the food is a mixed bag. Char siu (deeply rich roast pork splashed with Shaoxing wine) was divine, but the roast duck had sadly soggy skin. And at prices this steep, beef with pepper should be more than just slivers of dull meat accompanied by a few grinds from a pepper mill. To keep its globe-trotting clientele well watered, China Tang's wine list has a larger than average number of by-the-glass choices. A grüner veltliner was pleasantly sharp when combined with the sweet Cantonese flavours. Another plus? The adjoining cocktail bar: it's possibly the most stylish in London.

Babies and children welcome: high chairs. Booking advisable. Disabled: lift; toilet. Separate rooms for parties, seating 8-80. **Map 9 G7.**

Kai Mayfair

65 South Audley Street, W1K 2QU (7493 8988, www.kaimayfair.co.uk). Bond Street or Marble Arch tube. **Lunch served** noon-2pm Mon-Fri; 12.30-2.30pm Sat, Sun. **Dinner served** 6.30-10.30pm Mon-Sat; 6.30-10pm Sun. **Main courses** £16-£53. **Set lunch** £19 3 courses (£27 incl wine). **Credit** AmEx, DC, MC, V.

It's not only sceptics who reckon that dining at a Chinese restaurant in Mayfair usually means high prices for ordinary food. And, yes, apart from the set lunch menu, prices at Kai Mayfair conform to the stereotype. Hot and sour soup is a whacking £13, and don't even think about the wine list if you're on a budget. But during the past 20 years, owner Bernard Yeoh (who hails from Malaysia) has successfully introduced diners to a stylised take on Chinese cuisine. The ground-floor dining room, adorned with an elegant aquarium, exudes quiet self-confidence. At our meal, the kitchen showed an inventive streak from the off, with miso soup being paired with goji berries and boosted by a spicy kick. To follow, shredded lamb shank arrived with a yellow lentil purée: a tasty enough rendition, if oddly un-oriental. We had no reservations, however, about a splendid pan-fried sea bass with oyster sauce, finding each flavour to be distinctive: a hallmark of high-quality cooking. A refreshing almond curd encircled by dragon fruit and lychees concluded the meal. So, there is much to like at Kai – including the accommodating service.

Babies and children welcome high chairs. Booking advisable lunch; essential dinner. Separate rooms for parties, seating 6-12. Vegetarian menu. **Map 9 G7**.

★ Princess Garden

8-10 North Audley Street, W1K 6ZD (7493 3223, www.princessgardenofmayfair.com). Bond Street tube. **Lunch served** noon-4pm Mon-Fri; noon-4.30pm Sat, Sun. **Dinner served** 6.30-11pm Mon-Sat; 6.30-10.30pm Sun. **Dim sum served** noon-4pm daily. **Main courses** £7.50-£12. **Dim sum** £2.30-£3.80. **Set lunch** £12 per person (minimum 2). **Set dinner** £30-£85 per person (minimum 2). **Credit** AmEx, DC, MC, V.

Long known as a specialist in northern Chinese cuisine, Princess Garden also has a range of dim sum that stands comparison with London's best. As you would expect from the Mayfair address, the menu offers plenty of opportunities to splash out. Peking duck, lobster, shark's fin and abalone are all available in a range of northern, Cantonese and inventive fusion dishes. On a recent visit, the dim sum menu lived up to the restaurant's name: these little dumplings are fit for royalty. Enoki and beef cheung fun featured a perfectly steamed, cloud-light giant noodle wrapped around springy little mushrooms, tender beef and just enough water-chestnuts to create an interesting textural play. Chicken and mushroom steamed buns (baozi) were similarly light in texture, yet deep and rich in flavour. Popular for business lunches, the venue has an air of formality: light from two window-lined walls is carefully controlled; tables are discreetly distanced from one another; waiting staff are elegantly dressed and helpful. The fully stocked bar, above-average French wine list, fancy address, minimalist decor (dotted with Chinese antiques) and seamless service combine to make this an ideal place to impress your guests.

Babies and children welcome: high chairs. Booking advisable. Separate rooms for parties, seating 6-50. Takeaway service. **Map 9 G6**.

Dim sum

The Cantonese term 'dim sum' can be translated as 'touch the heart'. It is used to refer to the vast array of dumplings and other titbits that southern Chinese people like to eat with their tea for breakfast or at lunchtime. This eating ritual is simply known as 'yum cha', or 'drinking tea' in Hong Kong. Many of London's Chinese restaurants have a lunchtime dim sum menu, and at weekends you'll find them packed with Cantonese families. A dim sum feast is one of London's most extraordinary gastronomic bargains: how else can you lunch lavishly in one of the capital's premier restaurants for as little as £15 a head?

Restaurants used to cease serving dim sum at 4pm or 5pm, when the rice-based evening menus took over. These days, however, since dim sum became fashionable outside the Chinese community, several establishments serve them all day and into the night. Dim sum lunches at the weekend tend to be boisterous occasions, so they are great for children.

New World (*see p66*) in Chinatown serves dim sum in traditional Hong Kong-style, from circulating trollies. Some of the snacks are wheeled out from the kitchen after being cooked; others gently steam as they go or are finished on the trolley to order. The trolley system has the great advantage that you see exactly what's offered, but on a quiet lunchtime some of the food may be a little jaded by the time it reaches you. Other places offer snacks à la carte, so everything should be freshly cooked.

Dim sum menus are roughly divided into steamed dumplings, deep-fried dumplings, sweet dishes and so on. Try to order a selection of different types of food, with plenty of light steamed dumplings to counterbalance the heavier deep-fried snacks. If you are eating with a large group, make sure you order multiples of everything, as most portions consist of about three items. Tea is the traditional accompaniment. Musty bo lay (pu'er in Mandarin), grassy Dragon Well (long jing) or fragrant Iron Buddha (tie guan yin) are alternatives to the jasmine blossom that is usually served by default to non-Chinese guests. Waiters should leave the teapots filled throughout the meal; leave the teapot lid tilted at an angle or upside down to signal that you want a top-up.

Char siu bao: steamed bun stuffed with barbecued pork in a sweet-savoury sauce.
Char siu puff pastry or **roast pork puff**: triangular puff-pastry snack, filled with barbecued pork, scattered with sesame seeds and oven-baked.
Cheung fun: sheets of steamed rice pasta wrapped around fresh prawns, barbecued pork, deep-fried dough sticks, or other fillings, with a sweet soy-based sauce.
Chiu chow fun gwor: soft steamed dumpling with a wheat-starch wrapper, filled with pork, vegetables and peanuts.
Chive dumpling: steamed prawn meat and Chinese chives in a translucent wrapper.
Har gau: steamed minced prawn dumpling with a translucent wheat-starch wrapper.
Nor mai gai or **steamed glutinous rice in lotus leaf**: lotus-leaf parcel enclosing moist sticky rice with chicken, mushrooms, salty duck-egg yolks and other bits and pieces, infused with the herby fragrance of the leaf.
Paper-wrapped prawns: tissue-thin rice paper enclosing prawn meat, sometimes scattered with sesame seeds, deep-fried.
Sago cream with yam: cool, sweet soup of coconut milk with sago pearls and taro.
Scallop dumpling: delicate steamed dumpling filled with scallop (sometimes prawn) and vegetables.
Shark's fin dumpling: small steamed dumpling with a wheaten wrapper pinched into a frilly cockscomb shape on top, stuffed with a mix of pork, prawn and slippery strands of shark's fin.
Siu loon bao or **xiao long bao**: Shanghai-style round dumpling with a whirled pattern on top and a minced pork and soup filling.
Siu mai: little dumpling with an open top, a wheat-flour wrapper and a minced pork filling. Traditionally topped with crab coral, although minced carrot and other substitutes are common.
Taro croquette or **yam croquette**: egg-shaped, deep-fried dumpling with a frizzy, melt-in-your-mouth outer layer of mashed taro, and a savoury minced pork filling.
Turnip paste: a heavy slab of creamy paste made from glutinous rice flour and white oriental radishes, studded with wind-dried pork, sausage and dried shrimps, and fried.

Chinatown on the cheap

With its garish red lanterns and hotchpotch of low-priced restaurants playing cheesy Mandopop, Chinatown has long been a favourite haunt of local students, wandering tourists and cash-strapped diners. Broadly Cantonese menus are the norm among the budget establishments. Many of these lists contain Anglo-Canto takeaway fodder, and are further diluted by generic South-east Asian dishes, but there's good eating to be found if you know where to look.

Decor, ambience and service often leave much to be desired. Efforts at interior design are usually non-existent, while service is more about utility than smiles – at best brusque and efficient, at worst rude and sullen. And don't be surprised if you end up sharing tables with strangers. In general, you'll get better treatment if you eat at off-peak times, when staff will be less eager to slam your bill on the table and kick you out. It also pays to try a 'xie xie' or 'mm goi sai' – that's 'thank you' in Mandarin and Cantonese, respectively – after ordering. Even if you completely mangle the pronunciation, the attempt will usually be appreciated.

Receipts are often not itemised, and some places (HK Diner being one) have a minimum order per head – a fine-print condition that leaves unsuspecting diners irate. Check the menu beforehand, and ask for a receipt breakdown; very often it will have included the service charge.

At some restaurants, Mandarin or Cantonese speakers will receive Chinese-language menus that often contain a slightly different set of dishes. Savvier diners keen on more authenticity could ask for the Chinese menu, and hope that staff will provide a few translations. Alternatively, point at whatever your neighbouring Chinese diners are eating.

Baozi Inn

25 Newport Court, WC2H 7JS (7287 6877). Leicester Square tube. **Meals served** noon-10.30pm Mon-Thur, Sun; noon-11pm Fri, Sat. **Main courses** £6.50-£7.50. **No credit cards**.

At Baozi Inn, kitsch Communist Revolution decor meets northern Chinese street food tidied up for London. True to Sichuanese form, red is present in most dishes – if not as a slick of potent chilli oil, then in lashings of sliced or whole chillies. Beware of the generously portioned spicy beef noodles: the soup is topped with a layer of tongue-numbing chilli oil. Dan dan noodles, cucumber salad and crescent dumplings are all good choices, especially when accompanied by fresh, unsweetened hot soy milk. The kitchen occasionally gets things wrong, but when it's on song – which is often – the food is spicy, delicious and cheap.

Babies and children admitted. Bookings not accepted. Takeaway service. **Map 17 C4**.

Café de Hong Kong

47-49 Charing Cross Road, WC2H 0AN (7534 9898). Leicester Square tube. **Meals served** 11.30am-11pm Mon-Sat; 11am-10.30pm Sun. **Main courses** £5.90-£6.90. **Credit** (over £10) MC, V.

Not a French-style HK café, misleadingly enough, but a fun, buzzing diner just a few steps from Leicester Square tube station. This Chinese-student favourite serves Anglo-Canto fare with the odd British dish thrown in – noodle dishes, roast meats (decent, though nothing special), plus assorted snacks such as chicken wings, sesame prawn toasts and duck's tongues. Bubble teas, juices and grass jelly combos provide the liquid accompaniment. Food can be hit and miss, and occasionally a bit too greasy, but the café is certainly a worthwhile pitstop.

Takeaway service. Vegetarian menu. **Map 17 C4**.

Café TPT

21 Wardour Street, W1D 6PN (7734 7980). Leicester Square or Piccadilly Circus tube. **Meals served** noon-1am daily. **Main courses** £6.50-£22. **Set meal** £10-£19.50 per person (minimum 2). **Credit** AmEx, MC, V.

Given TPT's fast service and massive menu, with portions to match, you can forgive its slightly cramped seating (there's also an upstairs dining area) and occasional culinary misses. This is one of the friendlier, more relaxed Chinatown joints. Avoid the sloppy baked pork chop rice, and the posh pseudo-laksa, and order cold chicken strips with crunchy-tender jellyfish, sizzling stuffed beancurd, or beef ho fun fresh from the wok. The bubble teas and the sweet, silky beancurd dessert (chilled tau foo fah) are sublime, and pots of hot tea (plus refills) cost just 50p a head.

Available for hire. Babies and children welcome: high chairs. Takeaway service. Vegetarian menu. **Map 17 B5**.

Canton

11 Newport Place, WC2H 7JR (7437 6220). Leicester Square tube. **Meals served** noon-11.30pm daily. **Main courses** £5.50-£10. **Set meal** £11-£16. **Credit** AmEx, MC, V.

Yet another Chinatown stalwart intent on snappy, high-volume turnover, Canton is nevertheless still an excellent spot, especially for solitary dining. Food can be by turns heavily salted or remarkably bland (and, unforgivably, the roast meats are sometimes served stone cold). Skip the thick-skinned pork dumplings, and avoid drinking too much of the tongue-numbing broths (which taste like they contain much MSG). But when the tea is hot and a vast heap of tasty beef fried rice costs just £5, hungry, bleary-eyed travellers leave satisfied. Expect change from a tenner.

Available for hire. Babies and children welcome: high chair. Separate room for parties, seats 22. Takeaway service. **Map 17 C4**.

Cha Cha Moon

15-21 Ganton Street, W1F 9BN (7297 9800, www.chachamoon.com). Oxford Circus or Piccadilly Circus tube. **Meals served** 11.30am-11pm Mon-Thur; 11.30am-11.30pm Fri, Sat; noon-10.30pm Sun. **Main courses** £6-£8. **Set meal** £15 2 courses, £18 3 courses. **Credit** AmEx, MC, V.

Business is still brisk at Cha Cha Moon, but standards can be irritatingly inconsistent. We've been served a bland dish of chiu chow rice cakes, topped with pickled turnip and minced beef, and overcooked Taiwan noodles with brisket of beef and mustard greens – though with its seductive hint of five-spice powder, this dish was delicious. We also liked the sichuan wun tun, filled with prawns and chicken, which was pepped up by a garlicky chilli sauce. But it was the Wen Wen cocktail, a mix of peach and raspberry with a dash of vodka, that stole the limelight. Service has improved of late and the staff now seem more engaging.

Babies and children admitted. Bookings not accepted for fewer than 6 people. Disabled: toilet. Tables outdoors (6, courtyard). Takeaway service. **Map 17 A4**.

Four Seasons

12 Gerrard Street, W1D 5PR (7494 0870, www.fs-restaurants.co.uk). Leicester Square or Piccadilly Circus tube. **Meals served** noon-12.45am Mon-Sat; 11am-12.45am Sun. **Main courses** £7.50-£24. **Set meal** £14.50-£32 (minimum 2). **Credit** AmEx, MC, V.

The famed purveyor of the golden trio of roasted meats: duck, char siu (barbecued pork) and siew yoke (crispy belly pork). Any of them – or all three – on a plate with rice is reason enough to return for more of the same, but it's also worth trying other dishes on the extensive menu. Soya chicken is usually to be recommended, as are the stir-fried green beans with pork. Staff are particularly offhand during busy hours, and the meal-end plate of oranges is a not-so-subtle hint that there are other customers waiting.

Available for hire. Babies and children welcome: high chairs. Booking advisable. Takeaway service. Vegetarian menu. **Map 17 C4**.

For branches see index.

HK Diner

22 Wardour Street, W1D 6QQ (7434 9544). Leicester Square or Piccadilly Circus tube. Meals served 11am-4am daily. **Main courses** £5-£25. **Set meal** £10-£30 per person (minimum 2). **Minimum** £6. **Credit** MC, V.

Open until 4am every day, HK Diner is a favourite with students, the post-clubbing crowd and chef Jun Tanaka. It's charming, in a cheerful greasy-spoon kind of way. The café-style food is consistently decent, and some waiters aren't immune to smiles and

a little banter. But the real stars are the impeccably shaken bubble teas; for just £3.30 a pop, the HK original, black sesame or Japanese grape will send you straight to tapioca heaven. Have back-up choices in mind, though, as certain flavours are apt to run out. And watch out for the minimum £6 a head charge.
Available for hire. Babies and children welcome: high chairs. Takeaway service. Vegetarian menu. **Map 17 C4**.

Leong's Legends

4 Macclesfield Street, W1D 6AX (7287 0288, www.restaurantprivilege.com). Leicester Square or Piccadilly Circus tube. **Meals served** noon-11pm Mon-Thur, Sun; noon-11.30pm Fri, Sat. **Dim sum served** noon-5pm daily. **Main courses** £4.50-£18.50. **Dim sum** £1.90-£6.50. **Credit** (over £12) MC, V.
Arrive in the afternoon when this dark-panelled, teahouse-style Taiwanese specialist is half-empty, or risk queues and hurried dining. Select any of the following: xiao long bao (crab or the original pork); luscious, soup-filled baozi (an absolute steal at eight for £6.50); meltingly tender belly pork and rice (a fantastic, cheap lunch for £5.20); aubergine with mashed garlic and tao pan sauce; or the super-garlicky, salty-spicy chilli garlic crab, already cracked for convenient eating. We don't, however, recommend the congee. Dishes sometimes arrive at staggered intervals. Try to ignore the purist next to you moaning about how it's not all truly Taiwanese food, and then leave only marginally poorer.
Babies and children admitted. Bookings not accepted. Tables outdoors (2, pavement). Takeaway service. **Map 17 C4**.
For branch see index.

Wong Kei

41-43 Wardour Street, W1D 6PY (7437 8408). Leicester Square or Piccadilly Circus tube. **Meals served** noon-11.30pm Mon-Sat; noon-10.30pm Sun. **Main courses** £4.40-£8. **Set meal** £8.50-£13.50 per person (minimum 2).
No credit cards.
A faithful coterie of customers still visits the vast old restaurant known affectionately as 'Wonkies', in the nostalgic hope of being verbally abused by the waiters. Sadly, the rudeness was apparently (mostly) an act for the tourists; these days, the service is simply blunt and efficient – which is no bad thing in a multistorey restaurant with seating for scores of diners. The menu remains almost biblical in length, with dozens of stir-fries covering everything from pork to seafood. The rice can often be overcooked and the roast meats cold, but you do get free tea and huge portions for low prices.
Babies and children admitted. Disabled: toilet. Takeaway service. Vegetarian menu. **Map 17 B4**.

Leong's Legends

Paddington

Pearl Liang

8 Sheldon Square, W2 6EZ (7289 7000, www.pearlliang.co.uk). Paddington tube/rail. **Meals served** noon-11pm, **dim sum served** noon-4.45pm daily. **Main courses** £8.80-£60. **Dim sum** £3-£5. **Set meal** £25 per person (minimum 2); £38 per person (minimum 4). **Credit** AmEx, MC, V.
Far bigger and swankier than it appears from the concrete and glass development outside, Pearl Liang is an enticing prospect for Paddington's weary travellers. Its attractive, modern interior features dark floor tiling matched with brown walls and ceilings – the whole leavened by cubed spotlights, cool jazz, mirrors and a mural of blossoms; by the entrance is a cocktail bar. The multinational diners include several Chinese, for the Cantonese food here is proper stuff (trotters, jellyfish and all) and imaginative. Take the dim sum: pumpkin with mock shark's dumpling was a masterpiece of vegetarian artifice, transparent al dente noodles substituting for the shark's fin. Enjoyable too were the meaty pork and watercress grilled dumplings, the flavourful stock of the soup of the day (ham with carrot and lotus root) and, best of all, the abundant filling (prawns, egg, various meats) in the mini sticky rice in lotus leaf: the leaves kept moist by greaseproof paper, thus imparting fragrance and flavour – great value for £3.30. Only the bean pastry with prawns in abalone sauce was mundane. The main menu includes luxury ingredients (fresh abalone, lobster) prepared in various fashions (including sashimi-style), and classic hotpots. Serene service adds to the sense of well-being.
Babies and children welcome: high chairs. Booking advisable. Disabled: toilet. Separate room for parties, seats 40. Takeaway service. **Map 8 D5**.

Soho

Ba Shan

24 Romilly Street, W1D 5AH (7287 3266). Leicester Square tube. **Meals served** noon-11pm Mon-Thur, Sun; noon-11.30pm Fri, Sat. **Main courses** £7.90-£16.50. **Credit** AmEx, MC, V.
A notice from Chairman Mao, one of Hunan province's better-known sons, greets you on arrival at this Hunanese restaurant: 'If you don't eat chillies, you won't be a revolutionary.' Chillies, in their various Hunanese interpretations, feature prominently on the menu, which offers a wide range of fish, meat and vegetarian dishes from the region. Such authenticity is only to be expected when Fuchsia Dunlop (food writer, author of the *Revolutionary Chinese Cookbook* – and one-time *Time Out* reviewer) is Ba Shan's consultant. An appetiser of 'smacked cucumber', which looked more sliced than whacked into submission, was dressed in an addictive mixture of chilli, garlic, vinegar and sugar. The Chairman's favourite dish, red-braised pork belly, was as wobbly and melting as desired in its deep, beguiling juices. Peng's bean curd, the pieces steeped in a ground pork, black bean and chilli sauce, was equally as impressive in its depth and complexity of flavour. With mocked-up courtyard decor and classical Chinese music playing quietly in the background, Ba Shan (sibling to Barshu and Baozi Inn) makes for a special dining experience.
Babies and children admitted: high chairs. Booking advisable. Disabled: toilet. Separate room for parties, seats 12. **Map 17 C4**.

Royal China Club. See p69.

Barshu HOT 50

28 Frith Street, W1D 5LF (7287 6688, www.bar-shu.co.uk). Leicester Square or Tottenham Court Road tube. **Meals served** noon-11pm Mon-Thur, Sun; noon-11.30pm Fri, Sat. **Main courses** £8.90-£28.90. **Credit** AmEx, MC, V.

When it comes to Sichuan cooking, the gang of three – Barshu, Ba Shan and Baozi Inn, all under the same ownership – lead the London pack. Barshu, the original restaurant, is spread over three floors, but we prefer to sit at ground level. Although the dining area isn't large, the burly wooden furnishings and intricate wooden carvings add to the allure. Young, hip Chinese like the place too. Squeamish diners would do well to stay clear of some dishes, such as dry-wok ducks' tongues. Offal plays a big role, from pig's intestines to chicken gizzards, with all arriving bathed in searingly hot chilli. Jellyfish ribbons served with fresh chilli had more manageable heat, but sea bass, although it seemed tame on the menu, arrived with sizzling chilli oil complete with dozens of red chillies floating on top. Nevertheless, the fish was sweet and tender, and the flavours were staggeringly effective. We needed to cool down, but found no respite on the limited dessert menu, although the deep-fried golden-brown taro rolls were enjoyable. Service continues to be patchy, and it can be hard to extract a smile from the staff.

Babies and children welcome: high chairs. Booking advisable; essential Fri, Sat. Disabled: toilet. Separate room for parties, seats 24. **Map 17 C4.**

★ Yauatcha HOT 50

15 Broadwick Street, W1F 0DL (7494 8888, www.yauatcha.com). Leicester Square, Piccadilly Circus or Tottenham Court Road tube. **Dim sum served** noon-11.45pm Mon-Sat; noon-10.30pm Sun. **Dim sum** £4-£15. **Set meal** (3-6pm Mon-Fri) £14.44 per person (maximum 2). **Credit** AmEx, MC, V.

At first glance, Yauatcha may look like a swanky cocktail bar, and with its celebrity – or sometimes just attractive – guests, the place can often resemble a nightclub. Nevertheless, it also serves some of the capital's best and most innovative Cantonese food. Slide into a booth in the edgy ground-floor dining room, chicly accented with bright coloured lights and Chinese ceramics, or lounge around a table in the cavernous sexy brown room below. Here, you can sample the delights that first made the venue famous when Alan Yau opened it in 2004: top-quality dim sum that's served day and night. Yau has long since released control of the business, but standards remain high. Try the traditional har gau, the sea bass and lotus root congee, or experience the wonderful textural play in the three-mushroom cheung fun. As with the East-meets-West decor, so with the food: there's rhubarb tart for pud. Go for a cocktail if you like, or enjoy one of the long list of Chinese teas: traditionally brewed, iced or in smoothie form. The petits gateaux in the window are not just eye candy; they are French pastries with Chinese characteristics, and they are divine.

Available for hire. Babies and children admitted. Booking advisable. Disabled: lift; toilet. **Map 17 B3.**

West

Bayswater

Gold Mine

102 Queensway, W2 3RR (7792 8331). Bayswater or Queensway tube. **Meals served** noon-11pm daily. **Main courses** £7-£30. **Set meal** £15.50-£20.50 per person (minimum 2). **Credit** MC, V.

A queue had already built up at Gold Mine just before opening time for lunch. This bustling restaurant has become highly popular for its comfort food and, especially, its roast meats, which can be seen hanging in the open kitchen by the window. Decorated with red carpets, chairs in red fabric and large prints in gold frames, the dining room is virtually indistinguishable from many budget Chinese eateries found along Queensway and in Chinatown – though it's a fair bit larger than you'd reckon from the diminutive shopfront. Soon after its opening, the kitchen gained the reputation for producing the best roast meats in town, and after sampling a plate of roast duck, crispy pork and tender char siu we can endorse the belief. But going beyond these signature dishes paid few dividends. Stewed beancurd and crunchy pak choi would have been better served if the dish had not arrived in a surfeit of oil. A tender veal chop paired with a black pepper sauce was let down by over-salting and yet more oil. Complimentary fresh oranges – served by efficient if stony-faced staff – brought much welcome relief to all the oiliness.

Available for hire. Babies and children admitted. Booking advisable. Takeaway service. **Map 7 C6.**

★ Magic Wok

100 Queensway, W2 3RR (7792 9767). Bayswater or Queensway tube. **Meals served** noon-11pm daily. **Main courses** £6.50-£18. **Set meal** £14-£29 per person (minimum 2). **Credit** AmEx, MC, V.

Old school needn't mean complacency. Magic Wok has been conjuring up a fabulous assortment of Cantonese dishes from these seemingly unchanging, well-worn premises for decades, but the kitchen remains in prime form. We managed to bag a table in the brighter back area of the ground-floor dining room (preferable to the cramped front space or dull first floor), beneath a curious stain in the ceiling tiles. Large paintings of Chinese pastoral life cheer things up – as do the patient, friendly staff and the multinational hubbub of diners (many of them Chinese). The menu is huge and intriguing, offering the likes of stir-fried sea cucumber and dried fish-lip maw with black peppers. Best head straight for the main courses; a seafood platter starter was a mass of (albeit delectably) deep-fried creatures – langoustine, squid, prawns – around a disappointingly huge mound of crispy seaweed. Everything else was superb: the textural contrasts and fragrance of steamed chicken with dried lily and black fungus in lotus leaf; luscious, slippery aubergine with minced pork in hotpot (hotpots are highlights); the crunchy-fresh seasonal vegetables (ask for gai lan) with gelatinous preserved egg (and unadvertised crab meat). Go in a group and let rip.

Babies and children welcome: high chairs. Booking advisable dinner. Separate room for parties, seats 30. Takeaway service. Vegetarian menu. **Map 7 C6.**

Mandarin Kitchen

14-16 Queensway, W2 3RX (7727 9012). Bayswater or Queensway tube. **Meals served** noon-11.30pm daily. **Main courses** £6.90-£30. **Set meal** £11.90 per person (minimum 2); £20 per person (minimum 4). **Credit** MC, V.

Mandarin Kitchen's dining room is in dire need of a makeover. The cave-like ceiling, brown fabric and dim lighting would be fine if diners were bats. Staff in brown tops and groups of dark-suited Japanese men on expense accounts do nothing to lift the gloom. Thankfully, service was attentive and friendly on our visit – yet this hasn't always been the case. The restaurant has long been famed for lobster and seafood. However, our lobster noodles with ginger and spring onion, though acceptable, could no longer be said to set the London standard. It's worth enquiring about the 'fish of the day'; this time, we were rewarded by stir-fried venus clams in a garlicky sauce studded with fresh red chillies. The dish was a rare highlight in a meal that was overshadowed by some criminally overcooked mixed seafood in XO sauce. The scallops, prawns and squid were rubbery and the dish was swimming in oil; thank goodness for the accompanying perfectly cooked asparagus and straw mushrooms. None of these faults deters the hordes of queuing tourists (out-of-date guidebooks in hand) – but Mandarin Kitchen seems to be resting, nay slumped, on its laurels.

Babies and children welcome: booster seats. Booking advisable . Takeaway service. **Map 7 C7**.

Royal China

13 Queensway, W2 4QJ (7221 2535, www2.royal chinagroup.biz). Bayswater or Queensway tube. **Meals served** noon-11pm Mon-Thur; noon-11.30pm Fri, Sat; 11am-10pm Sun. **Dim sum served** noon-4.45pm Mon-Sat; 11am-4.45pm Sun. **Main courses** £7.50-£50. **Dim sum** £2.30-£5. **Set meal** £30-£38 per person (minimum 2). **Credit** AmEx, MC, V.

The Royal China chain (which also has branches in Marylebone, Fulham, Docklands and Harrow) is still the place to get high-quality, authentic dim sum at a reasonable price. This original branch does a roaring trade on a Sunday: the doors open at 11am, and the queue forms shortly after. It's worth the wait: for the price, the food is reliably good, and the newly renovated digs quite posh (elegant gold murals on black lacquer-lined walls show geese flying above dancing waves, and gold leaf covers much of the ceiling). Char siu buns lacked the one-dimensional sweetness of Chinatown versions, delivering airy steamed bread around tender barbecued pork. 'Royal China cheung fun' is a must-order selection of prawn, beef with water chestnut, and roast pork wrapped in wide rice noodles, all covered in sweet soy sauce. The specials are worth a try too. Clams with bean-curd-skin rolls offered a pleasant contrast in texture: juicy, sharp seafood (all things from the sea are a speciality here) sandwiched between crispy fried bean-curd skins. Similarly inventive were yam cakes with chunks of wind-dried meat, sitting under deep-fried glutinous rice and prawn croquettes: perfect comfort food. The staff's reputation for brusqueness seems unfair; on our visit, they were efficient in a busy dining room.

Babies and children welcome: high chairs. Booking advisable; not accepted lunch Sat, Sun. Separate rooms for parties, seating 20-40. Takeaway service. Vegetarian menu. **Map 7 C7**.

For branches see index.

Kensington

Min Jiang

10th floor, Royal Garden Hotel, 2-24 Kensington High Street, W8 4PT (7361 1988, www.min jiang.co.uk). High Street Kensington tube. **Lunch/dim sum served** noon-3pm, **dinner served** 6-10.30pm daily. **Main courses** £10-£48. **Dim sum** £3.60-£6. **Set lunch** (Mon-Fri) £20.50. **Credit** AmEx, MC, V.

It's quite a thrill to ascend to Min Jiang, situated on the tenth floor of the Royal Garden Hotel, and gaze at the sweeping views during the day. You can even catch a glimpse of Kensington Palace, with its newly landscaped garden. The serene dining room, decorated with elegant wooden lattices and Chinese vases, is a relaxing place to enjoy a quiet meal. The kitchen produces one of the best beijing ducks in town, and we can never resist the crispiness of its skin, which is served with three types of dip (the garlic paste with radish and tientsin cabbage being our favourite). The dim sum here is especially notable, but we plumped for the carte this time. Our clay pot of beef ribeye in a spicy Sichuan sauce was spot-on, and a dish of stir-fried tofu with seafood was kicked into life by a pungent fermented-chilli sauce. New on the menu, a soya pudding (similar to panna cotta), served with a consommé infused with the warmth of ginger, was made special by a topping of dried osmanthus flowers. Service, too, is well up to scratch, and often charm itself.

Babies and children welcome: high chairs; nappy-changing facilities. Booking advisable; essential Thur-Sun. Disabled: lift; toilet. Separate room for parties, seats 20. **Map 7 B8**.

Princess Garden. See p69.

South

Clapham

★ Mongolian Grill NEW

29 North Street, SW4 0HJ (7498 4448, www.mongolian-grill.co.uk). Clapham Common tube or Wandsworth Road rail. **Dinner served** 5-10.30pm Mon-Fri. **Meals served** 3-10.30pm Sat, Sun. **Main courses** £3.50-£10. **Set buffet** £12.50 all-you-can-eat. **Credit** MC, V.

Sitting incongruously in an old corner pub in the middle of Clapham, London's capital of convention, the Mongolian Grill is full of surprises. The dining room retains a relaxed, pubby atmosphere – a lick of red paint and a few dozen red lanterns serve as decoration – but the food is a million miles from typical Clapham high street fare. The eclectic menu offers dim sum, a range of food to grill on a hot plate at your table, or an invitation to the all-you-can-eat hotpot buffet. We recommend the latter option. Order half spicy soup and half mild for the cauldron in the middle of your table, pile your plate with thinly sliced beef and lamb, load up on cabbage, spinach, potatoes, fishballs, and anything else you fancy – and then get cooking. While the restaurant name suggests food of northern barbarians, the style is actually a hybrid of the western Sichuan-style hotpot, via Hong Kong, where the owner's family is from. While it's not strictly authentic (there were few Sichuan peppercorns in our spicy stock, and many of the vegetables – courgettes, field mushrooms – were more local favourites than traditional Chinese), the food is tasty. And at £12.50 for the all-you-can-eat buffet, it's a steal. There is a two-hour time-limit for the buffet, and booking is advisable on weekends and for large groups.

Babies and children welcome: high chairs. Booking advisable Sat, Sun. Takeaway service. **Map 22 A1**.

Gold Mine. See p73.

East

Docklands

Yi-Ban

London Regatta Centre, Dockside Road, E16 2QT (7473 6699, www.yi-ban.co.uk). Prince Regent or Royal Albert DLR. **Meals served** noon-11pm Mon-Sat; 11am-10.30pm Sun. **Dim sum served** noon-5pm daily. **Main courses** £4-£30. **Dim sum** £2.20-£4. **Set meal** £22-£38 per person (minimum 2). **Credit** AmEx, MC, V.

It's hard not to think of JG Ballard as you approach Yi -Ban: the driverless DLR trains that take you past overhead cable cars and the Dome; the walk along an empty road opposite City Airport. The first sight of Yi-Ban's exterior across the vast car park doesn't disappoint, its facade little more than a large concrete rectangle with a glass door. But once you make your way up the stairs it comes to life, opening into a bustling space with a spectacular view of planes taking off and landing across the dock. The menu we were given had all the standards you'd expect, from ma po bean curd to lemon chicken, but a query about our neighbouring table's dishes reveals another menu, the one handed to the numerous Chinese and Vietnamese diners. This is the one with a fine range of hotpots, as well as frogs' legs, intestines, bitter melon and tripe.

Pork belly hotpot with yam was well executed – the braising having rendered off much of the fat to leave slices of tender meat interleaved with yam. Aubergine, stuffed peppers and tofu had a deep, rich flavour, nicely offset by the steamed rice and a fresh, sparkling side order of garlic and pea shoots. There's an extensive dim sum menu, too. Note that the restaurant gets very busy at weekends, so do book.
Available for hire. Babies and children welcome: booster seats; high chairs; nappy-changing facilities. Booking advisable. Disabled: toilet. Separate room for parties, seats 30. Takeaway service. Vegetarian menu.

North East

Dalston

★ Shanghai Dalston

41 Kingsland High Street, E8 2JS (7254 2878, www.shanghaidalston.co.uk). Dalston Kingsland rail or 38, 67, 76, 149 bus. **Meals/dim sum served** noon-11pm daily. **Main courses** £5.50-£7.80. **Dim sum** £2.80-£4.50. **Set meal** £15.80-£19 per person (minimum 2). **Credit** MC, V.
Just north of Dalston Junction, Shanghai Dalston is a little bit of east London magic: the tiles and fittings of a Victorian pie and mash shop meeting a window display of hanging roast ducks, racks of ribs and crispy pork. The pie-shop booths and counter are still there at the front, but in recent years they've been joined by a large Buddha and the usual accoutrements of a neighbourhood Chinese restaurant. It's a mad – yet winning – cultural mash-up. Along with a menu of staples and some more unusual dishes, dim sum is available all day, though execution can be variable; the fillings of our har gau and siu mai were steaming-hot and delicious, but let down by soggy skins. Main dishes were more accomplished. Soft-shell crab (crispy and well seasoned), and twice-cooked pork (tender meat with chinese mushrooms), were both nicely presented and above the average high-street quality. From the lunch menu, the plate of duck and crispy pork on rice was a treat, and as good as you'd get in Chinatown. Afterwards, adventurous souls can work off their meal with a lively routine in one of the two bookable karaoke rooms.
Babies and children welcome: high chairs; nappy-changing facilities. Booking advisable. Disabled: toilet. Separate rooms for parties, both seating 45. Takeaway service. **Map 25 B5**.

North

Islington

Yipin China NEW

70-72 Liverpool Road, N1 0QD (7354 3388, www.yipinchina.co.uk). Angel tube or Highbury & Islington tube/rail. **Meals served** noon-10.30pm daily. **Main courses** £6.80-£14.90. **Set meal** (noon-5pm Mon-Fri) £5.50. **Credit** MC, V.
The food at this Hunanese restaurant is so convincingly authentic it could easily pass muster in China. Both Hunan and Sichuan cuisines rely on

Mongolian Grill. See p75.

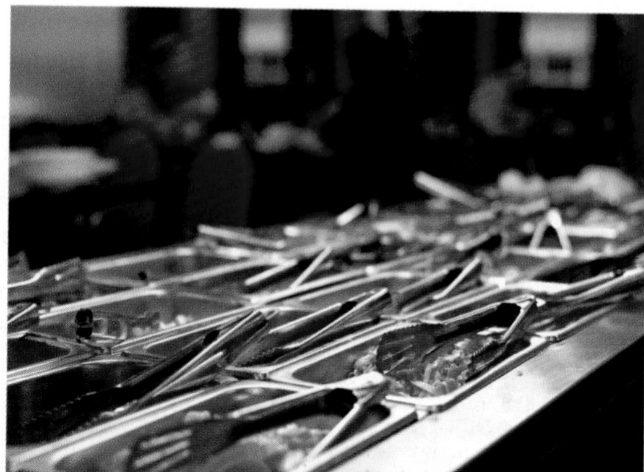

a serious amount of chilli – though many in China would insist that Hunan produces the most unforgivingly spiky dishes. Diners who balk at chilli heat and offal can find comfort in the clearly labelled Cantonese dishes, the delicious Hunanese smoked meats and fish, or in the red-braised pork, one of several stews fragrant with spices that also typify the south-central province's cuisine. Hunanese chef Geng makes no concessions to western tastes, boldly opening the menu's Hunan section with dry wok-cooked duck's tongues, and continuing with assorted fowl feet and innards. To start, spiced fungus contained chilled, springy wood-ear fungus, dotted with red chillies and raw minced garlic. Next, a perfectly prepared stir-fried dish of hand-torn cabbage with chilli and vinegar was a great example of Hunan's hearty peasant fare; slices of pork belly offered the perfect sweet balance to the sour vinegar. Judging by the sour sliced sea bass in pickled mustard soup, the Sichuan-style dishes are also excellent. Yipin's clean pink and white dining room won't win any design awards, but serving staff are charming and knowledgeable. A bright addition to London's Chinese repertoire.
Babies and children welcome: high chairs. Booking advisable. Disabled: toilet. Separate room for parties. Takeaway service. Vegetarian menu.

Yipin China

Outer London

Ilford, Essex

Mandarin Palace

559-561 Cranbrook Road, Ilford, Essex, IG2 6JZ (8550 7661). Gants Hill tube. **Lunch served** noon-3.30pm Mon-Sat. **Dinner served** 6-11.30pm Mon-Thur; 6pm-midnight Fri, Sat. **Meals served** noon-11.30pm Sun. **Dim sum served** noon-3.30pm Mon-Sat; noon-5pm Sun. **Main courses** £8.50-£30. **Dim sum** £2.50-£4.50. **Set meal** £24 per person (minimum 2); £29 per person (minimum 4). **Credit** AmEx, MC, V.

If *EastEnders* had a Chinese restaurant, it would be the Mandarin Palace. Clichéd Chinese motifs – jade-green ceramic screens, vases, dark woods and pretty lanterns – fill the restaurant, and there's even a (spotlessly clean) carpet underfoot, all of which makes the space feel comfortable and homely. It's a feeling heightened by the friendly staff, who chat and gossip with the numerous regulars. And the food is a delight. Set menus, including the likes of steamed fresh scallops and baked lobster, are tempting, as are dishes such as hotpot with jellyfish and crispy eel with honey sauce, but we visited on a Sunday, so opted for a mix of dim sum and main courses. Dim sum portions were generous, and included light-as-air cha siu bao, and plump, delicious har gau and siu mai. A plate of three mixed meats was tasty and plentiful. Vegetables are pricey, starting around £7, but are offset by distinctly good value in other dishes – the dim sum, in particular, is cheaper than in most West End restaurants, and served with a laid-back air that you rarely find in frantic Chinatown counterparts.
Available for hire. Babies and children welcome: high chairs. Separate room for parties, seats 50. Takeaway service; delivery service (over £25 within 2-mile radius). Vegetarian menu.
For branch see index.

East European

Full of vim and vitality, London's eastern European dining scene reflects the remarkable geopolitical events that have taken place in the region since the end of World War II. Here we corral cuisines from the Czech Republic eastwards to Russia, taking in cherished historical oddities such as the **Czechoslovak Restaurant** and the **Gay Hussar**, but also the manifestations of more recent developments. **Knaypa** and **Malina** cater at least in part to Hammersmith's Polish community – much invigorated since that country's entry into the EU. And one of this year's new openings, **Mari Vanna**, aims to pamper (with a caviar-tinged dose of nostalgia) the exceedingly wealthy Russians who are currently attracted to London; it's also a treat for the eyes and winner of the Best New Design gong in the Time Out 2012 Eating & Drinking Awards. Our other newcomer, **Colchis**, shows the increasing popularity of Georgian cuisine (and its wines) in the capital, offering sophisticated versions of a cooking style that marries eastern European and Middle Eastern influences.

Central

Knightsbridge

Mari Vanna NEW

2012 WINNER BEST NEW DESIGN

116 Knightsbridge, Wellington Court, SW1X 7PJ (7225 3122, www.marivanna.co.uk). Knightsbridge tube. **Lunch served** noon-3.30pm, **tea served** 3.30-5pm daily. **Dinner served** 7-11.30pm Mon-Sat; 7-10.30pm Sun. **Main courses** £10-£28. **Set dinner** £45-£75 4 courses. **Credit** AmEx, DC, MC, V.

Russian

Part of a Russian-owned chain, Mari Vanna seems aimed at nostalgic oligarchs – like its New York counterpart. It's named after a mythical babushka (grandmother), and comes replete with myriad objects evoking times past. There's ornate crockery, crystal from St Petersburg, lamps draped with fringed shawls, Lenin pins, an old accordion, the autographs of some very regal guests… A visit to the bathrooms (which feature old toilets with pull-chains and where Russian folk tales are played), is another adventure altogether. With so much going on, this could easily have been a Laika's dinner, but in the skilled hands of Russian-born, British-educated interior designer Yuna Megre, it's a marvel. And the welcome – once you're let in the locked entrance – is warm, the service solicitous and smiling. But how is granny's cooking? Very traditional, in the best sense. Excellent rye breads and nibbles whet the appetite. Pirozhki (small pasties) had attractive golden pastry and moist, juicy fillings (beef and pork, cabbage and chicken, sea bass). Blinis were exemplary too, and as delicate as the lace doilies adorning the tables. They arrived with smetana (sour cream), chopped egg, diced onion and salmon roe. To follow, beef stroganoff had strips of meat in a rich sauce of spiced sour cream, served with delectable kasha enhanced by wild mushrooms. What's not so good? The wine list is expensive, with few choices by the glass. Vodka may be a better option, or order kvass: a delicious low-alcohol drink made from fermenting rye bread, then flavoured with cranberry or raspberry juice. Afternoon tea is a cheaper option, and breakfast opening is planned.

Available for hire. Babies and children welcome: high chairs. Booking advisable. Separate room for parties, seats 14. **Map 8 F8.**

Soho

Gay Hussar

2 Greek Street, W1D 4NB (7437 0973, www.gayhussar.co.uk). Tottenham Court Road tube. **Lunch served** 12.15-2.30pm, **dinner served** 5.30-10.45pm Mon-Sat. **Main courses** £12.75-£17.75. **Set lunch** £19.50 2 courses, £22.50 3 courses. **Credit** AmEx, DC, MC, V.

Hungarian

Although the food here isn't bad, it's beside the point, as the Gay Hussar is an institution. Opened in 1953, it has operated as a canteen for Westminster politicians, as well as a useful spot for theatregoers, ever since. The interior is cosy, lined with political memoirs and Martin Rowson's caricatures. On a Monday night the crowd included a Labour MP, a Labour Lord, assorted apparatchiks and more than one table of Hungarians. The plate of Hungarian hors d'oeuvres is a good starting point, providing a taste of all the cold starters: highlights include goose and pork pâté, marinated herring in sour cream, cucumber salad, and smoked sausage and salami. Next comes goulash in various incarnations; the tasty veal goulash arrived with galuska (small dumplings not unlike gnocchi). Best dish of the evening was smoked goose breast with red cabbage and sólet (a bean and meat combo, called cholent in Jewish cuisine) – a rich, well-flavoured feast. Pancakes feature heavily for dessert; a mixed berry pudding (like a slightly grainy, heavy jelly) made a lighter finish. Drinks include Hungarian aperitifs and digestifs, plus a no-nonsense house red. Service is attentive, whether you're a first-timer, or an old friend.

Available for hire. Babies and children welcome: high chairs. Booking advisable dinner. Separate rooms for parties, seating 12 and 24. **Map 17 C3.**

South Kensington

Gessler Daquise

20 Thurloe Street, SW7 2LT (7589 6117, www.gessleratdaquise.co.uk). South Kensington tube. **Meals served** noon-11pm daily. **Main courses** £13-£24. **Set lunch** (noon-4pm Mon-Fri) £9 2 courses. **Credit** MC, V.

Polish

Mari Vanna

EAST EUROPEAN

In its 'modern' guise – this stalwart Polish restaurant was acquired by the Gessler family of Warsaw fame in 2008 – Daquise still attracts Polish regulars seeking the comfort of homely dumplings and pickles. The well-lit interior with its rustic-elegant stripped wooden floor, part-tiled walls and crisp napery caters just as readily to locals, tourists and the merely curious. The very correct maître d' can appear a mite stiff, but thawed as he witnessed us tucking into ladlefuls of sour rye soup, beef roulades, and pork fillet with a mound of barley groats. The chefs serving at table from searingly hot cast-iron pans could hardly have been cheerier. Our selection was a curate's egg: rather too literally in the case of a blue-ringed egg adorning the otherwise well-judged, delicious soup. Prune-stuffed roulades were terrific; plump pickled herring first-rate. However, a game and cranberry terrine was dense and dull, and the cured salmon had seen better days, though the crisp fried potato cakes were a mitigating delight. Desserts proved sound and filling, coffee so-so. Malty Polish beers and the house Gascon wine are gentle on both palate and purse, and herbal vodka chased away any discontent.

Available for hire. Babies and children admitted. Booking advisable. Separate room for parties, seats 40. Takeaway service. **Map 14 D10**.

West

Bayswater

Colchis NEW

39 Chepstow Place, W2 4TS (7221 7620, www.colchisrestaurant.co.uk). Bayswater or Notting Hill Gate tube.
Bar **Open/meals served** noon-midnight Tue-Sun. **Main courses** £3.50-£8.
Restaurant **Lunch served** noon-3pm, **dinner served** 6-11pm Tue-Sun. **Main courses** £10-£22.50.
Both **Credit** AmEx, DC, MC, V.
Georgian

Colchis is the ancient name for the Black Sea coast that is now western Georgia, and the menu lists an array of intriguing Georgian specialities, such as lobio (kidney bean stew, served with corn cakes) and pkhali (a vegetable paste made with walnuts, which is formed into balls). Grab a cocktail in the bar area – drinks such as negroni and gin martini are skilfully mixed – before moving on to the restaurant. A big mirror wall adorns the stylish charcoal-coloured interior, which is lined with yellow chairs and dark wooden tables. Khachapuri, Georgian cheese-bread, was fresh out of the oven – the soft flatbread slices inlaid with salty, stringy white cheese. Equally delicious were the khinkali: served on a slate, these chewy dumplings were filled with a moist mixture of minced meat and pork, and sprinkled with pomegranate seeds. Mains focus on grilled and roast meats; the vegetarian option is, rather unimaginatively, a mushroom risotto. Our mix of pork, lamb and veal skewers was excellent: juicy, flavoursome chargilled meat came with two dipping sauces – a spicy and a sweet one (made from dried plums). Georgian wines, both red and white, are available by the glass, and there are a few digestifs from the country too.

Available for hire. Babies and children admitted. Booking advisable Fri, Sat. Tables outdoors (3, terrace). **Map 7 B6**.

Hammersmith

Knaypa

268 King Street, W6 0SP (8563 2887, www.theknaypa.co.uk). Hammersmith tube.
Dinner served 6-10.30pm Mon-Fri. **Meals served** noon-10.30pm Sat; noon-9.30pm Sun. **Main courses** £10-£15. **Credit** AmEx, MC, V.
Polish

West London's Polish community is well served by restaurants purveying hearty soul food at reasonable prices, with Knaypa being a prime example. The popular steak tartare is an implausibly large plateful for a starter, and the sharing platters are ample for a family group, let alone a couple. Groups of any size are readily accommodated in two rooms of dramatic contrast. The ground-floor space has dark walls and tables, subdued lighting and bright red chairs (echoed by the rococo red frames of risqué posters). Downstairs takes you into a Silesian inn, with antlers replacing posters, and food served on wooden platters. Individual dishes proved more accomplished than the sharing platter. Krokiet (rolled, fried pancakes filled with tender sauerkraut and wild mushrooms) was a delightfully light and crisp first course, accompanied by a cupful of well-executed borscht; in the platter, advance cooking had rendered them leaden, and a smoked sheep's cheese was leathery. Traditional apple cake made a sound and filling dessert, though the mandarin segment garnishes seemed anachronistic. To finish, a glass of iced krupnik on the house was the kind of touch that ensures Knaypa's popularity.

Available for hire. Babies and children welcome: high chairs; nappy-changing facilities. Booking advisable weekends. Separate room for parties, seats 38. Vegetarian menu. **Map 20 A4**.

Malina

166 Shepherd's Bush Road, W6 7PB (7603 8881, www.malinarestaurant.com). Goldhawk Road or Hammersmith tube. **Dinner served** 6-11pm Mon-Fri. **Meals served** noon-11pm Sat, Sun. **Main courses** £9.90-£17.50. **Set lunch** (noon-3pm Sun) £12.50 2 courses, £13.50 3 courses. **Credit** AmEx, MC, V. Polish

Bright and inviting both outside and in, Malina somehow melds unprepossessingly with the shops at the Hammersmith end of Shepherd's Bush Road. This may account for its quietness on a recent Sunday lunchtime visit – certainly, neither the friendly welcome nor the delightful dishes merited empty seats. Encouragingly, however, an extensive Polish family were clearly enjoying themselves. The decor promises both homeliness and elegance, and the food perfectly fulfils the promise. Beetroot soup had brilliance of clarity and flavour, its dumplings as light and pillowy as the assorted pierogi. Ribbons of zesty apple added unanticipated brightness to another starter, tender pickled herring. There was particular deftness evident in the cooking of mushrooms – in tortellini, pierogi and a chanterelle sauce with pork fillet. If it's robust earthiness you're after, the heftily portioned meat dishes won't disappoint; the bigos, in particular, is a true trencherman's dish served in a three-bread 'bowl', with care and correctness once again exhibited in the near-melting, long-cooked sauerkraut. Desserts too can be as filling or light as you choose, with the raspberries that give the restaurant its name taking a leading role. This is Polish cuisine for enlightened and straitened times.

Available for hire. Babies and children welcome: high chairs. Booking advisable Fri, Sat. Separate room for parties, seats 10. **Map 20 C3**.

Kensington

Mimino

197C Kensington High Street, W8 6BA (7937 1551, www.mimino.co.uk). Kensington High Street tube. **Dinner served** 6-11pm Tue-Thur; 6pm-midnight Fri, Sat. **Main courses** £10-£16. **Credit** MC, V. Georgian

The jolly, eccentric vibe given out by this Georgian restaurant's website is sadly not matched by the nondescript surroundings of the slightly damp basement setting, nor by the nervous waiter. There's little decoration here – just white walls, faux-leather banquettes and dim lighting. The prime table sits in one corner under a half-hearted canopy of plastic grapes while a stuffed bird of prey eyes you from another corner. No doubt the atmosphere picks up on karaoke nights. The usual crowd consists of expats from the old Soviet regions, who come for authentic Georgian food. This draws influence from both Russian and Middle Eastern cooking but has its own distinctive taste, with heavy use of walnut, pomegranate and bitter herbs as well as sweet-sour fruits. Try meze dishes such as baked aubergine or spiced kidney beans with a creamy walnut sauce, or khachapuri – a much-loved pizza-like bread which is served here in many variations. Kebabs are a speciality too; smoky lamb was offset perfectly by a tart plum relish. Georgians prize their wine for its sweet, fruity flavours, so don't leave without trying a glass.

Available for hire. Babies and children welcome: high chairs. Booking advisable weekends. Takeaway service. **Map 7 A9**.

Shepherd's Bush

Tatra

24 Goldhawk Road, W12 8DH (8749 8193, www.tatrarestaurant.co.uk). Goldhawk Road tube.
Dinner served 6-10pm Mon-Thur; 6-11pm Fri. **Meals served** noon-11pm Sat; noon-10pm Sun. **Main courses** £9.70-£15.90. **Credit** AmEx, DC, MC, V. Polish

This newish addition to the west London slew of Polish/east European eateries belies its High Street location with something of a timeless east European club-room feel, all brick, dark wood and solid leatherette. A cheery bar offers the reassuring sight of multicoloured vodkas – the best way to start and finish a meal. Frozen rhubarb vodka proved an appetite-inducing aperitif; earthy beetroot the perfect foil to pungent pickled herring; a deeply fruity, tart blackcurrant version terrific with ice-cream or coffee. The young, friendly Polish couple who run Tatra are intent on injecting a touch of modernity to the anticipated stolid, traditional fare. So, while beef and smoked sausage goulash was as hearty and plate-filling as the golabki (cabbage stuffed with rice and pork), and potato pancakes the size of generous saucers made up for the relative lightness of smoked salmon, starters were a daintier proposition, and curiously garnished with streaks of balsamic glaze and herb-infused olive oil – which added little save eye appeal to nicely plump and butter-sauced pelmeni (Siberian dumplings), or an enlightened take on kaszanka (black pudding). Desserts are rich, sweet and unambitious; ice-box sorbets provide little competition to the toothsome caramel vodka.

Colchis. See p81.

Available for hire. Babies and children welcome: high chairs. Booking advisable weekends. Disabled: toilet. **Map 20 B2**.

South

Waterloo

Baltic HOT 50

74 Blackfriars Road, SE1 8HA (7928 1111, www.balticrestaurant.co.uk). Southwark tube. **Lunch served** noon-3pm Mon-Fri; noon-4.30pm Sat, Sun. **Dinner served** 5.30-11.15pm Mon-Sat; 5.30-11pm Sun. **Main courses** £10.50-£17. **Set dinner** (5.30-7pm, 10-11pm daily) £14.50 2 courses, £17.50 3 courses. **Credit** AmEx, MC, V. East European

Unassuming from the outside, Jan Woroniecki's bar and restaurant, crafted from an 18th-century coach builder's works, is a pleasure to step into. Conjuring up a timeless, somewhat Nordic aura, with an expanse of white walls, exposed timber and amber-themed decor, it's the perfect backdrop for sampling hearty fare from eastern Europe. Visiting on a quiet weekend lunchtime gave us ample opportunity to ogle the impossibly extensive list of vodkas, cocktails and punches. It's tempting to choose drinks first, then food to match. Orange-scented vodka, for instance, leads to thoughts of fish, and a beautifully roasted fillet of hake with a chunky broth of mushrooms and sorrel proved perfectly apt. Then again, if the food attracts your attention, you're bound to find a drink to suit; gloriously succulent, smoky and savoury black pudding (kaszanka) was perfectly partnered by a toasty, coffee-scented Icelandic porter. Portions are generous and execution rustic – though our pelmeni were delightfully light. Desserts proved mildly disappointing: a not-so-sour cherry no match for an otherwise competent brûlée; Hungarian chocolate cake correctly crunchy but lacking lusciousness. Dessert vodkas hit the mark, though, and a fruity rhubarb punch could readily replace pud.

Available for hire. Babies and children welcome; high chairs. Booking advisable. Disabled: toilet. Separate room for parties, seats 30. Tables outdoors (4, terrace). **Map 11 N8**.

South East

Elephant & Castle

★ Mamuska!

1st floor, Elephant & Castle Shopping Centre, SE1 6TE (3602 1898, www.mamuska.net). Elephant & Castle tube/rail. **Meals served** 7am-midnight Mon-Wed; 7am-12.30am Thur-Sat; 9am-midnight Sun. **Main courses** £5. **No credit cards.** Polish

Think of Polish home cooking and you're probably not imagining eating it somewhere like this: a simple yet swish café, stylishly and humorously branded. 'We have a vast wine selection', says the menu, 'one white, one red and even a rosé'. Orders are taken at the counter, and delivered swiftly to your table. The food is straightforward, and straightforwardly priced: starters £3, puddings the same, mains at £5. Eschewing that wine list for Zywiec and Tyskie beer, we began with a half portion of 'ruskie' pierogi (a satisfying mix of potato, onion and 'white cheese'), then got stuck into richly flavoured pork shoulder gulasz with mash, and slightly soggy fish cakes that were redeemed by a wonderful shaved cucumber and tomato salad with dill dressing. The nalesniki (folded pancakes with a sweetened ricotta-like cheese and chocolate sauce) seemed bland, but our appetite was by then on the wane. Mamuska!'s clientele reflects the Elephant & Castle setting – yes, several Polish diners watching the Polish news on the telly, but also Chinese, a cockney geezer, and a corner table of dressed-down business types. A highly enjoyable place to eat decent food at low prices.

Available for hire. Babies and children welcome: high chairs; nappy-changing facilities. Booking advisable. Takeaway service.

North

Camden Town & Chalk Farm

Trojka

101 Regents Park Road, NW1 8UR (7483 3765, www.troykarestaurant.co.uk). Chalk Farm tube. **Meals served** 8am-10pm Mon-Fri; 9am-10.30pm Sat, Sun. **Main courses** £8-£13.95. **Set lunch** (Mon-Fri) £5.95 1 course, £7.95 2 courses. **Credit** MC, V. Russian

Linger over a slice of cheesecake and coffee, observing the Primrose Hill yummy mummies in their natural habitat, or tuck into a full meal of well-prepared, inexpensive east European food – take your choice at this decent all-rounder. A relaxed Mitteleuropa vibe prevails at Trojka, with dark-wood furniture, red decor and a Chagall-like painting of a horse-drawn sleigh (the trojka) livening things up. Service is friendlier and more attentive than of old; a kindly Latvian waitress tried warning us off our favourite semi-sweet Georgian wine, having previously had customers who didn't take to it. The blini are top-notch: light, fluffy and fragrant from the nutty buckwheat flour. Enjoy them with herrings and sour cream, aubergine caviar or smoked trout. Vibrantly beetrooty Polish-style barszcz (clear, served with a floating dumpling) is also recommended. Next, well-stuffed mixed pierogi (filled with pork, cheese and potato, and sauerkraut and wild mushroom) will certainly warm you after a bracing walk up the hill. To finish, treat yourself to sweet cheese pancakes dusted with icing sugar. Entertainment is occasionally provided, but the gipsy violinist who appears some evenings isn't everyone's cup of tea.

Babies and children welcome: high chairs. Booking advisable dinner Fri, Sat. Entertainment: Russian folk music 8-10.30pm Fri, Sat. Tables outdoors (4, pavement). Takeaway service. **Map 27 A1**.

Highbury

★ Tbilisi

91 Holloway Road, N7 8LT (7607 2536). Highbury & Islington tube/rail. **Dinner served** 6-11pm daily. **Main courses** £8-£11. **Credit** AmEx, MC, V. Georgian

Set on an unpromising stretch of the Holloway Road, Tbilisi remains a good-value introduction to the delights of Georgian cookery (a popular cuisine across the former Soviet bloc, but rare in the UK). Few diners will fail to appreciate khachapuri (soft yeasty flatbread stuffed with cheese) and the intriguingly spiced salads of puréed aubergine, carrot, leeks and beetroot. A mixed plate is ideal for sharing. The kitchen's secret is the Georgian spice-mix of khmeli suneli, and the ubiquitous blend of marigold and crushed walnuts combined with fresh coriander – all good for vegetarians. For meat-eaters, warmly spiced lamb stews such as chanakhi

(long-braised with tomato and aubergine to tender perfection) are often a better bet than chicken dishes. Kharcho was disappointing; the soupy stew flavoured with tomato, plum paste and creamy ground walnuts was let down by chunks of chicken with a seemingly reheated taste and texture. Don't miss the Georgian wine; the great Kindzmarauli and Khvanchkara are something of an acquired taste with their rich, complex semi-sweetness, but there are also fresh whites such as Tsinandali and a lightly fruity Mtatsminda rosé. Like the restaurant itself, they're a refreshingly different experience.
Available for hire. Babies and children welcome: high chairs. Booking advisable Fri, Sat. Separate room for parties, seats 40. Takeaway service.

North West

St John's Wood

★ Tamada

122 Boundary Road, NW8 0RH (7372 2882, www.tamada.co.uk). Kilburn Park or St John's Wood tube, or Kilburn High Road rail. **Lunch served** 1-4pm Sat, Sun. **Dinner served** 6-11pm Tue-Sun. **Main courses** £9-£17. **Credit** AmEx, MC, V. Georgian

With its small shopfront entrance in a stylish street, Tamada looks like just another smart neighbourhood eaterie. Inside, photos of soaring Georgian mountains, naïve-art wall hangings and a soundtrack of soulful ballads are the only clues that you're about to encounter something special. Come here (or to the larger basement room) to feast on London's finest Georgian home-style cooking and drink luscious, rich, semi-sweet red wines such as Khvanchkara and Kindzmarauli – little known in the UK. Share a meze plate to savour ispanaki (herby steamed spinach, walnut and onion pâté studded with pomegranate seeds), lobio (tender, gently spiced red kidney beans with pounded walnuts), a pleasingly unctuous badrijani (aubergine salad) and a flavour-packed salat olivier (russian salad). But don't miss the stars in any Georgian culinary show – khachapuri (oozing melted white cheese) and the classic main course, khinkali: huge cushion-like dumplings made from the lightest dough, stuffed with juicy pork, beef and onions. Cut them open and swoon as the fragrant herb-inflected steam rises and juices seep out to make a tasty broth. Bliss.
Available for hire. Babies and children welcome: high chair. Booking advisable Fri, Sat. Separate room for parties, seats 28-35. Tables outdoors (4, pavement). Takeaway service. **Map 1 C1.**

West Hampstead

★ Czechoslovak Restaurant HOT 50

74 West End Lane, NW6 2LX (7372 1193, www.czechoslovak-restaurant.co.uk). West Hampstead tube. **Dinner served** 5-10pm Tue-Fri. **Meals served** noon-10pm Sat, Sun. **Main courses** £4-£12. **Credit** MC, V. Czech

Ever fallen in love with a place not for the food, but because of the all-round feel-good vibe? Czechs and Slovaks far from home probably really do crave those knedliky dumplings, but the rest of us are attracted by the wistful, nostalgic air. The Czechoslovak occupies a large, slightly scruffy house, where flock wallpaper, amateurish oil paintings and memorials to Czech/Slovak World War II servicemen create a 1970s social club feel. In the friendly bar or adjoining garden, enjoy Budvar and Pilsner Urquell on tap, or maybe a bottle of malty dark Budvar. And unless loud, big-screen Czech TV appeals, opt for the more formal front dining room, not the plainer back room. You could start with a deliciously sharp cabbage soup with smoked sausage or sample the brawn or pickled sausage (utopenec). The ubiquitous knedliky are good with beef and a creamed vegetable sauce, or try them with tasty roast goose and sauerkraut. Other choices include chicken and veal schnitzels – uninspiring, but good to soak up the beer. If you're keen to increase your cholesterol, don't hold back: a doughy apricot dumpling bathed in yoghurt with cinnamon sugar and whipped cream should do the trick.
Available for hire. Babies and children welcome: high chairs; nappy-changing facilities. Booking advisable weekends. Disabled: toilet. Tables outdoors (4, garden). Vegetarian menu. **Map 28 A3.**

Mamuska!

Menu

Dishes followed by (Cz) indicate a Czech dish; (G) Georgian; (H) Hungarian; (P) Polish; (R) Russian. Others have no particular affiliation.

Bigos (P): classic hunter's stew made with sauerkraut, various meats and sausage, mushrooms and juniper.
Borscht: beetroot soup. There are many varieties: Ukrainian borscht is thick with vegetables; the Polish version (**barszcz**) is clear. There are also white and green types. Often garnished with sour cream, boiled egg or mini dumplings.
Caviar: fish roe. Most highly prized is that of the sturgeon (beluga, oscietra and sevruga, in descending order of expense), though keta or salmon caviar is underrated.
Chlodnik (P): cold beetroot soup, bright pink in colour, served with sour cream.
Galabki, **golabki** or **golubtsy**: cabbage parcels, usually stuffed with rice or kasha (qv) and sometimes meat.
Golonka (P): pork knuckle, often cooked in beer.
Goulash or **gulasz (H)**: rich beef soup.
Kasha or **kasza**: buckwheat, delicious roasted: fluffy, with a nutty flavour.
Kaszanka (P): type of blood sausage that's made with buckwheat.
Khachapuri (G): flatbread; sometimes called Georgian pizza.
Kielbasa (P): sausage. Poland has dozens of widely differing styles.
Knedliky (Cz): bread dumplings.
Kolduny (P): small meat-filled dumplings (scaled-down pierogi, qv) often served in beetroot soup.
Koulebiaka, **kulebiak** or **coulebiac (R)**: type of pie made with layered salmon or sturgeon, with eggs, dill, rice and mushrooms.
Krupnik (P): barley soup, and the name of a honey vodka (because of the golden colour of barley).
Latke: grated potato pancakes, fried.
Makowiec or **makietki (P)**: poppy seed cake.
Mizeria (P): cucumber salad; very thinly sliced and dressed with sour cream.
Nalesniki (P): cream cheese pancakes.
Paczki (P): doughnuts, often filled with plum jam.
Pierogi (P): ravioli-style dumplings. Typical fillings are sauerkraut and mushroom, curd cheese or fruit (cherries, apples).
Pirogi (large) or **pirozhki** (small) **(R)**: filled pies made with yeasty dough.
Placki (P): potato pancakes.
Shashlik: Caucasian spit-roasted meat.
Uszka or **ushka**: small ear-shaped dumplings served in soup.
Zakuski (R) or **zakaski (P)**: starters, traditionally covering a whole table. The many dishes can include pickles, marinated vegetables and fish, herring, smoked eel, aspic, mushrooms, radishes with butter, salads and caviar.
Zrazy (P): beef rolls stuffed with bacon, pickled cucumber and mustard.
Zurek (P): sour rye soup.

Fish

Pristine marine life is the one common factor linking these enticing but disparate dining venues. Here, you'll find establishments both ancient and modern, the quintessentially British and the alluringly exotic – as well as celebrity hangouts and local favourites. Openings are a relative rarity, and this year's sole new entry, **Forman's**, is a venerable salmon-smoking firm that was forced to move to new premises by the construction of the Olympic Park. Our favourite seafood restaurant, **Bentley's Oyster Bar & Grill**, offers the best of old and new: premises and a history dating back nearly a century, married to outstanding modern cooking from Richard Corrigan, one of gastronomic London's top talents. Otherwise, try **J Sheekey** or **Scott's** for a sprinkling of stardust with your halibut; **Olivomare** (Sardinia) or **Chez Liline** (Mauritius) for a dash of foreign brio with your bivalves; or **Sweetings** for a generous helping of old London with your dover sole. The city's best chippies can be found in **Fish & Chips**, starting on p295. To find which species are certified as sustainable, consult the Marine Stewardship Council's website, www.msc.org.

Central

Belgravia

Olivomare

10 Lower Belgrave Street, SW1W 0LJ (7730 9022, http://olivorestaurants.com). Victoria tube/rail. **Lunch served** noon-2.30pm Mon-Fri; noon-3pm Sat, Sun. **Dinner served** 7-11pm Mon-Sat; 7-10.30pm Sun. **Main courses** £19.50-£22. **Credit** AmEx, MC, V.

Olivomare delivers very high quality at prices that, given its Belgravia location, are surprisingly unfrightening. The offering is 100% fish, largely Sardinian and ranges from very simple (fritto misto) to fairly elaborate stews, sautés and pasta sauces. From an order totalling nine dishes, eight were outstanding. Top marks to starters of baby octopus stew with chilli and bay leaves, and exquisite marinated anchovies served with accurately grilled vegetables. Two simple fish dishes – sea bream baked in salt, and sea bass baked with olives and vernaccia wine – were also perfectly timed. The only duff dish, oddly, was pasta: spaghetti with sea urchin sauce had apparently spent a while sitting under the hot lamp, resulting in a near-solid brick, the strands virtually impossible to disentangle. The Sardinian puddings are all worth exploring. There were a few slightly sour notes in service (our wine order was late being taken), but mostly it was charming and attentive. On the short wine list, go no further than the well-priced Sardinian bottles; if you find Terre Bianche from Sella e Mosca, order it and prepare to be dazzled. The decor has a maritime theme and is sleek and attractive. Sadly, the back room (particularly lovely) is noisy and hot when full, which Olivomare often is. When you offer quality this good in an area awash with money, what else can you expect?

Babies and children admitted. Booking advisable. Disabled: toilet. Tables outdoors (4, terrace). **Map 15 H10.**

City

Sweetings HOT 50

39 Queen Victoria Street, EC4N 4SA (7248 3062). Mansion House tube. **Lunch served** 11.30am-3pm Mon-Fri. **Main courses** £15-£33. **Credit** AmEx, MC, V.

A cherished City institution, Sweetings is one of London's last remaining proper lunchtime restaurants. It opened in 1889 and has barely changed since – thank goodness. The atmosphere is resolutely old-school; the waiting staff (now mainly Spanish, and dressed in white coats) appear to approach their jobs as vocations, while the custard-yellow, picture-lined walls and dark-wood decor evoke a spirit of yesteryear without seeming precious. City boys – mainly of the older variety – as well as a few tourists, come here to enjoy the classic fish dishes and the convivial spirit. The menu might not be startlingly original, but it's unlikely to disappoint anyone looking for simple, spanking-fresh fish dishes. Starters include scallops and bacon, prawn cocktail, and smoked eel, while mains largely consist of various fish fillets, which can be deep-fried, grilled or poached, and then served with lemon; all the usual species are here, from Cornish brill and dover sole to haddock, cod and plaice. Portions are huge, and supplemented by generous side plates of bread and butter. The chef's fish pie offers the rare chance of something more elaborate. Decent-enough side vegetables are something of an afterthought, and puddings are a public schoolboy's dream: crumble, spotted dick, bread and butter pudding, and baked jam roll. An unmitigated old-fashioned treat.

Available for hire. Bookings not accepted. Takeaway service. **Map 11 P6.**

Leicester Square

J Sheekey

28-32 St Martin's Court, WC2N 4AL (7240 2565, www.j-sheekey.co.uk). Leicester Square tube. **Lunch served** noon-3pm Mon-Sat; noon-3.30pm Sun. **Dinner served** 5.30pm-midnight Mon-Sat; 6-11pm Sun. **Main courses** £13.50-£39.50. **Set lunch** (Sat, Sun) £26.50 3 courses. **Cover** £2. **Credit** AmEx, DC, MC, V.

Open since the turn of the 20th century, Sheekey's – now owned by the Caprice group – had its heyday in swinging 1960s London, and remains a theatreland institution. Outwardly unassuming, it has an enviable pedigree that's quickly apparent upon entering. Black and white portraits of film and theatre stars line the walls, and the warren-like

interior houses discreetly placed tables. The decor is modest, and seemingly untouched by time. We opted for the grand, horseshoe-shaped Oyster Bar in the next-door building (added in 2008), which keeps conveniently long hours and has a more flexible booking policy. Dishes aren't cheap, but the range, freshness and presentation are impressive. As well as several varieties of oysters – West Mersea pearls, Lindisfarne rocks, fines de claire and Jersey rocks – the menu features classic seafood teamed with well-thought-out accompaniments. Razor clams come with chorizo and padrón peppers, Dorset crab with crushed avocado on toast, and tandoori tiger prawns are served with cucumber yoghurt. We particularly enjoyed daily specials of stone bass ceviche with plantain crisps, and crab bisque with cognac. Sheekey's fish pie is a renowned favourite. The wine list is long and varied (including 15 champagnes), and afters range from British classics (gooseberry pie, welsh rarebit) to adventurous concoctions such as the Cru Virunga chocolate crackle pot. Waiting staff are smartly suited and courteous, but not especially personable.
Babies and children welcome: colouring books; high chairs. Booking essential. Disabled: toilet. Vegan dishes. Vegetarian menu. **Map 18 D5.**

Mayfair

Scott's

20 Mount Street, W1K 2HE (7495 7309, www.scotts-restaurant.com). Bond Street or Green Park tube. **Meals served** noon-10.30pm Mon-Sat; noon-10pm Sun. **Main courses** £15-£42. **Cover** £2. **Credit** AmEx, MC, V.
Scott's offers an excuse to get dressed up and celebrity-spot. Outside, the smart set are helped from taxis by crisply dressed doormen. Inside, the tables are set around a dramatic marble oyster and champagne bar. Carpet walkways soak up clatter and celeb secrets; dark wood and red brown leather are lifted by white linen tablecloths and arty wall mirrors. There's an air of exclusivity about the place – and no wonder… these are Mayfair prices. Happily, staff are just as discreetly helpful whether you're ordering beluga caviar or fried squid. The menu is divided into sections: oysters, caviar, crustacea and molluscs, soups, smoked fish, starters and main courses. Our delicately flavoured smoked halibut had the texture of smoked salmon and was perfectly complemented by asparagus and fried oysters. Roasted cod too was a triumph, arriving with girolles, samphire and brown shrimps. Only puddings were a disappointment. Of a trio of desserts, the Pimm's jelly was the sole delight alongside a tasteless cheesecake and so-so almond tart. The extensive wine list spans European and New World vintages, but consult the website before visiting to get an inkling of the bill.
Babies and children welcome: high chairs. Booking essential. Disabled: toilet. Separate room for parties, seats 40. Tables outdoors (7, pavement). Vegetarian menu. **Map 9 G7.**

Piccadilly

★ Bentley's Oyster Bar & Grill HOT 50

11-15 Swallow Street, W1B 4DG (7734 4756, www.bentleysoysterbarandgrill.co.uk). Piccadilly Circus tube.
Oyster Bar **Breakfast served** 7.30am-noon Mon-Fri. **Meals served** noon-midnight Mon-Sat; noon-10.30pm Sun. **Main courses** £8.50-£50.
Restaurant **Lunch served** noon-2.45pm Mon-Fri. **Dinner served** 5.30-10.45pm Mon-Sat. **Main courses** £19-£38. **Set dinner**

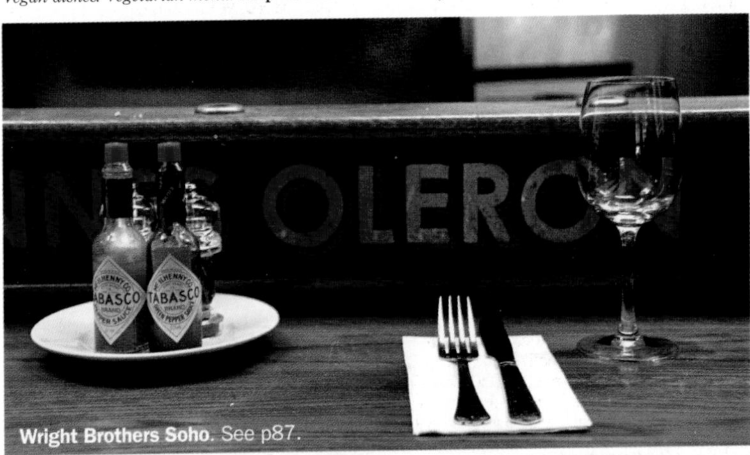

Wright Brothers Soho. See p87.

FISH

Sweetings. See p84.

(5.30-7.30pm Mon-Fri) £16.95 2 courses, £19.95 3 courses. **Cover** £2.
Both **Credit** AmEx, MC, V.

A deep reverence for heritage, combined with unsurpassed culinary credentials, has meant that chef-patron Richard Corrigan's 2005 overhaul of this 1916 grand dame has been an indisputable success. The art deco windows, grand wooden panelling, oak flooring and well-turned-out regulars all nod to the Bentley's of times past, while a reinvigorated menu and spruced-up decor bring the restaurant firmly up to date. Upstairs is the formal Grill restaurant, but we prefer the more relaxed ground-floor oyster bar. Here, scallop-shaped lamps, framed fish illustrations and the original marble oyster bar lined with red-leather chairs create a buzzing, sophisticated space. Corrigan's renowned soda bread (made with black treacle and buttermilk) makes for a delicious start. And while it would be rude not to order oysters (in season and supremely fresh), the menu offers such a tempting range of dishes – from scallop ceviche to classic fish pie – that it's almost impossible not to over-indulge. Specials of sea bass and caponata, and wild sea trout with samphire and verjus, were two outstanding seafood plates, the expertly balanced flavours and textures indicating world-class talent in the kitchen. Desserts of chocolate mousse and lemon steamed pudding with crème anglais were sensational, and the wine list doesn't disappoint. What's more, the formally dressed staff are fastidious, yet ready for a chat when time allows. Breakfasts are more kindly priced, and the pre-theatre set menus are excellent value too.
Available for hire. Booking advisable. Disabled: toilet. Dress: smart casual; no shorts. Separate rooms for parties, seating 14 and 60.
Map 17 A5.

FishWorks

7-9 Swallow Street, W1B 4DE (7734 5813, www.fishworks.co.uk). Piccadilly Circus tube.
Meals served noon-10.30pm Mon-Sat; noon-10pm Sun. **Main courses** £14-£19. **Set meal** (noon-7pm) £15 2 courses. **Credit** AmEx, MC, V.

After a heady few years of over-expansion and financial turmoil, FishWorks seems to have found its niche, with three branches in smarter parts of town. Each has a wet fish counter at the front, restaurant behind, with the airy Richmond outpost also offering a cookery school. The Mayfair branch is handsome and cleverly designed, thanks to dark wooden furniture, greeny-grey colours, and the nifty use of wine racks to divide up the space. Expect fellow diners to be business folk and a smattering of tourists. Fish (much of it from Devon and the south coast) is undeniably fresh and good quality – the seafood platters come piled high – but cooking can be mediocre. Spaghetti with palourde clams looked the part, though the essential brininess of the shellfish was missing – as were the promised flavours of chilli, garlic and parsley. And it featured unnecessary onions. A starter of crisp-fried baby squid with chilli was similarly muted, but whole sea bream stuffed with garlic and fennel was cooked just-so. Accompaniments cost extra, so with most main courses topping £15, the bill can escalate alarmingly. The drinks list specialises in white wine and fizz, although there are a few reds and beers too.
Available for hire. Babies and children welcome: children's menu; high chairs; nappy-changing facilities. Booking advisable. Disabled: toilet.
Map 17 A5.
For branches see index.

Geales

Soho

Wright Brothers Soho

13 Kingly Street, G7/G8 Kingly Court, W1B 5PW (7434 3611, www.thewrightbrothers.co.uk). Oxford Circus or Piccadilly Circus tube. **Meals served** noon-10.45pm Mon-Sat; noon-5pm Sun. **Main courses** £11-£32. **Credit** AmEx, MC, V.

White tiles, jade-green wood panels, high tables and chairs, and touches such as a coiled rope and old gramophone create a retro-nautical themed space that manages to be fresh, classy and evocative. Oysters are the stars, with seasonal varieties offered: Duchy natives, Carlingford, Colchester, Maldon and Brownsea Island on our visit in late spring. Dressings of apple, shallot and cider vinegar; caviar and crème fraîche; or ginger, chilli and soy sauce accompany the bivalves, and there are two types of caviar on the menu. These can all be enjoyed with a well-edited range of aperitifs, such as Pineau de Charentes (a fortified wine), champagne or white port. The shellfish house platter (containing oysters, prawns, langoustines, razor clams and more) makes a good sharing plate, but there are various fish dishes for those preferring the three-course format. Our roast pollock with chickpeas and aïoli – a daily special – was perfectly cooked, with a complementary blend of textures and flavours. Salmon and smoked haddock fish pie was gorgeously creamy with the right ratio of fish to potato. There are some token meat (steak, pork belly) and vegetarian (risotto) dishes too, but the fruits of the sea predominate. Desserts include caramel cream and biscotti, eton mess and sorbet from Gelupo, plus there's a selection of mainly English cheeses. Staff are friendly, efficient and patient.
Available for hire. Babies and children welcome: high chairs; nappy-changing facilities. Booking advisable. Disabled: toilet. Tables outdoors (9, courtyard). **Map 17 A4.**
For branch (Wright Brothers Oyster & Porter House) see index.

West

Notting Hill

Geales

2 Farmer Street, W8 7SN (7727 7528, www.geales.com). Notting Hill Gate tube.
Lunch served noon-3pm Tue-Fri. **Dinner served** 6-10.30pm Mon-Fri. **Meals served** noon-10.30pm Sat; noon-9.30pm Sun. **Main courses** £8-£29.50. **Set lunch** (noon-3pm Tue-Fri) £11.95 2 courses, £14.95 3 courses.
Credit AmEx, MC, V.

Someone had been at the salt cellar the night we dined at Geales – both battered pollock and fish pie had us gulping down water. A shame, as both were decent versions: the fish pie was a cheese, potato and fish medley, with one solitary prawn, topped with breadcrumbs; the large portion of firm pollock, cooked just so, was slightly overwhelmed by a vast wrapping of golden batter. This giant costs £10.75 (cod, haddock and sole hover around £12), but (OK) chips are cheekily priced separately – £3.45 for a modest helping. A tiny bowl of peas costs the same, meaning this chip shop classic comes in at £17.65. There's a short specials menu, plus a handful of grills and a macaroni cheese for refuseniks. Starters run from fish soup to Malden rock oysters; we liked the deep-fried whitebait and a hot-smoked salmon, pear and walnut salad, but loved the 'light bites' – bargain-priced pots of moreish vivid green olives; light pink, creamy taramasalata; and moreish pickled herring and anchovies, all at £2. Desserts are the usual mix of ice-creams and school puds. Decor is tastefully subdued, as is the clientele. There's a commitment to buying UK fish in season – for more details, see the website.
Babies and children welcome: children's menu; high chairs. Booking advisable Fri, Sat. Separate room for parties, seats 12. Tables outdoors (6, pavement). **Map 7 A7.**
For branch see index.

South East

London Bridge & Borough

Applebee's Café

5 Stoney Street, SE1 9AA (7407 5777, www.applebeesfish.com). London Bridge tube/rail. **Lunch served** noon-3.30pm Tue-Thur; 11.30am-4pm Fri; 11.30am-4.30pm Sat. **Dinner served** 6-10pm Tue-Thur, Sat; 6-10.30pm Fri. **Main courses** £11.50-£23. **Set lunch** £14.50-£17.50 2 courses. **Credit** MC, V.

Pescatarians only need apply: marine life dominates the menu here. Mains of tuna, sea bass and hake follow starters of prawns, whitebait or salmon sashimi – all market-fresh and simply prepared with minimal fuss. This formula has held Applebee's in good stead for years, and pleases Borough market-goers and tourists who drop by, but the restaurant could be resting on its laurels. During the day, the front area sells fresh fish while the kitchen behind prepares it. The cramped interior looks quite tired. Diners can sit close together on orange banquettes or at the bar overlooking the kitchen; outside on our visit, chairs were perched over a low kerb where sluice water from the fish counter had collected. Service, while friendly, was distracted – a mix up with dessert, a problem with the coffees, a wait for the bill – and the food, while competent, didn't wow. Our salad was lacklustre, the chips were OK, and the seafood linguine was adequate (though tomatoes that should have been pan-fried were almost raw). Minor quibbles, perhaps, but with mains costing £14-£24, and side dishes an additional £3.50, we expect more. Fish is fresh, but atmosphere, service and cooking could be fresher.

Available for hire. Babies and children admitted. Disabled: toilet. Tables outdoors (4, pavement). Takeaway service. **Map 11 P8**.

North East

South Woodford

Ark Fish Restaurant

142 Hermon Hill, E18 1QH (8989 5345, www.arkfishrestaurant.com). South Woodford tube. **Lunch served** noon-2.15pm Tue-Sat. **Dinner served** 5.30-9.45pm Tue-Thur; 5.30-10.15pm Fri, Sat. **Meals served** noon-8.45pm Sun. **Main courses** £12.25-£21.70. **Credit** MC, V.

The Ark is something of a local institution – much appreciated by everyone from local office workers at lunch to families on a night out. It's bright and airy, with lots of pale wood and big windows, and there's a bar that acts as a holding area when it's busy. The fish is quality stuff and everything is freshly prepared, including the caper-packed tartare sauce. Portion sizes are generous: two appetising starters (a plate of breaded scampi, and fresh anchovy and parmesan salad with croûtons) were ample for a table of four, especially as we knew how big the mains were. Many diners opt for the well-battered cod, haddock or plaice with chips, but there are plenty of alternatives, from seared scallops with garlic butter to a laden seafood platter, plus a handful of chicken and steak dishes for refuseniks. From the blackboard specials, we enjoyed a nicely grilled haddock with spinach and beurre blanc. Make it to pudding, and you'll find the likes of black forest trifle or sticky toffee pudding with custard. Service is solicitous and obliging: requests for shared plates and doggy bags are met with a smile.

Babies and children welcome: children's menu; high chairs. Bookings not accepted.

Hackney Wick

Forman's NEW

Stour Road, Fish Island, E3 2NT (8525 2365, www.formans.co.uk). Hackney Wick rail or Pudding Mill Lane DLR.

Bar **Open/snacks served** 5-9pm Thur, Fri; noon-5pm Sat, Sun.
Restaurant **Brunch served** 10am-2pm Sat. **Lunch served** noon-3pm Sun. **Dinner served** 7-9pm Thur-Sat. **Main courses** £11.50-£19.50.
Both **Credit** AmEx, MC, V.

When it was displaced by the development of the Olympic Park, London's oldest salmon smoker – established in the early 20th century to supply London's Jewish community with Baltic salmon – moved to a prime site just across the Lea Navigation from the Olympic Stadium. The snazzy new premises incorporate a restaurant and bar as well as the corporate headquarters and a spacious smokery with viewing gallery. But if the plan was to showcase the quality of the produce, it has slightly misfired. The menu features half a dozen routine Modern European dishes among which salmon features only incidentally. The mild London cure is served as a starter with accompaniments of sour cream, capers and red onion, which were rather tired on our visit; salmon and tuna sashimi with wasabi sauce was much nicer. Mains, of herb-crusted salmon and a smoked haddock fish cake, were OK, but nothing more. In playbook modern design – black spindly furniture, wood-strip flooring, open kitchen – the dining room, like the food, is nothing special, but it has a wall of windows and a small terrace offering great stadium views (ask when booking if you want a window seat), as does the nicer gallery-like bar next door.

Available for hire. Babies and children welcome: high chairs; nappy-changing facilities. Booking advisable. Disabled: lift; toilet. Separate rooms for parties, seating 80-350. Tables outdoors (3, terrace).

Forman's

North

Finsbury Park

Chez Liline

101 Stroud Green Road, N4 3PX (7263 6550, www.chezliline.co.uk). Finsbury Park tube/rail. **Lunch served** noon-3pm Sat. **Dinner served** 6.30-11pm Tue-Sun. **Main courses** £12.75-£22.75. **Set lunch** £10 2 courses. **Set dinner** £12.50 2 courses. **Credit** AmEx, MC, V.

There aren't many Mauritian restaurants in London, but we hope this might change after Shelina Permalloo won *Masterchef* 2012. Mauritian cuisine is a mash-up of French, Creole, Indian, Chinese and British traditions, and Chez Liline concentrates on seafood dishes (the same family owns the fish shop next door). The restaurant needs a makeover – it looks a bit 1970s Greek taverna – but locals know this joint by reputation, and head here for the food. Once seated, diners forget their surroundings and embark on a journey of taste sensation. Meat and vegetarian dishes are available on request, yet the menu is so packed with mouth-watering fish options, only pescaphobes could ignore them. We tried a simple but perfect warm squid and prawn salad, and also sampled scallops in a spicy mango sauce: these ingredients shouldn't work together, but the dish was sublime. To follow, you'd think a tamarind and coconut sauce might drown the subtle white barramundi, but not a bit of it. The French-style puddings are worth ordering too, if the hearty portions haven't defeated you.

Available for hire. Babies and children welcome: high chairs. Booking advisable. Tables outdoors (2, pavement).

French

London's French restaurants are streets, nay boulevards, ahead of most found in the rest of Britain. Elsewhere, clichés still predominate, with l'escargots, boeuf bourguignon, and crème brûlée presented with zestless cynicism, unyielding stuffiness and a sizeable profit margin to the provincial middle classes. In contrast, the best of the capital's Gallic dining venues have jettisoned the ooh-la-la, unless it's wrapped up in tongue-in-chic, retro clothing. Informality has freshened the scene too, with hushed reverence now mainly limited to the **Hotels & Haute Cuisine** operations (*see p131*).

London's links with the French capital are evident in the trend towards august Parisian brasseries, including the recently opened **Brasserie Zédel**, where good-value classics are provided in a grand belle époque setting by the team behind the **Wolseley** and the **Delaunay** (both of which are reviewed in our **Brasseries** chapter, starting on p39). Quality is spreading to the suburbs, shown by three of this year's openings: **Provender**, Max Renzland's accomplished new bourgeois brasserie in Wanstead; **Lawn Bistro**, a stylish take on modern French cookery in Wimbledon village; and **Garnier**, chef Eric Garnier's latest venture in Earl's Court. Other top spots this year are: **Bar Boulud**, **Chabrot Bistrot d'Amis**, **Chez Bruce**, **Les Deux Salons**, **Galvin Bistrot de Luxe**, **La Petite Maison** and **La Trompette**.

Central

Barbican

Morgan M

50 Long Lane, EC1A 9EJ (7609 3560, www.morganm.com). Barbican tube. **Lunch served** noon-2.30pm Mon-Fri. **Dinner served** 6-10.30pm Mon-Sat. **Main courses** £22.50-£26.50. **Set meal** (noon-2.30pm Mon-Fri; 6-7pm Mon-Sat) £23.50 2 courses, £25.50 3 courses; £48-£52 tasting menu (£75.50-£82 incl wine). **Credit** AmEx, MC, V.

After years on an Islington backstreet, Morgan Meunier moved his restaurant in late 2011. Little else has changed: inventive haute cuisine in tasteful surroundings remains the formula. The furnishings – in subdued shades of taupe and green – are a little more deluxe at the new premises, which are split between a basement (a less formal space, where smaller versions of dishes from the carte are served) and a ground-floor dining room where the main menu is served. There's also a tasting menu, and a fabulous 'from the garden' (vegetarian) menu. Meunier clearly has a way with vegetables – from the carte, butternut squash soup with rosemary and olive oil, with a centrepiece of wild mushroom tempura, was a triumph of punchy tastes, while an amuse-bouche of deconstructed borscht (beetroot soup and sorbet plus horseradish cream) was pretty much perfection. The short menu is seasonal; a winter menu highlight was Iken Valley venison (pot-roasted to a state of sublime taste and tenderness) with brilliantly realised accompaniments of farci of hare, sweet potato purée and sauce grand veneur (a classic game sauce). Roast pavé of turbot, with crayfish ravioli, ratatouille and lobster froth, is typical summer fare. All dishes are winningly presented, none more so than dark chocolate moelleux with milk sorbet and an armagnac 'drink'. The wine list is devotedly French but has a good range of prices, with bottles from lesser-known producers as well as big names. The dining experience won't suit everyone – the setting is too anodyne and the service too formal for that – but for foodies (and especially vegetarians) interested in modern haute cuisine, Morgan M is a must.

Available for hire. Babies and children admitted. Booking advisable. Dress: smart casual. Vegetarian menu. **Map 11 O5.**

Belgravia

Le Cercle

1 Wilbraham Place, SW1X 9AE (7901 9999, www.lecercle.co.uk). Sloane Square tube.
Bar **Open/snacks served** noon-midnight Tue-Sat.
Restaurant **Lunch served** noon-2pm, **dinner served** 5.30-10.45pm Tue-Sat. **Main courses** £9-£29. **Set lunch** £18.50 2 courses, £23.50 3 courses. **Set dinner** (5-7pm, 9.30-10.45pm) £18.50 2 courses, £23.50 3 courses.
Both **Credit** AmEx, MC, V.

A western partner of the Club and Comptoir Gascons in Smithfield, Le Cercle eschews its *confrères'* bustle for an atmosphere more suited to a spot just off Sloane Square – smart, multinational, a little brittle and very well heeled. Service is solicitous and the decor mellow, in a high-ceilinged basement with a long bar, clean lines, soft colours and semi-oriental details in the wall motifs and flower arrangements. On a mezzanine off the deep staircase is a romantically chic and snug lounge area. The carte and set dinner menus are suitably luxurious, but there are also more accessible lunch

Morgan M. See p89.

and pre- and post-theatre meals. Shorter menus in places like this often seem offered as a kind of obligation, and leave you wishing you'd splashed out on the carte, but there's none of that here. Exquisitely served vanilla salmon mousse had a fabulously expansive, complex flavour, and, to follow, vegetarian ravioli of two cheeses with braised chicory was magnificent, in a sumptuous truffle sauce (the kitchen clearly has a way with truffles: fittingly, given the group's Gascon roots). Overall, this was a gourmet experience disguised as a light lunch. The wine list is long, classy and mainly French, with a select range by the glass.
Available for hire. Babies and children welcome: high chairs. Booking advisable dinner and Sat, Sun. Disabled: lift; toilet. Dress: smart casual. Separate room for parties, seats 12.
Map 15 G10.

City

Le Coq d'Argent

No.1 Poultry, EC2R 8EJ (7395 5000, www.coqdargent.co.uk). Bank tube/DLR.
Brasserie **Lunch served** 11.30am-3pm Mon-Fri. **Main courses** £12-£18.50.
Restaurant **Breakfast served** 7.30-10am Mon-Fri. **Lunch served** 11.30am-3pm Mon-Fri; noon-3pm Sun. **Dinner served** 6-10pm Mon-Fri; 6.30-10pm Sat. **Main courses** £17.50-£24. **Set lunch** (Sun) £25 2 courses, £28 3 courses. **Set meal** (lunch Mon-Fri; dinner) £26 2 courses, £30 3 courses.
Both **Credit** AmEx, DC, MC, V.
Le Coq d'Argent's rooftop bar and restaurant are packed out on sunny after-work evenings, resulting in queues to catch the lift to the top (and to visit the loos, shared by dress-to-impress drinkers). The canopied outdoor eating area has views over the City to the Shard, while, indoors, the springy carpets, mahogany panelling and pale green leather armchairs give the plush feel of a cruise liner. Smartly dressed waiters weave their way through the sea of white shirts, serving snazzily presented nouvelle cuisine. Terrines were neat little blocks surrounded by tiny vegetables, while slightly dry pork cheeks had pig's ear crisps sticking jauntily out from (not very) truffle-flavoured mash. A fillet of bass came with an under-seasoned provençal casserole, and crème brûlée narrowly failed the crack test. Though portions are small, the food is rich; petits fours alongside coffees were a step too far, but our softly spoken waiter happily fashioned a doggy bag. Set menus are available, with special offers to attract weekend trade. The 56-page wine list has by-the-glass options divided between 'bar wines' and 'fine wines' in 125ml measures.
Available for hire. Babies and children welcome: high chairs. Booking advisable. Disabled: lift; toilet. Dress: smart casual. Tables outdoors (34, terrace).
Map 11 P6.

Lutyens

85 Fleet Street, EC4Y 1AE (7583 8385, www.lutyens-restaurant.co.uk). Blackfriars tube/rail or City Thameslink rail or bus 4, 11, 15, 23, 26.
Bar **Breakfast served** 7.30-10.30am, **meals served** noon-9pm, **drinks served** noon-midnight Mon-Fri. **Main courses** £12.50-£18.
Restaurant **Lunch served** noon-3pm, **dinner served** 6-10pm Mon-Fri. **Main courses** £12.50-£37. **Set lunch** £22 2 courses, £26 3 courses. **Set dinner** £18 2 courses, £22 3 courses.
Both **Credit** AmEx, MC, V.
Prepare to spend some time finding the entrance (a side door) to this classic Conran restaurant. The former Reuters building is a suitably grand home for an elegant 130-seat restaurant, bar, members' club and four private meeting-cum-dining rooms. For the most part, the dining room runs at a barely perceptible hum and is all clean lines and formal service. Despite the suited and booted clientele, our jeans and trainers didn't raise any eyebrows from the jovial waiting staff. The prices, on the other hand, are hair-raising in places; a tiny side dish of peas and beans, floating in a sea of melted butter, came in at £5. But the food was near-flawless and the prix fixe dinner is excellent value at £22 for three courses. For a dash of decadence, drop by instead for fish and chips with a glass of champagne, available in the bar every Friday evening for £17.50. Seafood is a forte of Conran restaurants; a very crabby chilled crab soup was the highlight of the meal, with succulent monkfish with clams and samphire coming a close second. Allergy-sufferers and fussy eaters, beware: an omission from the menu meant a fairy-light chocolate mousse came topped with an unadvertised praline tuile.
Available for hire. Babies and children welcome: high chairs. Booking advisable lunch. Disabled: lift; toilet. Dress: smart casual. Separate rooms for parties, seating 6-28. **Map 11 N6.**

Sauterelle

Royal Exchange, EC3V 3LR (7618 2483, www.sauterelle-restaurant.co.uk). Bank tube/DLR. **Lunch served** noon-2.30pm, **dinner served** 6-9.30pm Mon-Fri. **Main courses** £10-£35. **Set meal** £20 2 courses, £25 3 courses. **Credit** AmEx, MC, V.
Set on the mezzanine level of the swanky Royal Exchange complex, the interior windows of this stylish restaurant look down on the indoor piazza below, while those on the exterior look across to the grand Old Lady of Threadneedle Street. Despite the location, the atmosphere is relaxed, and favoured by groups of City ladies as well as gents. A short set menu offered excellent choices. Seared red mullet with pickled fennel, orange and pea shoots was brilliantly set off by a glorious beetroot purée. Salt marsh lamb on borlotti beans, peas and spinach with an aubergine purée was near perfection. The only disappointment was, ironically, a classic French dessert, tarte tatin, which came as an individual tart – a concept that just doesn't work – and with pastry that was too thin. As one would expect, the wine list is top-notch, with an excellent selection by the glass and carafe. Service was impeccable and very friendly. The only niggle was the over-styled 'designer' cutlery, which was uncomfortable to hold and had forks so narrow it was often difficult to get the food off the plate.
Babies and children welcome: high chairs. Booking advisable. Disabled: lift; toilet. Dress: smart casual. Separate room for parties, seats 26. Vegetarian menu.
Map 12 Q6.

Clerkenwell & Farringdon

Bistrot Bruno Loubet HOT 50

86-88 Clerkenwell Road, EC1M 5RJ (7324 4455, www.bistrotbrunoloubet.com). Barbican tube or Farringdon tube/rail. **Breakfast served** 7-10.30am Mon-Fri; 7.30-11am Sat, Sun. **Lunch served** noon-2.30pm Mon-Fri. **Brunch served** noon-3pm Sat, Sun. **Dinner served** 6-10.30pm Mon-Sat; 6-10pm Sun. **Main courses** £13.50-£21.50. **Credit** AmEx, MC, V.

One of the many plus points about BBL is that Bruno Loubet is firmly in the kitchen (easily seen from the dining room). His influence is clear on the menu too, from the aperitif (a Loubet-created infusion of lemon, orange, lavender and rosemary served with vermouth and soda) to the classy reimagining of French staples. The menu evolves through the year, but some dishes have become regulars, such as the must-try beetroot ravioli, rocket salad, fried breadcrumbs and parmesan, which on this visit was as good as ever. Watercress soup with soft poached egg was a summery success. Next, braised beef indochine, mango and herb salad was fabulous; so succulent it didn't need a knife, its richness offset by vibrant salad. Pan-fried sea bass with sweet potato gnocchi and chives was beautifully seasoned and cooked with precision. Desserts tread a similar line between classic and out-there, from apple tart with crème fraîche and cinnamon ice-cream to chilli-poached pineapple with passionfruit jelly and green tea sabayon. Decor is also a mixture of styles, but pleasantly so, and the large windows mean the room is full of light. Slightly odd service struck an off-note – supercilious and attempting to rush us through the meal, despite there being a few spare tables – but overall the Bistrot can be relied on, whatever the occasion.

Babies and children welcome: high chairs. Booking advisable. Disabled: toilet. Separate rooms for parties, seating 40-50. Tables outdoors (9, terrace). **Map 5 O4.**

Club Gascon

57 West Smithfield, EC1A 9DS (7796 0600, www.clubgascon.com). Barbican tube or Farringdon tube/rail. **Lunch served** noon-2pm Mon-Fri. **Dinner served** 6.30-10pm Mon-Thur; 6.30-10.30pm Fri, Sat. **Dishes** £12-£26. **Set lunch** £25 2 courses incl coffee or 3 courses. **Set dinner** £28 3 courses. **Set meal** £55 5 courses (£85 incl wine). **Credit** AmEx, MC, V.

Well-spaced tables, big flower arrangements and quirky tableware (asymmetric grey plates imprinted with floral patterns) adorn this smart dining room, which attracts business people and foodies with deep pockets. The set lunch (offering a very respectable choice of six dishes per course)

Brasserie Zédel. See p96.

is a way of sampling the south-western French cuisine without breaking the bank. A starter of marmite on toast revealed the restaurant's leftfield approach: two slices of toasted sourdough bread came with a pot of 'marmite' – foie gras pâté topped with salty marmite to be spread on the bread. A nice idea, but we wonder whether the French businessmen at the next table understood this *clin d'oeil*. The roast rabbit in our main course was far too pink – we complained and were immediately offered a replacement dish. The substitute beef onglet was sublime: heavily peppered, chargrilled slices came served on a plate brushed with lashings of own-made ketchup, which had an intense smoked wood taste. The aligot, a traditional dish from the south-west, was perfect: stringy, cheesy potato mash topped with crispy deep-fried kale and wild mushrooms. Faultless desserts showed why this establishment has a Michelin star: best was pink macaron, filled with a creamy rose mousse and tangy champagne-poached rhubarb, decorated with specks of raspberry jelly and brushstrokes of rhubarb jus. Uncharacteristically, service lacked attention to detail, but was friendly throughout.
Available for hire. Booking essential Thur-Sat. **Map 11 O5.**

Le Comptoir Gascon

61-63 Charterhouse Street, EC1M 6HJ (7608 0851, www.comptoirgascon.com). Barbican tube or Farringdon tube/rail. **Lunch served** noon-2.15pm Tue-Fri. **Brunch served** 9am-3pm Sat. **Dinner served** 7-9.45pm Tue, Wed, Sat; 7-10.45pm Thur, Fri. **Main courses** £11.50-£14. **Credit** AmEx, MC, V.

The most casual and least pricey member of the Club Gascon empire, the Comptoir focuses like its parent on the products of south-west France, and above all on the area's finest meats and wines. Naturally, it seems de rigueur to order anything involving pigs or duck, such as 'piggy treats' (a little slab of superlative charcuterie – toulouse sausage, black pudding, bayonne ham and more, all deliciously subtle yet punchy) or the 'classic duck burger', a rich, superior patty in a brioche-like bun (for added indulgence, this can be paired with the Comptoir's first-rate foie gras). The duck-fat-fried chips also have fans aplenty. By contrast, rabbit with apple and mustard was far less impressive, the meat so tenderised as to be almost mushy, and thin on flavour. Greenery is fairly scarce, but there are a few vegetarian dishes. Decor mixes bare brick and stylish details, tables are small and close together, and the restaurant is often packed. Service was friendly, though for somewhere with such special specialities many staff seemed ill-informed. A supremely smooth Gaillac red was one of several well-priced quality wines on an original list, bottles of which, like many meats, are available at the deli counter to take home.
Available for hire. Babies and children welcome: high chairs. Booking advisable. Tables outdoors (4, pavement). **Map 11 O5.**

Covent Garden

Clos Maggiore

33 King Street, WC2E 8JD (7379 9696, www.closmaggiore.com). Covent Garden or Leicester Square tube. **Lunch served** noon-2.15pm daily. **Dinner served** 5-11pm Mon-Sat; 5-10pm Sun. **Main courses** £15.50-£21.50. **Set meal** (lunch Mon-Fri; 5-6pm, 10-11pm Mon-Thur) £15.50 2 courses (£19.50 incl half bottle of wine), £19.50 3 courses (£23.50 incl half bottle of wine); (lunch Sat; lunch, 5-9.30pm Sun) £22.50 3 courses (£26.50 incl half bottle of wine). **Set dinner** (5-6pm Fri, Sat) £22.50 2 courses. **Tasting menu** (lunch daily; 5-10pm Mon-Sat; 5-9pm Sun) £59 (£98 incl wine). **Credit** AmEx, MC, V.

It's easy to see why this place has won a reputation as a 'romantic' restaurant: it's something like a cross between a gentlemen's club and a refined country inn. The light, flower-bedecked conservatory at the back and the moodily lit, wood-panelled rooms in the front are equally attractive. The romantic reputation pays off in an interesting way: Clos Maggiore feels distinctively relaxed and unshowy. We attributed this to a clientele consisting almost entirely of couples rather than money-splashing execs. Much of the food does full justice to the atmosphere. A boudin blanc of sweetbread and foie gras was subtly seasoned and very light in texture. Succulent roast loin rib of ibérico pork, heroically flavourful, came with classic petits pois à la française. Lower marks went to a rather bland Sicilian aubergine and fig caponata, and to a dish combining roast fillet and braised shoulder of lamb, pistachio cromesquis (croquette), chickpeas and carrots. It just didn't cohere as a single dish, and the effect was too rich. Even so, we'd happily return – it's just a lovely place to be. Unequivocal praise goes to the wine list, one of London's best: though stuffed with costly treasures, it makes a real effort to accommodate tight budgets and includes some interesting bottles. Seek advice from the authoritative but plain-talking sommelier. And note: the set lunch/pre- and post-theatre menu is an outstanding bargain.
Babies and children admitted. Booking advisable; essential weekends, 1 month in advance for conservatory. Separate room for parties, seats 23. Vegetarian menu. **Map 18 D4.**

★ Les Deux Salons

40-42 William IV Street, WC2N 4DD (7420 2050, www.lesdeuxsalons.co.uk). Charing Cross tube/rail. **Lunch served** noon-3pm Mon-Sat. **Brunch served** 10am-5pm Sun. **Tea served** 3-5pm daily. **Dinner served** 5-11pm Mon-Sat; 5-10.30pm Sun. **Main courses** £15.95-£23.95. **Set lunch** (Mon-Sat) £15.50 3 courses. **Set dinner** (4-6pm Mon-Sat) £15.95 2 courses, £17.95 3 courses. **Credit** AmEx, MC, V.

It may seem unfortunate that a prime site off Trafalgar Square is ardently French, but Anthony Demetre and Will Smith's homage to grand Parisian brasseries adds British class – and traditional afternoon teas – to the expected casserole of steak tartare and brass rails. Diners sit on lustrous banquettes at tables featuring crisp linens and heavy cutlery. Plentiful staff in prim striped aprons know the menu, and bring dishes quick as a flash. Start with a William IV cup comprising ginger liqueur, cranberry juice, lemonade and fruit; a request for house red brought a gutsy tempranillo, almost port-like in intensity. The carte ranges from hot dogs to foie gras, including wallet-friendly plats du jour such as fish pie and rabbit in mustard. A Josper grill churns out burgers, calf's liver, andouillettes and more. We opted for perfectly cooked roast halibut with a green vegetable 'salsa' featuring on-trend seaweeds. Anyone not following an Atkins diet must add a £3.95 side dish such as the dreamy gratin dauphinoise. Desserts are better than most in Paris; a long finger of Michelin-calibre gateau opera sang of dark caramel and espresso flavours. With brunch served only on Sundays, this is an all-day brasserie as long as your day begins at noon – pity, we'd like to see more of LDS's waffles and french toast.
Babies and children welcome: high chairs. Booking advisable. Separate rooms for parties, seating 10 and 25. **Map 18 D5.**

Mon Plaisir

21 Monmouth Street, WC2H 9DD (7836 7243, www.monplaisir.co.uk). Covent Garden tube. **Meals served** noon-11.15pm Mon-Fri. **Lunch served** noon-3pm, **dinner served** 5.45-11.15pm Sat. **Main courses** £16.95-£23.95. **Set lunch** £12.95 2 courses, £15.95 3 courses. **Set dinner** (5.45-7pm Mon-Sat; after 10pm Mon-Thur) £12.95 2 courses, £14.95 3 courses incl glass of wine and coffee. **Credit** AmEx, MC, V.

Set in Covent Garden, London's self-proclaimed oldest French restaurant attracts a mixture of tourists, businessmen, and students taking their parents out for a meal. It's a charming spot spread over four intimate rooms, all crammed with French bric-a-brac – the likes of vintage advertising signs, cockerels and antique brass kitchenware. While prices are on the steep side in the evenings, the lunchtime deal is an attractive budget option. Mon Plaisir's menu focuses on traditional French classics, so vegetarians may struggle here. Dishes such as garlic snails, onion soup, coq au vin and steak tartare may be regarded as clichés, but the execution at Mon Plaisir was faultless. A generous portion of cream of tomato soup was bursting with freshness and came adorned with crunchy bread croûtons. A salmon slice was cooked to perfection and served with a zingy tomato vinaigrette and buttery crushed potatoes. The highlight was a slice of apricot and almond tart – still slightly warm, the rustic pastry transported us straight to rural France. A real *plaisir*.
Babies and children welcome: high chairs. Booking advisable. Separate room for parties, seats 25. Vegetarian menu. **Map 18 D3.**

Fitzrovia

Elena's L'Étoile

30 Charlotte Street, W1T 2NG (7636 7189, www.elenasletoile.co.uk). Goodge Street or Tottenham Court Road tube. **Lunch served** noon-2.30pm Mon-Fri. **Dinner served** 6-10.30pm Mon-Sat. **Main courses** £15.75-£20.25. **Set meal** £20.95 2 courses, £25.95 3 courses. **Credit** AmEx, DC, MC, V.

Signed photos from many of Britain's best-loved actors line the walls at l'Etoile, forming a great sea of thespian endorsement that fills every available space. The restaurant itself has been around for over a century, and its aesthetic is firmly of the old school; etched glass, red banquettes and starched linen remain the order of the day. The food is resolutely classic too: a ham hock terrine starter with apple chutney and sauce vierge is straight from the Left Bank; and a delicate double-baked mushroom soufflé is a well-judged French staple, served with a cool twist of chive crème fraîche. Main courses satisfied without enthralling. A light, fresh salmon and leek fish cake arrived with mushy peas and an endive salad, and corn-fed chicken accompanied by a mini kiev and red wine sauce was hearty yet undistinguished. There's more imagination at work in the desserts. A light lemon tart came intriguingly topped with popping candy, and a hefty portion of rice pudding was decked

Bar Boulud

with great shavings of caramelised pineapple. Elena's faded grandeur and traditional dishes are part of its charm: this is a place for a nostalgic feed rather than an inspiring one.
Available for hire. Babies and children admitted. Booking advisable; essential lunch. Dress: smart casual. Separate rooms for parties, seating 10, 16 and 32. **Map 17 B1**.

Holborn

Cigalon

115 Chancery Lane, WC2A 1PP (7242 8373, www.cigalon.co.uk). Chancery Lane or Temple tube. **Lunch served** noon-2.45pm, **dinner served** 6-9.45pm Mon-Fri. **Main courses** £12.50-£21. **Set meal** £19.50 2 courses, £24.50 3 courses. **Credit** AmEx, MC, V.
A well-executed taste of Provence off Fleet Street, Cigalon breathes fresh, lavender-scented air into the area's traditional dining scene. While the chef's neat, modern take on traditional French dishes isn't going to start a revolution, the food is really very good. Curved booths with lavender-inspired upholstery surround clusters of businessmen; light fittings twirl in the arching roof space; and a hive-patterned lattice decorates the wall. You get the sense that every detail has been considered: from the waiters' ties that match the cushions, to the tastefully innovative Corsican wine list. Service was friendly and professional, as each course emerged from the open kitchen at the back of the restaurant. The set menu is good value for three outstanding yet uncomplicated courses. Black olive tapenade was topped with seasonal wild garlic, served with delicate, fresh bread. Chilled mint and lettuce soup was a real taste of summer, and crisp-skinned sea bream was impressive on top of fresh borlotti beans. Lavender appeared again in a delicious blackberry sorbet, served with a smooth, melting chocolate fondant. Closed at weekends, this is very much a City establishment that makes you feel you've escaped the city.
Available for hire. Booking advisable lunch. Babies and children welcome: high chairs. Dress: smart casual. **Map 11 N6**.

Knightsbridge

★ Bar Boulud

Mandarin Oriental Hyde Park, 66 Knightsbridge, SW1X 7LA (7201 3899, www.barboulud.com). Knightsbridge tube. **Lunch served** noon-3pm, **tea served** 3.30-5pm daily. **Dinner served** 5-11pm Mon-Sat; 5-10pm Sun. **Main courses** £12-£28. **Set meal** (lunch, 5-7pm) £23 3 courses; (3.30-5pm) £30 with tea or coffee. **Credit** AmEx, MC, V.
Bar Boulud may be within the luxurious Mandarin Oriental Hotel, and next door to One Hyde Park, London's most expensive apartment block, but you don't have to be minted to eat at this superb bistro. Framed photos of restaurants in Lyon and wine stains from prestige labels are indications of American celebrity chef Daniel Boulud's culinary compass. A winning informality emanates from the room, which is always busy; you can drink by the spacious bar, or perch next to the counter. Furnishings of oak and red leather add to the draw. We began with a tasty terrine of braised rabbit with asparagus and carrots, given an extra dimension by a splash of dijon mustard. Burgers here are among the best in town, and new this year is the 'BB', where the patty is topped by a layer of short-ribs (braised in red wine), a slice of foie gras and a truffle garnish; it's one hell of a burger and not to be missed. A gateau basque (light custard cake with brandied cherries) provided an enjoyable conclusion. The three-course lunch/early evening meal at £23 is great value, and there's a new 'Quatre Heures' afternoon menu where you can tuck into charcuterie and pâtisserie. We only wish the stellar wine list was more affordable.
Babies and children welcome: high chairs; nappy-changing facilities. Booking advisable. Disabled: toilet. Dress: smart casual. Separate rooms for parties, seating 16. **Map 8 F9**.

★ Chabrot Bistrot d'Amis

9 Knightsbridge Green, SW1X 7QL (7225 2238, www.chabrot.co.uk). Knightsbridge tube. **Lunch served** noon-3pm, **dinner served** 6.30-11pm Mon-Fri. **Meals served** noon-11pm Sat; noon-10pm Sun. **Main courses** £15.50-£34. **Set meal** (noon-3pm, 6.30-7pm) £12.50 1 course, £15.50 1 course incl glass of wine, £17.50 2 courses incl glass of wine. **Credit** AmEx, MC, V.
This incredibly charming place will have you thinking you're in Nîmes or Narbonne rather than a pedestrian alleyway five minutes from Harrods. The food is classic bistro fare, and the look – wood panelling, red and white table linen, dark aprons on waiting staff – maintains the illusion perfectly. But Chabrot is no bistro theme-park: this is seriously skilful cooking using high-quality ingredients. What's more, despite the locale, it doesn't even need to be expensive, and the succinct, all-French wine list gives ample scope (including 50cl carafes) under £25. We built a lunch mostly from the wonderful hors d'oeuvres ('served as ready'), which is an easy-going way to eat here. Nothing was less than excellent: snails swimming in garlicky butter, marrow bones split lengthwise for easy eating, a robust aubergine salad with soft goat's cheese,

deep-fried squid liberally dosed with spicy Espelette pepper (a fantastic dish). An artisanal charcuterie platter featured top-quality ham, lomo, saucisson, chorizo and rillettes. Some dishes are for two or three for special occasions (such as roast chicken with foie gras), and there is a daily 'formule' (main course with/without a glass of wine). The only sour note came from other diners: two young women who did their make-up at the table before departing. But that's not the management's fault, and certainly not enough to spoil a memorable meal at an exceptional restaurant.
Available for hire. Babies and children admitted. Booking advisable. Separate room for parties, seats 30. **Map 8 F9**.

Racine

239 Brompton Road, SW3 2EP (7584 4477, www.racine-restaurant.com). Knightsbridge or South Kensington tube. **Lunch served** noon-3pm Mon-Fri; noon-3.30pm Sat, Sun. **Dinner served** 6-10.30pm Mon-Sat; 6-10pm Sun. **Main courses** £16.50-£28.50. **Set meal** (lunch, 6-7.30pm Mon-Sat) £15.50 2 courses, £17.75 3 courses; (lunch, 6-7.30pm Sun) £18 2 courses, £20 3 courses. **Credit** AmEx, MC, V.
Aiming for the French bistro ideal, Racine comes close. It really does have a neighbourhood vibe, even if the neighbours are perfectly preserved couples of a certain age or well-mannered ex-pats of all ages. This isn't a snooty place, despite the moneyed location; the welcome is warm and the room unintimidating. The mirrors, leather banquettes, white linen and gleaming glassware are as comforting as the sight of 'daube de boeuf à la bourguignonne, pomme mousseline' on the carte. The prix fixe is good value: garlic and mint soup, roast lamb with creamed flageolets, and profiteroles with chocolate sauce made a generously portioned, well-flavoured supper. More interest came from that day's specials; a starter of ventrèche (like pancetta) with Jersey Royals and broad beans was a savoury treat, while roast quail with morteau sausage, tarbais (haricot) beans and herbs (from the main menu) also provided robust flavours and melting texture. There's lighter fare too: crab salad with herb omelette and horseradish, say, or skate with cider vinegar and parsley. The wine list, global but French-leaning, has plenty by the glass. Staff – there when you want them, invisible when you don't – ensure the place runs like clockwork.
Available for hire. Babies and children welcome: high chairs. Booking essential. Separate room for parties, seats 22. **Map 14 E10**.

Marylebone

★ Galvin Bistrot de Luxe

66 Baker Street, W1U 7DJ (7935 4007, www.galvinrestaurants.com). Baker Street tube. **Lunch served** noon-2.30pm Mon-Sat; noon-3pm Sun. **Dinner served** 6-10.30pm Mon-Wed; 6-10.45pm Thur-Sat; 6-9.30pm Sun. **Main courses** £16-£21.50. **Set lunch** £19.50 3 courses. **Set dinner** (6-7pm) £21.50 3 courses. **Credit** AmEx, MC, V.
Outstanding, knowledgeable staff and refined yet understated food supply the luxury to the Galvin brothers' informal Marylebone bistrot. When front of house know the finest details of how a tomato garnish is prepared (dried in the oven overnight, with a sprinkling of icing sugar, in this case), and confidently advise on wine pairings while making friendly, intelligent conversation – then you know you're in a fine-dining establishment. This is perhaps no surprise, coming from Michelin-starred brothers Chris and Jeff Galvin: two London chefs who continue to excel in the best of French cuisine. The menu is short, but still causes deliberation between the enticing seasonal plats principaux. Sea bass was crowned with a wafer-thin crisp skin, supported by braised cuttlefish and dense borlotti beans. Lightly poached cod was brought back to earth by mousseron mushrooms and intense black pudding. The puréed potatoes were quite simply the best we've tasted. Tarte tatin was homage to the finest points of this caramelised apple dessert, and the Valrhona chocolate delice came with a cheeky salted caramel ice-cream. Deserving of its accolades and its fiercely loyal following, Bistrot de Luxe brings a modern London touch to an undeniably French bistro experience. For more Galvin brothers food in more rarefied surroundings, try Galvin La Chapelle in Spitalfields.
Babies and children welcome: high chairs; nappy-changing facilities. Booking advisable. Disabled: toilet. Separate room for parties, seats 22. Tables outdoors (3, pavement). **Map 9 G5**.
For branches (Galvin Café a Vin, Galvin La Chapelle) see index.

Mayfair

La Petite Maison

54 Brooks Mews, W1K 4EG (7495 4774, www.lpmlondon.co.uk). Bond Street tube. **Lunch served** noon-2.30pm Mon-Fri; 12.30-2.45pm Sat; 12.30-3.30pm Sun. **Dinner served** 6-10.30pm

Mon-Sat; 6.30-9pm Sun. **Main courses** £13.50-£35. **Credit** AmEx, MC, V.
Like most top-end restaurants in France, La Petite Maison doesn't care a fig about dress codes. That's one reason that lunch here, in this London outpost of a famous Nice watering hole, is such a deeply enjoyable experience. Nearly everyone was dressed casually, and two large family groups made a happy noise in the centre of the room. At lunchtime, you really could be in Provence: two huge windows letting in lots of light, white walls, jolly Gallic prints. While the food can come at a price (most mains are over £20, and some are way over), the large choice of hors d'oeuvres allows you to put together a satisfying meal without breaking *la banque*. Two of us shared five, which was plenty. We had minor quibbles: thinly sliced octopus with lemon oil tasted great, but was too small to justify a price tag just short of £15, and excellent ratatouille didn't need pointless nuggets of feta cheese mixed in. Everything else was perfect, especially pissaladière (presented as five luscious rectangles) and petits farcis, tomatoes and courgettes with an earthy veal-based stuffing. The wine list starts just below £30 and is well chosen at every level. Service is wonderful: warm and attentive, and happy to see us linger. If you want cutting-edge cooking, go elsewhere. If you want real Provençal cooking in joyful surroundings, come here.
Babies and children welcome: high chairs. Booking advisable. Dress: smart casual. Tables outdoors (10, terrace). **Map 9 H6.**

Soho

FRENCH

Brasserie Zédel NEW

2012 RUNNER-UP BEST NEW RESTAURANT
20 Sherwood Street, W1F 7ED (7734 4888, www.brasseriezedel.com). Piccadilly Circus tube.
Bar **Open** 4.30pm-midnight daily.
Café **Open** 8am-midnight Mon-Sat; 11.30am-midnight Sun.
Brasserie **Meals served** noon-midnight daily.
Main courses £8-£17. **Set meal** £8.75 2 courses, £11.75 3 courses. **Credit** AmEx, MC, V.
Corbin and King, the restaurateurs behind the Wolseley (*see p42*) and the Delaunay (*see p40*), know how to run grand brasseries. When you combine this with a historic and impressive art deco setting – the former ballroom of a vast hotel at Piccadilly Circus – you already know you're in a destination restaurant. Yet rather than hiking the bill and making Brasserie Zédel 'exclusive', this time the duo have priced dishes low enough to make Café Rouge blush. You'll find set meal deals such as three courses for £11.75, and even an à la carte dinner for two might only come to £80 or so. The menu is resolutely old-school French; the £19.75 *formule* offers a starter of lamb's lettuce and beetroot, a choice of duck confit or grilled salmon for main course, and ice-cream or sorbet for dessert. The more interesting dishes are on the carte; choucroute alsacienne (a big heap of sauerkraut with hunks of salted pork, charcuterie and sausages) was a delight. Yet the very size of the Zédel – it's of ocean-liner dimensions – can count against the place. With an ever-changing relay of staff, we've found the service to be confused at times, and dishes don't always arrive *à point*.
Available for hire. Babies and children welcome: high chairs; nappy-changing facilities. Booking advisable. Disabled: lift; toilet. Entertainment: cabaret evenings; call for details. Vegan dishes. Vegetarian menu. **Map 17 B5.**

Garnier

Gauthier Soho

21 Romilly Street, W1D 5AF (7494 3111, www.gauthiersoho.co.uk). Leicester Square or Piccadilly Circus tube. **Lunch served** noon-2.30pm Mon-Fri. **Dinner served** 5.30-10.30pm daily. **Set meal** (lunch, 5.30-7pm) £18 2 courses (£26 with half bottle of wine), £25 3 courses (£33 with half bottle of wine). **Set meal** £40 3 courses, £50 4 courses, £60 5 courses; £70 tasting menu (£100-£130 incl wine); £60 vegetarian tasting menu (£90-£120 incl wine). **Credit** AmEx, MC, V.

Entry to this handsome Georgian townhouse requires the caller to press a buzzer: it sets the tone for a meal that is unapologetically exclusive, and at odds with the casual dining joints popping up all over Soho. The sumptuously furnished rooms are set over two floors, meaning the many waiters have to scuttle up and down flights of stairs every time a dish emerges from the basement kitchen – which is often, as multiple courses prevail. Although not quite the staid 'temple to gastronomy' many critics decry it as, Gauthier's exists for the food above all else. The cooking displays exacting French technique and inventive use of vegetables (something Provençal chef Alexis Gauthier is known for), but it often ends up too restrained to truly awe. A recent dish of belly pork with carrot, 'light chilli', coriander and coconut didn't display any of its advertised Asian influence; a ravioli of asparagus with bitter leaves was beautifully assembled, but too polite in flavour. Besides two tasting menus, the à la carte offers three, four or five courses from a fairly large list. There's also a reasonably priced lunch/early bird menu; but this is not somewhere to scrimp – such an intense level of service and finessed cooking doesn't come cheap.

Available for hire. Babies and children admitted. Booking advisable. Dress: smart casual. Separate rooms for parties, seating 4-40. Vegetarian menu. **Map 17 C4.**

South Kensington

Cassis Bistro

232 Brompton Road, SW3 2BB (7581 1101, www.cassisbistro.co.uk). South Kensington tube. **Meals served** 11.30am-11pm Mon-Sat; 11am-10.30pm Sun. **Main courses** £17-£29. **Credit** AmEx, MC, V.

We'll happily revisit Cassis time and again for its crispy farmhouse chicken: thick, juicy rounds of Devonshire chook that are sous-vided, rolled in herbs, pan-fried and then oven-baked. This triple cooking makes for an outrageously tasty dish, offset with a punchy jus and a healthy scattering of mushrooms. Other reasons to return to this slick, pretty Kensington bistro include the expertly mixed cocktails at the bar (half price 3-8pm; try the tangy apple berry gin), the clued-up service, the freshly baked sun-dried tomato focaccia served with high-octane olive oil, and the small but exquisite sea bass tartare starter (flavoured with goat's cheese and sesame). A recently installed chef from Italy has expanded the pasta and risotto section; we can heartily recommend his almond pesto spaghetti with nuggets of lobster. Desserts consist of monster soufflés made for two, and wonderful fresh tarts and clafoutis. The only downsides to Cassis are that it's far from cheap ('les plats' run from £17 to £29), and portion sizes are sometimes modest. Then again, given the quality of the food, service and atmosphere, it's pretty good value and a winning choice for an elegant dinner.

Available for hire. Babies and children welcome: high chairs; nappy-changing facilities. Booking advisable. Disabled: toilet. Tables outdoors (5, terrace). **Map 14 E10.**

West

Bayswater

Angelus

4 Bathhurst Street, W2 2SD (7402 0083, www.angelusrestaurant.co.uk). Lancaster Gate tube. **Meals served** 11am-11pm Mon-Sat; 11am-10pm Sun. **Main courses** £18-£33. **Set meal** (noon-6pm) £20 2 courses, £25 3 courses. **Credit** AmEx, MC, V.

Its location just north of Hyde Park, within earshot of the stables in the mews alongside, makes Angelus an appealing lunch spot, yet on our visit there was just one other couple eating. The dark wooden panelling, brown leather banquettes and red velvet drapes of this former pub add to a somewhat heavy atmosphere, and there's a gloomy cocktail bar to the rear. A choice of three menus – an all-day brasserie selection of brunch and pricey snacks (£11 for a cheese toastie), a fancy carte and a good-value set menu (with freshly baked bread, coffee and petits fours included) – is available until 6pm. While service can be over-attentive to the point of intrusive, chef Thierry Tomasin's cooking is perfectly judged; his light, lovely dishes do much to lift the mood. Asparagus with poached egg might have been rich, but the hollandaise was just sharp enough to create a balanced, elegant starter; salmon goujons were delicate, lightly battered slices with a wonderfully punchy tartare sauce. Own-made gnocchi with spring vegetables, top-notch goat's cheese and toasted hazelnuts made a beautiful medley. An evening visit might be more fun – but it won't come cheap.

Babies and children welcome: high chairs. Booking advisable. Disabled: lift; toilet. Separate room for parties, seats 22. Tables outdoors (5, terrace). **Map 8 D6.**

Chiswick

★ La Trompette

5-7 Devonshire Road, W4 2EU (8747 1836, www.latrompette.co.uk). Turnham Green tube. **Lunch served** noon-2.30pm Mon-Sat; 12.30-3pm Sun. **Dinner served** 6.30-10.30pm Mon-Sat; 6.30-9.30pm Sun. **Set lunch** (Mon-Sat) £27.50 3 courses; (Sun) £32.50 3 courses. **Set dinner** £42.50 3 courses. **Credit** AmEx, MC, V.

Nothing is out of place at this Chiswick stalwart, from the inch-perfect positioning of the wine glasses to the soothing grey-brown interior to the impeccable modern French food from chef Anthony Boyd. In business for over a decade, it's part of a winning triumvirate owned by Bruce Poole and Nigel Platts-Martin (the others are Chez Bruce in Clapham and the Glasshouse in Kew – *see p222*). The tablecloths may be starched, but not the atmosphere – as typified by the (mainly French) waiting staff. Crisp in their black aprons and ties, they were professional, knowledgeable and genuinely friendly. The fixed-price menu keeps things simple, but not cheap – all around us people were clearly celebrating. A recent meal was close to perfection, from a zingy, Asian-accented starter of seared tuna loin with a soy, sesame and citrus dressing to a refreshing finish of strawberry sherbet (halfway between sorbet and ice-cream) with black pepper meringue. In between came slow-roast pork belly with morteau sausage and earthy trompettes; and pan-fried black bream – moist flesh, crisp skin – with truffled creamy mash and a wonderfully complex sauce that involved smoked anchovy, brown shrimp, tiny capers and morello cherries. Thanks to head sommelier Matthieu Longeure, this is also a restaurant for wine lovers, with a wide-ranging list that's particularly strong on regional France.

Available for hire. Babies and children welcome: high chairs. Booking advisable. Disabled: toilet. Tables outdoors (7, terrace).

Le Vacherin

76-77 South Parade, W4 5LF (8742 2121, www.levacherin.co.uk). Chiswick Park tube/rail. **Lunch served** noon-3pm Tue-Sun. **Dinner served** 6-10.30pm Mon-Thur; 6-11pm Fri, Sat; 6-10pm Sun. **Main courses** £15-£21. **Set lunch** (Mon-Sat) £18.50 2 courses, £25 3 courses; (Sun) £25 3 courses. **Credit** AmEx, MC, V.

Very much a neighbourhood restaurant, Le Vacherin is reached across the park from Turnham Green tube, though the main view from its picture windows is of passing buses. The first and most upmarket of Malcolm John's stable of 'affordable fine dining' restaurants across south and west London, it's a slightly starchy place, with its smart cream and black frontage, 1980s-style sax music and rather stern service. The menu is classic (frogs' legs and snails both in attendance) with a robust edge (confit duck heart, veal kidney and roast bone marrow). We took advantage of an online 'anti-austerity' voucher, offering a 25% discount, but suspected the saving had been built into the prices. An asparagus starter may have been drizzled with truffle vinaigrette, but at £10.50 for spindly spears and an undercooked duck egg, did not seem good value. Pea velouté was so thick it took an age for the waiter to pour it into the bowl over a shrivelled gougère, which immediately turned soggy. While salt marsh lamb had a good flavour, the portion was meagre. Fortunately, an excellent blackberry soufflé and a more lively dining room ended the evening on a better note.

Available for hire. Babies and children welcome: high chairs; nappy-changing facilities. Booking advisable. Separate room for parties, seats 30.
For branch (Brasserie Vacherin) see index.

Earl's Court

Garnier NEW

314 Earl's Court Road, SW5 9BQ (3641 8323, www.garnier-restaurant-london.co.uk). Earl's Court tube or West Brompton tube/rail. **Lunch served** noon-3pm Mon-Sat; noon-3.30pm Sun. **Dinner served** 6.30-10.30pm Mon-Sat; 6.30-10pm Sun. **Main courses** £16.50-£49. **Set lunch** (Mon-Sat) £16.50 2 courses; (Sun) £21.50 2 courses. **Credit** AmEx, MC, V.

Eric and Didier Garnier, the brothers behind this recently opened venture, are no strangers to the restaurant scene. Eric's previous credits include running front-of-house teams at Racine and Koffmann's at the Berkeley, while Didier has earned an enviable reputation as proprietor of Chelsea's Le Colombier. Garnier is a spacious, slightly spartan dining spot, its walls lined with gold-framed mirrors and 1970s sitting room-style lighting. The tables are laid with simple, white

Les Deux Salons. See p93.

napery. However, it's the food that's the main player here. The restaurant flies the flag for retro bistro classics with a roll call of expertly executed staples: witness a juicy sirloin steak topped with glistening bone marrow butter and surrounded by sticky, meaty juices. An outstanding starter of pillowy gnocchi, lightly fried in nutty-tasting butter and tossed with sweet cherry tomatoes and chopped courgettes, finished with pecorino cheese and zesty mint, won us over. Next, a thick slab of marvellously bloody calves' liver was finished with warm peppery radishes, crunchy turnips, crisp fried sage and creamy onion purée. Even the chips were faultless – golden, piping hot and perfectly seasoned. Only dessert didn't quite deliver: strawberry parfait was let down by over-whipped cream in the mousse-like filling, though an intensely fruity scoop of strawberry sorbet pleased. Service is top-notch, and wines keenly priced, with a good range of half-bottles.
Available for hire. Babies and children admitted. Booking advisable. **Map 13 B11**.

Lawn Bistro. See p101.

Holland Park

Belvedere

Holland House, off Abbotsbury Road, in Holland Park, W8 6LU (7602 1238, www.belvedere restaurant.co.uk). Holland Park tube. **Lunch served** noon-2.15pm Mon-Sat; noon, 2.30pm Sun. **Dinner served** 6-10.15pm Mon-Sat. **Main courses** £12-£22. **Set meal** (lunch, 6-7pm Mon-Fri) £15.95 2 courses, £19.95 3 courses; (lunch Sat, Sun) £27.50 3 courses. **Credit** AmEx, MC, V.
The best thing about the Belvedere is its location, in a grand old building in Holland Park. Inside, you'll find an attractive, low-lit dining room tended by a charming restaurant manager, with a soundtrack provided by a talented pianist. The menu has a French slant, but also cherry-picks influences from across the Med, with the occasional detour to the UK (including a £17.50 fish and chips). Our food was solid and cheering, yet hardly innovative. A pleasant dish of seared scallops came with a tangy apple-laced salad; and a combination of poached duck egg with truffle and asparagus was hearty if unsubtle. Grilled Aberdeenshire ribeye with béarnaise sauce and thick chips was competently executed (for a Gallic thrill, you can choose to have it accompanied by snails and garlic sauce), and confit pork belly with sauerkraut was a pleasing, calorific treat. We finished with a filling, fruity blueberry financier edged with crème fraîche. The Belvedere has a loyal clientele of W8 regulars, who arrive to celebrate family occasions or seal business deals. They don't come to have their culinary envelopes pushed; straightforward, reliable comfort food is what they want, and that's exactly what they get.
Available for hire. Babies and children welcome: high chairs. Booking essential. Dress: smart casual. Separate room for parties, seats 20. Tables outdoors (8, terrace). Vegetarian menu. **Map 7 A8**.

South West

Wandsworth

★ Chez Bruce

2 Bellevue Road, SW17 7EG (8672 0114, www.chezbruce.co.uk). Wandsworth Common rail. **Lunch served** noon-2pm Mon-Fri; noon-2.30pm Sat, Sun. **Dinner served** 6.30-9.45pm Mon-Thur; 6.30-10pm Fri, Sat; 7-9pm Sun. **Set lunch** (Mon-Fri) £27.50 3 courses; (Sat, Sun) £35 3 courses. **Set dinner** £45 3 courses. **Credit** AmEx, DC, MC, V.
Turning 50? Promotion at work? Londoners looking to celebrate flock to the genteel suburban dining room of Chez Bruce, overlooking Wandsworth Common, in order to mark life's milestones at Bruce Poole's well-oiled operation. The elegant white dining room is dotted with tasteful contemporary art, and cleverly divided with mirrors and pillars to create intimate nooks in which to enjoy perfectly prepared French cuisine that exhibits influences from across Europe. There's no carte, just set menus, which change daily. At £45 for three courses, the set dinner isn't cheap. However, the finesse achieved by serving staff and kitchen make it a worthwhile expense. A deconstructed summer gazpacho, accented with hunks of buffalo mozzarella, borlotti beans and toasted almond chunks, was a typically complex dish that allowed prime seasonal ingredients to star. Pan-fried sea bream followed, cooked just-so and accompanied by juicy prawns, firm gnocchi dressed in pesto and baby seasonal vegetables; the plate was a masterpiece of simplicity, far greater in effect that the sum of its parts. For dessert, deep-fried pineapple with alphonso mango slices and rice pudding cooked in coconut milk was exactly in keeping with Chez Bruce's crowd-pleasing repertoire. The vast wine list (including several options by the carafe) offers opportunities to try regions often under-represented; we enjoyed a beautiful red and white from South Tyrol. Chez Bruce often comes top in polls of Londoners' favourite restaurants, and we won't disagree – it is indeed a treat.
Available for hire. Babies and children welcome lunch: high chairs. Booking essential. Disabled: toilet. Separate room for parties, seats 16.

Wimbledon

★ Lawn Bistro NEW

2012 RUNNER-UP BEST NEW LOCAL RESTAURANT

67 High Street, SW19 5EE (8947 8278, www.thelawnbistro.co.uk). Wimbledon tube/rail. **Lunch served** noon-2.30pm Mon-Sat; noon-3pm Sun. **Dinner served** 6.30-10.30pm Mon-Sat. **Set lunch** (Mon-Sat) £14.95, £19.50 2 courses, £18.95, £22.50 3 courses; (Sun) £29.50 3 courses. **Set dinner** (6.30-7.15pm Mon-Thur) £27.95 3 courses incl glass of wine; £32.50 2 courses, £37.50 3 courses. **Credit** AmEx, MC, V.

Wimbledon's chain-driven dining scene has bucked up considerably since the arrival of this swish outfit headed by Ollie Couillaud (one-time head chef at La Trompette). The wedge-shaped space, larger than it first appears, features olive and mushroom paintwork, dark wood furniture, large mirrors and subtle lighting. Staff didn't put a foot wrong on our visit. And the cooking, grounded in France, but with forays into Britain, Spain and North Africa, is very accomplished. Menus are fixed-price; lunch is a particular bargain, as it offers many of the same dishes that are available in the evening, alongside more casual fare such as croque monsieur with big chips and salad. To start, squid and watermelon salad, with fennel purée, chilli, garlic and ginger, was a scintillating combination of flavours and textures. And beautifully presented – as were all our dishes. Also excellent were mains of Gloucester Old Spot pork chop, and poached cod, the latter with green beans, ratte potatoes encased in aïoli, and a swirl of sauce nero (black from squid ink). By far the most popular dessert is baked alaska, dramatically set aflame at the table – it's designed for two, but could easily serve four. There's a well-chosen global wine list, plus beers from Wimbledon's very own By the Horns brewery.

Available for hire. Babies and children welcome: high chairs. Booking advisable. Disabled: toilet. Separate room for parties, seats 24.

South

Balham

Gazette

100 Balham High Road, SW12 9AA (8772 1232, www.gazettebrasserie.co.uk). Balham tube/rail. **Meals served** 8am-10pm daily. **Main courses** £8-£17. **Set lunch** (noon-5pm Mon-Fri) £10 2 courses, £13.50 3 courses. **Credit** AmEx, DC, MC, V.

It's easy to sneer at Gazette's 'posh brasserie by numbers' approach, where food is served on dainty boards or in dinky pails and the menu is almost comically Gallic (Voulez-vous les escargots? Soupe à l'oignon? Oui, bien sûr… you'll find them all here). But the venue is not trying to be anything other than a smart neighbourhood bistro, which it does rather well. Cooking is solid, rather than sensational, but when you factor in the attractive dining room and can-do attitude of the young staff (who welcome parties of pram-pushing mums as readily as starry-eyed young couples), it makes for a respectable package. The all-day menu caters for the masses: at lunchtime, we like the rich, cheese-laden soft omelettes and the 'Balhamoise', a savoury crêpe filled with spinach, tomato and superbly salty goat's cheese. Likewise, the excellent-value croque monsieur, while it won't win culinary prizes, equals anything on the Champs-Elysées. For dinner, more serious options come a-calling; our ribeye steak was correctly cooked, the miniature galvanised pot of matchstick fries a fitting accompaniment. A democratically priced Francophile wine list offers plenty by the glass, half-bottle or pichet.

Available for hire. Babies and children welcome: children's menu; crayons; high chairs; nappy-changing facilities. Booking advisable. Tables outdoors (4, terrace). Takeaway service. Vegan dishes.

For branch see index.

Battersea

Entrée

2 Battersea Rise, SW11 1ED (7223 5147, www.entreebattersea.co.uk). Clapham Junction rail. **Lunch served** noon-3.30pm Sun. **Dinner served** 6-10.30pm Tue-Sun. **Main courses** £14-£21. **Set meal** £20 2 courses, £24 3 courses. **Credit** AmEx, MC, V.

Chummy neighbourhood spot Entrée is one of the most popular venues on restaurant-heavy Battersea Rise. In the basement is a piano bar where musicians play at the weekends; on the ground floor is a dining room half plastered in cuttings from fin de siècle French magazines. As you tuck in to your amuse-bouche (we enjoyed a glass of rich cauliflower soup with a fluffy thyme roll), you can peruse adverts for 19th-century slimming aids, hair restoratives and Algerian decongestants. Scallop and crab lasagne was an inspired starter, alternating layers of seafood in an elegant beurre blanc. A main course of roasted duck was equally pleasing, matching thick wedges of crisp-skinned meat with date and shallot tarte tatin and chou farci (rich mince and bacon wrapped in cabbage). The only slight misfire on our visit was a rather low-impact swordfish served in a light Thai broth with strangely flavourless chunks of chorizo. Desserts include a series of creamy possets, fondants and panna cottas. Entrée keeps its tables full with the help of promotions such as BYOB nights on Tuesdays. The disadvantage to its deserved success is that noise ricochets around the room when it's full.

Babies and children admitted weekends. Booking essential Fri-Sun. Dress: smart casual. Separate room for parties, seats 20. **Map 21 C4.**

Androuet. See p103.

FRENCH

Waterloo

RSJ

33 Coin Street, SE1 9NR (7928 4554, www.rsj.uk.com). Waterloo tube/rail. **Lunch served** noon-2.30pm Mon-Fri. **Dinner served** 5.30-11pm Mon-Sat. **Main courses** £12-£19. **Set meal** £16.95 2 courses, £19.95 3 courses. **Credit** AmEx, DC, MC, V.

Opened in 1980 and named, bizarrely, after its dining room's lacklustre design rather than its beautifully executed traditional dishes or epic wine list, RSJ needs a makeover. The lighting is unsympathetic, the furniture utilitarian and the colour scheme ill-conceived. However, the kitchen produces food of great intensity of flavour, which honours tradition without being stodgy. A terrific starter featured chicken livers sautéed with heaps of lardons, doused with a spicy worcestershire-tinged sauce, and served with a fried egg on brioche. The rich food was ideally matched by a 2010 Quincy Dom des Ballandors, a sauvignon with impressive weight and ripeness. A giant portion of own-made ravioli with fresh crab and avocado arrived in a wonderfully rich bisque. Next, côte de boeuf was perfectly rare, as requested, flecked with rosemary, a flavour also used to sublime effect in the accompanying béarnaise. Puddings let the otherwise authentically Gallic menu down: no Frenchman ever requested spotted dick. RSJ is an oenophile's dream. Linger over the encyclopaedic, Loire-dominated list, or save time by ordering one of the dozen regularly changing by-the-glass options. A great pre- or post-theatre choice.

Available for hire. Babies and children admitted. Booking advisable. Separate rooms for parties, seating 25-40. Tables outdoors (5, terrace).

Map 11 N8.

Provender

East

Bethnal Green

Bistrotheque HOT 50

23-27 Wadeson Street, E2 9DR (8983 7900, www.bistrotheque.com). Bethnal Green tube/rail or Cambridge Heath rail or bus 55.

Bar **Open** 5.30pm-midnight Mon-Fri; 11am-midnight Sat; 11am-11pm Sun.

Restaurant **Brunch served** 11am-3.45pm Sat, Sun. **Dinner served** 6.30-10.15pm Mon-Thur, Sun; 6.30-10.45pm Fri, Sat. **Main courses** £15-£17. **Set dinner** (6.30-7.15pm, 9.45-10.15pm Mon-Thur, Sun; 6.30-7.15pm, 9.45-10.45pm Fri, Sat) £17.50 3 courses.

Both **Credit** AmEx, MC, V.

Bistrotheque was instrumental in putting the Hackney dining scene on the map. Hidden down an unassuming side street, it continues to draw those in the know for civilised dinners and excellent weekend brunches. Walking up the dark, battered staircase to the first-floor dining area feels a bit like entering an abandoned school, until the doors open to a buzzing industrial-chic space, with white tiled walls, vintage chandeliers, square marble tables and dark wooden chairs. But while the space evokes a Brooklyn eaterie, the menu draws elements from France and Britain – typical dishes include black bream with green sauce, steak tartare and rock oysters. Our quail starter was on the small side, but well prepared and presented. Mains of a half chicken with garlic oil and rocket, and cod with

FRENCH

fennel, radish and cooked celery, were both hugely enjoyable – cooked to perfection, with nicely complementary ingredients. The France-dominated wine list is also bound to please, while desserts are not to be missed – chocolate tart was heavenly, with top-notch shortcrust pastry. Service, meanwhile, is from trendily coiffed staff, who were friendlier and more engaged than we've experienced on previous visits. The restaurant's Manchichi Bar opened in early summer 2012, and is a great addition, offering oysters and champagne, cocktails and snacks.
Babies and children admitted: high chairs. Booking advisable. Disabled: toilet. Entertainment: pianist 11am-4pm Sat, Sun. Separate rooms for parties, seating 100-120.

Shoreditch

Boundary

2-4 Boundary Street, entrance at 9 Redchurch Street, E2 7DD (7729 1051, www.theboundary.co.uk). Shoreditch High Street rail. **Lunch served** noon-3.30pm Sun. **Dinner served** 6.30-10.30pm Mon-Sat. **Main courses** £20-£25. **Set meal** £19.50 2 courses, £24.50 3 courses. **Credit** AmEx, MC, V.

Shoreditch by way of the Champs-Elysées is the vibe at this upmarket French restaurant, which along with the scrubbed-up British caff Albion and a smart rooftop bar forms the dining options at Terence Conran's hip Boundary hotel. Stairs from pavement level head deep down to a basement, past artful street-art walls. Much thought has been put into making this potentially challenging space welcoming and stylish: lighting is perfect, and a display of bottles separates a 1950s-furnished bar from the dining space. From the glass-fronted open kitchen, chefs send out impeccable versions of French bistro classics – terrine de foie gras, soupe au pistou, lapin à la moutarde, escargots... all the stars are present and perfect. The pricing (and presentation) elevate a meal here above informality, although the prix fixe menu is good value; three courses cost £24.50, and include a choice from the likes of confit du canard, salmon with sauce vierge, and tarte au citron. Staff are effortlessly efficient, and there are some nice pieces of restaurant theatre: choose charcuterie, even from the set menu, and a selection is presented table-side on a trolley. The wine list is extensive, but a helpful sommelier dispenses advice.
Available for hire. Babies and children welcome: high chairs; nappy-changing facilities. Booking advisable dinner. Disabled: lift; toilet. **Map 6 R4.**

Les Trois Garçons HOT 50

1 Club Row, E1 6JX (7613 1924, www.lestroisgarcons.com). Shoreditch High Street rail. **Lunch served** noon-2.30pm Mon-Fri. **Dinner served** 6-9.30pm Mon-Thur; 6-10.30pm Fri, Sat. **Set lunch** £17.50 2 courses, £22 3 courses **Set dinner** £40.50 2 courses, £47 3 courses; £60 tasting menu (£99 incl wine), £75 tasting menu (£105 incl wine). **Credit** AmEx, MC, V.

It's in the shell of a Victorian pub, but no Victorian pub ever looked like this. When Les Trois Garçons opened in 2000, the talking point was the wildly eclectic decor – and it still wows today. A menagerie of taxidermy includes a giraffe, monkey and bejewelled sabre-tooth tiger; a handbag light installation hangs from the ceiling; and shelves are filled with an assortment of knick-knacks, curios and antiquities. To say it's cluttered would be wrong: the three boys behind the name are as accomplished interior designers as they are restaurateurs. All this ornamentation might overshadow the food, but the cooking is generally of a high standard. Dishes are based on classical French technique and quality ingredients, but the kitchen employs imaginative flourishes that demonstrate a sense of adventure. A seared scallop comes with burnt orange dressing and freeze-dried, crispy slices of pomelo; veal cutlet might be paired with sweetbread wun tuns, say, and roast lamb with a deeply flavoured 'croquette' of its shoulder. Although service is flawless and friendly, it's hard to justify the prices – two courses from the à la carte are £40.50. The fashionable crowd who pack LTG aren't here for value, that's for sure.
Available for hire. Booking essential. Children admitted over 12yrs. Separate room for parties, seats 10. **Map 6 S4.**

Spitalfields

Androuet NEW

Old Spitalfields Market, 107B Commercial Street, E1 6BG (7375 3168, www.androuet.co.uk). Liverpool Street tube/rail or Shoreditch High Street rail. **Lunch served** noon-2pm, **dinner served** 5-10pm Mon-Wed. **Meals served** noon-10.30pm Thur-Sat; noon-9.30pm Sun. **Main courses** £12-£20. **Credit** AmEx, MC, V.

This London outpost of Paris-based fromagerie extraordinaire Androuet is an implausibly chic cheese shop and bistro rolled into one. With graceful chandeliers and tall mirrors, it's both cosy and glamorous – despite the inevitable pong. Diners are surrounded by beautifully displayed goat's, cow's and sheep's cheeses, mostly from France and Britain but with a few Italian formaggi too. The house specialities are raclette and fondue; of the latter, there are two sorts – the traditional comté and emmental combo or a daily changing special blend (exemplary on our visit) served with charcuterie, cornichons and good bread for scooping up the golden, molten cheese. If you don't fancy a full meal, there's a build-your-own-cheeseboard option, excellent charcuterie, including a toothsome game terrine with pistachio, plus a selection of salads, starters and mains in which cheese has either star billing or a key supporting role. There's a cracking wine list too, with food-friendly bottles from top producers, including some biodynamic and 'natural' wines – all, like the cheeses, available to purchase and take away. Heaven on earth for cheese fiends.
Babies and children welcome: high chairs. Booking advisable Wed-Sun. Separate room for parties, seats 14. Tables outdoors (10, terrace). **Map 12 R5.**

North East

Wanstead

Provender NEW

2012 RUNNER-UP BEST NEW LOCAL RESTAURANT

17 High Street, E11 2AA (8530 3050, www.provenderlondon.co.uk). Snaresbrook tube. **Meals served** noon-9.30pm Tue-Thur; noon-10pm Fri, Sat; noon-5pm Sun. **Main courses** £9-£20. **Set meal** (Tue-Thur; noon-7pm Fri, Sat) £9.95 2 courses, £12.95 3 courses. **Credit** AmEx, MC, V.

This snappy Wanstead newcomer is the latest venture from Max Renzland, who ran a series of terrific French bistros in the suburbs in the 1990s. It's smart but relaxed, in looks, service and food. Wooden tables and chairs and (uncomfortable) banquettes are set against dark grey paintwork and bare brick walls; lampshades and cushions provide flashes of scarlet. The rear is quieter than the main room. Midweek, the place was bouncing with a lively local crowd, drawn by the classic 'bourgeois' brasserie food and the fair prices – the menu du jour is a particular bargain. Highlights included, to start, an intense aubergine bayildi and first-rate selection of charcuterie (featuring rosette de Lyon and goose and duck rillettes). To follow, an asparagus, pea, broad bean and goat's cheese risotto was perfectly textured, but the cheese overwhelmed the other flavours. Navarin d'agneu – a traditional stew of lamb and spring veg – was tasty even if the meat was overcooked. Timing was also an issue with the shrivelled frites, which had been left too long before serving. Redemption came with the desserts, uniformly fabulous, from an intense cassis sorbet and refreshing raspberry parfait to an ultra-rich chocolate tart. Aperitifs include pineau de charentes and assorted kirs, while the all-French wine list has plenty of choice by the glass and carafe.
Available for hire. Babies and children welcome: children's menu; crayons; high chairs; nappy-changing facilities. Booking advisable weekends. Disabled: toilet. Separate room for parties, seats 20. Tables outdoors (6, pavement).

North

Camden Town & Chalk Farm

L'Absinthe

40 Chalcot Road, NW1 8LS (7483 4848, www.labsinthe.co.uk). Chalk Farm tube. **Lunch served** noon-2.30pm Mon-Fri; noon-4pm Sat, Sun. **Dinner served** 6-10.30pm Tue-Sat; 6-9.30pm Sun. **Main courses** £9.50-£17.50. **Set lunch** (Tue-Fri) £10.95 2 courses, £13.95 3 courses; (Sun) £15.95 2 courses, £19.50 3 courses. **Credit** AmEx, MC, V.

Humour as dry as a croûton keeps this casual spot for *cuisine bourgeois* safely away from cliché. Staff brim with good cheer and kindness, and the lime-green decor is equally jolly and peppered with jokes (Sarkozy a notable victim). The menu barely changes from year to year, but is supplemented by specials – frogs' legs provençal, say, or moules with cream sauce and frites. Presentation is unpretentious and there's a sameness to main courses – both our orders arrived with identical piles of lettuce and sautéed potatoes – but, at these prices, *je ne regrette rien*. Buttery, garlic-laden snails served in a traditional terracotta escargot dish were as authentic as a Gallic shrug. Bavette steak, cut into chunks rather than sliced, was so heavily smothered with shallot gravy that it looked like a stew, but the beef was properly sweet and chewy. Best was pain perdu with silky, meaty-tasting mushrooms and perfectly poached egg. The cheapest red – Le Petit Mas grenache vin de pays – is a fruity, easy-drinking treat and, like several wines, available by the glass or pot lyonnaise (460cl). Premium bottles are offered at shop price plus £10 corkage, so the more you spend on, say, a 2007 or 2008 Burgundy, the better the deal.

Babies and children welcome: high chairs. Booking advisable. Separate room for parties, seats 24. Tables outdoors (5, pavement). **Map 27 B2**.

Highgate

Côte

2 Highgate High Street, N6 5JL (8348 9107, www.cote-restaurants.co.uk). Archway tube. **Meals served** 8am-11pm Mon-Fri; 9am-11pm Sat; 9am-10.30pm Sun. **Main courses** £8.95-£17.95. **Set meal** (noon-7pm Mon-Fri) £9.95 2 courses, £11.95 3 courses. **Credit** AmEx, MC, V.

Kudos to whoever handles the property side of this national chain, which has 18 branches in London's most bourgeois arrondissements – they find good sites and make the most of them. This spacious Highgate one benefits from a classy rear dining terrace, covered and heated for use year-round. The split-level interior has comfortable leather booths and eye-catching tilework. It attracts everyone from mums with babies to business people. Pitched as a value-for-money choice, Côte is nevertheless one of those places where the final bill can seem too high given the experience. Take care ordering: strengths include the halves of chargrilled Breton chicken with frites which, at £9.95, cost the same as a green vegetable risotto. Similarly, better to spend £14.95 on a 30-day-aged ribeye from Hereford cattle than £9.50 on steak haché – unless you want an expensive burger. Unlike in a true Parisian bistro, vegetarians have some good options, such as tomatoes breton (stuffed with a piquant goat's cheese mixture), mushroom crêpes and salades composées. The wine list is French, *naturellement*, and kindly offers 15 options under £20.

Babies and children welcome: children's menu; high chairs; nappy-changing facilities. Booking advisable. Disabled: toilet. Tables outdoors (15, terrace).

For branches see index.

Islington

Almeida

30 Almeida Street, N1 1AD (7354 4777, www.almeida-restaurant.co.uk). Angel tube or Highbury & Islington tube/rail. **Lunch served** noon-2.30pm Tue-Sat. **Dinner served** 5.30-10.30pm Mon-Sat. **Meals served** noon-3.30pm Sun. **Main courses** £9.50-£21.50. **Set dinner** £28.50 2 courses, £33.50 3 courses. **Set meal** (lunch Tue-Sat; 5.30-6.30pm, 10-10.30pm Mon-Sat) £15.95 2 courses, £18.95 3 courses. **Credit** AmEx, MC, V.

One of the D&D London stable, the Almeida remains unchallenged as the big hitter of Islington's (admittedly under-performing) restaurant scene. Understated assurance is its hallmark. The unshowy, calming dining room has an open kitchen at the rear and big front windows looking at the Almeida theatre opposite. The menu is modern French – duck breast with gratin dauphinois and green peppercorn sauce, crème brûlée with a warm madeleine – with the occasional flourish (cod brandade fritters with the vichyssoise, for example). Staff are charming, though we had to prise the menu du jour out of them. From this, pork and peppercorn rillettes was a generous portion, served with celeriac rémoulade; a main of braised beef cheek with mash, vegetables and red wine shallot sauce was meltingly good but too rich to finish. From the main menu, a vibrantly coloured starter of asparagus with poached duck egg and hollandaise looked and tasted a treat. Dish of the day – suckling pig with potato purée and spiced jus – was ideal on a cold day. So, a decent lunch: though we prefer the restaurant at night, when the room looks warmer, there's more buzz, and you've time to explore the cheese trolley.

Babies and children welcome: children's menu; high chairs; nappy-changing facilities. Booking advisable. Disabled: toilet. Separate rooms for parties, seating 10 and 20. Tables outdoors (8, pavement). Vegan dishes. Vegetarian menu. **Map 5 O1**.

North West

St John's Wood

L'Aventure

3 Blenheim Terrace, NW8 0EH (7624 6232, www.laventure.co.uk). St John's Wood tube or bus 139, 189. **Lunch served** 12.30-2.30pm Mon-Fri. **Dinner served** 7-11pm Mon-Sat. **Set lunch** £18.50 2 courses, £21.50 3 courses. **Set dinner** £31 2 courses, £39.50 3 courses. **Credit** AmEx, MC, V.

Save on that trip to the Loire and instead make your way to St John's Wood and enter this classic *restaurant bourgeois*. Virtually every French town has such a venue, with sharp white linen, gleaming glasses, and a fussily plush mix of soft seating, tapestries, prints, drapery and abundant fresh and dried flowers. Service, by the black-waistcoated young waiters, is très correct, Charles Aznavour croons away in the background, and the menu is hand-written in French only. L'Aventure is oblivious to fashion, but this doesn't bother an affluent, mostly older local clientele who can properly be described as devoted. The attraction is not just the traditional cosy comfort, but also the reliably satisfying food, such as, on our lunch menu, a smooth, rich nage (or broth) of mussels and scallops with saffron, followed by pan-fried quails with asparagus carefully offset against an accompanying tartine (or piece of toast) of full-flavoured foie gras. There's nothing exceptional here, but plenty of the kind of subtlety, attention to detail – fresh bread, delectable petits fours with coffee – and special flavours that won French cuisine its grand reputation in the first place. The extensive wine list is, of course, entirely French.

Available for hire. Babies and children admitted. Booking advisable dinner. Tables outdoors (6, terrace). **Map 1 C2**.

Outer London

Richmond, Surrey

Chez Lindsay

11 Hill Rise, Richmond, Surrey, TW10 6UQ (8948 7473, www.chezlindsay.co.uk). Richmond tube/rail.

Crêperie **Meals served** 11am-10.45pm Mon-Sat; noon-10pm Sun. **Main courses** £3.95-£11.50.

Restaurant **Meals served** noon-10.45pm Mon-Sat; noon-10pm Sun. **Main courses** £10.75-£25. **Set lunch** (noon-7pm Mon-Fri) £12.75 2 courses, £15.75 3 courses. **Set meal** (7-10.45pm Mon-Fri; noon-10.45pm Sat; noon-10pm Sun) £21.75 2 courses, £25.75 3 courses.

Both **Credit** MC, V.

Pleasingly unpretentious and ever so slightly haphazard, Chez Lindsay is a neighbourhood restaurant with wide appeal. Couples savour plates of oysters, while families tuck in to a pancake feast. Unstuffy (though by no means cheap) Breton food and drink is the focus, with buckwheat galettes a speciality and a range of bottled ciders that includes rosé and pear varieties. The wine list highlights the neighbouring Loire Valley, though the house selection is sourced from the south. Grands plats include interesting regional specialities around the £20 mark. La cotriade, a Breton fish stew with cabbage and potatoes, was gussied up with nuggets of lobster and a langoustine, but remained authentically bony. The liquor demanded to be mopped up, but bread had to be requested. Steak was tender and nicely charred, with skinny frîtes and perfect béarnaise. The sweet pancakes are less imaginative than the savoury, and mark-ups are staggering, particularly on flambéed options. Still, a simple beurre-sucre allowed the flavour of a good-sized crêpe to come through, and ice-creams, including vividly purple lavender and luxurious calvados flavours, were a treat. Approach the evening and weekend prix fixe with caution – it can work out more expensive than ordering off the carte.

Babies and children welcome: high chairs. Booking advisable Sat, Sun. Separate room for parties, seats 36.

Twickenham, Middlesex

Brula

43 Crown Road, Twickenham, Middx, TW1 3EJ (8892 0602, www.brula.co.uk). St Margarets rail. **Lunch served** noon-3pm daily. **Dinner served** 6-10.30pm Mon-Sat. **Main courses** £13.50-£25.50. **Set lunch** £15 2 courses, £19 3 courses. **Set dinner** £17 2 courses, £21 3 courses. **Credit** AmEx, MC, V.

Long the restaurant of choice in St Margarets for birthdays, family gatherings and other celebrations, Brula is looking slightly tired these days. The premises are romantic if old-fashioned: stained-glass windows, red velvet drapes and parquet flooring in the main room, plus a darker, cosier back room that's ideal for small groups. Bentwood chairs and white tablecloths provide that Parisian brasserie vibe. In addition to the carte, there's a good-value, prix-fixe regional menu (Provence in summer, Savoie in winter), occasional special menus (to celebrate Bastille Day, for example) and, admirably, even a vegetarian menu. Gallic standards (steak frites, snails, pissaladière, poulet à la Toulousaine) mix with British flavours and ingredients (Aberdeen Angus beef, roast trout with Jersey Royals) – and presentation is picture-perfect, with not a french bean out of place. Attentive service and a wine list that highlights the best of regional France aid the impression of an assured establishment. A shame, then, that unbalanced flavours marred our meal. To start, chicken liver parfait with Madeira jelly and onion marmalade was just too intense; in a main of barbecued lamb, the meat was tough and the herby flavours overpowered by an anchovy crouton, though the accompanying fennel purée was lovely. Also good: sardines à la provençale with sauce verte. Next time, we'll leave room for dessert, such as elderflower panna cotta, or chocolate mousse with toasted walnuts.

Available for hire. Babies and children admitted. Booking advisable. Separate rooms for parties, seating 8, 10 and 24. Vegetarian menu.

Gastropubs

When does a pub become a gastropub? And, for that matter, when does a gastropub become a restaurant? Since the 1990s, when the likes of the **Eagle** first began serving modern, high-quality food in a venerable boozer, the terms have gradually become blurred. Few pubs these days can survive without offering decent meals; and the urge to prise out drinkers to make room for more profitable diners has become irresistible at some establishments. To our minds, the best hostelries cater for all: giving imbibers an enticing choice of drinks (including real ales), the space for a natter and perhaps a pub quiz; and providing the hungry with freshly cooked, unfussy yet inventive nourishment. All too often a formula is followed, both in terms of decor (bare boards, mismatched furniture and all) and food (roast belly pork, lamb shank and mash, mundane tapas), but our favourite gastropubs are true London originals: the likes of Kentish Town's **Bull & Last** with its bucolic demeanour and own-cured provender; Dalston's resolutely pubby **Scolt Head**, where we were wowed by the potato and mustard lamb cakes; and Chiswick's spectacular **Duke of Sussex**, where you can dine under grand chandeliers on expertly wrought Spanish food. The section is ever-expanding: newcomers this year include the **Jugged Hare**, a meaty manifestation of the fast-growing Martin brothers' chain, and the **Lady Ottoline** and the **Pig & Butcher**, worthy siblings to the Princess of Shoreditch.

Central

Barbican

Jugged Hare NEW

49 Chiswell Street, EC1Y 4SA (7614 0134, www.thejuggedhare.com). Barbican tube or Moorgate tube/rail. **Open** 6.30am-11pm Mon-Wed; 6.30am-midnight Thur, Fri; 7am-midnight Sat; 7am-10.30pm Sun. **Breakfast served** 6.30-10.30am Mon-Fri; 7-11.30am Sat, Sun. **Lunch served** noon-3.30pm Mon-Fri; noon-4pm Sat. **Dinner served** 5.30-10.45pm Mon-Fri; 6-10.45pm Sat. **Meals served** noon-9.30pm Sun. **Main courses** £12-£27. **Set meal** (5.30-6.30pm, 9.30-11pm) £22 2 courses, £27 3 courses. **Credit** AmEx, MC, V.

Part of Ed and Tom Martin's ten-strong empire, the Jugged Hare has been handsomely done out, with a lovely oak floor, red leather seating and more than a scattering of stuffed and mounted animals. The bar is an idealised version of an old drinking haunt; pints of real ale (four on draught) are downed at tables fashioned from antique whisky barrels. Bar snacks are a cut-above: chips and gravy; pork crackling with apple sauce; venison scotch egg with cumberland sauce. Vegetarians will have got the message by now. Meat rules, with just one veggie dish of the day, though there's plenty of seafood on the dining-room menu (prettiest item: poached langoustine worthy of a still-life painting). Game is a feature: a perfectly cooked wood pigeon (from the rotisserie) was helped to star status by the accompanying lentils with dripping. Also good was a super-size wild boar and venison sausage, which we paired with a sprightly beetroot and fennel 'slaw. The kitchen can do delicate too – lemon junket with blood orange jelly was a dreamy finish. Bland bread was the only duff note. Dishes come from an open kitchen, a space that adds warmth and light to an already appealing dining room. Staff are well drilled, enthusiastic and knowledgeable about the menu and (impressive) wine list. Overall, there's a great sense of pride and attention to detail – nicely epitomised by the bespoke Jugged Hare bottled pale ale, commissioned from Sambrook's Brewery.
Available for hire. Babies and children welcome: high chairs. Booking advisable. **Map 5 P5.**

Bloomsbury

Lady Ottoline NEW

11A Northington Street, WC1N 2JF (7831 0008, www.theladyottoline.com). Russell Square or Chancery Lane tube. **Open** noon-11.30pm Mon-Sat; noon-10pm Sun. **Lunch served** noon-3.30pm, **dinner served** 6.30-10pm Mon-Sat. **Meals served** noon-8pm Sun. **Main courses** £9.95-£18.50. **Set lunch** (Mon-Fri) £15 2 courses, £19 3 courses. **Credit** AmEx, MC, V.

Full tables on a weekday evening are testimony to this buzzy gastropub's success since reopening in late 2011. Under the same owners as Shoreditch's Princess, the Victorian former boozer has been similarly renovated with an intelligent blend of smartness and old-pubbiness. The new name evokes Bloomsbury Groupie Lady Ottoline Morrell, and her famously large nose looks down from several photos. You can eat in the fairly noisy bar, or a snug upstairs dining room. Main menus are somewhat pricier than the gastropub norm, but more ambitious, with imaginative Mod-British combinations that on our visit would have been excellent if not for a few misses. In a salad of rare roast sirloin, pickles and wensleydale, the meat and cheese were great, but were presented in an overwhelming pile of rocket; to follow, wild

mushroom and summer bean tart with chargrilled fennel made for a lovely seasonal vegetarian choice, but was again heavily over-rocketed. Another main, slow-roasted pork belly, was juicy and tender, served with delicious braised cheek and roast carrots. Wines and beers are well chosen and well priced; service was friendly if rather ditzy. Skip the rocket addiction and this will be one to watch.
Babies and children welcome until 6pm: high chairs. Booking advisable lunch; dinner Thur, Fri. Separate rooms for parties, seating 10 and 60. Tables outdoors (3, pavement). **Map 4 M4.**

Norfolk Arms

28 Leigh Street, WC1H 9EP (7388 3937, www.norfolkarms.co.uk). Euston tube/rail. **Open** 11am-11pm Mon-Sat; noon-10.30pm Sun. **Lunch served** noon-3pm Mon-Fri; noon-4pm Sat. **Dinner served** 6-10.15pm Mon-Sat. **Meals served** noon-10.15pm Sun. **Tapas served** noon-10.15pm daily. **Main courses** £9.50-£13. **Tapas** £2-£12. **Credit** AmEx, MC, V.

Everything seems in place – relaxed environment, friendly staff, lively bar where some come simply to drink (draught Sagres or Theakston's XB, perhaps) – but somehow the Norfolk Arms didn't quite hit the spot on our last visit. How could you go wrong with a starter of Lyme Bay crab with ginger, chilli, honey, soy and sesame oil? There were just too many competing flavours. Goat's cheese crostini with mizuna and beetroot salad worked better, with a little less going on. Main courses didn't seem overpriced, as they sometimes can in the more self-regarding gastropubs, but marinated sea bream, roasted cherry tomato, peppers and fennel felt slightly like hard work, picking the whole fish apart. Free-range chicken breast, pardina lentils and red wine jus was a more successful combination. There was variety in the puddings, but our choice of apple and raspberry crumble was unwise – fine if you like your crumble oaty and pretend-healthy, not particularly if you don't. Service was good, yet a 12.5% charge for it was automatically added to the bill. We wanted to like the Norfolk Arms – and thought we would – more than we actually did.
Babies and children admitted: high chairs. Booking advisable. Separate rooms for parties, seating 10 and 20. Tables outdoors (9, pavement). **Map 4 L3.**

City

White Swan Pub & Dining Room

108 Fetter Lane, EC4A 1ES (7242 9696, www.thewhiteswanlondon.com). Chancery Lane tube. **Open** 11am-11pm Mon; 11am-midnight Tue-Thur; 11am-1am Fri. **Lunch served** noon-3pm, **dinner served** 6-10pm Mon-Fri. **Main courses** £14.50-£20. **Set lunch** (noon-1pm) £16 2 courses, £21 3 courses; (noon-3pm) £27 2 courses, £31 3 courses. **Credit** AmEx, MC, V.

Between Chancery Lane and Fleet Street, this outpost of the ETM empire (the Gun, the Botanist, the Jugged Hare and so on) is perfectly pitched at affluent local workers. It's a rebuild of an older pub of the same name on the site, and follows the model of the group's other venues: smartly traditional ground-floor bar with a small but well-kept selection of real ales (two Adnam's, one Wandle on our visit); rather posh dining room on the first, complete with tablecloths and attentive service. And tallying with our experience of other ETM pubs, the ambitious food is almost there – it reads very well on the menu, it looks fantastic on the plate, but afterwards there's a feeling something is missing. However, that's a minor criticism. Both our starters were delicate ensembles of summery igredients – a salad of young leek, carrot and scotched quail's egg with goat curd, and a mackerel fillet with mackerel tartar and pickled beetroot. Mains are mainly meaty, with the likes of stuffed saddle of rabbit, mutton with grilled tongue and wild garlic purée, or 45-day aged sirloin all making an appearance. Most evenings, the wood-panelled bar throngs with unwinding besuited professionals.
Available for hire. Babies and children admitted. Booking advisable. Separate room for parties, seats 52. **Map 11 N6.**

Clerkenwell & Farringdon

★ Eagle

159 Farringdon Road, EC1R 3AL (7837 1353). Farringdon tube/rail. **Open** noon-11pm Mon-Sat; noon-5pm Sun. **Lunch served** 12.30-3pm Mon-Fri; 12.30-3.30pm Sat; 12.30-4pm Sun. **Dinner served** 6.30-10.30pm Mon-Sat. **Main courses** £5-£15. **Credit** MC, V.

'An eagle for an Emperor,' the old poem goes. The pub named after that most regal of birds can

Jugged Hare. See p105.

certainly claim nobility of sorts. Perhaps the first to be given the 'gastro' tag, it maintains lofty standards to this day. The formula is simple. The left half of the bar (lining one wall of the single-room space) is given over to drinks; the right-hand side serves as a kitchen. Here, the day's offerings are chalked on blackboards, with ingredients on view in battered tins by the grill and stove: those bowls brimming with lemons, herbs and eggs aren't just for show. You might tend towards the pilaf or pasta, until you see what's on the grill – sardines, bream, Italian sausages. Blackboards imply rotation, but the menu has some stayers; bife ana, the pub's signature steak sandwich, is a constant. Turkish imam bayıldı, which pops up occasionally, is a dish of baked aubergine, coriander-spiked couscous and rich yoghurt. It's light and refreshing, in spite of the name ('the imam swooned'). There's a choice of four real ales, including (of course) Eagle IPA, plus a couple of guest brews. Be prepared to share a table, whether you're sitting under the high ceilings of the wood-panelled interior, or at one of the four pavement benches.
Babies and children admitted. Bookings not accepted. Tables outdoors (4, pavement). **Map 5 N4.**

Marylebone

Duke of Wellington

94A Crawford Street, W1H 2HQ (7723 2790, www.thedukew1.co.uk). Baker Street tube or Marylebone tube/rail. **Open** noon-11pm Mon-Sat; noon-10.30pm Sun. **Lunch served** noon-3pm Mon-Fri; noon-4pm Sat; 12.30-4.30pm Sun. **Dinner served** 6.30-10pm Mon-Fri; 7-10pm Sat; 7-9pm Sun. **Main courses** £13-£38. **Set lunch** (noon-1.30pm Mon-Thur) £14.95 2 courses. **Credit** AmEx, MC, V.

One of those smart venues that's more restaurant than pub (just a few seats at the bar), the Duke of Wellington attracts a well-heeled Marylebone clientele to enjoy food a tad more adventurous than the gastropub norm – roast veal and lobster salad with endives and a sweet dill dressing, say, or a truffled mozzarella starter – alongside the genre's regulars of fish, pork belly and confit duck. On a recent visit, pea and mint soup was full of flavour but watery; steamed prawns was a generous portion of meaty crustacea, with own-made mayo. A main of slow-roast lamb shoulder with pomegranate was exquisitely tender, with warm, mellow spicing and a subtle sweetness, served with nicely dressed salad. But provençal fish stew (mussels, prawns, octopus and hake hardly swimming in half a centimetre of fish stock) was disappointing. The kitchen got experimental with pudding, offering a chocolate and beetroot brownie with horseradish and mascarpone ice-cream. Instead, we shared a superb lime and chocolate crème brûlée. An excellent bottle of New Zealand sauvignon, a 12.5% service charge and a pound each for four bits of bread helped the bill to just under a ton.
Babies and children admitted: high chairs. Separate room for parties, seats 25. Tables outdoors (6, pavement). **Map 2 F5.**

Queen's Head & Artichoke

30-32 Albany Street, NW1 4EA (7916 6206, www.theartichoke.net). Great Portland Street or Regent's Park tube. **Open** 11am-11pm Mon-Sat; noon-10.30pm Sun. **Lunch served** noon-3pm Mon-Fri; 12.30-4pm Sat. **Dinner served** 6-10.30pm Mon-Sat. **Meals served** 12.30-10.15pm Sun. **Tapas served** noon-10.15pm Mon-Sat; 12.30-10.15pm Sun. **Main courses** £10-£16. **Tapas** £1.50-£12.50. **Credit** AmEx, MC, V.

A short step from Regent's Park and Fitzrovia, this fine old pub retains plenty of classic Victorian features – grand wooden panelling, lofty leaded windows – as a backdrop to its modern metropolitan gastropub identity. By contrast, a highlight of the menu is the long tapas list, which includes both excellent versions of Spanish favourites (creamy serrano ham croquettes, roasted peppers) and more pan-Mediterranean options, such as sweet potato and raisin couscous or bright, refreshing salads. Ingredients are consistently outstanding, and the range so broad that picking and choosing takes time. The shorter yet still imaginative Mod Euro main menu is also served in the bar, though to relax over a meal it's best to get a table in the cosy upstairs dining room, with its original fireplace. Dishes on the regularly changing list neatly avoid established gastropub routines, as in black pudding ravioli with a piquillo pepper sauce, or another Spanish-based option, baked hake with clams. Drink is also a draw, with a wine list that's short enough to be easily readable but still presents plenty of ably selected quality labels at below-average prices, along with a good mix of cocktails and beers (cask and others).
Babies and children welcome: high chairs. Separate room for parties, seats 50. Tables outdoors (6, garden; 8, pavement). **Map 3 H4.**

Lady Ottoline. See p105.

Pimlico

Orange Public House & Hotel

37 Pimlico Road, SW1W 8NE (7881 9844, www.theorange.co.uk). Sloane Square tube. **Open** 8am-11.30pm Mon-Thur; 8am-midnight Fri, Sat; 8am-10.30pm Sun. **Breakfast served** 8am-11.30am, **meals served** noon-9.30pm daily. **Main courses** £12.50-£16.50. **Credit** AmEx, MC, V.

Come Saturday evenings, folk squeeze into the Orange until its pips squeak, and the ground-floor bar seems constantly busy. With a casual vibe in its succession of elegantly attired adjoining rooms – and Adnams ale, Meantime lager and Aspall's cider on tap – this hostelry-cum-hotel makes a great pit-stop. The first-floor restaurant is decked out in the same style of weathered wood and tastefully taupe furnishings. An appealing menu covers a broad range of straightforward, well-executed comfort food. Crispy fried baby squid made a fresh, light opener to a meal. Wood-fired pizzas are a speciality, and we were impressed by the crust of a pizza packed with artichokes, olives, wild mushrooms and smoked mozzarella. Enjoyable too was a steak, Guinness and cheddar pie, the robust flavour of which helped take the chill off a cold day. The accompanying chunky chips were perfectly cooked: soft on the inside, crisp outside. Desserts are pricey at £7, but an orange and champagne jelly with blood orange sorbet was (wobbly) happiness on a

plate. To drink, there's an enticingly varied wine list, supplemented by beers and cocktails. Add staff who are always keen to assist, and it's small wonder the Orange is so popular – as are the other pubs in the Cubit House group, the Grazing Goat in W1, and the Pantechnicon and the Thomas Cubitt in SW1.
Available for hire. Babies and children welcome: high chairs; nappy-changing facilities. Booking advisable. Disabled: toilet. Separate rooms for parties, seating up to 75. Tables outdoors (5, pavement). **Map 15 G11.**

West

Chiswick

★ Duke of Sussex

75 South Parade, W4 5LF (8742 8801, www.thedukeofsussex.co.uk). Chiswick Park tube. **Open** noon-11pm Mon-Thur, Sun; noon-midnight Fri, Sat. **Meals served** noon-10.30pm Mon-Sat; noon-9.30pm Sun. **Main courses** £11-£17.50. **Credit** AmEx, MC, V.

Lively for the Sunday quiz night, this well-appointed pub has a large central counter in the main room, which leads to a dramatic dining room, thence the beer garden. That dining room is worth lingering over: half a dozen grand chandeliers hang from a lofty ceiling that's finished off with a kind of protruding greenhouse of skylights, decorated with cherubs. In such a setting, you might expect the food to struggle to make an impact, but the menu is both focused and inventive, having made a decisive shift towards Spain since our last visit. Of the 30 or so tapas and larger dishes, there was plenty to amuse us among the small plates alone. Razor clams with chilli and chorizo were simply presented, cascading out of their distinctive shells, done to a turn and packed with flavour; chipirones (baby squid) were similarly tender, with a slight crunch to the peppery batter. Other dishes – aubergine fritters; prawns with chilli and garlic under two slices of tomato bread; cecina flatbread with Pedro Ximénez sauce – were perfectly competent, if not sensational. Topped off with an ice-cold half bottle of fino, delivered by a warm, quick-witted waitress, this was an exceptional meal.
Babies and children welcome until 5pm: high chairs; nappy-changing facilities. Booking advisable dinner. Disabled: toilet. Tables outdoors (37, back garden; 3, front garden).

Roebuck

122 Chiswick High Road, W4 1PU (8995 4392, www.theroebuckchiswick.co.uk). Turnham Green tube. **Open** 11am-11pm Mon-Sat; noon-10.30pm Sun. **Lunch served** noon-4pm Mon-Fri; noon-5pm Sat, Sun. **Dinner served** 6-10pm Mon-Thur, Sun; 6-10.30pm Fri, Sat. **Main courses** £9.50-£18.50. **Set lunch** (Mon-Fri) £5 1 course. **Credit** AmEx, MC, V.

There's a degree of accomplishment here that's missing from many otherwise distinguished gastropubs. Perhaps the well-spaced chairs and tables to one side of the bar lend an air of Parisian-brasserie dignity that would be lost if the front sofas-and-slouching section extended further; perhaps it was just the combination of a leafy beer garden, a summer's day and a zingy lemon and ginger mojito. Duck egg with brown shrimps, unadvertised but welcome capers, samphire and sourdough toast made a perfect starter, while the wonderfully textured main of plump orzotto (pearl barley risotto), rendered an appetising green by its broad beans, only suffered from a degree too much parmesan. The menu is inventive – in the addition of slightly overpowering hazelnuts to asparagus with pea shoots, perhaps too much so – and due attention is given to details such as an excellent side of mash. The onglet could have been rarer, and offering a whole marrowbone to scrape out might be too much of a good thing, but the accompanying dressed parsley salad with thin rings of onion was superbly judged. Drinks on tap are also worth exploring: on this visit, Sharp's summer pilsner flavoured with thyme.
Available for hire. Babies and children welcome until 7pm: children's menu; high chairs; nappy-changing facilities. Disabled: toilet. Tables outdoors (20, garden; 3, pavement).

Ealing

Ealing Park Tavern

222 South Ealing Road, W5 4RL (8758 1879, www.ealingparktavern.com). South Ealing tube. **Open** noon-11pm Mon-Thur, Sun; noon-midnight Fri, Sat. **Lunch served** noon-3pm Mon-Fri; noon-4pm Sat. **Dinner served** 6-9.30pm Mon-Thur; 6-10pm Fri, Sat. **Meals served** noon-9pm Sun. **Main courses** £10-£15. **Credit** AmEx, MC, V.

There's no doubt that this is a popular pub. On a Sunday lunch visit, every table in the dining room was full with families, with drinkers packing the large main bar and garden. The draw is an unfussy atmosphere: this is a proper, old-fashioned boozer that may have leaned towards gastropub, but not forgotten its roots. There are nearly 20 wines by the glass, but real ales too (Sharps Doom Bar, say, or Brakspear's bitter), and Pimm's in the summer. Dark wood fittings mix with quirky pictures on the walls and mismatched tables. The open kitchen is a low point – more school canteen than appealing – and make sure you avoid the table spotlit by the glowing heat lamps of the servery. Service throughout remained inattentive. Food, on the other hand, was decent if not memorable. Modern gastropub dishes on a regularly changing menu include starters such as 'textures' of asparagus – a rather flavourless (but pleasant enough) green custard – with a seasonal salad of peas, broad beans and parmesan. Mains run from steak to wild mushroom risotto; our fish and chips had good fish but disappointingly stodgy chips. Finish with something from the English cheese menu.
Available for hire. Babies and children welcome until 6.30pm: high chairs; nappy-changing facilities. Disabled: toilet. Tables outdoors (20, garden).

Shepherd's Bush

Anglesea Arms

35 Wingate Road, W6 0UR (8749 1291, www.anglesea-arms.com). Goldhawk Road or Ravenscourt Park tube. **Open** 11am-11pm Mon-Sat; noon-10.30pm Sun. **Lunch served** 12.30-2.45pm Mon-Fri; 12.30-3pm Sat; 12.30-3.30pm Sun. **Dinner served** 7-10pm Mon; 7-10.30pm Tue-Sat; 6.30-9.30pm Sun. **Main courses** £13-£17. **Credit** MC, V.

From being one of the most popular gastropubs around a few years ago, the Anglesea Arms has become a bit so-what. We couldn't fault the staff the night we ate in the light-filled dining room (off the cosy, very pubby bar, where food is also served). Everyone, from barman to waitress, was charm itself, and a jug of tap water arrived on the table before we'd even asked. But the view of the open kitchen is not a glamorous one, and what came out of it was workaday too. Fish soup with all the trimmings seemed bland, through the rouille helped lift it; to follow, sea bream with courgette, artichoke, aubergine and sauce vierge was an excellent piece of fish held back by oily accompaniments. A flavoursome bavette steak, with decent chips and a nicely dressed watercress salad, proved the safer option. Own-made ice-creams (honeycomb, strawberry) and sorbets (passionfruit, blueberry) are a feature of the short dessert list. The choice of drinks is good, with bitters such as Harveys Sussex Best, and Otter from the Otter brewery; Weston's Old Rosie scrumpy from Herefordshire; and ten or so wines by the glass. So – a not-bad local, but in no way a destination gastropub.
Babies and children admitted. Tables outdoors (9, pavement). **Map 20 B3.**

Princess Victoria

217 Uxbridge Road, W12 9DH (8749 5886, www.princessvictoria.co.uk). Shepherd's Bush tube. **Open** 11.30am-11pm Mon-Thur, Sun; 11.30am-midnight Fri, Sat. **Lunch served** noon-3pm Mon-Sat; noon-4.30pm Sun. **Dinner served** 6.30-10.30pm Mon-Sat; 6.30-9.30pm Sun. **Main courses** £10.50-£16.50. **Set lunch** (Mon-Fri) £12.50 2 courses, £15 3 courses. **Credit** MC, V.

When this lovingly renovated former gin palace opened to critical fanfare in 2008, locals and White City BBC staff flocked to the spacious bar (serving first-rate, mostly meaty snacks) and elegant dining room – a leap up from the Bush's existing venues. Yet later that year, the Queen Adelaide sprang up down the road, followed by the beast that is the Westfield shopping mall, shifting the focus closer to the tube stations. On our latest visit here, we were alone in the dining area for most of the evening. With an impressive wine list (36 by the glass), three real ales on tap, and smart, sober panelling painted a drawing-room green, the Princess Victoria positions itself at the upper end of gastropubbery, yet prices remain on the whole reasonable. A light main course of own-made Thai sausages with fresh chilli dipping sauce and matchstick vegetables cost under £10, though we succumbed to additional chips: triple-cooked, chunky beauties. From the grill selection, our cheerful waiter recommended the hanger steak for its tenderness: the thinly sliced cut was a revelation. There are sharing boards of smoked fish and pork for more relaxed eating, along with a selection of rarely seen British cheeses.
Babies and children welcome: high chairs. Booking advisable. Separate room for parties, seats 60. Tables outdoors (10, garden).
Map 20 A2.

Queen Adelaide

412 Uxbridge Road, W12 0NR (8746 2573, www.thequeenadelaidew12.co.uk). Shepherd's Bush Market tube. **Open** noon-11pm Mon-Thur; noon-midnight Fri; 10am-midnight Sat; 10am-11pm Sun. **Breakfast served** 10am-noon Sat, Sun. **Lunch served** noon-4pm Mon-Fri; noon-5pm Sat. **Dinner served** 6-10.30pm Mon-Sat. **Meals served** noon-9.30pm Sun. **Main courses** £10.50-£17.50. **Credit** AmEx, MC, V.

Queen Adelaide feels a genteel world away from the bustling Uxbridge Road outside. Its smart, chandelier-lit dining room is separated from a

Brown Dog

buzzing pub by a large central bar, giving the dark wood-clad space a lively feel, even on quiet, midweek evenings. Harveys Sussex Best, plus two or three regularly changing guests, keep the ale drinkers merry. Most dishes on the daily-changing menu deviate little from the standard gastropub repertoire, though there are a few interesting surprises amid the beer-battered cod, Angus beef burger, weekend brunches and sticky toffee pud. Starters in particular pack a refined punch, with sautéed chicken livers made sweet by tart red grapes and sherry vinegar, and potted salt beef counterbalanced by watercress, apple and capers. The mains were altogether less impressive. A dish promising three types of lamb (spiced skewer, merguez and kofta) was generously sized, and the meat had been perfectly cooked, but a mound of shamefully bland couscous let the side down. Grilled sea bass was similarly marred by some flavourless truffle potatoes. Nevertheless, the Adelaide's friendly, proficient service and warm atmosphere make it a pleasant place to linger over a meal.
Available for hire. Babies and children welcome: children's menu; high chairs; nappy-changing facilities. Booking advisable. Disabled: toilet. Tables outdoors (12, terrace). **Map 20 A1**.

Westbourne Park

Cow

89 Westbourne Park Road, W2 5QH (7221 0021, www.thecowlondon.co.uk). Royal Oak or Westbourne Park tube. **Open** noon-11pm Mon-Sat; noon-10.30pm Sun. **Lunch served** noon-3.30pm, **dinner served** 6-10.30pm Mon-Fri. **Meals served** noon-10.30pm Sat; noon-10pm Sun. **Main courses** £10-£15. **Set lunch** (Sun) £24 2 courses, £26 3 courses. **Credit** MC, V.
Looks rate highly at this Notting Hill pub – as well they might, with a Conran running the show (Tom, son of Terence). Downstairs is a retro kitsch bar with a simple Anglo-Irish menu specialising in oysters, seafood platters and Guinness for a happy crowd of locals and tourists. On a recent Sunday lunch visit, we opted for the first-floor dining room where a more formal menu, also heavy on seafood, is served amid flock wallpaper hung with carefully mismatched artwork. Expect well-executed pub classics: a half pint of prawns with mayo were plump and juicy, fresh from Cornwall. Roasts were reasonable and served with all the trimmings, including impressively towering yorkshires with the beef, though rather let down by the dense roast spuds. Apple crumble, however, was exemplary. A focus on high-quality, seasonal ingredients cooked simply goes a long way, and we liked the touch of bringing fresh radishes with cold, creamy butter and Maldon salt to the table with the bread. Dishes are perhaps a little overpriced given that this is casual dining with slightly patchy service, but huge, steaming portions make amends.
Available for hire. Babies and children admitted (bar until 4pm; restaurant). Tables outdoors (2, pavement). **Map 7 A5**.

South West

Barnes

Brown Dog

28 Cross Street, SW13 0AP (8392 2200, www.thebrowndog.co.uk). Barnes Bridge rail. **Open** noon-11pm daily. **Lunch served** noon-3pm Mon-Fri; noon-4pm Sat, Sun. **Dinner served** 7-10pm Mon-Sat; 6-9pm Sun. **Main courses** £13.95-£16.95. **Credit** AmEx, MC, V.
Set on a quiet residential street amid the bijou railway cottages of Barnes, the Brown Dog

Duke of Sussex. See p108.

continues to flourish. It's a good-looking spot, with cream panelling, vintage metal signs, and daylight flooding in; at night, candles appear, the handsome copper globe lights above the bar reflect in the polished red ceiling, and the atmosphere becomes positively romantic. There's a small, sunny back yard too. Shame that the chunky wooden tables are rather awkward; a green banquette around the edge is more comfortable. The short, seasonal menu keeps things simple. On a Sunday lunch in spring, most starters involved no cooking: oysters, half pint of prawns, cured salmon with beetroot. Mains included Dorset crab salad with chunky chips, and fettuccine with radicchio, pine nuts and sultanas (a long-term favourite), but most diners were enjoying the full-blown roasts: poussin or 28-day-aged British sirloin. Rhubarb and ginger cheesecake with stem ginger crème fraîche was a delight. Ingredients are of a high quality and cooking more than competent, but prices are a bit of a shocker. Most mains cost over £15 and roast beef £18 – though that doesn't seem to deter the affluent locals. Real ale fans get two well-kept brews (Sambrook's Wandle and Twickenham Ale, on our visit) and there's an appealing wine list.
Available for hire. Babies and children welcome: high chairs. Booking advisable. Tables outdoors (12, garden). Vegetarian menu.

Chelsea

Cadogan Arms

298 King's Road, SW3 5UG (7352 6500, www.thecadoganarmschelsea.com). Sloane Square tube then bus 19, 22 or 319. **Open** 11am-11pm Mon-Sat; 11am-10.30pm Sun. **Lunch served** noon-3.30pm, **dinner served** 6-10.30pm Mon-Fri. **Meals served** noon-10.30pm Sat; noon-9pm Sun. **Main courses** £12-£24. **Credit** AmEx, MC, V.
While the bar, serving a decent if unremarkable beer selection including Adnams and Flying Scotsman, is closest to the King's Road action, a step down takes you to the hunting lodge-style dining room of this very west London outpost of the ten-strong, east London-slanted ETM pub group. With fish sourced from Billingsgate, Cumbrian shorthorn beef steaks for two, provenance flagged up at every opportunity (this is not just asparagus; this is Norfolk asparagus) and the prerequisite retro bar snacks (black pudding scotch egg, fish fingers), the Cadogan ticks all the right boxes, but does nothing outstandingly different. The decor – leather seating and hunting trophies – is similar to other pubs in the group. The menu is meaty, though a goat's cheese salad with popcorn-sweet candied walnuts, and a huge portion of tagliatelle with wild garlic and oddly chewy parmesan shavings were satisfying enough. 'Essex' ham hock did not appear to be glazed as stated and came with gravy rather than the advertised parsley sauce, making for a very salty dish. There were no specials available due to a function upstairs – which also explained the long wait times.
Available for hire. Babies and children welcome: children's menu; high chairs. Booking advisable. Separate room for parties, seats 50. **Map 14 E12.**

Lots Road Pub & Dining Room

114 Lots Road, SW10 0RJ (7352 6645, www.lotsroadpub.com). Fulham Broadway tube or Imperial Wharf rail. **Open** 11am-11pm Mon-Sat; noon-10.30pm Sun. **Lunch served** noon-3pm Mon; noon-4pm Tue-Sat; noon-5pm Sun. **Dinner served** 6-10pm Mon-Sat; 6-9.30pm Sun. **Main courses** £10-£17. **Set meal** (Mon, dinner Sun) £10 2 courses. **Credit** AmEx, MC, V.
Though Lots Road is within stumbling distance of Chelsea Harbour, it seemed unlikely that it was residents of the luxury development filling the tables here on our Monday evening visit. The large corner pub, part of the London-wide Food & Fuel chain, is tastefully decorated in pale green shades with feature wallpaper and standing lamps, but it's a little scuffed around the edges, and service can be perfunctory. Family groups and noisy post-work drinkers formed most of the crowd. The bargain start-the-week set meal is a definite draw. As with the main menu (which features sausage and mash and cheeseburger alongside specials such as chargrilled côte de boeuf, or sea bass with samphire), choices on the 'two courses for a tenner' deal aren't wildly exciting, but fit the bill for a no-fuss meal out with friends. Jugs of tap water are brought as a matter of course, allowing you to eat cheaply without feeling cheap. Both our starter of courgette, tomato and edam tart – a wobbly, custardy slice – and main course pea and mint risotto were under-seasoned, but generous portions. To drink, there are a few wines costing under £20 a bottle and Adnams on tap.
Available for hire. Babies and children welcome: children's menu; high chairs. Booking advisable lunch Sun. Disabled: toilet. **Map 21 A1.**

Pig's Ear

35 Old Church Street, SW3 5BS (7352 2908, www.thepigsear.info). Sloane Square tube then bus 19, 22 or 319.
Pub **Open** noon-11pm Mon-Sat; noon-10.30pm Sun. **Lunch served** 12.30-3pm, **dinner served** 6-10pm Mon-Fri. **Meals served** noon-10pm Sat; noon-7pm Sun. **Main courses** £10-£23.
Restaurant **Dinner served** 6-10pm Mon-Sat. **Meals served** noon-4pm Sun. **Main courses** £14-£23.
Both **Credit** AmEx, MC, V.
Tucked away down a quaint street, the lack of outdoor space keeps this neighbourhood boozer fairly quiet on warm evenings even when, as one punter noted on our visit, 'the whole of Chelsea is out and about.' It's surprisingly un-fusty in style, the walls covered in 1960s movie posters and music memorabilia, with Guinness adverts plastering the route to the lighter, smarter upstairs dining room. The ground floor is mostly given over to drinking,

with real ales (from Battersea's Sambrook's, plus guest appearances from the likes of Cardiff's Brains), and Symonds cider enjoyed by a multi-generational crowd; the dining area is tucked away in a slightly cramped, gloomy corner. The piggy theme is carried through from Uley Brewery Pig's Ear ale to the rustic pork board, which features a mammoth scotch egg, unctuous belly, tooth-testing crackling, rillettes, terrine (slightly overpowered by a big dollop of piccalilli) and sausage rolls. Each element was an excellent example of its type, refreshingly free of twists in common with the rest of the menu (ignoring the strange garnish of salted crisps on a chilled vichyssoise). We found the service to be similarly fuss-free, with the staff cheerful and accommodating.
Available for hire. Babies and children welcome (dining room): high chairs. Booking advisable dining room. **Map 14 E12.**

Fulham

★ Harwood Arms HOT 50

Corner of Walham Grove and Farm Lane, SW6 1QP (7386 1847, www.harwoodarms.com). Fulham Broadway tube. **Open/snacks served** 5-11pm Mon; noon-11pm Tue-Fri; noon-midnight Sat; noon-10pm Sun. **Lunch served** 12.30-4pm Sun. **Dinner served** 6.30-9.30pm Mon; 7-9pm Sun. **Meals served** 12.30-9.30pm Tue-Sat. **Main courses** £17-£19. **Set lunch** (Tue-Fri) £18 2 courses, £24 3 courses. **Credit** AmEx, MC, V.
We had high expectations of the Harwood Arms (it's part owned by Brett Graham from the Ledbury), and we weren't disappointed. Set in what was an old corner pub, in residential Fulham, it's now firmly at the restaurant end of the gastropub spectrum, though there are stools for perching at the bar to enjoy a pint of Young's London Gold or a house bloody mary (with own-made tomato juice and thyme and chilli vodka). The stripped-down country-chic decor is easy on the eye, and the atmosphere laid-back, though the informally dressed young staff are alert. The artfully arranged food takes things to a different level. Game is a speciality. Strangely, roe deer and walnut terrine with spiced chutney, chicory and caramelised onion bread, though highly moreish, didn't pack as much of a gamey punch as expected. In contrast, warm 'salad' of wood pigeon with creamed livers, bitter leaves and turnips was a full-flavoured delight. Next, cheek and jowl of Middlewhite pork with celeriac and white cabbage was Sunday lunch perfection, though we're not sure crackling – served as a thin sliver – should be so refined. Fish is also handled with aplomb: witness roast plaice on the bone with potted shrimp butter, smoked mash and cooked baby gem lettuce. We can heartily recommend a side order of crispy garlic potatoes; a bar snack of venison rissoles is also a must. Poached peach with lemon thyme, raspberry sorbet and salted almonds is typical of the classy puddings. Lucky old Fulham.
Available for hire. Babies and children welcome: children's menu; high chairs. Booking advisable. Vegetarian menu. **Map 13 A12.**

Putney

Spencer

237 Lower Richmond Road, SW15 1HJ (8788 0640, www.thespencerpub.com). Putney Bridge tube or Putney rail or bus 22, 265, 485. **Open** 11am-midnight Mon-Sat; 11am-11pm Sun. **Lunch served** noon-3pm Mon-Fri; noon-4pm Sat. **Dinner served** 6-10pm Mon-Fri; 5-10pm Sat. **Meals served** noon-9pm Sun. **Main courses** £9.75-£24.95. **Credit** AmEx, MC, V.
On a sunny afternoon, the Spencer's numerous tables on the edge of Putney Common are a joy, especially for families or dog owners. They're large, solid, well-designed tables too, far better than the pub norm. The pub's corner premises are pleasant enough, with big windows, grey-green wood panelling and the usual battered wooden tables and old school chairs; leather sofas and banquettes mark out the restaurant area. It all gets a bit noisy when busy, though, and there are no quiet corners in which to hide. Amiable bar staff deal efficiently with any queue, dispensing pints (three real ales plus standard lagers) or wine (a nicely priced list, with around 20 choices by the glass). Food is a please-all selection of standards, including assorted burgers, pies (shepherd's, fish), cumberland sausages and mash, chicken caesar salad and a few pasta dishes. Start with a classic prawn cocktail; finish with lemon tart or crème brûlée. It's not adventurous, but execution is better than you might expect. Crab, chilli and parsley linguine came with copious amounts of fresh crab, and was a nicely balanced mix of flavours, though strangely devoid of any oil. Fish pie was creamy and packed with salmon, but marred by a too-sharp sauce. Sunday brings roasts with all the trimmings.
Babies and children welcome until 9pm: high chairs; nappy-changing facilities. Disabled: toilet. Tables outdoors (8, pavement; 30, common).

Wimbledon

Earl Spencer

260-262 Merton Road, SW18 5JL (8870 9244, www.theearlspencer.co.uk). Southfields tube. **Open** 11am-11pm Mon-Thur; 11am-midnight Fri, Sat; noon-10.30pm Sun. **Lunch served** 12.30-2.30pm Mon-Sat; 12.30-3pm Sun. **Dinner served** 7-10pm Mon-Sat; 7-9.30pm Sun. **Main courses** £8.50-£14. **Set lunch** (Mon-Fri) £5.50-£10 1 course. **Credit** AmEx, MC, V.
Just the place for a well-pitched meal, the Earl Spencer is popular, yes, but has the distinct advantage of space. It feels every inch a proper Edwardian pub, the bar (with three real ales) bang in the middle of a cavernous room. The venue appeals to anyone who appreciates inviting food and

Prince Arthur. See p117.

GASTROPUBS

Canton Arms

audible conversation; it's so devoid of faddishness, and focused on decent grub, that the epithet 'gastropub' – with its increasing connotations of the assembly line – doesn't quite do it justice. Justin Aubrey's menu changes daily and is posted online like clockwork. Such care extends to the dishes themselves: prepped and primped, tweaked and tuned, always with the welcome addition of own-baked bread (no extra charge). A weekend lunch can stretch as long as you desire, no questions asked. Our moreish duck salad was polished off with unseemly haste. Chickpea fritters with salsa and sour cream, soft-centred and crisply coated, were splendid. To finish, a large helping of eton mess was on the tidy side, with its neat wedge of soft meringue, but respectable nonetheless. Denizens of SW18 are spoiled here: every neighbourhood should have an Earl Spencer.
Babies and children welcome: high chairs. Bookings not accepted lunch Sun. Separate room for parties, seats 70. Tables outdoors (10, patio).

Fox & Grapes

9 Camp Road, SW19 4UN (8619 1300, www.foxandgrapeswimbledon.co.uk). Wimbledon tube/rail then bus 93. **Open** noon-11pm Mon-Thur; 11am-midnight Fri, Sat; noon-10.30pm Sun. **Lunch served** noon-3pm Mon-Sat; noon-4pm Sun. **Dinner served** 6-9.30pm Mon-Sat; 6-9pm Sun. **Main courses** £13.50-£31.50. **Set lunch** (Mon-Sat) £17.50 2 courses, £19.50 3 courses. **Credit** MC, V.
What was once a locals' local has morphed into an altogether more gentrified outpost, still skirted by the wild tumble of Wimbledon Common. Ramblers and their dogs might hole up at the bar, but they're a little sidelined by the influx of diners nestled into spruced-up leather upholstery, brogues tip-tapping on the parquet flooring. The Fox & Grapes was opened under the watchful eye of Claude Bosi (of Hibiscus fame) in early 2011, and has established itself as the go-to pub for south-west Londoners craving Michelin-style sparkle. Claude's brother, Cedric, heads day-to-day operations, while Julian Ward runs the kitchen. The menu flashes a certain Brit-infused charm, with its Herefordshire snails, Cornish pollack and Wye Valley asparagus. It's easy to have a fine meal here, but less so a truly exceptional one, which, at these prices, matters. Guinea fowl breast was robust enough but served with over-salted saffron linguini. Fisherman's pie was more of a treat, piping hot in the skillet but lacking clout. Steaks are a speciality and tucking into the 28-day-aged ribeye should satisfy ardent carnivores. In short, this operation knows its market – high-end foodies – but doesn't always deliver.
Available for hire. Babies and children welcome: children's menu; high chairs; nappy-changing facilities. Booking advisable Thur-Sun.

South

Balham

Avalon

16 Balham Hill, SW12 9EB (8675 8613, www.theavalonlondon.com). Clapham South tube. **Open** noon-11pm Mon-Wed; noon-midnight Thur; noon-1am Fri, Sat; noon-10.30pm Sun. **Lunch served** noon-3.30pm Mon-Fri; noon-4pm Sat. **Dinner served** 6-10.30pm Mon-Sat. **Meals served** noon-9pm Sun. **Main courses** £9.50-£21. **Credit** AmEx, MC, V.
When the Avalon gastropub opened in 2008, discerning Balham folk felt they'd at last got the bar and dining room they deserved. This spacious and well-proportioned pub is lavishly decorated in a faux-Victorian way, with massive bars with a good selection of real ales, a comfortable and attractively decorated dining area, a big landscaped rear garden that was arguably London's best at the time, and even a summer-long barbecue station for people eating outside. The cooking was ambitious, even the barbecue menu was a thrill. But that's all changed. A couple of years into the operation, the dedicated barbecue station was mothballed, and the dining room's menu has been dumbed down to the expected steaks, burgers, and fish and chips. On our most recent visit, service was excellent, and the simplest items on the menu prepared to a good standard, reflecting the high prices. We enjoyed a grilled tuna salad (no snip at £15.75), but a more ambitious 'Thai spiced salmon' played it too safe, with a 'green papaya slaw' that was closer to a western-style creamy cabbage coleslaw, and the promised spice flavours very understated indeed. But for lovely beers (Hook Norton's Hooky, Skinner's Betty Stogs, Timothy Taylor Landlord) and a jolly atmosphere, Avalon is the posh pub to beat in SW12.
Babies and children welcome: children's menu; crayons; high chairs; nappy-changing facilities. Booking advisable weekends. Disabled: toilet. Entertainment: DJ 9pm Fri, Sat. Separate room for parties, seats 20. Tables outdoors (22, garden; 10, pavement; 10, courtyard).

Stockwell

Canton Arms NEW

177 South Lambeth Road, SW8 1XP (7582 8710, www.cantonarms.com). Stockwell tube. **Open** 5-11pm Mon; 11am-11pm Tue-Sat; noon-10.30pm Sun. **Lunch served** noon-2.30pm Tue-Sat; noon-4pm Sun. **Dinner served** 6-10pm Mon-Sat. **Main courses** £12-£15. **Credit** MC, V.
Canton Arms is an excellent place to while away a Sunday afternoon or indulge in a slap-up evening meal. Both the stripped-wood dining room, with its mismatched chairs, and the cosy bar retain a pubby sort of feel. The kitchen serves rustic, meaty dishes that are the essence of modern British cookery, occasionally with the addition of some Italian or French flair. To start, fish or meat terrines or warm seasonal salads are the perfect way to whet the palate. Next, share a slow-cooked joint, or opt for a lighter risotto or fish – the menu changes daily – and finish with a decadent chocolate pot with cream, or a tart crumble. The pub serves a pleasing range of beers, and also provides an extensive Old World wine list, but it's hard to find a bottle for under £20. Service may not be speedy, but it's amiable, and the place is child-, baby-, and dog-friendly, making it especially popular at weekends. The snug dining room, congenial staff and often-accomplished food will keep us coming back for more.
Babies and children welcome until 9pm: high chairs; nappy-changing facilities. Bookings not accepted. Tables outdoors (8, pavement).

Streatham

Manor Arms

13 Mitcham Lane, SW16 6LQ (3195 6888, www.themanorarms.com). Streatham rail or bus 249. **Open** 11am-11pm Mon-Fri; 10am-midnight Sat; noon-midnight Sun. **Lunch served** noon-3pm Mon-Fri; 11am-4pm Sat. **Dinner served** 6-10pm Mon-Sat. **Meals served** noon-9pm Sun. **Main courses** £9-£15. **Set lunch** (Mon-Fri) £10 2 courses, £14 3 courses. **Set dinner** (Mon-Fri) £12.50 2 courses, £15.50 3 courses. **Credit** AmEx, MC, V.
A perfectly circular dining area at one end of this whopper of a gastropub makes a distinguished feature, a curved banquette snaking round the perimeter and large tiled columns offering support. The bar dispenses the likes of Doom Bar and Wandle Ale. An open kitchen next to the bar smacks of confidence, and while the glorious Sunday roasts are a sight to behold, other dishes are not such hard-hitters. Roasted slip sole and seafood salad – a garden of mussels, whelks and prawns – looked impressive but didn't entirely work, owing to the hot/cold temperature combination. The signature lancashire macaroni cheese, golden and bubbling, was served with only a perfunctory herb salad. Service was spirited but slightly distracted, seemingly owing to the volume of children vying for attention, straddling leather sofas and playing ball. For a parent, the family-friendly attitude is a welcome change from the public froideur so often accorded under-tens in the UK. For a non-parent, it can feel a little like being hurled into an episode of *Outnumbered*. Activities across the week include storytime, Punch and Judy, and pop-up children's clothing shops. There's a kids' menu, naturally. No wonder it's won an award from Mumsnet.
Available for hire. Babies and children welcome: children's menu; high chairs; nappy-changing facilities. Booking advisable Sun. Disabled: toilet. Tables outdoors (20, garden).

Tooting

Antelope

76 Mitcham Road, SW17 9NG (8672 3888, www.theantelopepub.com). Tooting Broadway tube. **Open** 4-11pm Mon-Wed; 4pm-midnight Thur; 4pm-1am Fri; noon-1am Sat; noon-11pm Sun. **Lunch served** noon-4pm Sat; noon-5pm Sun. **Dinner served** 6-10.30pm Mon-Sat. **Main courses** £8.50-£15. **Credit** MC, V.
Seemingly sensitively restored, albeit not to any discernible decade, the Antelope is a vintage festival of a pub, a characterful sprawl of bar, dining room, games room and garden. The Antic Collective does a neat line in transforming ailing London pubs, and this is no exception. Its particular version of 20th-century austerity-chic incorporates everything from an old Singer sewing machine perched atop a dresser to a tankard collection and blowsy tabletop flowers that look as if they've been plucked from the nearest garden. There's lots to like about the Antelope, including the real ale choice: Purity's Ubu, Adnams' Lighthouse and four regularly changing guest beers. But service was haphazard and courses took a long time coming. Dishes are a gastropub roll-call, conducted with some finesse. Guinea fowl and ham hock terrine was good and robust, but would have benefited from bringing to room temperature. Broccoli fritters came piled high and so heavily battered that this dish may actually count as a minus figure from your 'five a day'. A bloody-mary burger was pleasingly spiced, while pan-fried sardines came with a piquant cucumber, dill and chilli salad. All in all, a little rough round the edges, but with the necessary hallmarks of a Brit eccentric in the making.

Available for hire. Babies and children welcome: high chairs. Booking advisable. Disabled: toilet. Separate room for parties, seats 150. Tables outdoors (20, garden).

Waterloo

★ Anchor & Hope

36 The Cut, SE1 8LP (7928 9898). Southwark tube or Waterloo tube/rail. **Open** 5-11pm Mon; 11am-11pm Tue-Sat; 12.30-5pm Sun. **Lunch served** noon-2.30pm Tue-Sat; 2pm sitting Sun. **Dinner served** 6-10.30pm Mon-Sat. **Main courses** £12-£20. **Credit** MC, V.

The Anchor & Hope has dominated Waterloo's gastronomic scene for over a decade, and is still among its highlights. The well-known 'no reservations' seating policy doesn't seem to deter punters, meaning that diners wanting to sample the robust seasonal British cooking must often wait in the pub area (separated from the restaurant by a heavy drape) until a table becomes free. Fortunately, decent draught ales and wines are on hand. On busy weekday evenings, things can get noisy, and some diners are seated at communal tables, so this isn't an ideal spot for an intimate dinner. But there's a convivial vibe, helped by pleasingly down-to-earth yet efficient staff. Maroon walls are hung with for-sale modern art, and heavily weathered wooden tables are surrounded by mismatched chairs – but don't mistake the A&H for a prosaic gastropub. It's always filled with chatter, and customers range from laddy City boys to thespians filling up before a visit to the nearby Old or Young Vic theatres. The nose-to-tail menu features dishes such as thinly sliced ox tongue with lentils, green sauce and mustard fruits; and braised suckling kid with bacon, fennel, chickpeas and aïoli. Vegetarian food is limited, but a flavourful chicory tart came with a rich concoction of dried ceps, cream and parmesan.

Babies and children welcome: high chairs. Bookings not accepted Mon-Sat; advisable Sun. Tables outdoors (5, pavement). **Map 11 N8.**

South East

Dulwich

Rosendale

65 Rosendale Road, SE21 8EZ (8761 9008, www.therosendale.co.uk). West Dulwich rail.
Bar **Open** noon-11pm Mon-Thur, Sun; noon-1am Fri, Sat. **Lunch served** noon-3.30pm Mon-Sat. **Dinner served** 6-10pm Mon-Thur; 6-10.30pm Fri, Sat. **Meals served** noon-9pm Sun.
Restaurant **Lunch served** noon-3.30pm Mon-Fri; noon-4pm Sat. **Dinner served** 6-10.30pm Mon-Sat. **Meals served** noon-9pm Sun.
Both **Main courses** £9-£16. **Credit** AmEx, MC, V.

The Rosendale is the only food-focused pub to serve West Dulwich; perhaps it's the lack of competition that has caused standards to slip despite this handsome establishment's refurbishment by the well-regarded Renaissance group. The sheer expanse of the dining area, while an appealing place to sit (bright by day, cosy yet elegant in the evening), is clearly challenging to fill with diners. On our last visit, we noted punters migrating from the bar area to share a bottle of wine and maybe a bar snack. Arriving at a quiet time, we nonetheless faced a considerable wait for our food. When the meal arrived, even the promising 'specials' had the air of weary, part pre-cooked standbys: stodgy risotto; 'pan-fried' duck with grey flesh and soggy, resilient skin; old-school cabbage. The 'summer fruit' tart owed its crisp, buttery pastry to last-minute assembly that threw up unhalved grapes and unripe mango. Wondering at the pub's popularity, we noted relaxed family groups populating the extensive, decked back garden with its dedicated toddlers' play area. Add fairly priced wines and decent cask beers to the mix and the Rosendale continues to fulfil a welcome, if not gastronomically exalted, function.

Babies and children welcome: high chairs; nappy-changing facilities; play area. Disabled: toilet. Separate rooms for parties, seating 25-100. Tables outdoors (40, garden).

East Dulwich

Palmerston

91 Lordship Lane, SE22 8EP (8693 1629, www.thepalmerston.net). East Dulwich rail or bus 185, 176, P13. **Open** noon-11pm Mon-Thur; noon-midnight Fri, Sat; noon-10.30pm Sun. **Lunch served** noon-2.30pm Mon-Fri; noon-3pm Sat, Sun. **Dinner served** 7-10pm Mon-Sat; 7-9.30pm Sun. **Main courses** £11-£16. **Set lunch** (Mon-Fri) £12.50 2 courses, £16 3 courses. **Credit** MC, V.

Eight or so years after reckoning East Dulwich was ready to embrace the gastropub trend, the team behind the Palmerston – notably ex-Bibendum head chef Jamie Younger – are justified in considering their handsome establishment a community stalwart. Declaring the provenance of the carefully sourced produce and the hanging age of the beef clearly goes down well with the customers, judging by the buzz on an early weekday evening. Both the banquette-lined bar area and the more formal wood-panelled room with its church chairs offer the same robust 'Brit-Med' menu, alongside decent real ales and a sound selection of wines by the glass. While certain dishes (such as Galloway Short Horn ribeye) are mainstays, others reflect seasonality. On our late-spring visit, wild garlic greens featured prominently alongside British asparagus, morel mushrooms and Jersey Royals. Sauces, condiments and garnishes pack a punch, and the olive-packed breads hold their own too. Desserts exhibit a lighter touch, whether modern or retro; arctic roll proved an irresistible medley of light sponge, creamy vanilla ice and tart berry preserve. The eclectic music may owe much to the 'Secret DJ' trend; exhibits by local artists provide more welcome distraction.

Babies and children welcome: high chairs; nappy-changing facilities. Booking advisable dinner; weekends. Tables outdoors (8, pavement). **Map 23 C4.**

New Cross

New Cross House

316 New Cross Road, SE14 6AF (8691 8875, www.thenewcrosshouse.com). New Cross or New Cross Gate rail. **Open** noon-midnight Mon-Thur, Sun; noon-1am Fri, Sat. **Meals served** noon-10pm Mon-Sat; noon-9.30pm Sun. **Main courses** £7-£10.50. **Credit** AmEx, MC, V.

Much thought has clearly gone into New Cross House's international menu of simple, appetising plates – 'foot-long' hot dog; warm beetroot, feta and horseradish tart; chorizo roast potatoes with confit chicken; sloppy salt beef bagels; juicy rosemary-marinated lamb kebabs with crisp salad; dahl with flatbreads. There are pizzas too, big and crispy and cooked in a wood-fired oven; and Ice Cream Union ice-creams, which come in left-field flavours such as coconut sorbet and Jack Daniel's. From the street, the building looks a smart, unassuming sort of place, more gentrified than some of its neighbours, but the interior goes on forever with a long, well-stocked bar, raised booths, a TV screen, table football, a piano and a dartboard. The pub is sibling to the Florence microbrewery in Herne Hill and East Dulwich's the Actress, so there are house beers such as Weasel and Bonobo on tap. We particularly love the playful photocopied 'wallpaper', which replicates the original Victorian tiling. Out back there's not just a beer garden, but a whole other world including a ping-pong table and a magical two-storey barn with comfy sofas and wood-fired heaters. A fun, friendly place with plenty going on.

Available for hire. Babies and children welcome: high chairs; nappy-changing facilities. Booking advisable Fri-Sun. Disabled: toilet. Tables outdoors (30, garden).

East

Docklands

Gun

27 Coldharbour, E14 9NS (7515 5222, www.thegundocklands.com). Canary Wharf tube or Blackwall DLR. **Open** 11am-midnight Mon-Sat; 11am-11pm Sun. **Lunch served** noon-3pm Mon-Fri; noon-4pm Sat, Sun. **Dinner served** 6-10.30pm Mon-Sat; 6.30-9.30pm Sun. **Main courses** £12.50-£28. **Credit** AmEx, MC, V.

A steady walk from Blackwall DLR or Canary Wharf, the Gun feels rather isolated on the Isle of Dogs, but it's a splendid gastropub. As we've come to expect from Martin brothers' ventures – which include the Cadogan Arms and the Chiswell Street Dining Rooms (*see p203*) – the food is amiable and accomplished. We tried stuffed rabbit leg with broad beans, peas, mushrooms and gnocchi in mustard and tarragon sauce, and herb and asparagus tagliatelle with parmesan – both flavourful enough, but the real hit for taste and texture was slow-roast Middle White pork belly with crushed Jersey Royals, glazed carrots and red wine jus. Service was charming and pleasingly swift; clearly staff are used to processing workday lunches. The layout is better for diners than drinkers; from the road, you enter a restaurant room with full napery, and heated dining tables fill an ample river terrace (opposite the O2 Centre). However, clusters of stools at high tables, and easy chairs with ankle-high tables in the back bar, as well as a pair of 'snugs', work fine for imbibers. Bar snacks (black pudding scotch egg, devilled whitebait) are a cut above too. In summer, the area beside the pub becomes a Portuguese barbecue.

Available for hire. Babies and children welcome: high chairs. Booking advisable. Disabled: toilet. Separate rooms for parties, seating 16 and 22. Tables outdoors (26, terrace). **Map 24 C2.**

Limehouse

Narrow

44 Narrow Street, E14 8DP (7592 7950, www.gordonramsay.com/thenarrow). Limehouse DLR. **Open** noon-11pm Mon-Sat; noon-10.30pm Sun. **Lunch served** noon-3pm Mon-Fri; noon-

Hundred Crows Rising. See p119.

Princess of Shoreditch

3.30pm Sat, Sun. **Dinner served** 6-10.30pm Mon-Sat; 6-10pm Sun. **Main courses** £10-£17. **Set meal** (lunch Mon-Sat; 6-10pm Mon-Thur, Sun; 6-7pm Fri, Sat) £18 2 courses, £22 3 courses. **Credit** AmEx, MC, V.
'Fine dining' promises the website of this Gordon Ramsay gastropub: it's either guilty of a bit of hyperbole, or the chef has forgotten the meaning of the phrase. Opened in 2007 and given a typical Ramsay smartening up, the Narrow has started to get a bit scuffed around the edges – not always a bad thing in a pub. But food on our last visit was distinctly variable, as was the service. Onion and cider soup was creamy and deeply flavoured, but its 'croutons' were no more than squares of bread rapidly getting soggy. Salt and chilli squid looked like a snack in its little dish. Beef and onion pie was better, although not exactly a challenge for the kitchen. A distracted waitress never brought us water, no offer to replenish empty wine glasses was forthcoming, and cutlery arrived after the main courses. But as pubs go, the prospect from the Narrow is hard to beat, especially at sunset – it's situated on a wide curve of the Thames, and an outdoor area and a conservatory look out to Canary Wharf and Rotherhithe. Ales are well kept and the wine list considered, so perhaps booze and views are its strongest suit.
Babies and children welcome: high chairs. Booking essential. Disabled: toilet. Separate room for parties, seats 18. Tables outdoors (36, riverside terrace).

Shoreditch

Princess of Shoreditch

76-78 Paul Street, EC2A 4NE (7729 9270, www.theprincessofshoreditch.com). Old Street tube/rail. **Open** noon-11pm Mon-Sat; noon-10.30pm Sun. **Lunch served** noon-3pm Mon-Fri; noon-4pm Sat. **Dinner served** 6.30-10pm Mon-Sat. **Meals served** noon-9pm Sun. **Main courses** £11.50-£19. **Set lunch** (Tue-Fri) £14 2 courses, £18 3 courses. **Credit** AmEx, MC, V.
Up the spiral staircase from the bustling downstairs bar, the dining room at the Princess is a good-looking, cosy space. A dozen linen-clothed tables – candlelit at night – are served by a small team of young, efficient staff. Choosing from a menu that included wild boar scotch egg, Chart Farm fallow deer and a host of seasonal goodies wasn't easy, but the kitchen more than fulfilled its remit. Rich ham hock, foie gras and pork knuckle terrine benefited from tangy piccalilli, and sour goat's cheese was a lovely foil for the sweetness of roasted red and yellow heritage beetroot. Mains of beer-battered fish and chips with mushy peas and tartare sauce, and Cornish brill with pea purée and black pudding were near perfect; the last ingredient slightly overpowered the purée, but it's a minor quibble. Simple but effective afters might be chocolate fondant with vanilla ice-cream, or an artisan cheese sold by the slice – the Lancashire 'strong bomb' is sensational. There's a choice of wine by the glass and carafe, as well a wide range of bottles (including five rosés), plus local beers, such as Wandle Ale from Sambrook's in Battersea, on tap. A top-notch operation, now joined by sister pub the Lady Ottoline in Bloomsbury.
Booking advisable. Children admitted until 6pm: high chairs. Separate room for parties, seats 40. Tables outdoors (3, pavement). **Map 6 Q4.**

North East

Dalston

★ Scolt Head

107A Culford Road, N1 4HT (7254 3965, www.thescolthead.com). Haggerston rail. **Open** noon-midnight daily. **Lunch served** noon-3pm Mon-Fri; noon-4pm Sat, Sun. **Dinner served** 6.30-10pm daily. **Main courses** £7.50-£16.50. **Credit** MC, V.
Some gastropub proprietors think that in order for their place to be more gastronomic it must appear less pubby. Thankfully, the Scolt Head doesn't make this mistake. A pub first and foremost, with a lively, young clientele, it's an unpretentious and relaxed spot. Staff are as friendly as they are efficient – and the food is fantastic. Starters range from tomato soup with pesto, to baked camembert with toast and cranberry sauce, via a rather intimidating-sounding pig's-head brawn with cornichons, chutney and toast. Main courses are even more robust. We enjoyed roast fillet of salmon with crushed new potatoes, asparagus and caper butter, but the great find was potato and mustard lamb cakes with poached egg, green beans and mint sauce. The combination of flavours, the lovely lean flakes of lamb, the egg, beans and mint: everything about the dish worked brilliantly. We were prepared for a drop in such exalted standards, but, astoundingly, a strawberry pavlova was just as good. With Leffe Blonde on draught and an excellent pinot grigio by the glass, this is everything a gastropub should be.
Available for hire. Babies and children welcome: high chairs; nappy-changing facilities. Booking advisable. Disabled: toilet. Entertainment (music nights; see website for details). Tables outdoors (9, garden). **Map 6 R1.**

Hackney

Prince Arthur

95 Forest Road, E8 3BH (7249 9996, www.theprincearthurlondonfields.com). Dalston Kingsland or London Fields rail or bus 38, 242, 277. **Open** 4-11pm Mon-Thur; 3-11pm Fri; noon-11pm Sat, Sun. **Lunch served** noon-4.30pm Sat. **Dinner served** 6-10pm Mon-Sat. **Meals served** noon-9pm Sun. **Main courses** £11-£23. **Credit** MC, V.
The Prince Arthur still has the feel of a neighbourhood pub, due in part to classic but attractive gastropub fittings of chunky wooden tables, dark-green leather stools and taxidermy on the walls. Indeed, many regulars choose to ignore the food and treat the place purely as a fine venue for a pint: perhaps of Adnams bitter, Bitburger lager or Symonds cider. The very British menu is reliable and solid, with high-quality ingredients used throughout, though dishes aren't especially original – or swift to change. Mainstays include starters of a half or full pint of prawns (served with mayonnaise), and pork, green peppercorn and garlic terrine. To follow, Adnams-battered haddock and chips, and ham hock with pease pudding and parsley sauce are normally present among the main courses. Vegetarians might go hungry if they're not tempted by the sole veggie main (Jerusalem artichoke risotto, on our last visit); traditional meat-based dishes dominate the repertoire. If that's your thing, you're likely to feel at home among the friendly locals, who range from twentysomething hipsters to groups of middle-aged, and mainly middle-class, locals who often come here on a Monday evening for the entertaining quiz.
Available for hire. Babies and children welcome: children's menu; high chairs; nappy-changing facilities. Booking advisable Sun. Disabled: toilet. Tables outdoors (4, pavement).

North

Archway

St John's

91 Junction Road, N19 5QU (7272 1587, www.stjohnstavern.com). Archway tube.
Bar **Open/meals served** 5-11pm Mon-Thur; noon-11pm Fri, Sat; noon-10.30pm Sun. **Main courses** £2.75-£12.50.
Restaurant **Lunch served** noon-3.30pm Fri; noon-4pm Sat, Sun. **Dinner served** 6.30-11pm Mon-Sat; 6.30-9.30pm Sun. **Main courses** £12.50-£19.
Both **Credit** AmEx, MC, V.
We've had mixed experiences here in recent years, but St John's was performing at its best on our recent Saturday lunch visit. Astute staff and a well-organised kitchen meant that the large birthday party on one side of the capacious dining room caused nary a blip in service. All the while a procession of good-looking Longhorn beef burgers, slow-roast pork bellies, and fish and chips were carried through to the attractive bar too. The sizeable blackboard menu stretches beyond gastropub faves to a River Cottage idyll, with dishes such as breaded Dorset snails and nettle purée; goose egg with chorizo and peas; and ox liver with bacon and cauliflower cheese. There's a couple of dishes for sharing, maybe on the chesterfield sofas, or in one of the U-shaped leather booths beneath the gallery of portraits that lend the room distinction. Estimable suppliers highlighted on the board above the semi-open kitchen include the source of flour for St John's bread. From the long list of desserts, own-made ices proved the best choice. A bar in the dining room allows convenient delivery of real ales (Cocker Hoop golden ale, Ruddles County and Hooky Bitter, on our visit), which seem a better deal than the 125ml glasses of wine.
Babies and children welcome: high chairs. Booking essential weekends. Tables outdoors (10, patio). **Map 26 B1.**

Crouch End

Queens Pub & Dining Room

26 Broadway Parade, N8 9DE (8340 2031, www.thequeenscrouchend.co.uk). Finsbury Park tube/rail then bus W7, or Crouch Hill rail. **Open** noon-11pm Mon-Thur, Sun; noon-midnight Fri, Sat. **Meals served** noon-10pm Mon-Sat; noon-9pm Sun. **Main courses** £9-£17.50. **Set meal** (noon-3pm Mon-Thur; noon-6pm Fri) £7.50 1 course. **Credit** AmEx, MC, V.
Glorious stained glass, floral ironwork, ornate plastering, mahogany panelling and many other details greet arrivals at the Queens. This magnificent piece of over-the-top Victoriana was built in 1899 to show respectable locals that a pub need not be anything down-at-heel. So big is it that the dining room and bar areas are separate, but equally spacious, and for smokers and summer visitors there's a courtyard garden too. Food adds to the allure. Able and friendly staff invite you to

settle in and feel at home, while the menu, rather than aiming for anything too ambitious, focuses on enjoyable versions of modern pub standards: great steaks; salmon and haddock fish cakes; delectable beer-battered fish and chips; and Jude's irresistible salted caramel ice-cream among the puds. De rigueur roasts are offered on Sundays, and though the weekday lunch specials have increased in price a little (from £5 to £7.50), they're still a bargain. The wine list shows the same enterprising generosity, with a well-chosen range at modest prices, and weekly special offers. What's more, the capacious bar has kept a real pub feel, with a very respectable array of international beers.
Babies and children admitted. Disabled: toilet. Separate room for parties, seats 50. Tables outdoors (10, garden).

Villiers Terrace

120 Park Road, N8 8JP (8245 6827, www.villiersterracelondon.com). Finsbury Park tube/rail then bus W7, or Hornsey rail. **Open** noon-11pm Mon, Tue, Sun; noon-midnight Wed; noon-1am Thur-Sat. **Meals served** noon-10.30pm daily. **Main courses** £11-£16.50. **Set menu** (noon-3pm, 6-7pm Mon-Fri) £10.50 2 courses, £14 3 courses. **Credit** MC, V.
For all its cocktail bar posturing (the choice of real ales here is, well, non-existent), this friendly spot is delightfully relaxed. Head to the paved beer garden if the chandeliers, gilt-framed mirrors and glittering wallpaper seem too prissy – that's where the blokes and kids were congregating on our recent visit. A change in the kitchen team has led to a fusion-fuelled menu, but for once that's a good thing, with well-judged dishes such as a pleasantly tepid sushi rice salad with samphire, hot-smoked salmon and pickled ginger among the seasonally inspired picks. You'll still find good British fare: ham hock salad with potato, watercress and egg, say, or grilled steak with horseradish butter. A confident burger came with sensational chips (also available with aïoli for snacking). There's a thoughtful children's menu taking in shepherd's pie, cumberland sausage, battered fish and pasta (£4.50 including ice-cream for dessert); staff are extremely good with little ones too. The international wine list starts at £16 a bottle, and classic cocktails are a mere £6.50 – underlining the overall impression that Villiers Terrace's target market is designer-heeled yummy mummies. That's not necessarily a criticism given the location, but worth noting if you don't fit the demographic.
Babies and children welcome: children's menu; high chairs; nappy-changing facilities. Booking advisable dinner Wed-Sun. Entertainment (DJs 10pm Fri, Sat). Separate room for parties, seats 50. Tables outdoors (20, garden; 10, terrace).

Finsbury Park

Old Dairy

1-3 Crouch Hill, N4 4AP (7263 3337, www.theolddairyn4.co.uk). Crouch Hill rail. **Open** noon-11pm Mon-Thur; noon-1am Fri, Sat; noon-10.30pm Sun. **Lunch served** noon-3.30pm Tue-Fri. **Dinner served** 6-10pm Mon-Fri. **Meals served** noon-10pm Sat; noon-9pm Sun. **Main courses** £11-£18. **Credit** AmEx, MC, V.
As the name suggests, the building was a Victorian dairy, which sets the tone both outside (there are some stunning friezes on the exterior walls) and inside this Real Pubs venture. Exposed brickwork and unusual angles create all sorts of cosy corners in what is actually a very large space, and locals of all ages come to enjoy the friendly welcome and above-average food. The weekday menu has dishes such as pan-fried sea bass and braised fennel with salsa verde, as well as pub classics (fish and chips, lancashire hotpot). On a Sunday lunchtime, roasts are the popular option. Beef was slightly more than medium rare – a small quibble about a great plate of food that included yorkshire puddings, bashed carrot and parsnip, a delectable pea, pak choi, mint and spring onion dish and horseradish cream. For pudding, our waitress directed us to the odd-sounding 'peanut butter parfait with strawberry jam'. It was one of the finest puddings we can remember eating, but it could do with a better name. A decent range of drinks includes a guest cider (Orchard Cornish cider, say); real ales such as Thunderbird from Cottage Brewing in Somerset or Windsor & Eton Brewery's Guardsman; and a global wine list with plenty by the glass.
Available for hire. Babies and children admitted until 7.30pm: children's menu; high chairs; nappy-changing facilities. Booking essential Sun. Disabled: toilet. Separate room for parties, (Mon-Sat) seats 50.

Islington

Duke of Cambridge

30 St Peter's Street, N1 8JT (7359 3066, www.dukeorganic.co.uk). Angel tube. **Open** noon-11pm Mon-Sat; noon-10.30pm Sun. **Lunch served** 12.30-3.30pm daily. **Dinner served** 6.30-10.30pm Mon-Sat; 6.30-10pm Sun. **Main courses** £13-£21. **Credit** MC, V.
Surprisingly, given the Duke's local, seasonal and organic emphasis, its blackboard menu doesn't list the provenance of ingredients. Nor, on a hot day, did a dish like pastry-topped beef pie with bashed neeps seem right for the time of year. Choose between the airy bare-boards bar – where you'll find a great variety of organic drinks – and the pleasingly poshed-up garden shed of a dining area. We arrived during a cauliflower glut. Caulis came in a ragoût, and with lemon sole, and the roast pork. A few florets even turned up, unadvertised, with the asparagus with pecorino and hazelnuts. Though cooking errs on the hefty side, as do prices, it's satisfying stuff. Beautifully pink cold roast beef salad had few puy lentils and more fregola than suggested. Rhubarb fool showed little evidence of the promised blackcurrant, and wasn't foolishly smooth enough – it was more compote with a topping of cream and crumble. Strips of chewy, smoky cuttlefish with a black olive relish, though, were typically full-flavoured and bigger than starter size. Expect also to find salad leaves with plenty of bite, punchy dressings, fat slices of terrific bread and plenty for vegetarians, as more evidence of commitment to sustainability.
Available for hire. Babies and children welcome: high chairs; nappy-changing facilities. Booking advisable. Separate room for parties, seats 50-60. Tables outdoors (4, pavement). **Map 5 O2.**

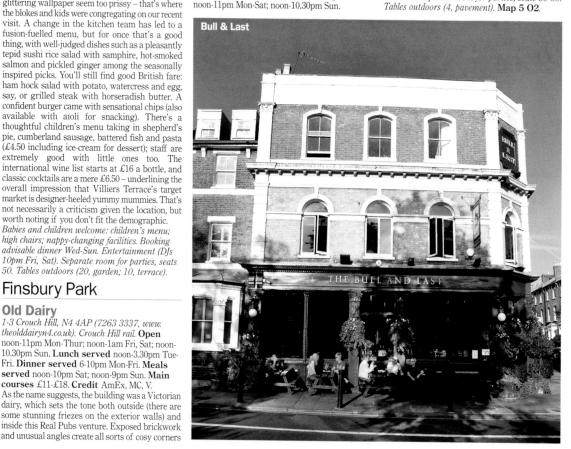

Bull & Last

Hundred Crows Rising NEW

58 Penton Street, N1 9PZ (7837 3891, www.hundredcrowsrising.co.uk). Angel tube. **Open** 9am-11pm, **meals served** 9am-10.45pm daily. **Main courses** £10-£19. **Credit** MC, V.

Once known as the Compass, this Islington boozer has been revamped (and refitted) and poetically renamed by the team behind nearby Elk in the Woods with all the usual gastropub elements. There's a bright, spacious wood-panelled interior; an inviting, innovative menu of British-based dishes, local ingredients and real ale; and a relaxed, convivial vibe. A starter of piping-hot corned beef hash was elevated by the kick of scotch bonnet peppers, while deep-fried anchovies were satisfyingly crisp and delicately salted. Main courses were less impressive. A pulled pork and beef burger with fried green tomatoes didn't quite work. The meat was too dry, while the garlic mayo wasn't pungent enough to offset the smokiness from a thick wedge of bacon. A slow-cooked beef stew hadn't quite been cooked slowly enough – its wonderfully tart rhubarb sauce, a spot-on match for mashed potato and spinach, was let down by chunks of chewy meat. Though savoury portions may have been small, our rich chocolate brownie was enormous. But size was this dessert's undoing – its edges were warm, crisp and winningly gooey, but it was cold in the centre. Prices are reasonable, service is efficient and the wine list covers all the bases, including some English whites and rosés.

Available for hire. Babies and children admitted. Booking advisable dinner. Disabled: lift; toilet. Tables outdoors (6, pavement). **Map 5 N2**.

Pig & Butcher NEW

80 Liverpool Road, N1 0QD (7226 8304, www.thepigandbutcher.co.uk). Angel tube. **Open** 5-11pm Mon-Wed; noon-midnight Thur; noon-1am Fri; 11am-1am Sat; 11am-11pm Sun. **Lunch served** noon-3pm Thur-Fri; noon-4pm Sat. **Dinner served** 6.30-10pm Mon-Sat. **Meals served** noon-9pm Sun. **Main courses** £11.50-£15.50. **Credit** MC, V.

The gutsy theme doesn't end with the name at this revamped pub from the team behind the Princess of Shoreditch and Lady Ottoline. Carcasses are butchered on site, allowing the kitchen to cook cuts from rare-breed animals at cheaper prices than normal. The meat is used in dishes such as own-cured bacon and black pudding salad with endive and orange; lamb shoulder with borlotti beans; or venison haunch with beetroot. And very good they are too, as was a plate of lentils, green beans and croûtons. Craft beer is a speciality, and comes mainly in bottles – there are more than 20, with many made in London from breweries such as Windsor & Eton, Hackney, Camden Town and Kernel; plus a couple from Scotland's Harviestoun and Brewdog. The wine list offers eight each of reds and whites by the glass, and avoids more obvious grapes in favour of imaginatively chosen examples. What's more, the place looks good; it has been given a handsome makeover, with a colour scheme of muted greys, assorted bits of paraphernalia on shelves, and huge windows.

Available for hire. Babies and children welcome (until 7pm dining room): high chairs; nappy-changing facilities. Booking advisable. Separate room for parties, seats 30-40. Tables outdoors (8, pavement). **Map 5 N1**.

Kentish Town

★ Bull & Last

168 Highgate Road, NW5 1QS (7267 3641, www.thebullandlast.co.uk). Kentish Town tube/rail then bus 214, C2, or Gospel Oak rail then bus C11. **Open** noon-11pm Mon-Thur; 9am-midnight Fri, Sat; 9am-10.30pm Sun. **Breakfast served** 9-11am Fri-Sun. **Lunch served** noon-3pm Mon-Fri; 12.30-4pm Sat, Sun. **Dinner served** 6.30-10pm Mon-Sat; 7-9pm Sun. **Main courses** £14-£28. **Credit** AmEx, MC, V.

It may seem as though a country pub complete with abundant hanging baskets has been plopped on to busy Highgate Road, but inside lies an edgy kitchen working sustainable practices into culinary magic. They cure their own meats and fish, churn a dazzling range of ices – even the oatcakes on the cheeseboard are made on site. This makes the Bull & Last special enough for a treat meal, though the rustic decor and modest dimensions are most suited to escapist weekday lunches. Service is usually very charming, but the slowness with which dishes arrive from the kitchen remains an aggravation. Characterful staples from summer menus include hearty English pea salad with pea fritters, goat's curd and Jersey Royals, and brown crab spaghettini with chilli and spring onion. For those not wanting the likes of slow-cooked beef cheek with spätzle, chard, ox tongue and prune, there are simple burgers, steaks and beer-battered fish, all with the superb triple-cooked chips. Desserts increasingly showcase the kitchen's inspired ice-cream flavours (lavender, black cherry and amaretti among them) and there's a stonking choice of English and French cheeses. A brief, punchy international wine list starts at £16 a bottle, while a pleasing choice of hand-pumped ales changes frequently and is strong on London breweries.

Babies and children welcome: high chairs; nappy-changing facilities. Booking advisable. Separate room for parties, seats 70. Tables outdoors (5, pavement). **Map 26 A3**.

Junction Tavern

101 Fortess Road, NW5 1AG (7485 9400, www.junctiontavern.co.uk). Tufnell Park tube or Kentish Town tube/rail. **Open** 5-11pm Mon-Thur; noon-11pm Fri, Sat; noon-10.30pm Sun. **Lunch served** noon-3pm Fri; noon-4pm Sat, Sun. **Dinner served** 6.30-10.30pm Mon-Sat; 6.30-9.30pm Sun. **Main courses** £12.50-£19.50. **Credit** MC, V.

With an enviable beer garden and bright conservatory, as well as bar and restaurant areas, this black-painted corner pub suits most moods and occasions. The jolly crew seem to take any excuse for a beer festival, and this year we arrived to find the bar piled with kegs bearing intriguing names. Even on a normal day's trading you'll be offered an impressive selection of real ales – there are five hand pumps and their output frequently changes, though Sambrook's Wandle and other London ales such as Redemption's Pale Ale are mainstays. France, South Africa and Spain find favour on the wine list; it starts at an approachable £15.50 per bottle. We like the relative serenity of Saturday brunch amid the cosily dark walls of the dining room. Go eggy with florentine, benedict, et al; opt for pancakes, pasta or something more substantial. Plaice fillet with crayfish butter was a delight, with sweet, juicy nuggets of shellfish and just-right greens. A thick pork chop had pan gravy that melded deliciously with the potatoes. Lemon posset with berries and shortbread was pick of the slightly disappointing desserts. Sundays see a wide choice of à la carte dishes offered in addition to the impressive roasts.

Babies and children admitted until 7pm: booster seats. Booking advisable weekends. Tables outdoors (20, garden). **Map 26 B4**.

Oxford

256 Kentish Town Road, NW5 2AA (7485 3521, www.theoxfordnw5.co.uk). Kentish Town tube/rail. **Open** noon-11.30pm Mon, Tue; noon-midnight Wed-Sat; noon-10.30pm Sun. **Lunch served** noon-3.30pm Mon-Fri; noon-4.30pm Sat. **Dinner served** 6-10pm Mon-Wed; 6-10.30pm Thur-Sat. **Meals served** noon-10pm Sun. **Main courses** £11-£15. **Credit** AmEx, MC, V.

One of the Real Pubs stable, the Oxford is clearly thriving, packed out on a Sunday lunchtime with big parties enjoying hearty roasts or choosing from a menu of posh gastropub fare. Dark grey walls, dark wood furniture and a dramatic oversized chandelier add up to a stylish interior. Staff were pleasant enough, but too rushed – it can take a while to order and get a drink – one of 20 or so wines by the glass, or a pint of Camden Town Brewery's Camden Hells lager, perhaps. The food can also be a bit hit and miss. Mussels came in a sauce where any hint of cider was overpowered by cream, but a plate of Spanish charcuterie with toasted Poilâne, cornichons and caperberries was fantastic: generous piles of chorizo; lean, chewy and intensely flavoursome lomo; and deliciously salty jamón. Inconsistency continued with the mains – pork, leek and ham hock pie with spring greens had a light shortcrust pastry lid covering a lip-smacking and moist filling, while a generous, well-grilled sea bass fillet on confit onion and fennel was again drowned by an excessively creamy sauce. Perfect fat chips did a lot to ease the pain. Lemon tart with undercooked pastry wasn't a touch on the M&S version. Truly a mixed bag.

Available for hire. Babies and children admitted until 8pm. Booking advisable dinner. Disabled: toilet. Entertainment(musicians 8.30pm Mon; quiz 7.30pm Tue; comedy 7pm Thur, Sat). Separate room for parties, seats 50. Tables outdoors (7, pavement). **Map 26 B5**.

Vine

86 Highgate Road, NW5 1PB (7209 0038, www.thevinelondon.co.uk). Tufnell Park tube or Kentish Town tube/rail. **Open** noon-11pm Mon-Wed, Sun; noon-midnight Thur-Sat. **Meals served** noon-10.30pm Mon-Sat; noon-9.30pm Sun. **Main courses** £10.50-£18. **Credit** AmEx, MC, V.

Now under the care of Real Pubs, this elegant Edwardian building may smack of formulaic thinking, but so what? It suits most occasions with its generous drinking and dining terrace, spacious front bar and separate rear restaurant. Ale enthusiasts will appreciate beers such as Truman's Swallow & Swift and Ruddles Best, while wine buffs will be equally pleased with their options. The menu is flexibility itself: cicchetti (Venetian-style bar snacks) that double as starters; generous plates of pasta that suit lunch or dinner; high-end mains alongside gastropub staples. Mostly, we've found the cooking impressive, especially the Sunday roasts, but on our last visit we ordered a clutch of favourites from the all-day cicchetti list to find them not only less good than before but entirely different

recipes. A blip? We hope so. Service is cheery and highly competent. Weekends can be overrun with families, but the tone is friendly; dim lighting helps make quiet weeknights in the bar cosy. Spells of hot weather are when this place really takes off – the numerous outdoor tables are a key draw.
Babies and children welcome: children's menu; crayons; high chairs; nappy-changing facilities. Booking advisable. Disabled: toilet. Separate room for parties, seating 35. Tables outdoors (20, garden; 20, terrace). **Map 26 A4.**

Muswell Hill

Clissold Arms

105 Fortis Green, N2 9HR (8444 4224, www.clissoldarms.co.uk). East Finchley tube. **Open** 9am-11pm Mon-Thur; 9am-midnight Fri, Sat; noon-11pm Sun. **Breakfast served** 9am-noon Mon-Sat. **Lunch served** noon-3pm Mon-Fri; noon-4pm Sat. **Dinner served** 6-10pm Mon-Fri; 6.30-10.30pm Sat. **Meals served** noon-9pm Sun. **Main courses** £10.25-£22.95. **Credit** AmEx, MC, V.

Muswell Hill couples, families and groups of friends regularly pack this large gastropub. Oddly, the Clissold doesn't have much competition locally, which might explain its high prices. On sunny days, the large, pretty terrace to the side feels like an escape to a Mediterranean isle (not only because of the Spanish cured meats, king prawns and other tapas-style dishes on the specials board). Tables under the large sheltered canopy introduce a boardwalk atmosphere. Inside, choose from the darker, cosier front bar (where Sambrook's Wandle Ale is among the cask beers) or the larger modern and airy back room. The evening menu combines gastropub classics, such as 28-day-aged beef and chips cooked in dripping, with Mediterranean dishes such as Catalan fish stew. At Sunday lunchtimes, the emphasis is on roasts, which come with a delicate portion of roast potatoes, root-vegetable mash and greens. Beef was medium-rare as requested; slightly undercooked tatties were the only disappointment. Pasta from the children's menu had fresh herby flavour. Star of the puddings was a perfect honey and vanilla panna cotta with a zingy passionfruit coulis. The Kinks played their first gig here, and a room is dedicated to the band.
Available for hire. Babies and children welcome: children's menu; high chairs; nappy-changing facilities. Booking advisable dinner Thur-Sat; lunch Sun. Disabled: toilet. Separate rooms for parties, seating 20 and 60. Tables outdoors (25, garden; 15, terrace).

North West

Hampstead

Horseshoe

28 Heath Street, NW3 6TE (7431 7206). Hampstead tube. **Open** 11am-11pm Mon-Thur; 11am-midnight Fri; 10am-midnight Sat; 11am-10.30pm Sun. **Brunch served** 11am-4pm Sat. **Lunch served** noon-3.30pm Mon-Fri. **Dinner served** 6-10pm Mon-Thur; 6-11pm Fri; 6.30-11pm Sat. **Meals served** noon-9pm Sun. **Main courses** £8-£26. **Set lunch** £8 1 course incl glass of wine. **Credit** AmEx, MC, V.

Look carefully at the Camden Town Brewery logo and you'll see a coloured horseshoe: it was in the basement of this field-to-fork gastropub that the business was born. Brews such as their Camden Ink stout and sparkling pale ale are, naturally, on tap here, but so too is a stellar range of other options, including Sierra Nevada, Little Creatures and Stiegl. Even rival London-born artisan brewer Kernel gets a nod. The estimable wine list starts at £4 for a glass of Kalius garnacha from Spain and rises to £80 a bottle for Billecart Salmon rosé – well, we are in Hampstead. If you're coming for the food, get here early or, better still, book. Sundays see pram-wielding customers queuing at the door before opening time; even on our weekday visit the almost-empty bar was busy come 2pm. The lunch deal (dish of the day – Camden-smoked salmon, bubble and squeak and mustard sauce, say – plus drink for £8) is a popular draw, as is the high-rise burger with a generous pail of chips. Pearl barley with goat's curd and courgette sounded like a salad, but arrived as a piping-hot orzotto topped with a crisp-crumbed courgette flower stuffed with molten goat's cheese. Frozen peanut butter parfait with raspberry jam toastie also struck an elegant note. The kitchen is very capable, but service could be more sprightly.
Available for hire. Babies and children welcome: high chairs; nappy-changing facilities. Booking advisable. Tables outdoors (2, pavement).
Map 28 B2.

Old White Bear NEW

1 Well Road, NW3 1LJ (7794 7719, www.theoldwhitebear.co.uk). Hampstead tube. **Open/tapas served** 5.30-11pm Mon; noon-11pm Tue-Thur; noon-11.30pm Fri, Sat; noon-10.30pm Sun. **Lunch served** noon-3pm Tue-Fri; noon-3.30pm Sat, Sun. **Dinner served** 6.30-10pm Mon; 5.30-10.30pm Tue-Sat; 5.30-9.30pm Sun. **Main courses** £12.50-£20.50. **Tapas** £4.50-£9.75. **Credit** AmEx, MC, V.

Decked out like a hipster's country-house hotel, this tucked-away spot has confidently distinguished itself from the slew of Hampstead gastroboozers with a discreet luxury vibe and highly

Pig & Butcher. See p119.

GASTROPUBS

accomplished kitchen. Don't roll up on Sundays expecting a cheap 'n' cheerful roast: lunch dishes are cooked, presented and priced like an upmarket restaurant, an impression underlined by the expensively attired crowd, though the charming ease of the staff forestalls stuffiness. You'll need to book well in advance too. When the kitchen is open, bar snacks such as sautéed chorizo with fennel seeds and lemon, and cod croquettes with aïoli, provide light alternatives to the likes of roast quails with creamed onions, sage, wild garlic and Madeira sauce. Desserts (chocolate marquis, sticky toffee pudding, lemon granita) are a strong point. Cheeses come from the esteemed La Fromagerie. Outside mealtimes, well-conceived (though still pricey) boards of antipasto and charcuterie provide gourmet sustenance. Even the regulars would prefer another couple of hand-pumps (the bar is tiny), but the wine list is fun and friendly, and staff make Pimm's a real treat by starting from scratch.
Babies and children welcome: high chairs; nappy-changing facilities. Booking advisable. Disabled: toilet. Separate room for parties, seats 10-14. Tables outdoors (5, pavement). **Map 28 C2.**

Wells
30 Well Walk, NW3 1BX (7794 3785, www.thewellshampstead.co.uk). Hampstead tube. **Open** noon-11pm Mon-Sat; noon-10.30pm Sun. **Lunch served** noon-3pm Mon-Fri; noon-4pm Sat, Sun. **Dinner served** 6-10pm Mon-Fri; 7-10pm Sat, Sun. **Main courses** £9.95-£18.95. **Credit** AmEx, MC, V.
A very Hampstead version of the modern pub, a short stroll from the Heath. Upstairs, the Wells' main dining areas feel like a proper restaurant, with distinctive, delicate furnishings – slightly Indian colours in one room, lighter shades and Chinese porcelain in another. The result is a relaxing and potentially romantic setting for a meal. The mostly British-European menus are strong on classic steaks, but also include such pub standards as cumberland sausages and mash, and more subtle options such as a fine sea bass with broad beans, chilli sauce and chorizo. There's nothing unusually innovative here, and menus could pay more attention to the seasons (a winter list was peculiarly heavy on salads), but dishes are nicely executed, with refined flavours. Hefty beef and chicken roasts are served for Sunday lunch, and the same menus (plus a few snacks) are also available in the ground-floor bar. Here, original features of the old Georgian inn are combined with elegant modern seating ideally suited to a clientele that has internalised the concepts of smart and casual. Packed at weekend lunchtimes, the bar is more peaceful during the week. There's not much choice for beer-drinkers, but the globally sourced wine list is serious business.
Babies and children welcome: children's menu; colouring books; high chairs; nappy-changing facilities. Disabled: toilet. Separate room for parties, seats 12. Tables outdoors (8, patio). **Map 28 C2.**

Kilburn

Salusbury
50-52 Salusbury Road, NW6 6NN (7328 3286). Queens Park tube/rail. **Open** 5-11pm Mon; noon-11pm Tue, Wed; noon-midnight Thur-Sat; noon-10.30pm Sun. **Lunch served** noon-2.30pm Tue-Fri; noon-3.30pm Sat, Sun. **Dinner served** 7-10.15pm Mon-Sat; 7-10pm Sun. **Main courses** £11.80-£16.40. **Credit** MC, V.
The Salusbury 'empire' takes up four shopfronts, starting with a pub that leads into the dining room, followed by a wine shop and deli, and ending with the 'Food Store': a casual, sit-in deli/café with patio seating, especially popular for its pizza. The dining room is a more sophisticated affair; mint-coloured walls with mirrors provide the backdrop for dark leather sofas under art-deco style lampshades. The menu is Italian and portions are big. Breton cider and Asahi beer are on the sizeable drinks list, along with plentiful Italian wines. To start, you can select antipasti or a primi piatti, such as paccheri pasta, which arrived a little too al dente on a fruity and light tomato sauce with dollops of creamy ricotta. As for mains, spatchcock baby chicken alla diavola was spicy yet lacked any deeper flavour – but the accompanying spring greens were tasty. Grilled swordfish was served with peperonata that was more of a flavoursome tomato-based soup containing pieces of pepper and some capers, rather than the expected rustic pepper stew. An excellent tiramisu went some way to restoring our faith in the kitchen's Italian credentials.
Available for hire. Babies and children welcome: high chairs. Tables outdoors (6, pavement).

Mill Hill

Adam & Eve
The Ridgeway, NW7 1RL (8959 1553, www.adamandevemillhill.co.uk). Mill Hill East tube then bus 240. **Open** noon-11pm Mon-Thur; noon-midnight Fri, Sat; noon-10.30pm Sun. **Lunch served** noon-3pm Mon-Fri; noon-5pm Sat, Sun. **Dinner served** 6-10pm daily. **Main courses** £10.95-£20. **Set lunch** (Sun) £20 3 courses. **Credit** AmEx, MC, V.
The apple of Mill Hill's eye, this elegant Edwardian pub features all the hallmarks of a classic gastropub conversion (grey-painted wood panelling, slouchy sofas, Tom Dixon lights) but throws in a Pizza East-style bistro extension and a large rear garden filled with generously proportioned tables. Monday night is curry night, Tuesdays feature 2-for-1 mains, while Fridays are for 'fish and fizz'. Yet there's a sense Adam and Eve is trying too hard to be all things to all people. We were offered a lengthy pizza menu, a printed list of specials and a sizeable à la carte with everything from charcuterie platters to slow-roast pork belly with mash and seasonal greens. Better to offer less and cook it better. Sea bass fillet came with yellowing broccoli, and the sad small burger was overdone, though the chips and pizza bread were good. We like the frosty tankards of real ales such as Butcombe Bitter, the friendly wine list and impressive choice of premium spirits – so, it seems, do the stylishly dressed couples frequenting the place. Service on our busy Thursday night visit was embarrassingly chaotic thanks to a lack of staff, though eventually more appeared and things improved.
Available for hire. Babies and children welcome: children's menu; high chairs; nappy-changing facilities. Booking advisable lunch Sat, Sun; dinner. Disabled: toilet. Separate room for parties, seats 70. Tables outdoors (12, garden).

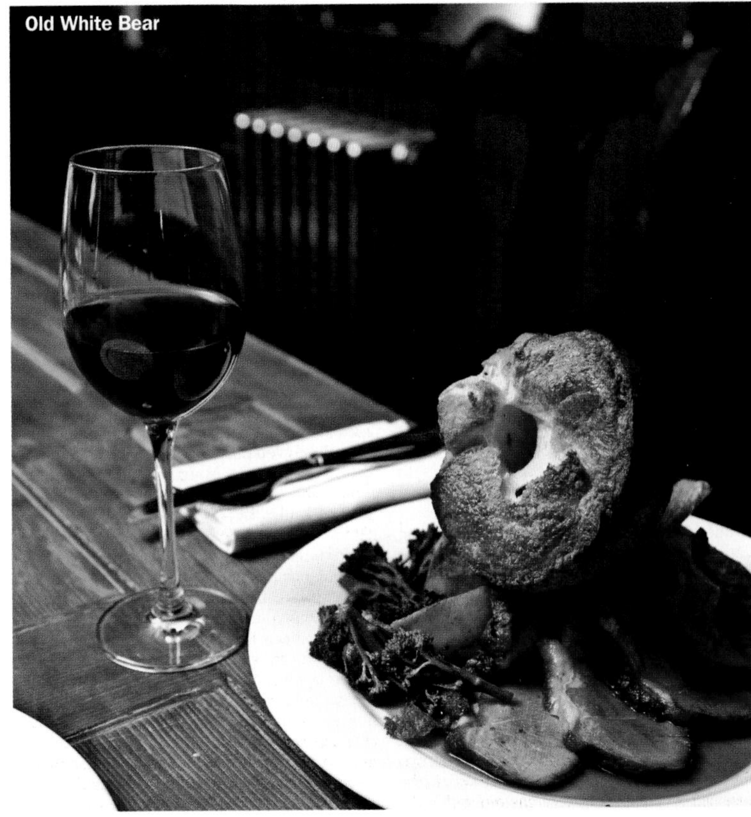
Old White Bear

Global

A keen knowledge of our city is key to winkling out the restaurants specialising in the capital's rarely found cuisines – and the sheer variety to be discovered is one of gastronomic London's glories. Few out-of-towners would think of exploring the unfashionable end of the Edgware Road in the expectation of finding Burmese food – served by the unprepossessing but consistently superb **Mandalay**. This section is also where you'll find the best of the city's Scandinavian, pan-Mediterranean and Afghan restaurants. Other star performers include those providing cooking that crosses national boundaries: the African-tinged Iberian food of **Eyre Brothers**; and the Austro-French pairing at **Bistro Délicat**. Read on, inwardly digest, and consume the world without breaching the M25.

Central

Clerkenwell & Farringdon

North Road

69-73 St John Street, EC1M 4AN (3217 0033, www.northroadrestaurant.co.uk). Farringdon tube/rail. **Lunch served** noon-2.30pm Mon-Fri. **Dinner served** 6-10.30pm Mon-Thur; 6-11pm Fri, Sat. **Main courses** £17-£28. **Set meal** (noon-2.30pm, 6-6.30pm Mon-Fri) £25 3 courses. **Credit** AmEx, MC, V. Scandinavian

The subdued surroundings – parquet floor, palette of low-key mushroom colours, subtle line drawings and gently flickering tea lights – do little to prepare diners for the excitement on the plate at North Road. Oversize and rather beautiful bare light bulbs add a playful note, which is carried through to the dishes: amuse-bouche of light-as-air pork scratchings, salty quail eggs nestled in hay, new potatoes stuffed with bakskuld (smoked fish) mayo in a pot lined with thyme. Mini bread rolls come in a small hessian bag, accompanied by caramelised and buttermilk butters. All delightful so far, as was a starter of scallops with sea buckthorn, buttermilk and strips of carrot. The dairy and sea combo continued – successfully – into a main of Cornish monkfish (and more bakskuld) with sea vegetables and seaweed butter. Less pleasing was Norfolk venison and smoked bone marrow (coated in ash) with beetroot and wild sorrel: a taste sensation too far, as the ash flavour dominated. Overall, there's much to be admired – particularly the commitment to British ingredients (many of them foraged) – and it's a treat to try such unfamiliar dishes. A note of caution for the lactose-intolerant: many dishes, and every dessert, contain milk. We devoured 'brunsviger' sponge and milk ice-cream: a divine, caramelised concoction. Unlike the Anglo-Danish menu, the wine list roams the globe; service is charm itself, though so heavily accented that we struggled to understand. Note that co-founder and chef Christoffer Hruskova left the business in summer 2012.

Available for hire. Babies and children admitted. Booking advisable. Disabled: toilet. Dress: smart casual. Separate rooms for parties, seating 10-24. **Map 5 O5.**

Edgware Road

★ ★ Mandalay HOT 50

444 Edgware Road, W2 1EG (7258 3696, www.mandalayway.com). Edgware Road tube. **Lunch served** noon-2.30pm, **dinner served** 6-10.30pm Mon-Sat. **Main courses** £5.50-£8.50. **Set lunch** £4.50 1 course, £6.50 3 courses. **Credit** AmEx, DC, MC, V. Burmese

At the wrong end of Edgware Road, as the Middle Eastern restaurants trail off, lies this unexpected gem. Mandalay's looks – half 'greasy spoon' with brown plastic tablecloths, half Burmese teahouse with wonkily hung pictures of the ancient city of Bagan on the walls – have remained unchanged for years. We wouldn't have it any other way; the place oozes a low-key charm that has garnered it a devoted following. The ten tightly packed tables are full each night with a mixture of students, Asiaphiles and expats (best make a reservation). Burma's food draws influence from its bordering countries (India, China and Thailand) and is rendered to a very high standard here, at bargain prices. A tangle of crisp beansprout fritters came with three dipping sauces: sour tamarind, salty soy and hot chilli. A chicken and shredded cabbage salad had earthy notes of turmeric and caramelised onion, though could have used a zip of lime. Both meat and vegetarian curries have deeply satisfying flavours and make a hearty meal with rice and nan. As the world's attention turns to Burma, this underrated cuisine could be ready for its moment in the spotlight.

Available for hire weekdays. Babies and children welcome: high chairs. Booking essential dinner. Takeaway service. **Map 2 D4.**

South Kensington

Madsen

20 Old Brompton Road, SW7 3DL (7225 2772, www.madsenrestaurant.com). South Kensington tube. **Open** noon-10.30pm Mon; noon-11pm Tue-Thur; noon-11.45pm Fri, Sat; noon-5pm Sun. **Lunch served** noon-4pm daily. **Dinner served** 4-9.30pm Mon; 4-10pm Tue-Thur; 4-10.45pm Fri, Sat. **Main courses** £11.50-£17.50. **Set lunch** £13.95 2 courses, £18.95 3 courses. **Set dinner** (5-7pm Mon-Sat) £16.50 2 courses, £20.95 3 courses. **Credit** MC, V. Scandinavian

This Scandinavian restaurant opposite South Ken tube station looks the part with its restrained decor of white walls, simple plywood furniture, classic Poul Henningsen light fittings and table-top tea lights. A red leather banquette adds a splash of colour along one wall; opposite is a display of Scandinavian cookery books (some for sale). Lunch options are limited, but include 'smushi' mini open sandwiches (smørrebrød), on dark rye or white

sourdough, with toppings such as Greenland prawns and sliced hard-boiled egg, smoked salmon and own-made mayo, or pork liver pâté. Despite good-quality ingredients, the results were rather dull, and parsley was no substitute for dill on the fishy versions. The set menu produced excellent, onion-marinated herring – our best dish – and a 'risotto' of pearl barley with västerbotten cheese that resembled a strongly flavoured, cheesy porridge: warming on winter nights, one imagines, but odd in August. To drink, there's akavit, wine, Swedish cider and some excellent – if pricey – craft beers from Nøgne Ø (Norway) and Nils Oscar (Sweden). Seasonal specialities include a Christmas buffet and a summer crayfish menu. Personable young staff are a bonus, but we wish Madsen would be a bit more adventurous – and offer more choice.
Available for hire. Babies and children welcome: children's menu; crayons; high chairs; nappy-changing facilities. Booking advisable dinner. Separate room for parties, seats 14. Tables outdoors (4, terrace). Takeaway service.
Map 14 D10.

South

Balham

★ Fat Delicatessen

7 Chestnut Grove, SW12 8JA (8675 6174, www.fatdelicatessen.co.uk). Balham tube/rail. **Meals served** 8am-8pm Mon-Wed; 8am-10pm Thur, Fri; 9am-10pm Sat; 11am-6pm Sun. **Main courses** £4-£8. **Credit** MC, V. Mediterranean

Multi-tasking to the max, the Fat Delicatessen is one part deli and wine shop and two parts breakfast, lunch and early-evening dining spot. It offers daily-changing specials of savoury tarts, salads and cakes alongside a selection of continental cheeses, breads and charcuterie boards. Three evenings a week, from Thursday to Saturday, the lights are turned down low and the deli's great ingredients are translated into a menu of inspiring small plates. The cooking is by way of Italy and France, though a Spanish influence dominates, most obviously in the tapas-style terracotta dishes in which the food is served. We enjoyed morcilla sausage on toast with an onion and piquillo pepper relish, and a tender baked aubergine covered in melted mozzarella. Brilliantly executed dishes continued to delight and surprise, especially an excellent pork belly confit on a bed of creamy, rosemary-scented fagioli beans, and a gratin of sweet braised fennel with a truffle-infused pecorino topping. Diners are seated informally among various jars of chutneys, sauces and other comestibles – all available to take home. A summer special, where drink-in wine was charged at in-store prices, made our already good-value bill a staggering bargain.
Available for hire. Babies and children welcome: high chairs. Booking advisable dinner Thur-Sat. Disabled: toilet. Takeaway service. Vegetarian menu.

Battersea

★ Bistro Délicat

124 Northcote Road, SW11 6QU (7924 3566, www.bistrodelicat.com). Clapham Junction rail then bus 319. **Meals served** 9.30am-3pm Tue-Fri; 9.30am-4pm Sat, Sun. **Dinner served** 6-10.30pm Tue-Sat. **Main courses** £11-£18. **Set meal** (11.30am-3pm Tue-Fri) £13.50 2 courses, £17.50 3 courses. **Credit** AmEx, MC, V. Austrian

Resembling the best sort of new-wave Viennese beisl (neighbourhood brasserie), Bistro Délicat has stylish, simple decor (white tiled walls at the front, black at the rear) and a welcoming vibe. The Austro-French menu starts with breakfast; toasted sourdough and bagels sit alongside savoury dumplings with scrambled egg and chives, bircher muesli and croque monsieur. Some of this menu is also available at lunch, alongside steak frites, nürnberger sausages with own-made sauerkraut (a softer, less acid version than the average shop-bought one) and a first-class bouillabaisse. The last also appears at dinner, together with a glorious tafelspitz – rump of beef cooked in consommé, with bone marrow, creamed spinach, rösti and sauces – and a superior beef goulash, served with spätzle and pickled gherkin. The generous portions – and the excellent bread – meant that a much-anticipated kaiserschmarrn (pan-fried soufflé-pancake pieces with roasted plum compote) was out of the question. The cheeseboard is sourced from Hamish Johnston, just up the road; coffee is taken seriously and carefully made. Like Kipferl (*see pxxx*), Bistro Délicat manages to serve Austrian wines at reasonable prices (along with some French bottles). A lovely local, with charming staff to match.
Available for hire. Babies and children welcome: children's menu; high chairs. Booking advisable Thur-Sun. Tables outdoors (5, pavement).
Map 21 C5.

South East

Crystal Palace

Mediterranea

21 Westow Street, SE19 3RY (8771 7327, www.mediterranea.co). Crystal Palace or Gipsy Hill rail. **Lunch served** noon-2.30pm Mon-Fri; noon-3.30pm Sat. **Dinner served** 6-10pm Tue-Thur; 6-11pm Fri, Sat. **Meals served** noon-10pm Sun. **Main courses** £9.90-£18.90. **Set dinner** (6-7.30pm Mon-Thur) £13.50 2 courses, £16 3 courses. **Credit** AmEx, MC, V. Mediterranean

A snapshot of the Mediterranean on a crowded high street, in which big smiles and a bright turquoise interior instantly boosted a grey Friday evening. A range of European dishes are offered alongside a core of Sardinian staples, including an excellent fish

North Road

stew that burst with a huge variety of fish and seafood mixed in with fregola (a couscous-like pasta made with semolina). A starter of thin slices of grilled pork belly with a perfectly balanced salsa verde was nearly outshone by a simple appetiser of crisp rosemary flatbread – which went down very nicely with a bottle of Ichnusa, a Sardinian beer. The dessert menu consists of old favourites – crème brûlée, cheesecake, panna cotta – but it's worth saving room for the more unusual sebada: just-melted pecorino cheese mixed with lemon zest, ensconced in warm pastry and drizzled with honey. Come 8pm, the locals started to pile in, ordering mainly from the separate pizza menu. Prices are reasonable and staff were knowledgeable about the more unfamiliar dishes and very accommodating – diners are left to linger as long as they wish.
Available for hire. Babies and children welcome: high chairs. Booking advisable weekends. Separate room for parties, seats 20. Vegetarian menu.

Gipsy Hill

Numidie

48 Westow Hill, SE19 1RX (8766 6166, www.numidie.co.uk). Gipsy Hill rail. **Dinner served** 6-11pm Tue-Sun. **Main courses** £8.95-£13.95. **Credit** AmEx, MC, V.
Algerian/French

Despite many competitors in the Crystal Palace triangle, this recently refurbished French-Algerian bistro has won local hearts. Colourful lampshades and glass lanterns throw beads of light on to the dining room's burnt-orange walls, creating a cosy atmosphere that complements an equally heartening, good-value menu. A starter of duck börek, with tender morsels of breast and a jammy relish inside crisp pastry, began the meal as it was set to continue. Couscous and tagines dominate the main courses, and a flavoursome merguez sausage came with fluffy steamed couscous and sweet pepper relish. Dessert, sumptuous cinnamon-spiced crêpes berber, arrived with toasted almonds, honey and ice-cream. Prepared in a tiny kitchen, the food was well cooked, beautifully spiced and easy on the eye. The wine list is notable too, containing popular European labels in addition to vintages from Lebanon and Morocco. Complimentary sweet mint tea, along with very amiable service, added to the informal, welcoming vibe. Downstairs is an intimate little bar, where diminutive cubby holes are ideal for quiet tête-à-têtes.
Available for hire. Babies and children welcome: high chairs. Booking advisable; essential Fri, Sat. Entertainment: musicians Wed, Fri.

East

Shoreditch

Eyre Brothers

70 Leonard Street, EC2A 4QX (7613 5346, www.eyrebrothers.co.uk). Old Street tube/rail. **Lunch served** noon-2.45pm Mon-Fri. **Dinner served** 6.30-10.45pm Mon-Fri; 7-11pm Sat. **Main courses** £15-£27.50. **Credit** AmEx, DC, MC, V. Iberian

David and Robert Eyre's restaurant, dedicated to the sterling ingredients and punchy flavours of the Iberian peninsula, turned ten in 2011. One reason for its continued success is that it manages to appeal to both sides of the Shoreditch/City demographic. The design helps: sturdy furnishings in polished wood and leather dominate the long narrow room, which is cleverly divided into sections to foster intimacy. Circular tables next to the street are perfect for groups. At the back is a long wooden bar: perch here for tapas or to sample the all-Iberian drinks list. This is not timid cooking: expect gutsy flavours, rustic presentation and hefty portions – you can even gorge on a Portuguese-style whole roast suckling pig, if you give them enough notice. The signature dish remains the acorn-fed Ibérico pork fillet, marinated in smoked paprika, thyme and garlic, then grilled medium rare. Served with roughly crushed patatas pobres, the pinkish meat was certainly tender, though some might find it overly spiced and too salty. Seafood looms large: hake and clams, bacalhau in various forms, and tiger prawns peri-peri (a nod to the brothers' Mozambique upbringing). Perfectly cooked tortilla with a ratatouille-like pepper stew was a commendable vegetarian main. Prices are on the high side, but amiable staff add to the convivial atmosphere.
Available for hire. Babies and children admitted. Booking advisable Thur-Sat. Disabled: toilet. **Map 6 Q4**.

North

Islington

Kipferl

20 Camden Passage, N1 8ED (7704 1555, www.kipferl.co.uk). Angel tube. **Open** 9am-10pm

GLOBAL

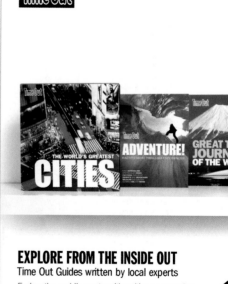

Tue-Sat; 10am-6pm Sun. **Main courses** £8.20-£16.80. **Credit** AmEx, MC, V. Austrian

Now firmly established in blond-wood premises stretching back off Camden Passage, Kipferl operates as a café during the day and more of a restaurant in the evening. The daytime menu starts with breakfasts and moves on to lunch, when there are snacks, soups (liver dumpling, goulash) and sausages: wiener (like a frankfurter), debreziner (slightly spicy) and käsekrainer (with cheese) appear in various combos – we relished a pair of debreziner with some fresh-tasting salads, rye bread and little pots of shredded horseradish and mustard. The main menu is available throughout the day, and offers satisfying platefuls such as rich-tasting beef goulash with own-made spätzle (egg noodles) or generously proportioned wiener schnitzel with parsley potatoes, cranberry sauce and mixed salad (you can hear the meat being pounded in the kitchen below). There are starters such as grilled goat's cheese on red lentil salad, or smoked trout on toasted rye, but we prefer to save ourselves for kaiserschmarrn, a dessert of chopped-up pancake served here with hot morello cherries. The short wine list is an all-Austrian affair, with plenty of tasting notes. There are Austrian beers too. Service is charming, and the welcoming atmosphere extends to canines – dog bowls are kept behind the counter. Kipferl also runs two daytime park cafés in Bloomsbury, in Coram's Fields and Gordon Square.

Available for hire. Babies and children welcome: high chairs; nappy-changing facilities. Booking advisable. Disabled: toilet. Tables outdoors (2, pavement). Takeaway service.

For branches see index.

Stoke Newington

El Olivo

24 Stoke Newington Church Street, N16 0LU (7254 7897). Stoke Newington rail or bus 38. **Meals served** 8am-midnight daily. **Main courses** £7.95-£14.95. **Set lunch** (noon-5pm) £5.95-£9.95 2 courses, £7.95 3 courses. **Credit** MC, V. Mediterranean

Paellas bristling with chicken, chorizo and seafood and served in the pan are the real deal here, popular with locals seeking a change of cuisine. A tapas bar in a Turkish stronghold, El Olivo only concedes defeat when it comes to the bread – which is not Spanish but lovely, warm, locally baked and indispensable for scooping up aubergine cooked to melting softness or tender albóndigas with red peppers. No surfeit of oil to mop up, mind. While tapas can be tired and oily, these taste fresh and perky. Black pudding with rice instead of oats was delightfully herby. More typical and tip-top were soft, bouncy calamares and slightly crisp patatas bravas. In contrast, padrón peppers could have done with a little longer on the grill, and the tortilla came topped with unnecessary salad-creamy aïoli. Tarta de santiago with vanilla ice-cream (nothing special) or flan coated with synthetic-tasting strawberry sauce aren't worth saving space for either. Gypsy-style violin music and a woody interior with wagon-wheel lights won't win awards for a cutting-edge environment, but pleasant service and well-priced wines, along with the savoury food, easily tip the balance in El Ol's favour.

Babies and children welcome: high chairs; nappy-changing facilities. Tables outdoors (2, pavement). Takeaway service. Vegetarian menu. **Map 25 C1.**

Eyre Brothers

North West

Kilburn

★ Ariana II

241 Kilburn High Road, NW6 7JN (3490 6709, www.ariana2restaurant.co.uk). Kilburn tube or Brondesbury rail. **Meals served** noon-11pm daily. **Main courses** £6-£12. **Set meal** £12.50 per person (minimum 2) 3 courses. **Unlicensed. Corkage** no charge. **Credit** MC, V. Afghan

Its pedigree may be glam (Ariana I is in Manhattan), but you'd never know it from this cosy little local fronting on to the Kilburn High Road. Behind the plate-glass window, Afghan tassels and framed photos adorn a simple dining area featuring black tiled flooring, brick walls and dark furniture. Sweet, enthusiastic and swift service brightens proceedings, as do the multicultural bunch of regulars – and the food. In addition to a raft of appetising-looking kebabs, the long menu holds plenty that is singularly Afghan. To start, aushak was a tangy triumph: delicate ravioli parcels filled with leeks, smothered with a tomato and mince sauce and dribbled with yoghurt. Further oomph was provided by a mint, chilli and lemon relish. A main course of kabuli palow consisted of a monumental mound of fluffy rice (the dry side of perfect) covering an entire, tender lamb shank and topped with sweet red strips of carrot, raisins and nuts, accompanied by a side dish of stewed kidney beans. Puddings, too, negotiate a line between the Middle East (baklava) and India (firnee, a yoghurt and nut confection). Low prices and a BYOB policy increase the appeal; we're eager to return.

Available for hire. Babies and children welcome: high chairs. Booking advisable Thur-Sun. Separate room for parties, seats 40. Takeaway service; delivery service (over £12 within 3-mile radius).

Outer London

Harrow, Middlesex

Masa HOT 50

24-26 Headstone Drive, Harrow, Middx, HA3 5QH (8861 6213). Harrow & Wealdstone tube/rail. **Meals served** 12.30-11pm daily. **Main courses** £5.95-£13. **Set meal** £23.95 (2 people); £33 (2-3 people); £55 (4-5 people). **Unlicensed. Corkage** no charge. **No credit cards.** Afghan

Not to be confused with Mazar, a rival eaterie across the road, Masa has long set the standard for the food of Afghanistan, a landlocked country which takes its culinary cues from its numerous neighbours. The kebabs are spiced like those in Pakistan, the pasta dishes originated in China and Uzbekistan, and the meze-style dips can also be found in Iran. These dips, known as bourani, were excellent; the fresh and flavoursome aubergine, spinach and courgette dishes topped with quroot (a slightly sour whey) are designed to be mopped up by soft, fluffy blankets of nan bread. The mains were impressive too. The national dish, qabali pilau, was a generous portion of moist pilau rice with almonds, carrots, raisins and lamb that fell from the bone. A lighter alternative is ashak, leek dumplings covered in yoghurt and minced meat. There's no alcohol licence, but there is dogh, a carbonated yogurt drink made with cucumber and mint, similar to Indian lassi. The good food, low prices and cheery service are somewhat undermined by the cold, formal atmosphere. A single chandelier hangs above heavy wooden furniture, and television is preferred to Afghan music.

Babies and children welcome: high chairs. Booking advisable Thur-Sun. Disabled: toilet. Takeaway service; delivery service (over £12 within 3-mile radius). Vegetarian menu.

COFFEE

In 19th century Viennese café's you were given a coffee colour palette – similar to this one. Guests were able to choose between very mild (light brown) to very strong (black) coffee.

CAFÉ LATTE or VERKEHRTER – espresso with lots of hot milk / £ 2.60

MELANGE is an espresso with hot milk – topped with milk foam / £ 2.30
with whipped cream / £ 2.60

CAPPUCINO is like a 'Melange' but a little stronger / £ 2.30

BRAUNER is an espresso with hot milk
Kleiner Brauner (small) / £ 1.80
Grosser Brauner (large) / £ 2.60

VERLANGERTER is like an 'Americano' – espresso with hot water / £ 2.20

SCHWARZER is a classic 'Espresso'
Kleiner Schwarzer (single) / £ 1.50
Grosser Schwarzer (double) / £ 1.90

Kipferl. See p125.

Greek

Crisis, what crisis? London's Greek restaurant scene has an enduring quality that might seem enviable to businesses back in the tumultuous homeland. Most venues major in Greek-Cypriot cuisine; if you're after the casserole dishes of the Greek mainland, head for **Greek Affair** and **As Greek As It Gets**. Innovation is rare in this section, and one of the most notable openings of the past 15 years, the **Real Greek** (which began trading as long ago as 1999), soon transformed into a chain and now exhibits many of the dreary characteristics that replication often entails. However, there is one bright newcomer this year: **Mazi** – let's hope it shakes London's more established Hellenic restaurants out of their complacency. As their brethren in Athens now realise, remaining static is not an option when the world around you is in transformation.

Central

Covent Garden

The Real Greek

60-62 Long Acre, WC2E 9JE (7240 2292, www.therealgreek.com). Covent Garden tube.
Meals served noon-11pm Mon-Sat; noon-10.30pm Sun. **Main courses** £2.50-£7.25. **Set mezédes** £26-£28 (minimum 2). **Credit** AmEx, MC, V.

With the original Hoxton Market restaurant of this Hellenic chain now closed, the Real Greek seems past its best. There's still life left at the Covent Garden branch, though. On a Monday night, the air buzzed with the intercontinental chatter of tourists, as slick, friendly staff served dishes speedily. Within 30 seconds of ordering, an aggressively garlicky bowl of melitzanosaláta was on the table. Ten minutes later, it was joined by the cinnamon aromatics of three tart, creamy tyrópitta; five minutes after that, a curiously bitter lamb souvláki arrived. The seating arrangement doesn't encourage lingering, with punters perched on bar stool-like seats and at high tables of varnished dark wood. Add the metal bucket of Mythos beer bottles that sits atop a cabinet, plus a prominent spirits display, and you have a venue that feels half-bar, half-restaurant. Typical decorative Greek touches are provided by big bunches of dried red chillies and net bags of garlic hanging in the window, a mini olive tree on the sill, and bottles of Cretan Latzimas olive oil joining the salt and pepper on tables. A perfectly pleasant place, well positioned for shoppers and sightseers, but not somewhere for a leisurely repast.

Babies and children admitted. Booking advisable. Separate room for parties, seats 15. Takeaway service. **Map 18 E3.**

For branches see index.

West

Bayswater

Aphrodite Taverna

15 Hereford Road, W2 4AB (7229 2206, www.aphroditerestaurant.co.uk). Bayswater, Notting Hill Gate or Queensway tube. **Meals served** noon-midnight Mon-Sat. **Main courses** £9.50-£23.50. **Set mezédes** £19 vegetarian, £22 meat, £31 fish per person (minimum 2). **Cover** £1. **Credit** AmEx, MC, V.

Stroll into this cosily chintzy eaterie and you might be forgiven for thinking you've entered some kind of 1980s Hellenic equivalent of the Geffrye Museum. Greek-Cypriot knick-knacks sit on every available surface. Oil-burning lamps top the tables; a huge bottle of Metaxa dominates the dark wooden bar; and mini bouzoukis, gourds, plaster Parthenons and Greek pottery frescoes combine to make a charmingly cluttered interior. Waiters – clad in the traditional garb of white shirts and black waistcoats, of course – are helpful and attentive, although perhaps slightly over-keen to sell the day's specials. The large menu features a substantial range of grills, steaks and meaty stews. A generous helping of kléftiko saw the unctuous lamb slip pleasingly from the bone, and a chunky serving of moussaká also impressed, coming topped with a thick cheese crust. However, calamares was just the wrong side of chewy, and the keftédes meatballs had an unpleasantly oniony tang to them. Don't worry if you don't have room for desserts afterwards; the meal ends with a complimentary portion of rose- and lemon-flavoured loukoúmi.

Available for hire. Babies and children welcome: high chairs. Booking advisable dinner. Tables outdoors (12, terrace). Takeaway service. Vegetarian menu. **Map 7 B6.**

Notting Hill

Greek Affair

1 Hillgate Street, W8 7SP (7792 5226, www.greekaffair.co.uk). Notting Hill Gate tube. **Lunch served** noon-3pm Thur-Sun. **Dinner served** 6-10.30pm. **Main courses** £10-£15. **Set meal** (lunch, 6-7pm) £9.50 2 courses, £11.50 3 courses. **Set mezédes** £14-£18. **Credit** AmEx, MC, V.

Standing apart from the Greek-Cypriot hegemony of the capital's Hellenic restaurants, this multi-floored eaterie is a breath of fresh air. Its menu is based on the cuisine of the Greek mainland and surrounding islands and is palpably different from the London norm. For instance, a starter of mixed dips shuns the customary basket of pitta for crusty white bread, and a portion of staggeringly tender calamares substitutes the typical deep-fried batter in favour of a rich, oily tomato sauce. The long menu also encompasses seldom-seen dishes such as yiouvetsi (meat, in this case lamb, baked in tomato sauce with orzo pasta) and hirino katsarolas (pork casserole in a tomato sauce). The grey-painted wooden interior produces a modern, contemporary feel, with half the seating capacity of the downstairs dining area made up of communal

Mazi

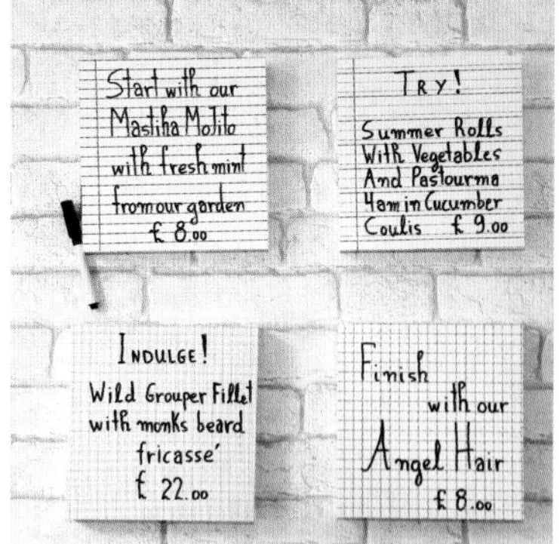
Start with our
Mastiha Mojito
with fresh mint
from our garden
£ 8.00
TRY!
Summer Rolls
With Vegetables
And Pastourma
Coulis £ 9.00
INDULGE!
Wild Grouper Fillet
with monks beard
fricasse'
£ 22.00
Finish
with our
Angel Hair
£ 8.00

tables topped with big vases of tulips. Upstairs, a slightly shabby roof terrace offers faded quarry tiling, rosemary bushes and bamboo fencing for alfresco dining. Service is relaxed and unobtrusive. As the Greek Affair never seems to be particularly full, it's a nice place to linger over a meal.
Available for hire. Babies and children welcome: high chairs. Booking advisable. Separate room for parties, seats 35. Tables outdoors (10, roof garden). Takeaway service. Vegetarian menu. **Map 19 C5**.

★ Mazi NEW

12-14 Hillgate Street, W8 7SR (7229 3794, www.mazi.co.uk). Notting Hill tube. **Lunch served** noon-3.30pm, **dinner served** 6.30-11pm Mon-Fri. **Meals served** noon-11pm Sat; noon-10pm Sun. **Main courses** £6-£25. **Credit** AmEx, MC, V.

As properly Greek as you'll find in London, this Notting Hill newcomer showcases both traditional dishes and the progressive cooking of leading restaurants in Mykonos and Athens, where its two consultant chefs are based. It's a simply but attractively furnished place – in what used to be Costas Grill – with eager, attentive service. Mazi's wine list is entirely Greek, sourced from new-wave producers as well as classic appellations such as Nemea, made from the indigenous agiorgitiko grape in the Peloponnese. Even Mazi's retsina is in the modern style: only lightly resinated and very palatable. Benchmark dishes such as Greek salad (horiátiki) were near-perfect. We especially like details such as the inclusion of rock samphire, the rustic hórta (wild greens) that Greeks call kritama. The dish presentation is a bit fancy-schmancy, with taramá served in a glass preserve jar, but we couldn't fault the freshness or quality of the spread, and the preserved lemon garnish was an inspired touch. Spanakópitta was deconstructed into sheets of filo pastry and a stew of spinach and feta, in the bottom of another jar, but the tastes and texture were spot-on. Matsata – rabbit stew with fresh pasta – also had correctly rustic flavours. For pudding, try the molten-centred tsoureki soufflé, made from brioche-like Easter bread. Paired with Greek-coffee ice-cream, it was an ingenious dish to finish an excellent meal.
Available for hire. Babies and children welcome: high chairs. Booking advisable Fri-Sun. Tables outdoors (9, garden). Vegan dishes. **Map 19 C5**.

South West

Earl's Court

As Greek As It Gets

233 Earl's Court Road, SW5 9AH (7244 7777, www.asgreekasitgets.co.uk). Earl's Court tube. **Lunch served** noon-3pm, **dinner served** 5-11pm Mon-Fri. **Meals served** noon-11pm Sat, Sun. **Main courses** £10-£15. **Credit** MC, V.

Strictly speaking, if this were as Greek as it gets, a traditional Hellenic homestead would be an interior-design showroom. This two-floor restaurant hangs around a chandelier-dominated alcove, its chic, black walls lined with artfully snapped portraits of black-clad elderly Greek women and red and gold wooden spoons. Mottled white marble tables are topped with vases of flowers. Were it not for a big orange map of Greece and a smattering of Greek

Menu

Dishes followed by (G) indicate a specifically Greek dish; those marked (GC) indicate a Greek-Cypriot speciality; those without an initial have no particular regional affiliation. Spellings on menus often vary.

Afélia (GC): pork cubes stewed in wine, coriander and other herbs.
Avgolémono (G): a sauce made of lemon, egg yolks and chicken stock. Also a soup made with rice, chicken stock, lemon and whole eggs.
Dolmádes (G) or **koupépia (GC)**: young vine leaves stuffed with rice, spices and (usually) minced meat.
Fasólia plakí or **pilakí**: white beans in a tomato, oregano, bay, parsley and garlic sauce.
Garídes: prawns (usually king prawns in the UK), fried or grilled.
Gígantes or **gígandes**: white butter beans baked in tomato sauce; pronounced 'yígandes'.
Halloumi (GC) or **hallúmi**: a cheese that is traditionally made from sheep or goat's milk, but increasingly from cow's milk. Best served fried or grilled.
Horiátiki: Greek 'peasant' salad made from tomato, cucumber, onion, feta and sometimes green pepper, dressed with ladolémono (a mixture of oil and lemon).
Hórta: salad of cooked wild greens.
Houmous, **hoúmmous** or **húmmus (GC)**: a dip of puréed chickpeas, sesame seed paste, lemon juice and garlic, garnished with paprika. Originally an Arabic dish.
Htipití or **khtipití**: tangy purée of matured cheeses, flavoured with red peppers.
Kalamári, **kalamarákia** or **calamares**: small squid, usually sliced into rings, with the pieces battered and fried.
Kataïfi or **katayfi**: syrup-soaked 'shredded-wheat' rolls.
Keftédes or **keftedákia (G)**: herby meatballs made with minced pork or lamb (rarely beef), egg, breadcrumbs and possibly grated potato.
Kléftiko (GC): slow-roasted lamb (often shoulder), served on the bone and flavoured with oregano and other herbs.
Kopanistí (G): a cheese dip with a tanginess traditionally coming from natural fermentation, but often boosted with chilli.
Koukiá: broad beans.
Loukánika or **lukánika**: spicy coarse-ground sausages, usually pork and heavily herbed.
Loukoumédes: tiny, spongy dough fritters, dipped in honey.
Loukoúmi or **lukúmi**: 'turkish delight' made using syrup, rosewater and pectin, and often studded with nuts.
Loúntza (GC): smoked pork loin.
Marídes: picarel, often mistranslated as (or substituted by) 'whitebait' – small fish best coated in flour and flash-fried.
Melitzanosaláta: grilled aubergine purée.
Meze (the plural is **mezédes**, pronounced 'mezédhes'): a selection of either hot or cold appetisers and main dishes.
Moussaká(s) (G): a baked dish of mince (usually lamb), aubergine and potato slices, topped with béchamel sauce.
Papoutsáki: aubergine 'shoes', slices stuffed with mince, topped with sauce that's usually béchamel-like.
Pourgoúri or **bourgoúri (GC)**: a pilaf of cracked wheat, often prepared with stock, onions, crumbled vermicelli and spices.
Saganáki (G): fried cheese, usually kefalotyri; also refers to anything (mussels, spinach) served in a cheese-based red sauce.
Sheftaliá (GC): little pig-gut skins stuffed with minced pork and lamb, onion, parsley, breadcrumbs and spices, then grilled.
Soutzoukákia or **soutzoúki (G)**: baked meat rissoles, which are often topped with a tomato-based sauce.
Soúvla: large cuts of lamb or pork, slow-roasted on a rotary spit.
Souvláki: chunks of meat quick-grilled on a skewer (known in London takeaways as kebab or shish kebab).
Spanakópitta: small turnovers stuffed with spinach, dill and often feta or some other crumbly tart cheese.
Stifádo: a rich meat stew (often made using beef or rabbit) with onions, red wine, tomatoes, cinnamon and bay.
Taboúlleh: generic Middle Eastern starter of pourgoúri (qv), chopped parsley, cucumber chunks, tomatoes and spring onions.
Taramá, properly **taramosaláta**: fish roe pâté, originally made of dried, salted grey mullet roe, but now more often smoked cod roe, plus olive oil, lemon juice and breadcrumbs.
Tavás (GC): lamb, onion, tomato and cumin, cooked in earthenware casseroles.
Tsakistés (GC): split green olives marinated in lemon, garlic, coriander seeds and other optional flavourings.
Tyrópitta (G): similar to spanakópitta (qv) but usually without spinach and with more feta.
Tzatzíki, **dzadzíki (G)** or **talatoúra (GC)**: a dip of shredded cucumber, yoghurt, garlic, lemon juice and mint.

recipe books in the window, you might struggle to identify the nationality of the cuisine served here. There's no doubting the heritage of the food, though, which tends more toward Greek than Cypriot dishes. Delicately fried cod came in a light batter with a serving of pungently garlicky skordalia; a platter of grilled meats arrived with an impressively aerated mustard mayonnaise and thick, chunky tzatzíki. Less successful was filo-wrapped feta, with a honey and ouzo coating that left it an unpleasant exercise in salty sweetness. Charcoal-flavoured keftédes lacked the requisite kick of onion and herbs. On our Friday night visit, the venue was curiously empty, with staff so untaxed they spent most of the evening chatting by the bar.
Available for hire. Babies and children welcome: high chairs. Booking advisable weekends. Tables outdoors (2, pavement). Takeaway service. **Map 13 B11.**

North East

South Woodford

George's Fish & Souvlaki Bar

164 George Lane, E18 1AY (8989 3970, www.georgesfishbar.co.uk). South Woodford tube. **Lunch served** noon-2.30pm Mon-Thur; noon-3pm Fri, Sat. **Dinner served** 5-10.30pm Mon-Sat. **Meals served** 1-9pm Sun. **Main courses** £11-£13.50. **Set lunch** £7.95-£10.95 2 courses. **Set mezédes** £22.50 per person (minimum 2). **Credit** MC, V.

It's all change at this chip-shop-cum-restaurant. While the tiles and takeaway prices of the chippy front space remain the same, the rear dining room has had a makeover. A long cream-coloured leather bench lines one side of the restaurant, and the rear wall is now all exposed slate, nicely mixing the chic and rustic. A jaunty soundtrack of Hellenic bouzouki music chirrups away in the background. The menu has remained constant: a mix of fish and chips and Cypriot cuisine that sees side orders of pickled eggs sitting alongside dishes of moussaká. A portion of dolmádes was filled with a pleasingly moist tomato and meat mix in typical Cypriot style, and a portion of herb-packed sheftaliá was nicely smoky. A Sunday offer of two courses for £10.95 sounded like good value. However, the serving of mixed starters was comically niggardly: a two-person portion of potato salad consisted of just one new potato cut into six chunks; and one course arrived with a side dish of only eight chips. Ordering à la carte has proven more successful in terms of portion size in the past.
Available for hire. Babies and children welcome: children's menu; high chairs; nappy-changing facilities. Booking advisable Thur-Sun. Tables outdoors (8, patio). Takeaway service.

North

Camden Town & Chalk Farm

Daphne

83 Bayham Street, NW1 0AG (7267 7322). Camden Town or Mornington Crescent tube. **Lunch served** noon-2.30pm, **dinner served** 6-11.30pm Mon-Sat. **Main courses** £10.75-£15.50. **Set lunch** £7.75 2 courses, £9.25 3 courses. **Set mezédes** £17.50 meat or vegetarian, £21.50 fish per person (minimum 2). **Credit** MC, V.

There's no doubting the charms of this family-run, Greek-Cypriot restaurant. Its three-floor layout takes in a cosy ground floor that's all floral-patterned booths and black and white photos of Cypriot village life. The first floor conjures up an authentic Mediterranean feel with its uneven whitewashed walls and tiled floors. Metal baskets of flowers that line the small, top-floor roof terrace (seating 20) help create a lovely summer spot for relaxed, atmospheric alfresco eating. Despite bucking the trend to serve gargantuan portions among the capital's Hellenic restaurants – many of Daphne's meals require the additional purchase of a side dish – this isn't always a case of quality over quantity. Three mini koubes (deep-fried wheat parcels stuffed with minced lamb) were crisp and aromatic, but a parsley-speckled portion of lounza ham was tough and dry, a grease-slicked spanakópitta sat in a puddle of oil, and both a portion of grilled fish skewers and lamb souvláki lacked the dishes' requisite smokiness. Service is nonetheless charming, with the bubbly, matronly restaurateur regularly rattling off quips about her homeland while taking customers through the menu.
Available for hire. Babies and children welcome: high chairs. Booking advisable. Tables outdoors (7, roof terrace; 2, veranda). Takeaway service. Vegetarian menu. **Map 27 D2.**

Lemonia

89 Regent's Park Road, NW1 8UY (7586 7454). Chalk Farm tube. **Lunch served** noon-3pm Mon-Fri; noon-3.30pm Sun. **Dinner served** 6-11.30pm Mon-Sat. **Main courses** £10.50-£15. **Set lunch** (Mon-Fri) £9.75 2 courses, £11.50 3 courses. **Set mezédes** £19.50 per person (minimum 2). **Credit** MC, V.

The only difference between a quiet and a busy night at this perennially packed eaterie is how long you have to wait at the bar for a table if you turn up without having booked. It's easy to see why the place is so popular. The multi-room interior's high ceilings create an atmosphere that means noise from the plethora of diners is buzzy rather than overpowering – particularly in the plant-strewn, botanical-garden-like conservatory. A large team of waiters bustles around, serving up dishes at impressive speed, tempered with a jocularity that avoids leaving you feeling rushed. A meze selection impressed with its range of cold dishes, including a pleasingly tangy taramosaláta and a melitzanosaláta zingy with lemon juice. The hot offerings didn't, unfortunately, sustain the quality, with a soft spanakópitta lacking the dish's requisite crispness, and calamares that leant towards the overcooked; but these were the only low points in a meal whose quality was high. Desserts shouldn't be missed: we particularly approve of the rich clove scenting of the galaktoboureko (custard pie) and the chunkily chopped pistachios in the baklava. The pavement tables add to the gaiety of Regent's Park Road in warm weather.
Babies and children admitted. Booking advisable. Separate room for parties, seats 40. Tables outdoors (6, pavement). Takeaway service. Vegetarian menu. **Map 27 A1.**

Kentish Town

Carob Tree

15 Highgate Road, NW5 1QX (7267 9880). Gospel Oak rail or bus C2, C11, 214. **Lunch served** noon-3pm, **dinner served** 6-10.30pm Tue-Fri. **Meals served** noon-10.30pm Sat; noon-9pm Sun. **Main courses** £3.20-£20. **Credit** MC, V.

The capital's Hellenic chain restaurants could take a lesson or two from the smart, contemporary decor to be found here. Floor-to-ceiling, swagged red curtains drape against stucco pillars, and a metallic graphic of a carob tree peps up a neutrally coloured dining area that's all taupes, creams and beech window frames. And in contrast to its multi-outlet rivals, Carob Tree has a menu containing several own-made treats. The sesame-seed studded falafel were so fragrant with lemon juice that it was almost a shame to use the accompanying tahini dip; and a portion of grilled Dutch calf's liver was juicy and succulent. On the other hand, a starter of pastourma (Cypriot beef sausage) was less impressive, leaning towards the wrong side of well done, and a grilled monkfish shashlik kebab lacked flavour. Towards the end of the evening, a chorus of 'happy birthday' blared from the speakers and the staff urged diners to serenade the celebrating punter. Throughout, service was impressively friendly, staff urging us to 'take our time' despite a dining room that was nearly full of local families chattering away in Greek. A corked glass of wine was replaced efficiently and apologetically.
Available for hire. Babies and children welcome: high chairs; nappy-changing facilities. Booking advisable. Disabled: toilet. Tables outdoors (10, garden). Vegetarian menu.

Wood Green

Vrisaki

73 Myddleton Road, N22 8LZ (8889 8760). Bounds Green or Wood Green tube. **Meals served** noon-11.30pm Mon-Sat; noon-9pm Sun. **Main courses** £10-£18. **Set mezédes** £19 per person (minimum 2). **Credit** AmEx, MC, V.

If you wanted a venue that sums up the unwritten rule about much of London's Hellenic restaurant scene, you couldn't do better than Vrisaki. From the chip shop frontage's metal deep-fat fryers, to the chiller cabinets packed with raw meat skewers, this ever-popular restaurant is very much a no-frills affair that attempts to coast on personality alone. The three-course set meze menu has a focus on quantity rather than quality, which means that while few dishes will impress, you'll barely be able to see your table under the weight of dishes that are piled on top. The selection of dips, herbed pulse salads and seafood medleys that make up the first course alone features no less than 16 plates. By the time the smoky pork kebabs, aromatic sheftaliá and fried quails' wings of the final course arrive, most diners are asking for takeaway boxes. Service is friendly and jovial, with wise-cracking, grandfatherly waiting staff ribbing customers about whether they're up to the task of finishing their meal. The pleasing community feel of the place is also enhanced by the background hum of customers chattering animatedly in Greek.
Available for hire. Babies and children welcome: high chairs. Booking advisable: essential weekends. Takeaway service.

Hotels & Haute Cuisine

Haute cuisine in a time of austerity could be seen as an indulgence bordering on the obscene – and if any diner becomes blasé about such establishments through over-exposure, perhaps the line has been crossed. (Out-to-impress corporate execs take note.) A meal at these stellar restaurants should be seen as a chance to experience a thought-provoking art form: a treat, certainly, but also a rich fund of culinary ideas – sometimes erudite, sometimes self-referential, sometimes playful. Impeccable execution is a given (or should be), so keeping all this in mind, the price of a haute cuisine lunch or dinner – often little more than a couple of tickets to a Chelsea home game – seems reasonable. Especially if the food is truly memorable. Flummery and charlatanism do exist, of course, but usually at restaurants pitched slightly lower than this level (though charging almost as much). Set menus are often the best way of getting a taste of haute cuisine venues without breaking the bank: ideally where the chefs produce equally innovative food but using less luxurious ingredients than found on the carte. So who are the best of the best? This year, our favourites are **Alain Ducasse**, **Gordon Ramsay**, the **Ledbury**, the **Greenhouse**, **Marcus Wareing**, **Pollen Street Social**, **Roganic**, **Sketch**, **Tom Aikens**, **Viajante** and newcomer **Dabbous** – gastronomic theatres in which to relish the cooking, and delight in the skill, of supremely talented chefs.

Central

Belgravia

Pétrus

1 Kinnerton Street, SW1X 8EA (7592 1609, www.gordonramsay.com/petrus). Knightsbridge tube. **Lunch served** noon-2.15pm, **dinner served** 6.30-10pm Mon-Sat. **Set lunch** £30 3 courses. **Set dinner** £65 3 courses. **Set meal** £75 tasting menu. **Credit** AmEx, MC, V.

The dining room at Pétrus exudes quiet self-confidence. Colours are pleasant on the eye, with dashes of claret and oyster-hued fabrics. There's a relaxed buzz in the room helped along by hospitable staff. At its centre is an eye-catching circular glass wine cabinet. A fritter of tête de cochon with gribiche sauce made a punchy opening to our meal. Next came a crispy skinned Cornish mackerel served with mackerel tartare, a splash of sour cream complementing the soft flesh of the fish, with pickled cucumber providing an enticing cool blast. The well-honed kitchen team is led by Sean Burbidge; it tends towards the conservative, with jiggery-pokery kept to a minimum. That said, a cep foam did appear on top of creamy wild mushroom and spinach wrapped in filo pastry, which accompanied a roasted breast of guinea fowl (Madeira jus adding a luscious end note). We were thrilled by the separate servings of three different coloured carrots and dauphinoise potatoes. Desserts aren't to be missed, and seasonal gariguette strawberries made a winning combination with Sauternes jelly, strawberry ice-cream and brown sugar beignets, the dish made still more ravishing by a jelly filled with liquid strawberry that oozed into our mouths. The charming Japanese sommelier helped us get the best from an impressive wine list filled with classic labels from around the globe. This place seems to get better with every visit.

Available for hire. Babies and children welcome: high chairs. Booking advisable. Disabled: toilet. Dress: smart casual. Vegetarian menu. **Map 9 G9**.

City

Bonds

Threadneedles, 5 Threadneedle Street, EC2R 8AY (7657 8088, www.theetoncollection.com). Bank tube/DLR or Liverpool Street tube/rail. **Breakfast served** 6.30-10am Mon-Fri; 7-11am Sat, Sun. **Lunch served** noon-2.30pm, **dinner served** 6-10pm Mon-Fri. **Main courses** £12.95-£26.50. **Set meal** (noon-2.30pm, 6-8pm) £19.95 2 courses, £23 3 courses. **Credit** AmEx, DC, MC, V.

With a winning combination of a Threadneedle location, majestic Victorian bank architecture and hotel convenience, it's little wonder that Bonds finds favour with City folk throughout the day: from crack-of-dawn breakfast, via cocktails and tapas 'during and after work', to weekday lunch and dinner, with afternoon tea affording leisurely meetings under the magnificent stained-glass atrium. No surprise either that the dining area is discreet, correct and hushed (even on a bright, hot

Pétrus. See p131.

summer's day the cool interior was chiaroscuro save for the occasional red glow), yet spacious, comfortable and opulent in its expanse of dark-wood flooring and wall panelling. What is unexpectedly welcome is the moderate pricing of the set menu for what is undoubtedly high-end dining. Remarkably, it's even possible to assemble a vegetarian selection from the carte at similar cost (the set meals don't always feature meat-free dishes). And while the enticing wine list is pre-austerity in its reach, the least expensive glasses are perfectly pleasing. The summer menu dishes produced by chef Stephen Smith proved delightful: opulent in their use of luxury ingredients (cream, truffles) and design-conscious plating, yet focused in their clarity, freshness and transformation of the humble (ham hock, carrots). An emphasis on seasonality, Britishness and sustainability shows an apt and modern sensibility. Inventiveness can lead to an occasional slip – the sweetness of candied carrot overrode all else in an otherwise earthy dish of truffled tortellini – but a happy absence of staidness seals the deal.

Available for hire. Babies and children welcome: high chairs. Booking advisable. Disabled: lift; toilet. Dress: smart casual. Separate rooms for parties, seating 8, 14 and 16. **Map 12 Q6.**

Fitzrovia

★ Dabbous NEW

2012 RUNNER-UP BEST NEW RESTAURANT

39 Whitfield Street, W1T 2SF (7323 1544, www.dabbous.co.uk). Goodge Street or Warren Street tube. **Meals served** noon-3pm, 5.30-11.30pm Tue-Sat. **Main courses** £11-£16. **Set lunch** (noon-2pm Tue-Sat) £22 3 courses, £26 4 courses. **Set meal** (noon-2pm, 6.30-9pm Tue-Sat) £54 tasting menu. **Credit** AmEx, MC, V.

Every so often a chef and restaurant pop up, seemingly from nowhere, and cause a sensation. In early 2012, that chef was Ollie Dabbous. His restaurant (pronounced 'Dabbou – the 's' is silent) first wowed the critics, then wowed the public; it's now nigh-on impossible to book a dinner table here. What the kitchen offers is gossamer-light cooking of the haute school, served in a modernist and hard-edged semi-industrial concrete space. Uncomplicated menu descriptions belie the wit and intricacy of the dishes: 'peas with mint' translated to a tiny ball of verdant pea granita suspended in a smooth and chilled pea soup, studded with fresh just-cooked peas and scattered with mint leaves and pea shoots. 'Rabbit pie', baked in a dinky bowl, saw tender pieces of white meat cooked in a marquis sauce (béchamel with French wholegrain mustard) then covered with a buttery, golden crust – with a baby carrot poking its head out just for fun. Finally, 'ripe peach in its own juice' showcased the fruit at its best, with sweet pieces of poached flesh in a puddle of heavily scented, coriander-spiked syrup. It's only a pity that on our visit, the waiting staff (efficient yet lacking confidence) did little to decode the barely comprehensible menu.

Available for hire. Babies and children welcome: high chairs. Booking advisable. Dress: smart casual. Vegetarian menu. **Map 17 B1.**

Pied à Terre

34 Charlotte Street, W1T 2NH (7636 1178, www.pied-a-terre.co.uk). Goodge Street or Tottenham Court Road tube. **Lunch served** noon-2.30pm Mon-Fri. **Dinner served** 6-10.45pm Mon-Sat. **Set lunch** £23.50 2 courses, £27.50 5 courses. **Set dinner** £80 3 courses. **Set meal** £99 tasting menu. **Credit** AmEx, MC, V.

A mite faded, but still enticing after some 20 years of plaudit earning and award gathering, Pied-à-Terre is currently showcasing the talent of Marcus Eaves, who left his training ground at sister restaurant L'Autre Pied in June 2011. The decor – mostly brown and beige, with occasional flashes of pinks and reds from glassware, artwork and floral decorations – feels muted and underwhelming; more dramatic touches are reserved for the private rooms. Best bet is to be ensconced in the cosy, almost intimate front room, with light filtering in from the street. Eaves is clearly determined not simply to maintain the style of pretty, intricately woven dishes, but to make a fair bid for the crown of 'London's best-value set lunch' – which is good news for (relatively) cash-strapped diners. Elaboration can quickly grow tiresome, however pretty the plates and the plating, but Eaves has a markedly delicate touch: in the implausibly fragile canapé wafers encasing droplets of zingy guacamole, for instance; or the lightest of foie gras mousses partnering smoked eel fillet, lifted by a slim shard of green apple. There are earthier notes to balance the near-abstraction: a truffled spelt risotto served amply in a chunky, resolutely rectangular dish; the brown flesh of poached sea bream and warm chunks of walnut bread. All is not faultless: loin of Middlewhite, clearly cooked without fat, was a suggestion rather than essence of porkiness; and salting can be heavy at times – stridently misplaced in a heavily saline caramel chocolate. Generosity even at set-meal level inspires forgiveness, however, as does the warmth of the staff, not least the sommelier, proudly displaying the provenance of the lowliest wines on an exhaustive list.

Babies and children admitted. Booking advisable; essential weekends. Dress: smart casual. Separate room for parties, seats 13. Vegetarian menu. **Map 17 B1**.

Roux at the Landau

The Landau, 1C Portland Place, W1B 1JA (7965 0165, www.thelandau.com). Oxford Circus tube. **Breakfast served** 7-10.30am Mon-Fri; 7am-noon Sat, Sun. **Lunch served** 12.30-2.30pm Mon-Fri. **Dinner served** 5.30-10.30pm Mon-Sat. **Main courses** £19-£42. **Set meal** (12.30-2.30pm, 5.30-7pm) £47.50 3 courses incl half bottle of wine, mineral water and coffee; £80 tasting menu (£140 incl wine). **Credit** AmEx, DC, MC, V.

The inviting design of its airy space, the smilingly solicitous staff, the restraint on intricacy of presentation – all indicate the Landau's move away from any stuffiness associated with high-end dining. Touches of Hispanic and Middle Eastern spicing and a penchant for own-made charcuterie similarly signal a modern outlook by the young Roux protégé, head chef Chris King. Nevertheless, the nomenclature, the daunting – if rather lovely – wine 'corridor' that leads to the dining room, and the likes of the silver-domed roast trolley confirm that this is a high-status restaurant, and a berth for clients who very much expect correctness. That said, it's not hard to relax into enjoying King's accomplished cuisine: whether via the tasting menus with suggested wine pairing (from that astounding cellar); the carte (which incorporates cleverly constructed dishes for two to share); or indeed the lunch and early evening set menus (with an optional half bottle of well-chosen wine). The set menus on our visit ran the gamut from delicacy (the lightest of Paris mushroom veloutés) to trencherman fare – an ample serving of outstanding suckling pig with milky, thyme-scented flesh and delicately crunchy crackling proving well worth the £5 supplement. Luxurious touches – flakes of summer truffle and swirls of bright saffron sauce counterpointing a deeply saline ham and confit chicken terrine – sat alongside upmarket peasant sustenance, with heart of summer cabbage and a bowlful of white beans lending considerable substance to a dish of crusted roast cod. Everything was deftly executed: a pastel pistachio panna cotta and essence of lavender ice vying for final honours with beautifully balanced petits fours. Judging by the genial banter, the soft-edged correctness in sumptuous surroundings clearly attracts many, admittedly well-heeled, devotees.

Available for hire. Babies and children welcome: high chairs. Booking advisable; essential weekends. Disabled: toilet. Dress: smart casual. Separate room for parties, seats 16. Vegetarian menu. **Map 9 H5**.

Holborn

Pearl Bar & Restaurant

Chancery Court Hotel, 252 High Holborn, WC1V 7EN (7829 7000, www.pearl-restaurant.com). Holborn tube.
Bar **Open** 11am-11pm Mon-Fri; 6-11pm Sat.
Restaurant **Lunch served** noon-2.30pm Mon-Fri. **Dinner served** 6-10pm Mon-Sat. **Set lunch** £19 1 course, £25 2 courses, £28 3 courses. **Set dinner** £38 1 course, £50 2 courses, £60 3 courses. **Set meal** £70 tasting menu (£120 incl wine).
Both **Credit** AmEx, DC, MC, V.

Pearl sits in an annexe of a deluxe hotel, housed in a striking building that was once the headquarters of Pearl Assurance. The beautiful grand dining room, complete with marble columns and a stylish bar, combines the best of Edwardian architecture with contemporary furnishings. The ambience is cleverly softened by warm shades of wood, cream leather and delicate hand-strung white pearls. Jun Tanaka has been the executive chef here since 2004, and he has been busy setting up gourmet catering van Street Kitchen of late. Pea foam and pea salad made a lovely prelude to our meal – though a soup spoon was too large for the dinky dish. Such little things matter at this level, and service too could have been sharper and more engaging. We continued in proper fashion with a vivacious mackerel fondant. This eye-catching dish came with superb smoked eel and mini-vegetables (turnips, carrots and cauliflower) served à la grecque circling the fondant. Tanaka's cookbook is entitled *Simple to Sensational*, and true to its front cover we were treated to a perfect Ely lamb wellington rounded off with minted peas and roasted Jersey Royals. We resisted the cheeses given the hefty £15 supplement, settling for a strawberry and champagne jelly topped with vanilla foam and crumble, which arrived in a glass compote jar; however, it turned out to be too sweet and playful for our liking. Fellow diners were corporate types, and the French-focused, pricey wine list is heavily geared to their expense accounts.

Available for hire. Babies and children welcome restaurant: high chairs. Booking advisable. Disabled: toilet. Dress: smart casual. Entertainment: pianist 7.30pm Wed-Sat. Separate room for parties, seats 12.
Map 18 F2.

Knightsbridge

The Capital

The Capital, 22-24 Basil Street, SW3 1AT (7591 1202, www.capitalhotel.co.uk). Knightsbridge tube. **Breakfast served** 7-10.30am Mon-Sat; 7.30-10.30am Sun. **Lunch served** noon-2.30pm daily. **Dinner served** 6.30-10.30pm Mon-Sat; 6.30-10pm Sun. **Main courses** £24-£40. **Set lunch** £24.50 2 courses, £39.50 3 courses. **Set meal** £70 tasting menu (£120 incl wine). **Credit** AmEx, DC, MC, V.

Operating as a hotel restaurant for some 40 years, the Capital knows its place as a refuge for the dedicated Knightsbridge shopper: it promises sophisticated French cuisine within an hour, but also offers an aura of hushed, unhurried calm for everyone else. The absence of piped muzak in the main dining room is welcome – though this does mean you might drop in on an Alan Bennett-esque monologue, as we inadvertently did on our last visit; long-standing clients are as at ease here as in their own sitting rooms. Cuisine and service are proudly French with frills, guéridon trolley at the ready, but that in no way signals absence of warmth from the smiling staff. There's a lightness of touch too, with markedly respectful treatment of vegetarian options, from head chef Jérôme Ponchelle. While the carte and tasting menus carry luxury ingredients (foie gras, wild sea bass and the like), with wine and whisky suggestions and prices to match, the weekday set lunch represents markedly good value and it seems churlish to cavil at elements that miss the mark. Nonetheless, the misses proved as marked as the hits on a summer set menu: while grilled halloumi with a medley of finely diced vegetables was impeccable, and the soft-shelled crab and tempura prawn addition to a well-judged gazpacho inspired, the pork fillet in a main course was tight fleshed, and somehow failed to marry with 'smoked' mash, roast peach and vibrant broccoli. The elements of a cinnamon ice, brownie and chunks of caramelised banana with an overly light chocolate sauce were well executed, but had the feel of hasty home-cooking assembly. Perfect petits fours and sound coffee, however, left all and sundry smiling.

Available for hire. Babies and children welcome: high chairs. Booking advisable. Disabled: toilet. Dress: smart casual. Separate rooms for parties, seating 10, 14 and 24. **Map 8 F9**.

Dinner by Heston Blumenthal

Mandarin Oriental Hyde Park, 66 Knightsbridge, SW1X 7LA (7201 3833, www.dinnerbyheston.com). Knightsbridge tube. **Lunch served** noon-2.30pm, **dinner served** 6.30-10.30pm daily. **Main courses** £26.50-£72. **Set lunch** (Mon-Fri) £36 3 courses. **Credit** AmEx, DC, MC, V.

Housed on the ground floor of the Mandarin Oriental hotel, Dinner does seem a little corporate in appearance. The main draw of the dining room is the futuristic glass-fronted kitchen, where you can watch the chefs at work. If you're after a cheaper version of the Fat Duck, then best keep saving your pennies – this is a rather different animal. The menu, devised by Heston Blumenthal and his right-hand man Ashley Palmer-Watts (who heads the kitchen), takes its essence from historical British dishes. With a bit of innovation, these are transformed into something befitting a fine-dining establishment. No meal here would be complete without trying the Tudor-inspired 'meat fruit'. It didn't disappoint: cool, unctuous chicken liver parfait came cloaked in a zingy mandarin jelly, which bore an impressive resemblance to the said fruit. With the exception of the umami-rich and slightly viscous cockle ketchup that accompanied our roast halibut, the mains, though all cooked with precision, lacked wow factor. On to the puds; our expectations were met by the much-lauded tipsy cake. The spit-roasted pineapple was intense and smoky, while the hot, sticky, custardy brioche made us feel a little nostalgic. Unselfconscious, friendly service helped make this a special night. The wine list is extensive, but predictably expensive, with bottles starting at £35.

Babies and children welcome: high chairs; nappy-changing facilities (hotel). Booking essential (3 months in advance). Disabled: toilet (hotel). Dress: smart casual. Separate rooms for parties, seating 6 and 10. Tables outdoors (15, terrace).
Map 8 F9.

Koffmann's

The Berkeley, Wilton Place, SW1X 7RJ (7107 8844, www.the-berkeley.co.uk). Hyde Park Corner or Knightsbridge tube. **Lunch served** noon-2.30pm Mon-Fri; noon-3pm Sat, Sun. **Dinner served** 6-10.30pm daily. **Main courses** £19-£34. **Set lunch** (Mon-Sat) £21.50 2 courses, £25.50 3 courses; (Sun) £22.50 2 courses, £26.50 3 courses. **Credit** AmEx, MC, V.

A new generation of diners, plus many long-time fans, have come here to experience the Gascony-based cuisine of the legendary Pierre Koffmann, since he came out of retirement and opened this brasserie in 2010. Koffmann, who earned three Michelin stars at his former restaurant, La Tante Claire, also trained some of Britain's most celebrated chefs. The swish dining room, with walls covered by textured wallpaper, can feel a little

buttoned-up for a brasserie. First-timers tend to go for the signature dishes – rich and gelatinous pied de cochon (pig's trotter stuffed with sweetbreads and morels) or pistachio soufflé. If you're on a budget, the set lunch is definitely worth exploring. We started with a smooth chicken liver terrine, which, with its flavours precisely balanced, exemplified the sort of technical skill that is honed in the best restaurants. Main courses of roasted monkfish with soya beans, and a tender roasted rump of lamb with aubergine stew, may not be the most adventurous of dishes, but the cooking never missed a beat. We were pleased, too, that vegetables continue to be included with the main courses (though extra portions are charged at £3 each). The meal ended on a high note with a raspberry soufflé that was sheer delight; we scraped the ramekin clean. The French wine list is voluminous, with 14 choices by the glass, and south-western labels to the fore. Service, crisp yet friendly, seemed more relaxed than we experienced a year ago.
Available for hire. Babies and children welcome: high chairs; nappy-changing facilities. Booking advisable. Disabled: toilet (hotel). Dress: smart casual. Separate room for parties, seats 16. **Map 9 G9.**

★ Marcus Wareing at the Berkeley

The Berkeley, Wilton Place, SW1X 7RL (7235 1200, www.the-berkeley.co.uk). Hyde Park Corner or Knightsbridge tube. **Lunch served** noon-2.30pm Mon-Fri. **Dinner served** 6-11pm Mon-Sat. **Set lunch** £30 2 courses, £38 3 courses (£50 incl 2 glasses of wine). **Set meal** £80 3 courses, £98 tasting menu, £120 chef's menu. **Credit** AmEx, DC, MC, V.
The glass-ball screens that shield kitchen from dining room may well be a cheeky reference to the abacus and how much it costs to eat here. Still, the lunchtime set menu includes enough extra treats to feel like you've splashed out. True, add water, wine and service and you'll likely spend over £70 per person, but then again, the trolley-wielding staff cosset guests to the max. The interior of burgundy and hessian, leather and velvet, smacks of tradition, yet there are modish details: the butter knives are so trendy you'll wonder which end to use to spread the delectable caramelised brown butter that comes with the choice of four own-made breads. An amuse-bouche of pineapple-tomato gazpacho made a delightful change from the norm, but the cherry tomatoes that arrived with our black olive-flecked burrata starter seemed more *ordinaire* than 'heritage'. Better was chargrilled bavette with girolles and oyster béarnaise: steak has never looked so pretty, and the tender juiciness of the chunks compensated for the modest portion. From the predominately French wine list (a whopping 800-plus bins), the sommelier chose Loire pinot blanc and a Fougères grenache-syrah to accompany the meal. Then came a tour de force of sweet finishes. Panna cotta was given a sophisticated edge with bitter tonka-bean spicing and a garnish of fresh almonds, peach and apricot; even better was the combination of fresh strawberries, streusel crumbs, passion-fruit foam and dense strawberry sorbet. Lunch ended with a choice of hunky dark chocolates and a relaxed Marcus Wareing emerging from the kitchen to chat with customers.
Available for hire. Babies and children welcome: high chairs. Booking essential. Dress: smart; jacket preferred. Separate room for parties, seats 12-16. Vegetarian menu. **Map 9 G9.**

One-O-One

101 Knightsbridge, SW1X 7RN (7290 7101, www.oneoonerestaurant.com). Knightsbridge tube. **Lunch served** noon-2.30pm Mon-Fri; 12.30-2.30pm Sat, Sun. **Dinner served** 6.30-10pm daily. **Main courses** £28-£39. **Set lunch** £17 2 dishes, £37 6 dishes. **Set dinner** £49 6 courses, £59 tasting menu (£89 incl wine). **Credit** AmEx, DC, MC, V.
Modern and smartly furnished, the dining room of One-O-One is a convivial place in which to spend time. Service, attentive as you'd expect, also helps make a meal here an event – as does the food. Pascal Proyart, who hails from Brittany, is one of London's best fish cooks. He made his first TV appearance on *Saturday Kitchen* in spring 2012 and this seems to have increased the footfall in his restaurant. At lunch, the prices of the 'petits plats' are a bargain (from £17 for two plates) and we were especially impressed by the sustainable fish menu. The cooking seamlessly switches from Asian to Mediterranean and French flavours. A wild Norwegian red king crab was cleverly matched with a sparkling mango and lime coriander tartare. A raviolo of braised wild octopus also came from the top drawer, and was sensationally stirred into life by a tomato cappuccino and a beautifully crafted red wine matelote. Meat dishes are equally wonderful; breast of Gressingham duck came with its leg served as a confit, plus baby pak choi, a ginger and carrot compote, and an orange sauce (giving a new take on duck à la orange). We basked in the moment with English rhubarb soaked in grenadine syrup and paired with vanilla bourbon panna cotta and a wicked white chocolate ice-cream infused with fresh mint. The wine list contains some tremendous bottles, though prices are dauntingly high.
Available for hire. Babies and children welcome: high chairs. Booking advisable Thur-Sun. Disabled: toilet. Dress: smart casual. Separate room for parties, seats 10. **Map 8 F9.**

Marylebone

★ Roganic

19 Blandford Street, W1U 3DH (7486 0380, www.roganic.co.uk). Baker Street or Bond Street tube. **Lunch served** noon-2.30pm, **dinner served** 6-9pm Tue-Sat. **Set lunch** (Tue-Sat) £29 3 courses, £35 3 courses incl 2 glasses of wine. **Set meal** £55 6 courses, £80 10 courses. **Credit** AmEx, MC, V.
An offshoot of Simon Rogan's esteemed L'Enclume in Cumbria, this slip of a restaurant has been cleverly promoted as a two-year pop-up. The result? A packed reservations book and cult status among a hip business crowd and catering's bright young things, despite mixed reviews at launch. The interior mixes rural charm (heritage green paint, tongue-and-groove panelling, small rooms and low ceilings) with retro chic; service strikes a similar note of easygoing formality. The staff's menu knowledge is admirable – as it needs to be with the likes of coal oil and liquorice curd on the menus. Diners choose from three, six or ten brow-raising courses. Diplomatically, the same is offered to vegetarians, perhaps not so difficult given that British natural ingredients are the kitchen's bedrock and none of the artistically presented dishes is complete without some leaf, seed, root or flower you didn't realise was edible. On our visit, ox-eye daisies lent a vegetal sweetness and bright colour to a plate of thumbnail-sized heritage potatoes poached in rapeseed oil and served with peas and burnet leaves. We loved the precision cooking of duck breast with sweetbreads, red orach and salt-baked turnips, and the exquisite delicacy of macerated strawberries with buttermilk, yoghurt and the aniseed kick of sweet cicely. The £29 lunch menu can include two glasses of paired wine for just £6 extra – great value. Given the complexity of the flavours on the plate, staff recommendations are the way to go here.
Available for hire. Babies and children admitted. Booking advisable. Dress: smart casual. Vegetarian menu. **Map 9 G5.**

Texture

34 Portman Street, W1H 7BY (7224 0028, www.texture-restaurant.co.uk). Marble Arch tube.
Bar **Open** noon-midnight, **lunch served** noon-2.30pm, **dinner served** 6.30-11pm Tue-Sat. **Main courses** £13.50-£85. **Set lunch** £19.90 2 courses, £24.90 3 courses.
Restaurant **Lunch served** noon-2.30pm, **dinner served** 6.30-11pm Tue-Sat. **Main courses** £27.50-£31.50. **Set lunch** £19.90 2 courses, £24.90 3 courses. **Set meal** £72-£76 tasting menu (£62 vegetarian).
Both **Credit** AmEx, MC, V.
Chef Agnar Sverrisson is from Iceland, but an Icelandic theme is more overt in the decorative detail – ice and fire paintings on the walls, and striking crockery in designs evoking rock and lava – than it is in Texture's very good fish-oriented food. The culinary influences are more broadly Scandinavian, and the ingredients are sourced for flavour and quality rather than slavish far-northern provenance. Veal comes from England, for example, and quail from Anjou – but king crab hails from Norway and lamb, when in season, from Iceland's unique pastures. Sverrisson surrounds these lynchpins prettily with mounds, puffs, puddles and scatterings of supporting ingredients. He infuses the whole with tastes familiar and teasingly obscure: salmon with mustard sauce recalled the berry wood in which it was (barely) smoked; Icelandic cod carried an undertow of tundra herbs. Eat carefully: the many flavours, ideas and elements can end up combining into something of a soup. The environment – a grand, high-ceilinged room with elaborate mouldings and well-spaced soft leather seating – and the assured service (though at the bar slightly inexpert) are on the approachable side of haute. That Texture is related to wine specialists 28°-50° is obvious from the lovingly compiled list, which has exceptional sections on riesling and pinot noir (worldwide) and some memorable bottles for under £40, as well as a range of champagnes offered at the bar.
Available for hire. Babies and children welcome: high chairs. Booking advisable. Disabled: toilet. Dress: smart casual. Separate room for parties, seats 16. Vegetarian menu. **Map 9 G6.**

Mayfair

★ Alain Ducasse at the Dorchester

The Dorchester, Park Lane, W1K 1QA (7629 8866, www.alainducasse-dorchester.com). Hyde Park Corner tube. **Lunch served** noon-1.30pm Tue-Fri. **Dinner served** 6.30-9.30pm Tue-Sat. **Set lunch** £55 3 courses incl 2 glasses of wine, mineral water, coffee. **Set dinner** £85 3 courses, £100 4 courses. **Set meal** £120 tasting menu (£215 incl wine), £180 seasonal menu. **Credit** AmEx, MC, V.

When you book a table here, they don't ask for your credit card number. Instead, they ask (a) whether you're celebrating a special occasion and (b) whether you have any dietary restrictions. That solicitous graciousness set the tone for our dinner at this triply Michelin-starred palace of haute cuisine. Yes, the expense at dinner is scary: over £100 a head for two courses without even beginning to approach the pricier territory on the wine list. But you get a lot for your money. Service was warm and not at all intimidating, and the food was fabulous. It arrived almost non-stop. A big bowl of gougères (cheesy pastry puffs) with apéritifs. Fabulous breads, heavenly butter. An exquisite amuse-bouche. And both starters and mains had us swooning. Presentation is high-art stuff, but flavours are anything but dainty. Spiced confit foie gras with lightly pickled vegetables was sensationally good. 'Cookpot' (like a covered mini-casserole) of vegetables, girolles and Montgomery cheddar was unbelievably flavourful – one of the best dishes we've ever eaten. Sea bass came with baby artichokes and a powerful but beautifully balanced black olive tapenade. Anjou pigeon, deftly dissected, was robustly sauced. The room and tables are decorated with tasteful opulence. The sommelier gave excellent advice. On our way out, a succession of staff bade us goodbye and, finally, gave us two little cakes in a fancy cardboard box 'for breakfast'. Note: the three-course set lunch is a relative bargain, and while the price is fixed, the choice is from the carte. Other restaurants in the Ducasse empire are far more expensive than this one, and for us, the expense here was justifiable as a once-in-a-lifetime experience.
Available for hire. Booking essential, 2 months in advance. Children over 10yrs admitted. Disabled: toilet (hotel). Dress: smart. Separate rooms for parties. Vegetarian menu. **Map 9 G7**.

Galvin at Windows

28th floor, London Hilton, Park Lane, W1K 1BE (7208 4021, www.galvinatwindows.com). Green Park or Hyde Park Corner tube. **Lunch served** noon-2.30pm Mon-Fri; 11.45am-3pm Sun. **Dinner served** 6-10.30pm Mon-Wed; 6-11pm Thur-Sat. **Set lunch** £25 2 courses, £29 3 courses (£45 incl half bottle of wine, mineral water and coffee). **Set dinner** £39-£65 3 courses. **Set meal** £95 tasting menu (£125 incl wine). **Credit** AmEx, DC, MC, V.

Make no mistake, the London Hilton-based residency of the Galvin brothers is a destination restaurant in every sense. Now in its fifth year of serving an international clientele, Galvin at Windows has all aspects of its operation sorted: from a finely honed selection of set menus to the 'View from the 28th Floor' postcards (which staff will post for you at no extra charge). Certainly, the panoramic view via floor-to-ceiling windows is a perennial draw. No doubt the impeccable service also plays its part in ensuring the venue's constant popularity; and the luxurious decor (all gold, beige and dark-wood panelling, with comfortable seating and spacing) can hardly displease; but it's the thoroughly enjoyable food and drink, with familiar Spanish and British elements, that's surely the thing. From a plethora of menus to suit various budgets, the 'Summer of Champagne' seasonal list – three courses including a glass of bubbly – was great value at just under £30. It may have featured 'humbler' fish, but both South Coast mackerel and Loch Duart salmon were top-notch: the former cured and barbecued, the latter crisp-skinned and

Dabbous. See p132.

pearlescent-fleshed. Neither was there an absence of luxury in the hugely flavourful ham hock and foie gras terrine with truffled mayonnaise; and an all-but-eton-mess take on strawberries and cream dessert featured the lightest of modernist touches in a meringue. Occasional pairings seemed misplaced or redundant – borlotti beans mirroring mussels felt too mealy a foil for the delicate salmon dish; Breton shortbreads an intrusion on perfect lemon posset. Seasoning proved assured, however, with trademark brightness and tang to the fore. A range of markedly well-priced wines by the glass had us reaching for more.
Available for hire. Babies and children welcome: high chairs. Booking advisable. Disabled: lift; toilet (hotel). Dress: smart casual. **Map 9 G8.**

Le Gavroche

43 Upper Brook Street, W1K 7QR (7408 0881, www.le-gavroche.co.uk). Marble Arch tube.
Lunch served noon-2pm Mon-Fri. **Dinner served** 6.30-11pm Mon-Sat. **Main courses** £25-£65. **Set lunch** £52 3 courses incl half bottle of wine, mineral water, coffee. **Set dinner** £110 tasting menu (£178 incl wine). **Credit** AmEx, DC, MC, V.
Given its setting, in a windowless basement with old-fashioned furnishings, you might not guess that this 46-year-old Mayfair stalwart is one of the capital's hottest tickets, with its reservations book filled three months ahead. Testament to the power of television, ever since exec chef Michel Roux Junior (who took over from his father Albert in 1991) became a judge on *Masterchef: The Professionals*, his profile has gone stratospheric. 'Le Gav' now attracts a mixed crowd: refined silver-topped regulars from the early days, and day-trippers who have saved up for 'sleb' cooking, filling the dining room with exuberant cackles. And save you must: starters and puds hover at the £25 mark (each), while mains average £50. By contrast, the £52 set 'business lunch', for three courses, wine, water and coffee remains exceptional value, particularly as it comes with complimentary amuse-bouche and just-baked breads. Cooking on our visit was sound, but not always spectacular. Most impressive was a tender roast guinea fowl nicely paired with a slab of creamy polenta, black olives adding to the intensity of the jus. A buttery piece of french toast with heady poached apricots, an almond-studded sugar snap and a dollop of amaretto ice-cream, took our breath away. On the other hand, a smoked eel starter was oddly topped with samphire, making it too salty, while a fillet of pollock with saffron aïoli, though well-judged, failed to excite. Service, save for the premature pouring of a not-yet-brewed tea, was an unstuffy, well-oiled machine.
Available for hire. Babies and children admitted. Booking essential. Dress: jacket; smart jeans accepted; no trainers. **Map 9 G7.**

★ Greenhouse

27A Hay's Mews, W1J 5NY (7499 3331, www.greenhouserestaurant.co.uk). Green Park tube. **Lunch served** noon-2.30pm Mon-Fri. **Dinner served** 6.30-11pm Mon-Sat. **Set lunch** £25 2 courses, £29 3 courses. **Set meal** £65 2 courses, £75 3 courses, £90 tasting menu. **Credit** AmEx, MC, V.
A change of chef in early 2012 (Antonin Bonnet out after six years; Arnaud Bignon in) has done nothing to detract from what is a fabulous dining experience at the Greenhouse. A la carte prices are still in keeping with the heart-of-Mayfair location (£65 for two courses), but, pleasingly, the set lunch menu remains as last year, at £29 for three courses – excellent value, and a fine way to ease yourself into this sumptuous world. Dishes arrive as beautiful ensembles, although with as much attention lavished on flavour as on appearance. French technique is applied to combinations of ingredients that cross continental boundaries for inspiration: on our recent visit, shrimp tartare was sharpened with tiny cubes of granny smith apple and draped in wafer-thin slices of radish for a memorable starter; another of girolles, enoki mushrooms and three quail eggs came with a startling yuzu jelly. Tasting menus (£90) take the experimentation levels higher, with the likes of scallops paired with tandoori masala and cabbage, or lamb with ras-el-hanout and aubergine. The wine list is notably lengthy, although lunches can be enlivened by the many appealing options by the glass. Service is smiling, unobtrusive and slick – this place really is flawless.
Available for hire. Babies and children admitted. Booking essential. Disabled: toilet. Dress: smart casual. Separate room for parties, seats 10. **Map 9 H7.**

Hélène Darroze at the Connaught

The Connaught, Carlos Place, W1K 2AL (3147 7200, www.the-connaught.co.uk). Bond Street tube. **Lunch served** noon-2.30pm Tue-Fri. **Brunch served** 11am-3pm Sat. **Dinner served** 6.30-10.15pm Tue-Sat. **Set lunch/brunch** £35 3 courses (£42 incl 2 glasses of wine). **Set meal** £80 3 courses, £95-£115 tasting menu (£160-£220 incl wine). **Credit** AmEx, DC, MC, V.
In this age of the celebrity chef, it's remarkable that Hélène Darroze maintains such a low profile. She's one of only a handful of women to have garnered multiple Michelin stars: her Parisian eaterie has one; this restaurant, two. In many ways, the Connaught is a reflection of Darroze's personality – sincere, thoughtful, restrained. Dark wood panelling and muted upholstery set the tone. Service is in the same vein: serious, though not dour, delivering plates of carefully crafted cooking that have roots in regional France and the Med. Warm breads and dainty amuse-bouche usher in an accomplished starter of cauliflower ravioli with roasted skate, the pasta and a crisp-skinned tail piece offset by morsels of crunchy florets, toasted hazelnut halves and parsley purée. Our main course was equally considered, with medallions of tender roast veal accompanied by miniature rolls of pan-fried polenta, Ligurian black olives and a warm salad of broad beans. A decadent pud of bitter chocolate ganache, wafer-thin gianduja (hazelnut and milk chocolate) biscuits and gold leaf might have been the grand finale, but for a generous selection of petits fours chosen from a trolley laden

Pied à Terre. See p132.

with candies and macarons. There are further trolleys: one for champagne; another for Armagnac; and a counter groaning with butter and cheese. The set lunch remains excellent value, although wallet-watchers be warned: on our visit, several dishes had supplements. The Francophile wine list is pitched at grown-ups with deep pockets; for best value, engage the genial sommelier, or order the lunch menu, when two (small) matched glasses cost just £7 extra. But be prepared to splash out. The Connaught is the kind of place where silver cloches are ceremoniously lifted from plates, and sauces are poured at table. Which suits the well-heeled clientele very nicely.
Available for hire. Babies and children welcome: high chairs. Booking advisable; essential weekends. Disabled: toilet (hotel). Dress: smart; no jeans or trainers. Separate room for parties, seats 16. Vegetarian menu. **Map 9 H7**.

Hibiscus

29 Maddox Street, W1S 2PA (7629 2999, www.hibiscusrestaurant.co.uk). Oxford Circus tube. **Lunch served** noon-2.30pm Mon-Sat. **Dinner served** 6.30-10pm Mon-Thur; 6-10pm Fri, Sat. **Set lunch** £33.50 3 courses. **Set dinner** £80 3 courses, £95-£105 tasting menu (£165-£185 incl wine). **Credit** AmEx, MC, V.
'Really weird, but really good.' Those words made an appearance at least three times during lunch here, a tribute to the playfully adventurous cooking of chef Claude Bosi. First, over an amuse-bouche of pineapple and hibiscus-flower cola; finally over a dessert of olive oil parfait with charlotte strawberry and basil. In between, there were so many surprises that we often found ourselves at a loss for words. Fruit enters the cooking in surprising ways, such as the strawberry sauce velouté embellishing an otherwise straightforward dish of roast cod with ratte potatoes and white asparagus, and the hint of pink grapefruit accompanying succulent pork belly cooked in hay. But it's not all innovation. Peas à la française (garnish for the pork) was textbook stuff, and bakewell tart was down-the-line traditional apart from its smear of cherry gel. All these dishes came from the three-course set lunch; ordering à la carte is a completely different proposition. Ingredients of the season are listed, and after discussing preferences and aversions with you, staff bring three, six or eight courses, chosen by the kitchen. Some would not like that slightly random approach, but we didn't hear any complaints – though that would probably have been impossible, as the tables are so blissfully far apart in a room that is plush, elegant and exceedingly soothing. The wine list offers little under £40, which is a shame but not surprising given the restaurant's brace of Michelin stars.
Babies and children welcome: high chairs. Booking essential. Disabled: toilet. Separate room for parties, seats 18. **Map 9 J6**.

Maze

10-13 Grosvenor Square, W1K 6JP (7107 0000, www.gordonramsay.com/maze). Bond Street tube. **Lunch served** noon-2.30pm, **dinner served** 6-11pm daily. **Main courses** £10-£20. **Set meal** (lunch daily; 6-7pm, 10-11pm Mon-Thur, Sun) £25 4 courses (£45 incl wine), £70 tasting menu (£120 incl drinks). **Credit** AmEx, MC, V.
Maze's split-level dining room is a sizeable, sociable space, especially the fabulous bar area. Handcrafted screens induce a maze-like effect, with classy touches such as cream leather, walnut finishes and splashes of mauve. The restaurant continues to be popular with both Londoners and visitors, and business was brisk during our visit. Service can be a little robotic and charmless, but we had fun browsing through the global wine list on an iPad, with prices starting at £28. Momentum was temporarily disrupted by the arrival of rather stale bread sticks, and a golden hash brown with pancetta and confit duck egg gussied up with a wild garlic sauce that lacked sparkle. Flavours were more vibrant in a tranche of sea bream teamed with fennel, green olives and a citrous vinaigrette. The kitchen then moved up a gear with a cross-cultural take on braised feather blade of beef lifted by paprika, served with pomme purée, shimeji mushrooms and a mildly spiced togarashi chilli jus. This was much better than the bland pork dumplings in a mushroom broth. To finish, a summery apple terrine was complemented by diced apple and rhubarb, and a refreshing custard ice-cream ensured a happy end to the meal. The cooking here has settled into a nice groove, but most of our dishes lacked pzazz; Maze appears to have lost some of its cutting edge – perhaps the introduction of a sushi bar (September 2012) will pep things up.
Available for hire. Babies and children welcome: high chairs. Booking essential. Disabled: toilet. Dress: smart casual; no trainers. Vegetarian menu. **Map 9 G6**.

★ Pollen Street Social

8-10 Pollen Street, W1S 1NQ (7290 7600, www.pollenstreetsocial.com). Oxford Circus tube.
Bar **Open** noon-midnight Mon-Sat.
Restaurant **Lunch served** noon-2.45pm, **dinner served** 6-10.45pm Mon-Sat. **Main courses** £24-£29.50. **Set lunch** £24 2 courses, £27.50 3 courses. **Set meal** £79 tasting menu.
Both **Credit** AmEx, MC, V.
The name suggests a club, of the accessible kind, but behind the narrow street frontage of Pollen Street Social lies an *Alice in Wonderland* complex of restaurant rooms showcasing the well-honed skills of Jason Atherton. Much has been written in praise of Atherton's food, and his creations continue to surprise and delight, but we're also astounded by the (welcome) flexibility that an establishment of this calibre is happy – indeed designed – to offer. A two-hour lunchtime slot allows you to go for a well-priced set menu, play around with the carte (just a couple of starters if that's what you're after) and repair to the dessert bar should the fancy take you. And then linger at the no-bookings social bar if sufficiently beguiled. Service is second to none in its friendliness, efficiency (there's quite a team in evidence), and willingness to inform, assist or stay in the background. Remarkably, even wines bought by the glass prompt a sample to ensure you're happy: a wise move, perhaps, given the unusual bottles offered, but also symbolic of a unique exchange between restaurant and diner. Our last visit saw happy deployment of artful simplicity, whether at set menu level (perfectly succulent square and cylinder of Dingley Dell pork belly and loin with simply outstanding mash) or the carte: tartare of fallow deer was perfect, needing no further accompaniment than its 'broken egg' sauce. Desserts carried more drama, but a sorbet of beetroot and strawberry with wild fruit and wafers of basil ash meringue was seamlessly well-balanced. Add-ons, from breads to chocolate 'pebbles', melded into one delightful experience. Elbow-room might be sparse, and the general buzz markedly loud, but no one seemed to mind in the least.
Available for hire. Babies and children welcome (restaurant): high chairs. Booking advisable. Disabled: toilet. Separate room for parties, seats 14. Vegetarian menu. **Map 9 J6**.

★ Sketch: Lecture Room & Library HOT 50

9 Conduit Street, W1S 2XJ (7659 4500, www.sketch.uk.com). Oxford Circus tube. **Lunch served** noon-2.30pm Tue-Fri. **Dinner served** 7-10.30pm Tue-Sat. **Main courses** £35-£55. **Set lunch** £30 2 courses incl coffee, £35 3 courses incl coffee, £48 3 courses incl half bottle of wine, mineral water. **Set meal** £75 vegetarian tasting menu, £95 tasting menu. **Credit** AmEx, MC, V.
If you have never ventured through the portals of Mourad Mazouz and Pierre Gagnaire's converted Georgian townhouse, prepare yourself by reading the legend on the website. 'Arrive with an open mind and imagine, if you will, a painting that never dries' is the exuberant invitation – and the reality does not disappoint. Catch the twinkling eye of Nathan the MD and he will take you on a tour of the crazily opulent spaces with the air of a guide to Hogwarts. Still, nothing can, nor should, distract from the no less exuberant cuisine of Gagnaire, and despite a carte that (justifiably) averages £40 each for starters and mains, you can drop in for a – relatively – 'rapide' lunch for less than this. You're unlikely, even, to begrudge a penny of the all-inclusive £48 deal given the quality of wine on offer. From the artful intrigue of the 'nibbles' – wafers you pull from a knife-block-like bed of sesame-scented 'sand' before dipping into essence of artichoke purée, for instance – via a symphony of starters that moved on our visit from a bright, citric lemon jelly with olive oil sorbet, via tastes sweet, salt and bitter to a crescendo of pungent foie gras mousse paired improbably with a disc of dark milk chocolate; to more familiar but no less meticulously executed mains (vegetarians get their full measure of magic) and desserts that again defy expectation, it is impossible not to smile with the delight of discovery. Were it simply a matter of artful deception and riotous colours, the whole show would grow tiresome; but the skill of Gagnaire's team is such that each section of the menu continually reawakens the palate. Amid the sensory riot, smooth service supplies a calm counterpoint.
Available for hire. Babies and children welcome: high chairs. Booking advisable. Dress: smart casual. Separate rooms for parties, seating 24 and 50. Vegetarian menu. **Map 9 J6**.

The Square

6-10 Bruton Street, W1J 6PU (7495 7100, www.squarerestaurant.com). Bond Street or Green Park tube. **Lunch served** noon-2.15pm Mon-Fri. **Dinner served** 6.30-10pm Mon-Fri; 6.30-10.30pm Sat; 6.30-9.30pm Sun. **Set lunch** (Mon-Sat) £30 2 courses, £35 3 courses. **Set dinner** £65 2 courses, £80 3 courses. **Set meal** £105 tasting menu (£170 incl wine). **Credit** AmEx, MC, V.
With its cultivated luxury and discreet (read: hard to find) doorway, the Square fits right into Conduit Street's moneyed aesthetic. In the hands of Philip Howard and Robert Weston, its food has been counted among London's best for more than a

decade, and we have regularly been impressed by the complexity and mastery of flavours. This time round, though, we encountered a rather average set lunch, which, even taking its pricing into account, wasn't a brilliant shop window for the à la carte. The best dish was a dramatic squid ink raviolo; the other starter, a slice of foie gras terrine with bean salad, was actively uninteresting. Mains, of cod with summer vegetable broth and potato purée, and lamb with borlotti beans, both exhibited first-rate ingredients and skills, but again failed to excite. The large room, decorated in shades of brown, is comfortable rather than directional, with well-spaced round tables draped with white linen, and cushioned chairs; it was half full when we visited. The wine list, from a carefully built-up cellar, offers little below £45 in 89 pages that concentrate on France's premium regions.
Available for hire. Babies and children admitted. Booking advisable. Disabled: toilet. Dress: smart; smart jeans accepted; no trainers. Separate room for parties, seats 18. Vegan dishes. Vegetarian menu. **Map 9 H7**.

Piccadilly

The Ritz

150 Piccadilly, W1J 9BR (7493 8181, www.theritzlondon.com). Green Park tube.
Bar **Open/meals served** 11.30am-midnight Mon-Sat; noon-10.30pm Sun. **Main courses** £20-£30.
Restaurant **Breakfast served** 7-10am Mon-Sat; 8-10am Sun. **Lunch served** 12.30-2.30pm daily. **Tea served** (reserved sittings) 11.30am, 1.30pm, 3.30pm, 5.30pm, 7.30pm daily. **Dinner served** 5.30-10.30pm Mon-Sat; 7-10pm Sun. **Main courses** £38-£49. **Set lunch** £35 2 courses, £45 3 courses. **Set tea** £40. **Set dinner** £50 3 courses, £65 5 courses; (Fri, Sat) £95 4 courses.
Both **Credit** AmEx, MC, V.
Stepping inside the Ritz restaurant, which opened in 1906, is like being transported back in time. The Louis XVI-inspired room is regally attired, with polished marble columns, thick-pile cerise carpet and dazzling chandeliers. Service is old-school and courtly, with staff formally greeting diners. We were informed at the time of booking that gentlemen were required to wear a jacket and tie: an inconvenience, but given such surroundings it would be incongruous not to dress up. High entry-level prices help ensure exclusivity; the lunch menu is £45 for three courses and the wine list rises quickly from a punishing £49. We opted for the five-course lunch at £65. After a stuttering start with lacklustre breads and amuse-bouche, our faith was restored by a refreshing chilled tomato consommé with tomatoes of various colours, and tender langoustines, followed by a rich ballotine of goose liver offset by peach coulis. The executive chef, John Williams MBE, keeps religiously to the culinary template laid down by Escoffier, but the cooking can feel too familiar – like upmarket event catering – and it lacked sparkle. There were slips too: our turbot, poached in butter, came with badly overcooked oxtail and was just saved by the lemon verbena sauce. Slow-cooked veal with white beans was tender yet bland, and the jus was salty. At least the final act was a good one: praline parfait arrived with a garnish of gold leaf, and an excellent mandarin sorbet. We loved the grandeur here, but felt the cooking was overshadowed by the setting.
Babies and children welcome: children's menu; high chairs. Booking advisable restaurant; essential afternoon tea. Dress: jacket; smart jeans accepted; no trainers. Entertainment: dinner dance Fri, Sat (restaurant); pianist daily. Separate rooms for parties, seating 16-60. Tables outdoors (8, terrace). **Map 9 J7**.

South Kensington

★ Tom Aikens

43 Elystan Street, SW3 3NT (7584 2003, www.tomaikens.co.uk). South Kensington tube.
Lunch served noon-2.30pm Mon-Fri. **Dinner served** 6.45-10.30pm Mon-Sat. **Main courses** £22-£32. **Set meal** (noon-1.45pm, 6.45-9.45pm) £60-£80 tasting menu. **Credit** AmEx, MC, V.
The look of Tom Aikens' eponymous restaurant has undergone a sea change, with Istanbul-based designer Hakan Ezer creating a deceptively simple aura wrought from canvas, wood and iron that is somehow evocative of the *Rime of the Ancient Mariner*. Food-related quotes are inscribed on the walls, adding to the sense of a timeless journey. Serving dishes have the solidity of shoreline stones, or jetsam washed up from another era. The delicacy of the first 'nibble' – an almost crystalline salt-cod dip served in a glass bubble bowl, alongside translucent wafers of white and purple potato – comes almost as a shock, while its saline clarity seems entirely apt. And so a quasi-poetic voyage of discovery goes on, from a bell-jar-contained duck egg sitting in a nest of smoking hay, seasoned with a deep-green swirl of sorrel sabayon, via a rock-pool of pearly cod in scallop-roe hued carrot dressing, to a 'washed up' symphony of chocolate foams, sand-like powders and smoky shells. Those in search of earthier, meatier flavours will find the likes – even at set lunch level – of tender-crisp confit pigeon legs, and utterly porcine pork belly; or the startling notes of porcini-flavoured butter and 'dehydrated' carrots that taste candied and earthy at once. Breads are inviting and plentiful, petits fours a superb array, wines well-chosen (with a good few available by the glass). We visited in the summer following the re-design; menus are set to change seasonally. Based on our last experience, we imagine that each will prove a revelation.
Available for hire. Booking advisable. Children admitted. Disabled: toilet. Separate room for parties, seats 10. Vegetarian menu. **Map 14 E11**.

West

Chiswick

Hedone

301-303 Chiswick High Road, W4 4HH (8747 0377, www.hedonerestaurant.com). Chiswick Park tube. **Lunch served** 12.30-2.15pm Fri, Sat. **Dinner served** 6.30-10pm Tue-Sat. **Set lunch** £19 2 courses. £25 3 courses. **Set dinner** £50 4 courses, £60 5 courses; £75 tasting menu (£134 incl wine). **Credit** AmEx, MC, V.
The cosy, sensual decor of Mikael Jonsson's characterful spot is a welcome change from the pearlised leather and silver vases of more uptight haute cuisine establishments. Deep-filled brown suede cushions, primitive-style paintings, and open brick- and stonework hit the right smart-casual tone for this unglamorous niche of the A315, but Hedone is not without pretensions. A continuing irritant is the wine list, which offers scant choice under £40 per bottle. The limited selection on the daily changing menu, however, is far more pleasurable; in essence, guests come to experience Jonsson's response to the finest produce available each morning. The price rises according to the number of courses ordered. As a bonus, you don't have to offer companions a taste because they're eating the same thing. Meals begin with own-made rustic bread of stunning deliciousness, served with such a generous hand it's difficult not to eat too much. Superb dishes on our summertime visit were a bulbous, tender poached oyster served in the shell with apple foam; a pretty assembly of slow-cooked duck's yolk with fresh almonds, girolles, apricot and white mayonnaise; and roast pigeon (its claws underlining the kitchen's uncompromising tone) with beetroot and cherries. Less pleasing was john dory with seaweed emulsion; magnifying glasses might have helped identify the rubbery scrap of fish swimming in tidal gloop. Desserts are OK – meringue discs stacked with lemon custard, lemon gel and accompanied by lemon sorbet, for example – but the kitchen's prime skill is in starter-style dishes and a few spartan mains.
Available for hire. Babies and children welcome: high chairs; nappy-changing facilities. Booking advisable. Disabled: toilet. Dress: smart casual. Separate room for parties, seats 16. Vegetarian menu.

Westbourne Grove

★ The Ledbury HOT 50

127 Ledbury Road, W11 2AQ (7792 9090, www.theledbury.com). Westbourne Park tube.
Lunch served noon-2.30pm Tue-Sat; noon-3pm Sun. **Dinner served** 6.30-10.30pm Mon-Sat; 7-10pm Sun. **Set lunch** (Tue-Sat) £30 2 courses, £35 3 courses; (Sun) £50 3 courses. **Set dinner** £80 3 courses; £95 vegetarian tasting menu (£145 incl wine), £105 tasting menu (£155 incl wine). **Credit** AmEx, MC, V.
On a busy weeknight, the Ledbury has all the relaxed bustle and hum of a hit French brasserie, yet as the international crowd and full reservations book shows, this edge-of-Notting-Hill spot has become a place of pilgrimage for lovers of fine dining. Chef Brett Graham is arguably Australia's most successful culinary export, but don't come expecting wattle table decorations and waiters in shorts – even the east-west fusion that characterised upmarket Australian cooking in the 1990s is almost imperceptible. Yes, there's Japanese herb shiso in the unmissable signature dish of flame-grilled mackerel with smooth avocado sauce; salted cherry blossom with roast leg and confit breast of pigeon; and kaffir lime in a mango millefeuille. But interesting ways with root veg (celeriac and beetroot baked in ash, for example) are just as typical. Flavours are thrillingly layered: witness a pre-dessert of olive oil panna cotta with hibiscus-poached peach and sweet cicely granita. Amid such creativity, classic French passionfruit soufflé with Sauternes ice-cream seemed tongue-in-cheek, yet was faultless nevertheless. The intense creamy filling of the vanilla tart was lent an acidic punch with a layer of blackcurrants, while blackcurrant leaf ice-cream added a tempering green note to the plate. Meat mains are elegantly butch, based on the likes of roebuck, Portland hogget, and cheek and jowl of pork. Wines start at £7 per glass; naturally, the charming sommeliers are happy to suggest wine pairings for each course. You'll find a good choice of beers too. We finished with Turkey Flat

Viajante

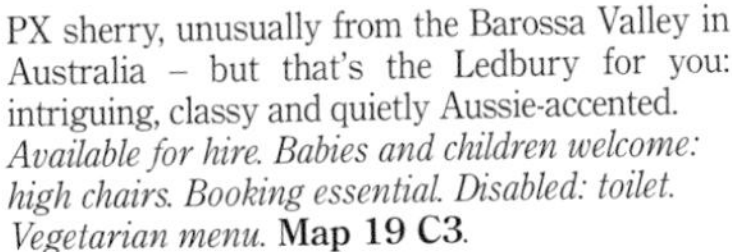
PX sherry, unusually from the Barossa Valley in Australia – but that's the Ledbury for you: intriguing, classy and quietly Aussie-accented.
Available for hire. Babies and children welcome: high chairs. Booking essential. Disabled: toilet. Vegetarian menu. **Map 19 C3**.

South West

Chelsea

★ Gordon Ramsay

68 Royal Hospital Road, SW3 4HP (7352 4441, www.gordonramsay.com). Sloane Square tube. **Lunch served** noon-2.15pm, **dinner served** 6.30-10.15pm Mon-Fri. **Set lunch** £45 3 courses. **Set meal** £95 3 courses, £125 tasting menu. **Credit** AmEx, DC, MC, V.
Gordon Ramsay's fortunes may rise and fall like those of great empires, but his namesake restaurant remains steady as a rock. The understated room was once home to Pierre Koffmann's celebrated La Tante Claire, but its current incarnation has been no less triumphant; for many years this was the only London restaurant to hold three Michelin stars (it was joined in 2010 by Alain Ducasse at the Dorchester). Elegant and intimate, with only a handful of tables, the carpeted room is quiet but for the hushed chatter of expectant diners. Given the celebrity chef's reputation, the menu is entirely lacking in ego, with no gimmicks, just a succession of visually stunning, technically astute dishes. An inventive starter of ravioli filled with smoked potato and a runny-middled poached egg came beautifully offset by roast chicken jus and delicate batons of warm cucumber. Equally memorable were pale medallions of rabbit loin wrapped in bayonne ham and served with a pretty assortment of broad beans, marjoram and confit tomato, ahead of a glorious twist on rhubarb and custard: an assembly of vivid pink macaron with a vanilla cream filling, poached stem pieces and a tart sphere of sorbet. The meal was punctuated by terrific 'freebies', such as just-baked mini-Poilâne rolls, frothy amuse-bouche, and impeccable petits fours, so if you're here for the set lunch, it's remarkably good value. The heavyweight wine list will impress even the haughtiest of oenophiles, showcasing coveted bottles from around the globe. While there are a handful of less expensive by-the-glass options, the majority are strictly for big spenders. Gracious, friendly staff, led by the charming maître d', attend to your every whim, be it sourcing signed souvenir menus or organising kitchen tours. As fine-dining experiences go, this teeters on flawless.
Available for hire. Booking essential. Children admitted. Dress: smart; jacket preferred.
Map 14 F12.
For branch see index.

East

Bethnal Green

★ Viajante HOT 50

Patriot Square, E2 9NF (7871 0461, www.viajante.co.uk). Bethnal Green tube/rail or Cambridge Heath rail. **Lunch served** noon-2pm Wed-Sun. **Dinner served** 6-9.30pm daily. **Set lunch** £35 3 courses (£53 with wine), £65 6 courses (£115 with wine), £80 9 courses (£145 with wine). **Set dinner** £90 12 courses (£170 with wine). **Credit** AmEx, MC, V.
Portuguese head chef Nuno Mendes works at a rarefied level of creativity that's often associated with pomp, ego and stratospheric prices. Here, it's all about the food – and exceptionally good value. The seating in the first of the restaurant's two rooms is angled towards the open kitchen, allowing diners to view not Ramsayesque drama but a focused team clinically tooling morsels of food into sublime presentations. There's no choice on the menu: a series of appetisers followed by three, six or nine courses are delivered in due course by staff who act as gastronomic tour guides, personal hosts and high priests. For this food elicits reverence. It's exploratory, disciplined and beautiful, stimulating both the mind and the senses. You might not like every dish, but some you will likely find revelatory. The appetisers set out the stall with startling flavours and textures: potato with yeast, pancetta and olive powder; or amaranth with sorrel, for example. Main courses are more overtly conventional – meat or fish with accompaniments – but they're intricately conceived: witness the sea bream with fennel and miso and caramel sauce, or strikingly pretty pluma (a Spanish pork cut served rare) with adobo and reconstructed tomatoes. Desserts (with a pre-dessert) return to the surprising-but-delicious theme: milk in several different molecular presentations, or jerusalem artichokes with chocolate soil and blood orange. The setting, a former town hall, retains its formality despite modern ceiling art and retro references, and the atmosphere is quiet and foodily serious (don't come for a raucous night out).
Available for hire. Booking advisable. Children over 11yrs admitted. Disabled: toilet. Separate room for parties, seats 16. Vegetarian menu.

Outer London

Richmond, Surrey

The Bingham

61-63 Petersham Road, Richmond, Surrey, TW10 6UT (8940 0902, www.thebingham.co.uk). Richmond tube/rail. **Breakfast served** 7-10am Mon-Fri; 8-10am Sat, Sun. **Lunch served** noon-2.15pm Mon-Sat; 12.30-4pm Sun. **Dinner served** 7-10pm Mon-Thur; 6.30-10.30pm Fri, Sat. **Set lunch** (Mon-Sat) £16 2 courses, £19.50 3 courses; (Sun) £38 3 courses. **Set meal** £45 3 courses, £65 tasting menu (£115 incl wine). **Credit** AmEx, DC, MC, V.
This boutique hotel occupies two Georgian houses overlooking the towpath just beyond Richmond Bridge, and is a charming spot in which to take temporary respite from the urban grind. The two dining rooms are serene; elegant but unshowy, with polished wood tables, modern chandeliers and gold tones, and french windows above the pretty garden. There are tables on the balcony too, while next door huge mirrors dominate the art deco-ish bar, decorated in shades of grey-silver. Assorted menus are available, from afternoon tea to dinner, with both à la carte and tasting menus, but the best value for money is offered by the set lunch. Choice is limited – just two options per course, and no luxe ingredients – but it's enough to get a feel for the skills of head chef Shay Cooper and his team. English pea and lemon verbena soup, served with an oozing slow-cooked duck egg and a sprinkling of edible flowers and herb sprigs, was a delicate, summery start. Of the mains, Cornish sea bream with sautéed squid was outclassed by a rich, flavour-packed risotto of roast garlic and girolles, with tiny globules of muscat vinegar contrasting with smooth, subtle belper knolle cheese. To finish, creamy passionfruit curd matched perfectly with zingy grapefruit sorbet and tiny chunks of citrus fruit, though the sprinkling of meringue pieces added little in terms of flavour. The colours – yellow curd, pink sorbet, white meringue – dazzled too. The young staff were charm personified: attentive and relaxed.
Available for hire. Babies and children welcome: children's menu; high chairs; nappy-changing facilities. Booking advisable Thur-Sun. Disabled: toilet. Dress: smart casual. Separate room for parties, seats 90. Tables outdoors (8, balcony). Vegetarian menu.

Indian

London's Indian restaurant scene has for many years been a jewel in the city's gastronomic crown. For both variety and quality, this is Europe's and quite possibly the world's premier city. The scene is constantly evolving, borrowing ideas from across the subcontinent (with Pakistani, Sri Lankan and East African Asian restaurants represented, along with those from regions throughout modern India) as well as creating home-grown innovations. Wembley, Tooting, Southall and Whitechapel remain hotspots for authentic, inexpensive Indian cookery – top practitioners include **Apollo Banana Leaf** (Tooting), **Brilliant** (Southall) and **Tayyabs** (Whitechapel) – but there are now several first-class establishments in central London: the likes of seafood specialist **Rasa Samudra**, elegant **Moti Mahal**, swish **Amaya** and innovative **Cinnamon Club**. The most recent phenomenon has been the growth of hip, low-priced venues specialising in Indian street food: sometimes self-consciously retro, sometimes aping the workers' cafés of urban India. Newcomer **Potli** follows the route pioneered by **Dishoom**, **Roti Chai** and **Delhi Grill**. This year's other new entries emphasise the tremendous choice now to be found: **Chakra** is an upmarket Modern Indian establishment; **Mr Chilly** majors in home-style, no-frills dishes from Pakistan; and **Cinnamon Soho** is top chef Vivek Singh's latest outlet for his creative take on the cuisine. To anyone with a yen for gastronomic adventure, a culinary exploration of subcontinental London is irresistible.

Central

Covent Garden

Dishoom

12 Upper St Martin's Lane, WC2H 9FB (7420 9320, www.dishoom.com). Leicester Square or Covent Garden tube. **Meals served** 8am-11pm Mon-Thur; 8am-midnight Fri; 10am-midnight Sat; 10am-10pm Sun. **Main courses** £1.70-£10.90. **Credit** AmEx, MC, V. Pan-Indian

Dishoom describes itself as 'a Bombay café in London' and is fashioned after that city's 'Irani' caffs, where a cup of spicy masala chai and small eats are always on offer. Design-wise, it could have all gone depressingly ersatz, but the ceiling fans and framed pictures of Bollywood stars make for a retro yet modern aesthetic. The place is undoubtedly a crowd-puller, open from breakfast (for egg, bacon or sausage nan rolls with chilli jam), straight through to lunch and dinner, with soups, salads, grills and curries. The menu also contains such Mumbai classics as vada pau (potato croquettes with sharp chutney in a fluffy Portuguese-style bun) and bhel (crunchy puffed rice with sharp tamarind chutney and pomegranate seeds), which tend to be better rendered than the fairly regulation kebabs and curries. Don't miss the thin, smoky roomali roti to mop up excellent black dahl, and enjoy it with a bhang lassi (without the ganja, of course) or a rose and cardamom lassi. Queues are common in the evening (reservations are taken for breakfast and lunch, but only for groups of six or more after 5.30pm); however, there's a bar downstairs, so waiting is no hardship.

Available for hire. Babies and children welcome: high chairs. Bookings not accepted for fewer than 6 people after 5.30pm. Disabled: toilet. Separate room for parties, seats 44. Tables outdoors (7, pavement). Takeaway service.
Map 18 D4.

★ Masala Zone

48 Floral Street, WC2E 9DA (7379 0101, www.masalazone.com). **Meals served** noon-11pm Mon-Sat; 12.30-10.30pm Sun. **Main courses** £8.50-£12.50. **Set meal** (noon-6.30pm) £9.20 2 courses. **Credit** AmEx, MC, V. Pan-Indian

This low-priced, canteen-like chain shares owners with Chutney Mary, Veeraswamy and Amaya – some of London's longest-running and best-respected Indian restaurants. There are now seven Masala Zones across town, each with the same plain furniture but its own distinctive look: old advertising posters in Islington; delicate line drawings by tribal artists at Soho. In this sizeable branch, tucked behind the Royal Opera House, scores of colourful Rajasthani puppets hang from the ceiling. Young staff in logoed T-shirts dealt well with solo lunchers and tourists. The pan-Indian menu features popular street snacks (hot and cold), meat grills, thalis and regional curries, from Goan prawn curry to Gujarati undhiyu and lentil khichadi, a hearty medley of sweet potato, purple yam, aubergine and dahl. Can't decide? Have a thali. Small metal containers hold assorted vegetable dishes, dahl, a choice of main curry (fish, veg or meat) plus rice or chapatis; our version featured tangy, tomatoey fish curry and fabulous pineapple chutney. Despite the fast-food nature of the operation, there's proper depth to the flavours, and the spicing is unabashed. You can eat well for surprisingly little money, especially if you choose the set menus, lunch deals or online offers.

Available for hire. Babies and children welcome: children's menu; crayons; high chairs; nappy-changing facilities. Booking advisable dinner. Disabled: toilet. Separate room for parties, seats 50. Tables outdoors (5, pavement). Takeaway service. Vegan dishes. Vegetarian menu.
Map 18 E4.
For branches see index.

★ Moti Mahal

45 Great Queen Street, WC2B 5AA (7240 9329, www.motimahal-uk.com). Covent Garden or Holborn tube. **Lunch served** noon-3pm Mon-Fri. **Dinner served** 5.30-11pm Mon-Sat. **Main courses** £9-£28. **Set lunch** £15 2 courses incl drink. **Set dinner** (5.30-11pm Mon-Thur; 5.30-6.45pm, 10-11pm Fri, Sat) £23 3 courses. **Set meal** £43 vegetarian (£63 incl wine); £49 tasting menu (£69 incl wine). **Credit** AmEx, MC, V. Modern Indian

The London outlet of Delhi's Moti Mahal restaurant group, extending over a ground floor and basement, is elegantly furnished with cream banquettes, chandeliers and white napery. Although the restaurant is a magnet for business types, it's also popular with tourists, romancing couples and families. The extensive menu covers pan-Indian classics, but also gives an imaginative nod to such gems as stuffed aubergine slices partnered with pear and clove chutney. Cooking is in the fine-dining league; highlights include distinctive curries – we recommend the aromatic warmth of Kashmiri rogan josh with its toasted fennel spicing, and the tartness of Goan fish curry, redolent with coconut, red chillies and tamarind. Kebabs are top-drawer too. Gilafi seekhs – pounded minced lamb, seasoned with cardamom and mace before being shaped around skewers and grilled over coals – worked well with lime-drenched cucumber wedges. Equally impressive was Amritsari tilapia, for its crisp gram-flour batter, seasoned with astringent carom seeds. Buttery black lentils are the real deal, crammed with rustic garlicky flavour that would doubtless win approval from a Punjabi trucker. Service is spot-on: attentive without being overbearing. The set dinner is an affordable taster of what's on offer here; it's also worth checking the website for special deals.

Available for hire. Babies and children welcome: high chairs. Booking advisable dinner. Separate room for parties, seats 35. Tables outdoors (5, pavement). Takeaway service. Vegetarian menu. **Map 18 E3**.

Sagar

31 Catherine Street, WC2B 5JS (7836 6377, www.sagarveg.co.uk). Covent Garden tube. **Meals served** noon-10.45pm Mon-Sat; noon-9.45pm Sun. **Main courses** £5.95-£14.95. **Set meal** (noon-8pm) £5.95. **Credit** AmEx, MC, V. South Indian vegetarian

The Covent Garden branch of this mini-chain celebrates South Indian vegetarian specialities from the state of Karnataka. Furnishings are a restrained mix of blond wood, occasional southern Indian ornaments, and wipe-clean tables; chefs seem to prefer to let their cooking do the talking. Dosais (rice and lentil pancakes) are some of the best in town, and star on the menu. For dramatic value, order a masala paper dosai, shaped into a gigantic hollow cone (almost 30cm at its widest point) and served with tart tamarind lentils (sambar), crushed potato and diced carrot masala mixed with fried curry leaves and mustard seeds, plus an astringent dollop of coconut and green chilli chutney. Beside southern specialities – like the spongy, steamed rice dumplings (idlis) – Sagar also covers Mumbai beach foods. We've found pani poori (crisp pastry globes filled with tamarind water) impressive, but bhel poori (a puffed rice snack cloaked in tamarind chutney) too soggy to recommend. However, prices are easy on the pocket and it's no surprise that Sagar is a hit with students.

Babies and children welcome: high chairs. Booking advisable Fri, Sat. Separate room for parties, seats 40. Takeaway service. Vegan dishes. Vegetarian menu. **Map 18 E4**.

For branches see index.

Fitzrovia

Rasa Samudra HOT 50

6 Dering Street, W1S 1AD (7629 1346, www.rasarestaurants.com). Oxford Circus tube. **Lunch served** noon-3pm Mon-Sat. **Dinner served** 6-10.30pm daily. **Main courses** £6.50-£12.95. **Set meal** £22.50 vegetarian, £25 meat, £30 seafood. **Credit** AmEx, MC, V. South Indian

Relocated to Dering Street, this flagship of Das Sreedharan's restaurant chain retains the signature cochineal-pink frontage, and the southern Indian artefacts remain prominent in the decor. The menu is popular with aficionados of South Indian cuisine who come here for the renowned Keralite cooking. Fish and seafood are specialities – as are the crunchy-snack appetisers, made with ground pulses and rice, and partnered by splendid own-made pickles. Dining here isn't for the timid. We loved our extremely peppery rasam: a steamy seafood broth, seasoned with mustard seeds and citrous curry leaves. Kingfish curry (kappayum meenum) benefited from a lovely fried onion masala, spiked with red chillies and softened by creamy coconut milk: a marvellous match with lime-drenched rice flecked with fried lentils. A pity the fish was overcooked, though. A simple but stunning thoran contrasted well with the richness of curries; the stir-fried cabbage, tastefully spiced with mustard seeds, was showered with coconut shreds. Kerala is also known for fiery meat dishes, but lamb curry was quite bland compared to the strident spicing in other dishes. Staff can be slow, although they're always well meaning.

Available for hire. Babies and children welcome: high chairs. Booking advisable. Takeaway service. Vegan dishes. Vegetarian menu. **Map 9 H6**.

For branches (Rasa, Rasa Express, Rasa Maricham, Rasa Travancore) see index.

Tayyabs. See p151.

Chakra. See p146.

INDIAN

Knightsbridge

Amaya HOT 50

Halkin Arcade, Motcomb Street, SW1X 8JT (7823 1166, www.amaya.biz). Knightsbridge tube. **Lunch served** 12.30-2.15pm Mon-Sat; 12.45-2.45pm Sun. **Dinner served** 6.30-11.30pm Mon-Sat; 6.30-10.30pm Sun. **Main courses** £19-£24. **Set lunch** £19.50-£32. **Set dinner** £45-£70 tasting menu. **Credit** AmEx, DC, MC, V. Modern Indian

An established destination for the smart Knightsbridge set, Amaya looks every inch the swish modern restaurant with its stylish open kitchen facing a gorgeous interior of terracotta statues, dark wooden fittings and glimmering chandeliers. It's owned by the Panjabi sisters (of Veeraswamy, Chutney Mary and Masala Zone fame), and the menu is a dramatic line-up of sophisticated tapas-sized morsels, along with more substantial curries. The cooks pay as much attention to dressing-up street food as to recreating authentic regal recipes. Favourites include dori kebab: ground lamb, spiced with an aromatic cardamom and mace masala, moulded on to a skewer and cooked over coals. Rustic fried lamb mince, studded with tender kidney, had a splendid base of sticky fried onions, spiced with astringent garlic, ginger and fiery red chillies. Vegetarian notables include watercress and fig griddle cakes, pomegranate raita and lightly seared tandoori broccoli. However, kebabs are the stars: prawns cloaked in a smoky, peppery marinade; lime-drenched grouper wrapped in pandan leaves; and rose-petal and chilli chicken bites. Save space too for the aromatic biriani, redolent of toasted spice and with a subtle floral fragrance. Service, although generally attentive, could be tighter at busy periods. *Booking advisable. Children admitted until 8pm. Disabled: toilet. Dress: smart casual. Separate room for parties, seats 14. Vegetarian menu.* **Map 9 G9**.

Haandi

7 Cheval Place, SW7 1EW (7823 7373, www.haandi-restaurants.com). Knightsbridge tube. **Lunch served** noon-3pm daily. **Dinner served** 5.30-11pm Mon-Thur, Sun; 5.30-11.30pm Fri, Sat. **Main courses** £6-£16. **Set lunch** £12.95. **Credit** AmEx, MC, V. East African Indian

It's not easy locating the tiny entrance to Haandi from the main Brompton Road. Our advice is to head for the Cheval Place entrance. The dining room has a kitchen on view to the rear and cane furniture; it's somewhat dark, and lacks much effort at interior design. However, considering the location, a short walk from Harrods, the prices are fair and the set lunch a steal. The North Indian food has an African slant (the firm has branches in Uganda, Kenya and Tanzania, as well as another London outlet), with tilapia fish tikka and mogo (fried cassava chips) among the starters. We kicked off dinner with a flaky roasted lentil popadom, followed by a delicious and smoky tandoori chicken served on the bone. The kitchen also came up trumps with fish makhani, which arrived clothed in a creamy and tangy tomato-based sauce. Vegetarian dishes get attention here too, and we enjoyed aloo chat (delicious crispy fried potatoes scattered with chillies) as well as tarka dahl, where the yellow lentils had a subtle hint of cumin. To finish, pistachio kulfi seemed a little too dense, however. Staff on our visit appeared to be beset by fatigue.

Available for hire. Babies and children admitted. Booking advisable. Separate room for parties, seats 30. Takeaway service; delivery service (over £10 within 2-mile radius). **Map 14 E9. For branch see index.**

Marylebone

★ Roti Chai

2012 RUNNER-UP BEST NEW CHEAP EATS
3-4 Portman Mews South, W1H 6HS (7408 0101, www.rotichai.com). Marble Arch tube.
Meals served noon-10.30pm Mon-Sat; 12.30-9pm Sun. **Main courses** £4.50-£8.50. **Credit** AmEx, MC, V. Pan-Indian

The name provides the clue: Roti Chai (bread, tea) is dedicated to serving inexpensive, café-style Indian food – along similar lines to Dishoom. It does so with some panache, in a stylish, contemporary setting. As you enter, you're faced with a counter stocked with colourful packets of Indian produce, and a serving hatch decorated with the vivid primary-coloured hues of retro street-food advertisements (emblazoned with statements like 'imli pani: finest ingredients'). The menu offers street snacks from across India: from the crisp bhel pooris of Mumbai beaches, to Gujarati steamed dokhla (a savoury sponge well matched with coconut chutney). Railway lamb curry was a light, punchy dish incorporating chunks of potatoes, while a bengali fish curry had been pungently flavoured with mustard seeds. A steaming hot, fluffy portion of roti was a highlight – as you'd expect, given the venue's name – although a glass tumbler of masala chai lacked depth of flavour, tasting of little other than cardamom. There's also a new 'dining room' menu containing the likes of chettinad chicken (from Tamil Nadu) and kozhikode seafood curry from Kerala. Service was thoroughly distracted on our trip, with staff forgetful and bringing the wrong dishes.

Available for hire. Babies and children welcome: high chairs; nappy-changing facilities. Booking advisable dinner. Disabled: lift, toilet. Vegan dishes. Vegetarian menu. **Map 9 G6.**

Trishna London

15-17 Blandford Street, W1U 3DG (7935 5624, www.trishnalondon.com). Bond Street tube.
Lunch served noon-2.45pm Mon-Sat; 12.30-3.15pm Sun. **Dinner served** 6-10.45pm Mon-Sat; 6.30-9.45pm Sun. **Main courses** £8-£20. **Set lunch** £15 2 courses, £18 3 courses, £21 4 courses. **Set dinner** (6-6.30pm Mon-Sat; 6.30-7pm Sun) £20 4 courses. **Credit** AmEx, MC, V. South Indian

When the well-heeled denizens of Marylebone go out 'for an Indian', they don't head to a mundane curry house. No, they reserve a table at Trishna, the London sister of a celebrated Mumbai restaurant popular with the Bollywood set. Here, bling is eschewed in favour of quietly sophisticated – spartan, even – surroundings: whitewashed walls, pale oak floors and designer light fittings. It's a suitably blank canvas for colourful, contemporary cooking. Presentation may be 'haute', but portions are anything but skimpy; on our visit, the so-called 'bites' were almost main course-sized. Highlights included a signature dish of delicate crab meat drenched in a buttery sauce with hints of garlic and plenty of black pepper; and roast guinea fowl, its fiery 'tikka' marinade of chilli, fennel and yoghurt complemented by the earthy notes of brown masoor lentils. Other dishes were less successful:

Pan-Indian menu

Spellings of Indian dishes vary widely; dishes such as gosht may appear in several versions on different menus as the word is transliterated from (in this case) Hindi. There are umpteen languages and several scripts in the Indian subcontinent, the most commonly seen on London menus being Punjabi, Hindi, Bengali and Gujarati. For the sake of consistency, however, we have tried to adhere to uniform spellings. The following are common throughout the subcontinent.

Aloo: potato.
Ayre: a white fish much used in Bengali cuisine.
Baingan: aubergine.
Bateira, **batera** or **bater**: quail.
Bengali: Bengal, before Partition in 1947, was a large province covering Calcutta (now in India's West Bengal) and modern-day Bangladesh. 'Bengali' and 'Bangladeshi' cooking is quite different, and the term 'Bengali' is often misused in London's Indian restaurants.
Bhajee: vegetables cooked with spices, usually 'dry' rather than sauced.
Bhajia or **bhaji**: vegetables dipped in chickpea-flour batter and deep-fried; also called **pakoras**.
Bhatura: deep-fried doughy discs.
Bhindi: okra.
Brinjal: aubergine.
Bulchao or **balchao**: a Goan vinegary pickle made with small dried prawns (with shells) and lots of garlic.
Chana or **channa**: chickpeas.
Chapati: a flat wholewheat griddle bread.
Chat or **chaat**: various savoury snacks featuring combinations of pooris (qv), diced onion and potato, chickpeas, crumbled samosas and pakoras, chutneys and spices.
Dahi: yoghurt.
Dahl or **dal**: a lentil curry similar to thick lentil soup. Countless regional variations exist.
Dhansak: a Parsi (qv) casserole of meat, lentils and vegetables, with a mix of hot and tangy flavours.
Dhaniya: coriander.
Ghee: clarified butter used for frying.
Gobi: cauliflower.
Gosht, **josh** or **ghosh**: meat, usually lamb.
Gram flour: chickpea flour.
Kachori: crisp pastry rounds with spiced mung dahl or pea filling.
Lassi: a yoghurt drink, ordered with salt or sugar, sometimes with fruit. Ideal to quench a burning palate.
Machi or **machli**: fish.
Masala or **masaladar**: mixed spices.
Methi: fenugreek, either dried (seeds) or fresh (green leaves).
Murgh or **murg**: chicken.
Mutter, **muter** or **mattar**: peas.
Nan or **naan**: teardrop-shaped flatbread cooked in a tandoor.
Palak or **paalak**: spinach; also called saag.
Paan or **pan**: betel leaf stuffed with chopped 'betel nuts', coconut and spices such as fennel seeds, and folded into a triangle. Available sweet or salty, and eaten at the end of a meal as a digestive.
Paneer or **panir**: Indian cheese; a bit like tofu in texture and taste.
Paratha: a large griddle-fried bread that is sometimes stuffed (with spicy mashed potato or minced lamb, for instance).
Parsi or **Parsee**: a religious minority based in Mumbai, but originally from Persia, renowned for its cooking.
Pilau, **pillau** or **pullao**: flavoured rice cooked with meat or vegetables. In most British Indian restaurants, pilau rice is simply rice flavoured and coloured with turmeric or (rarely) saffron.
Poori or **puri**: a disc of deep-fried wholewheat bread; the frying makes it puff up like an air-filled cushion.
Popadom, **poppadom**, **papadum** or **papad**: large thin wafers made with lentil paste, and flavoured with pepper, garlic or chilli. Eaten in the UK with pickles and relishes while waiting for the meal to arrive.
Raita: a yoghurt mix, usually with cucumber.
Roti: a round, sometimes unleavened, bread, thicker than a chapati (qv) and cooked in a tandoor or griddle. **Roomali roti** is a very thin, soft disc of roti.
Saag or **sag**: spinach; also called palak.
Tamarind: the pods of this East African tree, grown in India, are made into a paste that imparts a sour, fruity taste – popular in some regional cuisines, including Gujarati and South Indian.
Thali: literally 'metal plate'. A large plate with rice, bread, metal containers of dahl and vegetable curries, pickles and yoghurt.
Vadai or **wada**: a spicy vegetable or lentil fritter; **dahi wada** are lentil fritters soaked in yoghurt, topped with tamarind and date chutneys.
Vindaloo: originally, a hot and spicy pork curry from Goa that should authentically be soured with vinegar and cooked with garlic. In London restaurants, the term is usually misused to signify simply very hot dishes.
Xacuti: a Goan dish made with lamb or chicken pieces, coconut and a complex mix of roasted then ground spices.

the batter of our Trishna 'fish and chips' was a touch over-seasoned, while the squid in an otherwise excellent seafood salad (combining oily spiced Goan sausages with fruits de mer) was a little chewy. The multinational staff are accommodating and knowledgeable. Wine, too, is taken seriously, with an Old World-leaning list and an experienced sommelier to hand.
Available for hire. Babies and children welcome: high chairs. Booking advisable dinner. Separate room for parties, seats 12. Tables outdoors (3, patio). Vegetarian menu. **Map 9 G5**.

Mayfair

Benares

12A Berkeley Square House, Berkeley Square, W1J 6BS (7629 8886, www.benaresrestaurant.com). Green Park tube. **Lunch served** noon-2.30pm Mon-Sat; noon-2.45pm Sun. **Dinner served** 5.30-10.30pm Mon-Sat; 6-10pm Sun. **Main courses** £24-£54. **Set meal** (lunch, 5.30-6.30pm) £32 3 courses. **Credit** AmEx, DC, MC, V. Modern Indian

A magnet for expense-account suits, Benares is fronted by renowned chef Atul Kochhar. After this year's visit, however, we reckon Kochhar needs to keep a closer eye on kitchen affairs. The discreet entrance leads to a stylish first-floor bar: a spacious set-up where opulent artefacts and floating flowers compensate for a lack of natural light. In contrast, the adjacent dining area is more corporate in looks, with a neutral colour scheme. The menu offers Indo-European fusions, with varying results. Goan-style seared mackerel fillet – lightly steeped in a vinegary chilli-ginger paste before being sealed on a griddle – worked well with the astringency of a ginger and pounded sesame chutney and the fruity bite of pickled pears. But a first course of khasta murgh was hugely disappointing, little more than chopped chicken tikka mashed with potatoes and encased in dry, claggy pastry. At £16 a throw, we felt robbed. Lacklustre braised lamb shank dampened spirits further; it was reminiscent of a school-dinner stew with little trace of spices. Woes continued with an overcooked tandoori chicken breast partnered by soupy tomato and ginger sauce. Service, although well intentioned, was hardly slick either. We've had much better meals here in the past.
Available for hire. Babies and children welcome: high chairs; nappy-changing facilities. Booking advisable. Disabled: toilet. Dress: smart casual; no sportswear. Separate rooms for parties, seating 6, 10, 16 and 34. Takeaway service. Vegetarian menu. **Map 9 H7**.

Tamarind

20 Queen Street, W1J 5PR (7629 3561, www.tamarindrestaurant.com). Green Park tube. **Lunch served** noon-2.45pm Mon-Fri, Sun. **Dinner served** 5.30-11pm Mon-Sat; 6-10.45pm Sun. **Main courses** £17.95-£24.50. **Set lunch** (Mon-Fri) £18.50 2 courses, £20.50 3 courses, £28 tasting menu. **Set dinner** (5.30-6.45pm, 10.30-11pm) £28.50 3 courses. **Credit** AmEx, MC, V. Pan-Indian

An established fine-dining destination and a favourite with business types, Tamarind makes good use of an awkward (if large) basement space by clever positioning of speckled mirrors. Crisp white table linen accentuates the sophisticated chocolate tones of the decor. Head chef Alfred Prasad largely steers clear of flamboyant presentations, preferring instead to let the food – updated northern Indian classics in the main – do the talking. Crisp-fried slivers of tilapia, cloaked in lightly spiced gram-flour batter, were tastefully partnered with dabs of fresh mint chutney, elevating a street food staple into a stylish starter. To our minds, the makhani dahl here is among London's best; slow-cooked black lentils, infused with garlic and ginger, and enriched with cream, butter and tomatoes, made a splendid partner to hot nans. Not quite in the same league was an anaemic-looking chicken tikka, which needed a few seconds longer in the tandoor to develop a much-needed, smoky character. Thumbs up, though, to the rich Hyderabadi-style lamb biriani; fluffy basmati grains, streaked with saffron and coated in a cardamom and browned-onion masala, made a fine bed for the chunks of slow-simmered lamb. Yes, the atmosphere here is rather sedate, but the cooking is decent and service alert.
Babies and children welcome until 7pm: children's menu; high chairs. Booking essential. Takeaway service. Vegan dishes. Vegetarian menu. **Map 9 H7**.

Veeraswamy

Mezzanine Floor, Victory House, 99-101 Regent Street, entrance on Swallow Street, W1B 4RS (7734 1401, www.veeraswamy.com). Piccadilly Circus tube. **Lunch served** noon-2.30pm Mon-Fri; 12.30-2.30pm Sat; 12.30-2.45pm Sun. **Dinner served** 5.30-10.30pm Mon-Thur; 5.30-10.45pm Fri, Sat; 6-10.10pm Sun. **Main courses** £19.50-£36. **Set meal** (lunch, 5.30-6.30pm Mon-Sat) £17.75 2 courses; (lunch Sun) £24 3 courses. **Credit** AmEx, DC, MC, V. Pan-Indian

Billed as London's oldest surviving Indian restaurant (established 1926), Veeraswamy is accessed by a lift that opens into the light, airy, first-floor dining area. It's an elegant space decorated with coloured glass shades, silvery grilles, crisp table linen, and black and white photographs. Its owners, the Panjabi sisters, also oversee Amaya, Chutney Mary and the Masala Zone chain. The northern Indian dish of paneer labadar tikka (a tandoori spin on a sandwich) is here made with sliced fresh cheese filled with mint and toasted cumin chutney before being seared in the tandoor. We loved the way its wispy smoky crust yielded to the soft paneer within. Equally impressive, South Indian-style scallops were partnered with a tasty moilee sauce made from softened shallots, mustard, coconut cream and astringent ginger. Staying in the southern region, fruity pineapple curry, spiked with chilli, popped mustard seeds and peppery curry leaves, made a marvellous match with lemon-drenched rice. Only two side orders didn't hit the high notes; our nans were greasy, and an aubergine mash too salty. Service, however, is as smooth as Indian silk. Ask for a table by the window for a splendid view of bustling Regent Street below.
Babies and children admitted until 8pm. Booking advisable weekends. Disabled: lift; toilet. Dress: smart casual. Separate room for parties, seats 24. Vegan dishes. Vegetarian menu. **Map 17 A5**.

Soho

Cinnamon Soho NEW

5 Kingly Street, W1B 5PF (7437 1664, www.cinnamonsoho.com). Oxford Circus or Piccadilly Circus tube. **Meals served** 11am-11pm Mon-Sat; 11.30am-4pm Sun. **Main courses** £12-£17. **Set meal** (lunch, 5-7pm) £15 2 courses, £18 3 courses. **Credit** AmEx, MC, V. Modern Indian

Cinnamon Soho is a surprise if you're expecting curry-house portion sizes. Order plenty of dishes if you're hungry, because everything we tried was delicious, and we were left craving more. The location, a dark ground floor and basement on a lacklustre street, is less appealing. Also, the service on our visit was slow and ill-informed. But do go for the food: executive chef Vivek Singh's menu is highly innovative, as you'd expect from the chef behind the celebrated Cinnamon Club. A classic North Indian curry of karela chana (bitter gourd with chana dahl lentils) was topped with stuffed dudhi – an Indian marrow packed with lightly pickled, beetroot-coloured vegetable batons: ingenious. The all-day snacks were also fresh and well made: mathri are like the Rajasthani snack namak pare, crisp-fried wheat discs kneaded with ghee, flavoured with carom seed, served here with a slightly over-puréed aubergine dip. There are lots of balls too. Crab cake balls, tiny potato bondas, moist beef shami kebab – even tiny scotch quail eggs – all perfectly moist and marble-sized. These were encased in different batters, each served on delectable chutneys; a sensational starter, and one of the best dishes we've eaten this year. Even the sweets included beautiful petits fours of frozen golis ('goli' are small balls) in dark chocolate and chilli, and white chocolate and cardamom.
Available for hire. Babies and children welcome: high chairs. Booking advisable. Disabled: toilet. Dress: smart casual. Tables outdoors (3, pavement). **Map 17 A4**.

★ Imli

167-169 Wardour Street, W1F 8WR (7287 4243, www.imli.co.uk). Oxford Circus or Tottenham Court Road tube. **Meals served** noon-11pm Mon-Sat; noon-10pm Sun. **Tapas** £3.95-£9.95. **Set lunch** £8.50-£9.95. **Set dinner** (4-7pm) £12.95 2 courses. **Credit** AmEx, MC, V. Pan-Indian

Attracting local workers for lunch, and Soho explorers for dinner, Imli is an offshoot of Mayfair restaurant Tamarind ('imli' is Hindi for tamarind). The emphasis is on 'Indian tapas': small plates designed for sharing that focus on the subcontinent's varied street food. This means bhel poori, papdi chat and coriander vadai sit alongside more modern variants such as spicy battered squid, and tandoor-grilled meat, fish and vegetable dishes. There are special lunch deals, including nicely priced curry 'platters' and Indian sandwiches (aka 'naanwich'), a pre-theatre menu and usually a couple of special offers – check the website. In the main, it's good-value, competently executed food, if slightly dumbed-down for western tastes. Popadoms came with three excellent chutneys (beetroot, sweet mango, spicy tomato); tarka dahl was satisfying and flavourful; aloo mutter ki tikki ragda (potato, pea and ginger patties with chickpeas and tamarind chutney) was so-so. Decor has a blandly corporate feel, with dark wood tables, orange and red walls and large-format photos of Indian market vendors. Staff are welcoming but not always clued up about the food. Compared to newer, more fashion-conscious outfits such as Dishoom and Roti Chai, it all feels rather staid.
Available for hire. Babies and children welcome: children's menu; high chairs; nappy-changing facilities. Booking advisable Thur-Sat. Disabled: toilet. Separate room for parties, seats 45.

THREE OF THE VERY BEST
INDIAN RESTAURANTS

AMAYA

Offers a sophisticated innovative twist on Indian cuisine, with authentic flavours brought to life using 3 traditional grilling techniques in one of Knightsbridge's' coolest restaurants.

Open for lunch & dinner seven days a week

Halkin Arcade, Motcomb Street
Knightsbridge, London SW1

Telephone: 020 7823 1166

CHUTNEY MARY

Since 1990 Chutney Mary has transformed Indian cuisine in London, remaining true to authentic flavours while reflecting contemporary trends. In beautiful surroundings.

Open for dinner 7 days a week and lunch Sat/Sunday

535 Kings Road
Chelsea, London SW10

Telephone: 020 7351 3113

VEERASWAMY

World's oldest Indian restaurant
Classical Indian food beautifully served in sumptuous surroundings overlooking Regent Street.

Open for lunch and dinner 7 days a week

Mezzanine Floor, Victory House
99 Regent Street, London W1

Telephone: 020 7734 1401

Takeaway service; delivery service (over £20 within half-mile radius). Vegetarian menu. **Map 17 B3**.

Red Fort

77 Dean Street, W1D 3SH (7437 2115, www.redfort.co.uk). Leicester Square or Tottenham Court Road tube.
Bar **Open** 5pm-1am Tue-Sat.
Restaurant **Lunch served** noon-2.30pm Mon-Fri. **Dinner served** 5.30-11.30pm daily. **Main courses** £15-£18. **Set lunch** £14 2 courses. **Set dinner** (5.30-7pm) £16 2 courses incl tea or coffee.
Both **Credit** AmEx, MC, V. North Indian

This upmarket restaurant has been showcasing the more refined aspects of North Indian food since the early 1980s, and has outlasted the New Labour politicians who reportedly used it as a favoured meeting spot in the '90s. This association might make it seem like an expense-account sort of place – it's not cheap, and wine especially hammers the wallet – but it is possible to eat well here even if you're not on Mandelson money. Try the set lunch or pre-theatre menu if you're feeling frugal – the food is the same. It's accomplished Moghul court cooking with some pan-Indian influences: fine-minced seekh kebabs with tangy mint relish; the sort of chicken tikka and ochre-coloured, gingery bhuna gosht that reminds you how special these often bastardised dishes can be; and unusual items, such as baingan mirchi ka salan, quartered baby aubergines with peanut and tamarind sauce. Everything else that appears on the table, from the folded popadoms and dainty chutneys to steaming breads, is excellent. On special occasions, for which the flatteringly lit, elegantly neutral room is made, go à la carte for the likes of saffron lobster and aromatic spiced seafood. To paraphrase D:Ream, things couldn't get much better.

Available for hire. Babies and children admitted. Booking advisable. Dress: smart casual. Vegan dishes. Vegetarian menu. **Map 17 B3**.

Westminster

Cinnamon Club

Old Westminster Library, 30-32 Great Smith Street, SW1P 3BU (7222 2555, www.cinnamon club.com). St James's Park or Westminster tube.
Breakfast served 7.30-10am Mon-Fri. **Lunch served** noon-2.45pm, **dinner served** 6-10.45pm Mon-Sat. **Main courses** £14-£32. **Set meal** £22 2 courses, £24 3 courses. **Credit** AmEx, DC, MC, V. Modern Indian

On a quiet street, just across from the quaint Church House bookshop, the former Westminster Library is a glorious Grade II-listed red-brick building. Inside lies one of London's top Indian restaurants: the Cinnamon Club. Executive chef Vivek Singh makes masterful use of traditional herbs and spices and modern techniques to create elegant, innovative dishes. The kitchen's strength lies in game or lesser-seen cuts of meat. On our visit, this translated to a terrific starter of pan-fried lamb's brain with keema curry, the golden nuggets of tender offal beautifully matched by the warm spicing of curried lamb mince. Next came a trio of deliciously moist venison and prune kofta (meatballs), served over creamy black lentils and wilted spinach. A stunning dessert of wan, marinated strawberries suspended in a delicate strawberry jelly, quivering under a solitary fennel-scented wafer, proved a triumphant end to our meal. It's a great pity, given the standards of cooking, gracious service and grandeur of the building, that the dining room itself is bland, with the lighting overly bright. Although the structure's listed status prevents transformation, this top-flight restaurant desperately requires a redesign, to create a setting to match the inspiring food.

Available for hire. Babies and children welcome: high chairs. Booking advisable. Disabled: lift; toilet. Dress: smart casual. Separate rooms for parties, seating 30-60. **Map 16 K9**.

For branch (Cinnamon Kitchen) see index.

West

Hammersmith

Potli NEW

2012 RUNNER-UP BEST NEW LOCAL RESTAURANT

319-321 King Street, W6 9NH (8741 4328, www.potli.co.uk). Ravenscourt Park tube.
Lunch served noon-2.45pm Mon-Sat. **Dinner served** 6-10.30pm Mon-Thur; 6-11pm Fri, Sat. **Meals served** noon-10.30pm Sun. **Main courses** £6-£9.50. **Credit** AmEx, MC, V. Modern Indian

'Potli, an Indian market kitchen' is the full name of this yellow-fronted newcomer on Hammersmith's main drag, and the menu references some of India's most famous street-food bazaars, including Chandni Chowk in Delhi and Mumbai's Chowpatty Beach. Vintage film posters and tinplate advertisements have nostalgic appeal too, but otherwise you can ignore the concept and just enjoy the food. Which is indeed highly enjoyable. From top-notch samosa (lovely flaky pastry flavoured with carom seed) to Kerala fish curry (tilapia chunks simmered in a light, coconutty broth), it was hard to find fault. Five-lentil dahl was thick and tomatoey, with real depth of flavour. Portions are generous, so beware of over-ordering, especially as some dishes are very rich; shahi malai kofta produced two dense balls packed with cardamom, almonds and pistachio nuts, in a thick, nutty, creamy sauce. The room is split in two: a bar area and a main dining room, with seating at chunky dark-wood tables and a couple of large, semi-circular booths, with green and red accents in cushions and chair seats. To drink, there's wine, Indian beers, lassis and some Asian-inspired cocktails. Subdued lighting keeps the atmosphere intimate. Service on our evening visit was very polite and attentive to the diverse clientele: from Indian families to courting couples. At lunchtime, look out for some bargain-priced set deals.

Available for hire (lunch). Babies and children welcome: high chairs; nappy-changing facilities. Booking advisable dinner. Disabled: toilet. Separate room for parties, seats 30-35. Tables outdoors (6, pavement). Takeaway service; delivery service (over £15 within 2-mile radius). Vegan dishes. Vegetarian menu. **Map 20 A4**.

Kensington

Zaika

1 Kensington High Street, W8 5NP (7795 6533, www.zaika-restaurant.co.uk). High Street Kensington tube. **Lunch served** noon-2.45pm Tue-Sun. **Dinner served** 6-10.45pm Mon-Sat; 6-9.45pm Sun. **Main courses** £17-£29. **Set lunch** £12 1 course, £18.50 2 courses, £22.50 3 courses. **Set meal** (6-7pm Mon-Thur) £22.50 2 courses, £27 3 courses; £47-£62 tasting menu (£76-£99 incl wine). **Credit** AmEx, DC, MC, V. Modern Indian

Housed in a former bank sumptuously furnished with sweeping silk drapes, substantial antiques and impressive flower arrangements, Zaika attracts wealthy business folk and tourists. The kitchen aims high, with tasting menus, a menu gourmand, and the modern-Indian likes of masala foie gras, or scallops with coconut and lime foam. Cooking can be of a high standard, but it's too often inconsistent – and on our latest visit, service was surly. A lamb platter started the meal well, with a satisfyingly juicy seekh kebab seasoned with green chillies and coriander then grilled over coals. However, tandoori chops were tough and inadequately marinated, and equally dispiriting was a mini samosa filled with bland fried mince (we've had better at local cafés). Shredded tandoori rabbit, piled on to a mini nan, also disappointed, lacking any discernible spicing. Things picked up with the vegetarian thali; highlights included a splendid chopped okra masala, the crisp chunks cloaked in a garlicky tomato sauce. We also loved the soft pillowy cubes of paneer tossed with onions and peppers. Nevertheless, lacklustre basics (overcooked basmati rice and salty dahl) made us question the commitment of the team here.

Available for hire. Babies and children welcome: high chair. Booking advisable; essential weekends. Vegan dishes. Vegetarian menu. **Map 7 C8**.

Notting Hill

Chakra NEW

157-159 Notting Hill Gate, W11 3LF (7229 2115, www.chakralondon.com). Notting Hill Gate tube. **Lunch served** noon-3.30pm daily. **Dinner served** 6-11pm Mon-Sat; 6-10.30pm Sun. **Main courses** £7.95-£22.50. **Set lunch** (Sat, Sun) £16.95 buffet. **Set dinner** £60 4 courses. **Credit** AmEx, MC, V. Modern Indian

This new restaurant bucks the trend for budget-priced Indian street food with a fine-dining menu emphasising the 'royal' cooking styles of the Indian courts. Chakra is furnished in shades of biscuit-cream, with chandeliers, crisp napery and padded, dimpled walls creating a sophisticated vibe, and the siren-red outfits of the staff adding colour. A spectrum of cookery styles runs from the delicate cardamom-spiced kebabs favoured by the Nawab rulers of Lucknow to smoky game grills loved by the Rajputs in Rajasthan. Lamb chops – inspired by the Patiala palace kitchen in the Punjab – were well marinated in yoghurt, lemon juice and ginger, then cooked Punjabi-style over charcoal, delivering tenderness and robust flavours. Equally tasty, palak paneer was a faultless rendition: velvety-textured spinach purée, lightly seasoned with nutmeg and ginger, cradled pillows of paneer. A nod to London-style fusion cooking – griddle-seared garlic scallops anointed with garlic-chilli oil – was unremarkable. Like the rock-solid mango kulfi (frozen in a wafer-thin chocolate case and topped with mango compote), service might benefit from being warmed up a bit. Minor gripes aside, the cooking was top drawer, though prices are at the sharp end. On a weeknight, the place was busy with well-heeled locals and out-to-impress couples.

Available for hire. Booking advisable. Disabled: toilet. Separate room for parties, seats 26. Tables outdoors (2, pavement). Takeaway service. **Map 7 A7**.

TAMARIND
Let us change your perception of Indian food
As Tamarind enters its 16th year, the award-winning Indian restaurant, in the heart of Mayfair, continues to be instrumental in changing perceptions of the subcontinent's cuisine.
Tamarind offers beautifully balanced selection of signature classics complimented by an impressively extensive wine list, elegant décor and state of the art facilities.
A truly indulgent experience!
TAMARIND
For Reservations or
to find out more please visit
www.tamarindrestaurant.com
reservations@tamarindrestaurant.com
or call 020 7629 3561 20 Queen Street, Mayfair, London, W1J 5PR

Modern Indian Tapas
Imli offers authentic Indian street food sizzling with spices and full of fresh vibrant flavours
We serve it 'tapas-style' – perfect for sharing!
For the latest news, daily offers and monthly promotions visit our website www.imli.co.uk
For reservations
please call 020 7287 4243 or
info@imli.co.uk
imli
167-169 Wardour Street, Soho, London W1F 8WR
UNDERGROUND
Closest Tube: Piccadilly Circus/ Tottenham Court Rd

North Indian menu

Under the blanket term 'North Indian', we have included dishes originating in the Punjab (the region separating India and Pakistan), Kashmir and all points down to Hyderabad. Southall has some of London's best Punjabi restaurants, where breads cooked in the tandoor oven are often preferred to rice, marinated meat kebabs are popular, and dals are thick and buttery.

Bhuna gosht: a dry, spicy dish of lamb.
Biriani or **biryani**: a royal Moghul (qv) version of pilau rice, in which meat or vegetables are cooked together with basmati rice, spices and saffron. It's difficult to find an authentic biriani in London restaurants.
Dopiaza or **do pyaza**: cooked with onions.
Dum: a Kashmiri cooking technique where food is simmered in a casserole (typically a clay pot sealed with dough), allowing spices to permeate.
Gurda: kidneys.
Haandi: an earthenware or metal cooking pot, with handles on either side and a lid.
Jalfrezi: chicken or vegetable dishes cooked with fresh green chillies – a popular cooking style in Mumbai.
Jhingri, **jhinga** or **chingri**: prawns.
Karahi or **karai**: a small iron or metal wok-like cooking dish. Similar to the 'balti' dish made famous in Birmingham.
Kheema or **keema**: minced lamb, as in kheema nan (stuffed nan).
Kofta: meatballs or vegetable dumplings.
Korma: braised in yoghurt and/or cream and nuts. Often mild, but rich.
Makhani: cooked with butter (makhan) and sometimes tomatoes, as in **murgh makhani**.
Massalam: marinated, then casseroled chicken dish, originating in Muslim areas.
Moghul, **Mogul** or **Moglai**: from the Moghul period of Indian history, used in the culinary sense to describe typical North Indian Muslim dishes.
Pasanda: thin fillets of lamb cut from the leg and flattened with a mallet. In Britain, the term usually applies to a creamy sauce virtually identical to a korma (qv).
Punjabi: Since Partition, the Punjab has been two adjoining states, one in India, one in Pakistan. Lahore is the main town on the Pakistani side, which is predominantly Muslim; Amritsar on the Indian side is the Sikh capital. Punjabi dishes tend to be thick stews or cooked in a tandoor.
Roghan gosht or **rogan josh**: lamb cooked in spicy sauce; a Kashmiri speciality.
Seekh kebab: ground lamb, skewered and grilled.
Tandoor: clay oven originating in north-west India in which food is cooked without oil.
Tarka: spices and flavourings are cooked separately, then added to dahl at a final stage.
Tikka: meat, fish or paneer cut into cubes, then marinated in spicy yoghurt and baked in a tandoor.

South West

Chelsea

Chutney Mary

535 King's Road, SW10 0SZ (7351 3113, www.chutneymary.com). Fulham Broadway tube or bus 11, 22. **Lunch served** 12.30-2.45pm Sat, Sun. **Dinner served** 6.30-11.15pm Mon-Sat; 6.30-10.15pm Sun. **Main courses** £16.75-£31.50. **Set lunch** £24 3 courses. **Credit** AmEx, DC, MC, V. Pan-Indian

With leafy hanging baskets, palm-lined walls and a huge tree growing at its centre, Chutney Mary's conservatory remains one of London's loveliest dining spaces. The remainder of this large restaurant isn't as verdant, though classy upholstery and well-dressed tables are a constant. Over two decades, it has worked hard to keep up with the times, bringing in increasingly fashionable dishes, all served to a soundtrack of chilled-out beats. On our visit, however, cooking was mixed: a patty of finely minced duck, served with blueberry chutney, was overwhelmed by chilli. Better was a venison 'samosa': a thin pastry cone filled with warmly spiced ground meat, peas and sultanas, accompanied by cheffy squiggles of zingy mint sauce. Mains had similar highs and lows: a trio of giant tandoori prawns impressed (though at £10 per crustacean, you'd hope so), yet our curry sampler was undermined by bland rice (the promised 'aromatic spicing' undetectable) and overcooked okra. Service veers from polite to intrusive, but perhaps strangest of all, given the pedestrian cooking, is the secrecy over the menu, with staff forbidden to issues copies, and patrons banned from restaurant photography. Chutney Mary shares owners with upmarket Indian restaurants Veeraswamy and Amaya, as well as budget chain Masala Zone.

Available for hire. Babies and children welcome lunch; children admitted until 8pm: high chairs. Booking advisable; essential Thur-Sat. Dress: smart casual. Separate room for parties, seats 28. Vegan dishes. Vegetarian menu. **Map 13 C13.**

Painted Heron

112 Cheyne Walk, SW10 0DJ (7351 5232, www.thepaintedheron.com). Sloane Square tube then bus 11, 22. **Dinner served** 6-11pm Mon-Fri. **Meals served** 11am-11pm Sat, Sun. **Main courses** £13.50-£22. **Set brunch** (11am-5pm Sat, Sun) £20. **Set meal** £45 per person (minimum 2) 6 courses. **Credit** AmEx, MC, V. Modern Indian

A Cheyne Walk treasure, this discreet restaurant has deservedly built up a fan club of Chelsea residents, who come here for the adventurous menu inspired by classic culinary tradition. Dishes are well-thought through and carefully executed – if occasionally eyebrow-raising. Along with the staples, expect the likes of chilli-rosemary nan, or smoked chicken scented with southern spices, or even tandoori monkfish paired with rhubarb. An outstanding seafood platter included such stars as a mini dosa (rice and lentil pancake) filled with juicy flaked crab, and a lovely, lightly fried sea bass fillet kissed with coriander, green chilli and lime paste. Mains aren't usually as memorable; chicken breast stuffed with pickled limes, simmered in a browned onion-ginger masala with chickpeas, had too many discordant flavours. Strawberries, of all things, were given an extreme makeover to produce a surprisingly tasty curry; the berries, simmered in their own juice, were spiked with a kick of chilli and ginger and sharpened with lime: a splendid match for steamy lemon rice. On our visit, service needed to be more switched-on, to match the quality of the food. Check out the weekend brunches for a well-priced taster of what's on offer.

Available for hire. Booking advisable weekends. Babies and children welcome: high chairs; nappy-changing facilities. Disabled: toilet. Tables outdoors (3, pavement). **Map 14 D13.**

South

Tooting

★ Apollo Banana Leaf

190 Tooting High Street, SW17 0SF (8696 1423, www.apollobananaleaf.co.uk). Tooting Broadway tube. **Lunch served** noon-3pm, **dinner served** 6-10.30pm Mon-Thur. **Meals served** noon-10.30pm Fri-Sun. **Main courses** £3.50-£6.75. **Unlicensed. Corkage** no charge. **Credit** MC, V. Sri Lankan

Though Apollo Banana Leaf is marooned in a desolate no-man's land between Tooting Broadway and Collier's Wood, a seemingly endless parade of diners shuffled through its door on our midweek visit, filling first the main restaurant, then the neighbouring 'overflow' unit, before the three staff reluctantly began turning away punters. The attractions are threefold: a generous no-corkage BYO policy, recession-busting prices, and excellent cooking from Sri Lanka and South India. Short eats (street snacks) such as savoury lentil 'doughnuts' (vadais) or deep-fried, chilli-spiked fish cutlets are a good place to start, as are dosais (particularly the stuffed varieties), but the kitchen's true strength lies in its meat and fish curries. Our mutton curry saw tender meat in a deep, rich sauce with notes of fragrant cardamom. A whole white fillet of fish simmered in a creamy yet spicy coconut sauce also impressed. We teamed these with rice and traditional breads: a wholesome wholemeal chapati, and a chewy, buttery paratha (you won't find nans here). Tables are uncomfortably close, and service, though warm, can be painfully slow, but this unassuming spot remains one of the area's brightest stars.

Babies and children welcome: high chairs. Booking advisable weekends. Disabled: toilet. Takeaway service. Vegetarian menu.

East

Whitechapel

Café Spice Namaste

16 Prescot Street, E1 8AZ (7488 9242, www.cafespice.co.uk). Aldgate East or Tower Hill tube or Tower Gateway DLR. **Lunch served** noon-3pm Mon-Fri. **Dinner served** 6.15-10.30pm Mon-Fri; 6.30-10.30pm Sat. **Main courses** £12.50-£18.55. **Set meal** £35 3 courses. **Credit** AmEx, DC, MC, V. Pan-Indian

Given its location on a Whitechapel backstreet (well away from the well-trodden path towards Tayyabs), chef Cyrus Todiwala's enterprise is necessarily a destination restaurant – and even after 15 years, many seem more than happy to

Potli. See p146.

make the trip. The place made a name for itself with innovative, fresh takes on traditional pan-Indian cooking, as well as an emphasis on sustainability and local sourcing. The dining room is as bright/garish as ever (depending on your taste), but we can't help but feel certain aspects of the operation could do with an upgrade. Menus, for instance, were fading and dog-eared, and service could have been more personal. Although much of what we ate was far better than most Indian restaurants in London, not everything we ate was truly exciting. 'Mr Todiwala's' own-made pickles are lively and bursting with tart flavours, but the tomato and pumpkin sauce with fried prawns was one-dimensional; dhansak came with lamb on the bone and a thin but powerful gravy. The menu also takes in the varied likes of springbok bhuna, dosai, thali and venison tilla. Café Spice Namaste might not be the culinary phenomenon it once was, but it's still heartily recommended.
Available for hire. Babies and children welcome: high chairs. Disabled: toilet. Takeaway service; delivery service (over £15 within 2-mile radius).
Map 12 S7.

★ Lahore Kebab House

2 Umberston Street, E1 1PY (7488 2551, www.lahore-kebabhouse.com). Aldgate East or Whitechapel tube. **Meals served** noon-midnight daily. **Main courses** £6-£10.50. **Unlicensed. Corkage** no charge. **Credit** AmEx, MC, V.
Pakistani

There are three great places to eat Indian food in Whitechapel. Along with Tayyabs and Needoo, Lahore dishes out generous portions of brilliantly bold Punjabi grills, snacks and curries, and has been doing so for decades. A recent expansion has eased some of the queues that form on weekend evenings as crowds of hungry, in-the-know diners flock from near and far. They come for rich, powerfully spiced dahls and meat curries (some on the bone), piles of sweet onion bhajia, fiery grilled lamb chops and seekh kebabs, and fresh breads dripping with ghee. Everything is served in a rustic fashion, often in karahi on utilitarian metal stands, in keeping with the spartan (and spick-and-span) surroundings. It's not the kind of restaurant to take a date: large groups descend to take advantage of the bargain prices and BYO policy, and flatscreen TVs distract with IPL matches or Bollywood films. But for authentically vivid flavours in a no-nonsense setting, Lahore is hard to beat. The large open kitchen is a nice feature – nothing fuels the appetite while waiting for a table like watching the army of chefs kneading dough for the tandoor or manipulating skewers on the smoky grill.
Babies and children welcome: high chairs. Disabled: toilet. Takeaway service.
For branches see index.

★ Needoo Grill

87 New Road, E1 1HH (7247 0648, www.needoogrill.co.uk). Aldgate East or Whitechapel tube. **Meals served** 11.30am-11.30pm daily. **Main courses** £6-£6.50. **Corkage** no charge. **Credit** MC, V. Pakistani

Just round the corner from the perennially heaving, crowd-pleasing Tayyabs, and far from a million miles away in concept, Needoo Grill opened in 2009 and continues to be a more civilised provider of Punjabi grills, curries and snacks. The relative lack of queues also means it's a useful and speedy spot for takeaway. Over repeated visits, we've found the food consistently agreeable and the staff friendly,

South Indian menu

Much South Indian food consists of rice, lentil- and semolina-based dishes. Fish features strongly in non-vegetarian restaurants, and coconut, mustard seeds, curry leaves and red chillies are widely used. If you want to try South Indian snacks such as dosas, idlis or uppama, go at lunchtime, which is when these dishes are traditionally eaten, and they're more likely to be cooked fresh to order. In the evening, try the thalis and rice- and curry-based meals, including vegetable stir-fries such as thorans and pachadis.

Adai: fermented rice and lentil pancakes, with a nuttier flavour than dosais (qv).
Avial: a mixed vegetable curry from Kerala with a coconut and yoghurt sauce.
Bonda: spiced mashed potatoes, dipped in chickpea-flour batter and deep-fried.
Dosai or **dosa**: thin, shallow-fried pancake, often sculpted into interesting shapes; the very thin ones are called **paper dosai**. Most dosais are made with fermented rice and lentil batter, but variants include **rava dosai**, made with 'cream of wheat' semolina. **Masala dosais** come with a spicy potato filling. All variations are traditionally served with sambar (qv) and coconut chutney.
Gobi 65: cauliflower marinated in spices, then dipped in chickpea-flour batter and deep-fried. It is usually lurid pink due to the addition of food colouring.
Idli: steamed sponges of ground rice and lentil batter. Eaten with sambar (qv) and coconut chutney.
Kadala: black chickpea curry.
Kancheepuram idli: idli (qv) flavoured with whole black peppercorns and other spices.
Kappa: cassava root traditionally served with kadala (qv).
Kootu: mild vegetable curry in a creamy coconut and yoghurt sauce.
Pachadi: spicy vegetable side dish cooked with yoghurt.
Rasam: consommé made with lentils; it tastes both peppery-hot and tamarind-sour, but there are many regional variations.
Sambar or **sambhar**: a variation on dahl made with a specific hot blend of spices, plus coconut, tamarind and vegetables – particularly drumsticks (a pod-like vegetable, like a longer, woodier version of okra; you strip out the edible interior with your teeth).
Thoran: vegetables stir-fried with mustard seeds, curry leaves, chillies and fresh grated coconut.
Uppama: a popular breakfast dish in which onions, spices and, occasionally, vegetables are cooked with semolina using a risotto-like technique.
Uthappam: a spicy, crisp pancake/pizza made with lentil- and rice-flour batter, often topped with tomato, onions and chillies.
Vellappam: a bowl-shaped, crumpet-like rice pancake (same as appam or hoppers, qv, Sri Lankan menu).

even if the menu does little to differentiate itself from its local counterpart – it was opened by a former Tayyabs manager. What you get is meaty grills (mutton kebab, lamb chops, king prawns), a few street-food staples (samosa, pakora, paneer tikka roll), and stridently spiced curries ('daighi' dry lamb, dahls, karahi meat dishes). Take your time choosing and try some of the more unusual daily specials – lamb korma on Wednesdays, say, or nihari, made with slow-cooked lamb on the bone. Everything is good value, and there's no corkage on BYO. We wish Needoo aimed to be a bit more than a lookalike alternative to Tayyabs, but, even so, it's hard to fault for either execution or price.
Available for hire. Babies and children welcome: high chairs. Takeaway service. Vegetarian menu.

Tayyabs

83 Fieldgate Street, E1 1JU (7247 9543, www.tayyabs.co.uk). Aldgate East or Whitechapel tube. **Meals served** noon-11.30pm daily. **Main courses** £6.50-£25.80. **Unlicensed. Corkage** no charge. **Credit** AmEx, MC, V. Pakistani
Every year we feature this Punjabi grill, and every year it seems to be bigger and busier – as of 2012, the cellar and first floor of the former pub have been renovated and pressed into service to accommodate the endless stream of diners. Booking is essential, and we recommend an early evening or lunchtime visit, unless you're prepared to queue amid the crowds. So why the limitless popularity? Put simply, Tayyabs serves some of the best and cheapest Indian food in London, with a no-charge BYO policy to sweeten the deal. To start: juicy seekh kebabs, loaded with cracked coriander seeds and chilli; pakora dipped in yoghurt sauce; sizzling chicken tikka; and the dish that it's almost compulsory to order – hot, charred, gingery grilled lamb chops. For mains, full-flavoured curries (try the tomatoey chana masala, or the slow-cooked 'dry lamb'), often authentically dripping with ghee and unapologetically spicy, accompanied by tandoor-fresh breads. You'll struggle to spend £20 a head. We've heard reports of customers with bookings waiting ages for tables, service can be perfunctory, and there are often mere seconds between your last mouthful and the appearance of the bill. Nevertheless: an unmissable London dining experience.
Babies and children welcome: high chairs; nappy-changing facilities. Booking advisable. Disabled: toilet. Separate room for parties, seats 35. Takeaway service.

North East

Leytonstone

Mudra

715 Leytonstone High Road, E11 4RD (8539 1700, www.swadrestaurant.com). Leytonstone tube or Leytonstone High Road rail or 257, 66 bus. **Meals served** 5-11pm daily. **Main courses** £5-£6. **Credit** MC, V. South Indian
Although it's no longer a branch of Rasa, Mudra has maintained that estimable London-based Keralite mini-chain's commitment to dishes that transcend those of high-street curry houses. It's never a bad idea to tuck into the crunchy pre-meal snacks (including achappam and murukku) and half a dozen own-made pickles and chutneys while considering the menu. Here, populist concessions have begun to appear (vindaloos, chicken jalfrezi, prawn bhuna), but the emphasis remains on the likes of swaad erachi olathiyathu (a dry curry of stir-fried turmeric-marinated lamb with coconut) or kottayam fish moilee (a whole fish prepared with onion, tomato, ginger, green chilli and coconut milk), accompanied by a wide range of breads (not just dosa, chapati and paratha, but appam and poori). We'd recommend ironing out some vagaries of service – black-clad and unfailingly friendly though it is – and freshening the decor, which achieves the curious balancing act of being both energetically pink and a bit tired, rather than dumbing down the menu. Nonetheless, it's an enduring mystery why Mudra is so rarely full, and a source of considerable local anxiety. Should it close, the elegantly spiced, enticingly priced curries will be sorely missed.
Babies and children admitted. Booking advisable. Disabled: toilet. Takeaway service; delivery service (over £20 within 2-mile radius). Vegetarian menu.

North

Camden Town & Chalk Farm

Namaaste Kitchen

64 Parkway, NW1 7AH (7485 5977, www.namaastekitchen.co.uk). Camden Town tube. **Lunch served** noon-2.30pm, **dinner served** 5.30-11.30pm Mon-Thur. **Meals served** noon-11.30pm Fri, Sat; noon-11pm Sun. **Main courses** £7.50-£18.95. **Set lunch** £8.95 2 courses, £11.50 3 courses. **Credit** AmEx, MC, V. Modern Indian
Cream leather chairs and cocktail bars have become staples of London's modern Indian restaurants, but don't let the night-owl clichés of this aspirationally slick spot put you off. Inside, all is friendly, relaxed charm and, while the prices are on par with many a well-to-do neighbourhood curry house, the calibre of cooking is several notches above. Spicing is admirably diverse, ranging from the elegant subtlety of malai tikka (chicken marinated in cream cheese and homemade yoghurt) to the fiery laal maas (lamb with roast red chillies) from Rajasthan. Only our chingree samosas struck a coarse note, and they were tasty nonetheless. Vegetable sides of okra with mango, and baby aubergines flecked with sesame, mustard and curry leaves, sang with freshness. Crisp, bubbly date and ginger nan showed an intelligent grasp of flavour combining. To finish, there's a predictable round-up of tropical fruits, ices and Asian interpretations of classic French desserts. With Cobra lager on tap, wines starting at an affable £13.50 (for a bottle of Argentinian chenin-chardonnay), and the fun list of cocktails – our sweet Indian Tea flavoured with blackberry and lychee went down swiftly – Namaaste Kitchen deserves to become a Camden hotspot.
Available for hire. Babies and children welcome: high chairs. Booking advisable. Separate room for parties, seats 20. Takeaway service; delivery service (over £15 within 3-mile radius). Vegan dishes. Vegetarian menu. **Map 27 C3.**

Islington

★ Delhi Grill

21 Chapel Market, N1 9EZ (7278 8100, www.delhigrill.com). Angel tube. **Lunch served** noon-2.45pm, **dinner served** 6-10.30pm daily. **Main courses** £3.95-£8.95. **Credit** AmEx, MC, V. Punjabi

Islington's answer to a truckers' caff in the Punjab, this shabby-chic canteen is renowned for its earthy home-style cooking at prices that don't bite. Even on weekday evenings, the air is thick with smoky spices and the buzzy conversation of young professionals out for a masala-fix. Functional seating arrangements and Indian newspapers plastered across the walls are part of the rough-and-ready appeal, and are complementary to the reassuringly short menu of North Indian staples. There's even a guy making breads by the entrance. Although the tandoori platters are decent, we prefer to order the curries. Rogan josh, slowly simmered lamb cooked with fried onions, ginger and garlic, is spiked with aromatic spices and squished tomatoes: fabulous for its mellow flavour and best enjoyed with griddle-cooked chapatis. Keep an eye out too for blackboard specials; we love slow-cooked goat curry and spicy kidney beans. Vegetarians also get a look-in, with such gems as gingery black lentil dahl and quick-fried chopped okra. Service is well meaning, if at times a tad slow, but there's a steady supply of own-made dips and dunks to fill any gaps.
Available for hire. Babies and children admitted. Booking advisable Thur-Sat. Disabled: toilet. Takeaway service. Vegan dishes. **Map 5 N2**.

North West

Swiss Cottage

Eriki

4-6 Northways Parade, Finchley Road, NW3 5EN (7722 0606, www.eriki.co.uk). Swiss Cottage tube. **Lunch served** noon-2.30pm Mon-Fri, Sun. **Dinner served** 6-10.30pm daily. **Main courses** £10-£12. **Set lunch** £12.95 2 courses. **Credit** MC, V. Pan-Indian

A capacious venue, with an interior that evokes a grand Rajasthani Rajput setting: suitably palatial, with gold and maroon hues on the walls and carved, high-backed chairs. The menu is inspired by recipes from across India. To start, seekh kebab had the keema lamb mince perked up with mint and garam masala spices. There were scallops too (imported rarities in India), steamed with garlic and served in a curried green herb sauce. Breads such as parathas, kulchas and rotis are also worth trying; the pudina lachha paratha (flaky layers stuffed with mint leaves and baked in the tandoor) has a pungent flavour and is best teamed with one of the milder curries. Jhinga (prawn) curry was coloured by turmeric, the flavour of freshly grated coconut blended with spices making it a delightful main course. The drinks list is extensive and mango lassi was a real thirst quencher, with just the right level of sweetness. Service was friendly and well informed about the dishes – though 'jhinga curry from Bangalore' is likely to be novel to that city's inhabitants.
Available for hire. Babies and children admitted. Booking advisable. Takeaway service; delivery service (6-9.45pm, over £20 within 4-mile radius). Vegetarian menu. **Map 28 B4**.

Outer London

Edgware, Middlesex

★ Meera's Village NEW

36 Queensbury Station Parade, Edgware, Middx HA8 5NN (8952 5556). Queensbury tube. **Lunch served** noon-3pm Wed, Thur.

Gujarati menu

Most Gujarati restaurants are located in north-west London – mainly in Wembley, Sudbury, Kingsbury, Kenton, Harrow, Rayners Lane and Hendon – and they tend to be no-frills, family-run eateries.

Unlike North Indian food, Gujarati dishes are not normally cooked in a base sauce of onions, garlic, tomatoes and spices. Instead, they're tempered; whole spices such as cumin, red chillies, mustard seeds, ajwain (carom) seeds, asafoetida powder and curry leaves are sizzled in hot oil for a few seconds. The tempering is added at the start or the end of cooking, depending on the dish.

Commonplace items such as grains, beans and flours – transformed into various shapes by boiling, steaming and frying – are the basis of many dishes. Coriander, coconut, yoghurt, jaggery (cane sugar), tamarind, sesame seeds, chickpea (gram) flour and cocum (a sun-dried, sour, plum-like fruit) are also widely used.

Each region has its own cooking style. Kathiyawad, a humid area in western Gujarat, and Kutch, a desert in the north-west, have spawned styles that are less reliant on fresh produce. Kathiyawadi food is rich with dairy products and grains such as dark millet, and is pepped up with chilli powder. Kutchis make liberal use of chickpea flour (as do Kathiyawadis) and their staple diet is based on khichadi. In central Gujarat towns such as Baroda and Ahmedabad, grains are widely used; they appear in snacks that are the backbone of menus in London's Gujarati restaurants.

The gourmet heartland, however, is Surat – one of the few regions with heavy rainfall and lush vegetation. Surat boasts an abundance of green vegetables such as papadi (a type of broad bean) and ponk (fresh green millet). A must-try Surti speciality is undhiyu. Surti food uses 'green masala' (fresh coriander, coconut, green chillies and ginger), as opposed to the 'red masala' (red chilli powder, crushed coriander, cumin and turmeric) more commonly used in western and central regions.

The best time to visit Gujarati restaurants is for Sunday lunch, which is when you'll find little-seen regional specialities on the menu – but you will almost certainly need to book ahead.

Bhakarvadi: pastry spirals stuffed with whole spices and, occasionally, potatoes.
Bhel poori: a snack originating from street stalls in Mumbai, which contains crisp, deep-fried pooris, puffed rice, sev (qv), chopped onion, tomato, potato and more, plus chutneys (chilli, mint and tamarind).
Dhokla: a steamed savoury chickpea flour cake.
Farsan: Gujarati snacks.
Ganthia: Gujarati name for crisply fried savoury confections made from chickpea flour; they come in all shapes.
Ghughara: sweet or savoury pasties.
Kadhi: yoghurt and chickpea flour curry, often cooked with dumplings or vegetables.
Khandvi: tight rolls of 'pasta' sheets (made from chickpea flour and curds) tempered with sesame and mustard seeds.
Khichadi or **khichdi**: rice and lentils mixed with ghee and spices.
Mithi roti: round griddle-cooked bread stuffed with a cardamom-and-saffron-flavoured lentil paste. Also called **puran poli**.
Mogo: deep-fried cassava, often served as chips together with a sweet and sour tamarind chutney. An East African Asian dish.
Pani poori: bite-sized pooris that are filled with sprouted beans, chickpeas, potato, onion, chutneys, sev (qv) and a thin, spiced watery sauce.
Patra: a savoury snack made of the arvi leaf (colocasia) stuffed with spiced chickpea-flour batter, steamed, then cut into slices in the style of a swiss roll. The slices are then shallow-fried with sesame and mustard seeds.
Pau bhajee: a robustly spiced dish of mashed potatoes and vegetables, served with a shallow-fried white bread roll.
Puran poli: see mithi roti.
Ragda pattice or **ragada patties**: mashed potato patties covered with a chickpea or dried-pea sauce, topped with onions, sev (qv) and spicy chutney.
Sev: deep-fried chickpea-flour vermicelli.
Thepla: savoury flatbread.

Roti Chai. See p143.

Dinner served 6-10pm Mon-Thur. **Meals served** noon-10.30pm Fri, Sat; noon-10pm Sun. **Main courses** £5.99-£11.99. **No credit cards**. Gujarati vegetarian

Painted with gaudy murals showing Gujarati village life, and with staff wearing traditional dress, Meera's might seem an unpromising prospect – until the menu arrives. The list is encouragingly authentic, covering Gujarati classics plus a few South Indian snacks. Our friendly waiters (both recently arrived in this country) had difficulty explaining the dishes (which aren't annotated on the menu) in English. This is when set meals, such as thalis, come in useful. Meera's thalis arrive in shiny dishes on steel trays and are, in the true Indian way, all you can eat. When you finish a dish, the waiter tops it up until you ask him to stop. We were delighted with the spread: spicy chickpea stews, rich dahls and sambar with slightly sour notes of tamarind. Breads (poori, chapatis and thepla) were truly impressive. Queensbury's large East African Asian diaspora has had a strong influence on the menu, from mogo chips to corn masala. No alcohol is served, and this being a 'pure vegetarian' restaurant, no eggs are used either. To drink, try the wonderful chaas (cumin-spiced buttermilk) or the richer lassi. A meal costs around £15 per head, even less at lunchtime.

Available for hire. Babies and children admitted. Booking advisable. Takeaway service. Vegetarian menu.

Harrow, Middlesex

★ Mr Chilly NEW

344 Pinner Road, Harrow, Middx HA1 4LB (8861 4404, www.mrchilly.co.uk). North Harrow tube. **Meals served** noon-11.30pm Tue-Sun. **Main courses** £3.50-£7. **Set lunch** (noon-3pm) £6 2 courses. **Credit** MC, V. Pakistani

Brothers Riaz and Raza Ali have a great track record for producing modest destination restaurants, including Karahi King, Five Hot Chillies, Mirch Masala and Nauroz. (It's an unconventional business model – after building a cult following, they sell up and move on.) The dishes served, however, have remained virtually unchanged over the last decade. Mr Chilly caters to a local crowd who come here for home-style meals – slow-cooked dahls, onion-based meat masalas and soft griddle-cooked chapatis. This is classic dhaba food, the kind sold at roadside haunts in North India and Pakistan. The curries, especially those cooked on the bone, are first-rate. Deigi spring lamb, slow-cooked in a pot, arrived in a weathered and heat-scorched karahi; the tender lamb and smooth fried onion base simmered with toasted garlic, shredded ginger, red chilli and cardamom. Tandoori grills are less convincing: overcooked and unremarkable lamb chops lacked the expected garlicky punch and lemony tang. Although vegetarian dishes are not given top billing, mixed dahl had a pleasing green chilli kick, cut through with ginger. Turbo paneer tikka, one of the few 'modern' dishes, was an Indo-Chinese confusion of chewy, fried paneer doused in an oddball sweet-and-sour sauce. Stick to a stack of hot breads, dahl and masalas for an authentic rendition of no-frills northern cooking.

Babies and children admitted. Disabled: toilet. Tables outdoors (3, pavement). Takeaway service. Vegetarian menu.

★ Ram's

203 Kenton Road, Harrow, Middx HA3 0HD (8907 2022, www.ramsrestaurant.co.uk).

Cinnamon Soho. See p144.

INDIAN

Kenton tube/rail. **Lunch served** noon-3pm, **dinner served** 6-11pm daily. **Main courses** £4-£5. **Set meal** £22 (unlimited food and soft drinks). **Thalis** £4.99-£8.99. **Credit** MC, V.
Gujarati vegetarian
Surti vegetarian cuisine forms a highly cherished sub-section of Gujarati food, and Ram's has always been a prime exponent of this cooking style (along with sidelines in meat-free Punjabi and South Indian dishes). So it was a pity our meal failed to reach the exalted level of previous visits. Behind its plate-glass frontage (offering unparalleled views of the A4006 traffic), the restaurant has tiled flooring and high-backed leather chairs; proceedings are jazzed up by electric-blue fairy lights and two TVs playing Bollywood hits. Next door is a takeaway and sweet counter. Crispy snacks and street food dominate the starters, and kand (four slices of purple-hued potato in a spicy batter) arrived freshly fried with three small pots of chutney: fine, if a little dull. Next, Surti undhiyu was an interesting mix of bananas, three types of potatoes and beans – but dry to the point of aridity. Better was the khichadi, a nicely nutty mix of rice and mung beans, served, thankfully, with a pot of yoghurty kadhi gravy.

Sri Lankan menu

Sri Lanka has three main groups: Sinhalese, Tamil and Muslim. Although there are variations in the cooking styles of each community and every region, rice and curry form the basis of most meals, and curries are usually hot and spicy. The cuisine has evolved by absorbing South Indian, Portuguese, Dutch, Arabic, Malaysian and Chinese flavours over the years. Aromatic herbs and spices like cinnamon, cloves, curry leaves, nutmeg, and fresh coriander are combined with South-east Asian ingredients such as lemongrass, pandan leaves, sesame oil, dried fish and rice noodles. Fresh coconut, onions, green chillies and lime juice (or vinegar) are also used liberally, and there are around two dozen types of rice – from short-grained white varieties to several long-grained, burgundy-hued kinds.

Curries come in three main varieties: white (cooked in coconut milk), yellow (with turmeric and mild curry powder) and black (with roasted curry powder, normally used with meat). Hoppers (saucer-shaped pancakes) are generally eaten for breakfast with kithul palm syrup and buffalo-milk yoghurt, while string hoppers (steamed, rice-flour noodles formed into flat discs) usually accompany fiery curries and sambols (relishes).

Ambul thiyal: sour fish curry cooked dry with spices.
Appam or **appa**: see hoppers.
Badun: black. 'Black' curries are fried; they're dry and usually very hot.
Devilled: meat, seafood or vegetable dishes fried with onions in a sweetish sauce; usually served as starters.
Godamba roti: flaky, thin Sri Lankan bread, sometimes wrapped around egg or potato.
Hoppers: confusingly, hoppers come in two forms, either as saucer-shaped, rice-flour pancakes (try the sweet and delectable milk hopper) or as string hoppers (qv).
Idiappa: see string hoppers.
Katta sambol: onion, lemon and chilli relish; fearsomely hot.
Kiri: white. 'White' curries are based on coconut milk and are usually mild.
Kiri hodi: coconut milk curry with onions and turmeric; a soothing gravy.
Kuttu roti, **kottu** or **kothu roti**: strips of thin bread (resembling pasta), mixed with mutton, chicken, prawns or veg to form a 'bread biriani'; very filling.
Lamprais or **lumprice**: a biriani-style dish where meat and rice are cooked together, often by baking in banana leaves.
Lunnu miris: a relish of ground onion, chilli and maldives fish (qv).
Maldives fish: small, dried fish with a very intense flavour; an ingredient used in sambols (qv).
Pittu: rice flour and coconut steamed in bamboo to make a 'log'; an alternative to rice.
Pol: coconut.
Pol kiri: see kiri hodi.
Pol sambol: a mix of coconut, chilli, onions, maldives fish (qv) and lemon juice.
Sambols: strongly flavoured relishes, often served hot; they are usually chilli-hot too.
Seeni sambol: sweet and spicy, caramelised onion relish.
Sothy or sothi: another name for kiri hodi.
String hoppers: fine rice-flour noodles formed into flat discs. Usually served steamed (in which case they're dry, making them ideal partners for the gravy-like kiri hodi, qv).
Vellappam: appam (qv) served with vegetable curry.
Wattalappan or **vattilapan**: a version of crème caramel made with kithul palm syrup.

Service, pleasant at first, disintegrated later with staff chatting among themselves and ignoring us. At least the own-made kulfi (try the toasted cashew and almond version) provided a sweet finale. *Available for hire. Babies and children welcome: high chairs. Booking advisable weekends. Vegetarian menu.*

★ Saravana Bhavan

403 Alexandra Avenue, Harrow, Middx HA2 9SG (8869 9966, www.saravanabhavan.co.uk). Rayners Lane tube. **Meals served** 11am-10.20pm Mon-Thur; 11am-10.50pm Fri-Sun. **Main courses** £2.50-£7.95. **Credit** AmEx, MC, V. South Indian vegetarian

You could have a decent vegetarian spread at this no-frills community caff for little over a tenner for two people. No wonder the queue for eating here on a Saturday night often snakes out of the door. Once inside, park yourself at a wipe-clean table and peruse the South Indian menu. We suggest skipping the more esoteric innovations: the Indo-Chinese numbers, the northern Indian interpretations, and even the starters. Instead, order the dosas or the idlis. We usually opt for a masala dosa, stuffed with crushed potatoes, seasoned with mustard seeds and curry leaves. It is served, authentically, in a compartmentalised steel tray, with fresh coconut chutney and soupy tamarind and vegetable lentils (sambar). The paneer variation might be too greasy for some, but if proportions are your thing, then choose the paper masala dosa: it's enormous. Idlis are also served with chutney and sambar, although they're not always as light and spongy as they might be. Service is efficient and friendly, even when proceedings get (enjoyably) boisterous at weekends. *Babies and children welcome: high chairs; nappy-changing facilities. Bookings not accepted for fewer than 5 people. Disabled: toilet. Takeaway service. Vegetarian menu.*

For branches see index.

Southall, Middlesex

★ Brilliant

72-76 Western Road, Southall, Middx UB2 5DZ (8574 1928, www.brilliantrestaurant.com). Southall rail. **Lunch served** noon-3pm Tue-Fri. **Dinner served** 6-11.30pm Tue-Sun. **Main courses** £4.50-£14. **Credit** AmEx, MC, V. East African Indian

Over four decades and through several facelifts, Brilliant has been a consistent top performer, offering high-quality Punjabi food with Kenyan Asian flourishes. Its current guise verges on the nightclub-sassy, with TVs lining one wall, a shiny bar at one end, and linen-clad tables full of well-dressed diners from Southall and beyond. African ingredients appear in starters such as a superb fish pakora, where succulent tilapia is clothed in seductively spicy maize-flour batter. Most of the menu, though, consists of classic northern Indian dishes in expertly blended masalas that burst with flavour. Our three main course dishes – tarka dahl, aloo bringal and methi chicken – were all exemplary, the dahl thick and moreish, the potatoes and aubergine long-simmered yet not mushy, the chicken in a rich tomato sauce made zesty with fenugreek. Breads, especially the puffy bhatura, were good enough to eat on their own, but were even better with the six own-made pickles and chutneys provided. Our one caveat? Vegetables only come in main-course sizes, so Brilliant is best suited to group dining (as a centrepiece, try a half 'bowl' of palak lamb between six). Service is smart and prompt. *Available for hire. Babies and children welcome: high chairs; nappy-changing facilities. Booking advisable weekends. Separate room for parties, seats 120. Takeaway service. Vegetarian menu.*

★ New Asian Tandoori Centre (Roxy)

114-118 The Green, Southall, Middx UB2 4BQ (8574 2597, www.roxy-restaurant.com). Southall rail. **Meals served** 8am-10.30pm daily. **Main courses** £5-£6.50. **No credit cards.** Punjabi

Though you can still queue canteen-style for a carry-out here, the Roxy (as it's locally known) has come a long way since its days as a curry caff. Adjacent to the takeaway section is a spick-and-span dining room with vibrant paintings on the wall, and cream floor tiles; further on again is a still smarter room, where, behind frosted glass windows, local Punjabi families (both Sikhs and Muslims) eat at under-lit mock-marble round tables. Prompt staff keep things on track. Concentrate on the strengths of Punjabi cuisine and you're likely to relish your meal – so head for the tandoori dishes, the rich curries and the splendid array of breads. For starters, juicy, flavour-packed chunks of fish (coley) pakora were preferable to the bhel poori (which had rather hard, crisp shells), while the main course stars were creamy dahl makhani (served weekends only), the herb- and spice-flecked tomato sauce accompanying chicken kofta, and the wonderfully flaky reshmi nan and delicate roomali roti. Bengan bhartha (bland mashed aubergine,

Meera's Village. See p152.

served Tuesday and Saturday) was the one mundanity. But in all, the Roxy still rocks.
Available for hire. Babies and children welcome: high chairs. Booking advisable. Disabled: lift; toilet. Takeaway service. Vegan dishes. Vegetarian menu.

Wembley, Middlesex

★ Asher's NEW

224 Ealing Road, Wembley, Middx HA0 4QL (8795 2455). Alperton tube. **Meals served** noon-10pm daily. **Main courses** £3-£8. **No credit cards.** Gujarati vegetarian

Simplicity is key to the success of this family-run vegetarian thali house offering a limited selection of popular Gujarati classics. There are only three choices of generously portioned thalis to be had, and like every other customer on our visit, we ordered the Gujarati version. The chapatis, dahl, potato curry and rice – served, as they would be in India, in stainless-steel bowls and trays – tasted home-style and mild, more like dining at a Gujarati friend's home than in a restaurant. The à la carte menu offers other Gujarati delicacies too, such as khichadi, dahl bhajia and thepla. The full name of the enterprise is 'Asher's (africana) Vegetarian Thali House', which explains the presence on the menu of East African Asian snacks such as mogo (masala or plain cassava chips) and a few other recipes 'from Tanga' (in Tanzania), as our hostess told us in Hindi. The interior of the restaurant is of uncomplicated design, with cream-coloured walls adorned with a few bright posters of Hindu gods.
Babies and children admitted. Takeaway service. Vegan dishes. Vegetarian menu.

★ Sakonis HOT 50

129 Ealing Road, Wembley, Middx HA0 4BP (8903 9601). Alperton tube. **Breakfast served** 9-11am Sat, Sun. **Meals served** noon-10pm daily. **Main courses** £2-£6.99. **Set buffet** (breakfast) £4.50; (noon-4pm daily) £8.99; (6.30-10pm) £11.99. **Credit** MC, V.
Gujarati/South Indian vegetarian

From its prominent location on Ealing Road, Sakonis offers a broad menu of Gujarati, South Indian and Indo-Chinese food. The café-style interior features an impressive display of Indian sweets, snacks and a pan bar as you walk in. Gujarati street snacks figure prominently, but the restaurant has also evolved its own variations to the popular street food, chat. The farari chat and wada-like farari cutlet, for example, consisted of an interesting blend of deep-fried potatoes with spices. The main menu is predominantly Gujarati, but its version of that South Indian staple, idli, was laudable: the delightful soft rice cakes melted in the mouth. Mysore masala dosa – a crisp pancake stuffed with potato and vegetable mash infused with spices, accompanied by coconut chutney and sambar – was spiked with chilli heat. The chutney was blended to perfection with coconut, mustard seeds and fresh coriander leaves; the sambar was a little sweet and tangy in the Gujarati way, not with the strong coconut flavour and soup-like texture of South Indian sambars. There are many rice- and noodle-based dishes, and a popular buffet, too.
Available for hire. Babies and children welcome: high chairs. Takeaway service. Vegetarian menu.
For branch see index.

Sweets menu

Even though there isn't a tradition of serving puddings at everyday meals in South Asia, there is much ceremony associated with distributing sweetmeats at auspicious events, especially weddings and religious festivals. Desserts served at many Indian restaurants in London include the likes of gulab jamun, cardamom-scented rice pudding, creamy kulfi, and soft, syrup-drenched cheese dumplings. In the home, family meals don't often include a dessert; you're more likely to be treated to a platter of seasonal fruit. Winter warmers also have their place, including comforting, fudge-like carrot halwa, a Punjabi favourite and popular street snack. Winter is also the season for weddings, where other halwas, made with wholewheat flour, semolina, lentils and pumpkin, might be served.

Barfi: sweetmeat usually made with reduced milk, and flavoured with nuts, fruit, sweet spices or coconut.
Bibenca or **bibinca**: soft, layered cake from Goa made with eggs, coconut milk and jaggery (a brown sugar).
Falooda or **faluda**: thick milky drink (originally from the Middle East), resembling a cross between a milkshake and a sundae. It's flavoured with either rose syrup or saffron, and also contains agar-agar, vermicelli, nuts and ice-cream. Very popular with Gujarati families, faloodas make perfect partners to deep-fried snacks.
Gajar halwa: grated carrots, cooked in sweetened cardamom milk until soft, then fried in ghee until almost caramelised; usually served warm.
Gulab jamun: brown dumplings (made from dried milk and flour), deep-fried and drenched in rose-flavoured sugar syrup, best served warm. A traditional Bengali sweet, now ubiquitous in Indian restaurants.
Halwa: a fudge-like sweet, made with semolina, wholewheat flour or ground pulses cooked with syrup or reduced milk, and flavoured with nuts, saffron or sweet spices.
Jalebis: spirals of batter, deep-fried and dipped in syrup, best eaten warm.
Kheer: milky rice pudding, flavoured with cardamom and nuts. Popular throughout India (there are many regional variations).
Kulfi: ice-cream made from reduced milk, flavoured with nuts, saffron or fruit.
Payasam: a South Indian pudding made of reduced coconut or cow's milk with sago, nuts and cardamom. **Semiya payasam** is made with added vermicelli.
Rasgullas: soft paneer cheese balls, simmered and dipped in rose-scented syrup, served cold.
Ras malai: soft paneer cheese patties in sweet and thickened milk, served cold.
Shrikhand: hung (concentrated) sweet yoghurt with saffron, nuts and cardamom, sometimes with fruit added. A traditional Gujarati favourite, eaten with pooris.

Italian

The British middle classes' love affair with Italian cuisine shows no sign of abating – which is both a good and a bad thing for the Italian restaurant scene in the capital. Bad because, perhaps more than with any other cuisine in the city, you're liable to find grossly overpriced, mediocre cooking when making an unwise choice. Some of the worst culprits are staid affairs located in bland hotels, their expensive decor seeking to justify the hefty bill. Nevertheless, the compensations for this popularity are many. The capital has some stupendous Italian dining venues: from the sublime culinary skills exhibited by **Theo Randall at the InterContinental**, Angela Hartnett at **Murano** and the energetically imaginative Giorgio Locatelli at **Locanda Locatelli**, to the more classic delights of Bayswater's **Assaggi**, the vinous pleasures and regional specialities of Putney's **Enoteca Turi**, and the impeccably executed modern dishes at Bermondsey's **Zucca** – not forgetting (how could we?) the perfect simplicity and top-notch produce to be found at Hammersmith's **River Café**. A refreshing recent phenomenon has been the opening of more casual, inexpensive, independent establishments: 2010's **Trullo** being joined in the past year by **Lardo**. New too are **Polpo Smithfield**, latest branch of the on-trend, small-plates mini chain; and the lively Marylebone trattoria, **Briciole**. In short, choose carefully and *la dolce vita* can be yours.

Central

Belgravia

Il Convivio

143 Ebury Street, SW1W 9QN (7730 4099, www.etruscarestaurants.com). Sloane Square tube or Victoria tube/rail. **Lunch served** noon-2.45pm, **dinner served** 6.30-10.45pm Mon-Sat. **Main courses** £13.50-£24. **Set lunch** £17.50 2 courses. **Set dinner** £23.50 2 courses. **Credit** AmEx, MC, V.

Sitting in the conservatory tacked on to Il Convivio's Georgian premises, on a quietly plush backstreet, transported us back to a trattoria in Italy on a warm, sunny day. The deep-red walls of the dining room, bearing poetic quotations from Dante, provide an intimate feel, so it's a shame that the design (in general) and the cedar-wood furnishings (in particular) make the place feel rather outmoded. The restaurant never seems to be especially busy. Our meal got off to a good start with well-made focaccia and olive breads, but mistakes soon crept in with a chewy pappardelle with chicken livers and mushrooms, followed by an over-salted duck breast served with radicchio and an orange sauce. Disappointing, too, was the restaurant's rather oily signature dish of squid spaghetti with lobster. Thankfully, a side order of square-shaped courgette fritto and a delightful white espresso ice-cream studded with coffee beans saved the day. The lunch menu is fairly priced at £17.50 for two courses, but straying into the carte is a more costly affair – as you might expect when dining in Belgravia – and the serious Italian wine list will stretch bank balances further.

Available for hire. Babies and children admitted. Booking advisable dinner. Separate room for parties, seats 14. **Map 15 G10.**

For branch (Caravaggio) see index.

Olivo

21 Eccleston Street, SW1W 9LX (7730 2505, www.olivorestaurants.com). Sloane Square tube or Victoria tube/rail. **Lunch served** noon-2.30pm Mon-Fri. **Dinner served** 6-10.30pm Mon-Sat; 6.30-10.30pm Sun. **Main courses** £13-£23. **Set lunch** £23.50 2 courses, £28 3 courses. **Credit** AmEx, MC, V.

Olivo is part of a small group which includes a pizzeria, a seafood restaurant (Olivomare, *see p84*) and another focused on meat, plus a deli/wine shop – all around the Victoria/Belgravia borders. This restaurant, the mothership, specialises in Sardinian dishes. Decor is bright and colourful, in the island's traditional aquamarine and dark orange. The atmosphere is buzzy and convivial; the service welcoming and efficient. Intriguing dishes dot the menu, such as ricci de mare (iced raw sea urchins with crostini), roast rabbit wrapped in parma ham, and sebada (Sardinian cheese fritters with honey). Spaghetti bottarga – a creamy mound of pasta in a sauce of cheese and freshly grated grey mullet roe was an umami-packed delight, as was linguine al granchio, dressed with sautéed fresh crab meat, garlic, parsley and subtle, but evident, chilli. Although beef, veal and calves' liver are on the menu, seafood seems to be the forte: steamed sea bream with spinach was perfectly cooked and a plate-filling yellowfin tuna, chargrilled to exactly the degree requested. A delicious bottle of vernaccia and a generous and varied selection of Sardinian cheeses with walnuts and toasted ciabatta rounded off a memorable meal.

Babies and children admitted. Booking advisable. **Map 15 H10.**

For branches (Oliveto, Olivocarne) see index.

City

L'Anima

1 Snowden Street, EC2A 2DQ (7422 7000, www.lanima.co.uk). Liverpool Street tube/rail. *Bar* **Open/meals served** 9am-midnight Mon-Fri; 5.30-11pm Sat. **Main courses** £15-£33.

Restaurant **Lunch served** 11.45am-3pm Mon-Fri. **Dinner served** 5.30-11pm Mon-Fri; 5.30-11.30pm Sat. **Main courses** £15-£33. **Set lunch** £24.50 2 courses, £28.50 3 courses. *Both* **Credit** AmEx, DC, MC, V.

This large establishment, in a stark glass box on the ground floor of a modern city office building, is suitably stylish, with chrome and white leather armchairs set around circular tables, walls of brown porphyry and a limestone floor, chosen 'to evoke timeless luxury… for a comfortable, intimate and memorable experience'. Unfortunately, although memorable, if you're not tall the chairs don't foster a comfortable or intimate experience as conversing with companion(s) can require perching on their front edges. Service, however, is faultless and attentive, and the atmosphere convivial. The contemporary Italian food is excellent, employing the best of seasonal ingredients, imaginatively and perfectly cooked. For their prices, however, portions can seem a tad sparse – for £18, an albeit delicious and perfectly cooked starter of diver scallop with courgette flower stuffed with baccalà, anchovy sauce and chilli jam, consisted of one medium scallop with one smallish stuffed flower and a smear of jam. Another starter of summer salad was a delightful medley of crisp leaves, salad vegetables, fresh herbs and seasonal fruit, and a main of calves' liver with pancetta was cooked just so (if, again, not bounteous). Diners – City workers, by and large – presumably don't mind the mis-match between price and portion-size, leaving them free to savour the inventive menu.

Babies and children welcome: high chairs. Booking advisable. Disabled: toilet. Dress: smart casual. Separate rooms for parties, seating 6-15. **Map 6 R5.**

Clerkenwell & Farringdon

Polpo Smithfield NEW

2012 RUNNER-UP BEST NEW NO BOOKINGS RESTAURANT

3 Cowcross Street, EC1M 6DR (7250 0034, www.polpo.co.uk). Barbican tube or Farringdon tube/rail.

Bar **Open** 5.30-11.30pm Mon-Sat.
Restaurant **Meals served** noon-11.30pm Mon-Sat; noon-4pm Sun. **Dishes** £2-£9.50.
Both **Credit** AmEx, MC, V.

The newest branch of the Polpo mini-chain is one of our favourites. Grab a Campari-based cocktail in the romantic, intimate subterranean bar or up at the main cocktail counter (where you can also perch up and eat), or wait for a table in the buzzy dining area (you can't book in the evenings). Here, it's Polpo through and through: battered tiles meet exposed bricks, the floor is wood, the ceiling metal. Pipes are bare, as are the dangling lightbulbs; there's flattering lighting and a menu (offering the same dishes as at other branches, though they shift with the seasons) printed on brown paper. Highlights from the Italian-inspired small plates selection included mackerel tartare: a small mound fashioned from pieces of smoked fish, dulcet chunks of cucumber and tart Liliputian capers, served with tarta di musica (paper-thin shards of cracker bread) and a biting horseradish cream. A signature dish of pork and fennel meatballs was as good as ever: a trio of fat, juicy spheres spiked with tiny bursts of aniseed, in a puddle of mellow, slow-cooked pomodoro sauce. Salads can hold their own: we enjoyed the simple combination of bitter curly endive and mandolin-thin fennel with a lemony dressing and buttery whole almonds. Attractive, chatty waitstaff add to the appeal.

Available for hire. Babies & children welcome: high chairs. Booking advisable; not accepted after 4pm Mon-Sat. Tables outdoors (5, pavement). Vegan dishes. **Map 5 O5.**
For branches see index.

Covent Garden

Carluccio's Caffè

2A Garrick Street, WC2E 9BH (7836 0990, www.carluccios.com). Covent Garden tube.
Meals served 8am-11.30pm Mon-Fri; 9am-11.30pm Sat; 9am-10.30pm Sun. **Main courses** £8.95-£15.95. **Set meal** £9.95 2 courses. **Credit** AmEx, MC, V.

The flagship store is unmissable, thanks to its prime two-floor corner location, and boy is it popular. If the place is full, staff will take note of your requirements and leave you to browse in the next-door deli, collecting you when a table is ready. Best bets are the semi-circular banquettes around the edge; the central tables and chairs seemed cramped with no obvious place for coats and umbrellas, and the stylish aluminium ceiling lamps appear ominously close on a warm night. The atmosphere is buzzy and diners – a mix of theatre-goers, shoppers and out-of-towners – seemed happy with the experience. As were we – once seated, we felt under no pressure to move on, in spite of the bustle. The menu is an easy-going mix of pastas, salads, vegetarian options and assorted classics (fritto misto, grilled calf's liver). Our dishes scored well: perfectly cooked seabass (fried with tomato salsa and sautéed potatoes), al dente spaghetti (vongole) and chunky fishcakes. In fact, there's little to criticise here, though some prices are a little keen. In short – a winning formula, and not as soulless as many chains. *Forza!*

Babies and children welcome: children's menu; high chairs; nappy-changing facilities. Booking advisable pre-theatre. Disabled: toilet. Separate room for parties, seats 30. **Map 18 D4.**
For branches see index.

Fitzrovia

Sardo

45 Grafton Way, W1T 5DQ (7387 2521, www.sardo-restaurant.com). Warren Street tube. **Lunch served** noon-3pm Mon-Fri. **Dinner served** 6-11pm Mon-Sat. **Main courses** £12-£19.90. **Credit** AmEx, MC, V.

This longstanding Fitzrovia establishment feels like a neighbourhood ristorante transplanted to the West End. Sardinian specialities form the backbone of the menu and are served without excessive adornment. An outstanding own-made bread basket (a cover charge applies) included parchment-like carta di musica flatbread. Home-made herbed sausage seems an especially prized ingredient, making an appearance both with malloreddus pasta and as a main with endive and potato. Spaghetti bottariga, an intensely flavoured mullet roe, proved overpowering, but beef carpaccio draped over rocket and a generous portion of pecorino was a better manifestation of Sardo's focus on simplicity. Restraint is a keyword in the decor as well as the food – warm wood furnishings are accented with the odd mismatched mirror. The room is split into two, the front section with a small display bar leading into a cosier space separated by a heavy curtain. The dessert selection is a classic hit parade of tiramisu, panna cotta and gelati that suits Sardo's undemanding overall demeanour. It's an ideal venue for a date or a catch-up with a friend in mellow surrounds. Next door, sister venue Sardo Cucina offers more of a caffè experience.

Murano. See p161.

Briciole

Available for hire. Babies and children admitted. Booking advisable. Separate room for parties, seats 36. Tables outdoors (3, patio). **Map 3 J4.**

Knightsbridge

Zafferano

15 Lowndes Street, SW1X 9EY (7235 5800, www.zafferanorestaurant.com). Knightsbridge tube. **Lunch served** noon-3pm Mon-Fri; 12.30-3pm Sat, Sun. **Dinner served** 7-11pm Mon-Sat; 7-10.30pm Sun. **Main courses** £18-£30. **Set lunch** (Mon-Fri) £21 2 courses, £26 3 courses. **Credit** AmEx, DC, MC, V.

Zafferano has been serving some of London's most sophisticated Italian cooking for more than a decade. Sit in the bar area for a quick bite, or select from two dining rooms. We chose the cosy, serene front room, which is filled with the scent of lilies and decorated with terracotta walls and stripy banquettes. Service continues to be welcoming, although many of the experienced staff have left and the current team isn't the finished article. Chef Andy Needham may be British, but he absolutely gets Italian food. Impeccable ingredients and a sensitive balancing of flavours are his hallmarks, exemplified by our starter: a meltingly soft burrata cheese, perfectly offset by a piquant Sicilian aubergine caponata. Don't leave without sampling the pasta; chestnut tagliatelle provided a thrillingly nutty experience. Another winner is the chargrilled monkfish, its fleshiness cleverly counterbalanced by the sharpness of a julienne of courgettes and a touch of sweet chilli. To end, the tiramisu is rich and blissful: nothing like the travesties found in supermarkets. Wine is a highlight too, with only the high mark-ups marring a fabulous Italian list.

Babies and children welcome: high chairs. Booking essential. Disabled: toilet. Dress: smart casual. Separate room for parties, seats 20. **Map 15 G9.**

Marylebone

Briciole NEW

20 Homer Street, W1H 4NA (7723 0040, www.briciole.co.uk). Edgware Road tube. **Meals served** 11am-10.45pm daily. **Dishes** £3-£12. **Credit** AmEx, MC, V.

The capital's trattorias are a variable bunch, and the ones in central London are not always good value – but Briciole ('crumbs') has the sort of cooking and low prices that puts smiles on the faces of the whole famiglia. An offshoot of the fancier Latium, this former pub is more lively and convivial than its older sibling. To reach its two dining rooms you enter via a caffè-bar and deli, its back bar lined with bottles of Italian wines. Crumbs find their way into dishes, as in passatelli, a chicken soup from Emilia-Romagna with 'noodles' made from breadcrumbs, egg and just a hint of nutmeg. The dishes derive from many regions. Pizza fritta is a Neapolitan street snack of deep-fried pizza dough pasties filled with savoury ricotta and tomato. Meatballs are cooked Palermo-style; that is, with no breadcrumbs (giving the cured meat a firmer texture), and served with onions cooked down with vinegar to give the pleasing 'agrodolce' or sour-sweet flavours that are so distinctive in Sicilian cookery. Gnocchi filled with cheese, a special (made in Latium's kitchen, as are some other dishes), was terrific – firm on the bite, but melting on the inside. There's nothing hip about Briciole, but it's a little piece of Italy here in London.

Available for hire. Babies and children welcome: high chairs. Booking advisable. Disabled: toilet. Separate rooms for parties, both seating 16. Tables outdoors (5, pavement). Takeaway service. **Map 2 F5.**

★ Locanda Locatelli HOT 50

8 Seymour Street, W1H 7JZ (7935 9088, www.locandalocatelli.com). Marble Arch tube. **Lunch served** noon-3pm Mon-Sat; noon-3.30pm Sun. **Dinner served** 6.45-11pm Mon-Thur; 6.45-11.30pm Fri, Sat; 6.45-10.15pm Sun. **Main courses** £12.50-£31.50. **Credit** AmEx, MC, V.

The menu here contained none of the dishes we ate last year, a tribute to the restless, energetic spirit of chef Giorgio Locatelli. He oversees imaginative Italian cooking that has few peers in London, and despite his increasing prominence as a media star he remains committed to keeping his flagship restaurant fresh. You can order anything here and know that it's going to be outstanding. The approach is essentially simple: take the best ingredients and combine them with good taste and very great respect. Witness perfectly executed starters, a green bean salad with roasted red onion, parmesan and almonds, and a sublimely creamy purée of salt cod with a polenta crisp and a beautiful small salad. Pasta dishes were top-notch, especially busiate (own-made spirals) alla Trapanese, which used the Sicilian pesto variation: tomatoes, olives, capers, anchovies, mint and almonds. If the place has a fault, it's the prices, with not so much as a set lunch to soften the impact: mains such as roast monkfish with walnut and caper sauce, or roast organic chicken with grilled vegetables hover either side of £30. But the wine list can soften the hammer-blow to your credit card: as always, there are low-priced glasses available and a handful of bottles below or around £30. Some people don't care for the international-hotel decor but they should just look at each other, and at some of the best Italian food in London.

Available for hire. Babies and children welcome: high chairs; nappy-changing facilities. Booking advisable. Disabled: toilet. Dress: smart casual. Separate room for parties, seats 50. **Map 9 G6.**

Mayfair

Alloro

19-20 Dover Street, W1S 4LU (7495 4768, www.alloro-restaurant.co.uk). Green Park tube.
Bar **Open** noon-10pm Mon-Fri; 7pm-midnight Sat.
Restaurant **Lunch served** noon-2.30pm Mon-Fri. **Dinner served** 7-10.30pm Mon-Sat. **Main courses** £16-£20. **Set lunch** £29.50 2 courses, £35 3 courses. **Set dinner** £34 2 courses, £39 3 courses, £43 4 courses.
Both **Credit** AmEx, DC, MC, V.

Look beyond Alloro's restrained 'many shades of beige' interior and you'll find traditional Italian food that frequently transcends the London norm. The prix-fixe menu is full of seasonal and regional delights. A starter of creamy fresh burrata cheese was enlivened by shavings of salty bottarga (cured mullet roe – a Sardinian speciality), and balanced with earthier grilled slices of fennel. Freshly prepared pastas are a must here: delicate and perfectly cooked, they range from the deep and satisfying (taglierini with pigs' cheeks, asparagus and egg) to the light and almost sweet (ravioli with ricotta and spinach, surrounded by a smooth walnut sauce). Main courses can be, by contrast, slightly heavy. If there's a whiff of the corporate in the discreet dining room, blame the high proportion of business customers, and the fact that Alloro is owned by London Fine Dining Group, which has a collection of other somewhat sterile but similarly user-friendly restaurants, including Zafferano. Prices reflect the area, and aren't cheap, but the quality of the food, preparation and presentation make this a worthwhile splurge. Serving staff who show genuine warmth add to the attraction.

Available for hire. Babies and children welcome: high chairs. Booking advisable. Dress: smart casual. **Map 9 J7.**

Cecconi's

5A Burlington Gardens, W1S 3EP (7434 1500, www.cecconis.co.uk). Green Park or Piccadilly Circus tube. **Breakfast served** 7am-noon Mon-Fri; 8am-noon Sat, Sun. **Brunch served** noon-5pm Sat, Sun. **Meals served** noon-11.30pm Mon-Sat; noon-10.30pm Sun. **Main courses** £14-£28. **Credit** AmEx, MC, V.

Back in the 1970s, Enzo Cecconi wowed London's high society with the novelty of Venetian beef carpaccio and fresh pasta. Numerous incarnations later, this Mayfair institution clearly enraptures its rather more varied clientele. Flexibility is part of the appeal, as the kitchen offers week-round breakfasts, brunches, lunches, dinners and cicchetti (Venetian appetisers). On a recent visit we asked for a selection of hot and cold dishes, including a seasonal summer truffle pasta, to be brought at the same time – and they were, with impeccable timing. Service proved an efficient, unobtrusive delight throughout, and each course arrived in perfect condition. While the signature fresh pasta replete with truffle oil and shavings of truffle was a highlight, the carpaccio, drizzled with vibrant Ligurian olive oil and flaked with unimpeachable parmesan, came a close second. Pigs' cheeks were meltingly rich, polenta seductively soft. Silken meatballs and crunchy roast potatoes were clear kid-pleasers, while carafes of quaffable wine kept adults smiling. On summer days, tables spill on to reasonably secluded pavements; on dark evenings, the capacious, elegant bar is warm and inviting. Sumptuous yet relaxed, this old stalwart may well delight Londoners for decades to come.

Babies and children welcome: high chairs. Booking advisable. Disabled: toilet. Dress: smart casual. Tables outdoors (10, pavement terrace). **Map 9 J7.**

Murano

20-22 Queen Street, W1J 5PP (7495 1127, www.muranolondon.com). Green Park tube. **Lunch served** noon-2.30pm, **dinner served** 6.30-10.30pm Mon-Sat. **Set lunch** £25 2 courses, £30 3 courses. **Set meal** £65 3 courses, £75 4 courses, £80 tasting menu. **Credit** AmEx, MC, V.

Angela Hartnett's Mayfair outpost will confuse anyone who's looking for a purely Italian restaurant. The splendid wine list has more from France than from Italy, and the cooking too owes a great deal to France. But don't let that deter you. At £25 for two courses or £30 for three, the set lunch menu looks like one of London's greatest bargains given the luxurious table spacing, coolly elegant decor, and precise but cosseting service – and especially the food. Everything we ate was wonderful, beginning with exemplary breads and slices of salami and coppa as good as any we've

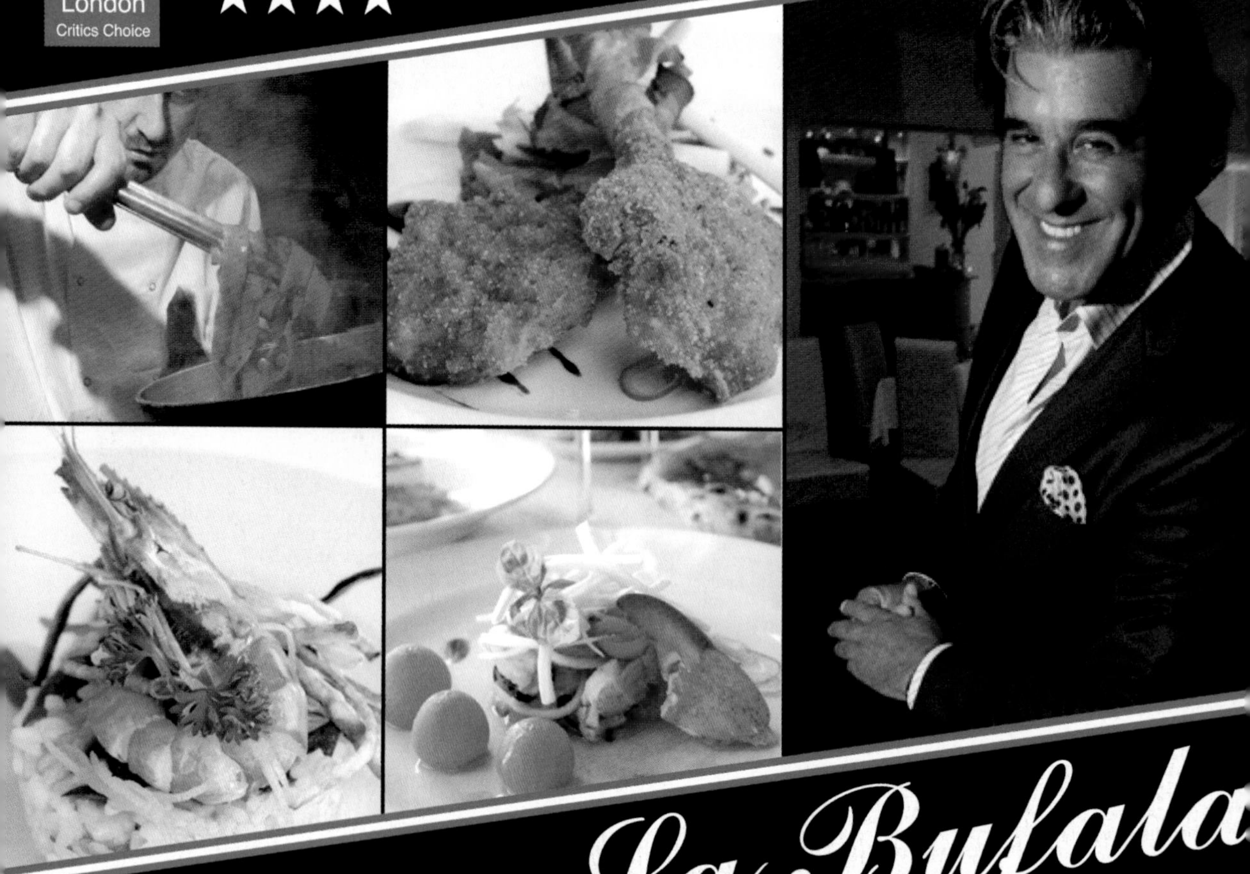

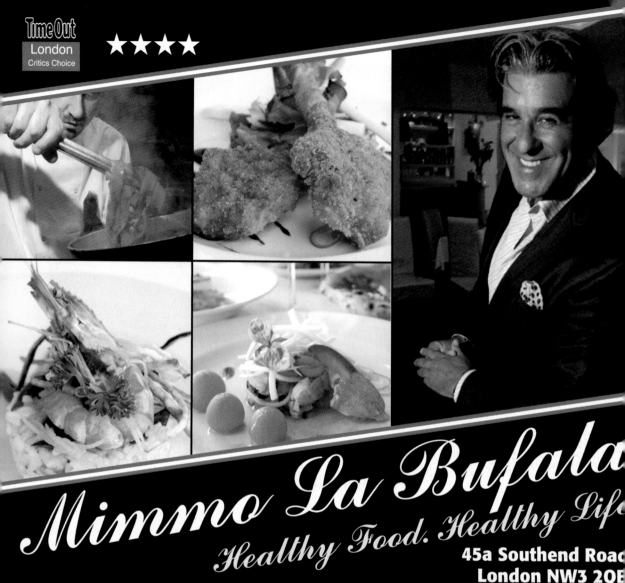

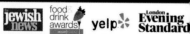

eaten in Italy. Then starters: a salad of perfect peaches, San Daniele prosciutto and burrata with startlingly fresh green beans; and tortelli filled with ricotta and courgette tucked under generous slices of smoked salmon. Mains kept up standards, in the form of wild mushroom tartlet topped with a perfect poached egg, and mackerel served two ways (roasted and tartare) with samphire and heavenly grilled sourdough. Two small complaints: the wine list scorns slim wallets (hardly anything below £35) and the espresso was carelessly made. Otherwise, we have nothing but praise for Murano. Nearby, two casually dressed gents enthusiastically worked through four courses and three bottles of wine. For a special occasion, we'd happily do the same.
Available for hire. Babies and children welcome: high chairs. Booking essential (1mth ahead for Fri & Sat dinner). Disabled: toilet. Separate room for parties, seats 12. Vegetarian menu. **Map 9 H8**.

★ Theo Randall at the InterContinental

1 Hamilton Place, Park Lane, W1J 7QY (7409 3131, www.theorandall.com). Hyde Park Corner tube. **Lunch served** noon-3pm Mon-Fri. **Dinner served** 5.45-11pm Mon-Sat. **Main courses** £28-£38. **Set meal** (lunch, 5.45-7pm, 9-11pm) £27 2 courses, £33 3 courses. **Credit** AmEx, DC, MC, V.

The name gives few clues, but there can be hardly an Italian food lover unaware that since 2007, following a long stint as head chef at the renowned River Café, Theo Randall has been turning out peerless Italian cuisine in this Mayfair hotel restaurant. No doubt the outstanding-value set lunches and early/late suppers aren't much of a secret either, but if you find a 'special deal' that includes a glass or two of wine from a dream list, seize the first opportunity to sample a sublime experience at unusually democratic pricing. The setting is as you'd expect: a sizeable space in shades of cream, brown and olive green, replete with leather and smoked glass. The staff are exceptional, their unfussy, smiling presence a relaxing joy. The wine (including prosecco and the 'lowliest' reds and whites) is as great as your budget allows; but the food, even at set-menu level, somehow continues to defy expectations. Generosity of spirit has something to do with it – focaccia is verdant with olive oil, ravioli impossibly plump, the finest prosciutto underscores even cooked dishes. Determined sourcing plays its part with the likes of datterini, camone and san marzano tomatoes complementing the finest British produce. Ultimately, though, it's breathtaking skill that renders guinea fowl skin so crisp, golden and scented, and fills the thinnest, buttery pastry shell with an impossible depth of gold-hued, zesty amalfi lemon cream. Simply sublime.
Available for hire. Babies and children welcome: children's menu; high chairs. Booking advisable. Disabled: lift; toilet. Dress: smart casual. Separate room for parties, seats 25. Vegetarian menu. **Map 9 G8**.

Pimlico

Tinello

87 Pimlico Road, SW1W 8PH (7730 3663, www.tinello.co.uk). Sloane Square tube or Victoria tube/rail. **Lunch served** noon-2.30pm, **dinner served** 6-10.30pm Mon-Sat. **Main courses** £16.50-£26. **Credit** AmEx, MC, V.

Lardo. See p169.

Tinello's contemporary Italian food is still pulling in the crowds – and not just from Kensington or Belgravia. The dark, industrial interior is fitted out with exposed brick walls and hanging metal table lamps, contrasting with the relaxed atmosphere that brothers Federico and Max Sali (formerly head chef and sommelier at Locanda Locatelli) have created. The list of primi is sprinkled with a few less common ingredients, such as nettle pappardelle with duck ragù; or vibrant, green borage risotto packed with piquant, salty pecorino cheese. Another primo of own-made spelt tagliatelle and subtly seasoned wild mushrooms offered just the right amount of resistance in the pasta. From the fish-heavy list of secondi, sweet-fleshed and succulent salt-baked sea bream sat slightly at odds with its avocado, almond and tomato accompaniment. Roast duck breast had also been skilfully cooked, though its orange sauce was a little sweet. The staff were attentive, and allowed us to stay long past our two-hour slot to enjoy a delicious glass of Amaro Averna digestif. Tinello's wine list also deserves a mention, for value (bottles start at £13.50) and variety.
Babies and children welcome: high chairs; nappy-changing facilities. Booking advisable. Separate room for parties, seats 26. Tables outdoors (2, pavement). **Map 15 G11**.

Soho

Bocca di Lupo

12 Archer Street, W1D 7BB (7734 2223, www.boccadilupo.com). Piccadilly Circus tube. **Lunch served** 12.30-3.45pm Mon-Sat; 12.45-3.45pm Sun. **Dinner served** 5.30-11pm Mon-Sat; 5.30-9pm Sun. **Main courses** £7-£25. **Credit** AmEx, MC, V.

Bocca di Lupo's menu takes you on a tour of Italy with a range of regional dishes and a few innovations. There's no need to stick to the traditional Italian structure of primo and secondo courses; if you prefer, you can choose the portion size and make it more of a mix-and-match meal. From the grill, baby cuttlefish was tender and juicy, while honey-marinated pork neck was earthy with a hint of sweetness. Both were treated simply, but to great effect in the way that Italian cooking does so well. A less traditional celeriac, pomegranate and pecorino salad with truffle oil was delicate and fresh. The snow crab in our pasta dish didn't quite sing as we'd hoped, however. If you're feeling adventurous, try the Calabrian sanguinaccio dessert – a bit like a chocolate and black pudding spread, it's odd, but not bad. Otherwise, there are more familiar options including ice-cream from the

restaurant's own gelateria (Gelupo – *see p303*). Noise levels increase once the evening is in full swing: a testament to the buzzing atmosphere. Staff are charming, attentive and pleased to offer advice on the food and wine.
Babies and children welcome: booster seats. Booking advisable. Disabled: toilet. Separate room for parties, seats 35. **Map 17 B4**.

South Kensington

Daphne's

112 Draycott Avenue, SW3 3AE (7589 4257, www.daphnes-restaurant.co.uk). South Kensington tube. **Lunch served** noon-3pm Mon-Fri. **Dinner served** 5.30-11.30pm Mon-Fri. **Meals served** noon-11.30pm Sat; noon-10.30pm Sun. **Main courses** £15-£30. **Set meal** (noon-3pm, 5.30-7pm Mon-Fri; noon-7pm Sat, Sun) £17.50 2 courses, £19.50 3 courses. **Credit** AmEx, DC, MC, V.

Daphne's faux-Tuscan decor, all exposed brick and bare plaster in tasteful shades of umber and sepia, has changed little since the restaurant's 1990s heyday – and neither has the menu, which remains conservatively Italianate. Which is no bad thing; there's evident care taken over the cooking. Pasta is freshly made each day, and our pappardelle with wild boar ragù had a lovely bouncy texture that complemented the rich meaty sauce. A starter of aubergine parmigiana would easily pass muster in Italy. Prices, though, would make a Tuscan contadino's eyes water – particularly for fish dishes (several are £24) on the à la carte – but they are probably deemed reassuringly expensive by the extraordinarily well-off customers of this fashionable district. Better value can be found on the set menu, which might include fresh mozzarella served with a whole deep-fried baby courgette with flower intact, and nicely al dente risotto primavera, made rich, we suspect, with large quantities of butter (slimming fashionistas, take note). Desserts play safe with the likes of sorbet and chocolate-based dolci. Service is gently solicitous and generally professional. Prices on the mostly Italian (and typically food-friendly) wine list seem reasonable, compared to the food.
Babies and children welcome: high chairs. Booking advisable. Separate room for parties, seats 40. **Map 14 E10**.

Westminster

Massimo

Corinthia Hotel London, 10 Northumberland Avenue, WC2N 5AE (7998 0555, www.massimo-restaurant.co.uk). Embankment tube.
Oyster Bar **Meals served** noon-11pm Mon-Sat. **Main courses** £8-£40.
Restaurant **Lunch served** noon-3pm, **dinner served** 6-10.30pm Mon-Sat. **Main courses** £16-£38. **Set meal** (noon-2.30pm, 6-7pm) £21.50 2 courses, £25 3 courses.
Both **Credit** AmEx, MC, V.

Even the business card at Massimo is solid and gold-embossed. The opulent David Collins' designed oyster bar and restaurant in the Corinthia hotel is all glistening gold and marble, tempered with deep, glossy brown and beige; the eye wanders from the magnificent lighting baubles to the wine wall-cabinets, from lunettes and candy-striped columns to each perfect detail of upholstery and napery. The food, fine as it is, cannot compete for attention. The international clientele are offered a wide-ranging Italian menu with a twist – perhaps more so than previously, following the eponymous chef's return to Rome. A carpaccio of tuna was more of a cured fillet with a medley of micro coriander leaves; a 'bruschetta' proved a painter's palette DIY job; torta della nonna contained an ethereal citrusy mousse rather than the dense lemon custard of tradition. All was virtually faultless, measured, and with just a touch of frisson. Service followed suit. If the pricing – not least of the wine – is hard to swallow, the outstanding breads, fine petits fours and unfussy detailing go far to sweeten the pill.
Available for hire. Babies and children welcome: high chairs. Booking advisable. Disabled: toilet. Dress: smart casual. Separate room for parties, seats 20. **Map 10 L8**.

Osteria dell'Angolo

47 Marsham Street, SW1P 3DR (3268 1077, www.osteriadellangolo.co.uk). St James's Park tube or bus 88.
Bar **Open** noon-10.30pm Mon-Fri; 6-10.30pm Sat.
Restaurant **Lunch served** noon-3pm Mon-Fri. **Dinner served** 6-10.30pm Mon-Sat. **Main courses** £18-£24.50. **Set lunch** £16.50 2 courses, £21 3 courses.
Both **Credit** AmEx, MC, V.

This expansive corner restaurant was around two thirds full on an August afternoon. When Parliament is sitting, it no doubt gets packed out – and it deserves to, because it's very good. Huge windows on two walls let plenty of light fall on the terracotta walls and crisp white linen, and from

ITALIAN

some tables you can watch the kitchen at work behind their window. The carte is not long, but it offers ample choice, at not-bad prices. The cooking has a few touches of contemporary daintiness (scallop and prawn carpaccio with spinach, radish and orange), but it is not fussy, and many dishes sit at the muscular southern-Italian end of the spectrum. We were mostly very pleased with our choices from the set lunch menu. Celeriac soup was frothy and flavourful, and prosciutto cotto with tangy, salty cacioricotta cheese made a great combination. Salmon with a fantastic tomato sauce came with perfectly sautéed spinach. A starter of mixed grilled vegetables, ordered as a main, featured a lip-smacking balsamic dressing. Puddings are taken very seriously, and come with individualised wine recommendations from an outstanding list, mostly Italian and offering plenty of bottles under £30. Service is efficient and friendly. A single flaw let the place down badly – salad leaves served with the prosciutto were distressingly gritty. A lapse indeed, but not enough to keep us from going back.
Babies and children welcome: high chairs; nappy-changing facilites. Booking advisable. Disabled: toilet. Dress: smart casual. Separate room for parties, seats 22. **Map 16 K10**.

Theo Randall at the InterContinental. See p163.

Quirinale
North Court, 1 Great Peter Street, SW1P 3LL (7222 7080, www.quirinale.co.uk). St James's Park or Westminster tube. **Lunch served** noon-2.30pm, **dinner served** 6-10.30pm Mon-Fri. **Main courses** £16-£28. **Set meal** (lunch, 6-7.30pm) £19 2 courses, £23 3 courses. **Credit** AmEx, DC, MC, V.
Clearly designed as a place for parliamentarians to conduct business, Quirinale has a small, bright subterranean dining room where deals can be made and broken, away from the inconvenience of daylight. However, this efficient operation also offers more relaxed diners the opportunity to indulge at their leisure in an impressive array of tempting traditional Italian food. Typical dishes draw on fresh, seasonal ingredients: scallop wrapped in pancetta with slices of black truffle on top, for instance, all served on a perfectly seasoned bed of mashed peas. But there can be slips in execution: the scallop and ham were slightly under-done; and a bowl of clams and spaghetti was surprisingly bland, lacking strong representation from the clams, tomatoes and bottarga visible on the plate. Attractive beige and gold decor, professional service and a lengthy Italian wine list, along with post-meal petits fours – all suggest an ambitious high-end restaurant. Yet while the dishes promise much in their conception, they don't always deliver. The lunch/pre-theatre set menu offers good value.
Available for hire. Babies and children admitted. Booking advisable lunch. **Map 16 L10**.

West

Bayswater

★ Assaggi
1st floor, 39 Chepstow Place, W2 4TS (7792 5501). Bayswater, Notting Hill Gate or Queensway tube. **Lunch served** 12.30-2.30pm Mon-Fri; 1-2.30pm Sat. **Dinner served** 7.30-11pm Mon-Sat. **Main courses** £18-£24. **Credit** MC, V.
It's some years since Assaggi was the hottest restaurant in London but, while tables are easier to secure, dining here remains a deservedly popular treat. The off-duty Notting Hill vibe and above-a-pub setting make it as well suited to long lunches as cosy romantic dinners. Decor is simple, with white walls, an old wooden floor, and colour coming from a spectacular flower arrangement and picture frames covered with bold fabric. Every meal begins with oil-smeared pane carasau and a couple of squares of focaccia. The wine list is brief but treat-packed; the cheapest white – Sardinian nuragus at £22.95 – is a reliable winner; spend more and you'll be rewarded with corresponding quality. The menu is much as it always has been, varying a little with the seasons but including perennials such as tagliatelle with herbs and walnuts, and grilled veal chop. Specials on our latest visit included john dory fillet with crushed potatoes and the slightly intrusive, bitter tang of spinach. We loved the slender finger of ricotta and herb crespelle cloaked in cream sauce and grilled to toasty perfection. Unfussy but well-executed desserts also tend to the classic: flourless chocolate torte, bavarese with espresso, a cheesecake. Service is friendly but unobtrusive – regulars, however, are treated like old friends.
Available for hire. Babies and children welcome: high chair. Booking essential. **Map 7 B6**.

Hammersmith

River Café HOT 50
Thames Wharf, Rainville Road, W6 9HA (7386 4200, www.rivercafe.co.uk). Hammersmith tube. **Lunch served** noon-2.15pm Mon-Fri; noon-2.30pm Sat; noon-3pm Sun. **Dinner served** 7-9pm Mon-Thur; 7-9.15pm Sat. **Main courses** £30-£37. **Credit** AmEx, DC, MC, V.

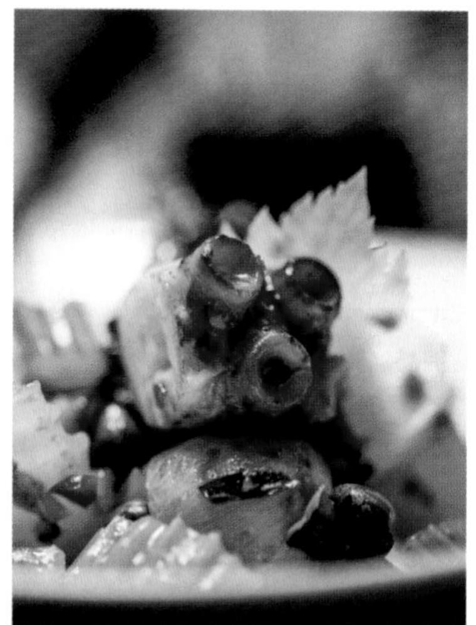

Polpo Smithfield. See p159.

Seemingly impervious to fashion or recession, the River Café is one of London's most name-checked restaurants, even after 25 years. And although the food is very good (and sourced with the utmost care), it's also eye-wateringly expensive – which makes the longevity even more noteworthy. Chargrilled marinated leg of lamb with carrots 'dada', roast red and golden beetroot, Italian spinach and salsa bagnet, for example, cost £35, which is at the low end for a main course here. It was a robust, satisfying dish, though not as gloriously charred as wild salmon with anchovy and rosemary sauce, plus chopped rocket, and fritti of courgette and lemon (also £35). Antipasti (seared squid with dried chilli, wild oregano, anchovy, tomato and fresh cannellini beans) and primi (fresh spinach tagliatelle with pork slow-cooked in Soave with rosemary and bay leaf) had more of a wow factor, and were generous portions. Panna cotta with grappa and raspberries was nice enough, but the selection of Italian cheeses may have been a better choice. The regional Italian wine list is every bit a match for the menu, and staff make a fine cocktail too. The light modern space has closely packed tables, and a huge wood-fired oven at one end. Big windows overlook a small patio with outdoor tables and a well-tended vegetable garden; beyond that is the river. Casually dressed young staff (in an assortment of bright T-shirts) help keep the atmosphere informal.
Babies and children welcome: booster seats; high chairs; nappy-changing facilities. Booking essential. Disabled: toilet. Separate room for parties, seats 18. Tables outdoors (15, terrace). **Map 20 C5.**

South West

Barnes

Riva

169 Church Road, SW13 9HR (8748 0434). Barnes or Barnes Bridge rail or bus 33, 209, 283. **Lunch served** 12.15-2.15pm Mon-Fri, Sun. **Dinner served** 7-10.30pm Mon-Sat; 7-9pm Sun. **Main courses** £13.50-£28.50. **Credit** AmEx, MC, V.

Not much changes at Riva, a fixture in Barnes for more than 20 years. If you're a frequent diner, who has no need of innovation, and who benefits from the warm welcome given to regulars, you'll be happy. An occasional visitor in search of a culinary treat will encounter courtesy, correctness and competence, gaze curiously at the olive walls punctuated with architectural prints, find well executed rustic/classic fare… and discover a slightly disproportionate hole in their pocket. Our platters of typical starters ran the gamut of cured meats, bruschetta, vitello tonnato and so on, evidencing solid, but not inspirational sourcing. Culatello, for example, was not the delectable treat it might have been – a surprise, as the main-course-size plate costs £24. Risotto with a tomato base and a sprinkling of seasonal vegetables was fine, but at £18 we were expecting more of a spark of excitement. Desserts, and wines, are more of a treat. The restaurant was very quiet on our lunchtime visit – little surprise when there's no set menu concession – giving Riva the air of a buzz-free bistro dressed uneasily in restaurant napery.
Babies and children welcome: high chairs. Booking essential dinner. Tables outdoors (3, pavement).

Chelsea

La Famiglia

7 Langton Street, SW10 0JL (7351 0761, www.lafamiglia.co.uk). Sloane Square tube then bus 11, 22, or bus 19. **Lunch served** noon-2.45pm, **dinner served** 7-11.30pm daily. **Main courses** £14-£30. **Cover** £1.85. **Credit** AmEx, MC, V.

If you like your Italian restaurants upmarket but theatrical, this eccentric Chelsea institution is the place to come; if you'd rather enjoy your pasta in peace, without waiters clapping loudly and barking across the room, you may be better off elsewhere. Tables sprawl through interlinking rooms, mostly tiled and all decorated in white and blue. The back area, where tourists seem to be relegated, is a curious indoor-outdoor space, covered in a striped awning with strings of lights and fake flowers. The Tuscan menu is as rambling as the place, with several variations on a theme (one type of pasta with summer truffles, another with truffle oil). The food on our most recent visit impressed less than the last; the bread was stale, nettle agnolotti were swamped in mascarpone, and roast wild boar with turnip tops was tired-looking, though the herby flavour was good. Service is odd – when ordering a bog-standard half-bottle of Orvieto Classico, we were asked if we were celebrating something. While the dessert trolley has retro charm, it was not wheeled in until all surrounding diners had caught up, and the roughly cut tarts could have done with cream on the side, especially at £7.25 a slice.
Babies and children welcome: high chairs. Booking advisable dinner & Sun. Tables outdoors (30, garden). **Map 13 C13.**

Osteria dell'Arancio

383 King's Road, SW10 0LP (7349 8111, www.osteriadellarancio.co.uk). Fulham Broadway or Sloane Square tube. **Lunch**

Zucca. See p169.

served noon-3pm Tue-Sun. **Dinner served** 6.30-11pm Mon-Sat; 6.30-9.30pm Sun. **Main courses** £17-£19.50. **Credit** AmEx, MC, V.
There's a decidedly old-school feel to this friendly neighbourhood Italian, with its colourful canvases and 1990s-throwback soundtrack. But lurking below the surface of what looks like an ordinary trat (albeit one with a posh postcode) is a very able kitchen, aided by great service. Chef Pierluigi Sandonnini hails from Piedmont, but he cooks like a Calabrian – and that's a compliment. Cicchetti (sharing plates) of crisply fried courgette, polpettine (little meatballs) served with a good tomato sauce, and octopus with 'nduja (the soft-textured, chilli-spiked Calabrian sausage) were spot-on: rustic yet refined. Pasta, made on the premises, is pleasing too. A proper carbonara with guanciale (pork jowl), firm tagliolini noodles and egg, unbesmirched by the sacrilege of cream, was just as you'd find it in Italy. Veal milanese and sea bass or salmon are regular mains on the seasonally changing menu. Desserts range from classics, such as tiramisu, to inventive dishes like panna cotta flavoured with sambuca liqueur, served with rhubarb and rosemary jam. The all-Italian wine list has excellent producers from Alto Adige to Sicily, with a few 'natural' wines and a decent by-the-glass selection. A justifiably popular spot.
Available for hire. Babies and children welcome: high chairs; nappy-changing facilities. Booking advisable dinner. Disabled: toilet. Separate room for parties, seats 35. Tables outdoors (12, terrace). **Map 14 D12**.

Putney

★ Enoteca Turi

28 Putney High Street, SW15 1SQ (8785 4449, www.enotecaturi.com). Putney Bridge tube or Putney rail or bus 14, 74, 270. **Lunch served** noon-2.30pm Mon-Sat. **Dinner served** 7-10pm Mon-Thur; 7-11pm Fri, Sat. **Main courses** £11.50-£24.50. **Set lunch** £17.50 2 courses, £20.50 3 courses. **Set dinner** (Mon-Thur) £27 2 courses, £32 3 courses. **Credit** AmEx, MC, V.
In Italy, an 'enoteca' usually refers to a wine shop or bar. The name of Giuseppe Turi's Putney gem – a rare independent on the chain-filled high street – flags up the 350-strong Italy-focused wine list, as do the bottles displayed in alcoves around the claret-red walls. It's easy to get carried away, with aperitifs such as the Venetian spritz (Aperol and prosecco), and top-class wines by the glass; the nero d'avola suggested with a rich duck ragù was £10. On the other hand, by-the-glass pairings and half-bottle carafes allow you to try excellent wines without forking out for the whole bottle. This is much more than a wine bar, however; the food is just as much of a draw. While service is warm, it is formal, and most come here for special occasions. The kitchen is not afraid of simplicity – delicate own-made ravioli shone in their butter coating, while a rustic (though artfully presented) antipasto featured an earthy dried broad bean purée on bruschetta. Calf's liver was tender, succulent and filling. Less familiar ingredients such as cime di rapa are helpfully explained by the knowledgeable waiting staff, keen to introduce regional specialities with origins ranging from Sardinia to Sicily.
Babies and children welcome: high chairs. Booking advisable. Disabled: toilet. Dress: smart casual. Separate rooms for parties, seating 18 and 30.

South East

Bermondsey

★ Zucca

184 Bermondsey Street, SE1 3TQ (7378 6809, www.zuccalondon.com). Bermondsey tube or London Bridge tube/rail. **Lunch served** noon-3pm Tue-Fri; noon-3.30pm Sat, Sun. **Dinner served** 6-10pm Tue-Sat. **Main courses** £14-£16. **Credit** AmEx, MC, V.
Inhabiting a street that's fast becoming populated with hip restaurants and shops, Zucca has been a destination local since 2010. Bookings are still hard to secure. The formula is simple and impeccably executed: modern Italian food based on top-notch ingredients at competitive prices, served by clued-up staff in contemporary surroundings. Wraparound windows offer great people-watching opportunities, as does the open kitchen running half the length of the room. The clean-lined interior is white with pumpkin-coloured accents to tie in with the restaurant's name. Minimalist furniture and a plush carpet mirror the simultaneous simplicity and luxury of the meals. A light starter of sea bass carpaccio was brightened by flecks of chilli and orange, and equalled by a salt cod and roasted tomato bruschetta sent out by the chef – a welcome mouthful of sea and sun. A forte is the extraordinary fresh pasta, including intensely golden-yellow taglierini with fresh peas, lemon and ricotta, as well as wonderful pillows of lamb-filled agnolotti. The sizeable portions are keenly priced for the excellent standard of food. Staff (neatly aproned) knew the menu well; we couldn't fault it and were planning the next visit before we left.
Available for hire. Babies and children welcome: high chairs. Booking advisable dinner. Disabled: toilet. Separate room for parties, seats 10.

Tower Bridge

Tentazioni

2 Mill Street, SE1 2BD (7237 1100, www.tentazioni.co.uk). Bermondsey tube or London Bridge tube/rail. **Lunch served** noon-2.45pm Mon-Fri. **Dinner served** 6-10.45pm Mon-Sat. **Main courses** £13.50-£45. **Set lunch** £11.95 2 courses incl drink, £15 3 courses incl drink and coffee. **Set dinner** £47.50 tasting menu (£68.50 incl wine). **Credit** AmEx, MC, V.
Tucked away in a handsome wharf near Tower Bridge, Tentazioni generates an atmosphere of warm elegance with burgundy walls, streamlined white leather chairs and moody abstract art. The menu spans Italy, taking in Venetian cicchetti, Ligurian trofie pasta tossed with vibrant pesto, potatoes and green beans, and unctuous Pugliese burrata (cream-filled mozzarella). The insipid cherry tomatoes accompanying the latter were a rare dud in an otherwise uniformly excellent parade of dishes. Dynamic creations for more adventurous palates dot the menu – you could encounter a starter of risotto with strawberry and balsamic, or decadent asparagus and truffle soup with poached duck egg. Pasta is a strong point, a highlight being beef and parma ham tortellini in a delicate broth. The cocoa and sugar sprinkling on a martini glass of tiramisu was theatrically set alight and the custardy goodness below offset by crunchy biscuits – a pleasantly unexpected variation on a classic. Smartly dressed staff provide polished service to well-to-do diners, dispensing personalised wine recommendations to groups of regulars. A seven-course tasting menu offers further indulgence. A contemporary yet intimate venue popular with those who can afford waterfront living.
Available for hire. Babies and children welcome: high chair. Booking advisable dinner Fri, Sat. Separate room for parties, seats 24. **Map 12 S9**.

East

Shoreditch

Fifteen

15 Westland Place, N1 7LP (3375 1515, www.fifteen.net). Old Street tube/rail. **Lunch served** noon-3pm, **dinner served** 6-10pm daily. **Main courses** £17.50-£23. **Set lunch** £26 2 courses, £30 3 courses, £36 4 courses. **Credit** AmEx, MC, V.
The same menu is now served throughout at Jamie Oliver's Fifteen: in the ground-floor trattoria and the basement restaurant. The trattoria is lighter, noisier and slightly more cramped than the restaurant, but the two modern spaces are similar. Eating downstairs allows diners to see the kitchen, where trainees on Oliver's admirable Apprentice Programme create the likes of Sicilian fisherman's stew or assemble magnificent platters of antipasti. Waiting staff displayed various degrees of nervousness and competency, but the young chefs passed with flying colours. Pappa al pomodoro (Tuscan tomato and bread soup) was an intense hit of flavour; a huge risotto primavera with peas, broad beans, courgettes, mint and pecorino was exemplary; pan-roasted, free-range Norfolk chicken with zucchini trifolati, rocket and salsa rosso crudo was another generous, tasty serving, with lots of courgette and tomato. To drink, a globe-trotting wine list has strong competition from interesting cocktails (an aperitivo of own-made raspberry gin, rhubarb juice and prosecco, say), English ales, and strawberry and vanilla lemonade. Prices are high – put that down to the cost of careful sourcing and the training, and be prepared to regard at least 20% of your bill as a charitable donation.
Available for hire. Babies and children welcome: high chairs; nappy-changing facilities. Booking essential restaurant. Disabled: toilet (trattoria). Dress: smart casual. **Map 6 Q3**.

North East

Hackney

Lardo NEW

205 Richmond Road, E8 3NJ (8985 2683, www.lardo.co.uk). London Fields rail. **Open** 11am-10.30pm Mon-Fri; 10am-10.30pm Sat; 10am-9pm Sun. **Brunch served** 10am-3pm Sat, Sun. **Lunch served** noon-3pm Mon-Fri. **Dinner served** 6-10.30pm Mon-Sat; 6-9pm Sun. **Main courses** £7.50-£14. **No credit cards**.
This trattoria and bar (inside the Arthaus studio/gallery/apartment complex), combines talented chefs with fuss-free, stripped-back design. The pizzas are excellent (though they have been known to run out), and the huge, domed, mirrored pizza oven is quite spectacular. The kitchen's other speciality is cured meats, all of which are processed in-house. So toppings include the likes of star anise salami, or juniper-scented speck ham with spinach, mozzarella and belper knolle, a pungent Swiss

cheese. Alternatives come in the form of small plates, some so small it makes sharing between more than two people tricky. But ingredient quality was exceptional. Scallop carpaccio with samphire and vivid olive oil; broad beans and pecorino with mint and lemon; and arancini (breadcrumbed and fried risotto balls) were all excellent. The short, all-European wine list presents an interesting range of styles – a Loire rosé, a grüner veltliner, a Picpoul de Pinet – as well as two proseccos by the glass. Service was inconsistent on our visit, but once Lardo can cope with the already-high demand, it will be a fine addition to the neighbourhood.
Available for hire. Babies and children welcome: high chairs; nappy-changing facilities. Booking advisable. Disabled: toilet. Tables outdoors (3, pavement). Takeaway service. Vegan dishes.

North

Archway

500 Restaurant

782 Holloway Road, N19 3JH (7272 3406, www.500restaurant.co.uk). Archway tube or Upper Holloway rail. **Lunch served** noon-3pm Fri, Sat. **Dinner served** 5.30-10pm Mon-Sat. **Meals served** noon-9.30pm Sun. **Main courses** £14.30-£16.80. **Credit** AmEx, MC, V.
Simpler than many restaurants but classier than a trat, 500 (named after the Fiat Cinquecento) is that all-too-rare find: an eaterie serving high quality food and interesting wines at prices far less than you might expect. Little has changed since opening, but it hasn't had to – save perhaps the humble decor of pale blue walls, blond and red wood furniture, and a mish-mash of paintings for sale. Pasta is fresh, made on site and served the very definition of al dente. Spaghetti with san marzano tomatoes, samphire and red mullet worked better than the oily special of tagliatelle with pesto and bottarga. Starters, being simple compositions such as smoked swordfish with melon and pea shoots, arrived faster than a Ferrari. Crab with raw courgettes and herby brown crabmeat dressing was full of punchy flavours. Service was slightly ditzy – forgetting to bring us water for the glasses on the table – but we enjoyed sipping the unusual white cannonau blend from Sardinia, one of many wines well under £20 a bottle. Finish with the feather-light pillow of tiramisu or a 500 coupe: vanilla-poached apricots with chocolate and hazelnut ice-cream.
Available for hire. Babies and children welcome: high chairs. Booking essential dinner. **Map 26 C1.**

Camden Town & Chalk Farm

La Collina

17 Princess Road, NW1 8JR (7483 0192). Camden Town or Chalk Farm tube. **Lunch served** noon-3pm, **dinner served** 6-11pm Mon-Fri. **Meals served** noon-11pm Sat, Sun. **Main courses** £12-£20. **Credit** AmEx, MC, V.
We were hoping for Kate Moss. We got Mike Atherton, fresh from a Lord's test match. La Collina is that kind of neighbourhood restaurant: friendly, relaxed, but with a certain flashiness for when the in-laws visit; great home-style cooking, but with stylish presentation and a depth of flavour; a short but balanced menu matched by a strong wine list. The menu is simplicity itself, with about half a dozen each of primo, pasta, carne and pesce, alongside seasonal daily specials. Pastas come in two sizes and you're free to order whatever, whenever, in proper Italian style. All of our meal hit the right notes: tagliatelle with crab in a tangy tomato sauce was rich but light enough for the crab to dominate; and a main of lamb chops, spinach and fried potatoes had been delicately scented with rosemary. Baccalà (salt cod) was light as air, a blast of sea-saltiness heightened by the tangy garlic and anchovy paste laced through it; and the artichoke served with spaghetti vongole complemented the clam flavours beautifully. To finish, the cannoli had too thick a casing, but the children tucking into the chocolate and pistachio-studded ricotta filling had no complaints.
Babies and children welcome: high chairs. Booking advisable. Separate rooms for parties, seating 15 and 25. Tables outdoors (15, garden). **Map 27 B2.**

Highbury

Trullo

300-302 St Paul's Road, N1 2LH (7226 2733, www.trullorestaurant.com). Highbury & Islington tube/rail.
Bar **Open/meals served** 6-10.30pm Thur-Sat. **Tapas** £2.50-£10.
Restaurant **Lunch served** 12.30-2.45pm Fri, Sat; 12.30-3pm Sun. **Dinner served** 6.30-10.15pm Mon-Sat. **Main courses** £14-£20.
Both **Credit** MC, V.
The young team behind Trullo have made a success of a difficult site just off Highbury Corner roundabout, and the place has settled down to being a super-popular local serving some of the best food in Islington. On a Saturday night the joint was jumping, with the two simply decorated floors (ground and basement) fully booked. Smiley staff expertly choreographed the melee – vital when most tables have two sittings – but, even so, we still had to stand at the basement bar for ten minutes. This was the one blot on an otherwise impeccable evening. The bar means cocktails (negroni, martini) in addition to an all-Italian wine list. The menu packs a lots of interest into a short space, and changes from day to day; a choice of antipasti included good pork neck carpaccio with smashed Italian peas and Selvapiana Estate olive oil, and a sprightly salad of broad bean, pecorino, little gem lettuce and mint. Primi featured tagliatelle with cuttlefish, chilli and garlic, and pappardelle with beef shin ragù – both produced appreciative murmurs. Creamy burrata with slightly under-seasoned chickpeas and a zingy Sicilian tomato bruschetta was a big portion that ultimately lacked star quality; better was Hampshire pork chop (from the charcoal grill; a chunky piece of meat for £16.50), with braised Florence fennel and salsa verde. On a hot night, melon granita took the dessert laurels, but caprese chocolate torte was good too, and there are Italian cheeses for £9. Prices are laudable, especially for the quality.
Babies and children welcome: high chairs; nappy-changing facilities. Booking advisable.

Islington

Jamie's Italian Islington

Angel Building, 403 St John Street, EC1V 4AB (3435 9915, www.jamieoliver.com/italian). Angel tube. **Meals served** noon-11pm Mon-Sat; noon-10.30pm Sun. **Main courses** £10-£18. **Credit** AmEx, MC, V.
Nobody could accuse Jamie Oliver of subtlety. Enter his Italian via the merchandising, past a deli counter hung with Parma hams and into a cavernous, industrial space. The open kitchen's rattling and clanging was more audible than our companions across the percussive zinc-topped table. Flavours are equally full on. A plank of crisp bruschetta glistening with oil included terrific toppings of chard and chilli, fennel and aubergine, pea purée, peas and pea shoots with ricotta. Bolognese was controversially carroty, on thick tagliatelle, but grilled free-range chicken on tomato sauce with olives, and black squid-ink angel hair pasta cooked perfectly al dente with scallops, capers, garlic and chilli, were more the business. Burger Italiano plays to the gallery. Parmesan-crusted polenta chips are irresistible. Dishes can be unsociably garlicky and chilli is ubiquitous, but if the seasoning turned up to 11 becomes a little relentless, it's all done with panache. British fish is typical of well-sourced ingredients. Ice creams and sorbets show more restraint than the boy-can't-leave-it-alone tiramisu with orange mascarpone and chocolate, or the brownie with raspberry and amaretto. An excellent Italian wine list (with an organic house white and red), beers and Italian-accented cocktails add to the occasion; the acoustics conspire against but don't spoil the enjoyment.
Available for hire. Babies and children welcome: children's menu; crayons; high chairs; nappy-changing facilities. Booking advisable dinner Fri, Sat. Disabled: lift; toilet. Tables outdoors (15, terrace). **Map 5 N3.**
For branches see index.

Outer London

Twickenham, Middlesex

A Cena

418 Richmond Road, Twickenham, Middx TW1 2EB (8288 0108, www.acena.co.uk). Richmond tube/rail. **Lunch served** noon-2pm Tue-Sun. **Dinner served** 7-10.30pm Mon-Sat. **Main courses** £14-£23.50. **Set lunch** (Sun) £21 2 courses, £25 3 courses. **Credit** AmEx, MC, V.
Grumpy service marred an otherwise enjoyable Sunday lunch at this neighbourhood Italian, though things cheered up considerably as the meal progressed (and the friendly boss appeared). The food made a better impression: starters included a rich roast cauliflower soup with chilli pangrattato (breadcrumbs) and parmesan, and a grilled aubergine and chilli bruschetta, though the latter lacked much kick. We also liked pork scallopine milanese with fried courgettes, herbs and lemon, and barbecued marinated Gressingham duck breast, with apricot dressing, watercress and pan-roasted potatoes with rosemary – all good value and skilfully prepared. Less impressive was a dish of Italian sausages with red peppers, onions, tomato and olive oil mash: remarkably bland, given the ingredients. The generous alcohol kick of a lovely crema di limone (lemon cream with strawberries, limoncello and mint) made a perky finish; taleggio and gorgonzola with apple and nuts also seemed popular. Surroundings are easy on the eye – from a single shopfront, the room opens out once past the bar and a few booth tables, into a restful, light space. The Italian wine list is clearly a labour of love, and coffee is excellent. In all, a local worth having.
Available for hire. Babies and children welcome: high chairs. Booking advisable.

Japanese

Japanese dining in London has blossomed like few other cuisines since the early editions of this guide. Back in the 1980s, dour, expensive restaurants for expat businessmen accounted for nearly all of the (precious few) venues. Now, we have glamorous headliners such as siblings **Zuma** and **Roka**, as well as plentiful low-priced sushi and noodle joints – Soho's **Koya** is our top choice for noodles, but other great options can be found in the Budget bites box (*see p172*) – and a wealth of specialist establishments in between. Fancy fusion? **Dinings** or glitzy **Nobu** will add some Latin pzazz to proceedings. Going for a grill? **Zuma**, **Roka** or budget-priced **Bincho** can supply skewers straight from the robata. Some sushi? You're spoilt for choice, with Kensington's **Yashin** and Ealing's **Atariya** our current favourites, though an honourable mention goes to Willesden's **Sushi-Say**. A bright new venture this year is **Okan**, a simple café in the cheap eats hotspot of Brixton Market, joining Covent Garden operator **Abeno Too** in specialising in okonomiyaki savoury pancakes.

Central

City

★ Moshi Moshi Sushi

24 Upper Level, Liverpool Street Station, EC2M 7QH (7247 3227, www.moshimoshi.co.uk). Liverpool Street tube/rail. **Meals served** 11.30am-10pm Mon-Fri. **Dishes** £1.90-£5. **Main courses** £10-£12. **Credit** MC, V.

Sustainability features large on the menu of this futuristic conveyor-belt sushi restaurant. Away from the counter, the centre of the space is dominated by wooden seating pods that resemble alien landing craft nestling on beds of pebbles. Mundanely, we sat in a bay window overlooking the platform for the Stansted Express. A commitment to local produce means the mackerel comes from Sussex, the salmon from Scotland and the shellfish from Cornwall or Mull. All very laudable. But also very restrictive, leaving just 13 options for nigiri sushi. With such impeccable credentials, the fish was superb. But there was something wrong with the rice, which managed to be both too hard and too soft at the same time, disintegrating into grain the moment you bit into it. This was such a uniform problem that we began to believe – wrongly – that the rice had been shaped by machine (as it can be in cheaper sushi joints in Japan). For a group night out with a touch of oriental urban style, Moshi Moshi has much to recommend it. Just don't expect the food to have as much impact as the decor.

Babies and children admitted. Disabled: toilet. Takeaway service; delivery service (over £25 within 4-mile radius). **Map 12 R5.**

Covent Garden

★ Abeno Too

17-18 Great Newport Street, WC2H 7JE (7379 1160, www.abeno.co.uk). Leicester Square tube. **Meals served** noon-11pm Mon-Sat; noon-10pm Sun. **Main courses** £9-£24. **Set lunch** (Mon-Fri) £11.80-£20.80. **Credit** MC, V.

Yaki-soba to the left of me, soba-rice to the right, om-soba (noodles wrapped in omelette) ahead… okonomiyaki may be the USP here, but the menu holds more. 'Osaka soul food' – Japan's answer to the Spanish tortilla – does occupy pride of place, and toppings range impressively from humble pork or pricey beef to veggie mushroom, lotus root and cheese or the ten-topping wonder that is the Kansai Special. However, some of the best dishes are to be found on the sidelines. Yaki-gyoza (asparagus, prawn and water chestnut dumplings) is a favourite; and beef kara-age (well-seasoned nuggets of fillet, crisp-fried on the outside, juicy-rare in the middle) has wowed in the past. Each table contains an embedded hotplate, but not everything is grilled there, so check when ordering if you've come for the teppan aspect. Staff are helpful, if sometimes stretched on Friday and Saturday nights when a modest queue may form. But whether lunching at a window table on a quiet Sunday afternoon or perching on an unforgiving wooden bench at the high central counter on a buzzing full-house night, you'll find that London's okonomiyaki pioneer is no one-trick pony.

Babies and children welcome: high chairs. Bookings not accepted. Takeaway service. **Map 18 C6.**
For branch (Abeno) see index.

Euston

Sushi of Shiori

144 Drummond Street, NW1 2PA (7388 9962, www.sushiofshiori.co.uk). Euston tube/ rail. **Lunch served** 11.30am-2.30pm, **dinner served** 5.30-10pm Tue-Sat. **Dishes** £4-£15. **Set lunch** £9.50-£17. **Set meal** £12-£50. **Credit** MC, V.

The saying 'small but perfectly formed' sums up Sushi of Shiori pretty well. With the sushi bar and two small tables, it seats eight diners at a push, so it's best to book. Behind the counter, the quiet chef prepares each dish to order, taking great care over every detail – from the garnishes to the pretty plates – while his wife attends to the customers. If you're feeling organised, pre-order the temari 'canapé' sushi and enjoy a clutch of dinky round rice balls topped with fresh fish, and just a touch of something else such as glistening salmon eggs or rich sea urchin. There's plenty to choose from on the à la carte menu too. Our sashimi selection featured silky minced horse mackerel wrapped in nori, and the sweetest sweet shrimp we've tried. A complex, smoky own-made hojicha (roasted green

Budget bites

Centre Point Sushi

1st floor, 20-21 St Giles High Street, WC2H 8LN (7240 6147, www.cpfs.co.uk). Tottenham Court Road tube. **Lunch served** noon-2.30pm, **dinner served** 6-10.30pm Mon-Sat. **Main courses** £8-£17. **Set lunch** £9-£13. **Credit** MC, V.

'Hidden gem' is a much-abused term, but in the case of this old-school sushi bar, it's completely appropriate. Accessed via a Korean-Japanese supermarket in the shadow of Centre Point, it deals in traditional dishes for salarymen, from made-to-order sushi to the selection of tempura or teriyaki. The set-price bento boxes are particularly popular with local office workers, who appreciate the tranquil atmosphere. Groups tend to head for the leather booths by the window, while solo diners and couples perch at the bar, watching the chefs at work.

Babies and children admitted. Booking advisable. Takeaway service. **Map 17 C2.**

Ittenbari NEW

84 Brewer Street, W1F 9UB (7287 1318, www.ittenbari.co.uk). Piccadilly Circus tube. **Meals served** noon-10.30pm Mon-Sat; noon-9.30pm Sun. **Main courses** £8.90-£15. **Set meal** £15.50. **Credit** MC, V.

The interior has changed little since the site was Men's Bar Hamine. The plain white-tiled walls, gaffer-taped air-conditioner vents and plastic tabletops will win few design plaudits. Service is similarly to the point, but friendly nonetheless. A ramen production line sees deep blue and red bowls filled with stock, either shio ('salt' – with seafood extract) or shoyu (with soy sauce). Thin wheat noodles, a slice of pork, half a soft-boiled egg, a scoop of spinach, bamboo shoots and spring onion complete the picture. The two stocks were pleasing, and the noodles springy, but the pork slice was undistinguished and the gyoza dumplings dry; however, for £8.90 a bowl, diners may be able to overlook any defects.

Available for hire. Bookings not accepted. Children admitted. Separate room for parties, seating 15. Takeaway service. **Map 17 A5.**

Kulu Kulu

76 Brewer Street, W1F 9TX (7734 7316). Piccadilly Circus tube. **Lunch served** noon-2.30pm Mon-Fri; noon-3.45pm Sat. **Dinner served** 5-10pm Mon-Sat. **Dishes** £1.75-£3.80. **Set meal** £5.20-£12.90. **Credit** MC, V.

The original branch of Kulu Kulu may be looking a tad tired, but it's as popular as ever, with queues often spilling on to Brewer Street. Keen pricing and a superb location are the main draws, as is the lively ambience. The conveyor-belt sushi can be hit and miss, with cheap farmed (though perfectly fresh) fish and sometimes stingy portions. Instead, order off-belt: Kulu Kulu was one of the first places to serve prawn tempura hand rolls, and these continue to be excellent. Staff are often stretched, and at busy times will shamelessly boot you out the instant you've stopped eating.

Bookings not accepted. Takeaway service. **Map 17 A5.**

For branches see index.

Necco

52-54 Exmouth Market, EC1R 4QE (7713 8575, www.necco.co.uk). Bus 19, 38, 55. **Meals served** noon-10pm Mon-Wed; noon-10.30pm Thur-Sat. **Main courses** £7.50-£12.50. **Set lunch** (noon-3pm) £5 bento box. **Credit** (over £10) MC, V.

If you share the Japanese penchant for all things *kawaii* (cute), then Necco is the place to go. Even the grout between the white tiles is pink. For a small café, the menu is ample: rice dishes, noodles, curries and green tea-laced desserts, as well as Japanese beers, teas and sakés. We weren't convinced by our sun-dried tomato, olive and cream cheese roll, but plump tako yaki (octopus balls) hit the spot. Service can be haphazard.

Available for hire. Babies and children admitted. Tables outdoors (3, pavement). Takeaway service. **Map 5 N4.**

Taro

10 Old Compton Street, W1D 4TF (7439 2275, www.tarorestaurants.co.uk). Leicester Square tube. **Meals served** noon-10pm Mon; noon-10.30pm Tue-Thur; noon-10.45pm Fri; 12.30-10.30pm Sat; 12.30-9.30pm Sun. **Main courses** £6.50-£9.90. **Set lunch** £6.90 incl tea. **Set meal** £11.90-£14 bento box. **Credit** MC, V.

You might think that the limited natural light in this basement canteen would put people off. Far from it – Taro's reputation for diminutive price tags and generous portions has made it popular with a wide spectrum of bargain-hunters. Clustering around chunky pine communal tables, diners order from a roll-call of traditional Japanese favourites, from sushi to noodles, plus teriyaki, katsu and tempura. It's surprisingly roomy, meaning that at all but the busiest times, staff are happy to leave you to it, appearing only occasionally to offer more drinks, such as cold bottles of Kirin or Asahi.

Babies and children welcome: high chairs. Booking advisable Fri, Sat. Takeaway service. **Map 17 C3.**

For branch see index.

Toku at Japan Centre

14-16 Regent Street, SW1Y 4PH (3405 1222, www.toku-restaurant.co.uk). Piccadilly Circus tube. **Meals served** noon-9.45pm Mon-Thur; noon-10pm Fri, Sat; noon-8.45pm Sun. **Main courses** £3-£26. **Set meal** (3-5.30pm Mon-Fri) £10.99 bento box. **Credit** MC, V.

Talk about playing to a tough crowd. Toku is the official restaurant of the Japan Centre. It's popular with local office workers too. While next door focuses on imported products and produce, Toku majors in fairly priced Japanese cooking of the highest order, from spankingly fresh sushi to traditional hot dishes of gyoza, teriyaki, noodles and donburi (one-bowl rice meals). Don't miss the delicately battered signature tempura.

Babies and children welcome: high chairs; nappy-changing facilities. Bookings not accepted Sat, Sun. Disabled: toilet. Tables outdoors (4, pavement). Takeaway service. **Map 17 B5.**

Tokyo Diner

2 Newport Place, WC2H 7JJ (7287 8777, www.tokyodiner.com). Leicester Square tube. Meals served noon-11.30pm daily. **Main courses** £8.50-£19.90. **Set lunch** (noon-6pm Mon-Fri) £8-£11.90. **Credit** MC, V.

A Japanese jewel in the heart of Chinatown, Tokyo Diner has a long-standing reputation for its affordable menu and friendly service. All the usual suspects are here, from soup noodles to sushi, as well as set lunch boxes and donburi, though you won't find any tuna – TD has taken an active sustainability stance on this. More café than canteen, the airy corner site has plenty of smaller tables if you don't care to share.

Babies and children welcome: high chairs. Bookings not accepted Fri, Sat. Takeaway service. **Map 17 C4.**

Tsuru

4 Canvey Street, SE1 9AN (7928 2228, www.tsuru-sushi.co.uk). Southwark tube. **Meals served** 11am-3.30pm Mon; 11am-9pm Tue-Fri; noon-9pm Sat. **Main courses** £8.20-£14.25. **Set meal** £6.40-£8.20 bento box. **Credit** AmEx, MC, V.

Tucked behind Tate Modern, the original branch of Tsuru proved such a success with the office crowd that it's spawned City offshoots near Liverpool Street and Bank. The signature dish is katsu curry, cooked for eight hours and served with pieces of golden breadcrumbed pork (Japanese schnitzel, if you like). It's worth exploring the rest of the menu, though, which ranges from hot dishes of gyoza and potato korokke (a type of croquette), to cold boxes of sushi or Japanese potato salad.

Available for hire. Babies and children welcome: high chairs. Disabled: toilet. Tables outdoors (5, pavement). Takeaway service. **Map 11 O8.**

For branches see index.

tea) ice-cream brought the meal to a happy conclusion. Drummond Street, a road better known for cheap Indian restaurants, holds a shining Japanese gem that would be just as at home in Tokyo. We'll be back for the chef's recommended (omakase) menu and a glass of saké.
Available for hire. Babies and children admitted. Booking advisable. Takeaway service. Vegetarian menu. **Map 3 J3.**

Fitzrovia

Nizuni
22 Charlotte Street, W1T 2NB (7580 7447, www.nizuni.com). Goodge Street or Tottenham Court Road tube. **Lunch served** noon-2.45pm Mon-Sat. **Dinner served** 6-10.45pm daily. **Main courses** £10-£15. **Set lunch** £8-£13. **Credit** AmEx, MC, V.
Nizuni has the same polished feel as its Korean counterpart Koba round the corner on Rathbone Street. The decor strikes an elegant balance between contemporary and classic Japanese style, while each dish arrives on well-considered crockery. The menu blends traditional and fusion elements, evident in a starter of yellowtail sashimi with avocado 'mousse' and truffle oil, which took the taste buds on a journey through layers of earthy, sweet and aromatic flavours. Next came a crowd-pleasing dish of crispy rock-shrimp tempura, lightly coated in a sweet chilli sauce. Beef nabe was another big hit: slippery noodles, soft tofu, Asian mushrooms and slices of beef simmered in a sweet and savoury broth. The only let-down was the sushi. The fish was fresh, but the chalky rice just didn't make the mark. We ended on a high, though, with a sticky chestnut cake offset by green tea ice-cream. Kirin beer (expensive at £4.20 a bottle) was our chosen accompaniment. Service waned a little towards the end, but staff were polite enough. If you feel like another drink after your meal, check out the cocktail bar in the basement.
Available for hire. Babies and children welcome: high chairs. Booking advisable Thur-Sat. Disabled: toilet. Separate room for parties, seats 20. Tables outdoors (4, pavement). Takeaway service. **Map 17 B1.**
For branch see index.

★ Roka HOT 50
37 Charlotte Street, W1T 1RR (7580 6464, www.rokarestaurant.com). Goodge Street or Tottenham Court Road tube. **Lunch served** noon-3.30pm Mon-Fri; 12.30-4pm Sat, Sun. **Dinner served** 5.30-11.30pm Mon-Sat; 5.30-10.30pm Sun. **Main courses** £4.50-£68. **Set meal** £50-£75 tasting menu. **Credit** AmEx, DC, MC, V.
Popularity is best displayed in a fish bowl, and Roka (younger sibling to Zuma) flaunts its assets through floor-to-ceiling glass. Anyone passing can see the robata grill edged with a chunky, knotted wood counter. Within lie bowls of pickles and garnishes wedged into crushed ice. It's a fine spot to watch the chefs – skewering magnificent stems of asparagus, perhaps, or tweezering bones from grilled black cod – while grazing on amazing savouries (robata-grilled scallops with wasabi cream made it into Time Out's 100 Best Dishes in London) and intriguing sweets (yoghurt and almond cake with toffee banana and tonka bean ice-cream). A lone portion of chu-toro – three slices rendered splendid against a shiso leaf and a crystal-clear boulder of ice upon a hillock of crushed ice – was beautiful to behold and exquisite to consume. Superb raw materials are key here, but shochu plays a major role too: stout glass jars of it line shelves, each dog-tagged with its owner-customer's name (often a local media exec). Then there's the 'sexy, subterranean' (Roka's words, not ours) Shochu Lounge, which offers the food menu plus Japan's answer to vodka. All served with faintly officious efficiency.
Babies and children welcome: high chairs; nappy-changing facilities. Booking advisable. Disabled: toilet. Tables outdoors (9, terrace). **Map 17 B1.**
For branch see index.

Soho Japan
52 Wells Street, W1T 3PR (7323 4661, www.sohojapan.co.uk). Oxford Circus tube.
Lunch served noon-2.30pm Mon-Fri.
Dinner served 6-10.30pm Mon-Sat.
Main courses £7.50-£20. **Credit** MC, V.
This is a Japanese restaurant that defies expectations from the moment you walk through the door. Current West End fashion dictates the presence of noren (short Japanese curtains) over the door, married to a cool interior with light wood panelling and paper screens. Here – and there's no getting away from it – you're in a curiously shaped Victorian pub that serves Japanese food. Behind the V-shaped bar lurks the kitchen, while diners cram together at pub tables overlooked by vintage beer advertisements that have survived at least three generations of owners. Atmospheric, it's not. Fortunately, the food is considerably fresher than the decor. On a weekday lunch, we sat elbow to elbow with office workers tucking into the reasonably priced specials that are helpfully tweaked to cater for British tastes (long on salmon and tuna sashimi and sushi, short on sea urchin and raw octopus). Grilled mackerel was juicy and succulent, while the beef in yakiniku don (beef in sauce on rice) was tender and well marinated. A side dish of agedashidofu (deep-fried tofu with sauce and spring onions) was prepared to perfection. At dinner, there's more emphasis on yakitori and beer than on sushi, which should go better with the surroundings.
Babies and children admitted. Booking advisable. Tables outdoors (3, pavement). Takeaway service. **Map 17 A2.**

Knightsbridge

★ Zuma
5 Raphael Street, SW7 1DL (7584 1010, www.zumarestaurant.com). Knightsbridge tube.
Bar **Open** noon-11pm Mon-Fri; 12.30-11pm Sat, Sun.
Restaurant **Lunch served** noon-2.45pm Mon-Fri; 12.30-3.15pm Sat, Sun. **Dinner served** 6-10.45pm Mon-Sat; 6-10.15pm Sun. **Main courses** £14.80-£70. **Set meal** £96. **Credit** AmEx, DC, MC, V.
It's hard to believe there is a recession when you enter Zuma. The bar and dining room of this ultra-chic destination crackle with sheer energy, and the

Koya. See p177.

Tonkotsu. See p177.

well-heeled diners seem to have no care in the world. The interior design is earthy, with stone flooring and cedar-wood furniture, but thankfully the hard wooden seats have now been tempered by soft cream leather. The invariably friendly staff manage to keep pace with the intense demand, although you'd expect this for the 13.5% service charge. Sushi and sashimi are of premier league quality, the raw tuna belly and sea urchin being notable gems. Our meal got off to a flying start with a small plate of asparagus cooked on the robata grill, made interesting by a golden wafu dressing. Ribeye beef, exactly medium-rare as requested, arrived with deep-fried garlic that melted in the mouth. Presentation is eye-catching, and quality has been consistently exemplary throughout several recent visits. Chocoholics, take note: the kitchen can conjure up a wicked chocolate fondant (ask for one even if it's not on the menu). An impressively diverse saké and wine list tops it all off.
Available for hire. Babies and children welcome: high chairs. Booking essential. Disabled: toilet. Separate rooms for parties, seating 12 and 14. **Map 8 F9.**

Marylebone

Dinings

22 Harcourt Street, W1H 4HH (7723 0666, www.dinings.co.uk). Marylebone tube/rail. **Lunch served** noon-2.30pm Mon-Fri. **Dinner served** 6-10.30pm Mon-Sat. **Main courses** £6-£28. **Set lunch** £14-£29. **Credit** AmEx, MC, V.
No one comes to this bunker-in-a-townhouse for airy spaces or pretty decor; Dinings lives or dies by what emerges from ex-Nobu chef Masaki Sugisaki's Latin-skewed kitchen. You can usually find space at the ground-floor sushi counter, but you'll need to book for the little basement. Exclusive, cosy or claustrophobic? That depends on your views about brutalist concrete and the audibility of everyone's conversation. Dinings' characteristic delectable titbits don't come cheap – epitomised by tiny 'tar-tar chips' (potato crisps cradling toppings of, for example, chopped raw tuna on jalapeño cream, or salmon and spicy miso) at £3-£4 per delicious crunch. Staff and customers generally hail from the West, while the globetrotting menu runs to char siu pork, Jersey royals, fiddlehead fern, truffle, foie gras and Korean spice alongside tuna, salmon and the renowned wagyu beef sushi. It makes for a disorientating read. Tender, charcoal-fragrant 'Santa Barbara shrimp' was a highlight, but wood pigeon intrigued then frustrated: grilled rare and quartered, it was tricky to chew off the bone and tasted of little. There are broadened horizons for dessert too, with the classy likes of balsamic vinegar and mirin ice-cream with still-hot strawberry tempura.
Available for hire. Babies and children admitted. Booking advisable. Takeaway service. Vegetarian menu. **Map 8 F5.**

Tomoe

62 Marylebone Lane, W1U 2PB (7486 2004, www.tomoe-london.co.uk). Bond Street tube. **Lunch served** noon-2.15pm Tue-Sat. **Dinner served** 6-10pm Mon-Sat. **Dishes** £1.90-£15. **Set lunch** £9.90-£22.50. **Minimum** (dinner) £15. **Credit** AmEx, MC, V.
Tomoe may be one of the more understated eating establishments on Marylebone Lane, but don't let that put you off. The kitchen can definitely knock up a decent plate of sushi, or any other Japanese

classic for that matter. The centrepiece of our meal was the own-made tofu. An earthenware pot was brought to the table atop a small brazier and we were told not to lift the lid for 20 minutes. After that our delicate, creamy tofu was ready to scoop out, and have dried bonito flakes, spring onion and sesame sauce added before being gobbled down. An unpretentious plate of grilled yuzu chicken was another success – crispy chicken, tangy citrus and a sprinkling of shredded purple shiso. Next came seared razor clams covered with enough fried garlic to dispatch a vampire; despite the pungency, the sweet flavour of the clams still won through. All the food arrived via a very squeaky dumb waiter, laboriously hoicked up and down by the staff. From the drinks list, draught Asahi or Kirin beer are popular with the regular stream of Japanese businessmen who kick back here, though there's saké, shochu and wine too.
Babies and children welcome: high chairs. Booking advisable dinner. Takeaway service. **Map 9 H6.**

Mayfair

Chisou

4 Princes Street, W1B 2LE (7629 3931, www.chisourestaurant.com). Oxford Circus tube. **Lunch served** noon-2.30pm, **dinner served** 6-10.15pm Mon-Sat. **Meals served** 1-9.30pm Sun. **Main courses** £12-£25. **Set lunch** £14.50-£20.50. **Credit** AmEx, MC, V.

Don't be misled by the modern interior: Chisou is pleasingly old-school, providing oshibori (hot flannels) and complimentary zensai (appetisers) before orders arrive on assorted chunky, artistic crockery. The extensive menu merits exploration, so allow time to consider lesser-spotted dishes such as ankimo ponzu (monkfish liver with citrus dressing) or inaniwa udon (a thin version of the slippery white noodles, served hot or cold). A la carte sushi at £2.50-£6 per piece may ring alarm bells if you're on a tight budget. Among the chef's recommendations, aubergine filled with minced chicken made a refreshing change from the usual miso treatment (nasu dengaku). Chicken and veg gyoza looked over-fried yet were well shaped and held an excellent filling. Puddings are classic too. This is the place to tell your daifuku (rice-flour cakes) from your dorayaki (red-bean pancake, including green tea mascarpone-filled). In the drinks department, Chisou is serious about saké: there's a double-page spread in the menu on the brewing process and categorisation. Staff, a cosmopolitan mix not unlike the clientele, sometimes seem uncomprehending, and there have been complaints of prompt service crossing over into premature plate-clearing, but we've yet to experience this.
Babies and children welcome: high chairs. Booking essential. Separate rooms for parties, seating 12-20. Tables outdoors (2, terrace). Takeaway service. **Map 9 J6.**

Nobu

1st floor, The Metropolitan, 19 Old Park Lane, W1K 1LB (7447 4747, www.nobu restaurants.com). Hyde Park Corner tube. **Lunch served** noon-2.15pm Mon-Fri; 12.30-2.30pm Sat, Sun. **Dinner served** 6-10.15pm Mon-Thur; 6-11pm Fri, Sat; 6-10pm Sun. **Dishes** £4-£35.75. **Set lunch** £33 bento box; £60, £70. **Set dinner** £80, £95. **Credit** AmEx, MC, V.

Yashin. See p178.

Nobu is no longer the exclusive celebrity haunt it once was; you're more likely to sit among business people and tourists than A-listers these days. All the signature dishes remain on the menu, including black cod with miso for an eye-opening £42. Endangered blue-fin tuna is here too, but you can opt for yellow-fin instead. Though a somewhat token gesture, we specified the yellow-fin in the 'hot miso (game) chips' topped with sweet, spicy raw tuna and scallop cubes. Next, the winning white-fish tiradito (a Japanese-Peruvian dish) balanced citrus sourness and chilli heat perfectly. Disappointingly, the wagyu and foie gras gyoza were greasy, lacking the hoped-for refinement. We ended on a high, though, with two knock-out desserts: a mind-bending rice pudding dish with chewy mochi balls, crispy rice crackers and saké sorbet; and tangy yuzu pie coated in buttery sablé biscuit crumbs. A five-cup saké tasting menu took us on a fun journey during the meal, ending on gold-flecked Honjozo Kinpaku-Iri. The service was faultless, with every last detail attended to – and watching the sun set over Hyde Park was definitely a bonus.
Babies and children welcome: high chairs. Booking advisable. Disabled: lift; toilet. Separate rooms for parties, seating 14-60. **Map 9 H8.**
For branch (Nobu Berkeley) see index.

Umu

14-16 Bruton Place, W1J 6LX (7499 8881, www.umurestaurant.com). Bond Street or Green Park tube. **Lunch served** noon-2.30pm Mon-Fri. **Dinner served** 6-11pm Mon-Sat. **Main courses** £13-£57. **Set lunch** £25-£45. **Set meal** £100. **Credit** AmEx, DC, MC, V.

The full Kyoto-style dining experience that Umu offers doesn't come cheap at £100 a pop for the kaiseki tasting menu. But if you've never tried it before, the succession of cured, raw, fried, simmered and grilled dishes – all intricately presented on pretty plates and finished off with rice or sushi – is definitely worth a whirl. Otherwise, there are sushi, sashimi and à la carte options to deliberate over, or you could go for one of the more reasonably priced set lunches. The four compartments in our lacquered bento box held crisp prawn tempura, cured fish with lightly pickled vegetables, some seriously good wild salmon sashimi, and tender simmered duck with pumpkin. The clear soup accompanying the bento was first-rate (salty, savoury, smoky and packed with Asian mushrooms), as was the innovative white asparagus sorbet that followed. Everything was rounded off with a toasty cup of genmaicha tea and a plate of petits fours that included delicate yuzu marshmallows. At night, we've found Umu's dark interior and atmosphere a little austere; during the day, it is lighter, more relaxed and even the chefs are up for a chat.
Babies and children welcome: high chairs. Booking advisable dinner. Disabled: toilet. Dress: smart casual. **Map 9 H7.**

Piccadilly

Yoshino

3 Piccadilly Place, W1J 0DB (7287 6622, www.yoshino.net). Piccadilly Circus tube. **Meals served** noon-9.30pm Mon-Sat. **Main courses** £6.80-£40. **Set meal** £20-£40 bento box. **Credit** AmEx, MC, V.

This hidden gem of a place is tucked away in a narrow alley off Piccadilly. Although it's been in business for more than 15 years, it looks as fresh and modish as a brand-new establishment. The ground floor has several small tables inside, canopied tables outside in summer, and a takeaway

counter that attracts a stream of well-heeled regulars. The main dining room is upstairs: minimalist decor, a high ceiling and huge windows give an airy feel. That the proprietor is a Japanese fish importer is evident in the superb quality of the seafood. Plump, crisp prawn tempura was just about the best you'll find, and tuna and salmon sashimi, topped with a micro-salad and served in lacquered trays, were also first-rate. Everything zings with flavour, from the tasty, wakame-packed miso soup topped with a whole poached prawn to the bracing green tea. The menu is focused on set meals, ranging in price from £10 upwards at lunch, though there are plans to offer more standalone dishes. What stands out above all is the warmth and attention of the service; on our visit, the smiling manager voiced a welcome and farewell to each and every takeaway customer.
Babies and children admitted. Booking advisable. Tables outdoors (8, pavement). Takeaway service. Vegetarian menu. **Map 17 A5**.

St James's

Matsuri

15 Bury Street, SW1Y 6AL (7839 1101, www.matsuri-restaurant.com). Green Park tube. **Lunch served** noon-2.30pm Mon-Sat; noon-3pm Sun. **Dinner served** 6-10.30pm Mon-Sat; 6-10pm Sun. **Dishes** £2.50-£10.50. **Main courses** £6.50-£55. **Set lunch** £25, £35 bento box; £39, £55. **Set meal** £35-£165. **Credit** AmEx, MC, V.

Teppanyaki, the Japanese iron-griddle cooking technique, is a bit like Marmite: you either love it or hate it. If you're under the age of 12, or enjoy pyrotechnics with your dinner, then Matsuri is definitely the place for you. The attractive underground dining room hosts a nightly influx of tourists and businessmen – mostly Japanese – who come to watch fish, vegetables and meat grilled by their own chef in front of their table. On our visit, the mixed seafood grill featured a decent range of fish (salmon, squid, scallops), but the fish and vegetables were extremely plain, and not tasty enough in their nude states to satisfy. Eating here isn't cheap, with the three-course set dinner costing £35, yet most diners opt to throw in an extra £5 for the mango and ice-cream dessert, for which your faithful chef is trotted out again, armed with a bottle of oil to create sky-high flames on the grill around your melting ice-cream, which is balanced precariously on the fruit. Previous visits to Matsuri have yielded impressive results from the small sushi counter, separate from the teppanyaki room. This is where we would spend our money.
Available for hire. Babies and children welcome: high chairs. Booking advisable. Disabled: toilet. Separate rooms for parties, seating 6-18. Takeaway service. Vegetarian menu. **Map 9 J8**.

Sake No Hana

23 St James's Street, SW1A 1HA (7925 8988, www.sakenohana.com). Green Park tube. **Lunch served** noon-3pm Mon-Fri; noon-4pm Sat. **Dinner served** 6-10.45pm Mon-Thur; 6-11.15pm Fri, Sat. **Main courses** £4-£37. **Set meal** £35-£60. **Credit** AmEx, MC, V.

Japanese architect Kengo Kuma has created an interior at Sake No Hana that MC Escher would be proud of. Escalators run continuously from the front desk to the striking first-floor dining room, where geometrically arranged maple wood batons line the walls and ceiling. Don't wait until the last minute for a trip to the loo, though: the lift taking you there is surely the slowest in the world. The menu is lengthy, but staff are happy to guide you through it, including how much to order. An unusual dish of crispy aubergine pieces with sweet sesame dressing and fresh figs got things off to a good start – the fruit counterbalancing the rich, earthy aubergine. Inside-out mooli and watercress sushi roll topped with minced wagyu and egg yolk made for an intense experience. Tori toban yaki was less inspiring, however; brought sizzling to the table, the chicken and mushroom dish had drama, but not enough flavour. Food is far from cheap and can be a little inconsistent, but dining here is definitely an experience. If you're out for a special occasion, stop off at the futuristic ground-floor bar beforehand for a decadent saké cocktail.
Available for hire. Babies and children admitted. Booking advisable. Disabled: lift; toilet. **Map 9 J8**.

Soho

★ Bincho

16 Old Compton Street, W1D 4TL (7287 9111, www.bincho.co.uk). Leicester Square or Tottenham Court Road tube. **Lunch served** noon-3pm Tue-Sat; 1-3.30pm Sun. **Dinner served** 5-11pm Mon-Sat; 5-10.30pm Sun. **Dishes** £1.50-£7. **Set lunch** £8.50-£9.50. **Set dinner** £25. **Credit** AmEx, MC, V.

At the centre of Bincho's dimly lit universe is the charcoal grill, where chefs ceaselessly prep and

JAPANESE

turn skewers of yakitori (from chicken breast and wing to liver and oyster) and kushiyaki (red meat, fish and veg). For making your budget stretch further, the Seven Samurai set is a winner (especially as à la carte skewers come as a minimum order of two). But if you're after culinary adventure, go out on a limb with gizzard and ginkgo nuts or explore off-skewer with whole grilled mackerel pike. Uncooked options include a refreshing salad of squid, salmon, mixed leaves and seaweed tossed in a yuzu (citrus) dressing. Brownie points for rapid-response staff and convivial surroundings, but we have been disappointed by the kushiyaki at off-peak times when perhaps the charcoal embers were not at their best. For a specialist, Bincho offers a surprising variety of meal endings: sweet East-meets-West desserts; savoury ochazuke (rice and toppings in a green tea broth); and even alcoholic Ichigo Plum – a cocktail of plum wine and strawberry purée over crushed ice that makes a splendid sorbet substitute.
Available for hire. Babies and children welcome: high chairs. Booking advisable. Disabled: toilet. Separate room for parties, seats 18. Takeaway service. **Map 17 C3.**
For branch see index.

★ ★ Koya HOT 50

49 Frith Street, W1D 4SG (7434 4463, www.koya.co.uk). Tottenham Court Road tube. **Lunch served** noon-3pm daily. **Dinner served** 5.30-10.30pm Mon-Sat; 5.30-10pm Sun. **Main courses** £6.70-£14.70. **Credit** AmEx, MC, V.
You can easily spot London's favourite Japanese noodle bar by the long queue regularly winding from its entrance. Fear not – there's a fairly rapid turnover at the shared wooden tables, and the food (authentic Japanese preparations using fresh, locally sourced vegetables, meats and fish) is well worth the wait. The menu stars udon noodles (chewy, thick white noodles made of wheat flour imported from Japan) in all their glorious possibilities: hot in soup, cold and served with hot soup, or cold served with cold sauce. There are also rice dishes and an impressive list of salads and sides. A vegetarian dish of cold udon noodles served with mushrooms in a walnut miso broth epitomised the glory of Koya: the noodles perfectly springy and the flavour of the soup simple but deeply savoury. Smoked mackerel with green leaves, served with hot udon in soup, allowed the fresh fish to dominate. Seasonal specials, listed on a blackboard, are well worth exploring; they often feature more exotic combinations than the regular menu. Koya's own ginger tea makes an ideal accompaniment to the salty food. Friendly staff can guide you through the dishes and advise.
Bookings not accepted. Vegan dishes.
Map 17 C3.

Sushi of Shiori. See p171.

So Japanese

3-4 Warwick Street, W1B 5LS (7292 0760, www.sorestaurant.com). Piccadilly Circus tube. **Lunch served** noon-3pm Mon-Fri. **Dinner served** 5.30-10.30pm Mon-Thur; 5.30-11pm Fri. **Meals served** noon-11pm Sat. **Main courses** £14-£28. **Set lunch** £6.95-£16. **Credit** AmEx, MC, V.
If you're after a quality plate of sushi, or a more decadent dining experience, So Japanese has something to offer. This guarantees a diverse mix of people in its contemporary dining room. For the sushi lover, it's always worth finding out what's on the specials board, and if you want to see the chefs at work, there's plenty of space at the counter. Squid nigiri were perfectly formed, while the tobiko (flying fish roe) in our gunkan maki popped pleasingly in the mouth. An inside-out tuna roll dotted with own-made spicy mayonnaise also went down well. For special occasions there's the likes of foie gras nigiri, grilled wagyu beef in miso, or plump, perfectly pan-fried scallops with shredded daikon and yuzu mayo. Less refined, but not to be knocked, our sweet, sticky tebasaki (tender chicken wings) scattered with sesame, came with a hot hand towel in case we got messy eating them. Service was unhurried, but friendly enough. There's a good selection of saké and shochu, and the tea is said to come from one of the oldest tea shops in Kyoto.
Available for hire. Babies and children welcome: high chairs. Separate room for parties, seats 6. Takeaway service. **Map 17 A5.**

★ Tonkotsu NEW

63 Dean Street, W1D 4QG (7437 0071, www.tonkotsu.co.uk). Leicester Square or Tottenham Court Road tube. **Lunch served** noon-3pm, **dinner served** 5-10.30pm Mon-Fri. **Meals served** noon-10.30pm Sat, Sun. **Main courses** £9-£11. **Credit** AmEx, MC, V.
The Tsuru sushi bar chain has made a radical departure with this, its latest restaurant: a dedicated noodle bar specialising in ramen. The menu covers a short yet impressive array of starters; try the pork gyoza or tofu hiyayakko (a large chunk of creamy-textured fresh tofu garnished with spring onions and dried fish flakes, which you bathe in a light soy sauce). 'Tonkotsu' refers to the slow-simmered pork belly stock that's a signature dish. Other options with which to combine your noodles include 'Tokyo Spicy': pepped-up pork stock in a combination of flavours

including salt and chilli. All ramen dishes come with eggs and vegetables, including the vegetarian dish of miso and shimeji mushroom ramen. It's not in the same league as udon-specialist Koya (*see p177*) in the neighbouring street, but this is nevertheless an essential stop-off for ramen fans.
Babies and children admitted. Bookings not accepted. Separate room for parties, seats 25. Tables outdoors (3, pavement). **Map 17 B4**.

West

Ealing

★ Atariya

1 Station Parade, Uxbridge Road, W5 3LD (8896 3175, www.atariya.co.uk). Ealing Common tube. **Lunch served** 11am-1.30pm, **dinner served** 4.30-9pm Tue-Sun. **Dishes** 60p-£3.20. **Set meal** £14-£20. **Credit** AmEx, MC, V.
Wherever London's discreetly growing Japanese community has put down roots, you'll find a branch of this small, unfussy sushi chain or its associated food stores. With its refrigerated counters and simple light wood decor, Atariya feels like the quintessential local sushi bar, as found in any Japanese town or suburb. The ordering system comes straight from Japan too. The waitress will bow, take your drinks order and leave you with a menu and a pen. You simply write down how many of each dish you require. The choice is impressive. Thanks, one suspects, to its largely Japanese clientele, Atariya offers foods that are rarely found in mainstream establishments, such as natto (pungent, fermented bean curd), uni (sea urchin) and awabi (abalone). The nigiri sushi was a delight, with the perfect amount of barely warm rice, and fish that melted away on the tongue. The sea bass, squid, sea bream and scallops – which can all be too chewy when poorly cut – were particularly good, while staples such as tuna, salmon and yellowtail were impeccably prepared, with just the right amount of wasabi. With enough chatter from the regular customers, you can close your eyes and be transported.
Babies and children welcome: high chairs. Booking advisable Fri, Sat. Takeaway service.
For branches see index.

Hammersmith

Tosa

332 King Street, W6 0RR (8748 0002, http://tosauk.com). Ravenscourt Park or Stamford Brook tube. **Lunch served** 12.30-2.30pm, **dinner served** 6-10.30pm daily. **Main courses** £7-£15. **Set lunch** £11. **Set meal** £30. **Credit** AmEx, MC, V.
First impressions of Tosa aren't great. You are more likely to be greeted by the sight of the chef smoking outside the shabby entrance than receive a warm welcome from the sometimes-indifferent waiting staff. Inside, the surroundings don't get much better – brown tiled floors, cheap wooden tables, paintwork in need of a touch-up. Having said that, we soon warmed to the atmosphere, as this is a place many clearly love. The restaurant bustled on a Monday night with a mixture of Japanese customers (a good sign) and locals who felt at home enough to throw their coats on the hooks by the door and ask for a seat at the counter. Try to follow suit: at the counter, in front of the open robata grill, you can watch the glazed skewers roasting. Food will come when it's ready, so share and explore, ordering lots of different little dishes (all reasonably priced). Sample, perhaps, the kombu onigiri, a triangle of sushi rice with a tangle of sweet seaweed in the centre, or shiso maki, a fantastic spiral of grilled pork loin layered with peppery shiso leaves.
Available for hire. Babies and children admitted. Booking advisable. Tables outdoors (4, pavement). Takeaway service. **Map 20 A4**.
For branch see index.

Kensington

★ Yashin

1A Argyll Road, W8 7DB (7938 1536, www.yashinsushi.com). High Street Kensington tube. **Lunch served** noon-2pm, **dinner served** 6-10.30pm daily. **Dishes** £30-£60. **Set lunch** £12.50-£60. **Credit** AmEx, MC, V.
In a discreet location just off Kensington High Street, Yashin has that modern eclectic look that's currently so hip. Highlights include black rabbit-shaped lamps atop Victorian-style mouldings on the walls. Behind the green-tiled sushi counter, a neon sign states 'without soy sauce – but if you want to', as the chefs disapprove of the salty sauce masking their sushi. Instead, the industrious throng of itamae (sushi chefs) finish their nigiri with a drizzle of truffle oil, a quick blast from a blowtorch or some other carefully considered garnish. And there's plenty other than sushi sets to explore on the menu. Our grouper 'carpaccio' saw the meaty fish beautifully balanced by tangy yuzu, a hint of chilli oil and pleasing little nuggets of toasted rice. An unusual eel and pineapple inside-out roll with a mango emulsion was an unexpected triumph, while the playful miso 'cappuccino' saw a satisfyingly complex miso soup arrive topped with tofu foam. A meal at Yashin may not be cheap, but it's an experience not to be missed – and we couldn't fault the service either. The restaurant takes its wine seriously too, though you won't find much under £30.
Available for hire. Babies and children welcome: high chair. Booking advisable weekends.
Map 7 B9.

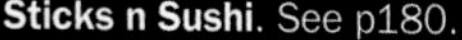

Sticks n Sushi. See p180.

Menu

Agedashidofu: tofu (qv) coated with katakuriko (potato starch), deep-fried, sprinkled with dried fish and served in a broth based on shoyu (qv), with grated ginger and daikon (qv).
Amaebi: sweet shrimps.
Anago: saltwater conger eel.
Bento: a meal served in a compartmentalised box.
Chawan mushi: savoury egg custard served in a tea tumbler (chawan).
Chutoro: medium fatty tuna from the upper belly.
Daikon: a long, white radish (aka mooli), often grated or cut into fine strips.
Dashi: the basic stock for Japanese soups and simmered dishes. It's often made from flakes of dried bonito (a type of tuna) and konbu (kelp).
Dobin mushi: a variety of morsels (prawn, fish, chicken, shiitake, ginkgo nuts) in a gently flavoured dashi-based soup, steamed (mushi) and served in a clay teapot (dobin).
Donburi: a bowl of boiled rice with various toppings, such as beef, chicken or egg.
Dorayaki: mini pancakes sandwiched around azuki bean paste.
Edamame: fresh soy beans boiled in their pods and sprinkled with salt.
Gari: pickled ginger, usually pink and thinly sliced; served with sushi to cleanse the palate between courses.
Gyoza: soft rice pastry cases stuffed with minced pork and herbs; northern Chinese in origin, cooked by a combination of frying and steaming.
Hamachi: young yellowtail or Japanese amberjack fish, commonly used for sashimi (qv) and also very good grilled.
Hashi: chopsticks.
Hiyashi chuka: Chinese-style ramen (qv, noodles) served cold (hiyashi) in tsuyu (qv) with a mixed topping that usually includes shredded ham, chicken, cucumber, egg and sweetcorn.
Ikura: salmon roe.
Izakaya: 'a place where there is saké'; an after-work drinking den frequented by Japanese businessmen, usually serving a wide range of reasonably priced food.
Kaiseki ryori: a multi-course meal of Japanese haute cuisine.
Kaiten-zushi: conveyor-belt sushi.
Karaage: deep-fried
Katsu: breaded and deep-fried meat, hence tonkatsu (pork katsu) and katsu curry (tonkatsu or chicken katsu with mild vegetable curry).
Kushiage: skewered morsels battered then deep-fried.
Maki: the word means 'roll' and this is a style of sushi (qv) where the rice and filling are rolled inside a sheet of nori (qv).
Mirin: a sweetened rice spirit used in many Japanese sauces and dressings.
Miso: a thick paste of fermented soy beans, used in miso soup and some dressings. Miso comes in a wide variety of styles: earthy, crunchy or smooth.
Miso shiru: classic miso soup, most often containing tofu and wakame (qv).
Nabemono: a class of dishes cooked at the table and served directly from the earthenware pot or metal pan.
Natto: fermented soy beans of stringy, mucous consistency.
Nimono: food simmered in a stock, often presented 'dry'.
Noodles: second only to rice as Japan's favourite staple. Served hot or cold, dry or in soup, and sometimes fried. There are many types, but the most common are **ramen** (Chinese-style egg noodles), **udon** (thick white wheat-flour noodles), **soba** (buckwheat noodles), and **somen** (thin white wheat-flour noodles, usually served cold as a summer dish – **hiyashi somen** – with a chilled dipping broth).
Nori: sheets of dried seaweed.
Okonomiyaki: the Japanese equivalent of filled pancakes or a Spanish omelette, whereby various ingredients are added to a batter mix and cooked on a hotplate, usually in front of diners.
Ponzu: usually short for ponzu joyu, a mixture of the juice of a Japanese citrus fruit (ponzu) and soy sauce. Used as a dip, especially with seafood and chicken or fish nabemono (qv).
Robatayaki: a kind of grilled food, generally cooked in front of customers, who make their selection from a large counter display.
Saké: rice wine, around 15% alcohol. Usually served hot, but may be chilled.
Sashimi: raw sliced fish.
Shabu shabu: a pan of stock is heated at the table and plates of thinly sliced raw beef and vegetables are cooked in it piece by piece ('shabu-shabu' is onomatopoeic for the sound of washing a cloth in water). The broth is then portioned out and drunk.
Shiso: perilla or beefsteak plant. A nettle-like leaf of the mint family that is often served with sashimi (qv).
Shochu: Japan's colourless answer to vodka is distilled from raw materials such as wheat, rice and potatoes.
Shoyu: Japanese soy sauce.
Sukiyaki: pieces of thinly sliced beef and vegetables are simmered in a sweet shoyu-based sauce at the table on a portable stove. Then they are taken out and dipped in raw egg (which semi-cooks on the hot food) to cool them for eating.
Sunomono: seafood or vegetables marinated (but not pickled) in rice vinegar.
Sushi: a combination of raw fish, shellfish or vegetables with rice – usually with a touch of wasabi (qv). Vinegar mixed with sugar and salt is added to the rice, which is then cooled before use. There are different sushi formats: **nigiri** (lozenge-shaped), **hosomaki** (thin-rolled), **futomaki** (thick-rolled), **temaki** (hand-rolled), **gunkan maki** (nigiri with a nori wrap), **chirashi** (scattered on top of a bowl of rice), and **uramaki** or **ISO maki** (more recently coined terms for inside-out rolls).
Tare: a general term for shoyu-based cooking marinades.
Tataki: meat or fish quickly seared, then marinated in vinegar, sliced thinly, and seasoned with ginger.
Tatami: a heavy straw mat – traditional Japanese flooring. A tatami room is usually a private room where you remove your shoes and sit on the floor to eat.
Tea: black tea is fermented, while green tea (**ocha**) is heat-treated by steam to prevent the leaves fermenting. **Matcha** is powdered green tea, and has a high caffeine content. **Bancha** is the coarsest grade of green tea, which has been roasted; it contains the stems or twigs of the plant as well as the leaves, and is usually served free of charge with a meal. **Hojicha** is lightly roasted bancha. **Mugicha** is roast barley tea, served iced in summer.
Tempura: fish, shellfish or vegetables dipped in a light batter and deep-fried. Served with tsuyu (qv), to which you add finely grated daikon (qv) and fresh ginger.
Teppanyaki: grilled on an iron plate. In modern Japanese restaurants, a chef standing at a hotplate (teppan) is surrounded by several diners. Slivers of beef, fish and vegetables are cooked and deposited on your plate.
Teriyaki: cooking method by which meat or fish – often marinated in shoyu (qv) and rice wine – is grilled and served in a tare (qv) made of a thick reduction of shoyu, saké (qv), sugar and spice.
Tofu: soy beancurd used fresh in simmered or grilled dishes, or deep-fried (**agedashidofu**, qv), or eaten cold (**hiyayakko**).
Tokkuri: saké flask – usually ceramic, but sometimes made of bamboo.
Tonkatsu: *see above* katsu.
Tsuyu: a general term for shoyu/mirin-based dips, served both warm and cold with various dishes ranging from tempura (qv) to cold noodles.
Umami: the nearest word in English is tastiness. After sweet, sour, salty and bitter, umami is considered the fifth primary taste in Japan, but not all food scientists in the West accept its existence.
Unagi: freshwater eel.
Uni: sea urchin roe.
Wakame: a type of young seaweed most commonly used in miso (qv) soup and kaiso (seaweed) salad.
Wasabi: a fiery green paste made from the root of an aquatic plant that belongs to the same family as horseradish. It is eaten in minute quantities (tucked inside sushi, qv), or diluted into shoyu (qv) for dipping sashimi (qv).
Yakimono: literally 'grilled things'.
Yakitori: grilled chicken (breast, wings, liver, gizzard, heart) served on skewers.
Zarusoba: soba noodles served cold, usually on a bamboo draining mat, with a dipping broth.
Zensai: appetisers.

OKAN
SET
LUNCH
6.50
☆Today's Okonomiyaki
☆Miso Soup
☆Salad
Weekdays only

Okan

South West

Putney

Chosan

292 Upper Richmond Road, SW15 6TH (8788 9626). East Putney tube or Putney rail. **Lunch served** noon-2.30pm Tue-Sun. **Dinner served** 6.30-10.30pm Tue-Sat; 6.30-10pm Sun. **Main courses** £3.30-£27.90. **Set lunch** £7.90-£13.90. **Set dinner** £18.90-£20.90; £20.90-£26.90 bento box. **Credit** MC, V.

Cosy, brightly lit and welcoming, Chosan brings the feel of an authentic Japanese family home to Putney. An elderly sushi chef works quietly behind an open bar, while softly spoken waitresses flutter around the tables. Every surface holds knick-knacks and mementos from the homeland – waving cats, teddy bear cushions, posters of Kyoto and even a fish tank. This quirky kitsch look, in stark contrast to the minimalist Japanese joints of central London, has garnered a loyal following of locals who are also attracted by the laid-back vibe and reasonable prices. There's something for everyone on the menu, from the familiar to the obscure. As well as fresh sushi and sashimi by the piece, you'll find izakaya favourites: from yakitori skewers to miso vegetables, comforting rice bowls and baskets of puffed-up vegetable and prawn tempura. We tried an unusual salad of royal ferns, which was silky and delicately flavoured, and a steaming pot of sukiyaki that had an intense sweet wine broth in which to cook generous slices of raw beef. Set menus will help those daunted by the large choice.

Babies and children admitted. Takeaway service.

Wimbledon

Sticks n Sushi NEW

36 Wimbledon Hill Road, SW19 7PA (3141 8800, www.sticksnsushi.com). Wimbledon tube/ rail. **Meals served** noon-10pm Mon, Tue, Sun; noon-11pm Wed-Sat. **Set meal** £6.50-£28; £28.50-£60 (minimum 2). **No credit cards.**

A Danish sushi chain, with nine branches in Copenhagen, and now one in Wimbledon. The cultural mix is not as strange as it might seem, the Danes being known for liking fish, clean flavours and simple aesthetics. It's a cavernous space, with a high brick wall on one side, and a huge curtain – printed to exactly match the facing brick wall – on the other. Danish chairs are integral to the design, as are the staff wearing black T-shirts printed with handy Danish words, and their English translations. Customers are greeted with what is supposed to be 'irrashaimase', the traditional greeting in Japanese restaurants – though the staff pronounced the word so badly, it took us a few repeats to realise what it was. The menus are aimed at neophytes: beautifully illustrated with photographs, and stripped of any challenging ingredients or dishes. To their credit, the sushi rice was excellent: warm and of fine quality. The sashimi too was fresh enough to serve in Japan. Presentation was consistently beautiful, with excellent use of colour contrasts. Attention to detail included good quality dipping sauces and miso soup – all made with care. For sushi novices, this is a terrific place to start; old hands may feel there's some excitement missing.

Babies and children welcome: children's menu; high chairs; nappy-changing facilities. Booking advisable dinner. Disabled: toilet. Takeaway service. Vegan dishes. Vegetarian menu.

South

Brixton

★ Okan NEW

2012 RUNNER-UP BEST NEW CHEAP EATS

Unit 39, Brixton Village Market, SW9 8PS (no phone, www.okanbrixtonvillage.com). Brixton tube/rail. **Lunch served** noon-3pm Wed-Fri; noon-4pm Sun. **Dinner served** 6-10pm Thur, Fri. **Meals served** noon-10pm Sat. **Main courses** £6.50-£8.25. **No credit cards.**

It might not be as busy as some of its Brixton Village counterparts, but Okan features some of the most unusual cuisine in the covered markets. Its focus on Japanese street food divides the menu into yaki soba noodle dishes and okonomiyaki – savoury pancakes with a flour, egg and shredded cabbage base. The latter are the highlight, topped with sesame-laced Japanese mayo (a thick, tangy, balsamic glaze-like sauce), dried seaweed and bonito fish flakes, which curl up into nothingness as you eat due to the heat from the pancake. It's a flavour combination that won't be to everyone's taste, but there's no denying the sweetness of the plump prawns that an Okan special was packed with – although the strips of processed-tasting squid were less impressive. Despite a smattering of framed Japanese prints, little wooden toys, and red and white paper lanterns, there's a very basic feel to the decor of wooden stools, scored tables and concrete floor in this tiny ex-industrial unit. The kitchen consists of a hotplate and sink behind a counter; you can't book; and they've only just obtained a licence to sell a small range of lager and saké. Nonetheless, there's a charm to the pared-back aesthetic. *Bookings not accepted.* **Map 22 E2.**

Clapham

Tsunami

5-7 Voltaire Road, SW4 6DQ (7978 1610, www.tsunamirestaurant.co.uk). Clapham North tube. **Lunch served** 12.30-4pm Sat, Sun. **Dinner served** 6-10.30pm Mon-Thur; 6-11pm Fri; 5.30-11pm Sat; 6-9.30pm Sun. **Main courses** £7.70-£19.50. **Set lunch** (Sat, Sun) £10.50. **Credit** MC, V.

On our weekend visit to Tsunami, smartly dressed thirtysomethings packed the place. This suburban sushi restaurant and cocktail bar has found a recipe for success and is sticking to it. The international waiting staff are warm and welcoming, the dining room glam but not intimidating, and the menu packed with modern Japanese crowd-pleasers. We began with a salad of beef tataki: seared slices of tender beef layered over rocket, beansprouts and red onion, dressed with sesame seeds and tangy, yuzu-based vinaigrette. Next, golden tempura-battered vegetables came in all textures, from soft sweet potato to chewy shiitake mushroom or crunchy lotus root. Sushi arrived beautifully presented on glazed earthenware, with slightly sweet, melt-in-the-mouth white tuna sashimi best enjoyed unadorned; dragon roll maki, combining sweet eel, avocado and tempura prawns, showed off the chefs' skills. The larger 'main course' section, dominated by meats in wasabi-based sauces, is somewhat tacky – head instead for the specials, where you might find crisp-skinned sea bass on a bed of braised gai lan (chinese broccoli). The small adjoining cocktail bar is a safe bet for pre- or post-prandial drinks.

Shimogamo. See p182.

Babies and children welcome: high chairs. Booking advisable; essential weekends. Takeaway service; delivery service (over £15 within 2-mile radius). **Map 22 B1.**
For branch see index.

North

Camden Town & Chalk Farm

Asakusa

265 Eversholt Street, NW1 1BA (7388 8533). Camden Town or Mornington Crescent tube. **Dinner served** 6-11.30pm Mon-Fri; 6-11pm Sat. **Main courses** £5.50-£13. **Credit** AmEx, MC, V.
Asakusa may not live up to the grandeur of its namesake Tokyo temple, but that doesn't stop this shabby little Camden restaurant from pulling in the crowds. The lack of windows and a low ceiling make the whole place a little dark, though the diminutive red, white and black dining room is far from sombre – as are the smiling staff. The long menu covers a range of classic dishes, including reasonable sushi and crisp vegetable tempura. For the budget-conscious, there are deals such as ginger pork or beef teriyaki, all served with rice and miso soup: a snip at around £8. If you're feeling adventurous, try some authentic (read: unusual) skewers from the specials menu. These include chicken gizzards and chicken skin as well as tamer options. Highlights of our most recent meal were super-fresh squid nigiri served with a sliver of shiso leaf; slow-simmered sweet and salty pork with a dab of fiery mustard; and chestnut ice-cream packed with nutty chunks to finish. We accompanied it all with a bottle of crisp Asahi Super Dry and some complimentary green tea.
Babies and children admitted. Booking advisable Thur-Sat. Takeaway service. **Map 27 D3.**

Shimogamo NEW

108 Parkway, NW1 7AN (7424 9560). Camden Town tube. **Lunch served** noon-2.30pm, **dinner served** 6-10pm Tue-Sun. **Main courses** £3.50-£20. **Set lunch** £10-£20. **Credit** AmEx, MC, V.
Kyoto's Shimogamo Shinto shrine is a place of quiet contemplation, so Shimogamo seems a suitable name for this small, relatively serene restaurant. The bland interior is just the sort of thing you find in the neighbourhood restaurants of suburban Kyoto (from where both the chef and owner hail). These neighbourhood joints try to cater for a variety of tastes under one roof, as does Shimogamo, which offers sushi and sashimi, sukiyaki (hotpots), teriyaki skewers, gyoza dumplings, Japanese salads, soba or udon noodles, and chef's specials. On our visit, the latter included beef hobayaki, a dish seldom seen in London. (Hoba, a type of Japanese magnolia, has a big, tough leaf that's used to wrap food before grilling it.) Here, it's cooked on a beautiful table-top hibachi grill. It's a good piece of table theatre, and resulted in almost autumnal flavours. Simple dishes such as sashimi are also artfully presented, and the quality was impeccable. Not all the dishes were such a success: deep-frying doesn't seem to be a strength, as vegetable tempura was indelicate, the batter claggy. A decent selection of sakés comes in a range of prices – *kampai*! (cheers!).
Babies and children welcome: children's menu; high chairs. Booking advisable. Tables outdoors (5, pavement). Vegetarian menu. **Map 27 C3.**

Crouch End

★ Wow Simply Japanese

18 Crouch End Hill, N8 8AA (8340 4539, www.wowsimplyjapanese.co.uk). Finsbury Park tube/ rail then bus W3, W7, or Crouch Hill rail. **Lunch served** noon-2.30pm Wed-Sat. **Dinner served** 6-10.30pm Mon-Sat; 6-10pm Sun. **Main courses** £7.80-£35. **Set lunch** £5.90-£8.90. **Credit** MC, V.
This neat, cream-walled box of a restaurant conveys 'Japanese' with the simplest of ornamentation: two folk masks between the arched windows, and a straw saké keg over the door. The main menu looks more traditional than the fusion-leaning repertoire offered when Wow opened in 2006, though there's still a welcome preponderance of garlic, chilli and coriander. The pungent garlic and spring onion on our beef tataki tasted so good with the silky slivers of rare meat that we felt reluctant to use the accompanying ponzu. And the garlic rice rocks. No wonder staff pop mint imperials on the salver with the bill. The specials list seems less special now that it features such workaday dishes as tori kara age (deep-fried chicken) alongside sea bass carpaccio. However, the bottom line is attractive, with bento lunches costing under £10 and dinner comfortably inside the £25-a-head zone. And Wow seems to suit any type of diner: pairs of friends, groups, couples, the odd single, families at weekends. Staff don't always know their stuff, but service is comfortably paced. This being Crouch End, the wine list includes a couple of organic labels.
Babies and children welcome: high chairs. Booking advisable. Takeaway service; delivery service (over £15 within 2-mile radius).

North West

Golders Green

Café Japan

626 Finchley Road, NW11 7RR (8455 6854). Golders Green tube or bus 13, 82. **Lunch served** noon-2pm Tue-Fri; noon-2.30pm Sat, Sun. **Dinner served** 6-10pm Tue-Sat; 6-9.30pm Sun. **Main courses** £9-£23. **Set lunch** £8.50-£15.50. **Set dinner** £14-£22. **Credit** MC, V.
Ownership has changed over the years (since 1996), but the name, decor and busy-ness are constants. On an all-bases-covered menu, highlights include soft-shell crab in batter with ponzu, and ika natto maki (squid, fermented soy bean and spring onion). Although the tare is too sweet, unagi features a generous blanket of eel over its traditional lacquered box of rice. Other decent grilled dishes include butterfish teriyaki and hamachi kama (salt-grilled yellowtail head). Sufficient waiting staff, smiling and eager, keep orders flowing smoothly between the close-quarters tables, sushi/grill counter and back kitchen. Children and Japanese dining novices get a helping hand with makeshift cheat chopsticks that utilise wadded napkins and elastic bands. New to the set-up is a loyalty card. Staid menu, ultra-basic dessert choice (green tea, azuki or chestnut ice-cream in a retro chrome bowl), After Eights with the bill, handwritten receipts – Café Japan can induce nostalgia, which appears to be what Golders Greeners want. Eat Tokyo around the corner does all right, Hi Sushi next door could do better, but Café Japan is doing great. So yes, you need to book.
Babies and children admitted. Booking advisable dinner; bookings not accepted lunch. Takeaway service.

Hampstead

Jin Kichi

73 Heath Street, NW3 6UG (7794 6158, www.jinkichi.com). Hampstead tube. **Lunch served** 12.30-2pm Tue-Sun. **Dinner served** 6-10.45pm Tue-Sat; 6-10pm Sun. **Main courses** £14-£16. **Set lunch** £9-£17. **Credit** AmEx, MC, V.
This neat, traditional eaterie set around a grill counter may lack the flashiness of many other restaurants in the heart of Hampstead, but it's enduringly popular with locals. The Hampstead sushi roll (inside-out, with prawn, watercress, avocado and egg) gives a wink to the luxuries of the moneyed classes, as does sakana nanban (premium fish including turbot, bream and sea bass deep-fried and marinated in vinegar). The wide-ranging menu covers everything from restrained ume cha (rice in fish stock soup) to hearty katsu curries. Zingy pork and shiso rolls, asparagus, and jumbo prawns are among the pleasures of the grill. We also enjoyed some crisp, pleasingly chewy and grease-free tempura vegetables (sweet potato, pumpkin, courgette, asparagus and more), plus succulent nasu-den (aubergine with sweet red miso sauce). Green tea (free of charge) was the right choice for lunch, but boozy possibilities include Japanese beers, plum wine and hot or chilled sake. The Japanese staff were patient, friendly and accommodating, offering honest advice about the size of our order; to be picky, our dishes should have arrived quicker. Diners range from mums with buggies (there is limited room for these in the cramped ground-floor space) to local workers who don't seem put off by the Hampstead pricing.
Babies and children welcome: high chairs. Booking advisable. Takeaway service. **Map 28 B2.**

Willesden

Sushi-Say

33B Walm Lane, NW2 5SH (8459 2971). Willesden Green tube. **Lunch served** noon-3.30pm Sat, Sun. **Dinner served** 6.30-10pm Wed-Fri; 6.30-10.30pm Sat; 6-9.30pm Sun. **Main courses** £7.20-£24.60. **Set dinner** £23.50-£39.50. **Credit** MC, V.
It may not look like much from the outside, but that hasn't stopped locals from cottoning on to just how good Sushi-Say is – the place is rarely empty. Following a warm welcome from the sushi chef, you're ushered into the long, simply adorned dining room. The no-nonsense matron is happy to talk you through the menu, which offers plenty of variety, including the usual tempura, teriyaki and noodle dishes: all done to a high standard. A mound of cold zaru soba noodles with a subtle soy-based dipping sauce proved perfect for a summer's day. Many opt for thickly sliced and perfectly fresh sashimi, or sushi. Surf clam nigiri was sweet and meaty with just a little resistance, while a salmon-skin maki was rich and earthy, if not as crisp as we'd expected. Don't be surprised by the absence of wasabi on the side of your rolls: the chef has already added it, and is confident he's used the right amount. If you join the ranks of the regulars, you can accompany a meal with your own bottle of saké kept behind the bar.
Babies and children welcome: high chairs. Booking advisable. Separate room for parties, seats 8. Takeaway service. Vegetarian menu.

Jewish

For the most varied choice of kosher dining establishments, you'll still need to visit the hotspots in the north-west of London, especially Hendon (NW4), Golders Green (NW11) and Edgware. Nevertheless, this year there has been some action in the previously near-moribund Jewish restaurant scene in central London. First, **Bevis Marks**, the most upmarket establishment in this section, has found a new home a short distance away from its synagogue namesake at the eastern edge of the City; and second, new venture **Deli West One** has opened in close proximity to **Reubens**, which was previously the only kosher eaterie in the West End. Like Reubens, the new arrival specialises in Ashkenazi cuisine, which has its roots in eastern Europe; chopped liver and salt beef are classics of the genre. **Mishkin's** (*see p24*) in Covent Garden also serves classic New York deli food, but is not kosher. The other main strand of Jewish cuisine is Sephardi cookery, originating in Mediterranean countries. **Dizengoff**, with its houmous, Israeli salads and baklava is one of the few London venues to offer a decent choice of these dishes.

However, most restaurants geared to Jewish diners in the capital do not offer Jewish food. Yes, they follow the strict rules of kashrut (so no mixing of dairy and meat, and no pork or shellfish), but their kitchens are influenced by a wide range of cooking styles. Witness this year's other newcomers: **Brasserie 103** serves a modern, globally influenced menu; **So Yo** is a popular new café with crêpes and salads in its repertoire; and **White Fish** offers an Asian/Med-influenced take on piscine cuisine.

Central

City

Bevis Marks Restaurant

3 Middlesex Street, E1 7AA (7247 5474, www.bevismarkstherestaurant.com). Aldgate tube or Liverpool Street tube/rail.
Bar **Open/meals served** noon-2.15pm Mon-Fri; 5.30-9pm Mon-Thur. **Main courses** £5.50-£12.50.
Restaurant **Lunch served** noon-2.15pm Mon-Fri. **Dinner served** 5.30-9pm Mon-Thur. **Main courses** £16.50-£27.95. **Credit** AmEx, MC, V.
This smart kosher restaurant has relocated from next to Bevis Marks synagogue into new, slightly nondescript premises. The plain interior has a bar where diners can snack (steak sandwich with tomato salsa, or salmon and cod pie) while perched on high stools, and a bigger dining section filled with white linen-clothed tables. Apart from some wallpaper and a flower arrangement, there's little decoration. The menu features classics alongside newer dishes. Chicken soup with matzo balls (just one little dumpling) lacked depth of flavour, and the matzo ball was pretty heavy, but the soup did have ample lockshen. Next, salt beef with 'frites' and beet with horseradish relish was better, a generous portion featuring fine salt beef, good relish and beautifully cooked chunky chips. But a starter of shredded salt beef, Thai herbs and noodle salad didn't convince, as the meat overpowered the other ingredients. We felt more kindly disposed towards a main of cured duck breast with smooth cauliflower mash and cranberry clove salsa. To finish, steamed apricot pudding with cardamom coconut custard was a sterling dessert, despite being dairy-free. Service is friendly and attentive. Overall, though, Bevis Marks will rarely entice anyone who doesn't require kosher food. Prices match those of London's best restaurants, while quality lags behind.
Available for hire. Babies and children admitted. Booking advisable lunch. Disabled: toilet. Kosher supervised (Shephardi). Separate rooms for parties, seating 8 and 24. Tables outdoors (4, pavement). Takeaway service. **Map 12 R6.**

Marylebone

★ Deli West One NEW

51 Blandford Street, W1U 7JH (7224 4033, www.thedelilondon.com). Bond Street tube.
Meals served 11am-10pm Mon-Thur, Sun; 11.30am-4pm Fri. **Main courses** £8.50-£10. **Credit** AmEx, MC, V.
This new deli/takeaway was started by four men (two of them New Yorkers) with a taste for genuine Jewish cookery, who set about creating an authentic deli in the heart of London. Busy staff behind the counter prepare real Ashkenazi food, with the owners promising it's as good as their mamma's. The short, value-for-money menu is aimed at local workers looking for a quick lunch. A 'Half & Half' deal offers any half-size home-cured meat sandwich with soup, salad or chopped liver: a more than adequate meal for less than the price of a main course elsewhere. The fat had been removed from the salt beef, so it lacked some flavour, but the tongue in a rye bread sandwich was succulent. The chicken soup (which tasted almost homemade) came with a massive matzo ball. We saw a honey-mustard turkey sandwich and a giant hot dog going past – they looked pretty enticing too. Side dishes are variable: an Israeli chopped salad was crunchy, but the coleslaw and pickle lacked flavour. Catering platters can also be ordered, and roast chicken and award-winning cholent are available for Shabbat. It's not exactly home cooking, but the chocolate brownies are brilliant.

Bevis Marks Restaurant. See p183.

Babies and children admitted. Booking advisable lunch. Kosher supervised (Beth Din). Tables outdoors (4, pavement). Takeaway service. **Map 9 G5.**

Reubens

79 Baker Street, W1U 6RG (7486 0035, www.reubensrestaurant.co.uk). Baker Street tube. **Lunch served** 11.30am-4pm Mon-Thur; 11.30am-3pm Fri. **Dinner served** 5.30-10pm Mon-Thur. **Meals served** 11.30am-10pm Sun. **Main courses** £9-£29. **Minimum** (restaurant) £10. **Credit** MC, V.

Deli West One (*see p183*) is now open around the corner, but Reubens is still holding its own – though the ground-floor cafeteria could do with a makeover. The cold blue walls and granite tables are unwelcoming, but the food is reliably haimische (home-style), appealing to those who like Ashkenazi staples. The menu is extensive, with sandwiches, shwarma, grills and burgers cooked to order, and attractive-looking salads on display. Downstairs in the pricier basement restaurant (with linen tablecloths and waiter service), you'll find more adventurous dishes: magret of duck, steak diane, beef wellington and sushi-grade tuna. Little changes: the salt beef is moist, and as flavourful as it can be with the fat removed. Prime-cut lamb chops (a generous serving) arrived perfectly chargrilled, with refreshing watercress and tomato on the side. Salads are appetising and fresh, especially the waldorf with walnuts and apple. Sautéed potatoes with fried onion make a pleasant change from chips (also available, of course). After soup and a large main course, few people have the appetite for apple strudel or hefty lockshen pudding. Instead, you could share a chocolate fondant with pistachio ice 'cream'.

Available for hire. Babies and children welcome: children's menu; high chairs. Booking advisable. Kosher supervised (Shephardi). Separate room for parties, seats 50. Tables outdoors (3, pavement). Takeaway service. **Map 3 G5.**

West

Shepherd's Bush

Isola Bella

Westfield London, W12 7SL (8740 6611, www.isolabella.co.uk). Wood Lane tube. **Meals served** *Summer* 10am-10pm Mon-Thur, Sun; 10am-5pm Fri. *Winter* 10am-10pm Mon-Thur, Sun; 10am-5pm Fri; 1hr after sabbath-10pm Sat. **Main courses** £8-£21. **Set lunch** £18 3 courses incl soft drink. **Credit** AmEx, MC, V.

Set in the airy Westfield shopping mall, Isola Bella doesn't advertise the fact that it is kosher, competing well with other elegant venues offering food all day. Tables are well spaced, and staff are cheery and efficient. The menu caters for morning shoppers wanting a Mediterranean-type breakfast – shakshouka (eggs poached in a spicy tomato sauce), eggs florentine – as well as late-night diners who can expect two distinct cuisines: Italian and Thai. There's a wide choice, with the emphasis on fish and fresh vegetables. Sandwiches (delicious hot bread from the in-store bakery) and salads are, like the soup casseroles, grand in size. A top-notch avocado and smoked salmon salad featured fresh ingredients in a pleasant dressing, but ko pangan stir-fried noodles lacked much oriental flavour. Fish dishes, such as whole sea bass, sizzling tuna or teriyaki salmon, looked appetising. Floored by the huge portions, we could only drool at the dessert menu. The cakes, flown in from Israel, include chocolate, cream, meringue, caramel and tiramisu. The himalaya gateau is a combination of nearly all of these. Next time, maybe...

Available for hire. Babies and children welcome: children's menu; high chairs; nappy-changing facilities. Booking advisable. Disabled: lift; toilet. Kosher supervised (Beth Din). Separate room for parties, seats 50. Takeaway service. Vegetarian menu. **Map 20 C1.**

For branch see index.

North West

Golders Green

Brasserie 103 NEW

103 Golders Green Road, NW11 8EN (8458 7273, www.brasserie103.com). Golders Green tube. **Meals served** noon-11pm Mon-Thur, Sun. **Main courses** £13-£29. **Set lunch** £11.95 2 courses. **Set meal** £16.90-£21.90 2 courses incl coffee. **Credit** AmEx, MC, V.

Mindful that there are nine other kosher establishments within a stone's throw, the new Brasserie offers sophistication and an ambitious menu that includes high-quality meat, fish and sushi, an impressive wine list and adventurous-sounding desserts. The venue seems poised to thrive, with its well-spaced tables already packed at every sitting. There's a buzz of expectant diners choosing from dishes rarely seen in kosher London: duck terrine, warm foie gras, salmon tartare. Starter salads, featuring the likes of tender chicken livers or quinoa and roast vegetables, come in generous portions. However, our grilled portobello mushrooms with pomegranate had too much apple miso dressing. To follow, hamburgers and grilled chicken with decent chips both got the thumbs up – though the fettuccine bolognese could have had a more savoury meat sauce, and both the veal milanese and an overcooked chocolate fondant needed more attention, given the premium prices charged. Families praise the chicken bento box. There's much to explore here: duck breast sous vide, an entire sushi menu, as well as sea bass or salmon tandoori. We're tempted to return, if only to try the passionfruit or praline mousse. Service was exemplary, and Sunday lunch is good value.

Available for hire. Babies and children welcome: children's menu; high chairs; nappy-changing facilities. Booking advisable. Disabled: toilet.

Kosher supervised (Beth Din). Tables outdoors (3, pavement). Takeaway service; delivery service (over £30 within 3-mile radius).

Dizengoff

118 Golders Green Road, NW11 8HB (8458 7003). Golders Green tube. **Meals served** noon-11pm Mon-Thur, Sun; noon-4pm Fri; 6pm-midnight Sat. **Main courses** £18-£21. **Set lunch** £7.95-£12.95 3 courses. **Set meal** £24.95-£26.95 3 courses. **Credit** MC, V.

Dizengoff's owner, Ami, made a good decision to close his nearby deli and revamp this main restaurant. The new pale decor, with low lighting, comfortable olive chairs and wooden tables, is welcoming. On a rainy weekday, the set lunch seemed a wise choice and individual dishes each turned out well. Chicken soup contained the required light knaidlach, and butter bean and barley soup had a warming depth of flavour. Houmous and the chopped liver can always be relied upon too. The 'Dizengoff special' consists of grilled chicken thighs, not over-spiced, served with moreish chips or flavoursome rice. Israeli salad is also included. Grilled lamb chops or steaks, stuffed vegetables and Greek-style baked lamb are among the choices at dinner. Each main course is served in a generous plateful, yet this style of classic Jewish food (sourced from the Mediterranean and the Middle East) doesn't leave you feeling over-full. The staff, speaking a dozen languages between them, communicate happily with the varied clientele, who frequently return to this favourite spot. Relaxing over baklava and mint tea, we judged this the pick of a street filled with kosher restaurants.

Babies and children welcome: children's menu; high chairs. Booking advisable weekends. Kosher supervised (Beth Din). Tables outdoors (3, pavement). Takeaway service; delivery service (phone for details).

La Fiesta

235 Golders Green Road, NW11 9ES (8458 0444, www.lafiestalondon.co.uk). Brent Cross tube. **Dinner served** 6-11pm Mon-Thur. **Meals served** noon-11pm Sun. **Main courses** £16-£50. **Credit** MC, V.

The decor at La Fiesta has changed again, with guitars and huge cowhides now hanging on the walls. Solid wooden tables are hefty enough to hold the braziers of hot coals that are brought to table by pleasant waitresses. The menu is now billed as Mexican rather than Argentinian, but it hasn't changed substantially and remains that of a South American grill (hence, you won't find mole, tacos or tortillas). To start, there are empanadas, chorizo and soups, but most diners head straight for the complimentary salad and the meat: entrecôte steaks or asado ribs; tender lamp chops or a brochette of mixed cuts – all sizzling hot and with appetising aromas. Portions are more than generous; chips just so. There's grilled chicken for those who don't want red meat; salmon or sea bass for fish eaters; but this is no place for vegetarians (vegetable dishes are limited to indifferent onion and pepper skewers or mushrooms in wine sauce). The main deal is the meat: charred outside, succulent within. Desserts include crêpes with parev ice-cream, but to our minds it would be better to end with a refreshing glass of lemon tea.

Available for hire. Babies and children welcome: children's menu; high chairs. Booking advisable. Disabled: toilet. Kosher supervised (Beth Din). Takeaway service.

So Yo

94 Golders Green Road, NW11 8HB (8458 8788, www.so-yo.co.uk). Golders Green tube. **Meals served** 8.30am-12.45am Mon-Thur, Sun; 8.30am-5.30pm Fri; 11pm-3am Sat. **Main courses** £7-£20. **Credit** AmEx, MC, V.

Billed as an espresso bar, this small restaurant is packed from morning to evening. Punters squeeze into closely set tables, illuminated by a stylish light made of tiny ice-cream spoons. You might need to shout above the noise to the occasionally surly waitress, but the range of dishes is encouraging. Breakfast with pancakes, french toast or omelettes continues until 3pm. A good choice is shakshouka: eggs poached in a spicy tomato sauce. In the afternoon, you could pop in for dessert crêpes or passionfruit mousse, with a freshly squeezed fruit juice. We braved the lunchtime crowds for a robust mushroom soup and well-filled savoury crêpe. Salads are stylish, especially the 'champagne' with blue cheese, grapes, raisins and pear, sprinkled with crunchy pumpkin and sunflower seeds. (We chose sesame dressing instead of the sweeter raspberry champagne version.) A quiche or sandwich would make a good prelude to So Yo's signature frozen yoghurt, where there's a choice of about 20 fruit and candy toppings. Food is fresh and lively, and brought quickly, but staff need to pay more attention to customers.

Available for hire. Babies and children welcome: children's menu; high chairs; nappy-changing facilities. Booking advisable. Kosher supervised (Federation). Separate room for parties, seats 50. Tables outdoors (4, pavement). Takeaway service.

Hendon

White Fish NEW

10-12 Bell Lane, NW4 2AD (8202 8780, www.whitefishrestaurant.co.uk). Hendon Central tube. **Lunch served** noon-2.30pm, **dinner served** 5-10.30pm Mon-Thur. **Meals served** noon-10.30pm Sun. **Main courses** £13-£20. **Set lunch** £9.95 2 courses incl soft drink. **Credit** AmEx, MC, V.

There's a measure of ambition at this family-run restaurant: photos of Billingsgate fish market in the 1940s line the walls; the wooden tables are well spaced, with comfortable leather chairs. Cooking takes place in full view, on state-of-the-art stainless-steel fryers and grills. Hand-fried crisps are offered as nibbles. Soup (choice of four) comes in large bowls; a well-judged gazpacho had a mound of cucumber and avocado at its centre. Fish features in a wide choice of dishes – from fish cakes and samosas for starters to main courses including kedgeree and Thai curries. Most popular is the standard fried fish served with chunky chips, though ours didn't quite come up to expectations. Nevertheless, salmon steak with new potatoes and tomato and basil salsa was perfectly grilled, and whole sea bass, plaice on the bone and spicy grilled sardines all looked like promising options. The extensive menu also includes vegetarian choices such as spring rolls, tempura and Thai noodles. The friendly waiter persuaded us to have dessert, so we finished with a large slice of own-made cheesecake and a cappuccino, promising to return another time.

Available for hire. Babies and children welcome: children's menu; high chairs. Booking advisable. Kosher supervised (Beth Din). Takeaway service; delivery service (over £15 within 2-mile radius).

Menu

Baklava: filo pastry layered with almonds or pistachios and soaked in scented syrup.
Borekas: triangles of filo pastry with savoury fillings like cheese or spinach.
Borscht: a classic beetroot soup served either hot or cold, often with sour cream.
Challah or **cholla**: egg-rich, slightly sweet plaited bread for the Sabbath.
Chicken soup: a clear, golden broth made from chicken and vegetables.
Cholent: a hearty, long-simmered bean, vegetable and (sometimes) meat stew, traditionally served for the Sabbath.
Chopped liver: chicken or calf's liver fried with onions, finely chopped and mixed with hard-boiled egg and chicken fat. Served cold, often with extra egg and onions.
Chrane or **chrain**: a pungent sauce made from grated horseradish and beetroot, served with cold fish.
Cigars: rolls of filo pastry with a sweet or savoury filling.
Falafel: spicy, deep-fried balls of ground chickpeas, served with houmous and tahina (sesame paste).
Gefilte fish: white fish minced with onions, made into balls and poached or fried; served cold. The sweetened version is Polish.
Kataifi or **konafa**: shredded filo pastry wrapped around a nut or cheese filling, soaked in syrup.
Kibbe, **kuba**, **kooba**, **kubbeh** or **kobeiba**: oval patties, handmade from a shell of crushed wheat (bulgar) filled with minced meat, pine nuts and spices. Shaping and filling the shells before frying is the skill.
Knaidlach or **kneidlach**: dumplings made from matzo (qv) meal and eggs, poached until they float 'like clouds' in chicken soup.
Kreplach: pockets of noodle dough filled with meat and served in soup, or with sweet fillings and eaten with sour cream.
Laffa: large puffy pitta bread used to enclose falafel or shwarma (qv).
Latkes: grated potato mixed with egg and fried into crisp pancakes.
Lockshen: egg noodles boiled and served in soup. When cold, they can be mixed with egg, sugar and cinnamon and baked into a pudding.
Matzo or **matzah**: flat squares of unleavened bread. When ground into meal, it is used to make a crisp coating for fish or schnitzel.
Parev or **parve**: a term describing food that is neither meat nor dairy.
Rugelach: crescent-shaped biscuits made from a rich, cream cheese pastry, filled with nuts, jam or chocolate. Popular in Israel and the US.
Shwarma: layers of lamb or turkey, cooked on a spit, served with pitta.
Worsht: beef salami, sliced thinly to eat raw, but usually cut in thick pieces and fried when served with eggs or chips.

Korean

Despite the number of Korean dining options in London steadily increasing of late, the cuisine is still passing under the radar of many of the capital's inhabitants. Which is highly gratifying for culinary adventurers keen to try this fascinating, chilli-rich food away from the folderols of fashion. The cooking style has much in common with the Japanese repertoire, though barbecuing is a mainstay, and delectable kimchi pickles pep things up further. And you don't have to travel far from the centre or spend a fortune to sample the genuine article. Some of the best Korean restaurants are clustered in the West End: Fitzrovia's **Koba** topping the pile, but modest establishments such as **Jindalle** usually coming up trumps too. To explore Korean cookery in greater depth, you'll need to head to 'Korea Town' in New Malden, on the city's south-western outskirts. Thousands of South Koreans have settled in the locality, and many businesses have their signs written in Hangul script as well as English. **Jee Cee Neh**, **Korea House** and **Korea Garden** are our current choices, though **Cah Chi** in nearby Raynes Park is worth a punt too.

Central

City

Ceena

13 St Bride Street, EC4A 4AS (7936 4941, www.ceena.co.uk). City Thameslink rail, Farringdon tube/rail or bus 17, 45, 46, 63. **Meals served** 11.30am-9.30pm Mon-Fri. **Main courses** £9-£16. **Set meal** £13.20-£17 3 courses. **Credit** AmEx, MC, V.

Despite the casual diner feel – high stools at a horseshoe counter wrapped around a tiny serving area – Ceena manages to serve classy fast Korean food. City slickers pop in for lunch, along with the odd bemused couple who look out of place but tuck in happily to some great staple dishes. Grills of kalbi, bulgogi and kochi (barbecued skewers, marinated in soy or red pepper sauce), and a small but coherent range of bibimbap are the orders of the day, either prepared at the end of the counter (lunchtime) or in the basement kitchen (evening), their freshness evident in both cases. Beef kalbi was tasty, moist and flavoursome, and a perfect foil to the two perfectly textured and seasoned bowls of cabbage and radish kimchi. The searing heat of a stone bowl filled with pork belly bibimbap produced wonderfully crisp crusted rice and a delicious cooked egg yolk. Staff were friendly, service swift, the menu short and the food gorgeous. What more could you want? Fellow diners in the evening, perhaps, when the emphasis is on takeaways and the staff power-walk out with large insulated bags – but the food can't be faulted.

Available for hire. Babies and children admitted. Booking advisable. Separate room for parties, seats 8. Tables outdoors (3, pavement). Takeaway service; delivery service (over £15 within 2-mile radius). Vegetarian menu. **Map 11 N6.**

Covent Garden

Naru

230 Shaftesbury Avenue, WC2H 8EG (7379 7962, www.narurestaurant.com). Tottenham Court Road tube. **Lunch served** noon-3pm, **dinner served** 6-10.30pm Mon-Sat. **Main courses** £8-£13. **Set dinner** £24.50-£34.50 3 courses. **Credit** MC, V.

Naru is one of the more reliable central London Korean restaurants. The menu describes itself as combining western and Korean styles, yet this is no Korea-lite. Presentation is considered and artful, but the dishes deliver a proper kick of spicy, sour and sweet flavours. The surroundings too are gentle on the eye; the walls of the long narrow room are hung with framed rice-paper calligraphy. There are chunky wooden tables, plus a few banquettes at the back (great for larger groups). The Asian pop, however, is anything but restful on the ear. All the Korean standards are on the menu: various sorts of bulgogi, bibimbap, noodle dishes and lots of warming, filling chigaes, combining tofu, pork, kimchi and vegetables. There are no table-top barbecues, though – all dishes are cooked in the downstairs kitchen. P'ajeon with kimchi was less spicy than some Korean pancakes we've tried, but crisp and hot. Bo ssam – tender, slow-cooked pork – was sweet and mellow, and worked well with a side dish of crunchy pickled cucumbers and a cooling Korean beer. Naru gets busy at lunchtime and pre- and post-theatre, but staff usually manage to keep smiling.

Babies and children admitted. Booking advisable Thur-Sat. Takeaway service. Vegan dishes. Vegetarian menu. **Map 18 D2.**

Fitzrovia

★ Koba HOT 50

11 Rathbone Street, W1T 1NA (7580 8825). Goodge Street or Tottenham Court Road tube. **Lunch served** noon-2.15pm Mon-Sat. **Dinner served** 6-10.30pm daily. **Main courses** £8-£11. **Set lunch** £6.50-£11.50. **Set meal** £25-£35. **Credit** AmEx, MC, V.

From the minimalist decor, to friendly service and meticulously prepared food, Koba is a slick operation. The industrial beige and black dining room is often bustling with all sorts of punters enjoying tender barbecued meat, crispy p'ajeon pancakes or attractively stacked Korean-style beef tartare, washed down with a Hite beer. Samsaek milssam proved a colourful choice: green, white and orange rice-flour pancakes stuffed with sweet simmered beef and earthy vegetables. An iron-pot stew of soft tofu with morsels of baby octopus came out sizzling in a tongue-tinglingly rich and

spicy broth. Deftly cooked on our table-top barbecue, the ossam bulgogi was another winner: pieces of creamy squid and pork belly in a chilli-packed, sweet and sticky sauce, which caramelised pleasingly on the grill. To round things off, a striking slate-grey bowl of black sesame ice-cream proved one of the best we've tried – deep, rich, sweet and smoky with just a hint of bitterness. Koba makes a great spot for anything from a business lunch or special-occasion feast to a casual dinner. We've yet to be disappointed.
Babies and children welcome: high chairs. Booking advisable. Disabled: toilet. Separate room for parties, seats 30. Takeaway service. **Map 17 B1.**

Holborn

Asadal

227 High Holborn, WC1V 7DA (7430 9006, www.asadal.co.uk). Holborn tube. **Lunch served** noon-2.30pm daily. **Dinner served** 6-10.30pm Mon-Sat; 6-10pm Sun. **Main courses** £8-£28. **Set lunch** £10-£15. **Set dinner** £20-£35 per person (minimum 2). **Credit** AmEx, MC, V.
If you weren't paying attention you could easily miss the entrance to Asadal, right next to Holborn tube station. Head down to the large, low-lit restaurant, and you're worlds away from the busy junction above. As well as the central dining room – often bustling with a mix of business people, shoppers and expat Koreans – there are a few more intimate booths and private rooms. You'll find all the classics on the menu, including chapch'ae, bulgogi beef and crispy p'ajeon. Arriving close to last orders on a lunchtime visit, we weren't given much time to choose our food, but ordering over, things relaxed. Yuk hwe arrived promptly: cool, savoury strands of raw beef, sweet pear and crushed pine nuts, all made unctuous with an egg yolk. The tolsot bibimbap came sizzling to the table, with just the right amount of crispy rice at the bottom and plenty of meat and veg on top, which we were trusted to mix ourselves. Unusually, there's no barley tea here, but you'll find plenty else to choose from on the drinks menu including Korean beer, soju and wine.
Babies and children welcome: high chairs. Booking advisable. Disabled: toilet. Separate rooms for parties, seating 6 and 12. Takeaway service. Vegetarian menu. **Map 18 E2.**

Leicester Square

Jindalle

6 Panton Street, SW1Y 4DL (7930 8881). Piccadilly Circus tube. **Meals served** noon-10.45pm daily. **Main courses** £6.90-£10.90. **Set lunch** £3.90-£8.90. **Set dinner** (5-9pm) £18.90-£24.90. **Credit** AmEx, MC, V.
Jindalle's location, just off Leicester Square in a street filled with cheap but cheerless eats, isn't a great start. Its exterior gives little inkling of what lies inside, but don't be put off: this small, unassuming barbecue restaurant offers very decent Korean food at moderate prices, served by quietly efficient staff who are happy to advise novices. Everything about the place is understated; the interior is pleasant rather than special, with oversized chairs cramming the long narrow space. Nevertheless, the predominantly Korean clientele park themselves at tables fitted with barbecues, usually opting for a set meal. Our choice, marinated beef, was part of an £8.90 pre-theatre special, which included rice, miso soup and a pretty trio of fermented salads; it was cooked to perfection by our waiter. In contrast, an accompanying kimchi pancake was greasy and bland, and barbecued belly pork, while tasty, was served plain and in a paltry portion. Still, a side of cabbage kimchi happily filled the hunger gaps. On the next table, three friends were sharing an immense and tempting-looking dumpling hotpot, but the huge selection of barbecued meats is what to choose in this genial space.
Babies and children welcome: high chairs. Booking advisable. Disabled: toilet. Vegetarian menu. **Map 17 C5.**

Asadal

Mayfair

Kaya

42 Albemarle Street, W1S 4JH (7499 0622, www.kayarestaurant.co.uk). Green Park tube. **Lunch served** noon-2.30pm, **dinner served** 6-10.30pm Mon-Sat. **Main courses** £9-£17. **Set lunch** £15 4 courses. **Set dinner** £45 4 courses. **Credit** AmEx, MC, V.
On the smarter end of the Korean food scene, Kaya has the refined atmosphere you'd expect from a restaurant around the corner from Cartier. The ground-floor dining room, frequented by expats, shoppers and (at weekends) families, is fitted out in calming cream and beige, with a vibrant mountain-scene mural topped with colourful palace-style roof eaves to greet you at the front. The basement is less glamorous, however, as you'll find out if you venture to the toilet. Highlights of the menu are perfectly crisp mandu dumplings with a subtle minced pork filling, succulent barbecue dishes, spicy stews and flavoursome bibimbap. You'll also find imperial elements such as the set ten-dish 'royal dinner' including gu shui pan: a lacquer box filled with tasty morsels of meat and veg that you wrap in rice-flour pancakes. On a recent visit, bo ssam – sliced pork belly wrapped in chinese cabbage with hot radish kimchi, salty shrimp sauce and sweet, spicy ssamjang (bean paste) – made a great sharing dish, though it's not for the chopstick novice. Service was impeccable as always, and our teacups were regularly topped up with free barley tea.
Babies and children admitted. Booking advisable. Disabled: toilet. Separate rooms for parties, seating 8 and 12. **Map 9 J7.**

Soho

★ Bi Bim Bap

11 Greek Street, W1D 4DJ (7287 3434, www.bibimbapsoho.com). Tottenham Court Road tube. **Lunch served** noon-2.30pm, **dinner served** 6-10.30pm Mon-Fri. **Meals served** noon-10.30pm Sat. **Main courses** £6.45-£9.95. **Credit** DC, MC, V.
'We love bibimbap' – that's the message spelled out by hundreds of Polaroids of happy, smiling diners covering the white walls of this bright, modern eaterie. Rightly so, as bibimbap is the signature dish here, available in ten versions, including chilli chicken, mixed seafood and 'nutritious' (vegetables, chestnuts, dates, ginseng and ginkgo). White rice comes as standard, but brown is also available. Both are served in a sizzling stone bowl, with plastic bottles of koch'ujang and denjang sauces on the side, so that customers can mix the ingredients to their own satisfaction. The short menu also features some salads and noodle dishes, plus assorted sides, such as kimchi pancake, pork and vegetable dumplings, and miso soup. Tolsot bibimbap (the classic version, of assorted vegetables, topped with a fried egg) was acceptable, though other West End Korean restaurants offer fresher ingredients and larger portions. A side of chilli squid was unappealing, however: dry, lacking chilli and tasting of barbecue seasoning. Drinks include Korean beer, plum wine, saké and ginseng tea. This isn't the place for a lingering meal, but it's ideal for a snappy lunch or dinner, with low prices and speedy service from young Korean staff.
Babies and children admitted. Bookings not accepted dinner Fri, Sat. Takeaway service. **Map 17 C3.**

★ Nara

9 D'Arblay Street, W1F 8DR (7287 2224). Oxford Circus or Tottenham Court Road tube. **Lunch served** noon-2.45pm, **dinner served** 5.30-10pm daily. **Main courses** £6.90-£13. **Set lunch** £6.90. **Set dinner** £9.90. **Credit** AmEx, MC, V.
While it ostensibly has one foot in Japan (and is named after the capital of Japan's Kansai region), it's Nara's Korean side that pulls in the punters. Cherry veneer tables are inlaid with covered grills (being electric, these have bulky bases that

Dotori

encroach on leg room) for barbecuing the likes of marinated ojingeo (squid) in soy sauce, or beef tongue in sesame oil. Cooking is generally good, but portions can be lacking. Our dolsot bibimbap played it safe with a fried, rather than raw egg, but was otherwise traditional, layering warm rice and seasoned, sautéed veg such as carrot and courgette in a hot stone bowl. But the paltry few pieces of dried-out beef seemed miserly. Likewise, a plate of salty, sticky seafood udon studded with plump mussels, shell-on shrimp and shelled prawns may have delivered on flavour, but was on the lean side. Both can be taken as part of a set lunch that includes miso soup, cold sides (such as bean sprouts in sesame oil) and slices of watermelon to finish, but though the parade of dishes may seem great value for the health conscious, arrive with an appetite and you may leave hungry.
Babies and children admitted. Takeaway service.
Map 17 B3.

South West

Raynes Park

★ Cah Chi

34 Durham Road, SW20 0TW (8947 1081, www.cahchi.com). Raynes Park rail or 57, 131 bus. **Lunch served** noon-3pm, **dinner served** 5-10.30pm Tue-Fri. **Meals served** noon-10.30pm Sat, Sun. **Main courses** £6-£14. **Set dinner** £20 3 courses. **Corkage** (wine only) £2. **Credit** MC, V.

Nearer the centre of London than New Malden's cluster of Korean restaurants, Cah Chi is only minutes away from Raynes Park railway station in a quiet residential street of mock-Tudor frontages, cherry trees and twitching net curtains. Yet the menu makes no concessions to its suburban setting, and is aimed at Korean diners with its barbecue tables and specials list that includes challenging dishes such as raw, fermented skate wing. Non-Korean diners are welcomed too, though, by smiling, English-speaking staff and a menu that has been considerately, though not accurately, translated into English – some pork and chicken dishes have been marked as 'vegetarian'. One of the signature dishes is soondae, a black pudding of sweet potato vermicelli and blood inside a casing of pig chitterlings. Although delicious, the intestinal smell is not to everyone's taste; in this case, order the soondae stir-fried with perilla leaves (called soondae-bokkeum). This dispels the soondae's aroma, and the heat can be adjusted by the addition of spicy chilli paste. The branch in Earlsfield has a more mainstream menu, and attracts many non-Korean customers.
Babies and children welcome: high chairs. Booking advisable. Separate room for parties, seats 18. Takeaway service.
For branch see index.

North

Finsbury Park

Dotori

3 Stroud Green Road, N4 2DQ (7263 3562). Finsbury Park tube/rail. **Lunch served** noon-2.50pm Tue-Sat. **Dinner served** 5-10.30pm Tue-Sun. **Main courses** £6.50-£15. **Set meal** £23 4 courses. **Credit** MC, V.

Menu

Chilli appears at every opportunity on Korean menus. Other common ingredients include soy sauce (different to both the Chinese and Japanese varieties), sesame oil, sugar, sesame seeds, garlic, ginger and various fermented soy bean pastes. Until the late 1970s, eating meat was a luxury in Korea, so the quality of vegetarian dishes is high.

Given the spicy nature and overall flavour of Korean food, drinks such as chilled lager or vodka-like **soju/shoju** are the best matches. A wonderful non-alcoholic alternative that's always available, although not always listed on the menu, is barley tea (**porich'a/borich'a**). Often served free of charge, it has a light, dry taste that works perfectly with the food. Korean restaurants don't usually offer desserts, though some serve orange or watermelon with the bill.

Spellings on menus vary hugely; we have given the most common.

Bibimbap or **pibimbap**: rice, vegetables and meat with a raw/fried egg dropped on top, often served in a hot stone bowl.
Bindaedok, **bindaedoek** or **pindaetteok**: a mung bean pancake.
Bokum: a stir-fried dish, usually including chilli.
Bulgogi or **pulgogi**: thin slices of beef marinated in pear sap (or a similar sweet dressing) and barbecued at the table; often eaten rolled in a lettuce leaf with shredded spring onion and fermented bean paste.
Chang, **jang** or **denjang**: various fermented soy bean pastes.
Chapch'ae or **chap chee**: mixed vegetables and beef cooked with transparent vermicelli or noodles.
Cheon, **jeon** or **jon**: meaning 'something flat'; this can range from a pancake containing vegetables, meat or seafood, to thinly sliced vegetables, beancurd or other ingredients, in a light batter.
Cheyuk: pork.
Chigae or **jigae**: a hot stew that contains fermented bean paste and chillies.
Gim or **kim**: dried seaweed, toasted and seasoned with salt and sesame oil.
Gu shul pan: a traditional lacquered tray that has nine compartments containing individual appetisers.
Hobak chun or **hobak jun**: sliced marrow in a light egg batter.
Japch'ae, **japchae** or **jap chee**: alternative spellings for chapch'ae (qv).
Jjim: fish or meat stewed for a long time in soy sauce, sugar and garlic.
Jeongol or **chungol**: casserole.
Kalbi, **galbi** or **kalbee**: beef spare ribs, marinated and barbecued.
Kimchi, **kim chee** or **kimch'i**: fermented pickled vegetables, usually chinese cabbage, white radishes, cucumber or greens, served in a small bowl with a spicy chilli sauce.
Kkaktugi or **kkakttugi**: pickled radish.
Koch'ujang: a hot, red bean paste.
Kook, **gook**, **kuk** or **guk**: soup. Koreans have an enormous variety of soups, from consommé-like liquid to hearty broths of noodles, dumplings, and meat or fish.
Ko sari na mool or **gosari namul**: cooked bracken stalks with sesame seeds.
Mandu kuk or **man doo kook**: clear soup with steamed meat dumplings.
Naengmyun or **neng myun**: cold noodle dishes, usually featuring thin, elastic buckwheat noodles.
Namul or **na mool**: vegetable side dishes.
Ojingeo: squid.
P'ajeon, **pa jeon** or **pa jun**: flour pancake with spring onions and (usually) seafood.
Panch'an: side dishes; they usually include pickled vegetables, but possibly also tofu, fish, seaweed or beans.
Pap, **bap**, **bab** or **pahb**: cooked rice.
Pokkeum or **pokkm**: stir-fry; common types include **cheyuk pokkeum** (pork), **ojingeo pokkeum** (squid).
Shinseollo, **shinsonro**, **shinsulro** or **sin sollo**: 'royal casserole'; a meat soup with seaweed, seafood, eggs and vegetables, all of which is cooked at the table.
Teoppap or **toppap**: 'on top of rice'; for example, **ojingeo teoppap** is squid served on rice.
Toenjang: seasoned (usually with chilli) soy bean paste.
Tolsot (or **dolsot**) **bibimbap**: tolsot is a sizzling hot stone bowl that makes the bibimbap (qv) a little crunchy on the sides.
Tteokpokki: bars of compressed rice (tteok is a rice cake) fried on a hotplate with veg and sausages, in a chilli sauce.
Twaeji gogi: pork.
T'wigim, **twigim** or **tuigim**: fish, prawns or vegetables dipped in batter and deep-fried until golden brown.
Yach'ae: vegetables.
Yuk hwe, **yukhoe** or **yukhwoe**: shredded raw beef, strips of pear and egg yolk, served chilled.
Yukkaejang: spicy beef soup.

With its winning neighbourhood restaurant feel, small, sweet Dotori offers a Korean-Japanese combo that is half sashimi, sushi and donburi, and half bibimbap, kimchi and bulgogi. You'd be hard-pressed to say which cuisine they do better. Dumpling soup comprising a meaty stock, two large vegetable-stuffed dumplings and an assortment of veg was a steal at £2.50, and a perfect warm-up to the mains. Another starter, agedashi tofu, four cubes of beancurd dusted in cornflour, deep fried and served in a delicate tentsuyu broth, was also a knockout. Yukhoe dolsot bibimbap – shredded raw beef, raw egg, rice and vegetables – was served in a piping hot stone bowl, and mixed at the table. It made a hearty, warming but also fresh-tasting dish. Doenjang jjigae, a Korean stew in a soybean paste broth with vegetables and tofu, served with rice, was another delicious bargain at £7. Around us, crammed-in fellow diners seemed equally impressed with light tempura and beautifully composed sashimi. A generous meal for two came in at less under £30. Do book for dinner – Dotori gets busy, and we saw prospective diners being turned away.
Babies and children admitted. Booking advisable dinner. Takeaway service. Vegetarian menu.

Outer London

New Malden, Surrey

★ Jee Cee Neh

74 Burlington Road, New Malden, Surrey, KT3 4NU (8942 0682). New Malden rail. **Lunch served** noon-3pm, **dinner served** 6-11pm Mon, Tue, Thur, Fri. **Meals served** 11.30am-10.30pm Sat, Sun. **Main courses** £7-£13. **Credit** (over £20) MC, V.

Known for serving some of the most authentic Korean food in London, Jee's still has a surprisingly residential feel. Locals congregate after work to put the world to rights over a few choice dishes and a bottle of soju. Not all of the staff speak perfect English, but what they lack in language, they more than make up for with their warm and welcoming spirit. Delicious panch'an, such as delicate own-made cabbage kimchi or earthy fried mushrooms in sesame oil, come to the table almost as soon as you arrive in the shabby beige dining room – as does an obligatory cup of porich'a tea. Our subtle chapch'ae contained chunky vegetable batons and juicy strips of marinated beef, while a hot and sour kimchi chigae concealed tender chunks of pork below a sea of soft chinese cabbage and firm tofu. The only let down was a dish of stir-fried octopus in a dark, red, spicy sauce, which was tasty enough, but rather chewy. In all, Jee Cee Neh's reputation is well deserved, and at these prices, your wallet won't take a big hit either.
Available for hire. Babies and children welcome: high chairs. Separate room for parties, seats 20. Takeaway service.

Korea Garden NEW

73 Kingston Road, New Malden, Surrey, KT3 3PB (8336 1208). New Malden rail. **Lunch served** noon-2.30pm Tue-Sat. **Dinner served** 6-10.30pm Tue-Sun. **No credit cards.**

As with many of the Korean restaurants in New Malden, this place has a decidedly residential feel. Locals congregate here to catch up over a hot bowl of bibimbap and a glass of Korean beer, or a cup of barley tea, while K-pop blares out across the brown and white dining room. Warming hotpots filled with tender meat, seafood or tofu are a big draw. Another is the table-top charcoal barbecue, guaranteeing a satisfyingly smoky finish to your bulgogi or kalbi beef. Each table is fitted with an industrial-looking, metal extractor fan, which doubles as a spotlight so that you can see exactly what you're eating. Spicy stir-fried squid (ojingeo pokkeum) came in generous, tender chunks, coated in a well-balanced sticky, red sauce. A refreshing bowl of cold naengmyun soup was packed with sweet, tangy, pickled radish, chewy soba noodles and thinly sliced beef brisket. A small dish of fresh, crunchy mustard leaf kimchi that arrived as part of our free panch'an is also worthy of mention. Service came with a shy, but friendly, smile.

Korea House

Ground floor, Falcon House, 257 Burlington Road, New Malden, Surrey, KT3 4NE (8942 1188). Motspur Park rail. **Lunch served** noon-3pm Mon, Tue, Fri. **Dinner served** 6-11pm Mon-Fri. **Meals served** noon-11pm Sat, Sun. **Main courses** £6.50-£50. **Set meal** £10 per person (minimum 2). **Credit** MC, V.

Formerly known as Hankook, Korea House has changed its name, but apparently not much else. The staff assured us that the chef and owner were the same, and the decor is untouched too. There's a dimly lit dining room in the middle with the odd Korean mask on the wall, and a couple of tranquil tatami rooms to the side. As for the unglamorous location on a busy B road, there's not much staff can do about that. On a recent Saturday lunchtime visit, the place was pretty empty, but this isn't always the case. It's often buzzing with local families and businessmen making the most of the reasonably priced barbecue, sashimi, stir-fries and, of course, the soju. A spicy beef rib hotpot packed a punch: the beef falling off the bone, mixed with tender chinese cabbage in a boiling bowl of fiery broth. A generous heap of gunmandu fried dumplings satisfied appetites, while the jellyfish and prawn salad in sweet mustard dressing left our noses tingling. If you're after a relaxed night out, a few Korean beers and a full belly, Korea House can definitely oblige.
Available for hire. Babies and children welcome: high chairs. Booking essential dinner Fri, Sat.

Jee Cee Neh

Malaysian, Indonesian & Singaporean

As we went to press, the future of one of Malaysian London's swankiest culinary stars was uncertain. **Awana** had departed from its Sloane Avenue premises, but had yet to announce a new venue (consult its website, www.awana.co.uk, for the latest news). Meanwhile, the long-established **Singapore Garden** remains the sole top-end restaurant in this section, producing classy renditions of Chinese, Malaysian and Singaporean cuisine. At the street-food end of the spectrum, we welcome **East/West**, a tiny outlet in Chinatown that serves authentic Indonesian dishes.

There was also a spruce-up this year for **New Fook Lam Moon**, also in Chinatown, and for the mid-range **C&R Restaurant** in Bayswater, one of the few London venues where you can try fish-head soup. Otherwise, there are still relatively few practitioners of this flavour-packed, fusion cuisine in the capital: a pity, as the combination of styles – including Nonya (also called Peranakan) food, which is an amalgamation of Chinese and Malay cookery – has created some classic dishes. Laksa and satay are barely the start of a cuisine with a wealth of influences.

Central

Barbican

★ Sedap

102 Old Street, EC1V 9AY (7490 0200, www.sedap.co.uk). Old Street tube/rail. **Lunch served** 11.30am-2.30pm Mon-Fri. **Dinner served** 6-10.30pm daily. **Main courses** £6.80-£8. **Set lunch** £7.80-£8.80 2 courses. **Credit** MC, V.

Upon arrival at Sedap, we were warmly greeted in Penang-Hokkien dialect by the owner Mary Khoo, who moved here from Notting Hill in 2009. Her family members continue to run the restaurant: from the stove all the way to front-of-house. Black furniture and olive-green walls add a sense of style to proceedings, as do neat touches such as a glass display cabinet showcasing antique tea sets. We kicked off with a seafood char mee (stir-fried yellow noodles), which was packed with deep-fried shallots and minced garlic giving long-lasting flavour. Sedap is known for its Nonya cooking – a fusion of Malay and Chinese cuisines – and the typical hot and sour flavours were exemplified by a curry tumis, which arrived in a sturdy copper bowl. Inside, we found a tasty, soft and fleshy sea bream accompanied by okra. To finish, the own-made Nonya kueh (brightly coloured cakes) are difficult to resist. Accompanying the kueh with a glass of warm, sweet teh tarik ('pulled tea') would doubtless bring back happy memories to Malaysian expats. The good-value lunch menus are also worthy of inspection.

Available for hire. Babies and children admitted. Booking advisable dinner. Separate room for parties, seats 14. Takeaway service; delivery service (over £10 within 1-mile radius).
Map 5 P4.

Chinatown

★ East/West NEW

1st floor, 57 Charing Cross Road, WC2H 0NE (07 531 378329, www.eastwestoriental.com). Leicester Square or Tottenham Court Road tube. **Meals served** noon-9pm Mon-Sun. **Main courses** £4-£5. **No credit cards.**

While there's nothing exotic about East/West's location, a messy shopping centre on the edge of Chinatown, it could hardly feel any more Asian. The neighbouring stalls selling cutesy toys and kitschy accessories set the scene, but the authentic Indonesian cooking steals the show. There's no menu as such, just a choice of the four or five dishes picked for that day. And at this price – a tenner will comfortably feed two people – it really is a steal. In a kitchen tucked behind the kind of wooden pushcart used by street food vendors in Jakarta, the

convivial owner prepares a faithful version of bakso, a Javanese soup of spongy meatballs in a clear, flavoursome broth. Other dishes are prepared off-site and heated upon order, but there's no doubting their freshness and authenticity. Nasi padang combines coconut rice with several items including rendang (tender, flaky beef simmered for six hours in coconut milk), sayur lodeh (a spicy vegetable stew), batagor (fried fish dumplings) and several varieties of sambal (chilli sauce). If the spice is overbearing, a dessert of glutinous black rice in coconut cream makes a cool finish. Be prepared to wait at peak times – there are only three tables.
Babies and children admitted. Takeaway service. **Map 17 C4.**

New Fook Lam Moon

10 Gerrard Street, W1D 5PW (7734 7615). Leicester Square or Piccadilly Circus tube. **Meals served** noon-11pm Mon-Sat; noon-10pm Sun. **Main courses** £11.50-£27. **Credit** MC, V.
We visited shortly after the dining rooms here had been spruced up. Little could have been done to the snug space, but welcome modern touches include smart brown walls, wooden tables and gold-coloured chairs. Fortunately, the roast meat counter at the front has been left untouched. This is essentially a Hong Kong-style Cantonese café, and it's now even more difficult to spot the Malaysian dishes among the standard Cantonese fare on the lengthy menu. Our waiter was clueless, so we asked for assistance from the head waiter, who turned out to be very helpful. There are around a dozen Malaysian options, some appearing only on a separate lunch menu. We were delighted that bak kut teh – pork ribs in herbal soup, a delicious concoction – is still available. We also lapped up a curry laksa, featuring mixed seafood, vermicelli, beansprouts and bean curd; the curry and coconut sauce had a lovely deep flavour, but the squid was rubbery. Morning glory with a spicy belacan (shrimp sauce) was also a winner. Although the variety of Malaysian dishes is limited, quality remains high – it's a nostalgic reminder of good home cooking in the Straits.
Babies and children welcome: high chairs. Booking advisable. Takeaway service. **Map 17 C4.**

Rasa Sayang

5 Macclesfield Street, W1D 6AY (7734 1382, www.rasasayangfood.com). Leicester Square or Piccadilly Circus tube. **Meals served** noon-10.30pm Mon-Thur, Sun; noon-11.30pm Fri, Sat. **Main courses** £6.90-£17.80. **Credit** AmEx, MC, V.
Street food from the Straits, low prices and a location amid the commotion of Chinatown draw a ready supply of customers – including Malaysian expats – to this worthwhile pit-stop. Try to squeeze into the ground-floor dining area, a brighter and buzzier space than the basement room. Tables are packed closely together, so this is not a place to linger. We lapped up a popular breakfast dish of chee cheong fun (flat rice noodles, like the Chinese dim sum favourite of cheung fun) served with a spicy sauce topped with dried shallots. The authentic flavours of that Malay staple, nasi goreng istimewa (fried rice served with chicken satay, fried egg and prawn crackers), transported us back to a street stall in Kuala Lumpur. Equally irresistible was the squidgy texture of ondeh-ondeh (glutinous rice balls filled with caramelised palm sugar), but beware: piercing the rice balls hard with a fork can result in a sudden spurt of palm sugar that may

Rasa Sayang

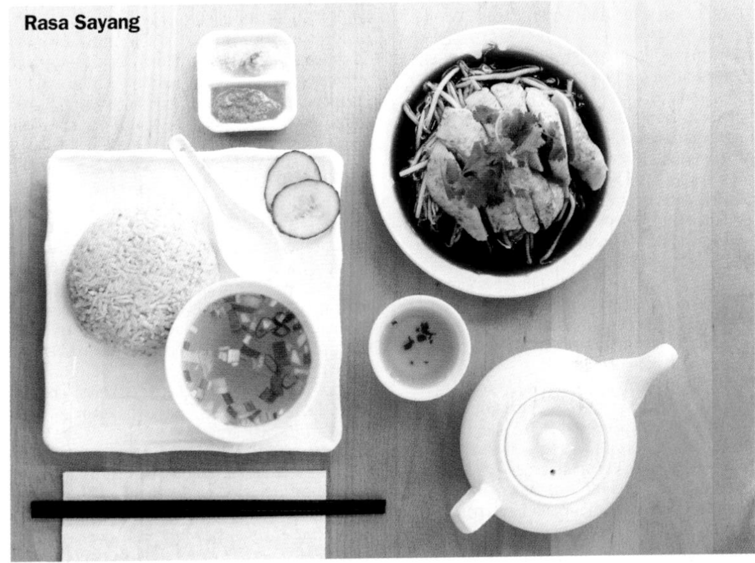

MALAYSIAN, INDONESIAN & SINGAPOREAN

Menu

Blachan, **belacan** or **blacan**: dried fermented shrimp paste.
Char kway teow or **char kwai teow**: a stir-fry of rice noodles with meat and/or seafood with dark soy sauce and beansprouts. A Hakka Chinese-derived speciality of Singapore.
Gado gado: a salad of blanched vegetables with a peanut-based sauce.
Gula melaka: palm sugar, an important ingredient with a distinctive caramel flavour added to a sago and coconut-milk pudding of the same name.
Hainanese chicken rice: poached chicken served with rice cooked in chicken stock, light chicken broth and a chilli-ginger dipping sauce.
Ikan bilis or **ikan teri**: tiny fish, often fried and made into a dry sambal (qv) with peanuts.
Laksa: a noodle dish with either coconut milk or tamarind as the stock base.
Mee: noodles.
Mee goreng: fried egg noodles with meat, prawns and vegetables.
Nasi ayam: rice cooked in chicken broth, served with roast or steamed chicken and a light soup.
Nasi goreng: fried rice with shrimp paste, garlic, onions, chillies and soy sauce.
Nasi lemak: coconut rice on a plate with a selection of curries and fish dishes topped with ikan bilis (qv).
Nonya or **Nyonya**: the name referring to both the women and the dishes of the Straits Chinese community.
Otak otak: a Nonya (qv) speciality made from eggs, fish and coconut milk.
Pandan leaves: a variety of the screwpine plant; used to add colour and fragrance to both savoury and sweet dishes.
Peranakan: refers to the descendants of Chinese settlers who first came to Malacca (now Melaka), a seaport on the Malaysian west coast, in the 17th century. It is generally applied to those born of Sino-Malay extraction who adopted Malay customs, costume and cuisine, the community being known as 'Straits Chinese'. The cuisine is also known as Nonya.
Rendang: meat cooked in coconut milk.
Roti canai: a South Indian/Malaysian breakfast dish of fried unleavened bread served with a dip of either chicken curry or dal.
Sambal: there are several types of sambal, often made of fiery chilli sauce, onions and coconut oil; it can be served as a side dish or used as a relish.
Satay: there are two types – **terkan** (minced and moulded to the skewer) and **chochok** ('shish', more common in London). Beef or chicken are the traditional choices, though prawn is now often available too. Satay is served with a rich, spicy sauce made from onions, lemongrass, galangal, and chillies in tamarind sauce; it is sweetened and thickened with ground peanuts.

end up on your neighbour's lap. Pearl milk 'bubble' tea makes a suitably frivolous accompaniment; on cold days, try a cup of sweet, warming teh tarik. Service is diligent but casual, adding to the easy-going atmosphere.
Babies and children admitted. Booking advisable. Separate room for parties, seats 30. Takeaway service. **Map 17 C4.**

West

Bayswater

C&R Restaurant

52 Westbourne Grove, W2 5SH (7221 7979, www.cnrrestaurant.co.uk). Bayswater tube.
Meals served noon-10.30pm Mon, Wed-Fri; noon-11pm Sat; noon-10pm Sun. **Main courses** £7.50-£24. **Set meal** £16 vegetarian, £19 meat per person (minimum 2). **Credit** AmEx, MC, V.
This year, the dining room at C&R looks much more attractive, with freshly painted walls (still in magnolia) and the former tacky artwork replaced by red lanterns hanging from the ceiling. The menu is extensive, criss-crossing China and Thailand as well as Malaysia. Specials include a Malaysian delicacy rarely found in London restaurants: fish-head soup with rice vermicelli. We started with chicken satay, which was rather ho-hum although the accompanying peanut sauce was well made. Mee goreng (selected from a list of 18 noodle dishes) arrived as a hillock of yellow noodles stir-fried with prawns, beancurd, beansprouts and egg cooked in a tomato-based sauce. The dish could have done with a spicier kick, and the prawns had an unpleasant iodine aftertaste. Much better was the boo-boo cha cha: an exotic name for boiled yam and sweet potato served with rich coconut milk. Although the cooking here rarely sets the pulse racing, the food has a broad appeal – as evidenced by the restaurant's continuing popularity (although we suspect that this has as much to do with the relaxed vibe).
Babies and children welcome: high chairs. Takeaway service; delivery service (within 2-mile radius). **Map 7 B6.**
For branch (C&R Café) see index.

Satay House

Paddington

Satay House

13 Sale Place, W2 1PX (7723 6763, www.satay-house.co.uk). Edgware Road tube or Paddington tube/rail. **Lunch served** noon-2.30pm, **dinner served** 6-10.30pm daily. **Main courses** £5-£18.50. **Set meal** £16.90-£27.90 per person (minimum 2). **Credit** AmEx, MC, V.
Still going strong after 40 years, Satay House's popularity remains undiminished judging from our recent visits to its well-patronised premises. Unfortunately, service can easily take a wrong turn when the tables fill with customers. The dining room has a modern feel, created by wooden flooring and modish red and grey walls. Hibiscus (the Malaysian national flower) makes an appearance in motifs throughout. This is the place to try murtabak, a savoury crêpe filled with minced lamb. Chicken satay had a pleasant barbecued flavour, but was let down by a watery peanut sauce. Stir-fried beansprouts with salted fish is also a good bet. Mee goreng (stir-fried vermicelli) was a reasonably satisfying dish, although the flavour dial had been turned down a little low, and we could have done without the stringy pieces of beef. Nevertheless, it's good to note that dishes were much less oily than on previous visits. To finish, we happily shared ais kacang, a brightly coloured mélange of red beans, black jelly and sweetcorn topped with shaved ice.
Available for hire. Babies and children welcome: high chairs. Booking advisable. Separate room for parties, seats 35. Takeaway service. Vegetarian menu. **Map 8 E5.**

North West

Swiss Cottage

★ Singapore Garden

83A Fairfax Road, NW6 4DY (7624 8233, www.singaporegarden.co.uk). Swiss Cottage tube.
Lunch served noon-2pm Mon-Sat; noon-4pm Sun. **Dinner served** 6-10pm Mon-Thur, Sun; 6-10.30pm Fri, Sat. **Main courses** £10-£30. **Set meal** £30-£40 per person (minimum 2). **Minimum** (dinner) £15 per person. **Credit** AmEx, MC, V.
The long-running Singapore Garden continues to be London's prime destination for upmarket Straits cooking. It's a plush, large space with modern furnishings, where Anna, the ever-smiling manager, keeps a watchful eye over the service team. The menu lists a selection of Chinese food alongside popular dishes from Singapore and Malaysia. An enjoyable opener to a meal (especially popular with children) is kueh pie tee – crispy pastry in the shape of top hats, filled with tasty prawns, chicken and bamboo shoots. Tofu goreng, deep-fried beancurd paired with a satay sauce, is a fine vegetarian option. We loved the crisp, punchy, deep-fried, five-spice pork rolls. Noodle dishes are good too; we happily tucked into a generous plateful of fried sa ho fun (stir-fried flat rice noodles served with char siu, beef, prawns and fish cake) that exuded real 'wok hay' (a lovely caramelised flavour caused by the quick sizzle in the wok). To finish, few expats can resist the flavour combination of coconut milk and palm sugar, and we polished off every last bit of a sago melaka.
Babies and children admitted. Booking essential. Disabled: toilet. Takeaway service; delivery service (within 1.5-mile radius). **Map 28 A4.**

Middle Eastern

Gauging the quality of a Middle Eastern restaurant is easy. Look to the breads: they should be fresh from the oven, perfectly weighted, scorched and doughy in all the right places, and good enough to eat by themselves. Look to the rice: no other cuisine does this staple better; if you find moist, light, free-flowing grains, you know you're on to a winner. And look to the kebabs: seared, tender and juicy meats that need no saucing indicate plenty of talent in the kitchen. That's not to say there's little else in the cuisine worthy of mention. Middle Eastern food is richly varied, encompassing the multifarious dips and snacks that make up a meze feast and reach their pinnacle in Lebanese cooking – our long-time favourite practitioner of which is **Maroush I** – and the gorgeously tangy stews of Persian cuisine, where this year we've awarded top marks to two Iranian restaurants: **Behesht** and **Sufi**. The latest arrival is Fitzrovia's **Honey & Co**, which augments Israeli cookery with dishes from across the region, including the culinary traditions of Jewish immigrants from Algeria, Morocco and Iraq. Other takes can be found at **Zengi** (pan-Middle Eastern), **Abu Zaad** (Syrian) and **Mesopotamia** (Iraqi) – all also sited away from the Middle Eastern heartland of Edgware Road.

Central

Edgware Road

★ Maroush I

21 Edgware Road, W2 2JE (7723 0773, www.maroush.com). Marble Arch tube. **Meals served** noon-11.30pm daily. **Main courses** £12.95-£18. **Credit** AmEx, DC, MC, V.
Lebanese

The name Maroush is synonymous with London Lebanese restaurants, and this is the original branch of the chain. There are a few tables on the ground floor, but the main restaurant in the basement has a nightclub feel, with entertainment every evening. Even on our Wednesday visit, things got pretty lively with soul standards and a belly dancer. But there was no compromise with the food, which was outstanding. From the big bowl of salad vegetables at the beginning to the free pastries and fruit at the end, the meal was little short of ideal (the only exception being the bread, which was leathery pitta instead of freshly baked discs warm from the oven). Silky-smooth houmous beiruti was given a kick by a perfect balance of added chilli and spices. It made a good match for lemony tabouleh and a homely fuul. Chicken livers sautéed with lemon were pillow-soft, with a hint of pink in the middle, the thin sauce adding a citrous tang. A main course of lamb grill was beautifully tender. What's more, the staff managed the combination of eating and entertainment with politeness and aplomb. A very good night out.

Babies and children welcome: high chairs. Booking advisable. Entertainment: belly dancers and musicians 9.30pm daily. Separate room for parties, seats 25. Takeaway service; delivery service (over £20 within 2-mile radius). **Map 8 F6.**

For branches (Beirut Express, Maroush, Maroush Gardens, Randa) see index.

Fitzrovia

Honey & Co NEW

25A Warren Street, W1T 5LZ (7388 6175). Warren Street tube. **Meals served** 7.30am-7pm daily. **Main courses** £8.50-£12.50. **Credit** MC, V. Middle Eastern

Honey & Co is run by an Israeli husband and wife team with an impressive pedigree: Itamar Srulovich (husband) was head chef at Ottolenghi (*see p50*), and Sarit Packer (wife) was both head of pastry at Ottolenghi and executive chef at NOPI (*see p228*). The place is stacked with own-produced comestibles, including the breads and pastries displayed in the window, jars of exotic jams and preserved lemons. Itamar describes the homely, daily changing menu as 'food from the Middle East': not merely Israeli, but drawing on roots from the entire region. Dishes, alive with colour and texture, sometimes include non-kosher ingredients such as prawns. We kicked off with tiny meze dishes, each one showing care and attention to detail. Highlights included beetroot marinated in Corinthian wine vinegar, the tang offset by oregano. No less impressive was watermelon salad: the sweet, juicy pieces of fruit were a foil to creamy, salty feta, with pistachios, chilli and mint adding crunch, punch and zing. Beautifully textured falafels were exceptional, as was slow-baked lamb shank served with couscous and zhough (a Yemeni spice paste). What this small, plain venue lacks in wall colour, larger-than-life Itamar makes up for tenfold in charm. Tables are hard to come by, so book early.

Available for hire. Babies and children admitted. Booking advisable. Tables outdoors (2, pavement). Vegan dishes. **Map 3 J4.**

Holborn

Hiba

113 High Holborn, WC1V 6JQ (7831 5171, www.hiba-express.co.uk). Holborn tube. **Meals served** noon-11.30pm daily. **Main courses** £9.95-£14.95. **Set meal** £8.95-£10.95 1 course. **Set meze** £35-£65. **Credit** AmEx, MC, V.
Lebanese

Bright and modern, with striking yellow walls and big red hanging lampshades, Hiba is a Holborn lunchtime favourite, doing a brisk trade in meze dishes, wraps and freshly squeezed juices. It's popular and relaxed in the evening too (although there's no alcohol), despite the regular rumbles from the Piccadilly Line below. The menu contains a

Honey & Co. See p195.

varied selection of Lebanese standards, with grills as well as a meze list. From the latter, we tried a lemony batinjan el-rahib; a crisp fattoush salad with crunchy toasted pitta squares, warmed by signature sumac spice; and a classic fuul medames – warm, homely and comforting, with lashings of olive oil to mix in with the beans. Lentil soup was a sound rendition too. To follow, a main course of king prawns was served with flavoursome Lebanese rice (cooked with oil and vermicelli), but the shellfish were distinctly average, and the accompanying tahini made an odd companion. Stick to the classics, though, and you can enjoy some great Lebanese food at prices far lower than in the flashy places of Edgware Road.
Available for hire. Babies and children welcome: high chairs. Takeaway service; delivery service (over £15 within 4-mile radius). Vegetarian menu. **Map 18 F2**.

Marylebone

Levant

Jason Court, 76 Wigmore Street, W1U 2SJ (7224 1111, www.levant.co.uk). Bond Street tube. *Bar* **Open** 5pm-midnight Mon-Thur; noon-2am Fri, Sat; noon-midnight Sun. *Restaurant* **Meals served** noon-11pm Mon-Thur, Sun; noon-midnight Fri, Sat. **Main courses** £13-£19.50. **Set lunch** £9.95 2 courses. **Set meal** £28-£50 3 courses; £50 kharuf feast.
Both **Credit** AmEx, MC, V. Lebanese

It's certainly worth booking ahead at Levant. Early on a weekday evening, the restaurant almost empty, you may still be condemned to a small corner table crammed in by the kitchen door if you don't have a reservation. The alternative is the bar, but the drinks tables are scarcely large enough to hold a meal. Early birds can take advantage of the two-for-one cocktail deal; try fresh, fruity mango and passionfruit mojitos. Opulent velvet drapes, brocade cushions, seductive lighting from filigree lanterns and friendly, attentive staff create a good impression, but the soundtrack of loud dance music jars somewhat – especially as most diners are over thirty. Middle Eastern rhythms only take over when belly dancers shake their stuff. If the pricey set menus don't appeal, consult the carte to find the usual houmous, tabouleh and fattoush, but also some surprises: silky fried courgette purée with a crispy topping was tasty but stunningly salty; baby squid with chilli and coconut lacked crunch yet was otherwise OK. A well-presented mixed grill of tender chicken, lamb and cinnamon-scented lamb köfte served with vermicelli-flecked rice and crunchy salad was also seriously over-salted. Must try harder.
Booking advisable. Entertainment: belly dancer 8.30pm Mon-Thur; 8.30pm, 11pm Fri-Sun. Separate room for parties, seats 10-12. Takeaway service. Vegetarian menu. **Map 9 G6**.

Mayfair

Noura Mayfair

16 Curzon Street, W1J 5HP (7495 1050, www.noura.co.uk). Green Park tube. **Meals served** 11.30am-11.30pm daily. **Main courses** £14-£18. **Set meal** £32-£45 (minimum 2). **Credit** AmEx, MC, V. Lebanese

The swanky, suave Belgravia branch was the Noura chain's first London outpost and remains its flagship. Next door, Noura Lounge is a contemporary lounge bar and restaurant. Noura Knightsbridge is a café and deli, while this branch, Noura Mayfair, has a basement lounge bar hosting 'Lebanese nights' (musicians and belly-dancing) on Fridays and Saturdays. Upstairs, the restaurant is a neutral and rather boring-looking rectangle. It was almost empty on a recent visit, which did nothing to dispel an aura of gloom. Neither did the lack of accoutrements you might expect in this kind of place. Instead of the big bowl of salad vegetables, ready for diners to chop and dip, we had to make do with a measly bowl of olives and pickles; also absent was the constant replenishing of discs of warm, own-made bread. Most of our food was fine, though nothing was exciting and some dishes were below par, such as the pale and insipid batata harra and oily makanek sausages. Houmous shawarma, on the other hand, was thick and full of flavour, dotted with little squares of lamb, and manakish zaatar (warmed pitta bread with oil and zaatar spice) was well executed too. But much of the enjoyment of a Lebanese meal, at least in a restaurant in this price band, is down to buzz and sense of occasion. Without it, the food didn't add up to much.

Available for hire. Babies and children welcome: high chairs; nappy-changing facilities. Booking advisable. Separate room for parties, seats 30. Tables outdoors (4, pavement). Takeaway service; delivery service (over £21 within 1-mile radius). Vegetarian menu. **Map 9 H8.**

For branches see index.

Al Sultan

51-52 Hertford Street, W1J 7ST (7408 1155, www.alsultan.co.uk). Green Park or Hyde Park Corner tube. **Meals served** noon-11pm daily. **Main courses** £13.50-£20. **Cover** £2. **Minimum** £20. **Credit** AmEx, DC, MC, V. Lebanese

Don't come to Al Sultan in search of Arabian high jinks, though the extensive menu of hot and cold meze and grills rarely disappoints. Formal but friendly service at this classic Lebanese restaurant seems to suit the wealthy Mayfair crowd, staff from the nearby Saudi Embassy and a few wandering tourists. Between five and six meze dishes make a good meal for two, alongside the pile of fresh salad vegetables, olives and bread that arrive automatically (£2 cover). Alternatively, substitute two of them with a grill for quite a feast. All the usual dishes are here: subtly smoky moutabal; crunchy kibbeh stuffed with cinnamon-scented minced lamb and pine nuts; juicy, well-spiced sujuk; and scrumptious muhamara (roughly chopped nuts vibrantly flavoured with rich red peppers and piquant pomegranate molasses: a texture and flavour sensation). Fuul moukala (green broad beans, supposedly in a herby lemon dressing) was served too cold, lacking any citrous zing. Great Lebanese wines such as Château Musar come at a hefty price, but more affordable wines feature too. A complimentary plate of fresh honeyed pastries makes a nice finishing touch, as does the possibility of an apple-scented shisha at an outdoor table. A reassuringly reliable restaurant.

Available for hire. Babies and children welcome: high chairs. Booking advisable dinner. Tables outdoors (4, pavement). Takeaway service; delivery service (over £35 within 4-mile radius). Vegetarian menu. **Map 9 H8.**

Soho

Yalla Yalla

1 Green's Court, W1F 0HA (7287 7663, www.yalla-yalla.co.uk). Piccadilly Circus tube. **Meals served** 10am-11pm Mon-Sat; 10am-10pm Sun. **Main courses** £8.50-£13.75. **Credit** MC, V. Lebanese

Soho's lively little Lebanese hub continues its success, judging by the numbers who cram around the tables in the distinctive yellow, black and white interior. At the back is a counter stacked with ready-made wraps to take away. This cheery café is a world away from staid traditional Lebanese restaurants. There's none of the formality (or the space), but the standard of food is just as high. On a recent visit, we loved the tangy stickiness of sawda djej (melt-in-the-mouth chicken livers), which, in this version, came in a dark sauce sweet with pomegranate seeds. Falafel made a great contrast: soft, cushiony insides and crisp shells, served with a generous portion of tahini. They went well with the dense, garlicky houmous too. Manakish zaatar was perfect – pitta bread drizzled with olive oil and dusted with lemony zaatar spice, warmed in the oven just enough to let the flavour flood out – simple but delicious. Yalla Yalla is popular as a lunch spot – and staff can get overwhelmed – but it's open in the evening too, and serves grills and mains alongside the meze all day. It also has an extensive, largely Lebanese, wine list and cocktails.

Babies and children welcome: nappy-changing facilities. Bookings not accepted for fewer than 10 people. Tables outdoors (2, pavement). Takeaway service. **Map 17 B5.**

For branches see index.

Budget bites

Comptoir Libanais

65 Wigmore Street, W1U 1PZ (7935 1110, www.lecomptoir.co.uk). Bond Street tube. **Meals served** 8am-10.30pm Mon-Sat; 8am-9.30pm Sun. **Main courses** £5.95-£8.45. **Credit** MC, V. Lebanese

Bright, fun and full of local workers having lunch, Comptoir Libanais is part-canteen, part-delicatessen. One wall is lined with shelves containing preserves and other imported goods. The rest of the space is taken up with colourful tables and chairs. Dishes are clearly displayed behind the counter, and there are plenty to choose from: salads, tagines, wraps, and mountains of glistening pastries and baklava. Service is personable even during the lunchtime rush, but while the decor is appealing, the standard of cooking is no better than the Middle Eastern caffs of the Edgware Road. Fruit juices come in a variety of interesting and vitamin-packed flavours, with apple, mint and cucumber a highlight.

Available for hire. Babies and children welcome: high chairs. Bookings not accepted lunch; for fewer than 6 at dinner. Tables outdoors (5, pavement). Takeaway service. **Map 9 H6.**

For branches see index.

Fresco

25 Westbourne Grove, W2 4UA (7221 2355, www.frescojuices.co.uk). Bayswater or Royal Oak tube. **Meals served** 8am-11pm daily. **Main courses** £5.95-£9. **Set meze** £11.50. **Credit** MC, V. Lebanese

Light and airy Fresco is furnished with bright yellow walls and rustic wooden furniture. The kitchen rustles up salads and sandwiches for customers swinging past for a quick takeaway, plus cooked meals for those sticking around and taking a seat. Huge portions of meatballs arrived with potatoes, rice and salad, and mixed meze plates came packed with falafel, tabouleh, moutabal garnished with pomegranate seeds, houmous, stuffed vine leaves and aubergine in yoghurt. The juice machine whirs almost constantly as the efficient, friendly staff make juices and refreshing fruit milkshakes. A perfect place to refuel.

Takeaway service. Vegetarian menu. **Map 7 B6.**

For branches see index.

Pilpel

38 Brushfield Street, E1 6AT (7247 0146, www.pilpel.co.uk). Liverpool Street tube/rail. **Meals served** *Summer* 10am-8pm Mon-Fri; noon-6pm Sun. *Winter* 10am-8pm Mon-Thur; 10am-4pm Fri. **Main courses** £4.25-£5.85. **Unlicensed. No credit cards.** Middle Eastern

It may look like an American chain, but Uri Dinay's bijou falafel and houmous bar has become a firm favourite among connoisseurs of the Middle East's fried chickpea dumplings. There are a few tables and chairs for diners who want to eat in (and watch the goings-on at Old Spitalfields Market), but this is mostly back-to-the-office fare, which suits Liverpool Street denizens nicely. You can eat very well for a fiver, or pay a little more and get extra toppings (egg, guacamole, feta, aubergine), and have your dish served in a container with pitta on the side instead of shaped into a wrap. For a change from falafel, try the sabich (houmous, aubergine, egg, tabouleh and salad in pitta). Drinks (no alcohol) include own-made lemonade.

Babies and children admitted. Takeaway service. Vegetarian menu. **Map 12 R5.**

For branches see index.

Ranoush Juice

43 Edgware Road, W2 2JE (7723 5929, www.maroush.com). Marble Arch tube. **Meals served** 8am-3am daily. **Main courses** £3-£10.50. **No credit cards.** Lebanese

Ranoush is all about getting in and out. A few stools, metallic tables and chairs line one side, while the other is filled with juicing machines, huge turning kebab grills and piles of sticky baklava behind the counter. Pay at the till, then watch as flatbreads are filled with shawarma skewers of lamb or chicken, gherkins and tomatoes and served with serious speed. Hot and cold meze are available for those opting to sit in, and there are a couple of tables at the front for watching busy Edgware Road over a fresh fruit juice until the early hours.

Bookings not accepted. Takeaway service. **Map 8 F6.**

For branches (Maroush Ranoush, Ranoush Juice) see index.

West

Bayswater

Hafez

5 Hereford Road, W2 4AB (7221 3167, www.hafezrestaurant.co.uk). Bayswater tube or 328 bus. **Meals served** noon-11.30pm daily. **Main courses** £7.50-£15.90. **Credit** MC, V. Iranian

Opened in 1983, Hafez is one of London's oldest Iranian restaurants, but it's also one of the most modern. The square dining room is bright and airy, with ample space between tables, and big windows overlooking Notting Hill's leafy backstreets. There's some eye-catching decor courtesy of Iranian-born designer Ali Siavoshi – light fittings made from recycled chair legs and cutlery, a series of colourful abstract paintings – alongside a few more traditional Persian artworks (even a framed silk tie sporting a map of Iran), but nothing that detracts from the familial living-room feel of the place. It's a popular spot with locals, and justifiably so. Owner and head chef Farshid Ziafat's family opened the original Nayeb, Iran's most famous kebab restaurant, in 1875 (it's now a chain). High-quality ingredients help raise Hafez's game: the herbs in the sabzi-o panir (mixed greens and feta) were fresh and fragrant; a main of ghorm-e sabzi (lamb stew with kidney beans) featured some unusually powerful dried limes. But kebabs are the real stars here, as you'd expect: the meat is marinated and grilled to perfection, and served (as in Nayeb) with grilled tomatoes and some of the lightest, fluffiest rice imaginable.

Available for hire. Babies and children welcome. Booking advisable. Tables outdoors (3, terrace). Takeaway service. Vegetarian menu. **Map 7 B6**.

Al Waha

75 Westbourne Grove, W2 4UL (7229 0806, www.alwaharestaurant.com). Bayswater or Queensway tube. **Meals served** noon-11.30pm daily. **Main courses** £11-£17. **Set lunch** £13.50-£15. **Set dinner** £22 per person (minimum 2) 2 courses, £26 per person (minimum 2) 3 courses. **Cover** £1.50. **Minimum** (dinner) £13.50. **Credit** MC, V. Lebanese

A welcome haven from frenetic Westbourne Grove, Al Waha brings a fresh, light touch to the usual Lebanese meze delights, along with friendly service. Bold but spare modern Syrian calligraphy designs hang around the dining room. Arabic divas provide an atmospheric, throbbing soundtrack. A selection of three or four meze dishes, a shared main course and warm, puffy flatbread make a good, reasonably priced meal for two. If you can't manage it all, staff will happily pack up your leftovers to take home. Try the fresh, herby, lemon-dressed green broad beans (fuul moukala), perfect deep-fried kibbeh maklieh (their deliciously crunchy bulgar-wheat shells stuffed with cinnamon-infused lamb and onions), and salatate al rahib (smoky roasted aubergine and tomato salad). Omnivores will love the mixed grill of tender chunks of slightly pink lamb, gently spiced minced lamb köfte, and chicken cubes served with a salad of onions and tomatoes – lip-smackingly tasty. Al Waha has a great drinks list featuring various Lebanese wines, from the aromatic, oaky white Château Ksara to the majestic Château Musar rouge. Finish with rich honeyed pastries with walnuts and pistachios, and fresh mint tea or bittersweet Lebanese coffee.

Babies and children welcome until 7pm. Booking advisable; essential dinner. Tables outdoors (4, patio). Takeaway service; delivery service (over £20 within 3-mile radius). **Map 7 B6**.

Chiswick

Faanoos II

472 Chiswick High Road, W4 5TT (8994 4217, www.faanoosrestaurant.com). Chiswick Park tube. **Meals served** noon-11pm Mon-Thur, Sun; noon-midnight Fri, Sat. **Main courses** £3.80-£10.95. **Credit** AmEx, MC, V. Iranian

This second branch of Faanoos takes the rustic charms of the popular East Sheen original even further. The walls are set with mock Middle Eastern windows and clad with straw that in places peels away to reveal bare brick beneath; there are arches inlaid with turquoise tiles and hung with paintings of rural Iranian life; and shelves are laden with Persian memorabilia, including old teapots, a Tehran number plate and countless variations on the lantern from which the restaurant takes its name. The overall effect can border on the Disney Iran Experience, should such a thing exist, but then authenticity isn't Faanoos's strong suit. The food is cheap even compared to the Iranian restaurant norm, but it's wise to stick to the standards. A starter of masto khiar (yoghurt with mint and chopped cucumber) is a creamy accompaniment to a basket of taftoon bread hot from the oven, while kebabs are a safe alternative to stews that we've sometimes found to be short on meat and under-seasoned. The citrus- and saffron-marinated chicken joojeh and the minced lamb koobideh, served either with rice or wrapped in hot bread, are both reliable.

Available for hire. Babies and children welcome: high chairs. Booking advisable Fri, Sat. Tables outdoors (1, pavement; 4, garden). Takeaway service.

For branch see index.

Maida Vale

Kateh

5 Warwick Place, W9 2PX (7289 3393, www.katehrestaurant.co.uk). Warwick Avenue tube. **Lunch served** noon-4pm Sat. **Dinner served** 6-11pm Mon-Sat. **Meals served** noon-9.30pm Sun. **Main courses** £11-£17.50. **Credit** AmEx, MC, V. Iranian

Kateh is a hit with locals, packed to the rafters even on a recent midweek visit. The location, a leafy side street beside a popular pub, helps fill the place, as does the fact that the narrow space is not much bigger than a large living room. Decoration is limited to a couple of Persian tapestries and a few colourful lamps; there's also a private dining room downstairs and a rear garden terrace. The menu offers modern twists and classic Persian fare: starters include jigar (grilled calf's liver with fresh parsley) and a crumbly kookoo mahi fish and potato cake. A main of ghorm-e sabzi (lamb and kidney bean stew) was rich and generous, though we missed the addition of dried limes in our serving; khoresht gheymeh bademjan (lamb and aubergine stew with split peas) was satisfyingly smoky, but the split peas were undercooked. Our only real gripe was being told we'd need to vacate our table before we'd had a chance to consider dessert, having been given no warning at the outset of a time limit on our sitting.

Available for hire. Babies and children welcome: high chairs. Booking advisable. Separate room for parties, seats 10-12. Tables outdoors (3, terrace). Takeaway service. **Map 1 C4**.

Olympia

Mohsen

152 Warwick Road, W14 8PS (7602 9888). Earl's Court tube or Kensington (Olympia) tube/rail. **Meals served** noon-midnight daily. **Main courses** £15-£20. **Unlicensed. Corkage** no charge. **No credit cards**. Iranian

We've long been fans of Mohsen, a restaurant whose success depends largely on the 'ain't broke/don't fix it' formula that many of its peers ignore. Little has changed over the years: the blink-and-miss-it façade, sandwiched between two moribund boozers; the tightly packed, functional tables; the laminated menus and the walls decorated with dog-eared Iranian tourist posters. The warm welcome remains equally undiminished: in a culture where restaurant dining is seen as a poor substitute for a decent home-cooked meal, Mrs Mohsen's happy banter with customers old and new lends the feel of a dinner party. And the food is still very good. Hot starters include dishes uncommon in London's Iranian restaurants: fried chicken liver with mushrooms, tender ox tongue and nourishing ash-e jow (a provincial barley soup). A list of daily-changing specials offers the likes of Monday's zereshk polo ba morgh (a quarter of a chicken served with bitter-sweet barberry-spiked rice), though there's always a list of expertly marinated kebabs; the barg (lamb fillet), served with rice and a grilled tomato, is superb, and goes well with a plate of own-made torshi (mixed sour pickle).

Babies and children admitted. Takeaway service. **Map 13 A10**.

Shepherd's Bush

★ Abu Zaad

29 Uxbridge Road, W12 8LH (8749 5107, www.abuzaad.co.uk). Shepherd's Bush Market tube. **Meals served** 11am-11pm daily. **Main courses** £5-£14. **Unlicensed** no alcohol allowed. **Credit** MC, V. Syrian

It may look rather forbidding, the windows on its corner site obscured by black bars, and it may not be a beauty inside either – a reproduction of an Old Damascene street scene dominates the brown walls – but Abu Zaad is a real neighbourhood hangout, popular with everyone from Somalian women to Arab families and young hipsters. Cheap, honest and very good food is the draw, as well as the genuinely friendly service, making for a pleasant vibe even when the place is quiet. Syrians share many dishes with their Lebanese neighbours. A lunchtime meze selection included a huge helping of sprightly tabouleh; fuul medames served with tahini and tons of lemony olive oil; and plump, generous kibbeh shamieh (the crunchy shell of cracked wheat contrasting with the spicy minced lamb within). Meze dishes cost around £3-£4, while mains are even more of a bargain at £6-£7. In addition to the usual grills, you'll find some dishes rarely seen on restaurant menus: the likes of molokhia (lamb cooked with molokhia leaves – jew's marrow – to produce a distinctive, slightly sticky, stew) or spiced

grilled chicken with frika (fried bulgar). Freshly squeezed juices make a splendid accompaniment. *Babies and children welcome: high chairs. Booking advisable weekends. Separate room for parties, seats 36. Takeaway service.* **Map 20 B2.**
For branch see index.

★ Sufi

70 Askew Road, W12 9BJ (8834 4888, www.sufirestaurant.com). Hammersmith tube then 266 bus. **Meals served** noon-11pm daily. **Main courses** £6.50-£13.50. **Corkage** £5. **Credit** MC, V. Iranian

While many of its contemporaries go out of their way to emulate the canteen feel of Tehran's downtown chelo kebab houses, Sufi is a restaurant in the conventional sense. This is one of the few places in London that capably blends authentic Persian cuisine with an intimate environment that's as suited to romantic liaisons as family reunions. The walls are hung with Middle Eastern musical instruments, calligraphic bronze art and the occasional framed painting of a wizened Sufi cleric. Candles illuminate the linen-clad tables after dark; and a traditional clay oven by the front door turns out soft and seeded taftoon bread. The latter makes a perfect accompaniment to a bowl of ash-e reshteh, a creamy noodle and bean soup that's among the best we've had in the capital. Kebabs are expertly grilled, but this is one place where it's worth experimenting: the khoresht-e fesenjan (chicken with chopped walnuts and pomegranate molasses) is incredibly flavourful, and there are some excellent fish and even vegetarian dishes. There's also an unusually decent wine list, including some punchy reds from Lebanon's Château Ksara.
Babies and children welcome: children's menu; high chairs. Separate room for parties, seats 40. Takeaway service; delivery service (over £20 within 3-mile radius). **Map 20 A2.**

Yalla Yalla. See p197.

South

Tooting

★ Meza

34 Trinity Road, SW17 7RE (07722 111299). Tooting Bec tube. **Meals served** noon-11pm Tue-Sat; 1-10pm Sun. **Main courses** £7.50-£9.50. **Set meze** £16. **No credit cards.** Lebanese

Meza is so popular – and tiny, with room for only 15 customers – it's necessary to book well in advance. The menu consists of hot and cold meze dishes and grilled meat mains, and everything we sampled was excellent. Fatayer pastries were packed with fragrant spinach and onion; stuffed vine leaves were slightly dry but improved with a dab of olive oil; and the makdous (pickled aubergines stuffed with walnuts) were beautifully presented – they're typically served whole, but these were halved and covered in pomegranate seeds. The houmous wasn't as light and creamy as most versions in Beirut, but there's something to be said for a Lebanese chef going easy on the oil. With crisp bulgar wheat shells and moist minced lamb interiors, the kebbe were tremendous, and the shish taouk was grilled to juicy perfection and served the proper way, with an unhealthy dollop of garlic cream. The wine list features affordable Lebanese bottles, and it's great to see beer from Lebanese Brew, one of the Arab world's newest microbreweries. The setting is nondescript and the service slightly rushed, but the superb food makes Meza a gem.
Available for hire. Babies and children welcome: high chairs. Booking advisable dinner. Takeaway service.

East

Spitalfields

Zengi

44 Commercial Street, E1 6LT (7426 0700, www.zengirestaurant.co.uk). Aldgate East tube. **Meals served** noon-11pm daily. **Main courses** £2.50-£14. **Credit** AmEx, MC, V. Iraqi

With its laid-back attitude and extensive menu mixing Iraqi, Lebanese, Syrian and Turkish influences, Zengi remains a popular option with young Londoners looking for something more sustaining than a sandwich before hitting nearby bars in Spitalfields. Most tend to gather on the functional ground floor, a room dominated by an open kitchen in which chefs turn kebabs on coals and retrieve breads and turkish pizzas from the specialised oven. There's a non-committal mix of generic Middle Eastern decoration upstairs – framed prints, engraved metal tables, shisha pipes (available to those willing to brave the arguably more carcinogenic air of the pavement tables on Commercial Street) – but also a quieter, more comfortable basement room with intimate alcove seating. We've found the meze dishes here to be hit and miss in the past, but our choices on a recent visit were consistently good: moutabal was rich and pleasingly smoky, böregi featured crisp filo pastry and melting cheese and spinach fillings, and the crisp, saffron-infused rice shells of Iraqi haleb kibbeh broke open to reveal pleasantly spiced mincemeat within. A main course of chicken shish taouk was artfully marinated and

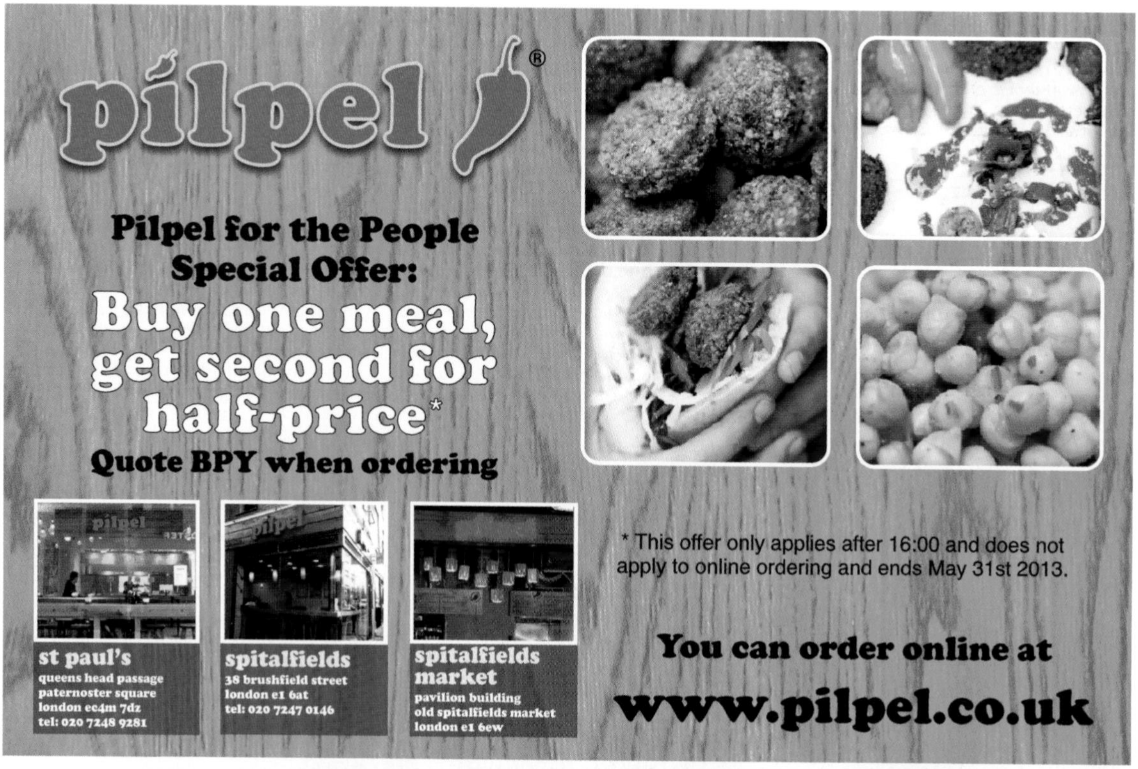
pilpel®
Pilpel for the People
Special Offer:
Buy one meal, get second for half-price*
Quote BPY when ordering
st paul's
queens head passage
paternoster square
london ec4m 7dz
tel: 020 7248 9281
spitalfields
38 brushfield street
london e1 6at
tel: 020 7247 0146
spitalfields market
pavilion building
old spitalfields market
london e1 6ew
* This offer only applies after 16:00 and does not apply to online ordering and ends May 31st 2013.
You can order online at
www.pilpel.co.uk

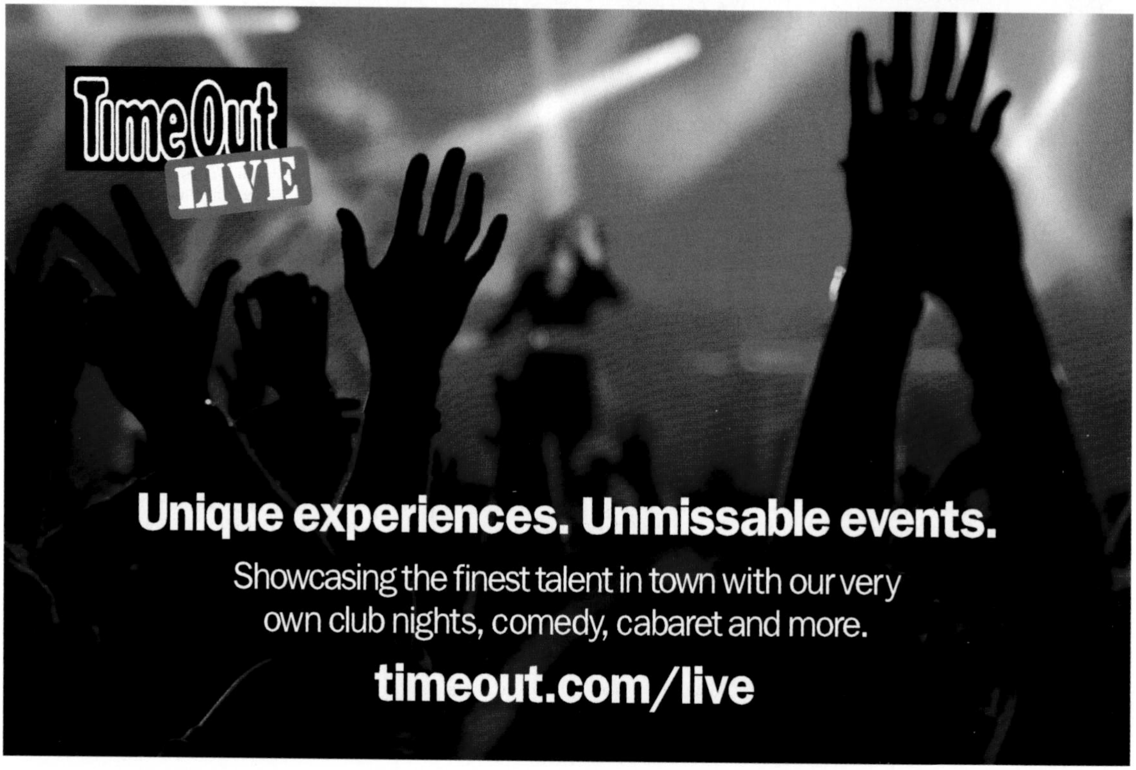
Time Out
LIVE
Unique experiences. Unmissable events.
Showcasing the finest talent in town with our very own club nights, comedy, cabaret and more.
timeout.com/live

grilled, while mint tea with carrot and saffron halwa made a refreshing culinary coda.
Available for hire. Babies and children admitted. Booking advisable. Tables outdoors (3, pavement). Takeaway service; delivery service (over £15 within 2-mile radius). **Map 12 S5.**

North

Archway

Gilak

663 Holloway Road, N19 5SE (7272 1692). Archway tube or Upper Holloway rail. **Meals served** 11am-10.30pm Mon-Fri; noon-10.30pm Sat, Sun. **Main courses** £6.99-£14.50. **Set meal** £42 (minimum 4). **Credit** MC, V.
Iranian
Iranian restaurants aren't known for their culinary variation, which makes the regional emphasis of this north London outpost all the more commendable. The menu focuses on dishes from the Gilan region of northern Iran, a cluster of coastal towns bordering the Caspian Sea. It's an area that also influences the restaurant's decor, minimal though this is – a fishing net strung across the ceiling, a few framed prints of boats and Iranian beaches. The single, caff-sized room holds only a handful of tables and chairs. Staff on our visit were happy to explain some of the more obscure dishes, including the 'Gilak special' starter, a hunk of smoked mackerel served with walnuts and broad beans, which are then rolled together in bread to create an interesting combination of flavours and textures. We also loved the sour-sweet contrast of zeytoon parvardeh (green olives in a punchy walnut and pomegranate marinade). A main of lemon and saffron-marinated joojeh chicken kebab was moist and flavoursome, but it was the regional morgh-e torsh that stole the show: a side of chicken in a sour herb and lemon sauce served with saffron-tinted rice.
Available for hire. Babies and children welcome: high chairs. Booking advisable. Disabled: toilet. Takeaway service; delivery service (over £15 within 2-mile radius). **Map 26 C1.**

Camden Town & Chalk Farm

Tandis

73 Haverstock Hill, NW3 4SL (7586 8079). Chalk Farm tube. **Meals served** noon-11.30pm Mon-Thur, Sun; noon-midnight Fri, Sat. **Main courses** £8.90-£14.90. **Credit** AmEx, MC, V.
Iranian
One of the few Iranian places in London offering glamorous interior design and an atmosphere more in keeping with a Modern European restaurant, Tandis features romantic dark wood furniture, bare brick walls embellished with painted symbols, and a large mirrored and backlit bar – appropriate, given the unusually good wine list. An intimate rear room sports leather booth seating, though we opted for a spot by the big windows overlooking Haverstock Hill. Food was generally excellent, and refreshingly authentic given the restaurant's upmarket ambience. A starter of sabzi-o panir was a heaped plate of fresh mixed herbs cut with crumbly blocks of feta and walnuts, while kookoo sabzi (herb omelette) was wonderfully aromatic and rich with olive oil. To follow, khoresht geymeh

Menu

See also the menus in **North African** and **Turkish**.

MEZE

Baba ganoush: Egyptian name for moutabal (qv).
Basturma: smoked beef.
Batinjan or **bazenjan el-rahib**: aubergine mashed with olive oil, garlic and tomato.
Batata hara: potatoes fried with peppers and chilli.
Falafel: a mixture of spicy chickpeas or broad beans, ground, rolled into balls and deep fried.
Fatayer: a soft pastry, filled with cheese, onions, spinach and pine kernels.
Fattoush: fresh vegetable salad containing shards of toasted pitta bread and sumac (qv).
Fuul or fuul medames: brown broad beans that are mashed and seasoned with olive oil, lemon juice and garlic.
Kalaj: halloumi cheese on pastry.
Kibbeh: highly seasoned mix of minced lamb, cracked wheat and onion, deep-fried in balls. As meze it is often served raw (**kibbeh nayeh**) like steak tartare.
Labneh: cream cheese made from yoghurt.
Moujadara: lentils, rice and caramelised onions mixed together.
Moutabal: a purée of chargrilled aubergines mixed with sesame sauce, garlic and lemon juice.
Muhamara: dip of crushed mixed nuts with red peppers, spices and pomegranate molasses.
Sambousek: small pastries filled with mince, onion and pine kernels.
Sujuk: spicy Lebanese sausages.
Sumac: an astringent and fruity-tasting spice made from dried sumac seeds.
Tabouleh: a salad of chopped parsley, tomatoes, crushed wheat, onions, olive oil and lemon juice.
Torshi: pickled vegetables.
Warak einab: rice-stuffed vine leaves.

MAINS

Shawarma: meat (usually lamb) marinated then grilled on a spit and sliced kebab-style.
Shish kebab: cubes of marinated lamb grilled on a skewer, often with tomatoes, onions and sweet peppers.
Shish taouk: like shish kebab, but with chicken rather than lamb.

DESSERTS

Balkava: filo pastry interleaved with pistachio nuts, almonds or walnuts, and covered in syrup.
Konafa or **kadayif**: cake made from shredded pastry dough, filled with syrup and nuts, or cream.
Ma'amoul: pastries filled with nuts or dates.
Muhallabia or **mohalabia**: a milky ground-rice pudding with almonds or pistachios, flavoured with rosewater or orange blossom.
Om ali: bread pudding, often made with filo pastry and including nuts and raisins.

IRANIAN DISHES

Ash-e reshteh: soup with noodles, spinach, pulses and dried herbs.
Ghorm-e sabzi: lamb with greens, kidney beans and dried limes.
Halim bademjan: mashed chargrilled aubergine with onions and walnuts.
Joojeh or **jujeh**: chicken marinated in saffron, lemon and onion.
Kashk, **qurut** or **quroot**: a salty whey.
Kashk-e bademjan: baked aubergines mixed with herbs and whey.
Khoresht-e fesenjan or **fesenjoon**: chicken cooked in ground walnut and pomegranate sauce.
Kuku-ye sabzi: finely chopped fresh herbs with eggs, baked in the oven.
Masto khiar: yoghurt mixed with finely chopped cucumber and mint.
Masto musir: shallot-flavoured yoghurt.
Mirza ghasemi: crushed baked aubergines, tomatoes, garlic and herbs mixed with egg.
Sabzi: a plate of fresh herb leaves (usually mint and dill) often served with a cube of feta.
Salad olivieh: like a russian salad, includes chopped potatoes, chicken, eggs, peas, gherkins, olive oil and mayonnaise.

bademjan (lamb, aubergine and split pea stew) was close to perfection, as was the accompanying saffron-tinted rice, but the meat in a baghali polo ba mahicheh (lamb shank with broad bean and dill-infused rice) was a touch dry. The only other duff note came via the overpowering piano music on the stereo: off-putting, given the mere handful of customers on a quiet weekday lunchtime.
Available for hire. Babies and children welcome: high chairs. Booking advisable Fri, Sat. Separate rooms for parties, seating 14-30. Tables outdoors (7, terrace). Takeaway service; delivery service (over £15 within 3-mile radius).

North West

Cricklewood

Zeytoon

94-96 Cricklewood Broadway, NW2 3EL (8830 7434, www.zeytoon.co.uk). Cricklewood rail. **Meals served** 12.30-11pm daily. **Main courses** £5.95-£11.95. **Set meze** £14.95. **Credit** AmEx, MC, V. Afghan
With its coloured windows, sculpted doors and shaded shisha terrace book-ended by illuminated trees, Zeytoon is an oasis of exoticism amid the otherwise mundane surrounds of Cricklewood Broadway. Inside, no corner has been cut in embellishing the orientalist fantasy: brick alcoves are painted with scenes depicting dream-like Persian women in the ancient poetic tradition; doorways are hung with tasselled rugs; ceilings are set with coloured chandeliers. Chunky wooden tables and chairs are spread over two rooms. The menu mixes dishes from Iran and Afghanistan; of the former, salad shirazi is a cold starter of diced chicken, eggs, potatoes and gherkins in citrus mayonnaise, while masto musir blends thick yoghurt with finely chopped shallots. There are various stews and an intimidating list of lamb and chicken kebabs, plus the traditional Persian workers' breakfast of kaleh pacheh (a broth of lamb's head and trotters), though we'd recommend the Afghan qabli polow (lamb shank with carrot, raisin and almond-infused brown rice): the house dish, and pretty unbeatable. On the downside, the restaurant can be awkwardly quiet – and staff tend towards the surly.
Available for hire. Babies and children welcome: high chairs. Booking advisable. Disabled: toilet. Separate room for parties, seats 100. Tables outdoors (6, pavement). Takeaway service.

Kensal Green

★ Behesht

1082-1084 Harrow Road, NW10 5NL (8964 4477, www.behesht.co.uk). Kensal Green tube/rail. **Meals served** noon-11.30pm daily. **Main courses** £5.95-£9.95. **Unlicensed** no alcohol allowed. **Credit** MC, V. Iranian
Top-notch Iranian food is not the only thing going for Behesht, which is also a walk-through gallery in the Persian storytelling tradition. Its maze-like warren of rooms features sculpted wooden walls and ceilings lined with weathered Iranian carpets; there are shelves laden with decorative daf drums and hand-beaten copper pots, cabinets filled with dolls and ram skulls and old Persian pipes; the babble of fountains is punctuated by the occasional squawk of the house parrot. We started our meal with a generous portion of smoky mirza ghasemi (mashed aubergine with garlic, eggs and tomato) and ash-e reshteh (a rich winter soup thickened with beans and noodles, and topped with whey). A main of baghali polo ba mahicheh was flawless: a mountain of rice spiked with dill and broad beans and served with a tomato and saffron-marinated lamb shank. Ghorm-e sabzi (lamb stew with greens, kidney beans and dried limes) was the best example we've tasted outside of an Iranian home. Save room for falooda (frozen rosewater and starch noodles) or pistachio-studded bastani ice-cream. If there's a restaurant serving more authentic Iranian cuisine in the capital, we've yet to find it.
Babies and children welcome: high chairs; nappy-changing facilities. Booking advisable. Disabled: toilet. Separate rooms for parties, seating 30-120. Takeaway service. Vegetarian menu.

West Hampstead

Mahdi

2 Canfield Gardens, NW6 3BS (7625 4344). Finchley Road tube. **Meals served** noon-11pm daily. **Main courses** £4.90-£12.90. **Set lunch** (buffet) £7.90. **Credit** MC, V. Iranian
The original Mahdi was a revelation when it first opened on Hammersmith's King Street, the authenticity of its cooking and the gargantuan portions quickly becoming talking points among the capital's Persian expats. Our most recent visit was to the NW6 outpost, which was packed with local Iranians: always a good sign. Great efforts have been made to emulate the feel of an Iranian chelo kebab restaurant – the windows set with coloured glass, the walls with brick arches housing Persian tapestries, a head-high samovar overlooking proceedings from one corner – but there's an air of functionality, something not helped by the closely packed tables or the slightly frantic staff. For all that, the menu is one of the most extensive you'll find in London, including rarities such as tah chin (an indulgent rice-cake starter with cream, saffron, eggs and barberries) and abgoosht, a slow-cooked worker's stew of lamb, potatoes and beans. Kebabs are wonderfully tender and bigger than a baby's arm, while one-pot dishes such as lubia polo (rice with lamb and green beans) come in portions fit to feed a small family. Expect to leave with leftovers.
Available for hire. Babies and children welcome: high chairs. Takeaway service. **Map 28 B3.**
For branch see index.

Outer London

Wembley, Middlesex

Mesopotamia

115 Wembley Park Drive, Wembley, Middx HA9 8HG (8453 5555, www.mesopotamia.ltd.uk). Wembley Park tube. **Dinner served** 5.30-11.30pm Mon-Sat. **Main courses** £7-£14. **Set meal** £19.95-£24.95 (minimum 2) 3 courses. **Credit** AmEx, MC, V. Iraqi
Complimented on the flavoursome tomatoes in a portion of fattoush, Suha Holmyard, co-owner of this modest yet lavishly attired Iraqi restaurant, smiled and said simply: 'We choose.' Similar care was evident in other meze dishes: smoky baba ganoush as soft as an aubergine fool; houmous smooth and subtly bitter; fuul medames with tang and bite. Falafel were plump and perfectly fried. Next, an Iraqi main of beef guss apparently included tahini and cumin, although pepper and citrus were the loudest notes. An accompanying mound of rice was feather light. Köfte-like lamb meatballs came with chunks of potato in a rich curried tomato sauce. Lebanese labels are highlights of the wine list, and Arabian cardamom coffee made a wonderful, aromatic end to the meal, the spice seeming to redouble the caffeine's effects. The interior is heady too, inspired by Babylon: billowing, Bedouin tent-effect ceiling; urns and sand-coloured walls with lion shapes in relief; a huge dresser so ornate it might house religious relics. Yet despite the escapist decor, Mesopotamia's food still provides ample distraction – as it would even if served on the forecourt of the petrol station outside.
Available for hire. Babies and children welcome: high chairs. Booking advisable Fri, Sat. Takeaway service. Vegetarian menu.

Gilak. See p201.

Modern European

In the early days of London's restaurant revolution, through the 1990s, the term 'Modern European' was coined to describe the innovators and risk-takers: those establishments with talented chefs whose imaginations transcended the bounds of national cuisines and (French-based) culinary edicts. London's position as a world city gave them ready access to ingredients from around the globe. Over the years, a new canon has been created: grounded in British cookery, but with ample influences from France, Italy and (increasingly) Spain – as well as from further afield. The wilder areas of experimentation have largely been left to the fusion specialists (for which, *see p226* **Pan-Asian & Fusion**) and the gastronomic laboratories of a few trailblazing haute cuisine practitioners (*see p131* **Hotels & Haute Cuisine**). But that's not to say today's cohort of Modern European restaurants has become staid. Talent and inventiveness course through this section, no more so than in our favourite 'red star' venues: **10 Greek Street**, a new venture producing low-key excellence in Soho; **Café Anglais**, Rowley Leigh's assured Bayswater brasserie-restaurant; the **Exhibition Rooms**, a consistently top performer in Crystal Palace; Philip Howard's exceptional Kensington outfit, **Kitchen W8**; the **Orrery**, producing exquisitely prepared nourishment in Marylebone; the **Oxo Tower Restaurant, Bar & Brasserie**, where superb river views are complemented by sophisticated cooking; and Mayfair's **Wild Honey**, with its effortless attainment of first-class quality. Along with 10 Greek Street, our other new arrival this year is **Abbeville Kitchen**, creating robust Anglo-Med food in Clapham. They join this outstanding collection of some of the capital's most popular, and classy, dining venues.

Central

Barbican

Chiswell Street Dining Rooms

56 Chiswell Street, EC1Y 4SA (7614 0177, www.chiswellstreetdining.com). Barbican tube or Moorgate tube/rail. **Lunch served** 11.30am-3.30pm, **tea served** 3.30-6pm, **dinner served** 6-10.45pm Mon-Fri. **Main courses** £12.50-£27. **Set meal** £38-£50 3 courses. **Credit** AmEx, MC, V.

Unlike other Martin Brothers' ventures, Chiswell Street Dining Rooms isn't much of a pub (though you can drink in the roomy bar, where beer and wine are taken seriously), and the dining room feels like a restaurant, with prices to match. The decor here is less in-your-face (no taxidermy, for a start) and more lounge-like than the Jugged Hare (*see p105*) – the gastropub that's also attached to the Montcalm London City hotel. Colours are subdued, chairs nicely padded; staff are friendly and professional. What was slightly below-par on our visit was the food. Coq au vin, served with excellent savoy cabbage and creamed potato, was more like three chicken pieces recently introduced to gravy, while a main course salad of smoked barbary duck breast was dominated by its salad cream-like dressing and (unexpectedly candied) walnuts. These dishes hovered around £15; even pricier were the likes of grilled fillet of Cornish brill (£27) – too much for what is merely competent cooking. The bar menu might be the more attractive option, including charcuterie plates, cheeseboards, and steak sandwiches (though even these are £15) – or look out for one of the generous special offers.
Available for hire. Babies and children welcome: high chairs; nappy-changing facilities. Booking advisable. Disabled: toilet. Separate rooms for parties, seating 10, 30, 40, 45 and 60. **Map 5 P5.**

Belgravia

Botanist

7 Sloane Square, SW1W 8EE (7730 0077, www.thebotanistonsloanesquare.com). Sloane Square tube. **Breakfast served** 8-11.30am Mon-Fri; 9-11.30am Sat, Sun. **Lunch served** noon-3.30pm Mon-Fri; noon-4pm Sat, Sun. **Tea served** 3.30-6pm, **dinner served** 5.30-10.45pm daily. **Main courses** £15-£46. **Set dinner** (5.30-6.30pm, 10-10.45pm) £21 2 courses, £26 3 courses. **Credit** AmEx, MC, V.

Sloane Square's Botanist is one of the upmarket ventures of gastropub-meisters the ETM Group, the force behind the Gun, the Well and other fashionable venues. In accordance with the location, however, it eschews any pubbiness in favour of a cocktail-bar-cum-restaurant feel. Shining metalwork and creamy leather dominate in the buzzy bar, while tall windows and subtle lighting make the dining room an airy, comfortable space, artfully decorated with images of botanical specimens. Service was bright and charming. The menu makes an appealing read, and our meal was, well, pleasant, yet nothing more: the kind of thing you'd expect in any half-decent gastropub, but at a substantially higher price. Fresh asparagus came with a 'vinaigrette' that was really a bland herb dressing,

Dock Kitchen. See p210.

while a prawn and herb cocktail – one of a few retro-Brit favourites on the list – was, again, inoffensive, but served too cold. Duck confit with bacon and puy lentils had decent flavour, and a rather potato-heavy salmon fish cake with spinach and beurre blanc was unexceptionally enjoyable too. The hefty flash-the-cash wine list adds substantially to the bill, although prices don't seem to deter the area's recession-proof clientele.
Babies and children welcome: high chairs; nappy-changing facilities. Booking advisable. Disabled: toilet. Dress: smart casual. Tables outdoors (4, pavement). **Map 15 G10**.

Bloomsbury

Giaconda Dining Room

9 Denmark Street, WC2H 8LS (7240 3334, www.giacondadining.com). Tottenham Court Road tube. **Lunch served** noon-2.15pm Tue-Fri. **Dinner served** 6-9.15pm Tue-Sat. **Main courses** £12-£14. **Cover** £1.50. **Credit** AmEx, MC, V.

Giaconda is a one-of-a-kind restaurant – a totally unpretentious, tiny, anti-decor dining room, serving serious, French-based food. But by September 2012, the restaurant will have been reconfigured, the kitchen (and loo) upgraded, and the whole place expanded into a back room. While there'll be more space, the food is set to remain the same. This is often traditional and fairly uncompromising, with a good deal of offal featured on the laminated menu – the likes of baked tripe with butter beans and paprika; poached ox tongue with parsley, bread and lentil salad; and a quintessential Giaconda starter of crisped pigs' trotters with potato and egg mayonnaise. On a recent visit, our starter of warm smoked salmon with celeriac was a well-flavoured, smoky hunk rather than slices. Risotto of the day with saffron and squash had some skilfully subtle flavours and a consistency that was spot on. Braised guinea fowl with red wine sauce and polenta was a little more ordinary, but no one could say a word against the huge, indulgent helping of eton mess. Wines are a well-curated, all-European collection, and staff are as friendly and unstuffy as the surroundings.
Available for hire. Babies and children admitted. Booking advisable. Separate room for parties, seats 30. **Map 17 C3**.

Paramount

101-103 New Oxford Street, WC1A 1DD (7420 2900, www.paramount.uk.net). Tottenham Court Road tube.
Bar **Open** 8am-1.30am Mon-Wed; 8am-2.30am Thur-Sat; noon-4pm Sun.
Restaurant **Breakfast served** 8-10.30am Mon-Fri. **Lunch served** noon-3pm daily. **Dinner served** 6-11pm Mon-Sat. **Main courses** £14.50-£25.50. **Set lunch** (Mon-Fri) £23.50 2 courses incl glass of wine, £28.50 3 courses incl glass of wine. **Set dinner** £30 3 courses incl cocktail.
Both **Credit** AmEx, MC, V.

Completed in the year England won the World Cup, Centre Point is now home to the kind of restaurant where you might hope to spot premiership footballers. The 360-degree viewing gallery and cocktail bar on the 33rd floor is dramatic, and the restaurant (plus additional bar space) one floor below buzzes with chatter and a sense of occasion. Cooking is ambitious, with a lot of combinations per plate; seared scallop with crab tortellini, curry oil, green apple salad, carrot and coriander purée is a typical starter. Beef carpaccio with horseradish panna cotta, pickled vegetables, capers and bone marrow was a good stab at a theme, with sweet miniature pickled carrots and a zesty horseradish; it was pleasant, but the carpaccio was a little bland. A main course hake fillet was also slightly drab, but enlivened by the tang of chorizo, while a trio of pork (cheek, pie and belly) had some good elements, especially the pastry on the mini pork pie, but the belly pork lacked verve and again, was a trifle dull. Overall, dishes rarely amounted to more than the sum of their many parts. However, staff were charming, the joint was jumping (this is not a place for a quiet dinner à deux) and it's not every night you get to eat with a panorama of London before you.
Babies and children welcome (restaurant): high chairs. Booking essential. Disabled: lift; toilet. Dress: smart. Separate rooms for parties, seating 16-30 and 150. **Map 17 C2**.

City

Prism

147 Leadenhall Street, EC3V 4QT (7256 3888, www.harveynichols.com/restaurants). Bank tube/DLR or Liverpool Street tube/rail.
Bar **Open** 11am-11pm, **lunch served** 11.30am-3pm Mon-Fri. **Main courses** £10-£14.
Restaurant **Lunch served** noon-3pm, **dinner served** 6-10pm Mon-Fri. **Main courses** £18-£25. **Set meal** £24.50 2 courses, £29.50 3 courses.
Both **Credit** AmEx, DC, MC, V.

Part of the Harvey Nichols family, Prism occupies the former Bank of New York building on Leadenhall Street. The restaurant is housed in the grand, neo-classical banking hall, complete with pillars, high ceilings and stucco. On one side, near the long bar, is an informal area with red sofas; the rest of the space has tables. Unfortunately, when the place is (almost) empty, as it was on our visit, diners are dwarfed and conviviality is almost impossible – though staff assured us that lunches and winter evenings are busier. Confident cooking, with good ingredients combined with flair and originality, marked our meal. From the (very good-value) set menu, a cube of luxurious, dense duck confit was topped with gorgeously flavoured green beans wrapped in pancetta. On the side was a little dollop of sweet apple sauce. Equally good was a simple starter of melt-in-the-mouth, just-cooked trout, served with samphire. A main of roast chicken came with a flavoursome jus, and was beautifully presented with a circle of vivid peas and green broad beans. And a pudding of mini churros with a small cup of chocolate sauce made for a lighthearted, wickedly indulgent end to the meal. Staff were friendly and competent – doing their bit to inject some vitality into a cavernous space. The bar in the vaults below is a cosier spot, with a less expensive menu.
Babies and children welcome: high chairs. Booking advisable. Disabled: toilet. Separate rooms for parties, seating 23 and 45. Vegetarian menu. **Map 12 Q6**.

Clerkenwell & Farringdon

Smiths of Smithfield

67-77 Charterhouse Street, EC1M 6HJ (7251 7950, www.smithsofsmithfield.co.uk). Barbican tube or Farringdon tube/rail.
Café-bar **Open** 7am-11pm Mon-Wed; 7am-midnight Thur, Fri; 9.30am-midnight Sat; 9.30am-5pm Sun. **Meals served** 7am-4.45pm Mon-Fri; 9.30am-4.45pm Sat, Sun. **Main courses** £5.50-£10.50.
Wine Rooms **Dinner served** 6-10.45pm Tue, Wed; noon-11pm Thur, Fri; 12.30-11pm Sat. **Main courses** £5-£10.
Dining Room **Lunch served** noon-2.45pm Mon-Fri. **Dinner served** 6-10.45pm Mon-Sat. **Main courses** £12-£28.
Top Floor restaurant **Lunch served** noon-2.45pm Mon-Fri; 12.30-3.45pm Sun. **Dinner served** 6-10.45pm Mon-Sat. **Main courses** £16-£30.
All **Credit** AmEx, MC, V.

MasterChef judge John Torode's huge Smithfield venue tries to be all things to all people, and largely succeeds: it's packed nightly with a sometimes boisterous crowd, a mix of City spillover and local office workers. The ground floor houses a bustling bar, which serves snacks such as hot dogs and sliders; the first-floor 'wine rooms' offers small plates and a large wine list; then there's a casual restaurant and, above that, a more formal dining room (Top Floor) with great views. The lower levels have an exposed, industrial feel that is beginning to look a little dated (as is the house habit of writing everything within inverted commas – as in 'toilets'), but the food is still of a high standard, as we discovered at a recent meal on the second floor. Mini chorizos with chickpea purée was a great accompaniment to menu perusal. An Indian spiced chicken was beautifully juicy and fragrant, well matched by yoghurt and cucumber salad and flatbread. Red meat is a cornerstone of the menu – chargrilled rib steak with chips and watercress was a perfect marriage of texture and flavour. Service is friendly enough under often busy circumstances.
Babies and children welcome (restaurant): high chairs; nappy-changing facilities. Disabled: lift; toilet. Entertainment (ground floor): DJs 7pm Thur-Sat. Separate rooms for parties, seating 12 and 24. Tables outdoors (4, pavement; 8, terrace). **Map 11 O5**.

Covent Garden

L'Atelier de Joël Robuchon

13-15 West Street, WC2H 9NE (7010 8600, www.joel-robuchon.com). Leicester Square tube.
Bar **Open** noon-2am Mon-Sat; noon-10.30pm Sun.
Ground floor **Lunch served** noon-2.30pm Mon-Sat. **Dinner served** 5.30-10.30pm Mon-Sat; 5.30-10pm Sun. **Main courses** £15-£55. **Set meal** (noon-2.30pm, 5.30-6.30pm) £28 2 courses, £32 3 courses, £40 4 courses.
1st floor **Lunch served** noon-2.30pm, **dinner served** 6-11.30pm Mon-Sat. **Main courses** £15-£55.
All **Credit** AmEx, MC, V.

The multi-storey Robuchon complex (informal La Cuisine on the first floor, bar on the second and Atelier at ground level) is bang in the middle of the West End, but nothing about it says 'London'. The Atelier is a link in a dozen-strong international chain from the French chef-restaurateur, all sharing the smart if slightly dated bento-box aesthetic of shiny reds and blacks, square central bar, low light and striking curio cabinets; this one has a feature wall of tumbling creeper. It's a nightclub look that doesn't play so well at lunchtime, when the crowd can be small. They're missing out: while Robuchon's philosophy of season and terroir is no longer innovative, his standards and quality control remain high, and the set lunch, with the usual haute cuisine trappings, is the most economic way to sample it. An amuse-bouche of foie gras with a port reduction was a masterclass in taste and texture (and an advert for the considerably more expensive and sophisticated à la carte); the menu proper used simpler ingredients but with impeccable technique: a soft-boiled egg that melted into piperade and parsley oil with a snap of tuile and fizz of spice; an onglet that was impeccably cut and cooked and prettily served on lemony polenta. The wine list is the connoisseur's document you'd expect, and the staff as able.
Available for hire. Babies and children welcome: high chairs; nappy-changing facilities. Booking advisable; essential dinner. Disabled: toilet. Dress: smart casual. Vegetarian menu. **Map 17 C3**.

The Ivy

1 West Street, WC2H 9NQ (7836 4751, www.the-ivy.co.uk). Leicester Square tube.
Meals served noon-11.30pm Mon-Sat; noon-10.30pm Sun. **Main courses** £11.50-£34.50. **Set meal** (2.30-6pm, 10-11.30pm Mon-Thur; noon-10.30pm Sun) £21.75 2 courses, £26.25 3 courses. **Cover** £2. **Credit** AmEx, DC, MC, V.

The Ivy may no longer be the people-watching destination of old; but it's hard to imagine that the food served to club members is more perfectly executed than the 'downstairs' fare of the main restaurant. Yes, prices are quite steep for a place where neither fashionistas nor culinary fireworks are at play – but it's hard to find fault with ambience, food or service, and there is much to commend all three. On a wet and windy Sunday lunchtime, the place was as packed as ever and buzzing with the sound of enjoyment (even the waiters were joshing behind the scenes). From families tucking into roast and trimmings to couples cracking open the fizz, the mix was as eclectic as the global cuisine, all bathed in a stained glass glow. Our own pick 'n' mix ordering – burger and chips for the teen, one set meal, a selection of starters – was deftly and smilingly accommodated, with a finger bowl surreptitiously slipped across to the cutlery ignorer. Their millionth burger it might be, but it was seared and medium-rare perfection. Verdant broad bean soup, a rainbow of heirloom tomatoes, simple roast chicken, the dessert tasting plate – all were spot on. Long may it stay stalwart.
Babies and children welcome: high chairs. Booking essential, 4-6 weeks in advance. Separate room for parties, seats 60. Vegan dishes. Vegetarian menu. **Map 18 D4**.

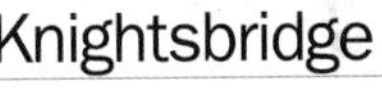

Knightsbridge

Fifth Floor

Harvey Nichols, Knightsbridge, SW1X 7RJ (7235 5250, www.harveynichols.com/restaurants). Knightsbridge tube.
Café **Breakfast served** 8am-noon, **lunch served** noon-3.30pm, **dinner served** 6-10.30pm Mon-Sat. **Brunch served** 11am-5pm Sun. **Tea served** 3-6pm daily. **Main courses** £9.50-£15.
Restaurant **Lunch served** noon-2.45pm Mon-Thur; noon-3.45pm Fri, Sat. **Brunch served** noon-4pm Sun. **Tea served** 2.30-5.30pm Mon-Sat; 3-5pm Sun. **Dinner served** 6-10.30pm Mon-Sat. **Main courses** £19.50-£26. **Set meal** £20 2 courses, £25 3 courses.
Both **Credit** AmEx, DC, MC, V.

Wild Honey. See p207.

10 Greek Street. See p209.

The entrance you use to access Fifth Floor will colour your impression of the place. Come through the shop itself, past an area of more informal dining in the food hall, and you'll notice the sophisticated market elements – a menu that picks out fresh ingredients from the field, farm and sea. Come straight up in the lift from the street and you'll enter through the bar, which dazzles with white leather, lime green walls and loud music. The restaurant itself is decorated in neutral taupe, simple and stylish under a fantastic domed, latticed ceiling. It ties modern and classic together well for a moneyed crowd who don't mind the inflated prices and enjoy the flourish of a champagne trolley being wheeled to their table. Portions are small and light, and use seasonal ingredients in classic combinations. A dish of marinated beef came in carpaccio-thin slices with green leaves and a punchy cream dressing – excellent. On the other hand, a fennel upside-down tart with truffle dressing lacked any finesse and was under-seasoned. You'd expect better for the price: on current form, Fifth Floor is more suitable for a shopping trip lunch than a special dinner.
Babies and children welcome: children's menu; high chairs; nappy-changing facilities. Disabled: lift; toilet. Tables outdoors (15, café terrace). **Map 8 F9.**

Marylebone

L'Autre Pied

5-7 Blandford Street, W1U 3DB (7486 9696, www.lautrepied.co.uk). Baker Street tube.
Lunch served noon-2.30pm Mon-Sat; noon-3.30pm Sun. **Dinner served** 6-10pm Mon-Sat. **Main courses** £26-£30. **Set meal** (noon-2.30pm Mon-Sat; 6-7pm daily) £22 2 courses, £25 3 courses. **Set lunch** (Sun) £29.50 3 courses. **Credit** AmEx, MC, V.

What it lacks in elbow room and statement design, L'Autre Pied makes up for with precision fine dining – the kind that makes you stop mid-conversation to murmur appreciative ahs and mmms. Andy McFadden's menu at this bijou version of sister restaurant Pied à Terre conjures up dainty yet intense dishes, at more accessible prices than its grown-up sibling (especially good value are the set menus). A riot of ingredients is packed into every mouthful, so a starter of beetroot risotto brought goat's cheese, tapioca, ras el hanout and a micro hit of balsamic into the fray. Mains are likewise accomplished balancing acts: a poached duck egg served with asparagus, tomato, onion seeds and crab bisque was the simplest dish on offer. Haunch of roe deer had a satisfyingly sweet counterpoint, courtesy of tea-marinated prunes. In short, you need to like a certain level of complexity to get the most out of L'Autre Pied. And while the culinary artistry does the talking, the decor takes a back seat. A kind of modest chinoiserie punctuated by rosewood tables free of starched tablecloths, it lends itself to a casualness not usually associated with such consummate cooking.
Babies and children welcome: high chairs. Booking advisable. Separate room for parties, seats 16. Tables outdoors (3, pavement). Vegan dishes. Vegetarian menu. **Map 9 G5.**

★ Orrery

55 Marylebone High Street, W1U 5RB (7616 8000, www.orrery-restaurant.co.uk). Baker Street or Regent's Park tube. **Lunch served** noon-2.15pm, **dinner served** 6.30-10.15pm daily. **Set lunch** £22.50 2 courses (£38.50 incl wine),

£25 3 courses (£41.50 incl wine). **Set dinner** £48 3 courses, £55 6 courses, £59 tasting menu (£104 incl wine). **Credit** AmEx, DC, MC, V.
Dining at the Orrery takes place in the slim rectangular space of a converted stable block, a floor above street level and bathed in light from a glorious string of arched windows and skylights. And despite being so central, the views are bucolic and villagey, thanks to the well-tended church grounds opposite. Service is not overly formal, but can feel a little intrusive. It's a shame as Igor Tymchyshyn's dishes are so exquisitely prepped and preened that they make a big impression, no fussing required. A starter of smooth asparagus velouté was extravagantly poured at the table, while the seafood raviolo emerged from a moat of delightful shellfish bisque. Shoulder of lamb arrived as a turret of braised, shredded meat, threatening to topple as soon as the fork struck, and adorned with crisped potato fanned out like a peacock's tail. A super-fresh sea bass fillet was more modestly proportioned. Desserts are equally impressive, or there are cheeses from the trolley; coffees and teas include a refill. The wine list is a serious read, sprinkled with a few wallet-friendly bottles. Take your time – it's worth it. Hang out in the dinky bar or, better still, dine on the roof terrace if weather permits.
Available for hire. Babies and children welcome: high chairs; nappy-changing facilities. Booking essential. Disabled: toilet. Dress: smart casual. Separate room for parties, seats 16. Tables outdoors (5, roof terrace). Vegetarian menu. **Map 3 G4.**

Mayfair

Sotheby's Café

Sotheby's, 34-35 New Bond Street, W1S 2RT (7293 5077, www.sothebys.com/cafe). Bond Street or Oxford Circus tube. **Breakfast served** 9.30-11.30am, **lunch served** noon-2.45pm, **tea served** 3-4.45pm Mon-Fri. **Main courses** £15-£21.50. **Set tea** £8.25-£21.25. **Credit** AmEx, DC, MC, V.
Not a café at all, but a small restaurant serving breakfast, lunch and afternoon tea in a space that looks like it's been tipped out of a rather elegant old train compartment. The windowless room is all mirror and wood, though half the tables spill across into the plush but bland main corridor of the auction house. These foyer tables give you a good view of the comings and goings of the delightfully posh Sotheby's clientele. The lunch menu is short and adventurous: three starters and three mains, one apiece for carnivores, piscivores and vegetarians. Chopped duck liver pâté was generous but disappointing, the elements plonked on to the plate with little care, its flavour equally utilitarian. A main of devilled quail looked and tasted better, delicately cooked to the requisite pinkness, and accompanied by delicious cornbread and a perfectly ripe avocado and tomato salad. Goat's cheese soufflé looked equally enticing as it went past. Prices are a touch expensive, with a rocket and parmesan side salad at £5.50 feeling like a particularly cheeky ask, though balanced by a more reasonable £5.75 for perfect eton mess.
Babies and children admitted. Booking advisable. Closed 2 weeks Aug. Disabled: toilet. **Map 9 H6.**

★ Wild Honey HOT 50

12 St George Street, W1S 2FB (7758 9160, www.wildhoneyrestaurant.co.uk). Bond Street or Oxford Circus tube. **Lunch served** noon-2.30pm Mon-Sat; noon-3pm Sun. **Dinner served** 5-11pm Mon-Thur; 5-11.30pm Fri, Sat; 5.30-10.30pm Sun. **Main courses** £17.50-£19.50. **Set lunch** £21.95 3 courses. **Set dinner** (5-6.30pm) £22.95 3 courses. **Credit** AmEx, MC, V.
The team at Wild Honey make it all seem effortless: the place is a happy blend of grand decor and easy-going atmosphere; the cooking is top-notch; and from the initial cheery welcome to the final helping-on of coats, service is a model of charm and efficiency. From a dinner that ranged from the pretty delicacy of Dorset crab with avocado and Italian leaves, to the robustness of guinea fowl and foie gras boudin blanc with peas, broad beans and pancetta (both starters), only a main course bouillabaisse failed to wow. The soup had depth of flavour, and good accompaniments, but contained fish only (no seafood), and was quickly cold. Much more satisfying was a generous breast of Limousin veal with caramelised onion and anchovy, and Cornish cod with peas, broad beans and ridiculously tasty boneless chicken wings. English pear clafoutis with vanilla ice-cream was a dreamily good pudding. All wines on the globe-trotting list come by the 250ml carafe as well as the bottle. Wild Honey was the second of three restaurants opened by Anthony Demetre and Will Smith (after Arbutus, and before Les Deux Salons). Each is different in look and feel, but all exude quality.
Available for hire. Babies and children welcome: high chairs. Booking essential. **Map 9 H6.**

Piccadilly

Criterion

224 Piccadilly, W1J 9HP (7930 0488, www.criterionrestaurant.com). Piccadilly Circus tube. **Lunch served** noon-2.30pm, **dinner served** 5.30-11.30pm Mon-Sat. **Main courses** £16-£28.50. **Set meal** (lunch, 5.30-7pm, 10-11.30pm) £19 2 courses, £29 3 courses. **Credit** AmEx, MC, V.
Given its location, plumb on Piccadilly Circus, the Criterion needs to make a splash to distinguish itself. Does it manage the feat? On first impressions, wow. The spectacular interior (created 1874) is an uninhibited celebration of neo-Byzantine craziness: a huge hall, resplendent in white marble fittings, decorative archways and a glorious golden mosaic ceiling. HG Wells, Churchill, Lloyd George and Bertrand Russell dined here. Look closer, though, and the image becomes slightly tarnished – the drab carpeting, the hotel-lounge chairs in the front bar, the deadening muzak. Likewise the food. The carte reads well, containing prime steaks, roasted rack of lamb, and lemon sole with truffle mash and brown shrimp beurre blanc. The wine list, arranged by style, is pleasing too. And our set lunch began splendidly with exemplary duck-egg benedict with parma ham. But a main of salmon on samphire screamed out for some lemony tang, and we struggled to discern gooseberry flavour in a sugary gooseberry tart (albeit well matched with tangy fruit and blackberry sorbet). Service was also curate's eggy: the waiting staff epitomising charm and efficiency; less so the kitchen team, whose roars and oaths could clearly be heard – a reminder, perhaps, of when Marco Pierre White ran the show here.
Babies and children welcome: high chairs. Booking advisable. Disabled: toilet. Dress: smart casual. Separate room for parties, seats 70. **Map 17 B5.**

St James's

Avenue

7-9 St James's Street, SW1A 1EE (7321 2111, www.theavenue-restaurant.co.uk). Green Park tube.
Bar **Open** 11am-11pm Mon-Fri; 5.45-11pm Sat.
Restaurant **Lunch served** noon-3pm Mon-Fri. **Dinner served** 5.45-11pm Mon-Sat. **Main courses** £13.50-£20.50. **Set lunch** £19.50 2 courses, £23.50 3 courses. **Set dinner** (5.45-7pm, 9.30-11pm) £17.50 2 courses, £21.50 3 courses.
Both **Credit** AmEx, DC, MC, V.
In a part of town characterised by gentlemen's clubs, purveyors of gourmet foodstuffs and fogeyish fashion outlets, Avenue offers a contrastingly contemporary look, in a large, bright and airy – if potentially cold – white space with lofty ceilings, swathes of red, and changing exhibitions of modern paintings for sale. Tables are spread over two levels, and there's a long, sleek, well-stocked cocktail bar. It's a big space to fill, and the management has responded to current times with various promotions and set menus, including a post-theatre meal (from 9.30pm) as well as the usual pre-theatre deals. Food is a light, fresh Mod Euro mix, very attractively presented. A starter of English asparagus featured first-rate main ingredients perfectly prepared, although the accompanying truffle vinaigrette lacked the punch of top-notch truffles; a goat's cheese salad included an original mix of different radishes. To follow, pea risotto with real violets – flavourless, but undeniably pretty – was lovely and smooth, and we also enjoyed a very tender marinated chicken breast. Service is welcoming, and the wine list intelligently wide-ranging. Also gratifying is the bill, which is far less painful than the St James's norm.
Available for hire. Babies and children admitted. Booking advisable. Disabled: toilet. Separate room for parties, seats 20.
Map 9 J8.

Le Caprice

Arlington House, Arlington Street, SW1A 1RJ (7629 2239, www.caprice-holdings.co.uk). Green Park tube. **Meals served** noon-midnight Mon-Fri; 11.30am-midnight Sat; 11.30am-11pm Sun. **Main courses** £15.75-£32. **Set dinner** (5.30-6.45pm, after 10.15pm) £19.75 2 courses, £24.25 3 courses. **Cover** £2. **Credit** AmEx, DC, MC, V.
Shiny black and chrome fixtures and fittings, which nod to art deco, set the scene at Le Caprice, the slinky celebrity bolthole off Piccadilly. This cornerstone of upscale chain Caprice Holdings comes with a 30-year reputation to maintain – and that reputation is only partly for the food. Everyone from Liz Hurley to Peter Stringfellow dines here, in a room that borders on the intimate – but any notion of earwigging is usually dispelled by the exuberant pianist. Customers tend to dress up, oozing wealth, if not always sophistication. The à la carte menu is on the pricey side for such classic, comfort food as salmon fish cake with buttered spinach and sorrel sauce (a signature dish), a Caprice burger or ribeye with béarnaise sauce. But the theatre menu is good value. A starter of pan-fried duck egg on toast came with delicate fingers of tender asparagus. Fillet of bream with fregola salsa and pesto was a pleasant main, while veal and artichoke ragù was overseasoned yet moreish. No fireworks then, but an enduringly reliable place to see and be seen.

Dock Kitchen occupies one floor of furniture designer Tom Dixon's headquarters, which are in a former warehouse overlooking the Grand Union Canal. The restaurant combines guest chefs and themed, just-discovered-this menus with a casual, café-style vibe evocative of the River Café. Its fans don't seem to mind that it charges top West End prices for dishes that most of us can easily make from one of chef (and *Telegraph* cookery columnist) Stevie Parle's cookbooks. Current culinary trends and ingredients are used for inspiration, with varying degrees of success. A starter plate of tomato salad (£7.50) was garnished with freekeh, purslane, sumac and 'flowers from the garden', the resulting collision of flavours saved by the excellent quality of the ripe, plump tomatoes. £18.50 brought a bowl of watery stew of white fish chunks; this was advertised as coming with clams, but four of the six shells were empty. The dabbling in oriental cuisines can be similarly hit or miss; our tandoor flatbread was pale and undercooked. Still, the tables outdoors overlooking Innocent drink company HQ across the canal can be a lovely spot on a warm day. Be warned that the restaurant seems perpetually over-subscribed, with frequent table-turning, and note that the Kitchenette bar on the floor below serves drinks and bar food from 5.30pm to midnight on Fridays and Saturdays.

Available for hire. Babies and children welcome: high chairs; nappy-changing facilities. Booking advisable. Disabled: toilet. Separate room for parties, seats 25. Tables outdoors (6, terrace).

Notting Hill

Notting Hill Brasserie

92 Kensington Park Road, W11 2PN (7229 4481, www.nottinghillbrasserie.com). Ladbroke Grove or Notting Hill Gate tube.

Lunch served noon-3pm daily. **Dinner served** 6.30-11pm Mon-Sat; 6.30-10.30pm Sun. **Main courses** £19.50-£25.50. **Set lunch** (Wed-Sat) £15.50 2 courses, £19.50 3 courses; (Sun) £29.50 2 courses, £36.50 3 courses. **Credit** AmEx, MC, V.

When is a brasserie not a brasserie? When it's the Notting Hill Brasserie. From the moment you set foot inside, you'll see this is no casual diner, but a high-end restaurant designed to relieve you of your bonus and/or trust fund. The sumptuous front bar (complete, on many nights, with piano player) gives way to a flatteringly low-lit dining room, where the linen is starched, the surroundings elegant and the staff ultra-polite. The globe-trotting wine list offers decent by-the-glass options. The kitchen is ambitious, using purées, emulsions and luxury ingredients – yet it doesn't always deliver. Our two-stage seafood starter showed potential, beginning with a mound of delicate crab and avocado salad on wafer-thin crispbread, but it was let down by bland, fridge-cold tuna tataki. A main course of juicy lamb with roasted sweetbreads and various sauces, blobs and squiggles (from gutsy green olive tapenade to sweet, plump raisins) showed a more deft hand. Unfortunately, pud, a cloying rhubarb and rosewater cheesecake with an impenetrable base, also fell short of the mark. Such inconsistency, given the considerable prices, would normally sound a restaurant's death knell, but wealthy Notting Hillbillies keep returning.

Babies and children welcome: high chairs. Booking advisable. Entertainment: jazz/blues musicians 7pm daily, lunch Sun. Separate rooms for parties, seating 12 and 32. **Map 7 A6**.

South West

Barnes

Sonny's Kitchen

94 Church Road, SW13 0DQ (8748 0393, www.sonnyskitchen.co.uk). Barnes or Barnes Bridge rail, or bus 33, 209, 283.

Bar **Lunch served** noon-3.30pm daily. **Brunch served** 10am-4pm Sat; 10am-noon Sun. *Restaurant* **Lunch served** noon-3pm daily. **Dinner served** 7-10.30pm Mon-Thur; 7-11pm Fri, Sat. **Set dinner** (Mon-Thur) £16.50 2 courses, £19.50 3 courses. *Both* **Main courses** £16.50-£19.50. **Set lunch** (Mon-Sat) £14.50 2 courses, £16.50 3 courses; (Sun) £18.50 2 courses, £22.50 3 courses. **Credit** AmEx, MC, V.

Barnes institution Sonny's has turned into Sonny's Kitchen, courtesy of restaurateur Rebecca Mascarenhas and chef Philip Howard, who have collaborated previously on Kitchen W8 in Kensington. The basic layout is unchanged, though the look is more casual, with white tiles and mirrors on the walls and pale wood tables free of tablecloths. The sunken rear area is as noisy as ever, thanks to the low ceiling and ever-vociferous locals, and the eclectic art collection remains. It's the menu that has changed most. Italian influences are strongest – including three pastas, three pizzas – but Spainish, North American, Middle Eastern and British flavours and ingredients feature too. There's enough meat to stock a butcher's and fishy offerings from octopus to cod, but the balance seems awry: half the starters were vegetarian, but none of the mains apart from one pizza and one pasta. Our dishes varied. Best was dessert: a rich, tangy lemon posset, served with two light beignets oozing elderflower sauce. And a main of barbecued baby back ribs was as it should be: sweetish, tender meat, with simple sides of potato skins and sour cream. But tomato and crushed olive pizza with flaked saltcod, lemon zest and rocket pesto was a disaster; the topping sounded intriguing, but what transpired – brittle dough, no olives, chunks of normal (not salt) cod, too much lemon zest – verged on the inedible. It was early days in the new incarnation and the menu will no doubt settle down; we'd also ditch the naff logo aprons.

Available for hire. Babies and children welcome: children's menu; high chairs. Booking advisable (restaurant). Separate room for parties, seats 18.

Kitchen W8. See p210.

Chelsea

Bluebird

350 King's Road, SW3 5UU (7559 1000, www.bluebird-restaurant.co.uk). Sloane Square tube then bus 11, 19, 22, 49, 319. **Lunch served** noon-2.30pm Mon-Fri. **Brunch served** noon-3.30pm Sat, Sun. **Dinner served** 6-10.30pm Mon-Sat; 6-9.30pm Sun. **Main courses** £13.50-£25. **Set meal** (lunch, dinner Mon-Thur, Sun; lunch, brunch, 6-7pm, 9.30-10.30pm Fri, Sat) £20 2 courses, £25 3 courses. **Credit** AmEx, DC, MC, V.

The ground-floor café and shop at Bluebird seem to be thriving, while, in comparison, the large first-floor restaurant seemed a bit purposeless on our evening visit. The plum and silver decor – which looks like something a second-rate boutique hotel might consider stylish – looks rather dated, though the room is successfully divided into sections (including a bar area), which gives the vast space intimacy. The menu is a bit of a mish-mash: some brasserie dishes (steak tartare, escargots à la bourguignon); a few British classics (fish and chips, chicken and mushroom pie); a handful of international offerings (monkfish curry, summer vegetable tagine); and some frankly depressing vegetarian options (mushroom risotto, spinach and ricotta cannelloni). A starter of gazpacho was a decent, though stunningly garlicky, version. After that, it was hard to appreciate the nuances of salt-marsh lamb rump with piedmontese pepper, salsa verde and olive tapenade, good though it was. We could tell that it had more oomph than the cold poached organic salmon – a small, very average portion saved by a zingy samphire and cucumber salad and a side of golden chips. A nice-enough vanilla cheesecake with blueberry compote pretty much summed up the experience – OK, but nothing special, and a long way from being value for money.

Available for hire. Babies and children welcome:high chairs; nappy-changing facilities. Booking advisable. Disabled: lift; toilet. Separate rooms for parties, seating 10-110. Tables outdoors (25, courtyard). Vegetarian menu. **Map 14 D12**.

Henry Root

9 Park Walk, SW10 0AJ (7352 7040, www.thehenryroot.co.uk). Fulham Broadway tube then bus 211, 414. **Open** 11am-midnight daily. **Meals served** noon-10.45pm Mon-Fri; 9.30am-10.45pm Sat; 9.30am-8.45pm Sun. **Main courses** £12-£28. **Set lunch** (noon-4pm Mon-Fri) £11 1 course incl drink. **Credit** AmEx, MC, V.

Named after a fictional letter-writer and decorated like someone's living room, with books, trophies and photos lining an alcove beside the open kitchen, Chelsea's Henry Root hovers just the right side of clever-clever. Everything has been chosen either for its stylishness or quirkiness, from gilt-framed postcards of risqué Edwardian ladies to Laguiole knives and pretty blue teacups. Ingredients are equally carefully sourced, but less eclectic; besides a charcuterie selection, the menu has a strong British slant. The all-day Sunday roasts are, however, a bit of a red herring: by 2.30pm on our visit, beef was off and pork came with a yorkshire instead of crackling; by 3.30pm, the restaurant was deserted. Of the more inventive dishes, spiced lamb rump looked impressive on its spring vegetable salad, but was slightly overpowered by big chunks of feta. Wild thyme gave honeycomb parfait a beguiling scent, but didn't stop it being over-sweet, as was the panna cotta. Waitresses in lumberjack shirts are smiley and efficient, though we couldn't help but gulp when told a bottle of French cider would be the same price as prosecco – that'll be £30.

Available for hire. Babies and children welcome: high chairs. Disabled: toilet. Tables outdoors (4, pavement). **Map 14 D12**.

Medlar

438 King's Road, SW10 0LJ (7349 1900, www.medlarrestaurant.co.uk). Fulham Broadway tube or bus 11, 22. **Lunch served** noon-3pm daily. **Dinner served** 6.30-10.30pm Mon-Sat; 6.30-9.30pm Sun. **Set lunch** (Mon-Fri) £26 3 courses; (Sat, Sun) £30 3 courses. **Set dinner** (Mon-Sat) £39 3 courses; (Sun) £30 3 courses. **Credit** AmEx, MC, V.

Budding restaurateurs take note: Medlar's seasonal menu and wine list are close to perfection, guaranteed to pique the interest of reviewers, and, more importantly, attract a crowd. Yes, an extra vegetarian starter and main (there's currently just one of each) wouldn't go amiss, but otherwise read and drool: lamb's tongue with lentil salad and mustard fruits; roast hake with summer bean ragoût and palourde clams; redcurrant sorbet with lemon madeleines; 14 globally sourced wines by the glass, carafe and bottle (from a vast list). So, does the execution measure up? Well, mostly. Presentation is generally excellent, as is textural variation. Take, for instance, a colourful crab raviolo starter with samphire, brown shrimps and bisque sauce; or, to follow, assiette of pork (tender confit, delightfully oozing rissoles, crunchy crackling) with peas, girolles and anchovies. A moist, light raspberry and frangipane tart was pleasing too. And yet, portions are small, carbohydrates a rarity (we demanded more bread), and flavours occasionally misjudged – halibut ceviche with avocado, keta and squid had an unpleasantly sweet aftertaste. Behind cordoned-off pavement tables and window screens that partially alleviate the King's Road traffic, the interior is stylishly neutral in tone: all greys, greens and bare boards. Chelsea's lunching ladies put their world to rights here, waited on by exemplary staff. Fine tuning could work wonders.

Babies and children welcome lunch: high chairs. Booking essential. Dress: smart casual. Separate room for parties, seats 14. Tables outdoors (3, pavement). **Map 14 D12**.

South

Battersea

Ransome's Dock

35-37 Parkgate Road, SW11 4NP (7223 1611, www.ransomesdock.co.uk). Battersea Park rail or bus 19, 49, 319, 345. **Brunch served** noon-5pm Sat; noon-3.30pm Sun. **Meals served** noon-11pm Mon-Fri. **Dinner served** 6-11pm Sat. **Main courses** £11.50-£24. **Set brunch** (Sun) £22.50 3 courses. **Set meal** (noon-7.30pm Mon-Fri) £16 2 courses. **Credit** AmEx, DC, MC, V.

A south London fixture, Ransome's Dock has been around for more than 20 years. The riverside location is appealing (even if this stretch of the Thames isn't the most stunning) and, in warmer months, tables on the outdoor terrace are great for watching life drift past. The chef-proprietor owners, Martin and Vanessa Lam, seem to take an 'if it ain't broke, don't fix it' attitude, so while the restaurant retains a loyal following, it hasn't quite kept pace. The decor (purple walls, faux-parquet wooden floors) and the Anglo-French menu now seem a bit outdated. For starters, there may be the likes of pork and duck rillettes with Poilâne toast, or goat's cheese crostini. Breads, from Sally Clarke, are excellent. Our mains, plump spinach and ricotta gnocchi (attributed on the menu to Elizabeth David) with butter and fried sage leaves, were simple but nicely flavoured. Pink-cooked duck breast with pardina lentils and peas, though, was rather soupy, with indistinct flavours. Service is friendly and the wine list (one of the best, and best-value, in the capital) remains as strong as ever; time taken perusing its depths is well spent, revealing gems from around the wine-making globe.

Available for hire. Babies and children welcome: high chairs. Booking advisable. Disabled: toilet. Tables outdoors (10, terrace). **Map 21 C1**.

Tom Ilic

123 Queenstown Road, SW8 3RH (7622 0555, www.tomilic.com). Battersea Park or Queenstown Road rail. **Lunch served** noon-2.30pm Wed-Sun. **Dinner served** 6-10pm Tue-Sat. **Main courses** £11.50-£15.50. **Set meal** £12.50 1 course, £15.50 2 courses, £19.50 3 courses. **Credit** AmEx, MC, V.

In the hands of Tom Ilic, chef-proprietor of this Battersea stalwart, the preparation of pork is akin to an art form: transformed into chops, loins, rillettes and sausages of marvellous variety, flavour and texture. Slow-cooked pigs' cheeks, nestled on mashed potato like a piglet on straw, is a soft-textured, deep-flavoured starter. Ilic's signature dish, a 'degustation' of pork, combines rare-cooked loin, slow-cooked belly and black pudding with apple, offset by a mound of sharp pickled cabbage. The menu may be a meat-fest (top-quality lamb and beef also appear), but there's always a veggie starter and a main, and the fish cooking is accomplished. Crab tart with gruyère, leek and chive hollandaise, topped with a poached egg, hit the spot and super-fresh scallops were seared on the outside, perfectly pearlescent within. Desserts such as classic tarte tatin should fill any gaps. The repertoire hasn't changed much for some time, and the cooking is beginning to seem old-school – as is the somewhat formal decor of heavy red chairs and beige walls. Nevertheless, service is clued-up and friendly and the place remains popular; it's very good value for cooking of this calibre.

Available for hire. Babies and children welcome: high chairs. Booking advisable weekends.

Brixton

Upstairs

89B Acre Lane, entrance on Branksome Road, SW2 5TN (7733 8855, www.upstairslondon.com). Clapham Common tube or Brixton tube/rail. **Dinner served** 6-9.30pm Tue, Wed; 6.30-10pm Thur-Sat. **Set dinner** £28 2 courses, £35 3 courses, £40 4 courses. **Credit** AmEx, MC, V.

Not a restaurant as you'd usually know it, Upstairs does indeed occupy the top two floors of a house, with a cosy cocktail bar off the first landing and an equally intimate, ten-table dining room above. Beyond this, it suffers something of an identity crisis. Is it a trendy Brixton speakeasy, as the hidden entrance via buzzer suggests, or a posh restaurant, with amuse-bouches and prices steeper

than its many stairs? You must book in advance, and order a minimum of two courses from the three-choice-per-course set menu. Dark wooden tables and black chairs are sleek and modern, the toilets excessively mood-lit, but carpets are worn and coats haphazardly hang along the hallway. Service is charming, yet explanations of every dish feel laboured. The cooking is also a little try-hard, featuring one too many cubes of jelly, from beetroot to elderflower. Our vegetarian choice was a pretty arrangement of saffron spätzle (fried dumplings) with an over-sweet red pepper sauce. Lamb rump with goat's cheese and apricot was a rustic, rich, more successful dish. Desserts arrived attractively plated, but raspberries and cherries were unripe and Kahlúa granita contained great lumps of ice. In conclusion: not quite special enough for the special-occasion prices.
Available for hire. Babies and children admitted. Booking advisable Tue-Fri; essential Sat.
Map 22 C2.

Clapham

★ Abbeville Kitchen NEW

2012 WINNER BEST NEW LOCAL RESTAURANT

47 Abbeville Road, SW4 9JX (8772 1110, www.abbevillekitchen.co.uk). Clapham South tube.
Open/snacks served noon-11pm Mon-Fri; 9am-11pm Sat; 9am-10pm Sun. **Breakfast served** 9-11am Sat, Sun. **Lunch served** noon-3pm Mon-Sat; 1-3.30pm Sun. **Dinner served** 6.30-10.30pm Mon-Sat; 6-10pm Sun. **Main courses** £11-£17. **Credit** AmEx, MC, V.
This Clapham newcomer is so on-trend, in looks, menu and vibe, it wouldn't be out of place in the middle of Soho. A few pavement tables and a fold-back frontage give way to a long thin room furnished in a retro-distressed manner, all bare light bulbs, knackered dining chairs and fabric-lined walls. Ex-school stools are lined up next to the bar; at the rear is the (slightly whiffy) open kitchen. Bare tables, Duralex glasses and paper napkins set the casual tone, as do the friendly but efficient staff (all good-looking young men on our visit). Menu descriptions are terse – 'razor clams, cucumber, tomatoes and lettuce', 'Hereford veal, soft polenta and parmesan' – with no hint of cooking techniques. Many diners (a varied lot on our visit, in age and fashionability) were sharing a series of smaller plates, rather than having the standard starter/main; there are also a few dishes designed for two. All our food was tremendous, from excellent bread to a simple bowl of boiled red potatoes with minty butter to buttermilk pudding (similar to panna cotta) with gooseberries and toasted hazelnuts. The aforementioned veal and polenta was exquisite comfort food, the meat falling-off-the-bone tender, with an intense gravy and a large mound of cheesy polenta. The wine list is thoughtfully compiled and fairly priced; there are sherries, Breton cider and Clapham Pale Ale, too.
Babies and children welcome: high chairs. Disabled: toilet. Tables outdoors (4, pavement).
Map 23 A3.

Trinity

4 The Polygon, SW4 0JG (7622 1199, www.trinityrestaurant.co.uk). Clapham Common tube.
Lunch served 12.30-2.30pm Tue-Fri; noon-2pm Sat; noon-4pm Sun. **Dinner served** 6.30-10.30pm Mon-Sat. **Main courses** £17-£28. **Set lunch** (Tue-Sat) £20 2 courses. **Set meal** (Tue-Sat) £45 tasting menu (£75 incl wine). **Cover** £1.50 lunch, £2 dinner. **Credit** AmEx, MC, V.
Has Adam Byatt taken his eye off the ball? In 2012, Trinity's chef/patron opened Bistro Union (*see p45*), a brilliant casual diner on Clapham's Abbeville Road, but his elegant main restaurant – long a favourite with our reviewers – is showing cracks. On our visit, service was inconsistent, with inattentive juniors undermining the warmth and can-do attitude of their more experienced colleagues. The kitchen fared better, delivering pretty plates of modern Anglo-French cooking. We enjoyed an intricate starter of charred mackerel with a parcel of cucumber-wrapped shrimp and a light oyster mayonnaise. Chunky rhubarb and apple crumble in a ramekin showed that simplicity is also a forte. In between, however, crisp-skinned pollock with soft, fleshy mussels and sautéed baby leeks was overwhelmed by an excess of sea-salty samphire. Heavy, oily sourdough from the bread basket was similarly disappointing. Perhaps most galling, though, was that breads, a pre-starter of radishes and cod roe, and filtered tap water – all of which came across as 'nice touches' – appeared on our bill as a cover charge, a disingenuous practice we thought had disappeared with the ark. We hope Trinity (still popular with locals) returns to its glory days soon.
Available for hire. Babies and children admitted. Booking essential. Disabled: toilet. **Map 22 A1**.

Waterloo

★ Oxo Tower Restaurant, Bar & Brasserie

8th floor, Oxo Tower Wharf, Barge House Street, SE1 9PH (7803 3888, www.harveynichols.com/restaurants). Southwark tube or Waterloo tube/rail.
Bar **Open** 11am-11pm Mon-Wed; 11am-11.30pm Thur-Sat; noon-10.30pm Sun. **Meals served** noon-11pm Mon-Sat; noon-10pm Sun. **Main courses** £6-£12.
Brasserie **Lunch served** noon-3pm Mon-Sat; noon-3.30pm Sun. **Dinner served** 5.30-11pm Mon-Sat; 6-10pm Sun. **Main courses** £13-£33. **Set meal** (lunch, 5.30-6.15pm, after 10pm Mon-Fri; 5.30-6.15pm Sat; 6-6.30pm, after 9pm Sun) £24.50 2 courses; £29.50 3 courses.
Restaurant Lunch served noon-2.30pm Mon-Sat; noon-3pm Sun. **Dinner served** 6-11pm Mon-Sat; 6.30-10pm Sun. **Main courses** £22-£35. **Set lunch** £35 3 courses.
All **Credit** AmEx, DC, MC, V.
Escape the ordinary by contemplating superb vistas from the Harvey Nichols-run eating spots on the top floor of the Oxo Tower: river traffic by day, or St Paul's and the glittering City at night. If it's chilly, look out through panoramic windows; when it's warm, sit out on a stunning terrace. The biggest differences between the brasserie at the western end and the restaurant at the other (separated by a chic, sleek cocktail bar) are in noise levels, seat-softness and spaciousness. Food in the restaurant comes with extra refinement, but there's no lack of sophistication in the seasonal brasserie menu, with options such as (outstanding) scallops with chorizo and butter bean cassoulet, or roast venison in green peppercorn oxtail sauce offset by celeriac and cranberries. The vegetarian choice, too, is imaginative. Exemplary service, charming and on the ball, adds to the enjoyment, and the wine list offers both classy celebration labels and Harvey Nick's exceptional house wines. Prices can be lofty, in both restaurant and brasserie, but aren't exaggerated for this blend of quality and setting. Set menus are even a bargain by current standards.
Available for hire. Babies and children welcome: children's menu; high chairs. Booking advisable. Disabled: lift; toilet. Entertainment (brasserie): jazz lunch Sat, Sun; 7.30pm daily. Tables outdoors (50, brasserie terrace; 40, restaurant terrace). Vegan dishes. Vegetarian menu.
Map 11 N7.

Skylon

Royal Festival Hall, Belvedere Road, SE1 8XX (7654 7800, www.skylon-restaurant.co.uk). Waterloo tube/rail.
Bar **Open/snacks served** noon-11pm daily.
Brasserie **Meals served** noon-10.45pm daily. **Main courses** £12.50-£25.
Restaurant **Lunch served** noon-2.30pm Mon-Sat; noon-3.30pm Sun. **Dinner served** 5.30-10.30pm Mon-Sat. **Set lunch** (Mon-Sat) £24.50 2 courses, £28.50 3 courses; (Sun) £25.50 2 courses, £29.50 3 courses. **Set dinner** £40 2 courses, £45 3 courses; £59 tasting menu (£106 incl wine).
All **Credit** AmEx, DC, MC, V.
With splendid views across the Thames from an expansive window frontage, Skylon benefits from an enviable location at the Royal Festival Hall, attracting a mix of well-to-do tourists, corporate clients and romancing couples. It's a spacious set-up, divided into three destinations with a raised central bar separating the fine dining space from a more laid-back brasserie. Whether you're perching by the bar, tucking into steak and fries at the grill, or marking an occasion with a fine dining meal – it is the marvellous vistas that make this venue so memorable. Cooking, although good in parts, can be uneven at the sharply priced restaurant. A starter of deconstructed chicory tart tatin, sharpened with the fruity tang of orange vinaigrette made a tasty match with toasted walnut and roquefort salad – a triumph of complementary and contrasting flavours. We were also satisfied with delicately steamed sea bream fillets partnered with the crunch of white winter radish and an inspired sticky red wine reduction. Less impressive was the complex melange of sautéed red mullet fillets, teamed with saffron risotto, preserved lemons, shellfish sauce and an olive fricassée. Service needs to be more attentive – especially during busy evenings.
Available for hire. Babies and children welcome: children's menu; high chairs. Booking advisable. Disabled: lift; toilet. Vegetarian menu.
Map 10 M8.

South East

Crystal Palace

Exhibition Rooms

69-71 Westow Hill, SE19 1TX (8761 1175, www.theexhibitionrooms.com). Crystal Palace rail.
Bar **Open/snacks served** 5.30-11pm Mon-Thur; 5.30pm-1am Fri, Sat.
Restaurant **Lunch served** noon-4pm Fri, Sat. **Dinner served** 5.30-10pm Mon-Thur; 5.30-10.30pm Fri, Sat. **Meals served** noon-9pm Sun. **Main courses** £11-£23. **Set lunch** £8

Abbeville Kitchen

1 course. **Set dinner** (5.30-7pm Mon-Fri; 5-6.30pm Sat) £12 2 courses, £15 3 courses. *Both* **Credit** AmEx, MC, V.
Consistency has been the watchword at the Exhibition Rooms since this well-turned-out restaurant and bar first opened in 2009 (when it won Time Out's Best Local Restaurant award). The menu consists of no-nonsense classic dishes – oysters with tabasco, ribeye with bordelaise sauce, beer-battered haddock, pear tarte tatin. Food is skilfully cooked and handsomely presented; sparklingly fresh ingredients appear in sensible flavour combinations. The quality of meat in particular is excellent, so Sunday lunch is a high point. On our latest visit, a plate of roast beef with all the trimmings could not be faulted. The regular Tuesday 'steak night' offers great value for money too, with a rump or a tuna steak costing just £11.95 including a glass of wine or bottled beer. Exposed brick, pale green walls, mismatched furniture (with plenty of room between tables), and huge light-catching chandeliers create a relaxed environment: leisurely enough for a weekend brunch, smart enough for a family lunch and intimate enough for a romantic night out. Downstairs, a lounge bar (which opens on to a decked courtyard) has regular DJs and a varied choice of cocktails.
Babies and children welcome Mon-Thur; until 7pm Fri, Sat: children's menu; high chairs; nappy-changing facilities. Booking advisable; essential weekends. Disabled: toilet. Tables outdoors (9, courtyard).

Greenwich

Inside

19 Greenwich South Street, SE10 8NW (8265 5060, www.insiderestaurant.co.uk). Greenwich rail/DLR. **Lunch served** noon-2.30pm Tue-Fri; noon-3pm Sat, Sun. **Dinner served** 6.30-11pm Tue-Sat. **Main courses** £12.95-£18.95. **Set lunch** (Mon-Fri) £12.95 2 courses, £17.95 3 courses; (Sat, Sun) £18.95 2 courses, £23.95 3 courses. **Set dinner** (6.30-11pm Tue-Thur; 6.30-8.30pm Fri, Sat) £19.95 2 courses, £24.95 3 courses. **Credit** AmEx, MC, V.
One of the few Greenwich restaurants operating above chain level, Inside is an unassuming spot, plainly decorated apart from changing displays of local art. On a Saturday night, diners ranged from a big family group to couples on dates, all tucking into a reliable menu that occasionally shows flashes of inspiration, as in roast cod with chickpea, chilli and chorizo cassoulet and tomato and smoked paprika coulis. A baked, spiced paneer filo parcel also far exceeded expectations of a vegetarian main course. Simple works well too – an adjoining table seemed happy with a textbook grilled ribeye with big chips, roast garlic mayo and rocket salad. Starters contain a similar mix of safe (risotto, goat's cheese salad) and adventurous (five-spice chicken, coconut and coriander spring rolls with dipping sauce); best was a flavoursome carrot soup. The generous cheese plate would be our choice to finish, but the sweet-toothed will enjoy warm chocolate fudge cake with vanilla ice-cream and cinnamon tuile. Professional, if eager, service comes with a smile. The drinks list has something for everyone, from locally brewed Meantime pale ale to a delicate provençal rosé. Chef-proprietor Guy Awford also runs the nearby Guildford Arms pub and dining room.
Available for hire. Babies and children admitted. Booking advisable. Disabled: toilet.

Brawn. See p220.

London Bridge & Borough

Delfina

50 Bermondsey Street, SE1 3UD (7357 0244, www.thedelfina.co.uk). London Bridge tube/rail. **Breakfast served** 8-11am, **lunch served** noon-3pm Mon-Thur. **Meals served** 8am-10pm Fri. **Main courses** £9-£18.95. **Set lunch** £25 6 dishes (minimum 2). **Credit** AmEx, DC, MC, V.

Little has changed at this hangar of a gallery/restaurant but, in this case, that's a good thing. The space – white, light, airy, with enormous Howard Hodgkin-style wall art – is filled with functional white tables, blue architecturally designed chairs and '80s-style lapis blue glasses, all giving it a slightly retro look. It's understandably popular for business lunches, as tables are well spaced and prices are keen for the quality of the food. Service was a little slow, but when the food arrived it was very good indeed. We ordered from the prix fixe and à la carte menus and enjoyed pretty much every dish. The trio of beetroot with creamed curd, pear and walnut dressing was a wonderful combination of individual tastes and textures, and a main of globe artichoke, parmesan polenta and creamed wild mushrooms was a similarly well-balanced plateful. Over-salty samphire accompanying otherwise excellent scallops and pan-fried cod was the only downside. Puddings include lemon meringue pie, own-made sorbets and ice-creams, and a bargain Neal's Yard cheese selection with crackers and chutney for £6.95. A short global wine list includes a rosé from Kent's Chapel Down.

Available for hire. Babies and children admitted: high chairs; nappy-changing facilities. Booking advisable. Disabled: toilet. Separate room for parties, seats 250. Tables outdoors (8, pavement). **Map 12 Q9**.

Magdalen

152 Tooley Street, SE1 2TU (7403 1342, www.magdalenrestaurant.co.uk). London Bridge tube/rail. **Lunch served** noon-2.30pm Mon-Fri. **Dinner served** 6.30-10pm Mon-Sat. **Main courses** £13.50-£20. **Set lunch** £15.50 2 courses, £18.50 3 courses. **Credit** AmEx, MC, V.

Magdalen (pronounced Magdalen, not Maudlin – it backs on to a street of the same name) is the best kind of neighbourhood restaurant. Smart yet unstuffy, it can do both special-occasion suppers and casual lunches with aplomb. The claret-hued room with its dark wooden floors, small marble-topped bar and a few linen-clad tables isn't out of the ordinary, but the cooking consistently hits the spot. The modern British menu takes seasonal produce and injects it with Mediterranean flavours. New-season garlic soup combined a smooth, subtle base with a heady drizzle of intense garlic oil and thin crispbreads smothered in fresh crumbly goat's cheese. Main courses, though modestly proportioned, were equally thoughtful: soft-poached duck rested on creamy polenta with al dente asparagus spears for dipping; and summery fish stew came in a copper pan, allowing us to smother the giant aïoli-topped croûton at will. To close, Campari and orange sorbet delivered a sharp, well-judged bite. The Old World-dominated wine list plays it safe, but offers a handful of decent sherries and several options by the carafe to keep things current. Factor-in relaxed, clued-up staff and it's no wonder Magdalen is such a local hit.

Oxo Tower Restaurant, Bar & Brasserie. See p214.

Available for hire. Babies and children admitted. Booking advisable. Disabled: toilet. Separate rooms for parties, seating 8-35. **Map 12 Q8**.

Tower Bridge

Blueprint Café

Design Museum, 28 Shad Thames, SE1 2YD (7378 7031, www.blueprintcafe.co.uk). Tower Hill tube or Tower Gateway DLR or London Bridge tube/rail or bus 47, 78. **Lunch served** noon-2.45pm daily. **Dinner served** 6-10.45pm Mon-Sat. **Main courses** £12.50-£21. **Set lunch** £15 2 courses, £20 3 courses. **Set dinner** £18 2 courses, £23 3 courses. **Credit** AmEx, DC, MC, V.

The Blueprint Café has a lot going for it – fantastic river views, handsome design and great service. The food, however, fell short of the promise of the chic surroundings and under-delivered for the ambitious prices (mains hover around £20). New head chef Mark Jarvis, formerly of haute cuisine restaurant Texture, was settling in on our visit with artily plated dishes that were good rather than outstanding. Cromer crab in mayonnaise on a slick of avocado purée was overly rich, as was an unctuous risotto that arrived with sliced courgette rather than courgette flowers as listed on the menu, although strands of luminous saffron did brighten the mascarpone-heavy dish. Gloucester Old Spot pork loin featured flavourful but far from crispy crackling and waxy mash. Despite this, the overall experience at this smart venue is more than agreeable, thanks to the pleasant, polished staff and elevated riverside location, complete with mini binoculars on each table. Organic and biodynamic wines are featured on the wine list. The spruce design is in keeping with a restaurant on top of the Design Museum; clientele ranges from gallery-goers to ladies who lunch. Part of the D&D London group.

Available for hire. Babies and children welcome: high chair. Booking advisable dinner. Disabled: lift; toilet (in museum). Tables outdoors (4, terrace). **Map 12 S9**.

Le Pont de la Tour

Butlers Wharf Building, 36D Shad Thames, SE1 2YE (7403 8403, www.lepontdelatour.co.uk). Tower Hill tube or Tower Gateway DLR or London Bridge tube/rail.

Bar & grill **Lunch served** noon-3pm Mon-Fri; noon-4pm Sat, Sun. **Dinner served** 6-10.30pm Mon-Sat; 6-10pm Sun. **Main courses** £11.50-£22.

Restaurant **Lunch served** noon-3pm Mon-Fri; noon-4pm Sat, Sun. **Dinner served** 6-11pm Mon-Sat; 6-10pm Sun. **Main courses** £22-£46. **Set lunch** £37.50 2 courses, £44.50 3 courses.

Both **Credit** AmEx, DC, MC, V.

One of D&D London's stable of sleek, metropolitan restaurants, Le Pont de la Tour boasts expert staff, French-biased cuisine and, best of all, a stunning view of Tower Bridge. It should be the perfect venue for a special date, but the slightly cold atmosphere means it's probably best suited to corporate dinners. The quality of ingredients and near-faultless execution were clear, although at times it's all a bit joyless. It's also expensive – even the cheapest starter (mushroom consommé) comes in at £9.50, while even the earthier mains, such as sautéed calf's liver with pommes mousseline, alsace bacon and sauce diable, are over £20. Yellow fin tuna salad niçoise – a succulent seared loin served rare on top of potato, basil and poached quail's

Paramount. See p204.

eggs – followed by assiette of raspberries (a delicate jelly, creamy raspberry parfait, and refined raspberry coulis) made a delicious summer meal, without quite matching the price tag. Saffron passionfruit crumble had more wow factor, and we loved the amuse-bouche of truffled choux buns. More fun can perhaps be had eating the likes of Toulouse sausage with lyonnaise potatoes from the bar and grill menu. A serious wine list is aimed at City pockets, though affordable bottles are dotted here and there.
Available for hire. Babies and children welcome: high chairs. Booking advisable. Entertainment (bar & grill): pianist 6pm Tue-Sun. Separate rooms for parties, seating 22 and 26. Tables outdoors (22, terrace). **Map 25 S8**.

East

Bethnal Green

Corner Room

Town Hall Hotel, Patriot Square, E2 9NF (no phone, www.townhallhotel.com). Bethnal Green tube. **Lunch served** noon-4pm, **dinner served** 6-10.30pm daily. **Main courses** £10-£15. **Set lunch** (noon-3pm Mon-Fri) £17 2 courses, £21 3 courses. **Credit** AmEx, MC, V.

The more affordable and informal of Nuno Mendes' two restaurants in the Town Hall boutique hotel is nevertheless almost as much of a culinary adventure as the Michelin-starred Viajante. No bookings are taken, so you'll probably wait for a table, but the bar on the ground floor is a smart, stylish space for an apertif and some olives. Once seated in the small, quietly arty – though slightly lacking in atmosphere – corner dining space, an amuse-bouche will prepare you for the start of a creatively put-together menu. Dishes change regularly with the seasons, but normally feature lots of seafood options, such as sea bass ceviche with fennel, octopus with smoked potato and hazelnut milk, or cod with clam porridge. Meat dishes, along the lines of neck of lamb with wild garlic and grains, keep your taste buds on their toes, while Mendes' Iberian heritage is often apparent in the ingredients – we particularly enjoyed Iberico pork served with Portuguese bread pudding. Presentation is as important as flavour here, with the modern-art-on-a-plate approach continuing to wow punters. For the price, these are exciting eats; but beware of the final bill – the short but well-chosen wine list here is more high-end, with the cheapest bottle costing £28 on our last visit.
Available for hire. Babies and children welcome: high chairs. Bookings not accepted dinner. Disabled: lift; toilet. Separate room for parties, seats 9-16. Vegetarian menu.

Palmers

238 Roman Road, E2 0RY (8980 5590, www.palmersrestaurant.net). Bethnal Green tube/rail or 8 bus. **Dinner served** 6-10.30pm Mon-Sat. **Meals served** noon-9pm Sun. **Main courses** £9.50-£16.50. **Set meal** (Mon-Thur) £15 2 courses, £25 3 courses. **Credit** AmEx, MC, V.

This family-run joint is a surprisingly impressive local gem, given its incongruous location across from a particularly grey, brutalist Bethnal Green estate. The simple, unpretentious space is made welcoming by the genial owner, who runs the place with his sons and creates the kind of warm atmosphere that attracts return customers. The menu is equally thoughtful, offering such hearty treats as smoked sprats with lemon mayonnaise alongside adeptly executed crowd-pleasers such as steak with chunky chips and fresh chimichurri sauce. The veggie staple of falafel was a commendable version, the patties moist, pleasantly spiced and served with butternut purée and a sweet and salty beetroot and feta salad. Other popular dishes on the night included lamb burger with tsatsiki, and duck breast with orange gnocchi. Do leave room for dessert. A pair of stupendous sorbets married the classic cocktail ingredients of peach with prosecco, and cherry with bourbon, to delectable effect. The standard of cooking is made even better value by the bountiful servings, making this an exemplary local that deserves to do well.
Available for hire. Babies and children welcome: high chairs. Booking advisable weekends. Disabled: toilet. Takeaway service.

Docklands

Plateau

Canada Place, Canada Square, E14 5ER (7715 7100, www.plateau-restaurant.co.uk). Canary Wharf tube/DLR.
Bar & grill **Meals served** noon-10.30pm Mon-Sat. **Main courses** £12-£22. **Set meal** £13.50 2 courses and glass of wine, £15 2 courses, £18 3 courses.
Restaurant **Lunch served** noon-3pm Mon-Fri. **Dinner served** 6-10pm Mon-Sat. **Main courses** £14-£29.50. **Set meal** £22 2 courses, £25 3 courses.
Both **Credit** AmEx, DC, MC, V.

First impressions of Plateau do it few favours: after the brisk reception greeting, we sipped cocktails in a bar where the crisp low furniture, acres of space and somewhat sterile minimalism put us in mind of a hotel lobby. When we were shown to our tables, however, the modern conservatory aspect of the building came into its own – the view down from the fourth floor into the square is impressive enough, but the real fun is looking up through the roof into the nest of skyscrapers that reach above – and our waitress was so unaffectedly pleasant and obliging that even the business-like surroundings warmed up. The food was mostly a bit meek – heavily smoked mackerel lightened with a too-gentle horseradish cream; a tasty, soothing but very mash-based fish pie; and startlingly white plaice fillet given too little kick by capers and parsley. From the good-value Express Menu (two courses and glass of the house wine for £13.50), a baby spinach, crouton and parmesan salad of which little was, rightly, expected, was followed by a tender, flavour-packed but insufficiently crisped rectangle of belly pork with puréed bubble and an exquisitely rich jus. Even so, the whole experience was really rather engaging.
Available for hire. Babies and children welcome: children's menu; high chairs; nappy-changing facilities. Booking advisable. Disabled: lift; toilet. Dress: smart casual. Separate rooms for parties, seating 16 and 25. Tables outdoors (17, terrace). Vegetarian menu. **Map 24 B2**.

Medlar. See p213.

Shoreditch

Brawn

49 Columbia Road, E2 7RG (7729 5692, www.brawn.co). Hoxton rail or bus 48, 55.
Lunch served noon-3pm Tue-Sat; noon-4pm Sun. **Dinner served** 6-10.30pm Mon-Thur; 6-11pm Thur-Sat. **Main courses** £16-£27.50. **Set lunch** (Sun) £25 3 courses, £30 incl cheese. **Credit** MC, V.

Brawn is the second offering from the team behind Terroirs (and most recently, Soif), and is nicely pitched to appeal to a hip east London crowd without alienating other diners. Staff are young and attentive, and there's a contented buzz about the place. The decor is unfussy: two rooms with whitewashed walls and simple furniture. Likewise, the terse menu: 'Cod's roe £4', for example, doesn't do justice to the deluxe taramasalata that appears. Dishes are made to share. From a selection labelled 'Pig' we tried moreish pork rillettes; from 'Cold', hand-chopped Tuscan-style beef was steak tartare by any other name, and equally good. Less full-on options might be swiss chard with Cantabrian anchovies and lemon, or buffalo mozzarella with olive oil and capers. The 'Hot' choice included excellent clams with lemon and garlic, and gone-in-a-flash cauliflower cheese. Unmissable crêpes with salted caramel butter are among the short list of puddings. Much care is taken over provenance: cheese comes from Androuet (Spitalfields) and the wonderful bread from E5 Bakehouse (London Fields). 'Natural' wine is showcased on the drinks list, with most bottles produced by small, committed growers; it certainly makes for an interesting choice.
Babies and children welcome: high chairs; nappy-changing facilities. Booking advisable. Disabled: toilet. Separate room for parties, seats 30. **Map 6 S3**.

Spitalfields

The Luxe

109 Commercial Street, E1 6BG (7101 1751, www.theluxe.co.uk). Liverpool Street tube/rail or Shoreditch High Street rail.
Café-bar **Open** 8am-midnight Mon-Thur, Sun; 8am-1am Fri, Sat. **Meals served** 8.30am-4.30pm Mon-Sat; 9.30am-4.45pm Sun. **Main courses** £7.50-£11.50.
Restaurant **Lunch served** noon-3pm Mon-Fri; noon-4pm Sun. **Dinner served** 6-10.45pm Mon-Sat. **Main courses** £13-£15.
Both **Credit** AmEx, DC, MC, V.

This gargantuan enterprise includes a busy ground-floor brasserie, a quieter first-floor restaurant, a private dining room and a basement music bar. A take-away kiosk takes advantage of the Spitalfields Market location, plying the crowds with portable food such as hot dogs and quality burgers. The focus on meat continues indoors. The more casual of the dining spaces is the ground floor, which takes its cue from the dominating central bar. It's also a buzzing brunch spot, though the standard of food was disappointing. Pancakes were leathery and unforgivably undercooked in places, while the ratio of sausage to starch on a plate with waffles and french toast was mean – a single, mediocre sausage is stingy for a carnivore-baiting restaurant. Choices are fleshed out by big sandwiches (salt beef, steak, fish finger) and substantial salads. Milkshakes are spot-on, and alcoholic versions enhance the posh burger bar aspect of the Luxe's multiple identities. The more formal restaurant upstairs deals in grills and straightforward Mod Euro dishes. The clientele is more City than Shoreditch, erring towards the middle of the road rather than the cutting edge. Young staff work to a soundtrack of mid 1990s pop that intensifies the Luxe's lack of charm.
Available for hire. Babies and children welcome: high chairs; nappy-changing facilities. Booking advisable restaurant; not accepted café. Disabled: lift; toilet. Separate rooms for parties, seating 30-50. Tables outdoors (3, pavement). Takeaway service. **Map 12 R5**.

Victoria Park

Empress

130 Lauriston Road, E9 7LH (8533 5123, www.empresse9.co.uk). Mile End tube then bus 277 or 425. **Brunch served** 10am-noon Sat, Sun. **Lunch served** noon-3.15pm Mon-Sat. **Dinner served** 6-10.15pm Mon-Sat. **Meals served** noon-9.30pm Sun. **Main courses** £12-£17. **Credit** MC, V.

In 2011 , the Empress lost 'of India' from its name along with its previous corporate owners. The all-rounder café/bar/restaurant is now in the hands of a small, dedicated team who are on a mission to turn it into a culinary destination, albeit one with a neighbourhood vibe and pricing. On the evidence of our last visit, they're on the way. Chef Elliot Lidstone's short, unpretentious menu mixes snacks and modern-brasserie dishes for the coffee and drinks crowd with more cheffy dishes. Snails with

Glasshouse. See p222.

Petersham Nurseries Café. See p222.

bone marrow were extremely good, untypically smooth and subtle; braised pork was more interesting than its name, being a roundel of pulled pork with a crust of extreme savouriness served on bulghur wheat. A mysterious absence of side dishes resulted in the veg served beneath good trout being repeated, but at least they were properly seasonal (chard and peas in May). The large corner room is comfortable, with huge windows, lots of red banquette seating, white walls dotted lightly with art and a long bar, but when weather allows, the outside seating on a wide pavement is where the buzz is. Staff are engaged and engaging, but we recommend waiting for table service rather than ordering drinks at the bar (slower in the long run).
Available for hire. Babies and children welcome: children's menu; high chairs; nappy-changing facilities. Booking advisable Fri-Sun. Disabled: toilet. Tables outdoors (8, pavement). Vegan dishes.

Wapping

Wapping Food HOT 50

Wapping Hydraulic Power Station, Wapping Wall, E1W 3SG (7680 2080, www.thewapping project.com). Wapping tube or Shadwell DLR. **Brunch served** 10am-noon Sat, Sun. **Lunch served** 1-4pm Sat, Sun. **Dinner served** 6.30-10.30pm Mon-Fri; 7-10.30pm Sat. **Main courses** £15-£22. **Credit** AmEx, MC, V.

Dining under the soaring ceilings, original green tiles and industrial-sized chains of a defunct hydraulic power station is part of the appeal here. Tables are set among old machinery that's softened to magical effect with dozens of candles after dusk. The unique space also features a bright, airy entrance dining area that's good for lunches, and a cavernous, spooky art gallery at the back. A small selection of art magazines and books completes the Wapping Project's triple purpose. The place attracts an urbane crowd. The daily changing, seasonal menu is broadly Modern European. Scallop carpaccio with salty, tangy slices of lime-spritzed peach was a high point. To follow, onglet with roast potatoes was characteristically straightforward, as was a pea and yoghurt pilaf, which nonetheless could have been enhanced by another element on the plate. Tempting cocktails are offered before and after the meal; a banana split martini in place of dessert was like a tasty adult milkshake. Prices are steep and the food on this occasion was little above average, but the spectacular setting garners bonus points since an evening in such an unusual venue is bound to stick in the memory.
Available for hire. Babies and children welcome: high chairs; nappy-changing facilities. Booking essential Wed-Sun. Disabled: toilet. Entertainment: performances and exhibitions; phone for details. Tables outdoors (20, garden).

Whitechapel

Whitechapel Gallery Dining Room

Whitechapel Gallery, 77-82 Whitechapel High Street, E1 7QX (7522 7888, www.whitechapel gallery.org/dining-room). Aldgate East tube. **Lunch served** noon-3pm Tue-Sat; noon-3.45pm Sun. **Dinner served** 6-9.30pm Wed-Sat. **Main courses** £10.50-£15.95. **Credit** AmEx, MC, V.

The warm, intimate Dining Room is a welcome contrast to the urban grit of Whitechapel High Street. Soft lighting and mellow wood (including a lovely parquet floor) give the place a comfortable vibe that's backed by chatty but efficient service. The menu, overseen by Angela Hartnett, makes a lively read. Nibbles include canapé-size bites of whipped goat's curd with roast garlic, while small plates run from a rich assembly of asparagus with perfectly poached egg, smoky ham and parmesan to a more abstemious (verging on bland) roast beetroot, toasted walnut and mustard leaf salad. Next, a special of shepherd's pie with a cheesy potato topping and tenderstem broccoli tasted delightfully homemade; sea trout with a sublime caponata was another hit. In contrast, a slightly dry, rather flavourless onglet with insipid horseradish crème fraîche disappointed, though the accompanying onion rings were a beignet-like triumph. Pear and almond tart seemed a bit so-what, whereas the ice-creams and sorbets were wonderful, especially the salted caramel – and they're only £1.65 a scoop. A compact drinks list covers much ground, and includes a highly drinkable house red (by the bottle, carafe and glass), Meantime beers and leaf teas.
Available for hire. Babies and children welcome: high chairs; nappy-changing facilities. Booking advisable. Disabled: toilet. Separate room for parties, seats 14. **Map 12 S6.**

North

Camden Town & Chalk Farm

Odette's

130 Regent's Park Road, NW1 8XL (7586 8569, www.odettesprimrosehill.com). Chalk Farm tube or bus 31, 168, 274. **Lunch served** noon-2.30pm Tue-Fri; noon-3pm Sat, Sun. **Dinner served** 6.30-10.30pm daily. **Main courses** £11.50-£25. **Set meal** (lunch Tue-Fri; 6-7pm daily) £17 2 courses, £20 3 courses; (lunch Sat, Sun) £22 2 courses, £25 3 courses; £50 tasting menu (£45 vegetarian tasting menu). **Credit** AmEx, MC, V.

Odette's is a great place to dine alfresco – either in the secluded walled garden or at one of the pavement tables with added people-watching possibilities. Inside, the decor is contemporary country house – soothing greys, greens and modern florals – not very North London, and all the more charming for it. With TV chef Bryn Williams at the helm, expectations are high. Many dishes hark back to his Welsh origins – try his *Great British Menu*-winning roast turbot, braised oxtail, cockles and samphire. To start, crab lasagne was sublime – feather-light, silky pasta with meaty crab custard, crispy baby squid and rich, salty-sweet shellfish sauce. A crispy-coated duck egg oozing super-yellow yolk on to truffle salad with asparagus was a textural delight. A main of salmon with sprouting broccoli was lifted by intensely flavoured potted shrimp risotto. With such good cooking on display, an undistinguished artichoke en croûte with a strangely insipid confit of tomato and aubergine

was all the more disappointing. Similarly, white chocolate arctic roll with raspberries and mint was not much superior to the original '70s Findus favourite. More consistency is needed, but given the polished service and mostly great food in such lovely surroundings, a return visit is guaranteed.
Babies and children welcome: high chairs. Booking advisable. Separate room for parties, seats 20. Tables outdoors (5, garden; 4, pavement). Vegetarian menu. **Map 27 A2**.

York & Albany

127-129 Parkway, NW1 7PS (7388 3344, www.gordonramsay.com/yorkandalbany). Camden Town tube. **Breakfast served** 7-10.30am Mon-Fri; 7-11.30am Sat, Sun. **Lunch served** noon-3pm Mon-Fri; 12.15-3pm Sat. **Dinner served** 6-11pm Mon-Sat. **Meals served** noon-8.30pm Sun. **Main courses** £15-£22. **Set meal** (lunch, 6-7pm Mon-Sat) £18 2 courses, £21 3 courses. **Credit** AmEx, MC, V.
This fine Georgian pile beside Regent's Park may once have been a pub, but there's not much pub-like about its current incarnation within this Gordon Ramsay complex, housing a bar, restaurant, elegant 'townhouse hotel' and even an upmarket deli and takeaway pizza counter. The bar area is delightfully airy, with seductively soft leather sofas for extended lounging over a cocktail; dining rooms, divided between a light space by a small patio and a tomb-like basement, are similarly mellow, featuring muted colours and antique details. In contrast, the menu retains an informal feel, with burgers and (apparently highly regarded) pizzas alongside more intricate dishes. Head chef Colin Buchan and his team aren't afraid to take risks: rabbit ravioli with peas, bacon, marjoram and butter sauce was a difficult combination carried off to perfection, exuberantly rabbity and buttery; salmon ceviche with beetroot and avocado was deliciously refreshing. The same blend of subtle skills and rich flavour came through in our mains, a perfectly tender pork chop in cider gravy, and almost nutty-flavoured pollock with orecchiette pasta. Service was charming and very obliging. In all, this was a comfortable and, yes, mellow experience: one Ramsay outlet providing quality at accessible prices.
Babies and children welcome: high chairs. Booking advisable Thur-Sun. Disabled: toilet. Separate rooms for parties, seating 24 and 70. Tables outdoors (6, pavement). **Map 3 H1**.

Finsbury Park

Season Kitchen

53 Stroud Green Road, N4 3EF (7263 5500, www.seasonkitchen.co.uk). Finsbury Park tube/ rail. **Dinner served** 5.30-10.30pm Tue-Sun. **Main courses** £10.95-£15.95. **Credit** MC, V.
Surrounded by nondescript shops, Season Kitchen is easy to miss, but a growing band of devotees beat a path to its door. Plain brown wrapping paper serves as tablecloths, wine lists come in Muji-style white zip-up folders, tealights balance on piles of cookbooks and waiting staff are glam but friendly, making for a stylishly quirky vibe. The menu showcases seasonal, carefully sourced produce at quite modest prices – wedges of mildly smoked salmon with orange and Chinese-style crispy seaweed were sublime; equally as good was unctuous roasted bone marrow offset by coarse flakes of sea salt, radishes and parsley. Mains of tender miso-glazed aubergine with nutty sesame-infused wild rice and lightly home-pickled cucumber, flecked with chilli, and a simple lamb casserole with a gently herbed broth, were further demonstration of the kitchen's skills. A rich chocolate pot delicately spiked with rosemary, with black pepper biscotti and a beautifully executed eccles cake (perfect pastry, filling not too sweet) with a buttermilk and delicately orange-flower-scented parfait were a fine finish. There's a short list of 'natural' wines. A little corner of gastronomic heaven in Finsbury Park.
Available for hire. Babies and children welcome: high chairs. Booking advisable. Tables outdoors (4, garden).

Islington

Frederick's

Camden Passage, N1 8EG (7359 2888, www.fredericks.co.uk). Angel tube. **Lunch served** noon-2.30pm, **dinner served** 5.45-10.30pm Mon-Sat. **Main courses** £12.50-£26. **Set meal** (lunch; dinner Mon, Tue; 5.45-7pm Wed-Sat) £15.50 2 courses, £19 3 courses. **Credit** AmEx, MC, V.
An Islington institution in an 1830s building dating from the days of Frederick, Duke of Sussex, this bar and restaurant is a popular venue for the neighbourhood's rites of passage: weddings, civil partnerships, bar mitzvahs. One attraction is the 'secret' back garden, which lies beyond the 1970s conservatory extension (hung with gaudy paintings) where most dining takes place. Another is a great wine list (wide ranging, well priced and with ample choice by the glass), which rather puts the food in the shade. Granted, the set menu probably didn't show the kitchen's full range, though starters were engaging: cockles in sweetly stewed shallots, and a halloumi salad with ribbons of carrot and courgette, perky with herbs. To follow, spanking fresh mackerel (not cleaned quite thoroughly enough to remove the bitter innards), and a plump breadcrumbed chicken escalope with aïoli and scanty purple sprouting broccoli, made up in generosity what they lacked in excitement. The French-accented carte doesn't go in for surprises (or much for vegetarians), but treats prime protein such as scallops, dover sole, Welsh lamb and fillet of beef carefully. Good bread, teardrop-shaped truffles with coffee, long white tablecloths and old-fashioned French service account for prices the cooking doesn't quite justify.
Available for hire. Babies and children welcome: children's menu; high chairs. Booking advisable weekends. Separate rooms for parties, seating 16 and 30. Tables outdoors (12, garden). **Map 5 O2**.

Outer London

Kew, Surrey

Glasshouse

14 Station Parade, Kew, Surrey, TW9 3PZ (8940 6777, www.glasshouserestaurant.co.uk). Kew Gardens tube/rail. **Lunch served** noon-2.15pm Mon-Sat; 12.30-2.45pm Sun. **Dinner served** 6.30-10.30pm Mon-Sat; 7-10pm Sun. **Set lunch** (Mon-Sat) £27.50 3 courses; (Sun) £32.50 3 courses. **Set dinner** £42.50 3 courses. **Credit** AmEx, MC, V.
A classy local that has equal appeal for business diners, dates and family groups, all of which were in evidence on a sunny summer lunchtime. The place is aptly named – many windows let the light stream in; what wall space is left is taken up with modern paintings. There's more art on the plate – sashimi of hand-dived scallop with ponzu dressing, prawn beignet and wasabi (a starter) was strikingly served in a scallop shell. Disappointingly, with the exception of a well-flavoured main of miso-glazed pork belly with spring greens, shiitake and pork pastille, soy and enoki mushrooms, most dishes we tried looked better than they tasted. Neither a prettily arranged char-grilled mackerel fillet with celeriac and apple remoulade, bacon and smoked cod roe, nor a still-life of roast wood pigeon with pommes sarladaise, turnips, poached pear and spiced jus (to follow), were more than the sum of their ingredients, though both were nice enough. Fabulous, super-fruity sorbets (orange, mango and lemon) and an above-average chocolate mousse (Valrhona chocolate, served with iced coffee, milk ice-cream and nougatine) made a good finish. Professional service comes with a smile. All in all, there's a lot to like about the Glasshouse – fingers crossed for more culinary excitement next time around.
Available for hire. Babies and children welcome: high chairs. Booking advisable. Dress: smart casual.

Richmond, Surrey

Petersham Nurseries Café HOT 50

Church Lane, off Petersham Road, Richmond, Surrey, TW10 7AG (8940 5230, www. petershamnurseries.com). Richmond tube/ rail then 30 mins walk or bus 65.
Tea house **Open** 9am-5pm Tue-Sat; 11am-5pm Sun.
Café **Lunch served** 12.30-3pm Tue-Sun. **Main courses** £19.50-£29.50.
Both **Credit** AmEx, MC, V.
Housed in an old greenhouse, Petersham Nurseries is a fantasy of the Garden of England, mixed up with Tuscan farmhouse furniture and Indian artefacts, which under chef Skye Gyngall's stewardship garnered volumes of critical praise. Following her departure in 2012, Greg Malouf, previously a guest chef, was hired. Malouf, like Gyngell, is an Aussie who likes to play with expectations and culinary styles – he's supplemented, rather than replaced, Gyngell's menu. So the bright, Mediterranean colours and flavours, assembled from impeccably sourced ingredients (such as buffalo ricotta with golden beetroot, rocket and purple basil), remain. On our visit, new dishes better reflecting the cook's true abilities included an exceptional starter of charred rabbit on a parsnip skordalia, while one of the few Arabic touches was a signature Malouf dish of 'bisateeya' (pastilla) of duck. An explosion of flavour, it saw tender duck meat, moist from an egg custard made with almond, coriander and parsley, wrapped tightly in pastry and dusted with icing sugar for the Moroccan combination of sweet and savoury. The richness was offset by a white cabbage and dried mint salad: another Malouf family recipe. Seasonal pavlova was a delight, with iridescent pink rhubarb draped over a firm meringue, and a layer of lemon posset replacing the usual whipped cream. The only sour note is the pricing, which has remained uncomfortably high.
Available for hire. Babies and children welcome: high chairs; nappy-changing facilities. Booking essential, 1 month in advance. Disabled: toilet.

North African

The stars of London's small North African eating-out scene occupy opposite ends of the price spectrum, but both have an honoured position in the history of the city's restaurants. **Adam's Café** in Shepherd's Bush was among the capital's first joint-use dining venues, serving greasy-spoon caff standards during the day, but transforming itself into an excellent Moroccan-Tunisian bistro by night; and **Momo** almost single-handedly made this cuisine fashionable among the Mayfair glitterati, seducing A-listers with its harem-like furnishings and impeccable couscous. Sadly, the Momo effect hasn't permeated through the city, and London's one other glamorous North African establishment, Pasha, closed in the past year. Nevertheless, its place in the guide has been taken by our first Algerian representative, Brixton's homely **Khamsa**.

Central

Edgware Road

Sidi Maarouf

56-58 Edgware Road, W2 2JE (7724 0525, www.maroush.com). Marble Arch tube. **Meals served** noon-12.30pm Mon-Sat; noon-midnight Sun. **Main courses** £14-£18. **Set meal** £30-£35 4 courses. **Credit** AmEx, DC, MC, V.

The only non-Lebanese outpost of the Maroush chain offers an atmospheric experience, especially at the weekend when belly dancers strut their stuff under billowing silk canopies and dimly lit lanterns. But we have doubts about the authenticity of the food. Adequate zaalouk (spicy aubergine) and taktouka (green pepper and tomato) dips were served with poppy-seed rolls, a bizarre offering from a North African restaurant. A request for Moroccan bread resulted in a plate of cold pitta rather than the warm, thick, crusty khobz we expected. The briouats were excellent – don't miss the spinach and goat's cheese version – and the pastilla impressed with its light casing and toothsome minced chicken filling. But the kofta tagine disappointed: the meatballs lacked flavour, the tomato sauce was bland, and the poached egg had been hard-boiled by the time it reached the table. Ultimately, this is a Lebanese interpretation of a Moroccan restaurant. Levantine bottles dominate the wine list, the beer is Al-Maza rather than Speciale Flag or Casablanca, and Lebanese standards such as moutabel feel like anomalies on the menu. Service is a little brusque and prices are too high. Your best bet is briouats, drinks and shisha on the terrace.

Available for hire. Babies and children welcome: high chairs. Booking advisable. Entertainment: belly dancer 9.30pm, 10.30pm Thur-Sun. Tables outdoors (6, pavement). **Map 8 F6.**

Marylebone

Original Tagines

7A Dorset Street, W1U 6QN (7935 1545, www.original-tagines.com). Baker Street tube. **Meals served** 11am-11pm Mon-Fri; 2-11pm Sat. **Dinner served** 6-11pm Sun. **Main courses** £12.95-£15.95. **Set lunch** £11.50 2 courses. **Credit** AmEx, MC, V.

While this Baker Street stalwart rarely lets us down, it's never excited us much either. Its seemingly incurable Achilles' heel is its lack of atmosphere. On a Wednesday evening, we found an empty, slightly tatty venue, barely livened up by some dated Moroccan tourism posters. It struggles to match the atmosphere of an average London living room, never mind the thriving medinas of Marrakech and Fez. The food is solid but uninspired. There's nothing wrong with the houmous or the grilled halloumi (although £6.30 for seven pieces seems excessive), but the chicken pastilla was poor. It should be a thick round pie made with ouarka, a thin filo-like pastry, but this was flat, square and doughy, and the chicken and almond topping (as opposed to filling) was too dry. The kedra tagine was a partial success; the chicken was perfect, and the pine nuts and prunes contributed texture and sweetness, but an overdose of caramelised raisins overwhelmed the saffron and ginger in the broth. Couscous royale, meanwhile, got the lamb and vegetables spot-on, but the sauce was bland. There's a decent wine list (with house bottles from £11.95) and staff are friendly, but this restaurant is in desperate need of something fresh.

Available for hire. Babies and children welcome: high chairs; nappy-changing facilities. Booking advisable. Separate room for parties, seating 40. Tables outdoors (5, pavement). Takeaway service. Vegetarian menu. **Map 3 G5.**

Mayfair

★ Momo HOT 50

25 Heddon Street, W1B 4BH (7434 4040, www.momoresto.com). Piccadilly Circus tube. **Lunch served** noon-2.30pm, **afternoon tea served** 12.30-5.30pm Mon-Sat. **Dinner served** 6.30-11.30pm daily. **Main courses** £17-£28. **Set lunch** £15.50 2 courses, £19.50 3 courses. **Set dinner** £45-£55 3 courses incl cocktail. **Credit** AmEx, DC, MC, V.

Still London's most glamorous Moroccan restaurant, Momo attracts a fair smattering of beautiful people alongside couples on special dates, hen parties and business types. The soundtrack of classic Maghrebi beats and attractive young francophone waiting staff create a seductive buzz. Sexy Marrakech-style interiors, sparkling with light from intricately latticed mashrabiya-style windows and ornate metalwork lanterns, add to the allure. Tables are small and tightly packed, but somehow this rarely seems an imposition. Enjoy deliciously light, carefully crafted starters such as juicy prawns wrapped in crispy shredded kataifi pastry with a sour-sweet mango and tomato salsa, or scrumptious pan-fried scallops with a piquant salsa verde, before moving on to Moroccan classics such as lamb tagine with pears and prunes. But the main attraction has to be the near-perfect couscous: silky

fine grains served with vegetables in a light cumin-scented broth, with tender, juicy chicken, plump golden raisins, chickpeas and harissa – all served separately so you can mix them as you please. Such delights coupled with a pricey wine list result in a hefty bill, so Momo needs to iron out the galling little niggles such as the shabby dark toilets and the occasionally inattentive service.
Available for hire. Babies and children admitted. Booking advisable weekends. Vegetarian menu.
Map 17 A4.
For branch (Mô Café) see index.

West

Bayswater

Couscous Café

7 Porchester Gardens, W2 4DB (7727 6597). Bayswater tube. **Meals served** 6-11.30pm daily. **Main courses** £9.95-£15.95. **Licensed. Corkage** no charge. **No credit cards.**

Couscous Café certainly isn't lacking in charm. A cosy, warm eaterie tucked down a side street, it's full of instruments, trinkets, shisha pipes and carpets, with lanterns hanging from a bamboo ceiling. Staff are smiley, and the dancey North African music fits the bill. The food, however, is somewhat hit and miss. Dips of mechouia (roasted pepper and tomato), zaalouk (aubergine) and shakshouka (tomato and egg) were let down by lukewarm pitta bread, not the warm, round crusty bread usually offered at Moroccan restaurants. With its delicate filo casing and subtly sweet minced chicken stuffing, the pastilla would have been perfect had it not been for the pesky presence of a small bone. It's a rich and sugary dish, so we'd suggest ordering a starter-sized portion. Dolma tagine (vegetables stuffed with minced lamb) required more meat and more spark – the tomato sauce was plain and the large boiled potato had barely been stuffed. A side portion of 'Moroccan bread' was disappointing; it seemed neither particularly Moroccan nor particularly fresh. Pluses include an impressive and well-priced list of wines from Morocco and Tunisia, and a rare London outing for Casablanca beer.
Babies and children admitted. Table outdoors (1, patio). Takeaway service. **Map 7 C6.**

Shepherd's Bush

Adam's Café

77 Askew Road, W12 9AH (8743 0572, www.adamscafe.co.uk). Hammersmith tube then 266 bus. **Breakfast served** 7.30am-2pm Mon-Fri; 8.30am-2pm Sat. **Dinner served** 7-11pm Mon-Sat. **Set dinner** £12.50 1 course incl mint tea or coffee, £15.50 2 courses, £17.95 3 courses. **Licensed. Corkage** (wine only) £3.50. **Credit** AmEx, MC, V.

Every night, Adam's Cafe pulls off a transformation worthy of Clark Kent. By day it's a greasy spoon serving sandwiches and fry-ups. But at night the candles come out, the music comes on, and the North African vibe seems entirely natural. It's an impressive trick, and one which owners Abdel and Frances Boukraa have pulled off for over 15 years now. The pricing is simple and sensible: £12.50 for one course, £15.50 for two and £17.95 for three. Our starters were enjoyable if unexpected: crêpe aux fruits de mer was covered in melted cheese like a seafood quesadilla; and the brik à l'œuf, a Tunisian breakfast dish, was a deep-fried, fan-shaped crêpe with a poached egg at its centre. Chicken tagine with apricots benefited from a punchy, fruity broth and was given crunch by almonds, while gargoulette, a traditional Tunisian stew, was even better – the succulent lamb came in a thick tomato sauce spiced up by harissa chilli paste. All meals come with pickled vegetables and meatballs. Service is friendly and efficient, and the wine list includes North African varieties (£3.50 corkage fee for BYO).
Babies and children admitted. Tables outdoors (5, patio). Takeaway service. Vegetarian menu.
Map 20 A1.

South

Brixton

Khamsa NEW

140 Acre Lane, SW2 5UT (7733 3150, www.khamsa.co.uk). Brixton tube/rail. **Lunch served** noon-4pm Sun. **Dinner served** 6-10.30pm Mon-Sat. **Main courses** £10.90-£13.90. **Unlicensed. Corkage** no charge. **Credit** MC, V.

Khamsa is a homely neighbourhood eaterie run by a couple who quit their jobs to pursue their goal of making Algerian cuisine better known. It's an exceptionally pretty spot with intricate handmade crockery, colourful pillows and curtains, timber-panelled walls and blackboard menus. The marvellous meze selection (£12, large enough for two) includes velvet-smooth zaalouk (aubergine and

Adam's Café

Momo. See p223.

walnut paste), beetroot salad with fennel and anchovies, garlicky chickpeas topped with spicy meatballs, lentil and bulgar wheat salad, and a light yet flavoursome couscous salad. The mains weren't so impressive. Fish tagine came wrapped in silver foil, which aided temperature control, but made it cumbersome to eat, and the salmon lacked flavour. The 'modern couscous' dish featured a fantastically punchy broth, fresh vegetables, succulent grilled chicken and a spicy merguez sausage, but was let down by chewy pieces of lamb. Service was generally pleasant, but we were alarmed by the owner's stern tone when he asked why we were photographing the food. You can bring your own booze (no corkage), or there's a range of fruit juices.
Available for hire. Babies and children admitted. Booking advisable. **Map 22 C2.**

North

Finsbury Park

★ Le Rif

172 Seven Sisters Road, N7 7PX (7263 1891). Finsbury Park tube/rail. **Meals served** 8am-10pm Mon-Fri; noon-10pm Sat, Sun. **Main courses** £4-£6. **Unlicensed** no alcohol allowed. **No credit cards.**

It's tough finding a tagine for under a tenner in this town. But at Le Rif, only one dish on the extensive menu costs more than £5. This Finsbury Park eaterie isn't remotely atmospheric, although there's much to be said for a North African restaurant free of Arabic cliches. Instead, it caters to a local lunchtime crowd, many of whom eschew the North African offerings for sandwiches, jacket potatoes and spaghetti bolognaise. While such options seem bland compared to the Moroccan dishes the friendly owner can speedily conjure up, the starters were nothing special: a mild lentil, chickpea and rice soup; and houmous with olives and flatbread. The mains were excellent, though. With a combination of spinach, olives, potato, aubergine and lemon, the fish tagine got that balance of sweet and savoury flavours absolutely correct. Couscous royale was every bit as successful, with tender, succulent chunks of chicken and lamb in a subtly spicy broth. There's only one way to end a great Moroccan meal – with pastries and a cup of fresh mint tea – although it does feel a little surreal to pour tea from a beautiful brass pot in a Finsbury Park caff.
Babies and children admitted. Tables outdoors (5, patio). Takeaway service.

Menu

North African food has similarities with other cuisines; see the menu boxes in **Middle Eastern** and **Turkish**.

Brik: minced lamb or tuna and a raw egg bound in paper-thin pastry, then fried.
Briouats, **briouettes** or **briwat**: little envelopes of deep-fried, paper-thin ouarka (qv) pastry; can contain ground meat, rice or cheese, or be served as a sweet, flavoured with almond paste, nuts or honey.
Chermoula: a dry marinade of fragrant herbs and spices.
Couscous: granules of processed durum wheat. The name is also given to a dish where the slow-cooked grains are topped with a meat or vegetable stew; couscous royale usually involves lamb, chicken and merguez (qv).
Harira: lamb, lentil and chickpea soup.
Harissa: very hot chilli pepper paste flavoured with garlic and spices.
Maakouda: spicy potato fried in breadcrumbs.
Merguez: spicy, paprika-rich lamb sausages.
Ouarka: filo-like pastry.
Pastilla, **bastilla** or **b'stilla**: an ouarka (qv) envelope with a traditional filling of pigeon, almonds, spices and egg, baked then dusted with cinnamon and powdered sugar. Chicken is often substituted for pigeon.
Tagine or **tajine**: a shallow earthenware dish with a conical lid; it gives its name to a slow-simmered stew of meat (usually lamb or chicken) and vegetables, often cooked with olives, preserved lemon or prunes.

Islington

Maghreb

189 Upper Street, N1 1RQ (7226 2305, www.maghreb-restaurant.com). Highbury & Islington tube/rail. **Meals served** 6-11.30pm Mon-Thur; 5-11.30pm Fri-Sun. **Main courses** £7.95-£13.95. **Set dinner** £12.95 2 courses, £16.95 3 courses. **Credit** AmEx, MC, V.

A trusty stalwart, Maghreb has a slightly tired air these days, though charming staff and fair prices make it reasonable for a local evening out. On our last visit, starters of za'luk (cumin-infused mashed aubergine with tomatoes and lemon) and juicy grilled merguez sausages with lentils were fine, but lacked just-prepared freshness. A sanitised version of pastilla – flaky pastry pie traditionally made with squab pigeons, bones and all, sprinkled with icing sugar, but here stuffed with cinnamon, chicken and almonds served on a green salad – was a hit. But chicken tagine with olives and preserved lemons (a standard that any Moroccan restaurant should get right) was disappointing: plenty of chicken, but mainly dried-out breast with a reheated flavour. A couple of the generous glasses of drinkable house wine were needed for lubrication. The menu attempts some modern twists; venison tagine with redcurrants and caramelised quince just seems wrong. A shorter menu with freshly cooked, simpler dishes would greatly improve quality here.
Available for hire. Babies and children welcome: high chairs. Booking advisable. Takeaway service. **Map 5 O1.**

Pan-Asian & Fusion

Like no other of the world's major cities, London is ideally placed for culinary experimentation. Recipes flow freely across cultural boundaries in this most multinational of metropolises, helped by a ready supply of ingredients from around the globe. Historical links with the Indian subcontinent, Malaysia and Hong Kong mean that there is no shortage of Asian chefs in the city, and the growth of the capital's Japanese, Thai and Vietnamese dining scenes has added still more ideas into the pot. Fusion cuisine can throw up some unpalatable hotchpotches of incompatible ingredients, but in the right hands, it produces startlingly original and exciting dishes. New Zealander Peter Gordon at the **Providores & Tapa Room** has long been at the helm of this movement, and his creations continue to thrill. A similarly well-honed culinary sensibility is on display at pan-Asian specialist **Champor-Champor**, the **Modern Pantry** (run by Anna Hansen, previously of the Providores) and **L'Etranger** – which manages to conjure up gastronomic gold from the unlikely combination of French and Japanese cuisines. Pan-Asian and Fusion has proved a great crowd-pleaser over the past decade, leading to the success of trendy joints such as Will Ricker's **Eight Over Eight** and its siblings, and the top-end **Sketch**.

Central

Clerkenwell & Farringdon

The Modern Pantry

47-48 St John's Square, EC1V 4JJ (7553 9210, www.themodernpantry.co.uk). Farringdon tube/rail.
Café **Breakfast served** 8-11am Mon-Fri. **Brunch served** 9am-4pm Sat; 10am-4pm Sun. **Meals served** noon-10pm Mon; noon-10.30pm Tue-Fri. **Dinner served** 6-10.30pm Sat; 6-10pm Sun.
Restaurant **Brunch served** 9am-4pm Sat; 10am-4pm Sun. **Lunch served** noon-3pm Tue-Fri; noon-4pm Sat, Sun. **Dinner served** 6-11pm Tue-Sat.
Both **Main courses** £15.50-£22.50. **Set lunch** (Mon-Fri) £20 2 courses; (Sun) £20 2 courses, £25 3 courses. **Credit** AmEx, MC, V.

The on-plate magic at the Modern Pantry – fabulous ingredients conjured into inventive combinations by Anna Hansen's very capable kitchen – is beautifully balanced by the calm setting. Spread over two floors, plus some attractive outdoor tables, it's all lovely clean lines in a gentle colour palette of white and grey, and works equally well for brunch or dinner. Pleasant, engaged staff add to the feel-good vibe, as does the regularly changing aperitif (chilli espresso martini had a delightful kick). Not every dish works – in kimchee-marinated roast lamb rump, with goat's curd, samphire, smoked almond and beetroot salad and smoked anchovy dressing, the ingredients fought a losing battle against the dominance of saltiness – but when they do, the results are glorious. We relished every mouthful of another main: roast persian-spiced poussin with aubergine, currant, red onion and coriander salad, sweetcorn and ginger mash, and neri goma (Japanese sesame paste) cream. Starters of Vietnamese-style peanut soup with coriander pesto, and sweetcorn, date and feta fritters with rose and pomegranate molasses yoghurt were less showy, but flavour-packed nonetheless, though the fritters were a little heavy. Desserts are less out-there, though even the affogato comes with cinder toffee ice-cream. An excellent range of drinks includes craft beers, a global wine list, cocktails and assorted teas. A great restorative for the jaded London palate.

Available for hire. Babies and children welcome: high chairs. Booking essential weekends. Disabled: toilet. Separate room for parties, seats 40. Tables outdoors (13, square). **Map 5 O4.**

Fitzrovia

Bam-Bou

1 Percy Street, W1T 1DB (7323 9130, www.bam-bou.co.uk). Goodge Street or Tottenham Court Road tube.
Bar **Open** 5.30pm-1am Mon-Sat.
Restaurant **Meals served** 11am-11pm Mon-Sat. **Main courses** £8-£15.75. **Set meal** (noon-7pm Mon-Fri; 5.30-7pm Sat) £12.50 2 courses.
Both **Credit** AmEx, MC, V.

Set across several floors of a Fitzrovia townhouse, Bam-Bou holds various elegant dining and meeting rooms, and the Red bar on the third floor. It's smartly decked out in a low-key way, with subtle Asian theming and subdued lighting, as befits a restaurant that's part of Caprice Holdings (the group that also owns the Ivy, Scott's and Daphne's). Service is self-assured and on the ball. The menu ranges across Thai, Chinese and Vietnamese dishes, taking in the likes of spiced slow-roast duck with plum sauce and sugar-snap peas (too rich to finish) and a lovely, unctuous yellow curry with squash, aubergine and pleasingly textured tofu. There are noodle bowls, salads, soups and, on Mondays, dim sum. A hot and sour soup, served as an amuse-bouche, hit the spot, and nibbles such as steamed edamame with spiced sea salt, and huge prawn crackers with chilli sauce, were worth ordering. Not every dish succeeds – while ground beef in wild pepper leaves were tasty morsels, salt and pepper squid was well flavoured but limp – but generally this is quality stuff, justifying the West End prices, such as £5.50 for passionfruit panna cotta or a chocolate and tamarind pot.

Available for hire. Babies and children admitted. Booking advisable Thur-Sat. Separate rooms for parties, seating 8-20. Tables outdoors (4, terrace). **Map 17 B1.**

Gloucester Road

★ L'Etranger

36 Gloucester Road, SW7 4QT (7584 1118, www.etranger.co.uk). Gloucester Road tube.
Lunch served noon-3pm Mon-Fri. **Brunch served** noon-3pm Sun. **Dinner served** 5.30-11pm Mon-Sat; 5.30-10pm Sun. **Main courses** £16.50-£32.50. **Set lunch** £16.50 2 courses, £21 3 courses. **Set dinner** £21 2 courses, £25 3 courses; £75-£95 tasting menu. **Credit** AmEx, MC, V.

True to its name, this dark, chic restaurant is the outsider on a busy road otherwise occupied by charity shops, posh delis and quirky specialists. Inside, a world of glossy minimalism awaits, with black lacquer tables and grey leather walls. Thoughtful, attentive staff serve a modish French-Japanese menu that mostly favours high-end hits from both cuisines (scallop sashimi or miso black cod; terrine of foie gras or Charolais fillet steak), but also remarkably good Eurasian food. Our house 'fish and chips' translated as tempura-fried fillets served with crisp french fries, roughly puréed peas, a lightly wasabi-spiked mayo and pickled ginger. Equally memorable was a pimped-up starter of eggs benedict with crispy pancetta, asparagus and tarragon-scented béarnaise. Pudding – pleasingly light, moussey lime and lemongrass cheesecake on a dense biscuit base – maintained standards. Sexy lighting makes the restaurant great for dates, though business dinners can be safely conducted by the large glass windows. Prices are steep, but the weekday lunch menu remains exceptional value. With both a wine shop and a new wine bar next door, L'Etranger's vinous collection is impressive, encompassing scores of famed crus, a bucketload of champagne, and various sakés.
Available for hire. Babies and children welcome: high chairs. Booking advisable. Separate room for parties, seats 20. **Map 13 C9.**

Marylebone

★ The Providores & Tapa Room HOT 50

109 Marylebone High Street, W1U 4RX (7935 6175, www.theprovidores.co.uk). Baker Street or Bond Street tube.
The Providores **Lunch served** noon-2.45pm Mon-Fri. **Brunch served** noon-2.45pm Sat, Sun. **Dinner served** 6-10.30pm Mon-Sat; 6-10.15pm Sun. **Main courses** (lunch) £17-£25. **Set dinner** £33 2 courses, £47 3 courses, £57 4 courses, £63 5 courses. **Cover** (brunch) £1.50.
Tapa Room **Breakfast/brunch served** 9-11.30am Mon-Fri; 10am-3pm Sat, Sun. **Meals served** noon-10.30pm Mon-Fri; 4-10.30pm Sat; 4-10pm Sun **Tapas** £2-£14.40.
Both **Credit** AmEx, MC, V.

There's an 'upstairs, downstairs' element to this perennially popular café and restaurant. The kitchen is run by the inimitable Peter Gordon, who's famed for brave, yet never foolhardy cooking combinations that few other chefs would dare to imagine (and he's an Officer of the New Zealand Order of Merit, to boot). On the ground floor is the Tapa Room, a casual space open (almost) all day, serving breakfast, lunch and dinner (no bookings); upstairs is the more formal restaurant (reservations advisable). The Tapa Room – so called for the decorative Pacific Island cloths hung on the walls – is where to head for start-the-day-treats such as muffins, classy breakfast fry-ups or the likes of turkish eggs with yoghurt and hot chilli butter (delicious). Later, the all-day menu offers small plates such as a glazed duck-filled bun with chilli jam, or salad of seared beef with pomelo, green papaya and tamarind caramel. There's always an element that surprises, but the dishes really work; expect queues on farmers' market days. Upstairs at Providores, the kitchen notches up a gear with dishes such as smoked coconut tamarind laksa with fish dumpling and soba noodles. The New Zealand-only wine list is sublime, from the solid sauvignon blancs and pinot noirs to beguiling curiosities such as Kiwi grüner veltliner.
Available for hire. Babies and children welcome: high chairs; nappy-changing facilities. Booking advisable Providores; bookings not accepted Tapa Room. Disabled: toilet. Tables outdoors (3, pavement). **Map 9 G5.**

Mayfair

Sketch: The Gallery

9 Conduit Street, W1S 2XG (7659 4500, www.sketch.uk.com). Oxford Circus tube.
Dinner served 6.30-11pm Mon-Sat. **Main courses** £12-£32. **Credit** AmEx, MC, V.

'Why have less when you can have more?' is the attitude at Sketch, Pierre Gagnaire's wonderfully OTT gastronomic playground for well-heeled scenesters. Now a decade old, the Gallery had a revamp in early 2012, with input from Turner Prize-winning artist Martin Creed. Creed's work is everywhere. You'll be sitting on, eating off and drinking from Work No.1343, a collection of mismatched chairs and tables, laid with a hotchpotch of cutlery and glasses. Gagnaire has overhauled the menu, but has kept the trademark global vibe, drawing on influences from Japan, Italy, Spain and Britain – all underpinned by French cuisine. Modern classics, such as the 63°C egg, conceived by French chemist Hervé This, are a strong suit, but Asian-inspired dishes don't always hit such culinary high notes. There's a proper sense of creativity to the menu, from a sea bass paillard

The Modern Pantry

with artichokes and seaweed to the playful 'big mac' dessert – a lemongrass macaroon on sweet wine jelly with grapefruit marmalade. It isn't cheap, but if you scour the menu, you'll find items less taxing to the wallet. The wine list is imaginatively chosen, and service is sweet and switched-on. Ten years on, this is still a place with wow factor. For the high-end Lecture Room & Library, *see p137*; for more casual dining – and afternoon tea – try the third space at Sketch, the Parlour.
Available for hire. Babies and children welcome: high chairs; nappy-changing facilites. Booking essential. Disabled: toilet. Entertainment: DJs 10pm-2am Thur-Sat. Separate rooms for parties, seating 150. **Map 9 J6.**
For branch (Parlour) see index.

Soho

NOPI HOT 50

21-22 Warwick Street, W1B 5NE (7494 9584, www.nopi-restaurant.com). Piccadilly Circus tube. **Breakfast/lunch served** 8am-2.45pm, **dinner served** 5.30-10.30pm Mon-Fri. **Meals served** 10am-10.30pm Sat; 10am-3.30pm Sun. **Main courses** £8-£13. **Credit** AmEx, MC, V.
The big brother of the Ottolenghi cafés (*see p50*), NOPI has the same sense of culinary adventure found in Yotam Ottolenghi's cookery books. Its largely white ground floor is softened by brass fittings and lampshades; the look continues in the basement, where there are communal tables and an open kitchen. A diverting drinks list includes several cocktails. The menu advises choosing three small sharing plates each, though it's possible to have a three-course meal. The best dish from the veg list was a thrilling five-spice tofu with tomato and cardamom passata and braised aubergine. There was a long hiatus before mackerel on nettle vichyssoise and apple, topped by wasabi fish roe, appeared (a slightly murky disappointment), together with two top-quality dishes: wild sea bream with smoked labneh and shards of preserved lemon, and twice-cooked baby chicken with little bowls of chilli sauce and lemon myrtle salt. Six dishes, plus a shared pudding and one glass of wine, came to more than £90 at lunch – spend less and you'll leave peckish. There's admirable passion and ambition, but the cost, combined on this occasion with a snippy waitress, uneven dish pacing and confusion over the booking, left us disappointed.
Available for hire. Babies and children welcome: high chairs. Booking advisable dinner. Dress: smart casual.
Map 17 A4.

NOPI

Spice Market

W London, 10 Wardour Street, W1D 6QF (7758 1088, www.spicemarketlondon.co.uk). Leicester Square tube. **Breakfast served** 7-11am Mon-Fri; 8-11.30am Sat, Sun. **Lunch served** noon-2.45pm, **dinner served** 5-10.45pm daily. **Main courses** £26-£40. **Set lunch** £15-£20. **Set dinner** £48 tasting menu. **Credit** AmEx, MC, V.
The notion of offering an entire continent's cuisines may seem odd, but that's what Jean-Georges Vongerichten's London restaurant attempts, echoing his New York Meatpacking District establishment in the somewhat less salubrious environs of Leicester Square… albeit in the highly salubrious W hotel. Vongerichten's menu reads like a whirlwind tour of Asia, with the space a plush Asian-themed assembly of dark woods and burnished metals, and the service the formal kind you'd expect at a W. The venue looks pricey, and it is, but £17.50 for an unremarkable chicken curry was unjustified, despite its gorgeous presentation. In a selection of lunchtime bento boxes, the flavours and textures were confused and indistinct. A dish billed as green papaya salad, charred long beans, tomatoes and cashews came without the beans, which were replaced by copious flecks of an unidentifiable white goo. Lobster summer roll was zesty, yet we struggled to find even a hint of lobster; spiced chicken samosa was bland; and a red curried duck was mistaken for chicken and tasted like a supermarket ready meal. Odd successes – including a steamed red snapper with shiitake mushrooms, ginger and tarragon that was fresh and perfect – did just enough to merit Spice Market's inclusion in this guide.
Available for hire. Babies and children welcome: high chairs; nappy-changing facilities. Booking advisable. Disabled: toilet. Dress: smart casual; no sportswear. Separate room for parties, seats 40. Vegetarian menu. **Map 17 C5.**

West

Ealing

★ Tuk Cho NEW

2012 RUNNER-UP BEST NEW CHEAP EATS
28-30 New Broadway, W5 2XA (8567 9438, www.tukchoealing.co.uk). Ealing Broadway tube/rail. **Meals served** noon-11pm Mon-Sat; noon-10.30pm Sun. **Main courses** £6-£9. **Credit** AmEx, MC, V.
Despite it being the only branch of Tuk Cho in existence, this South-east Asian street-food specialist feels very much like a chain in the making. The slick design of the vast dining area makes the place seem rather like a Wagamama for the backpacker crowd. Post-industrial decor – poured concrete floors, weathered wooden floorboards – is offset by rustic furnishings that range from distressed ornate garden furniture to rickety-looking wooden chairs and benches upholstered in a mish-mash of cutesy patterned fabrics. The menu is arranged into various salads, stir-fries, curries, noodle-based dishes, rice plates and street snacks. A dish of Vietnamese bun cha hanoi noodles was topped by fragrant lemongrass pork patties, yet was marred by tough pork slices. Desserts, however, were outstanding; a banh chuoi nuong (soft sponge banana cake) contrasted nicely with a topping of crisp coconut shavings. The inclusion of popular Japanese dishes (yaki udon noodles, chicken katsu) suggests that the owners'

Tuk Cho

eyes are firmly fixed on mass-market appeal, rather than authenticity. But before the concept is rolled out, the service needs some tweaking; on our visit, it was very difficult to attract the attention of staff. *Babies and children welcome: children's menu; crayons; high chairs; nappy-changing facilities. Bookings not accepted. Disabled: toilet. Tables outdoors (2, pavement). Takeaway service.*

South West

Chelsea

Eight Over Eight

392 King's Road, SW3 3UZ (7349 9934, www.rickerrestaurants.com). Sloane Square or South Kensington tube. **Lunch served** noon-3pm Mon-Fri; noon-4pm Sat; 12.30-4pm Sun. **Dinner served** 6-10.45pm Mon-Sat; 6-10.30pm Sun. **Main courses** £10-£36. **Credit** AmEx, DC, MC, V.

This swish Chelsea restaurant is part of Will Ricker's mini-chain of stylish pan-Asian eateries. Elegant oriental lampshades hang from the ceiling of the airy black and white dining room, which is populated by a clientele dressed in the expected chinos or cocktail dresses. The only departure from the polished aesthetic is the use of disposable tablecloths, which are whipped away after every course – not a bad idea considering all the dipping sauces served. The menu includes everything from sushi to dumplings, curries to barbecue dishes – all cooked to a high standard. Highlights of our meal included a generous portion of pad thai (one of the best we've found in London), and the restaurant's signature salt and chilli squid, which was attractively presented in a newspaper cone. Also enjoyable was duck and watermelon salad with refreshing sprigs of mint and coriander, all coated in a hoi sin dressing – though it was a little on the sweet side. To drink, there's Asian beer, wine, saké or tea and a reasonably priced cocktail menu. Our attentive suited and booted waiter was keen on a joke, such as telling us with a twinkle in his eye that the next-door table had settled our bill.

Available for hire. Babies and children admitted. Booking advisable dinner. Dress: smart casual. Separate room for parties, seats 18. Vegan dishes. **Map 14 D12.**

For branches (Cicada, E&O, Great Eastern Dining Room, XO) see index.

South East

Herne Hill

★ Lombok

17 Half Moon Lane, SE24 9JU (7733 7131). Herne Hill rail or bus 37. **Dinner served** 6-10.30pm Tue-Sun. **Main courses** £6-£8. **Credit** MC, V.

Herne Hill residents are constantly complaining about the (surprising) paucity of good restaurants in their postcode. Perhaps they just take Lombok

Best oriental chains

Banana Tree

103 Wardour Street, W1F 0UQ (7437 1351, www.bananatree.co.uk). Oxford Circus, Piccadilly Circus or Tottenham Court Road tube. **Meals served** noon-11pm Mon-Sat; noon-10.30pm Sun. **Main courses** £5.95-£10.80. **Credit** AmEx, DC, MC, V.

Offering modish spaces with communal wooden tables, what started out as Banana Leaf Canteen in Battersea has expanded across the capital, with all branches now known by one single name: Banana Tree. The menu describes the food as being from 'Indochina', an old name for the peninsula that includes Vietnam, Laos and Cambodia, but, in fact, the selection here fearlessly mixes up the distinct cuisines of Thailand, Vietnam and Malaysia. Service is speedy, designed to keep tables turning. Cooking is usually excellent, but a recent visit to the new Soho branch proved disappointing, with a dish of 'tamarind crispy fish with a Thai basil glaze' and a classic Vietnamese pho (rice noodle soup) both lacking the subtle touches we'd normally have expected.

Babies and children welcome: nappy-changing facilities. Bookings not accepted for fewer than 6 people; not accepted Thur-Sat. Disabled: toilet. Vegan dishes.
Map 17 B4.
For branches see index.

dim t

56-62 Wilton Road, SW1V 1DE (7834 0507, www.dimt.co.uk). Victoria tube/rail. **Meals served** noon-11pm Mon-Sat; noon-10.30pm Sun. **Dim sum** £3.60-£3.85. **Main courses** £7.95-£9.95. **Credit** AmEx, MC, V.

With its dark, slick interiors, dim t has the oriental swagger of an A-list establishment, but with a much more affordable price-tag. Unfortunately, the cooking doesn't always live up to expectations, particularly in the selection of dim sum that leads the charge: on recent visits, pastry has been thick and doughy, while fillings were bland. Elsewhere, the menu is a pick 'n' mix of popular pan-Asian fare, from crispy duck with pancakes to Thai green curry or stir-fried yaki soba. After dark, the compact choice of exotic cocktails is a draw, while weekends cater more to families. There are just five outlets, but they span the city, from London Bridge via Fitzrovia to Hampstead.

Babies and children welcome: children's menu; high chairs; nappy-changing facilities. Booking advisable. Disabled: toilet. Takeaway service. Vegan dishes.
Map 15 J10.
For branches see index.

Feng Sushi

1 Adelaide Road, NW3 3QE (7483 2929, www.fengsushi.co.uk). Chalk Farm tube. **Meals served** 11.30am-10pm Mon; 11.30am-10.30pm Tue, Wed; 11.30am-11pm Thur, Fri; noon-11pm Sat; noon-10pm Sun. **Main courses** £7-£18. **Set meal** £12 bento box. **Credit** MC, V.

Banana Tree

While its competitors shout loudly, Feng Sushi quietly goes about its business, consistently delivering on quality. Taking its cues from both traditional and modern Japanese kitchens, the menu includes stalwarts such as nigiri, maki and tempura, as well as more fashionable options, such as tuna tartare on pickled cucumber with a yuzu and miso dressing, or seasonal specials such as crispy battered pollock served with a Japanese salsa verde. It's not cheap, but with MSC certification as well as numerous organic or brown rice variations, you're sure to come away feeling virtuous. Branches pop up in all sorts of useful places, from the South Bank to Notting Hill.

Babies and children admitted. Disabled: toilet. Takeaway service; delivery service (over £12 within 3-mile radius). **Map 27 B1.**
For branches see index.

Itsu

118 Draycott Avenue, SW3 3AE (7590 2400, www.itsu.com). South Kensington tube. **Meals served** noon-11pm Mon-Sat; noon-10pm Sun. **Main courses** £3-£8. **Set meal** £4.50-£9.99 bento box. **Credit** AmEx, MC, V.

Itsu has more than 30 takeaway outlets across the capital, which do a roaring lunchtime trade, but only two proper restaurants: in Notting Hill and at this Brompton Cross branch (the original, opened back in 1997). The ground floor is home to a traditional conveyor belt, albeit with less-than-traditional plates: Vietnamese-inspired rice-paper rolls packed with fresh herbs and chilli crab; seaweed salad with seared tuna; or sashimi 'new style' with strips of ginger and a sesame dressing. The upstairs bar – a more peaceful daytime option – comes with waiter service: order from the conveyor menu or a made-to-order list (crispy baby squid, teriyaki-marinated grilled eel). Be warned: the bill can mount.

Babies and children welcome: high chairs; nappy-changing facilities. Bookings not accepted. Takeaway service; delivery service (over £20 within 3-mile radius).
Map 14 E10.
For branch see index.

Ping Pong

45 Great Marlborough Street, W1F 7JL (7851 6969, www.pingpongdimsum.com). Oxford Circus tube. **Dim sum served** noon-midnight Mon-Sat; noon-10.30pm Sun. **Dim sum** 95p-£6.69. **Set meal** £9.95-£36. **Credit** AmEx, MC, V.

Credited with bringing dim sum to the masses, this, the original branch of Ping Pong, opened in 2005. Since then, it has spawned almost a dozen offshoots across the West End and a few outlying areas, all with the same attractive formula of smart, sexy surroundings, decent cocktails and a large selection of the popular steamed parcels – available all day. Standards can be wobbly, with dumplings all too often coming with thick, claggy pastry – it's best to head for dishes that don't require as much finesse, such as Vietnamese prawn paper-rolls, or the signature honey-glazed ribs.

Babies and children welcome: high chairs; nappy-changing facilities. Bookings not accepted for fewer than 8 people. Disabled: toilet. Takeaway service. **Map 17 A3.**
For branches see index.

Wagamama

1 Ropemaker Street, EC2Y 9AW (7588 2688, www.wagamama.com). Moorgate tube/rail. **Meals served** 11.30am-10pm Mon-Fri. **Main courses** £6.75-£13. **Credit** AmEx, MC, V.

Everyone has their favourite Wagamama dish, and this branch of the nation's favourite noodle bar can cater for the lot. Whether it's a slurpy, soupy bowl of chicken (a generous portion of wheat noodles in broth, topped with thick slabs of breast meat), a huge mound of colourful stir-fried udon studded with chicken, prawns and veg, or one of the increasingly popular rice bowls, you're unlikely to leave hungry. Even so, many diners also indulge in side plates of gyoza, breaded prawns or chicken yakitori.

Babies and children welcome: children's menu; high chairs. Disabled: toilet. Takeaway service. Vegan dishes.
Map 12 Q5.
For branches see index.

Yo! Sushi

52 Poland Street, W1F 7NQ (7287 0443, www.yosushi.com). Oxford Circus tube. **Meals served** noon-11pm Mon-Sat; noon-10.30pm Sun. **Dishes** £1.80-£6. **Credit** AmEx, DC, MC, V.

Yo! Sushi's Poland Street branch is where many Londoners got their first taste of conveyor-belt dining. With its loud music and call buttons for service, Yo! Is quirky and fun, but not for sushi aficionados. Special offers and free refills of soft drinks and soup make it popular with wallet-watchers, while the menu constantly reinvents itself, with innovative specials (scallop katzu, salmon and tobiko tartare) supplementing a wide range of sushi, tempura and teriyaki.

Babies and children welcome: high chairs; nappy-changing facilities. Disabled: toilet. Takeaway service. Vegetarian menu.
Map 17 A3.
For branches see index.

for granted; after all, it's been churning out the same superb South-east Asian staples for years. Friendly, family-run and low-key in design – the small room of cloth-covered tables is still dominated by an old-school dark wood bar – the place is always packed on a Friday and Saturday night. The menu covers classic dishes from across the region, taking in Myanmar, Vietnam, Malaysia, Indonesia, Thailand… The Singapore chilli crab was singularly impressive, if messy to eat: a whole crustacean served with an explosion of crispy noodles and a thick, sweet sauce of ginger, onion and spices. Thai green curry is no namby-pamby creamy-coconut dish – it really packs a punch. Waiters will steer those less in love with chilli towards milder dishes such as the chef's special, padang chicken – still a complex compilation of sweet, citrussy and spicy flavours. Starters were nice enough but overshadowed by the mains, though the house ice-creams and sorbets provided a refreshing end to the meal.

Babies and children admitted. Booking essential weekends. Takeaway service. **Map 23 A5.**

London Bridge & Borough

★ Champor-Champor

62-64 Weston Street, SE1 3QJ (7403 4600, www.champor-champor.com). London Bridge tube/rail. **Lunch served** noon-2.30pm Mon-Fri. **Dinner served** 6-10.30pm Mon-Sat. **Main courses** £12-£20. **Credit** AmEx, MC, V.

This funky little restaurant, long a *Time Out* favourite, is under new management – and we're happy to report that standards have been maintained. The food is as good, and the service as solicitous as ever. Indeed, little seems to have changed: the acres of exotic Thai silks and Indonesian fabrics, the teak, incense, candles and little Buddha statues still cast their calming spell. 'Champor-champor' is a Malaysian expression that translates roughly as 'mix and match': an apt description of the menu, which combines cooking styles and ingredients from throughout East and South-east Asia. Many dishes have their roots in Thai-Malay cookery and there are a few western touches too, as in chicken liver and green peppercorn pâté with melba toast and mango chutney. This pick-and-mix style could easily go horribly wrong, but the cooking is brilliantly executed and the clever combinations really work. Seared scallops were cooked just-so, served with salty-crisp bits of bacon and sour-sharp apple – a great combination. Vegetarians are also well cared for; a spicy yellow young banana curry with turmeric had depth of flavour and a potent kick. Save room for the desserts such as chocolate and chilli cheesecake.

Available for hire. Babies and children welcome: high chairs. Booking advisable. Separate room for parties, seats 8-12. Takeaway service. **Map 12 Q9.**

Eight Over Eight. See p229.

Outer London

Barnet, Hertfordshire

★ Emchai

78 High Street, Barnet, Herts, EN5 5SN (8364 9993, www.emchai.co.uk). High Barnet tube. **Lunch served** noon-2.30pm daily. **Dinner served** 6-11pm Mon-Thur; 6pm-midnight Fri, Sat; 5-10pm Sun. **Main courses** £4.20-£8.90. **Set meal** £15-£18.50 per person (minimum 2). **Credit** AmEx, MC, V.

With its jade-green walls, curvy black plastic chairs and white-painted birdcages, Emchai cuts a dash on Barnet High Street. Practised, efficient service and pretty, Japanese-style coordinated crockery add further degrees of sophistication without losing the warmth that characterises a much-loved, long-standing local restaurant in which most customers seem to be remembered or greeted by name. The not-quite-Chinese menu includes the likes of venison in black pepper sauce (a reliable winner) and laksa, as well as plenty of please-all sweet-and-sour dishes and aromatic crispy duck. Moist fillets of fresh salmon were used to excellent effect in a tangy, chilli-laden sambal sauce. Also luscious was Sichuan beancurd with an even-handed dose of the region's trademark numbing peppercorns. A special of salt and spicy beansprouts was not as interesting as it sounded – more a limp, mildly spiced side dish or pickle than a starter – but we enjoyed the competent satay chicken. Child-friendliness extends from plastic cutlery, bowls and trainer chopsticks to advising which noodle dish is best for young palates. Several wine bottles under £25, including our pleasing white Rioja at £17.90, keep the adults happy.

Available for hire. Babies and children welcome: high chairs. Booking advisable weekends. Disabled: toilet. Takeaway service.

Spanish & Portuguese

Spanish cookery has been one of the most dynamic, exciting cuisines of recent years, symbolised by the startling creations of nueva cocina in the Basque Country and the likes of Ferran Adrià (of the now-closed El Bullí) in Catalonia. You won't yet find any such cutting-edge gastronomic laboratories among London's Spanish restaurants, but that's not to say innovation doesn't exist. Take the first-rate **Opera Tavern**, for instance, where classic Spanish tapas are combined with Italian-accented dishes using expertly sourced British ingredients. And there's ambition aplenty at South Ken's classy **Cambio de Tercio**, the hugely popular Soho tapas bar **Barrafina** and hip Camberwell hangout **Angels & Gypsies**. That the capital's Spanish dining scene – and more especially its tapas-bar scene – is in rude health is evidenced by the number of new openings this year. Welcome to Brixton's **Boqueria Tapas**, winner of our Best New Cheap Eats award for 2012; **Copita**, serving imaginative and traditional snacks in Soho; **Donostia**, a Basque-accented tapas joint in Mayfair; **Fat of the Land**, bringing Catalan tapas to Marylebone; **Pizarro**, José Pizarro's bang-on-trend new Bermondsey venue; **Tapas Revolution**, in the unlikely setting of Westfield shopping centre; and Stoke Newington's **Trangallan**, where the tapas have a pleasingly rustic edge.

In contrast to their Iberian neighbours, most of London's Portuguese restaurants tend to stick firmly to tradition: meat with chips; fish with boiled potatoes, plus a few more interesting bacalhau (salt cod) dishes and meat or seafood stews – not forgetting the delectable pastries served in the pastelaria. An exception is **Portal**, where head chef Jeronimo Abreu imaginatively updates traditional cuisine, with often-superb results.

SPANISH

Central

Bloomsbury

Cigala

54 Lamb's Conduit Street, WC1N 3LW (7405 1717, www.cigala.co.uk). Holborn or Russell Square tube or bus 19, 38, 55, 341. **Meals served** noon-10.45pm Mon-Fri; 12.30-10.45pm Sat; 12.30-9.45pm Sun. **Main courses** £12.50-£19. **Set lunch** (noon-3pm Mon-Fri) £17.50 2 courses, £19.50 3 courses; (12.30-4.30pm Sat, Sun) £16 3 courses. **Credit** AmEx, DC, MC, V.

It's now a Lamb's Conduit institution, but Cigala has worked hard to keep itself fresh and appealing. The venue remains both buzzy and busy, with crowds spilling out on to the notably capacious pavement seating-area in summer. The menus (tapas/starters and main courses, both seafood-heavy) make a good stab at ticking various Iberian boxes, from the ubiquitous (pimientos de padrón, tortilla, meatballs, cured ham, patatas bravas), to the regional (a couple of Basque and Andalusian dishes), to the culinarily creative. On the plate, though, the food is something of a modern British take on Spanish cookery: nice, but a little too polite. Own-made chorizo sausages were tasty, yet too spindly to pack a good, fatty punch; baked crab was cautious with its cayenne, brandy and parsley flavourings; and arroz negra with squid was as good as you'd get from a Valencia seaside stall (it's classic beach fare), but lacked a decent slug of olive oil. Amicable, attentive staff, a well-annotated wine list (including a decent rosé section, a clutch of sherries and Basque txakoli by the glass), and simple wood and white decor make eating here unfailingly pleasant.

Available for hire (bar). Babies and children welcome: high chairs. Booking advisable. Separate room for parties, seats 26. Tables outdoors (11, pavement). Vegan dishes. Vegetarian menu. **Map 4 M4.**

Clerkenwell & Farringdon

Morito

32 Exmouth Market, EC1R 4QE (7278 7007, www.morito.co.uk). Angel tube or Farringdon tube/rail or bus 19, 38, 341. **Tapas served** noon-4pm, 5-11pm Mon-Sat; noon-4pm Sun. **Tapas** £1-£9.50. **Credit** MC, V.

Fat of the Land. See p236.

Moro's little sibling, next-door to big sis and exuding the same 'Moorish' vibe, serves some of the best-conceived small plates in town. The Moorish thing pulls in influences from southern Spain, Turkey and the Levant; the spicy results can be revelatory – even if the wipe-clean, orange surrounds and cramped seating don't make for the most comfortable dining experience. Perusal of the wine list, which explores Spain's vinous nooks and crannies, aids relaxation. If you can get a stool, perch at the central bar to watch the chefs at work. Our star dish – crisp, cinnamon-spiced bits of lamb atop creamy aubergine, with chickpea purée and pine nuts – was an object lesson in mixing spices and textures. Cadiz-style chicharrones (meaty pork scratchings), with a sprinkling of sea salt, were simple and satisfying, as were salt-cod croquetas and mildly flavoured, soft sweetbreads with piquillo pepper. Puntillitas (deep-fried baby squid) were hot and fresh, but mouth-puckeringly over-seasoned with sour sumac – as was our grilled courgette salad. Ultra-fresh flatbreads and lightly leavened rounds are well worth the £2.50-per-basket price tag. The small dishes can be pricey, though, and be prepared to queue (no bookings taken at dinner).
Available for hire. Babies and children welcome: high chairs. Bookings not accepted dinner. Disabled: toilet. Tables outdoors (3, pavement). Vegan dishes. **Map 5 N4**.

★ Moro HOT 50

34-36 Exmouth Market, EC1R 4QE (7833 8336, www.moro.co.uk). Angel tube or Farringdon tube/rail or bus 19, 38, 341.
Bar **Open/tapas served** 12.30-10.30pm Mon-Sat; 12.30-2.45pm Sun. **Tapas** £3.50-£14.50. *Restaurant* **Lunch served** noon-2.30pm Mon-Sat; 12.30-2.45pm Sun. **Dinner served** 6-10.30pm Mon-Sat. **Main courses** £16.50-£21. *Both* **Credit** AmEx, DC, MC, V.
A well-established favourite on civilised Exmouth Market, Moro is renowned for its high-quality Spanish/North African food, simply cooked and presented with a twist. On our last visit, we were disappointed to be seated in the small conservatory-like area around the corner at the back, as the main restaurant has much more buzz. But the food, and the helpful staff, more than compensated. Starters of chargrilled squid with grilled pepper salad, lemon and capers, and broad bean, green almond and zataar (a Middle Eastern spice blend) salad with mojama (thinly sliced air-dried tuna), blew us away with their punchy flavours – the squid, in particular, was sublime. Wood-roasted chicken with onion, sumac and pine nut salad, and chargrilled sea bass with spiced rice and fried okra in yoghurt with pomegranate, also more than lived up to their lengthy descriptions. The expertly balanced flavours were enhanced by the extraordinary variety of textures: sensual dining of the highest order. For dessert, yoghurt cake with pistachios and pomegranate shouldn't be missed. The Spanish-oriented wine list is divided by style (crisp and dry, fruity, and so on), and includes plenty of sherries, dessert wines and ports. If the restaurant is full, eat from the excellent tapas menu while perched on a stool at the bar.
Available for hire. Babies and children welcome: high chairs. Booking advisable. Disabled: toilet. Tables outdoors (7, pavement). Vegan dishes. **Map 5 N4**.

Covent Garden

★ Opera Tavern

23 Catherine Street, WC2B 5JS (7836 3680, www.operatavern.co.uk). Covent Garden tube.
Tapas served noon-3pm, 5-11.30pm Mon-Sat; noon-3pm Sun. **Tapas** £2.55-£14.95. **Credit** AmEx, DC, MC, V.
Little distinguishes this former pub (dating from 1879) from its siblings Salt Yard and Dehesa, but the differences are to be applauded. The south-east Covent Garden location itself feels like a golden ticket, and there's a ground-floor bar that welcomes pre-theatre drinkers. Centre stage is an open grill producing smoky-tasting chorizo, burgers of ibérico pork and foie gras, and succulent little lamb cutlets. Upstairs is a cosy yet glamorous restaurant serving the mix of Spanish- and Italian-inspired tapas for which the group is rightly regarded. However, sustainable British produce plays an increasing role in the repertoire (wild Cornish bass, Old Spot pork belly, heritage carrots) and consequently some dishes take on a fusion sensibility, such as crispy soft-shell crab with radish, celery, watercress and horseradish aïoli. Purists, though, will be satisfied with classic tortilla, patatas bravas and artisan-made charcuterie and cheeses. We like the easy-going friendliness of the knowledgeable staff. They're very good chatting about the wines, though the enticing, well-written list provides plenty of help to get you started. As might be expected, there's an appealing choice of sherries, with all ten available by the glass, starting at £4.50.
Babies and children welcome (dining room): high chairs. Booking essential. Dress: smart casual. Separate room for parties, seats 45. Tables outdoors (3, pavement). Vegan dishes. **Map 18 E4**.

Fitzrovia

Barrica

62 Goodge Street, W1T 4NE (7436 9448, www.barrica.co.uk). Goodge Street tube. **Tapas served** noon-11.30pm Mon-Fri; 1-11.30pm Sat. **Tapas** £1.95-£10. **Credit** AmEx, MC, V.

Tall stools, a marble-top bar (where diners nibble on croquetas and toasted almonds), muted yellow walls, and a chatter of Spanish coming from the front-of-house staff – you could be forgiven for enjoying yourself at Barrica. Much like in Spain, the tapas portions here are large enough to satisfy, yet small enough and pitched at the right price for you to order more. Jamón hangs from the ceiling, and black and white tiled flooring offsets dark wooden features; an inviting little bodega of wine is on show. The exclusively Spanish wine list features grapes from smaller producers, such as albariño from Galicia. It's also ideal for experimentation, with more than 24 wines available by the glass, plus fino, manzanilla and amontillado sherries. Pick from classic cold tapas, or daily changing specials from the grill, for a real taste of Spain. Tortilla was rich with egg, just that satisfying side of squishy, with a contrast of sweet red onions against a dusting of salt. Pimientos de padrón lacked spice, but grilled chorizo made up for that. Duck was seared on an oak grill, with tender flesh that melted into whipped cherry butter on toast.

Available for hire. Babies and children admitted. Booking advisable Tue-Sat. Tables outdoors (2, pavement). **Map 17 A1.**

Fino

33 Charlotte Street, entrance on Rathbone Street, W1T 1RR (7813 8010, www.finorestaurant.com). Goodge Street or Tottenham Court Road tube. **Tapas served** noon-2.30pm, 6-10.30pm Mon-Fri; 6-10.30pm Sat. **Tapas** £2-£25. **Credit** AmEx, MC, V.

Sam and Eddie Hart know how to create a stylish dining experience, and Fino continues to be a hugely popular choice for lovers of good food where budget isn't an issue. The decor is a blank canvas, with simple, clean lines, neutral tones and a smattering of colourful modern art. This allows diners to get on with it, and the atmosphere is buzzing most evenings. Customers – couples, friends, colleagues – are dressed up and in some cases dressed down, but in this hip venue anything goes. The modern Spanish menu is enticing, with renowned dishes such as papery courgette flowers stuffed with garlicky goat's cheese, or crisp roasted pork belly. Authentic tortilla with a runny centre arrives topped with chorizo or black pudding; mouth-watering ribeye steak is paired with melting picos cheese. Drinks are a forte too, with an extensive list of Spanish wines, sherry (as you might expect) and cocktails. There's a separate bar, should you want to continue your evening. Tables in the centre of the room or the booths offer the best vantage points, so ask when you book.

Available for hire. Babies and children welcome: high chairs. Booking advisable. Disabled: lift; toilet. **Map 17 B1.**

Salt Yard

54 Goodge Street, W1T 4NA (7637 0657, www.saltyard.co.uk). Goodge Street tube. **Open** noon-11pm Mon-Fri; 5-11pm Sat. **Tapas served** noon-3pm, 5.30-11pm Mon-Thur; 5-11pm Fri, Sat. **Tapas** £4.75-£9. **Credit** AmEx, DC, MC, V.

Over the past couple of years, London has seen countless tapas joints open, but Salt Yard – one of the pioneers of the capital's new Spanish scene, and forefather of Dehesa and Opera Tavern – remains among the best. This understatedly handsome, rather small venue was full for our weekend visit (including the counter seats towards the front window and along the bar), and maintained a pleasant hubbub all night. Although there are always notable Italian touches on the regularly changing menu, among them minor variations on stuffed courgette flowers or a fine affogato, the kitchen's skill and attention to sourcing really come to the fore in pitch-perfect Spanish tapas. Sample, for instance, the justly named 'classic' tortilla (which maintained its structure despite being oozingly moist) or the simple selection of three types of manchego. Adventures into more unusual flavour combinations – perhaps a warm potato and beetroot salad with nettle pesto, say, or a scallop carpaccio – rarely disappoint. For wine, a faintly sparkling Basque txakoli rosé was an intriguing if not entirely successful recommendation, partly undermined by a barely functional aerating pouring spout. And our waitress, clearly new to the job, was struggling a little, but some discreet steering by a senior colleague kept the occasion good-humoured.

Available for hire. Babies and children admitted (restaurant). Booking essential. Tables outdoors (4, pavement). **Map 17 A1.**

For branch (Dehesa) see index.

King's Cross

Camino

3 Varnishers Yard, Regent Quarter, N1 9FD (7841 7331, www.camino.uk.com). King's Cross tube/rail.

Bar **Open** noon-midnight Mon-Wed; noon-1am Thur-Sat; noon-11pm Sun. **Tapas served** noon-4pm, 4.30-11pm daily.

Restaurant **Tapas served** noon-3pm, 6-11pm Mon-Fri; noon-4pm, 6-11pm Sat; noon-4pm Sun. **Set meal** £14.95 tasting menu (minimum 2).

Both **Tapas** £2.75-£39.50. **Credit** AmEx, MC, V.

The Spanish hotspot that is Camino is a little tucked away. It's certainly a capacious venue, consisting of two big bar rooms, a restaurant, an outside terrace and sherry haven, Bar Pepito. Furnishings are of simple natural materials (wooden floors and panelling, leather chairs) offset

Donostia. See p236.

SPANISH & PORTUGUESE

by colourful Spanish posters and, in one bar, a gigantic map of Spain. Even on a Sunday lunchtime, the vibe is upbeat, with music playing. Staff are extremely warm, although service on our visit was a little slow at times. The menu provides various options – tapas, platters, a tasting menu and, at weekends, tempting brunches with a Spanish twist. We ordered a platter with beautifully tender fried squid, crisp ham croquetas, fried chorizo, crab pâté and marinated peppers: a flavoursome, well-executed choice that perhaps might have benefited from fewer oily options. The wine list offers a good choice by the glass, carafe and bottle (handy if your tastes differ from those of your dining companions). The informal, fun atmosphere makes Camino a great place to come with a group for a lively night out.
Available for hire. Babies and children welcome (before 6pm Thur-Sat): high chairs; nappy-changing facilities. Booking advisable. Disabled: toilet. Tables outdoors (10, garden; 4, pavement). **Map 4 L3.**
For branches see index.

Marylebone

Fat of the Land NEW

35 New Cavendish Street, W1G 9TR (7487 3030, www.thefatoftheland.co.uk). Bond Street, Oxford Circus or Regent's Park tube. **Tapas served** 10am-10pm daily. **Tapas** £5.50-£22. **Credit** AmEx, MC, V.

The latest pub from the crew behind the Queen's Head & Artichoke (*see p107*) and the Norfolk Arms (*see p106*) has more fashionable decor than at either sibling: black and grey meets expensive oak and exposed brick (though the hams swaying in the window are a common feature). The compact, Catalan-slanted tapas menu is equally modish. There's a smart and airy upstairs dining room, and a lively ground-floor bar in which we sipped sherry (a fine oloroso from Hidalgo) and a cold pint of draught Mahou lager. Having spied a spice-crusted and spatchcocked baby chicken that smelled as good as it looked, we ordered one. But when it arrived, it was the pale cousin to the earlier bird. Still, the meat was juicy, while the accompaniment of sweet prunes and toasted pistachios (a twist on the traditional Catalan mix of raisins and pine nuts), set over wilted spinach, worked well. A trio of ham croquetas and a classic tortilla were properly cooked. A small bowl of escalivada (a sort of Catalan ratatouille) was decent, but not outstanding; ditto a cold dish of broad beans and baby squid (swimming in their own ink). FOTL may already be buzzing with well-heeled residents and workers, but if it wants to stand shoulder to shoulder with the exceptional Spanish restaurants of nearby Fitzrovia, it'll need to work a bit harder.
Available for hire. Booking advisable. Disabled: toilet. **Map 9 H5.**

Mayfair

Donostia NEW

10 Seymour Place, W1H 7ND (3620 1845, www.donostia.co.uk). Marble Arch tube. **Open** 6-11pm Tue; 12.30-11pm Wed-Sat; 12.30-3.30pm Sun. **Credit** MC, V.

Donostia – San Sebastián in Basque – is a place of pilgrimage for food lovers. Besides internationally acclaimed avant-garde restaurants such as Mugaritz or Arzak, it is also home to older dining traditions. The tapas bars, in particular, are renowned for their appetising pintxos (skewered tapas) and bonhomie. Calling your restaurant Donostia when you have no Basque heritage is asking for trouble, but chef Tomasz Baranski has made a decent stab of it. He used to be in charge of the kitchen at Barrafina, and this link is clear in the clean lines of Donostia, which has a large entrance bar serving pimped-up bar food, plus (bookable) tables. Start with a glass of txakoli, a slightly fizzy, low-alcohol wine. Food highlight was the tortilla; fresh from the hotplate, it was molten in the centre and filled with spinach and salt cod. Cod is a major building block of Basque cuisine; cod cheeks are considered a delicacy, and here you can have the slithery jowls in a classic pil pil sauce, rich in olive oil, garlic and a little chilli garnish. Not everything is such good quality. The romesco sauce served with a pork fillet was a letdown – bland and lacking punch. And don't arrive too hungry, or you'll ramp up a hefty bill. There's much diversion and enjoyment to be had from the wine list, though, as the owners have been collecting unusual wines from Spain and beyond.
Available for hire. Babies and children welcome: high chairs. Booking advisable dinner. Tables outdoors (2, pavement).
Map 8 F6.

★ El Pirata

5-6 Down Street, W1J 7AQ (7491 3810, www.elpirata.co.uk). Green Park or Hyde Park Corner tube. **Meals served** noon-11.30pm Mon-Fri. **Dinner served** 6-11.30pm Sat. **Main courses** £13.95-£17.95. **Tapas** £1.90-£10.95. **Set tapas** (noon-3pm) £10.25 2 dishes incl glass of wine; £16.35 8 dishes. **Credit** AmEx, MC, V.
El Pirata is a neat little tapas bar off the leafy streets of Green Park. Staff, food and ambience are all effortlessly authentic; the only reminder you're in England is the need to book to get a table. The main restaurant on the ground floor feels like an intimate, upmarket tapas bar with dark wooden interiors and alfresco dining. Downstairs is more informal for groups; simple whitewashed walls evoke an old-school tapas establishment. The set menu is an easy and good-value way to navigate the extensive tapas list. Classics including croquetas, calamares and jamón sit alongside less expected offerings of bean stew from northern Spain, grilled lamb cutlets, or kidneys in sherry wine. The classics were done to perfection; it's surprisingly hard to find good tortilla even when eating out in Spain, yet El Pirata's tortilla is very good indeed. Prawns in spicy garlic oil were succulent and seaside-fresh, and cured meats

Copita

SPANISH & PORTUGUESE

included a rich paprika chorizo and smooth slices of lomo. A gazpacho was cool, creamy and among the best we've tasted. The wine menu is an Iberian epic, but the house red works perfectly if you're just after an honest glass of wine to accompany delicious tapas.
Babies and children admitted. Booking advisable dinner. Separate room for parties, seats 65. Tables outdoors (4, pavement). Takeaway service. **Map 9 H8**.

Soho

★ Barrafina HOT 50

54 Frith Street, W1D 4SL (no phone, www.barrafina.co.uk). Leicester Square or Tottenham Court Road tube. **Tapas served** noon-3pm, 5-11pm Mon-Sat; 1-3.30pm, 5.30-10.30pm Sun. **Tapas** £2-£18.50. **Credit** AmEx, MC, V.
Any preconceptions about tapas bars being pleasant but unmemorable places with routine menus are dispelled by this slick offshoot of Fitzrovia's Fino. Barrafina is very much a bar, the only seating being stools around an L-shaped bar in gleaming steel, behind which chefs display their skills in grilling seafood and assembling complex salads with stunning panache. The tapas, supplemented by larger specials, are truly exceptional. Careful sourcing of impeccable ingredients, especially seafood and Spanish cold meats, is the key to quality here, but there's no shortage of cooking ability either. Ham croquetas were superbly creamy, while morcilla with fried quail's eggs and roasted piquillo peppers was sumptuously suave. The pleasure continued with tortilla stuffed with deliciously meaty prawns and peppers, and a salad of radishes, cherry tomatoes and fabulously fresh, fragrant fennel, delicately balanced by a subtle citrus dressing. The same expert attention informs the wine list: conveniently short but with an excellent mix of superior modern Spanish wines by the glass or bottle. The only problem is in grabbing one of the 23 stools, as the place is generally packed from opening time to last orders. Staff, though, deal with the constant flow with admirably friendly efficiency.
Babies and children admitted. Bookings not accepted. Tables outdoors (4, pavement). **Map 17 C3**.

Copita NEW

26 D'Arblay Street, W1F 8EP (7287 7797, www.copita.co.uk). Oxford Circus tube. **Open** 11am-11pm Mon-Fri; noon-11pm Sat. **Tapas served** noon-4pm, 5.30-10.30pm Mon-Fri; 1-10.30pm Sat. **Tapas** £2.95-£6.95. **Credit** AmEx, MC, V.
Black and white floor tiles evoke a traditional Seville tapas bar, with diners perching around tall wooden tables. The tiled walls make it rather noisy, but there are a few tables outside if you prefer quieter surroundings. Staff were easy-going and jovial, and particularly enthusiastic about the sherry menu. Standards such as almonds, cheeseboards and chorizo de bellota are on the menu, but there are more original pairings too, which change frequently – on our visit, these included kohlrabi and apple salad, and mussel croquettes. Miniature violet artichokes were perfectly grilled, crisp at the end of each leaf. Ajoblanco was an addictive cold soup of puréed garlic, almonds and breadcrumbs, served with sweet chunks of beetroot, peanuts and fresh dill.

Tapas Revolution. See p239.

Marinated lamb was a mini roast dinner, served just medium rare with glazed carrots and black olives. Servings are on the small side (as they tend to be in Spain), so you may need three or four dishes per person. The wine list is well informed, and all wines come by the glass; Copita encourages you to have several little glasses (or copitas) with each tapas. Do try the sherries on offer, and even a glass of pacharán sloe berry liqueur as a digestif.
Available for hire. Babies and children admitted. Bookings not accepted dinner. Tables outdoors (3, pavement). **Map 17 B3**.

Tapas Brindisa Soho

46 Broadwick Street, W1F 7AF (7534 1690, www.brindisa.com). **Open** noon-11pm Mon-Sat; noon-10pm Sun. **Tapas served** noon-10.45pm Mon-Sat; noon-9.45pm Sun. **Tapas** £1.50-£21.50. **Credit** AmEx, MC, V.
Brindisa's Soho incarnation has all the atmosphere of a traditional Spanish establishment, but with a London edge. Classic tapas such as grilled octopus or chorizo in a red wine reduction are very well executed, while imaginative dishes such as air-cured tuna with pear, or honey-soaked baked cheese, make a new mark on the tapas circuit. The air-cured tuna loin is cut using a charcuterie slicer, so it's as thin as ibérico ham, but comes with an alluring taste of the sea. Coupled with pear slices and a glug of good oil, this was our favourite dish. Tortilla with chorizo was earthy and deliciously gooey, and clams stewed with white beans made a rustic dish to mop up with sourdough bread. Spanish touches abound: from the endearing staff to cutlery stacked in Spanish paprika tins on each table. Sit at the back, right in the heart of the action next to the grills; dine more formally in the main part of the restaurant; or sit at the bar, indulge in the impressive Spanish wine list, and chat to bar staff for a true tapas experience.
Babies and children welcome: high chair. Bookings not accepted dinner. Disabled: toilet. Tables outdoors (2, pavement). **Map 17 A3**.
For branches (Casa Brindisa, Tapas Brindisa) see index.

South Kensington

★ Cambio de Tercio

163 Old Brompton Road, SW5 0LJ (7244 8970, www.cambiodetercio.co.uk). Gloucester Road or South Kensington tube. **Lunch served** noon-3pm daily. **Dinner served** 7-11.30pm Mon-Sat; 7-11pm Sun. **Main courses** £13.90-£32. **Credit** AmEx, DC, MC, V.
With its warm Spanish welcome, a vibrant colour scheme of pinks, yellows and oranges, and surreal artwork adorning the walls, a visit to Cambio de Tercio is certainly a vivid experience. Fortunately, the menu has as much colour as the setting: it's full of top-notch modern cooking with plenty of imagination. A starter of smoked raw tuna with scallops, crisp endive and asparagus was a sign of good things to follow. Starters double as tapas, so you can opt for three or four, or move on to a main. Both options are worthwhile, with tapas allowing you to sample a range of the chefs' skilfully constructed dishes. Melt-in-the-mouth sweet braised oxtail is a must for meat lovers, while tomatoes marinated in oloroso sherry and roasted for eight hours are not to be missed. Desserts were equally impressive, as were the mini cones of cinnamon-flecked crema catalana and rich dark truffles that came with coffee. To drink, there's an extensive choice of wines listed by region, along with sherries and cava. High prices make this somewhere to go for a special occasion, but the ambience, culinary skill and service make you feel you're getting good value.
Available for hire. Babies and children admitted. Booking advisable dinner. Separate room for parties, seats 20. Tables outdoors (3, pavement). **Map 13 C11**.

Capote y Toros

157 Old Brompton Road, SW5 0LJ (7373 0567, www.cambiodetercio.co.uk). Gloucester Road or South Kensington tube. **Tapas served** 6-11.15pm Tue-Sat. **Tapas** £4.50-£22. **Credit** AmEx, MC, V.

Sit against the wall at Capote y Toros and you can view the bar, barrels, bottles and the Old Brompton Road; sit facing it and you see so many pictures of bulls, bullfighters and other loads of old bull, it's all hard to take in – though the hanging 'bulls' heads' are of basketwork rather than the real thing. The smallest offshoot of the Cambio de Tercio restaurant next door and Tendido Cero opposite, this venue is described as a 'ham and sherry bar', so seating is limited. A prime attraction is the chance to explore the Cambio group's remarkable (if pricey) wine list, with fine bottles from nearly every Spanish region and, especially, an encyclopaedic range of sherries. Very fine ibérico ham and other meats feature highly on the (bizarrely naff-looking) menu, but there are also more intricate modern tapas such as salmon tartare with garlic and oil, a smooth salt cod brandade and a goat's cheese salad made special by irresistible Pedro Ximénez sherry dressing. The young Spanish staff are perkily friendly in tapas-bar style, though you wonder if they could offer advice about the £500 Priorats or Ribera del Dueros on the wine list.
Babies and children admitted. Bookings not accepted. Tables outdoors (1, pavement). **Map 13 C11.**

Tendido Cero

174 Old Brompton Road, SW5 0BA (7370 3685, www.cambiodetercio.co.uk). Gloucester Road or South Kensington tube. **Tapas served** noon-2pm, 6.30-11pm daily. **Tapas** £4-£14. **Credit** MC, V.

Middle in size of the three near-adjacent branches of the Cambio de Tercio clan, Tendido Cero is also mid-point in style: bigger and more comfortable than Capote y Toros, more bustling and tapas-oriented than the flagship Cambio de Tercio restaurant. It broadly shares the impressively wide-ranging Spanish wine stock and similar smartly modern but bullfight-obsessed decor, with one wall lined by giant images of pouting matadors. The tapas are, again, more intricate than at Capote, less refined than the Cambio creations. Best of all were the simplest and most traditional, first-rate padrón peppers with all the right bittersweet flavours. Chicken croquettes were smooth and satisfying, while the 'new' patatas bravas were an enjoyably stylish take on an old favourite: neatly formed little crispy potato barrels topped with delicate aïoli. Other tapas had a few low notes: in grilled asparagus with romesco sauce, the main ingredient was of a high quality, but the romesco lacked tang; nicely meaty meatballs were also let down by a bland sauce. Staff are fast and cheery, although some had an annoying tendency to push us towards more expensive bottles on the wine list.
Available for hire. Babies and children welcome: booster seats. Booking advisable dinner Wed-Sat. Tables outdoors (4, terrace). **Map 13 C11.**
For branch (Tendido Cuatro) see index.

West

Bayswater

El Pirata Detapas

115 Westbourne Grove, W2 4UP (7727 5000, www.elpiratadetapas.co.uk). Bayswater tube. **Tapas served** noon-3pm, 6-11pm Mon-Fri; noon-11pm Sat, Sun. **Tapas** £3-£7. **Set tapas** £20 7 dishes, £25 8 dishes. **Credit** AmEx, MC, V.

This offshoot of Mayfair's El Pirata has a much trendier look and buzzier feel than its long-running parent. The food style was set by young former chef Omar Allibhoy (ex-student of mega-chef Ferran Adrià at El Bullí in Catalonia), who has now moved on to his own venture at Tapas Revolution. Any connection with El Bullí can raise awesome expectations of culinary pyrotechnics; frankly, these won't be met here, but what you will get is refined, artfully prepared tapas well above the norm – at the same price as dead-ordinary elsewhere. The renowned serrano ham croquettes are gorgeously creamy, and the mojo picón (a Canary Islands equivalent of brava sauce) with fried potatoes was both smooth and deceptively punchy. A mushroom risotto made with socarrat (the slightly burnt rice left over in a paella pan, apparently) had an original, toasty flavour, and our only problem with the black rice with squid and aïoli was a paucity of garlic. Wines aren't neglected, with a list that runs from quality house bottles to some of the finest new Spanish labels. Detapas is deservedly popular and often packed, but staff keep things coming with a laconic, very Spanish lack of fuss.
Available for hire. Babies and children welcome: high chairs. Booking advisable. Separate room for parties, seats 30. Takeaway service. Vegan dishes. **Map 7 B6.**

Shepherd's Bush

Tapas Revolution NEW

The Balcony, Westfield London, W12 7GB (no phone, www.tapasrevolution.com). Shepherd's Bush tube/rail. **Tapas served** 11am-10pm Mon-Sat; 11am-9pm Sun. **Tapas** £3.50-£8.25. **Set meal** £11 per person (minimum 2). **Credit** AmEx, DC, MC, V.

You might not expect to find good tapas in the middle of a shopping centre, but that's what Tapas Revolution, run by Omar Allibhoy (formerly of El Pirata Detapas in Westbourne Grove) manages to offer. This small, circular tapas bar might not start a revolution, but it does manage to capture a sense of Spain, with the metal bar-top, Spanish service and good tapas. We loved the sangría, and actually overheard two other diners asking for the secret of their recipe (Cointreau and sweet fruit including strawberries and pear cut into small pieces, apparently). Chicken cooked in saffron and cumin had a Spanish-Moorish influence, and oven-roasted chorizo was crisp, with just the right amount of oil to be soaked up with bread. Vegetable pisto stew was unremarkable, however, as was the paella, but the patatas bravas were a confident interpretation of a classic tapas dish. The location may seem a bit bizarre and lacking in atmosphere – beside large shops and an oversized cinema – but this is a great place to refuel with a glass of wine and some nibbles after a shopping spree.
Babies and children welcome: nappy-changing facilities (shopping centre). Bookings not accepted. Disabled: lift; toilet (shopping centre). Vegetarian menu. **Map 20 C1.**

South

Battersea

Lola Rojo HOT 50

78 Northcote Road, SW11 6QL (7350 2262, www.lolarojo.net). Clapham Junction rail. **Tapas served** noon-3pm, 6-10.30pm Mon-Thur; noon-10.30pm Fri-Sun. **Tapas** £4-£15.50. **Credit** MC, V.

Stylish, funky Lola Rojo brings a bit of Barcelona to Battersea. It's a tiny place decorated in black, red and white, with a raised sharing table in the main dining room, chic white tables and chairs throughout and, outside, a few stools. The latter are ideal in summer for perching with a glass of chilled Rueda while nibbling tapas. It's easy to compose a small meal or a grand feast from among the fish, meat and 'cured' tapas, small starters and unmissable rice dishes. Catalan flavours are to the fore, such as the rustic bread with all i oli (Catalan for aïoli) that kicked off our meal. Young artichokes were cooked in the Jewish-Roman style – flattened and deep-fried to perfect crunchiness. Deep-fried

Boqueria Tapas. See p241.

mushrooms, stuffed with manchego cheese, arrived with punchy romesco sauce. Black rice with squid, the colour of a vampire's cape, was flavoured with squid ink, but the saffron all i oli was garlicky enough to keep Dracula at bay. Lola Rojo isn't without faults. Tables are cramped and service can be brusque under pressure. Even so, it's justifiably popular. The excellent wine list explores lesser-known regions, showcasing some of the best contemporary Spanish wine making.
Babies and children welcome: booster seats. Tables outdoors (16, terrace). Takeaway service.
Map 21 C5.

Brixton

Boqueria Tapas NEW

2012 WINNER BEST NEW CHEAP EATS
192 Acre Lane, SW2 5UL (7733 4408, www.boqueriatapas.com). Clapham North tube or Brixton tube/rail. **Tapas served** 5-11pm Mon-Thur; noon-11.45pm Fri, Sat; noon-10pm Sun. **Tapas** £3.90-£7.90. **Credit** AmEx, MC, V.
The traditional and the contemporary combine to fine effect at this newbie Brixton tapas joint. Near the entrance is a stylish bar lined with aluminium stools, where little globe spotlights hang low over the counter, and vases of lilies and gigantic Rioja bottles decorate the surfaces. The small rear dining room comes complete with a skylight. The menu offers modern twists on tapas such as enjoyably slimy aubergine cannelloni, and a parsnip crisp-topped roast pork dish rendered stunningly refreshing by a little ball of lemon sorbet melting into a pool of apple sauce. The 'tradicionales' selection was less impressive, including a dry, bland tortilla, plus ham and cheese croquetas that consisted of a dribble of liquid sitting at the bottom of a virtually empty breadcrumb shell. Our Sunday visit saw the service quite distracted, with the sole waiter leaving the dining room for up to 30 minutes at a time. However, there's no faulting the ingredient quality: a fried portion of cod in sweet tomato sauce flaked apart tenderly; and the delicious, deep flavour of a complimentary starter of rosemary-scattered olives set a high standard that was continued throughout much of the meal.
Babies and children welcome: high chairs. Booking advisable. Disabled: toilet. Separate room for parties, seats 50. Takeaway service.
Map 22 C2.

Vauxhall

Rebato's

169 South Lambeth Road, SW8 1XW (7735 6388, www.rebatos.com). Stockwell tube.
Bar **Open/tapas served** 5.30-10.45pm Mon-Fri; 7-11pm Sat. **Tapas** £3-£10.
Restaurant **Lunch served** noon-2.30pm Mon-Fri. **Dinner served** 7-10.45pm Mon-Sat. **Main courses** £12-£19. **Set meal** £21.50 3 courses.
Both **Credit** AmEx, MC, V.
Rebato's is strictly old school. At the front is a bar area, all dark wood and red-upholstered seating, good for drinks and tapas; behind is a formal restaurant with white tablecloths. Both spaces enjoy service from professional older waiters of a type now rare in London. The timeless theme continues with the food. All the tapas standards are here, along with mains like sauté of kidneys with sherry, and spicy pork meatballs. We sat in the quiet restaurant to enjoy some herby charcoal-grilled rabbit pieces, garlicky oyster mushrooms, big fat prawns with garlic dip, a generous mixed salad, well-flavoured batatas bravas and croquettas with spinach and pine. Portions were generous for tapas, there was a profusion of olive oil and garlic: nothing anaemic here, all great tastes and satisfying, if not especially filling. We decided to finish our meal with something sweet. And yes, Rebato's has a sweet trolley, from which we chose traditional flan (crème caramel). We only had one gripe. Rebato's may old-fashioned, but we weren't happy to be presented with an indecipherable bill scrawled on various bits of paper stapled together. With drinks and pudding, our bill wasn't negligible – it would have been good to have seen what we were paying for.
Available for hire. Babies and children admitted. Booking advisable. Vegetarian menu.
Map 16 L13.

South East

Camberwell

★ Angels & Gypsies

29-33 Camberwell Church Street, SE5 8TR (7703 5984, www.angelsandgypsies.com). Denmark Hill rail or bus 36, 185, 436. **Lunch served** noon-3pm Mon-Fri; noon-3.30pm Sat; noon-4pm Sun. **Dinner served** 6-10.30pm Mon-Thur, Sun; 6-11pm Fri, Sat. **Tapas** £3.50-£12. **Credit** AmEx, MC, V.
South London hipsters continue to pack out this buzzing, bijou restaurant, making booking essential. Dark wooden tables, pews, and chairs bearing cross motifs are arranged around a tiled horseshoe bar, with stunning stained-glass windows looming over proceedings. Atmospheric, low lighting adds to the ecclesiastical vibe. But there's more to Angels & Gypsies than stylish decor, as hinted at by legs of serrano ham on display, and blackboards listing wines and specials. The menu combines Spanish classics with more imaginative creations, so dishes such as scallops, ginger oloroso and ibérico ham share space with gambas al ajillo and traditional tortilla. Food arrives on rustic crockery. Prawn croquetas with tender morsels of meat and a spiky habanero salsa hit the mark, while a meatball with melting manchego in its centre, surrounded by a tomatoey broth, was as unexpected as it was delicious. To drink, there's an interesting selection of wines, sherry and cava as well as an extensive list of rums from South America and the Caribbean. Prices are reasonable and the dress code casual. Camberwell has lucked out at last.
Available for hire. Babies and children welcome: high chairs. Booking advisable. Separate room for parties, seats 25. Takeaway service. Vegan dishes. **Map 23 B2**.

Herne Hill

Number 22

22 Half Moon Lane, SE24 9HU (7095 9922, www.number-22.com). Herne Hill rail or bus 3, 37, 68. **Tapas served** 5-11pm Thur, Fri; noon-3pm, 5-10.30pm Sat; noon-9.30pm Sun. **Tapas** £3-£10. **Credit** MC, V.
Sleek dark furnishings, contemporary art for sale and deep olive-green walls create a stylish feel in this narrow but cosy venue. Number 22's classy demeanour reflects its menu, which uses high-quality ingredients to create a modern take on tapas, and throws in a few more substantial dishes to boot. Prices aren't cheap, but the atmosphere is far from pretentious and staff will help you select a good spread of food. The menu is refreshed daily, with seasonal ingredients given their due. Purple sprouting broccoli with garlic and chorizo made a delicious tapa and worked well as a foil to more fatty (but no less delicious) dishes of fried monte enebro cheese and jamón serrano croquetas. Meat comes from well-known local butcher William Rose; veal cheeks with a provençal sauce made an interesting addition to the menu on this occasion. On Sundays, three types of paella are served, so if you happen to catch a sunny day, head for the sweet little courtyard at the back, which is ideal for enjoying a leisurely Cruzcampo along with seafood, meat or vegetarian rice. An intimate little restaurant that's ideal for couples or small groups of friends.
Available for hire. Babies and children welcome: high chairs. Booking advisable. Tables outdoors (6, patio). Vegan dishes.
Map 23 A5.

London Bridge & Borough

José

104 Bermondsey Street, SE1 3UB (7403 4902, http://joserestaurant.co.uk). Borough tube or London Bridge tube/rail. **Tapas served** noon-10.30pm Mon-Sat; noon-5.30pm Sun. **Tapas** £3.50-£9.50. **Credit** AmEx, MC, V.
In Spain, a tapas bar isn't defined only by serving small portions, but also by being part of a bar-crawl scene that's as much about atmosphere as food and drink. José is the real deal here. It's tiny and no-frills – a corner property with a pretty tiled bar, a couple of Formica-like tables and some barrels to put drinks on – but the staff curate their crowd brilliantly, giving parched cyclists water, lone lunchers some sherry chat, and evening parties at least a couple of square feet to call their own. For it's often standing room only here, and no bookings are taken, so arrive early if you want a seat. From the short menu, the classics (jamón ibérico, chorizo, tortilla, croquetas and patatas bravas) all hold their own. The grilled dishes are almost brutally simple, involving only a transfer of whatever looked good in the market that day from a cold cabinet on the counter to the grill behind – and some well-judged seasoning. On our last visit, pluma ibérica (a cut of pork served rare), and sea bream were both delicious. There's a list of beyond-the-obvious sherries and wines by the glass to accompany.
Babies and children admitted. Bookings not accepted. Disabled: toilet. **Map 12 Q9**.

Pizarro NEW

2012 RUNNER-UP BEST NEW NO BOOKINGS RESTAURANT
194 Bermondsey Street, SE1 3TQ (7378 9455, www.pizarrorestaurant.com). Borough tube or London Bridge tube/rail.
Bar **Open** noon-11pm daily.
Restaurant **Lunch served** noon-3pm, **dinner served** 6-11pm Mon-Fri. **Meals served** noon-11pm Sat; 10am-10pm Sun. **Main courses** £11-£18.
Both **Credit** AmEx, MC, V.
The gentrification of Bermondsey Street marches on, with Pizarro (and its more casual sibling José) having joined the front line. Though Spanish chef José Pizarro's reputation was built at the casual Brindisa tapas bars (where he was co-founder and

Pizarro. See p241.

exec chef), this restaurant showcases his classier side. The interiors take traditionally rustic elements – warm woods, exposed bricks, open kitchen – and lend them a sophisticated touch; all smooth, polished edges and designer lighting. Likewise, the kitchen takes classic Spanish dishes and moves them upmarket (though the result is not without flaws). We enjoyed the velvety centres of our dinky ham croquetas (in spite of the scant jamón) alongside a sea-salty trio of just-cooked razor clams, served straight from the plancha with morsels of chorizo. But to follow, dainty slabs of terrific rosemary-scented lamb were undermined by a bed of Puy lentils (studded with braised celery, carrots and onions) which had been wincingly over-salted. Happily, a joyful pud – airy chocolate sorbet on two thin slices of brownie, scattered with pieces of cherry, strawberry and mint – marked a return to form. Given the small portions, prices are rather stiff, but there's a strong selection of sherry and Iberian wines, and staff are knowledgeable and charming.
Babies and children welcome: high chairs. Bookings not accepted dinner; Sat, Sun. Disabled: toilet. Dress: smart casual. Separate room for parties, seats 8-10.

East

Docklands

Ibérica Food & Culture

12 Cabot Square, E14 5NY (7636 8650, www.ibericalondon.co.uk). Canary Wharf tube/DLR. **Tapas served** 11.30am-11pm Mon-Sat; noon-5pm Sun. **Tapas** £3.50-£12.50. **Set lunch** (noon-4pm) £16 3 courses. **Credit** AmEx, MC, V.

This glamorous new branch of Ibérica has a spacious, airy feel that blends well with the glass towers and moneyed streets of Canary Wharf, yet it conveys a real sense of Spain. A large bull's head hangs on the wall behind the basement bar, and white slatted walls recall Spanish-style shutters. The space feels contemporary but rooted – as does the menu, which blends traditional dishes with 'nuevo' flourishes. Chef César Garcia cooks with confidence, and on our visit it was the nuevo dishes that excelled. Highlights of the tapas menu were crisp, fried spring onions with zesty, lemony aïoli; mushroom caps stuffed with melting bone marrow; cute, slider-like Ibérica pork burgers; and a simple but sublime 'asparagus toast' layered with slow-cooked onions and cheese. Trad takes on cheese and ham croquetas (heavy, bland) and Galician-style octopus (somewhat flavourless) were less successful. Desserts are nothing special. If celebrating, you could give 24-hours' notice and order a roast suckling pig, but should you just need a quick gap-filler, there's a chic jamón and sherry bar at ground level. The wine list contains excellent finds from lesser-known quality-led regions of Spain, such as Valdeorras and Somontano.
Babies and children welcome: high chairs; nappy-changing facilities. Booking advisable Mon-Fri. Disabled: toilet. Separate room for parties, seats 40. Takeaway service. **Map 24 B2.**
For branch see index.

Shoreditch

Laxeiro

93 Columbia Road, E2 7RG (7729 1147, www.laxeiro.co.uk). Hoxton rail. **Tapas served** noon-3pm, 7-11pm Tue-Fri; 11am-4.30pm, 7-11pm Sat; 9am-4.30pm Sun. **Tapas** £4.50-£7.95. **Credit** AmEx, MC, V.

Contemporary Columbia Road feels like one of those twee, fake streets in a film shoot. Among the chichi little accessories and homeware shops, the art galleries and the restaurants and cafés, Laxeiro fits right in – complete with local artwork, blond wooden furniture, Farrow & Ball paintwork and friendly staff. Would that the dishes matched up to this idyll. On a long menu, they certainly sounded tempting, and authentic too: paella, morcilla, pisto and fabada were all offered, with meat-free snacks including such staples as tortilla and pimientos de padrón. We ordered the lot, and more besides, excited by the positive buzz of the busy restaurant despite the early evening hour. Sadly, it all left something to be desired: rubbery tortilla; near-cold morcilla rice sausage; lukewarm pisto topped by a plasticky egg; greasy pimientos; and a tomato and onion salad that was tired and tasteless. The fabada was too close to baked beans for our liking, but was at least hot – our only dish that was. A shame… with the rise in popularity of small plates, the East End could really use a decent tapas joint.
Babies and children welcome: high chairs. Booking advisable; not accepted Sun. Tables outdoors (3, pavement). Takeaway service. Vegan dishes. **Map 6 S3.**

North East

Stoke Newington

Trangallan NEW

61 Newington Green, N16 9PX (7359 4988, www.trangallan.com). Canonbury tube/rail or bus 21, 73, 141, 341. **Open** 6.30-11.30pm Tue-Sat; 12.30-3pm Fri-Sun. **Tapas served** 7-10.30pm Tue-Sat; 12.30-3pm Fri-Sun. **Tapas** £4-£13. **Credit** MC, V.

A one-time social club, given a vintage-themed makeover by four Stoke Newington residents, and reopened as a hybrid venue: an intimate, candle-lit tapas restaurant on the ground floor, and performance space and bar in the tiny basement. Its daily-changing menu lists mainly rustic Spanish tapas. Our salami board was generously piled with five meats, including chorizo, jamón and a sobrassada – a soft Mallorcan 'sausage' that tasted

of smoked paprika, served like paté in a glass jar. Offbeat options include a modern twist on the classic tortilla, served deconstructed in a martini glass (a layer of melting onions, then another of potato purée, topped with a runny egg yolk), but the kitchen's strength lies in more homely dishes. We enjoyed a hearty stew of tender pork cheeks on a bed of borlotti beans; pan-fried sea bass with jerusalem artichokes; and traditional dessert of crème caramel. One of the founders is an ex-sommelier, and the wine list reflects this with a good selection of sherries by the glass, as well as natural wines and coverage of new Spanish regions.
Available for hire. Babies and children welcome: high chairs. Booking advisable. Separate room for parties, seats 25. Tables outdoors (7, terrace). Vegan dishes. **Map 25 A4**.

Walthamstow

Orford Saloon

32 Orford Road, E17 9NJ (8503 6542). Walthamstow Central tube/rail. **Tapas served** 6-10.30pm Tue-Fri; 10am-3pm, 6-10.30pm Sat; 10am-3pm, 6-9.30pm Sun. **Tapas** £4.15-£7.25. **Credit** MC, V.

A narrow corridor of a venue, with a conservatory out the back, the Orford Saloon conjures up a little piece of Spain in the middle of Walthamstow. Tiled floors and tables, juicy manzanilla olives, dishes served as soon as they're ready – the only thing lacking from this Iberian dining experience was sunshine. It's a popular local, and during our visit the place was bustling with couples, families, and a few folk having a drink at the little bar. The fact that there are two sittings is further indication that you'd be wise to book ahead. The menu covers all the expected repertoire, including three versions of paella (for which there's a 45-minute wait). Our choices were mostly excellent. Spicy, juicy langostinos pil pil; good judías verdes (green beans) with jamón; and moreish patatas bravas were all winners. However, the tortilla wasn't moist enough and the calamares' 'special batter' didn't convince either. Service is knowledgeable and solicitous; the staff cheerily offered us extra bread for mopping up the juices. The Spanish wine list – which includes some fine sherries – merits praise too.
Babies and children welcome: high chairs. Booking advisable. Disabled: toilet. Tables outdoors (2, pavement).

North

Camden Town & Chalk Farm

El Parador

245 Eversholt Street, NW1 1BA (7387 2789, www.elparadorlondon.com). Mornington Crescent tube. **Tapas served** noon-3pm, 6-11pm Mon-Thur; noon-3pm, 6-11.30pm Fri; 6-11.30pm Sat; 6.30-9.30pm Sun. **Tapas** £4.20-£8.20. **Credit** MC, V.

Don't be deceived by the size of the diminutive, yellow dining room at El Parador, there's a basement room too – albeit a little gloomy. Locals come back time and again for this long-established restaurant's eclectic tapas selection and welcoming atmosphere. Among the 30-odd dishes, tortilla, sumptuously soft in the middle, always makes a sound choice, as do the hot chorizo with butter beans and the El Parador-style fried hake. You'll find a few more unusual options too (such as chicken livers with Japanese shimeji mushrooms), and no shortage of non-meat tapas. Particular favourites are the chargrilled padrón peppers with flaky salt, the roasted butternut squash with feta, and the garlicky broad bean dip (puré de habas). A word of warning about the seasoning: it's a little hit and miss. Ordering anything with chilli or harissa in it can be rather like a game of Russian roulette. Take advantage of the 'two for one tapas' offer at lunchtime and be sure to bag yourself a garden seat in the summer, and maybe a glass or two of sherry.
Babies and children admitted. Booking advisable for 3 or more. Separate room for parties, seats 30. Tables outdoors (12, garden). Vegan dishes. Vegetarian menu. **Map 27 D3**.

Tufnell Park

Del Parc

167 Junction Road, N19 5PZ (7281 5684, www.delparc.co.uk). Archway or Tufnell Park tube. **Dinner served** 7.30-10.30pm Wed-Sat. **Tapas** £6-£10. **Credit** MC, V.

Slightly raised above the cosy front and back dining rooms, Del Parc's chef can be seen putting together the stream of tapas you'll shortly enjoy. This is an unusual restaurant in that there's no menu. You'll be asked about any dietary restrictions when booking; after that, your meal is in the chef's hands. Our most recent visit began well with four fat and incredibly tender escabeche mussels, presented neatly on a slate, as if marching with cocktail sticks for bayonets. Stuffed gordal olives were another success, but the cold mushrooms needed more spice. Mackerel infused with vanilla on a beetroot and potato salad was an imaginative hit, and juicy king prawns and moroccan meatballs delicious, but heritage tomato salad and pistou (like ratatouille) weren't especially memorable. You get to choose your own drinks, of course; we couldn't resist a bottle of the Asturian Sidra 'El Gaitero' from a list that includes four sherries. The atmosphere is notably warm and chatty, with interesting chilled Hispanic tunes in the background and some arty touches (a vast wooden relief of a woman's face by the entrance). This, perhaps more than the food, keeps locals thronging back.
Booking advisable; essential weekend. Tables outdoors (5, pavement). **Map 26 B2**.

Trangallan

Morito. See p233.

PORTUGUESE

Central

Clerkenwell & Farringdon

★ Portal

88 St John Street, EC1M 4EH (7253 6950, www.portalrestaurant.com). Barbican tube or Farringdon tube/rail. **Lunch served** noon-3pm Mon-Fri. **Dinner served** 6-10.15pm Mon-Sat. **Main courses** £14-£24. **Credit** AmEx, MC, V.

In contrast to the urban trendiness of Clerkenwell, Portal feels like a breath of fresh air. The main restaurant – with its floor-to-ceiling windows and big skylights looking on to a tiled courtyard – is the place where London cool meets Mediterranean terrace. Decor is monochrome, exposed brick and air-con pipes, punctuated by framed wine labels, tall vases of corks and other wine paraphernalia. Wine and port lovers will find plenty to tempt on the almost exclusively Portuguese list. Food is excellent. A starter of perfectly poached egg with al dente asparagus and creamy serra cheese was stunning both in appearance and flavour. To follow, braised bisaro, a cross between pig and boar, had tender, succulent flesh that was beautifully complemented by the chorizo açorda (a bread stew). We finished with textbook Portuguese custard tarts, with crisp flaky pastry and smooth filling, served with a smear of rich dark chocolate, a citrous brandy snap and cinnamon ice-cream – indicative of the presentation and detail in each of the dishes. Portal's location attracts a mainly dressed-up work clientele. For a less formal experience, opt for the tapas menu in the bar.

Available for hire. Babies and children welcome: high chairs; nappy-changing facilities. Booking advisable. Disabled: toilet. Separate room for parties, seats 14. Tables outdoors (5, patio). **Map 5 O4**.

Knightsbridge

O Fado

50 Beauchamp Place, SW3 1NY (7589 3002, www.ofado.co.uk). Knightsbridge or South Kensington tube. **Lunch served** noon-3pm, **dinner served** 6.30-10.30pm Mon-Sat. **Main courses** £15.99-£20.95. **Set lunch** (Mon-Fri) £14.95 2 courses incl coffee. **Cover charge** £2.50. **Credit** AmEx, MC, V.

The fado singers were on holiday when we visited O Fado, so we had to make do with the slightly less romantic sound of a man plugging away on his electric keyboard. While that sounds twee, it worked with the venue's faded grandeur and slightly outdated decor. The restaurant is set below street level, in among flashier neighbours. The food is good, but in a homemade, informal kind of way; caldo verde (Portuguese cabbage soup) is among the starters. Chargrilled sardines were salty and evocative of summer holidays, but piri-piri chicken really was just chicken and chips. The chicken was well cooked, but the sauce tasted one-dimensional. The bread was also slightly dry. Seafood risotto was the most impressive dish: packed full of squid, mussels, lobster claws and clams. Desserts run from Portuguese-style rice pudding to crêpe suzette; there are also cheese and fruit selections. Accompany it all with Vinho Verde, a very young and slightly sparkling white wine from northern Portugal.

Available for hire. Babies and children admitted until 6.30pm. Booking advisable; essential dinner weekends. Vegetarian menu. **Map 14 F9**.

Pastelaria

Those coffee shop stalwarts, pastéis de nata or custard tarts, are perhaps the most recognisable dish in Portuguese cuisine. These places sell them, along with a range of other traditional pastries and bica (Portuguese espresso).

Café Oporto

62A Golborne Road, W10 5PS (8968 8839). Ladbroke Grove or Westbourne Park tube or bus 23, 52. **Open** 7.30am-7pm Mon-Sat; 8am-5pm Sun. **Snacks** £1-£3.50. **No credit cards.**

This corner site is larger than Lisboa Pâtisserie, its rival on the opposite side of the road, and has a more relaxing vibe that's great for people-watching and grazing *en famille*. The counter is well stocked with sandwiches, but we prefer the savoury pastries (salt cod, chicken, cheese) or a toasted cheese and ham croissant.

Babies and children admitted. Tables outdoors (3, pavement). Takeaway service. **Map 19 B1**.

Funchal Bakery

141-143 Stockwell Road, SW9 9TN (7733 3134). Stockwell tube. **Open** 7am-7pm daily. **Snacks** £1-£5. **Credit** MC, V.

Reflecting the Stockwell area's Madeiran immigrants (Funchal is the capital of Madeira), this friendly, functional spot offers keenly priced groceries and deli items plus cut-above cakes. We're very fond of the bolo con arroz. Expats gather to watch football on the TV in the café.

Babies and children admitted. Takeaway service. **Map 22 D1**.

Lisboa Pâtisserie

57 Golborne Road, W10 5NR (8968 5242). Ladbroke Grove or Westbourne Park tube or bus 23, 52. **Open** 7am-7.30pm daily. **Snacks** 75p-£2.65. **Credit** MC, V.

A friendly spot – with delicious baking that attracts customers from some distance away, and inevitable queues – though the humble environs may surprise first-timers. For a change from custard tarts, try the scrumptious orange and coconut cake or a custard doughnut. Savouries include salt cod croquettes, and ham and chorizo pastries; the breadcrumbed pork and chicken escalopes also win plaudits.

Babies and children admitted. Tables outdoors (3, pavement). Takeaway service. **Map 19 B1**.

For branches see index.

South

Brixton

Lisboa Grill

256A Brixton Hill, SW2 1HF (8671 8311, www.lisboagrill.net). Brixton tube/rail or bus 45, 109, 118, 250. **Meals served** 7-10.30pm Mon-Fri; noon-10.30pm Sat, Sun. **Main courses** £7.50-£14. **Credit** MC, V.

Renowned in Brixton for its piri-piri chicken, we found Lisboa Grill slightly underwhelming on our visit. The service was slow, although friendly when it came, and the food wasn't special enough to justify the wait. There are actually three parts to Lisboa Grill; the takeaway section at the front, the café (where we ate) to the left, and a more formal dining room painted with traditional Portuguese scenes behind. They all have the same menu, although the dining room seems to have more ambience – low beams and intimate lighting – compared to the basic café. Grilled chicken was good, but the piri-piri sauce was dull. Bacalhau gomez de sa was an immense portion of flaked salted cod, boiled potatoes and hard-boiled egg baked with onions. This is old-style comfort food from Porto, served with black olives and a small salad, and a little too much oil. The own-made caramel flan portions are also enormous (share one between two), and come with a light and runny caramel sauce.

Available for hire. Babies and children welcome: high chairs. Booking advisable weekends. Disabled: toilet. Tables outdoors (5, garden). Takeaway service. **Map 22 D3**.

Vauxhall

Casa Madeira

46A-46C Albert Embankment, SE11 5AW (7820 1117, www.madeiralondon.co.uk). Vauxhall tube/rail. **Meals served** *Coffee shop* 6am-9pm daily. *Restaurant* noon-11pm Mon-Fri, Sun; noon-1am Sat. **Main courses** £6.95-£15.95. **Tapas** £3-£5.95. **Credit** (over £5) AmEx, MC, V.

Caught between Vauxhall train lines and the Albert Embankment is a little Portuguese community, complete with a café, restaurant and mini-supermarket. The fact that they are all owned by the same man just adds to the tight-knit feel, as people sit on the green area outside and wander in and out of the connected shops. The restaurant in the middle – Casa Madeira – serves the most formal food, but even then it is very much Portuguese home-style cooking. Order the chouriço assado and the chorizo arrives in a flaming clay dish; very theatrical, delicious and crisp. Bacalhau à brás is not for the faint-hearted as, much like in Portugal, it arrives as a slightly greasy and formidable pile of salt cod, scrambled eggs, onions and fried potatoes. Servings here are more than generous, so order accordingly. The house steak comes with delicious Portuguese-style round chips, and covered in gravy. Give the flan (crème caramel) a miss, and instead save yourself for the lovely Portuguese custard tarts from the deli in the supermarket.

Babies and children admitted. Booking advisable weekends. Entertainment: musicans 7pm Fri, Sat. Tables outdoors (40, pavement). Takeaway service. **Map 16 L11**.

For branches (Bar Madeira, Café 89, Madeira Café, Pico Bar & Grill) see index.

Steakhouses

Being forced to respond to its troubled history of the 1990s put British beef ahead of the game. Provenance is of prime importance, and any steakhouse worth its salt should be able to detail the source of its meat – the breed, the region and very often the farm. And that's before we even mention the ageing of the cuts. So, how is this first-rate beef presented? All too often British steakhouses try to emulate their US counterparts, but the tremendous success of the excellent **Hawksmoor** – now with three branches, in the City, Covent Garden and Spitalfields – shows there is a demand for a home-grown take on the concept. Otherwise, our recommended establishments range from the neighbourhood appeal of Wimbledon's **Butcher & Grill**, to the classy Canary Wharf outpost of **Goodman**. Of course, superb beef can be found outside the steakhouse genre; consult our **Latin American** section (*see p31*) for the best Argentinean steak, and top-notch cuts are to be had near London's famous wholesale meat market at **Top Floor at Smiths** (*see p205* **Smiths of Smithfield**).

Central

City

Butcher at Leadenhall

6-7 Leadenhall Market, EC3V 1LR (7283 1662, www.butcheratleadenhall.com). Bank tube/DLR.
Breakfast served 8-11am Mon-Fri. **Lunch served** 11.30am-3pm Mon-Wed; 11.30am-4pm Thur, Fri. **Main courses** £10.50-£25. **Credit** MC, V.

A butcher's counter, a grill alongside, and a few cheap aluminium tables: if you saw this set-up in any other market or shopping centre, you might walk right on by. But this is grand old Leadenhall Market, and everything basks in the maroon-and-gold glow of Horace Jones' 19th-century design. There are no starters: just nibbles such as marcona almonds, olives and artichokes. Our waitress recommended the minute steak or pork chop, but a quick glance at the display counter and we were snagged by the aged-looking ribeye. Its 250g came in a thin slab, yet despite our request for medium-rare, the pink was nearly gone to brown. The 'vegetable of the day' was a jumble of button mushroom slices. Bretby lamb and Packington pork are advertised, so we asked where the beef was from. 'England', came the reply. Not good enough for a meat specialist. Service was casual and tinged with banter as befits a market environment. For dessert, there's ice-cream or a cheese plate from the unit next door. The takeaway service (11.30am to 3pm) offers burgers, a 'butcher's hot dog' and roast pork or salt beef bagels.

Available for hire. Babies and children welcome: high chairs. Bookings not accepted. Tables outdoors (22, market). Takeaway service.
Map 12 Q7.

High Timber

8 High Timber Street, EC4V 3PA (7248 1777, www.hightimber.com). Mansion House tube.
Lunch served noon-3pm, **dinner served** 6.30-10pm Mon-Fri. **Main courses** £13.25-£29. **Set lunch** £16.50 2 courses, £20 3 courses. **Credit** AmEx, DC, MC, V.

A City steakhouse is never going to set tongues wagging with its culinary innovation, but High Timber provides enough encouragement for non-pinstripe-wearers to venture in. Unrestrained chunks of modern art liven up a rather bland, new-build room, but the real views are over the river to Tate Modern and Shakespeare's Globe. Tables and chairs are of bare wood; music is quiet enough not to startle, staff are professional without being chatty. There's nothing here to alarm the client, which can make for a slightly tame experience on a quiet evening. But the steaks are very good, the cooking assured. Meat is charred to perfection (rib eye, sirloin) and expertly seasoned, and clearly comes from well-bred cows. The only adornment is a grilled tomato and a mushroom, although sauces are available – £2.80 for garlic and parsley butter seems a bit opportunistic, though. Chunky chips – fried at least twice for crunch – were excellent too, arriving in a neat little metal basket. Otherwise, the mainly meaty menu offers the likes of sausage and mash, rack of lamb and cured salt beef. The wine cellars are vast, and, reflecting the restaurant's ownership, big on South African labels.

Available for hire. Babies and children admitted. Booking advisable. Disabled: toilet. Separate rooms for parties, seating 10 and 18. Tables outdoors (4, riverside). **Map 11 O7.**

Covent Garden

★ Hawksmoor Seven Dials HOT 50

11 Langley Street, WC2H 9JJ (7420 9390, www.thehawksmoor.co.uk). Covent Garden tube.
Lunch served noon-3pm Mon-Sat; noon-4.30pm Sun. **Dinner served** 5-10.30pm Mon-Thur; 5-11pm Fri, Sat. **Main courses** £15-£30. **Set meal** (noon-3pm, 5-6.30pm, 10-10.30pm Mon-Fri) £22 2 courses, £25 3 courses. **Credit** AmEx, MC, V.

This former fruit warehouse is now carnivore central in Will Beckett and Huw Gott's confidently expanding empire, and the bar a place of pilgrimage in its own right for cocktail geeks. Winner of Time Out's Best New Restaurant award in 2011, the discreetly fronted basement location is elevated to a high-end destination with a characterful interior of reclaimed materials and the fan-boys' zeal for premium meats and other taste sensations. The bad news is, with a similar appreciation of gustatory pleasures (a couple of cocktails, say, followed by

crab or lobster, sirloin and side dishes, wine and pudding), dinner here can easily set you back £100 a head. The good news is the express menu (ideal pre-theatre when tables are easy to snare) offers two courses for £22 and three courses for £25 – and still allows enjoyment of fine Ginger Pig Longhorn ribeye (a more-than-strictly-needed 250g), and bone marrow with onions. Desserts here, in our experience, don't benefit from the same obsessive attention to detail as the beef dripping chips, kimchi burger, hot dogs or historic anti-fogmatics – still, there's the post-prandial cocktail list to peruse, featuring the likes of Climpson's espresso martini. The most recent branch to open is the glamorous City-outpost, Hawksmoor Guildhall.
Available for hire. Babies and children welcome: high chairs. Booking advisable. Disabled: lift; toilet. **Map 18 D4.**
For branches see index.

Marylebone

Le Relais de Venise L'Entrecôte

120 Marylebone Lane, W1U 2QG (7486 0878, www.relaisdevenise.com). Bond Street tube. **Lunch served** noon-2.30pm Mon-Thur; noon-2.45pm Fri; 12.30-3.30pm Sat, Sun. **Dinner served** 6-10.45pm Mon-Thur; 6-11pm Fri; 6.30-11pm Sat; 6.30-10.30pm Sun. **Set meal** £21 2 courses. **Credit** AmEx, MC, V.
Le Relais de Venise's 'customer path', as marketers would have it, doesn't involve many opportunities for diversion. Queue, sit, order drinks (small wine list, odd beer selection – Beck's or Cusqueña). Specify rare, medium or well-done meat. Eat bread and a salad – soft lettuce, mustardy dressing, a few walnut bits. Eat a steak (brought in two parts to keep it warm) with fries and the house sauce (a secret recipe, but surely containing garlic, mustard and peppercorns). Eat dessert, if you wish. Pay and leave. There is only one main dish here, and it is served to hordes of diners every day; yes, there are places to get better steak in London, but nowhere does it with such an intensely French spectacle. Black-and-white-clad waitresses provide clockwork service; crammed-in tables ensure a buzzy atmosphere; the mirrors, light fittings and banquettes create a creditable likeness of a Parisian brasserie. It's an in-and-out experience, but a highly popular one, and as fast food goes, you won't find much better in this city.
Babies and children welcome: high chairs; nappy-changing facilities. Bookings not accepted. Disabled: toilet. **Map 9 G5.**
For branches see index.

Mayfair

Maze Grill

10-13 Grosvenor Square, W1K 6JP (7495 2211, www.gordonramsay.com/mazegrill). Bond Street tube. **Breakfast served** 6.45am-10.30am, **meals served** noon-11pm daily. **Main courses** £13.50-£28. **Set meal** (noon-6.30pm Mon-Thur, Sun; noon-4pm Fri, Sat) £21 2 courses, £24 3 courses. **Credit** AmEx, MC, V.
They may share an entrance hall and name, but the grill version of Maze couldn't be less like its haute cuisine sibling across the corridor. This, the younger of the two restaurants (opened in 2008), is a Mayfair take on a New York steakhouse, with designer lighting against a backdrop of olive leather and oak floors. Staff in pristine black aprons

Hawksmoor Guildhall

glide around the tables, serving luxurious cuts of meat on attractive wooden boards. If the 'market price' (read: 'if you have to ask what this costs, you can't afford it') of the Creekstone prime USDA or Wagyu ninth-grade beef makes you nervous, don't be put off; there are bargains to be had, such as a straightforward 8oz onglet or the deservedly popular burger. Our burger was a juicy, pink-middled patty served in a toasted sesame bun with tomato, lettuce, thick-cut bacon and melted cheese. Sadly, the dish preceding it, a 'small plate' of salt and pepper squid, had taken its moniker too literally, arriving so wincingly over-seasoned that both we, and an adjoining table, had to send it back. Well-drilled staff help soften the blow, as does the long, varied wine list.
Babies and children welcome: children's menu; high chairs; nappy-changing facilities. Booking advisable. Disabled: toilet. Separate room for parties, seats 12. **Map 9 G6.**

West

Olympia

Popeseye Steak House

108 Blythe Road, W14 0HB (7610 4578, www.popeseye.com). Kensington (Olympia) tube/rail. **Dinner served** 7-10.30pm Mon-Sat. **Main courses** £9.95-£55.95. **No credit cards.**
When a restaurant's offer consists mainly of just one foodstuff, it has to be done well. And when that one thing is steak, a dish increasingly attracting serious attention from dedicated restaurateurs in London, there's no room at all for slip-ups. Popeseye's basic surroundings – fairy lights, a few paintings of cows – is mirrored in its limited-choice menu: steak and chips. You can at least pick sirloin, fillet or popeseye (the Scots term for rump), all served with chips, and there's salad for £3.95 if you're concerned about vitamin intake. A bowl of good black olives is provided, with ashtrays on the tables in which to deposit the stones – an odd sight. On a recent visit, a quiet Wednesday evening, our 12oz popeseye was cooked past its requested medium rare, almost rendering every other aspect of this review pointless. But here they are: the long list of big 'n' bold red wines are all chosen to stand up to the steaks, but the only one available by the glass, an unidentified house Chilean, was merely passable. If the hankering for a hefty hunk of meat hits in Hammersmith, this is a good option, but it's not worth a haul across town.
Available for hire. Babies and children admitted. Booking advisable Thur-Sat. **Map 20 C3.**
For branch see index.

South West

Wimbledon

Butcher & Grill

33 High Street, SW19 5BY (8944 8269, www.thebutcherandgrill.com). Wimbledon tube/rail then bus 93. **Lunch served** noon-3.30pm, **dinner served** 6-10pm Tue-Fri. **Meals served** 9am-10pm Sat; 9am-5pm Sun. **Main courses** £12.50-£22. **Credit** AmEx, MC, V.
From the stylised paintings of butchers' hooks to the blue and white colour scheme echoing a traditional butcher's apron, Butcher & Grill does everything short of flying a banner saying 'Vegetarians beware'. At first glance, all you see is the butcher's counter up front, but behind it is a large frill-free space, with exposed brick walls, chunky wooden tables, and that all-important grill. This being Wimbledon Village, provenance is king; the livestock, we are told, comes from Highfields Farm in the Kent and Sussex Weald, where the sheep are English breeds and cattle are pure-bred Sussex stock: no steroids or GM feed here, thank you. Reassured, you can plunge into a meaty menu that includes baby back ribs, calf's liver, devilled kidneys, chops and – naturally – steak, plenty of it. There are a handful of seasonal mains, but the grill is where it's at. Lamb loin chops had a delicious flavour; a rump steak was every bit as hearty as you'd hope. Anything from the grill comes with a choice of sauce: béarnaise, green peppercorn, salsa verde and so on. Tuesday is the busiest night; with 50% off the price of all beef steaks, you'll want to arrive early.
Available for hire. Babies and children welcome: children's menu; high chairs; nappy-changing facilities. Booking advisable. Disabled: toilet. Tables outdoors (2, pavement).
For branch see index.

Butcher & Grill

East

Docklands

★ Goodman Canary Wharf

3 South Quay, E14 9RU (7531 0300, www.goodmanrestaurants.com). Canary Wharf tube/DLR or South Quay DLR. **Meals served** noon-10.30pm Mon-Sat. **Main courses** £14-£70. **Credit** AmEx, MC, V.
Over the footbridge from the Canary Wharf hub, Goodman is nonetheless well situated, with plenty of upholstered seating in window booths from which to view the dock, as well as a few outdoor tables at the bar end of the restaurant. Our waiter was warm, informative and reassuringly averse to upselling – despite being immensely proud of Goodman's supremely high-quality meat. He duly paraded 'the meat tray' for our admiration (a plate of four chunky steaks, beautifully marbled and offered both on and off the bone), yet gave no sign of disappointment when we opted for the lunch deal (three courses for £19) rather than one of the luxury cuts: £45 for a 400g fillet – much more should you essay the blackboard detailing today's finest. The flesh lived up to the schtick: unctuously fatty, deep, juicy 9oz Black Label sirloin steak, served with thick, foamy béarnaise on the side and functional, if slightly too dense, chips, all accompanied by a 2009 Château Bellevue Bordeaux that was wonderfully tannic and of exemplary length. And one final good taste in the mouth: we were alerted to the fact the tip was already included in the price. Good man.
Babies and children welcome: high chairs. Booking advisable Thur-Sat. Disabled: toilet. Separate room for parties, seats 8. Tables outdoors (patio). Takeaway service.
Map 24 B2.
For branches see index.

Burger joints

Byron

222 Kensington High Street, W8 7RG (7361 1717, www.byronhamburgers.com). High Street Kensington tube. **Meals served** noon-11pm Mon-Thur; noon-11.30pm Fri; 11am-11.30pm Sat; 11am-10.30pm Sun. **Main courses** £6.50-£10.50. **Credit** AmEx, MC, V.

An upmarket burger chain with more than 20 branches in London, Byron has found success by paying attention to all areas of its operation. The spaces are clean, light and attractive; staff are welcoming and good with kids. The menu has burgers centre stage (including chicken and vegetarian choices) and all come with lettuce, tomato, red onion, pickle and mayo. Further toppings include bacon, avocado, roasted red pepper, portobello mushroom, jalapeño and various cheeses (such as monterey jack). For sauces, choose from chilli, spicy barbecue, aïoli, tomato mayonnaise, blue cheese or Byron's own. The only other main-course options are salads (cobb and caesar among them). Quality is good, and service generally speedy. A similarly well-considered drinks list runs from apple juice and Oreo cookie milkshake to wine; beers (from small breweries) include a Byron pale ale, from Camden Town Brewery.

Babies and children welcome: children's menu; high chairs; nappy-changing facilities. Bookings not accepted lunch Sat & Sun. Disabled: toilet. Tables outdoors (4, pavement). Takeaway service. **Map 7 A9.**

For branches see index.

★ Dirty Burger NEW

79 Highgate Road, NW5 1TL (no phone, www.eatdirtyburger.com). Kentish Town tube. **Meals served** 7am-midnight Mon-Thur; 7am-1am Fri; 9am-1am Sat; 9am-11.30pm Sun. **Main courses** £3.50-£5.50.

After wandering round several London locations, this Soho House operation finally settled in the back of the former Grand Union pub, in a corrugated-steel shack with salvage yard furnishings. You order from a counter: the menu lists a burger, sides of crinkle-cut fries and onion fries – and that's it. Plus sausage/bacon and egg rolls (served until 11am) and assorted drinks, including milkshakes and Camden Pale Ale on draught. Our burger was sensational. The patty is a blend of several cuts, including ribeye and bavette. Cooked all the way through, it was served in a tasty toasted roll with pickles, tomato, lettuce, cheese and a condiment that contains – inter alia – French and American mustards and mayonnaise. The side dishes were, if anything, even better. The chips are irregularly cut and triple-cooked à la mode de Heston Blumenthal (poach, blanch, fry). The onions are red onions, in shreds, deep-fried with a cider tempura batter. On their first Friday, Dirty Burger tweeted that they were giving away free burgers for one hour. They ended up serving 550. We're not surprised.

Babies and children admitted. Takeaway service. **Map 26 A4.**

Gourmet Burger Kitchen

121 Lordship Lane, SE22 8HU (8693 9307, www.gbk.co.uk). East Dulwich rail. **Meals served** noon-10pm Mon-Thur, Sun; noon-11pm Fri, Sat. **Main courses** £4.95-£11.95. **Credit** AmEx, MC, V.

When Gourmet Burger Kitchen was launched in Battersea by a trio of New Zealanders in 2001, it seemed a revolutionary concept – chunky, juicy burgers with multiple imaginative toppings, served in the sort of environment that was a real step-up from typical fast-food joints, while remaining laid-back and almost funky. The chain was just ahead of the curve when it came to posh burger joints and profited: by 2010 there were more than 50 restaurants and the company was bought by Nando's. And now? Well, while there are still sweet touches – free monkey nuts at the East Dulwich branch – there's also something rather tired about the enterprise, from the faux-Pop Art on the walls to the fine-but-not-amazing burgers. The cheeseburger comes in 4oz and 6oz versions, and is as unmemorable as the fries; more imaginative options such as the Kiwiburger (beetroot, egg, cheddar, pineapple, salad) seem like Pizza Hut-style novelties. Inevitably, perhaps, GBK has crystallised into being what it always probably was: just another fast-food joint, with a more expensive than usual menu. Good enough, but the revolution is most certainly over.

Babies and children welcome: children's menu; crayons; high chairs; nappy-changing facilities. Disabled: toilet. Tables outdoors (4, terrace). Takeaway service.

For branches see index.

★ Haché

153 Clapham High Street, SW4 7SS (7738 8760, www.hacheburgers.com). Clapham Common tube. **Meals served** noon-10.30pm Mon-Thur; noon-11pm Fri, Sat; noon-10pm Sun. **Main courses** £6.95-£16.95. **Credit** DC, MC, V.

A burger joint with a distinctly continental approach, Haché even offers the option of brioche buns, or smelly French cheeses to match the meat. This branch is the third in a smart chain that started out well in 2004 and has had a few years since to fine-tune the menu. It's more a restaurant than a fast-food place and even has chandeliers. The menu is much more creative than most, with chicken, duck and good vegetarian alternatives. Try the reblochon burger, where the distinctively aromatic

Honest Burgers

STEAKHOUSES

Meat Market

cheese adds a wonderful, gooey quality to the dish. High-quality beef mince is cooked as requested; brioche works surprisingly well with it. The frites are thin and properly crisp, and all the other details are correct. A falafel blue cheese burger – one of four vegetarian choices – is better than it sounds, the patty well spiced and moist, topped with melting stilton. We found the service cheery and the atmosphere jolly. Of Clapham's many low-budget dining options, this is one of the best.
Babies and children welcome: children's menu; crayons; high chairs. Bookings not accepted (6.30-11pm Fri, Sat). Tables outdoors (2, pavement). Takeaway service. **Map 22 B2.**
For branches see index.

★ Honest Burgers

Unit 12, Brixton Village Market, Coldharbour Lane, SW9 8PR (7733 7963, www.honest burgers.co.uk). Brixton tube/rail. **Lunch served** noon-4pm Mon-Fri, Sun; noon-5pm Sat. **Dinner served** 6-10.30pm Thur-Sat. **Main courses** £6.50-£8.50. **Credit** MC, V.
While Honest Burgers might not be the most exciting restaurant in Brixton Village, it certainly feels like the one most likely to branch out into London-wide success. That's a tribute to a simple concept, strong branding and sensational food, making this tiny space consistently busy and doing for Brixton's burgers what Franco Manca did for its pizzas. You'll struggle to find a more memorable burger anywhere in London – the meat is 35-day dry-aged British chuck steak from Ginger Pig and packs more bang between the buns than seems possible. You can top it with stilton or bacon (or both) if you choose, but just make sure you get a load of the chips: thrice-cooked, stunningly crispy and covered in rosemary salt. There's a chicken sandwich and vegetarian fritter – plus occasional specials – but the basic burger is done so well, it seems foolish to try anything else. Decor is simple wood and stone with an open kitchen taking up most of the space, and there are thoughtful touches such as the cute box the bill comes in. It is, like the restaurant as a whole, a superb package.
Babies and children admitted. Bookings not accepted. Takeaway service. **Map 22 E2.**
For branch see index.

Meat Market NEW

The Mezzanine, Jubilee Market Hall, Tavistock Street, WC2E 8BE (no phone, www.themeatmarket.co.uk). Covent Garden tube. **Meals served** noon-11pm daily. **Main courses** £6-£30. **Credit** AmEx, MC, V.
The latest fast-food joint from Yianni Papoutsis, burger god to the Twitterati, Meat Market makes a concerted effort to keep tourists at bay, employing a series of off-putting pictures of greasy takeaway fare at its bare, concrete street entrance. There's no table service: just order at the till and collect your food once your name is called. Our giant £7 'ripper' hot dog, with its soggy bun and excess of mustard, was a let-down, but a side of 'poppaz' (jalapeño peppers stuffed with cheese, breaded then deep fried) helped even the score. As for those burgers – our sloppy, juicy 'dead hippy' saw two patties of top-notch ground beef layered with finely chopped onion, tangy gherkin, melted cheese, lettuce, tomato and plenty of 'secret sauce'. The place has a cult following, and it's easy to see why.
Available for hire. Babies and children admitted. Bookings not accepted. Takeaway service. **Map 18 E4.**

Tommi's Burger Joint NEW

58 Marylebone Lane, W1U 2NX (07717 207770, http://burgerjoint.co.uk). Bond Street tube. **Meals served** 11.30am-9.30pm Mon-Fri; noon-9.30pm Sat. Main courses £5.30-£7.95. **Set meal** £8.90 1 course incl drink. **Credit** AmEx, MC, V.
Restaurateur Tomas 'Tommi' Tómasson has added a London outpost to his five-strong chain of Icelandic burger joints. As with everything here, the vibe is ultra-casual. Dishes are scribbled on pieces of cardboard and pinned above the counter, drinks are kept in an unlocked fridge (pay, then help yourself), and there's even a workaday coffee dispenser for a free cup of joe. Not forgetting the obligatory exposed brickwork, industrial venting, old movie posters and loud music. The menu reflects the back-to-basics vibe, with just a few burgers, sodas and shakes available. When your food is ready, one of the cooks will take a break from the fryers to bring it over. The mostly Icelandic staff are a ruggedly handsome bunch – if they weren't flipping burgers, they'd probably be advertising Fisherman's Friends. Our cheeseburger passed muster: a pink-middled patty of chunky mince, topped with a molten square of processed cheese and served in a soft bun with red onion and salad. The pricier steak burger (made with a higher grade of mince) was noticeably juicier, while fries were properly skinny, crunchy and salty.
Babies and children welcome: children's menu; high chairs. Takeaway service. **Map 9 H6.**

Thai

Thai cuisine in London suffers from an image problem. Too many restaurants serve a toned-down, rough approximation of the cooking, where authentic ingredients are replaced by cheap alternatives (despite a vague similarity in appearance, garden peas taste nothing like the bitter pea aubergines that enhance the flavour of several true Thai dishes). Nevertheless, good Thai food does exist in our city: from the haute cuisine creations of David Thompson at **Nahm** (though the restaurant seems to have slipped off its exalted perch of late), via the well-executed classics emerging from the kitchen at **Sukho** in Parsons Green, to the unexpectedly authentic dishes to be found at the **Heron** pub in Bayswater. Modern Thai restaurants, such as **Rosa's** or the **Busaba Eathai** chain, have also rekindled interest in the cuisine. Beautiful venues are an additional draw, and restaurants such as **Patara** and **Blue Elephant** provide exotically attired interiors ideal for romance.

Central

Belgravia

Nahm HOT 50

The Halkin, Halkin Street, SW1X 7DJ (7333 1234, www.nahm.como.bz). Hyde Park Corner tube. **Lunch served** noon-2.30pm Mon-Fri. **Dinner served** 7-10.45pm Mon-Sat; 7-9.45pm Sun. **Main courses** £17.50-£26.50. **Set lunch** £25 2 courses, £30 3 courses. **Set dinner** £60 3 courses. **Credit** AmEx, MC, V.

David Thompson's restaurant in the 'sanctuary of discretion' of Belgravia's chicest boutique hotel, the Halkin, is indeed an 'inimitable experience' – but the place lost its Michelin star in 2011. As chefs complain, this can depend as much on the loos as the food, and having to walk into the entrance hall, through the bar and downstairs to the toilets might seem unglamorous. The restaurant is wood-panelled and quietly stylish – if somewhat corporate – and lightened by a wall of windows overlooking a leafy garden. Service combines total professionalism with warmth. The menu has been criticised for Thompson's insistence on not indicating the degree of heat for each dish. This remains the case, yet staff now seem better able to inform diners. A scallop salad with asian celery, thai basil and peanut nahm jim sauce was tasty, but the shellfish lacked perfect texture. Stir-fried cuttlefish with green peppercorns and young ginger was a pleasure, though the serving seemed skimpy. To finish, a dessert of Thai wafers with golden noodle meringue, sesame seeds and glacé fruit (the only pudding without coconut) proved something of a non-event. Perhaps loss of the coveted star has blunted Nahm's edge.

Available for hire. Babies and children welcome: high chairs; nappy-changing facilities (hotel). Booking advisable. Disabled: toilet. Dress: smart casual. Separate room for parties, seats 30. Vegetarian menu. **Map 9 G9.**

Bloomsbury

Busaba Eathai

22 Store Street, WC1E 7DS (7299 7900, www.busaba.com). Goodge Street or Tottenham Court Road tube. **Meals served** noon-11pm Mon-Thur; noon-11.30pm Fri, Sat; noon-10pm Sun. **Main courses** £7-£12.50. **Credit** AmEx, MC, V.

Busaba was an instant hit back in 1999 when restaurateur Alan Yau (also the creator of Wagamama, Hakkasan and Yauatcha) opened the original branch on Wardour Street. Yau's no longer involved, but the chain retains its appeal. Size probably matters; compared to some corporate sharks, it's a minnow (just nine London outlets) and the Store Street branch, in particular, feels more like a one-off than a cog in a machine. Brooding good-looks – dark teak furniture and walls, oversized lampshades, incense – help, and the communal tables are big enough to make sharing less irritating. The modern Thai menu covers stir-fries, wok-cooked noodles, grilled meat and the ever-popular curries. Instead of starters, there are sides such as chicken wings or vegetable springs rolls. Green veg curry is always dependable, with a creamy intensity of flavour and plenty of sliced chillies; som tam (green papaya salad) had an eye-watering zinginess; chilli-inflected red lamb curry went wonderfully with fragrant lychees. Drinks include some inventive juices and smoothies, Thai beers and saké. Well-drilled staff keep things ticking over smoothly. Not everything works, though: the non-spicy dishes can be dull, we resent paying extra for rice, and prices keep climbing – Busaba is no longer a bargain.

Available for hire. Babies and children welcome: high chairs. Bookings not accepted. Disabled: toilet. Separate room for parties, seats 22-24. Tables outdoors (12, pavement). Takeaway service. **Map 17 B1.**

For branches see index.

Covent Garden

Suda

23 Slingsby Place, WC2E 9AB (7240 8010, www.suda-thai.com). Covent Garden or Leicester Square tube. **Meals served** 11am-10.30pm Mon-Wed; 11am-11pm Thur-Sat; noon-10.30pm Sun. **Main courses** £7.50-£9.95. **Set lunch** £7.50. **Credit** AmEx, MC, V.

Opened by the Patara chain in 2010 in St Martin's Courtyard, Suda makes a perfect pit-stop for a quick lunch or dinner. The venue is set over two storeys and has a contemporary feel, with views on the first floor of the open kitchen. Regional Thai food is the speciality, so as well as the ubiquitous curries there are a few more unusual dishes. Highlights include various versions of that street-food classic, som tam (spicy green papaya salad),

here served with cherry tomatoes and nuts plus a choice of grilled meats; we tried the version with crisp-skinned barbecued chicken. The salad had a decent chilli kick by western standards, but could have done with a splash more fish sauce. Pork and crab crackers (essentially spring rolls) were also enjoyable, with well-seasoned meat and crisp pastry, while sizzling sea bass with red curry sauce was flecked with fragrant slivers of lime leaf. There are plenty of interesting drinks, including fruity smoothies, equally fruity cocktails and Thai beer. With lunchtime specials at £7.50 (for curry or pad thai with veg and rice-wrapper rolls), Suda can be very good value too.
Available for hire. Babies and children welcome: children's menu; high chairs; nappy-changing facilities. Booking advisable weekends. Disabled: lift; toilet. Tables outdoors (4, pavement). Takeaway service. **Map 18 D4.**

Edgware Road

Heron NEW

Basement, 1 Norfolk Crescent, W2 2DN (7706 9567). Edgware Road or Marble Arch tube or Paddington tube/rail. **Meals served** 1-11pm daily. **Main courses** £7.50-£18. **No credit cards.**

The Heron is an ordinary estate pub, with an extraordinary Thai restaurant in a basement karaoke room. You won't find the usual Thai top 30 dishes here; instead, the cooking is the sort of thing found as street food or in ramshackle café-bars in small-town Thailand. The menu is lengthy – more than 100 dishes – with an entire page devoted to various som tams (spicy papaya salads), nam toks (salads containing sliced meats) and larbs (spicy minced meat and rice salads). We tried a basic som tam but with added salted crabs, the tiny black shells of these rice-paddy inhabitants uncooked but fermented in salt water. The resulting flavours were pure Thailand: hot and sweet, but also salty and zingy with fresh lime juice and the sharp-tasting green papaya. Better still though was the larb pla, a dish from the Isan region that borders Laos. Catfish had been shredded and deep-fried, tossed with chilli, lime dressing and other spices, and topped with roasted peanuts; the result was an explosion of sour, hot and then salty. Having been warned that the dishes were authentically fiery, we ordered our dishes 'mild'. The result was high-street-Thai strength; next time, we'll try a few dishes 'medium'. There is much, much more to explore on this menu, and we look forward to going back. Eat before 9pm unless you appreciate Thai pop karaoke.
Babies and children admitted. Booking advisable. Takeaway service. **Map 8 E5.**

Marylebone

Chaopraya Eat-Thai

22 St Christopher's Place, W1U 1NP (7486 0777, www.eatthai.net). Bond Street tube. **Meals served** noon-11pm daily. **Main courses** £10.50-£23.95. **Set lunch** £13.95-£15.95 bento box. **Set dinner** £30-£40 per person (minimum 2-6). **Credit** AmEx, MC, V.

Chaopraya is a restaurant with pretensions. The walls are burnished gold in parts, boldly patterned in others and highly adorned throughout the ground-floor dining room. The basement is simpler, bigger, but also rather darker. The food, a mix of familiar favourites and the chef's own inventions, is also embellished with the likes of carved vegetable flowers and little heaps of western salad leaves. A bowl of tom yam koong, served on an oversized rectangular plate, was appropriately hot and sour, and packed with plump prawns. Another starter of pan-fried scallops with the chef's 'homemade spicy sauce' tasted of little other than black pepper – the scallops totally masked. Green chicken curry put things back on track, though, with interesting herbal notes. Our pad thai also had plenty of wow-factor thanks to the skilful lattice-work omelette it was wrapped in. Chaopraya's location makes it the perfect stop-off for a post-shopping meal, but the West End postcode does mean that prices are a little higher than average. The staff seemed rather uninterested on our visit, though perhaps this was down to a less than busy restaurant.
Babies and children welcome: high chairs. Takeaway service. Vegetarian menu. **Map 9 G6.**

Suda

Soho

★ Patara

15 Greek Street, W1D 4DP (7437 1071, www.pataralondon.com). Leicester Square tube. **Lunch served** noon-2.30pm Mon-Sat. **Dinner served** 6.30-10.30pm daily. **Main courses** £13-£24. **Set meal** £38. **Credit** AmEx, MC, V.

Patara (meaning 'gracious lady'), an international chain created by Khun Patara Sila-On and her family from humble beginnings as a Bangkok ice-cream parlour, has branches in Geneva, Vienna, Taipei, Singapore and Beijing. There are also four in London, the most recent in Greek Street being the flagship. 'Gracious' is indeed the watchword, with rich, darkly elegant, subtly lit interiors and finely carved wood decoration. Welcoming staff are prompt and attentive yet unobtrusive. A starter of assorted rice-paper rolls with prawns, crab meat and five-spiced duck was disappointing, seemingly prepared much earlier and kept overlong in the fridge, but the piquant lime and chilli sauce redeemed matters. To follow, king scallops sautéed in chilli paste and sweet basil was simply superb: an ample serving of perfectly cooked, fat, juicy cushions in a nectar-like gravy. Stir-fried asparagus in garlic and oyster sauce was equally faultless and the sauce plate-lickable. To top it all, steamed fragrant rice was just about the most perfectly cooked, individually-grained rice ever, and made the perfect vehicle for such ambrosial liquids. Baked banana with coconut ice-cream, like most Thai desserts, seemed an anticlimax after such savoury delights.
Available for hire. Babies and children admitted. Booking advisable. Disabled: toilet. Vegetarian menu. **Map 17 C3.**
For branches see index.

★ Rosa's

48 Dean Street, W1D 8BF (7494 1638, www.rosaslondon.com). Leicester Square or Tottenham Court Road tube. **Meals served** noon-11pm Mon-Sat; noon-10.30pm Sun. **Main courses** £5.99-£15.99. **Credit** AmEx, MC, V.

The name is coincidental (it belonged to the caff previously occupying the restaurant's original Spitalfields site), but it seems appropriate for this cheery, low-key endeavour, run by an English husband/Thai wife team. The scarlet frontage is echoed inside by red stools and lampshades; otherwise it's all pale plywood furniture and corrugated-effect panelling. The basement has slightly bigger tables. It's not comfortable and there's zero atmosphere, but the emphasis is on speedy, casual budget dining, whether it's local workers at lunch or Soho explorers for dinner. The lengthy menu covers all the standards – fish cakes, spicy-sour soups, salads, stir fries and curries – with dishes marked with one, two or three chillies to indicate heat. Portions are generous, so you could cut costs by sharing a starter: 'fresh' spring rolls (similar to Vietnamese rice paper rolls) produced four hefty pieces. Green vegetable curry included proper Thai aubergines and big chunks of tofu; we've had better but it was a perfectly acceptable rendition. Best of all was a mouth-tingling, eye-wateringly hot som tam (shredded papaya salad with prawns, long beans, cherry tomatoes and cashew nuts and copious lime) – despite being only a two-chilli dish. To drink, there's an assortment of teas (hot and cold) and Chang beer.

Babies and children admitted. Booking advisable. Tables outdoors (2, pavement). Takeaway service; delivery service (over £15 within 2-mile radius). Vegetarian menu. **Map 17 C4.**
For branches see index.

Patara. See p253.

West

Bayswater

Nipa

Lancaster London Hotel, Lancaster Terrace, W2 2TY (7262 6737, www.niparestaurant.co.uk). Lancaster Gate tube.
Bar **Open** 10am-10pm daily.
Restaurant **Lunch served** noon-2pm Mon-Fri. **Dinner served** 6.30-10.30pm Mon-Sat. **Main courses** £9.50-£15.50. **Set meal** £29-£34 4 courses.
Both **Credit** AmEx, DC, MC, V.

Nipa has the polished feel you'd expect from a hotel restaurant: immaculately turned out staff; fresh flowers on every table; and a rich, carved-wood interior dotted with shiny trinkets. If you manage to bag one of the window tables, you also get a great view of Hyde Park. The food is attractively presented with the obligatory vegetable flowers. An abundant starter of sweet minced chicken and peanuts in sticky rice-paper parcels deserved its position on the list of recommended dishes. Wrapped at table in lettuce leaves with a few sprigs of coriander, it was a taste and textural treat. The crab fried rice, flecked with onion and egg, was another good choice, with plenty of juicy chunks of crab meat. A grilled aubergine and prawn salad was the perfect dish for a hot day – light and refreshing with ample lime and fish sauce. Other diners included hotel guests and a group of friends enjoying a special occasion with a bottle of fizz. As the staff are friendly and the atmosphere relaxed, Nipa makes a good spot for a casual meal, as well as for any special event.

Babies and children welcome: high chairs; nappy-changing facilities (hotel). Booking essential Fri, Sat. Disabled: toilet (hotel). Dress: smart casual. Vegetarian menu. **Map 8 D6.**

Earl's Court

Addie's Thai NEW

121 Earl's Court Road, SW5 9RL (7259 2620, www.addiesthai.co.uk). Earl's Court tube. **Lunch served** noon-3pm, **dinner served** 6-10.30pm daily. **Main courses** £5.59-£13.95. **Credit** MC.

'What time are you leaving?' was the greeting on arrival at Addie's. This Earl's Court institution, highly popular with the youth of Thailand's high society in London, has become so busy that table-turning is commonplace. The ground-floor booth seating is packed most evenings, though on our visit the basement room – sometimes used as a karaoke bar – was empty. It's the food, not the service or slightly gloomy decor, that's the draw. The dishes are good versions of what you find in Bangkok: spicy noodle soups, stir-fries, noodle dishes, street food from the north-east. We were delighted to find unusual crab dishes on the menu; the long arms of raw blue swimming crab marinated in lemon juice and fish sauce was a highlight (fingers and napkins required). Surprises litter the menu, such as Shanghai noodles, which turned out to be a salad of translucent sheets of mung bean mixed with vegetables from the East (cloud-ear mushroom) and West (lettuce). There was delicacy in some details, such as the egg lace enveloping the pad thai. No such delicacy with the service, though: with five minutes of our 90 still to go, we were told to leave the table.

Babies and children admitted. Booking advisable. Takeaway service; delivery service (over £15 within 1-mile radius). **Map 13 B10.**

Hammersmith

★ 101 Thai Kitchen NEW

352 King Street, W6 0RX (8746 6888, www.101thaikitchen.com). Stamford Brook tube. **Lunch served** noon-3pm daily. **Dinner served** 6-10.30pm Mon-Thur, Sun; 6-11pm Fri, Sat. **Main courses** £6.50-£14.95. **Credit** AmEx, MC, V.

A few minutes from Stamford Brook tube, this unassuming family-run restaurant offers relatively inexpensive but fairly authentic food from the north-eastern Thai region of Isarn ('101' is the translation of 'Roi Et', an Isarn province known for the 11 satellite towns around its main city). The region's food is fairly spicy and, in place of fish sauce, uses pla ra (a paste of fermented salted freshwater fish) and plenty of lime juice. The atmosphere of the brightly painted room is inviting and comfortable, the staff pleasant, and tables reassuringly dotted with South-east Asian diners. A platter of mixed starters for two was satisfying, if predictable: spring rolls, grilled baby chicken wings, sweetcorn cakes and prawn toast. A dish of curried soft-shell crab with celery and spring onions consisted mainly of scrappy claw bits, but was tasty and nicely crunchy. Grilled sea bass with turmeric and garlic had a perfectly crisp exterior yet remained deliciously moist inside. Fried rice packed with prawns, and nicely suffused with chilli, garlic and holy basil, set everything off well. A short but cleverly selected wine list offers nothing over £15.95, though the choice of only two Thai beers seemed minimal.

Available for hire. Babies and children welcome: children's menu; high chairs. Booking advisable. Takeaway service; delivery service (over £15 within 2-mile radius). **Map 20 A4.**

Shepherd's Bush

★ Esarn Kheaw

314 Uxbridge Road, W12 7LJ (8743 8930, www.esarnkheaw.com). Shepherd's Bush Market tube or 207, 260, 283 bus. **Lunch served** noon-3pm Mon-Fri. **Dinner served** 6-11pm daily. **Main courses** £7.95-£10.95. **Credit** MC, V.

It doesn't look like anyone has changed the decor at Esarn Kheaw since the restaurant first opened its doors in 1992. The kitsch, minty-green dining room (with dark wooden timbers in patterns along the walls) is hung with slightly faded clippings of past awards, as well as the obligatory pictures of the Thai royal family. Despite the furnishings, the venue has a loyal local following – and justifiably so, as the kitchen prepares some impressive authentic north-eastern (Esarn) dishes. One such example is a bamboo-shoot salad laced with hot, smoky, dried chilli, sesame seeds and plenty of fish sauce. It didn't look like much, but the dish certainly packed a punch: seriously savoury and spicy too. Ask for it mild if you don't cope well with chilli,

Heron. See p253.

and the same goes for the papaya salad. Own-made Esarn sausage (another speciality) was garlicky, sour and rich with fatty pork, while a more typical red chicken curry looked the part with slightly bitter pop-in-the-mouth pea aubergines and a decent balance of hot, sweet and salty flavours. The staff can be abrupt at times, but they're very well meaning with it.
Babies and children welcome: high chairs; nappy-changing facilities. Booking advisable. Takeaway service. **Map 20 B1**.

South West

Fulham

Blue Elephant

Waterside Tower, The Boulevard, Imperial Wharf, Townmead Road, SW6 2UB (7751 3111, www.blueelephant.com/london). Fulham Broadway tube then 391 bus or Imperial Wharf rail. **Lunch served** noon-2.30pm Mon-Sat; noon-4.30pm Sun. **Dinner served** 6-10.30pm Mon-Thur, Sun; 6-11pm Fri, Sat. **Main courses** £18-£28. **Set meal** £45-£55 4 courses. **Buffet** (Sun) £30. **Credit** AmEx, DC, MC, V.
After 25 years on Fulham Broadway, this ever-popular Thai has moved to new riverside premises at Imperial Wharf (formerly occupied by Blue Elephant's fancier offshoot Saran Rom). The development itself has yet to find its soul, but stepping through the doors of the restaurant transports you to another world. A stylish mix of teak furniture, acid-green walls and an abundance of jungle greenery helps bring the banqueting halls of Bangkok to Fulham. In the words of the effusive manager, while the old restaurant emulated a Thai village, the new is a Thai palace. There's an updated menu to match, with a mix of traditional and modern dishes as well as tasting menus. Some dishes, such as an enoki mushroom and vermicelli salad, sang with hits of lime and garlic, and a duck breast laab had a perfect balance of strong chilli heat and fresh mint. Others, such as the house spring rolls, felt a little tired, with a too-sweet dipping sauce and meagre filling. Still, staff are eager to please and keen for feedback from customers to help smooth the move. The outdoor terraces should prove a hit in good weather.
Available for hire. Babies and children welcome: high chairs. Booking advisable. Disabled: lift; toilet. Separate room for parties, seating 50-100. Tables outdoors (20, terrace). Takeaway service. Vegetarian menu. **Map 21 A2**.

Parsons Green

★ Sukho

855 Fulham Road, SW6 5HJ (7371 7600, www.sukhogroups.com). Parsons Green tube. **Lunch served** noon-3pm, **dinner served** 6.30-11pm daily. **Main courses** £11.25-£18.95. **Set lunch** £12.95 2 courses. **Credit** AmEx, MC, V.
This unassuming spot dishes up some of the best Thai food in west London to a crowd of upmarket Fulhamites. Expect a friendly welcome from the traditionally dressed staff, who remain attentive throughout. It's not the best place for intimate conversation as you sit elbow-to-elbow with your neighbours on small, tightly packed tables, but it has an easy charm and stylish surroundings. White walls are enlivened with dark wooden screens and colourful raw-silk panels; starched

Menu

Spellings are subject to considerable variation. Word divisions vary too: thus, kwaitiew, kwai teo and guey teow are all acceptable spellings for noodles.
Thailand abandoned chopsticks in the 19th century in favour of chunky steel spoons and forks. Using your fingers is usually fine, and essential if you order satay sticks or spare ribs.

STARTERS
Khanom jeep or ka nom geeb: dim sum. Little dumplings of minced pork, bamboo shoots and water chestnuts, wrapped in an egg and rice pastry, then steamed.
Khanom pang na koong: prawn sesame toast.
Kratong thong: tiny crispy batter cups ('top hats') filled with mixed vegetables and/or minced meat.
Miang: savoury appetisers with a variety of constituents (mince, ginger, peanuts, roasted coconut, for instance), wrapped in betel leaves.
Popia or porpia: spring rolls.
Tod mun pla or tauk manpla: small fried fish cakes (should be lightly rubbery in consistency) with virtually no 'fishy' smell or taste.

SOUPS
Poh tak or tom yam potag: hot and sour mixed seafood soup.
Tom kha gai or gai tom kar: hot and sour chicken soup with coconut milk.
Tom yam or tom yum: a hot and sour soup, smelling of lemongrass. Tom yam koong is with prawns; tom yam gai with chicken; tom yam hed with mushrooms.

RICE
Khao, kow or khow: rice.
Khao nao: sticky rice.
Khao pat: fried rice.
Khao suay: steamed rice.
Pat khai: egg-fried rice.

SALADS
Laab or larb: minced and cooked meat incorporating lime juice and other ingredients such as ground rice and herbs.
Som tam: a popular cold salad of grated green papaya.
Yam or yum: refers to any tossed salad, hot or cold, but it is often hot and sour, flavoured with lemon and chilli.
Yam nua: hot and sour beef salad.
Yam talay: hot and sour seafood salad (served cold).

NOODLES
Generally speaking, noodles are eaten in greater quantities in the north of Thailand. There are many types of kwaitiew or guey teow noodles. Common ones include sen mee: rice vermicelli; sen yai (river rice noodles): a broad, flat, rice noodle; sen lek: a medium flat noodle, used to make pad thai; ba mee: egg noodles; and woon sen (cellophane noodle): transparent vermicelli made from soy beans or other pulses. These are often prepared as stir-fries.
Common noodle dishes are:
Khao soi: chicken curry soup with egg noodles; a Burmese/Thai dish, referred to as the national dish of Burma.
Mee krob or mee grob: sweet crispy fried vermicelli.
Pad si-ewe or cee eaw: noodles fried with mixed meat in soy sauce.
Pad thai: stir-fried noodles with shrimps (or chicken and pork), beansprouts and salted turnips, garnished with ground peanuts.

CURRIES
Gaeng, kaeng or gang: the generic name for curry. Yellow curry is the mildest; green curry (gaeng keaw wan or kiew warn) is medium hot and uses green chillies; red curry (gaeng pet) is similar, but uses red chillies.
Jungle curry: often the hottest of the curries, made with red curry paste, bamboo shoots and just about anything else to hand, but no coconut cream.
Massaman or mussaman: also known as Muslim curry, because it originates from the area along the border with Malaysia where many Thais are Muslims. For this reason, pork is never used. It's a rich but mild concoction, with coconut, potato and some peanuts.
Penang, panaeng or panang: a dry, aromatic curry made with 'Penang' curry paste, coconut cream and holy basil.

FISH & SEAFOOD
Hoi: shellfish.
Hor mok talay or haw mog talay: steamed egg mousse with seafood.
Koong, goong or kung: prawns.
Maw: dried fish belly.

linen table runners and napkins complete the polished look. The menu contains thoughtfully chosen dishes where flavours are perfectly balanced: sourness enhanced by heat, sweetness tempered by saltiness. Much thought, too, has been given to presentation, and we even liked the carved flower garnishes, which elsewhere can look offputtingly reused. An unusual dish of vegetable tempura worked well with a tangy roasted coconut sauce, while a classic red beef curry was executed impeccably. We loved the skewers of pork grilled in pandan leaves, and a stir-fry of minced chicken perfumed with basil was spot-on too. Sukho has two sister restaurants: Suk Saran in Wimbledon and Suksan in Chelsea.
Babies and children admitted. Booking advisable. Takeaway service.
For branches (Suk Saran, Suksan) see index.

Putney

Thai Square

2-4 Lower Richmond Road, SW15 1LB (8780 1811, www.thaisquare.net). Putney Bridge tube or bus 14, 22.
Bar **Open/snacks served** noon-11pm Mon-Thur; noon-2am Fri, Sat; noon-10.30pm Sun. *Restaurant* **Lunch served** noon-3pm, **dinner served** 6-11pm Mon-Fri. **Meals served** noon-11pm Sat; noon-10.30pm Sun. **Main courses** £5.50-£14.95. **Set dinner** £25-£35 per person (minimum 2) 3 courses.
Both **Credit** AmEx, MC, V.
We get the impression that this London-wide chain of upmarket Thai restaurants trades more on its impressive locations than on singular food. Occupying the stunning Putney Bridge building, which stands alone, ship-like, on the water's edge, this branch is one of the most striking. The downstairs cocktail bar has a clubbish vibe (great when full, a bit bleak on a weeknight), while the upstairs restaurant is minimalist so as not to distract from the uninterrupted view of the Thames. An extensive menu covers all the bases, with a few pan-Asian favourites thrown in for good measure; diners looking for authenticity may be disappointed. The benchmark dish of green curry was passable, yet lacked a certain depth of flavour; a chef's special, described as thinly sliced chargrilled duck breast with exotic tamarind sauce, arrived instead as a piece of crispy aromatic duck (also on the menu) drowned in a sickly syrup with none of the sour notes of tamarind to cut the richness. We hope the kitchen raises its game, as the high prices warrant more than just a great view.
Available for hire. Babies and children welcome: high chairs. Booking advisable Fri, Sat. Disabled: lift; toilet. Tables outdoors (8, patio). Takeaway service. Vegetarian menu.
For branches see index.

South

Brixton

★ KaoSarn

Brixton Village Market, Coldharbour Lane, SW9 8PR (7095 8922). Brixton tube/rail.
Lunch served 12-3.30pm Tue-Sun. **Dinner served** 3.30-10pm Tue-Sat; 3.30-9pm Sun. **Main courses** £6.90-£11.50. **Unlicensed. Corkage** no charge. **No credit cards.**
Relishing its position amid the energetically hip scene that is Brixton Market, KaoSarn is one of the best providers of victuals hereabouts. The kitchen conjures up impressive food with complex and authentic flavours that you can only dream of finding at Thai restaurants charging twice the price elsewhere in London. A typically gutsy dish is a soup of pleasingly fiery, sour and pungent fish-flavoured stock, hosting two giant prawns in a tempura batter, along with rice noodles, light and airy pork meatballs, dense and smooth fish balls, crunchy beansprouts and chillies galore. Factor in incredible value, friendly and helpful service, the charming straw light fixtures and the vibrant bustle of the market (where left-leaning mums with prams are replaced by hipsters grooving to live music as day turns into night) – and this is a place worth crossing town for. KaoSarn may not be for everyone, however; its corner location on the edge of the market leaves alfresco diners exposed not just to the elements, but also to the motley crew of passers-by.
Babies and children admitted. Booking essential dinner. Tables outdoors (10, market). Takeaway service. **Map 22 E2.**
For branch see index.

Blue Elephant. See p257.

South East

South Norwood

Mantanah

2 Orton Building, Portland Road, SE25 4UD (8771 1148, www.mantanah.co.uk). Norwood Junction rail. **Lunch served** noon-3pm Sun. **Dinner served** 6-11pm Tue-Sun. **Main courses** £6.50-£13.95. **Set lunch** £7.95 3 courses. **Set dinner** £18 per person (minimum 2) 3 courses, £25 per person (minimum 2) 4 courses. **Credit** MC, V.
'Don't judge a book by its cover' – there couldn't be a more appropriate phrase for Mantanah. Although the decor is understated (with dark wooden panelling and Thai embroidery) and the station-side location unprepossessing, the food is anything but unremarkable. Standard options such as pad thai or green chicken curry are no doubt good here, but it's worth exploring the hefty menu further. An excellent northern-style slow-simmered pork belly and peanut curry was spicy, savoury and just a little sour from chunks of pickled garlic; and green papaya salad was laced with as much fish sauce and fresh, red chilli as you'd expect from any Thai street-food stall. A word of warning: the kitchen doesn't hold back on the heat, so if you can't take too much chilli, let staff know you want something mild, or be prepared to dampen the flames with plenty of Singha beer. A great destination for good-value, authentic Thai food and charming staff.
Available for hire. Babies and children admitted: high chairs. Booking advisable. Takeaway service; delivery service (over £15 within 3-mile radius). Vegetarian menu.

North

Tufnell Park

★ Charuwan

110 Junction Road, N19 5LB (7263 1410, www.charuwan.co.uk). Archway or Tufnell Park tube. **Dinner served** 6-10.30pm daily. **Main courses** £5.95-£8.95. **Set dinner** £19.50 3 courses. **Credit** MC, V.
North London lacks good Thai eateries, so this longstanding family-run spot is as refreshing as lemongrass tea on a steamy tropical afternoon. The Lanna pavilion-style wood interior, serene buddhas and angular white leather furniture may not exactly transport you to Chiang Mai, but they do at least feel removed from the Junction Road. Service is confident, but lacked warmth and speed on our latest visit. The menu offers a greatest hits selection of Thai cooking, plus some intriguing chef's specialities such as 'snow prawns' (stuffed with minced chicken and topped with egg whites). Wine options lack thrills but are keenly priced. Steamed fish with pickles, plum and fresh ginger was exquisitely light yet full of flavour. Correctly fiery yum woon sen (glass noodle salad with pork, shrimp, chilli and lime) continued the good work. Less satisfactory was aubergine stir-fried with black bean sauce: a chewy, bitter letdown thanks to too little time in the wok, but we couldn't fault the sticky, comforting rice.
Babies and children welcome: high chairs. Takeaway service; delivery service (over £15 within 3-mile radius). Vegetarian menu.
Map 26 B2.

Turkish

Turkish dining in London has reached maturity – but it hasn't lost sight of its vibrant youth. Budget cafés and grills started appearing towards the end of the 1980s, mostly in the Turkish enclaves of Dalston and Harringay. Several prospered as Londoners from outside those communities came to relish the excellent kebabs, fresh flatbreads and zesty meze dishes to be found (as well as the low prices). The message was spread across the city, as branches and new enterprises opened both north and south (though the west has still to catch up). Still later, the concept was turned into a business opportunity by the **Tas** chain, and a march upmarket was undertaken by the likes of **Ishtar** in Marylebone, **Kazan** in Pimlico and **Quince** in Mayfair (where a fusion version of the cuisine is being forged by a Bulgarian-born TV chef). Nevertheless, some of the most cherished Turkish eateries remain the old guard: the basic cafés devoid of flimflam and furbelows, where superb cooking still draws the crowds. Take a bow, **Mangal Ocakbasi** and **19 Numara Bos Cirrik I**.

Central

Clerkenwell & Farringdon

★ Tas

37 Farringdon Road, EC1M 3JB (7430 9721, www.tasrestaurants.co.uk). **Meals served** noon-11.30pm Mon-Sat; noon-10.30pm Sun. **Main courses** £8.45-£12.90. **Set meal** £9.95 2 courses; £19.95 3 courses incl coffee (minimum 2 people). **Set meze** £10.95 (minimum 2 people). **Credit** AmEx, DC, MC, V.

The interior of this branch of Tas has a satisfying solidity. Gothic-looking chandeliers hang down between great wooden ceiling beams. Stout wooden chairs have a medieval look; cool rustic tiles line the floor. It's as if to reassure diners: the restaurant may be part of a chain, but it has deep culinary roots. Initial fears about the menu's unwieldy length were dispelled by the starters. A dish of artichokes (enginar) and broad beans was remarkably generous in size. The hearts seemed fresh rather than preserved, and were well matched to their light tomato and dill dressing. Another starter, mücver, had an improbable, pleasing lightness despite the frying and the feta within. Standards dipped a little with the mains. Karışık ızgara, a kebab sampler, should have arrived singing from the grill, yet the cooking didn't seem fresh. A dollop of spicy sauce was needed to enliven the experience. Vegetarian fasulye kavurması looked exhausted, with the green beans drained of much colour, yet the flavours came through with some vibrancy. A guitarist who played traditional music throughout the evening did himself proud; the maestro behind the charcoal grill needs to up his game.

Available for hire. Babies and children welcome: high chairs. Booking advisable. Disabled: toilet. Separate room for parties, seats 45. Takeaway service. **Map 5 N5.**

For branches (EV Restaurant, Bar & Delicatessen, Tas, Tas Café, Tas Pide) see index.

Fitzrovia

Özer

5 Langham Place, W1B 3DG (7323 0505, www.sofra.co.uk). Oxford Circus tube.

Bar **Open** noon-11pm daily.

Restaurant **Breakfast served** 8am-noon, **meals served** noon-11pm daily. **Main courses** £8.95-£23.95. **Set meal** (noon-7pm) £12.95; (7-11pm) £13.95.

Both **Credit** AmEx, MC, V.

This flagship of Huseyin Özer, who also runs the Sofra chain, aims to appeal to tastes acquired in other holiday destinations as well as Turkey. Hence, along with an accessible Turkish selection, there's Thai-style stir-fry, and black cod in miso as pioneered at Nobu. This ought to count against Özer, but doesn't as it's stylishly done, keenly priced and doesn't miss a beat. There's a happy babble from shoppers, workers, and people dating and celebrating in the long, smart dining room (with a maître d' gatekeeper), and the comfortable front bar. Mixed meze was beautifully presented on a glass plate with perky versions of falafel, houmous, börek, bulgar and nut salad, tabouleh and, best of all, tender broad beans on yoghurt – all lined up in neat blobs. Bread was lovely, fluffy and wholemeal. A lightness of touch extends even to grills like lamb meatballs: a good half-dozen delicately flavoured patties with rice and grilled vegetables. Prawns in coconut and ginger sauce was surprisingly pleasing too. Wines, including the refreshing Turkish house, are decently priced; tables (draped in heavy linen) are generously spaced; service is excellent. An impressive outfit, and understandably very popular.

Available for hire. Babies and children welcome: high chairs; nappy-changing facilities. Booking advisable. Disabled: toilet. Tables outdoors (5, pavement). Takeaway service. **Map 9 H5.**

For branches (Sofra) see index.

Marylebone

Ishtar

10-12 Crawford Street, W1U 6AZ (7224 2446, www.ishtarrestaurant.com). Baker Street tube. **Meals served** noon-11pm Mon-Thur, Sun; noon-11.30pm Fri, Sat. **Main courses** £9.95-£15.95. **Set lunch** (noon-6pm) £8.95 2 courses. **Set meal** £25-£27.50 3 courses. **Set meze** £8.95. **Credit** MC, V.

As much a neighbourhood restaurant as a Turkish venue – albeit for an upmarket 'hood – Ishtar is packed with well-groomed Marylebone families and

Mangal Ocakbasi. See p262.

groups. The ground floor is stylish, warm and welcoming, and there's plenty more space under the arches in the basement. In the open kitchen, chefs apply a deft touch to a menu that has much more than dips and grills to recommend it. Hence there was a zesty lightness to the virtually carb-free, heavily parsleyed tabouleh. Köfte were neat but a little factory-perfect. Adana kebab was distinctively lemony, garlicky and peppery, while the more unusual meyveli kuzu (lamb soft and sweet from slow-cooking with apricot, pear and almond, with orange couscous) was a rich treat. Food arrived almost disconcertingly quickly, yet there was no rushing. Such well-paced service would be particularly welcome at lunch when the decent-sized menu strays beyond the light interpretations of Turkish, to the middle-of-the-road likes of smoked salmon or goat's cheese salad. Puddings, including the crème caramel-like kazandibi, inspiringly matched with coconut ice-cream, rounded off dinner beautifully. Ishtar is a fun, well-run crowd-pleaser that doesn't dumb down the cuisine.
Babies and children welcome: high chairs; nappy-changing facilities. Booking advisable Thur-Sat. Disabled: toilet. Entertainment: musicians Wed-Sat; belly dancer Fri, Sat. Separate room for parties, seats 120. Tables outdoors (6, pavement). Takeaway service. Vegetarian menu. **Map 2 F5.**

Mayfair

Quince

May Fair, Stratton Street, W1J 8LT (7915 3892, www.quincelondon.com). Green Park tube.
Breakfast served 7-10.30am Mon-Fri; 7.30-11am Sat, Sun. **Lunch served** 12.30-3pm Mon-Fri; 1-4pm Sat, Sun. **Afternoon tea served** 2.30-5pm, **dinner served** 6-10.30pm daily. **Main courses** £14.50-£29. **Credit** AmEx, DC, MC, V.

Quince opened in 2011 to plentiful reviews thanks to Bulgarian-born TV chef Silvena Rowe taking charge at the May Fair hotel's streetside restaurant. Her personal take on Ottoman cuisine adds modish flavours that appeal to ingredient-literate restaurant goers. Hence there's avocado houmous with tahini, black sesame and coconut dukkah; fattoush with burrata and za'atar. Though dishes are often beautiful – dainty micro leaves on lamb, orange baklava with pomegranate and orange oil, wonderfully matched with pistachio ice-cream, girlishly garnished with a pansy – the kitchen doesn't put appearance above substance. Flavours are zesty and inspired: feta and lemon dressing, and grapefruit with jumbo prawns; smoky aubergine more conventionally paired with pomegranate sharpness. Starters aren't stingy, but mains require padding out with sides such as rice with wild blueberries, pistachios and lemon balm. There was no sign of Rowe in the open kitchen, and some dishes could have done with a beadier eye on seasoning. Squid batter was greasy and the slow-cooked lamb had a very salty sauce. Enervating music and a plush Byzantine interior direct the spotlight to the food, so lapses in star quality are more apparent. The tea menu is delightful, but beware the cost of cocktails.
Available for hire. Babies and children welcome: high chairs. Booking essential. Disabled: toilet. Dress: smart casual. Separate room for parties, seats 46. Tables outdoors (6, pavement).
Map 9 H7.

Pimlico

Kazan

93-94 Wilton Road, SW1V 1DW (7233 7100, www.kazan-restaurant.com). Victoria tube/rail.
Lunch served noon-3pm Mon-Fri; noon-4.30pm Sat, Sun. **Dinner served** 5.30-10pm Mon-Sat; 5.30pm-9.30pm Sun. **Main courses** £11.95-£15.95. **Set meal** £14.95 2 courses. **Set meze** £34.95. **Credit** MC, V.

When asked for a Turkish white wine recommendation, our waitress raised her eyebrows knowingly. 'Do you want to try?' she asked. But the Çankaya she brought was excellent, as was the food to come. We were initially dispirited, as a vegetarian meze wasn't the bountiful plateful that Turkish restaurants often deliver. However, Kazan clearly doesn't need to seduce with portion size: all seats were taken on a weekday evening. Each meze was modest in quantity, inviting us to savour rather than shovel. Houmous was simple and smooth, in contrast to the smoky baba ganoush of baritone depth. Biting into domes of expertly fried falafel brought a hit of coriander seed. Börek were freshly fried, kısır was generously nutty and tabouleh light. A main of hünkar beğendi had us raising our eyebrows like the droll waitress earlier, but this was a reaction of delight; the lamb and aubergine stew was superb, blurring the boundary between smoky and sweet. A toothsome Ottoman grill – a mix of various kebabs, poussin and sausage – also showed that the chefs aren't afraid of the meat-over-charcoal basics.
Available for hire. Babies and children welcome: high chairs. Booking advisable Thur-Sat. Disabled: toilet. Takeaway service. **Map 15 J11.**

North East

Dalston

★ Mangal II

4 Stoke Newington Road, N16 8BH (7254 7888, www.mangal2.com). Dalston Kingsland rail or 76, 149, 243 bus. **Meals served** noon-1am Mon-Sat; noon-midnight Sun. **Main courses** £8.45-£15.45. **Credit** AmEx, MC, V.

Can you judge a restaurant by its decor? Mangal II's red interior walls certainly suit the intense atmosphere of the place. With tables packed like lily pads on a pond, waiters stretch awkwardly behind diners' backs to lay down plates. For some, this might feel like 'buzz'; others will prefer the quieter basement space. A mixed meze seemed rather pick 'n' mix, with a powerful tarama heaped next to kısır, houmous, a rich cacık, çalı fasulye (green beans in tomato sauce) and a couple of tired,

Iznik. See p263.

stuffed vine leafs. A tweaked arrangement was served to another table. Arnavut ciğeri can be a wonderful, spiky battle between raw onion and sticky liver, but here the meat had been cooked timidly. The crunchy salad accompanying a delicious çöp şiş kebab was excellent, as was the abundant warm bread. Yoğurtlu lamb beyti – cubed bread and meat slathered in rich tomato sauce (and even richer yoghurt) – was as pleasingly rib-sticking as it should be. All four of the vegetarian dishes are aubergine-based, but there are also simple grilled mackerel and sea bass options.
Babies and children welcome: high chairs. Booking advisable weekends. Takeaway service. **Map 25 C4.**

★ Mangal Ocakbasi

10 Arcola Street, E8 2DJ (7275 8981, www.mangal1.com). Dalston Kingsland rail or 67, 76, 149, 243 bus. **Meals served** noon-midnight daily. **Main courses** £9.50-£13.50. **Corkage** no charge. **No credit cards.**

This backstreet grill has featured in every *Time Out Eating & Drinking* guide since it opened more than 20 years ago. It's certainly doing something right to draw diners away from the numerous Turkish restaurants up and down Dalston's main drag – but it's far from flashy. The first thing you see on entering the slightly worn space is the cabinet of skewers: cubed and minced lamb, chops and ribs, chicken wings and fillets, quail. There are even a few vegetables, though this is definitely a destination for meat eaters. Next to this display of flesh is the six-foot charcoal grill, billowing smoke and overseen by a chef kept constantly busy twirling skewers and stoking the flames. Pretty much everything on the menu is worth ordering, but the beyti and adana kebabs (minced lamb) are particularly juicy and flavoursome, matched perfectly by fresh Turkish bread (free) and tart salad. Starters are fairly standard – meze, lahmacun and so on – and do a good job of setting the scene for the main event. There's no charge for BYO (although Mangal is licensed to sell alcohol), which, along with the superb and good-value food, ensure the place is heaving most nights.
Available for hire. Babies and children welcome: high chairs. Booking advisable. Takeaway service. **Map 25 C4.**

★ 19 Numara Bos Cirrik I

34 Stoke Newington Road, N16 7XJ (7249 0400, www.cirrik1.co.uk). Dalston Kingsland rail or 76, 149, 243 bus. **Meals served** noon-midnight daily. **Main courses** £7.50-£10.50. **Licensed. Corkage** £1-£5. **Credit** MC, V.

One of many Turkish restaurants lining Stoke Newington Road, 19 Numara is a hardy perennial. It's among the strip's more popular joints, and we've yet to experience a slip in its high standards. There's a good range of traditional starters: the likes of imam bayıldı, patlıcan soslu (aubergines and green peppers in a tomato sauce, served cold) and mücver. You'll also find plenty of dips: ıspanak tarator (purèed spinach and yoghurt), houmous and tarama. Be careful when ordering, as one thing that gives this place an edge over its competitors is the little plates of salad – onions with pomegranate sauce, finely chopped mixed salad, and another onion salad – that come gratis with main courses. Mains are reliably good: lamb şiş is succulent, the full mixed kebab (for two to three) is enormous, and iskender kebabs are generous and flavoursome. The atmosphere is convivial too. Customers these days are as likely to be trendy young Dalstonites as Turkish families, but everyone usually has a good time, helped along by friendly service. As with elsewhere in the area, prices have risen over the past few years, but 19 Numara still feels like good value.
Available for hire. Babies and children welcome: high chairs. Booking advisable. Separate room for parties, seats 40. Takeaway service. Vegetarian menu. **Map 25 C4.**
For branches see index.

North

Finsbury Park

Petek

94-96 Stroud Green Road, N4 3EN (7619 3933). Finsbury Park tube/rail. **Meals served** 2-11pm Mon-Thur; noon-11pm Fri-Sun. **Main courses** £8.60-£17.80. **Set meal** £9.45-£10.85 2 courses. **Set meze** £7.85-£9.85 per person (minimum 2). **Credit** AmEx, MC, V.

Out of the way for much of London, Petek depends on enthusiastic local trade – and our busy visit suggests it's pitching things just right. Gorgeous warm bread appeared with a spicy red dip and fat olives, to settle stomachs upset by the torment of choice. The list of cocktails fluttered its eyelashes at anyone keen to make a night of it. And, above all, our waitress was charming and efficient – even when calmly correcting a mistake we'd made over our wine order. As on previous visits, the food

arrived in industrial quantities. A huge 'Petek special' was the pick of our most recent meal: three unctuous meats (charcoal-grilled chicken cubes, and lamb done two ways, as shish köfte and cubed), a dome of tasty rice, mixed salad with pomegranate sauce, and lemon mayonnaise. The 'vegetarian kebab salad', which proved to be a neat combination of feta, grilled halloumi, peppers, rocket and spinach, only disappointed with its chewy overcooked portobello mushrooms. Beneath a hundred multicoloured ceiling lamps, and with simple tea-lights on each table, Petek conjures up an atmospheric night out.
Babies and children welcome: high chairs. Tables outdoors (3, pavement). Takeaway service.

Harringay

★ Hala

29 Grand Parade, Green Lanes, N4 1LG (8802 4883, www.halarestaurant.co.uk). Manor House tube then bus 29. **Meals served** 7am-2am daily. **Main courses** £3.50-£11.50. **Credit** AmEx, MC, V.

Hala may be a simple eat-in or takeaway joint, but it has always been smart. Waiting staff wear black waistcoats and yellow ties, while the ladies sitting in the window hand-rolling gözleme (filled crêpes) sport matching white T-shirts and hair nets. A revamp has reinvigorated the place a little, but the food and the welcome remain blessedly unchanged. Everything has visual pzazz. Our waiter scooped froth on to a glass of ayran, before poking a pink straw through the lot. Excellent mixed meze came in a colourful arrangement on the plate: houmous as grainy as grits sat next to a relatively restrained tarama; butter-rich cacık nudged a mellow aubergine salad (patlıcan salatası). Cubes of fresh white cheese and some zingy but mild ezme (tomato salad) completed the picture. The three 'daily dishes' – stews and pasta – can be served as a mix. Knowing Hala's generosity, you'd end up with more than your fair share of each. But the grill is the main attraction. Even if the alinazik was short on puréed aubergine, it mattered little, so succulent was the lamb. Mixed kebab platters come on huge plates, and there are a couple of grilled fish options.
Available for hire. Babies and children welcome: high chairs; nappy-changing facilities. Disabled: toilet. Takeaway service. Vegetarian menu.

Highbury

Iznik

19 Highbury Park, N5 1QJ (7354 5697, www.iznik.co.uk). Highbury & Islington tube/ rail or 4, 19, 236 bus. **Meals served** 10.30am-11pm daily. **Main courses** £10-£15. **Set meal** (Mon-Fri) £12.95 2 courses, £15.45 3 courses. **Credit** AmEx, MC, V.

Making the same decorative gestures as its many competitors – multiple lamps, evil eyes of dramatically different sizes and functions – Iznik is nonetheless a notch upmarket: witness the extravagant fretwork door and the two modish ceramic vases in the shape of Turkish dresses. The lighting is gentle, the seating clearly restaurant rather than canteen, and the service proud to a point just short (but acceptably short) of officious. A slightly underpowered fava bean purée, served with lovely warm flatbread, was casually prettified with a sprinkle of red chilli flakes and green dill. Pirasa mücveri (leek and feta fritters) provided a pleasing mix of surface crunch and interior juiciness, and came with richly flavoured kısır, but were served on tatty shreds of iceberg. The same mistake (more tired leaves) was made with the hünkar beğendi, where tender braised lamb sat on a deliciously smoky aubergine purée with well-flavoured bulgar wheat. A surprisingly effective karides sote (sautéed tiger prawns with chilli and garlic, served with a creamy sauce and cold tomatoes) also suggested a care in the combination of flavours that wasn't matched by consistency of presentation.
Available for hire. Babies and children welcome: high chairs. Booking advisable; essential weekends. Takeaway service.

Islington

Antepliler

139 Upper Street, N1 1PQ (7226 5441, www.anteplilerrestaurant.com). Angel tube or Highbury & Islington tube/rail. **Meals served** noon-11pm daily. **Main courses** £9.50-£13.90. **Credit** MC, V.

A dazzlingly white-shirted greeter whisks diners off busy Upper Street into Antepliler's nightclubby, chandelier-lit interior – or, if you're lucky and it's summer, back out on to a pavement table. From a menu boasting the köfte, stews and pastries that make the Anatolian city of Antep famous, there's plenty to tempt. Highlights of the mixed meze were sesame-studded falafel; lowlights were stodgy cabbage dolma. Given that köfte are a feature of the menu, ours were surprisingly chewy, but forgivably so: sweetly stewed with shallots infused with the refreshing sourness of pomegranate, in this Antep speciality. Antep salad – a tart, wet mix of finely chopped tomato, onion, parsley, walnut and pomegranate – also made a piquant change from the norm. Bread, puffed up like a football, was flourished with a heat warning: typical of the charming service. All the cooking might not have the delicacy of the mother-of-pearl marquetry tabletops, but presentation is artful and Antepliler turns a meal into an occasion. A delightful spot.
Available for hire. Babies and children welcome: high chairs. Tables outdoors (4, pavement). Takeaway service. **Map 5 O1.**
For branch see index.

Pasha

301 Upper Street, N1 2TU (7226 1454, www.pasharestaurant.co.uk). Angel tube or Highbury & Islington tube/rail. **Meals served** noon-11.30pm Mon-Sat; noon-11pm

Zara. See p264.

TURKISH

Menu

It's useful to know that in Turkish 'ç' and 'ş' are pronounced 'ch' and 'sh'. So şiş is correct Turkish, shish is English and sis is common on menus. Menu spelling is rarely consistent, so expect wild variations on everything given here. See also the menu boxes in **Middle Eastern** and **North African**.

COOKING EQUIPMENT

Mangal: brazier.
Ocakbaşı: an open grill under an extractor hood. A metal dome is put over the charcoal for making paper-thin bread.

MEZE DISHES & SOUPS

Arnavut ciğeri: 'Albanian liver' – cubed or sliced lamb's liver, fried then baked.
Barbunya: spicy kidney bean stew.
Börek or böreği: fried or baked filo pastry parcels with a savoury filling, usually cheese, spinach or meat. Commonest are muska or peynirli (cheese) and sigara ('cigarette', so long and thin).
Cacik: diced cucumber with garlic in yoghurt.
Çoban salatası: 'shepherd's' salad of finely diced tomatoes, cucumbers, onions, perhaps green peppers and parsley.
Dolma: stuffed vegetables (usually with rice and pine kernels).
Enginar: artichokes, usually with vegetables in olive oil.
Haydari: yoghurt, infused with garlic and mixed with finely chopped mint leaves.
Hellim: Cypriot halloumi cheese.
Houmous kavurma: houmous topped with strips of lamb and pine nuts.
Imam bayıldı: literally 'the imam fainted'; aubergine stuffed with onions, tomatoes and garlic in olive oil.
Işkembe: finely chopped tripe soup; an infallible hangover cure.
Kısır: usually a mix of chopped parsley, tomatoes, onions, crushed wheat, olive oil and lemon juice.
Kizartma: lightly fried vegetables.
Lahmacun: 'pizza' of minced lamb on thin pide (qv).
Mercimek çorbar: red lentil soup.
Midye tava: mussels in batter, in a garlic sauce.
Mücver: courgette and feta fritters.
Patlıcan: aubergine, variously served.
Pide: a term encompassing many varieties of Turkish flatbread. It also refers to Turkish pizzas (heavier and more filling than lahmacun, qv).
Pilaki: usually haricot beans in olive oil, but the name refers to the method of cooking not the content.
Piyaz: white bean salad with onions.
Saç: paper-thin, chewy bread prepared on a metal dome (also called saç) over a charcoal grill.
Sucuk: spicy sausage, usually beef.
Tarator: a bread, garlic and walnut mixture; havuç tarator adds carrot; ıspanak tarator adds spinach.
Yayla: yoghurt and rice soup (usually) with a chicken stock base.
Yaprak dolması: stuffed vine leaves.

MAIN COURSES

Alabalik: trout.
Güveç: stew, which is traditionally cooked in an earthenware pot.
Hünkar beğendi: cubes of lamb, braised with onions and tomatoes, served on an aubergine and cheese purée.
İçli köfte: balls of cracked bulgar wheat filled with spicy mince.
İncik: knuckle of lamb, slow-roasted in its own juices. Also called kléftico.
Karni yarik: aubergine stuffed with minced lamb and vegetables.
Mitite köfte: chilli meatballs.
Sote: meat (usually), sautéed in tomato, onion and pepper (and sometimes wine).

KEBABS

Usually made with grilled lamb (those labelled tavuk or piliç are chicken), served with bread or rice and salad. Common varieties include:
Beyti: usually spicy mince and garlic, but sometimes best-end fillet.
Böbrek: kidneys.
Çöp şiş: small cubes of lamb.
Döner: slices of marinated lamb (sometimes mince) packed tightly with pieces of fat on a vertical rotisserie.
Halep: usually döner (qv) served over bread with a buttery tomato sauce.
İskender: a combination of döner (qv), tomato sauce, yoghurt and melted butter on bread.
Kaburga: spare ribs.
Kanat: chicken wings.
Köfte: mince mixed with spices, eggs and onions.
Külbastı: char-grilled fillet.
Lokma: 'mouthful' – boned fillet of lamb (beware, there's a dessert that has a similar name!).
Patlıcan: mince and sliced aubergine.
Pirzola: lamb chops.
Şiş: cubes of marinated lamb.
Uykuluk: sweetbread.
Yoğurtlu: meat over bread and yoghurt.

DESSERTS

Armut tatlısı: baked pears.
Ayva tatlısı: quince in syrup.
Kadayıf: cake made from shredded pastry dough, filled with syrup and nuts or cream.
Kazandibi: milk pudding, traditionally with very finely chopped chicken breast.
Kemel pasha: small round cakes soaked in honey.
Keşkül: milk pudding with almonds and coconut, topped with pistachios.
Lokum: turkish delight.
Sütlaç: rice pudding.

Sun. **Main courses** £7.95-£14.95. **Set meal** £20.95 3 courses. **Set meze** lunch £9.95, dinner £12.95 (minimum 2). **Credit** AmEx, MC, V.
Although no longer Upper Street's most soigné Turkish restaurant, Pasha still draws a crowd, and its tightly packed tables overflow on to the pavement in summer. The attraction? Smart, highly professional staff, and Turkish cooking that's skilfully executed, if sometimes toned down for high-street tastes. Yes, the imam bayıldı in our meze wasn't as richly sauced or smoky as usual, and the crisp yet salty börek arrived, oddly, with a South-east Asian chilli sauce. But other dishes produced murmurs of pleasure: chicken livers, sweet and sour with red onion and pomegranate, were piquant perfection; mücver fritters were deliciously soft and fluffy. Grilled sardines with an onion salad sweetened with sumac were another class act. Next, instead of predictable grills, try more unusual meat dishes such as duck with pomegranate and walnuts, or melting lamb baked with aubergines. More stops than usual are pulled out for dessert, with chocolate brownies, pistachio ice-cream and raspberry sauce vying with baklava and cinnamon ice-cream. To drink, there are cocktails, champagnes and a short but decent wine list. So, Pasha may not have the rough charm of completely authentic Turkish establishments, but it gets its version just right for the location.
Available for hire. Babies and children welcome: high chairs. Booking advisable. Tables outdoors (4, pavement). Takeaway service. **Map 5 O1.**

North West

Belsize Park

Zara

11 South End Road, NW3 2PT (7794 5498). Belsize Park tube or Hampstead Heath rail.
Meals served noon-11.30pm daily. **Main courses** £9-£15. **Credit** AmEx, MC, V.
At its best, Zara is a bonhomous neighbourhood joint producing Anatolian specialities and popular grills for loyal locals. Lunchtime deals help keep the weekday trade steady and, with the french doors pulled back, the front room is a pleasant spot to enjoy the bustle of South End Green. The sky-lit rear section is more intimate with its shelf of books, decorative musical instruments and gilt mirrors, but the advantage is diminished by its proximity to the loos and kitchen; the terracotta floor tiles are noisy too. We felt a little forgotten back there, but staff were pleasant enough. The workaday set meze is reasonable value, yet offers no surprises; try supplementing it with tender grilled curls of squid in lip-smacking pan gravy, or the moist, deliciously spicy sausages. We particularly enjoyed the thin-shelled, deep-fried köfte with juicy lamb interior. Larger appetites can follow with main courses such as islim kebab (diced lamb wrapped with aubergine, peppers and tomatoes), güveç chicken (baked with vegetables) and kuzu firin (baked lamb). Turkish vintages are the best choices on the wine list and not expensive; full-bodied Çankaya (made with indigenous Turkish grapes emir and narince) is a reliable choice.
Available for hire. Babies and children welcome: high chairs. Booking essential weekends. Tables outdoors (2, pavement). Takeaway service. Vegetarian menu. **Map 28 C3.**

Vegetarian

Do London's vegetarians get a raw deal? Well, yes and no. First, to dispense with the pun, raw food is increasingly making its crunchy presence felt, with the opening of two new cafés. Both **42° Raw** and **Wild Food Café** operate in the West End and at the budget end of the spectrum, recreating rice (from tiny chopped vegetables), bread (from cold-pressed seeds) and even lasagne (thin layers of veg with cashew 'cream'). If they're successful, doubtless we'll see some higher-end practitioners starting up. London's old guard of dedicated vegetarian restaurants may be small in number, but most continue to thrive. The City's excellent **Vanilla Black** has sprouted a cheaper Holborn café, **Orchard**, and Hammersmith favourite the **Gate** (set to recommence trading in autumn 2012 after a refurbishment) has opened a new, Middle Eastern-slanted branch in Islington.

Compared to those in many western capitals, meat-free diners in London are in clover. The cuisines of South India and Gujarat are fertile areas to explore (*see pp140-157*), but there are also plenty of delectable vegetarian meze dishes offered by Middle Eastern restaurants (*see pp195-202*). You want posh? An increasing number of top chefs are catering for non-meat eaters, so head for the delights of the **Hélène Darroze at the Connaught** (*see p136*), **Morgan M** (*see p89*) and **Murano** (*see p161*) and ask for their vegetarian menus. Something more experimental? Consult the Pan-Asian & Fusion chapter (*see pp226-232*) for eclectic, bold flavours from the likes of **Modern Pantry**, **NOPI** and the **Providores & Tapa Room**.

Central

Chancery Lane

★ Vanilla Black

17-18 Tooks Court, off Cursitor Street, EC4A 1LB (7242 2622, www.vanillablack.co.uk). Chancery Lane tube. **Lunch served** noon-2.30pm Mon-Fri. **Dinner served** 6-10pm Mon-Sat. **Set lunch** £18.50 2 courses, £23.50 3 courses. **Set meal** £26 2 courses, £35 3 courses. **Credit** AmEx, MC, V.

Vanilla Black staked out a niche in meatless haute cuisine in 2008 and hasn't wavered since, in standards or appeal. Diners come to this sophisticated space for business meetings, smart lunches and memorable dinners. Adornments are limited to streamlined chandeliers, muted paint colours, solid wood furniture, tasteful flower arrangements and starched linens – it could seem austere, but the charming, attentive staff help create a thoroughly pleasing dining experience. The understated interior is a stark contrast to the fireworks created on the plate, where unconventional, imaginative combinations of textures and flavours are showcased. Savoury mushroom mousse was presented with tarragon pancakes, bright pea purée, refreshing fennel and a palate-awakening fizzy grapefruit foam. A painterly dessert of burnt orange marshmallow (made with a vegetable gel in place of gelatine) surprised with sweet and crisp parsnip tendrils, though the parsnip purée was less successful. The hit rate is usually high, especially given the numerous different elements to be savoured in each dish. The set menus, especially at lunch, are exceptionally good value for cooking of this exalted standard. Recently opened offshoot Orchard (*see below*), which caters to a lunchtime crowd in Holborn, is also worth checking out.

Babies and children admitted. Booking advisable. Disabled: toilet. **Map 11 N6.**

Holborn

Orchard NEW

11 Sicilian Avenue, WC1A 2QH (7831 2715, www.orchard-kitchen.co.uk). Holborn tube. **Meals served** 8am-8pm Mon-Sat. **Main courses** £7.95-£9.95. **No credit cards.**

A cheaper, more casual spin-off from the accomplished, upmarket Vanilla Black (*see above*), this homely, retro-styled café can be found on traffic-free Sicilian Avenue. A counter near the entrance displays the day's sandwiches, salads, and cakes such as 'parsnip loaf with Horlicks icing', or orange-flavoured madeleines (served for breakfast, with warm chocolate sauce). A 'mug of soup with a sarnie' had freshly fried croûtons and chive oil garnishing the leek and potato soup; the sandwich bread was wholemeal and well textured, filled with sharp cheddar, chunky chutney and the red shock and crunch of baby beetroot leaves. A 'savoy cabbage pudding' used the textured leaf to provide a pretty wrap for the cheddar-laced centre; the accompanying heritage potatoes were blue spuds, and a slick of creamed celeriac and a red wine reduction made a handsome main course. Desserts are even more impressive: the innocent-sounding 'golden syrup pudding' was a neat tower, garnished with blobs of 'burnt' satsuma and whipped cream, which had a whiff of cinnamon. Another winner was the russet apple tart with butterscotch sauce. It's a pleasant surprise to find an excellent vegetarian café drawing on British ingredients and traditions with such delicious results.

Babies and children admitted. Bookings not accepted. Tables outdoors (8, pavement). Takeaway service. Vegan dishes. **Map 18 E1.**

Orchard. See p265.

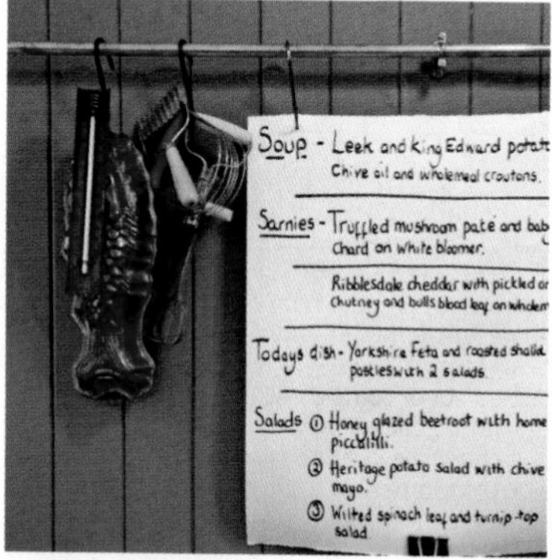

King's Cross

★ Itadaki Zen

139 King's Cross Road, WC1X 9BJ (7278 3573, www.itadakizen.com). King's Cross tube/rail. **Meals served** 6-10pm Mon-Thur; 6-10.30pm Fri, Sat. **Main courses** £6.50-£12. **Set meal** £15 3 courses, £21 4 courses. **Credit** MC, V.

Japanese, vegan, and organic? No wonder Itadaki Zen is the first of its kind in Europe. But despite operating from a narrow pool of ingredients, the predominately noodle/tofu/seaweed menu impresses with its range of tastes and textures. Grilled spring rolls with soft mashed tofu filling were a welcome change to the usual greasy, stringy sort, while the 'kakiage' tempura for a main had the same salty, crisp, golden, gorgeous smack as chips on Brighton pier, and came with fluffy rice. Our oh-so-casual waiter (dressed in jogging bottoms, no less) perfectly matched the restaurant's tone, with its frayed tie-dye hessian curtains and bunches of wheat swaying lazily from the ceiling. The Zen-like lack of music, chatter or even ticking clocks made us wary of slurping our udon noodles too loudly, although some may enjoy the tranquillity. All puddings are sugar-free on principle, which made the pumpkin cake with tofu cream too savoury for us, tasting as it did of Irish potato farl. Instead, maybe try a pungent sasou tea, made from bamboo leaf and buckwheat, which promises to soothe a weak stomach. Probably a good thing, after three courses of tofu.

Available for hire. Babies and children welcome: high chair. Separate room for parties, seats 14. Takeaway service. Vegan dishes. **Map 4 M3**.

Mayfair

★ Tibits

12-14 Heddon Street, W1B 4DA (7758 4110, www.tibits.co.uk/e). Oxford Circus or Piccadilly Circus tube. **Meals served** 9am-10pm Mon-Wed; 9am-11.30pm Thur-Sat; 11.30am-10pm Sun. **Buffet** lunch £2.10 per 100g; dinner £2.30 per 100g. **Credit** MC, V.

This small Swiss chain updates the buffet concept with a modern feel. Essentially a pimped-up salad bar, it's popular as a rest stop for shoppers. There's outdoor seating in a courtyard dubbed 'the Regent Street Food Quarter', and several punters were just treating it as a bar. It's less pretentious than its neighbours and perhaps that's what draws the crowds – the place was buzzing on a midweek evening. Staff explain the concept as you enter – pile up a plate (or takeaway container) on the central buffet boat and pay by weight, minus a free bread roll. For the Mayfair location, prices aren't bad, though the large choice of dishes can make it easy to overload your plate. Prices per 100g vary depending on the time of day, moving upwards from breakfast. Thirty-odd salads and hot dishes span the globe in their influences, and could include flavoursome coconut and tofu curry, crisp samosas, creamy gratins and pasta bakes made with organic eggs and cheese. Salads were fresh and embraced a varied array of produce from celeriac to chickpeas. The minimal selection of desserts (slabs of cheesecake and sticky toffee pudding) looked unappetising, but in general Tibits has hit on a successful formula.

Babies and children welcome: crayons; high chairs; nappy-changing facilities. Bookings not accepted for fewer than 8. Disabled: lift; toilet. Separate room for parties, seats 50. Tables outdoors (18, terrace). Takeaway service. Vegan dishes. **Map 17 A4**.

Soho

Mildreds

45 Lexington Street, W1F 9AN (7494 1634, www.mildreds.co.uk). Oxford Circus or Piccadilly Circus tube. **Meals served** noon-11pm Mon-Sat. **Main courses** £8-£10.50. **Credit** MC, V.

Only Lady Luck can get a table at Mildreds during peak hours, so if, like the rest of Soho, you want dinner at London's coolest vegetarian restaurant, be prepared to wait – you can't book. It's more the style of the place that attracts the crowds than its food; laid-back (but quick and friendly) waiters sport funky hairdos and tattoos, and noisy diners sit elbow-to-elbow on squishy banquettes. Beneath the cool exterior lies a relatively simple, rustic menu. To start, try asparagus with poached egg and shavings – nay, 'chunks' – of parmesan (expensive, at £6.25), or smoky dips with flatbread. The mains don't really extend beyond burritos, stir-fries, salads and the like, although each dish is made innovative by its ingredients. A quinoa, pea and leek burger was fresh and big in flavour, if a little dry: more basil mayo next time, please! By far the best dish was a side of sweet potato fries. With dreamy, creamy flesh and charred, chewy skin, they were best eaten in great quantity, dunked in sour cream. Runner-up was a very rich truffle torte, dotted with sharp raspberries and served with two forks – it was far too big for just one.

Babies and children welcome: high chairs. Bookings not accepted. Separate room for parties, seats 14. Tables outdoors (2, pavement). Takeaway service. Vegan dishes. **Map 17 A4**.

West

West Kensington

★ 222 Veggie Vegan

222 North End Road, W14 9NU (7381 2322, www.222veggievegan.com). West Kensington tube or West Brompton tube/rail or 28, 391 bus. **Lunch served** noon-3.30pm, **dinner served** 5.30-10.30pm daily. **Main courses** £7.50-£10.50. **Set lunch** £7.50 buffet. **Credit** MC, V.

Don't be misled by the name – everything at this North End Road eaterie is 100% vegan, and even raw foodists are welcome. A high ceiling and pretty lanterns are the only features to a cramped dining area: the niche food is the attraction, which is enough to entice a crowd of young, groovy diners every evening. Bean and tofu pancake to start was as light as the starchy ingredients would allow, but tasted bland and needed accompanying swigs of (good) organic English lager. For mains, though, a tropical mix of raw pumpkin and courgette noodles with fresh coconut and zingy lime sauce soon won us back, especially when coupled with such smiley service. It's hard to escape pungent dairy substitutes for pudding; the chocolate gateau was too far removed from the gooey loveliness non-vegans are used to. Maybe try the intriguing 'raw' spice island pie instead, a multi-textured cashew cream cheesecake on a crumbly coconutty base. The best dishes are those that champion fresh

Budget bites

Beatroot

92 Berwick Street, W1F 0QD (7437 8591, www.beatroot.org.uk). Oxford Circus, Piccadilly Circus or Tottenham Court Road tube. **Meals served** 9.15am-9pm Mon-Fri; 11am-9pm Sat. **Main courses** £4.30-£6.50. **Credit** MC, V.

For a fast, wholesome lunch, try this long-time favourite tucked next to the veg stalls of Berwick Street Market. Cartons come in three sizes, to be filled with a mix of tasty, freshly made salads and hot dishes (ten of each), on display behind a glass counter. Stalwarts include creamy coconutty dahl, lentil and mushroom shepherd's pie, organic rice salad with tamari soy sauce and seaweed, mini 'sausage' rolls or simple blanched broccoli – it's surprising how much you can cram in. Most people take away, but there are a few seats in the shabbily colourful interior, beneath the bird mobiles and bulbous orange lampshade, and more on the pavement outside. Friendly staff are kept busy chopping ingredients, replenishing dishes or whirring up juices and smoothies. Coffees and teas, vegan cakes (including hefty flapjacks made with hemp seed), and soft drinks by the likes of Purdey's and Fentimans are also available.

Babies and children admitted. Tables outdoors (5, pavement). Takeaway service. Vegan dishes. **Map 17 B3.**

Food for Thought

31 Neal Street, WC2H 9PR (7836 0239, www.foodforthought-london.co.uk). Covent Garden tube. **Meals served** noon-8pm Mon-Sat. **Lunch served** noon-5pm Sun. **Main courses** £4.90-£8. **Minimum** (noon-3pm, 6-7.30pm Mon-Sat) £3.50. **No credit cards.**

Celebrating its 40th birthday in 2014, Food for Thought is a phenomenon – still occupying the same cramped Neal Street premises, still serving an array of nourishing, flavourful grub at low prices, still packed out every lunchtime. The pine furniture and chunky stoneware plates have a 1970s vibe too. The menu changes daily, with soup, quiche, three hot mains – perhaps stir-fried veg with rice, or zingy cauliflower, spinach and pea curry – assorted salads, desserts and cakes. Vegan, wheat-free and gluten-free options are marked, but this isn't the place for protein faddists or superfood obsessives; expect hearty, carb-laden fare with a Mediterranean or Asian tinge. And expect hefty portions: the scones (savoury and sweet versions) are almost indecently large. For takeaway, head to the ground floor; to eat in, descend the steep stairs, order and pay for your food at the kitchen counter, and pray there'll be somewhere to sit. Staff are perfunctory and you'll need cash.

Babies and children admitted. Bookings not accepted. Takeaway service. Vegan dishes. **Map 18 D3.**

42° Raw NEW

6 Burlington Gardens, W1S 3ET (7300 8059, www.42raw.co.uk). Piccadilly Circus tube. **Meals served** 8.30am-6pm Mon-Fri. **Main courses** £7-£11. **Credit** MC, V.

Set within the rear entrance hall of the Royal Academy, this new café defies expectations by creating familiar-sounding dishes out of completely raw ingredients. Our 'Thai noodles' were ribbons of carrot and courgette in a raw coconut curry sauce, while the 'bread' in a sandwich was not baked, but made out of cold-pressed seeds. We were especially impressed by a stunning-looking lasagne: layers of thin vegetable slivers were teamed with cashew cream (a raw take on the classic béchamel), tomato sauce and parsley pesto and were topped with sunflower seeds; the taste was unexpectedly sweet and nutty. From the pretty cake display, a chewy 'cupcake' had been made with almond flour, dates, cashews and agave syrup, and came with a vegan icing of cashews and coconut oil. We found the service to be rather slow, so it might be unwise to visit if you're in a hurry.

Babies and children admitted. Bookings not accepted. Disabled: toilet. Tables outdoors (18, terrace). Takeaway service. Vegan dishes. **Map 9 J7.**

Wild Food Café NEW

1st floor, 14 Neal's Yard, WC2H 9DP (7419 2014, www.wildfoodcafe.com). Covent Garden tube. **Meals served** noon-5pm Mon-Wed, Sun; noon-10pm Thur-Sat. **Main courses** £4.50-£11.50. **Credit** MC, V.

Occupying the space that was once home to the World Food Café, this café above Neal's Yard now focuses on serving 'raw' food. Diners sit around the open kitchen, watching chefs employ futuristic techniques to create raw sandwiches, raw desserts and even a daily-changing soup (warmed to no more than 40°C and served at body temperature). We enjoyed the gentle spicing and depth of flavour of a raw 'red thai curry', served at room temperature with either raw 'ryce' (tiny chopped veg), or the real, conventionally cooked stuff. There is plenty more for non-raw diners too, from 'steaming hot' options such as 'provençal stew', or toasted sourdough sandwiches in lieu of 'raw bread'. Sandwich toppings are equally raw and intriguing, from pistachio falafel to raw squash and hemp houmous or coconut and almond 'cheeze'.

Available for hire. Babies and children welcome: high chair. Booking advisable (5-10pm Thur-Sat). Takeaway service. Vegan dishes. **Map 18 D3.**

42° Raw

ingredients and don't rely on substitutes. Near-£6 is too expensive for a lacklustre starter, but the all-you-can-eat lunchtime buffet is fantastic value.
Available for hire. Babies and children welcome: high chairs. Booking advisable. Takeaway service. Vegan dishes. **Map 13 A12.**

North

Camden Town & Chalk Farm

Manna

4 Erskine Road, NW3 3AJ (7722 8028, www.mannav.com). Chalk Farm tube or bus 31, 168. **Lunch served** noon-3pm Sat, Sun. **Dinner served** 6.30-10.15pm Tue-Sun. **Main courses** £10-£14. **Credit** AmEx, MC, V.
Even on weekday nights, this relaxed yet rather formal restaurant has several tables reserved by off-duty Primrose Hill-ites: friends catching up, yoga bunnies sharing boyfriend woes, romantic dates and birthday get-togethers. Few customers are confirmed vegetarians, which is a tribute to the quality and heartiness of the cooking. Portions are large, and help compensate for the steep pricing – expect to pay £15 for a main course, £8 for dessert. Dishes range from veggie caff staples to creative concoctions such as a delicious special of tempeh-filled cabbage rolls with Thai-style dipping sauce. A popular option is to choose four items from the mezes and sides to make your own main course; the flexible menu also offers a pasta, risotto and soup of the day. Burrito of white beans was distinguished by tangy smooth tomatillo and chunky pineapple salsas. Good malbec, from the entirely organic wine list, made a satisfying match. Dessert disappointed: it sounded like a tahini-flavoured pot of chocolate and arrived as an unattractive, over-rich pot of chocolate-flavoured tahini cream. Service is friendly, unobtrusive and proper, which suits the casual elegance of the glittery flora-themed room. The skinny front conservatory is a prime target on grey days.
Babies and children welcome: high chairs; children's menu. Booking essential weekends. Tables outdoors (2, conservatory). Takeaway service. Vegan dishes. **Map 27 A1.**

Islington

Gate

370 St John Street, EC1V 4NN (7278 5483, www.thegaterestaurants.com). Angel tube. **Brunch served** 10am-3pm Sat, Sun. **Meals served** noon-11pm Mon-Fri; 3-11pm Sat, Sun. **Main courses** £13-£15.50. **Set meal** (noon-3pm, 6-10.30pm) £12.50 2 courses. **Set meze** (noon-11pm Mon-Fri; 3-11pm Sat, Sun) £4-£15. **Credit** AmEx, MC, V.
First established in the late 1980s in Hammersmith, the Gate has finally opened a second branch in Islington, morphing in every respect to match its far-trendier surroundings. The only thing not modern and breezy about this vegetarian restaurant (a former Victorian butcher's) is the ornate, listed tiling on one side of the room – a unique feature that reflects the equally original menu. Food here has a Middle Eastern twist, far more ethnic than its Hammersmith sister. Pick from either the meze menu – fritters bursting with salty feta flavour; tart mushroom ceviche; featherlight artichoke tempura – or the carte, which refreshingly avoids using meat substitutes. Squeaky halloumi drizzled in a tikka marinade to start was well cooked, but a little mean in portion size for £6.50. For mains, asparagus rotolo (a cheesy roll-up of Mediterranean vegetables and thyme potato) was as light as soufflé, and Thai favourites were piled high in a spicy summer salad, topped with an abundance of crushed peanuts. Friendly but uninformed waiters need more time to get used to the menu, and although our seasonal crumble with crème anglaise did the job, we would have preferred an extra round of meze instead.
Available for hire. Babies and children welcome: high chairs; nappy-changing facilities. Booking advisable. Disabled: toilet. Vegan dishes.
Map 5 O3.
For branch see index.

Gate

Vietnamese

Not so long ago, Londoners in search of genuine Vietnamese cookery looked wistfully across the Channel to Paris. No longer. First came the Vietnamese people – refugees and others – many of whom settled in east London, or more particularly around Shoreditch and Hackney. After a while they opened eating places near their homes, initially for others in their community. Then Shoreditch became trendy, the Kingsland Road became the 'pho corridor' and the rest is history. Except that history continues down its jaunty path, and the Vietnamese dining scene is starting to embark on its next phase of development: the diaspora away from the heartland. Thus you can now sample the cuisine in Hammersmith at **Saigon Saigon** and in Finchley at **Khoai Café** and **Vy Nam Café**. In addition, two of the most successful east London practitioners have opened branches elsewhere in the capital: **Cây Tre** in Soho, and **Mien Tay** in Battersea. Nevertheless, the Kingsland Road remains the prime hunting ground for top-notch pho – and is the home of our long-time favourite Vietnamese establishment, **Song Que**.

Central

Soho

Cây Tre

42-43 Dean Street, W1D 4PZ (7317 9118, www.caytresoho.co.uk). Leicester Square tube. **Meals served** noon-11pm Mon-Thur; noon-11.30pm Fri, Sat; noon-10pm Sun. **Main courses** £8-£11. **Set meal** £22.50 3 courses (minimum 2). **Credit** MC, V.

Cay Tre's Shoreditch branch was closed for a refurb at the time of review, leaving the newer Soho outpost flying the flag for creative, mainly southern Vietnamese cooking. The long, narrow room feels a world apart from the in-out caffs of the 'pho mile' on Kingsland Road; the slick, contemporary, monochrome design is enticing and devoid of any bamboo-and-conical-hat clichés. The cooking is also a lot more colourful and innovative than the standard spring rolls and pho (although both here are superb, the pho available in eight versions). Staff can be a bit bullish when it comes to upselling: our waitress more or less told us we were having the special starter of steamed, dumpling-like rolls with ground pork and a fragrant dipping sauce (it was excellent). Also great were main courses of dong du lamb, a rich, spicy, Indian-accented curry with aubergine, and roast pork belly, stuffed with sweet curry leaves. Other unusual dishes include surf clams with lemongrass and chilli, ox cheek 'au vin' with cinammon and cardamom, and black mushroom hotpot. Although the Vietnamese staples are great, variation executed with this level of skill is always welcome.

Babies and children welcome: nappy-changing facilities. Booking advisable. Disabled: toilet. Takeaway service. **Map 17 B4.**

For branches (Cây Tre, Viet Grill) see index.

West

Hammersmith

Saigon Saigon

313-317 King Street, W6 9NH (0870 220 1398, www.saigon-saigon.co.uk). Ravenscourt Park or Stamford Brook tube. **Lunch served** noon-2.30pm Mon-Fri; noon-3pm Sat; 12.30-3pm Sun. **Dinner served** 6-10pm Mon, Sun; 6-11pm Tue-Thur; 6-11.30pm Fri, Sat. **Main courses** £6.95-£15. **Credit** MC, V.

In contrast to the riches of east London, there's a dearth of Vietnamese joints churning out fantastic low-priced food in the west of the city. Saigon Saigon, on the quiet end of King Street, partially fills the gap with its extensive menu of classics that allows locals to feast on pho, bun and cook-your-own steamboats amid attractive surroundings (white walls, dark wood, ethnic gold). Room divisions create an intimacy that belies the large space, and tables can spill on to the wide pavement in summer. Expect hits and misses with the food; staff aren't enthusiastic enough to steer your choices. Portions are generous and full of fresh ingredients, but the same flavours appear repeatedly across dishes, which can lead to monotony if you order a few to share. There's generally a liberal use of fried shallots, a restraint with the chilli, and a sweet, lacklustre nuoc cham sauce that seems to come with everything. Still, this is a pleasant place to get your South-east Asian fix without the need to venture east.

Available for hire (bar). Booking advisable. Babies and children welcome: high chairs. Tables outdoors (4, pavement). Vegetarian menu. **Map 20 A4.**

South East

Surrey Quays

★ Café East

Surrey Quays Leisure Park, 100 Redriff Row, SE16 7LH (7252 1212, www.cafeeast.co.uk). Canada Water tube/rail or Surrey Quays rail. **Lunch served** 11am-3pm, **dinner served** 5.30-10.30pm Mon, Wed-Fri. **Meals served** 11am-10.30pm Sat; noon-10pm Sun. **Main courses** £6-£7.50. **Unlicensed** no alcohol allowed. **No credit cards**.

In-the-know fans of pho seek out this hard-to-find restaurant for authentic and good-value Vietnamese cooking. Café East is in a remote corner of a leisure complex, and if you're not driving

involves a dispiriting walk across a car park. Inside, it's not much to look at – plain walls, paper tablecloths, plastic crockery – but the largely young, South-east Asian crowd who flock here nightly don't seem to care. Take a ticket from a waitress at the door and wait for your number to be called. Once seated, you're presented with a mercifully brief menu that covers the classics: soups, rolls (both fried and fresh), cold noodle dishes with grilled meats. There are a few lesser-seen dishes too, such as goi cuon (spring rolls with ground rice and shredded pork skin) and cha hue, sausage-style sliced meatloaf. All soups are offered with spicy or regular base stock. Portions are huge (order austerely), but staff will box up leftovers. No alcohol is served, and signs pointedly state that tap water won't be provided, so choose a refreshing coconut water or che ba mau jelly drink. Consistently one of London's best Vietnamese dining experiences. Note that the restaurant is usually closed for about a month from late July.
Babies and children welcome: high chairs. Bookings not accepted. Disabled: toilet. Takeaway service.

East

Shoreditch

★ Mien Tay

122 Kingsland Road, E2 8DP (7729 3074, www.mientay.co.uk). Hoxton rail. **Lunch served** noon-3pm, **dinner served** 5-11pm Mon-Sat. **Meals served** noon-10pm Sun. **Main courses** £6-£12.50. **Credit** MC, V.

Not much changes at family-run Mien Tay. It's still one of the least fancified restaurants in the Kingsland Road Vietnamese enclave; decor in the odd two-room set-up could be generously described as 'homely', although more realistically it's in sore need of a sprucing up. Service is still brisk, occasionally warm. But, reassuringly, the food is still brilliant: this remains one of the best (and best-value) places to eat Vietnamese in London. Don't visit without ordering the barbecued quail – a quartered and blackened bird, marinated in spices and honey, and served simply with a chilli and herb salad, and an aromatic dipping salt. Cutlery is definitely not required. The menu focuses on the cuisine of south-west Vietnam, although there are dishes from elsewhere: the pho is a fine version, if a bit too liberally speckled with sliced red onion. A speciality is the whole 'hard-fried' fish, served with green mango: perfect for picking over with chopsticks. Seafood hotpots are also popular. If you can ignore the worn-out surroundings – and crowds of diners do so every night – Mien Tay's a winner.
Babies and children welcome: high chairs. Disabled: toilet. Takeaway service. **Map 6 R3.**
For branch see index.

★ Song Que 

134 Kingsland Road, E2 8DY (7613 3222, http://songque.co.uk). Hoxton rail. **Lunch served** noon-3pm, **dinner served** 5.30-11pm Mon-Fri. **Meals served** 12.30-11pm Sat, Sun. **Main courses** £4.80-£11.80. **Credit** (over £10) MC, V.

There are several restaurants of note in the Vietnamese hotspot on Kingsland Road, but the stalwart Song Que, found slightly away from the pack up towards Haggerston, is somewhere that stands out over repeat visits. The corner site with its large windows and effortless decor doesn't do much to excite the senses as you wait for a table (as is inevitable if you haven't booked), and it's true that the attitude of the hustling staff is more functional than friendly. But the food is good enough to overlook hospitality shortcomings, and prices haven't risen disproportionately with popularity. The menu is a formidably extensive list of dishes from the north and south of Vietnam, as is common in most such restaurants. You could visit every day for a year and eat a different dish, but classics are brilliantly executed. The beef pho – warming, subtly spiced, generous with the meat – is one of the best bowlfuls in London, while the likes of chargrilled quail; fragrant ground beef in betel leaf; fried and fresh rolls; bun cha (grilled pork mince with noodles); and fruity, chilli-laden salads are consistently superb.
Babies and children welcome: high chairs. Booking advisable. Disabled: toilet. Vegetarian menu. **Map 6 R3.**

North East

Dalston

★ Huong-Viet

An Viet House, 12-14 Englefield Road, N1 4LS (7249 0877). Dalston Junction or Haggerston rail or 67, 149, 236, 242, 243 bus. **Lunch served** noon-3pm, **dinner served** 5.30-11pm daily. **Main courses** £6.90-£11.30. **No credit cards.**

VIETNAMESE

Set in the premises of a longstanding Vietnamese community centre, behind a hedge and indicated only by a small sign, Huong-Viet feels like a bit of a secret. It's well known, though, among locals looking for Vietnamese food a little north of the main Shoreditch drag. Inside, the windowless space has an intimate, homely feel. When things get busy, the staff can become abrupt and some dishes can be average, but on the whole the place is lively and fun. Starters such as traditional Vietnamese pancakes, spring rolls and crispy seaweed give on to a long list of mains, including pork with aubergine and garlic, sizzling prawns with ginger and spring onion, and more unusual barbecue dishes such as prawns wrapped in pork. Vietnamese special salad had grated crudités with a little pineapple, topped with crushed peanuts – a combination that was pleasantly sweet, zingy and crunchy. Rice vermicelli with seafood, lemongrass and chilli was a big bowlful, with plenty of seafood, including scallops, subtle spicing, and mint adding a distinctive edge. Good, honest, flavourful food – and good value too.
Babies and children welcome: high chairs. Booking advisable weekends. Disabled: toilet. Separate rooms for parties, both seating 30. Takeaway service.

Hackney

★ Green Papaya

191 Mare Street, E8 3QE (8985 5486, www.green-papaya.com). London Fields rail or 26, 48, 55, 277, D6 bus. **Dinner served** 5-11pm Tue-Sun. **Main courses** £5-£8. **Credit** MC, V.

Over in the trendier side of Hackney, Kingsland Road's Vietnamese restaurants draw in the crowds, but here in Mare Street there's a more casual vibe – and this homely place is the pick of the bunch. The walls are a deep Communist red, dotted with watercolours of the homeland; the furniture is basic and unselfconsciously scuffed. There's a new printed menu this year, which showcases dishes from the north of the country, and the specials include a few lesser-seen treats – venison with coconut and shallot, say, or wing bean salad, or thit bo xao ot (stir-fried beef with cumin and chilli). We were delighted with everything on our most recent visit, including deep-fried squid with spring onion and a light dipping sauce, and a superb banh tom – sweet potato rösti with prawns, here appearing as a pan-sized cake cut into slices. The pho is a gratifying bowl, and even at £6.50 isn't shy with the rare beef. A steady stream of locals troop in of an evening for relaxed dinners, takeaways and a chat with the friendly boss.
Babies and children welcome: high chairs. Booking advisable. Disabled: toilet. Takeaway service.

Tre Viet

247 Mare Street, E8 3NS (8986 8885, www.treviet.co.uk). London Fields rail or 26, 48, 55, 277, D6 bus. **Meals served** noon-11pm Mon-Thur, Sun; noon-11.30pm Fri, Sat. **Main courses** £4.70-£13. **Set meal** £19 per person (minimum 2) 3 dishes. **Credit** MC, V.

A gentle spruce-up has brought even more bamboo latticing and a delicate wall-sized mural to this local favourite. No change to the food, though: it remains as reliable and tasty as ever. Away from the weekend mania of Shoreditch's Vietnamese corridor, this Hackney Central restaurant has managed to develop its own buzzy, mixed crowd of faithfuls, thanks in no small part to the arrival of the Hackney Picturehouse cinema virtually opposite. A clientele consisting of families, groups of friends and couples keeps the patient, helpful staff busy with questions about a menu that ranges from ever-popular peking duck, hearty pho soups and fresh, fat summer rolls, to a great selection of stewed hotpots, sizzling meats and seafood dishes. We tried a wonderfully crunchy and perfectly cooked crispy soft-shelled crab, and chilli salt and pepper squid that ranked among the best we've tasted. A £19 set menu brings together some of Tre Viet's best dishes, with a nicely varied range of mains. Alternatively, given the consistently strong selection, you could let the movie you've just seen inspire your choices. We've never had a dud dish yet.
Booking advisable weekends. Disabled: toilet. Takeaway service.
For branch (Lang Nuong) see index.

Cây Tre. See p269.

Menu

Vietnamese cookery makes abundant use of fresh, fragrant herbs such as mint and sweet basil; it also utilises refreshing, sweet-sour dipping sauces known generically as nuoc cham. Look out for spices such as chilli, ginger and lemongrass, and crisp root vegetables pickled in sweetened vinegar.

Some dishes are assembled at the table in a way that is distinctively Vietnamese. Order a steaming bowl of pho (rice noodles and beef or chicken in an aromatic broth) and you'll be invited to add raw herbs, chilli and citrus juice as you eat. Crisp pancakes and grilled meats are served with herb sprigs, lettuce leaf wraps and piquant dipping sauces. Toss cold rice vermicelli with salad leaves, herbs and hot meat or seafood fresh from the grill. All these dishes offer an intriguing mix of tastes, temperatures and textures.

Aside from the pronounced Chinese influence on Vietnamese culinary culture, there are hints of the French colonial era (in sweet iced coffee, for example, and the use of beef), along with echoes of neighbouring South-east Asian cuisines. Within Vietnamese cooking itself there are several regional styles; the mix of immigrants in London means you can sample some of the styles here. The food of Hanoi and the north is known for its street snacks and plain, no-nonsense flavours and presentation. The former imperial capital Hue and its surrounding region are famed for a royal cuisine and robustly spicy soups; look out for Hue noodle soups (bun bo hue) on some menus. The food of the south and the former Saigon (now Ho Chi Minh City) is more elegant and colourful, and makes much greater use of fresh herbs (many of these unique to Vietnam), vegetables and fruit.

Banh cuon: pancake-like steamed rolls of translucent fresh rice pasta, sometimes stuffed with minced pork or shrimp (reminiscent in style of Chinese cheung fun, a dim sum speciality).
Banh pho: flat rice noodles used in soups and stir-fries, usually with beef.
Banh xeo: a large pancake made from a batter of rice flour and coconut milk, coloured bright yellow with turmeric and traditionally filled with prawns, pork, beansprouts and onion. To eat it, tear the pancake apart with your chopsticks, roll the pieces with sprigs of herbs in a lettuce leaf, and dip in nuoc cham (qv).
Bo la lot: grilled minced beef in betel leaves.
Bun: rice vermicelli, served in soups and stir-fries. They are also eaten cold, with raw salad vegetables and herbs, with a nuoc cham (qv) sauce poured over, and a topping such as grilled beef or pork – all of which are tossed together at the table.
Cha ca: North Vietnamese dish of fish served sizzling in an iron pan with plenty of dill.
Cha gio: deep-fried spring rolls. Unlike their Chinese counterparts, the wrappers are made from rice paper rather than sheets of wheat pastry, and pucker up deliciously after cooking.

Chao tom: grilled minced prawn on a baton of sugar cane.
Goi: salad. There are many types in Vietnam, but they often contain raw, crunchy vegetables and herbs, perhaps accompanied by chicken or prawns, with a sharp, perky dressing.
Goi cuon (literally 'rolled salad', often translated as 'fresh rolls' or 'salad rolls'): cool, soft, rice-paper rolls usually containing prawns, pork, fresh herbs and rice vermicelli, served with a thick sauce similar to satay sauce but made from hoi sin mixed with peanut butter, scattered with roasted peanuts.
Nem: north Vietnamese name for cha gio (qv).
Nom: north Vietnamese name for goi (qv).
Nuoc cham: the generic name for a wide range of dipping sauces, based on a paste of fresh chillies, sugar and garlic that is diluted with water, lime juice and the ubiquitous fish sauce, nuoc mam.
Nuoc mam: a brown or pale liquid derived from fish that have been salted and left to ferment. It's the essential Vietnamese seasoning, used in dips and as a cooking ingredient.
Pho: the most famous and best-loved of all Vietnamese dishes, a soup of rice noodles and beef or chicken in a rich, clear broth flavoured with aromatics. It's served with a dish of fresh beansprouts, red chilli and herbs, and a squeeze of lime; these are added to the soup at the table.
Rau thom: aromatic herbs, which might include Asian basil (**rau que**), mint (**rau hung**), red or purple perilla (**rau tia to**), lemony Vietnamese balm (**rau kinh gioi**) or saw-leaf herb (**ngo gai**).
Tuong: a general term for a thick sauce. One common tuong is a dipping sauce based on fermented soy beans, with hints of sweet and sour, often garnished with crushed roasted peanuts.

North

Finchley

★ Khoai Café

362 Ballards Lane, N12 0EE (8445 2039, www.khoai.co.uk). Woodside Park tube or 82, 134 bus. **Lunch served** noon-3.30pm, **dinner served** 5.30-11.30pm daily. **Main courses** £5-£11.25. **Set lunch** £5.95 1 course, £8.45 2 courses. **Credit** AmEx, MC, V.

In an area lacking culinary excitement, Khoai Café is a reliable and useful local. Behind its strident green frontage is a spacious, modern and spotless restaurant with shiny tiled floor, blond wood furniture and soothing pale walls in buttermilk and toffee tones. Over several years, we've enjoyed decent meals and takeaways here – and at the Crouch End original – but the kitchen wasn't on top form during our latest visit. A few things we ordered (bo la lot, Saigon beer) were unavailable, and greasy prawn toast arrived at the table instead of prawn satay. Cooking lacked verve too: morning glory was stir-fried with garlic and oyster sauce to an unappealing grey-green colour; chewy white fish arrived in a gloopy caramel sauce; and Vietnamese cuisine's enticing array of sparky herbs seemed limited to coriander and mint. Still, service was courteous and accommodating as usual, and we revelled in a turmeric-yellow crispy golden crêpe generously studded with large prawns and slices of delicious barbecue pork. Hue and Hanoi lagers are perfectly acceptable alternatives to Saigon; there's also a reasonable choice of inexpensive wines, plus intensely sweet own-made lemonade for those wanting to skip the booze.

Available for hire. Babies and children welcome: high chairs. Disabled: toilet. Takeaway service.

For branch see index.

Vy Nam Café

371 Regents Park Road, N3 1DE (8371 4222). Finchley Central tube. **Lunch served** noon-3pm, **dinner served** 5-11pm daily. **Main courses** £6.80-£13. **Credit** AmEx, MC, V.

Spread over two floors, this homely restaurant filled with glass and basket-weave furniture brings a hint of the tropics to a suburban Finchley high street. Takeaway trade seems to be roaring, thanks not least to the near-tube location. Dine-in custom on our recent visit ranged from elderly local couples to young Vietnamese students. There's a sense that the repertoire has been restrained since launch (freshly squeezed juice combos, for example, were on the printed menu but not available), though in other respects Vy Nam keeps standards high. Lotus root and prawn salad laden with sesame seeds and shredded mint was simple yet punchy. A tureen of superb crab and egg stew, generous with shellfish and rich with tomato, showcased the French colonial influence on Vietnamese cuisine and offered a flavourful yet unfiery alternative to our chilli-laden vermicelli noodle salad and spicy chicken curry. Vietnamese special fried rice was undistinguished, but comforting nonetheless; more adventurous diners can opt for sizzling goat, or frogs' legs. Vietnamese beers and kind service add to the attraction of what is a very welcome destination amid Finchley's all-too pedestrian dining options.

Available for hire. Babies and children welcome: high chair; nappy-changing facilities. Booking advisable weekends. Disabled: toilet.

Cheap Eats

Budget

London dining doesn't have to cost an arm and a leg – though you might need to go out on a limb to find the best budget venues. Throughout this guide we've used a green star symbol (★) to denote inexpensive eateries, where it's possible to buy a three-course meal for around £25 a head. Many of these are in less affluent areas: the Indian restaurants of Tooting or Whitechapel, for instance, or the Turkish cafés of Dalston. Here, we've listed some of our favourite budget establishments – encompassing caffs, diners, bistros and more – including a few that are sited in otherwise expensive districts such as the City or Kingston (home of the new branch of Bavarian specialist **Stein's**). Two of our top spots this year embrace the old and the new: the fabulous century-old East End café **E Pellicci**, and the hip original Soho branch of **Hummus Bros**. We also love the dinky rice balls at Kentish Town's new **Arancini Factory** and the cut-price global cooking at Battersea's **Galapagos Bistro-Café**. Also worth a visit is the **Vincent Rooms** (Westminster Kingsway College, Vincent Square, SW1P 2PD, 7802 8391, www.westking.ac.uk, map 15 J10): head here in term time for high-quality, low-priced meals prepared and served by the college's catering students.

Central

City

Café Below

St Mary-le-Bow, Cheapside, EC2V 6AU (7329 0789, www.cafebelow.co.uk). St Paul's tube or Bank tube/DLR. **Meals served** 8am-3pm Mon-Fri. **Main courses** £3.50-£7.50. **Credit** MC, V.

This long-running café in the crypt beneath St Mary-le-Bow Church in the heart of the City has returned to serving just breakfast and lunch after a stint of also opening in the evening. Descend the stone stairs and queue at the kitchen counter for hot dishes (lamb burger or salmon fish cakes, perhaps), salads (rice, puy lentil and mushroom) or sandwiches (Porterford sausages and onion marmalade). It's busy for takeaway lunches, but many people eat in – at the crammed wooden tables in the rough-walled crypt itself, or outside in the courtyard. Avoid the 1-2pm slot if you want to be sure of a seat. Cooking is hearty rather than refined, and vegetarians fare well (the café was veggie-only for years) with the likes of courgette and feta filo pie with salad leaves: tasty, but on the watery side. Puds – such as comforting rhubarb crumble and custard, or a slice of rich, mousse-like chocolate espresso tart – are worth a punt. Prices have risen, so it's no longer such a bargain, but oft-replenished jugs of tap water with mint and lemon halves are a welcome touch.

Available for hire. Babies and children welcome: high chairs. Booking advisable lunch. Tables outdoors (20, churchyard). Takeaway service. Vegan dishes. Vegetarian menu. **Map 11 P6.**

Clerkenwell & Farringdon

Little Bay

171 Farringdon Road, EC1R 3AL (7278 1234, www.little-bay.co.uk). Farringdon tube/rail. **Meals served** noon-midnight Mon-Sat; noon-11pm Sun. **Main courses** £7.95-£11.95. **Credit** MC, V.

The Farringdon branch of this cut-price chain looks vaguely like a Greek taverna until you see the menu, which is in French (and English). What's most striking, however, are the prices. With all starters at £2.65 and mains only £5.95, entering Little Bay is like stepping back in time. Soup of the day, carrot and coriander, was really rather good, while grilled chicken satay was perfectly edible – but not really satay as we know it, despite the crunchy peanut-butter sauce. Roast spiced fillet of salmon with couscous and chickpeas was good, even if the chickpeas didn't really suit the other ingredients; no such problems with roast duck breast with butternut squash, red cabbage and a honey-ginger sauce. If you don't overdo it on rich main courses, you might feel like a slice of apple cake, profiteroles or some chocolate log (all desserts cost £2.65). Decent beers and wines are available, although they'll bump the bill up as they're not quite as wallet-friendly as the food. Service is welcoming and efficient. On Sundays, there's roast beef or pork, at slightly higher prices.

Babies and children welcome: high chairs. Booking advisable. Disabled: toilet. Separate room for parties, seats 120. **Map 5 N4.**

For branches see index.

Covent Garden

Canela

33 Earlham Street, WC2H 9LS (7240 6926, www.canelacafe.com). Covent Garden tube. **Meals served** 10.30am-10.30pm Mon-Sat; 10.30am-8.30pm Sun. **Main courses** £5-£12. **Credit** (over £7) MC, V.

Most of the menu at this little Brazilian/Portuguese café is on show in the cold cabinet, including quiches, salads, Brazilian cheese bread, and the likes of vegetarian lasagne or meatballs in tomato sauce waiting to be heated up. Half the space is taken up with puddings and cakes, such as the chocolate mud cake (served warm) or the classic Portuguese custard tart. There's also soup of the day, plus dishes such as Mozambique chicken curry (a rather dull, one-note dish, served with rice) and the excellent Brazilian version of feijoada (a stew of black beans and smoked meats, here served with rice, farofa – toasted manioc flour – and what resembles a chunky version of pork scratchings). Soft drinks include fresh mint tea and juices, plus Guaraná and other fizzy options, and, of course,

coffee. In the daylight Canela's small red and black premises look slightly in need of a spruce-up, but at night the Portuguese wines and caipirinhas come into their own and the chandelier and the huge gilt mirror look less out of place. Staff are charming, whatever the hour.
Babies and children admitted. Tables outdoors (4, pavement). Takeaway service. **Map 18 D3.**

Soho

★ Hummus Bros
88 Wardour Street, W1F 0TJ (7734 1311, www.hbros.co.uk). Oxford Circus or Tottenham Court Road tube. **Meals served** noon-10pm Mon-Wed; noon-11pm Thur-Sat; noon-9pm Sun. **Main courses** £3.50-£8.60. **Credit** AmEx, MC, V.
'Give peas a chance' is the cheeky slogan for this laid-back snack bar devoted to the humble chickpea or, more precisely, its creamy offshoot, houmous. This Soho shop, with its shiny red communal tables, bench seating and large windows overlooking Wardour Street, is the original. There are also branches in Holborn and near St Paul's; we'd be happy to see them everywhere. Order and pay for your meal at the counter; at lunchtime, the queue for takeaways snakes out on to Wardour Street. You'll get a bowl of silky-smooth houmous, with a dollop of tahini, a sprinkling of paprika and two warm wholemeal pittas (regular size – just one pitta with the small), plus a topping of your choice. Chunky slow-cooked beef, perhaps, or juicy guacamole with red peppers and red onions, or our favourite: mashed, cumin-scented fava beans. You can add a side salad – options include zingy tabouleh made with plenty of parsley, or barbecued aubergine – or customise your plate with extras such as tortilla chips, carrot sticks or hard-boiled egg. Fresh mint and ginger lemonade is the perfect match for the Middle Eastern flavours, or there are coffees and juices. The young, international staff keep things moving smoothly.
Babies and children welcome: high chairs. Bookings not accepted. Takeaway service. Vegan dishes. Vegetarian menu. **Map 17 B3.**
For branches see index.

Leon
36-38 Old Compton Street, W1D 4TT (7434 1200, www.leonrestaurants.co.uk). Tottenham Court Road tube. **Meals served** 8.30am-10pm Mon-Wed; 8.30am-11pm Thur; 8.30am-1am Fri; 11am-1am Sat; noon-10pm Sun. **Main courses** £3.95-£6.75. **Set dinner** (6pm-close Mon-Sat) £27.50 2 courses (2 people). **Credit** AmEx, MC, V.
This fun, fairly fast-food chain continues to impress with its inventive range of wraps, salads, rice boxes and soups, building on a reputation for healthy, global cuisine that's both inexpensive and appealing. Part of Leon's charm lies in its well-designed interiors, and this branch is particularly attractive, with big window tables giving a ringside view of Old Compton Street's lively goings-on, and a cosy book-lined basement offering space for quiet contemplation. At the counter, choice is made difficult by a wide array of dishes that all sound good. On the whole, they are: a superfood salad featured crunchy broccoli and cucumber mixed with lots of peas and quinoa, ripe avocado, feta and fresh mint, and a side of baked fries provided a commendably grease-free boost of carbs. Soups are flavoursome and stuffed with fresh ingredients: a red pepper and wensleydale was silky and filling, the cheese adding a nice sharp touch to the sweet peppers. Not everything works – unless you're under 12, we'd advise steering clear of the fish fingers and meatballs – but for its dedication to sustainably sourced ingredients and a menu of good home-style cooking, Leon stands out.
Babies and children welcome: children's menu; high chairs; nappy-changing facilities. Disabled: toilet. Separate room for parties, seats 50. Tables outdoors (4, pavement). Takeaway service. Vegetarian menu. **Map 17 C4.**
For branches see index.

Pierre Victoire
5 Dean Street, W1D 3RQ (7287 4582, www.pierrevictoire.com). Tottenham Court Road tube. **Meals served** noon-11pm Mon-Wed, Sun; noon-11.30pm Thur-Sat. **Main courses** £9.90-£14.90. **Set lunch** (noon-4pm) £9.90 2 courses. **Set dinner** (4-7pm) £12.90 2 courses. **Credit** AmEx, MC, V.
Enter this bijou Soho bistro and you're greeted by a whiff of garlic and a big frog statue smiling down from the back of the room. Walls are decorated with colourful amateur paintings, depicting rural France, while rustic wooden tables are adorned with a bottle of red – ready to be popped open if diners decide to wine and dine. The two-course lunch/dinner deal, priced at £9.90/£12.90 respectively, is a real bargain in the world of Soho dining. Choose your starter and main from an extensive menu that features French classics such as goat's cheese salad, steak frites and sole meunière. There are also quite a few dishes that lean towards gastropub grub – you'd never spot cumberland sausages with mash in a Paris brasserie. A starter of garlic mussels was a fine twist on the traditional snail version, mimicking the original in texture and with a garlicky punch. The gratin dauphinois that accompanied a confit duck leg was perfect, with thin layers of creamy potato, while the red cabbage with sultanas made this dish proper French comfort food. Generous portions and a pristine presentation rendered the low price tag even more appealing. A Frenchman would definitely give his *accord*.
Babies and children welcome: high chairs. Booking advisable. Separate room for parties, seats 25. Tables outdoors (2, pavement). **Map 17 B3.**

Stockpot
18 Old Compton Street, W1D 4TN (7287 1066). Leicester Square or Tottenham Court Road tube. **Meals served** 9am-11.30pm Mon, Tue; 9am-midnight Wed-Sat; noon-11.30pm Sun. **Main courses** £3.95-£9.10. **Set meal** £7.10 2 courses. **No credit cards.**
Soho restaurants open and close all the time, but Stockpot somehow remains. Known for its wallet-friendly, filling food, the restaurant attracts a diverse clientele. From Japanese tourists to groups of elderly ladies enjoying a pre-theatre meal and local workers reading the papers while tucking into a hearty lunch, Stockpot unites them all. The nostalgia-packed dishes are served in tacky, old-school surroundings – a wooden interior with varnished tables and sticky plastic menus adds to the experience – that seem stuck in the 1960s, but charmingly so. Choose from the likes of fried liver with mash, beef stroganoff and banana split. Food lacks pretensions: a generous slab of creamy fish pie came served with a side of two veg – bland and unsalted, but who's complaining when prices hover around the £6 mark? Add friendly and speedy service to the mix, and you see why Stockpot remains a Soho institution. The two other Stockpot restaurants in the West End have no connection to this one.
Babies and children admitted. Tables outdoors (2, pavement). Takeaway service. **Map 17 C3.**

South

Battersea

Galapagos Bistro-Café
169 Battersea High Street, SW11 3JS (8488 4989). Clapham Junction rail. **Meals served** 9.30am-9.30pm Tue-Sat. **Main courses** £7.50-£9.95. **Set lunch** (noon-4pm) £10.95 2 courses, £13.95 3 courses. **Set dinner** (6.30-9.30pm) £12.95 2 courses, £15.95 3 courses. **Credit** MC, V.
Years before a long-necked chain began trampling on the terrain of 'world food', this tiny neighbourhood bistro was quietly going about its business. Here you can go globe-trotting through the likes of Moroccan lamb tagine, a Corsican beef stew or escalope of chicken Milanese, all without dusting off your passport. Interiors are low-budget but homely, the laminate flooring and faded upholstery spruced up with colourful cushions and ceiling-hung miniature glitter balls, while a mosaic of a turtle gives a nod to the eponymous group of Pacific islands. On our visit, a starter of gyoza with a dense pork, ginger and chive filling hit all the right notes, as did a well-spiced and fragrant curry of chicken, lentils and split peas. Elsewhere, there are café staples, from breakfasts and burgers, though special mention should go to the large collection of intriguing own-made preserves, from whiskey marmalade to spiced courgette and fennel chutney. Our waitress may have been a little vacant, but the Ecuadorian owner was charming and chatty. Galapagos Bistro-Café brings much-needed cheer to a tired street.
Available for hire. Babies and children admitted. Booking advisable. Tables outdoors (2, pavement). Takeaway service.

East

Bethnal Green

★ E Pellicci
332 Bethnal Green Road, E2 0AG (7739 4873). Bethnal Green tube/rail or bus 8. **Meals served** 7am-4pm Mon-Sat. **Main courses** £6.40-£8.20. **Unlicensed. Corkage** no charge. **No credit cards.**
You go to Pellicci's as much to dine on the atmosphere as the food. Opened in 1900, and still in the hands of the same family, this Bethnal Green landmark has an almost-opulent appearance that conjures up some mythical caff culture where the spoons were silver rather than greasy. The gobsmacking decor – chrome and Vitrolite outside, wood panelling with deco marquetry, Formica tabletops and stained glass within – earned the café a Grade II listing in 2005. The food (steadfastly everyday) is prepared with pride by Mama Maria, queen of the kitchen since 1961. Her children, Anna and Nevio Junior, serve it up with a wink. You might wonder at how the staff are on first-name terms

with so many customers, until they start using yours. It's this vibrant welcome (and occasional mickey-taking) that makes the place so special. Recommended are the fry-ups, spaghetti 'Toscana', Friday fish 'n' chips, and desserts from bread pudding to Portuguese pasteis de nata.
Available for hire. Babies and children welcome: high chairs. Bookings not accepted. Tables outdoors (4, pavement). Takeaway service.

North East

Stoke Newington

Blue Legume

101 Stoke Newington Church Street, N16 0UD (7923 1303, www.thebluelegume.co.uk). Stoke Newington rail or bus 73, 393, 476. **Meals served** 9.30am-11pm Mon-Sat; 9.30am-6.30pm Sun. **Main courses** £7.95-£11.95. **Credit** (Mon-Fri) MC, V.

A noticeboard crammed with adverts for gardeners and yoga classes reinforces Blue Legume's local vibe. You get the sense that everyone eating here lives within a five-minute radius. Weekends see a younger crowd healing hangovers with a standard breakfast menu. Grilled cumberland sausages, crispy hash browns, tiny button mushrooms, smoked bacon, a perfectly poached egg and a dollop of baked beans populated a generous plate. Thick scotch pancakes soaked up a pool of maple syrup, while the scrambled eggs were rich with cream. The coffee was served too hot, and could have been better brewed, but it did the trick. Order the delicious fresh orange juice or a vegetable juice for a healthy counterpart to the all-day breakfast. Blue Legume also does lunch and dinner, offering everything from burgers to lamb shank with mash. A small conservatory out the back is light and verdant and there are street-side tables out front. Staff, although obviously busy, were friendly and responsive. There are now three Blue Legumes, in Stokey, Islington and, the newest, Crouch End.
Babies and children welcome: high chairs. Booking advisable dinner. Tables outdoors (5, pavement). Takeaway service. **Map 25 B1.**
For branches see index.

North

Camden Town & Chalk Farm

Marine Ices

8 Haverstock Hill, NW3 2BL (7482 9003, www.marineices.co.uk). Chalk Farm tube. **Lunch served** noon-3pm, **dinner served** 6-11pm Tue-Fri. **Meals served** noon-11pm Sat; noon-10pm Sun. **Main courses** £6.95-£15.55. **Credit** MC, V.

This traditional Italian spot may lack the slickness of the family-friendly chains, yet staff have an easy-going way with bambini that makes visits a pleasure. Testament to this Chalk Farm institution's popularity with little ones was the large Hello Kitty-themed party being prepared in one of the dining rooms on our visit. Staff were happy to let our children roam the premises once they'd had enough of the high chairs – just as well, frankly, because service on a quiet lunchtime should have been much speedier. Kids' portions of pasta, at £7.10, aren't the cheapest in town, but would easily sate a teenager. Penne amatriciana was spiced for the more sophisticated young palate and featured plenty of bacon strips; spaghetti pomodoro and ravioli are other reliably tasty options. Pick of the lengthy menu for adults was generous linguine agli scampi, featuring large, succulent prawns in a creamy tomato sauce. As the name suggests, you can't leave without having ice-cream – the value is in the versatile, build-your-own sundaes. The wide variety of flavours, hot and cold sauces, fruit and chunky, crunchy bits is fun to choose from and, inevitably, a headily rich finish to a meal.
Babies and children welcome: high chairs; nappy-changing facilities. Booking advisable weekends. Takeaway service. **Map 27 B1.**

Islington

Le Mercury

140A Upper Street, N1 1QY (7354 4088, www.lemercury.co.uk). Angel tube or Highbury & Islington tube/rail. **Meals served** noon-midnight Mon-Sat; noon-11pm Sun. **Main courses** £8.95. **Credit** AmEx, MC, V.

This old-timer has been an Upper Street fixture for many years, with its tried-and-trusted formula of cod-French bistro food at bargain prices (all starters cost £3.95, all mains £8.95), served over three floors in a candlelit setting. And it still pulls in the crowds – the place was packed on a Saturday night. After our meal, though, we were left wondering why. Admittedly, it wasn't yet dark enough outside for candlelight to cast its magic glow, but Le Mercury seemed like a worn and cynical operation. First, tables are uncomfortably closely packed. Second, the food was extremely average. From the totally trad menu – foie gras and grilled goat's cheese for starters, cassoulet and roast pork for mains – moules marinière was fine if ordinary, while ravioli de la mer was dull. Mains were worse. A meanly thin steak, although tender, came with a packet-like gravy that was nothing like the advertised shallot sauce; frites were the saving grace. 'Gateaux de poissons', aka fish cakes, tasted like a supermarket version. So, while £8.95 may be cheap for a main course, it really wasn't good value. Le Mercury seems like a restaurant past its sell-by date.
Available for hire. Babies and children welcome: high chairs. Booking advisable weekends. Separate room for parties, seats 50. **Map 5 O1.**

Kentish Town

Arancini Factory NEW

115 Kentish Town Road, NW1 8PB (3648 7941, arancinibrothers.com). Kentish Town tube/rail. **Meals served** 8am-4pm Mon-Fri; 10am-5pm Sat, Sun. **Main courses** £4-£7.80. **No credit cards.**

Sicily's fried risotto balls (gluten-free here) are the mainstay of this retro-chic caff, a factory outlet for the market stall and event-catering team known as Arancini Brothers. The new venture is a welcome player in the re-hipification of Kentish Town; its eat-in option attracts everyone from lunching builders to laptop-wielding media types. The open kitchen at the back, surrounded by boxes of market-fresh produce, offers just two varieties of the little brown nuggets – original (vegetarian) and mushroom and zucchini (vegan) – but many ways in which to enjoy them. Wrapped in a tortilla with slow-roast chicken or bacon, perhaps. With a hot stew of meat, or aubergine and peppers; on a salad; by the handful. Want something else? There's an enticing display of filled bagels and sandwiches and baked goods by the window. A savoury cheddar and leek muffin was dry and bitter-tasting, but we adored the sweet, soft apple and cinnamon variety with crusty love handles bursting over the paper case. Quality coffees at keen prices keep customers rolling in. There's outdoor seating at the rear and a spacious loo too.
Available for hire. Babies and children admitted. Tables outdoors (6, garden). Takeaway service. Vegan dishes. **Map 11 P6.**

Leon. See p275.

BUDGET

Stein's

North West

Hendon

Nando's

Brent Cross Shopping Centre, Prince Charles Drive, NW4 3FP (8203 9131, www.nandos.co.uk). Brent Cross tube. **Meals served** 11am-8pm Mon-Fri; 11am-7pm Sat; noon-6pm Sun. **Main courses** £6-12. **Credit** AmEx, MC, V.

Nando's is slightly barmy and deliberately contrary. If it were family it would be a dear eccentric uncle. The format (sit down, then order at the counter, and then sit down again) isn't rocket science, but it does seem to disconcert the brightest minds. And when you're ensconced in a luxurious booth at one of the plusher branches, being allowed to go and refill your Diet Coke feels bizarrely decadent. Why do punters return in their thousands? They'd say it was for the peri-peri; we reckon it's the chicken and chips. It's definitely not the £3.55 ratatouille. Plucky staff deal well with harassed parents too. If Hugh Fearnley-Whittingstall hasn't persuaded you to eat more of the bird than just its breast, take note: the grill is kinder to marinated halves and quarters than it is to Nando's white meat. Still, we've enjoyed the breast with salad and mayo in a juicy tortilla wrap (though at £6.90 each, these make Pret seem cheap). We also like the fact that chicken livers in a bun are offered here – hardly beak-to-tail-feather eating, but a welcome start.

Babies and children welcome: children's menu; high chairs; nappy-changing facilities. Bookings not accepted. Disabled: toilet. Takeaway service. Vegetarian dishes.

For branches see index.

Outer London

Kingston, Surrey

Stein's

56 High Street, Kingston, Surrey KT1 1HN (8546 2411, www.stein-s.com). Kingston rail. **Meals served** noon-11pm Mon-Sat; noon-10pm Sun. **Main courses** £7-£16. **Credit** AmEx, MC, V.

Stein's Bavarian-style 'beer garden' next to the river in Richmond has been a hit for some years; this is its new, second outpost. There's no grass, but the view from either of the decked terraces, overlooking a leafy section of the Thames, is as pretty as any in Munich's Englischer Garten. If it's too cold for outdoors, the inside is tricked out in rustic ski chalet chic, all rough-hewn woods and chintzy carved hearts, while staff wear lederhosen and dirndls (his and hers Bavarian dress). We kicked off with weisswurst, a local speciality. Ours were terrific: two soft, springy sausages of finely minced pork and veal poached in a delicate broth and correctly served with a freshly-baked pretzel and süßer Senf (sweet mustard). A classic pork schnitzel (beaten, breadcrumbed and fried until golden brown), may have originated in Austria, but came with a south German potato salad with a dressing of oil, vinegar and mustard. A bland slab of pork shoulder with red cabbage failed to excite, but a terrific sweet dumpling filled with poached apricots and a buttery breadcrumbed topping ended the meal on a high. Some dishes take longer to prepare, so if you're time-pressed, check before ordering. Traditional steins of helles and dunkles (pale and dark lagers) come courtesy of Munich breweries Paulaner and Hacker-Pschorr, while weissbier (cloudy wheatbeer) is by Erdinger; wines tour Germany, Austria and Italy.

Available for hire. Babies and children welcome: children's menu; high chairs; nappy-changing facilities; play area. Bookings not accepted for fewer than 6 people. Disabled: toilet. Separate room for parties, seats 50. Tables outdoors (16, river terrace). Takeaway service.

For branch see index.

Cafés

London's cafés – and we don't mean the greasy spoon caffs, the best of which can be found in our **Budget** section (*see p274*) – form a dynamic part of the city's eating and drinking scene. We especially like the fact that café spaces offer a relatively affordable arena for experimentation by young chefs and entrepreneurs. Some of these ventures evolve into brasseries as the day progresses, witness Herne Hill's **Lido Café**, Vauxhall's **Brunswick House Café**, **No 67** in Camberwell, **Salvation Jane** in Shoreditch and **La Fromagerie** in Marylebone. We've listed them here because customers are able to pop in at any time of day for an excellent cup of tea (or coffee) and a choice of delicious baked goods. Cafés are often sited in the most curious of locations – from Brunswick House Café's bolt-hole on the edge of a major traffic interchange, to the rustic setting of both **Frizzante@Mudchute** and **Frizzante@Hackney City Farm**, via the Regent's Canal perch of **Towpath**. Among the newcomers this year is a café of a very different type: the London branch of a smart Turkish chain, **Kahve Dünyasi**, in Piccadilly. This chapter should be read in conjunction with **Coffee Bars** (*see p290*), as many cafés listed below take coffee very seriously, notably **Workshop Coffee Co**, **Lantana**, **Fernandez & Wells** and **Tina, We Salute You**.

Central

City

Bea's of Bloomsbury

One New Change, 83 Watling Street, EC4M 9BX (7242 8330, www.beasofbloomsbury.com). St Paul's tube. **Open** 8am-7pm Mon-Fri; noon-7pm Sat, Sun. **Main courses** £5-£10. **Afternoon tea** (2.30-7pm Mon-Fri; noon-7pm Sat, Sun) £17, £24.50 with champagne. **Credit** (over £5) AmEx, MC, V.

Following the success of its Bloomsbury operation, Bea's has opened a slip, or strip, of an outlet in the City's New Change shopping centre. Order from the counter in the corridor-sized room and head upstairs to a similar space just wide enough for a length of banquette seating covered in devoré velvet in jewel-like colours of turquoise, pink and gold. The end table offers a glimpse of St Paul's, and industrial-looking exposed air-conditioning is softened by quirky coffeepot and teapot light fittings. Early birds can enjoy excellent fruit salads, sourdough toast and croissants; for lunch, there are filled toasties; and the counter of cakes, meringues and cupcakes baked by the four chefs at the Bloomsbury kitchen make for sweet accompaniments to a long list of teas and coffees. A handy place for a swift meeting, Bea's also offers afternoon tea for £17. If you can't leave the office, order a box of six cupcakes for £15, but to celebrate that multimillion-pound merger, it has to be the champagne tea at £24.50.

Available for hire. Booking advisable. Takeaway service. **Map 11 P6.**

For branches see index.

Clerkenwell & Farringdon

Clerkenwell Kitchen

27 Clerkenwell Close, EC1R 0AT (7101 9959, www.theclerkenwellkitchen.co.uk). Angel tube or Farringdon tube/rail. **Open** 8am-5pm Mon-Fri. **Main courses** £4.80-£12. **Credit** (over £5) MC, V.

It might be catering for the lunch-hour rush, but Clerkenwell Kitchen is equally suited to those wishing to enjoy a longer break. For the time-pressed customer, doorstep sandwiches can be ordered to take away from the bar. Round the corner, though, is the dining room, all clean lines and bright light with its floorboards, white walls and exposed brick. Dishes are mainly European in origin and change daily, perhaps inspired by a morning flick-through of the collection of cookery books on shelves around the door. It's simple food, executed with confidence and elegance. Devilled crab linguine, for example, was an accomplished combination of pasta and crab meat dressed with chilli and generous amounts of butter, lemon and parsley. The meze platter also showed care: smoky aubergine purée, herby tabbouleh, a sliver of goat's cheese tart, and cubes of feta, tomato and beetroot to finish the dish off. The courtyard is a real draw in good weather.

Babies and children welcome: high chairs. Disabled: toilet. Tables outdoors (8, courtyard). Takeaway service. **Map 5 N4.**

J&A Café

4 Sutton Lane, EC1M 5PU (7490 2992, www.jandacafe.com). Barbican tube or Farringdon tube/rail. **Breakfast served** 8-11am, **lunch served** noon-3.30pm Mon-Fri. **Brunch served** 9am-3pm Sat. **Tea served** 3.30-5.45pm Mon-Fri; 3-4pm Sat. **Main courses** £3.50-£10.50. **Credit** MC, V.

A cute little café, hidden down an alleyway and based in an old diamond-cutting factory. Delicious breakfasts are a forte: the choice runs from pastries, granola and fresh fruit to big bacon sarnies and egg dishes, such as the mighty eggs royale (english muffin, organic smoked salmon, perfectly cooked poached eggs and hollandaise). Freshly baked Irish soda bread is perfect for mopping up the full english breakfast, while the Clonakilty black pudding is our favourite from the extras list. Accompany all this with a large mug of tea or not-bad coffee. Lunch features sandwiches (roast chicken, ham and cheddar) and salads, plus a daily pie, soup and stew. An array of cakes changes on a daily basis. Decor is a mixture of homely chic combined with exposed brick walls; out in the small cobbled courtyard, there are a few retro tables under white bunting. *Available for hire. Babies and children welcome: high chairs. Disabled: toilet. Tables outdoors (13, courtyard). Takeaway service.* **Map 5 O4.**

Workshop Coffee Co

27 Clerkenwell Road, EC1M 5RN (7253 5754, www.workshopcoffee.com). Farringdon tube/rail. **Open** 7am-6pm Mon, Sun; 7am-10pm Tue-Sat. **Main courses** £4.50-£15. **Credit** AmEx, MC, V.

Perhaps better known for its coffee (roasted on site), Workshop has extended its opening hours, and now serves food into the evening. On the ground floor, tables are close together, with the coffee roaster and large barista counter occupying a big chunk of the space. In the evening, a good selection of bar snacks (pig-skin grissini with apple sauce, corn 'frittettes' with spiced yoghurt) is served here, while upstairs there's a short dinner menu. From this, the Dexter burger looked like a cartoon version, with a picture-perfect brioche bun, a slab of comté and some chipotle mayo. Deep-fried ratte potatoes were a treat. Wild mushroom pithivier was nicely crisp, and accompanied by pea laksa. Breakfasts are just as tempting: toasted banana bread, with date and orange jam and espresso mascarpone, for example. Decor is spacious and light, with long tables for groups and an elegant bar; industrial exposed brick is softened by flower arrangements on each wooden tabletop. Finish with a house roast, such as Juana Mamani from Bolivia.

Available for hire. Babies and children admitted. Booking advisable; bookings not accepted brunch Sat, Sun. Disabled: toilet. Separate room for parties, seats 60. Takeaway service. **Map 5 O4.**

For branch see index.

Euston

Peyton & Byrne

Wellcome Collection, 183 Euston Road, NW1 2BE (7611 2138, www.peytonandbyrne.com). Euston Square tube or Euston tube/rail. **Open** 9.45am-6pm Mon-Wed, Fri, Sat; 9.45am-10pm Thur; 10.45am-6pm Sun. **Main courses** £3.50-£9.50. **Credit** MC, V.

Over the past few years, Peyton & Byrne has established something of a museum café empire. This airy outlet of the Brit-themed chain sits in the foyer of the Wellcome Collection. Pass through the bag check at the entrance and grab a seat on the stylish, candy-coloured furniture. A mouthwatering array – including savoury pies, mountains of salads, and trays filled with sweet baked treats – is displayed at a long deli counter. Food can be hit and miss. A bland-tasting cauliflower and coconut soup came with a slice of limp sandwich bread. Better proof of their baking credentials came with a lamb pie – a crisp, buttery crust encased a flavoursome lamb ragoût. Sweet treats are definitely the main attraction; the own-made cakes, heavily frosted cupcakes and innumerable cookies are hard to resist. A smallish slice of apple and blackberry flapjack turned out to be more of an apple tart, sprinkled with cinnamon oatmeal crumble, while a giant chelsea bun was filled with dark chocolate specks (instead of the usual sticky currants). Not traditional, but good.

Babies and children welcome: high chairs; nappy-changing facilities. Disabled: lift; toilet. Takeaway service. **Map 4 K4.**

For branches see index.

Fitzrovia

Lantana

13 Charlotte Place, W1T 1SN (7637 3347, www.lantanacafe.co.uk). Goodge Street tube. **Open** 8am-6pm Mon-Fri; 9am-5pm Sat, Sun. **Breakfast served** 8-11.30am, **lunch served** noon-3pm Mon-Fri. **Brunch served** 9am-3pm Sat, Sun. **Main courses** £5-£12.50. **Credit** AmEx, MC, V.

You have to be up for the ride at Australian-run Lantana. With the music loud, every table filled and the staff clearly enjoying each other's company immensely, the service can be as laid-back as the atmosphere. Through the commotion, though, appears some excellent food. Smoked haddock, pea and lemon risotto showed an impressive balance of the ingredients' three contrasting flavours suffused through some perfectly cooked rice. Inside a ciabatta roll was a mound of shredded pork belly, crisped up to an appropriate level of indulgence; successfully bringing the two together in happy union was a sneaky chilli mayonnaise. Lantana's cakes and pastries selection is accomplished too, with hummingbird and hello dolly cakes joining the more quotidian brownies, blondies and banana bread on the stand. The breakfast and weekend brunch menus are equally impressive and the coffee is definitely worth a pit-stop – there's a takeaway kiosk attached next door. With such interesting and well-executed food and drink, a touch of the slap-dash is perfectly acceptable. Lantana's new offshoot, Salvation Jane (*see p285*), is open into the evenings, and has a bar and menu reflecting that fact.

Babies and children admitted. Tables outdoors (2, pavement). Takeaway service. **Map 17 B1.**

Scandinavian Kitchen

61 Great Titchfield Street, W1W 7PP (7580 7161, www.scandikitchen.co.uk). Oxford Circus tube. **Open** 8am-7pm Mon-Fri; 10am-6pm Sat; 10am-4pm Sun. **Main courses** £5.95-£8.95. **Credit** AmEx, MC, V.

Such is the popularity of this Nordic café and specialist grocery shop with both expats and local office-workers, you'll be lucky to find a seat at lunchtime. There's always a couple of hot dishes (meatballs or a hot dog, perhaps), but most people opt for the open sandwiches and salads temptingly displayed behind the glass counter. Choose three for £5.95, five for £8.95: maybe prawns and sliced boiled egg, with a dab of mayo and a sprig of dill; salmon and cucumber; Swedish grève cheese with radish – all served on dark rye or lighter, stone-ground bread. Beetroot and apple, and a slightly odd-tasting winter 'slaw, are typical salads, and there are usually little pots of lip-smackingly tasty pickled herring. Coffee is excellent, as you'd expect, and the good-looking cakes are a must-try, especially the apple, cinnamon and custard version. At the back of the rather cluttered room, beneath paper garlands of Swedish, Norwegian and Danish flags, are shelves laden with groceries, including pepparkakor ginger biscuits, tinned and pickled herring, cheese, crispbreads galore and a large array of sweets: from liquorice pipes to Plopp chocolate. Friendly staff are happy to advise.

Babies and children welcome: high chairs; nappy-changing facilities. Takeaway service; delivery service (over £35). **Map 9 J5.**

Holborn

Fleet River Bakery

71 Lincoln's Inn Fields, WC2A 3JF (7691 1457, www.fleetriverbakery.com). Holborn tube. **Open** 7am-7pm Mon-Fri; 9am-5pm Sat. **Main courses** £6.50-£8. **Credit** AmEx, MC, V.

This café increases in popularity all the time, and with good reason. At lunchtime, office workers queue up for the daily specials, which get tweeted about as soon as they come out of the kitchen. Typical is a substantial dish, such as lamb and courgette meatballs with a yoghurt sumac dressing, served with salads (herbed quinoa and a light coleslaw, say). Other options include frittatas, quiches, wraps and sandwiches – all on display as you come in. As the name suggests, baked goods

Nordic Bakery. See p281.

are a highlight: melt-in-the-mouth 'duffins', doughnut-like muffins with a hint of nutmeg, come covered in cinnamon sugar. Lemon pie was also delicious; we liked the sprinkling of roasted coconut on the meringue topping. Attention to detail can be seen in the drinks list too, which runs to wine (off-sales available), craft beers from Kernal Brewery and Monmouth coffee. Have your meal in one of the two rustic rooms, kitted out with mismatched tables and chairs, at the back.
Babies and children welcome: high chairs. Tables outdoors (6, pavement). Takeaway service. **Map 18 F2**.

Knightsbridge

Serpentine Bar & Kitchen

Serpentine Road, Hyde Park, W2 2UH (7706 8114, www.serpentinebarandkitchen.com). Hyde Park Corner tube. **Open** *Summer* 8am-9pm daily. *Winter* 8am-5pm daily. **Main courses** £4.90-£18. **Credit** AmEx, MC, V.

The uninterrupted view over the Serpentine makes this Benugo-run café a great place to kick back for an hour or two. Designed by Patrick Gwynne in the 1960s for Charles Forte (when it was called the Dell), the building looks like the bottom layer of an enormous pagoda and has floor-to-ceiling windows that offer perfect sightlines of frenetic boat and pedalo activity. On a sunny day, the outdoor terrace packs out. Customers are also lured in by the juicy 8oz beefburgers (with all the trimmings) coming off the barbecue. Tourists and families commandeer trestles or small tables, while deck chairs fill up with newspaper readers and the odd sunbather. The menu covers a host of breakfast options, soup with crusty bread, salads, fish and chips, sandwiches, wood-fired pizzas and a few specials, such as sea bass with crushed potatoes and buttered spinach. Quality is good, but prices are high (pizzas £11.50-£12.50, salads all more than a tenner). Kids love the ice-cream cart by the entrance, while adults appreciate the Citröen van converted into a gin bar.
Babies and children welcome: children's menu; high chairs; nappy-changing facilities. Bookings not accepted. Disabled: toilet. Tables outdoors (45, terrace; 20 balcony). **Map 8 E7**.

Marylebone

★ La Fromagerie HOT 50

2-6 Moxon Street, W1U 4EW (7935 0341, www.lafromagerie.co.uk). Baker Street or Bond Street tube. **Open** 8am-7.30pm Mon-Fri; 9am-7pm Sat; 10am-6pm Sun. **Main courses** £6-£15. **Credit** (over £5) AmEx, MC, V.

In an ideal world, we'd all be able to afford to live the La Fromagerie life, being served delicious morsels by a team of bright young things amid shelves and counters laden with exquisite groceries. Prices aren't so steep that occasional visits aren't possible, to sample a carefully selected seasonal cheese board, say, or a dish from the café menu, such as rare roast beef with horseradish crème fraîche, a smoked salmon plate, or the generous ploughman's – superior French gammon, Keen's cheddar, pickled onions, a slightly too-polite piccalilli and good bread. A tart of asparagus, caprini tartufo (an Italian goat's cheese) and thyme with a side of delightfully sweet roast cherry tomatoes made a perfect light summer lunch. Come for breakfast (cheese and ham toastie, boiled egg and soldiers, pastries or a cheese plate) or tea (Valrhona chocolate flourless cake, apple and cinnamon muffins) or for ice-cream (made specially for La Fromagerie, using organic Ivy House milk, which is also sold in the shop). There's a short wine list, chosen with the same care as the produce. For a final example of the meticulous sourcing, take a look at the cheese room before you leave.
Available for hire (evenings Mon-Thur). Babies and children admitted. **Map 3 G3**.
For branch see index.

Piccadilly

Kahve Dünyasi NEW

200 Piccadilly, W1 9HU (7287 9063, www.kahvedunyasi.com/en). Piccadilly Circus tube. **Open** 7am-9pm daily. **Main courses** £1.50-£6. **Credit** MC, V.

The first British outpost of a Turkish chain of coffee shops, Kahve Dünyasi has taken to its large Piccadilly premises like a duck to water. It's packed much of the time – little wonder, given the winning formula of colourfully wrapped chocolates (boxes are for sale), a wide variety of coffees and milkshakes (many with lashings of whipped cream), plus ice-cream (a mastic-flavoured variety provides a hint of the cafe's eastern origin), chocolate fondue and cakes, all at prices that are extremely competitive for the area. The cakes look mass-produced (the menu says 'homemade'), but are tasty enough. We liked the chocolate caramel cake; alternatives range from chocolate soufflé to carrot. The house speciality of iced turkish coffee is like a grown-up milkshake, strong, but with plenty of coffee ice-cream, milk and chocolate. Amid all this are a few baguettes and mini quiches, but, really, it's all about the sweet stuff. Waitress service adds a touch of occasion to a low-spend, cheerful treat.
Babies and children welcome: high chairs. Bookings not accepted. Takeaway service. **Map 17 A5**.

Soho

Hummingbird Bakery

155A Wardour Street, W1F 8WG (7851 1795, www.hummingbirdbakery.com). Oxford Circus or Tottenham Court Road tube. **Open** 9.30am-8pm Mon-Sat; 10am-7pm Sun. **Main courses** £2-£4. **Credit** (over £5) AmEx, MC, V.

Fernandez & Wells

The Soho branch of this successful mini-chain is a busy spot; there are also branches in Notting Hill, South Ken, Spitalfields and Islington. Most customers come here for the colourful frosted cupcakes, which are displayed in long glass cabinets, alongside whoopee pies, tiered American cakes and varieties of brownies. Raspberry cheesecake brownie has to be the most indulgent version – a dense chocolate brownie base topped with a baked cream cheese layer and finished off with whipped raspberry cream – delicious. Red velvet is still the best-selling flavour of cupcake, though customers are encouraged to try out new creations from the daily changing specials. On our visit, it was a 'tea cake', a chocolate sponge with pieces of digestive biscuit. Verdict? Too dry. The moister black-bottom cupcake, available any time, was a much better choice. Note that this branch doesn't have many seats, and much of the business is in take-outs (gift boxes are available).
Babies and children admitted. Takeaway service. **Map 17 B3.**
For branches see index.

Maison Bertaux

28 Greek Street, W1D 5DQ (7437 6007, www.maisonbertaux.com). Leicester Square, Piccadilly Circus or Tottenham Court Road tube. **Open** 9am-10.30pm Mon-Sat; 9am-8pm Sun. **Main courses** £3.60-£4.75. **Credit** (over £7.50) AmEx, V.
Maison Bertaux is a blessed relief from identikit coffee chains – the interior is painted cream and pale blue, and, in Diamond Jubilee year, festooned with bunting and royal ephemera. There's an upright piano wedged into the tiny ground floor, and art on the walls of the first-floor room. The window is packed with top-notch baked goods, from creamy fruit tarts to sultana scones. Coffee has improved, but is still no match for the wave of passionate coffee specialists sweeping across London, and service can be chaotic – we'd finished a (delicious) ham and cheese croissant by the time coffee arrived, and no one seemed to be manning the till. Maison Bertaux is best seen as a little piece of Soho history – allowing its faults to be seen as idiosyncrasies, and the steep price of a coffee and croissant to be marked down as payment for experiencing a relic.
Babies and children admitted. Tables outdoors (7, pavement). Takeaway service. **Map 17 C4.**

Nordic Bakery

14A Golden Square, W1F 9JG (3230 1077, www.nordicbakery.com). Piccadilly Circus tube. **Meals served** 8am-8pm Mon-Fri; 9am-7pm Sat; 10am-7pm Sun. **Main courses** £3.25-£4. **Credit** MC, V.
'Dark rye bread. Cinnamon buns. Coffee' reads the sign (Helvetica, of course) in the picture window of this stylish Finnish café. That pretty much sums it up. Flat circular sandwiches of tasty dark rye bread enclose fillings such as prawn, smoked salmon, ham and cheese, or hard-boiled egg and herring (the last with a tangy mustard sauce). The cinnamon buns are dark, sticky and hefty. Coffee is well made and strong. There are no hot dishes, but other baked options include rye muffins, Karelian pies filled with rice or mashed potato, or hefty boston cake – similar to the aforementioned bun, but topped with flaked almonds. A few deli items are available too, including jams, cordials (lingonberry, Arctic cloudberry), that addictive rye bread and the Nordic Bakery cookbook. Creatives from what remains of Soho's adland pack the place, drawn no doubt by its clean-lined good looks: pine panelling, a muted colour scheme of dark blue, grey and black (even the staff are colour-coded, with denim aprons over black) and classic Scandinavian tableware.
Babies and children admitted. Takeaway service. **Map 17 A4.**
For branches see index.

Strand

Fernandez & Wells

East Wing, Somerset House, Strand, WC2R 0RN (7420 9408, www.fernandezandwells.com). Temple tube. **Open** 8am-10pm Mon-Fri; 10am-10pm Sat; 10am-8pm Sun. **Tapas** £5-£12. **Credit** AmEx, MC, V.
This newest branch of the thriving mini-chain is also the biggest: four rooms in the east wing of Somerset House, and very attractive rooms they are too, displaying light wood, clean lines and minimal decoration. The formula is the same here as elsewhere, with emphasis on very good coffee and simple food whose selling point is the quality of raw ingredients (mostly Iberian but also Italian). Already familiar with the excellent jamón and salami, we decided to give the on-display sandwiches a go – and lived to regret it. They appeared to have been sitting around for a while, and seemed distinctly tired – dried, cracking cheese, staling bread. They weren't terrible, just boring. Baked goods were much better, and the coffee was the real star. F&W buys from Has Bean, and its espresso blend has good fruity notes and a pleasantly long aftertaste even without sugar. A piccolo was smaller than most, with lovely creaminess. The wine list is not exactly cheap, but it is concise and of a high quality. You could easily spend a happy lunchtime or evening here, as long as you stick to the strong points.
Available for hire. Babies and children welcome: nappy-changing facilities. Disabled: toilet. Tables outdoors (7, terrace). **Map 10 M7.**
For branches see index.

West

Ladbroke Grove

Books for Cooks

4 Blenheim Crescent, W11 1NN (7221 1992, www.booksforcooks.com). Ladbroke Grove tube. **Open** 10am-6pm Mon-Wed, Fri, Sat; 10am-5.30pm Thur. **Lunch served** noon-2pm Tue-Fri; 11.30am-2pm Sat. **Set lunch** £5 2 courses, £7 3 courses. **Credit** MC, V.
So popular is the bargain lunch in the tiny café at the back of this specialist cookbook shop that regulars start lurking from 11.45am to secure a table. From the small open kitchen, co-owner Eric Treuillé puts recipes (one starter, one main) from the cookbook(s) of the day to the test. There's no choice – until it comes to pudding, when there's an array of must-try cakes – but the standard of cooking is high. We enjoyed both a flavoursome sweet-smelling pistou soup (taken from *The Little Paris Kitchen* by Rachel Khoo), and a hearty chicken and chorizo stew. Vegetarians have to make do with starter and cake, and white wine lovers must go elsewhere: only red wine from Eric's own biodynamic vineyard is served. If you want to recreate the dishes yourself, pick up the cookbook on your way out, or sign up for the regular cooking classes offered upstairs.
Bookings not accepted. **Map 19 B3.**

Westbourne Grove

Tom's Deli

226 Westbourne Grove, W11 2RH (7221 8818, www.tomsdelilondon.co.uk). Notting Hill Gate tube. **Open** 8am-6.30pm Mon-Sat; 9am-6.30pm Sun. **Main courses** £10-£12. **Credit** (over £5) MC, V.
Enter Tom's through a mini sweetshop of retro delights: flying saucers, liquorice and bars of delicious chocolate. The basement deli has posh cupboard treats, fine charcuterie and cheeses – as well as, come lunchtime, hot dishes such as fish curry or lasagne, and a variety of salads. Climb up a few stairs to the café-diner, which continues the retro theme with a clutch of booths with Formica tables bearing bottles of HP sauce and Heinz ketchup, and walls covered in advertising memorabilia and the odd Shepard Fairey or Banksy print. The soundtrack is an equally old-school Bowie/Stones/American blues mash-up. The simple menu consists mainly of breakfasts – which accounts for the venue's popularity with Notting Hillbillies at the weekend. Alongside the full english, and a vegetarian version, there are a dozen different ways with eggs. Unfortunately, not all are a success. The kitchen's use of tinned tomatoes in the 'Turkish Steamer' (eggs steamed on a bed of tomato with wilted spinach, feta and yoghurt) made the dish far too watery. To drink, decent Kimbo coffees give way in the evening to bloody marys, Meantime Pale Ale and Pilsner, and wines.
Babies and children welcome: high chairs. Tables outdoors (6, garden; 2, terrace). Takeaway service. **Map 7 A6.**

South West

Barnes

★ Orange Pekoe

3 White Hart Lane, SW13 0PX (8876 6070, www.orangepekoeteas.com). Barnes Bridge rail or bus 209. **Meals served** 7.30am-5.30pm Mon-Fri; 9am-5.30pm Sat, Sun. **Main courses** £4.70-£8.50. **Credit** AmEx, MC, V.
The metal pavement tables have been upgraded, but little else has changed at this charming tea salon. The front room holds the coffee machine, a counter laden with cakes and pre-made sandwiches, and tea paraphernalia for sale – including loose leaf teas in smart black and gold canisters. Venture further in for more seating; white-painted brickwork, a skylight and pretty wallpaper make the most of the rather cramped space. Serving staff are young and very polite; this is Barnes, after all. Food varies from breakfast items such as own-made muesli and pastries to variations on the eggs benedict/florentine theme, a daily soup, platters (vegetarian, pâté, ploughman's) or miniature pies with salad. 'Pekoe royal' brought a toasted muffin, each half topped with baby spinach leaves and a perfectly poached egg, with a huge swirl of dill-flecked smoked salmon on the side. Full-blown afternoon tea is also served (star performer: the scones), but many customers come just to sample the myriad different teas. A separate book lists the types available (black, white, yellow, green, oolong, plus herbal infusions); a pot, of any kind, costs just £3.60, an absolute bargain considering the quality, and a fantastic way to experiment. There's a separate booklet for the 'real trade' coffee too.

Babies and children welcome: crayons; high chairs; nappy-changing facilities. Tables outdoors (7, pavement). Takeaway service.

Fulham

Fulham Palace Café

Bishop's Avenue, SW6 6EA (7610 7160, www.fulhampalace.org). Putney Bridge tube. **Open** 9am-5pm daily. **Main courses** £8.50-£9. **Credit** AmEx, MC, V.

Just up from Putney Bridge, Fulham Palace was the country residence of the Bishops of London for over 12 centuries. Now the splendid remains, mixing Tudor, Georgian and Victorian architecture, are open to the public, along with this café, set in the graceful former drawing room. The main attraction lies beyond the tall windows: a terrace overlooking a vast lawn, surrounded by a handsome wall and towering historic trees. Families love it because it's safe for scampering children – and also next door to Bishops Park with its recently renovated playground and 'beach'. Standard breakfast fare, from croissants to a full english, is followed by a short lunch menu that includes 'platters' of fish, ham or vegetables, a few salads, and hot dishes such as grilled salmon or Old Spot sausages with chips. There's also a kids' menu and, later on, proper afternoon tea. Sadly, the food doesn't match the setting – we experienced underdone poached eggs, overdone bacon, poor coffee – and prices are high, with burger and chips costing nearly a tenner. Note that you can't book the terrace tables.

Babies and children welcome: children's menu; high chairs; nappy-changing facilities. Bookings not accepted Sat, Sun. Disabled: toilet. Tables outdoors (8, terrace).

South

Balham

Trinity Stores

5-6 Balham Station Road, SW12 9SG (8673 3773, www.trinitystores.co.uk). Balham tube/ rail. **Open** 8am-8pm Mon-Fri; 9am-5.30pm Sat; 9.30am-5pm Sun. **Main courses** £3.75-£9.55. **Credit** (over £5) AmEx, MC, V.

Forget that it's overlooked by Balham station: Trinity Stores is the fantasy of an idyllic country café. Furniture is a mix-and-match of farmhouse and vintage, staff are youthful and enthusiastic, and the soundtrack is ultra laid-back. It stocks only the finest deli goods, from the Rare Tea Company's silver tip leaves to saffron strands from Brindisa, all lovingly displayed on open wooden shelves, in wicker baskets or in old-fashioned wooden crates. The chiller cabinet holds top-notch 'basics', be they organic tomatoes, thick-cut bacon or free-range eggs. If eating in, choose from made-to-order breakfasts (cinnamon porridge, a full english) or from a counter of cured meats, cheeses and picnic foods. We enjoyed the depth of flavour and crunchy casing of a black pudding scotch egg, while a slice of quiche, combining bites of salty feta with generous chunks of soft, sweet pumpkin and wilted spinach in an excellent crumbly pastry, was equally memorable. Sadly, the slice of passionfruit cake that came next was bland and sickly. The only other grumble is the prices, which are definitely more town than country.

Available for hire. Babies and children welcome: high chairs. Takeaway service.

Clapham

Breads Etcetera

127 Clapham High Street, SW4 7SS (07717 642812). Clapham Common or Clapham North tube. **Open** 10am-10pm Tue-Sat; 10am-4pm Sun. **Main courses** £5.50-£12. **No credit cards.**

Putting bread at the centre of its offering – literally – this bakery-cum-café keeps an enormous basket of loaves on a counter-top in the middle of the room. Inside, you'll find freshly baked bread, from everyday white or wholemeal to more artisan options of rye or olive, with one thing in common: they're all sourdough-based. Tables are kitted out with retro Dualit toasters. The idea is to help yourself, cutting off as many different slices as you dare, and toast them at your table. This 'DIY' option doesn't come cheap – £6.50 is a lot for a spot of toast – so for better value, order one of the slightly dearer all-day breakfasts, and get the bread for 'free'. We largely enjoyed our full english, featuring nicely charred thick-cut bacon, herby mushrooms and own-made beans, though the sausage was fatty and cheap. No matter: the bread is excellent, and an occasion in itself. There are other nice touches: the kitchen doesn't poach eggs, but it will soft-boil them and shell them for you, just like nanny would do. Note: it's cash only.

Babies and children admitted. Bookings not accepted. Tables outdoors (2, pavement). Takeaway service. **Map 22 B2.**
For branch see index.

Macaron

22 The Pavement, SW4 0HY (7498 2636). Clapham Common tube. **Open** 7.30am-7pm daily. **Main courses** £2.85-£4.50. **No credit cards.**

Macaron is a charming French pâtisserie and café on a prime location overlooking Clapham Common. It's a favourite spot for the area's many well-to-do couples and young parents, who drop in for a coffee or one of the excellent pastries, glazed fruit tarts or brownies. The croissants, in particular, are among the best in London, and the five-cereal bread, rye bread and pain au levain (sourdough) are also excellent. The pastry chef is often visible in the pastry kitchen at the back, demonstrating that everything from the viennoiserie to the ice-creams are freshly made. The savoury menu is brief, but the filled sandwiches use good ingredients. As Macaron is consistently busy, be warned that service, from charming all-French staff, can be disorganised; on our many visits, we have had orders lost or forgotten, or the bill added up wrongly by mistake.

Tables outdoors (3, pavement). Takeaway service. **Map 22 A2.**

Vauxhall

Brunswick House Café

30 Wandsworth Road, Vauxhall Cross, SW8 2LG (7720 2926, www.brunswickhousecafe.co.uk). Vauxhall tube/rail. **Open** 8.30am-5pm Mon; 8.30am-5pm, 6.30-10.30pm Tue-Fri; 10am-5pm, 6.30-10.30pm Sat; 10am-5pm Sun. **Main courses** £4-£16. **Credit** MC, V.

Part of the joy of Brunswick House Café lies in its setting: a lone Georgian mansion, marooned amid a tangle of A-roads and modern high-rise blocks near Vauxhall station. It shares its premises with architectural salvage company Lassco, whose finds furnish the bar and dining room – a beguiling jumble of church pews, chandeliers, antique tables and maritime flags, with price tags attached. If the decor is all about excess, the kitchen favours simplicity, with a daily changing one-page menu and a focus on seasonal ingredients: spring lamb sweetbreads with bacon and kohlrabi, perhaps, or a feather-light soufflé of new season asparagus, sprinkled with pea shoots and chives. Standards are high, though portions can be on the small side, so it's wise to order a few plates to share. A short but thoughtful wine list offers plenty by the carafe, while the cocktails are top-notch: old-fashioned sazeracs, sours and negronis, mixed with a practised hand. Come the weekend, the emphasis shifts to sturdy brunches (Old Spot bacon and egg butties, kippers on sourdough toast), which draw a loyal following; whenever you're planning to visit, it's best to book ahead.

Available for hire. Babies and children welcome: nappy-changing facilities. Booking advisable brunch, dinner. Tables outdoors (11, patio). Takeaway service. **Map 16 L12.**

South East

Camberwell

No 67

South London Gallery, 67 Peckham Road, SE5 8UH (7252 7649, www.southlondongallery.org). Bus 12, 36 or 171. **Breakfast served** 9am-11.30pm, **lunch served** noon-3.30pm Tue-Fri. **Brunch served** 10am-3.30pm Sat, Sun. **Dinner served** 6.30-10pm Wed-Sat. **Main courses** £9.80-£13.80. **Credit** AmEx, MC, V.

Hip as it is, this area isn't blessed with smart restaurants serving innovative food, which makes No 67 such a revelation. Housed in the refurbished South London Gallery, by day it's a delightful café serving tarts, salads, nice cakes and good coffee, with tables spilling out into an airy modern extension and a pretty garden. In the evenings (Wed-Sat), the low-key townhouse becomes an intimate dining room, a chic space on a domestic scale, decked out in muted greys and with low lighting, where cultured south Londoners sip bellinis and Camden Brewery beers. The reasonably priced seasonal menu is modern and creative, with dishes such as morcilla-stuffed pork belly, rabbit three ways, and plaice with samphire, followed by own-made buttermilk pudding and boozy strawberries and in-house rye bread ice-cream. And if you've been out all night at one of Peckham's art squat parties, what better way to revive than a weekend brunch of kippers, spanish eggs and chorizo, or waffles oozing with maple syrup, all washed down with a bloody mary.

Available for hire. Babies and children welcome: high chairs; nappy-changing facilities. Disabled: toilet. Tables outdoors (6, terrace; 5, garden). Takeaway service. **Map 23 B2.**

Deptford

Deptford Project

121-123 Deptford High Street, SE8 4NS (07545 593279, www.thedeptfordproject.com). Deptford rail or Deptford Bridge DLR. **Open** 9am-5.30pm Mon-Sat; 10am-4.30pm Sun. **Main courses** £1.50-£6.95. **No credit cards.**

Since its arrival in 2008, a disused train carriage has become part of the fabric of Deptford High

Lido Café

Street. Thanks to a collaborative art project, both the disused railway yard and the carriage itself were transformed, the latter housing a surprisingly cosy café and the yard hosting open-air film screenings and other events. The colourful, partly covered decking area has a surprise waiting in the shed at one end – a WC masquerading as a shrine to Elvis. The café is popular with families for early brunches and lunches, so you may find that the menu becomes more limited after about 1pm on weekends. On our visit, the soup and specials had run out, but helpful staff were ready to suggest additions that could be made to the available dishes. Baked potatoes and sandwiches with an array of toppings and fillings form the backbone of the menu, along with a choice of salads. No need to stop for a full meal, however – excellent coffee, fresh juices and generous wedges of own-made cakes make it a good pit-stop.
Babies and children welcome: high chairs; nappy-changing facilities. Disabled: toilet. Tables outdoors (11, terrace). Takeaway service.

East Dulwich

Blue Mountain Café
18 North Cross Road, SE22 9EU (8299 6953, www.bluemo.co.uk). East Dulwich rail. **Open** 9am-6pm Mon-Sat; 10am-6pm Sun. **Main courses** £4.50-£8. **Credit** MC, V.
An East Dulwich institution and a key fixture on busy North Cross Road, Blue Mountain's quirky mosaic frontage adds a splash of colour and a dash of fun to the area. The organic Full Monty fry-ups are as famous as Blue Mountain itself – double sausage, bacon, egg, tomato, mushrooms, toast and a tea or coffee (with a veggie option too) – and there's a nice line in high-cal comfort cakes such as chocolate fudge, banoffee pie and carrot. But there's also good value to be had from the lunch menu, which includes fish cakes, a meze platter, a seriously meaty burger (with fat jacket chips), and assorted salads and sandwiches. A blackboard displays more sophisticated daily specials such as grilled trout, but if you're hungry, the jerk chicken with rice and peas will set you up for anything (and be sure to order some plantain on the side). Changing art exhibitions by south London artists, and a crammed noticeboard add to the busy vibe; this is a friendly café at the heart of the local action.
Babies and children welcome: children's menu; high chairs; nappy-changing facilities. Disabled: toilets. Separate room for parties, seats 10. Tables outdoors (5, garden; 5, terrace).
Map 23 C4.
For branch see index.

Luca's
145 Lordship Lane, SE22 8HX (8613 6161, www.lucasbakery.com). East Dulwich rail. **Open** 9am-5pm Mon-Sat; 9am-4.30pm Sun. **Main courses** £3.50-£7.50. **Credit** AmEx, MC, V.
A prime position on Lordship Lane, with sunny pavement tables, a secluded courtyard out back and plenty of space for buggies in between, makes this a popular spot for stay-at-home parents and homeworkers who can pass significant chunks of their day here. Location aside, the other big draw is the cakes. Dedicated to Austrian pâtisserie, the long counter and display cabinet are heaped with fat cinnamon buns; fruit crumble slices; rich moist sachertorte; spiced carrot cake; baked cheesecake... but there's also room for a few other favourites, such as scones and croissants. The breakfast and light lunch menu is of the eggs benedict/full English/ granola/croque monsieur variety, with a few daily specials and soups. These have the bonus of Luca's own crusty breads, which are also available to buy (many people come in just to pick up their rye loaves and bloomers). Service comes with a smile (apart from the owner). Our advice is to visit in the morning, as by mid-afternoon those post-yoga mums have polished off most of the goodies.
Available for hire. Babies and children welcome: nappy-changing facilities. Tables outdoors (5, garden; 5, pavement). Takeaway service.
Map 23 C4.

Herne Hill

★ Lido Café
Brockwell Lido, Dulwich Road, SE24 0PA (7737 8183, www.thelidocafe.co.uk). Herne Hill rail or Brixton tube/rail then bus 37. **Open** *Summer* 8am-6pm Mon, Tue, Sun; 8am-11pm Wed-Sat. *Winter* 9am-6pm Mon, Tue, Sun; 9am-11pm Wed-Sat. **Main courses** £11.50-£15.95. **Credit** MC, V.
As befits a café attached to one of south London's best-loved outdoor swimming pools, the Lido Café is light, fresh and very chilled. It's a simple white space, flooded with light, opening out on to a decked area of poolside tables, occupied by swimmers as well as dry-side diners. If the squishy sofas and attentive service don't help you relax, then the soothing music (Goldfrapp, Nick Drake), potted palms and fresh-cut flowers will. The monthly menu is designed with love, care and boundless enthusiasm for seasonal British produce, stretching from the breakfast menu of eggs benedict, fry-ups and blueberry buttermilk pancakes (plus a cheeky weekend prosecco) through light lunch dishes (smoked haddock fish cakes, meaty burgers, seasonal tarts, and a juicy pulled-pork bap), to sophisticated evening dinners. Alternatively, you could just pop in for a seriously good coffee, a wicked slice of cake and a few lengths of front crawl. This was judged Time Out's Best Park Café 2011, but it's so much more than that.
Available for hire. Babies and children welcome: children's menu; high chairs; nappy-changing facilities. Disabled: toilet. Tables outdoors (10, terrace). Takeaway service. Vegan dishes.
Map 22 E1.

Peckham

Petitou
63 Choumert Road, SE15 4AR (7639 2613, www.petitou.co.uk). Peckham Rye rail. **Open** 9am-5.30pm Mon-Sat; 10am-5.30pm Sun. **Main courses** £6.60-£7. **Credit** MC, V.
There are destination cafés and there are community cafés. Petitou is the latter. If you're looking for somewhere comfortable to ensconce yourself while you tap on your laptop or breastfeed your baby, this is the place. If you want local art and junk shop furniture in a peaceful leafy street, you'll feel right at home. And if you like healthy comfort food served with a smile and somewhere that positively welcomes children and vegetarians, then sit right down. The menu is all about old favourites such as Marmite on toast, own-made quiche, scrambled egg and bowls of soup, with nice touches like the salad selection served with warm flatbreads. Gooey carrot cake and plates of pastries sit next to a guilt-inducing range of cereal bars, so the choice is between you and your conscience. In this upwardly-mobile corner of Peckham, there is probably more exciting food to be had, and almost certainly more serious coffee, but few places with as big a heart.

Babies and children welcome: high chairs. Tables outdoors (5, pavement). Takeaway service. Vegan dishes. **Map 23 C3**.

East

Docklands

Frizzante@Mudchute

Mudchute Park & Farm, Pier Street, E14 3HP (3069 9290, www.mudchutekitchen.org). Mudchute DLR. **Open** 9.30am-4.50pm Tue-Sun. **Main courses** £2.50-£9. **Credit** MC, V.

Frizzante, the company that runs the lovely café at Hackney City Farm, took on Mudchute Kitchen in spring 2011 (having already taken over the café at Surrey Docks City Farm). You'll find the café in the middle of Mudchute City Farm, a short walk from Mudchute DLR station. It's a world away from the towers of Canary Wharf, which poke up over the fields to the north. The café looks as it always did, with wooden tables, shelves of books, white walls and posters about Isle of Dogs inhabitants. The kitchen is noticeably better organised, however. Most customers are family groups, here to pet and feed the animals, and the food reflects this. The kids' menu includes scrambled egg or beans on toast and a variety of pastas, while adults are offered a hearty meat dish, plus salad, soup and pasta options. The coffee is excellent and the small selection of cakes and Italian ice-creams superb. Staff are friendly (once you've got their attention) and seem very relaxed about people eating their own picnics on the large terrace overlooking the stables.

Babies and children welcome: children's menu; high chairs; nappy-changing facilities. Disabled: toilet (farm). Tables outdoors (20, courtyard). Takeaway service. **Map 24 C4**.

Shoreditch

Frizzante@Hackney City Farm

Hackney City Farm, 1A Goldsmith's Row, E2 8QA (7739 2266, www.frizzanteltd.co.uk). Hoxton rail. **Lunch served** 10am-4pm Tue-Sun. **Dinner served** 7-10pm Thur. **Main courses** £5-£17. **Credit** MC, V.

Come to this City Farm café on a weekend at your peril; toddlers rule the roost inside and out, and while the food is appealing, nearby Broadway Market or Columbia Road offer better, more original cooking without having to eat it in a crèche. But come in the evening and it's a different matter. Then, the shabby space comes into its own, with candles and strings of coloured bulbs bringing out the natural warmth of the wooden decor. The menu is much the same as its daytime counterpart – all-day breakfasts, pastas, salads and roasts – but on Thursdays, an ambitious *agriturismo* menu offers a small selection of rustic dishes such as own-made pappardelle with asparagus, peas and pecorino, rabbit stew, stuffed squash, and seared duck salad. The quality of both the produce and cooking is variable, and some dishes are overpriced at around £16, but on a warm evening you can get a very real sense of eating in an idyllic Italian hillside trattoria, despite being yards away from Hackney Road. Don't come hungry though – courses are served around 45 minutes apart, and with no bread or nibbles to munch on, it's a long night.

Available for hire (autumn and winter only). Babies and children welcome: children's menu; high chairs; nappy-changing facilities. Booking advisable dinner. Disabled: toilet. Tables outdoors (10, park). **Map 6 S3**.

Jones Dairy Café

23 Ezra Street, E2 7RH (7739 5372). Hoxton rail. **Meals served** 9am-3pm Fri; 9am-4.30pm Sat; 8am-3pm Sun. **Main courses** £3-£8. **No credit cards**.

Jones Dairy sits on a narrow cobbled side street off Columbia Road, its interior a charming one-time stable with a huge, picturesque stove occupying one corner and a tiny counter another. It's a ramshackle affair, all mismatched tables and chairs, and the kind of granny crockery you'd once have found on Brick Lane for pennies. Outside, a few equally rickety tables are perfect for sunny days – unless it's a Sunday, when the parade of people tottering along with huge plants from Columbia Road Flower Market can be overwhelming. Daily specials (written on a board) include smoked salmon with fennel and orange salad, and flaky, crumbly pasties and rolls, while mainstays include a range of all-day breakfasts, from traditional fry-ups to the likes of Mersea Island oysters and Norfolk herring kippers. All are excellent, come with bread and butter (you can help yourself to jams and preserves from a tray), are reasonably priced and served by friendly staff, making the experience a retro one in the best sense.

Babies and children welcome: high chairs. Tables outdoors (4, pavement). Takeaway service. **Map 6 S3**.

Ozone Café NEW

11 Leonard Street, EC2A 4AQ (7490 1039, www.ozonecoffee.co.uk). Old Street tube/rail.
Open 7.30am-5pm Mon-Fri; 9am-4pm Sat, Sun. **Main courses** £5-£11. **Credit** AmEx, MC, V.
Ozone started life in New Zealand, then opened in London as a coffee roaster in 1998, and as a café in March 2012. It's already a popular spot, and often has a long queue for takeaways. Understandably so – it's an impressive place occupying two floors of a converted industrial building, with a nicely grungy feel, especially in the downstairs rooms where tables have a view of the roastery. Service is friendly, and the menu covers all the bases from granola, through eggs, to proper main courses. Food displays strong Mediterranean, Asian and Middle Eastern influences. A vegetable broth flavoured with soy, sesame and ginger was light yet deeply flavourful. An earthy-coloured kedgeree had a perfect poached egg replacing the hard-boiled egg of the traditional version. There's lots by the glass on the all-Kiwi wine list, and a better-than-average set of soft drinks including teas and milkshakes. Strangely enough, the coffee was the sole let-down. A flat white was fine, but the only filter coffee available was woefully weak and barely hot. A glitch, we're sure, but an odd one in such a quality-conscious outfit.
Available for hire. Babies and children welcome: high chairs. Booking advisable; bookings not accepted Sat, Sun. Disabled: toilet. Separate room for parties, seats 16. **Map 6 Q4.**

Salvation Jane NEW

1 Oliver's Yard, 55 City Road, EC1Y 1HQ (7253 5273, www.salvationjanecafe.co.uk). Old Street tube/rail. **Open** 7.30am-5pm Mon; 7.30am-10pm Tue-Fri; 9am-5pm Sat, Sun. **Meals served** 8am-3pm Mon-Fri; 9am-3.30pm Sat, Sun. **Dinner served** 6-9.30pm Tue-Fri. **Main courses** £3-£12. **Credit** MC, V.
A new sibling for Antipodean café Lantana, just off Old Street roundabout, Salvation Jane is not only bigger than its sibling, it's also open longer hours. A large display counter at the entrance is reserved for takeaways, while a spacious dining room is tucked away at the back. There are brunch-style dishes, such as french toast with maple syrup, bacon and fried bananas; lunch sees sandwiches, salads and more substantial mains with an Australian influence; in the evening there's a selection of small plates. At lunch, corn fritters on a bed of rocket came with bacon (to our regret, not crisp) and chilli jam – a good sweet-savoury combo. Confit duck leg with crisp skin and moist and flavoursome meat lost points for an oddly bland 'slaw of red cabbage, fennel and raisin. Cakes are a highlight, and the window is stacked with mouth-watering sweet treats. A cherry ripe slice (a homage to the Aussie chocolate bar of the same name) had biscuit base topped with a red glacé cherry and coconut mixture, covered with a thick chocolate layer – enough to make any expat nostalgic.
Available for hire. Babies and children admitted. Disabled: toilet. Tables outdoors (5, courtyard). Takeaway service. Vegan dishes. **Map 6 Q4.**

Spitalfields

Nude Espresso

26 Hanbury Street, E1 6QR (07804 223590, www.nudeespresso.com). Liverpool Street tube/rail or Shoreditch High Street rail.
Open 7am-8pm Mon-Fri; 9.30am-7pm Sat, Sun. **Main courses** £4-£9.50. **Credit** AmEx, MC, V.
On a sunny Saturday morning, Nude was a sea of milky foam, artfully feathered on a non-stop procession of cups. The long, light room was packed out, and not just with hip caffeinistas but parents and young children too. Despite the crowds, solo customers were allowed to sit at tables for two and watch the world go by. Nude takes its food ever more seriously. The brunch/lunch menu was imaginative, and very popular: half a dozen plates of ricotta pancakes, with roasted grape and pomegranate molasses went by us in 20 minutes, and much else besides. As we went to press, plans were afoot for offering a dinner menu. That will surely be popular, both here and at the newer branch in Soho. Coffee? Our espresso was well-made from Nude's own East blend: bracing and nicely bitter, needing just a pinch of sugar to make the balance perfect. It could have been hotter, but that's the problem almost everywhere and not a major complaint. Brunch at Nude is definitely an occasion worth getting dressed for.
Babies and children admitted. Bookings not accepted. Tables outdoors (2, pavement). Takeaway service. Vegan dishes. Vegetarian menu. **Map 12 S5.**
For branch see index.

Tea Smith

6 Lamb Street, E1 6EA (7247 1333, www.teasmith.co.uk). Liverpool Street tube/rail.
Open 11am-6pm daily. **Afternoon tea** £20. **No credit cards.**
Get to know the national drink in more depth by booking in for afternoon tea at this little café. Take a seat at the long red bar, and one of the knowledgeable staff will serve – and explain – several different styles of tea. You get some exquisite cakes too. White tea (using the lightest of all leaves, picked when young) was served first as a palate cleanser, along with a delicious cinnamon palmier. Next, an energising Korean green tea, renowned for its nuttiness, came with a miso and walnut biscuit with matcha (ground green tea leaves) and honey. The third tea was a floral oolong – somewhere between green and our more familiar black tea – from the mountains of Taiwan. Its slightly grassy scent was followed by a warm, frothy matcha tea, served in a bowl and passed around the table, in the traditional manner. A final oolong was a smoky, long-roasted leaf, said to aid digestion. A pleasant and informative experience – the only jarring note was the incongruous soundtrack (Van Halen and T-Rex to the fore).
Babies and children admitted. Takeaway service. **Map 12 R5.**

Victoria Park

Pavilion Café

Victoria Park, Crown Gate West, E9 7DE (8980 0030, www.the-pavilion-cafe.com). Mile End tube then bus 277, 425. **Meals served** *Summer* 8am-4pm Mon; 8am-8pm Tue-Sun. *Winter* 8am-4pm daily. **Main courses** £4-£9. **Credit** MC, V.
The domed pavilion on Victoria Park's boating lake is nowadays a fine café, populated (during weekends at least) as heavily by young Hackney trendies as rampaging family groups. Proceedings were given a lovely lilt on our latest visit by an understated jazz trio. All the tables were outside (covering fair acreage), so it was possible to grab a seat even in the midday rush – though we would gladly have queued for the food. From an extensive all-day breakfast menu (three types of eggs benedict, kippers, pancakes, things on toast, three variations on full english), we plumped for the Farmhouse (fried egg on toast, magnificent black pudding, sausage, bacon and disappointingly flavourless own-made baked beans). Of the select lunch list (two burgers, salad, BLT on focaccia with aïoli), a beetroot, ricotta, puy lentil and watercress salad needed a more aggressive cheese or heavier seasoning, but was accompanied by excellent focaccia with frills of shaved courgette baked on top. Cakes were a hit: chocolate brownie a mite dry, but not oversweet; grapefruit brioche a pleasantly grown-up surprise. Best of all, the pretty young waitresses were well drilled and knowledgeable.
Babies and children welcome: children's menu; high chairs; nappy-changing facilities. Bookings not accepted. Disabled: toilet. Tables outdoors (20, park). Takeaway service.

North East

Clapton

Venetia

55 Chatsworth Road, E5 0LH (8986 1642). Homerton rail or bus 242, 308. **Open** 8am-5pm daily. **Main courses** £4-£4.85. **Credit** MC, V.
This pretty little café, along with a crêperie and a deli, forms a foodie triangle on Chatsworth Road. The demographic changes as the day goes on: it's popular with mums and babies mid-morning, does a brisk lunchtime trade with workers, then fills up with laptop users through the afternoon, before finally emerging as an after-school spot. A short menu covers pastries and cakes (lemon drizzle, cupcakes), substantial sandwiches and toasties, own-made soup and a salad at lunch, and decent Fairtrade coffee all day. Service is friendly and solicitous – help with awkward buggies a speciality – and the noticeboard, carrying details of flute lessons and tai chi classes, along with the 10% discount for NHS and nearby Beaufort School staff, signals that this is very much a locals' café. An outside area comes into its own in the summer.
Babies and children welcome: high chairs; nappy-changing facilities; toys. Tables outdoors (6, garden). Takeaway service.

Dalston

Tina, We Salute You

47 King Henry's Walk, N1 4NH (3119 0047, www.tinawesaluteyou.com). Dalston Kingsland rail or bus 38. **Open** 8am-5pm Mon; 8am-7pm Tue-Fri; 10am-7pm Sat, Sun. **Main courses** £4-£6. **No credit cards.**
Set in the backstreets of Dalston, this place is essentially a neighbourhood café, offering good coffee, a friendly welcome and a short, simple blackboard menu: chilli-sprinkled avocado or own-made baked beans on toast, say, or pancakes piled with fruit. The hot breakfast pide is about as elaborate as it gets: a slab of Turkish flatbread filled with egg mayonnaise, cheese, ham, spinach and chilli jam; a cure for the most sinister of hangovers. Early arrivals can choose from a handful of pavement tables, the sagging sofa and armchair in one corner or the square communal table, with its

Salvation Jane. See p285.

teapot of flowers, stack of newspapers and help-yourself pots of jams and honey; a narrow window seat accommodates the overflow. The laid-back, anything-goes attitude extends to the decor, with a different local artist given free rein to paint on the walls and install their work for two-month stints; the back wall, meanwhile, functions as an ad-hoc loyalty scheme, scrawled from floor to ceiling with regulars' names and a star for every coffee they've bought. Remember to bring cash as there's no card machine, and look out for JH Lynch's kitschly suggestive portrait of Tina by the counter.
Babies and children admitted. Bookings not accepted. Disabled: toilet. Tables outdoors (3, pavement). Takeaway service.

Hackney

Wilton Way Café NEW

63 Wilton Way, E8 1BG (7249 0444, www.londonfieldsradio.com). Hackney Central rail or bus D6, 48, 106, 254. **Open** 8am-5pm Mon-Fri; 8am-6pm Sat; 9am-6pm Sun. **Main courses** £2.50-£5.50. **No credit cards.**

Independently owned Wilton Way Café is home to a steady stream of twenty- to thirtysomethings, some with kids, others with laptops. Stylish recycling – such as the converted apple crates turned into tables on wheels that slide neatly under benches – is the order of the day. Curvy, corrugated iron-clad counters are laden with cakes and pastries, while in the corner stands the London Fields radio station equipment (it's hosted from here). Food is quality stuff: suppliers include local E5 Bakehouse, Brindisa and Ginger Pig. Those in a hurry grab a coffee (beans supplied by nearby Climpson & Sons) from a list that includes an excellent flat white; those stopping to eat can chow down on a selection of delicious toast-based snacks, including portobello mushroom with goat's curd on sourdough, served with peppery rocket and a sprinkle of chilli flakes.
Babies and children admitted. Entertainment: live radio station. Tables outdoors (4, pavement). Takeaway service.

Hackney Wick

Counter Café

Stour Space, 7 Roach Road, E3 2PA (07834 275920, www.thecountercafe.co.uk). Hackney Wick tube/rail or bus 488. **Open** 7.30am-midnight daily. **Main courses** £3.50-£9. **Credit** AmEx, MC, V.

Counter Cafe retains much from its original boho incarnation up the road – alt-folk sounds, rough floor, tables of recycled wood blocks and a row of cinema seats – but feels more grown up now it's settled into the River Lea side of the Stour Space gallery. The staff are cool yet faultlessly charming, but not always efficient – most recently, a lost ticket meant a wait of nearly an hour. When breakfast did arrive, it was up to its normal high standards: skinny but flavour-packed sausages, thick rashers, a dense potato cake, glossy scrambled eggs, and a trademark spicy, garlicky mix of tomatoes and white beans, eased down with a punchy long black. The rest of the menu runs from muesli to enticing pies (pork, apple and fennel; moroccan lamb, aubergine and mint). The once superlative view of the Olympic Stadium is much diminished by three-storey prefabs on the far bank, but new folding tables on river-level decking outside are perfect for observing the coots. Expect the place to be busy at weekends, when tapas is served until late.
Available for hire. Babies and children admitted. Bookings not accepted before 6pm. Disabled: toilet. Tables outdoors (4, pavement; 20, canal). Takeaway service.

Haggerston

Towpath HOT 50

Regent's Canal towpath, between Whitmore Bridge and Kingsland Road Bridge, N1 5SB (no phone). Haggerston rail or bus 67, 149. **Open** *Mar-Nov* 8am-dusk Tue-Fri; 9am-dusk Sat, Sun. **Main courses** £3-£8. **No credit cards.**

A few years ago, no one would have given a café by Hackney's Whitmore Bridge, accessible only from the Regent's Canal towpath, much chance of survival. Now, the Towpath has a swanky neighbour (Waterline, *see p62*). But the simplicity of Towpath remains hugely appealing: four shallow units opening on to the canal, one for the kitchen, one for hot drinks, cakes and orders, and two to sit in when you don't fancy one of the uncovered tables. The food (off a chalkboard) is very good despite the restrictions of the kitchen: we enjoyed a peppery crusted pork tenderloin served with grilled green peppers, their slight chilli heat mitigated by mint and parsley, all with a punchy jus. The cakes are lovely – especially the delightfully sharp raspberry tart, crunchy outside, moist within. Hot chocolate, served in a small glass, was rich-flavoured but frothily light. We had to wait half an hour for Saturday lunch, but coots on the canal and passing cyclists and dog-walkers are excellent entertainment.
Available for hire. Babies and children admitted. Bookings not accepted. Tables outdoors (10, towpath). **Map 6 R1.**

North

Camden Town & Chalk Farm

Lanka

71 Regent's Park Road, NW1 8UY (7483 2544, www.lanka-uk.com). Chalk Farm tube. **Open** 9am-6.30pm Tue-Sat; 9am-5pm Sun. **Main courses** £5-£12. **Credit** AmEx, MC, V.

Despite a queue that spills out on to the pavement, this tiny cake shop and tea salon oozes serenity. Exposed brickwork combined with pristine white walls offers a blank canvas for the pretty pâtisserie and desserts. Some are traditional, others have a Japanese twist, such as the green tea bread and butter pudding. The assiette of desserts is the best way to sample as many of these exquisite creations as possible, and is a great showcase for the talents of chef-patron Masayuki Hara. Of the selection – all matched with own-made vanilla ice-cream – the standouts were a delicious miniature chocolate sponge roll and a delightful rhubarb mousse tart. The mostly Japanese staff are friendly and unobtrusive, and will happily advise on the tea menu, which lists an extensive selection of exclusive infusions from the Euphorium Tea Salon in Sri Lanka. All loose tea is Ceylon based and served in stylish glass teapots. Monmouth coffee is also on offer.
Babies and children admitted. Tables outdoors (2, pavement). Takeaway service. **Map 27 A2.**

Finsbury Park

Boulangerie Bon Matin

178 Tollington Park, N4 3AJ (7263 8633, www.boulangeriebonmatin.co.uk). Finsbury Park tube/rail. **Open** 7am-6.30pm daily. **Main courses** 80p-£5.90. **Credit** MC, V.

French pâtisseries are rare on the streets of Finsbury Park, so Boulangerie Bon Matin's pretty window display is a nice surprise. As the name suggests, this café is more of a morning venue, with the kitchen closing at 3.30pm, but until then, warm sandwiches, quiches and salads are on offer alongside a breakfast and brunch menu. From a range of cakes and pastries that runs from fruit tarts to chocolate gateaux, the blueberry financier caught our eye; this little almond-flour based cake was light but moist, with a juicy blueberry-filled centre. Cheesecake was pleasant though a little dry. Breads are another speciality; the choice includes various types of rye as well as a traditional french stick. The café's bare brick walls display work by local artists, and there's a lovely light-filled extension at the back. One final plus – the coffee is worth ordering; enjoy it while flicking through one of the many newspapers supplied.
Available for hire. Babies and children welcome: high chairs. Takeaway service.

Highgate

Pavilion Café

Highgate Woods, Muswell Hill Road, N10 3JN (8444 4777). Highgate tube. **Open** 9am-1hr before park closing daily. **Main courses** £6-£10. **Credit** AmEx, MC, V.

This café has a captive market and knows it. Set in a clearing surrounded by the ancient trees of Highgate Wood, sporting a large terrace inside a picket fence, it's pure English idyll. Families, joggers and walkers (with or without dogs) are its main customers, and it's easy to see why complaints about service never register – a steady stream of punters continues to arrive despite long waits for attention, food and bills. On a chilly lunchtime, with very few tables occupied, we still waited almost 50 minutes for our main courses, while later arrivals were already on their pudding. The menu lists the usual standards (burger and chips, pitta and dips, pasta), but the specials board tries harder. We oped for roast salmon steak stuffed with soft cheese and chives, and paprika-marinated rump steak with chips. Both were decently cooked, although the salmon was a stingy portion, padded out by a mountain of potatoes. More pleasing was lemon polenta cake (and their plum muffin is a local legend). If you're in a hurry, the kiosk round the side serves ice-creams, coffees and snacks speedily in summer.
Babies and children welcome: children's menu; crayons; high chairs; nappy-changing facilities. Disabled: toilet. Tables outdoors (30, garden). Takeaway service. Vegetarian menu.

Hornsey

Haberdashery

22 Middle Lane, N8 8PL (8342 8098, www.the-haberdashery.com). Turnpike Lane tube or Crouch Hill or Hornsey rail. **Open** 8am-6pm Mon-Fri; 9am-6pm Sat, Sun. **Main courses** £5.95-£9.50. **Credit** AmEx, MC, V.

Although the Haberdashery only opened in 2010, it has established itself as a Crouch End institution,

Kahve Dünyasi. See p280.

complete with regular musical evenings, a once-a-month bazaar and the like. Its artful retro styling sees bunting strung across the room, mismatched vintage crockery on display shelves, and fireplace tiles decorating the walls. There's also art for sale. But it's more than a pretty face – the food is good too. Breakfast and weekend brunches (full english, breakfast baguette, porridge) segue into lunch: mains such as Scandinavian meatballs and two sides (earthy beetroot 'slaw and summery confit tomato and leaf salad, say) or minted grilled halloumi, or soup of the day and hearty sandwiches. Drinks include cordials, fresh juices, coffee (from Italian roasters Bristot) and tea (a wide range from W Martyn in Muswell Hill). Baking is also a strong point; try one of the daily changing flowerpot-baked breads or one of the splendid cakes. We gave the wheat-free almond sponge filled with mascarpone and blackberries the thumbs-up.
Available for hire. Babies and children welcome: children's menu; high chairs; nappy-changing facilities. Tables outdoors (12, garden; 2, pavement). Takeaway service.

Muswell Hill

Feast on the Hill

46 Fortis Green Road, N10 3HN (8444 4957, www.feastcaterers.co.uk). Highgate tube then bus 43, 134. **Open** 8.30am-5pm Mon-Wed, Sun; 8.30am-10pm Thur-Sat. **Main courses** £6-£12. **Set lunch** (Mon-Fri noon-4pm) £7.95 1 course incl drink. **Credit** MC, V.

The café part of this café/deli operation is a popular haunt for locals and packs out at lunchtime with diners reeled in by the £7.95 special deal. This buys a drink and a dish, such as hearty meat lasagne in a sea of tomato sauce or fish cake with salad. (Busier locals can opt to have it delivered.) The space, with its Farrow & Ball walls, bentwood chairs and wooden tables, is light and appealing, but, thanks to poor acoustics, not great for an intimate chat. Prices are reasonable, portions are large and service is warm and friendly. The menu of burgers, panini and all-day breakfasts – from full fry-ups to eggs benedict and muesli – is supplemented by items from the deli next door – the soup, tarts (a choice of three) and meat and vegetable lasagne. Later on, Feast segues into an evening venue, when tablecloths and a more upmarket menu appear, though the good value remains: £11.95 for two courses.
Babies and children welcome: children's menu; high chairs. Disabled: toilet. Tables outdoors (4, pavement). Takeaway service.

Newington Green

That Place On the Corner

1-3 Green Lanes, N16 9BS (7704 0079, www.thatplaceonthecorner.co.uk). Canonbury rail or bus 73, 141, 341. **Open** 9.30am-5.30pm Mon-Fri; 9am-2.30pm Sat. **Main courses** £3.95-£6.95. **Credit** MC, V.

This is probably the only café in London with a door policy: an adult must be accompanied by a child to enter. The aim is to create a home-from-home atmosphere for local families. A giant doll's house, groaning book shelves, floor cushions and an extensive dressing-up wardrobe means children can play while parents snatch a chat over coffee in this light and pleasant space. Owners (local mums Sam and Ginny) and their staff are chatty with children and friendly to their carers; regulars get Monopoly

money to spend as cash on their next visit. They've thought of everything: toddler portions, bibs, bottle warmers, purées and a help-yourself cold water urn with tap. The menu features freshly cooked, healthy ingredients, and dish quality has improved since our last visit – beetroot and feta salad was excellent. Kids get several pasta options (own-made pesto, tomato and basil, bolognese), bangers and mash, a burger and so on. Service can be a bit haphazard (they completely forgot our child's meal), but the all-round generosity of spirit makes up for it.
Available for hire. Babies and children welcome: children's menu; colouring books; crayons; high chairs; nappy-changing facilities; toys. Disabled: toilet. Takeaway service. **Map 25 A4.**

North West

Hampstead

Brew House

Kenwood House, Hampstead Lane, NW3 7JR (8341 5384, www.companyofcooks.com). Archway or Golders Green tube then bus 210. **Open** *Apr-Sept* 9am-6pm daily (7.30pm on concert nights). *Oct-Mar* 9am-dusk daily. **Main courses** £4.75-£9.95. **Credit** AmEx, MC, V.
Company of Cooks' tried-and-tested formula at the Brew House, the cafeteria at Kenwood House, remains the same. The flagstone floors and high ceilings inside the old kitchen wing make for a din on busy weekends. Choose from the limited menu at the hotplate (full english breakfasts, then sausage and veg, quiche and salad or soup and bread for lunch) or fresh and well-filled doorstep sandwiches in the chiller cabinet. The hotplate is a less attractive option during quieter weekdays as food sits around for longer. The coffee is unremarkable, but there's a selection of quality cakes available (we're partial to the unusually spicy carrot cake and the gooseberry and elderflower cheesecake). The Brew House is an institution frequented by old and young, wellied and well heeled, and the tiered, sheltered terrace is one of the prettiest spots in north London. Despite its limitations, locals always come back for more. Company of Cooks runs cafés at other tourist sites across London, including the Imperial War Museum, Greenwich Park and Hyde Park.
Available for hire. Babies and children welcome: children's menu; high chairs; nappy-changing facilities. Separate room for parties, seats 120. Tables outdoors (50, garden). Takeaway service. Vegetarian menu. **Map 28 C1.**

Kensal Green

Gracelands

118 College Road, NW10 5HD (8964 9161, www.gracelandscafe.com). Kensal Green tube. **Open** 8.30am-5pm Mon-Fri; 9am-4.30pm Sat; 9.30am-3.30pm Sun. **Main courses** £7-£12.95. **Credit** AmEx, MC, V.
The large terrace out front, the partially covered garden, the airy interior and informal atmosphere attract all sorts to Gracelands. Families love it because there's also a toy and children's book area; in the pretty backyard, kids group together to play hide-and-seek along the mews. Others come for refreshment after visiting Gracelands Yard (a creative holistic centre). The food at the café was always good, but they've really sorted out the service since our last visit. Now it's calm, friendly and knowledgeable instead of chaotic. Breakfasts and brunches are popular, as is the salad bar fronting the open kitchen. Red cabbage coleslaw, roasted parsnip, carrot and butternut squash salad, chick pea medley and green bean salad are typical choices. Hearty quiches taste just-cooked, while the cake selection is small but well formed, with the double chocolate cheesecake and lime and coconut cake both scoring top marks. There are cooked breakfasts and pasta options for kids, and a large soft drink selection that includes smoothies. Coffee now comes from Caravan, and you can taste the improvement.
Babies and children welcome: children's menu; high chairs; nappy-changing facilities; play area; toys. Tables outdoors (5, pavement; 8, garden). Takeaway service.

Ozone Café. See p285.

Coffee Bars

Londoners – and London – have come a long way since the time when instant coffee was ubiquitous. Back in that insipid era, only the odd Italian or Greek café stood out as a rich brown oasis in a grey desert. These days, the level of expertise of much of the drinking public has approached connoisseurship. Do the best beans come from Brazil, Nicaragua, Costa Rica or elsewhere? Does a La Marzocco or a Synesso machine have the edge? And what about the roasting? Likewise, the London coffee bar scene has responded, with a variety of dedicated, independent enterprises that grind the global chains into dust. This is still a dynamic sector, with great new bars popping up frequently. This year we welcome Covent Garden's **Salt**, and Battersea's excellent **Birdhouse** (run, like many of the city's best caffeine joints, by Australians). Birdhouse immediately joins our list of favourite coffee bars that also includes **Monmouth**, near London Bridge, **Prufrock** on Leather Lane, and Fitzrovia's **Kaffeine**. Elsewhere in this guide you'll encounter other purveyors of great coffee, most notably **Fernandez & Wells** (*see p281*) **Nude Espresso** (*see p285*) and **Caravan** (*see p39*). Here, we give the best a good roasting.

Central

Bloomsbury

Espresso Room

31-35 Great Ormond Street, WC1N 3HZ (07760 714883, www.theespressoroom.com). Russell Square tube. **Open** 7.30am-5pm Mon-Fri. **No credit cards.**

Some people have wardrobes that are larger than the Espresso Room – a dozen people would make the place feel crowded. ER has been wowing customers since opening in 2010. It's completely focused on coffee, made in a lovingly cared-for La Marzocco machine. Beans are from Square Mile and Has Bean, with Square Mile providing the espresso (Red Brick) when we visited. This is a powerful blend, but there is sweetness in there too, carefully preserved in brewing. Had the crema not been just a little bit thin, it would have been a perfect cup. Food is minimal: one sandwich, a soup of the day (Moroccan chicken on our visit), baked sweet things. The famous children's hospital is just across the road, and academics from nearby university campuses also feature among the clientele. Service is from a pair of baristas who display warmth and friendliness in addition to technical skills. ER proves that small is indeed beautiful.

Babies and children admitted. Tables outdoors (6, pavement). Takeaway service. **Map 4 L4.**

Chancery Lane

Department of Coffee & Social Affairs

14-16 Leather Lane, EC1N 7SU (no phone, www.departmentofcoffee.co.uk). Chancery Lane tube. **Open** 7am-6pm Mon-Fri; 10am-4pm Sat, Sun. **Credit** (over £5) MC, V.

A Supremes compilation was playing on the sound system when we came here, and just about every aspect of the place made us hear a symphony. The decor is especially welcoming, with some of the most evocative bare-brick walls you've seen outside Pompeii. Service was ultra-friendly. Espresso and piccolo (espresso with foamed milk) were both well made on a La Marzocco machine that was carefully tended between coffees, and foamed milk applied with care. Beans come from assorted suppliers, with a constantly changing roster. At lunchtime there's a varied selection of sandwiches, and baked goodies are made both here and elsewhere (including the excellent Primrose Bakery). Our brownie and plum cake were outstanding, though the brownie seemed pricey given its size. Our only other grumble is that the espresso arrived at too low a temperature: slightly weird, since it was just a ten-second walk from the machine to our table. But there's an epidemic of under-hot espresso in London at the moment, so this is hardly a unique problem. Nor is it important enough to prevent another visit to this charming venue.

Babies and children admitted. Separate room for parties, seats 12-20. Tables outdoors (3, market). Takeaway service. **Map 11 N5.**

★ Prufrock Coffee

23-25 Leather Lane, EC1N 7TE (7242 0467, www.prufrockcoffee.com). Chancery Lane tube. **Open** 8am-6pm Mon-Fri; 10am-5pm Sat; 10am-4pm Sun. **Credit** AmEx, MC, V.

This is the second branch of the highly respected Shoreditch original (a tiny bar at the front of a men's clothing store: no chairs, you just stand there or take away). The Leather Lane operation couldn't be more different. It's a large, airy space with plenty of comfortable seating, and is clearly designed for people who want to take their time. Which we did, with the happiest of results. This branch uses mostly Square Mile beans and one of two prototypes of a Dutch-made 'Spirit' espresso machine, given by the manufacturers for testing and feedback before rolling it out for production. The coffee is excellent, though the espresso (like so many) wasn't hot enough. For those who don't want espresso or espresso with milk, top-notch brewed coffees are made using several different methods, including the increasingly popular Aeropress. Whether sweet or savoury, food is good, with prices that – while not exactly low – are in line with competitors. Even amid stout competition, Prufrock continues to shine.

Available for hire. Babies and children admitted. Disabled: toilet. Takeaway service. **Map 11 N5. For branch see index.**

Clerkenwell & Farringdon

Brill

27 Exmouth Market, EC1R 4QL (7833 9757, www.clerkenwellmusic.co.uk). Angel tube or Farringdon tube/rail. **Open** 7.30am-6pm Mon-Fri; 9am-6pm Sat; 11am-4pm Sun. **No credit cards**.

In the mid 1990s, with sales of CDs sliding, Jeremy Brill, owner of the tiny music shop here, decided he could subsidise the business by selling coffee. Coffee came to be increasingly important, and in 2011 the shop was refurbished to create a coffee bar that also sells CDs (and a bit of second-hand vinyl). The result is a little gem. For one thing, the staff play great music. For another, they show real enthusiasm for everything they do, including serving customers. The small choice of food is of a high quality; there are a few savouries (notably bagels), but baked goods dominate. The one downer on our visit was an espresso that had deficient crema. But they use a good blend from Union Coffee Roasters and a bit of training could solve the problem quickly. In the meantime, we wouldn't hesitate to choose Brill even if Exmouth Market is jam-packed with coffee purveyors. Why? All those smiling faces. The sweet back garden. And where else can you browse the music shelves, and pick up anything from Johnny Cash to Ornette Coleman while waiting for your cup to appear?

Babies and children admitted. Tables outdoors (3, pavement; 4, garden). **Map 5 N4**.

Dose Espresso

70 Long Lane, EC1A 9EJ (7600 0382, www.dose-espresso.com). Barbican tube. **Open** 7am-5pm Mon-Fri; 9am-4pm Sat. **Credit** MC, V.

This tiny place near Smithfield Market can barely seat a dozen people, and that gives the barista plenty of time to concentrate on each cup. Which she did with happy results on our visit. The espresso was a single-origin Brazilian (from Square Mile) called Fazenda do Sertão, and it made a really memorable cup: sweet notes preserved with a backbone of pleasing acidity. Served properly hot, it required no sugar. Dose trains its staff well in the use of the big La Marzocco machine, and it clearly has a happy relationship with Square Mile, which supplies most of the beans (there are a few guest coffees as well). Most of the tables occupy an L-shaped space giving equally good views of the bar and the big window, past which office workers walk – many of them ending up in here for their dose. There's very little food: cereal, toast, yoghurt and a few filled croissants. So you're unlikely to come for lunch, but that isn't the point here. The point is the coffee. And the point is well made.

Babies and children admitted. Takeaway service. **Map 11 O5**.

Covent Garden

Salt NEW

34 Great Queen Street, WC2B 5AA (7430 0335, www.saltwc2.co.uk). Covent Garden or Holborn tube. **Open** 7.30am-7pm Mon-Fri; 10am-7pm Sat. **Credit** MC, V.

There's much to like about Salt. For one thing, it looks great: white walls, bare wooden floors, tables and chairs made by the East London Furniture company from reclaimed wood, big windows looking on to the street, cosy back room. Service is friendly and skilled, and the barista tended his small La Marzocco conscientiously. Baked goods are made in-house, there's a varied selection of teas, and food includes sandwiches, a daily stew and some very popular salads. We just wish our sandwich had been better made. Billed as mozzarella with serrano ham, it contained insipid cheese, and ham cut from the knuckle-end, so it was dominated by fat and gristle: impossible to bite off a mouthful gracefully. But the ciabatta roll was good, and greater attention would eliminate the faults. Our espresso made up for them. All beans come from Square Mile, and the seasonal Red Brick blend produced a typically assertive, bracing (and well-made) brew. Anyone working nearby should regard Salt as a lunchtime sweet-spot – especially when the staff sort out their sandwich blips.

Babies and children admitted. Tables outdoors (2, pavement). Takeaway service. **Map 18 E3**.

Fitzrovia

★ Kaffeine

66 Great Titchfield Street, W1W 7QJ (7580 6755, www.kaffeine.co.uk). Oxford Circus tube. **Open** 7.30am-6pm Mon-Fri; 9am-6pm Sat; 9.30am-5pm Sun. **Credit** (over £6) MC, V.

Kaffeine remains as popular as ever: there was barely a spare seat on a rainy Friday lunchtime. Staff coped brilliantly, taking pains to be helpful and friendly to customers and colleagues alike. The attractive room of muted earth tones and exposed brick is similarly warm and welcoming. Food has always been taken seriously here and is stronger than ever, far exceeding mere café grub. Think heritage tomato salad with watercress, sea purslane and hedge garlic, or pulled pork belly on candied beetroot and radicchio. There are good-looking sandwiches and a tart of the day; on our visit, the large selection of baked goods was constantly replenished from the kitchen downstairs. Dozens of elegantly feathered milky drinks went past us, and the essentials of machine maintenance were observed rigorously. Our espresso (Square Mile beans from a Synesso machine) was of fine quality, sweet and rounded, though it wasn't hot enough by the time it reached us (a common problem these days). If there is a complaint about Kaffeine, it's that you feel guilty for dawdling when there's a queue for tables.

Available for hire. Babies and children welcome: high chair. Takeaway service. Vegan dishes. **Map 9 J5**.

Tapped & Packed

26 Rathbone Place, W1T 1JD (7580 2163, www.tappedandpacked.co.uk). Tottenham Court Road tube. **Open** 8am-7pm Mon-Fri; 9am-7pm Sat. **Credit** AmEx, MC, V.

T&P used to buy beans from several roasters, but has narrowed the field down to just one: Has Bean. Happily, there has been no fall-off in quality as a result. This top-notch Fitzrovia hangout remains a coffee-lover's haven, whether you want espresso-based drinks (Simonelli machine), or brewed coffees made in a drip cone or the increasingly popular Aeropress. When we went, the Aeropress specialist

Prufrock Coffee

Salt. See p291.

was not around. We contented ourselves with a drip Nicaraguan, the drip unrushed and the beans excellent (single-origin, as were both of the other filter choices). Sandwiches and baked goods are all made on the premises and reasonably priced. The decor is plain and attractive: dark wood in the benches, tables and flooring contrasting with the magnolia-hued paint on the walls (which would benefit from a fresh coat). Beans and coffee hardware are sold to take away, and service comes with a big smile and willingness to talk. All in all, we love this place.
Babies and children admitted. Takeaway service. **Map 17 B2.**
For branch see index.

Soho

Flat White

17 Berwick Street, W1F 0PT (7734 0370, www.flatwhitecafe.com). Leicester Square, Oxford Circus or Tottenham Court Road tube. **Open** 8am-7pm Mon-Fri; 9am-6pm Sat, Sun. **No credit cards.**

While its baby sister Milk Bar seems in need of freshening up, Flat White is as perky as a spring lamb. The place is rarely without a good crowd, yet the smiling and efficient baristas cope easily with demand. The Square Mile espresso blend is better suited to milky drinks than the dark stuff, unless you like the high-octane roasting style, but a flat white and a cappuccino showed off the blend to its best effect: creamy sweetness carefully balanced with the hefty bitterness of the roast. And the cappuccino was of a tasteful size, not one of the great big buckets that lesser places throw at you. On our visits, the food has included enticing sandwiches and salads, as well as baked goods; if you can bag a table at lunchtime, you'll be set fair for a relaxed, enjoyable stay. In the morning or afternoon, if demand for tables isn't too great, you can settle in for a leisurely session.
Babies and children admitted. Takeaway service. Vegan dishes. **Map 17 B4.**

Milk Bar

3 Bateman Street, W1D 4AG (7287 4796). Leicester Square or Tottenham Court Road tube. **Open** 8am-7pm Mon-Fri; 9am-6pm Sat, Sun. **No credit cards.**

It's dark inside the Milk Bar, even during the day; that's what you get when you paint the walls black. The music is quite loud, which may be a plus when the room is crowded but is incongruous when just a handful of tables are occupied. This place is all about coffee, like its progenitor Flat White. The espresso (from a bespoke Square Mile blend) that emerged from the La Marzocco machine was exceptionally bracing, high-roast in profile with minimal fruit and body. You would have to be very brave to drink it without sugar. But that's beside the point, because it's really designed, we suspect, for the milky drinks that most people order. (There's even an espresso milkshake.) Food consists of an all-day brunch, heavy on eggs (try the Turkish menemen), plus a few sandwiches and own-made baked beans. The range of baked goods when we visited was decidedly limited; it looked like an afterthought. Some staff wore great big smiles, matched in their conversation, but one rather sullen face spoiled some of the effect. Milk Bar feels a little tired. It could use some livening up.
Babies and children admitted. Takeaway service. **Map 17 C3.**

Tapped & Packed. See p291.

Sacred

13 Ganton Street, W1F 9BL (7734 1415, www.sacredcafe.co.uk). Oxford Circus tube. **Open** 7.30am-8pm Mon-Fri; 10am-8pm Sat; 10am-7pm Sun. **Credit** AmEx, MC, V.

Very little has changed at this, the original branch of Sacred, since our last visit. Loyal fans will feel that's a good thing, and we're largely inclined to agree, but not completely. The small ground-floor and larger basement rooms are both cosy and welcoming in a 'bare brick and wood' kind of way. Staff are friendly and give well-informed advice about the baked goods that dominate the choice of food. The quality is generally very sound, but two complaints we have made in past years have gone unaddressed. One: our espresso (from Sacred's own beans) was less than hot and the crema had lost a good part of its foaminess (assuming the foam was there to begin with). Two: sandwiches were tired-looking by mid-afternoon – a turn-off even if you're sticking to the sweet stuff. Which we did, very happily, in the form of an ace brownie. Sacred is good, make no mistake. But it could be a bit better. Note to tea-lovers: this place has its own blends. Loose tea, no bags, high quality.
Available for hire. Babies and children admitted. Tables outdoors (6, pavement). Takeaway service. **Map 17 A4.**
For branches see index.

South

Battersea

★ Birdhouse NEW

123 St John's Hill, SW11 1SZ (7228 6663, www.birdhou.se). Clapham Junction rail. **Open** 7am-4pm Mon-Fri; 9am-5pm Sat, Sun. **Credit** (over £6) MC, V.

Slate-grey walls, floorboards, utilitarian-industrial seating, minimal decor – Birdhouse couldn't look more on-message contemporary. It has become a comfortable perch for the local flock, and they were out in force on a weekday morning. Staff take a quiet, unflashy pride in making first-rate coffee. All beans come from Climpson & Sons, whose Central American seasonal blend, expertly brewed to create a startlingly luxurious crema, sang with rich, complex chocolate flavours. We haven't had a better espresso in Rome or Naples. During a brief lull in service, the barista comprehensively wiped down his La Marzocco machine and nearby work surfaces; lesser baristas might be so thorough only at the end of service. Baked goods, made on the premises, reflect the owners' Australian origins: anzac cake, banana bread, dense chocolate brownies and the like. Breakfasts look good. Sandwiches have a Spanish tilt, as in lomo with caramelised onions and ibérico cheese. Food is reasonably priced, and service is so artlessly warm that you could miss its precise professionalism. Reports of long weekend queues don't surprise us.
Babies and children admitted. Takeaway service. **Map 21 B4.**

South East

London Bridge

★ Monmouth Coffee

2 Park Street, SE1 9AB (7940 9960, www.monmouthcoffee.co.uk). London Bridge tube/rail. **Open** 7.30am-6pm Mon-Sat. **No credit cards.**

There was a sizeable queue at this, the larger of Monmouth's two outlets. When the woman in front of us asked for a skinny latte, she was told politely that Monmouth uses only whole milk. This says a lot about the company's ethos: do things properly and ignore fashions. Well-made espresso and derivatives (including a terrific iced latte) are served here, but brewed coffees are the stars: take your pick

from Monmouth's peerless single-origin selection, or choose its suggestion of the day. Food consists of a small range of top-notch baked goods (some from Sally Clarke's bakery), plus bread and jam for self-service at the one sizeable table; most seating is at small tables or stools along counters. In warm weather, the crowds overflow on to the pavement. When leaving, we asked one of the staff about the most expensive coffee (a Brazilian winner of the prestigious Cup of Excellence awards). She instantly offered us a free taste, giving a learned discourse on brewing methods while she made it. If you're crazy about coffee, visit Monmouth. See how it's done properly
Babies and children admitted. Takeaway service.
Map 11 P8.
For branch see index.

East

Shoreditch

Allpress Espresso

58 Redchurch Street, E2 7DP (7749 1780, http://uk.allpressespresso.com). Liverpool Street tube/rail or Shoreditch High Street rail. **Open** 8am-5pm daily. **Credit** (over £5) MC, V.
The owners call this popular place Allpress Espresso, but that does a disservice to one of its really distinguished features: a small group of brewed coffees. Excellent beans (we had a single-origin Costa Rican) are roasted on the premises, in the big roaster that sits behind a glass wall to the right of the door. Two days a week you can watch the roasting, or attend a roasting class if you're really serious about your beans. The generous cup came out piping hot, and had proper creamy smoothness. An espresso was a little less successful, its crema going flat and not as hot as it should have been; sitting around while the Costa Rican finished dripping might have been the problem. Every single sandwich looked like something we would like to eat, and a couple of plates of scones with fresh berries, jam and clotted cream were food fit for the gods. Hot chocolate was a dream: chocolate pieces sitting at the bottom of a glass of hot milk. Stir, slurp, swoon. Allpress is always crowded, and it's easy to see why.
Babies and children admitted. Disabled: toilet. Takeaway service. **Map 6 S4.**

Shoreditch Grind

213 Old Street, EC1V 9NR (7490 7490, www.shoreditchgrind.com). Old Street tube/rail.
Open 7am-8pm Mon-Fri; 9am-6pm Sat; 10am-6pm Sun. **Credit** AmEx, MC, V.
Shoreditch Grind has acquired a good reputation since its founding in 2011, and there's much to admire. The high-ceilinged space has a striking view of Silicon Roundabout. And food and drink are mostly up to scratch. Cappuccino and a piccolo (espresso and foamed milk in roughly equal proportions) were both competently made and served hot. Espresso was below that standard, with a weak crema and a little too highly roasted for our taste, but baked goods (apricot tart and raspberry crumble muffin) were outstanding even compared to the generally high baking standards of London coffee bars. However, the Grind was let down by a certain lack of TLC in service. We were offered paper cups on one visit, even for coffee to be drunk on the premises. The barista looked a little hang-doggish; there was some sloppy wiping of the steam wand on the La Marzocco machine. Used coffee cups and other detritus sat on tables too long, even with staff passing by. Polish up the service and this turns into a place that does full justice to the location.
Babies and children admitted. Takeaway service.
Map 6 Q4.

Birdhouse. See p293.

Spitalfields

Taylor Street Baristas

1A New Street, EC2M 4TP (7929 2207, www.taylor-st.com). Liverpool Street tube/rail.
Open 7am-5pm Mon-Fri; 10am-4pm Sun.
No credit cards.
The Liverpool Street branch of this seven-strong chain was heaving the day we visited, and as you would expect from the area, much of the chatter concerned high finance: 'What's in it for you?' 'Has the M&A team run the numbers yet?' Despite the location, in a rather dreary shopping arcade, the place manages to convey a bit of boho charm. Attractive dark wood flooring, big windows and some eccentric wall decorations all help. As does the presence of non-money clientele, earnestly deep in coffee, cakes and conversation. TSB buys most of its beans from Union Coffee Roasters, the source of its very high-roasted espresso blend. Some would find this blend just a bit too dangerously dark, and the crema died pretty quickly. But the cup arrived decently hot (a rarity nowadays) and a dose of sugar corrected the balance. With milk in any form, the blend comes into its own. Guest beans are from Square Mile and Has Bean: single-origin coffees for conventional brewing. The edible offering – cakes, sandwiches, salads – isn't large but it's good, and staff are well informed.
Babies and children admitted. Takeaway service.
Map 12 R5.
For branches see index.

North West

Hampstead

Ginger & White

4A-5A Perrin's Court, NW3 1QS (7431 9098, www.gingerandwhite.com). Hampstead tube.
Open 7.30am-5.30pm Mon-Fri; 8.30am-5.30pm Sat, Sun. **Credit** MC, V.
There are better sources of cake within a muffin's throw, but Hampstead has taken this affable coffee bar to heart; near closing time on a recent visit, staff were sending a small queue of disappointed locals away as the espresso machine had been switched off. Mercifully, the tourist crowd hasn't caught on to it yet. A hiply distressed Union Jack watches over the vaguely familiar actors and glossy-haired lovelies tapping on their laptops while sipping Square Mile lattes. There's a communal table inside, but the pavement tables (with elegant felt rugs) beneath the fashionably dark brown awning are the most prized, though staff tend to be lax serving them. The pipsqueak kitchen offers the likes of sausage and cheddar frittata, own-made baked beans on sourdough toast, and punchy salads of lentils and ham; quality is good and ingredients carefully sourced, but the pricing is ambitious. We like the fact that they will grind beans for home use – many high-end coffee bars refuse. Success has led to new branches in Belsize Village and Soho.
Babies and children welcome: high chairs. Tables outdoors (4, pavement). Takeaway service. Vegan dishes. **Map 28 B2.**
For branches see index.

Fish & Chips

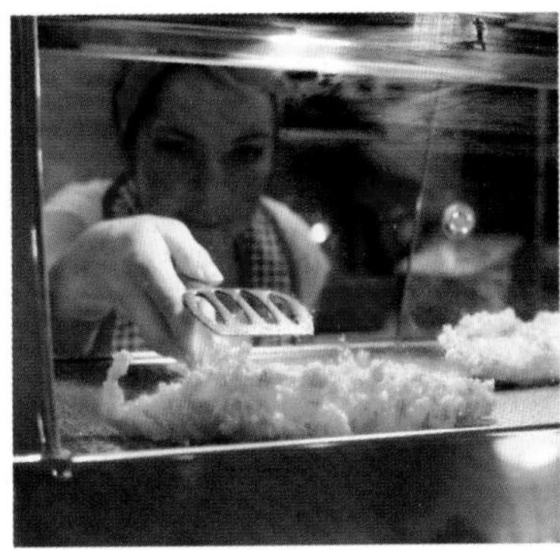

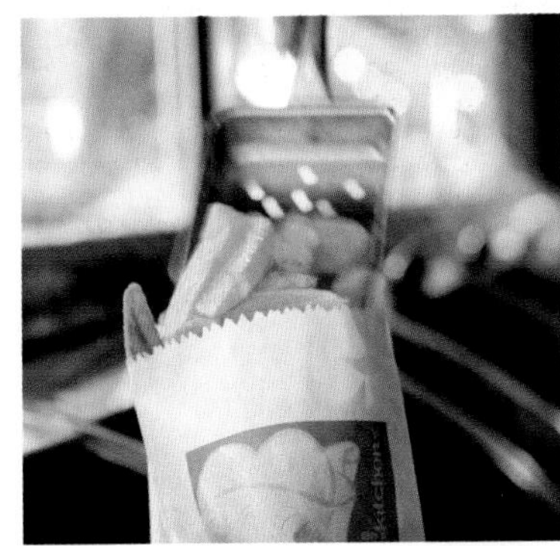

Britain's national dish (or at least a prime contender for the honour) is in rude health, judging by London's restaurants dedicated to fish and chips: the standard throughout this section is high. From a large pool, we've landed the best chippies in town: those producing the crispest, lightest batters encasing the freshest, gently steamed fish, along with chips that are crunchy on the outside, comfortingly soft within – and not forgetting the mushy peas. There's a pleasing mix of the old school (**Fryer's Delight**, **Rock & Sole Plaice** and **Golden Hind** among them) and the new here, but this year our favourite chip shops have all come from the new wave (with the exception of the excellent **Fish Central**) – congratulations to the recently opened East Sheen branch of **fish! kitchen**, Victoria Park's **Fish House**, and **Kerbisher & Malt** of Hammersmith. We've also tried to highlight the establishments aiming to buy at least some of their fish from sustainable sources, so our plaudits go to **Golden Union Fish Bar** (despite using the 'where possible' caveat), **Kerbisher & Malt**, **Brady's**, **Fish Club** and **Sea Cow**. For restaurants providing a wider range of marine life on their menus, *see p84* **Fish**.

Central

Barbican

★ Fish Central

149-155 Central Street, EC1V 8AP (7253 4970, www.fishcentral.co.uk). Old Street tube/rail or bus 55, 243. **Lunch served** 11.30am-2.30pm Mon-Fri. **Dinner served** 5-10.30pm Mon-Thur; 5-11pm Fri. **Meals served** noon-10.30pm Sat. **Main courses** £9.90-£19.50. **Credit** AmEx, MC, V.

A smart restaurant and takeaway in a nondescript shopping precinct in the no-man's land between Barbican and Islington, Fish Central defies all expectations. It's a treat to eat in the white-painted dining room, whether you're having lobster (a perfectly cooked beast, with plenty of juicy flesh) or hake and chips (one of many blackboard specials, with nicely bronzed fries and flaky white fish encased in just-so batter). Staff are busy but attentive, and diners receive little extras such as refreshing watermelon (to finish) or moreish own-made houmous and bread. Full-on starters include fish soup, prawn cocktail and greek salad. Fish (cod, haddock, plaice, skate, and so on) can be deep-fried, grilled or cooked in matzo meal; dover sole and salmon can be chargrilled, as can steaks and lamb chops. Sides are good too; we plumped for mushy peas over rocket and tomato salad. Booking is strongly advised – the place was buzzing on a Tuesday night, and we just managed to snag a table next to a large family group. The crowds are deserved: Fish Central tries that little bit harder than most.

Babies and children welcome: children's menu; high chairs; nappy-changing facilities. Booking advisable dinner Thur-Sat. Separate room for parties, seats 60. Tables outdoors (4, pavement). Takeaway service. **Map 5 P3.**

Bloomsbury

North Sea Fish Restaurant

7-8 Leigh Street, WC1H 9EW (7387 5892, www.northseafishrestaurant.co.uk). Russell Square tube or King's Cross tube/rail. **Lunch served** noon-2.30pm, **dinner served** 5.30-10.30pm Mon-Sat. **Main courses** £9.95-£21. **Credit** MC, V.

This long-established restaurant not far from St Pancras comes with a towering reputation, but, be warned, its prices can be just as lofty. The interior resembles a Cotswold village tearoom, with what looks like an old hotel bar plonked in the middle. Service is efficient, friendly and attentive without being intrusive. Starters, mains and desserts are varied and the bar well-stocked. Prawns in spicy batter (a special) was good value, and own-made cod fish cakes well above average. The hoo-ha, though, is all about the fish – and here size matters. A plate of Scottish salmon was nothing short of huge, and surely not for one person (it was). Other fish portions come in normal or jumbo size – normal would be considered 'large' in any other chippy – but the quality was only slightly above average. A portion of peas was enough for three, but the chips were disappointing: anaemic and floppy. The North Sea needs to sharpen up its act, or be superseded by the new breed of chippies.

Babies and children welcome: children's menu; high chairs. Booking advisable Thur-Sat. Separate room for parties, seats 40. Takeaway service. **Map 4 L4.**

Covent Garden

Rock & Sole Plaice

47 Endell Street, WC2H 9AJ (7836 3785). Covent Garden tube. **Meals served** 11.30am-10.30pm Mon-Sat; noon-9.30pm Sun. **Main courses** from £10. **Credit** MC, V.

The prime Covent Garden location means Rock & Sole Plaice is often packed. The menu makes a lot of the restaurant being the site of London's third-ever chippie (established 1871); while the claim seems a bit overplayed, the quality of the product is beyond question. Both the large-cut chips – a plentiful portion – and the crisp batter were well executed, and the fish inside flaky. Other options include pies, sausages and standard sides (mushy peas, baked beans). This isn't glamorous dining – there are steel-tube chairs, and West End show posters line the walls – but the tables, inside and out, were full by 7pm on our midweek visit. The

Kerbisher & Malt

prices smell slightly of a tourist trap, though: a piece of battered fish starts at £13.50. Also, when we asked about the shop's stance on sustainable sourcing, we were met with blank expressions from a first, and then a second, waiter.
Babies and children welcome: high chairs. Separate room for parties, seats 40. Tables outdoors (7, pavement). Takeaway service. **Map 18 D3**.

Holborn

Fryer's Delight

19 Theobald's Road, WC1X 8SL (7405 4114). Holborn tube or bus 19, 38, 55. **Meals served** noon-11pm Mon-Sat. **Main courses** £4.75-£7.65. **Unlicensed**. **Corkage** no charge. **No credit cards**.
This Italian-run chip shop has been in business for over 40 years. Takeaway is, of course, available, but if you choose to eat in (at lunch), you should expect to share one of the five Formica-topped tables sandwiched by two-seater benches (in the evenings the place is more sparsely occupied). The menu is standard stuff. Fish cakes are indifferent, while the half chicken is a magnificent meaty specimen – but this place really is all about the fish. Fillet of cod may not have been the biggest serving, but the fish was superb: clearly fresh, chunky, firm and thinly coated in the lightest and most flavoursome batter. Fish is cooked 'skin-on' and a request to have it removed was declined by the waitress, but accepted by the cook. Chip butty aficionados, take note: the doorstep bread and butter makes construction tricky – a roll is a better choice. Proudly displaying an old newspaper cutting declaring it to be the third-best chippy in the UK, the Fryer's Delight is still a contender.
Babies and children admitted. Takeaway service. **Map 4 M5**.

Marylebone

Golden Hind

73 Marylebone Lane, W1U 2PN (7486 3644). Bond Street tube. **Lunch served** noon-3pm Mon-Fri. **Dinner served** 6-10pm Mon-Sat. **Main courses** £6.30-£10.50. **Minimum** (dinner) £5. **Unlicensed**. **Corkage** £1. **Credit** AmEx, MC, V.
Having expanded into a bright, airy second room, the Golden Hind felt rather quiet when we arrived for a late lunch. With the fish, chips and peas separately priced, you'll easily shell out a tenner, but tables of workmen, ladies-about-town and suited gentlemen suggest the venue's appeal is pretty broad, testament to nearly a century's expertise – the list of owners since 1914 (a total of five) is at the back, near the decommissioned vintage fryer. After the disappointment of our properly strong builder's tea arriving in a mere cup rather than a mug, the main event was pleasing. A 'small' haddock was, as anticipated, overhanging the plate, tight in its crisp batter sleeve (though the flesh was quite soggy), and accompanied by little pots of ketchup and fairly bland tartare sauce. Mushy peas were tasty and excessively green, as tradition dictates, and although the chips arrived lukewarm and chewy, they came up nicely under a drizzle of vinegar. Starters such as feta cheese fritters or breaded calamares are preferable to a dessert of heavy bread and butter pudding and flavourless custard.
Babies and children welcome: high chairs. Takeaway service. **Map 9 G5**.

Sea Shell

49-51 Lisson Grove, NW1 6UH (7224 9000, www.seashellrestaurant.co.uk). Marylebone tube/rail. **Meals served** noon-10.30pm Mon-Sat. **Main courses** £12-£30. **Credit** AmEx, MC, V.
When fire destroyed the interior in 2009, the 40-year-old Sea Shell was suddenly the best known 'celebrity fish diner' in London – but unable to capitalise on its fame thanks to the extensive building and refurbishment work required. Things were a little glossier and more upmarket on reopening but largely the same – and that's still the case. The eye-catching black and white marble checked floor is matched with smart chairs and etched glass screens. Colour comes from Harry Bilson's exuberant paintings, which evoke sun-filled days in the nearby Regent's Park, and a sparkling blue aquarium that charms everyone. Crisp-battered haddock came with chips in a modish white pot. Lovely fish pie featured a flavourful cream sauce with parsley, chive, mushroom and tomato. A side of steamed spinach was correctly bouncy – we could have had it creamed, or instead ordered green beans, or broccoli with chilli and garlic. The wine list is fun, reasonably priced and helpfully annotated. Look out for special offers, such as two courses for £15 from 5pm to 7pm, or seasonal discounts in the takeaway, which can be less than half the price of eating in the restaurant.
Babies and children welcome: children's menu; high chairs; nappy-changing facilities. Booking advisable Thur-Sat. Disabled: toilet. Tables outdoors (8, pavement). Takeaway service. **Map 2 F4**.

Soho

Golden Union Fish Bar

38 Poland Street, W1F 7LY (7434 1933, www.goldenunion.co.uk). Oxford Circus tube. **Meals served** 11.30am-10pm Mon-Sat. **Main courses** £4.50-£7.50. **Credit** AmEx, MC, V.
For a fish and chip shop just off Oxford Street, on a Friday night, Golden Union seemed surprisingly devoid of tourists in search of some classic British food. The sit-down area was full, though, and

it's clear why: a laid-back atmosphere and accomplished deep-frying. Those who choose the takeaway option miss out on the place's well-pitched and unpretentious retro decor of tiled walls, plastic table-tops and tomato-shaped ketchup dispensers, as well as friendly service from fleet-footed waitresses. Freshly fried batter was wonderfully crisp and the fish inside tender and flaky. Chips were less impressive: not too greasy, but unexceptional. Other traditional standards are offered (sausages, pies and so on), but on our visit sticking to the battered options was more rewarding – the fish cake was a bit dry. The menu states that, where possible, fish is sustainably sourced, and pollock and coley are available alongside omnipresent cod and haddock.
Babies and children welcome: children's menu; high chairs; nappy-changing facilities. Bookings not accepted lunch Fri. Disabled: toilet. Takeaway service. **Map 17 A3**.

Victoria

Seafresh Fish Restaurant

80-81 Wilton Road, SW1V 1DL (7828 0747, www.fishandchipsinlondon.com). Victoria tube/rail. **Lunch served** noon-3pm, **dinner served** 5-10.30pm Mon-Fri. **Meals served** noon-10.30pm Sat. **Main courses** £10.75-£25.95. **Set lunch** £12.25 2 courses incl tea or coffee. **Credit** AmEx, MC, V.

A popular restaurant and takeaway that manages to appeal to both locals and tourists. At £12.25 (for lunch; at dinner it's £13.25), the set menu of cod or haddock and chips with peas, bread and butter, dessert and a hot beverage is good value. Fish can be grilled to order, but we stuck to the classic version. While the batter of the deep-fried cod was a tad oily, the fish was nicely flaky and moist. The fat chips were a bit pale and could have done with another turn in the fryer, and such generous portions need bigger plates. A refreshing fruit salad had freshly sliced banana, kiwi, orange and strawberry. Away from the set menu, there's smoked salmon, taramasalata, prawn cocktail or deep-fried whitebait to start, followed by skate, scampi or fish cakes, as well as a few grilled meat dishes (steak, lamb chops) and salads (prawn, roast chicken). A lightly themed room has wooden furniture and a ship's wheel on the wall; friendly service keeps things ticking over smoothly.
Available for hire. Babies and children welcome: high chairs. Booking advisable. Takeaway service. **Map 15 J10**.

West

Bayswater

Mr Fish

9 Porchester Road, W2 5DP (7229 4161, www.mrfish.uk.com). Bayswater or Royal Oak tube. **Meals served** 11am-11pm daily. **Main courses** £6.25-£12.95. **Set lunch** (11am-3pm) £6.95 2 courses, £7.95 3 courses. **Credit** AmEx, MC, V.

Seemingly transplanted from some British coastal town, this local chippy carries off its kitsch aquamarine decor and irony-free retro menu (avocado and prawns, scampi bites and spotted dick) with nostalgic charm. The all-day, every day Senior Citizen's Special might account for a large proportion of the covers, but the takeaway counter bustles with locals of every age, impressed by a broad choice of fish (including lemon sole, sea bass and rock) and moreish, chunky chips that come without finger-drenching grease. Grilled fish, as well as breadcrumb or matzo meal coatings, are available for the health conscious, but the deliciously light and crispy batter is worth indulging in – even if some of the accompanying condiments, particularly a thin tartare sauce, are a poor complement.
Available for hire. Babies and children welcome: children's menu; high chair. Takeaway service.
Map 7 C5.
For branch see index.

Hammersmith

★ Kerbisher & Malt

164 Shepherd's Bush Road, W6 7PB (3556 0228, www.kerbisher.co.uk). Hammersmith tube. **Lunch served** noon-2.30pm, **dinner served** 4.30-10pm Tue-Fri. **Meals served** noon-10pm Sat; noon-9pm Sun. **Main courses** £4-£8.60. **Credit** MC, V.

This sleek, modern establishment opposite Brook Green brings the old-fashioned chip shop bang up to date. It's small but stylish, with monochrome photos on white-tiled walls, and metal seating around a chunky communal table; there's also a couple of pavement tables. Visit early evening and you can expect a constant flow of customers, some to eat in, some for takeway. Fish is cooked to order, and can be battered, grilled or breaded; most go for the traditional batter – and rightly so, thanks to a light, crispy coating and succulent flesh. A sustainable approach means there's coley and pollock alongside haddock and cod. Alternatives include calamari, whitebait and a very decent fish cake that has the right fish-to-potato ratio and a slightly chewy exterior. Crushed potato and red onion salad was tasty, but a tiny portion compared to a standard helping of excellent, double-fried chips. The battered pickled onion rings and own-made mushy peas have many fans too, and everything tastes freshly made. Drinks include Fentimans botanical beverages, a brief wine list and Meantime bottled beers. Such has been K&M's success that a new branch opened in Ealing in summer 2012.
Babies and children welcome: children's menu; high chairs. Bookings not accepted dinner Fri. Tables outdoors (2, pavement). Takeaway service. **Map 20 C3**.
For branch see index.

South West

East Sheen

★ fish! kitchen

170 Upper Richmond Road West, SW14 8AW (8878 1040, www.fishkitchen.com). Mortlake rail. **Dinner served** 5-10pm Tue-Thur. **Meals served** noon-10pm Fri, Sat. **Main courses** £10.95-£16.95. **Set meal** £12.95 2 courses. **Credit** AmEx, MC, V.

This is a branch of the original posh fish and chip restaurant in Kingston, and a cousin of the even posher fish! restaurant at Borough Market. We like this outpost a lot, not least because it's a bit unexpected in suburban East Sheen. A modern, well-designed interior extends to a menu that goes far beyond the usual deep-fried fare; upmarket options include grilled tuna steak or whole grilled lobster. The seafood is all responsibly sourced, and the basics are done beautifully: pert fish, crisp batter, firm and flavourful chips. It's the freshness of the fish that really stands out, though: the operation shares owners with Jarvis the Fishmonger, the Kingston-based, top-quality restaurant supplier. What's more, thanks to this connection, if you give them 48 hours notice they can source any in-season fish and cook it however you'd like it. If you have room for anything beyond a main course – portions are on the large side – there are also desserts such as affogato or fruit crumble and custard. The well-considered drinks list majors on white wine, but there's also French cider and some fizz.
Available for hire. Babies and children welcome: children's menu; crayons; high chairs; nappy-changing facilites. Booking advisable. Disabled: toilet. Tables outdoors (6, pavement). Takeaway service.
For branches see index.

Wandsworth

Brady's

513 Old York Road, SW18 1TF (8877 9599, www.bradysfish.co.uk). Wandsworth Town rail. **Lunch served** 12.30-2.30pm Fri, Sat. **Dinner served** 6.30-10pm Tue-Thur, Sat; 6.30-10.30pm Fri. **Main courses** £7.85-£12.95. **Credit** MC, V.

It may be miles from the ocean, but Brady's is something of a seaside hut. Surroundings are spartan, with pale-toned tongue-and-groove walls, mermaids painted on to mirrors, and a faint whiff of vinegar in the air. There's plenty from the grill (including swordfish, tuna and brill), though battered options are more limited: just cod, haddock, plaice or sustainable Scottish saithe (a type of coley). On our visit, a moist piece of haddock came parcelled in golden batter, though the portion was a little mean. Chips were just as good: crunchy on the outside, fluffy in the middle, and plenty of them. Mains come book-ended by retro starters (smoked salmon, pint of prawns) and equally old-school desserts (treacle tart, bread and butter pudding). These go down a storm with the upper-crust locals, who can't get enough of the back-to-basics Brady's approach – perhaps they're re-living bygone summer holidays. If it's your first visit, beware: the warmest reception is reserved for the regulars.
Babies and children welcome: children's menu; high chairs. Takeaway service. **Map 21 A4**.

South

Battersea

Fish Club

189 St John's Hill, SW11 1TH (7978 7115, www.thefishclub.com). Wandsworth Town rail. **Dinner served** 5-10pm Mon. **Meals served** noon-10pm Tue-Sun. **Main courses** £6.70-£14.95. **Credit** AmEx, MC, V.

If only every neighbourhood chippy were like Fish Club. This unpretentious joint has no airs and graces, but combines good, honest cooking with sincere and accommodating service. Sauces and sides play second fiddle here: the fish is where it's at. On our visit, stubby little haddock fish cakes fresh from the fryer came studded with tiny capers and chopped dill, though the accompanying 'saffron' mayo (with no discernable saffron flavour)

was surplus to requirements. Next up, coley was proof, if you needed it, that in the right hands this sustainable swimmer should never be called cod's poor cousin. Cooked to perfection, its light and crispy golden batter gave way to a moist, flaky fillet; on the side was a generous portion of decent old-school chips. Once again, the sauce disappointed: the tartare could have done with a little more 'tart'. Elsewhere, there are blackboard specials, pies, and posh prawn and chorizo kebabs, all delivered in a bright, retro space tricked out with black and white floor tiles and turquoise walls. There's even a tiny courtyard out back.
Babies and children welcome: children's menu; high chairs. Disabled: toilet. Tables outdoors (3, courtyard; 2, pavement). Takeaway service. **Map 21 B4.**
For branch see index.

Waterloo

Masters Super Fish

191 Waterloo Road, SE1 8UX (7928 6924). Southwark tube or Waterloo tube/rail. **Lunch served** noon-3pm Tue-Sat. **Dinner served** 5.30-10.30pm Mon; 4.30-10.30pm Tue-Thur, Sat; 4.30-11pm Fri. **Main courses** £7.25-£16. **Set lunch** £7 1 course incl soft drink, tea or coffee. **Credit** MC, V.
This long-standing chippy resembles a retro greasy spoon, with exposed brickwork offset by turquoise walls peppered with prints of soap stars and comedians of yesteryear. Although known for its popularity with cabbies, the takeaway counter was empty and the dining room eerily quiet on a Wednesday lunchtime. Specials available included mackerel and turbot, but we opted for the more traditional cod and scampi. Our efficient waitress delivered complimentary appetisers, which were as retro as the decor: baguette slices and a few cooked prawns (with roe). The scampi was rather overwhelmed by its batter, but the cod arrived perfectly cooked, with pleasingly crisp batter. Hand-cut chips (a little soggy in places) were piled high, and helped along by own-made gherkins, pickled onions and jugs of ketchup and tartare sauce. Portions verge on the unconquerable in size; a 'half chips, half salad' option is also available. Worth considering if you happen to be in the area, attending a play at the Young or Old Vic, perhaps, but not one to go out of your way for.
Babies and children welcome: children's menu; high chairs. Bookings not accepted Fri. Takeaway service. **Map 11 N9.**

South East

Dulwich

Sea Cow

37 Lordship Lane, SE22 8EW (8693 3111, www.theseacow.co.uk). East Dulwich rail or bus 176. **Meals served** noon-10pm Mon, Sun; noon-11pm Tue-Sat. **Main courses** £8.50-£10. **Credit** MC, V.
The Sea Cow has been plying its trade for nearly a decade; it was part of the vanguard of modern fish and chip shops, but the menu doesn't seem to have developed since then and lacks the excitement of newer street food. In addition to the standard battered cod/haddock/plaice/coley and chips, dishes include crab cakes, sea bass, gambas al pil pil, calamares, grilled sardines and minted mushy peas. The commitment to sustainable sourcing is admirable, and the fish is well cooked with pleasingly crispy batter. We think the chips aren't as tasty as traditional fried-in-dripping ones, though some people will prefer them this way. The interior aims for bare-wood beach-hut chic, with work by local artists on the walls, but the back of the restaurant can be a bit dark and gloomy. Bonuses include the fact that it's licensed, and has an astonishingly good-value 'kids eat free till 4pm' deal at the weekend.
Babies and children welcome: children's menu; high chairs. Takeaway service. **Map 23 C4.**

Herne Hill

Olley's

65-69 Norwood Road, SE24 9AA (8671 8259, www.olleys.info). Herne Hill rail or bus 3, 68, 196. **Lunch served** noon-3pm Tue-Sun. **Dinner served** 5-10pm Tue-Sat; 5-9pm Sun. **Main courses** £5.50-£19.50. **Set meal** (noon-3pm, 5-7pm) £5.50 1 course. **Credit** AmEx, MC, V.
Firmly established as one of London's finest chippies, Olley's has barely shifted from a successful formula that has served it nicely for well over a decade. There's the occasional innovation, of course – the presence of Innis & Gunn beer on the drinks menu is probably the most welcome – but otherwise this is a cracking, no-nonsense fish and chip restaurant, serving fat, crispy chips, epic fillets of a dozen types of fish, and big dollops of ice-cream for afters. You can have your fish grilled if you prefer, or plump for one of the celeb options;

Poppies

the Lord Archer Experience ('tart not included') is a good indicator of how long things have been ticking over. Decor is an unusual mix of Greek taverna and the maritime, but the dining area is a big, clean space and the waiting staff are quick to entertain any children that may be in your party. Sustainability doesn't get much of a mention, but that just adds to the old-fashioned charm of the place. Still, if you don't want cod, there's plenty else from which to choose.
Babies and children welcome: children's menu; crayons; high chairs; nappy-changing facilities. Booking advisable weekends. Disabled: toilet. Separate room for parties, seats 40. Takeaway service. **Map 23 A5.**

Lewisham

Something Fishy

117-119 Lewisham High Street, SE13 6AT (8852 7075). Lewisham rail/DLR. **Meals served** 9am-5.30pm Mon-Sat. **Main courses** £4-£7.25. **No credit cards.**
For longer than most locals can remember, this Lewisham High Street institution has been serving hearty cooking at rock-bottom prices. The no-frills cafeteria counter is staffed by a troupe of cheery ladies, who dispense teas and coffees from an industrial-sized urn in the corner. High standards are maintained by cooking fish to order. Deep-fried cod was encased in a gloriously crisp batter, benefiting from its swift fryer-to-diner trajectory. The accompanying chips were satisfyingly chunky, soft in the middle with crisp outer edges. Our pie and mash was as traditional as it comes, the flaky pastry and gargantuan portion of potato soaking up a ladle or two of dark, rich gravy. With a prime spot in the town centre, Something Fishy serves as a popular meeting place for Lewisham shoppers, many of whom were packed tightly into the plastic seats, catching up over a milky coffee or two. The interior is charmingly dated, producing the feeling of a bygone era; order eels and liquor to complete the nostalgic experience.
Babies and children welcome: children's menu; high chairs. Tables outdoors (5, pavement). Takeaway service.

East

Spitalfields

★ Poppies HOT 50

6-8 Hanbury Street, E1 6QR (7247 0892, www.poppiesfishandchips.co.uk). Aldgate East tube or Liverpool Street tube/rail. **Meals served** 11am-11.30pm Mon-Sat; 11am-10.30pm Sun. **Main courses** £9.90-£15.90. **Credit** AmEx, MC, V.
Poppies serves fish and chips as they were meant to be, but probably never were. Fine fillets of haddock, plaice, rock and the rest arrive in crisp batter, flesh firm to the fork, chips soft but never limp. No wonder the food's so good – the proprietor, Pops Newland, has been frying fish in the area all his life. The premises follow a bright, retro theme, with a 1950s jukebox kicking out doo-wop hits, shelves of mementos (including an Underwood typewriter) and a strip of Cockney rhyming-slang phrases and translations around the wall like a Plimsoll Line to save you from sinking into the sea of Hackney trendies hereabouts. The takeaway counter at the door even serves your tucker in a traditional twist of newspaper, but Poppies isn't

fish! kitchen. See p297.

at all backward-looking. Attention is paid to sustainability of the fish, fresh from Billingsgate, and the menu is broad enough to entice a slightly more upmarket clientele; as well as jellied eels and saveloys, you can enjoy whole lemon sole or cumbrian sticky toffee pudding. There are also Meantime bottled beers, soft drinks from Fentimans, and even a short wine list – running through the prices up to Chapel Down fizz.
Available for hire. Babies and children welcome: children's menu; high chairs. Booking advisable. Takeaway service. **Map 12 S5.**

Victoria Park

★ Fish House

128 Lauriston Road, E9 7LH (8533 3327, www.fishouse.co.uk). Mile End tube then 277 bus. **Meals served** noon-10pm Mon-Fri; 11am-10pm Sat, Sun. **Main courses** £8.95-£12.95. **Credit** AmEx, MC, V.
A bright, lively restaurant just yards from Victoria Park, Fish House elevates the labours of a chippy to an art form. Friendly staff serve your choice of cod (fat or thin), haddock, rock, plaice or scampi and chips, with proper mushy peas and tartare sauce – all of it nigh-on perfect. Batter is crunchy, light and grease-free, containing juicy chunks of cod; the chips are crisp and fresh, thanks to the near constant stream of customers at the smart white-tiled takeaway counter. To its left, the modern restaurant offers a stunning selection of fish dishes at excellent prices, from a tempting daily specials board. On our visit, this included lobster bisque and whole dressed crab salad, as well as mains such as baked gurnard with saffron, tomatoes, mussels and basil, and pan-fried hake steak with samphire and palourde clams (a huge, beautifully cooked portion, and a snip at £12.50). A blackboard above the takeaway counter lists the provenance of the fish, all of which are approved by the Marine Conservation Society. Puddings are equally well thought-out, with seasonal produce and own-made ice-cream figuring prominently.
Babies and children welcome: children's menu; crayons; high chairs; nappy-changing facilities. Booking advisable dinner Fri; Sat, Sun. Tables outdoors (8, pavement). Takeaway service.

North East

Dalston

Faulkner's

424-426 Kingsland Road, E8 4AA (7254 6152). Haggerston rail or bus 67, 149, 242. **Lunch served** noon-2.30pm Mon-Fri. **Dinner served** 5-10pm Mon-Thur; 4.30-10pm Fri. **Meals served** 11.30am-10pm Sat; noon-9pm Sun. **Main courses** £10-£18.90. **Set meal** £16.90 2 courses. **Credit** MC, V.
As shops, restaurants and pubs up and down Kingsland Road fall to the army of hipsters making this part of London their home, Faulkners soldiers on in a defiantly old-school way. The takeaway side does a brisk trade; on the right is a surprisingly formal restaurant, with quaintness added by mock wooden beams, a fish tank and dimpled windows. The food is similarly from a bygone age (as is the soundtrack – Phil Collins, Jennifer Rush). To start, there's prawn cocktail, scampi, fish cakes, rollmops or mussels. Catch of the day (cod, haddock, plaice, rock, salmon) is fried in batter or matzo meal, or grilled. Accompaniments are chips or boiled potatoes, and a standard portion of mixed veg. All

this, plus the heavy napkins, net curtains and service from a weary old waiter, should be a classic nostalgic dining experience – the problem is that the food isn't quite as good as it should be. Chips are a little wan, tartare sauce all mayo and no punch. A grilled plaice was generous but slightly soggy. Tradition is fine, but it's not always enough.
Babies and children welcome: children's menu; high chairs; nappy-changing facilities. Booking advisable weekends. Disabled: toilet. Takeaway service. **Map 6 R1.**

Stoke Newington

Sutton & Sons

90 Stoke Newington High Street, N16 7NY (7249 6444, www.suttonandsons.co.uk). Stoke Newington rail. **Meals served** noon-10pm Mon-Thur; noon-10.30pm Fri, Sat. **Main courses** £5.90-£12.50. **No credit cards.**
Sutton & Sons is a friendly local chippy, serving ethically sourced fish (from its own fishmonger), whether deep-fried and crispy or healthy with a salad. Sit outside on wooden benches with the 67 bus whizzing past, or cosy up next to the fryer in the white-tiled dining area. The menu may feature impressive loin of swordfish, grilled seasonal fish or half a dozen Maldon oysters, but Sutton's equally excels at classic cod and chips, haddock or battered sausage. Fresh trout was impeccably grilled so the pink flesh remained tender against a crisp skin, drizzled in lemony garlic oil. Chips were a little dry at first, but a good douse of vinegar brought them back to life. Mushy peas had the right ratio of mush to peas, and the batter was a deep golden crisp bubble around chunks of fresh white cod. Staff are lovely, and home delivery is available every day except Fridays, when the shop is bursting with the regular Friday fish-supper crowd.
Booking advisable. Babies and children welcome: children's menu; high chairs. Tables outdoors (3, pavement). Takeaway service; delivery service (over £15 within 3-mile radius). **Map 25 C2.**

North

Finchley

Two Brothers Fish Restaurant

297-303 Regent's Park Road, N3 1DP (8346 0469, www.twobrothers.co.uk). Finchley Central tube. **Lunch served** noon-2.30pm, **dinner served** 5.30-10.15pm Tue-Sun. **Main courses** £12.95-£25.95. **Credit** AmEx, MC, V.
An appropriately named north London institution, run by Mel and Nari Atwal, that feels as comfortable and familiar as a much-loved sofa. The New England-inspired interior is looking more shabby than chic these days, but staff are wonderfully cosseting to harassed parents, and are happy to entertain children for a few minutes while mum and dad try to eat. Specials such as chickpea soup, avocado and artichoke salad, moules marinière, and monkfish and scallop ragoût provide diversion for regulars, but most are here for the main event: deep-fried fish fillets that stretch right off the plate. Battered is good, matzo better. The fat chips were a touch pale on our visit but lip-smacking nonetheless. Fish are delivered daily from Billingsgate: you'll find all the basics plus premium lines best grilled (dover sole, halibut steak and whole sea bass and bream). There's a good choice of seafood starters (cod roe in butter, sardines with herbs and garlic, jellied eels), and a few uninspiring desserts (bread and butter pudding, Irish cream cheesecake) – but so what? We can't imagine anyone having room to fit them in.
Babies and children welcome: high chairs. Booking advisable. Takeaway service.

Highgate

Fish Fish

179 Archway Road, N6 5BN (8348 3121). Highgate tube. **Dinner served** 5-9.30pm Mon-Fri. **Meals served** noon-10.30pm Sat, Sun. **Main courses** £9.95-£17.50. **Credit** MC, V.
Is it a posh chippy or a fish restaurant? Is it Greek or Turkish? Is it in Highgate or Archway? The prices say Highgate, but the location is a bit of a walk from the tube station of that name towards Archway (at least it's downhill). The nautical decor and profusion of nets is somehow more Greek taverna than either chip shop or seafood restaurant, but the advertised beer is Turkish Efes. In fact, the friendly staff are Georgian (there are clues on the menu in the shape of anchovies in the eastern Black Sea style, as well as Georgian casseroles). Choose from grilled sea bass, sea bream, salmon, tuna, swordfish, sole, halibut or turbot, with prices starting around £13. There's a narrower range for poached or pan-fried, and to get your fish in batter, it's cod or haddock only. Lightly battered cod and grilled swordfish steak, both cooked to perfection, came with excellent non-greasy chips and generous helpings of mixed salad with plenty of fresh chopped dill. The menu also offers meat, pasta and vegetarian dishes, and children's portions of cod or fish fingers. It's not the cosiest place (nor the cheapest), but the welcome is warm.
Available for hire. Babies and children welcome: high chairs; nappy-changing facilities. Tables outdoors (20, garden). Takeaway service.

Muswell Hill

Toff's

38 Muswell Hill Broadway, N10 3RT (8883 8656, www.toffsfish.co.uk). Highgate tube then bus 43, 134. **Meals served** 11.30am-10.30pm Mon-Sat. **Main courses** £11.95-£24.95. **Set meal** £8.95 1 course incl tea or coffee. **Credit** AmEx, DC, MC, V.
The cosy dark wood-panelled interior and sepia prints hark back to Victorian London but Toff's isn't quite that old: it was founded by Greek-Cypriot Andrea Toffali in 1968 and remains undisputed king of the Muswell Hill dining scene. Battered fish is the staple – egg and matzo costs an additional 75p, grilled is £1 extra. Salad garnish comes as standard, and there's an offer to replenish the already generous portions of chips. The groundnut oil is changed nightly and given to farmers for recycling – a key factor in the superior flavour. We appreciated having alternatives to fish such as chicken and sausage for fussy kids. The wine list isn't as lively or extensive as it could be – surprising given the middle-class 'hood. Opt instead for a Becks or Keo beer. The ground floor restaurant is a little cramped but the tone is cheerfully unpretentious; there's upstairs seating amid similar decor when things are especially busy, but it does feel remote. Better to enjoy the bustling takeaway queue and cooks' banter.
Babies and children welcome: children's menu; crayons; high chairs. Disabled: toilet. Separate rooms for parties, seating 20 and 24. Takeaway service.

North West

Belsize Park

Oliver's

95 Haverstock Hill, NW3 4RL (7586 9945, www.oliversfishandchips.com). Chalk Farm tube. **Meals served** noon-10.15pm Tue-Sun. **Main courses** £9.20-£11.45. **Credit** AmEx, MC, V.
Classic fish and chips are the main draw at Belsize Park's upmarket chip shop. Fish comes battered, covered in matzo meal or grilled. There's also an interesting specials board: on our visit, options included salmon with new potatoes, creamed onions and cabbage; tuna with sweet potato gratin and papaya salad; and sea bass with parsnip purée and spinach and orange dressing. The latter was a delicate dish, expertly put together, and battered fish and chips didn't disappoint either. Friendly staff were incredibly patient with two children who kept changing their minds, but no one could confirm whether the fish was line-caught. The bright, narrow restaurant has white walls and unfussy furniture; a splash of green tiles around the open kitchen creates a focal point. There's alcohol (wine, bottled beer) as well as tea and coffee. As well as takeaways, Oliver's also offers home deliveries, which can be ordered online. A thoroughly modern fish and chip restaurant, then, but one which brings all the right traditions into the present day.
Babies and children welcome: high chairs. Booking advisable. Separate room for parties, seats 20. Tables outdoors (2, pavement). Takeaway service; delivery service (over £15 within 3-mile radius). **Map 28 C4.**

West Hampstead

Nautilus

27-29 Fortune Green Road, NW6 1DU (7435 2532). West Hampstead tube/rail then bus 328. **Lunch served** 11.30am-2.30pm, **dinner served** 4.30-10pm Mon-Sat. **Main courses** £10.50-£22.50. **Credit** MC, V.
We've always found this kitsch, almost-Cricklewood spot friendly, but on our last visit realised we were the only people in the room not kissed hello by the staff. Should we take it personally? More likely it reflects the regularity with which well-to-do locals visit. Retired couples seem to be the backbone of the clientele but you're as likely to sit in a busy restaurant amid families with school-age kids, flatmates and one or two fish-frying mavens (this place has something of a cult following). Nautilus overcomes its workaday menu and old-fashioned interior (boat pictures, pine panels, condiment trays decorated with fruit) with expert, accurate cooking and a generous hand with portions. One quirk – there's no battered fish: it's matzo or grill only. Prices are on the high side too. Try plaice fried on the bone for a fantastically fresh, light and minerally-tasting supper. The Greek ownership sees taramasalata, houmous and Mediterranean-style salads in the mix alongside the expected pickles, peas and coleslaw. The drink and dessert options are undistinguished – forget the sweet stuff and relish those complimentary extra chips instead.
Babies and children welcome: children's menu; high chairs. Booking advisable. Disabled: toilet. Takeaway service. **Map 28 A1.**

Ice-cream Parlours

A sweet treat for children, or a sexed-up seductive aid to romance? Ice-cream has always been both, and London's parlours embrace the dual aspects of this cold comfort-food. In recent years, family classics such as **Marine Ices** (*see p276*) have been joined by venues where adults can also get their kicks – and our favourite, top-rated establishments all come from this latter, grown-up batch: the likes of adventurous newcomer **Gelateria 3bis** at Borough Market (try the gooseberry gelato), Camden's fabulously experimental **Chin Chin Laboratorists** (where the staff wear white lab coats) and Sicilian-accented **Gelupo** in Soho (where the ewe's milk ricotta with sour cherry is a current favourite). New parlours continue to open, but Italian gelateria still dominate the sector.

Central

Charing Cross

Gino Gelato

3 Adelaide Street, WC2N 4HZ (7836 9390, www.ginogelato.com). Charing Cross tube/rail. **Open** noon-10.30pm Mon-Thur, Sun; noon-11.30pm Fri, Sat. **Credit** MC, V.

Wedged between Charing Cross and Trafalgar Square and just south of Leicester Square, Gino Gelato is worth knowing about for post-theatre or pre-train pit stops. For those wanting to hang around there's a bank of seating, as well as a few stools outside. The main wall of the small, brightly lit interior proclaims the place's credentials, including all-natural ingredients and organic milk. The line-up of ice-creams and sorbets changes regularly and they are all made by the in-house machine. Flavours range from the classic to the more unusual; all the ones we tried had an impressive depth and intensity, especially the dark chocolate. Pistachio had a lovely savoury nut flavour; both almond and rosewater, and pear and cinnamon had an addictive delicacy, but the stand-out scoop was strawberry and balsamic vinegar – a wonderful balance of flavours. If you discover a favourite, you can take home a cartonful.

Takeaway service. Vegan dishes. **Map 18 D5.**

Covent Garden

La Gelatiera NEW

27 New Row, WC2N 4LA (7836 9559, www.lagelatiera.co.uk). Leicester Square or Covent Garden tube or Charing Cross tube/rail. **Open** *Summer* 11am-10.30pm Mon; 11am-11pm Tue-Thur; 11am-11.45pm Fri, Sat; 11.30am-9.30pm Sun. *Winter* 2-10.30pm Mon; 11am-11pm Tue-Thur; 11am-11.45pm Fri, Sat; 11.30am-9.30pm Sun. **Credit** MC, V.

Imaginative – rather than daft – flavours give La Gelateria an edge in an increasingly crowded market. Chocolate and chilli had a huge kick; 'kibana', a mix of kiwi fruit and banana, was a brilliant match (and vegan); sour cherry and meringue was another blissful union, dotted with chunks of chewy fruit; vanilla was good and creamy. Only a slightly underwhelming latte flavour didn't live up to the high standard set by the rest. Ices are made from carefully sourced seasonal ingredients, with no additives. They are served in small, funky premises by super-enthusiastic staff. Also offered are cakes and pastries, and coffee – which, like the ice-cream, is treated with due respect. Through a glass floor, you can see into the basement 'laboratory' where the magic happens.

Takeaway service. Vegan dishes. **Map 18 D4.**

Gelatorino

2 Russell Street, WC2B 5JD (7240 0746, www.gelatorino.com). Covent Garden tube. **Open** 11am-9pm Mon-Wed; 11am-11pm Thur-Sat; 11am-8pm Sun. **No credit cards.**

Gelatorino's website promises many exciting flavours, all made on site and without any artificial colours and preservatives. Sadly, none of the more interesting ones, such as cinnamon and orange or 'breakfast in Turin' (coffee with chocolate chip) were available on our visit, so we had to opt for a more classic selection: a very creamy chocolate chip, a nutty gianduja and a dense dark chocolate. All were fine tasting and spot-on in their velvety smooth texture, but the outstanding flavour was fig ripple, a rich, cream-based ice-cream with strands of juicy figs. We also liked that for £3 you get three different flavours (one more than most other ice-cream parlours offer); staff are happy to offer tasting spoonfuls too. As you sit at a little side bar or at one of the tables at the back, you can watch two old-fashioned Italian ice-cream machines working their magic. Italian biscuits, chocolates and nougat are also sold.

Babies and children welcome: high chairs. Tables outdoors (3, pavement). Takeaway service. Vegan dishes. **Map 18 E4.**

Icecreamists

Market Building, Covent Garden Market, WC2E 8RF (8616 0721, www.theicecreamists.com). Covent Garden tube. **Open** 11am-10pm daily. **Credit** MC, V.

At Icecreamists, good-looking staff dressed in black military-style uniforms, complete with caps, serve you in front of black walls with a neon pink 'God save the cream' scribbled across. What was exciting when it first opened now seems a bit gimmicky, but names such as 'sex, drugs and choc 'n' roll' are much more fun than 'milk chocolate' (which it actually is). You're enticed to try different flavours, such as popcorn, aka 'smack, crack and pop'. The creamy gelato-style ice-cream is excellent, but the sundaes are a bit of a let-down. The 'rock 'n' royal ice-cream sandwich' turned out to be two rather dry giant chocolate chip cookies with an ice-cream flavour of your choice in between. The ice-cream to

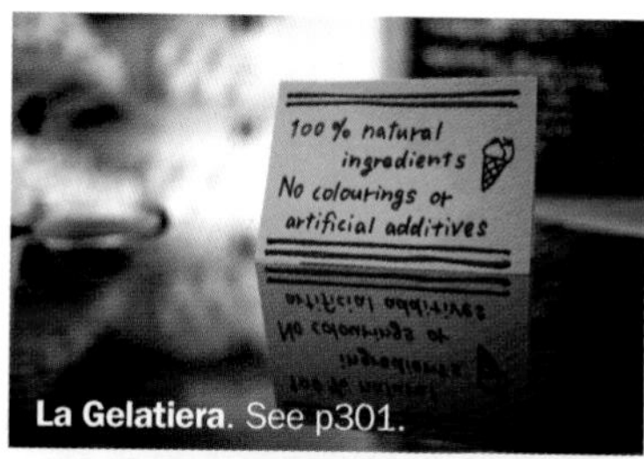

La Gelatiera. See p301.

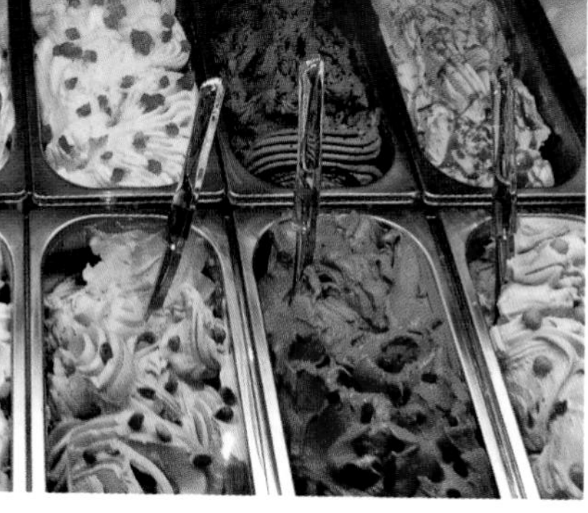

cookie ratio didn't work and we regretted not having chosen one of the alcoholic ice-cream cocktails instead. Prices match the Covent Garden Market location; sundaes, for example, start at £9.95, but you can take away one of the black ice-cream cones more cheaply.
Babies and children admitted. Tables outdoors (16, market). Takeaway service. Vegan dishes. **Map 18 E4**.

Scoop

40 Shorts Gardens, WC2H 9AB (7240 7086, www.scoopgelato.com). Covent Garden tube. **Open** noon-10.30pm Mon-Thur; noon-11pm Fri-Sun. **Credit** AmEx, MC, V.
Scoop doesn't wear its sourcing lightly: the flavours board opposite the counter resembles an ingredient superstar roll-call, listing Gran Cru single-origin cocoas, Piedmontese tonda gentile hazelnuts, both *planifolia* and *tahitensis* vanilla pods, Chilean sultanas and Sri Lankan and Indonesian cinnamon. For some flavours, this attention to detail stands out: tè verde (with matcha powder from Kyoto) tasted impressively of green tea before gelato, and pistachio (with nuts from Bronte, the pistachio capital of Italy) was salty before creamy. Other classic Italian gelato flavours, which dominate the selection here, included a powerful amaretto and a deep Ecuadorian cioccolato fondente, though for something even darker, try the cioccolato extra fondente sorbet. Scoop parlours are decorated in a beige, brown and orange colour palette; limited seating at this branch means that most patrons end up spilling out on to the street or wandering away with their selections.
Takeaway service. Vegan dishes. **Map 18 D3.**
For branches see index.

Knightsbridge

Ice Cream Parlour at Harrods

2nd floor, Harrods, 87-135 Brompton Road, SW1X 7XL (7893 8959, www.harrods.com). Knightsbridge tube. **Open** 10am-7.30pm Mon-Sat; 11.30am-5.30pm Sun. **Credit** AmEx, MC, V.
Morelli's retro ice-cream bar is a cross between an 1950s American diner and a quaint English tearoom, tucked next to the Prosecco bar in Harrods. You can choose to sit at a table, or on an old-fashioned chrome stool by the bar, from where it's fascinating to watch the desserts being hand-assembled in front of you. The sundaes aren't cheap (£11.95-£19.95), but they're satisfyingly grand, towering high with fresh fruit, nuts, sauces and whipped cream. The ice-cream is of a fair quality, the vanilla especially creamy; the cookie pieces in the 'cookies 'n' cream' scoop were soft and chewy, with plenty of chocolate chunks. Flavours range from the classic (rum and raisin) to the more unusual (mango). On our visit, service was quite slow considering the number of staff, and the ice-cream, although presented stylishly, seemed no better than good-quality brands available in supermarkets. There are no madcap creations here, just old-fashioned sundaes and jugs of hot fudge sauce. Given the high prices, we reckon there needs to be something more to make a visit worthwhile.
Babies and children welcome: high chairs; nappy-changing facilities. Disabled: lift; toilet. Takeaway service. Vegan dishes. **Map 14 F9**.

Mayfair

Freggo

27-29 Swallow Street, W1B 4QR (7287 9506, www.freggo.co.uk). Piccadilly Circus tube. **Open** 8.30am-10pm Mon-Thur; 8.30am-midnight Fri, Sat; 9am-8pm Sun. **Credit** AmEx, MC, V.
As Regent Street curves into Piccadilly Circus, take a side-step into Swallow Street – an apt name for an ice-cream parlour. Freggo's decor is gaudy-nightclub purple and silver, and the music slightly offputting, though the outdoor seats are pleasant. The choice of ice-cream and sorbet was a tad limited, and (good heavens!) no toppings were available, but Freggo's Argentinian roots shone through in the dulche de leche and chocolate chip, and passionfruit cheesecake options. At £4 for two scoops, it's quite expensive, and our servings were too rich and the flavours too similar-tasting. However, the mini macaroons – crumbly biscuits with a smooth vanilla, strawberry or chocolate filling – were delicious. Freggo also offers South American-style empanadas, frittatas and cakes, along with shakes, coffees and juices.
Tables outdoors (2, pavement). Vegan dishes. **Map 17 A5**.

Soho

Amorino

41 Old Compton Street, W1D 6HF (7494 3300, www.amorino.com). Leicester Square or Piccadilly Circus tube. **Open** noon-midnight Mon-Thur, Sun; noon-1am Fri, Sat. **Credit** MC, V.
This London outpost of an international chain is surprisingly small and cosy: ideal for a quick treat, but not for lingering. Unlike many of the capital's ice-cream parlours with their bright and gaudy decor, Amarino looks traditionally and typically Italian. Jars of biscotti are on display, and wooden furniture adds to the warmth of the interior. Ice-creams are organic and free from preservatives, or artificial flavourings and colours. A wide range of flavours includes fruits such as alphonso mango or banana. Ices made from the rich Argentinian dessert, dulche de leche, are also popular. The simple classics are good too: pistachio gelato had an intense nutty flavour with a pleasant hint of saltiness. We were also impressed with the raspberry ice, made from Willamette berries (a North American variety) – the texture was dense and smooth, with every mouthful bursting with flavour. There are various qualities and styles of dark chocolate ice-creams too. Service is prompt and on-the-ball, as it needs to be on this busy central thoroughfare.
Tables outdoors (2, pavement). Takeaway service. **Map 17 B4**.

★ Gelupo HOT 50

7 Archer Street, W1D 7AU (7287 5555, www.gelupo.com). Piccadilly Circus tube. **Open** noon-11pm Mon-Thur; noon-1am Fri, Sat; noon-10pm Sun. **Credit** MC, V.

Brainchild of Jacob Kennedy (executive chef of hit Italian restaurant Bocca di Lupo, *see p163*), this sunny spot adds a scoop of Sicily to the south side of Soho, though you'd be hard-pressed to find ices this good even in Acireale or Catania. Friendly staff offer tasters of any flavour of interest – and there will be plenty of those, with 20 or so freshly made each day. Ewe's milk ricotta with sour cherry is a particular favourite, as is monte bianco (rum, chestnut and bitter chocolate) and the refreshing mint granita, which tastes nothing like toothpaste. Do try a sugar-crusted brioche stuffed with gelato (it's a traditional breakfast in Sicily, honest); the ice-cream melting into the bun seems to make the pleasure even guiltier. Gelupo also offers a cut-above range of chunky sandwiches filled with trending ingredients such as squacquerone (fresh Italian cream cheese) and 'nduja (spreadable spicy sausage). Sit at the stools near the front or head to the rear deli benches where shelves are lined with a connoisseur's selection of olive oils, pasta and booze.

Takeaway service. Vegan dishes. **Map 17 B4.**

South Kensington

Oddono's

14 Bute Street, SW7 3EX (7052 0732, www.oddonos.co.uk). South Kensington tube. **Open** 10am-11pm Mon-Thur, Sun; 10am-midnight Fri, Sat. **Credit** AmEx, MC, V.

The ice-cream reigns supreme in this quintessential old-school gelateria in South Kensington. Staff natter in Italian, while mothers gently reprimand their children in French – it all makes for a rather cosmopolitan and pleasant atmosphere. Some 15 flavours of ice-cream and sorbet are on offer, using natural ingredients. Some change weekly: make sure you're there for the salted caramel, hazelnut chocolate, and cookies and cream editions – creamy but not too heavy. Strawberry sorbet was also exquisite, using real fruit and minimal sugar. If you've got a sweet tooth and lunchtime descends, try a couple of scoops on a warm cinnamon waffle with extra chocolate sauce. For dessert, you can take home a sizeable gelati cake (banoffee pie and Oreo cakes were staring smugly at us from behind the glass), followed by a chilled affogato (Illy coffee and vanilla ice-cream).

Tables outdoors (2, pavement). Takeaway service. Vegan dishes. **Map 14 D10.**

For branches see index.

West

Ladbroke Grove

Dri Dri Gelato

189 Portobello Road, W11 2ED (3490 5027, www.dridrigelato.com). Ladbroke Grove or Notting Hill Gate tube. **Open** noon-10.30pm Mon-Thur, Sun; 11am-11pm Fri, Sat. **Credit** MC, V.

A neat little gelato bar, gaily decorated in shades of orange and pink, selling ice-creams and sorbets made on the premises from carefully sourced ingredients. Every day, the ices are mixed and frozen at the same time, so the air is smoothly absorbed – whatever happens, it works. We perched on a couple of the bar stools, and made light work of a salted caramel ice-cream (a smooth, sweet hit), a pink grapefruit sorbet (a delightfully sharp contrast to the caramel), an extra-noir chocolate sorbet (an excellent special, almost creamy enough to be an ice-cream), and an espresso ice-cream (our pick of the bunch). Other flavours included melon, strawberry, pistachio and stracciatella; there are a few cocktails, as well as coffee and tea. Charming service adds to the all-Italian experience.

Takeaway service. **Map 19 B3.**

For branch see index.

Zazà Gelato NEW

195 Portobello Road, W11 2ED (07796 968025, www.zazagelato.eu). Ladbroke Grove or Notting Hill Gate tube. **Open** 10.30am-18.30pm Mon-Thur; 10.30am-midnight Fri, Sat; noon-7pm Sun. **Credit** MC, V.

Part of a growing family-run chain, this Neapolitan gelateria attracts plenty of customers, despite competition from branches of the longer-established Gelato Mio and Dri Dri Gelato. The ice-cream flavours range from white chocolate to specials such as hazelnut coffee, while the sorbets – lemon, orange, strawberry – are sharp, fruity and refreshing. Our coconut gelato had a desiccated coconut garnish and a pleasing aftertaste. The textures of these ices tended towards frozen, rather than the creamy consistency associated with some Italian gelateria. An impressive variety of gelati cakes is also on display: hazelnut, pistachio or other flavours on a sponge base, topped with whipped cream. Insulated boxes protect the cakes from melting for up to 30 minutes. Note that space here is limited, making this more of a takeaway joint than some; there are also kiosks in Canary Wharf and Westfield London, and more planned.

Babies and children welcome: high chairs; play area. Tables outdoors (2 pavement). Takeaway service. Vegan dishes. **Map 19 B3.**

South East

London Bridge & Borough

★ Gelateria 3bis NEW

4 Park Street, SE1 9AB (no phone). London Bridge tube/rail. **Open** 8am-10pm Mon-Sat; 10am-6pm Sun. **Credit** MC, V.

Tucked between Neal's Yard Dairy and Monmouth Coffee at Borough Market, 3bis is an Italian gelateria that excels in creamy gelato and refreshing sorbets. Step inside and watch the line-up of gelato machines churning out new flavours. There's an emphasis on creamy, milky ones, from fior di panna ('cream' ice-cream) to panna cotta. While the classics (such as chocolate or pistachio) are not neglected, the team likes to experiment. A caramel-coloured liquorice gelato surprised with an initial burst of intense coffee notes, which then merged into the familiarly strong hit of anis. As for whoever dreamt up the idea of making gooseberry gelato, they deserve a big *baci*. Sorbets are also worth sampling: strawberry was delightfully fresh and zingy. A chocolate tap on the counter means your ice-cream pot can be enhanced with a dollop of liquid milk chocolate at the bottom. Cutesy surroundings (white walls, wooden floors and tables, pastel-coloured metal chairs) make this a welcoming place to sit down for a lick of summer.

Babies and children admitted. Takeaway service. **Map 11 P8.**

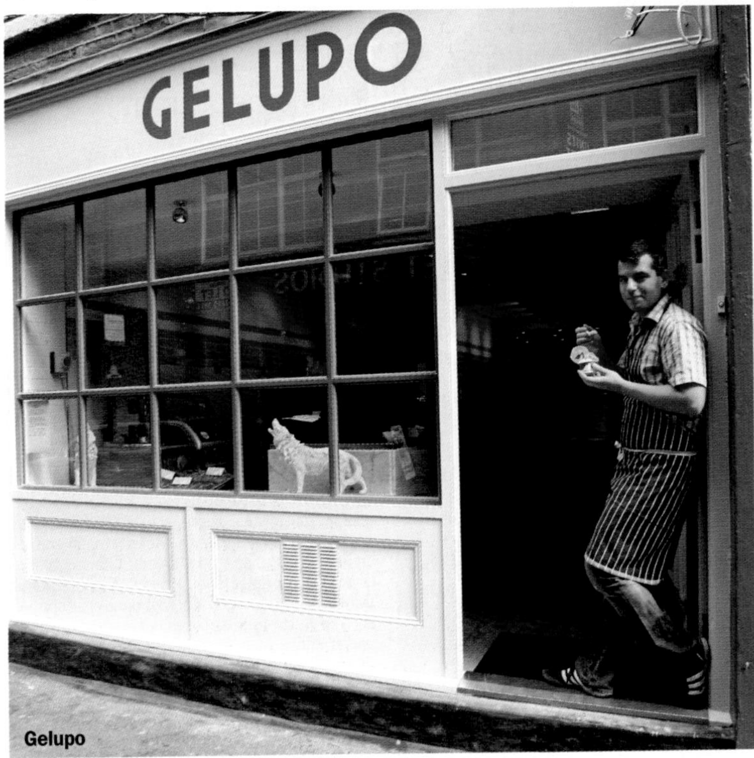

Gelupo

North

Camden Town & Chalk Farm

★ Chin Chin Laboratorists

49-50 Camden Lock Place, NW1 8AF (07885 604284, www.chinchinlabs.com). Camden Town tube. **Open** noon-7pm Tue-Sun. **No credit cards.**

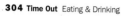

On any Sunday, some of London's most highly regarded haute cuisine chefs can be found seeking, er, inspiration at this cramped, crazy spot where staff in white lab coats freeze ice-cream and sorbet to order using liquid nitrogen. The daily-changing flavours are churned in a row of KitchenAid mixers and the billowing clouds that spill over the counter make fun viewing. You then choose toppings from the range of wacky sprinkles (grilled white chocolate, green tea peanut brittle, caramelised pretzels) or classic sauces (chocolate, raspberry, salted caramel), though staff will advise on ideal matches. Recipes are carefully conceived – even vanilla is anything but plain, made with caramelised unrefined cane sugar and Pondicherry vanilla beans. Proper dark chocolate, containing 80% couverture, is a paragon. Novelty of the day was truffle popcorn ice-cream, made by infusing finely chopped fresh white truffle in the custard base – it worked, despite a distinct savoury edge. We marvelled at the creaminess of dairy-free barbecued pineapple sorbet, an elegant ice more at home in a fine dining restaurant than the middle of Camden Market. Presumably one of those famous chefs has 'borrowed' that idea already too…

Babies and children admitted. Tables outdoors (3, pavement). Takeaway service. Vegan dishes. **Map 27 C1.**

Gelateria 3bis. See p303.

North West

Belsize Park

Gelato Mio

204 Haverstock Hill, NW3 2AG (7998 9276, www.gelatomio.co.uk). Belsize Park tube. **Open** 11am-10.30pm daily. **Credit** AmEx, MC, V.

Read the fine print and you'll see Gelato Mio calls itself a pasticceria and gelateria, which accounts for the personable comforts that on some days may give this place the edge over its epicurean rivals in central London, or the local coffee shop. This branch offers free Wi-Fi and, unlike many ice-cream parlours, has plenty of space inside for relaxing or wielding a pram; in good weather, the pavement tables and swing are the hotspots, whether you're amusing a toddler or charming a first date. The gelato is good, but veer away from the fabulously dark cioccolato to specials such as tarte tatin, and the flavours are comparatively mild, indistinct and oversweet. You won't go wrong if you stick with classics such as hazelnut, stracciatella (choc chip) and amarena (cherry). There are also breakfasty pastries and own-baked cookies to enjoy with reliable Illy coffee. Gelato celebration cakes require 48 hours' notice. The take-home tubs are pricey, but why grab and go when this leafy neighbourhood is so good for people-watching?

Babies and children welcome: high chairs. Disabled: toilet. Tables outdoors (8, pavement). Takeaway service. **Map 28 C3.**
For branches see index.

Hampstead

Slice of Ice

8 Flask Walk, NW3 1HE (7419 9908, www.slice-of-ice.co.uk). Hampstead tube. **Open** *Summer* 11am-7pm Mon-Fri; 11am-10pm Sat, Sun. *Winter* 11am-7pm daily. **Credit** AmEx, MC, V.

We've enjoyed this place in the past, but on our last visit were 'greeted' by an agitated young man screeching 'Takeaway only, takeaway only! We close at seven,' as we entered. It wasn't yet 6.30pm. For a Saturday evening in peak summer, an ice-cream parlour in the centre of touristy Hampstead Village needs to be better prepared. Fortunately, there's much to like about this lime green- and white-painted spot. The ice-cream isn't made on site, but is sourced from Il Gelato di Ariela, a first-rate artisan manufacturer in north London. Choice is wide, but don't expect innovation: flavours tend to be Italian classics of the type that make yoghurt gelato look daringly modern – think pistachio, mint choc chip, lemon. Still, once tried, the dark chocolate sorbet is unmissable, and the 'malaga' (rum and raisin) suitably adult. Any variety can be made into a decadent shake for £4. Care is taken to offer allergy sufferers something to delight. The cakes, chocolates, tea and coffee, all hailing from London and surrounds, are of high standard too.

Babies and children welcome: high chairs. Disabled: toilet. Takeaway service. Vegan dishes. **Map 28 C2.**

Outer London

Richmond, Surrey

Gelateria Danieli

16 Brewers Lane, Richmond, Surrey, TW9 1HH (8439 9807, www.gelateriadanieli.com). Richmond tube/rail. **Open** *Summer* 10am-10pm Mon-Sat; 11am-6pm Sun. *Winter* 10am-6pm Mon-Sat; 11am-6pm Sun. Times may vary, phone to check. **No credit cards.**

In a lane that's close to Richmond Green, Gelateria Danieli is a tiny shop with a thriving takeaway business. In warm weather, you can head off with a mouth-watering scoop of the flavour of the day and bask in the sun on the grass nearby. Apart from regular flavours such as milk chocolate, pistachio or tiramisu, there are seasonal ones: on our visit, a mango gelato. This had a fresh, intense taste; we were surprised to find staff were using the kesar ('saffron') variety of mango, a popular variety in Gujarat – sweeter than the more usual alphonso. A take on that British classic, the bakewell tart, had a pleasantly jammy tang. More refreshing was crema siciliana, a rich ice-cream with candy-like crystallised orange and orange syrup. Gelateria Danieli also offers several sorbets, and cone options such as gluten-free rice cones. Service was attentive and friendly, with the staff happy to let you try flavours and help you make your choice. A small branch also opened in the West End in 2012.

Takeaway service.
For branches (Danieli on the Green, Gelateria Danieli) see index.

Pizza & Pasta

Simple inexpensive food, yes, but easy to do well? For too long, London's pizza market was dominated by the chains, with the few local independent operators getting business where they could. Then, in 2008, **Franco Manca** opened in Brixton, giving Italianate care to the sourcing of ingredients and, above all, the texture of the pizza bases. It has rightly thrived, opening new branches in east and west London, and has also led to other operators raising their game, including promising new Portobello Road joint, **Saporitalia**, the hip new pizzeria near the Olympic Park, **Crate Brewery**, and Kensal Green's recently opened branch of Ealing's Santa Maria, **Sacro Cuore**. As for pasta restaurants, timing of the main ingredient (al dente, please!) and first-class raw materials hold the key to success. Specialists are thin on the ground – London could do with a pasta-joint version of Franco Manca – but **Pasta Plus** can knock up decent cannelloni.

Central

Clerkenwell & Farringdon

Santoré

59-61 Exmouth Market, EC1R 4QL (7812 1488). Farringdon tube/rail or bus 19, 38, 341. **Meals served** noon-11pm daily. **Main courses** £7.65-£15.95. **Set lunch** (noon-3pm) £9.95 2 courses. **Set dinner** (3-6pm) £12.95 2 courses. **Credit** AmEx, MC, V.

A lively trattoria, done out in earthen shades, with a long list of classic pizzas all cooked in a wood-fired oven. A napoletana was nicely singed (if a little soggy in the middle) and deliciously heavy on the anchovies. For larger groups (or appetites), pizzas are available by length. A host of alternatives runs from pan-fried calves' liver in butter and sage, served with balsamic vinegar and crispy potatoes, to a range of pastas. Penne sicilia – cheese-topped and baked with aubergine and Italian sausage – disappointed: it was nice enough, but a bit bland and served lukewarm. Much better was a piping hot, flavour-packed starter, tegamino di melanzane (baked aubergines with tomato, parmesan and basil sauce). To finish, affogato was given extra zing by a dash of amaretto. The wine list is matched by a set of cocktails, including a very decent negroni. Staff run the gamut from friendly to over-eager, but deal well with a busy, noisy room.

Available for hire. Babies and children welcome: booster seats. Tables outdoors (10, pavement). Takeaway service; delivery service (over £10 within 3-mile radius). **Map 5 N4.**

Euston

Pasta Plus

62 Eversholt Street, NW1 1DA (7383 4943, www.pastaplus.co.uk). Euston tube/rail. **Lunch served** noon-2.30pm Mon-Fri. **Dinner served** 5.30-10.30pm Mon-Sat. **Main courses** £7-£18. **Credit** AmEx, MC, V.

Neither the location nor the frontage appear very promising at first, but look beyond appearances for decent Italian food at a good price. A weekday evening was busy with tourists and regulars in the know. The plain interior is a little unimaginative, but the many windows at the back lift the room. Although bruschetta was made with flavoursome olive oil and a good sprinkling of oregano, the bread beneath was lacklustre. Next, salmon tagliatelle came with mushrooms and spring onions in a creamy sauce; equally delicious was plump cannelloni. From a small list of salads, and meat and fish dishes, pan-roasted guinea fowl with Italian-style roast potatoes and vegetables proved an excellent choice. We ended the meal with tiramisu: we planned to share one between two, but liked it so much we ordered a second.

Available for hire. Babies and children welcome: high chairs. Separate room for parties, seats 26. Tables outdoors (2, pavement). **Map 4 K3.**

Mayfair

Rocket

4-6 Lancashire Court, off New Bond Street, W1S 1EY (7629 2889, www.rocketrestaurants.co.uk). Bond Street or Oxford Circus tube. *Bar* **Open** noon-11pm Mon-Sat; noon-10pm Sun. **Meals served** noon-10pm Sun. *Restaurant* **Lunch served** noon-3pm, **dinner served** 6-11pm Mon-Fri. **Meals served** noon-11pm Sat. *Both* **Main courses** £8-£17. **Credit** AmEx, MC, V.

Rocket is a distinctly upmarket take on a pizzeria. This Mayfair branch attracts a smart clientele, drawn in summer to the tables outside in the narrow alley. Service is from well-groomed waitresses. Walk inside to the bar; the spacious and airy restaurant is on the first floor. There's a Californian slant to the menu, with grills and big, lavish salads (one has St Agur and goat's cheeses, pear, olives, little mozzarella balls, pesto, peas, tomato, avocado salsa, beetroot and toasted seeds; another is a version of surf and turf) in addition to pizzas. But on a recent visit, most customers were here for the pizzas. One of the simpler versions, topped with anchovy, chilli, olives, tomato, mozzarella and capers was a great, lively combination of flavours, with a lovely chilli kick. Another with salami, chorizo, ham, pancetta, roasted chilli, tomato and mozzarella was heavily laden (no stinting here) and equally good. Dough in both was thin but not brittle. All in all, these were top-quality pizzas – they're a few quid more expensive than is typical, but worth it.

Babies and children welcome: high chairs. Booking advisable. Separate rooms for parties, seating 10 and 26. Tables outdoors (7, pavement). **Map 9 H6.**

For branches see index.

Saporitalia

West

Ladbroke Grove

Rossopomodoro

184A Kensington Park Road, W11 2ES (7229 9007, www.rossopomodoro.co.uk). **Meals served** noon-11.30pm daily. **Main courses** £11-£16. **Set lunch** £9.99 1 course incl drink. **Credit** AmEx, MC, V.

This Neapolitan pizza specialist now has five branches in London. The W11 establishment was bustling with parties of Italian women on our visit: a good sign, but it did mean we had to wait for service, having to make do with a wink on occasion, while our waiter entertained the ladies. Luckily, the food was worth waiting for. Moist, crispy tiellina (dough balls with tomato, parmesan and basil pesto) put Pizza Express's rather dry efforts to shame, and meatballs were intensely flavoured. There's a choice of 14 pizzas, and they look and taste authentically Neapolitan. The classic margherita was as mouthwatering as the massese with its spicy salami, and there are four chef's specials to tempt the curious. There are also ten pasta dishes and half a dozen salads. The beer is Moretti – nicely chilled – and there's a short Italian wine list. The restaurant is snug, warm and colourful, with bare-brick walls and vivid canvases. The loyalty card is not the only reason we'll be back.

Babies and children welcome: children's menu; high chairs; nappy-changing facilities. Booking advisable. Tables outdoors (4, pavement). Takeaway service. **Map 19 B3.**

For branches see index.

Saporitalia NEW

222 Portobello Road, W11 1LJ (7243 3257). Ladbroke Grove tube. **Meals served** noon-11pm daily. **Main courses** £5.50-£17.95. **Set lunch** £10.50 2 courses. **Credit** AmEx, MC, V.

Saporitalia is a firmly traditional place, with an all-Italian staff and a great many native customers. The interior has a trompe-l'œil Italian street scene painted on to the rear walls, while young pizzaioli in white aprons and hats work their craft, spinning dough and sliding pizzas in and out of the wood-fired oven on long-handled wooden peels. Passata is spread with a wooden spoon, olive oil poured from the long spout of a copper can. The time from the pizzas leaving the oven to hitting the customers' tables is barely two minutes. On our visit, the dough of our 'Saporita' was crisp and flavoursome, not soggy; the tomato sauce was light, and no more than molten mozzarella was required by way of embellishment. The menu extends beyond pizza to simple grills (our sardines had nicely blackened skin) and salads – including some meltingly sweet aubergines – from a buffet table. There are pasta dishes and other Italian classics but, essentially, this is a pizzeria – and an excellent one at that. A word of warning: service on our visit was inattentive, and the atmosphere hectic.

Available for hire. Babies and children welcome: children's menu; high chairs. Booking advisable. Separate room for parties, seats 35. Takeaway service. Vegan dishes. Vegetarian menu. **Map 19 B2.**

Maida Vale

Red Pepper

8 Formosa Street, W9 1EE (7266 2708, http://theredpepper.net). Warwick Avenue tube. **Dinner served** 6.30-11pm Mon-Fri. **Meals served** 11am-11pm Sat; 11am-10.30pm Sun. **Main courses** £9-£21. **Credit** MC, V.

A neighbourhood favourite, Red Pepper is split over ground floor and basement. The tables are a little cramped but the relaxed atmosphere makes everyone feel at home. The owner is Neapolitan, and the pizzas (also available to take away) do him proud. Thin, crispy bases are topped with Italian ingredients such as bresaola, fior di latte and San Danielle ham; a basilico (a margherita with fresh basil and mozzarella) went down a treat. The menu also features own-made pasta, and daily changing specials such as marinated lamb steaks with baby artichoke, green olive and sun-dried tomato salad. The juicy steak was grilled just-so and the accompaniments were a good foil, if a rather stingy portion. We also like the zabaglione semifreddo and the well-priced wine list.

Babies and children admitted. Booking essential. Separate room for parties, seats 25. Tables outdoors (2, pavement). Takeaway service. **Map 1 C4.**

Westbourne Grove

Mulberry Street

84 Westbourne Grove, W2 5RT (7313 6789, www.mulberrystreet.co.uk). Bayswater or Royal Oak tube. **Meals served** noon-midnight Mon-Sat; noon-11pm Sun. **Main courses** £7.55-£14.95. **Credit** AmEx, MC, V.

Don't expect to leave this modern, clean-cut, diner-style restaurant any more enlightened as to what makes a pizza 'New York' in style. What matters is that the main act is well thought out, with a thin crust and a chewy base. This crisp outer ring surrounds a smattering of almost anonymous sauce topped by a thin layer of evenly spread cheese – neither intrusive enough to take away from the fresh, chunky toppings. Starters span both ends of the satisfaction spectrum, from dismal pizza-style garlic bread (burnt in the middle, overly crunchy on the edge, with a paltry spread of garlic butter and raw garlic chunks) to fantasic meatballs. You get four of them, split in half and immersed in a tasty tomato sauce – it would be difficult to do better in London. Service is young, friendly and efficient, and staff cope well with the invariably busy weekends when large groups nestle into the six-seater booths.

Babies and children welcome: high chairs; nappy-changing facilities. Booking advisable. Disabled: toilet. Separate room for parties, seats 30. Takeaway service; delivery service (over £20 within 5-mile radius). **Map 7 B6.**

South West

Fulham

Napulé

585 Fulham Broadway, SW6 5UA (7381 1122, www.madeinitalygroup.co.uk). Fulham Broadway tube. **Lunch served** noon-3.30pm Sat, Sun. **Dinner served** 6-11pm Mon-Thur; 6-11.30pm Fri, Sat; 6-10.30pm Sun. **Main courses** £6.50-£16. **Credit** MC, V.

There's something of a rustic feel to this Fulham pizzeria (part of the small Made in Italy family), with its chequered tablecloths, tiled floor, exposed brickwork and greenery – although the clientele is firmly south-west London. There are tried and trusted pasta dishes (spaghetti carbonara, ravioli with spinach and ricotta) along with some main-course salads, but it's the pizzas, from a wood-fired oven, that are the main draw. After we ordered, a large wooden trestle was placed on our table. Our choices – capricciosa, with mozzarella, sausage, mushroom, artichoke and ham; and diavola, with mozzarella, salami and mushroom – were served pizzametro-style (by the metre), as one long pizza, on a wooden board that rested on the trestle. We were given plates, but there was really no room for them. The pizzas were generously portioned, with chewy thin crusts – good, but not outstanding. We were less happy when the bill arrived: a jug of tap water appeared as sparkling water at £3.20, we were charged for two mixed salads (we'd commented on the generous portion, served on a single plate) and a 250ml glass of sauvignon blanc turned out to have cost a staggering £7.80.

Babies and children welcome: high chairs. Booking advisable. Separate room for parties, seats 14. Takeaway service. **Map 13 A13.**

For branches (Luna Rossa, Made In Italy, Santa Lucia) see index.

South

Balham

Ciullosteria

31 Balham High Road, SW12 9AL (8675 3072, www.ciullosteria.com). Clapham South tube or Balham tube/rail. **Dinner served** 6-11pm Mon-Thur; 6-11.30pm Fri, Sat. **Meals served** noon-10.30pm Sun. **Main courses** £7-£20. **Credit** MC, V.

From the enthusiastic welcome on entering to the complimentary shot of limoncello on leaving, Ciullosteria had the canny knack of making us feel like treasured regulars on our first visit to its intimate little premises. An eagerness to please extends to the sheer range of dishes offered. Italian favourites of pizza and pasta feature alongside a selection of meat and fish: from calf's liver to sea bream. Our antipasti starter was a mix of mortadella, prosciutto and bresaola, lifted by a side helping of marinated tomatoes and artichokes. Chilli-flecked, grilled spatchcock of baby chicken served with morsels of deep-fried courgette followed. Portion sizes are challenging. There's a 'big is bellissimo' ethos here and we struggled to finish an otherwise excellent beef carpaccio and truffle oil pizza. What makes the place stand out from the crowd is its five-star service. We appreciated the bottle of tap water, placed on each table as a matter of course, and the option of

Crate Brewery. See p310.

Dabbous astonished with its cutting-edge cooking (*see p132*), and its downstairs cocktail bar sets out to do the same. There are plenty of unorthodox ingredients, and at times the combinations look forbidding: the Giddy Up contains tequila, bramley and gage slider (traditional sloe-infused cider from Devon), elderflower cordial, lemon juice and camomile-infused acacia honey topped with Sierra Nevada IPA. But other drinks stay closer to classicism, and you can always order off-menu if you're feeling timid. Three out of four cocktails were top-notch, especially the superb oak-aged negroni and the 2091210 (gin, Aperol and citrus juices topped with cream soda). The bar has the same stripped-back industrial decor as the restaurant, with bare walls that do a great but unwelcome job of bouncing noise all over the shop. Service was sweet and solicitous, and bar snacks a cut above. A very good place, but check ingredients attentively.
Available for hire. Disabled: toilet. **Map 17 B1**.

Hakkasan

8 Hanway Place, W1T 1HD (7927 7000, www.hakkasan.com). Tottenham Court Road tube. **Open** noon-12.30am Mon-Wed; noon-1.30am Thur-Sat; noon-midnight Sun. **Credit** AmEx, MC, V.
The newer, Mayfair branch of this seriously smart Fitzrovia Chinese restaurant (*see p67*) and bar has stolen some of the limelight from its sibling, which is now more than a decade old. But we still prefer this original outpost of what has now become an international chain. The long, thin strip of a bar behind the Chinese screens continues to look glamorous, and the cocktails are still superb. Premium spirits are used, the bar staff are well trained and there is a definite homage to the East with drinks such as the Hakka (with regular saké) or the plum sour (with plum saké). Don't be put off by the frosty door staff, the dark descent to the basement or the bevy of hostesses asking about your booking (not actually required for the bar): it's worth the perseverance, and has less of a press of people than many newer bars operating at this level.
Available for hire. Babies and children admitted until 7.30pm. Booking advisable. Disabled: lift; toilet. Entertainment: DJs 9pm Thur-Sat. Function room (65 capacity). **Map 17 C2**.

King's Cross

Booking Office

St Pancras Renaissance London Hotel, NW1 2AR (7841 3540, www.bookingofficerestaurant.com). King's Cross or St Pancras tube/rail. **Open** 6.30am-2.45am daily. **Credit** AmEx, DC, MC, V.
As part of the architect George Gilbert Scott's 1873 Midland Grand Hotel at St Pancras station, this former railway booking office was designed to instil in passengers a sense of awe at the power and wonder of the railways. These days, it serves as an equally awe-inspiring bar, and its refit has made the most of the Victorian splendour. The drinks demonstrate equal attention to detail, with a cocktail list, created by great London mixers Nick Strangeway and Henry Besant, that shows a deep respect for the history of British drinking. Sours, fizzes and cobblers are represented, but perhaps most exciting are the punches, served with dash from handmade copper mugs. The bar snacks are less impressive – this is a railway station bar, after all – and the service isn't all it might be, but the setting makes up for this shortcomings. For the Gilbert Scott restaurant, *see p53.*
Available for hire. Babies and children admitted. Disabled: toilet. Tables outdoors (27, terrace). **Map 4 L3**.

VOC

2 Varnishers Yard, Regents Quarter, N1 9AW (7713 8229, www.voc-london.co.uk). King's Cross tube/rail. **Open** 5pm-1am Mon-Thur; 5pm-2am Fri, Sat. **Credit** AmEx, MC, V.
This small, stylish cocktail bar in the busy Regents Quarter of King's Cross is yet another by the chaps behind Purl and Worship Street Whistling Shop. It looks like Phileas Fogg's front room, with cartography adorning the brick walls, swashbuckling busts, telescopes and cosy candlelight. It takes its name and 17th-century maritime theme from the Vereenigde Oost-Indische Compagnie, more commonly known as the Dutch East India Company. Back in the 1800s, punches were a big deal in the colonies and one of the earliest examples of a mixed drink. The punches packed here, however, run a gamut of styles. Some are individually bottled; others are aged in new and ex-sherry casks and dangle in mini barrels from the ceiling. There's an array of bottle-matured cocktails decanted into apothecary-style vessels. Each bottled is wax-sealed, then individually labelled with the date of creation and priced accordingly – the older, the dearer.
Available for hire. Booking advisable. Disabled: toilet. Tables outdoors (2, pavement; 4, terrace). Wireless internet. **Map 4 L3**.

Knightsbridge

Mandarin Bar

Mandarin Oriental Hyde Park, 66 Knightsbridge, SW1X 7LA (7235 2000, www.mandarinoriental.com/london). Knightsbridge tube. **Open** 10.30am-1.30am Mon-Sat; 10.30am-12.30pm Sun. **Credit** AmEx, DC, MC, V.
The well-established bar of Knightsbridge's Mandarin Oriental now operates partly as a holding pen for people waiting to bag a walk-in table at the hotel's high-profile restaurant, Dinner by Heston Blumenthal (*see p67*). But this only adds to the frisson; it's a great place for people-watching, and the service here is well drilled and charming – as you'd expect from a five-star outfit. The floor is as shiny as a banker's pearl cufflink, and the size of the cocktails bespeaks an era that recession forgot. They're not bad, either: a bit sweet (five spoonfuls is a lot of sugar, even for a caipirinha) but well balanced, and portions really are huge. There's no obligatory service charge, which, given that the staff are splendid and the crisps are replenished at five-minute intervals, is a pleasant surprise.
Disabled: toilet (hotel). Dress: smart casual. **Map 8 F9**.

Marylebone

Artesian

Langham Hotel, 1C Portland Place, W1B 1JA (7636 1000, www.artesian-bar.co.uk). Oxford Circus tube. **Open** noon-2am Mon-Sat; noon-midnight Sun. **Credit** AmEx, DC, MC, V.
The Langham Hotel is one of those high-ceilinged, marble-pillared palaces that many well-padded visitors, yet few resident Londoners, seem to visit. But it's worth getting your best togs on just to admire David Collins's handsome bar design. The result blends grand Victorian decadence (marble bar, soaring inset mirrors) with modern details

Mark's Bar. See p315.

Bar Américain

(purple snakeskin-effect leather seats, carved pagoda-style back bar). As if that's not enough, world-renowned bartender Alex Kratena has won more awards for his mixology skills than Michael Phelps has gold medals. Service is faultless, and the drinks list is divided into categories such as 'rum de luxe', 'tonic and gin', 'heritage' and 'Artesian classics'. The only catch is that such opulence and perfection doesn't come cheap, with most cocktails starting at around £15, excluding service.
Available for hire. Babies and children admitted until 6pm. Disabled: toilet (hotel). Wireless internet. **Map 9 H5**.

Purl

50 Blandford Street, W1U 7HX (7935 0835, www.purl-london.com). Bond Street tube.
Open 5-11.30pm Mon-Thur; 5pm-midnight Fri, Sat. **Credit** AmEx, MC, V.
The first bar from the people who went on to create the Worship Street Whistling Shop, VOC and Dach & Sons, Purl was a clear taste of things to come. It uses the speakeasy feel and look that is now de rigueur everywhere, but pairs this with some excellent bar skills.The list of cocktail creations is divided between molecular mixology and a confident mastery of the classics. The former often have spectacular presentation, with smoke, unusual glassware, balloon popping and clever sleight of hand. Drinks change frequently, but options might include a Backward Bellini – a lavender-soaked sugarcube topped with prosecco, finished with pomegranate foam; or a marmalade vodka with Aperol and bitters, with a 'juniper oil burner'.
Available for hire. Booking advisable. **Map 9 G5**.

Mayfair

Coburg Bar

The Connaught, Carlos Place, W1K 2AL (7499 7070, www.the-connaught.co.uk). Bond Street or Green Park tube. **Open** 11am-11pm Mon, Sun; 11am-1am Tue-Sat. **Credit** AmEx, MC, V.
There's no velvet rope barring your way to the Connaught hotel's destination bar, and no strict door policy: you can just walk straight on in. What's more, once you've done so, the service will be faultless. The room oozes sophistication, with modern touches (grey velvet wingback chairs, black glass tables) that enhance the historic character of the space.The drinks list charts the evolution of the cocktail, with each drink – the greatest hits of the last two centuries, more or less – well worth the considerable expense. Tip-top nibbles are free of charge; better, a tiny skewer of iced fruit on a silver dish appears with each cocktail as a palate-cleanser. Luxurious, elegant and discreet, the Coburg Bar is everything a good hotel bar should be. But if it's just not 'scene' enough for you, the hotel's other, noisier and busier bar (the Connaught) is just a stroll away down the corridor.
Available for hire. Disabled: toilet. Wireless internet. **Map 9 H7**.

Piccadilly

Bar Américain

Brasserie Zédel, 20 Sherwood Street, W1F 7ED (7734 4888, www.brasseriezedel.com). Piccadilly Circus tube. **Open** 4.30pm-midnight daily.
Credit AmEx, MC, V.
A message to all aspiring bartenders considering a leap on to the already overcrowded Prohibition/1930s-theme bandwagon: this is how you do it properly. Brasserie Zédel (*see p96*) is a new venture from the chaps behind the Wolseley (*see p42*) and the Delaunay (*see p40*), and is housed in what used to be the Atlantic Bar & Grill. A short list of mixed drinks ('classic' and 'house') are faithful to the golden age of cocktails. There's a martini, a manhattan and a mint julep, as well as a fabulous sazerac; fancier creations include a beautifully balanced Belle Zédel (with vodka, crème de myrtille, rose liqueur and rhubarb bitters among its constituents), or a spiky Spritz Américain, with champagne, grapefruit liqueur and bitters. They all cost £9.75 – even those charged with bubbly – and come with trays of olives and cashews. This, coupled with the attentive service and the fact you'll be drinking in one of the most truly opulent bars in London, is excellent value.
Available for hire. Disabled: lift; toilet.
Map 17 B5.

Powder Keg Diplomacy. See p318.

St James's

Dukes Bar

Dukes, 35 St James's Place, SW1A 1NY (7491 4840, www.dukeshotel.com). Green Park tube.
Open 2pm-midnight Mon-Thur; noon-midnight Fri, Sat; 4pm-midnight Sun. **Credit** AmEx, MC, V.
Dukes Hotel has changed hands a few times in recent years, but one thing remains unchanged: this is the hotel bar to visit for a martini. Well-mannered waiters flick dry vermouth into an iced glass, fill it with gin or vodka (various premium options, all priced accordingly) and then drop in a sliver of lemon peel. Simple, but wonderful. Sipping a drink amid the murmur of the very adult clientele , while munching nuts and Puglian olives, is one of the most elegant drinking experiences in London. If you're looking for a hipster bar, look elsewhere; with its engravings and fringed chairs, this tiny but comfortable space resembles a Georgian railway carriage, and the atmosphere is surprisingly sober.
Dress: smart casual. Tables outdoors (4, garden). Wireless internet. **Map 9 J8**.

Soho

Mark's Bar

Hix, 66-70 Brewer Street, W1F 9UP (7292 3518, www.marksbar.co.uk). Piccadilly Circus tube. **Open** 11am-1am Mon-Sat; 11.30am-midnight Sun. **Credit** AmEx, DC, MC, V.
It's impossible to recommend Mark's Bar without first pointing out that this basement space (a previous winner of Time Out's Best New Bar Award) is still one of the hardest places in London to get a seat. Bookings are not taken, but arrive at the right time, sweet-talk the receptionist, and you might be lucky. This initiation only makes you want to linger longer once esconced in a padded leather sofa in the rakishly dim room. The cocktail list was originally created by Nick Strangeway with a similar emphasis on ingredient provenance to that preached by restaurateur Mark Hix in his restaurant upstairs (*see p54*): you might see drinks made with the likes of Kentish redcurrants, sea buckthorn and rhubarb. Historically revived mixed drinks also feature heavily: step back to the golden age of bartending with a Criterion Milk Punch, a Scoff Law Cocktail or a Pegu Club.
Available for hire. Babies and children admitted until 5pm. Bookings not accepted. Disabled: toilet. Wireless internet. **Map 17 A4**.

Milk & Honey

61 Poland Street, W1F 7NU (7065 6840 ext 6, www.mlkhny.com). Oxford Circus tube. **Open** *Non-members* 6-11pm Mon-Sat (2hrs max, last admission 9pm). *Members* 6pm-3am Mon-Sat.
Credit AmEx, DC, MC, V.
This, the popular myth has it, has always been one the best cocktail bars in London. It might be, but it's hard to tell unless you have night vision like an owl – the lighting is turned down so low you'll need to borrow a candle to read the drinks list, let alone see your drink, and you may not even recognise your drinking companions across the table. And then there's the difficulty of getting in. It's a members' club most of the time, although the rest of us can book a table in the early evening for up

Best new beer bar

Brewdog

The beer taps are almost unrecognisable from the average high-street chain pub. When you discover that the landlord Dan Fox was for years manager of the White Horse in Parsons Green, it becomes clear this pub holds beer in extremely high esteem. Five of the pumps dispense the fine products of the London Brewing Company, made on the premises – a zesty raspberry wheat beer, say, or Beer Street best bitter. A merry evening could easily be whiled away with these alone, but keg fonts advertise the likes of Sierra Nevada Torpedo and Veltins Pilsener. The well laid-out list of bottles isn't the longest in town, but wins over with its descriptions. You'll find several unusual imports from Great Divide and Odell in the US, as well as cans from Kona. *Babies and children welcome: children's menu; crayons; high chairs; nappy-changing facilities. Booking advisable Thur-Sun. Disabled: toilet. Separate room for parties, seats 60. Tables outdoors (12, terrace).*

Crown & Anchor

2012 WINNER BEST NEW BEER BAR

246 Brixton Road, SW9 6AQ (7737 0060, www.crownandanchorbrixton.co.uk). Stockwell tube or Brixton tube/rail. **Open** 4.30pm-midnight Mon-Thur; 4.30pm-1am Fri; noon-1am Sat; noon-11pm Sun. **No credit cards.**

The Jolly Butchers in Stoke Newington is a stop-off on every beer buff's ultimate pub crawl, so news that its owners had taken over this public house south of the river was greeted with glee. The no-frills restoration stripped things back to bare brick and gave the wraparound windows smart gunmetal-grey frames; the most exciting feature though is the lengthy bar and its endless fonts (or so it seems – there are seven real ales from the cask, and 14 keg beers and ciders). The breweries you'll see

Brewdog

2012 RUNNER-UP BEST NEW BEER BAR

113 Bayham Street, NW1 0AG (7284 4626, www.brewdog.com). Camden Town tube or Camden Road rail. **Open** noon-11.30pm Mon-Thur; noon-midnight Fri, Sat; noon-10.30pm Sun. **Credit** MC, V.

We were midway through explaining to a drinking chum the difference between his half of Henley Dark porter and our Zeitgeist black lager when the barmaid glanced over from the pint she was pouring. 'You've got them the wrong way round,' she said. She hadn't served us, the beers were in identical glasses, they looked exactly the same – how could she tell? Such an insouciantly cool observation is testament to Brewdog staff's knowledge (and irreverent attitude). The Scottish craft brewery's London outpost is an initiation into the exciting and groundbreaking world of craft beer, but never feels intimidating. Admit to bar staff you've no idea where to start and they'll gladly guide you through the list, offering tasters. And what a list it is – every one of Brewdog's beers on keg draught (with occasional guests) and bottle, from the smooth, amber 5am Saint to the quadruple IPA Sink the Bismarck at 41% abv. Fridges hold a selection from other microbreweries, mainly from the US (the likes of Stone, Evil Twin and Anchor, although there's plenty from the Scandic Mikkeller and Nøgne Ø too). English beer producers barely get a look-in – almost certainly a typical Brewdog provocation. *Available for hire. Babies and children admitted. Disabled: toilet. Function room (60 capacity).* **Map 3 J1.**

Bull

2012 RUNNER-UP BEST NEW BEER BAR

13 North Hill, N6 4AB (8341 0510, www.thebullhighgate.co.uk). Highgate tube. **Open** noon-11pm Mon-Wed, Sun; noon-midnight Thur-Sat, Sun. **Credit** AmEx, MC, V.

First impressions would suggest the Bull is just another suburban gastropub, in a very nice part of Highgate. But look closer and you'll spot much enamelled beer memorabilia on the walls, and garlands of hop flowers on the beams. You might also catch a glimpse of the Willy Wonka tubing and brass vats of the brewing equipment.

Bull

Crown & Anchor

represented regularly are Redemption, Dark Star, Magic Rock, Camden Town, Brewdog, Brooklyn and Kernel; bottles take a more global approach and include a fair few Belgians. Clued-up staff are keen to recommend and offer tasting notes and samples. What makes this pub really stand out is the way it bridges the apparent divide between Camra-endorsed real ale and its hip young cousin, craft beer. Bearded note-takers and bearded hipsters should feel equally at home, as will their female companions: the Crown & Anchor – friendly, unpretentious and devoted to the cause – is also a very nice place to sink a drop.
Babies and children welcome: children's menu; high chairs. Disabled: toilet. Tables outdoors (8, pavement). Wireless internet.

Railway Tavern

2012 RUNNER-UP BEST NEW BEER BAR
2 St Jude Street, N16 8JT (0011 1195). Dalston Kingsland rail. **Open** noon-11pm Mon-Sat; noon-10.30pm Sun. **Credit** MC, V.
The Railway Tavern, on a residential street in Dalston, is essentially a local – but, to its credit, drinkers from farther afield will travel to visit. The owners of the Pineapple in Kentish Town returned this pub to its original name and gave it a thoughtful, mid-century-style makeover, with a few bits of artful railway ephemera here and there. Food is Thai; musicians frequently play. But the beer selection is something special, and is served with a dedication that prospective London publicans would do well to emulate. There are six regularly changing real ales on tap, and they're often made in London – from Redemption, Brodie's or the East London Brewing Company, for instance. On the recently expanded keg taps are Meantime London Lager, König Pilsner, Black Isle Porter and Brewdog's 5am Saint. The bottles pay homage to the microbrewing nous of the Americans, with the likes of Brooklyn, Anchor and Sierra Nevada, although there are a good few Europeans too. This is also a place to sample the latest hop explosions from Bermondsey's cult Kernel Brewery. No mainstream sops for the unadventurous sipper in sight, and brews are served in handled, dimpled pint mugs: magic.
Babies and children admitted. **Map 25 B4.**

Railway Tavern

to two hours – as long as you reserve at least a day in advance, and arrive before 9pm. However, if you're prepared to put up with all that ballyhoo, this is a great place for perfectly executed classic cocktails. We were impressed with our negroni, not least by our bartender enquiring about our preferences of gin and vermouth combinations. Be warned that the electricity saved on the lighting seems to be diverted to the fierce air-conditioning; jackets, or at least warm clothing, are a good idea.
Booking essential for non-members. Function rooms (50 capacity). **Map 17 A3.**

West

Notting Hill

Lonsdale

48 Lonsdale Road, W11 2DE (7727 4080, www.thelonsdale.co.uk). Ladbroke Grove or Notting Hill Gate tube. **Open** 6pm-midnight Tue-Thur; 6pm-1am Fri, Sat. **Credit** AmEx, MC, V.
This well-established bar has been an unwavering champion of well-made cocktails as other Notting Hill bars have come and gone. The 'London contemporary classics' offer the best in British mixes from recent times, such as the elderflower martini (Zubrowka bisongrass vodka stirred with apple juice and elderflower cordial for £8.75), though there is also a page devoted to modern classics created by legendary bartender Dick Bradsell, which includes the Wibble, the Bramble and a rose petal martini. Mixing and service are fittingly old-school, and the setting – a sun-catching front terrace, a long bar counter and wide, candlelit main seating area at the back – remains a very attractive proposition.
Babies and children admitted until 9pm. Disabled: toilet. Entertainment: DJs 9pm Thur-Sat. Function room (75-80 capacity). Tables outdoors (5, terrace). **Map 19 C3.**

South

Battersea

Lost Society

697 Wandsworth Road, SW8 3JF (7652 6526, www.lostsociety.co.uk). Clapham Common tube, Wandsworth Road rail or bus 77. **Open** 5-11pm Tue, Wed; 5pm-1am Thur; 5pm-2am Fri; 2pm-2am Sat; noon-11pm Sun. **Credit** AmEx, MC, V.
Run by the same crew as the Lost Angel in Battersea and Citizen Smith in Putney, this is one of south London's longest-established bars; in the 1980s, it was home to the Tearoom des Artistes. Its evergreen appeal is clear: a louche vibe, a great music policy, affordable drinks (£4.50 for some cocktails) and friendly staff. The list covers classics, mojitos, martinis and sours, plus a few of the bar's own more leftfield creations. Part of the premises have been rebranded as the Blind Tiger, a supposedly 'secret' restaurant (in reality, heavily promoted by Lost Society), which also has its own bar and has been decorated in – you guessed it – a wacky, decadent speakeasy style.
Babies and children admitted until 5pm. Entertainment: music 8pm Fri; DJs 9pm Fri, Sat. Tables outdoors (4, front garden; 5, back garden). **For branches (Citizen Smith, Lost Angel) see index.**

Powder Keg Diplomacy

147 St John's Hill, SW11 1TQ (7450 6457, www.powderkegdiplomacy.co.uk). Clapham Junction rail. **Open** 4pm-midnight Mon-Fri; 10am-midnight Sat, Sun. **Credit** AmEx, MC, V.

Despite the colonial name and portrait of Queen Victoria at the front door, the bar area isn't overtly imperial – there's wallpaper with prints of cavorting animals, lightbulbs in cages and studded leather seating. The cocktails are equally well considered. Cordials, syrups, liqueurs and mixers are own-made and used in mixed drinks that draw heavily on ingredients from every corner of the former Empire. The Bee's Knees uses American Blue Coat gin, lemon juice and honey from the Hive in Wandsworth. It's worth donning your pith helmet and puttees for the trip to deepest, darkest Battersea (if you're not already stationed nearby).

Babies and children welcome: high chairs; nappy-changing facilities. Booking advisable. Tables outdoors (3, pavement). **Map 21 B4**.

Clapham

Rookery

69 Clapham Common Southside, SW4 9DA (8673 9162, www.therookeryclapham.co.uk). Clapham Common or Clapham South tube. **Open** 5-11pm Tue,Wed; noon-11pm Thur; noon-midnight Fri, Sat; 12.30-10.30pm Sun. **Credit** MC, V.

This voguish, speakeasy-style bar and diner was inspired by New York's Lower East Side, and is of a type now common to central London – but this one's in Clapham. Rookery does Brit food (*see p59*) and beers very well, but also makes a go of cocktails from the well-stocked back bar of spirits. The cocktails veer towards the classic – gimlet, sidecar, white russian – and are all the better for it. Best of all though, they only cost in the £5 to £6 range. Rookery also has a west-facing canopied outdoor area, overlooking – albeit across the busy A24 – the green space of Clapham Common.

Babies and children welcome: high chairs. Booking advisable. Separate room for parties, seats 30. Tables outdoors (8, terrace). **Map 22 A3**.

Callooh Callay

East

Shoreditch

Book Club

100-106 Leonard Street, EC2A 4RH (7684 8618, www.wearetbc.com). Old Street tube/rail or Shoreditch High Street rail. **Open** 8am-midnight Mon-Wed; 8am-2am Thur, Fri; 10am-2am Sat; noon-midnight Sun. **Admission** *Club* free-£10. **Credit** MC, V.

This busy but commendable bar-club comprises one expansive room – divided by a wall with an oval hole in the middle, giving the illusion that half of Hoxton is here – and a small pool room downstairs. Cocktails are scrawled up in black felt-tip on white tiles by the bar, most in the £7 range and with in-joke names; perennial favourites include the Shoreditch Twat (Jägermeister, tequila and chartreuse shaken with an egg) and the Don't Go to Dalston (vodka, raspberry and cherry). And if you can't be bovvered with that, there are jugs of cocktails such as Pimm's, iced teas or Hoxton Triomphe, flavoured with elderflower. Come here for the scene, if nothing else.

Babies and children admitted until 8pm. Entertainment: bands/DJs 7pm Thur-Sat. Function room (100 capacity). Wireless internet. **Map 6 R4**.

Callooh Callay

65 Rivington Street, EC2A 3AY (7739 4781, www.calloohcallaybar.com). Old Street tube or Shoreditch High Street rail. **Open** 6pm-midnight Mon-Wed, Sun; 6pm-1am Thur-Sat. **Credit** AmEx, DC, MC, V.

This landmark of the Shoreditch bar scene takes its inspiration from a line in Lewis Carroll's poem 'Jabberwocky' and tends to divide visitors. Many simply adore it; others find it pretentious. We're not sure that the silly names of the cocktails, the Marmite-tinged number (the Marmageddon) or another flavoured like a black forest gateau will be for everyone, but mostly, the drinks meet with approval, and the list has won international awards. In the main bar room, with its low, purple seating, said drinks are served from a long bar counter by savvy staff featured in the childhood photos pinned to the wall. The handsome, backroom Jubjub Members' Bar, hidden behind a heavy wardrobe door (not a looking glass, but a nice touch) is more atmospheric than the front space (refreshingly, membership is based on appreciation of drinks rather than money). This being Shoreditch, DJs spin at weekends.

Booking advisable Thur-Sat. Disabled: toilet. Entertainment: DJs 8pm Fri, Sat. Function rooms (20-60 capacity). Wireless internet. **Map 6 R4**.

Happiness Forgets

8-9 Hoxton Square, N1 6NU (7613 0325, www.happinessforgets.com). Old Street tube/rail or Shoreditch High Street rail. **Open** 5.30-11pm Mon-Sat. **Credit** MC, V.

This tiny basement has such low light that torches ought to be provided to aid with reading the drinks list. But low light makes the room – dark walls and dark wooden floorboards – just that much more appealing. What's more, the cocktails are fabulous: innovative but with impeccable taste and a sure grasp of fundamentals. Two gin-based drinks, the French Pearl (shaken with fresh mint, lime and a dash of absinthe) and Mar*Tea*Ni both possessed flawless balance. Served in icy, frosted coupes, they stayed cold for 30 minutes. Minor complaint: the sound system was turned up to full whack. Apart from that, we remember Happiness Forgets with unalloyed pleasure. And a mixed crowd (mercifully free of Shoreditch poseurs) seemed to share that feeling. True happiness.

Booking advisable. Wireless internet. **Map 6 R3**.

Nightjar

129 City Road, EC1V 1JB (7253 4101, www.barnightjar.com). Old Street tube/rail. **Open** 6pm-1am Mon-Wed, Sun; 6pm-3am Thur-Sat. **Credit** AmEx, MC, V.

This glam basement hangout has almost everything going for it. Service is wonderful. It doesn't get overcrowded because, being table-service only, there's no standing. And it does fabulous things with alcohol. A beautifully garnished singapore sling aged in wood was well balanced and complex, and a gin fizz (ordered off-menu) was textbook stuff. But Nightjar lets itself down with a huge drinks list that can intimidate even seasoned cocktail-hounds: it's organised by era, and ingredients lists are not just lengthy but often baffling. Would you know what to expect from the Kinloch Special: cheddar-matured Scotch, pomelo jelly, fig perfume and oolong infusion with lemon juice? It's just a bit too cerebral. Yet the advice is good and the talent undeniable. Make sure you book, and don't be afraid to order something classic.

Booking advisable Tue-Sun. Disabled: toilet. Entertainment: musicians 9.30pm Tue-Sat. **Map 6 Q4**.

Worship Street Whistling Shop

63 Worship Street, EC2A 2DU (7247 0015, www.whistlingshop.com). Old Street tube/rail. **Open** 5pm-midnight Tue, Wed; 5pm-1am Thur; 4pm-2am Fri, Sat. **Credit** AmEx, MC, V.

This is the epitome of bar trends circa 2011 – a semi-secret location, Victoriana, reinterpretations of classic British drinks. Worship Street Whistling Shop does them all, and does them very well. The cellar room is darkly Dickensian in looks, full of cosy corners, leather armchairs and select

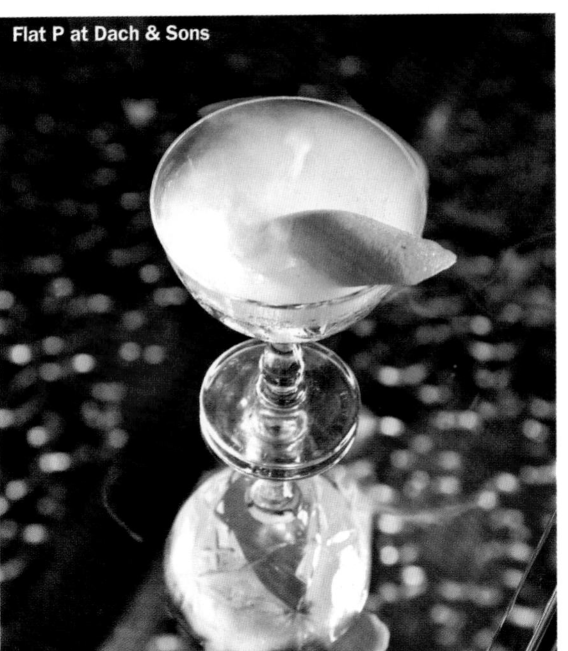

Flat P at Dach & Sons

antiquities. In the back is a windowed laboratory – worthy of a Jekyll and Hyde fantasy – crammed with equipment modern and antiquated, used to create the wondrously described ingredients that constitute the cocktails. The list is updated every few months, but you may find 'chip pan bitters', 'Hereford soil distillate', or 'high pressure hydrosol' used as ingredients. Many come with explanatory annotations; all are used to create original and stimulating drinks around the £10 mark (although the 'Living Cocktail', with *Penicilium roquefortii* (from blue stilton cheese), 'biologically aged', costs £20). Customers appear divided on the issue of service, but on our visits, it has never been anything less than professional.
Babies and children admitted until 7pm. Booking advisable Fri, Sat. Function room (10 capacity). **Map 6 Q4**.

Spitalfields

Hawksmoor

157 Commercial Street, E1 6BJ (7426 4856, www.thehawksmoor.com). Shoreditch High Street rail. **Open** noon-midnight Mon-Fri; 11am-midnight Sat; 11am-8.45pm Sun. **Credit** AmEx, MC, V.
All three of Hawksmoor's bars would be worthy of inclusion here (the others are in Covent Garden, *see p246*, and the City), but this year's refurbishment of the Spitalfields branch's basement has created a separate arena to indulge in the exquisite cocktails. Hawksmoor's bartenders are some of the most highly trained in London, and in this cosy and brick-vaulted space present a small but focused list that includes a contender for one of our favourite cocktails ever – Shaky Pete's Ginger Brew, with gin, ginger, lemon and London Pride beer. A monthly changing 'specials' section is curated by one of the personable staff – you might find the powerful-sounding Gangster Grappa, which involves the Italian firewater, cognac, Campari, plum sherbet and lemon. All mixes are priced fairly – usually less than a tenner – and are always models of restraint, balance and invention.
Available for hire. Babies and children admitted. Disabled: toilet. Wireless internet. **Map 6 R5**.

Mayor of Scaredy Cat Town

12-16 Artillery Lane, E1 7LS (7078 9639, www.themayorofscaredycattown.com). Liverpool Street tube/rail or Shoreditch High Street rail. **Open** 5-11pm Mon-Thur; noon-11.30pm Fri, Sat; noon-10.30pm Sun. **Credit** AmEx, MC, V.
One of several new 'secret' speakeasies, this one is a basement bar beneath Breakfast Club (*see p47*) in Spitalfields. The entrance is the one that looks like a big Smeg fridge door, located in the BC's dining area. Venture inside and you'll find a quirky, dimly lit cocktail bar clad in exposed brick and wood: it's all a bit like a cabin from *Twin Peaks*. The drinks menu makes an amusing mockery of more self-conscious 'underground' venues. The cocktails, consisting of classics and house specials, are well-crafted on the whole – we liked the chilli and lemongrass margarita.
Available for hire. **Map 12 R5**.

North

Islington

69 Colebrooke Row

69 Colebrooke Row, N1 8AA (07 540 528593, www.69colebrookerow.com). Angel tube. **Open** 5pm-midnight Mon-Wed, Sun; 5pm-1am Thur; 5pm-2am Fri, Sat. **Credit** AmEx, MC, V.
This tiny bar opened in mid 2009, and is overseen by Tony Conigliaro, widely considered to be one of London's top bartenders and cocktail experts. With just a handful of seats, the understated, intimate space proves a fine environment in which to enjoy the pristine cocktails (peach and figleaf bellini, martinis made with 'woodland bitters', rhubarb gimlet), mixed with quiet ceremony. The attention to detail includes impeccably attired staff, handwritten bills and tall glasses of water poured from a cocktail shaker, which add to the sense of occasion. At £9 for most house cocktails, the prices are very fair. Note that the small room is rammed at peak times.
Available for hire. Booking advisable. Entertainment: pianist 8pm Thur, 10pm Fri. Wireless internet. **Map 5 O2**.

North West

Hampstead

Flat P at Dach & Sons

68 Heath Street, NW3 1DN (7433 8139, www.dachandsons.com). Hampstead tube. **Open** 11am-11pm daily. **Credit** AmEx, DC, MC, V.
On the ground floor is a NYC-style American craft beer bar and US fast-food joint. Walk straight through, following the signs to the toilets, then the pointing finger signs, up via the residential stairwell to the cocktail bar behind the door marked 'Flat P', behind which is the Purl bar (Hampstead branch). This is where you'll find the Fluid Movement team, who also run Purl and the Worship Street Whistling Shop, doing what they do best: cocktail alchemy. From the list of half a dozen intriguing-sounding blends, Mr Hyde's Fixer Upper arrives with a smoke-filled bottle that you use to top up your glass of aged rum. Ingredients seem outlandish – smokes, foams, even 'Talisker atomised blue cheese' – and are mainly for theatrical effect, but, importantly, the flavour and aroma combinations work. The 'burbs have never seen anything like this before, and therein lies its problem – it is already oversubscribed.
Babies and children welcome: high chairs. Bookings not accepted. Function room (35 capacity). Tables outdoors (5, terrace). **Map 28 C2**.

Eating & Entertainment

Few, if any, world cities can match London for its exhilarating breadth of dining possibilities and its wealth of entertainment options. But what happens when these two dynamic aspects of the city's life are combined? Here you'll find gypsy swing tunes matched with beef bourguignon at Battersea's **Le Quecum Bar**; burlesque served with lamb rump or finger sandwiches at **Volupté** in the City; and steak dinners coupled with Latin dancing classes at **Salsa** on the Charing Cross Road. Want jazz with your risotto? **Ronnie Scott's** is as renowned as the world-famous stars it frequently attracts. Something more bizarre? You can eat in the pitch dark at **Dans Le Noir**, dine in a simulated jungle in the **Rainforest Café** or even don lederhösen to yodel, while preparing for the würst at **Tiroler Hut**.

Blues, jazz & soul

Blues Kitchen

111-113 Camden High Street, NW1 7JN (7387 5277, www.theblueskitchen.com). Camden Town tube. **Open** noon-midnight Mon, Tue; noon-1am Wed, Thur; noon-3am Fri; 11am-3am Sat; 11am-1am Sun. **Meals served** noon-11pm Mon-Fri; 11am-11pm Sat, Sun. **Music** *Bands* 9.30pm Mon-Thur; 10pm Fri, Sat; 7pm Sun. *DJs* 1am-3am Fri, Sat. **Main courses** £8-£15. **Admission** Gigs free; £4 after 10pm Fri; £5 after 9pm Sat. **Credit** MC, V.

Musicians play nightly at the Blues Kitchen in Camden, a bar-restaurant that prides itself on its huge bourbon collection and classic American South dishes such as pulled pork, fried chicken and barbecued ribs from the in-house barbecue pit. Past acts include the Mystery Jets, Band of Skulls and the Caezars.

Available for hire. Booking advisable. Babies and children welcome until 7pm: high chairs. **Map 27 D3.**

Dover Street

8-10 Dover Street, W1S 4LQ (7629 9813, www.doverst.co.uk). Green Park or Piccadilly Circus tube. **Open** 6pm-3am Mon-Thur; 7pm-3am Fri, Sat. **Dinner served** 6pm-midnight Mon-Wed; 6pm-1am Thur; 7pm-1am Fri, Sat. **Music** *Bands* 9.30pm, 11pm Mon; 10pm, midnight Tue, Wed; 10.45pm, midnight Thur-Sat. *DJs* until 3am Mon-Sat. **Main courses** £15.95-£25.95. **Set dinner** £32.50-£48.50 3 courses incl service, music. **Admission** (after 10pm) £7 Mon; £8 Tue; £12 Wed; £15 Thur-Sat. **Credit** AmEx, DC, MC, V.

Three atmospheric bars, all decked out in black and white fashion prints, where a Modern European menu is served until late: the likes of seared scallops, fillet steak with shaved truffle, or asparagus risotto. Here you can listen to jazz, swing, soul and funk bands, before dancing away the rest of the night to Dover Street's resident DJ.

Booking advisable; essential weekends. Dress: smart casual. Separate rooms for parties, seating 20-100. **Map 9 J7.**

Green Note

106 Parkway, NW1 7AN (7485 9899, www.greennote.co.uk). Camden Town tube. **Dinner served** 7-9.30pm Wed, Thur, Sun; 7-10pm Fri, Sat. **Music** 9-11pm Mon-Fri, Sun; 8-11pm Sat. **Tapas** £2.50-£4.95 **Admission** £4-£15. **Credit** MC, V.

Serving an inventive selection of vegetarian world tapas, salads and dips (including an array of vegan choices), and decorated with the bold folk-icon portraits of artist Twinkle Troughton, this Camden organic food paradise has played host to acts including Johnny Flynn and Amy Winehouse.

Babies and children admitted: high chair. Booking advisable. Vegan dishes. Vegetarian menu. **Map 27 C3.**

Jazz After Dark

9 Greek Street, W1D 4DQ (7734 0545, www.jazzafterdark.co.uk). Leicester Square or Tottenham Court Road tube. **Open** 2pm-2am Tue-Thur; 2pm-3am Fri, Sat. **Meals served** 2pm-midnight Tue-Sat. **Music** 9pm Mon-Thur; 10.30pm Fri, Sat. **Tapas** £4.50-£10.95. **Set meal** £10.95 3 courses. **Admission** £5 Tue-Thur; £10 diners, £15 non-diners Fri, Sat. **Credit** AmEx, DC, MC, V.

There's a slight Amy Winehouse theme to this late-night Soho jazz restaurant, where you can try an Amy's Platter of fried chicken, meatballs and chicken wings while downing a Back to Black cocktail. There are also 'naughty' mixes to drink, such as a Kick in the Balls or a Between the Sheets, and food features Spanish tapas as well as English favourites such as fish and chips or lamb shanks – perfect for accompanying the musicians who play almost every night.

Available for hire. Booking essential Fri, Sat. Dress: smart casual. Tables outdoors (2, pavement). **Map 17 C3.**

Jazz Café

5-7 Parkway, NW1 7PG (7688 8899, www.meanfiddler.com). Camden Town tube.

Open 7pm-2am daily. **Meals served** varies; phone for details. **Music** daily; phone for details. **Main courses** £16.50. **Set meal** £26.50 2 courses. **Admission** varies; phone for details. **Credit** MC, V.
An inventive, Louisiana-inspired menu – including a black-eyed bean stew and fried baby chicken with creole sauce – is served up in the balcony restaurant overlooking the Jazz Café's stage, where jazz, funk, world and soul musicians perform. This venue is renowned for hosting the biggest names in the jazz and soul world before they become famous. The restaurant is open only on event nights.
Booking advisable. Disabled: toilet. **Map 27 D2.**

Pizza Express Jazz Club

10 Dean Street, W1D 3RW (0845 602 7017, www.pizzaexpresslive.com). Tottenham Court Road tube. **Meals served** *Club* 7-11pm daily. *Restaurant* 11.30am-midnight Mon-Sat; 11.30am-11.30pm Sun. **Music** 8.30-10.30pm Mon-Thur; 9-11pm Fri, Sat; 8-10pm Sun. **Main courses** £6.50-£10.95. **Admission** £15-£25. **Credit** AmEx, DC, MC, V.
Jazz musicians play seven days a week at this laid-back venue, with previous artists including Norah Jones and Scott Hamilton. Big names are liberally mixed with new talent in the line-up. Pizza Express's usual repertoire of reliable, reasonably priced food is on the menu.
Babies and children welcome (restaurant): high chairs. Disabled access. Booking advisable. Takeaway service. **Map 17 B3.**

Le Quecum Bar

42-44 Battersea High Street, SW11 3HX (7787 2227, www.quecumbar.co.uk). Clapham Junction rail. **Open** 6pm-midnight Mon, Fri-Sun; 7pm-midnight Tue-Thur. **Meals served** 6-10pm Mon-Fri; 7-10pm Tue-Thur. **Music** varies Mon, Sun; 8pm Tue-Sat. **Main courses** £6-£15. **Admission** varies Mon, Sun; free Tue; £5 after 8pm Wed-Sat. **Membership** £60/yr. **Credit** AmEx, MC, V.
Le Quecum in Battersea claims to be the world's only venue dedicated to the Django Reinhardt gypsy swing genre. Spend an evening here to experience a 1930s Parisian night out, including a classic French menu (beef bourguignon, pâté and the like). All are welcome to bring an instrument to the free Tuesday Gypsy Swing Jam, while there are ticketed concerts on Sundays and Mondays.
Booking advisable Fri, Sat. Dress: smart casual. Tables outdoors (5, garden). **Map 21 B2.**

Ronnie Scott's

47 Frith Street, W1D 4HT (7439 0747, www.ronniescotts.co.uk). Leicester Square or Tottenham Court Road tube. **Open** 6pm-late Mon-Thur; 6-10pm, 10.30pm-3am Fri, Sat; noon-4pm, 6pm-1am Sun. **Meals served** 6pm-1am Mon-Sat; noon-4pm, 6-11pm Sun. **Music** 7.30pm-2am Mon-Thur; 7.15pm-3am Fri, Sat; 1.30-4pm, 8pm-midnight Sun. **Main courses** £15.40-£28.50. **Admission** (non-members) £20-£40. **Membership** £175/yr. **Credit** AmEx, MC, V.
A delightful slice of music history, Ronnie Scott's is one of London's oldest jazz clubs and continues to host renowned artists such as Billy Cobham and Kenny Garrett. A wide range of dishes is served – from fish pie to saffron and broad bean risotto, via sevruga caviar. Standards of culinary execution might vary, but the jazz is unswervingly hot.
Available for hire. Booking advisable. Disabled: toilet. Dress: smart casual. Over-14yrs admitted if accompanied until midnight; all ages admitted Sun lunch. **Map 17 C3.**

606 Club

90 Lots Road, SW10 0QD (7352 5953, www.606club.co.uk). Earl's Court tube then bus C3 or Sloane Square tube then bus 22. **Open** 7-11.30pm Mon; 7pm-12.30am Tue, Wed; 7-11.30pm Thur; 8pm-1.30am Fri, Sat; 12.30-4pm, 7-11.15pm Sun. **Meals served** 7-11pm Mon-Thur; 12.30-3.30pm, 7-10.30pm Sun; 8pm-midnight Fri, Sat. **Music** 8.30pm Mon, Thur, Sun; 7.30pm Tue, Wed; 9.30pm Fri, Sat. **Main courses** £9.70-£19.50. **Admission** (non-members) £8-£12. **Membership** £95 1st yr, £60 subsequent yrs. **Credit** AmEx, MC, V.
A basement club, established in 1976, which prides itself on booking the best of British jazz music. The menu is inspired by European and Middle Eastern influences, and changes weekly, but expect dishes such as baked teriyaki salmon, roast lamb rump and own-made houmous, as well as Sunday lunch. The club's licence means non-members can only drink alcohol with meals, and are admitted at weekends only if they're eating.
Available for hire. Babies and children admitted. Booking advisable Fri, Sat. **Map 13 C13.**

Burlesque

Brickhouse

152C Brick Lane, E1 6RU (7247 0005, www.thebrickhouse.co.uk). Liverpool Street tube/rail or Shoreditch High Street rail. **Open** 6pm-late Tue, Wed; 6pm-3am Thur, Fri; 6.30pm-3am Sat. **Dinner served** 6.30pm-midnight Tue, Wed; 6.30pm-2am Thur-Sat. **Main courses** £15-£22.50. **Set dinner** £22.50 2 courses, £32.50 3 courses. **Credit** MC, V.
A Brick Lane supper club that stages dinner cabarets every night, showcasing performances of burlesque, circus, comedy and music in a modern venue. Dining takes place on split levels, with views overlooking the performance space. The menu holds enticements such as grilled sea bream with fried samphire and zefirino peppers, and wild rice and gorgonzola salad.
Available for hire. Booking advisable. Disabled: toilet. Entertainment: live acts, DJs 9pm daily. **Map 6 S5.**

Volupté

7-9 Norwich Street, EC4A 1EJ (7831 1622, www.volupte-lounge.com). Chancery Lane tube. **Open** 4.30pm-1am Tue, Wed; 4.30pm-3am Thur, Fri; 2pm-3am Sat; 2-6pm Sun. **Dinner served** 6.15-10pm Tue-Sat. **Tea served** 2.30pm Sat. **Dinner prices** £55 3 courses (incl show) Tue, Wed; £58 3 courses (incl show) Thur-Sat. **Admission** £14-£42. **Membership** £150/yr. **Credit** AmEx, MC, V.
Walls swathed in red velvet and silk, and a retro bar and dining room provide the background for this cabaret supper club, which stages a variety of acts including musicians and burlesque shows. As you take in a performance, try a vintage-inspired cocktail such as the Ernest Hemingway-created Death In The Afternoon, or enjoy the tempting Saturday 'Afternoon Tease', an afternoon tea selection of finger sandwiches, cakes and tea, served on antique china. The dinner menu provides a range of traditional dishes: foie gras or asparagus preceding beef sirloin or lamb rump.
Available for hire. Booking essential. Dress: smart casual. Entertainment: cabaret 8pm Wed-Fri; 2.30pm, 7pm, 10pm Sat; 3pm Sun. **Map 11 N5.**

Latin

Nueva Costa Dorada

47-55 Hanway Street, W1T 1UX (7631 5117, www.costadoradarestaurant.co.uk). Tottenham Court Road tube. **Open/meals served** noon-3am Mon-Sat. **Main courses** £9.95-£16.45. **Credit** MC, V.
With its tables arranged around the stage, this Spanish restaurant concentrates on creating a party atmosphere. Flamenco shows take place from Thursday to Saturday, and Spanish music acts

Green Note

appear every week. The food is authentic if rarely adventurous: share a paella, choose from the simple à la carte, or dive into the large range of assorted tapas plates (calamares, jamón serrano, cheese. Top it off with a glass of sangria or one of Costa Dorada's exclusively Spanish wines.
Available for hire. Babies and children admitted until 11pm. Entertainment: flamenco shows 8.30pm Thur, 10pm Fri, Sat; DJ 11pm Fri, Sat. **Map 17 B2.**

Salsa!

96 Charing Cross Road, WC2H 0JG (7379 3277, www.barsalsa.info). Leicester Square or Tottenham Court Road tube.
Bar **Open** 5pm-2am Mon-Thur; 5pm-3am Fri, Sat; 5pm-1am Sun.
Café **Open** 10am-5pm Mon-Sat. **Snacks served** noon-5pm Mon-Sat. **Main courses** £4.95-£5.45.
Restaurant **Meals served** 5-11pm daily. **Main courses** £8.99-£11.50.
Bar & Restaurant **Admission** £4 after 9pm Mon-Thur; £2 after 7pm, £4 after 8pm, £8 after 9pm, £10 after 11pm Fri, Sat; £4 after 8pm Sun.
All **Credit** AmEx, MC, V.
Dance classes take place here every evening from just £5, with levels from beginner to pro; Latin-themed cocktails are available to ease any embarrassment. Test out the tapas selection or pick from main dishes of Latin-inspired chicken, steak and burgers as you get into the party mood. Musicians play on Saturday nights.
Booking advisable; essential weekends. Dress: smart casual. Entertainment: dance classes 7pm or 8pm, DJs 9.30pm, daily. Tables outdoors (14, pavement). **Map 17 C3.**

Music & dancing

Roadhouse

35 The Piazza, WC2E 8BE (7240 6001, www.roadhouse.co.uk). Covent Garden tube.
Open 5.30pm-3am Mon-Sat; 6.30pm-1.30am Sun. **Meals served** 5.30pm-1.30am Mon-Sat; 5.30pm-midnight Sun. **Main courses** £8.25-£17. **Admission** £5 after 10pm Mon-Wed, Sun; £7 after 10pm Thur; £10 after 9pm Fri; £5 after 8pm, £12 after 9pm Sat. **Credit** AmEx, MC, V.
Dream of being a rock star but don't have the time, skill, or other band members? Well, at Roadhouse you can fulfil your desires with 'Rockaoke', an alternative karaoke where customers perform their favourite songs with a live backing band. Diner-style food takes in burgers, steaks and a cajun grill, and the drinks list is extensive. Bands, DJs and the Flair bartending championships add to the lively, US-style atmosphere.
Booking advisable. Dress: smart casual. Entertainment: bands/DJs times vary daily. **Map 18 E4.**

Tiroler Hut

27 Westbourne Grove, W2 4UA (7727 3981, www.tirolerhut.co.uk). Bayswater or Queensway tube. **Open** 6.30pm-1am Tue-Sun. **Dinner served** 6.30pm-12.30am Tue-Sun. **Main courses** £14.50-£17.50. **Set meal** (Tue-Thur, Sun) £25.50 3 courses; (Fri, Sat) £29.50 3 courses. **Credit** AmEx, MC, V.
The hills are alive with the sound of cowbells. In this Alpine ski-chalet of a restaurant, host Joseph encourages you to yodel, sing and laugh as he entertains with the Tirolean Cowbell Show. The authentic Austrian fare includes sweet and sour herring, stuffed cabbage and bratwurst, while the bar is well stocked with Austrian and German wines and beers (you can even drink from a stein). Warm up your vocal cords and prepare to yodel.
Available for hire. Babies and children admitted. Booking essential. Entertainment: cowbell show times vary Tue-Sun. **Map 7 B6.**

One-offs

Dans Le Noir?

30-31 Clerkenwell Green, EC1R 0DU (7253 1100, www.danslenoir.com/london). Farringdon tube/rail. **Lunch served** by appointment. **Dinner served** (fixed sittings) 6.30-7.30pm, 9-9.30pm Mon-Thur; 6.30-7.15pm, 9.15-10pm Fri, Sat; 6.45-8pm Sun. **Set dinner** £42 2 courses; £51 3 courses. **Credit** AmEx, MC, V.
A dining experience that aims to re-evaluate perceptions of taste. Here you eat in total darkness, so it's the taste, smell and texture of the food that you're discovering. In the bar, you select one of four top-secret colour-coded menus – red (meat), blue (fish), green (vegetarian) and white (chef's special) – before being led into the completely dark dining room by one of the restaurant's blind guides/waiters. It's a unique, sensory food adventure that also gives money to blind charities. Don't worry, the toilets are not in the dark.
Booking essential. Children admitted. Disabled: toilet. Separate room for parties, seats 60. **Map 5 N4.**

Lucky Voice

52 Poland Street, W1F 7LR (7439 3660, www.luckyvoice.co.uk). Oxford Circus tube. **Open/meals served** 5.30pm-1am Mon-Thur; 3pm-1am Fri, Sat; 3-10.30pm Sun. **Main courses** £7.50. **Credit** AmEx, MC, V.

Food (pizzas and snacks) is not the main event here. No, this is a revolution in karaoke bars, with nine private 'pods' where groups of between four and 12 people can belt out a classic. It's perfect for those usually too shy to have a go, as only friends will be watching. A fun cocktail list should chase away any lingering inhibitions. With almost a million songs, from Beyonce to Iron Maiden, on the play list, there's ample opportunity to grab the microphone and pretend you're wowing Wembley.

Booking essential. Entertainment: karaoke pods for hire, £5-£10/hr per person. Over-21s only.

Map 17 A3.

For branch see index.

Rainforest Café

20 Shaftesbury Avenue, W1D 7EU (7434 3111, www.therainforestcafe.co.uk). Leicester Square or Piccadilly Circus tube. **Meals served** noon-10pm Mon-Fri; 11.30am-10pm Sat; 11.30am-10pm Sun. **Main courses** £14-£22.50. **Credit** AmEx, MC, V.

If you ever wanted to dine in the jungle, surrounded by chattering monkeys, colourful parrots and the odd thundering elephant – but without all the airports and mosquito spray – then this is the kids-oriented next best thing. There's a large children's menu (activity packs at an additional £3) and animatronic animals that spring to life at regular intervals as you dine from a varied selection of pasta, burgers, seafood, salads and more. You might even visit the shop where kids can pick up a memento of their adventure on the way home. No advance bookings are taken, but a priority seating system operates online (where the next available table is yours within a certain time slot).

Babies and children welcome: children's menu; crayons; high chairs; nappy-changing facilities. Entertainment: face painting weekends & school hols. Separate rooms for parties, seating 11-100.

Map 17 B5.

Troubadour

263-267 Old Brompton Road, SW5 9JA (7370 1434, www.troubadour.co.uk). West Brompton tube/rail. **Open** *Club* 8pm-midnight Mon-Wed, Sun; 8pm-2am Thur-Sat. *Café* 8am-midnight daily. **Food served** noon-10.30pm daily. **Main courses** £6.50-£14.95. **Credit** AmEx, MC, V.

Steeped in music history, this venue has played host to some of the world's greatest artists, from Sammy Davis Jnr and Jimi Hendrix gigs to Led Zeppelin jam sessions. The ground-floor café, with its stained glass and wood panelling, serves a range of omelettes, burgers and seafood; there's also a salad bar operating from noon until 4pm. The basement club presents a varied programme, with musicians, DJs and poetry nights from Monday to Saturday. There's also a rentable apartment (the Garret) upstairs and a wine bar/shop next door that holds regular tastings.

Available for hire. Babies and children welcome (café): high chair. Booking advisable. Entertainment: bands 7.30pm Mon-Sat. Separate rooms for parties, seating 15-32. Tables outdoors (8, garden; 6, pavement). Takeaway service (salad bar). **Map 13 B11.**

Tiroler Hut

Opera

Bel Canto

Corus Hotel Hyde Park, 1 Lancaster Gate, W2 3LG (7262 1678, www.lebelcanto.com). Lancaster Gate tube. **Dinner served** 7-11pm Wed-Sat. **Set dinner** (incl show) £44 2 courses, £51 3 courses, £60.75 4 courses. **Credit** MC, V.

Inside the Corus hotel on the edge of Hyde Park, Bel Canto serves traditional French cuisine – the likes of foie gras or beef fillet – in a beautiful dining room filled with musical instruments and opera costumes. It's the staff, however, who are the special event. Tables are served by trained opera singers who pause and perform classic opera favourites every 15 minutes, aiming to create a wonderful (and unique) dining experience.

Available for hire. Booking essential. Children admitted. Disabled: lift; toilet. Dress: smart casual.

Map 8 D7.

Sarastro

126 Drury Lane, WC2B 5QG (7836 0101, www.sarastro-restaurant.com). Covent Garden or Holborn tube. **Meals served** noon-10.30pm Mon-Thur, Sun; noon-11.15pm Fri, Sat. **Main courses** £10.25-£25.85. **Set lunch** (noon-6.30pm Mon-Sat) £14.50 2 courses. **Set meal** £29.95 3 courses. **Credit** AmEx, DC, MC, V.

Musicians from London's opera houses and across the world come to perform some of the most popular arias here, while diners choose from the Mediterranean-Turkish menu. There are ten uniquely decorated opera boxes lining the walls, each in a different style (rococo, Gothic, Ottoman), complete with velvet drapes and theatrical props.

Babies and children welcome: high chairs. Booking advisable. Disabled: toilet. Entertainment: opera, string quartet 8.30pm Mon, 2.30pm, 8.30pm Sun; swing & motown vocalist 8.15pm Thur. **Map 18 F3.**

Wine Bars

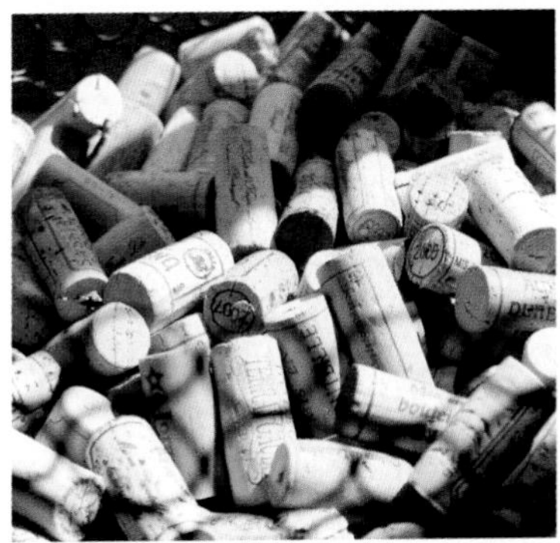

London has for many decades been a world centre for the wine trade: we have the thirst, if not the vineyards. Trends are made here, with different wine-making countries coming into and falling from fashion. For the past few years, 'natural' wines have been in vogue: fermented grape juice with little added or taken away. **Terroirs** was a pioneer in this sector, but **Bar Battu** (one of our current favourites) is an equally firm advocate. Since the advent of gastropubs and their spruced-up wine lists, wine bars have had a fight on their hands. The best have responded by also serving great food, with menus often fashioned into providing ideal vinous accompaniments: top-notch charcuterie, and prime specimens of cheese, for instance. Some, such as **28°-50°**, also offer wine flights: groups of taster samples built around a theme, giving an excellent opportunity for getting to know a region or collection of vintages. Other establishments incorporate an off-licence, so you can give a glass a test-run, then, if you're pleased with the results, buy a bottle to take home – **Vinoteca** is a fine example of this enoteca model, and now has three outlets in central London.

Central

City

★ Bar Battu

48 Gresham Street, EC2V 7AY (7036 6100, www.barbattu.com). Bank tube/DLR. **Open** 11.30am-11pm, **meals served** noon-9pm Mon-Fri. **Main courses** £10.50-£24.50. **Set meal** £17.50 2 courses, £19.50 3 courses. **House wine** from £17.50 bottle, from £4 glass. **Credit** AmEx, MC, V.

In a corner of the City that's dull before 5pm and dead after, this anomalously characterful and charming wine bar is good enough to attract customers well into the night. It's an advocate of natural wines, but not didactically so; an exceptionally interesting and well-presented list (divided into taste categories, such as 'salty and mineral whites') also includes worthwhile standard wines from around the world. Wine lovers and traders are among the crowd, but they're of the unstuffy variety, comfortable with the informal (but switched-on) service and decor. The long, brick-walled room has a slightly 1970s retro feel, to go with Battu's signature *Pink Panther* typeface. You might expect the modern English/French/Spanish food to play only a supporting role – but there's serious talent in the kitchen, and alongside easy-eating charcuterie platters and steak frites are some more involved main dishes whose subtle rendition belies their hearty composition: double pork chop with potato, piquillo and wild garlic leaf salad, for example; or roast cod with girolles, chard and tarragon butter. Yes, the tables are a little close together, especially if there's a big party in, but the flip side to this is a good buzz.

Available for hire. Babies and children admitted. Booking advisable lunch. Disabled: toilet. **Map 11 P6.**

Clerkenwell & Farringdon

Cellar Gascon

59 West Smithfield, EC1A 9DS (7600 7561, www.cellargascon.com). Barbican tube or Farringdon tube/rail. **Open** noon-midnight, **tapas served** noon-2.30pm, 6-11pm Mon-Fri. **Tapas** £4.50-£7.50. **Set lunch** £9.50 1 course, glass of wine and coffee, £12.50 2 courses, glass of wine and coffee. **House wine** from £19.50 bottle, from £2.75 glass. **Credit** AmEx, MC, V.

The Cellar inhabits a sliver of a corner site in the shadow of the more substantial Club Gascon (*see p91*), and these days it appears to occupy a similar position in the Gascon hierarchy. The place feels untended, its brown decor and uncomfortable high bucket-chair and bench seating in need of updating. It lacks direction too; we've been well served by keen young staff, but haven't noticed a manager. The food is in Gascon's small-plate style (which works well with wine), comprising of much charcuterie and other shareable nibbles, including foie gras. It's rich, but, though regional, not terribly interesting or demanding of the kitchen – apart from the dish of the day, which features in the £9.50 set lunch (along with a glass of wine and a coffee); this might be bouillabaisse or, as on our last visit, some very good slow-cooked pork on mash. The Cellar still has a noteworthy wine list that ranges expertly around south-west France's styles and regions, including some interesting aperitifs. However, wine aficionados seem to have moved on (or perhaps they now come just for the occasional tasting evenings), leaving the place largely to tourists and trysters – and not too many of those.

Available for hire. Babies and children admitted. Tables outdoors (3, pavement). **Map 11 O5.**

Marylebone

28°-50° Wine Workshop & Kitchen

15-17 Marylebone Lane, W1U 2NE (7486 7922, www.2850.co.uk). Bond Street tube. **Open** noon-11pm Mon-Wed; noon-midnight Thur-Sat; noon-10.30pm Sun. **Lunch served** noon-2.30pm Mon-Sat; noon-3pm Sun. **Dinner served** 6-10pm Mon-Wed; 6-10.30pm Thur-Sat; 6-9.30pm Sun. **Main courses** £11.95-£16. **House wine** from £20 bottle, £2.20 glass. **Credit** AmEx, MC, V.

This second branch of the 'wine workshop & kitchen' opened a couple of years after the Fetter Lane original, just as we went to press, and was gently evolving as it learned about its new

Bags packed, milk cancelled, house raised on stilts.

You've packed the suntan lotion, the snorkel set, the stay-pressed shirts. Just one more thing left to do – your bit for climate change. In some of the world's poorest countries, changing weather patterns are destroying lives.

You can help people to deal with the extreme effects of climate change. Raising houses in flood-prone regions is just one life-saving solution.

Climate change costs lives.
Give £5 and let's sort it *Here & Now*

www.oxfam.org.uk/climate-change

Oxfam is a registered charity in England and Wales (No.202918) and Scotland (SCO039042). Oxfam GB is a member of Oxfam International.

Be Humankind **Oxfam**

constituency. The two locations look very different – Fetter Lane is a basement decorated in a simple, lightly rustic style, with no natural light, but a warm atmosphere. Marylebone Lane occupies a flatiron corner site with an expanse of windows and spare, striking modern decor: a central metal bar bristling with glassware and surrounded by powder-blue chairs; unvarnished tables, flower arrangements, industrial lights and duct pipes. Only the wine lists and menu are similar. Wine lists in the plural: one offers a frequently changing, interesting selection of around 30 relatively young wines by the glass, carafe and bottle, starting with a flight or other themed grouping; the other, more serious bottles from collectors for whom 28°-50° acts as an agent – a clever system. Food is simple and appetising, with grills, cheese and meat plates common to both and a slant to the French evident at the slightly dearer Fetter Lane and to salads and luxury (foie gras, oysters) at Marylebone.
Babies and children welcome: high chairs. Booking advisable Fri, Sat. Disabled: toilet. Separate room for parties, seats 15. **Map 9 G5.**
For branch see index.

Soho

Vinoteca HOT 50

53-55 Beak Street, W1F 9SH (3544 7411, www.vinoteca.co.uk). Oxford Circus tube. **Open** noon-11pm Mon-Sat; noon-10.30pm Sun. **Meals served** noon-10.30pm Mon-Sat; noon-10pm Sun. **Main courses** £10-£21. **House wine** £15.50 bottle, £2.70 glass. **Credit** AmEx, MC, V.
Much like its siblings in Farringdon and Marylebone, the third branch of Vinoteca is somewhere you come to drink wines that are off the beaten track and distinctive, from independent producers. On our latest trip, the menu listed the likes of a pinot blanc from West Sussex, an organic dry Vouvray from the Loire Valley, and a tannat from Uruguay. They're also all available to take away in bottles. Unlike in some wine bars, food is an even match for the wine, and vice versa. Bread is baked every day on the premises, and continental cured hams are cut to order on a hand-cranked 1950s Berkel slicer. Big windows look on to busy Beak Street; brick walls display vast vintage European advertising posters; and the furniture is all comfortable dark wood. Steamed mussels and clams arrived in a tomato and chorizo broth with caper berries. A small plate of mackerel saw beautifully grilled fillets offset by an interesting pile of rhubarb, chilli and lovage. All dishes come with a wine-by-the-glass suggestion, and the young and trendy staff are happy to offer informed advice.
Babies and children welcome: high chairs. Booking advisable. Disabled: toilet. **Map 17 A4.**
For branches see index.

Strand

Terroirs HOT 50

5 William IV Street, WC2N 4DW (7036 0660, www.terroirswinebar.com). Charing Cross tube/ rail. **Open** noon-11pm, **lunch served** noon-3pm, **dinner served** 5.30-11pm Mon-Sat. **Main courses** £13-£15. **House wine** £17 bottle, £4.75 glass. **Credit** AmEx, MC, V.
Terroirs positions itself as an evangelist for natural wines, but is equally valued for the quality of its informal French cooking and its buzzy atmosphere. Gastronomes, the wine trade and in-the-know pre-theatre diners fill the split-level bistro-style space.

28°-50° Wine Workshop & Kitchen. See p325.

That the wine list is 27 pages long and the menu is written on a table mat doesn't reflect the priorities here. The dozen or so small plates, plus cheese and charcuterie and main-course specials, offer good options for both hunger- and thirst-driven customers. They're generally well made, but on our latest visit, some disappointed. The beetroot served with goat's curd and walnuts was tasteless, and clams and garlic undercooked. Potted shrimp on toast, wild garlic soup and an £8 steak tartare were good enough to compensate. The wines, sourced from small traditional, creative and experimental natural producers in primarily France and Italy, are a joy, and the wine of the month is reliably fascinating (amphora-aged, for example). Our only complaint is that with just 15 available by the glass, smaller parties don't get to sample the wide variety. Staff are bright and engaged, but there can be delays at busy times.
Babies and children admitted. Booking advisable. **Map 18 D5**.

West

Notting Hill

Kensington Wine Rooms

127-129 Kensington Church Street, W8 7LP (7727 8142, www.greatwinesbytheglass.com). Notting Hill Gate tube. **Open** noon-midnight, **meals served** noon-10.45pm daily. **Main courses** £13-£24. **House wine** £19 bottle, £3.40 glass. **Credit** AmEx, MC, V.
KWR is thoroughly modern in using dispensers to keep wine fresh for longer, so allowing single glasses to be served and thus facilitating experimentation. In contrast, its handsome, light-filled premises retain a comfort and clubbability that refer back to wine trade tradition. Usually busy, the venue seems to have become an unofficial clubhouse for a fairly smart Notting Hill crowd who drop by for everything from an aperitif and tapa to an evening blowout. The full house on our previous visit suggested that the below-par food and patchy service were a temporary faltering, as the management later contacted us to explain. This time, with new head chef Patrick Strauss and a clued-up maître d', the restaurant had rediscovered its high standards. A prawn and chorizo pot (also on the tapas-like bar menu) was stuffed with flavour, and foie gras was paired successfully with pineapple chutney. Main courses of pork belly in mustard and tarragon sauce, and sea bass with a chorizo crust, were excellent, the former served on a broth of early-season vegetables of distinct and delicate flavour, and the latter working well with the suggested Neudorf (New Zealand) pinot noir.
Babies and children welcome: high chairs. Booking advisable dinner. **Map 7 B7**.
For branch (Fulham Wine Rooms) see index.

South East

East Dulwich

Green & Blue

36-38 Lordship Lane, SE22 8HJ (8693 9250, www.greenandbluewines.com). East Dulwich rail. **Open** 11am-11pm Mon-Thur; 11am-midnight Fri; 10am-midnight Sat; noon-5pm Sun. **Meals served** noon-10pm Mon-Sat; noon-4pm Sun. **Main courses** £5-£12.50. **House wine** £21.75 bottle, £4.30 glass. **Credit** MC, V.
Green & Blue is a rarity of a wine bar, the product of South African-born Kate Thal's mission to create wine 'epiphanies' at affordable, high-street reach. The pleasant two-room space, open-fronted on balmy evenings, is as much a shop as a bar-restaurant, with an improbable number of carefully documented vinous discoveries (majoring on the boutique and the 'natural') lining the shelves of the bar area. On certain evenings, diners can book a 'wine trolley'; on others, secure a bottle off the shelf at shop price; and an interesting selection is available as standard by large or small glass, carafe or bottle. So far, so good; indeed, very good – but the transformation from shop/bar/deli to more fully fledged bistro has not yet hit its mark. Chef Simon Barnett (previously of Balham's Fat Delicatessen) brings a strong Hispanic influence to the table, from the likes of cecina and boquerones to more fully fledged dishes such as a light, Moro-inspired borani of beetroot and goat's cheese. Oily fish and cured meats predominate; heartier offerings – red mullet with a 'ragoût' of runner beans, lamb shoulder with a variant of caponata – evidence good buying, but were, on our visit, a tad dull in both colour and flavour, and prevented some truly remarkable wines from singing as they might. Desserts are standard bistro/café-bar fare, and include Gelupo ices; dessert wines are again a step into a higher realm.
Available for hire. Babies and children welcome until 7pm: high chairs; nappy-changing facilities. Booking advisable weekends. Disabled: toilet. **Map 23 C4**.

Vinoteca. See p327.

Maps & Indexes

The following maps highlight London's key restaurant areas: the districts with the highest density of good places to eat and drink. They show precisely where each restaurant is located, as well as major landmarks and tube stations.

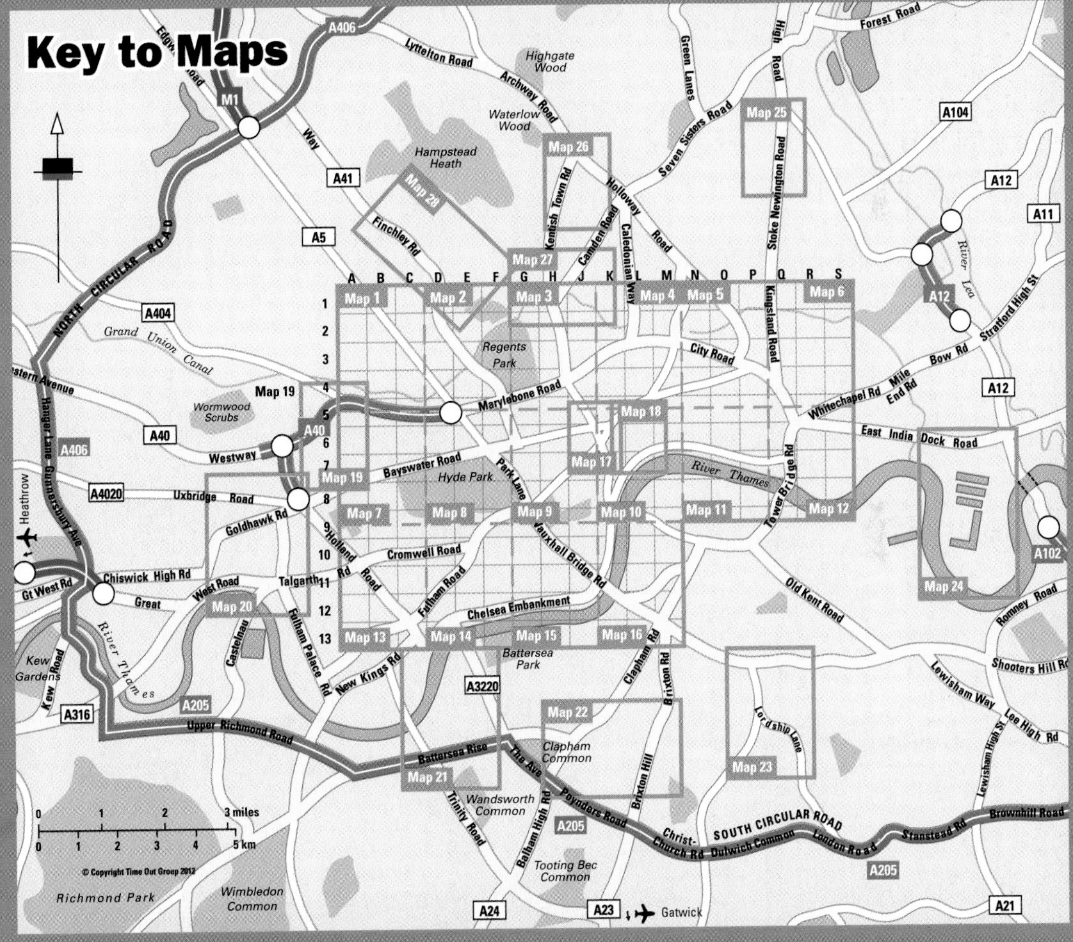

Queen's Park & Maida Vale

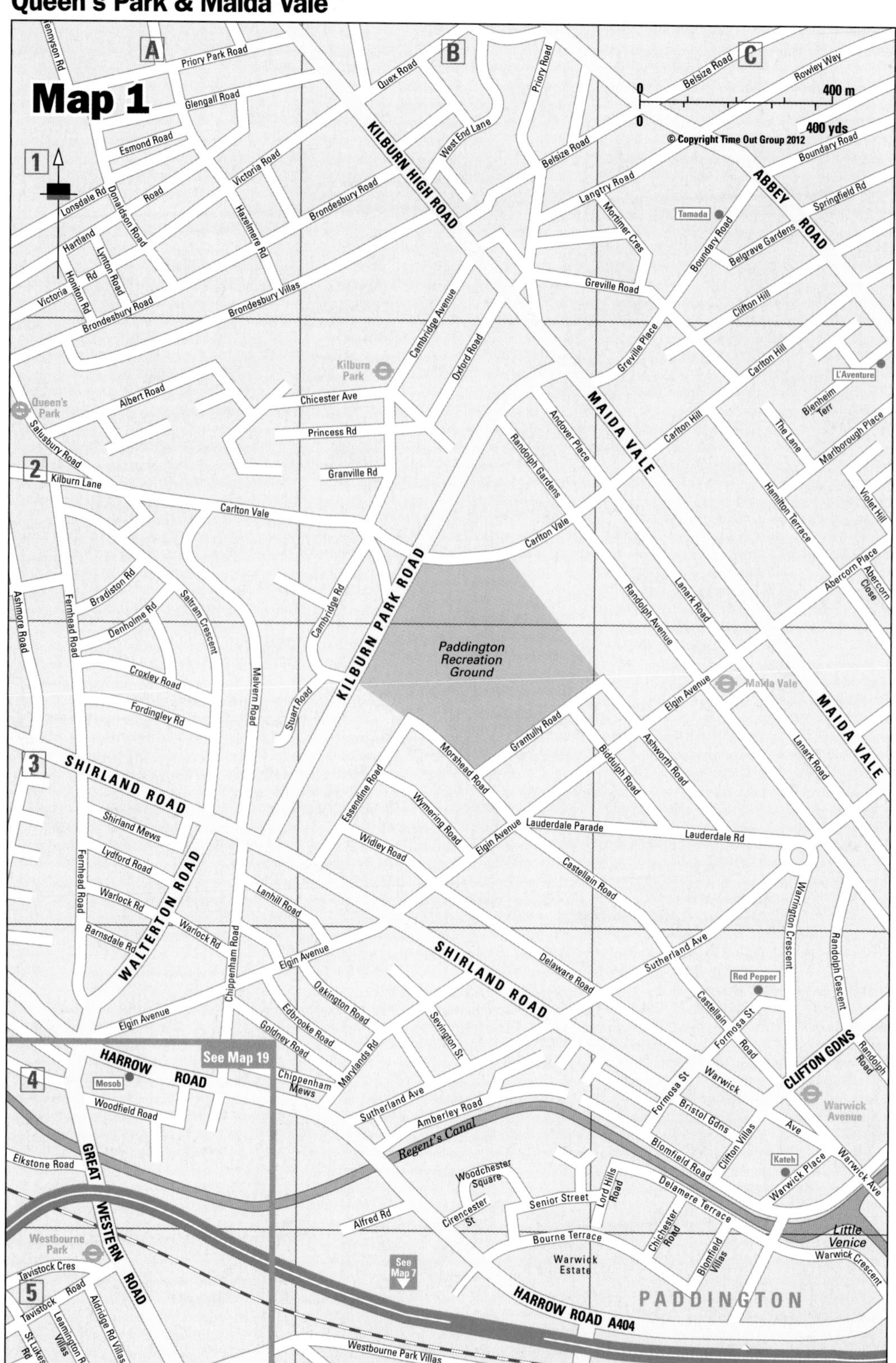

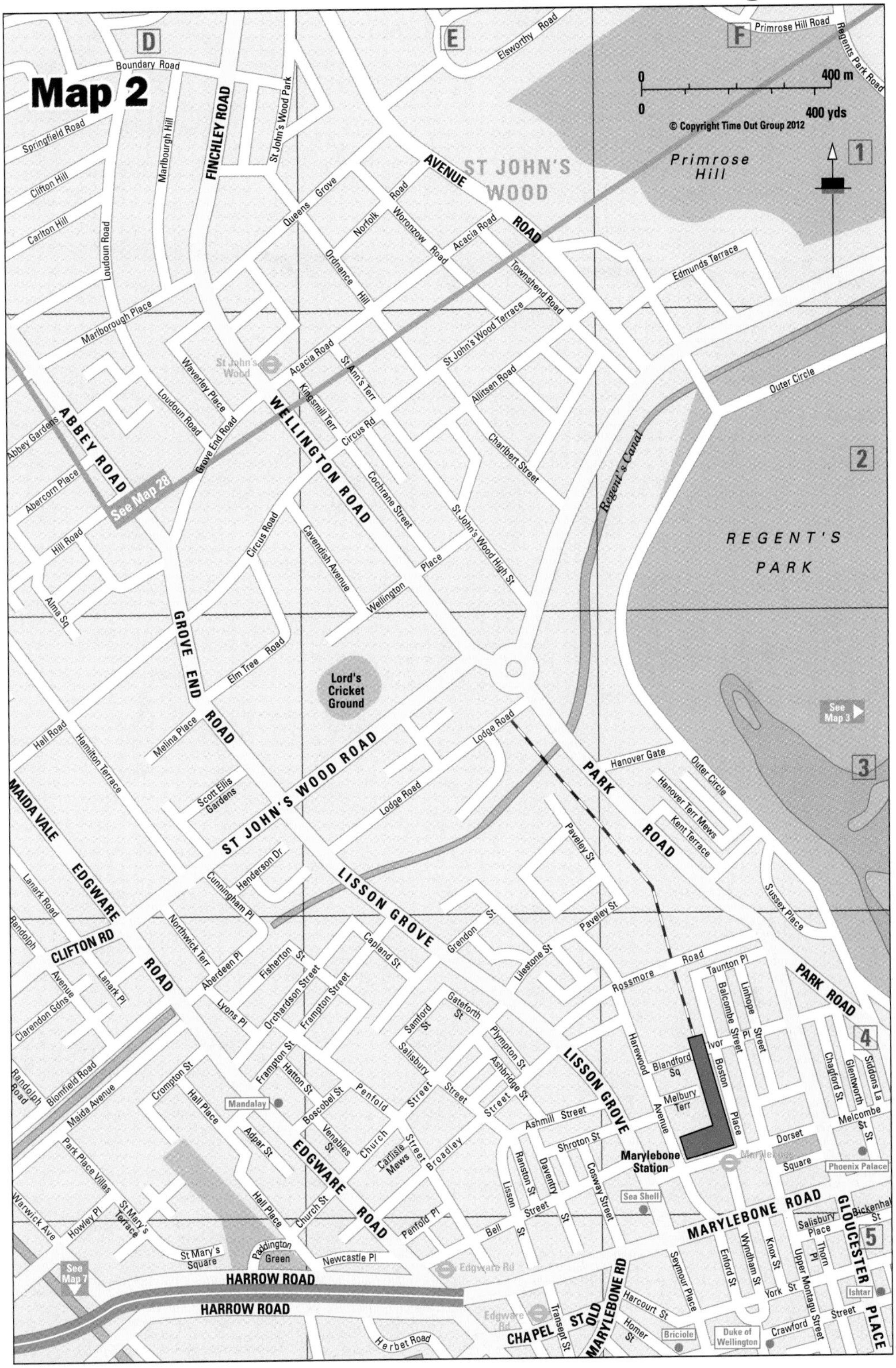

Map 2

D E F
1 2 3 4 5
0 400 m
0 400 yds
© Copyright Time Out Group 2012

ST JOHN'S WOOD
Primrose Hill
REGENT'S PARK
Lord's Cricket Ground

Boundary Road
Springfield Road
Clifton Hill
Carlton Hill
Marlborough Hill
Loudoun Road
FINCHLEY ROAD
St John's Wood Park
Queens Grove
Norfolk Road
Woronzow Road
Acacia Road
AVENUE ROAD
Elsworthy Road
Primrose Hill Road
Regents Park Road
Edmunds Terrace
Townshend Road
Ordnance Hill
Marlborough Place
St John's Wood Terrace
Allitsen Road
Outer Circle
Regent's Canal
Charlbert Street
St John's Wood
Acacia Road
St Ann's Terr
Kingsmill Terr
Circus Rd
Waverley Place
Loudoun Road
Grove End Road
ABBEY ROAD
Abbey Gardens
Abercorn Place
See Map 28
WELLINGTON ROAD
Cochrane Street
St John's Wood High St
Hill Road
Circus Road
Cavendish Avenue
Place
Wellington
Alma Sq
GROVE END ROAD
Elm Tree Road
See Map 3
Hall Road
Hamilton Terrace
Melina Place
ST JOHN'S WOOD ROAD
Lodge Road
Hanover Gate
Outer Circle
PARK ROAD
Hanover Terr Mews
Kent Terrace
MAIDA VALE
Scott Ellis Gardens
Paveley St
EDGWARE ROAD
Lanark Road
Henderson Dr
Cunningham Pl
LISSON GROVE
Sussex Place
Randolph Avenue
CLIFTON RD
Northwick Terr
Aberdeen Pl
Fisherton St
Capland St
Grendon St
Paveley St
Lilestone St
Rossmore Road
Taunton Pl
PARK ROAD
Lanark Pl
Clarendon Gdns
Lyons Pl
Orchardson Street
Frampton Street
Samford St
Gateforth St
Plympton St
Balcombe Street
Linhope Street
Ivor Pl
Harewood Avenue
Blandford Sq
Boston Place
Melbury Terr
Chagford St
Glentworth St
Siddons La
Randolph Road
Blomfield Road
Crompton St
Maida Avenue
Frampton St
Hatton St
Mandalay
Salisbury Street
Ashbridge St
Penfold Street
Ashmill Street
Shroton St
Dorset Square
Melcombe St
Phoenix Palace
Park Place Villas
Hall Place
Boscobel St
Venables St
Church Street
Carlisle Mews
Broadley Street
Ranston St
Daventry St
Cosway Street
Marylebone Station
Marylebone
Aspar St
Warwick Ave
Howley Pl
St Mary's Terrace
Hall Place
Church St
Penfold Pl
Lisson Street
Bell Street
Sea Shell
MARYLEBONE ROAD
GLOUCESTER PLACE
Salisbury Place
Bickenhall St
Thorn Pl
St Mary's Square
Paddington Green
Newcastle Pl
Edgware Rd
Seymour Place
Enford St
Wyndham St
Knox St
Upper Montagu Street
York St
Ishtar
See Map 7
HARROW ROAD
HARROW ROAD
Herbet Road
CHAPEL ST
Transept St
OLD MARYLEBONE RD
Harcourt St
Homer St
Briciole
Duke of Wellington
Crawford Street

MAPS

Camden Town & Marylebone

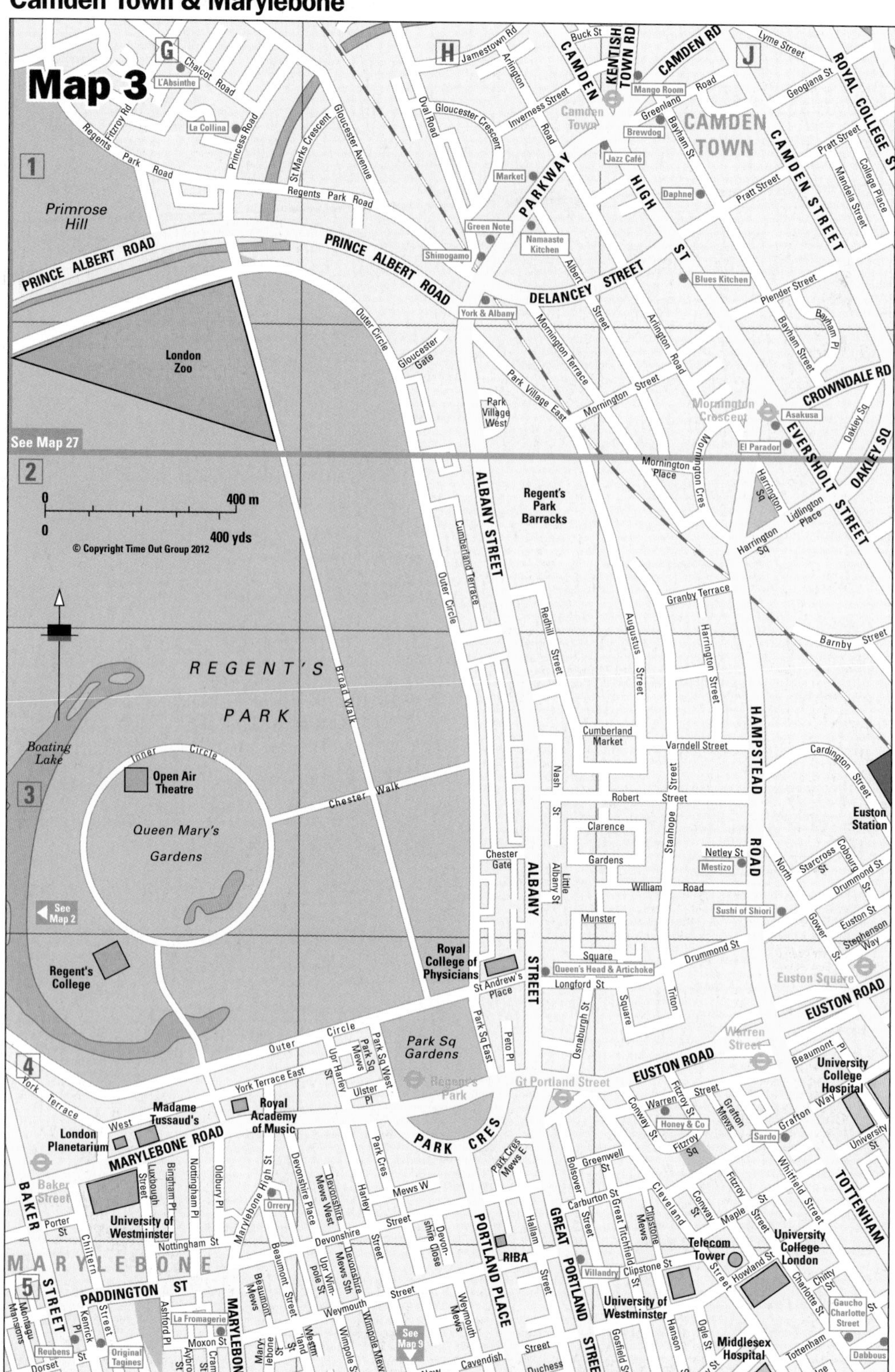

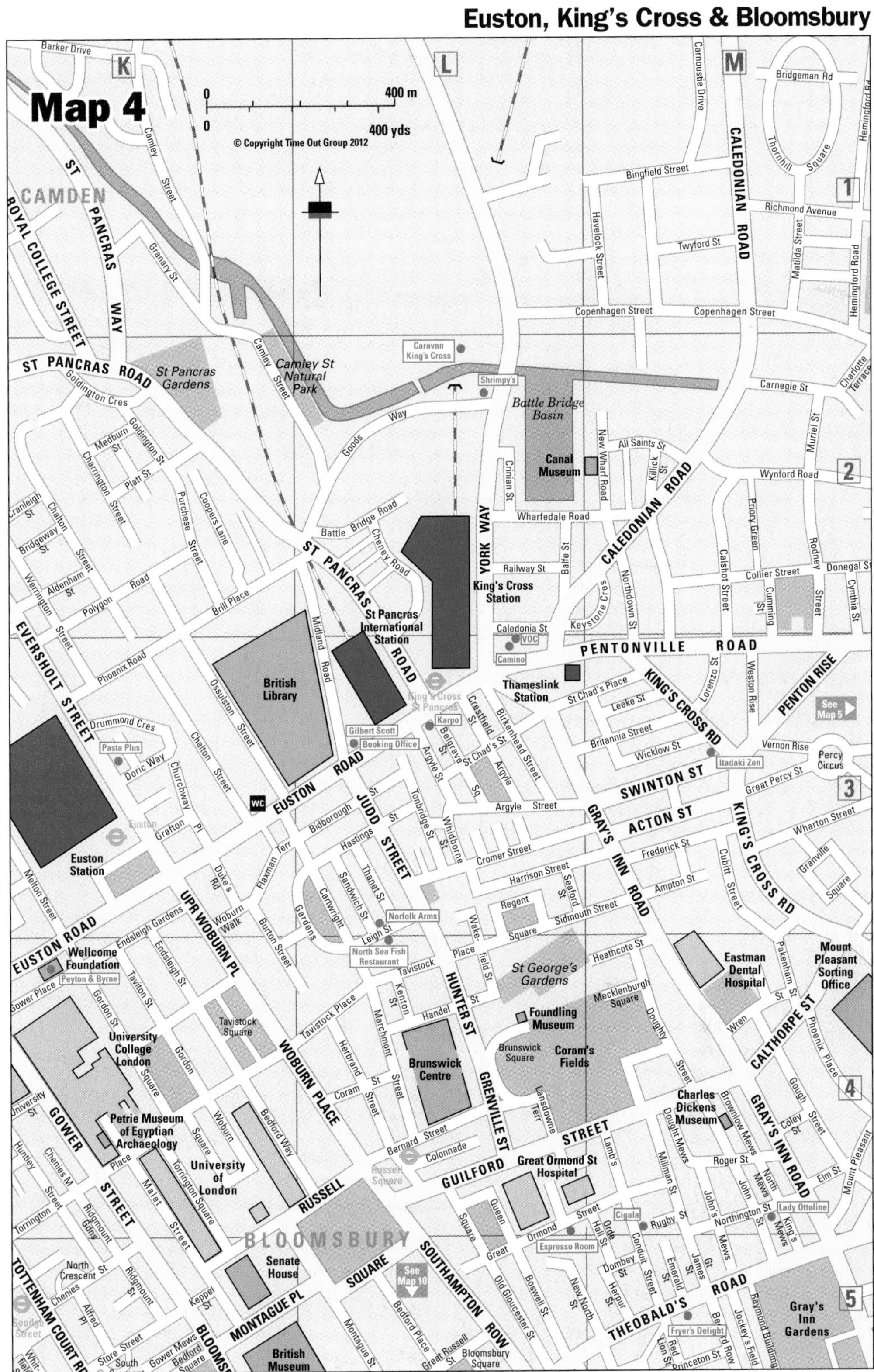
Map 4
0 400 m
0 400 yds
© Copyright Time Out Group 2012
K
L
M
CAMDEN
ST PANCRAS WAY
ROYAL COLLEGE STREET
St Pancras Gardens
Camley St Natural Park
Battle Bridge Basin
Canal Museum
CALEDONIAN ROAD
King's Cross Station
St Pancras International Station
British Library
Thameslink Station
PENTONVILLE ROAD
KING'S CROSS RD
EUSTON ROAD
Euston Station
EVERSHOLT STREET
Wellcome Foundation
University College London
Petrie Museum of Egyptian Archaeology
University of London
Senate House
British Museum
BLOOMSBURY
St George's Gardens
Foundling Museum
Brunswick Centre
Coram's Fields
Charles Dickens Museum
Great Ormond St Hospital
Eastman Dental Hospital
Mount Pleasant Sorting Office
Gray's Inn Gardens
GRAY'S INN ROAD
GOWER STREET
TOTTENHAM COURT RD
RUSSELL SQUARE
WOBURN PLACE
SOUTHAMPTON ROW
THEOBALD'S ROAD
GUILFORD STREET
SWINTON ST
ACTON ST
PENTON RISE
See Map 5
See Map 10
1
2
3
4
5

MAPS

Islington, Clerkenwell & Farringdon

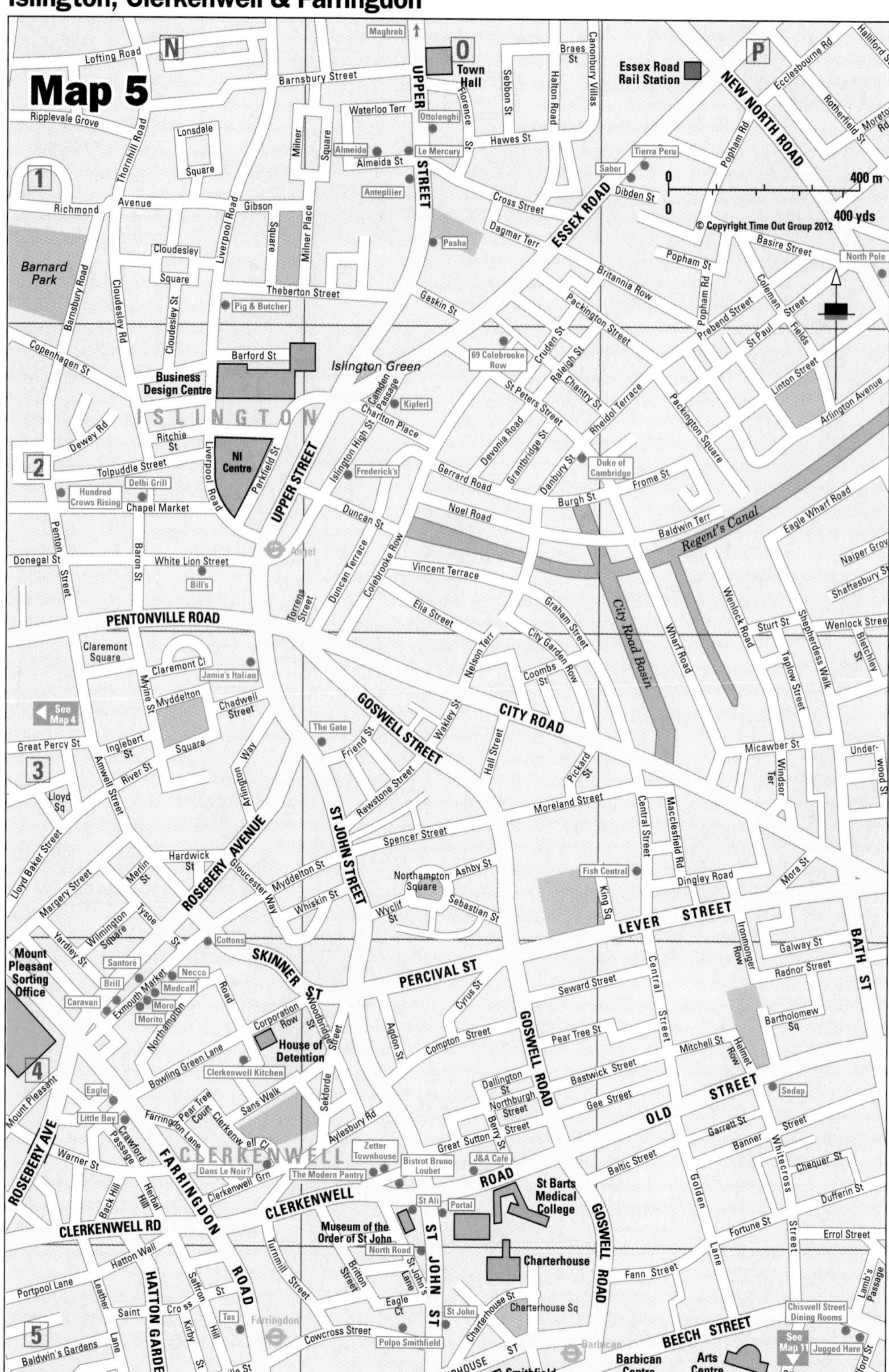

MAPS

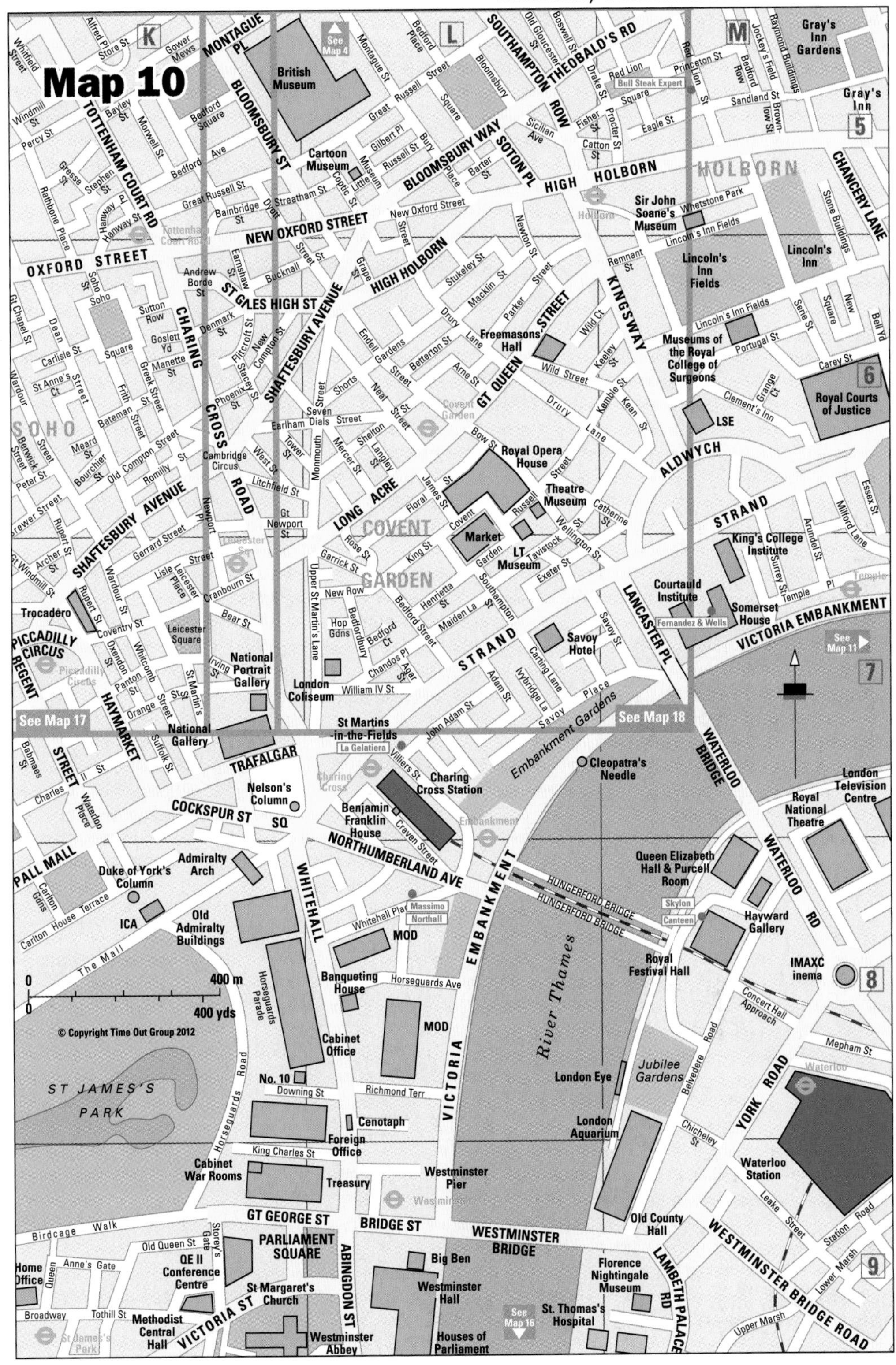
Map 10
K
L
M
British Museum
Cartoon Museum
Sir John Soane's Museum
Lincoln's Inn Fields
Lincoln's Inn
Gray's Inn Gardens
Gray's Inn
Museums of the Royal College of Surgeons
Royal Courts of Justice
LSE
Freemasons' Hall
Royal Opera House
Theatre Museum
Market
LT Museum
King's College Institute
Courtauld Institute
Somerset House
Savoy Hotel
Trocadero
Leicester Square
National Portrait Gallery
London Coliseum
National Gallery
St Martins -in-the-Fields
Nelson's Column
Charing Cross Station
Benjamin Franklin House
Cleopatra's Needle
Duke of York's Column
Admiralty Arch
ICA
Old Admiralty Buildings
MOD
Banqueting House
Cabinet Office
No. 10
Cenotaph
Foreign Office
Cabinet War Rooms
Treasury
Westminster Pier
London Eye
London Aquarium
Jubilee Gardens
Royal Festival Hall
Queen Elizabeth Hall & Purcell Room
Hayward Gallery
Royal National Theatre
London Television Centre
IMAXC inema
Waterloo Station
Old County Hall
Florence Nightingale Museum
St. Thomas's Hospital
Big Ben
Westminster Hall
Houses of Parliament
Westminster Abbey
St Margaret's Church
QE II Conference Centre
Home Office
Methodist Central Hall
PARLIAMENT SQUARE
ST JAMES'S PARK
River Thames
SOHO
COVENT GARDEN
HOLBORN
See Map 4
See Map 11
See Map 16
See Map 17
See Map 18
0
400 m
400 yds
© Copyright Time Out Group 2012
MAPS

City, Waterloo & Borough

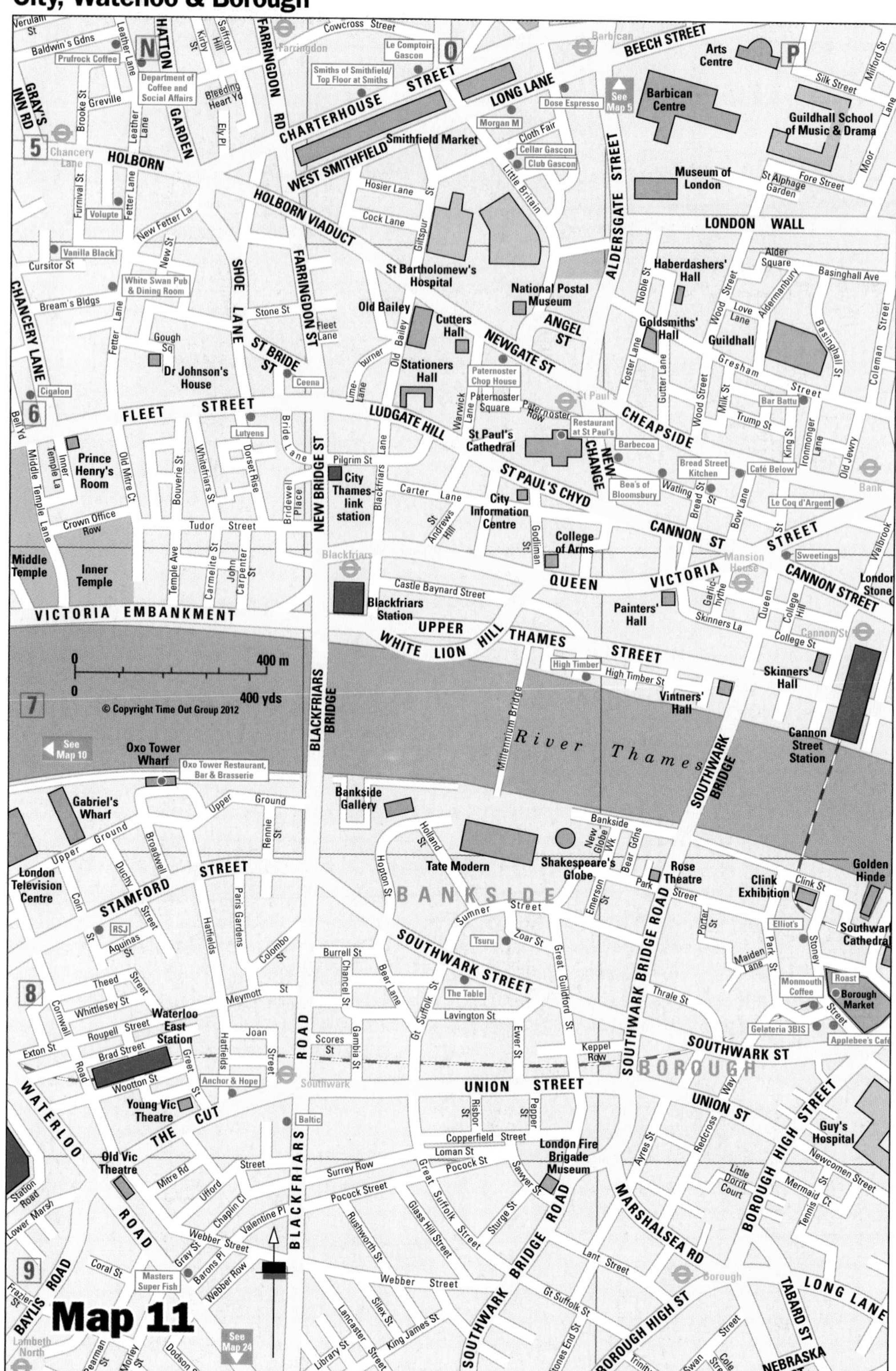

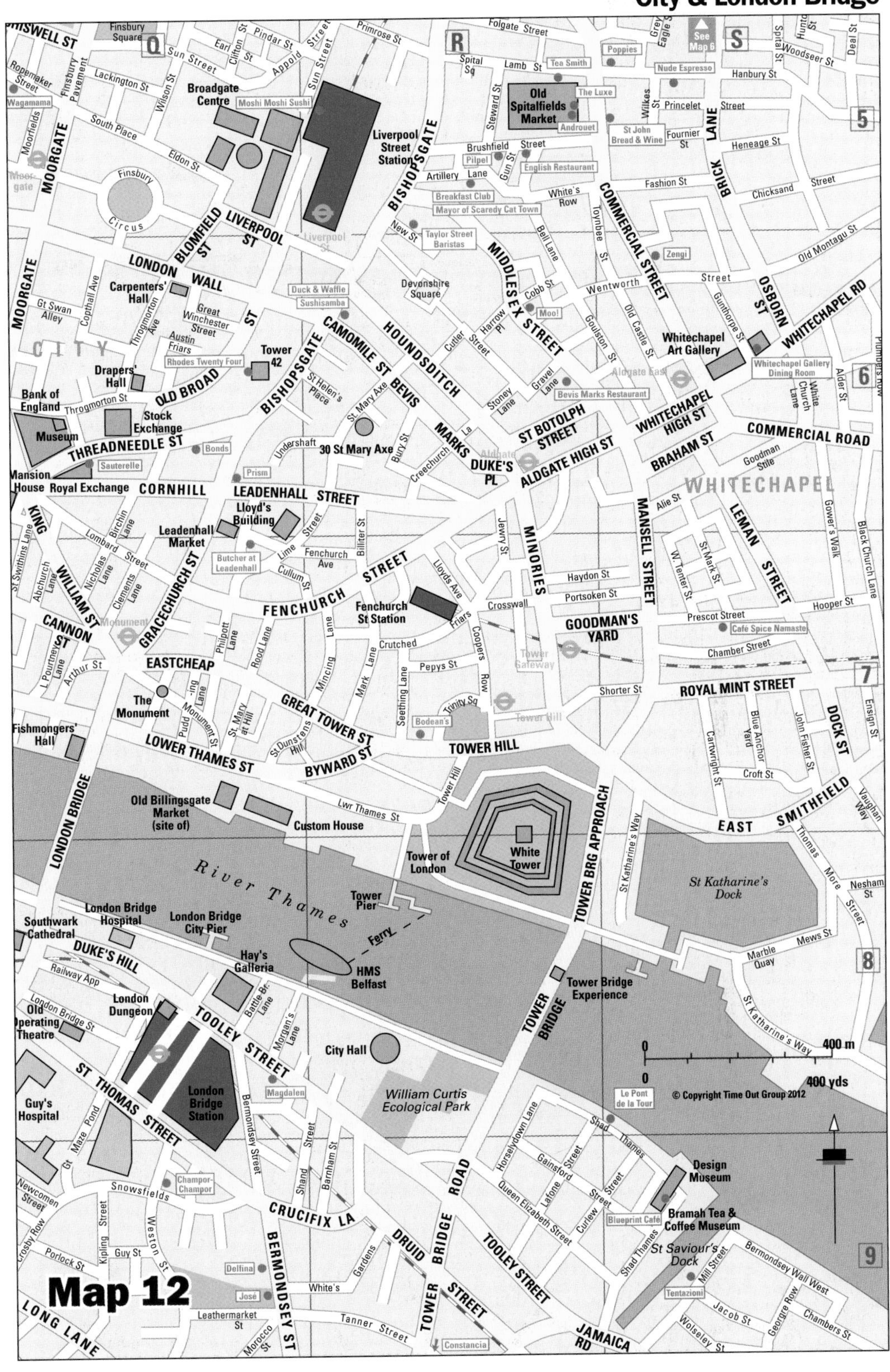
Map 12
Liverpool Street Station
Broadgate Centre
Old Spitalfields Market
Finsbury Circus
Bank of England
Stock Exchange
Royal Exchange
Lloyd's Building
Leadenhall Market
Tower 42
30 St Mary Axe
Fenchurch St Station
The Monument
Tower of London
White Tower
St Katharine's Dock
River Thames
HMS Belfast
City Hall
London Bridge Station
Tower Bridge
Design Museum
Whitechapel Art Gallery
WHITECHAPEL
CITY
© Copyright Time Out Group 2012

See Map 6

Earl's Court, Gloucester Road & Fulham

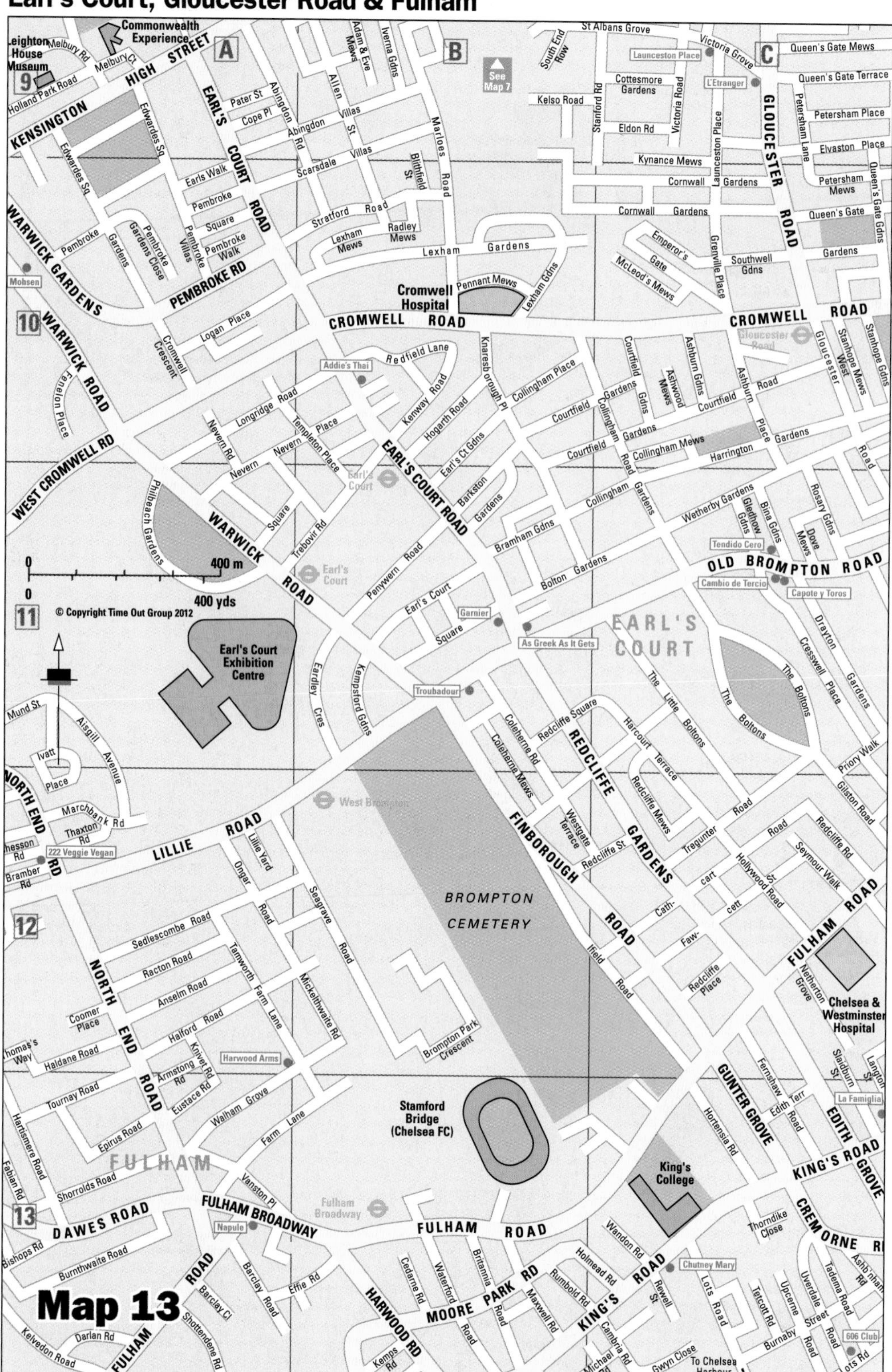

MAPS

Knightsbridge, South Kensington & Chelsea

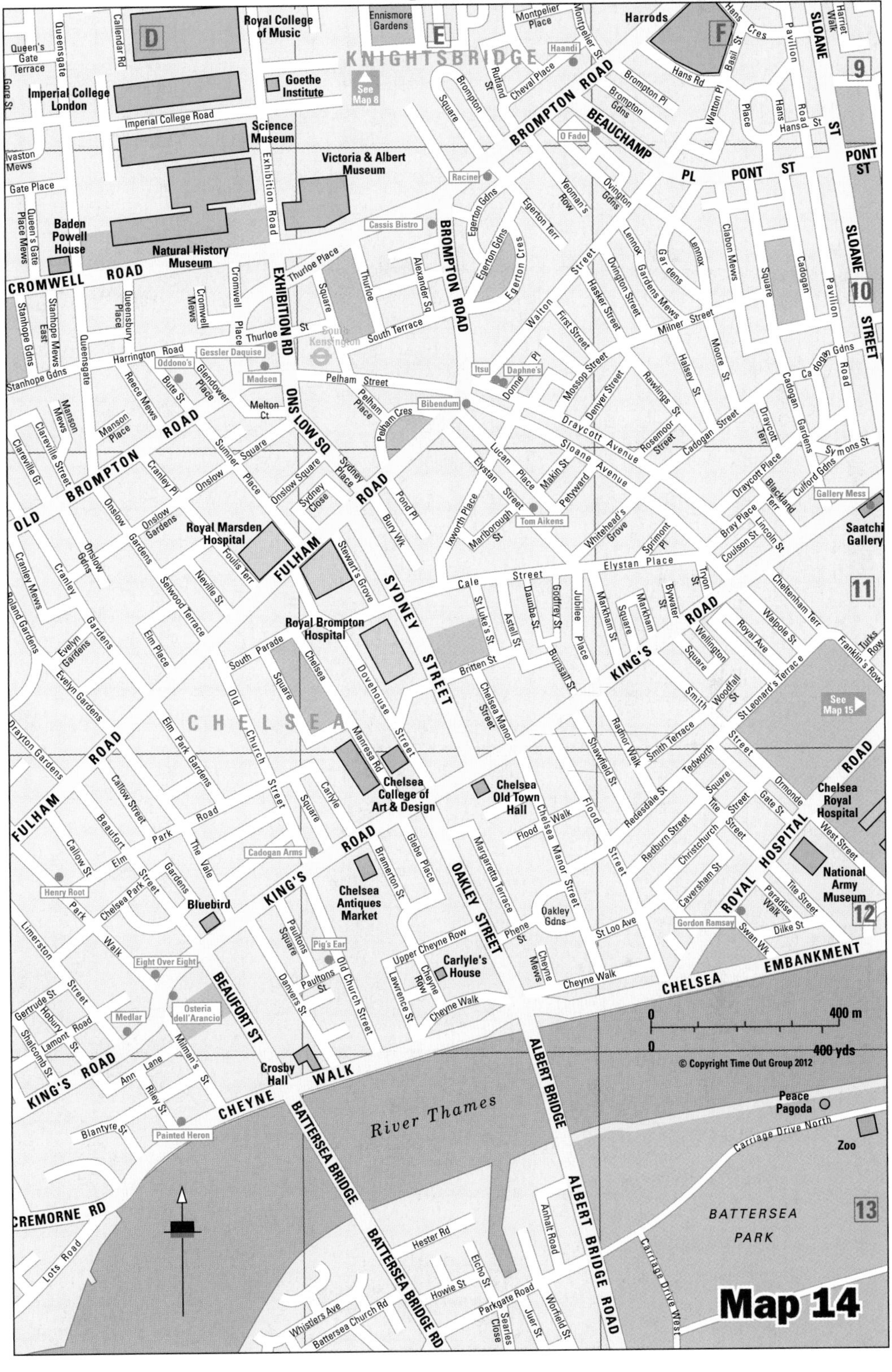

Map 14

Royal College of Music
Imperial College London
Goethe Institute
Science Museum
Victoria & Albert Museum
Natural History Museum
Baden Powell House
Harrods
Royal Marsden Hospital
Royal Brompton Hospital
Chelsea College of Art & Design
Chelsea Old Town Hall
Chelsea Antiques Market
Carlyle's House
Bluebird
Crosby Hall
Saatchi Gallery
Chelsea Royal Hospital
National Army Museum
Peace Pagoda
Zoo
Battersea Park
River Thames
CHELSEA
KNIGHTSBRIDGE

© Copyright Time Out Group 2012

MAPS

Belgravia, Victoria & Pimlico

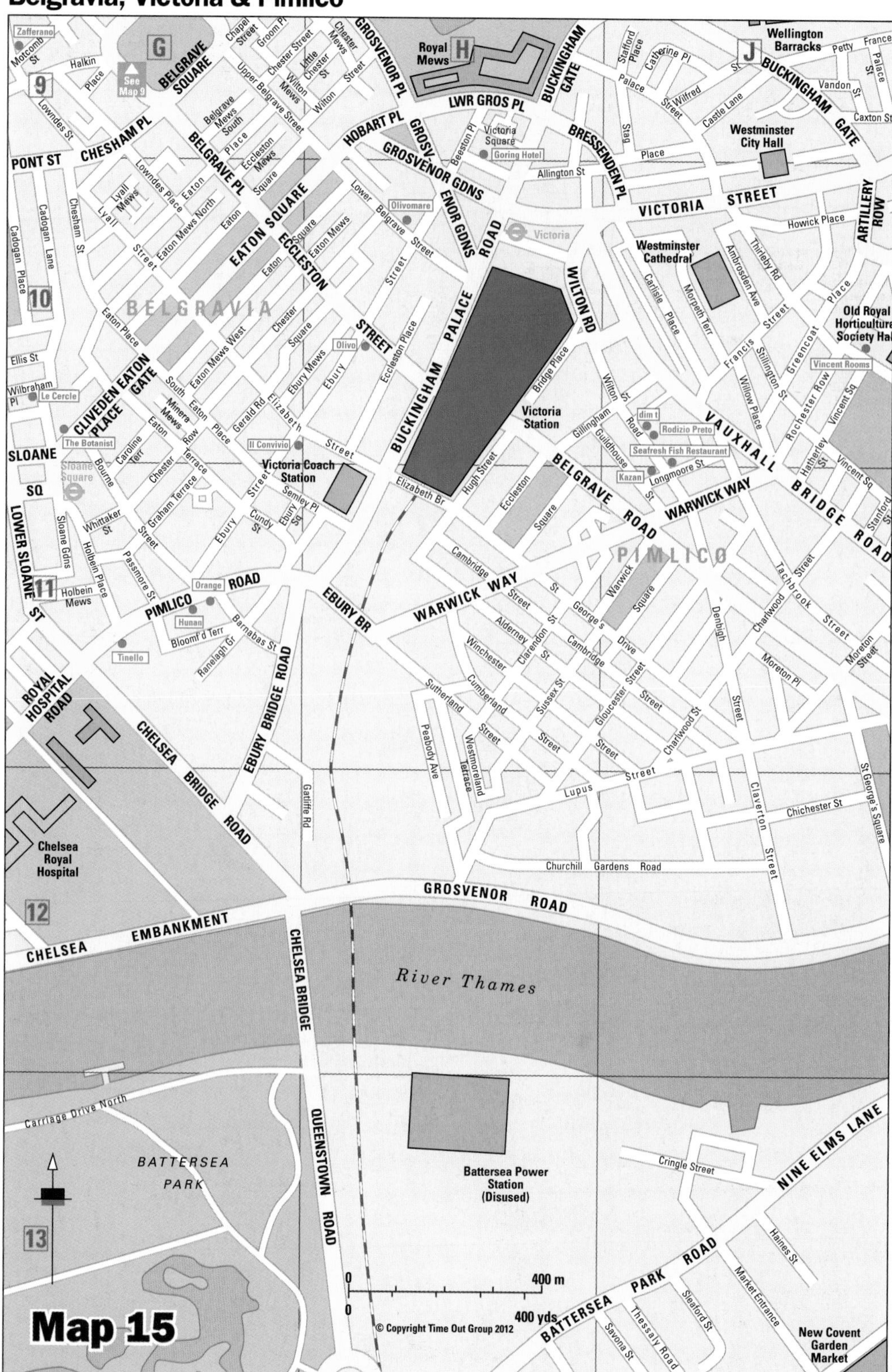

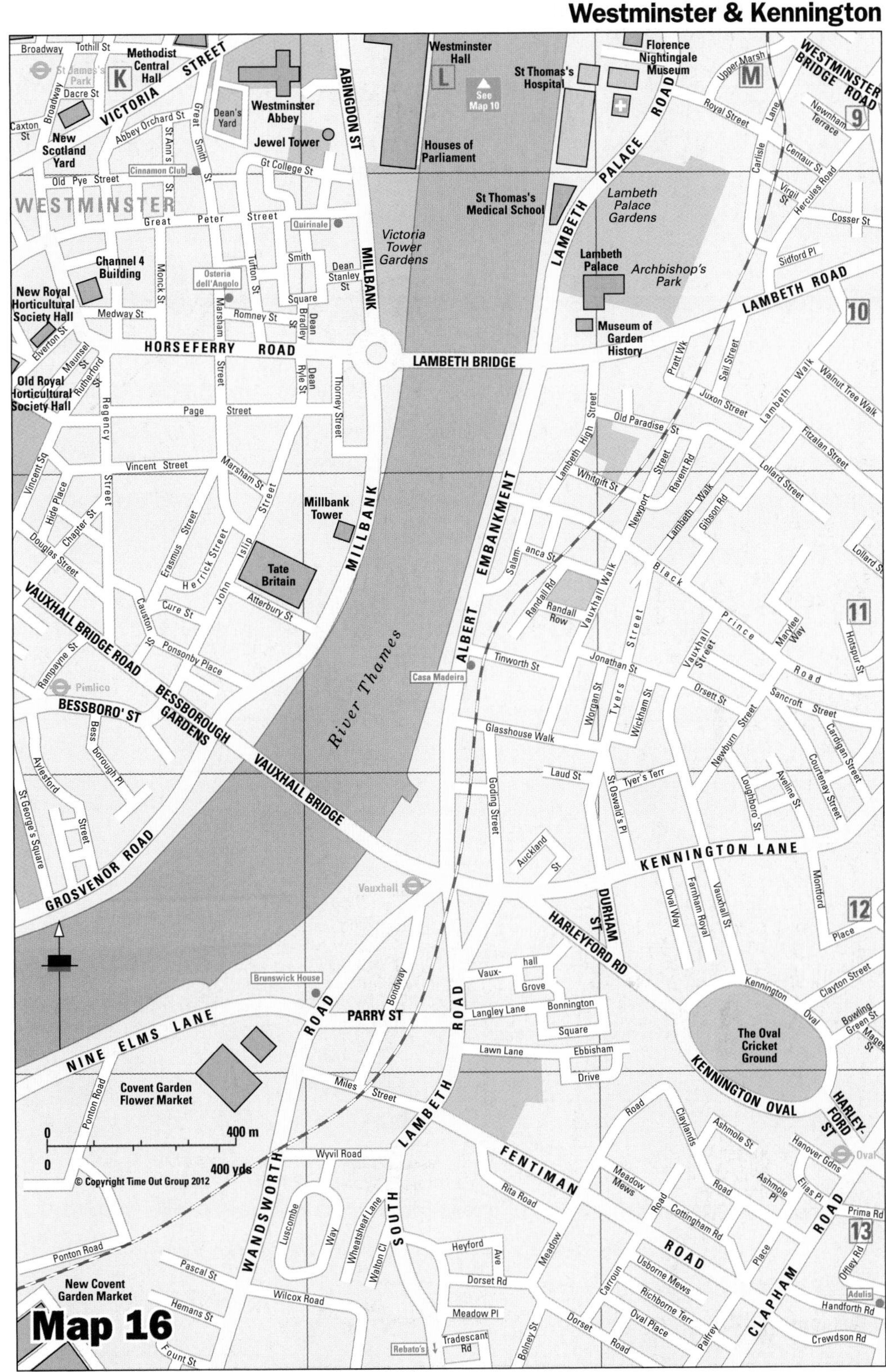
Map 16
Westminster Abbey
Houses of Parliament
Westminster Hall
St Thomas's Hospital
Florence Nightingale Museum
Methodist Central Hall
New Scotland Yard
WESTMINSTER
Victoria Tower Gardens
Lambeth Palace
Lambeth Palace Gardens
Archbishop's Park
Museum of Garden History
St Thomas's Medical School
Jewel Tower
Channel 4 Building
New Royal Horticultural Society Hall
Old Royal Horticultural Society Hall
Millbank Tower
Tate Britain
River Thames
LAMBETH BRIDGE
VAUXHALL BRIDGE
ALBERT EMBANKMENT
MILLBANK
HORSEFERRY ROAD
VICTORIA STREET
LAMBETH ROAD
LAMBETH PALACE ROAD
WESTMINSTER BRIDGE ROAD
VAUXHALL BRIDGE ROAD
GROSVENOR ROAD
NINE ELMS LANE
KENNINGTON LANE
KENNINGTON OVAL
HARLEYFORD RD
FENTIMAN ROAD
CLAPHAM ROAD
SOUTH LAMBETH ROAD
WANDSWORTH ROAD
The Oval Cricket Ground
Covent Garden Flower Market
New Covent Garden Market
Cinnamon Club
Quirinale
Osteria dell'Angolo
Casa Madeira
Brunswick House
Rebato's
Adulis
Vauxhall
Pimlico
St James's Park
Oval
See Map 10
0 400 m
0 400 yds
© Copyright Time Out Group 2012

MAPS

Fitzrovia, Soho & Chinatown

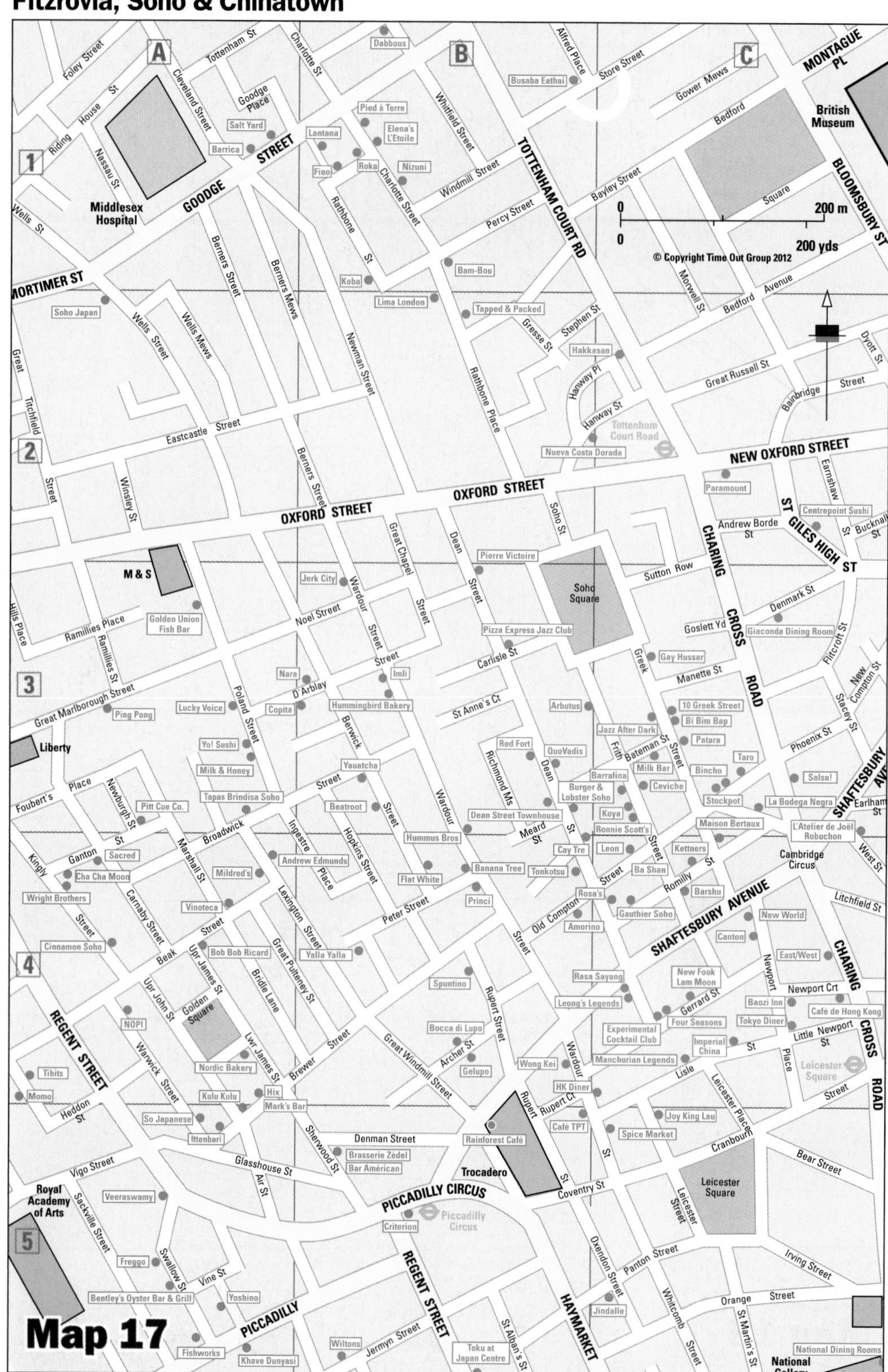

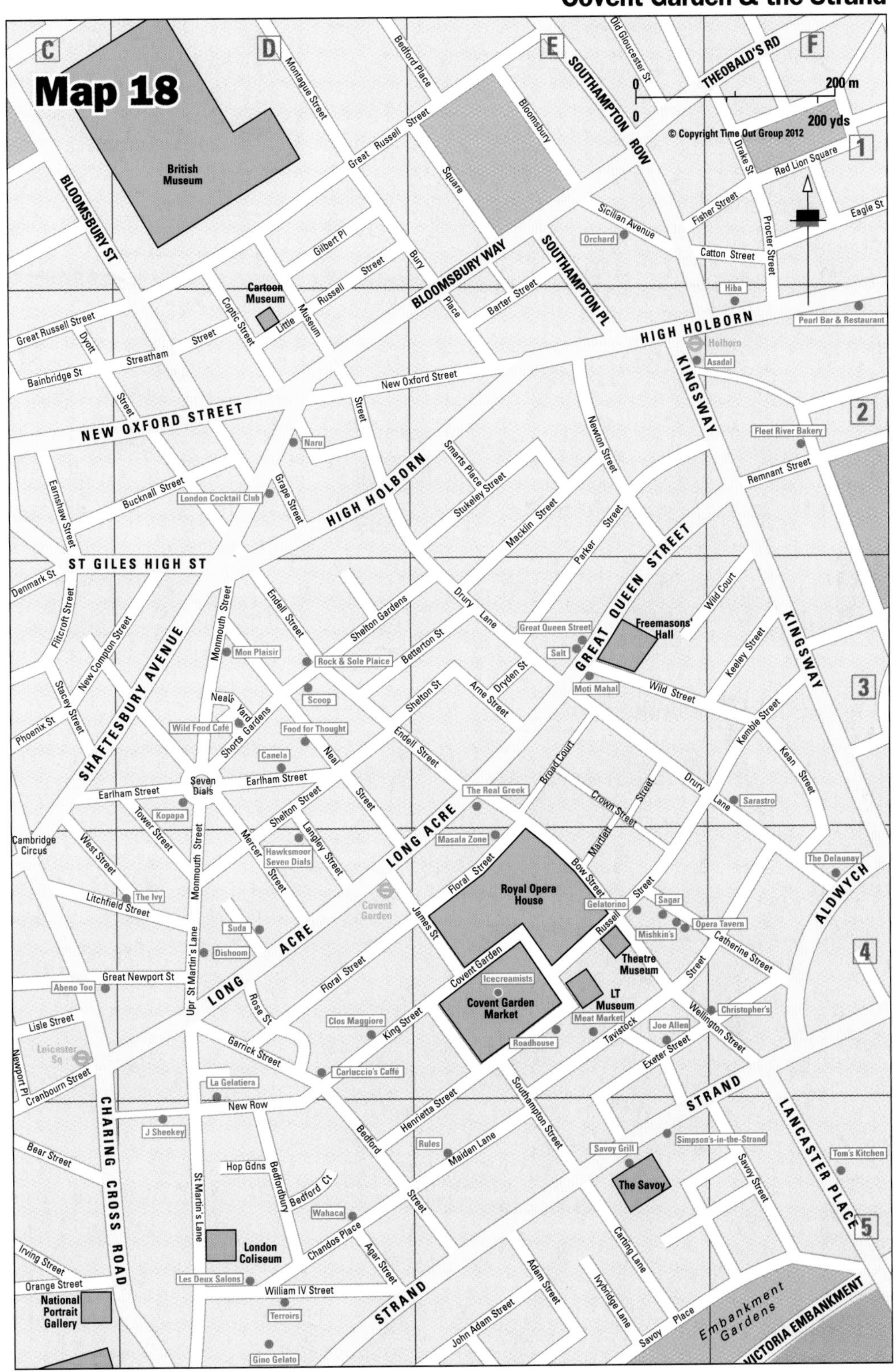
Map 18
C
D
E
F
1
2
3
4
5
0
200 m
200 yds
© Copyright Time Out Group 2012
British Museum
Cartoon Museum
Montague Street
Bedford Place
Great Russell Street
Bloomsbury Square
Southampton Row
Old Gloucester St
Theobald's Rd
Drake St
Red Lion Square
Fisher Street
Eagle St
Procter Street
Catton Street
Sicilian Avenue
Orchard
Hiba
Pearl Bar & Restaurant
Bloomsbury St
Bloomsbury Way
Southampton Pl
Barter Street
Bury Place
Gilbert Pl
Russell Street
Little Russell Street
Museum Street
Coptic Street
Dyott Street
Streatham Street
Bainbridge St
High Holborn
Holborn
Asadal
Kingsway
New Oxford Street
Newton Street
Fleet River Bakery
Remnant Street
Naru
Grape Street
London Cocktail Club
Bucknall Street
Earnshaw Street
Smarts Place
Stukeley Street
Macklin Street
Parker Street
Great Queen Street
St Giles High St
Denmark St
Flitcroft Street
New Compton Street
Stacey Street
Phoenix St
Shaftesbury Avenue
Monmouth Street
Endell Street
Shelton Gardens
Drury Lane
Wild Court
Freemasons' Hall
Great Queen Street
Salt
Mon Plaisir
Rock & Sole Plaice
Betterton St
Dryden St
Arne Street
Shelton St
Moti Mahal
Wild Street
Keeley Street
Kemble Street
Kean Street
Neal's Yard
Scoop
Wild Food Cafe
Shorts Gardens
Food for Thought
Neal Street
Canela
Seven Dials
Earlham Street
Broad Court
The Real Greek
Crown Street
Martlett Court
Sarastro
Cambridge Circus
Kopapa
Tower Street
West Street
Mercer Street
Langley Street
Hawksmoor Seven Dials
Long Acre
Masala Zone
Floral Street
Royal Opera House
Bow Street
Russell Street
Gelatorino
Sagar
Opera Tavern
The Delaunay
Aldwych
Catherine Street
The Ivy
Litchfield Street
Covent Garden
Suda
Dishoom
James St
Mishkin's
Theatre Museum
Great Newport St
Abeno Too
Upr St Martin's Lane
Rose St
Icecreamists
Covent Garden Market
LT Museum
Meat Market
Christopher's
Wellington Street
Lisle Street
Leicester Sq
Newport Pl
Cranbourn Street
Garrick Street
Clos Maggiore
King Street
Roadhouse
Tavistock Street
Joe Allen
Exeter Street
Carluccio's Caffè
La Gelatiera
New Row
Charing Cross Road
Henrietta Street
Southampton Street
Strand
Lancaster Place
J Sheekey
Bedford Street
Simpson's-in-the-Strand
Tom's Kitchen
Bear Street
Rules
Maiden Lane
Savoy Grill
Savoy Street
Hop Gdns
Bedfordbury
Bedford Ct
The Savoy
St Martin's Lane
Wahaca
Carting Lane
London Coliseum
Chandos Place
Agar Street
Irving Street
Orange Street
Les Deux Salons
William IV Street
Adam Street
Ivybridge Lane
Savoy Place
Embankment Gardens
Victoria Embankment
National Portrait Gallery
Terroirs
John Adam Street
Gino Gelato

Hammersmith & Shepherd's Bush

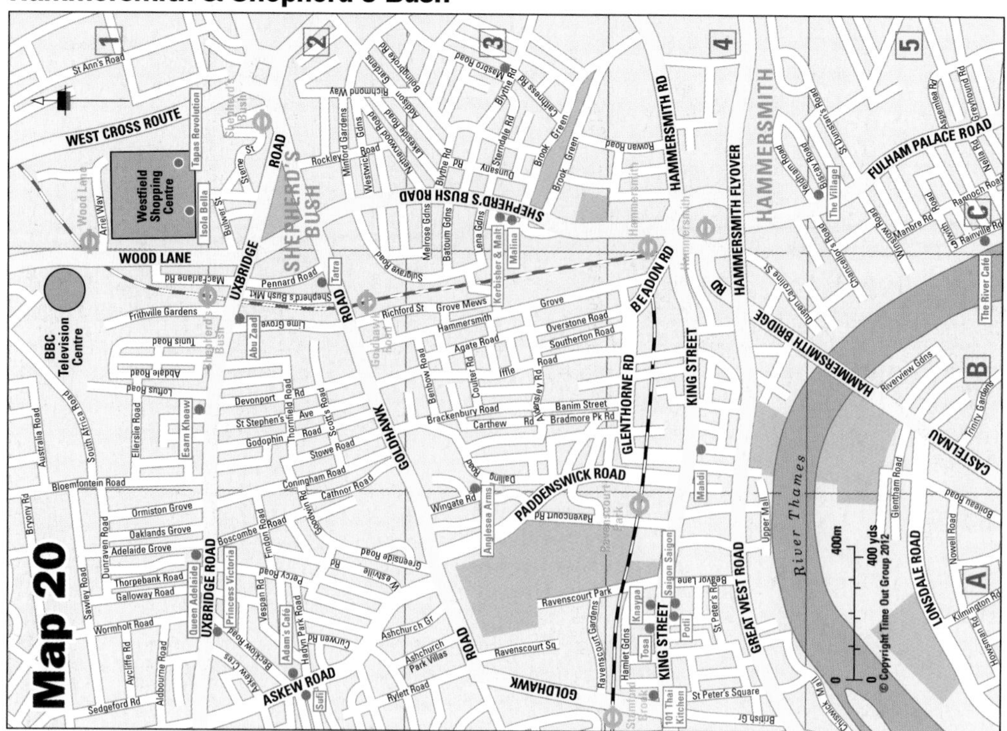

Notting Hill & Ladbroke Grove

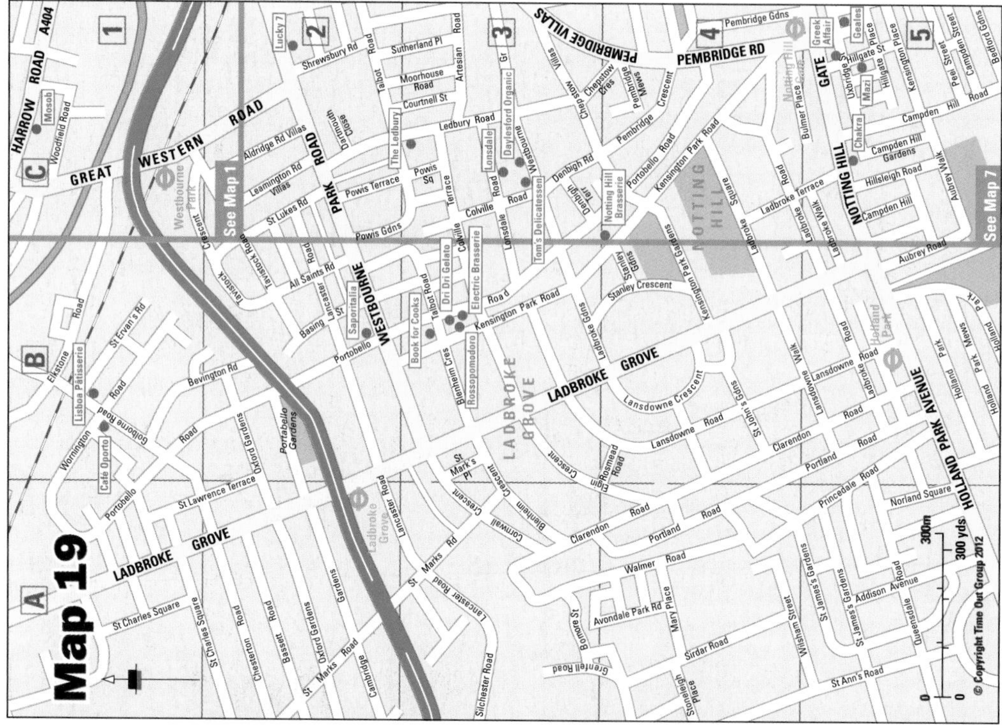

Clapham & Brixton

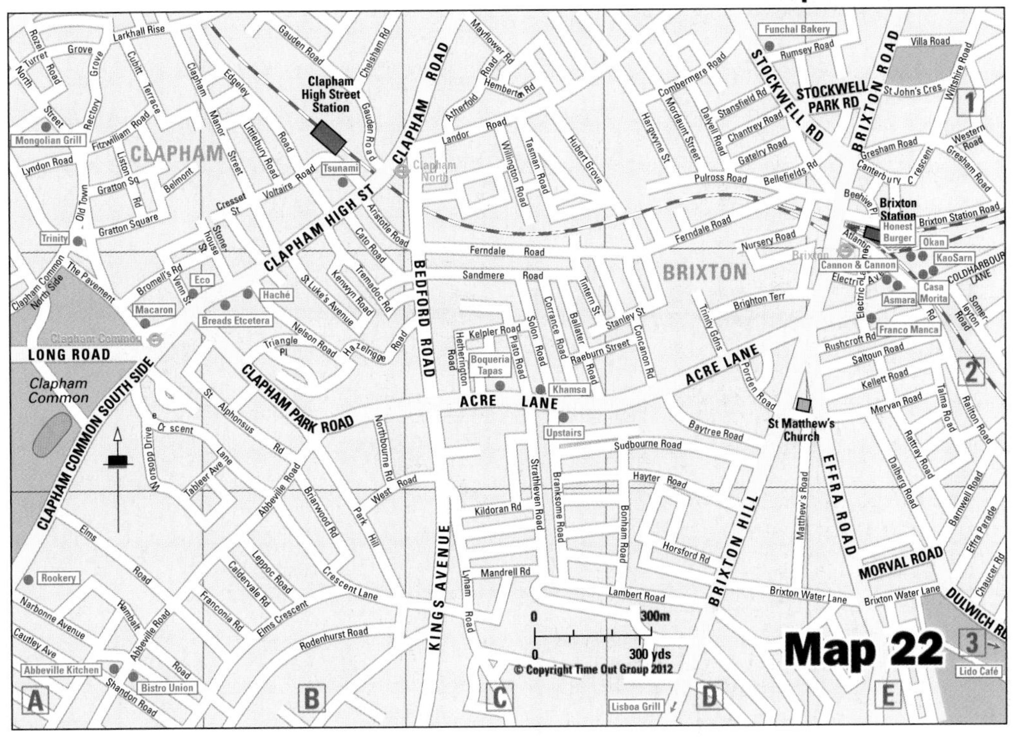

Battersea & Wandsworth

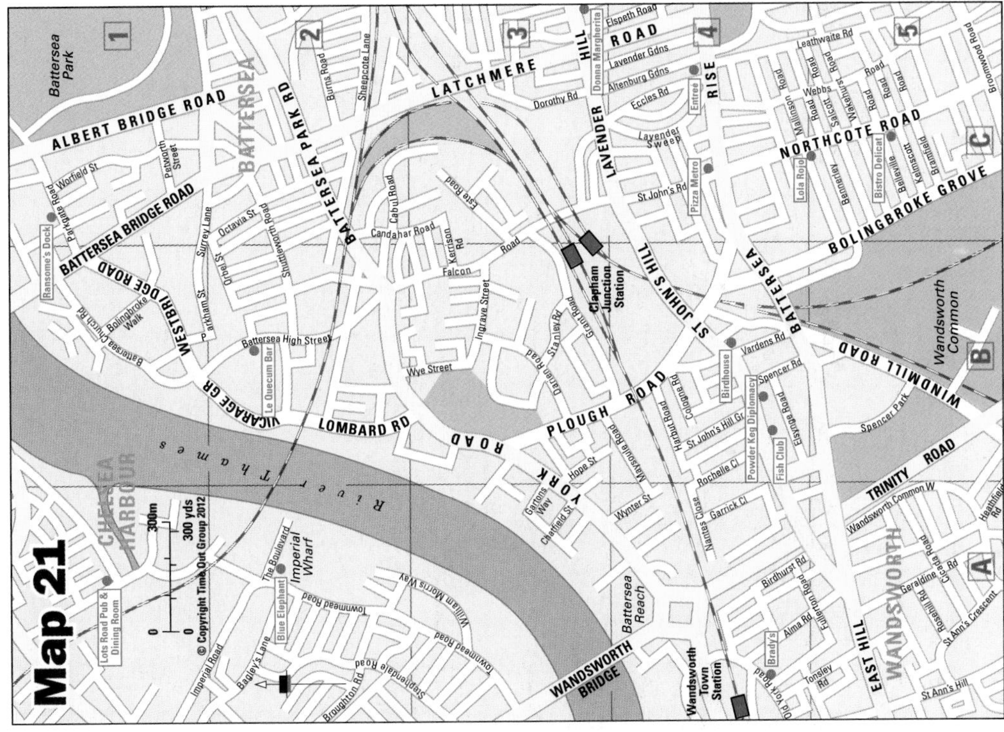

MAPS

Docklands

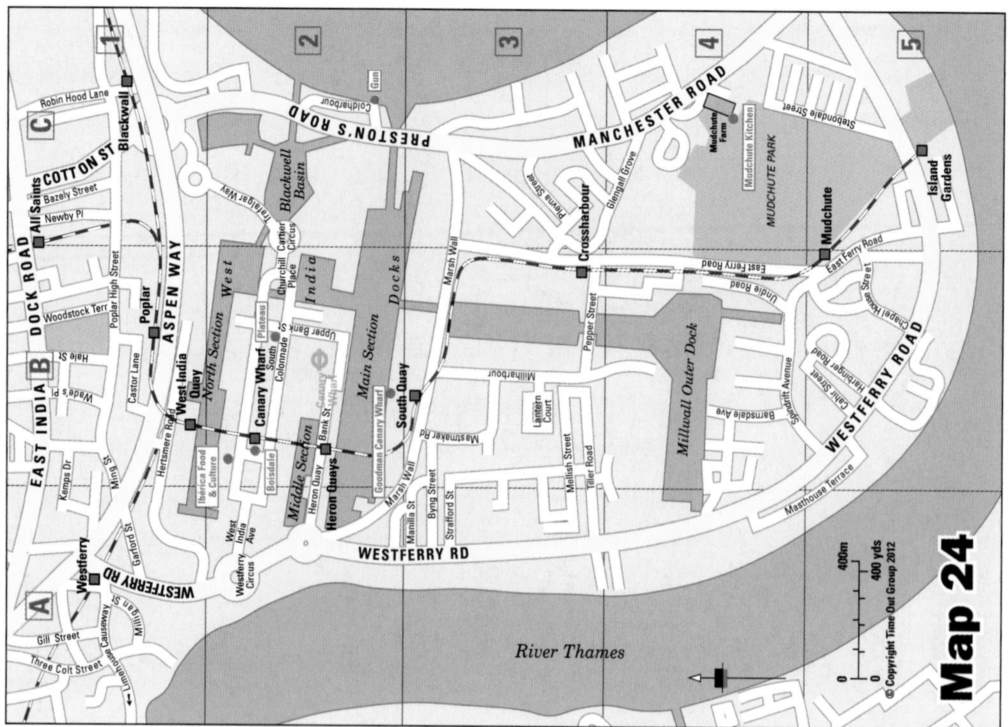

Camberwell & Dulwich

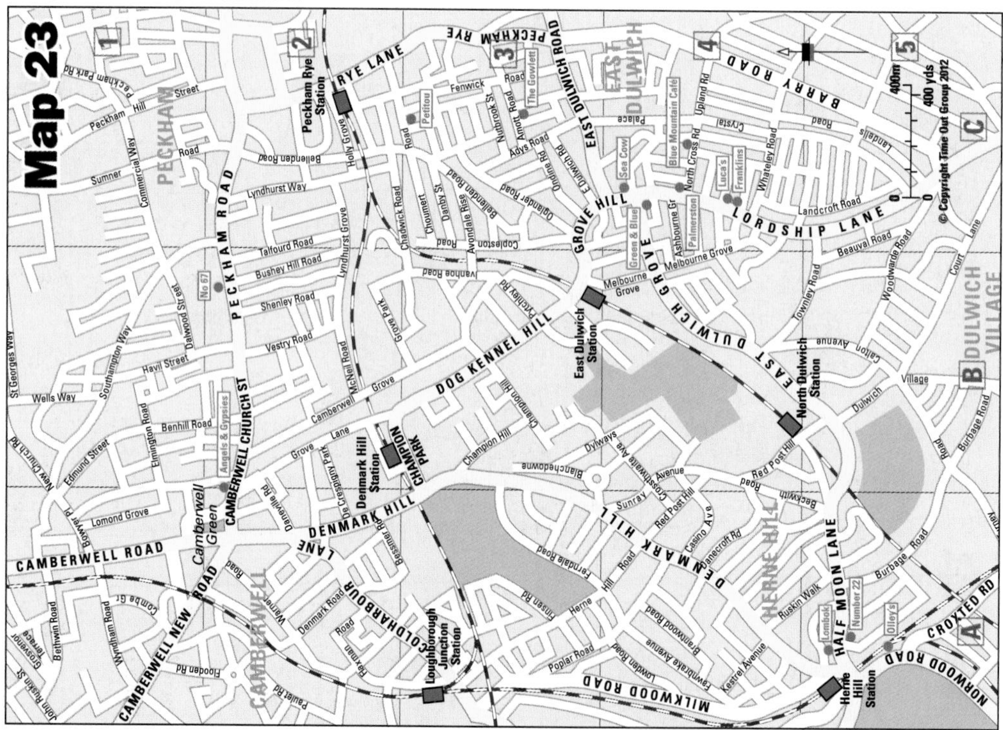

Kentish Town & Archway

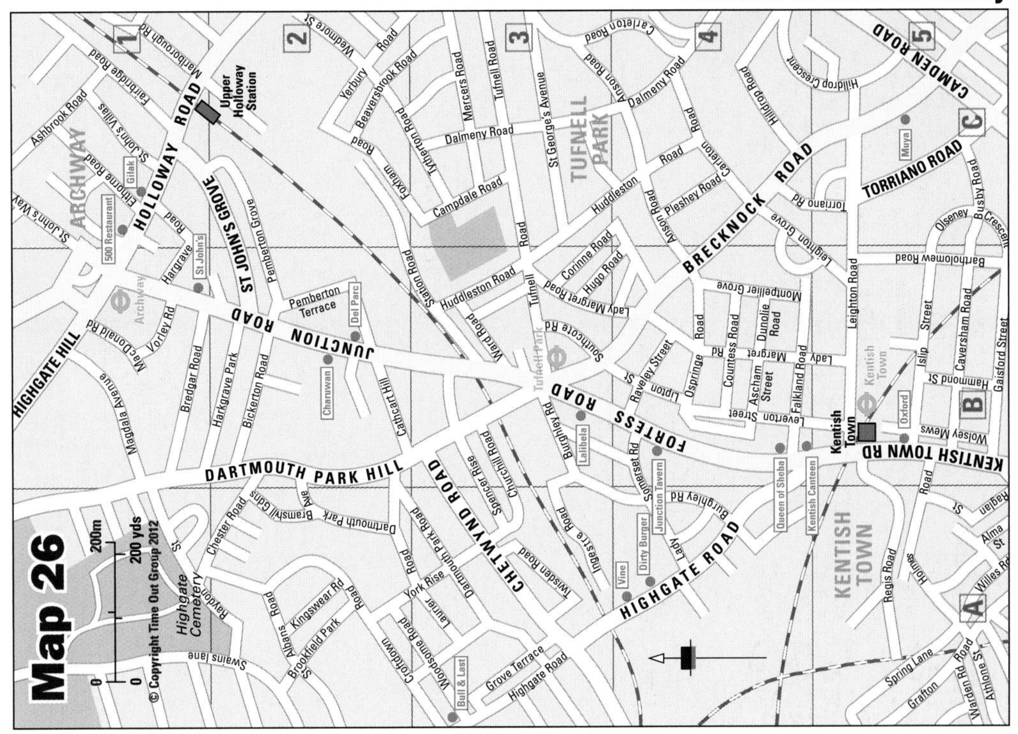

Dalston & Stoke Newington

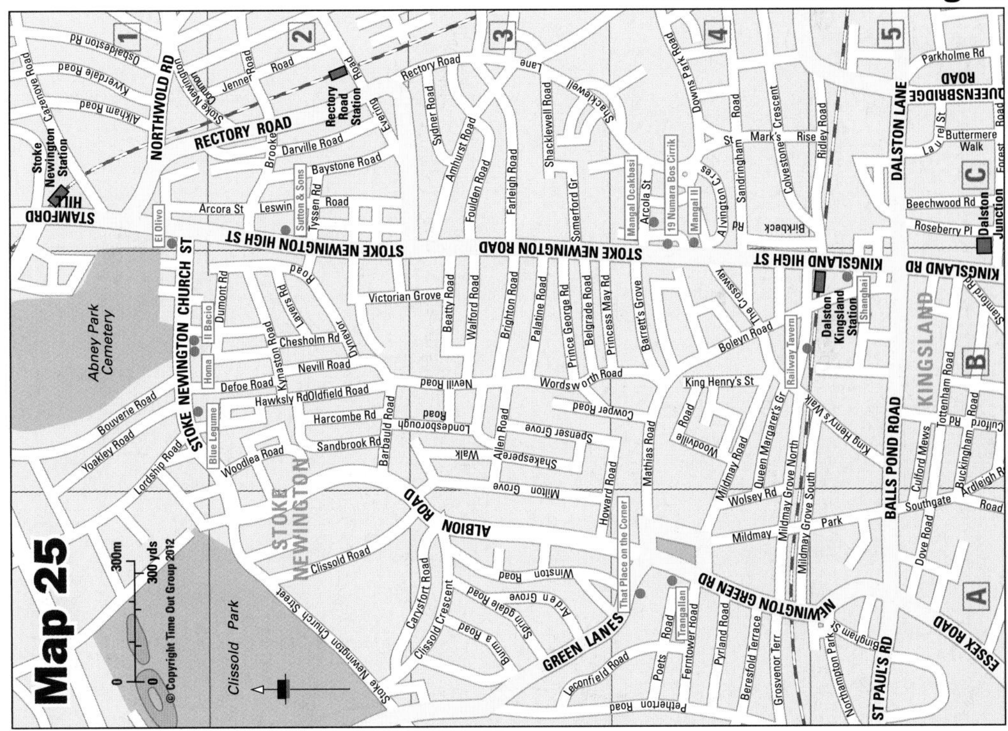

MAPS

Hampstead & St John's Wood

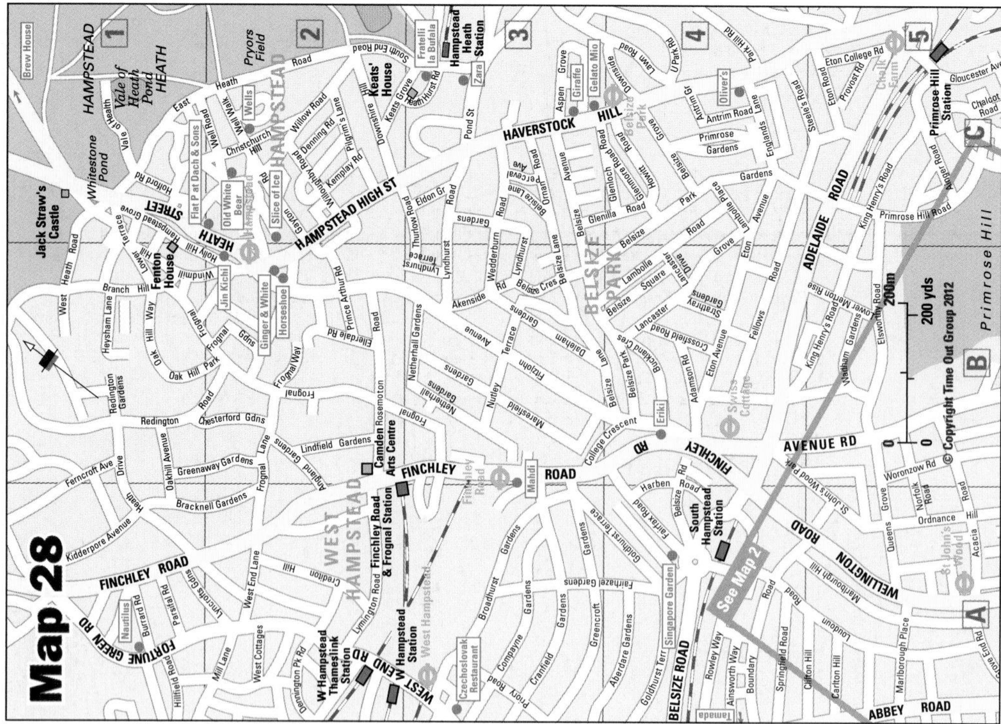

Camden Town & Chalk Farm

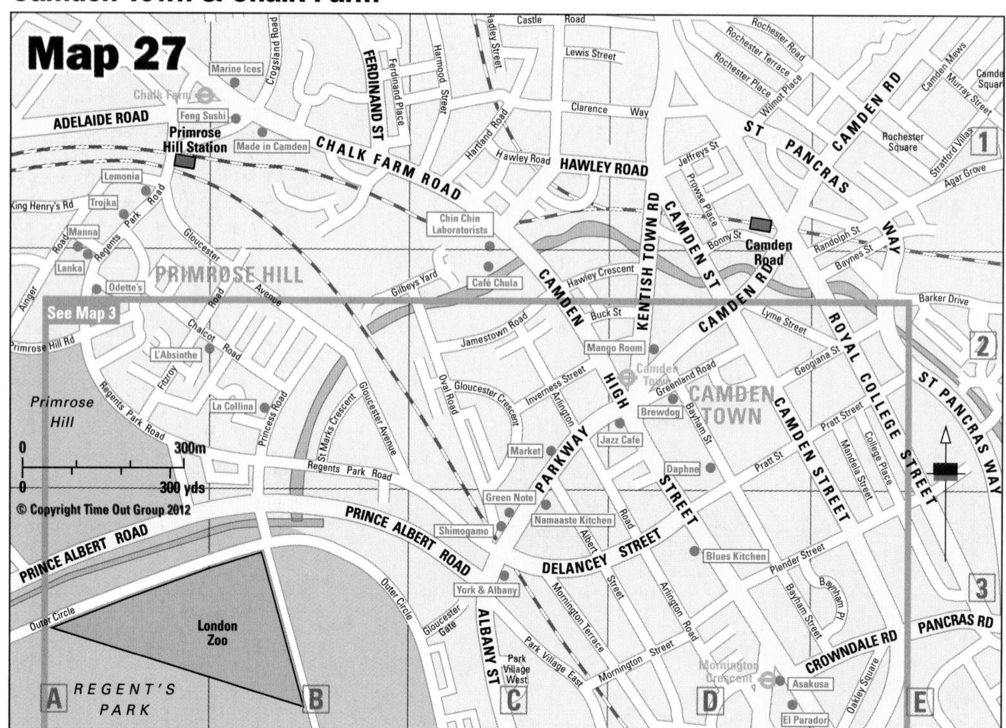

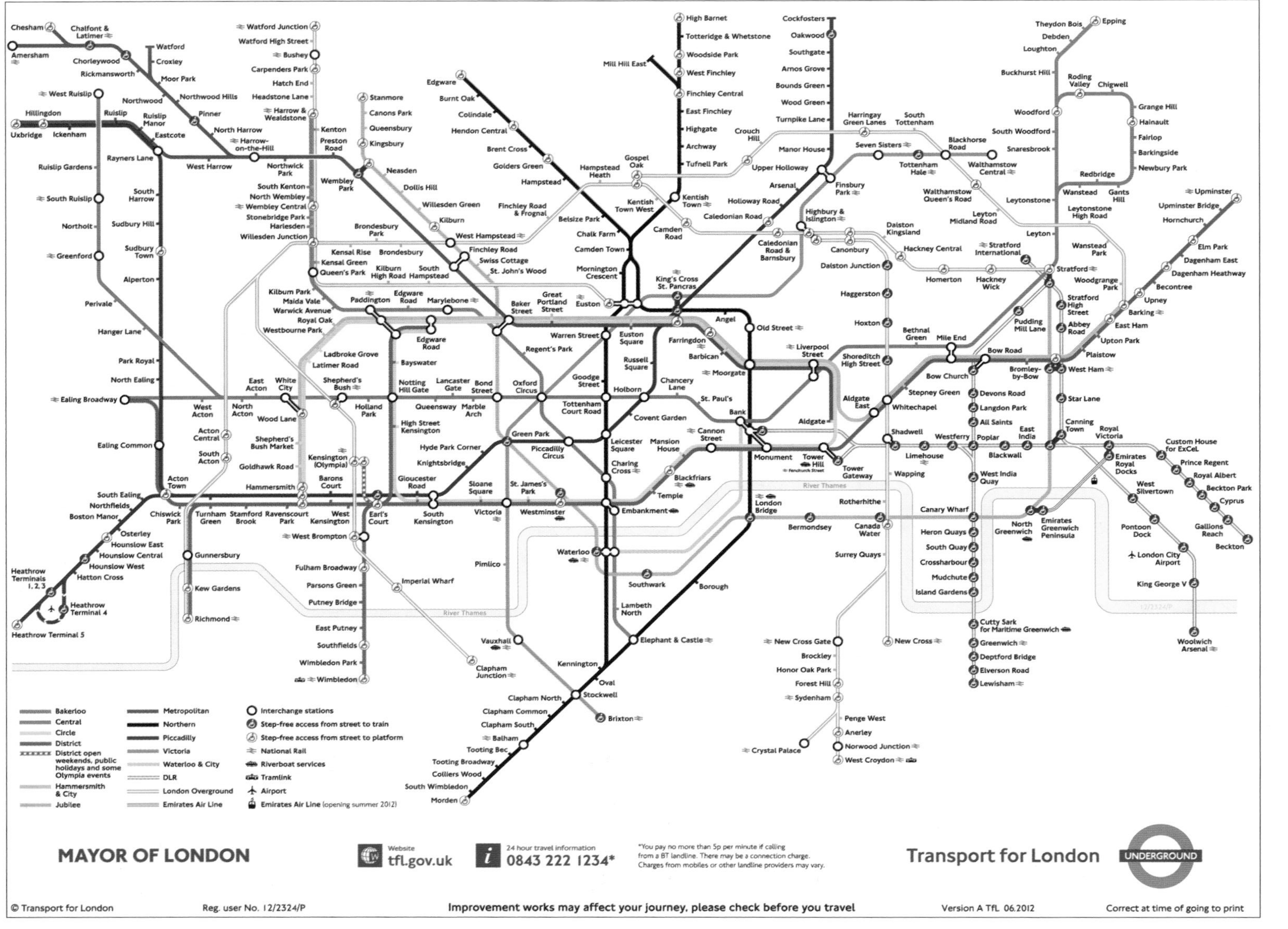

Transport for London
UNDERGROUND
MAYOR OF LONDON
Website
tfl.gov.uk
24 hour travel information
0843 222 1234*
*You pay no more than 5p per minute if calling from a BT landline. There may be a connection charge. Charges from mobiles or other landline providers may vary.
Bakerloo
Central
Circle
District
District open weekends, public holidays and some Olympia events
Hammersmith & City
Jubilee
Metropolitan
Northern
Piccadilly
Victoria
Waterloo & City
DLR
London Overground
Emirates Air Line
Interchange stations
Step-free access from street to train
Step-free access from street to platform
National Rail
Riverboat services
Tramlink
Airport
Emirates Air Line (opening summer 2012)
River Thames
© Transport for London
Reg. user No. 12/2324/P
Improvement works may affect your journey, please check before you travel
Version A TfL 06.2012
Correct at time of going to print

Area Index

Colliers Wood

Branches

Nando's
Tandem Centre, Tandem Way, SW19 2TY (8646 8562).

Covent Garden

Branches

Bill's
13 Slingsby Place, St Martin's Courtyard, WC2E 9AB (7240 8183).
Busaba Eathai
44 Floral Street, WC2E 9DA (7759 0088).
Byron
33-35 Wellington Street, WC2E 7BN (7420 9850).
Byron
24-28 Charing Cross Road, WC2H 0DT (20 7557 9830).
Byron
1A St Giles High Street, WC2H 8AG (7395 0620).
Canteen
21 Wellington Street, WC2E 7DN (7836 8368).
Côte
17-21 Tavistock Street, WC2E 7PA (7379 9991).
Côte
50-51 St Martin's Lane, WC2N 4EA (7379 9747).
Gourmet Burger Kitchen
13-14 Maiden Lane, WC2E 7NE (7240 9617).
Jamie's Italian Covent Garden
11 Upper St Martin's Lane, WC2H 9FB (3326 6390).
Kulu Kulu
51-53 Shelton Street, WC2H 9HE (7240 5687).
Monmouth Coffee Company
27 Monmouth Street, WC2H 9EU (7379 3516).
Nando's
66-68 Chandos Place, WC2N 4HG (7836 4719).
Peyton & Byrne
1 St Giles High Street, WC2H 8AG 422 1451).
Polpo Covent Garden
6 Maiden Lane, WC2E 7NA (7836 8448).
The Real Greek
60-62 Long Acre, WC2E 9JE (7240 2292).
Rossopomodoro
50-52 Monmouth Street, WC2H 9EP (7240 9095).
Sacred
12-14 Long Acre, WC2E 9LP.
Sofra (branch of Özer)
36 Tavistock Street, WC2E 7PB (7240 3773, www.sofra.co.uk).
Thai Square
166-170 Shaftesbury Avenue, WC2H 8JB (7836 7600).
Union Jacks
4 Central St Giles Piazza, 1 St Giles High Street, WC2H 8LE (3597 7888).
Union Jacks
5 North Hall, Covent Garden Piazza, WC2E 8RA (3640 7086).
Wagamama
1 Tavistock Street, WC2E 7PG (7836 3330).
Wahaca
66 Chandos Place, WC2N 4HG (7240 1883).

The Americas

Christopher's p23
18 Wellington Street, WC2E 7DD (7240 4222, www.christophersgrill.com).
Joe Allen p24
13 Exeter Street, WC2E 7DT (7836 0651, www.joeallen.co.uk).
Mishkin's p24
25 Catherine Street, WC2B 5JS (7240 2078, www.mishkins.co.uk).

Bars

London Cocktail Club p312
224A Shaftesbury Avenue, WC2H 8EB (7580 1960, www.londoncocktail club.co.uk).

Brasseries

Kopapa p41
32-34 Monmouth Street, WC2H 9HA (7240 6076, www.kopapa.co.uk).

British

Rules p52
35 Maiden Lane, WC2E 7LB (7836 5314, www.rules.co.uk).

Budget

Canela p274
33 Earlham Street, WC2H 9LS (7240 6926, www.canelacafe.com).

Coffee Bars

Salt p291
34 Great Queen Street, WC2B 5AA (7430 0335, www.saltwc2.co.uk).

Eating & Entertainment

Roadhouse p322
35 The Piazza, WC2E 8BE (7240 6001, www.roadhouse.co.uk).
Sarastro p323
126 Drury Lane, WC2B 5QG (7836 0101, www.sarastro-restaurant.com).

Fish & Chips

Rock & Sole Plaice p295
47 Endell Street, WC2H 9AJ (7836 3785).

French

Clos Maggiore p93
33 King Street, WC2E 8JD (7379 9696, www.closmaggiore.com).
Les Deux Salons p93
40-42 William IV Street, WC2N 4DD (7420 2050, www.lesdeuxsalons.co.uk).
Mon Plaisir p93
21 Monmouth Street, WC2H 9DD (7836 7243, www.monplaisir.co.uk).

Greek

The Real Greek p127
60-62 Long Acre, WC2E 9JE (7240 2292, www.therealgreek.com).

Ice-cream Parlours

La Gelatiera p301
27 New Row, WC2N 4LA (7836 9559, www.lagelatiera.co.uk).
Gelatorino p301
2 Russell Street, WC2B 5JD (7240 0746, www.gelatorino.com).
Gino Gelato p301
3 Adelaide Street, WC2N 4HZ (7836 9390, www.ginogelato.com).
Icecreamists p301
Covent Garden Market, WC2E 8RF (8616 8694, www.theicecreamists.com).
Scoop p302
40 Shorts Gardens, WC2H 9AB (7240 7086, www.scoopgelato.com).

Indian

Dishoom p140
12 Upper St Martin's Lane, WC2H 9FB (7420 9320, www.dishoom.com).
Masala Zone p140
48 Floral Street, WC2E 9DA (7379 0101, www.masalazone.com).
Moti Mahal p141
45 Great Queen Street, WC2B 5AA (7240 9329, www.motimahal-uk.com).
Sagar p141
31 Catherine Street, WC2B 5JS (7836 6377, www.sagarveg.co.uk).

Italian

Carluccio's Caffè p159
2A Garrick Street, WC2E 9BH (7836 0990, www.carluccios.com).

Japanese

Abeno Too p171
17-18 Great Newport Street, WC2H 7JE (7379 1160, www.abeno.co.uk).

Korean

Naru p186
230 Shaftesbury Avenue, WC2H 8EG (7379 7962, www.narurestaurant.com).

Modern European

L'Atelier de Joël Robuchon p205
13-15 West Street, WC2H 9NE (7010 8600, www.joel-robuchon.com).
The Ivy p205
1 West Street, WC2H 9NQ (7836 4751, www.the-ivy.co.uk).

Spanish & Portuguese

Opera Tavern p234
23 Catherine Street, WC2B 5JS (7836 3680, www.operatavern.co.uk).

Steakhouses

Hawksmoor Seven Dials p246
11 Langley Street, WC2H 9JJ (7420 9390, www.thehawksmoor.co.uk).
Meat Market p251
The Mezzanine, Jubilee Market Hall, Tavistock Street, WC2E 8BE (www.themeatmarket.co.uk).

Thai

Suda p252
23 Slingsby Place, WC2E 9AB (7240 8010, www.suda-thai.com).

Vegetarian

Food for Thought p267
31 Neal Street, WC2H 9PR (7836 0239, www.foodforthought-london.co.uk).
Wild Food Café p267
1st floor, 14 Neal's Yard, WC2H 9DP (7419 2014, www.wildfoodcafe.com).

Cricklewood

Middle Eastern

Zeytoon p202
94-96 Cricklewood Broadway, NW2 3EL (8830 7434, www.zeytoon.co.uk).

Crouch End

Branches

Blue Legume
130 Crouch Hill, N8 9DY (8442 9282).
Khoai Café
6 Topsfield Parade, N8 8PR (8341 2120).

Cafés

Haberdashery p287
22 Middle Lane, N8 8PL (8342 8098, www.the-haberdashery.com).

Gastropubs

Queens Pub & Dining Room p117
26 Broadway Parade, N8 9DE (8340 2031, www.thequeenscrouchend.co.uk).
Villiers Terrace p118
120 Park Road, N8 8JP (8245 6827, www.villiersterracelondon.com).

Japanese

Wow Simply Japanese p182
18 Crouch End Hill, N8 8AA (8340 4539, http://wowsimplyjapanese.co.uk).

Croydon, Surrey

Branches

Little Bay
32 Selsdon Road, Croydon, Surrey, CR2 6PB (8649 9544).
Nando's
26 High Street, Croydon, Surrey, CR0 1GT (8681 3505).
Nando's
Croydon Valley Leisure Park, Hesterman Way, Croydon, Surrey, CR0 4YA (8688 9545).
Wagamama
4 Park Lane, Croydon, Surrey, CR0 1JA (8760 9260).
Yo! Sushi
House of Fraser, 21 North End Road, Croydon, Surrey, CR0 1TY (8181 4495).

Crystal Palace

Brasseries

Joanna's p46
56 Westow Hill, SE19 1RX (8670 4052, www.joannas.uk.com).

Global

Mediterranea p123
21 Westow Street, SE19 3RY (8771 7327, www.mediterranea.co).

Modern European

Exhibition Rooms p214
69-71 Westow Hill, SE19 1TX (8761 1175, www.theexhibitionrooms.com).

Dalston

Branches

Nando's
148 Kingsland High Street, E8 2NS (7923 3555).

The Americas

Duke's Brew & Que p29
33 Downham Road, N1 5AA (3006 0795, www.dukesjoint.com).

Brasseries

A Little of What You Fancy p47
464 Kingsland Road, E8 4AE (7275 0060, www.alittleofwhatyoufancy.info).

Cafés

Tina, We Salute You p285
47 King Henry's Walk, N1 4NH (3119 0047, www.tinawesaluteyou.com).

Chinese

Shanghai Dalston p76
41 Kingsland High Street, E8 2JS (7254 2878, www.shanghaidalston.co.uk).

Fish & Chips

Faulkner's p299
424-426 Kingsland Road, E8 4AA (7254 6152).

Gastropubs

Scolt Head p117
107A Culford Road, N1 4HT (7254 3965, www.thescolthead.com).

Turkish

Mangal II p261
4 Stoke Newington Road, N16 8BH (7254 7888, www.mangal2.com).
Mangal Ocakbasi p262
10 Arcola Street, E8 2DJ (7275 8981, www.mangal1.com).
19 Numara Bos Cirrik I p262
34 Stoke Newington Road, N16 7XJ (7249 0400, www.cirrik1.co.uk).

Vietnamese

Huong-Viet p270
An Viet House, 12-14 Englefield Road, N1 4LS (7249 0877).

Deptford

Cafés

Deptford Project p282
121-123 Deptford High Street, SE8 4NS (07545 593279, www.thedeptfordproject.com).

Docklands

Branches

Byron
2nd floor, Cabot Place East, E14 4QT (7715 9360).
Camino Canary Wharf
28 Westferry Circus, E14 8RR (7239 9077).
Canteen
Park Pavilion, 40 Canada Square, E14 5FW (0845 686 1122).
Caribbean Scene Royale
ExCeL Marina, 17 Western Gateway, Royal Victoria Dock, E16 1AQ (7511 2023).
Carluccio's Caffè
Reuters Plaza, E14 5AJ (7719 0101).
Gaucho Canary
29 Westferry Circus, E14 8RR (7987 9494).
Goodman Canary Wharf
3 South Quay, E14 9RU (7531 0300).
Gourmet Burger Kitchen
Jubilee Place, E14 5NY (7719 6408).
Jamie's Italian Canary Wharf
2 Churchill Place, E14 5RB (3002 5252).
Leon
Cabot Place West, E14 4QS (7719 6200).
Nando's
Jubilee Place, off Bank Street, E14 5NY (7513 2864).
Nando's
Cabot Place East, E14 4QT (3200 2096).
Le Relais de Venise l'entrecôte
18-20 Mackenzie Walk, E14 4PH (3475 3331).
Rocket
2 Churchill Place, E14 5RB (3200 2022).
Roka
4 Park Pavilion, 40 Canada Square, E14 5FW (7636 5228).
Royal China
30 Westferry Circus, E14 8RR (7719 0888).

Taylor Street Baristas
8 South Colonnade, E14 4PZ.
Wagamama
Jubilee Place, 45 Bank Street, E14 5NY (7516 9009).
Wahaca
Park Pavilion, 40 Canada Square, E14 5FW (7516 9145).

British

Boisdale Canary Wharf p60
Cabot Place, E14 4QT (7715 5818, www.boisdale.co.uk).

Cafés

Frizzante@Mudchute p284
Mudchute Park & Farm, Pier Street, E14 3HP (3069 9290, www.frizzanteltd.co.uk).

Chinese

Yi-Ban p75
London Regatta Centre, Dockside Road, E16 2QT (7473 6699, www.yi-ban.co.uk).

Gastropubs

Gun p114
27 Coldharbour, E14 9NS (7515 5222, www.thegundocklands.com).

Modern European

Plateau p219
Canada Place, Canada Square, E14 5ER (7715 7100, www.plateau-restaurant.co.uk).

Spanish & Portuguese

Ibérica Food & Culture p242
12 Cabot Square, E14 5NY (7636 8650, www.ibericalondon.co.uk).

Steakhouses

Goodman Canary Wharf p249
3 South Quay, E14 9RU (7531 0300, www.goodmanrestaurants.com).

Dulwich

Gastropubs

Rosendale p114
65 Rosendale Road, SE21 8EZ (8761 9008, www.therosendale.co.uk).

Wine Bars

Green & Blue p328
36-38 Lordship Lane, SE22 8HJ (8693 9250, www.greenandbluewines.com).

Ealing

Branches

Carluccio's Caffè
5-6 The Green, W5 5DA (8566 4458).
Côte
9-10 The Green, High Street, W5 5DA (8579 3115).
Gourmet Burger Kitchen
35 Haven Green, W5 2NX (8998 0392).
Kerbisher & Malt
53 New Broadway, W5 5AH (8840 4418).
Nando's
1-2 Station Buildings, Uxbridge Road, W5 3NU (8992 2290).
Nando's
1-5 Bond Street, W5 5AP (8567 8093).
Santa Maria
15 St Mary's Road, W5 5RA (8579 1462, www.santamaria pizzeria.com).

Gastropubs

Ealing Park Tavern p108
222 South Ealing Road, W5 4RL (8758 1879, www.ealingparktavern.com).

Japanese

Atariya p178
1 Station Parade, Uxbridge Road, W5 3LD (8896 3175, www.atariya.co.uk).

Pan-Asian & Fusion

Tuk Cho p228
28-30 New Broadway, W5 2XA (8567 9438, www.tukchoealing.co.uk).

Earl's Court

Branches

Byron
242 Earl's Court Road, SW5 9AA (7370 9300).
Gourmet Burger Kitchen
163-165 Earl's Court Road, SW5 9RF (7373 3184).
Masala Zone
147 Earl's Court Road, SW5 9RQ (7373 0220).
Nando's
204 Earl's Court Road, SW5 9QF (7259 2544).
Wagamama
180-182 Earl's Court Road, SW5 9QG (7373 9660).

Eating & Entertainment

Troubadour p323
263-267 Old Brompton Road, SW5 9JA (7370 1434, www.troubadour.co.uk).

French

Garnier p97
314 Earl's Court Road, SW5 9BQ (3641 8323, www.garnier-restaurant-london.co.uk).

Greek

As Greek As It Gets p129
233 Earl's Court Road, SW5 9AH (7244 7777, www.asgreekasitgets.co.uk).

Spanish & Portuguese

Capote y Toros p237
157 Old Brompton Road, SW5 0LJ (7373 0567, www.cambiodetercio.co.uk).

Thai

Addie's Thai p255
121 Earl's Court Road, SW5 9RL (7259 2620, www.addiesthai.co.uk).

Earlsfield

Branches

Cah Chi
394 Garratt Lane, SW18 4HP (8946 8811).
Carluccio's Caffè
537-539 Garratt Lane, SW18 4SW (8947 4651).

East Dulwich

British

Franklins p59
157 Lordship Lane, SE22 8HX (8299 9598, www.franklinsrestaurant.com).

Cafés

Blue Mountain Café p283
18 North Cross Road, SE22 9EU (8299 6953, www.bluemo.co.uk).
Luca's p283
145 Lordship Lane, SE22 8HX (8613 6161, www.lucasbakery.com).

Fish & Chips

Sea Cow p298
37 Lordship Lane, SE22 8EW (8693 3111, www.theseacow.co.uk).

Gastropubs

Palmerston p114
91 Lordship Lane, SE22 8EP (8693 1629, www.thepalmerston.net).

Steakhouses

Gourmet Burger Kitchen p250
121 Lordship Lane, SE22 8HU (8693 9307, www.gbk.co.uk).

East Ham

Branches

Saravana Bhavan
300 High Street North, E12 6SA (8552 467).

East Sheen

Branches

Faanoos
481 Upper Richmond Road West, SW14 7PU (8878 5738).

Fish & Chips

fish! kitchen p297
170 Upper Richmond Road West, SW14 8AW (8878 1040, www.fishkitchen.com).

Edgware Road

Branches

Abu Zaad
128 Edgware Road, W2 2DZ (8749 5107).
Beirut Express
112-114 Edgware Road, W2 2JE (7724 2700).
Maroush Gardens
1-3 Connaught Street, W2 2DH (7262 0222).
Maroush III
62 Seymour Street, W1H 5BN (7724 5024).
Maroush IV
68 Edgware Road, W2 2EG (7224 9339).

Global

Mandalay p122
444 Edgware Road, W2 1EG (7258 3696, www.mandalayway.com).

Middle Eastern

Maroush I p195
21 Edgware Road, W2 2JE (7723 0773, www.maroush.com).
Ranoush Juice p197
43 Edgware Road, W2 2JE (7723 5929, www.maroush.com).

North African

Sidi Maarouf p223
56-58 Edgware Road, W2 2JE (7724 0525, www.maroush.com).

Thai

Heron p253
Basement karaoke room of the Heron, 1 Norfolk Crescent, W2 2DN (7706 9567).

Edgware, Middx

Branches

Haandi
301-303 Hale Lane, Edgware, Middx, HA8 7AX (8905 4433).
Nando's
137-139 Station Road, Edgware, Middx, HA8 7JG (8952 3400).

Indian

Meera's Village p152
36 Queensbury Station Parade, Edgware, Middx, HA8 5NN (8952 5556).

Elephant & Castle

Branches

Nando's
Metro Central, 119 Newington Causeway, SE1 6BA (7378 7810).

East European

Mamuska! p82
1st floor, Elephant & Castle Shopping Centre, SE1 6TE (3602 1898, www.mamuska.net).

Enfield, Middx

Branches

Nando's
2 The Town, Enfield, Middx, EN2 6LE (8366 2904).

Euston

Branches

Nando's
The Piazza, Euston Station, NW1 2RT (7387 5126).
Rasa Express
327 Euston Road, NW1 3AD (7387 8974).

Cafés

Peyton & Byrne p279
Wellcome Collection, 183 Euston Road, NW1 2BE (7611 2138, www.peytonandbyrne.com).

Japanese

Sushi of Shiori p171
144 Drummond Street, NW1 2PA (7388 9962, www.sushiofshiori.co.uk).

Pizza & Pasta

Pasta Plus p305
62 Eversholt Street, NW1 1DA (7383 4943, www.pastaplus.co.uk).

Finchley

Branches

Nando's
Great North Leisure Park, Chaplin Square, N12 0GL (8492 8465).
Tosa
152 High Road, N2 9ED (8883 8850).
Yo! Sushi
02 Centre, 255 Finchley Road, NW3 6LU (7431 4499).

Fish & Chips

Two Brothers Fish Restaurant p300
297-303 Regent's Park Road, N3 1DP (8346 0469, www.twobrothers.co.uk).

Vietnamese

Khoai Café p272
362 Ballards Lane, N12 0EE (8445 2039, www.khoai.co.uk).
Vy Nam Café p272
371 Regents Park Road, N3 1DE (8371 4222).

Finsbury Park

Branches

Il Bacio Highbury
178-184 Blackstock Road, N5 1HA (7226 3339).

Fish

Chez Liline p88
101 Stroud Green Road, N4 3PX (7263 6550, www.chezliline.co.uk).

Gastropubs

Old Dairy p118
1-3 Crouch Hill, N4 4AP (7263 3337, www.theolddairyn4.co.uk).

Korean

Dotori p189
3 Stroud Green Road, N4 2DQ (7263 3562).

Modern European

Season Kitchen p222
53 Stroud Green Road, N4 3EF (7263 5500, http://seasonkitchen.co.uk).

North African

Le Rif p225
172 Seven Sisters Road, N7 7PX (7263 1891).

Turkish

Petek p262
94-96 Stroud Green Road, N4 3EN (7619 3933).

Fitzrovia

Branches

Byron at The Black Horse
Black Horse, 6 Rathbone Place, W1T 1HL (7636 9330).
Côte
5 Charlotte Street, W1T 1RE (7436 1087).
dim t
32 Charlotte Street, W1T 2NQ (7637 1122).
Ibérica Food & Culture
195 Great Portland Street, W1W 5PS (7636 8650).
London Cocktail Club
61 Goodge Street, W1T 1TL (7580 1960).
Nando's
2 Berners Street, W1T 3LA (7323 9791).
Nando's
57-59 Goodge Street, W1T 1TH (7637 0708).
Nando's
190 Great Portland Street, W1W 5QZ.
Peyton & Byrne
Heals, 196 Tottenham Court Road, W1T 7LQ (7580 3451).
Ping Pong
48 Eastcastle Street, W1W 8DX (7079 0550).
Ping Pong
48 Newman Street, W1T 1QQ (7291 3080).
Sacred
Kiosk, Torrington Place, off Gower Street, WC1E 6EQ (07726 500 171).
Sagar
17A Percy Street, W1T 1DU (7631 3319).
Tapped & Packed
114 Tottenham Court Road, W1T 5AH (7580 2163).
Tsunami
93 Charlotte Street, W1T 4PY (7637 0050).
Wahaca
19-23 Charlotte Street, W1T 1RL.
Yalla Yalla
12 Winsley Street, W1W 8HQ (7637 4748).

Italian

River Café **p165**
Thames Wharf, Rainville Road, W6 9HA (7386 4200, www.rivercafe.co.uk).

Japanese

Tosa **p178**
332 King Street, W6 0RR (8748 0002, www.tosauk.com).

Thai

101 Thai Kitchen **p255**
352 King Street, W6 0RX (8746 6888, www.101thaikitchen.com).

Vietnamese

Saigon Saigon **p269**
313-317 King Street, W6 9NH (0870 220 1398, www.saigon-saigon.co.uk).

Hampstead

Branches

Carluccio's Caffè
32 Rosslyn Hill, NW3 1NH (7794 2184).
Côte
83-84 Hampstead High Street, NW3 1RE (7435 2558).
dim t
3 Heath Street, NW3 6TP (7435 0024).
Feng Sushi
280 West End Lane, NW6 1LJ (1435 1833).
Gaucho Hampstead
64 Heath Street, NW3 1DN (7431 8222, EC3V 0BL).
Giraffe
46 Rosslyn Hill, NW3 1NH (7435 0343).
Wagamama
58-62 Heath Street, NW3 1EN (7433 0366).

Bars

Flat P at Dach & Sons **p319**
68 Heath Street, NW3 1DN (7433 8139, www.dachandsons.com).

Cafés

Brew House **p289**
Hampstead Lane, NW3 7JR (8341 5384, www.companyofcooks.com).

Coffee Bars

Ginger & White **p294**
4A-5A Perrin's Court, NW3 1QS (7431 9098, www.gingerandwhite.com).

Gastropubs

Horseshoe **p120**
28 Heath Street, NW3 6TE (7431 7206).
Old White Bear **p120**
1 Well Road, NW3 1LJ (7794 7719, www.theoldwhitebear.co.uk).
Wells **p121**
30 Well Walk, NW3 1BX (7794 3785, www.thewellshampstead.co.uk).

Ice-cream Parlours

Slice of Ice **p304**
8 Flask Walk, NW3 1HE (7419 9908, www.slice-of-ice.co.uk).

Japanese

Jin Kichi **p182**
73 Heath Street, NW3 6UG (7794 6158, www.jinkichi.com).

Pizza & Pasta

Mimmo La Bufala **p310**
45A South End Road, NW3 2QB (7435 7814).

Harringay

Branches

Antepliler
46 Grand Parade, Green Lanes, N4 1AG (8802 5588).

Turkish

Hala **p263**
29 Grand Parade, Green Lanes, N4 1LG (8802 4883, www.halarestaurant.co.uk).

Harrow, Middx

Branches

Nando's
300-302 Station Road, Harrow, Middx, HA1 2DX (8427 5581).
Nando's
309-311 Northolt Road, Harrow, Middx, HA2 8JA (8423 1516).
Royal China
148-150 Station Road, Harrow, Middx, HA1 2RH (8863 8359).
Sakonis
5-8 Dominion Parade, Station Road, Harrow, Middx, HA1 2TR (8863 3399).

Global

Masa **p126**
24-26 Headstone Drive, Harrow, Middx, HA3 5QH (8861 6213).

Indian

Mr Chilly **p154**
344 Pinner Road, Harrow, Middx, HA1 4LB (8861 4404, www.mrchilly.co.uk).
Ram's **p154**
203 Kenton Road, Harrow, Middx, HA3 0HD (8907 2022, www.rams restaurant.co.uk).
Saravana Bhavan **p154**
403 Alexandra Avenue, Harrow, Middx, HA2 9SG (8869 9966, www.saravana bhavan.co.uk).

Hendon

Branches

Atariya
31 Vivian Avenue, NW4 3UX (8202 2789).

Budget

Nando's **p277**
Brent Cross Shopping Centre, Prince Charles Drive, NW4 3FP (8203 9131, www.nandos.co.uk).

Jewish

White Fish **p185**
10-12 Bell Lane, NW4 2AD (8202 8780, www.whitefishrestaurant.co.uk).

Herne Hill

Cafés

Lido Café **p283**
Brockwell Lido, Dulwich Road, SE24 0PA (7737 8183, www.thelidocafe.co.uk).

Fish & Chips

Olley's **p298**
65-69 Norwood Road, SE24 9AA (8671 8259, www.olleys.info).

Pan-Asian & Fusion

Lombok **p229**
17 Half Moon Lane, SE24 9JU (7733 7131).

Spanish & Portuguese

Number 22 **p241**
22 Half Moon Lane, SE24 9HU (7095 9922, www.number-22.com).

Highbury

Branches

La Fromagerie
30 Highbury Park, N5 2AA (7359 7440).
StringRay Café
36 Highbury Park, N5 2AA (7354 9309).

The Americas

Garufa **p38**
104 Highbury Park, N5 2XE (7226 0070, www.garufa.co.uk).

East European

Tbilisi **p82**
91 Holloway Road, N7 8LT (7607 2536).

Italian

Trullo **p170**
300-302 St Paul's Road, N1 2LH (7226 2733, www.trullorestaurant.com).

Turkish

Iznik **p263**
19 Highbury Park, N5 1QJ (7354 5697, www.iznik.co.uk).

Highgate

Branches

dim t
1 Hampstead Lane, N6 4RS (8340 8800, www.dimt.co.uk).

Bars

Bull **p316**
13 North Hill, N6 4AB (8341 0510, http://thebullhighgate.co.uk).

Cafés

Pavilion Café **p287**
Highgate Woods, Muswell Hill Road, N10 3JN (8444 4777).

Fish & Chips

Fish Fish **p300**
179 Archway Road, N6 5BN (8348 3121).

French

Côte **p104**
2 Highgate High Street, N6 5JL (8348 9107, www.cote-restaurants.co.uk).

Holborn

Branches

Gelateria Danieli
222 Shaftesbury Avenue, WC2H 8EB (7240 1770).
Hummus Bros
Victoria House, 37-63 Southampton Row, WC1B 4DA (7404 7079).
Nando's
9-10 Southampton Place, WC1A 2EA (7831 5565).

The Americas

Bull Steak Expert **p31**
54 Red Lion Street, WC1R 4PD (7242 0708, www.thebullsteak expert.com).

British

Great Queen Street **p53**
32 Great Queen Street, WC2B 5AA (7242 0622).

Cafés

Fleet River Bakery **p279**
71 Lincoln's Inn Fields, WC2A 3JF (7691 1457, www.fleetriver bakery.com).

Fish & Chips

Fryer's Delight **p296**
19 Theobald's Road, WC1X 8SL (7405 4114).

Hotels & Haute Cuisine

Pearl Bar & Restaurant **p133**
Chancery Court Hotel, 252 High Holborn, WC1V 7EN (7829 7000, www.pearl-restaurant.com).

Korean

Asadal **p187**
227 High Holborn, WC1V 7DA (7430 9006, www.asadal.co.uk).

Middle Eastern

Hiba **p195**
113 High Holborn, WC1V 6JQ (7831 5171, www.hiba-express.co.uk).

Vegetarian

Orchard **p265**
11 Sicilian Avenue, WC1A 2QH (7831 2715, www.orchard-kitchen.co.uk).

Holland Park

Branches

Gelato Mio
138 Holland Park Avenue, W11 4UE (7727 4117).
Giraffe
120 Holland Park Avenue, W11 4UA (7229 8567).

French

Belvedere **p99**
Holland House, off Abbotsbury Road, in Holland Park, W8 6LU (7602 1238, www.belvedererestaurant.co.uk).

Holloway

Branches

Sacred
Highbury Studios, 8 Hornsey Street, N7 8EG (7700 1628).

Hornchurch, Essex

Branches

Mandarin Palace
197-201 High Street, Hornchurch, Essex, RM11 3XT (01708 437 951).
Nando's
111-113A High Street, Hornchurch, Essex, RM11 1TX (01708 449537).

Ilford, Essex

Branches

Nando's
I-Scene, Clements Road, Ilford, Essex, IG1 1BP (8514 6012).

Chinese

Mandarin Palace **p77**
559-561 Cranbrook Road, Ilford, Essex, IG2 6JZ (8550 7661).

Islington

Branches

Banana Tree
412-416 St John Street, EC1V 4NJ (7278 7565).
Blue Legume
177 Upper Street, N1 1RG (7226 5858).
Breakfast Club
31 Camden Passage, N1 8EA (7226 5454).
Byron
341 Upper Street, N1 0PB (7704 7620).
Carluccio's Caffè
305-307 Upper Street, N1 2TU (7359 8167).
Côte
5-6 Islington Green, N1 2XA (7354 4666).
The Diner
21 Essex Road, N1 2SA (7226 4533).
Giraffe
29-31 Essex Road, N1 2SA (7359 5999).
Lucky Voice
173-174 Upper Street, N1 1RG (7354 6280).
Masala Zone
80 Upper Street, N1 0NU (7359 3399).
Nando's
324 Upper Street, N1 2XQ (7288 0254).
Thai Square
347-349 Upper Street, N1 0PD (7704 2000).
Wagamama
N1 Centre, 39 Parkfield Street, N1 0PS (7226 2664).
Yo! Sushi
N1 Centre, 39 Parkfield Street, N1 0PS (7359 3502).

The Americas

North Pole **p29**
188-190 New North Road, N1 7BJ (7354 5400, www.thenorthpolepub.co.uk).
Sabor **p38**
108 Essex Road, N1 8LX (7226 5551, www.sabor.co.uk).
Tierra Peru **p38**
164 Essex Road, N1 8LY (7354 5586, www.tierraperu.co.uk).

Bars

Railway Tavern **p317**
2 St Jude Street, N16 8JT (0011 1195).
69 Colebrooke Row **p319**
69 Colebrooke Row, N1 8AA (07540 528593, www.69colebrookerow.com).

Brasseries

Bill's **p50**
9 White Lion Street, N1 9PD (7713 7272, www.bills-website.co.uk).
Ottolenghi **p50**
287 Upper Street, N1 2TZ (7288 1454, www.ottolenghi.co.uk).

Budget

Le Mercury **p276**
140A Upper Street, N1 1QY (7354 4088, www.lemercury.co.uk).

Chinese

Yipin China **p76**
70-72 Liverpool Road, N1 0QD (7354 3388, www.yipinchina.co.uk).

French

Almeida **p104**
30 Almeida Street, N1 1AD (7354 4777, www.almeida-restaurant.co.uk).

Gastropubs

Duke of Cambridge **p118**
30 St Peter's Street, N1 8JT (7359 3066, www.dukeorganic.co.uk).
Hundred Crows Rising **p119**
58 Penton Street, N1 9PZ (7837 3891, www.hundredcrowsrising.co.uk).

Advertisers' Index

Please refer to relevant sections for addresses/telephone numbers.

A-Z Index

C

D

E

F

G

H

Moshi Moshi Sushi p171
24 Upper Level, Liverpool Street Station, EC2M 7QH (7247 3227, www.moshimoshi.co.uk). Japanese
Mosob p20
339 Harrow Road, W9 3RB (7266 2012, www.mosob.co.uk). African
Moti Mahal p141
45 Great Queen Street, WC2B 5AA (7240 9329, www.motimahal-uk.com). Indian
Mr Chilly p154
344 Pinner Road, Harrow, Middx, HA1 4LB (8861 4404, www.mrchilly.co.uk). Indian
Mr Chow p67
151 Knightsbridge, SW1X 7PA (7589 7347, www.mrchow.com). Chinese
Mr Fish p297
9 Porchester Road, W2 5DP (7229 4161, www.mrfish.uk.com). Fish & Chips
Mr Fish
51 Salusbury Road, NW6 6NJ (7624 3555). Branch
Mudra p151
715 Leytonstone High Road, E11 4RD (8539 1700, www.swadrestaurant.com). Indian
Mulberry Street p306
84 Westbourne Grove, W2 5RT (7313 6789, www.mulberrystreet.co.uk). Pizza & Pasta
Murano p161
20-22 Queen Street, W1J 5PP (7495 1127, www.muranolondon.com). Italian
Muya p22
13 Brecknock Road, N7 0BL (3609 0702, www.muyarestaurant.com). African

N

Nahm p252
Halkin Street, SW1X 7DJ (7333 1234, www.nahm.como.bz). Thai
Namaaste Kitchen p151
64 Parkway, NW1 7AH (7485 5977, www.namaastekitchen.co.uk). Indian
Nando's p277
Brent Cross Shopping Centre, Prince Charles Drive, NW4 3FP (8203 9131, www.nandos.co.uk). Budget
Nando's
26 High Street, Croydon, Surrey, CR0 1GT (8681 3505). Branch
Nando's
9-25 Mile End Road, E1 4TW (7791 2720). Branch
Nando's
114-118 Commercial Street, E1 6NF (7650 7775). Branch
Nando's
120 Middlesex Street, E1 7HY (7392 9572). Branch
Nando's
Cabot Place East, E14 4QT (3200 2096). Branch
Nando's
Jubilee Place, off Bank Street, E14 5NY (7513 2864). Branch
Nando's
1A Romford Road, E15 4LJ (8221 2148). Branch
Nando's
366 Bethnal Green Road, E2 0AH (7729 5783). Branch
Nando's
Westfield Stratford, 2 Stratford Place, Montifichet Place, E20 1EJ (8519 4459). Branch
Nando's
552 Mile End Road, E3 4PL (8981 9867). Branch
Nando's
148 Kingsland High Street, E8 2NS (7923 3555). Branch
Nando's
Level 1 South, Cheapside Passage, One New Change, EC4M 9AF (7248 0651). Branch
Nando's
2 The Town, Enfield, Middx, EN2 6LE (8366 2904). Branch
Nando's
300-302 Station Road, Harrow, Middx, HA1 2DX (8427 5581). Branch
Nando's
309-311 Northolt Road, Harrow, Middx, HA2 8JA (8423 1516). Branch
Nando's
137-139 Station Road, Edgware, Middx, HA8 7JG (8952 3400). Branch
Nando's
420-422 High Road, Wembley, Middx, HA9 6AH (8795 3564). Branch
Nando's
I-Scene, Clements Road, Ilford, Essex, IG1 1BP (8514 6012). Branch
Nando's
Odeon, Longbridge Road, Barking, Essex, IG11 8RU (8507 0795). Branch
Nando's
37-38 High Street, Kingston, Surrey, KT1 1LQ (8296 9540). Branch
Nando's
324 Upper Street, N1 2XQ (7288 0254). Branch
Nando's
12-16 York Way, N1 9AA (7833 2809). Branch
Nando's
Great North Leisure Park, Chaplin Square, N12 0GL (8492 8465). Branch
Nando's
139-141 Stoke Newington Church Street, N16 0UH (7923 1019). Branch
Nando's
Hollywood Green, Redvers Road, off Lordship Lane, N22 6EJ (8889 2936). Branch
Nando's
106 Stroud Green Road, N4 3HB (7263 7447). Branch
Nando's
The Piazza, Euston Station, NW1 2RT (7387 5126). Branch
Nando's
57-58 Chalk Farm Road, NW1 8AN (7424 9040). Branch
Nando's
Tesco Extra, Great Central Way, NW10 0TL (8459 6908). Branch
Nando's
02 Centre, 255 Finchley Road, NW3 6LU (7435 4644). Branch
Nando's
227-229 Kentish Town Road, NW5 2JU (7424 9363). Branch
Nando's
252-254 West End Lane, NW6 1LU (7794 1331). Branch
Nando's
308 Kilburn High Road, NW6 2DG (7372 1507). Branch
Nando's
658-660 Kingsbury Road, NW9 9HN (8204 7905). Branch
Nando's
111-113A High Street, Hornchurch, Essex, RM11 1TX (01708 449537). Branch
Nando's
Metro Central, 119 Newington Causeway, SE1 6BA (7378 7810). Branch
Nando's
225-227 Clink Street, SE1 9DG (7357 8662). Branch
Nando's
108 Stamford Street, SE1 9NH (7261 9006). Branch
Nando's
The O2, Millennium Way, SE10 0AX (8269 2401). Branch
Nando's
UCI Cinema Complex, Bugsby's Way, SE10 0QJ (8293 3025). Branch
Nando's
Bugsby's Way, SE10 0QJ (8293 3025). Branch
Nando's
16 Lee High Road, SE13 5LQ (8463 0119). Branch
Nando's
88 Denmark Hill, SE5 8RX (7738 3808). Branch
Nando's
74-76 Rushey Green, SE6 4HW (8314 0122). Branch
Nando's
9-11 High Street, Sutton, Surrey, SM1 1DF (8770 0180). Branch
Nando's
1A Northcote Road, SW11 1NG (7228 6221). Branch
Nando's
116-118 Balham High Road, SW12 9AA (8675 6415). Branch
Nando's
148 Upper Richmond Road, SW15 2SW (8780 3651). Branch
Nando's
6-7 High Parade, Streatham High Road, SW16 1EX (8769 0951). Branch
Nando's
224-226 Upper Tooting Road, SW17 7EW (8682 2478). Branch
Nando's
Southside Shopping Centre, SW18 4TF (8874 1363). Branch
Nando's
1 Russell Road, SW19 1QN (8545 0909). Branch
Nando's
Tandem Centre, Tandem Way, SW19 2TY (8646 8562). Branch
Nando's
17 Cardinal Walk, Cardinal Place, SW1E 5JE (7828 0158). Branch
Nando's
107-108 Wilton Road, SW1V 1DZ (7976 5719). Branch
Nando's
59-63 Clapham High Street, SW4 7TG (7622 1475). Branch
Nando's
204 Earl's Court Road, SW5 9QF (7259 2544). Branch
Nando's
Fulham Broadway Retail Centre, Fulham Road, SW6 1BY (7386 8035). Branch
Nando's
117 Gloucester Road, SW7 4ST (7373 4446). Branch
Nando's
234-244 Stockwell Road, SW9 9SP (7737 6400). Branch
Nando's
2-4 Hill Rise, Richmond, Surrey, TW10 6UA (8940 8810). Branch
Nando's
1-1A High Street, Hounslow, Middx, TW3 1RH (8570 5881). Branch
Nando's
The Chimes Centre, High Street, Uxbridge, Middx, UB8 1LB (01895 274277). Branch
Nando's
58-60 Notting Hill Gate, W11 3HT (7243 1647). Branch
Nando's
Westfield London, W12 7GF (8834 4658). Branch
Nando's
284-286 Uxbridge Road, W12 7JA (8746 1112). Branch
Nando's
46 Glasshouse Street, W1B 5DR (7287 8442). Branch
Nando's
10 Frith Street, W1D 3JF (7494 0932). Branch
Nando's
57-59 Goodge Street, W1T 1TH (7637 0708). Branch
Nando's
2 Berners Street, W1T 3LA (7323 9791). Branch
Nando's
113 Baker Street, W1U 6RS (3075 1044). Branch
Nando's
190 Great Portland Street, W1W 5QZ. Branch
Nando's
63 Westbourne Grove, W2 4UA (7313 9506). Branch
Nando's
Royal Leisure Park, Kendal Avenue, W3 0PA (8896 1469). Branch
Nando's
187-189 Chiswick High Road, W4 2DR (8995 7533). Branch
Nando's
1-2 Station Buildings, Uxbridge Road, W5 3NU (8992 2290). Branch
Nando's
1-5 Bond Street, W5 5AP (8567 8093). Branch
Nando's
9-10 Southampton Place, WC1A 2EA (7831 5565). Branch
Nando's
The Brunswick, Marchmont Street, WC1N 1AE (7713 0351). Branch
Nando's
66-68 Chandos Place, WC2N 4HG (7836 4719). Branch
Napulé p307
585 Fulham Broadway, SW6 5UA (7381 1122, www.madeinitaly group.co.uk). Pizza & Pasta
Nara p187
9 D'Arblay Street, W1F 8DR (7287 2224). Korean
Narrow p114
44 Narrow Street, E14 8DP (7592 7950, www.gordonramsay.com/thenarrow). Gastropubs
Naru p186
230 Shaftesbury Avenue, WC2H 8EG (7379 7962, www.narurestaurant.com). Korean
National Café
East Wing, National Gallery, Trafalgar Square, WC2N 5DN (7747 2525, www.thenationalcafe.com). Branch
National Dining Rooms p55
Sainsbury Wing, National Gallery, Trafalgar Square, WC2N 5DN (7747 2525, www.peytonandbyrne.co.uk/ the-national-dining-rooms). British
Nautilus p300
27-29 Fortune Green Road, NW6 1DU (7435 2532). Fish & Chips
Necco p172
52-54 Exmouth Market, EC1R 4QE (7713 8575, www.necco.co.uk). Japanese
Needoo Grill p149
87 New Road, E1 1HH (7247 0648, www.needoogrill.co.uk). Indian
New Asian Tandoori Centre (Roxy) p156
114-118 The Green, Southall, Middx, UB2 4BQ (8574 2597, www.roxy-restaurant.com). Indian
New Cross House p114
316 New Cross Road, SE14 6AF (8691 8875, www.thenewcrosshouse.com). Gastropubs
New Fook Lam Moon p193
10 Gerrard Street, W1D 5PW (7734 7615). Malaysian, Indonesian & Singaporean
New World p66
1 Gerrard Place, W1D 5PA (7434 2508, newworldlondon.com). Chinese
Nightjar p318
129 City Road, EC1V 1JB (7253 4101, www.barnightjar.com). Bars
19 Numara Bos Cirrik I p262
34 Stoke Newington Road, N16 7XJ (7249 0400, www.cirrik1.co.uk). Turkish
19 Numara Bos Cirrik II
194 Stoke Newington High Street, N16 7JD (7249 9111). Branch
19 Numara Bos Cirrik III
1-3 Amhurst Road, E8 1LL (8985 2879). Branch
19 Numara Bos Cirrik IV
665 High Road, N17 8AD (8801 5566). Branch
Nipa p255
Lancaster London Hotel, Lancaster Terrace, W2 2TY (7262 6737, www.niparestaurant.co.uk). Thai
Nizuni p173
22 Charlotte Street, W1T 2NB (7580 7447, www.nizuni.com). Japanese
Nizuni Go
39 Marylebone Lane, W1U 2NP (7935 2000). Branch
No 67 p282
South London Gallery, 67 Peckham Road, SE5 8UH (7252 7649, www.southlondongallery.org). Cafés

S

T

U

V

W

X

Y

Z